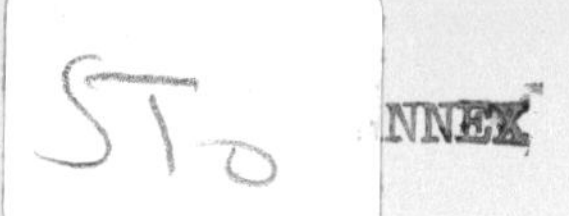

EMPLOYMENT AND WAGES IN THE UNITED STATES

THE TWENTIETH CENTURY FUND

THE TRUSTEES of the Fund choose subjects for Fund studies and underwrite the expenses of each project. The authors, however, assume full responsibility for the findings and opinions in each report.

EMPLOYMENT AND WAGES SURVEY OF THE TWENTIETH CENTURY FUND

COMMITTEE ON EMPLOYMENT AND WAGES *

The following special committee was appointed by the Fund to formulate a report containing constructive policies to deal with some of the major problems disclosed by the research findings of this survey. The Committee's report, for which it is solely responsible, is contained in Chapter 45.

LLOYD K. GARRISON, *Chairman*

Lawyer, Paul, Weiss, Rifkind, Wharton & Garrison
Formerly Chairman, National War Labor Board

SOLOMON BARKIN

Director of Research
Textile Workers Union of America

HARRY A. BULLIS

Chairman of the Board
General Mills, Inc.

WALDO E. FISHER

Professor of Industrial Relations
Wharton School of Finance and Commerce
University of Pennsylvania

E. L. OLIVER

Labor Bureau of Middle West

SUMNER H. SLICHTER

Lamont University Professor
Harvard University

LOUIS STARK

Editorial Writer
The New York Times

LAZARE TEPER

Director, Research Department
International Ladies' Garment
Workers' Union

HAROLD L. ZELLERBACH

President, Zellerbach Paper Company

---

* William A. Hughes, President, New Jersey Bell Telephone Company, and Anna M. Rosenberg, formerly Assistant Secretary of Defense, were originally members of the Committee, but resigned before participating in either the deliberations or the conclusions of the Committee.

EMPLOYMENT AND WAGES SURVEY OF THE TWENTIETH CENTURY FUND

RESEARCH STAFF

The following special research staff is solely responsible for the research findings included in Chapters 1 to 44 inclusive.

W. S. WOYTINSKY
Research Director

THOMAS C. FICHANDLER
Collaborator

MORRIS C. BISHOP
Collaborator

MARY ROSS GANNETT
Editorial Assistant

CONTRIBUTORS

PHILIP ARNOW
ROBERT M. BALL
WITT BOWDEN
KARL DE SCHWEINITZ
H. M. DOUTY
LOUIS J. DUCOFF
W. DUANE EVANS
JUDITH GRUNFEL
FRANZ HUBER
JOSEPH KOVNER
E. R. LIVERNASH
HARRY OBER
ELINOR PANCOAST
BARKEV S. SANDERS
IRVING H. SIEGEL
COLLIS STOCKING

EMPLOYMENT AND WAGES IN THE UNITED STATES

by W. S. WOYTINSKY

AND ASSOCIATES

THE TWENTIETH CENTURY FUND

NEW YORK · 1953

Library of Congress Catalog Card Number: 53–7170

MANUFACTURED IN THE UNITED STATES OF AMERICA
BY THE LORD BALTIMORE PRESS, BALTIMORE, MARYLAND

FOREWORD

EMPLOYMENT AND WAGES are, of course, supremely important to almost everyone. Our whole way of life is dependent on our income. Our breadwinners, at least, spend a very large part of their waking time in their places of employment. It is only natural, therefore, that books without number have been written on these subjects and on their many special parts and aspects.

But there has been a great need for a comprehensive factual survey, within the covers of a single volume, of the working people of the United States and their conditions of labor: the size, make-up and distribution of the labor force; the various occupations represented and the numbers of workers employed in each; the ebb and flow of employment and unemployment; the wages that American workers are paid and how their wages are determined; their hours of labor and other working conditions and the regulations and controls that government has imposed upon them; labor unions and the role they play in the vast drama of wages and employment; the underpinnings of insurance which have been set up to make the worker's life more secure; and finally, the relation of all these basic facts to the operation of the economy as a whole.

This volume represents an attempt to meet this urgent need and to do so in a way that will create not merely a still picture of the situation as of here and now, but a moving one that shows past trends and projects these trends into the future. Nor is this study purely one of facts and statistics. The authors have summarized and analyzed the theories of leading economists to explain the demand for labor and the flow of wages — a useful feature for any discussion of future wage policies.

As part of the research on which this report is based a canvass was made of the opinions of leading labor and management representatives on various aspects of collective bargaining policies and practices. The results of this poll were published in mimeographed form for limited distribution in March 1949 under the title "Labor and Management Look at Collective Bargaining." The principal findings of that report are incorporated in the appropriate chapters of the present volume.

A specially recruited staff prepared this volume with the aid of outside contributors. The special staff consisted of the Research Director, W. S. Woytinsky, who was responsible for the plan and execution of the whole project, and two assistant directors: Thomas C. Fichandler, who prepared the chapters on labor unions and unemployment (Chapters 18–21 and 32–33), and Morris C. Bishop, who was responsible for the preliminary study and report on labor and management opinions. Each of the outside contributors (listed on page v) was selected from among experts in each field, and had wide freedom in planning his chapter, within the general framework of the project, and in expressing his personal judgments.

As usual with its major studies, the Fund appointed a special committee to review the factual findings of the staff and to formulate a program of action in the public interest to deal with the problems disclosed by the research. The members of the Committee on Employment and Wages were carefully chosen so that the point of view of both labor and management should be represented by knowledgeable persons representative of each group. The Committee also includes eminent economists and others not committed to either side but intimately familiar with the field. Under the chairmanship of Lloyd K. Garrison, distinguished lawyer and formerly Chairman of the National War Labor Board, this Committee has explored some of the leading problems of wage determination and employment and has developed constructive policies to meet them.

The composition of the Committee makes its report especially important and significant. Here were leaders on both sides of some of the most hotly controversial questions of our time and others with wide experience and strong opinions of their own who owed allegiance to neither side. This group met around the table and corresponded over a period of many months with complete good will and with a common purpose of finding as much agreement as possible on future policies in the public interest. That, in itself, is heartening in these days of heightened emotional tensions. All the members signed the report. That, too, is evidence of the vitality of our democratic way of life — as are the various dissents of individual members expressed in footnotes to the report and broader supplementary statements. The divergence of these opinions highlights the unsolved problems in labor-management relations.

The Fund presents this volume in the hope that it will prove to be a storehouse of useful facts for those, both in private industry and in government, who have a practical stake in labor-management relations and for those who are less directly concerned but realize the pressing national importance of the subject. Also, the Fund hopes that the leadership which the Committee has given in its report may point the way to wider agreement between management, labor and the public on policies which are truly in the interests of the nation as a whole.

The Fund recognizes the great contribution which the Research Director and his associates and the members of the Committee have made in this crucial field and deeply appreciates their cooperation in this important venture.

EVANS CLARK, *Executive Director*
The Twentieth Century Fund

330 WEST 42 STREET
NEW YORK 36, N. Y.
FEBRUARY 2, 1953

PREFACE

This volume presents facts as the Research Director and his associates see them. Insofar as the interpretation of fact requires a definite economic philosophy, the report rests on the concept of our economy as a vigorous and dynamic system, able to grow and develop. In the light of this theory the parties which meet each other in collective bargaining appear as adversaries in the bargaining process but as partners in the broad field of production and economic progress.

The Director of the study is deeply in debt to his collaborators in this project, particularly for their cooperation in the final shaping of the report — always the most difficult task in projects of this sort. The Director is also deeply indebted to Dr. J. Frederic Dewhurst, the Fund Economist, for his advice in different phases of the project and for his critical comments on the draft of most chapters; to Mrs. Mary Ross Gannett for editorial help; to Dr. Ewan Clague, who read the whole manuscript before it went to the printer; and to the following persons who gave their comments on parts of the manuscript: Mr. Solomon Barkin, Dr. Waldo E. Fisher, Dr. Paul R. Hays, Mr. K. James Ralph, Dr. Leonard Rosenfeld.

W. S. Woytinsky
Research Director

CONTENTS

PART ONE

WAGES: THEORY, TRENDS AND OUTLOOK

PART TWO

THE INSTITUTIONAL SETTING

PART THREE

EMPLOYMENT AND UNEMPLOYMENT

PART FOUR

WAGES AND EARNINGS

COMMITTEE REPORT

APPENDICES

FIGURES

APPENDIX NOTES

APPENDIX TABLES

PART I

WAGES: THEORY, TRENDS AND OUTLOOK

PART II

THE INSTITUTIONAL SETTING

PART III

EMPLOYMENT AND UNEMPLOYMENT

PART IV

WAGES AND EARNINGS

PART I

WAGES: THEORY, TRENDS AND OUTLOOK

Chapter 1

WAGE THEORIES *

A WAGE DISPUTE is more than a clash of interests: often it is also a clash of ideas. Among labor leaders as well as among employers, opinions on the issue at stake may differ. Their judgments may be affected not only by differences in the position of each group but also by differences in appraising the situation. In the heat of a wage dispute, neither party is inclined to bring into the open doubts and dissensions within its own ranks. Conventional clichés, mutual accusations, exaggerated arguments and half-truths replace dispassionate discussion. Paul H. Douglas has applied to the field of wage disputes the words of Matthew Arnold:

> And we are here as on a darkling plain
> Swept with confused alarms of struggle and flight,
> Where ignorant armies clash by night.

Lack of a widely accepted theory of wages that could serve both parties as a common frame of reference contributes largely to "confused alarms" in wage disputes. Except for the general concept of the law of supply and demand, and the old observation of Adam Smith that "the workmen desire to get as much, the masters to give as little as possible," [1] no generally accepted theory of wages has been integrated into our social and economic philosophy. Some people even question whether wage theories contribute much to the understanding of everyday wage problems.

Clarification of certain topics related to the theory of wages, however, is essential in this report. In recent years, spokesmen of both labor and management have used theoretical arguments with great insistence in crucial labor disputes. If their supporting evidence from economic science has failed to bring a prompt settlement of the controversy, the fault may have been in the selection of arguments and the judgment of their value. On the other hand, the sound labor-management relations in many plants investigated by the National Planning Association [2] reflect acceptance by both parties of definite fundamentals in approaching the wage problem. It is true that the pattern of industrial relations depends less on theoretical principles than on the psychological climate prevailing in an industry or an individual plant — in other words, on the spirit in which labor and management approach their tasks. But agreement on fundamentals in wage theory can be a step toward establishing the desirable spirit in labor-management relations.

Wages as the Price of Labor

From a purely economic point of view, the wage is the price of labor. Like other prices, it is determined by the interplay of demand and supply, the competition between buyers and sellers, and, ultimately, the cost of reproducing the labor force. Despite this conceptual similarity, wages differ from commodity prices; for labor is unique among things that are sold, bought and priced.

Differences between Wages and Commodity Prices

The main distinction between labor and other things sold and bought in our economic system is that labor cannot be separated from the personality of the seller. When a manufacturer sells his product, the transaction ends his relationship to the object sold. But labor necessarily continues to be a part of the worker's personality.

Another important difference between wages and commodity prices is that the level of wages directly affects the welfare of the greater part of the population. Adam Smith long ago recognized the significant role of wages in the economic system. Workers, he wrote, make up by far the greater part of every great society, and

* By W. S. Woytinsky.

1. Adam Smith, *An Inquiry into the Nature and Causes of the Wealth of Nations,* Black, Edinburgh, 1863, p. 30.

2. Committee on the Causes of Industrial Peace under Collective Bargaining, Case Studies, 1948–1950.

what improves the circumstances of the greater part "can never be regarded as an inconveniency to the whole."

The third important difference between wages and prices is in the procedure for their determination. On a typical commodity market, the sellers do not approach the buyers with a request for higher prices and the buyers do not announce to the sellers the price they intend to pay. The sellers establish the prices. When they believe it to their advantage, they simply reprice their merchandise, advertising a cut in price and trying to make a raise inconspicuous. After having established the new price, they neither argue nor fight with buyers but wait and study their reaction. In manipulating prices — and, if necessary, production — the producers have a clearly defined objective, to maximize their profits.

In wage determination the procedure is very different. Unless the wage rates have been bargained collectively and determined by a contract, they are fixed by the employers as buyers of services. The workers, as sellers, then must choose between accepting the job at the wage offered or rejecting it. In practice, the choice is made either through labor turnover, when workers leave underpaid and unattractive jobs for better positions, or through collective walkouts — a feature of wage determination that has no exact parallel in the formation of prices on commodity markets.

When we speak about the struggle between sellers and buyers on a commodity market, the word "struggle" is used metaphorically. Normally, relations between sellers and buyers in a department store or a corner grocery have nothing in common with the strife characteristic of wage negotiations. This contrast in the psychology of the parties in price and wage determination is illustrated by a comparison of the walkout of an angry housewife from a store with the walkout of embittered workers from a plant.

Theoretically, a walkout of workers or a general lockout means that because of lack of agreement between the buyers and the sellers of labor, the purchase cannot be carried through, just as happens when a grocer refuses to sell a housewife a pound of butter at the price she is willing to pay. But the economic and social implications of the two situations differ greatly. Rarely does the disagreement between the grocer and the housewife become of concern to the community. A walkout of workers, however, often affects a wide circle of persons who are not directly involved in the dispute. A strike may eventually disorganize and paralyze the economic life of the nation. In planning a walkout a labor union naturally picks the time and the place that give it the best chance to win. Its strategy is to strike in such a way as to cause the most harm to the other party, and the "other party" may eventually include the whole community.

A strike, of course, is an expensive and wasteful method of settling a dispute. Often a strike costs both parties many times the value of the object of their disagreement.

Few dislike strikes more than the leaders of strong and firmly established unions. The situation is somewhat different in unions that want to display their strength and resoluteness before their rank-and-file members, their employers and the public. Even such unions, however, are as reluctant to assume responsibility for a strike as employers are reluctant to take responsibility for a lockout. Thus mutual accusations of unwillingness to bargain in good faith and to try to understand the other party have become common in labor conflicts.

From a broader point of view, however, collective bargaining appears pointless unless each party is entitled to reject the other's offer. The threat of an interruption in the employment relationship is ultimately the principal factor that compels each party to listen to the opposing arguments and to make concessions. This threat is somewhat analogous to a producer's risk of losing outlets for his merchandise if his price is too high.

The special role of wages as contrasted to other prices in our economic system is reflected in the attitude of the government toward wage determination. Apart from national emergencies and the support of certain prices by tariffs and subsidies, the government does not interfere directly in setting prices, least of all in their downward revision by producers. But it does participate in the procedures leading to the setting of wages. Without assuming direct responsibility for particular wage rates, it requires that contracts be negotiated in good faith, agreed on, signed and honored by both parties, and renewed at the proper time. The government also prohibits the hiring of children, limits employment of women, prescribes "fair labor practices," establishes minimum wages, supervises work conditions, and so on.[3]

Most of these matters can also be settled by union agreements. By making them the subject of legislation and administrative regulation, society excludes them from the scope of negotiation between labor and management.

The mechanism of wage determination is also affected by the character of the bargaining parties. The modern labor union as a party in collective bargaining has no counterpart on the commodity markets. It is not a collective seller of labor but, rather, a political body representing individual workers, speaking and signing — with certain exceptions — in their name. Although its main function is traditionally wage negotiation, it also keeps other objectives in sight. Its ultimate aim is neither to maximize the total take-home pay of all workers nor to maximize wage rates or employment.[4] The aim includes, rather, growth and perpetuation of the union's influence among workers and defense of its prestige in the community.

As time goes on, the purely political functions of labor unions, supported by educational campaigns and outright propaganda, become increasingly important. A union discovers that sometimes it can do more for its members through use of its political weight than through negotiations with employers. On the other hand, employers, conscious of the goals of union policy, develop a strategy of wage negotiation sometimes aimed at weakening the union, sometimes toward using the union's influence for stabilizing industrial relations. They also learn to use the political influence of unions in support of their own claims upon Congress and the current administration. Thus, the simple test of bargaining power over the negotiation table becomes a complicated game in which each side has a great variety of possible moves.

To sum up, the particular characteristics of labor and wages, compared with other commodities and prices, make the labor market distinctly different from commodity markets. So deep are these divergences that the general theory of prices proves insufficient, and in many cases useless, for understanding labor market phenomena.

3. Cf. Chapters 11–17.
4. A. M. Ross, "The Trade Union as a Wage-Fixing Institution," *American Economic Review,* September 1947, and "Dynamics of Wage Determination under Collective Bargaining," *American Economic Review,* December 1947.

Origin of Conflicting Wage Theories

Wages and prices differ in still another important way. The relationship between seller and buyer on a commodity market is comparatively simple, while the relationship between labor and management is extremely complicated and changes as time goes on.

In the eighteenth century the terms "workers" and "the poor" were synonymous. In our times, labor signs itself with a capital L and is a leading power in our society. These extremes are separated by long years of social and political strain. Disputes over the theory of wages in this period have reflected the clashes between labor and capital. It is natural that the wish has been father to the thought in doctrines developed in the heat of conflict. When labor and management have coined slogans and developed theories in support of their claims, they have often used the same words with different meanings and have cited the same facts but interpreted them differently.

Conflicting wage theories can best be understood in relation to the conditions under which they were born. Wage theories developed in periods of economic stagnation, at times of great pressure from overpopulation and growing poverty, differ basically from wage theories formulated in an expanding economy. Similarly, wage theories originated in the heat of violent class struggles are very different from those that answer problems of a democratic community in which labor is a stout supporter of freedom and order.

The succession of wage theories in the past two centuries may seem chaotic. The same ideas, with minor variations in wording, have appeared on the scene, sunk into oblivion, and returned to life. The same theories, with variations in details, have been used by labor as arguments against management and by management as arguments against unions. The picture becomes less chaotic when wage theories are classified in accordance with the economic and social climate in which they were conceived and developed.

Types of Wage Theories

A wage theory always deals with two groups of problems: the over-all level of wages, and differentials in the remuneration of various groups of workers. The emphasis can shift from one issue to another, but the general scope of the questions remains the same.

To answer these questions an economist must study and interpret the facts. The broader his field of observation, the greater the probability that he will give different interpretations to different groups of facts. If he is good enough to be remembered in textbooks, he will be classified as an eclectic in the same niche with Adam Smith, in whose works at least five conflicting doctrines have been traced — doctrines centering on the subsistence minimum, the wage fund, exploitation, bargaining and productivity.

The question arises whether these doctrines are distinctly different theories of wages, each one standing on its own feet, or only generalizations that supplement one another.

Take, for instance, the doctrine of the "subsistence minimum." It is rooted in the soil of France, where it was originally developed by the Physiocrats, long before the great revolution. Adam Smith mentioned it casually, along with other observations on the behavior of wages. Malthus made it a part of his gloomy picture of mankind condemned to misery because of the tendency of population to grow faster than the means of subsistence. Lassalle converted it into a weapon for fighting the capitalist society. It has since served as a part of various theories critical of the existing system. Obviously, in the long list of subsistence-wage theories, only the name of the doctrine has remained the same, while its meaning has undergone fundamental changes.

Different interpretations have also been given to the "bargaining" doctrine, which has appeared in the history of economic thought sometimes as a simple description of the mechanism of wage determination (Adam Smith), sometimes as a marching song of labor unions, and sometimes as an accusation that unions are undermining the economic system.

History shows a similar course for wage doctrines centering on the "wage fund" and on "productivity."

To make sense, the classification of wage theories should be based, not on the emphasis they give to the different factors in wage determination, but on their relation to trends in wages. The fundamental distinction is between theories of economic growth and theories of economic stagnation.

This distinction is crossed, however, by another cleavage — the theories' relation to the clash of interests in wage determination. An economist can align himself with management or espouse the cause of labor or try to keep himself aloof from both. All three attitudes can be professed by both optimistic and pessimistic wage theorists.

WAGE THEORIES OF THE CLASSICAL SCHOOL

The classical school of economics was divided between optimistic and pessimistic appraisals of the new industrial system. Adam Smith was the troubadour of the triumphal advance of capitalism, and *The Wealth of Nations* (1776) is full of exuberant optimism. David Ricardo and Malthus were spokesmen of the gloom that prevailed in England at the time of the French Revolution and the Napoleonic Wars. Nassau Senior marked the return of prosperity and the revival of optimism.

Adam Smith

Despite its primitive techniques of production and transportation, the economic system described by Adam Smith has much in common with the modern economy. It is full of dynamism, contradictions and hopes, and this quality makes the author's views particularly interesting to modern readers.

Adam Smith did not think much of the subsistence-wage doctrine universally accepted by his predecessors.[5] For him, the tendency of wages to fall to the subsistence minimum was self-evident, but only as one of many tendencies that are checked by other forces.

After casual mention of the subsistence-wage theory, Adam Smith remarks:

> There are certain circumstances, however, which sometimes give the labourers an advantage, and enable them to raise their wages considerably above [the subsistence] rate; evidently the lowest which is consistent with common humanity.[6]

He then describes such circumstances. He first rejects the notion that wages are raised artificially by "combinations" of workers.

> The masters, being fewer in number, can combine much more easily. . . . We rarely hear . . . of the combinations of masters, though frequently of those of workmen. But whoever imagines, upon this account, that masters rarely combine, is as ignorant of the world as of the subject. Masters are always and everywhere in a sort of tacit, but constant and uniform combination, not to raise the wages of labour above their

5. See Appendix Note 1.
6. Smith, *op. cit.,* p. 31.

actual rate. . . . We seldom . . . hear of this combination, because it is the usual, and one may say, the natural state of things, which nobody ever hears of. Masters too sometimes enter into particular combinations to sink the wages of labour even below this rate. These are always conducted with the utmost silence and secrecy, till the moment of execution, and when the workmen yield, as they sometimes do, without resistance, though severely felt by them, they are never heard of by other people. Such combinations, however, are frequently resisted by a contrary defensive combination of the workmen; who sometimes too, without any provocation of this kind, combine of their own accord to raise the price of their labour. Their usual pretenses are sometimes the high price of provisions; sometimes the great profit their masters make by their work. But whether their combinations be offensive or defensive, they are always abundantly heard of.[7]

All in all, Adam Smith concludes, "in disputes with their workmen, masters must generally have the advantage." And yet wages tend to rise above the subsistence level. They rise for the simple reason that "the demand for those who live by wages . . . increases with the increase of national wealth . . ." [8] "The liberal reward of labour . . . , as it is the necessary effect, so it is the natural symptom of increasing national wealth." [9]

Thus, without discarding the old subsistence theory, Smith gave it a new interpretation.

Every species of animals naturally multiplies in proportion to the means of their subsistence. . . . The liberal reward of labour, by enabling them to provide better for their children, and consequently to bring up a greater number, naturally tends to widen and extend those limits. . . . It is in this manner that the demand for men, like that for any other commodity, necessarily regulates the production of men . . .[10]

To the population argument in support of high wages, Adam Smith adds the efficiency argument.

The liberal reward of labour, as it encourages the propagation, so it increases the industry of the common people. . . . A plentiful subsistence increases the bodily strength of the labourer; and the comfortable hope of bettering his condition, and of ending his days perhaps in ease and plenty, animates him to exert that strength to the utmost. Where wages are high, accordingly, we shall always find the workmen more active, diligent, and expeditious, than where they are low . . .[11]

7. *Ibid.,* p. 30.
8. *Ibid.,* p. 31.
9. *Ibid.,* p. 33.
10. *Ibid.,* p. 36.
11. *Ibid.,* p. 37.

Smith's approach to the doctrine of the wage fund was characterized by the same optimistic and dynamic spirit.

It is evident [that] the demand for those who live by wages . . . cannot increase but in proportion to the increase of the funds which are destined for the payment of wages. These funds are of two kinds; first, the revenue [of employers] which is over and above what is necessary for the maintenance [of their families]; and, secondly, the stock [of independent workmen] which is over and above what is . . . sufficient to purchase the materials of [their] own work and to maintain [themselves].[12]

Thus, the total amount of wages received by workers is determined by the amount of money employers are willing to spend on labor. This fact does not preclude the possibility that wages will rise as time goes on, but it implies that there is always a fairly rigid limit to their rise. As Adam Smith put it, "the demand for those who live by wages [that is, the fund available for payment of wages] . . . necessarily increases with the increase of the revenue and stock of every country, and cannot possibly increase without it." [13]

Nassau Senior

The wage-fund doctrine was further elaborated by Nassau Senior half a century later. In his "Lectures on the Rate of Wages," Senior starts with this definition:

The quantity and quality of the commodities obtained by each labouring family during a year must depend on the quantity and quality of the commodities directly or indirectly appropriated during the year to the use of the labouring families . . .; or, to speak more concisely, *on the Extent of the Fund for maintenance of Labourers, compared with the Number of Labourers, to be maintained.*[14]

It will be noticed that Senior speaks here of *real* wages and visualizes the wage fund as the workers' share in current production. He rejects as fallacious the contention that wage rates are determined by the ratio of the amount of capital or total national product to the number of workers.[15] He denies that the rate of wages is diminished by the introduction of ma-

12. *Ibid.,* p. 31.
13. *Loc. cit.*
14. Nassau William Senior, "Three Lectures on the Rate of Wages," delivered before the University of Oxford in Easter term, 1830, Murray, London, 1831, p. 19. The same statement (with the last part of the sentence italicized) is repeated in Senior's *Political Economy,* Griffin, London, 1850, p. 153.
15. *Political Economy,* p. 154.

chinery[16] or by the importation of foreign commodities.[17] He condemns the theory that the unproductive consumption of landlords and capitalists is beneficial to the laboring classes because it furnishes them with employment.[18] Senior insists that the wage fund is determined by two factors, and only two: (1) the productiveness of labor in the direct or indirect production of the commodities used by the laborer; and (2) the number of persons directly or indirectly employed in the production of these commodities.[19]

Senior's wage-fund theory is so close to modern economic thinking that one is surprised to find it in a time-yellowed tiny volume bearing the name of a man who became widely known as the spokesman of big business.

Senior in this phase of his career was representative, however, of the great economic writers of the first half of the nineteenth century. They were aloof from the clashes between workers and masters and more often than not sympathized with the underdogs.

The situation changed in the middle of the century under the impact of Chartism in England, the revolutionary upheavals in continental Europe in 1848, and the emergence of the socialist movement. This period was surprisingly lacking in developments in economic science, especially in wage theory.

WAGE THEORIES IN AN EXPANDING ECONOMY

In the latter part of the nineteenth century, American writers developed some new ideas on the theory of wages. Francis Walker was the most outstanding among them.

Francis Walker

Walker's wage theory was originally developed as a rebuttal of the notion that the rise of wages is limited by the amount of money employers have for hiring workers[20] and rested on American experience.

Of the wage-fund theory he said:

> That English writers should have been misled, by what they saw going on around them, into converting a generalization of insular experience into a universal law of wages, is not greatly to be wondered at. But that American writers should have adopted this doctrine, in simple contempt of what they saw going on around them, is, indeed, surprising.[21]

The core of Walker's theory was that wages are paid, not from capital, but from current product. Capital and current product oppose each other as the past, "whose accumulations have been plundered by class legislation and wasted by dynastic wars," opposes the present and the future, "always larger, freer, and more fortunate." For Walker, this was more than a literary flourish.

> If capital furnishes the measure of wages [he contended], then . . . no increase of energy, intelligence, and enterprise on the part of the laboring class can add to, as no failure on their part can take from, their present remuneration . . . If production furnishes the measure of wages . . . then the wage classes are entitled to the immediate benefit of every improvement in science and art, every discovery of resources in nature, every advance in their own industrial character.[22]

This concept of the source of wages was the cornerstone of Walker's social philosophy:

> Every invention in mechanics, every discovery in the chemical art, no matter by whom made, inures directly and immediately to [the] benefit [of workers], except so far as a limited monopoly may be created by law, for the encouragement of invention and discovery.[23]

Alfred Marshall

Similar ideas, but in a more generalized form and without the pro-labor bias with which Walker could be charged, were developed by Alfred Marshall, head of the neoclassical school of theoretical economics in Great Britain.[24] He introduced the modern mathematical technique used in analyzing shifts and changes in the economic system. A discussion of his full contribution to economic science is, however, outside the scope of the present study.

Marshall approached the problem of wages as one of a continually changing distribution of an increasing social dividend:

> Our growing power over nature makes her yield an ever larger surplus above necessaries; and this is not

16. *Ibid.,* pp. 162–68.
17. *Ibid.,* p. 168.
18. *Ibid.,* pp. 169–73.
19. *Ibid.,* p. 174.
20. This was the wage-fund theory as formulated — and later abandoned — by John Stuart Mill. Expressed in this way, the theory had nothing in common with the ideas of Senior on the "real" fund of wages.
21. Francis Walker, *The Wages Question: A Treatise on Wages and the Wages Class,* Holt, New York, 1891 (originally published in 1876), p. 142.
22. *Ibid.,* p. 411.
23. Francis Walker, *Political Economy,* 3d edition, Holt, New York, 1888, p. 251.
24. Alfred Marshall, *Principles of Economics,* 8th edition, Macmillan, London, 1920.

absorbed by an unlimited increase of the population. There remain therefore the questions: What are the general causes which govern the distribution of this surplus among the people? . . . What share of the general flow is turned to remunerate [labor]? [25]

Marshall answered the question of how the national dividend is distributed by the so-called marginal-value theory.

The alert business man is ever seeking for the most profitable application of his resources, and endeavouring to make use of each agent of production up to that margin, or limit, at which he would gain by transferring a small part of his expenditure to some other agent. [This] principle of substitution so adjusts the employment of each agent that, in its marginal application, its cost is proportionate to the additional net product resulting from its use.[26]

Because of these continual adjustments the wages of every class of labor tend to be equal to the net product due to the additional labor of the marginal laborer of that class. In other words, a businessman, before spending an additional $1,000, tries to figure out what use of his money promises the largest net return: hiring new workers, purchasing new tools or equipment, or using the money for some other purpose.

Marshall recognized that this general law of wages has by itself no real meaning; for in order to estimate the net return of a new outlay, the businessman has to take into consideration all the conditions of production other than wages — alternative outlay on tools and so on.[27] But he thought that the mechanism of adjustment of wages and other expenses was properly described by the principle that "every agent of production, land, machinery, skilled labor, unskilled labor, etc., tends to be applied in production as far as it profitably can be." [28]

Marshall was no less an advocate of high wages than was Adam Smith. He pointed out that continually rising wages not only tend to increase the efficiency of labor and to augment the national product, but also contribute to the growth of a healthy and vigorous population and meet the moral requirements vital for our civilization.

Marshall's marginal theory implies that the level of the wages of each group of workers and the average level of earnings of the working classes are determined by conditions of production — more specifically, by the relative contributions of the various factors used in production. If wages rise above this level, employment of marginal workers becomes uneconomical for the owners of capital, and employment is bound to decline.

Without minimizing the clash of interests of owners and workers over the distribution of the national dividend, the marginal-value theory stresses the identity of their interests in the field of production:

Capital in general and labor in general co-operate in the production of the national dividend, and draw from it their earnings in the measure of their respective [marginal] efficiencies. Their mutual dependence is of the closest; capital without labor is dead; the laborer without the aid of his own or someone else's capital would not long be alive. Where labor is energetic, capital reaps a high reward and grows apace; and, thanks to capital and knowledge, the ordinary laborer in the western world is in many respects better fed, clothed and even housed than were princes in earlier times. . . . The prosperity of each [capital and labor] is bound up with the strength and activity of the other; though each may gain temporarily, if not permanently, a somewhat larger share of the national dividend at the expense of the other.[29]

The marginal-productivity theory of wage determination has found wide acceptance in recent years all over the world. In the United States it has been carried forward and developed by many distinguished economists, among whom Paul H. Douglas [30] is probably the best known.

THEORY OF COLLECTIVE BARGAINING

The marginal-value theory has become the starting point of almost every discussion on wage theory in recent years and, with some reservation, may be regarded as the modern version of the classical supply-and-demand formula. Its wide acceptance, however, does not eliminate controversy about such problems as labor unions, collective bargaining, strikes and arbitration of labor disputes — problems interwoven with wage determination not only in everyday practice but also in theory.

Nearly all wage theorists since Adam Smith have noticed the effect of "combinations" on wage determination. For the author of *The Wealth of Nations,* collective action of workers and of masters was part of the normal contest between buyers and sellers. His successors were

25. *Ibid.,* p. 504.
26. *Ibid.,* pp. 514–15.
27. *Ibid.,* p. 518.
28. *Ibid.,* p. 521.
29. *Ibid.,* p. 544.
30. See Appendix Note 1.

more inclined to stress the negative role of workers' combinations in restricting the free play of demand and supply. With the growth of labor unions, a reappraisal of their role in wage determination became urgently necessary. The theory of collective bargaining developed in this country by John Bates Clark met this need.[31]

John Bates Clark

Clark's theory was inspired by economic progress in the United States, activities of the Knights of Labor, and rising wages.

> The historical fact of the past three hundred and fifty years [he wrote] has been that real wages have declined for three centuries and advanced for a half century. . . . There has been a vast increase in the quantity of wealth produced; and this fact may have sufficed to increase the laborer's reward without any enlargement of his proportionate share of the [product]. Whether the division is, at the present day, taking place on terms more favorable to the laborer than those which ruled fifty years ago is of far less consequence than the question whether the present principle of division is one which must yield permanently better results than the old one. That real wages are high this year is of little importance in comparison with the fact that they are adjusted by a process which promises to make them higher next year, and still higher in the years following . . .[32]

In a modern democratic society, wages are determined, according to Clark, by collective bargaining by labor unions, in contrast to individual bargaining by workers in the past.

> The old principle of division rendered gross injustice inevitable; the present principle makes equity possible. . . . A maximum of justice in distribution is attained where the brute forces are evenly matched, and where moral influences are efficient. A minimum of justice results where brute forces are unequal, and moral forces wanting.[33]

Using the same argument as Smith, Clark points out that without organization workmen cannot resist the pressure of capitalists, and he concludes: "The distributive phenomena of the past have been distinctly those of unbalanced competition." [34] The worker's condition has improved in the past half century, thanks to

> centralization and an intense struggle for existence. Of the two possible causes of higher wages both have been in action in recent years; there has been more to divide, and the division has been made under more equal conditions. . . . Massed labor has been pitted against massed capital. . . . The equality has been secured, not by restoring competition on the side of capital, but by suppressing it on the side of labor.[35]

Clark was aware of the dangers of ultimate "centralization."

> [If] one corporation produced the entire supply of a particular article, while a trades union controlled the entire labor force available for its production, actual competition would be at an end. . . . The adjustment, if left to be effected by crude force, would produce disturbances too disastrous to be tolerated, and arbitration on a comprehensive scale would be a prime necessity.[36]

He stressed the fact that combinations of workers, despite their growing strength, still lagged behind the concentration of capital. Employers, he pointed out, can counter the demand for a wage increase by curtailing production, and

> the reaction of this fact upon the reward of labor is direct and resistless; no combination of workmen can undo the depressive effect upon their own wages of the presence of a large force of idle men. Upon the men thrown out of employment the effect of curtailed production is obvious; it is equally so upon society. It means pauperism, crime, embittered contests, and an added strain upon republicanism. . . . The only outcome consistent with peace will be arbitration under governmental authority. . . . The problem of the future is the extent to which movements now in progress will actually go. . . .
>
> The present state of industrial society is transitional and chaotic. . . . The relation between "capital and labor" is not what it was yesterday, nor what it will be tomorrow. The crudeness of the transitional system has begotten lawlessness. . . . Individual competition . . . has . . . practically disappeared. It ought to disappear; it was, in its latter days, incapable of working justice. The alternative regulator is moral force, and this is already in action . . . though it is in the infancy of its distinctively social development. The system of individualistic competition was a tolerated and regulated reign of force; solidarity, even in its present crude state, presents the beginning of a reign of law.[37]

In stressing collective bargaining as the central problem of wage theory, John Bates Clark was half a century ahead of his time.

A. C. Pigou

Just as Walker and Marshall both contributed to the development of the modern concept of wages as the share of labor in current, continu-

31. John Bates Clark, *The Philosophy of Wealth, Economic Principles Newly Formulated,* 2d edition, Ginn, Boston, 1892.
32. *Ibid.,* pp. 131–32.
33. *Ibid.,* p. 132.
34. *Ibid.,* p. 133.
35. *Ibid.,* pp. 134–35.
36. *Ibid.,* p. 137.
37. *Ibid.,* pp. 147–48.

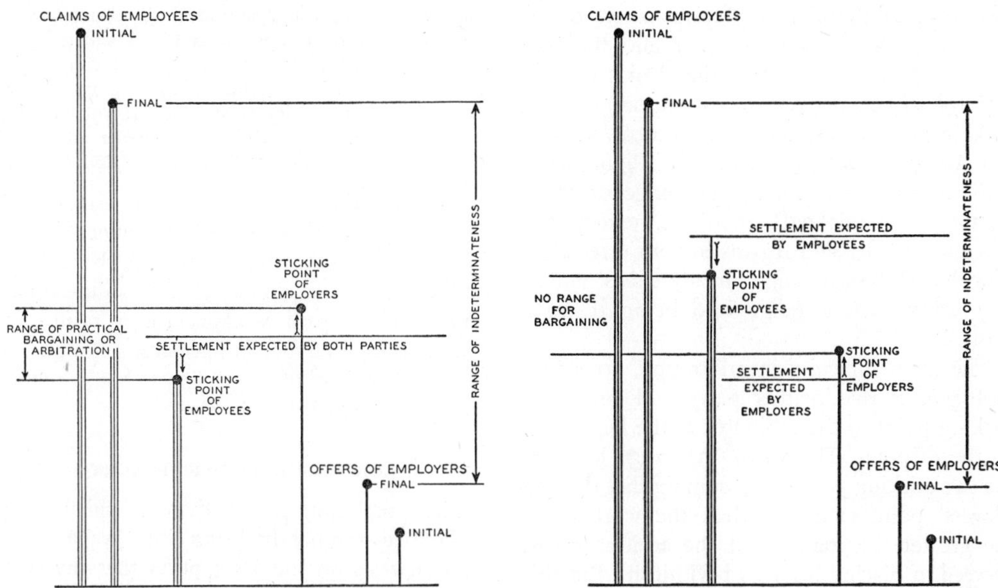

A. Identical Expectations of Employees and Employers B. Divergent Expectations of Employees and Employers

FIGURE 1. MECHANISM OF WAGE NEGOTIATION

This figure illustrates two typical situations in wage disputes, according to Pigou's theory. In both cases, the dispute starts from initial claims and offers, which are soon replaced by final claims and offers. The gap between final claims and offers is described as the *range of indeterminateness*.

In case A, both parties expect the same settlement in the event of a strike. The *sticking point* of employers is somewhat above the anticipated level of settlement; the *sticking point* of workers is somewhat below this level. The distance between the two points represents the range of practical bargaining or arbitration.

In case B, the anticipations of the two parties are far apart, perhaps because they suspect each other of bluffing. Therefore the *sticking point* of employees is much higher than that of employers and there is no range for bargaining.

ally growing production, so the theory of collective bargaining originally formulated by Clark was elaborated and presented in a generalized form much later by the British scholar, A. C. Pigou.

Collective bargaining of wages starts, according to Pigou, from a *range of indeterminateness* between the rates desired by union and employer. The upper limit of workers' claims is set by fear of the adverse effect of an excessive raise of wages on employment. The lower limit of wage rates desired by employers is determined by the possible adverse effect of extremely low rates on the supply of labor. Besides these limits, each party has, at the opening of negotiation, a *sticking point* beyond which it does not intend to retreat without a fight. For workers, this point is usually lower than their claims; for employers, it is higher than their offer.[38] When the workers' sticking point is lower than the employers', the range between the two points constitutes the *range of practical bargaining*. (See Figure 1, A.) When, however, the sticking point of workers is higher than that of employers, the issue cannot be settled without a fight. (See Figure 1, B.)

If both sides have similar expectations about the way in which the fight will end, the sticking point of workers must be lower than that of employers, the range between them being determined by the anticipated cost of the fight to both parties. But an inverse situation develops when the anticipations of the two parties are widely different — for example, when each party suspects the other of bluffing or when one side seeks a showdown in the hope of weakening the other side. In this event, the sticking point of the workers is likely to be higher than that of the employers, and there is no range for either practical bargaining or arbitration.

Usually, the rising strength of labor unions, by increasing the cost of the fight to employers and improving the workers' chance of success, tends to raise both sticking points. Similarly,

38. Of course, each party may change its views on the sticking point as negotiations go on.

the rising strength of employers lowers them. If both parties become stronger and the cost of the fight increases while the chance of success for either party remains unchanged, the sticking point of workers moves downward and that of employers upward. As Pigou says, "Within the limits set by the range of indeterminateness this will, therefore, extend the range of practicable bargains in both directions, provided that such range already exists, and it may bring such a range into being if none exists."

The main difficulty in arbitration, according to Pigou, is that neither party will reveal its sticking point to the arbitrator at the beginning of the dispute. The wider the range between the two sticking points — assuming that the employers' point is higher than the workers' — the greater the chance that the arbitrator will succeed in placing his award within it. But this is not always the outcome in negotiations in which both parties are bluffing.[39]

Pigou terms wages "fair" if they conform to the marginal-utility theory, that is, if they are equal to the value of the marginal net product of a group of workers.[40] He believes that an artificial raise of "fair" wages, in the specified sense of the term — even if they are below the "living wage" level — would be detrimental to the social dividend, but he argues strongly for raising "unfair" wages.

Pigou distinguishes two types of unfair wages: (1) wages that, though not below the marginal net product of the particular group of workers, are lower than the marginal product of similar workers elsewhere in the nation, that is, lower than "fair" wages of other workers with similar qualifications; (2) wages lower than the marginal net product of the workers to whom they are paid. In both such cases a raise in wages promotes the general welfare.

> In the first case, interference designed to force wages up to the fair level benefits the national dividend by contributing to a better distribution of employment among industries and enterprises. [In the second,] if the exploiting employers were persons of the ordinary competence of their grade, interference, which forced up the wages paid by them to the fair level, would simply compel them to hand over to workpeople profits formerly exacted from them. . . . As a matter of fact, however, exploitation of this kind is much more often practiced by incompetent or badly situated employers, who, without it, could not maintain themselves in business, than by competent and well-situated men . . . and the prevention of exploitation would tend to hasten their defeat at the hands of more efficient rivals. . . . External interference to prevent that type [of exploitation] . . . is desirable in the interest of the national dividend as well as upon other grounds.[41]

To use the language of collective bargaining, Pigou rejects the low-profit argument in defense of low wages but recognizes the validity of the high-profit argument as justification of claims of low-paid workers for a raise. He stresses the point that in bargaining, unions, to ensure a fair level of wages, must claim amounts appreciably above this level.

PURCHASING-POWER THEORY

The purchasing-power theory, which labor spokesmen frequently bring into wage negotiations, rests on the assumption that the community as a whole is interested in full employment and an adequate flow of purchasing power. Since workers generally spend all their earnings for necessaries of life, the argument goes, each dollar in the wage envelope represents active purchasing power. Capitalists, on the other hand, spend part of their profits and put part aside as savings. The spokesmen for this theory argue that wage increases and curtailment of profits are therefore the best defense against unemployment and depression, and that rising unemployment is a proof that wages must be adjusted upward.

Although this reasoning is often labeled as the wage theory of labor unions, it can hardly be considered a theory at all. In fact, all its tenets are questionable. Workers do not necessarily spend all their earnings, and there is no extravagance in their claim for wages that will permit them some savings either for a rainy day or for durable goods — for example, for the purchase of a home ("saving-wages," as William Green has called them). On the other hand, outlays of employers, including investments, often exceed their current profits. A shift of money from employers' pockets to workers' will not necessarily increase the active purchasing power in the community.

An increase of wages in relation to profits may be desirable for the "general welfare" or for other reasons. But if this is so, the arguments in favor of a new pattern of distribution

39. A. C. Pigou, *The Economics of Welfare,* 4th edition, Macmillan, London, 1933, pp. 450–61.
40. *Ibid.,* p. 549.
41. *Ibid.,* p. 563.

of the national income should be made clear and discussed on their merits. Indeed, such arguments may prove convincing to those who reject the purchasing-power theory of wages as fallacious.

Four Principles of Wage Theory

The preceding survey of the wage theories that have been offered by leading economists in the past two centuries is limited to theories that presume an expanding economy and can be applied, therefore, to our time — a period of economic growth.[42] Despite its fragmentary character, however, this survey permits some few generalizations.

It shows that the controversies of our day in the field of wage theory are not new. Discussion of such problems as subsistence minimum, fair and unfair wages, the origin of wage differentials, exploitation, "combinations," surplus workers, unrestricted or limited competition, strikes, the interference of government in labor disputes, and so on is very old indeed. As time goes on, these controversial issues change their form and appear in new guises. The transformation takes place so slowly, however, that we continue to use old terms in speaking of phenomena that, in the words of John Bates Clark, are no longer what they were yesterday or what they will be tomorrow.

42. For wage theories based on the ideas of economic stagnation and unavoidable collapse, see Appendix Note 1.

Moreover, all wage theories based on belief in the dynamic character of the economic system have much in common. They agree, in fact, on four principles:

First, that wages represent the share of labor in the continually growing social product and rise with the growth of production.

Second, that wages are not paid out of some special fund, profits, or any source whatever other than current production.

Third, that, despite the special character of the labor force as compared with commodities bought and sold in our economic system, wages as the price of labor are controlled by the same economic forces as other prices — the interplay of supply and demand, reproduction cost, marginal utility, bargaining power.

Fourth, that labor unions ("combinations" in the time of Adam Smith) are the mainspring that moves the mechanism of supply and demand in wage determination.

A long list of great names — from Adam Smith and Nassau Senior to Marshall and Pigou — can be called as witnesses in support of these four principles. Each of the principles summarizes a long chain of observations; each suggests definite conclusions. On the other hand, these principles do not in themselves show how high the wages of this or that group of workers should be; nor do they show what is fair or unfair in the existing wage structure or in the claims of labor and the counteroffers of employers.

Chapter 2

THE POSTWAR ECONOMY *

The contrasting views of Adam Smith and Malthus, Ricardo and Marshall were determined largely by changes in the economic climate of England. In the United States the prosperity of the 1920's brought an outburst of untempered optimism in our economic literature; the great depression gave rise to the theory of economic maturity; the postwar boom has revived ideas of the predepression era. Our approach to wage problems in the coming decade or two will likewise be determined by the economic climate of that time.

We cannot visualize that future in terms of year-to-year estimates of employment, production, prices, wages, profits and so on; the unknown factors are too numerous, and the margin of error in such forecasts is too wide. Experience in economic forecasting during the past decade is not encouraging. Most of the predictions proved so completely off the beam that it is difficult now to give credit even for the estimates that have been vindicated by events: May they not have been right for the wrong reasons or by pure coincidence?

Long-range economic predictions are particularly dangerous. There is no way to foresee the international conditions that will determine this country's exports and its outlays for defense. There is likewise no way to predict taxes, management of the national debt, behavior of labor unions, attitudes of the business community, and so on. We can assume the usual succession of ups and downs in the volume of economic activities, but uncertainty remains about such questions as when a setback will come, how long it will last, when the revival will begin, and how soon a new downturn will follow.

In view of these limitations of economic forecasting, the following discussion is restricted to the most general features of the present economic era.

Economic Growth or Stagnation

In recent years the emphasis in public discussion of the economic outlook has changed repeatedly. When World War II was coming to an end, discussion centered about the question, How severe will unemployment be after munitions factories are closed and 12 million men are released from the armed forces? Next, attention shifted to the question, How long can the inflationary boom last? In 1949, when a depression seemed to be around the corner, the problem appeared to be, How severe will the depression be and how long will it last?

Now in the 1950's, for the first time since the end of the war, perhaps for the first time since the economic collapse in 1929, there is broad consensus among economic experts that our economic system is in good shape and that the outlook, at least for the near future, is decidedly favorable. For wage policy, the crucial question is whether the prosperity will last, with minor setbacks, a comparatively long time, say a decade or two, or whether it is a purely temporary phenomenon and will be succeeded by a long spell of economic stagnation and mass unemployment. In other words, the question whether our economy is still growing or has passed the peak is far from new. As early as 1776, Adam Smith wrote in *The Wealth of Nations:*

> During the past hundred years, five years have seldom passed away in which some book or pamphlet has not been published . . . pretending to demonstrate that the wealth of the nation was fast declining, that the country was depopulated, agriculture neglected, manufactures decaying, and trade undone. Nor have these publications been all party pamphlets, the wretched offspring of falsehood and venality: Many of them have been written by very candid and very intelligent people, who wrote nothing but what they believed, and for no other reason but because they believed it.[1]

Belief that the English economy was decaying rested on the observation of "the declension either of certain branches of industry or of certain districts of the country, things which sometimes happen though the country in general be in great prosperity." [2]

* By W. S. Woytinsky.

1. Adam Smith, *An Inquiry into the Nature and Causes of the Wealth of Nations,* Black, Edinburgh, 1863, p. 14.
2. *Ibid.*

In the 1930's such declines occurred in the United States on an unprecedented scale in all industries and all districts, and the unexpectedness of the setbacks greatly strengthened their impact on public opinion. The Committee on Recent Economic Changes expressed the opinion then prevailing in the nation when it declared in 1929, in its report to the President's Conference on Unemployment:

> We have the power to produce and the capital to bring about exchange between the producing and consuming groups. We have communication to speed and spread the influence of ideas. We have swift and dependable transportation. We have an educational system which is steadily raising standards and improving tastes. We have the sciences and arts to help us. We have a great national opportunity. . . . We seem only to have touched the fringe of our potentialities. . . . Our situation is fortunate, our momentum is remarkable.[3]

The printer's ink in the report to the Conference was still wet when the collapse of the New York stock market announced a sharp turn of the road. The nation awoke to the realization that it was living in a fog of unwarranted self-confidence and self-admiration. The shock was painful. Prosperity appeared, in retrospect, as a mirage. Mass unemployment, an economic system disorganized and unable to recover its balance, scarcity and privation in the midst of powerful but idle means of production — these made up the bitter reality.

From this disillusionment was born the theory of economic maturity and stagnation, the theory that the United States had reached a stage of development at which its economy could no longer employ all its available labor force and make full use of natural resources; that from then on, it was condemned to chronic depression unless its equilibrium was maintained by artificial measures.

Alvin H. Hansen, the most influential proponent of this theory, pointed to four characteristics as indicating economic maturity: the rapid decline in population growth; the decline in outlets for investments in the frontier regions and abroad; the absence of new industries requiring substantial investments; and the tendency of the wealthy groups of population to put aside more money than capital formation could currently absorb.[4]

It is obvious, however, that the validity of the theory did not depend on the validity of all four characteristics. The essential point was the contention that, for one reason or another, the United States had reached a stage of development at which its economy could not expand fast enough to absorb its growing labor force. Such a statement would be valid if it were shown that in the coming years no jobs were in sight for the annual addition to the labor force and for workers replaced by machines. But such a contention can hardly be substantiated.

The Population Factor

The controversy about the economic repercussions of a growing or a declining population cannot be settled here. For the purpose of the present study, it suffices to examine recent trends in population growth in the United States.

Population growth in this country tended to taper off until the middle of the 1930's, but since then the trend has been upward. The birth rate shrank from 25 per thousand population at the time of World War I to less than 17 per thousand in 1935–1936. Then came an upturn: by 1941 the birth rate regained all the loss it had incurred since 1929. In 1946 it was at the level of 1919–1920 and in 1947 it was higher than at any time since 1914; it dropped only slightly in 1948–1950 and was rising again in 1951. (See Appendix Table 1 and Figure 2.) Extrapolation of the trend for 1915–1935 gives a rate for 1949 close to 13 births per thousand population; actually the rate in that year was 24 per thousand.

The changes in the rate of surplus of births over deaths have been even more impressive. This rate declined slowly during World War I, dropped to a low during the influenza epidemic of 1918, reached a new peak of 12.7 per thousand population in 1921, and shrank to 5.1 in 1936. A projection of the 1921–1936 trend would indicate for 1947 a surplus of births over deaths of approximately 4 per thousand; actually the rate increased rapidly after

3. Committee on Recent Economic Changes, *Recent Economic Changes in the United States,* McGraw-Hill, New York, 1929, Vol. I, pp. xvi, xvii and xxii.

4. Alvin H. Hansen, *Fiscal Policy and Business Cycles,* Norton, New York, 1941. See also *Investigation of the Concentration of Economic Power,* Hearings before the Temporary National Economic Committee, May 1939, 76th Cong., 1st sess., Part 9, pp. 3497 ff. For critical appraisal of the theory see George Terborgh, *The Bogey of Economic Maturity,* Machinery and Allied Products Institute, Chicago, 1945.

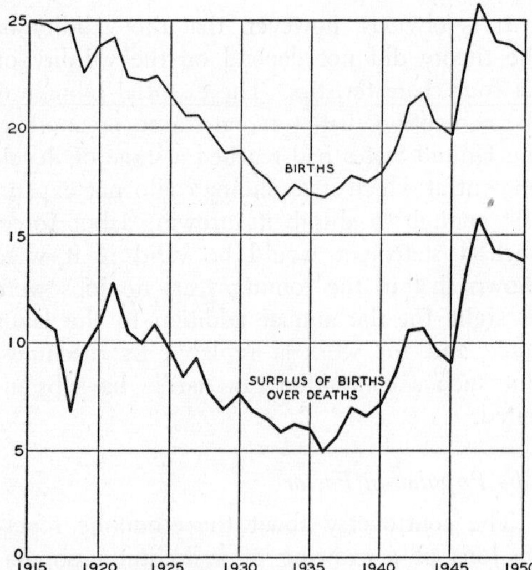

FIGURE 2. BIRTHS AND SURPLUS OF BIRTHS OVER DEATHS, PER THOUSAND POPULATION, 1915–1950

Source: Appendix Table 1.

1937, reached an unprecedented peak of nearly 16 per thousand in 1947, and was around 14 per thousand in 1948–1950.

Thus, contrary to the theory of tapering off of population growth, the United States now has a very high birth rate and an exceptionally high surplus of births over deaths. The upturn in natality since the middle of the 1930's cannot be dismissed as a wartime flare. Unquestionably the attitude toward rearing children has changed radically, though it is not easy to explain why.

It is generally accepted that the decline in the birth rate during the 1930's was largely due to the depression, which temporarily brought the rate far below the level to which it would otherwise have dropped because of the practice of birth control. If the depression had been the only cause of the downswing in births, however, economic recovery might have brought the rate back to the predepression level, say 20 per thousand, assuming that the practice of birth restriction had not progressed since 1929. Actually, after 1945 the birth rate rose to 24 and more per thousand. Much of the rise was caused by factors associated with the war; but even these, combined with the upturn in business conditions, do not account for all of the increase in recent years.

A more satisfactory explanation is that planned parenthood starts necessarily with a situation in which many families have more children than they wish. Since the desire of such families to have children has already been satisfied, the birth rate in this section of the population drops temporarily to almost zero. In this initial period, the number of second, third and subsequent births, and hence the average birth rate in the nation also, tends to fall below the level at which it will be stabilized after birth control becomes common practice. Apparently this was the situation in the United States and many European countries during the late 1920's and early 1930's.

If this hypothesis is correct, birth rates in the coming decade or two are unlikely to drop below 20–22 per thousand, and the absolute number of births will hardly be less than 3 to 3.5 million a year.[5]

If it is true that the declining birth rate in the 1920's and early 1930's had an unfavorable effect on the economic growth of this nation, the reversal of the demographic trend should be favorable for economic development in coming years. There will be a growing demand for educational facilities in the 1950's, and a growing demand for new houses, furniture and household equipment accompanying the growing number of marriages in the 1960's. And as a result of these marriages, a new upswing of births can be expected later in that decade. There will also be an acceleration in the growth of the labor force, but the influx of new workers will naturally come later than the increase in births.

Total population in the United States will not grow in the years ahead at as high a rate as before World War I, in the time of mass immigration. The growth of the labor force in the 1950's will lag, also, because of the low natality in the 1930's; but, in contrast to the past, the new entrants will consist overwhelmingly of boys and girls graduated from American schools and better adjusted to the environment than the new workers brought to the shores of this country in the past.

The Frontier and Foreign Markets

The contention of believers in the maturity doctrine that the frontier has closed and that

5. These figures assume a much higher fertility than that assumed in the new high-fertility projection by P. K. Whelpton ("Forecasts of the Population of the United States, 1945–1975," Bureau of the Census, 1947, p. 30). The difference is approximately 700,000–1,000,000 births a year.

foreign trade also offers fewer economic outlets for investment than formerly is of questionable validity.

The western frontier of the United States was never before as wide open to labor and capital as it is now. Between 1940 and 1950, the population of the three Pacific states increased as much as in the preceding quarter century, mainly through immigration from eastern and central states. (See Table 1.) At the same time, hundreds of thousands of men were moving along other historical routes of internal migration, from regions with comparatively low standards of living and high birth rates toward regions of low natality and particularly rapid economic expansion.

From the viewpoint of economic growth an open "frontier" means opportunity for those who, in search of improvement, are ready to change residence and site of work. It is true that the frontier, in this sense, was closed in the 1930's, when work opportunity in the West was as poor as in the East. But the situation has changed since then. The "frontier" has been reopened, and this is another favorable factor in the economic outlook for coming years.

The United States depends on foreign countries for certain foodstuffs and raw materials such as tropical fruits, coffee, cacao, sugar, wool, furs, silk, wood pulp and paper, rubber, industrial diamonds, manganese, tin, copper, nickel, asbestos, nitrates. There is no indication that the United States domestic market cannot absorb all its products, but prospects for exports are less certain. They depend on the progress of recovery in the countries devastated by the war, the economic development of underdeveloped areas, the achievement of international peace, and on the price structure in this country and abroad, as well as other factors.

There is, however, no evidence that this nation needs to export more merchandise than is necessary to cover its imports. Nor is there any evidence that it will be unable to trade its goods for goods it needs and cannot find within its borders.

Investment Outlets in New Industries

More than a century ago, Karl Marx contended that, because of dwindling outlets for investment, the capitalist system had exhausted its capacity to develop productive forces. This doctrine was further elaborated by his disciples and became the foundation of their theories of business cycles, colonial exploitation and the unavoidability of imperialistic wars. Other economic theories have shifted, since the end of the eighteenth century, between unlimited optimism and gloomy apprehension. The gloomy state of mind found expression in the doctrine of tapering off in technological progress and decline in outlets for capital investment.

TABLE 1

POPULATION OF THE PACIFIC STATES, 1870–1950 [a]

(*In Thousands*)

Year	Total	Increment since Preceding Census
1870	675	231
1880	1,115	440
1890	1,888	773
1900	2,417	529
1910	4,192	1,775
1920	5,567	1,375
1930	8,194	2,627
1940	9,733	1,539
1950	14,487	4,754

a. Includes Washington, Oregon and California.

Source: Census data.

One of the most interesting early proponents of the maturity doctrine was Carroll Wright, Commissioner of Labor under President Cleveland, who published in 1886 a striking appraisal of the state of economic affairs in the United States and the world. After exhaustive study of economic conditions here and abroad, Dr. Wright concluded that the rapid progress of the preceding fifty years would not again be repeated and that the economy of the western world had reached maturity. He said:

> In England, Belgium and France the railroads and canals that are really needed have been built. . . . In Holland the great works are completed; Amsterdam is united to the sea, . . . there are no longer urgent works to be undertaken, and the reward of capital . . . is not sufficient to tempt lenders. . . . Italy and Spain . . . are now provided with railroads, while the products moved and the revenues derived from capital invested are notoriously inferior to what was expected. . . . Harbors and rivers are sufficiently developed, and warehouses, water and gas works, tramways, etc., are largely provided for. The Pyrenees and the Alps are tunnelled, and a sufficient network of international communication established. In England railroad building cannot be extended . . . to absorb much capital or much labor. In Russia the principal lines of railroad have been built . . . and it is not likely that further construction will take place except for strategical purposes. Germany is provided with a full network of railroads, and the facilities for transportation are in excess of actual needs. Austria is in

much the same condition as Germany, and Turkey also has as many railroads as can be used. In the United States the mileage of new railroads constructed has been out of all proportion to the increase of products to be carried. The Suez Canal has been built, terrestrial and transoceanic lines of telegraph have been laid, and the merchant marine has been transformed from wood to iron. Today the carrying service of nations, and especially of the great marine nation, England, is overstocked to a far greater extent than the industries. On all sides one sees the accomplished results of the labor of half a century. . . . the discovery of new processes . . . will undoubtedly continue . . . but it will not leave room for a marked extension, such as has been witnessed during the last fifty years, or afford . . . a remunerative employment of the vast amount of capital . . . created during that period. The market price of products will continue low, no matter what the cost of production may be. The day of large profits is probably past. There may be room for further intensive, but not extensive, development of industry . . .[6]

These were the thoughtful conclusions of an honest, competent and intelligent scholar. Yet, at that time the economic system we know was still in early childhood. Although it already had steel at its disposal, it had not learned how to use it. Although it had discovered electricity, it did not know what to do with it. The petroleum industry was in its infancy, and transportation was still effected by horses and clumsy coal-fed steam engines. Industrial chemistry and scientific methods in agriculture and forestry were unknown.

President Franklin D. Roosevelt gave the same sort of picture in his pamphlet "Looking Forward," published in 1933 at the depth of depression:

Our physical economic plant will not expand in the future at the same rate at which it has been expanded in the past. We may build more factories but the fact remains that we have enough to supply all our domestic needs, and more if they are used. With those factories we can now make more shoes, more textiles, more steel, more radios, more automobiles, more of almost everything, than we can use.

Roosevelt was right in saying that at the time he wrote there was no outlet for private investments in this country. That was a purely temporary phenomenon, however, and an era of unprecedented expansion lay ahead. (See Table 2.)

Investment is the most flexible of economic activities. It is one of the best indicators of the current state of the economy but a very deceptive indicator of long-range trends. In

TABLE 2

GROSS PRIVATE DOMESTIC INVESTMENTS, 1929–1950

(*In Billions*)

Year	Total	New Construction	Producers' Durable Equipment	Change in Business Inventories
1929.....	$15.8	$7.8	$6.4	$1.6
1930.....	10.2	5.6	4.9	—0.3
1931.....	5.4	3.6	3.2	—1.4
1932.....	0.9	1.7	1.8	—2.6
1933.....	1.3	1.1	1.8	—1.6
1934.....	2.8	1.4	2.5	—1.1
1935.....	6.1	1.9	3.4	0.9
1936.....	8.3	2.8	4.5	1.0
1937.....	11.4	3.7	5.4	2.3
1938.....	6.3	3.3	4.0	—1.0
1939.....	9.9	4.9	4.6	0.4
1940.....	13.9	5.6	6.1	2.3
1941.....	18.3	6.8	7.7	3.9
1942.....	10.9	4.0	4.9	2.1
1943.....	5.7	2.5	4.1	—0.9
1944.....	7.7	2.8	5.7	—0.8
1945.....	10.7	3.9	7.5	—0.7
1946.....	28.7	10.3	12.3	6.1
1947.....	30.2	13.9	17.1	—0.8
1948.....	42.7	17.7	19.9	5.0
1949.....	33.0	17.3	19.0	—3.2
1950.....	48.9	22.1	22.5	4.3

Source: Survey of Current Business, National Income Supplement, 1951, p. 150.

the early phase of the postwar expansion, the volume of investment reached an all-time peak. There is, of course, no evidence that the demand for private investments will continue at this level; it will probably fluctuate in a fairly wide range, reflecting changes in business conditions and outlook. But temporary contraction will not signify maturity of our economic system.

Just now, our economy is in process of transformation. Industry is shifting from natural to synthetic raw materials; urban areas are undertaking the long-postponed task of replanning and rezoning in accord with new systems of transportation; geographic shifts of population and capital require a large volume of building construction. All these factors tend to widen the outlets for capital investment.

Danger of Oversaving

The forecasts of economic collapse and mass unemployment immediately after World War II were largely based on the theory that people in the United States are inclined to save more than the national economy can absorb for investment. This theory has been thoroughly discredited by the course of economic development, but it has not been completely abandoned

6. 1886 report of the Commissioner of Labor.

and remains a cliché in publications of the International Labor Office and some labor unions.

The doctrine can be stated as follows: Under the existing pattern of income distribution, the wealthy classes in the United States do not spend all their income; the proportion of disposable income that is saved increases with the rising wealth in the nation; the United States has become, therefore, an excess-savings country; its annual savings tend to outrun its needs for investment; the widening deflationary gap is bound to lead to rising unemployment unless it is filled by public investments, surplus of exports over imports, and similar measures.[7]

This reasoning would be convincing if the rate of savings in the United States tended to increase and to outrun the needs for investment. The truth is that during the depression of the 1930's savings were negative, in the sense that withdrawals of old savings exceeded accumulation of new savings. Later, during recovery and especially during the war — under pressure of budgetary deficits, rationing and price control — private savings increased faster than income. After the end of the war, part of the savings flowed back into the channels of consumption, and current net savings declined sharply. (See Table 3.) At no time has there been a negative correlation between the rate of savings and economic growth.

The pattern of savings in the next decade or two will depend on a number of economic, political and psychological factors, partly controversial, partly unpredictable. This much, however, is fairly certain: the economic history of the United States and of other countries furnishes no example of economic stagnation caused by an excess of savings.

TABLE 3

PERSONAL INCOME AND SAVINGS, 1929–1950

(*Dollar Figures in Billions*)

Year	Personal Income	Disposable Personal Income after Taxes	Personal Savings	Ratio of Savings to Disposable Income
1929.....	$85.1	$82.5	$3.7	4.5
1930.....	76.2	73.7	2.9	3.9
1931.....	64.8	63.0	1.8	2.9
1932.....	49.3	47.8	−1.4	−2.9
1933.....	46.6	45.2	−1.2	−2.6
1934.....	53.2	51.6	−0.2	−0.5
1935.....	59.9	58.0	1.8	3.0
1936.....	68.4	66.1	3.6	5.4
1937.....	74.0	71.1	3.9	5.5
1938.....	68.3	65.5	1.0	1.5
1939.....	72.6	70.2	2.7	3.8
1940.....	78.3	75.7	3.7	4.9
1941.....	95.3	92.0	9.8	10.6
1942.....	122.7	116.7	25.6	21.9
1943.....	150.3	132.4	30.2	22.8
1944.....	165.9	147.0	35.4	24.1
1945.....	171.9	151.1	28.0	18.5
1946.....	177.7	158.9	12.0	7.6
1947.....	191.0	169.5	3.9	2.3
1948.....	209.5	188.4	10.5	5.6
1949.....	205.1	186.4	6.3	3.4
1950.....	224.7	204.3	10.7	5.2

Source: Survey of Current Business, National Income Supplement, 1951, p. 151.

New Work Opportunities

The current version of the theory of economic maturity is that, despite a continuous rise of national income, production and profits, this country is unable to provide enough jobs for a half million or more additional workers each year. This is another way of saying that per capita consumption in this country is bound to lag behind output per worker. Both historical experience and logic tend to contradict this theory.

Assuming an over-all rise in the productivity of labor by 2 or 3 per cent a year, an advance in per capita consumption at the same rate would mean that demand for labor (work opportunities) would keep pace with the growth of population. It is fairly probable, however, that the nation will use technological progress not only to increase production but also to shorten work hours and gain more leisure. For example, an advance of 30 per cent in the productivity of labor in a decade can be split between a 20 per cent increase in output per worker and a 10 per cent cut in weekly hours of work.[8] Such a split would be in line with past trends and would help solve the problem of providing work opportunities for the increasing number of workers.

Since agriculture is unlikely to provide additional jobs, employment of the annual increase in the labor force depends wholly on openings in nonagricultural establishments (including the government). Though the demand for labor

7. See, for example, *The Maintenance of High Levels of Employment during the Period of Industrial Rehabilitation and Reconversion* (1945) and *Public Investment and Full Employment* (1946), International Labor Office, Montreal.

8. Cf. J. Frederic Dewhurst and Associates, *America's Needs and Resources,* Twentieth Century Fund, New York, 1947, pp. 20–21 and 695.

TABLE 4

EMPLOYMENT IN NONAGRICULTURAL ESTABLISHMENTS, 1935–1950 [a]

(*In Thousands*)

Industry	1935	1940	1945	1946	1947	1948	1949	1950
Total	28,848	34,762	39,786	41,235	43,007	43,923	42,564	44,250
Manufacturing	8,904	10,882	15,186	14,493	15,215	15,285	14,172	14,951
Mining	840	927	829	871	938	986	915	919
Contract construction	866	1,285	1,135	1,739	2,060	2,274	2,129	2,342
Transportation, communication and other public utilities	2,736	2,970	3,797	3,976	4,051	4,077	3,891	3,918
Trade	5,164	6,479	6,857	8,127	8,574	8,832	8,725	8,904
Finance	1,182	1,345	1,326	1,511	1,553	1,609	1,623	1,689
Services	4,376	5,156	4,998	5,223	5,503	5,621	5,645	5,930
Government (excluding the armed forces)	4,780	5,718	5,658	5,295	5,113	5,239	5,464	5,597

a. Number of full-time equivalent employees as estimated by the Department of Commerce in national income computations, excluding armed forces and permanent United States residents employed by foreign governments and international organizations.

Source: Survey of Current Business, National Income Supplement, 1951, pp. 180–81.

by this sector of the economy seemed fairly well satisfied in 1940, at about 35 million (excluding the armed forces), it rose to 43.9 million in 1948 and to 44,250,000 in 1950.

Employment in the various industries does not increase at the same rate each year. Between 1935 and 1950, manufacturing and construction showed the most uneven growth in demand for labor. (See Table 4.) Similar fluctuations may be expected in the future.

Moreover, the maintenance of a high level of employment does not require that all industries increase personnel. Apart from an extraordinary demand for labor by defense industries, it is possible that for several years manufacturing of civilian goods may absorb fewer workers than in 1950 while employment in building construction, services and finance will rise. In some later period, employment in construction may decline while factories — especially in heavy industries — hire more labor. The necessary condition of a high level of employment is not a strictly proportionate expansion of employment in all industries, but a sufficient growth of total per capita demand for goods and services, including capital equipment — in other words, a sufficient rise in the nation's standard of living.

PATTERNS OF A POSTWAR ECONOMY

In appraising the probable economic setting of wage determination in coming years, the characteristics of a postwar economy should be kept in mind. The general pattern of such an economy has been described by Leonard P. Ayres as follows:

> Great wars are accompanied by prosperity and followed by depression. The simple rule is that the war is accompanied by a period of exceptional business activity. . . . It is followed by a sharp and usually short period of hard times which we may designate as the primary postwar depression. This gives way to a rapid recovery and a period of active business expansion, which in turn is displaced by a long and severe period of subnormal activity which we may term the secondary postwar depression.[9]

The United States completed the primary postwar readjustment in 1949. The setback was short and not very hard this time but it fulfilled essentially the same role as the much more severe depression in 1921. In the middle of 1949 it gave way to a rapid postwar expansion. How soon will it be displaced by a "long and severe" secondary postwar depression? According to Ayres, the postwar expansion can last a long time

> but eventually it destroys itself. . . . Apparently it takes about fifteen years for the events . . . to run their course. It takes about ten years for the developments that intervene between the peak of wartime prices and the beginning of the secondary postwar depression.[10]

Going back as far as the Revolutionary War, Ayres points out that each of this country's major wars (including the Mexican War in 1846 and the Spanish War in 1898) has been followed by a major business depression ten years later. He presents this observation, however, as "an interesting fact, rather than an important one in economics." He is more positive in appraising the chain of events that ties

9. Leonard P. Ayres, *The Economics of Recovery,* Macmillan, New York, 1933, p. 15.
10. *Ibid.,* p. 21.

the secondary depression as the final phase of the postwar cycle with the war as its originating cause.

> The fundamental principle is that the huge and abnormally distributed material and financial demands of a great war must inescapably disrupt and disorganize any system of production and distribution. . . . The true lesson of [the depression of the 1930's] is that we cannot afford any more great wars.[11]

This appraisal may be objected to in two ways. First, it tends to reduce the economic impact of a war to the dislocation of prices. Second, it plays down the importance of the new factors that appear on the scene between the end of the war and the collapse of the postwar prosperity. Apart from these objections, the observation that a postwar expansion is not an affair of a few years but lasts a decade or more is correct. Expansion lasted more than a decade after World War I, despite the most unfavorable conditions — an orgy of speculation, a weak financial structure and chronic depression in agriculture. A comparison of the economic scene after the two world wars suggests that the new postwar expansion will last longer and will not necessarily end in the same way as the prosperity of the 1920's.

The Economic Scene after World War II

The present economic scene is in certain respects similar to that after 1921, in other respects substantially different.

The task of reconversion after World War II was essentially the same as after World War I: demobilization of industry and of the armed forces; redistribution of manpower and other resources; readjustment of hours of work, prices, wages and taxes; relaxation and eventual repeal of wartime controls. The difference lies in the economic conditions at the outbreak of war, the economic strain during the war, and the economic and political setting of subsequent developments.

World War I was preceded in this country by a period of prosperity. According to Warren M. Persons, from November 1900 to November 1914 the United States had 75 months of prosperity and only 22 months of trough, while in the remaining 71 months the economic system was moving from one extreme to the other.[12]

11. *Ibid.*, p. 24.
12. Warren M. Persons, *Forecasting Business Cycles*, Wiley, New York, 1931, p. 198.

On the average, the level of production in this period was somewhat above the "normal" indicated by the long-range trend.

In contrast, World War II arrived on the heels of a long and severe depression. Recovery was far from complete when the war broke out in Europe, and at the end of 1941 the United States still had almost 4 million unemployed workers. The availability of idle human and technical resources helped solve the double task of raising a huge army and building up the industrial plant to provide a world arsenal of democracy. The war economy could be developed as a superstructure above peacetime civilian production "as usual," with a minimum of regulations and controls and a high level of civilian consumption.

In addition the prewar depression has proved a salutary preventive to an inflationary boom during the war and in the reconversion period. Because liquid assets of individuals and financial reserves of business enterprises were depleted during the depression, wartime savings were less "hot" than they would have been if the war boom had followed a spell of prosperity.

On the other hand, the backlog demand for civilian goods developed during the war was added to that carried over from the depression — as, for example, in housing and in the production of automobiles.

In 1925 the United States had nearly 20 million registered motor vehicles. If the average life of a car is set at eight years, 2.5 million new cars were needed each year to replace obsolete vehicles and maintain a stable number. An addition in the number of cars of 2 to 3 per cent annually was required to keep pace with population growth and the rise of national wealth. All in all, 3 million motor vehicles were probably enough to maintain motor traffic at the existing level. The demand, however, was not saturated; the number of cars on highways and streets increased steadily. (See Table 5.) In 1929, 26.5 million cars were registered. Assuming again the average life of a car to be eight years, an annual output of 4 million was required to keep traffic at the level it had reached and to provide additional cars in accordance with the growing population and rising national income.

In the decade 1930–1939, automobile factories turned out 31 million cars, 9 million less than the "normal" demand. The wartime stop-

TABLE 5

FACTORY SALES OF MOTOR VEHICLES, 1923–1950

(*In Millions*)

Year	Sales	Year	Sales
1923	4.0	1937	4.8
1924	3.6	1938	2.5
		1939	3.6
1925	4.3		
1926	4.3	1940	4.5
1927	3.4	1941	4.8
1928	4.4	1942	0.4 [a]
1929	5.4	1943	0.0 [a]
		1944	0.1 [a]
1930	3.4		
1931	2.4	1945	0.4 [a]
1932	1.4	1946	3.1
1933	1.9	1947	4.8
1934	2.8	1948	5.3
		1949	6.2
1935	3.9		
1936	**4.5**	1950	8.0

a. Excluding military vehicles.

Source: Statistical Abstract, 1950, p. 487; for 1949 and 1950, *Survey of Current Business.*

page of production of cars for private use resulted in an additional cumulative deficit of approximately 15 million. The reconverted automobile industry did not start with an effective demand for 24 million new cars; part of the deficit had been absorbed by curtailment of traffic during the war and longer use of vehicles. The effective backlog was, however, greater than that built up during the war; it was a combined effect of the prewar depression and the war. This explained the tremendous expansion of the automobile industry and all related industries after the reconversion, in 1949–1950.

The same reasoning applies to building construction and other lines of production of durable goods. The conclusion is inescapable: the expansive forces originated by World War II were greatly augmented by the prewar depression.

The Strain of War

The momentum of postwar expansion depends on the duration and intensity of the economic strain of the war. In 1945 the United States had more than 12 million men under arms, as compared with 4.2 million on Armistice Day in 1918. World War I lasted 19 months for this country; World War II, from Pearl Harbor to V-J Day, 44 months.

The economic strain of the two wars may be measured by the war expenditures and their ratio to national income. World War II has cost this country approximately $360 billion, as compared with an outlay of $35 billion for World War I. In terms of national income, the United States has spent approximately two years' average income this time, as compared with an outlay of six months' income for the preceding war.

The strain of World War II had deep impacts on the economic system. For the economic outlook, the most important are the accumulation of backlog demand for consumer and capital goods and of savings and business reserves, and the change in the position of farmers.

Backlog Demand and War Savings

Our wartime economy was characterized by liberal remuneration of workers and business for their contribution to national defense, combined with allocation of raw materials, restriction of production of consumer goods, rationing of certain commodities, and selective price control. Such a system necessarily leads to accumulation of backlog demand on the one hand and of purchasing power on the other. The backlog demand after the war included not only houses, cars, household equipment and clothing, but also capital equipment, maintenance and repair works, and inventories of producers, wholesalers and retailers. Purchasing power was accumulated in the form of savings and business reserves.

With minor corrections, consumer savings and financial reserves accumulated during a war amount to the earnings and gains of individuals and corporations that were not spent either for consumption or for investment. In the flow of national income they equal the difference between the payments by government to individuals and corporations and the amount of money the government extracts from the private sector of the economy by taxes and similar levies. In other words, consumer savings and liquid reserves of enterprises accumulated during a war are in balance with the surplus of public expenditures over tax receipts or the growth of public debt.

According to this measurement, World War II left liquid assets of approximately $216 billion in the hands of consumers and business enterprises, as compared with $22 billion stored during the preceding war. In relation to current national income, the accumulated purchasing power this time was approximately three and a half times that after the Armistice in 1918. In brief, this time the United States entered the postwar cycle with savings of unprecedented magnitude, widely distributed among the population.

Although one must allow for a considerable margin of error in computations of this type, it is likely that by the end of the war about 50 per cent of all households had savings at least equal to their prewar annual income, 10 to 15 per cent had saved the equivalent of six to eleven months of their prewar earnings, an equal proportion had the equivalent of six months' income or less, and only 25 per cent had no appreciable financial reserves.

When the war ended, liquidation of savings contributed to the inflationary rise of prices. Low-income consumers were naturally the first to use up their wartime savings. At the same time the real value of savings that were not spent was reduced by the decline in the purchasing power of the dollar. Thus the distribution of savings is less favorable at present than at V-E Day.

Wartime saving did not transform the United States into a nation of capitalists nor did it eliminate poverty or iron out economic inequality. Savings, however, have brought a new feeling of security to many households, and this is a potent factor in the present economic picture.

Theoretically, only small amounts of savings can be added to current expenditures. When consumers are ready to spend more than their current earnings, prices must go up unless dissavings in one economic sector are counterbalanced by savings in another sector or by high taxes and partial liquidation of the national debt. Essentially, the stored purchasing power that flows back to the market is an antideflationary factor, but it can also create an inflationary pressure on prices. It is difficult to foresee how long the effect of wartime savings will be felt. It is fairly certain, however, that it will last much longer than after World War I.

The Position of Farmers

Agriculture was the weakest spot in the United States economy in the 1920's; it is now one of the strongest. Both world wars brought a rise in agricultural prices followed by a boom in farm real estate, but the World War I gains were short-lived.

From 1915 to 1920, the mortgage debts of farmers rose from $6.7 billion to $12.3 billion and their non-real-estate debts from $1.6 billion to $3.9 billion. The subsequent collapse of farm real-estate speculation wiped out all the book gains of farmers without reducing their liabilities.

This time, apart from the rise in the value of farm real estate, livestock, machinery, crops stored on and off farms, and household equipment, farmers have increased their financial assets and reduced their debts.[13]

The strengthened financial position of agriculture, combined with protection of parity prices by the federal government and support of farmers under the soil conservation program, makes an agricultural depression like that in the 1920's and 1930's highly improbable for many years to come.

Institutional Changes

The period after World War II differs from the early 1920's in the system of public laws and regulations that tend to channel economic activities and protect certain groups of the population and form the institutional setting of the labor market. Some of the institutional changes directly related to the labor market and wage determination, which are discussed in Part II, will be briefly summarized here.

Protection of Veterans

The task of reintegrating men released from the armed forces into civilian life was particularly serious this time because of the large number of veterans, the long duration of service (for many, four or five years), the unbearable strain to which many of the men were exposed, and the fact that many youths entered the armed forces without previous experience in regular civilian work. There was imminent danger that the war would leave the nation with throngs of war-weary, mentally crippled young men. To meet this danger, a vast program of aid to veterans was developed.[14]

Long before the war ended, measures were taken to help servicemen in planning for post-

13. *The Balance Sheet of Agriculture, 1947,* Department of Agriculture, August 1947.

14. See Chapter 13.

war occupations. Trained social workers were assigned to each military hospital and each separation center. Facilities were provided for veterans who wished to receive vocational training or to continue their education. Readjustment allowances were granted to those needing time to find suitable jobs. Loans were granted to those who intended to start a business or buy a home.

These measures were added to such veterans services as medical care, physical rehabilitation, disability compensation, pensions, retirement pay and National Service Life Insurance. The record of veterans in jobs, their academic achievements and the surprisingly low proportion of psychoneurotic cases among them suggest that the program has been a success.

Social Security

The social security program, a heritage of the interwar period and to some extent of the great depression, has had a deep influence on the postwar economic outlook.

A self-sustaining social security system cannot act on the flow of purchasing power as directly as can relief payments and purely fiscal measures, including public deficit spending. Neither old-age and survivors insurance nor disability and health insurance is very responsive to changing business conditions. Moreover, in the next decade the existing federal old-age and survivors insurance system, even after amendment, will probably remove more purchasing power from circulation than it will restore through benefits. Only unemployment insurance will pay out, in bad years, more than it collects, but its net disbursements will constitute only a small fraction of losses in wages and national income. Furthermore, the surplus of benefit payments over contributions in the unemployment insurance system develops only gradually in the early phase of a depression and declines or disappears completely in its more advanced phase, after most of the laid-off workers have exhausted their benefit rights.

The real importance of the social security program is that it gives workers what the name "social security" promises — the feeling of security supported by a social organization. The confidence it inspires helps people keep their courage and self-respect and helps prevent the social disintegration resulting from fear and despair. More specifically, unemployment insurance, by temporarily protecting idle human resources from rust and decay, preserves the most precious economic asset of a nation.

Economic Controls

The great depression gave rise to new controls in the United States designed to preserve economic equilibrium and prevent major dislocations. In addition to protection of farmers' earnings, two measures enacted in the early 1930's warrant mention: control over the stock exchanges and insurance of bank deposits.

Control over stock exchange operations, combined with the sobering effect of losses in the early 1930's, has tended to eliminate speculation from the early phase of postwar expansion. During the inflationary boom stock prices have advanced only moderately, lagging behind the general rise in prices and business expansion. The situation may change in the future, but a new orgy of speculation on margin, like that in 1928–1929, is not likely to develop so long as existing laws and regulations remain in force. Likewise, a new rush on banks like that of March 1933 is not very probable so long as bank deposits are insured by the Federal Deposit Insurance Corporation.

The Danger Points

The postwar developments described in the preceding pages favor a long period of comparatively smooth economic growth. This, however, is only one side of the picture: lack of stability is also characteristic of a postwar economy.

A long war breaks the continuity of economic relationships. It destroys the traditional relations between men, enterprises, economic areas and nations, and it makes obsolete the old structure of exchange rates, prices, wages, production and consumption standards. Before a new equilibrium is developed, the whole system is particularly exposed to the danger of dislocations and its future is uncertain.

Sumner H. Slichter, in an analysis of the problems and prospects of the American economy,[15] enumerates ten points that may justify fear for the future of our economy: drop in population growth; possible decline in the proportion of gainful workers to total population; curtailment

15. Sumner H. Slichter, *The American Economy: Its Problems and Prospects,* Knopf, New York, 1948.

of work hours; growing scarcity of natural resources; decline in the spirit of enterprise and in the willingness of business managers to take chances; a growing number of customs and rules that impede flexibility of business enterprises; make-work rules of unions; possible decline in the rate of technological discovery; shift in demand from commodities to services; and tax and wage policies that impede the accumulation of capital.

For three reasons he does not share these fears:

> In the first place, some of the reasons given for expecting a decline in the increase in output are open to question. In the second place, others are of minor importance. Finally, there are some conditions that will tend to cause output to grow even more rapidly in the future than in the past.[16]

In the final analysis, Slichter finds only two important grounds for doubting the optimistic case: (1) the possibility that the community will be unwilling to reform tax laws so as to avoid stiff penalties on enterprise and (2) the possibility that the strong and aggressive trade-union movement and public hostility to price increases will prevent adequate expansion of certain industries.[17]

With certain reservations, Slichter looks ahead to a reformed capitalist system maintaining the present rate of industrial progress and doubling the standard of living every forty years or less.[18]

In a more general way, the danger points during this beginning phase of postwar expansion can be reduced to the factors that threaten to make the economic system rigid and brittle and the social conflicts that threaten to interrupt its smooth operation.

Rigidity of Prices and Wages

The danger of manipulation of prices by powerful business combinations was recognized in our legislation as early as 1890 in the Sherman Antitrust Act. Monopolies were, however, too strong to be curbed by law. Progressive concentration of economic power went on during World War I, and in the 1930's under the NRA. And the last war has given new power to the leading financial and industrial groups.[19] In brief, the scope of free prices in our economy has been steadily declining, and that of managed prices has been steadily increasing. This trend has been paralleled in the structure of wages.

The new postwar cycle begins with a system of prices and wages more resistant to downward pressures than ever in the past. This new tendency did little harm in the early phase of postwar expansion. Agricultural prices were soaring because of the exceptionally favorable supply-demand situation rather than because of the parity floor below them. Some prices were pushed up by the rise of wages; in some industries, controlled by a monopolistic concern (aluminum for instance) or by a few huge corporations (automobiles for instance), wholesale prices were deliberately kept below the free-market level. The moderate price inflation that resulted did not prevent the smooth progress of demobilization and primary postwar adjustments. This does not mean, however, that monopolistic practices in the determination of prices and wages cannot become a real threat to postwar expansion.

Rigid prices can influence economic equilibrium for good or ill. A precipitous fall of prices in the early phase of an economic setback can touch off a deflationary spiral and endanger sectors of the national economy that are not in need of a downward price adjustment. Falling prices often become carriers of the germs of depression.[20] In such circumstances, control over the prices of certain commodities by powerful concerns can prove salutary. On the other hand, the fact that some prices are kept stable while others are diving may lead to serious economic dislocations. In this respect, excessive rigidity of agricultural prices at a time of sharp decline in industrial production is as dangerous as their excessive flexibility. But the most dangerous aspect of price rigidity is that it tends to weaken competition among industrial products and individual firms and discourages the efforts of business management to improve production methods. Similarly, the rigidity of wages tends to weaken the incentive to individual effort on the part of workers.

16. *Ibid.*, p. 172.
17. *Ibid.*, p. 179.
18. *Ibid.*, p. 214.
19. Cf. *Economic Concentration and World War II*, Report of the Smaller War Plants Corporation to the Special Committee to Study Problems of American Business, U.S. Senate, 79th Cong., 2d sess., 1946.
20. W. S. Woytinsky, *The Social Consequences of the Economic Depression*, International Labor Office, Geneva, 1936, pp. 301 ff.

Social Clashes

Our economic system is extremely elastic, as industrial mobilization, all-out war and reconversion have amply demonstrated. At the same time it is vulnerable, a fact the great depression dramatized. There is no evidence, however, that the economy of the United States cannot grow at the same rate as in the past or at an even greater rate. But will it grow fast enough to satisfy the claims of its people for a rising standard of living and work opportunities?

The actual speed of economic expansion will depend on the political and psychological climate, largely on the patterns of relations between labor and management, between the business community and government. The significance of these factors for the long-range economic outlook cannot be overemphasized. From this point of view, a shortsighted and aggressive policy of business management toward unions is as dangerous as an aggressive policy of labor toward management; a public policy hostile to labor is as harmful as a policy hostile to business. Ultimately, the way to prosperity in coming years is through reconciliation of the conflicting interests and opinions of labor and management in conformance with the interests of the community.

CHAPTER 3

TRENDS IN PRODUCTION *

IF LABOR AND MANAGEMENT can agree to approach the problem of determining wages as a matter of allocating the growing social product, their next step will be to ascertain the approximate amount to be allocated. A definite assumption about the long-range trends in production and national income is therefore a requirement for a farsighted wage policy.

The problem of determining long-range economic trends presents a twofold difficulty. First, the measurement of long-range trends presumes observations covering a long span of time and statistical information for periods for which, actually, only scattered and fragmentary records are available. Second, once the long-range trends of the past have been established, there remains a broad field of controversy about their interpretation and projection into the future.

LOOKING BACKWARD

In scrutinizing the records of the past it must be kept in mind that the future never duplicates the past. The postwar economy of the 1950's will probably differ from that of the 1920's, just as the economic scene in the 1920's differed from that in the 1890's. However, the record of the past, though it does not foreshadow future developments, helps in visualizing them.

Past performance must be carefully appraised, of course, with special attention to the particular period surveyed. For example, future economic trends should not be estimated solely from the experience of 1919–1929 or 1929–1939, since both periods are too short and were exceptional in the economic history of the United States. Similarly, a projection into the future of a straight line running from 1920, immediately after World War I, to 1940, the eve of this country's entry into World War II, is not very instructive, because of the economic dislocations between these dates. Observations covering longer periods, including good and bad times, peace and wars, are more conclusive. A trend that prevailed through a long period and has neither leveled off nor been reversed is at least suggestive of future developments, though reservations and corrections may be necessary in using it as a basis for projection.

It is difficult to measure the speed of economic growth over a long period — from the Civil War to our time, for example — because of gaps in the statistical records. Aside from the decennial censuses, economic statistics before the turn of the century are limited to scattered records of output and consumption of a few raw materials, railroad traffic, bank activities, imports and exports.[1] However, these records have been used successfully by Carl Snyder, Edwin Frickey, Robert F. Martin, the Cleveland Trust Company, the American Telephone and Telegraph Company and others for long-range indexes of business activity and national income. Conclusions drawn from these studies are internally consistent and in substantial agreement with one another.[2]

Industrial Production, 1860–1914

An appraisal of the long-range trends in industrial production can conveniently begin with the indexes prepared by Edwin Frickey on the basis of the spadework of the National Bureau of Economic Research and the Economics Department of Harvard University.

Frickey's survey of the trend in production in the United States covers the period from the beginning of the Civil War to the outbreak of World War I.[3] It records changes in the physical volume of manufacturing production (for durable and nondurable goods separately) and in transportation and communication, and combines the two indexes in a general index of

* By W. S. Woytinsky.

1. See the list of Production Series and Their Dates of Commencement, in Arthur F. Burns, *Production Trends in the United States since 1870,* National Bureau of Economic Research, New York, 1934, pp. 12–13.

2. Wesley C. Mitchell, *Business Cycles: The Problem and Its Setting,* National Bureau of Economic Research, New York, 1927, pp. 330–48.

3. Edwin Frickey, *Production in the United States, 1860–1914,* Harvard University Press, Cambridge, 1947.

industrial and commercial production.[4] (See Appendix Table 2.) The most important of Frickey's indexes are reproduced in Figures 3 and 4.

One of Frickey's main preoccupations was to ascertain whether or not the rate of growth of production in this period was slowing down. He started with the hypothesis of a gradually declining rate of growth and fitted a trend line to each series in such a way as to measure the speed of growth in the early phase of the period and its change in the later phase.[5] The results of a test of five series are shown in Table 6.

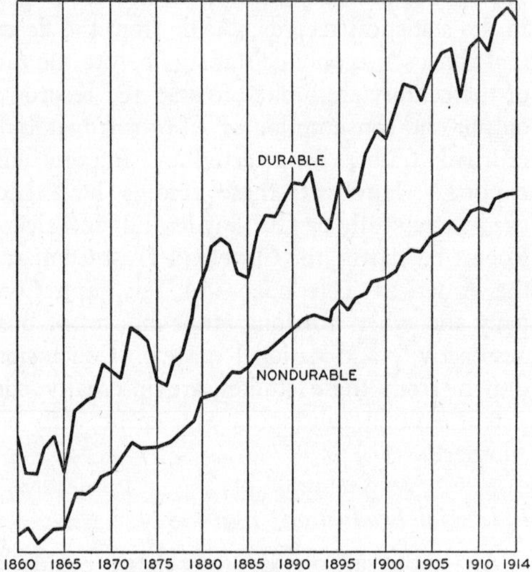

FIGURE 3. FRICKEY'S INDEXES OF THE VOLUME OF MANUFACTURING PRODUCTION, 1860–1914

Source: Edwin Frickey, *Production in the United States, 1860–1914,* Harvard University Press, Cambridge, 1947.

The indexes in this figure and in Figures 4 and 5 are plotted on a logarithmic vertical scale. A curve plotted in this way has the same slope when the index changes in the same proportion, regardless of the level on which the change occurs. Thus, a change from 100 to 110 is represented by the same slope as changes from 50 to 55 or from 500 to 550. The position of the curves in relation to each other (for example, the fact that the curve of durable commodities tops that of nondurable, or the curve of industrial and commercial production is plotted above that of manufacturing) is irrelevant. Only the direction of each curve in each period of time counts.

The dotted lines in Figure 4 indicate the long-range trend of each series. They are not perfectly straight but indicate a very slight, almost negligible retardation of growth.

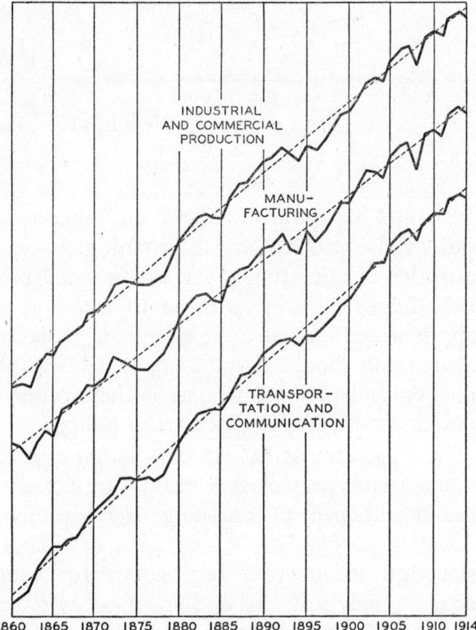

FIGURE 4. FRICKEY'S INDEXES OF THE VOLUME OF INDUSTRIAL AND COMMERCIAL PRODUCTION, 1860–1914

Source: Edwin Frickey, *Production in the United States, 1860–1914,* Harvard University Press, Cambridge, 1947.

TABLE 6

ESTIMATED AVERAGE ANNUAL PERCENTAGE GROWTH IN PRODUCTION, 1860–1914

Item	Average Annual Rate of Growth	Average Annual Retardation of Growth
All industrial and commercial production	5.38	0.007
Manufacturing	4.95	None
Durable goods	5.90	None
Nondurable goods	4.50	None
Transportation and communication	5.82	0.014

Source: Edwin Frickey, *Production in the United States, 1860–1914,* Harvard University Press, Cambridge, 1947, pp. 60, 66, 118 and 128.

Retardation in the growth of industrial and commercial production at 0.007 per cent a year is practically negligible; it suggests that the annual rate of growth conforming to the long-range trend averaged 5.53 per cent in 1860–1870 and 5.23 per cent in 1904–1914. The indicated retardation in the growth of transportation and

4. Frickey's method is developed in his *Economic Fluctuations in the United States,* Harvard University Press, Cambridge, 1942.

5. The method used for this purpose is fitting a second-grade parabola to the logarithms of the index numbers, such as those represented graphically in Figures 3 and 4. In such a formula one member represents the prevailing trend at a selected point while the other member characterizes the retardation (or acceleration) of the growth. If the second member turns out to be close to zero, this shows that there was no consistent change in the speed of growth.

communication activities suggests that the long-range trend would comprise an average annual gain of 6.13 per cent in the first decade and 5.51 per cent in the last.

Frickey's production indexes permit more than one interpretation, however. They show, for example, that during the postwar expansion after the Civil War (1865–1873), manufacturing production was advancing at an annual rate of 6.44 per cent and total industrial and commercial production at 6.67 per cent.[6] If this period is excluded, the annual advance is somewhat less than the average from 1860 to 1914. (See Table 7.)

Comparison of Frickey's index of manufacturing production with the decennial censuses shows that the growth of production in the period surveyed was due to growing factory employment and rising output per worker. There were periods of rapid growth in factory employment with only moderate gains in the productivity of labor as well as times when technological progress outran the growth in employment. In the first decade (1859–1869) all gains were due to the growth of the working force; in the 1890's per capita output was rising almost as rapidly as the working force; after the turn of the century, technological progress was three times as important in bringing about increased production as growth in the number of factory workers. (See Table 8.)

Output of Finished Goods, 1879–1939

Frickey's observations are supplemented by the survey of production of finished goods prepared by William N. Shaw for the National Bureau of Economic Research.[7] In this study "finished commodities" are defined as all products of farming, fishing, mining and manufacturing that have reached the stage at which they will be used by ultimate consumers without further fabrication, including also such commodities as machinery and equipment intended for multiple use in production and with an average life of three or more years.[8]

TABLE 7

ESTIMATED AVERAGE ANNUAL PERCENTAGE GROWTH IN PRODUCTION, 1860–1914, 1865–1873 AND 1874–1914

Item	1860–1914	Postwar Expansion 1865–1873	1874–1914
All industrial and commercial production	5.38	6.67	5.07
Manufacturing ..	4.95	6.44	4.65

Source: Based on Edwin Frickey, *Production in the United States, 1860–1914,* Harvard University Press, Cambridge, 1947.

TABLE 8

AVERAGE DECENNIAL PERCENTAGE GROWTH IN PRODUCTION, NUMBER OF WORKERS AND OUTPUT PER WORKER IN MANUFACTURING, 1859–1909

Period	Production	Number of Workers	Output per Worker
1859–1869	56	56	0
1869–1879	44	33	8
1879–1889	83	56	17
1889–1899	51	25	21
1899–1909	66	15	44

Source: For number of workers, Census data; for production, Frickey's indexes.

TABLE 9

AVERAGE ANNUAL PERCENTAGE GROWTH IN PRODUCTION, BY GROUPS OF FINISHED GOODS, 1879–1939

Commodity	Rate of Growth
All finished commodities	3.2
Consumers' perishable goods	2.9
Consumers' semidurable goods	2.9
Consumers' durable goods	4.7
Producers' durable goods	3.6

Source: William N. Shaw, *Finished Commodities since 1879, Output and Its Composition,* Occasional Paper No. 3, National Bureau of Economic Research, New York, August 1941, p. 10.

Shaw found an appreciable difference in the rates of growth in production of various groups of finished goods. (See Table 9.) These rates are lower than in Frickey's indexes, partly because of differences in coverage, classification and methods of computation and partly because Shaw has included the depression decade of the 1930's. According to Shaw's series, the annual rate of advance in production of all finished goods would average 3.8 per cent for the period 1879–1914, as compared with Frickey's average rate of 4.65 per cent for growth in manufac-

6. Computed by fitting a straight line to the logarithms of Frickey's indexes (*op. cit.,* pp. 54 and 127).

7. William N. Shaw, *Finished Commodities since 1879, Output and Its Composition,* Occasional Paper No. 3, National Bureau of Economic Research, New York, August 1941.

8. In this definition the word "finished" does not apply solely to the degree of processing; it indicates as well the use to which an article is put. Flour, for example, is considered finished if it is to be consumed in households, in institutions, in service establishments like hotels, or in government agencies or enterprises; it is considered unfinished if it is to be consumed by a factory engaged in making bread or other products for which flour is a raw material. A barrel of apples destined for home consumption is included in estimates of finished commodities, whereas apples shipped to a commercial bakery are excluded.

turing production from 1874 to 1914. Aside from this, Shaw's series show the same trends as Frickey's indexes. The average annual rate of growth in output of all finished goods changed from decade to decade but did not slow down before 1929. (See Table 10.)

TABLE 10

AVERAGE ANNUAL PERCENTAGE GROWTH IN PRODUCTION OF FINISHED GOODS, DECADE TO DECADE, 1879–1928

Decade	Rate of Growth
1879–1888 to 1889–1898	2.9
1889–1898 to 1899–1908	4.6
1899–1908 to 1909–1918	3.4
1909–1918 to 1919–1928	4.3

Source: William N. Shaw, *Finished Commodities since 1879, Output and Its Composition,* Occasional Paper No. 3, National Bureau of Economic Research, New York, August 1941, p. 16.

Production of Goods and Services, 1899–1939

Comprehensive statistics on trends in production, employment and output per worker have been computed by the National Bureau of Economic Research and analyzed by Solomon Fabricant and George J. Stigler.[9] (See Appendix Table 3.) The industries covered by this survey — agriculture, mining, manufacturing, electricity, gas, steam railroads — employed two thirds of the national labor force in 1899 and slightly less than half in 1939. Changes in output, employment and productivity of labor over the period 1899–1939 are shown for these industries as a group in Table 11. Stigler points out that the changes are underrated because insufficient allowance is made for qualitative improvements in products and are overrated because no allowance is made for decline in production within the household. He believes that the first bias is the more important.

TABLE 11

INDEXES OF PRODUCTION, EMPLOYMENT AND OUTPUT PER WORKER, 1909–1939 COMPARED WITH 1899[a]

(*1899 = 100*)

Item	1909	1919	1929	1939
Production	146	195	283	289
Employment	129	153	150	130
Output per worker	113	127	189	222

a. Agriculture, mining, manufacturing, electricity, gas, steam railroads.

Source: George J. Stigler, *Trends in Output and Employment,* National Bureau of Economic Research, New York, 1947, p. 3.

The average annual rate of growth over the four decades has been

for total output	2.7 per cent
for employment	0.7
for output per worker	2.0

These average rates are not typical, however, for they are largely affected by the low level of employment in 1939. A comparison of average annual rates of gain or loss, decade by decade, is more instructive. (See Table 12.)

TABLE 12

AVERAGE ANNUAL PERCENTAGE RATE OF GROWTH OR DECLINE IN PRODUCTION, EMPLOYMENT AND OUTPUT PER WORKER, BY DECADE, 1899–1939

Decade	Production	Employment	Output per Worker
1899–1909	+3.9	+2.7	+1.2
1909–1919	+2.9	+1.7	+1.2
1919–1929	+3.8	—0.2	+4.0
1929–1939	+0.2	—1.4	+1.6

Source: Computed from Table 11.

The course of employment was the most erratic, rising in two decades and declining in the other two. The gains in output per worker were the most consistent. Output per man-hour has certainly increased at a higher rate than output per worker, probably at an annual rate averaging close to 2.4 per cent through the four decades.

Gains in production have varied widely from industry to industry and from year to year. (See Appendix Table 3 and Figure 5.) Manufacturing and mining advanced until 1929, but suffered severe setbacks in the 1930's. Steam railroads were losing ground after World War I. Output of electricity continued to increase — although at a reduced annual rate — during the depression.

A straight extrapolation of the trends of 1899–1939 into the future would be misleading because the observation period starts with a good year and ends with a year in which this country had not yet recovered from the great depression and had about 9 million unemployed. What appears in Figure 5 as a gradual leveling-off of the rate of growth was actually a dent inflicted in the secular upward trend by the depression of the 1930's.

In manufacturing, the annual rate of increase of total output, according to Fabricant, averaged 4.3 per cent before World War I (1899–1915)

9. Solomon Fabricant, *Labor Savings in American Industry, 1899–1939,* Occasional Paper No. 23, National Bureau of Economic Research, New York, November 1945; George J. Stigler, *Trends in Output and Employment,* National Bureau of Economic Research, New York, 1947.

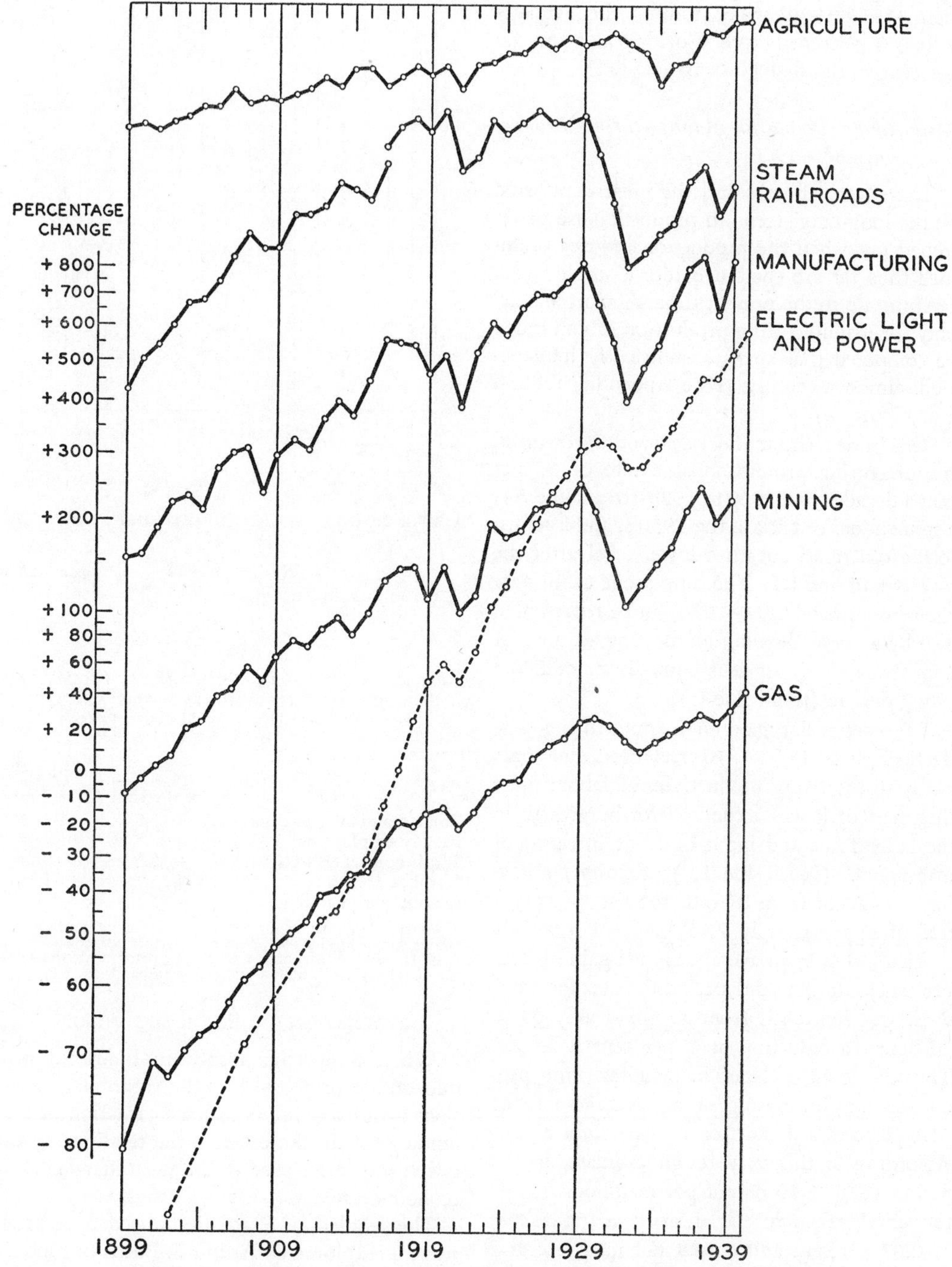

FIGURE 5. STIGLER'S INDEXES OF OUTPUT IN SIX INDUSTRIES, 1899–1939

Source: George J. Stigler, *Trends in Output and Employment,* National Bureau of Economic Research, New York, 1947.

Like Figures 3 and 4, this chart shows indexes of production plotted on a logarithmic vertical scale. The position of the curves in relation to one another is irrelevant. The rate of change in period of time and at any level of the plot is measured by the scale on the left, which is intended to be used as a movable ruler.

and 5.4 per cent in the period of postwar expansion (1919–1929). For mining the averages were 5.0 per cent before World War I and 5.5 per cent in the first postwar decade.[10]

Long-Range Trend in Manufacturing Production, 1860–1950

The effects of wars and the great depression on the long-range trend in production are partly ironed out when the production indexes examined thus far are combined into a single index reaching up to the present time. Unfortunately, only for manufacturing production can an index be computed that spans a sufficiently long period, almost a century. (See Appendix Table 4 and Figure 6.)

This index shows fairly smooth growth in manufacturing production at a rate of 57 per cent a decade from 1860 to 1929 (trend line A), a tremendous setback in the 1930's, and a return to the old trend but on a lower level after the war (trend line B). The long-range trend over the whole period 1860–1950 can be represented also by a curve showing an average advance of approximately 4 per cent annually or 48.8 per cent a decade (trend line C).

The spectacular gain in manufacturing production since 1860–1870 has been due only partly to the rising productivity of labor; more than half of it was accounted for by growth in the labor force and input of labor in terms of man-hours. (See Table 13.) Factory employment advanced from 1870 to 1950 at an average rate of approximately 27.5 per cent a decade (which indicates an average annual gain of 2.46 per cent). In the same period the average work week was shortened from approximately 63 to 40 hours, a reduction of 5 per cent a decade. Thus the input of labor in manufacturing production was increasing at an average rate of 21.1 per cent a decade, or 1.94 per cent a year. According to this very rough estimate, in the period 1870–1950 output per man-hour of factory employment rose at an average annual rate of 2.07 per cent and output per man-year at a rate of 1.55 per cent.[11]

10. These rates are computed by fitting straight lines to the sections of Figure 5 by the method of least squares.

11. The rates of annual growth of output are close to 1.86 per man-hour and 1.40 per man-year when output is prorated over all factory employees rather than production workers only.

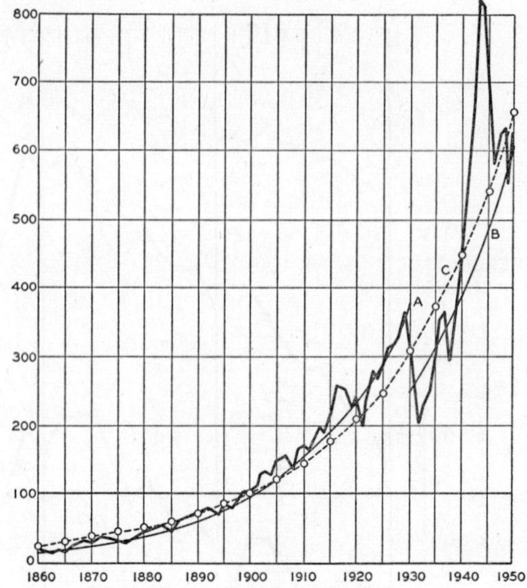

FIGURE 6. INDEX OF MANUFACTURING PRODUCTION, 1860–1950

(*1899 = 100*)

Source: Appendix Table 4.

TABLE 13

AVERAGE DECENNIAL AND ANNUAL CHANGES IN PRODUCTION, EMPLOYMENT, HOURS AND OUTPUT PER MAN-HOUR IN MANUFACTURING, 1870–1950

Item	Percentage Change per Decade	Percentage Change per Year
Total manufacturing output.	+48.8	+4.05
Factory employment	+27.5	+2.46
Work hours per week......	— 5.0	—0.51
Man-hours	+21.1	+1.94
Output per man-hour......	+22.9	+2.07

Source: For manufacturing output, Appendix Table 4; for factory employment, the number of factory wage workers in 1869 (Census of Manufactures) is compared with the number of factory production workers in midyear 1950.

RETARDATION IN ECONOMIC PROGRESS

When long-range trends in industrial production are projected into the future, two questions arise; one refers to the retardation in economic growth, the other to the relationship between industrial production and other fields of economic activity.

The problem of retardation in economic progress was explored by Arthur F. Burns in a monograph published by the National Bureau of Economic Research in 1934.[12] This study has become a classic, and not much can be added to its findings. The gist, as summarized by

12. Arthur F. Burns, *Production Trends in the United States since 1870,* National Bureau of Economic Research, New York, 1934.

Wesley C. Mitchell in his introduction to the volume,

is that rapid growth in general production and decline in the rate of growth of individual industries go together. The latter is as characteristic of a progressive state as the former. The incessant introduction of new commodities restricts the increase in the demand for old commodities. The faster these new industries expand at first the greater is this restrictive influence, and the harder it is to sustain their own rates of growth for long. Doubling output each year may be feasible when a novel product wins favor; but a continuation of that rate of growth for a generation or two would mean the marketing of impossible quantities. Changes in methods also lead to retardation. For example: "The increasing replacement of farm work animals by automobiles and tractors has resulted in a rapid retardation in the production of horses and mules, has tended to retard the lumber industry, and has released millions of acres of crop land—which means that the increasing mechanization of agriculture has contributed to the retarded growth of certain of its branches, especially the production of oats and hay." Similarly, the coal industry is suffering from improved methods of combustion in railway locomotives and electric power plants. Reclamation of raw materials checks the increase in the demand for fresh production . . . Further, new products and new processes exert a retarding influence upon other parts of the system by attracting to themselves portions of the capital, labor and materials which might have been used to sustain the growth of older industries. . . . inventions may accelerate the rate of growth, but once the reorganization has been accomplished retardation reappears. Finally, industries which experience retardation are prone to organize in self-defence; in particular they resort to technical research and more intensive salesmanship. Insofar as these efforts prosper they increase the pressure upon all other industries, limiting the expansion of the latter's markets and so strengthening the forces tending toward retardation.[13]

Burns stresses the fact that a declining rate of growth is a salient feature of the long-range histories of industries.

Barring structural changes, the course of the life history of a typical industry may be divided into a number of "stages." But irrespective of the number of stages of industrial development that may be distinguished, or how they may be defined, given stages will be found to differ in duration and intensity from industry to industry, as will the relative durations of the several stages. Thus, the stage of industrial "nascence" was long in the beet-sugar and cottonseed-oil industries, but short in the aluminum and rayon industries. The stage of industrial "maturation" extended over several centuries in the lumbering industry, over several decades in the wire-nail industry, but only over several years in the miniature-golf industry. The stage of "decadence" has been rather long in the whaling industry, but brief in the iron-rail industry. Nor are the stages of industrial decline often symmetrical with the stages of advance. So diverse are the patterns of the development of industries that only this rule of uniformity can be allowed: an industry tends to grow at a declining rate, its rise being eventually followed by a decline.[14]

He remarks also that

there are substantial grounds for believing that the life histories of industries are becoming shorter. An increasing share of our production is assuming the form of "luxuries," "superfluities," and "style goods." The demand for such products is determined in large part by caprice, and does not have the stability which staples enjoy.[15]

Retardation in the growth of particular industries does not imply, however, a leveling-off of the growth of the whole economic system.

The tendency of individual industries to grow at a declining rate has become an outstanding expression of the progressiveness of the American economy. This tendency indicates that . . . a fairly regular and orderly transformation in the pattern of national production has accompanied the rapid growth in its volume.[16]

After a careful analysis of the existing over-all measurements of total production Burns concludes that

if there has been any decline in the rate of growth in the total physical production of this country, its extent has probably been slight, and it is even mildly probable that the rate of growth may have been increasing somewhat.

He is more positive in judgment about the over-all trends in production per capita of population:

. . . we know definitely that population has grown at a declining percentage rate; it follows, therefore, that if total physical production has experienced retardation, the production per capita has experienced retardation at a lower rate, and that if the rate of retardation of total physical production has been less than that of population, the production per capita has been growing at an increasing percentage rate.

And he makes still another reservation:

. . . while it may be true that the percentage rate of growth in our total physical production has been declining, that does not mean necessarily that our "economic welfare" — even if we should view the physical volume of production as the sole factor in economic welfare — has been growing at a "declining rate." [17]

Burns' conclusions may have seemed sanguine and bold in 1934, when the philosophy of eco-

13. *Ibid.*, pp. xvi–xvii.

14. *Ibid.*, pp. 172–73.
15. *Ibid.*, p. 173.
16. *Ibid.*, p. 174.
17. *Ibid.*, pp. 279–80.

nomic maturity was spreading like wildfire through this country. In the light of more recent developments, his findings appear sober and rather conservative.

A declining rate of growth after a certain point is the general law in individual industries, just as it is in organic growth. But within the limited span of our experience, covering sixty to ninety years, there has been no retardation in the economic growth of the United States, and there is no indication that progress will level off in coming years.

Trends in Manufacturing and Other Industries

Continual changes in consumption habits and in the quality and types of products prevent precise measurement of changes in the volume of the total social product.[18] There is no escape from this dilemma. A comprehensive index of production must cover commodities and services that cannot readily be measured by volume; but the more an index is loaded with such items, the wider is its margin of error. With some reservation, one can accept at face value the index of industrial production of the Federal Reserve Board or of Frickey; but there is no reliable and generally accepted yardstick for measuring all the goods and services produced in the nation.[19]

The best substitute for such a measure is national income adjusted to changes in prices. But the result depends largely on the price index used as deflation factor, and there are serious doubts whether the aggregate national income prorated over the population and divided by the conventional cost-of-living index is a proper expression of real per capita income. Despite this criticism, it would be unwise to reject adjusted national income as an approximate over-all measure of economic progress. Imperfect tools must often be used in economic analysis, and national income adjusted to prices serves as an auxiliary device along with direct measurement of the volume of production.

Direct measurement of total national production has two main difficulties: many types of economic activities cannot be measured in physical units; and some others have been measured only in recent years, so that the long-range trends in their production cannot be ascertained. Practically, the problem is how to shift from direct measurement of output in mining, manufacturing, agriculture, railroads and utilities, to trends in other less tangible goods and services constituting more than a third of the social dividend. One approach is to compare trends in these activities with those for which the long-range trend can be measured with reasonable accuracy. Since the trends in manufacturing production have been better explored than any other, it seems logical to start with them.

Frickey's indexes provide some information of this sort. They show that from 1860 to 1914 the volume of services provided by transportation and communication increased at a higher annual rate than manufacturing production (5.82 and 4.95 per cent a year respectively). Indexes of the National Bureau of Economic Research (Fabricant-Stigler) reveal a similar relationship. If proper weight is given to private transportation and services related to automobile traffic, it appears that the volume of transportation and communication services was growing faster than manufacturing output.

On the other hand, agricultural output increased at a lower annual rate. The Day-Persons index of "total production," embracing agriculture, mining and manufacturing, therefore lags behind the index of manufacturing production alone.[20]

The volume of services provided by domestic wholesale and retail trade tends to keep pace with the output of finished products or to outrun it. It keeps pace with production in so far as all finished merchandise is distributed among consumers through the channels of trade; it has a somewhat higher rate of growth in so far as it provides additional services in terms of more comfort, greater choice, delivery to consumers' homes, and so on.

18. In composite indexes such as those discussed in the preceding pages, many items can be measured only in dollars (as "value added" or price of finished products) or by input of labor (as in some production indexes of the Federal Reserve Board). In the first case, the index must be adjusted to changing prices; in the second, to changes in the productivity of labor. Such adjustment introduces new sources of uncertainty into the computation: Only rarely does the price index used for "deflating" a series answer all the requirements of precision and cover all commodities and services, and it is still more difficult to adjust production indexes based on input of man-hours of labor to changes in output per man-hour.

19. Cf. Chapter 4.

20. Warren M. Persons, *Forecasting Business Cycles,* Wiley, New York, 1931; cf. Burns, *op. cit.,* p. 263.

In the long run, the volume of such services as transportation, communication, trade and finance is likely to increase faster than the output of manufacturing industries, while the output of mining and agriculture lags behind.

When only services directly purchased by consumers are recorded, this form of consumption seems to advance less rapidly than consumption of commodities.[21] The picture changes, however, when services provided by government are added to those purchased directly by consumers.[22]

All in all, it seems justifiable to assume that the long-range trend in production of all goods and services in the past eighty or ninety years did not differ much from the trend in manufacturing production and that any difference in rate of growth falls within the margin of error of measurement.

On the other hand, the share of services (including those provided by government) in employment increased considerably from 1870 to 1940 in comparison with that of manufacturing, but this trend has been reversed in more recent years. A comparison of the shares of services in national income and employment indicates that output per worker in service industries lagged behind that in manufacturing. The lag was not very significant, however, and can hardly be measured with the rough tools at our disposal.

At first, the contention that productivity of labor in service industries has kept pace with productivity of factory labor seems contrary to the well-known contrast between the use of mechanical power in manufacturing and transportation and the lack of mechanization in most of the service industries. There is, however, ample evidence of the increase in output per worker in services, especially professional services. Obviously the services provided by physicians have been increased tremendously by improved methods of communication and transportation like the telephone and the automobile, and by new techniques of preventive and curative medicine, new drugs, better organization of hospitals, and so on. Similarly, new techniques in recreation industries (movies, records, broadcasting, television) have multiplied the volume of their services to consumers. Even in domestic service, laundries and beauty shops, new techniques have largely replaced old methods of work.

To sum up, there is no evidence that the long-range trend in output per worker differs substantially for service industries and industries in which output can be directly measured in physical units. Allowing for a margin of error, the rate of progress for the whole United States economy from 1870 to 1950 has probably been the same as for manufacturing or for all commercial and industrial activities: an increase in output per man-hour averaging 22.9 per cent a decade or 2.07 per cent a year.

21. According to the surveys of Personal Consumption Expenditures by Type of Product published annually by the Department of Commerce, the share of "services" in consumer outlays dropped from 40.2 per cent in 1929 to 29 per cent in 1946. *National Income Supplement to Survey of Current Business,* July 1947.

22. If the services of federal, state and local governments to the people are measured by the value of goods and services purchased by government and this value is added to private consumer outlays, the share of "services" in total outlays, excluding business services, amounted to 42.6 per cent in 1929 and 42.2 per cent in 1946.

CHAPTER 4

TRENDS IN NATIONAL INCOME *

THE MONEY ECONOMY is Janus-faced: Its operations appear not only as production, transformation and exchange of commodities and services but also as money transactions that find their expression in the flow of national income. Similarly, the clash of interests in allocating the social dividend among the various factors in production appears also as a struggle for shares of the national income.

SIZE OF NATIONAL INCOME

Official statistics of national income go back no further than 1929. The two decades they cover include the great depression, recovery, mobilization, all-out war, reconversion and the postwar boom. In this period short-range dislocations have overshadowed secular developments. To appraise the long-range trends in the size and structure of national income, official statistics must be supplemented by private estimates, such as Kuznets' series of estimates for 1919–1938 and Martin's for 1799–1938.

Besides having methodological differences, these series differ in degree of reliability. The further back a series goes, the wider is its margin of error. Estimates for the nineteenth century rest on fairly thin information, and those for periods before the Civil War are particularly questionable.

Trend in National Income, 1869–1929

According to Martin's estimates,[1] from 1869 to 1919 national income, adjusted to the cost of living, rose approximately 4 per cent a year. (See Figure 7, Trend A.) After the setback in 1920–1921, progress was resumed at the same annual rate but on a lower level. (See Figure 7, Trend B.)

Martin's estimates of the long-range trend in adjusted national income can also be represented as a growth at an annual rate of 4.5 per cent in the period 1869–1909 and 2.3 per cent in the period 1909–1929. If this measurement is used, it appears that real national income increased until 1909 at about the same rate as the volume of manufacturing or total industrial and commercial production as estimated by Frickey (Appendix Table 2). The two series show significant divergence, however, after 1909.

A similar discrepancy appears when real income derived from manufacturing production as estimated by Martin (Figure 8) is compared with Frickey's index of production. This discrepancy probably arises from the conventional method of estimating real income by "deflating" nominal income by a price index. In the long run, and especially in periods when prices are widely dispersed, this method usually gives a distorted picture of the changes in the volume of goods and services that real income is supposed to measure.[2]

---

* By W. S. Woytinsky.

1. The series on national income computed by Robert F. Martin for the National Industrial Conference Board (*National Income in the United States, 1799–1938,* National Industrial Conference Board, New York, 1939) is restricted until 1910 to years immediately preceding the decennial censuses; beginning with that year, it shows the year-to-year change in national income (total and per capita) at current prices and with adjustment to cost-of-living and wholesale (or general) price indexes. (See Appendix Table 5.) The study also contains many distributions of national income by industrial origin and distributive shares. (See Appendix Tables 6 and 7.)

2. The source of the bias is in the method of weighting divergent changes in prices of individual commodities in proportion to their assumed significance in the consumer's household or in the whole economy. The weights established when an index is being constructed remain unchanged as long as the index is maintained, the assumption being that the consumer, or the community as a whole, uses the same merchandise in the same proportions year in and year out. Consumption habits change, however, as time goes on. New articles appear on the market and replace old ones. New merchandise often begins its career as a luxury accessible only to the rich and gradually finds its way to broader circles of consumers until it becomes a necessity. This has been the story of electric lighting, the gas range, the telephone, the car, the radio set, all kinds of electrical household appliances, aluminum, rayon, nylon and so on. As the costs and prices of new articles fall, their consumption increases. The rise in demand makes mass production possible, and successive cuts in price open broader outlets.

Similarly, the relative positions of staple commodities in the consumer's budget tend to shift in inverse

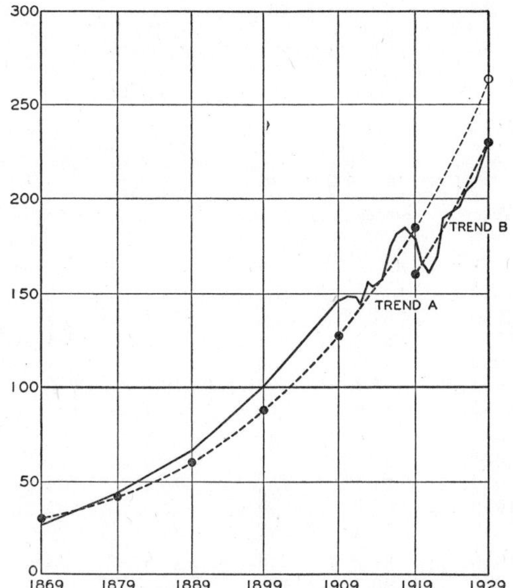

FIGURE 7. INDEX OF NATIONAL INCOME, ADJUSTED TO COST OF LIVING, 1869–1929

(*1899 = 100*)

Source: Computed from Appendix Table 5.

Trend in National Income, 1919–1938

The estimates of national income from 1919 to 1938 developed by Simon Kuznets for the National Bureau of Economic Research [3] differ from Martin's estimates in details, but they show the same trend. (See Table 14 and Appendix Tables 8 and 9.)

If the twenty years covered by Kuznets are considered as a continuous period, it appears that the secular trend in national income was completely masked by the short-range ups and downs. For example, the index of national income adjusted to the consumers' price index [4] shows a succession of movements: a rise until 1929, a steep fall to the low in 1932–1933, and a new rise ending in a setback in 1938. (See Figure 9.) No consistent trend can be deduced from such diverse shifts within so short a period.

Trend in National Income, 1929–1950

According to the Department of Commerce, national income amounted to $87.4 billion in

TABLE 14

NATIONAL INCOME, 1919–1938

(*In Billions*)

Year	At Current Prices	At Average 1935–1939 Prices	Year	At Current Prices	At Average 1935–1939 Prices
1919..	$65.9	$53.2	1929..	$87.8	$71.7
1920..	76.4	53.3	1930..	77.6	65.0
1921..	60.3	47.2	1931..	60.3	55.5
1922..	61.5	51.3	1932..	42.6	43.6
1923..	72.9	59.8	1933..	41.8	45.2
1924..	73.4	60.1	1934..	49.5	51.7
1925..	77.8	62.0	1935..	54.4	55.5
1926..	82.8	65.5	1936..	62.7	63.2
1927..	81.4	65.6	1937..	70.1	68.3
1928..	83.4	68.0	1938..	64.9	64.4

Sources: Current national income as estimated by Simon Kuznets, *National Income and Its Composition, 1919–1938,* National Bureau of Economic Research, New York, 1941, pp. 163–64. The current figures are adjusted to the Bureau of Labor Statistics "consumers' price index," formerly known as "cost-of-living index."

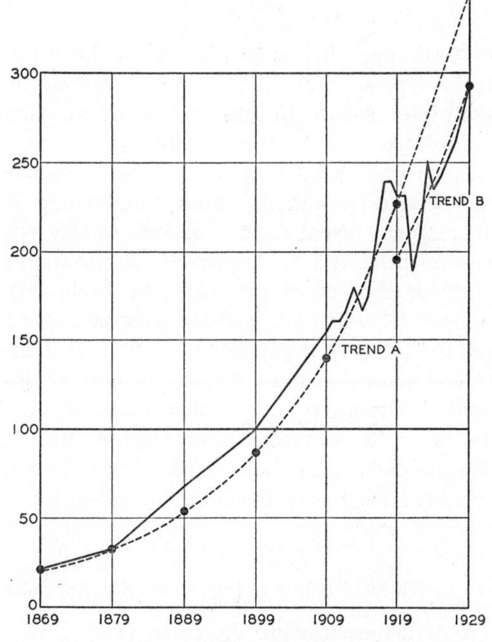

FIGURE 8. INDEX OF INCOME FROM MANUFACTURING, ADJUSTED TO COST OF LIVING, 1869–1929

(*1899 = 100*)

Source: Computed from Appendix Table 6.

direction to changes in price. Of two competing articles, the one for which prices are being cut gains ground. Since each consumer continually adjusts his consumption pattern to get more for his money, in the long run each dollar he spends brings him more than he would have got if he had followed a set pattern in his spending. Thus, when prices go up, a price index of the conventional type tends to overstate the loss in the purchasing power of money; when prices go down, it understates the gain. As long as prices fluctuate within a fairly narrow range, the resulting bias is negligible, but in periods of marked price changes it becomes considerable. This probably explains the downward bias of Martin's figures for adjusted national income during and after World War I in comparison with the index of industrial production.

3. Simon Kuznets, *National Income and Its Composition, 1919–1938,* National Bureau of Economic Research, New York, 1941.

4. All responsibility for this adjustment is the writer's.

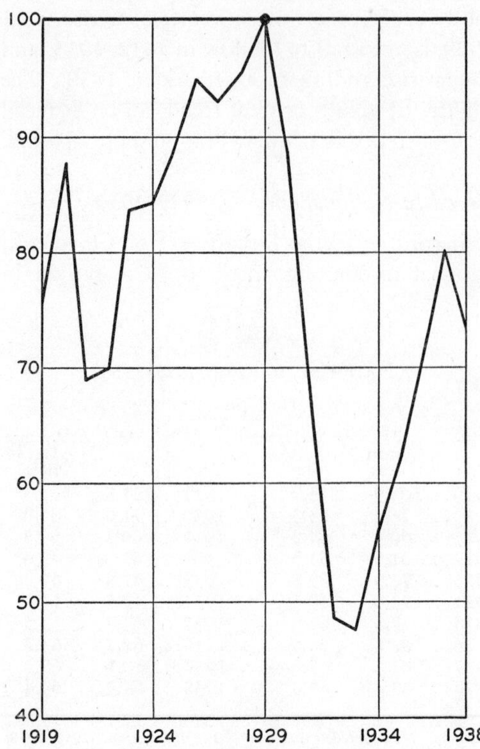

FIGURE 9. INDEX OF NATIONAL INCOME, ADJUSTED TO CONSUMERS' PRICE INDEX, 1919–1938

(*1929 = 100*)

Source: Based on Appendix Table 8.

TABLE 15

NATIONAL INCOME AND INCOME FROM MANUFACTURING, ADJUSTED TO CONSUMERS' PRICE INDEX, 1929–1950

Year	National Income		Income from Manufacturing	
	Amount (*In Billions, at 1935–1939 Prices*)	Index (*1929 = 100*)	Percentage of National Income	Index (*1929 = 100*)
1929....	$71.3	100	25.2	100
1930....	62.8	88	24.4	85
1931....	54.2	76	21.1	63
1932....	42.7	60	17.3	41
1933....	42.8	60	19.1	46
1934....	50.8	71	22.5	63
1935....	57.9	81	23.5	76
1936....	65.3	92	25.0	91
1937....	71.7	101	26.2	104
1938....	66.8	94	22.3	83
1939....	73.0	102	24.7	100
1940....	81.2	114	27.5	124
1941....	98.7	138	31.7	174
1942....	117.7	165	33.0	216
1943....	137.3	193	34.2	261
1944....	146.5	205	32.9	268
1945....	142.3	200	28.4	224
1946....	129.4	181	27.1	195
1947....	124.8	175	29.9	207
1948....	130.5	183	30.1	218
1949....	128.2	180	29.1	207
1950....	139.6	196	31.0	241

Source: Based on Appendix Table 10. The writer takes all responsibility for the adjustment of the original figures to consumer prices.

1929, dropped below $40 billion at the depth of the depression of the 1930's, and reached the $200 billion mark in 1947.[5] Because of wide fluctuations in prices, these figures do not reflect correctly the changes in the volume of goods and services produced. More enlightening is the ratio of current national income to the consumers' price index, despite the shortcomings of this method of adjustment. (See Table 15.)

From 1929 to 1950, deflated national income (at 1935–1939 prices) almost doubled. It increased somewhat more than the volume of industrial output. (Cf. Appendix Table 4.) On the other hand, income from manufacturing, likewise deflated by the consumers' price index, fluctuated more than the index of production.[6]

In 1939 both adjusted national income and the volume of manufacturing production were at the same level as in 1929. On a per capita basis the 1939 level meant a setback of approximately 7 per cent rather than the rise that could have been expected from the long-range trend. Thus the United States entered the war with national income and industrial production far below the trend line. The fabulous growth of production during the war was largely a catching-up process.

In the five years 1939–1944 the nation doubled its income (adjusted to prices) and more than doubled industrial output, but it could hardly have achieved these results if the starting point had not been so low. Besides mobilizing idle reserves of manpower and industrial capacity, the country shifted from 40 hours to more than 48 hours of work a week and let housewives, children and youths leave homes and classrooms for workshops and assembly lines.

The wartime economy was so completely different from the peacetime that it is difficult

5. *National Income Supplement to Survey of Current Business,* July 1947; *Survey of Current Business,* National Income Number, July 1948. See Appendix Tables 10 to 13.

6. At the depth of the depression (1932), when the production index dropped to 54 (1929 = 100), the index of adjusted income from manufacturing fell to 41; in 1943–1944, when the production index rose to 221–225, the index of adjusted income from manufacturing rose to 261–268.

to determine how real were the gains in production and "real earnings" announced by wartime statistics. It seems, however, that the response of the United States to the challenge of the war offset the losses the economic system suffered in the 1930's and brought production back close to the long-range trend line. If national income had been advancing steadily since 1919 at a rate of 4 per cent a year (see Figure 7, Trend B), by 1950 it would have reached roughly $160 billion, at 1935–1939 prices. Actually it was somewhat below this figure. The lag may have been partly due to the bias in the method of deflating national income by the price index. If this is corrected, the average rate of growth of real national income in the past two decades was close to 4 per cent annually.

As in the trend of industrial production,[7] this progress was largely due to the growth of population and labor force. Adjusted national income per capita of population increased from 1929 to 1949 by approximately 48 per cent, an average annual gain of approximately 2 per cent.

In measuring the growth of production per man-hour worked, size of the labor force, level of employment, and shortening of the work week must be taken into account. According to official estimates, the number of persons engaged in economic activities on a full-time basis [8] increased from 45.7 million in 1929 to 57.3 million in 1949 and 58.8 million in 1950.[9] In manufacturing industries the work week went down from an average of 44.2 hours in 1929 to 39.2 hours in 1949 and increased again to 41.4 by the end of 1950. Hours of work in nonmanufacturing industries were also reduced after 1929 — in some instances less drastically but in others, such as mining, even more. Assuming that the reduction in hours per week from 1929 to 1950 averaged 6 per cent for the nation as a whole, the total number of hours worked may have increased from 1929 to 1950 by 21 per cent. This suggests that adjusted national income per man-hour worked rose approximately 62 per cent from 1929 to 1950, an average annual gain of 2.6 per cent.

Over-All Trend, 1849–1950

When the Department of Commerce index of national income for 1929–1950 is combined with Martin's estimates going back to 1849, adjusted national income appears to have been more than thirty times as large in 1950 as in the middle of the nineteenth century. In the same span of time, however, population increased more than sixfold. Thus real income per capita of population in 1950 was approximately 4.7 times higher than a century ago. This figure indicates an advance of approximately 1.56 per cent a year. If the measurement starts with 1879, however, the average annual gain is close to 2 per cent. The rate would be reduced to approximately 1.8 per cent if adjusted national income is prorated over the population of working age. It would be raised to 2.3 per cent if the curtailment of weekly work hours is taken into account and national income is prorated over man-hours of work.

Distribution of National Income by Industry

The shares of national income originating in various industries are determined by the distribution of economic resources (employment and capital investments), on the one hand, and the structure of prices and wages, on the other. Both factors are in turn affected by the interplay of long-range economic forces, cyclical ups and downs in business activity, and various short-range influences. It is not always possible to disentangle these factors.

Though the distribution of national income has fluctuated somewhat erratically in the past two decades, the trends enumerated below are clearly discernible in the period from 1799 to 1929. (See Figure 10 and Appendix Table 6.)

1. Until the last decade of the nineteenth century, the relative shares of agriculture and transportation and communication in private national income steadily declined.

2. By the turn of the century, these trends leveled off. In 1919 the share of agriculture in the national income was practically the same as in 1879 or 1899. The share of mining and manufacturing continued to increase while the share of trade and services declined and that of transportation and communication did not change appreciably.

3. In the decade from 1919 to 1929 the share of agriculture fell from 22.9 per cent to 12.7 per cent, that of mining and manufacturing remained about the same, and services made substantial gains.

7. See Chapter 3.
8. Excluding unpaid family workers.
9. Estimates of the Department of Commerce.

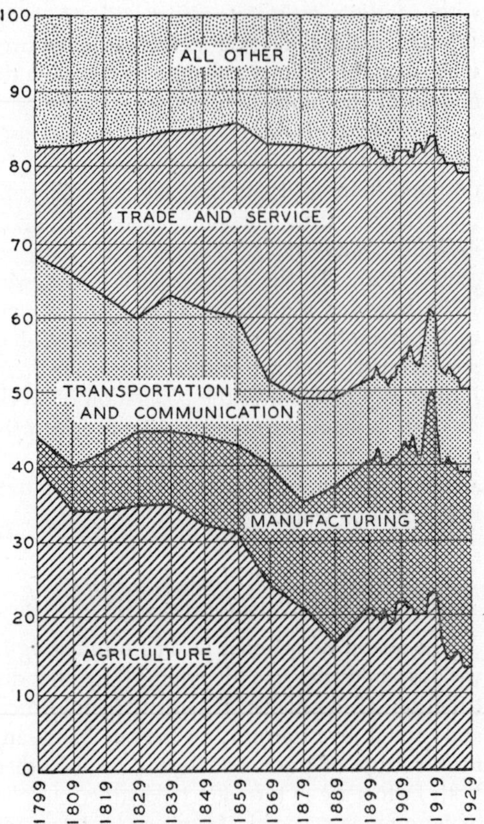

FIGURE 10. PERCENTAGE DISTRIBUTION OF NATIONAL INCOME, BY INDUSTRY, 1799–1929

Source: Robert F. Martin, *National Income in the United States, 1799–1938,* National Industrial Conference Board, New York, 1939. Cf. Appendix Table 6.

From 1929 to 1950 the share of agriculture in total national income fell from 9.2 per cent to 7.4 per cent; that of mining, manufacturing and building construction increased from 31.8 to 38.2 per cent, and that of services (including trade and transportation but excluding government) declined from 52.4 per cent to 44.3 per cent.

Recent Changes

Recent changes in the distribution of national income by industrial origin have been dominated by the succession of the depression, the economic revival, the defense and armament programs, the war economy, the demobilization and the postwar boom; they fail to show any consistent long-range trend. (See Figure 11 and Appendix Table 11.)

Even the widespread notion that government's share in the national income has been continually rising requires serious qualification. It is true that the ratio of public expenditures and taxes to national income has increased. This item, however, includes transfer payments, which are not a component part of national income. After exclusion of transfer payments, it appears that the share of government in national income amounted to 5.9 per cent in 1929, averaged 12.3 per cent in the period 1932–1939, jumped to 20.5 per cent in 1945, went down to 8.8 per cent in 1948, increased again to 10.1 in 1949, and amounted to 9.8 in 1950. During the twenty-two years 1929–1950, in only two years, 1929 and 1930, was the relative share of government in national income lower than in 1948.

The downward trend in the relative share of agriculture that prevailed until 1932 has leveled off in recent years, but there is no evidence to indicate whether or not agriculture will continue to hold its present comparatively favorable position. The share of manufacturing and mining increased from 18.9 per cent in 1932 to 35.8 per cent in 1943. It was 32.5 per cent in 1948 and 33.1 in 1950 as compared with 27.6 per cent in 1929. The combined share of wholesale and retail trade, finance, insurance and real estate was 30 per cent in 1929, 26.9 per cent in 1948 and 26.6 in 1950.

It is a matter of opinion whether all these changes were temporary or have reflected some long-range trend. But even if they are interpreted as long-range shifts, they should hardly be projected into the future.

DISTRIBUTIVE SHARES OF NATIONAL INCOME

According to Martin's estimates, the relative size of the major distributive shares of national income fluctuated within a very narrow range in the periods 1899–1919 and 1921–1937. In the first of these periods, wages and salaries represented between 57.6 and 62.2 per cent of total realized private production income; there was a slight upward trend, from an average of 58.6 per cent in 1899–1902 to 60.2 per cent in 1916–1919. The combined share of entrepreneurial income (including income of farmers), interest, net rent and royalties declined in the same period from an average of 41.5 per cent in 1899–1902 to 39.8 per cent in 1916–1919. (See Figure 12.)

After World War I the share of wages and salaries rose considerably. According to Martin's

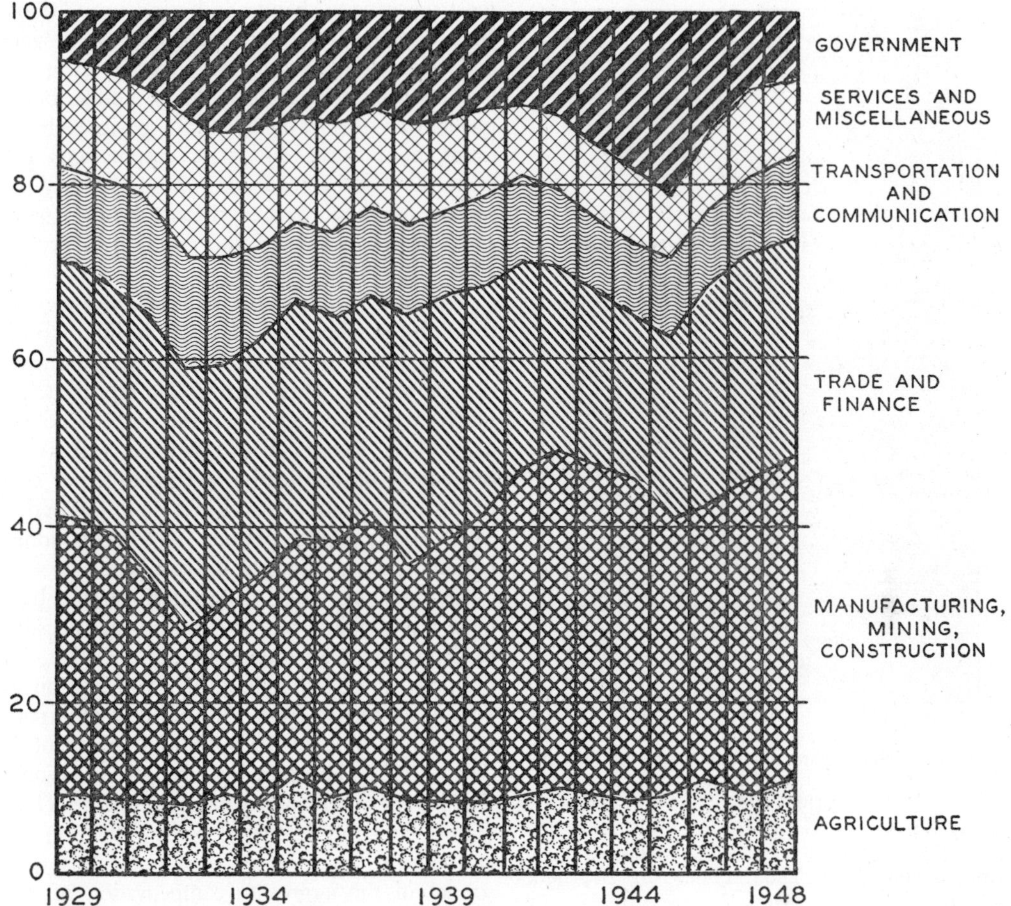

FIGURE 11. PERCENTAGE DISTRIBUTION OF NATIONAL INCOME, BY INDUSTRIAL ORIGIN, 1929–1948
Source: Appendix Table 11.

estimates, it has fluctuated most of the time between 66 and 68 per cent since 1921. Although for the period 1929–1937 Martin's series does not agree in all details with the official national income statistics of the Department of Commerce, his observation of the increase in the share of wages and salaries since World War I nevertheless deserves attention.

That war brought considerable gains to organized labor both in membership and prestige and in wage rates. Success was short-lived, however, and after the Armistice labor lost most of its battles. Precisely at this time, in a period of setbacks and stagnation in the labor movement, the share of wages and salaries in national income went up.

This change was probably due to the combined effect of several factors: as the farmers' share in national income shrank, the share of wages and salaries was bound to increase; with the progressive concentration of industrial enterprise, managerial functions shifted from owners to salaried officers; with the development of corporative organization of business, a part of the profits of owners took the form of salaries for services rendered to the corporation or partnership; the relative share of interest, net rent and royalties in the national income was reduced by the war and postwar inflation.

Effects of Business Cycles

Official statistics of national income show that the relative share of wages and salaries tends to increase in depression and to decline in prosperity. The share of wages and salaries in private national income [10] advanced from 55.5 per

10. Private national income is defined as national income excluding compensation of government employees.

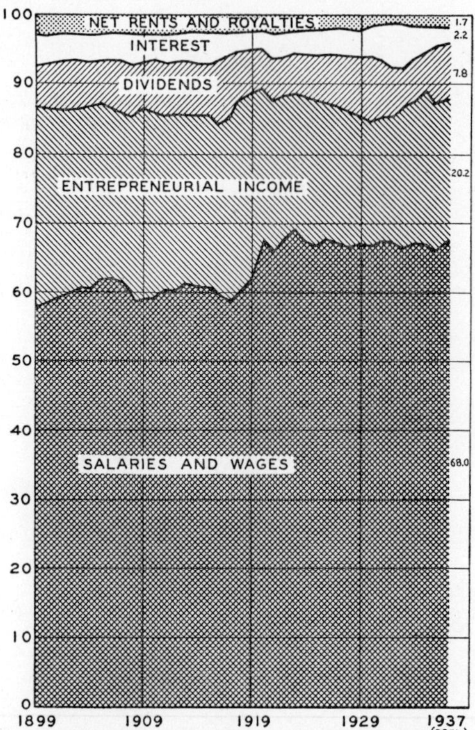

FIGURE 12. PERCENTAGE DISTRIBUTION OF PRIVATE NATIONAL INCOME, BY DISTRIBUTIVE SHARES, 1899–1937

Source: Robert F. Martin, *National Income in the United States, 1799–1938,* National Industrial Conference Board, New York, 1939. Cf. Appendix Table 7.

cent in 1929 to more than 70 per cent in 1932–1933, shrank again in the recovery period, and continued to decline until 1942, with only one appreciable interruption, in the recession year 1938. (See Appendix Tables 12 and 13.) Apart from fluctuations during the war, there has been a perfect negative correlation between business conditions and the share of wages and salaries in the national income. (See Table 16 and Figure 13.)

Corporate profits, especially undistributed profits (after tax and dividend payments), are most sensitive to changes in business conditions. In bad years they often drop to zero; in very bad times they become negative. During the two decades from 1929 to 1948, undistributed profits were negative eight times, positive eleven times, zero once. In 1929, corporations put aside $2.6 billion; during 1930–1938 they absorbed losses of $20.2 billion; during 1939–1950 they accumulated $86.7 billion in profits. (See Table 17.)

The net balance of undistributed profits through the whole period, $69.1 billion, is misleading, however; for the losses occurred during the depression, when each dollar represented a much larger real value than the postwar dollars of profits. Losses of corporations (after disbursement of dividends) averaged 5 per cent of current private national income in the period 1930–1938; in the period 1939–1950, undistributed profits averaged 4.6 per cent.

Changes in other distributive shares have been less striking, and it is not always possible to determine their immediate cause. What, for example, caused the share of compensation of employees to rise from 55.5 per cent of private national income in 1929 to 60.4 per cent in 1949–1950? The growing strength of unions? The labor-friendly policy of government? These factors probably exercised some influence, but at the same time the share of managerial personnel in the aggregate compensation of employees was also increasing. Moreover, from 1929 to 1950, total compensation of employees increased in almost exactly the same proportion as proprietary income including corporate profits, but excluding rent and net interest. In fact, compensation of employees increased from $50.8 billion to $153.3 billion, or 202 per cent, while proprietary income went up from $24.2 billion to $72.2 billion, or 198 per cent. (See Appendix Table 12.)

The most important real change in the distribution of private national income, it appears, was the drop of net interest from 8 per cent

TABLE 16

PERCENTAGE DISTRIBUTION OF PRIVATE NATIONAL INCOME, SELECTED PERIODS, 1929–1950

Type of Income	1929	Average 1932–1933	Average 1942–1943	Average 1949–1950
Total	100.0	100.0	100.0	100.0
Compensation of employees	55.5	70.1	57.1	60.4
Proprietors' and rental income	24.0	20.7	23.3	20.8
Corporate profits	12.5	— 5.6	16.8	16.2
Net interest	8.0	14.7	2.8	2.5

Source: Appendix Table 13.

TABLE 17

UNDISTRIBUTED CORPORATE PROFITS, 1929–1950

Year	Amount, in Billions	Percentage of Private National Income	Year	Amount, in Billions	Percentage of Private National Income
1929..........	$2.6	3.2	1940..........	$ 2.4	3.3
1930..........	—3.0	— 4.4	1941..........	4.9	5.3
1931..........	—5.4	—10.1	1942..........	5.1	4.3
1932..........	—6.0	—16.4	1943..........	6.2	4.3
1933..........	—2.4	— 7.1	1944..........	6.1	4.1
1934..........	—1.6	— 3.8	1945..........	3.8	2.6
1935..........	—0.6	— 1.2	1946..........	8.1	5.1
1936..........	—0.3	— 0.5	1947..........	12.0	6.7
1937..........	0.0	0.0	1948..........	13.5	6.6
1938..........	—0.9	— 1.5	1949..........	9.8	5.0
1939..........	1.2	1.9	1950..........	13.6	6.3

Source: Based on Appendix Tables 12 and 13.

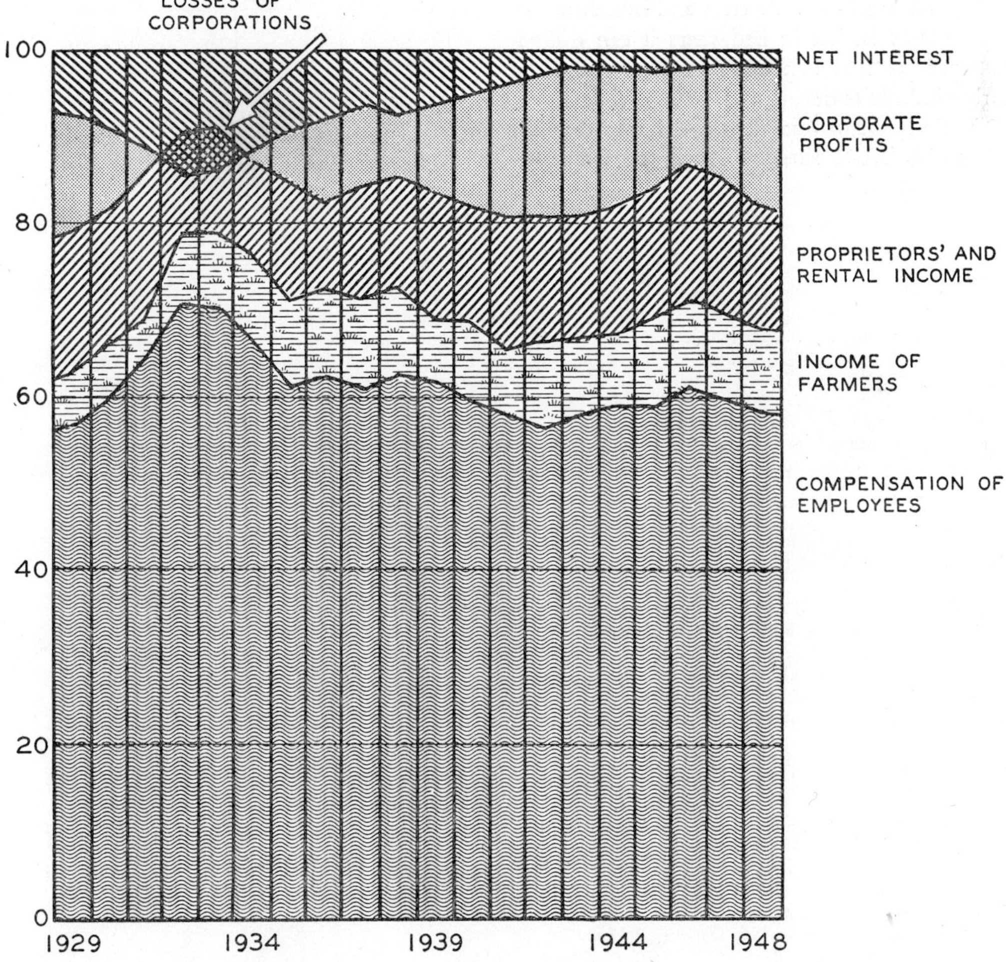

FIGURE 13. PERCENTAGE DISTRIBUTION OF PRIVATE NATIONAL INCOME, BY DISTRIBUTIVE SHARES, 1929–1948

Source: Appendix Table 13.

to 2.5 per cent of the total. The difference was shared by employees and employers.

Employees' Share, by Industry, 1929–1950

Wages and salaries constitute approximately 18 per cent of income originating in agriculture; somewhat less than 30 per cent in finance, insurance and real estate; 60 per cent in wholesale and retail trade and in communication and public utilities; 65 per cent in manufacturing and in mining; and about 75 per cent in transportation. (See Appendix Table 14.) The percentages vary appreciably from year to year, increasing during declines in business and decreasing in good times. (See Figure 14.)

The remarkable feature of the ratio of wages to income in single industries and broad industrial groups is that in bad years it can exceed 100 per cent, as happened in most manufacturing industries during 1932–1933. (See Table 18.) Such a situation does not imply that all other distributive shares disappeared from the

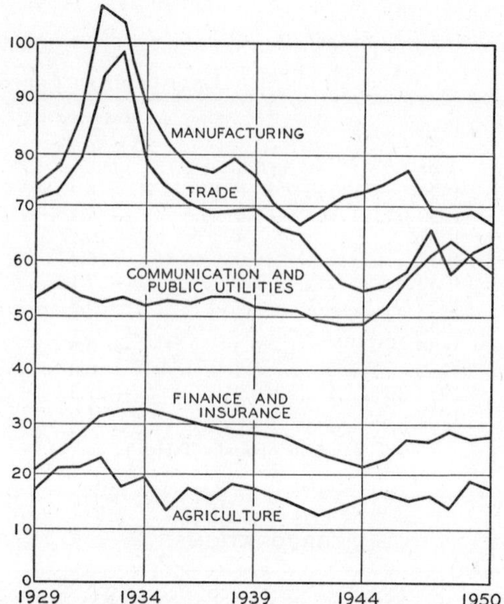

FIGURE 14. WAGES AS PERCENTAGE OF INCOME, SELECTED INDUSTRIES, 1929–1950

Source: Appendix Table 14.

TABLE 18

RATIO OF WAGES AND SALARIES TO INCOME ORIGINATING IN SELECTED INDUSTRIES, 1929, 1932, 1933 AND 1947–1950

Industry	1929	1932	1933	1947	1948	1949	1950
MINING	72.2	100.4	103.6	72.3	61.3	63.8	62.7
Metal	41.8	252.4	126.8	53.0	48.9	53.1	49.3
Anthracite	91.6	100.7	101.5	87.2	80.7	83.5	82.3
Bituminous and other soft coal	93.4	108.4	109.4	80.0	72.4	75.0	71.9
Crude petroleum and natural gas	66.0	76.4	90.8	65.9	48.8	54.4	54.2
Nonmetallic	63.3	104.0	112.2	73.6	65.4	64.1	67.8
MANUFACTURING	73.1	106.7	103.5	69.3	69.1	69.3	66.8
Food and kindred products	72.6	77.8	84.7	63.0	65.6	67.8	70.2
Tobacco manufactures	55.0	27.3	52.1	55.0	47.5	45.2	41.5
Textile mill products	81.1	107.7	128.6	61.1	67.7	76.6	78.4
Apparel and other finished fabric products	84.8	113.6	107.0	72.7	83.3	83.8	89.3
Lumber and timber basic products	83.3	150.0	163.1	70.9	68.5	76.6	71.5
Furniture and finished lumber products	90.1	119.0	137.2	88.5	80.3	84.1	85.3
Paper and allied products	76.4	101.1	96.2	57.3	63.3	66.7	63.2
Printing and publishing	78.2	95.1	90.8	73.2	76.9	79.0	79.0
Chemicals and allied products	58.5	74.1	61.0	60.1	55.9	54.6	52.9
Products of petroleum and coal	23.8	122.7	876.5	36.6	26.3	32.3	29.4
Rubber products	78.9	115.9	136.9	72.0	76.3	76.9	88.0
Leather and leather products	81.7	95.4	112.6	78.8	80.2	86.0	88.4
Stone, clay and glass products	77.3	193.5	109.1	70.9	71.0	70.0	64.2
Iron and steel and their products	71.1	174.9	117.9	68.9	72.2	72.7	64.0
Nonferrous metals and their products	70.5	104.6	132.9	71.3	74.4	70.7	74.4
Machinery, except electrical	73.4	164.1	116.0	78.2	75.2	73.6	70.9
Electrical machinery	82.0	117.2	109.4	77.5	76.6	72.5	62.2
Transportation equipment, except automobiles	82.6	131.5	134.8	95.5	90.5	86.2	83.3
Automobiles and automobile equipment	70.2	219.6	91.4	67.5	62.7	54.2	48.8
Miscellaneous	74.9	135.2	113.5	84.3	82.8	78.8	80.8

Source: Survey of Current Business, National Income Supplement, 1951, pp. 158–61. Cf. Appendix Table 14.

scene at that time. It indicates only that at the depth of a depression, losses of corporations may exceed dividends, rents, net interest and entrepreneurial withdrawals.

In petroleum and coal products, for example, wages and salaries were 23.8 per cent of income in 1929, 122.7 per cent in 1932, and 876.5 per cent in 1933. At first sight the last relationship seems improbable, but this is how it developed: In 1933 the petroleum and coal industry paid out to employees $149 million and to stockholders $120 million. In addition $11 million was paid in taxes, $24 million in interest and $5 million was received by employees as supplements to wages and salaries. The total of $309 million, however, did not originate in the industry but was largely covered from reserves of corporations: $171 million from liquid reserves (as negative undistributed profits) and $121 million from the value of inventory (inventory valuation adjustment). Thus, the net income originating in the industry amounted to only $17 million and the wage-to-income ratio for the operating year: $149 million ÷ $17 million = 876.5 per cent.

No "normal" wage-to-income ratio is, therefore, applicable to all industries. The ratio varies from industry to industry in accordance with differences in capital structure (capital investment per worker), and it also varies from year to year under the impact of changes in profits.

CHAPTER 5

TRENDS IN WAGES AND HOURS *

TRENDS IN EARNINGS and wage rates, in dollars and cents, can be traced with approximate accuracy for a century. Fairly dependable information about year-to-year changes in real wages covers somewhat more than half a century. For the decades from 1840 to 1890, the general upward trend of real wages is apparent but the many fluctuations are difficult to trace. If due consideration is given to the limitations of the available data, analysis of developments in the earlier periods may contribute to an understanding of long-range trends in the economy of the United States.

Information on wages and prices, especially on retail prices, before 1840 is so slight that widely differing conclusions have been drawn from the data. For 1840–1890, more or less continuous data are available. (See Appendix Table 15.) Among the measures of changes in real wages in this period are the indexes constructed by Alvin H. Hansen, Harold G. Moulton, Rufus S. Tucker, and the Federal Reserve Bank of New York.[1] All these indexes rely mainly on the *Report on Wholesale Prices, Wages and Transportation* prepared by the Senate Committee on Finance (Aldrich Committee).[2] Before this committee was authorized, in 1891, to make a survey of wages and prices, the government had made no consistent or continued effort to collect such data. The experts of the committee had to start from scratch, and their report affords evidence that they proceeded "with every precaution to secure the greatest possible degree of accuracy."[3]

Hourly Earnings

Data on wages, hours and prices provided by the committee, supplemented by Mitchell's index of cost of living for 1860–1880, show gains in real hourly earnings in each decade from 1840 to 1890 except the 1870's and an exceptionally rapid rise from 1880 to 1890. (See Table 19; cf. Figure 15.) These changes reflect the composite effects of industrial progress, repercussions of war, and changes in business conditions and prices. The increase of more than 90 per cent in money earnings adjusted by the "cost-of-living" index is probably a fairly close approximation; the changes within the period, as shown in Table 19, are probably less dependable.

The index of hourly earnings adjusted by the cost-of-living index rose from 81.5 in 1840 to 156.9 in 1890 (1860 = 100), an average growth of 1.3 per cent a year. Progress was very slow in the first half of the period under survey and faster in the second: if 1865 is taken as the division point, the rate of annual growth of adjusted hourly earnings averaged 0.5 per cent in 1840–1865 and 2.2 per cent in 1865–1890. The extreme difference in these rates of change was caused in part by the depressed wartime level of real wages in 1865.

Hours of Work

The Aldrich Committee report also provided detailed information on daily hours by occupation and establishment and summarized it for

---

* By Witt Bowden, Bureau of Labor Statistics, U.S. Department of Labor. Opinions expressed in this chapter are those of the author and not necessarily of the agency with which he is associated.

1. See Alvin H. Hansen, "Factors Affecting the Trend of Real Wages," *American Economic Review*, March 1925, p. 32; Harold G. Moulton, *Income and Economic Progress*, Brookings Institution, Washington, 1935, pp. 181–82; Rufus S. Tucker, "Real Wages under Laissez-Faire," *Barron's Weekly*, October 23, 1933, p. 7; the index of the Research Department of the Federal Reserve Bank of New York.

Cf. W. S. Woytinsky, *Earnings and Social Security in the United States*, Committee on Social Security, Social Science Research Council, Washington, 1943, Appendix Tables, pp. 32–33.

2. *Report on Wholesale Prices, Wages and Transportation*, Senate Committee on Finance, S.Rept. 1394, 52d Cong., 2d sess., 1893.

3. Actual collection of the data was largely under the supervision of Carroll D. Wright, Commissioner of Labor of the recently created Bureau of Labor (later the Bureau of Labor Statistics). The indexes of wages and prices were constructed by R. P. Falkner, Professor of Statistics at the University of Pennsylvania. Certain criticisms and refinements of the data were made later by Professor Wesley C. Mitchell and others, and Mitchell constructed independently an index of cost of living for 1860 to 1880. See Wesley C. Mitchell, *Gold, Prices, and Wages under the Greenback Standard, 1860–1880,* University of California Press, Berkeley, 1908.

TABLE 19

INDEXES OF NOMINAL HOURLY EARNINGS, PRICES AND ADJUSTED EARNINGS, 1840–1890

Period	Nominal Hourly Earnings [a]	Prices: Wholesale	Prices: "Cost of Living"	Hourly Earnings Adjusted by: Wholesale Price Index [b]	Hourly Earnings Adjusted by: "Cost-of-Living" Index [b]
		Indexes (*1860 = 100*)			
1840	79.6	116.8	97.7	68.2	81.5
1850	87.0	102.3	89.2	85.0	97.5
1860	100.0	100.0	100.0	100.0	100.0
1870	175.0	142.4	150.0	122.9	116.7
1880	152.8	106.9	132.0	142.9	115.8
1890	185.0	92.3	117.9	200.4	156.9
		Percentage Change			
1840–1860	+ 25.6	−14.4	+ 2.4	+ 46.6	+22.7
1860–1890	+ 85.0	− 7.7	+17.9	+100.4	+56.9
1840–1890	+132.4	−21.0	+20.7	+193.8	+92.5

a. Derived from the Aldrich Committee's index of weighted day rates and index of hours per day.
b. Neither of these indexes should be viewed as an adequate index of real wages, because there is no genuine index of prices paid by wage earners as consumers. The first index undoubtedly exaggerates both the fluctuations and the over-all rise in real wages; the second exaggerates the fluctuations and may somewhat minimize the over-all rise.

Sources: Report on Wholesale Prices, Wages and Transportation, Senate Committee on Finance (Aldrich Committee), S.Rept. 1394, 52d Cong., 2d sess., 1893, and Wesley C. Mitchell, *Gold, Prices, and Wages under the Greenback Standard, 1860–1880,* University of California Press, Berkeley, 1908.

single industries and for all industries covered by the report.[4]

Few records were available for the earlier years of the period, but twenty-one industries were included by 1860. The committee found that in 1840 the prevailing length of the working day (weighted by estimated employment) averaged 11.4 hours for the nine industries included and ranged from 9.3 hours in the white-lead industry to 14 hours in cotton goods.

In 1890 the average for the twenty-one industries was 10 hours, with the shortest work day — 9.3 hours — in municipal public works and the longest — 12 hours — in the ale, beer and porter industry and in paper manufacturing. Thus, on the average, hours of work were reduced by 12.3 per cent in fifty years. The report describes this change as "hardly so considerable as might have been expected," and expresses the view that there had probably been a somewhat greater reduction in hours of employment as a whole than in the establishments and industries surveyed.[5]

Hours and Wages in 1890

The Aldrich Committee was concerned primarily with tracing the trends of wages, although the committee's report contains detailed occupational wage-rate data. On the basis of this and other information, Paul H. Douglas has estimated the general average of hourly earnings in 1890 at 21.1 cents. His estimate of average annual earnings of workers generally in that year was $486. Standard or normally scheduled hours of work in 1890 were computed at 58.4 hours a week.[6] The Douglas figure of hourly earnings is substantially above the actual average, because of the emphasis in the available data on above-average occupational rates. The average annual wage of workers in manufacturing as derived from censuses of manufacturing was $445 in 1889 as compared with $247 in 1849.

Wages after 1890

Wage trends since 1890 can be traced with greater precision, owing to the relative abundance of statistical data. About that time the Bureau of Labor began to collect information on wages and prices on a systematic basis. Originally, the retail price statistics were restricted largely to foods, but by using supplementary data on other consumer prices, Douglas was able to construct his cost-of-living index for 1890–1913. The period since then is covered by the Bureau of Labor Statistics index.

Despite serious gaps in the available data and their limited comparability, the two indexes

4. *Report,* pp. 178–79.
5. *Ibid.,* pp. 179–80.

6. Paul H. Douglas, *Real Wages in the United States, 1890–1926,* Houghton Mifflin, Boston, 1930, pp. 205, 208, 391.

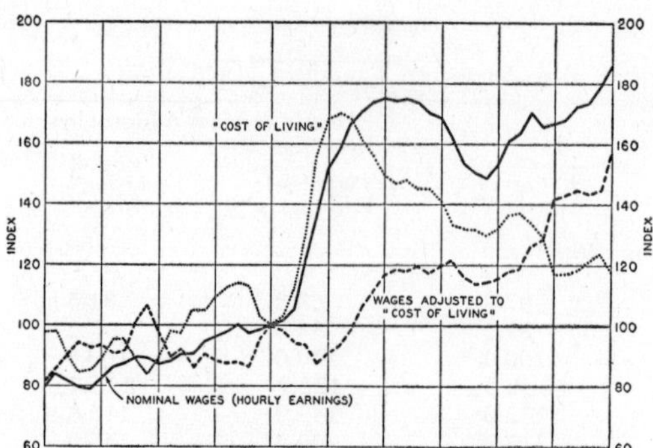

FIGURE 15. INDEXES OF HOURLY EARNINGS, COST OF LIVING AND ADJUSTED WAGES, 1840–1890

(*1860 = 100*)

Source: Table 19.

Falkner constructed for the Aldrich Committee two indexes of wage rates per day. One was a simple average of the indexes of all occupational day rates, each occupational rate representing the average rate in a particular establishment. The other index was constructed by combining the occupational indexes for each industry and weighting the industry indexes by estimated industry employment at ten-year intervals. The latter series is reproduced in Figure 15 as the index of nominal wages (hourly earnings).

For adjustment of nominal wages to changing prices, the committee used two indexes. Its wholesale price index (used in Table 19) is a simple or unweighted average of the indexes of wholesale prices of commodities for which data were available in 1891. This is the widely used index of wholesale prices published by the Bureau of Labor Statistics. (See *Report on Wholesale Prices, Wages and Transportation,* Senate Committee on Finance [Aldrich Committee], S.Rept. 1394, 52d Cong., 2d sess., 1893, Part I, pp. 90–94.) The committee's experts concluded, however, that the closest approximation to the trend of consumer prices was the wholesale price index adjusted to take account of differences in family consumption. The separate commodity wholesale price indexes were, therefore, weighted by the estimated volume of family consumption of the articles included in the index. Commodities for which consumption estimates were not available and items such as rents were omitted. Although the committee did not describe the weighted index as a cost-of-living index, it was designed to approximate as closely as possible the trend in retail prices.

A detailed study of available price data by Mitchell revealed that the committee's weighted price index was not satisfactory for the period during and immediately after the Civil War. Probably the best available indication of the trend of consumer prices for the entire period 1840–1890 is the committee's weighted wholesale price index to 1860, Mitchell's cost-of-living index for 1860–1880, and the committee's weighted index linked to Mitchell's index for 1880–1890 ("Cost of Living" index in Figure 15).

linked to each other permit approximate measurement of general trends in nominal and real wages.

Four major measures of wage changes since 1890 deserve attention: (1) the composite wage index (basically, the average of hourly earnings); (2) the index of union hourly rates in the building trades; (3) the index of average weekly earnings of wage earners in manufacturing; and (4) the index of full-time equivalent average annual earnings of nonfarm wage earners and salaried employees. (See Appendix Table 16.) Each series exemplifies distinctive aspects of the trends of wages and salaries. (See Table 20.)

Average nominal wages increased from fivefold to more than sevenfold between 1890 and 1947, according to the various indexes in Table 20. Increases in real wages were retarded, however, by the rise in prices, which almost tripled over the same period. Changes in the several series of nominal wages and salaries were far from uniform. Because of reduction of the length of the work week, weekly and annual earnings rose less than hourly earnings. Short-term variability was affected by many factors, depending on the measure of wages. Wage rates as well as average hours of work and the composition of employment have been particularly elastic in manufacturing.

Price Fluctuations

Wholesale prices rose much more sharply than consumers' prices during the wartime and postwar periods of inflation and declined more during periods of deflation. All in all, however, from 1890 to 1947, consumers' prices rose 197 per cent as compared with a rise of only 170 per cent in wholesale prices.[7] (See Appendix Table 17 and Figure 16.)

Real Wages

Changes in real wages (money wages adjusted by the consumers' price index) are traced in Table 21 and Figure 17 and in Appendix Table 18. Before World War I, union workers in the building trades made significant gains in real wage rates, and the composite wage-rate index also rose; in contrast, real weekly earnings in manufacturing and real full-time annual earnings were lower in 1914 than in 1890. Between those years, wages lagged behind the general advance in national income; part of this lag, however, may be explained by the comparatively large gains in real wages during the 1880's, in the period of relative prosperity after the pro-

7. A similar difference in the trends of wholesale and retail prices was observed in 1840–1890.

TABLE 20

INDEXES OF NOMINAL WAGES AND SALARIES AND PRICES, 1890–1947

Period	Composite Wage [a]	Union Hourly Rates in the Building Trades [b]	Average Weekly Earnings of Wage Earners in Manufacturing [c]	Full-Time Equivalent Average Annual Earnings of Nonfarm Hired Workers [d]	Wholesale Prices [e]	Consumers' Prices [f]
			Index (*1926 = 100*)			
1890	29.6	22.8	34.2	37.8	56.2	42.4
1914	46.0	41.8	44.7	47.3	68.1	56.8
1920	99.1	79.3	106.7	97.9	154.4	113.4
1923	94.6	83.7	96.6	95.5	100.6	96.4
1926	100.0	100.0	100.0	100.0	100.0	100.0
1929	103.7	105.4	101.5	103.8	95.3	96.9
1932	88.0	94.1	69.2	84.6	64.8	77.2
1939	111.3	113.3	96.8	96.9	77.1	78.6
1947	203.9	167.5	202.7	189.7	151.8	125.9
			Percentage Change			
1890–1914	+ 55.4	+ 83.3	+ 30.7	+ 25.1	+ 21.2	+ 34.0
1914–1923	+105.7	+100.2	+116.1	+101.9	+ 47.7	+ 69.7
1923–1929	+ 9.6	+ 25.9	+ 5.0	+ 8.7	− 5.3	+ 0.5
1929–1932	− 15.1	− 10.7	− 31.8	− 18.5	− 32.0	− 20.3
1932–1939	+ 26.5	+ 20.4	+ 39.9	+ 14.5	+ 19.0	+ 1.8
1939–1947	+ 83.2	+ 47.8	+109.4	+ 95.8	+ 96.9	+ 60.2
1890–1947	+588.9	+634.6	+492.7	+401.9	+170.1	+196.9

a. Basically an index of average hourly earnings. For the period from 1890 to 1913 it follows Douglas' series, described by him as an index of "average hourly earnings in all industry" — meaning all industry for which available data seem to warrant estimates. This index appears to be broadly representative of changes in basic wages and salaries, including farm wages. See Paul H. Douglas, *Real Wages in the United States, 1890–1926*, Houghton Mifflin, Boston, 1930, pp. 204–07. The index prepared by the Research Department of the Federal Reserve Bank of New York was linked, after minor adjustments, to the Douglas index for 1890–1913.

b. This is an index of changes in basic rates but it is far from typical of general wage changes. It combines an index constructed by Douglas for 1890–1907 with a Bureau of Labor Statistics index for more recent times. See *Real Wages*, p. 135; Bureau of Labor Statistics, Bulletin No. 910, 1947, p. 2.

c. Derived, for 1890 to 1913, from estimates by Douglas of the average annual earnings of wage earners and, for 1914 to 1947, from the Bureau of Labor Statistics series. Both series are adjusted for comparable coverage.

d. Derived from the Stanley Lebergott series. See his article entitled "Earnings of Nonfarm Employees in the United States, 1890–1946," *Journal of the American Statistical Association*, March 1948, pp. 74–93.

e. The Bureau of Labor Statistics index.

f. The Douglas index, 1890 to 1913, linked to the Bureau of Labor Statistics index.

longed depression of the preceding decade, often described as the secondary postwar depression after the Civil War.

Noteworthy gains in real wages were made after World War I. Prices temporarily outran wages, but between 1920 and 1923 the greater fall in prices than in wages netted appreciable gains in real earnings. During the prosperous years 1923–1929, real wages continued to advance, but very slowly except for union workers in the building trades, whose rates rose much faster, in contrast to the losses they had suffered in World War I.

Basic rates and full-time annual earnings, adjusted for price changes, continued to advance even in the depression years, but real weekly earnings in manufacturing declined; the combined effects of lowered nominal wage rates and reduced hours more than offset the advantage of lower prices. After 1932, the indexes of real wages shown in Figure 17 and Table 21 indicate a consistent rise to 1947 except in union hourly rates in the building trades. The index for those trades rose from a point considerably below the others in 1920 to a higher level in 1939 and then declined, in contrast to the upward trend of the other series. Year-to-year changes occasionally show slight downturns.

The adjusted composite wage index is in many respects the most significant single measure of changes in real hourly earnings in the nation. (See Figure 18.)

Hours of Work after 1890

The full-time work week of 60 hours in 1890 in manufacturing, bituminous coal mining and steam railroads had decreased to 40, 35 and 48 hours, respectively, in 1940. Union agreements in the building and the printing trades provided for similar cuts in the normal work schedules in these trades. (See Appendix Table 19.)

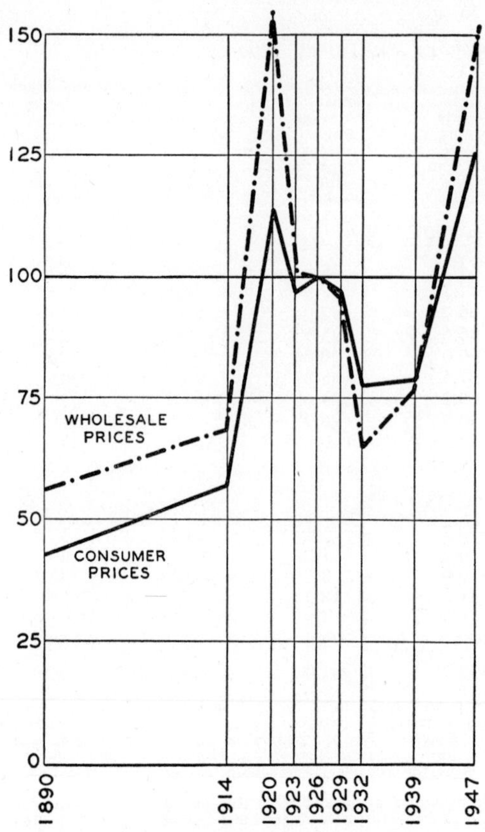

FIGURE 16. INDEXES OF WHOLESALE PRICES AND CONSUMER PRICES, SELECTED YEARS, 1890–1947

(*1926 = 100*)

Source: Table 20.

For simplicity of presentation, the price data are plotted on this chart only for especially important years. No significant fluctuations occurred between 1890 and 1914. The inflation originated by World War I reached its climax in 1920; the fall in prices during the primary postwar depression was followed by a spell of relative price stability in 1923–1929 and another fall in 1930–1932. The year 1939 was the crucial prewar year and marked the beginning of a new rise, similar to that in 1914–1920.

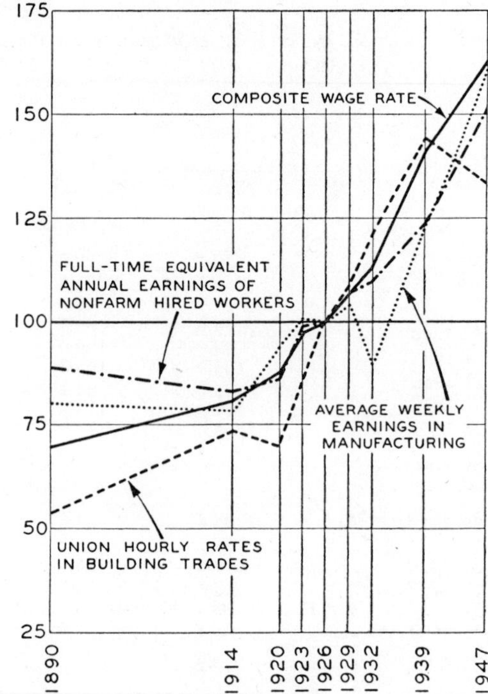

FIGURE 17. INDEXES OF REAL WAGES AND SALARIES, SELECTED YEARS, 1890–1947

(*1926 = 100*)

Source: Table 21.

As in Figure 16, the four indexes of wages, adjusted to the cost of living, are plotted only for selected years.

Average weekly hours (computed by taking into account the effects of overtime and of hours of work less than the full-time or scheduled work week) varied widely from year to year during the period 1909–1947. (See Table 22.) The low averages in bituminous coal mining for the earlier years were largely due to part-time operation of the mines; the average number of days worked was 209 in 1909, 145 in 1932, 202 in 1940. In 1944, the higher level of operations, combined with overtime, raised the average work week in coal mining far above the 1944 standard or straight-time week of 35 hours.

The standard work week was reduced gradually before 1929 and rapidly in the 1930's, by union agreements and by legislation (the civil service laws and the Fair Labor Standards Act of 1938). The 40-hour standard was generally adopted, and this was continued throughout the wartime period, with premium pay for overtime. A good many workers, however, retained a straight-time week of more than 40 hours, notably in local transit and service establishments. Railroad workers did not obtain the 40-hour straight-time work week until 1949. Some union agreements now provide for a standard week of less than 40 hours, notably in the clothing industries and the building and printing trades. In bituminous coal mining, the 35-hour straight-time week (excluding travel time in the mine before 1944) was raised in 1947 to 40 hours, including travel time and also a "staggered" thirty-minute period for lunch.

TABLE 21

INDEXES OF WAGES AND SALARIES ADJUSTED TO CONSUMERS' PRICE INDEX, 1890–1947

Period	Composite Wage	Union Hourly Rates in the Building Trades	Average Weekly Earnings of Wage Earners in Manufacturing	Full-Time Equivalent Average Annual Earnings of Nonfarm Hired Workers
	Index (*1926 = 100*)			
1890	69.8	53.8	80.7	89.2
1914	81.0	73.6	78.7	83.3
1920	87.4	69.9	94.1	86.3
1923	98.1	86.8	100.2	99.1
1926	100.0	100.0	100.0	100.0
1929	107.0	108.8	104.7	107.1
1932	114.0	121.9	89.6	109.6
1939	141.6	144.1	123.2	123.3
1947	162.0	133.0	161.0	150.7
	Percentage Change			
1890–1914	+ 16.0	+ 36.8	− 2.5	− 6.6
1914–1923	+ 21.1	+ 17.9	+27.3	+19.0
1923–1929	+ 9.1	+ 25.3	+ 4.5	+ 8.1
1929–1932	+ 6.5	+ 12.0	−14.4	+ 2.3
1932–1939	+ 24.2	+ 18.2	+37.5	+12.5
1939–1947	+ 14.4	− 7.7	+30.7	+22.2
1890–1947	+132.1	+147.2	+99.5	+68.9

Source: Computed from Table 20.

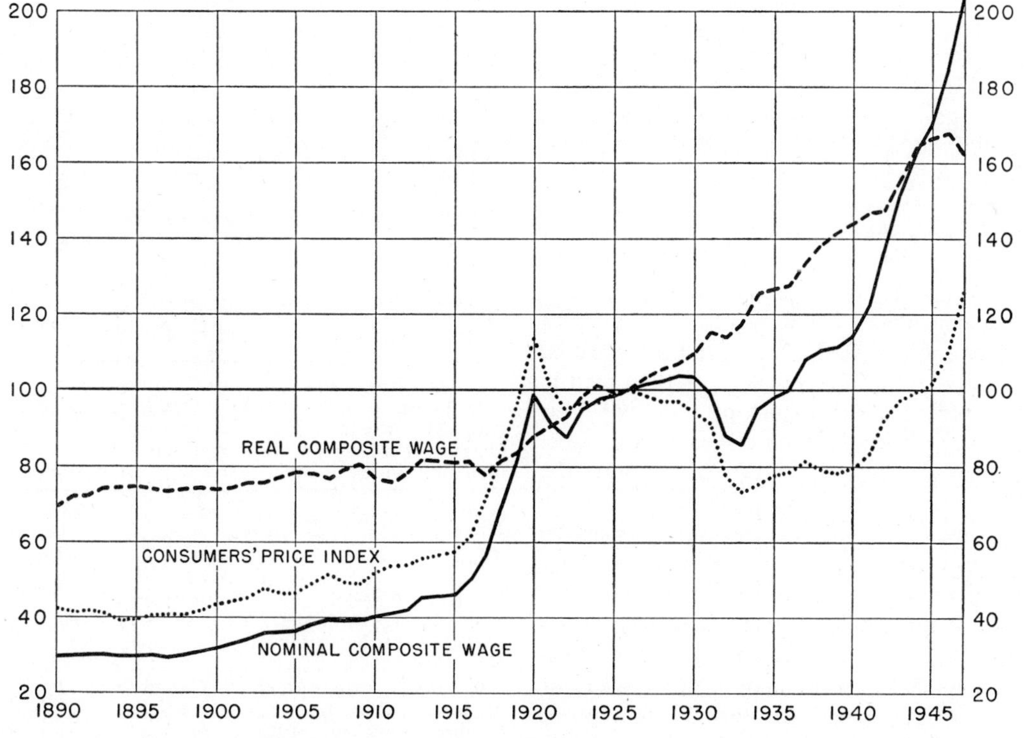

FIGURE 18. COMPOSITE INDEXES OF NOMINAL AND REAL WAGES, 1890–1947 (*1926 = 100*)

Sources: Appendix Tables 16, 17 and 18.

TABLE 22

AVERAGE WEEKLY HOURS IN MANUFACTURING, BITUMINOUS COAL MINING AND STEAM RAILROADS, 1909–1947

Year	Manu-facturing	Bituminous Coal Mining	Steam Railroads
1909.........	51.0	37.8	53.9
1932.........	38.3	27.2	38.9
1940.........	38.1	28.1	44.0
1944.........	45.2	43.4	49.1
1947.........	40.3	40.6	46.3

Source: Bureau of Labor Statistics series. Steam railroad figures are derived from Interstate Commerce Commission reports; the average is that of employees reported on an hourly basis; the count of employees is the number on the payrolls during the month; the hours are hours paid for. In bituminous coal mining, hours before 1944 exclude travel time in the mine; beginning in 1944, hours include travel time and a "staggered" lunch period of thirty minutes.

A Century of Progress

The index of real hourly earnings for 1840–1890 (Table 19) and the composite real wage index for 1890 to 1947 (Table 21), combined, show striking variations in the rate of growth of wages in the United States.

In the period before 1890, the fluctuations in the Civil War decade, the lack of any net gains in the 1870's, and the sharp rise in the 1880's are especially worthy of note. However, the statistics for 1840–1890, which are based on fragmentary information on wages and prices, probably overstate the year-to-year variation in real wages. The economy as a whole was then largely a local and even a nonmarket economy. Workers depended on money wages less than they do now and relied more on household and local production. The actual conditions of living were, therefore, more stable than the recorded short-run ups and downs in wages in relation to prices would suggest.

There was, nevertheless, a greater fluctuation in real wages in the period 1860–1890 than in later periods. The impact of the Civil War and the resulting inflation depressed real wages below the prewar level. After the war, the downward adjustment of prices, the sharp rise in business activity, and westward expansion combined to raise real wages. Owing to a long and severe depression, real wages failed to advance in the decade after 1872. During 1880–1890, real wages rose because of a strong demand for labor resulting from the recovery of business and the continued westward movement. It was in the decade of the 1880's that unions first achieved noteworthy national influence.

The composite wage index adjusted to consumers' prices shows a remarkably small increase during the three decades after 1890 and a strikingly rapid advance thereafter. The increase from 1890 to 1919 was only 20 per cent — 0.6 per cent a year. In contrast, the rise from 1919 to 1947 was 94 per cent — 2.4 per cent a year. Several factors accounted for this difference in trends.

1. The increase immediately after 1890 was slow because of the unusually rapid advance in the preceding decade.

2. During the period 1890–1919, production per man-hour grew rather slowly.[8]

3. A large part of the increment of national income in this period was absorbed by investments in railroads, urban expansion, mines, land settlement and the like. These developments, and wartime needs toward the end of the period, limited the output of consumption goods and thus restricted the rise in the real earnings of workers.

4. The bargaining position of labor was highly unfavorable as a result of the rise of corporations, the influx of foreign workers, and the thwarting of labor organization. The flood of immigration abated somewhat in the 1890's but increased rapidly after the turn of the century, when the annual number of immigrants exceeded a million in six of the ten years 1905–1914. Most of the immigrants at that time came from low-wage areas of southern and eastern Europe and settled mainly in urban areas. Earlier immigrants had come largely from northern and western Europe; they had been assimilated more easily; and they had settled to a larger extent in sparsely populated rural areas.[9]

8. Man-hour output in manufacturing increased only 35 per cent from 1899 to 1919, as compared with 131 per cent during the two succeeding decades. Output per worker (which was affected by reductions in hours) in six industries (manufacturing, mining, electric light and power, gas, steam railroads, agriculture) rose 27 per cent from 1899 to 1919, in contrast to 75 per cent from 1919 to 1939. See Solomon Fabricant, *Labor Savings in American Industry, 1899–1939,* Occasional Paper No. 23, National Bureau of Economic Research, New York, November 1945, p. 46; George J. Stigler, *Trends in Output and Employment,* National Bureau of Economic Research, New York, 1947, p. 3.

9. *Statistical Abstract of the United States, 1944–45,* p. 109; E. A. Ross, *The Old World in the New,* Century, New York, 1914, p. 314. In reference to obstacles in the way of unionism and collective bargaining before World War I, see H. A. Millis and R. E. Montgomery, *Organized Labor,* McGraw-Hill, New York, 1945, pp. 76–130.

5. In recent years the bargaining position of workers has been strengthened by collective bargaining, minimum-wage and social security legislation.

Over the past one hundred years the rise in real wages, although subject at times to lags and even setbacks, has been an integral part of the country's economic growth and the advances in technology and productivity. The best available measures indicate that the real hourly wage of the ordinary worker in 1947 was at least four times as high as in 1847.

There was a striking difference, however, between the early part of this period and more recent times. Real wages doubled from 1847 to 1914 and doubled again from 1914 to 1947. The average annual rate of advance was 1.05 per cent in the first 67 years and 2.1 per cent in the subsequent 33 years.

Social Gains

The wage index used here is primarily an index of hourly earnings. The indicated increase in real wages is, therefore, larger than the increase in real weekly or annual earnings. Workers have taken some of their gains in the form of more leisure and some in the form of goods and services. As much as one third of the time devoted to work in 1840 is now available for leisure, and the adjusted wage per worker is not far from three times as large as in 1840.

Questions arise regarding the basic worth of leisure and purchasing power today and a hundred years ago. To what extent may changes in real wages and hours of work be viewed as indicating changes in well-being? [10]

A much wider range of goods has become available to workers, and improvements have been made in health and life expectancy, material comforts, education and recreation, civil and political rights. Many of these improvements in the status of the worker relate to intangibles, and, although vitally dependent on income and leisure, they can hardly be compared with gains in wages, measured in dollars, and gains in leisure, measured in hours.

As to reductions in working time, it can be questioned whether an hour of work in a modern factory or office is more or less life-consuming than an hour of work a century ago. Have mechanization and specialization increased or diminished job satisfaction and enjoyment of work? What is the significance, for the well-being of the worker, of the change from a handicraft society to mass production and a market economy?

---

10. *Monthly Labor Review,* Thirty-fifth Anniversary Issue, July 1950, especially the articles "The Worker and His Job" and "Changes in Modes of Living."

CHAPTER 6

CYCLICAL VARIATIONS IN THE ECONOMIC SYSTEM *

ECONOMIC GROWTH in the United States has been characterized by a series of rapid gains interrupted by spells of stagnation and loss. Since the eighteenth century, western civilization has progressed along a boom-and-bust course.

Business cycles have been described hundreds of times, but their origin still remains one of the most controversial issues in economic science.[1] Moreover, the existing theories of the business cycle are not mutually exclusive. Although they differ greatly in emphasis, they all recognize that the intermittent ups and downs in production, employment, prices, national income and so on are caused by the interplay of many factors. Because these forces operate in different combinations, the rhythm of business cycles is never perfect. Perhaps the term "cycle," which suggests a rhythmic movement, is somewhat misleading, but in the past century not a single decade has elapsed without appreciable fluctuation in the economic climate and in the rate of economic progress.

Each attempt to project the economic trends of the past into the future, therefore, must take this fact into account: average annual rates of growth exist only in our imagination. Actual rates have always fluctuated around these averages, and sometimes the range of fluctuation has been wide enough to overshadow, temporarily, the long-range trend.

VOLUME OF PRODUCTION

The cyclical rhythm in economic progress affects various fields of economic activity differently. Manufacturing and transportation are particularly sensitive to the business cycle.

Manufacturing

At a very rough approximation, the long-range trend in manufacturing output in the United States from 1860 to 1950 can be described as a growth at an annual rate of 4 per cent through the whole period, as shown in Figure 6. A somewhat better fit is obtained if the trend is represented as an advance at a rate of 5 per cent a year from 1860 to 1914, at somewhat less than 4 per cent a year from 1914 to 1940, and at a somewhat higher annual rate thereafter. (See Figure 19, A.)

The actual volume of production, however, has deviated widely from the trend line. In the seventy years 1860–1929 it was within 5 per cent of the hypothetical trend value 30 times; it deviated from this value by 6 to 10 per cent 25 times and by 11 per cent or more 15 times. After 1929 the range of deviation was much wider.

The amplitude of cyclical variations in the volume of manufacturing production can be measured in terms of the percentage increase from the low to the peak in periods of expansion and the percentage decline from the peak to the new trough in periods of contraction. (See Table 23.) Thus measured, growth in manufacturing production shows fifteen cycles of unequal duration and amplitude from 1862 to 1946.[2] Of these cycles, seven lasted 2 to 4 years; five, 5 to 8 years; and three, 9 to 11 years. All the comparatively long cycles occurred before the turn of the century. Cycles of moderate duration (5 to 8 years) have prevailed since the outbreak of World War I.

For the whole period surveyed, the average duration of a business cycle, from trough to

* By W. S. Woytinsky.

1. Wesley C. Mitchell distinguished twenty-four types of theories of business cycles. See *Business Cycles: The Problem and Its Setting,* National Bureau of Economic Research, New York, 1927, pp. 50–53. Elmer Bratt describes thirteen schools of thought. See *Business Cycles and Forecasting,* 3d edition, Irwin, Chicago, 1948, p. 161. Gottfried Haberler classifies the most popular cycle theories in nine groups. See *Prosperity and Depression: A Theoretical Analysis of Cyclical Movements,* 3d edition, Columbia University Press, New York, 1946, pp. 14 ff.

2. Since Table 23 is based on the production index unadjusted to the long-range trend in production, it does not register some minor setbacks that are evident in Figure 19, B, where changes in production are related to the long-range trend.

A. Index of Manufacturing Production and Its Trend
(*1899 = 100*)

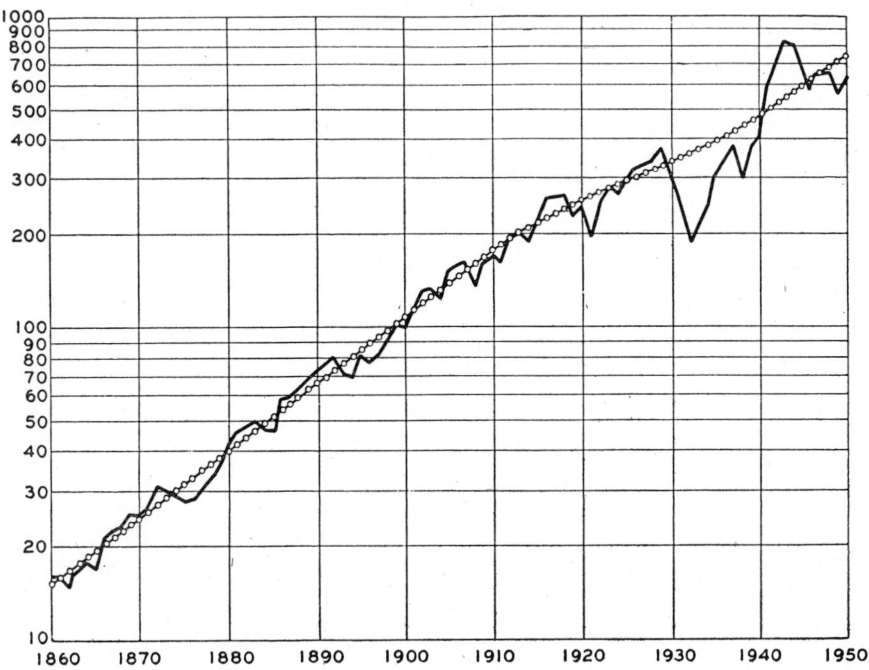

B. Annual Deviations as Percentage of Trend Level
(*Trend = 100*)

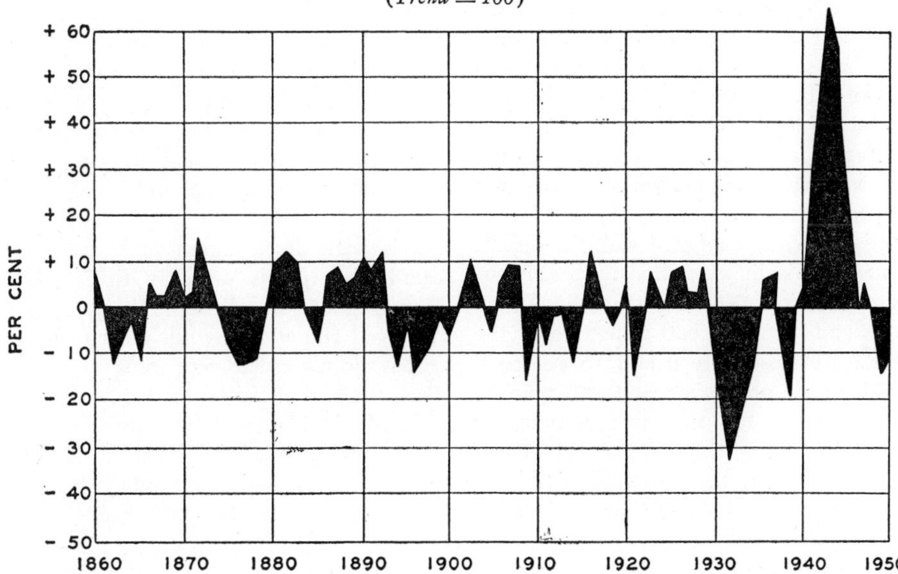

FIGURE 19. DEVIATION OF ANNUAL MANUFACTURING PRODUCTION FROM THE TREND LEVEL, 1860–1950

Source: Appendix Table 4.

The index of manufacturing production is plotted at the top of the chart on a logarithmic vertical scale, so that the same percentage growth is represented by the same slope of the curve, regardless of the level on which the growth takes place. The trend for the period from 1860–1914 is represented by a straight line, which indicates a steady rate of annual advance (5 per cent a year). After 1914 the trend is indicated by a freehand line rising at a rate of somewhat less than 4 per cent a year until 1940 and at a somewhat higher rate thereafter. At the bottom of the chart deviations of the production index from the hypothetical trend value are represented as a percentage of that value.

TABLE 23

CYCLICAL VARIATIONS IN MANUFACTURING PRODUCTION, 1862–1946

Trough		Peak		Duration, in Years [a]			Percentage Change	
Year	Index of Production (1899 = 100)	Year	Index of Production (1899 = 100)	From Trough to Peak	From Peak to Trough	From Trough to Trough	From Trough to Peak	From Peak to Trough
1862	15	1864	18	2	1	3	+ 20	− 6
1865	17	1872	31	7	4	11	+ 82	−10
1876	28	1883	50	7	2	9	+ 79	− 6
1885	47	1892	79	7	2	9	+ 68	−14
1894	68	1895	81	1	1	2	+ 19	− 4
1896	78	1903	128	7	1	8	+ 64	− 5
1904	122	1907	159	3	1	4	+ 30	−18
1908	130	1910	169	2	1	3	+ 30	− 5
1911	161	1913	199	2	1	3	+ 24	− 7
1914	186	1916	259	2	3	5	+ 39	−14
1919	222	1920	242	1	1	2	+ 9	−20
1921	194	1923	280	2	1	3	+ 44	− 5
1924	266	1929	364	5	3	8	+ 37	−46
1932	197	1937	376	5	1	6	+ 91	−22
1938	295	1943	820	5	3	8	+178	−31
1946	566							

a. The measurement of duration of business cycles and their phases in years is very rough, of course. There are, however, no records available on monthly variations in volume of manufacturing production in the early part of the period surveyed.

Source: Appendix Table 4.

trough, was 5.6 years—3.9 years of rise and 1.7 years of decline; since the beginning of this century, however, the cycles have become somewhat shorter, averaging 4.7 years — 3 years of rise and 1.7 years of decline. Excluding the period since 1929, the average cycle since 1862 has lasted 5.4 years, with 3.7 years of rise and 1.7 years of fall. On the average, the rise lasts about twice as long as the fall.[3]

The average amplitude of variation for the period as a whole is an advance of 54 per cent (as compared with the trough) followed by a loss of 14 per cent (compared with the peak). Average rates of gain were almost precisely the same in the period 1860–1894 and in 1894–1946, 54 and 51 per cent respectively; the average rates of loss were 8 and 16 per cent. If the volume of production at the beginning of the rise is set at 100, the index mounted to approximately 154 at the culmination of the cycle and fell back at the next trough to 132, a level close to that indicated by the secular trend.

Thus for almost ninety years, embracing fifteen cycles, manufacturing production has gone forward at about this average pace: a rise to a peak 54 per cent above the preceding trough, followed by loss of 41 per cent of the gain in the next setback.

Cyclical ups and down are heavily concentrated in certain industries. Minor setbacks are often limited to production of capital goods — industrial equipment and machinery. Next in variability come durable and semidurable consumer goods, luxuries, building materials and so forth. A long and severe depression finally affects all industries, but manufactures of durable goods are struck first and suffer most.

From 1860 to 1914, production of durable goods went down eleven times, production of nondurable goods only six times. Losses in durable goods, in relation to the preceding peak, averaged 18 per cent, while those in nondurable goods did not exceed 6 per cent. In round numbers, the typical pattern of variation in production of durable goods was three years of rise with a total gain of 65 per cent followed by two years of fall, leaving the production index more than 30 per cent above the preceding trough. (See Figure 20.)

Nonmanufacturing Industries

Cyclical ups and downs in commerce, transportation and communication are of about the same severity as those in manufacturing production. (See Figure 21.) The pattern of the cycle in manufacturing industries can therefore be applied to the whole field of industrial and

3. The rise in a cycle as measured here includes the time of slow advance, which lags behind the secular trend. A business index showing the relation of economic activities to the hypothetical trend would designate such time as "fall."

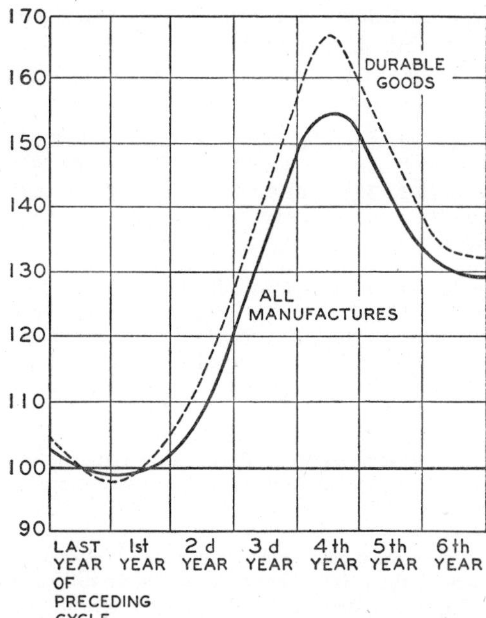

FIGURE 20. TYPICAL VARIATION OF MANUFACTURING PRODUCTION THROUGH A SIX-YEAR BUSINESS CYCLE

(*Production at Low Point at Beginning of Cycle = 100*)

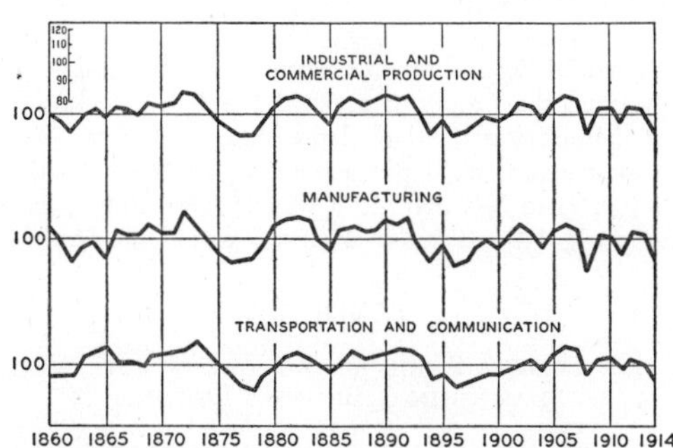

FIGURE 21. PERCENTAGE DEVIATION OF THE VOLUME OF INDUSTRIAL AND COMMERCIAL PRODUCTION FROM THE LONG-RANGE TREND, 1860–1914

Source: Edwin Frickey, *Production in the United States, 1860–1914,* Harvard University Press, Cambridge, 1947.

commercial activities, which embraces about half of our economy. The other half includes agriculture, building construction, governmental services, professional services (such as education, recreation, medical care, religious and other nonprofit organizations) and personal services. Most of these activities are either only slightly sensitive to the business cycle or react in their own way and not in the pattern typical of manufacturing.

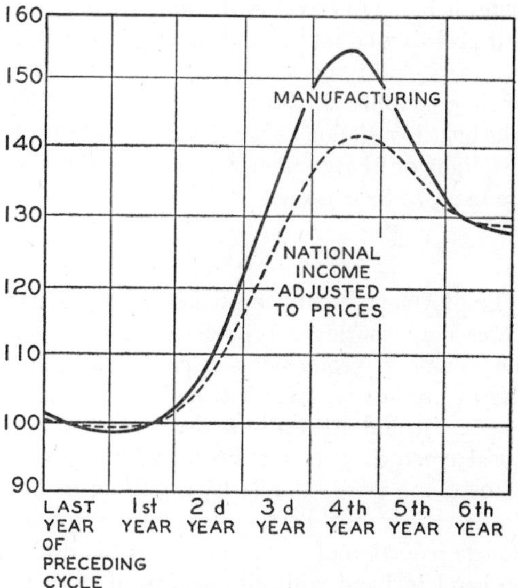

FIGURE 22. TYPICAL VARIATION OF MANUFACTURING PRODUCTION AND NATIONAL INCOME ADJUSTED TO PRICES THROUGH A SIX-YEAR BUSINESS CYCLE

(*Production, National Income and Prices at Low Point at Beginning of Cycle = 100*)

Farmers suffer heavy losses during a depression as a result of falling prices, but they do not reduce production. Building construction may be paralyzed by a severe and long depression but it is controlled essentially by its own cycle, which often embraces several short business cycles. On the other hand, activities such as recreation, art and personal services contract when business conditions are bad and expand with a general revival.

As a group, all these activities tend to expand in good times and contract in bad times, but their fluctuation is considerably narrower than that of manufacturing. Probably it does not exceed a third of the range of fluctuation in manufacturing output.[4] The amplitude of the typical cyclical variation in total production in the United States, therefore, is likely to be about a third less than the amplitude of variation in manufacturing. (See Figure 22.)

"Typical" patterns deduced from past experience do not, of course, foreshadow the shape of future business cycles. No cycle exactly duplicates the preceding one, or even the average of the preceding ten or fifteen cycles. Some of the business cycles through which the United

4. This rate is found by weighting nonindustrial activities affected by business cycles against those manifesting no cyclical fluctuation.

States is likely to travel in the next twenty years will probably be longer and others shorter than five years, and some will have a larger, others a smaller, amplitude. Still, the patterns around which such variations were clustered in the past cast light on those patterns around which they are likely to be clustered in the future.

EMPLOYMENT

Employment usually fluctuates within a narrower range during a business cycle than does the volume of production. A particularly rapid rise in production from a trough to a peak of prosperity, and especially a rise in time of national emergency, is accompanied by extension of overtime work. Similarly, a setback in production does not necessarily cause a proportionate reduction of employment; layoffs usually go hand in hand with elimination of overtime and spreading of part-time work.

In manufacturing industries, for example, average weekly hours of work increased from 34.6 in 1934 to 45.2 in 1944 and declined to 40.3 in 1947. Thus the average work week was nearly a third longer at the peak of the war effort than in 1934, and it was reduced by more than 10 per cent after the war ended.[5]

Sharing the Work

The principle of limited work sharing in bad times is widely recognized by labor unions and management. In the course of the canvass of labor and management opinions made in connection with the present study, union leaders were asked: "Suppose that during a general decline in business fewer man-hours of work were available in a particular plant. What would you suggest to management should be done in that case?" Thirteen said they would recommend sharing the work with no layoff, 17 would begin layoffs after limited work sharing, 10 favored layoffs without spreading the work, and 6 would seek a cut in hours with maintenance of the weekly take-home pay.[6] (See Table 24.)

The plan most often recommended was for work sharing at first, followed by layoffs if the amount of work available for each employee fell below a certain level. Some union officials would not favor sharing the work if hours dropped below 32 a week; others would continue work sharing until the work week was cut to 24 or even 20 hours. The following statements are typical:

> The only agreement for sharing work in depression that we'd stand for would be to reduce the hours from 40 to 32 — and we'd do that very reluctantly. And we wouldn't rotate men — we don't like that, either.

> Most of our agreements call for reduction in hours in cases like that. But in no case can hours be reduced to less than the equivalent of three full days' work. If that limit is reached and there still isn't enough work for all, we'd begin layoffs from the bottom of the lists.

> We recommend work sharing to a certain extent. We reduce the work week to 30 hours before any layoffs.

> I guess we'd have to share the work. But we'd only share to the point where each man could still earn a living wage. Beyond that point, we'd have to agree to layoffs.

> We'd probably suggest that the hours of work be decreased rather than have any layoffs. But there'd probably be a floor of 32 hours. And if that was not sufficient to take up the slack, then employers would have to start layoffs.

> It would depend on the depth of the depression. If it seemed the proper step, we'd share the work. We did that during the last depression. But if we have to do it again, we'll put a floor under hours, so they can't drop to less than 20 a week. If we didn't share the work, I don't know what we would do. I think

TABLE 24

UNION LEADERS FAVOR LIMITED OR STRAIGHT WORK SHARING IN A BUSINESS DECLINE

Question: Suppose that during a general decline in business fewer man-hours of work were available in a particular plant. What would you suggest to management should be done in that case?

Response	Number of Unions	Union Members: Number, in Thousands	Union Members: Percentage of Total
Number of respondents	52	11,523	100.0
Recommendation to management:			
Layoffs	27	6,049	52.5
After limited work sharing	17	4,753	41.2
Immediate	10	1,296	11.2
Straight work sharing	13	3,103	26.9
Reduced hours at same take-home pay	6	875	7.6
No recommendation	6	1,496	13.0

Source: W. S. Woytinsky and Associates, *Labor and Management Look at Collective Bargaining,* Twentieth Century Fund, New York, 1949, p. 211.

5. *Handbook of Labor Statistics,* 1947 edition, Bulletin No. 916, Bureau of Labor Statistics, 1948, p. 54.

6. W. S. Woytinsky and Associates, *Labor and Management Look at Collective Bargaining,* Twentieth Century Fund, New York, 1949, p. 210.

we'd probably have to make a decision after we knew exactly what is involved.

Share the work. We did it during the last depression. But then we reduced hours way down. Many of our members only worked 12 hours a week. If a depression happened again, I think we'd draw the line at 24 hours.[7]

Among the labor leaders who were canvassed, however, a strong minority opposed work sharing, while other union presidents advocated unrestricted work sharing as a lesser evil than layoffs.

The opinions of management were just as divided. (See Table 25.) Moreover, some management spokesmen who favored work sharing referred to the provisions in their labor contracts.

Under our contract we lay off temporary workers in order of seniority and rotate the work among the regular union members down to 32 hours a week.

The contract provides for equalization of work—"share and share alike." We would rotate weeks or half weeks, and so forth.

We stagger the work. There is a provision in our contract which says that work must be equally divided between pieceworkers and week-workers.

We would drop from a five-day week to a four-day week. Usually that would take care of it. However, if that was not enough, we'd call in the union leaders and sit down with them to determine whether we'd have a further sharing of work or a layoff. This, of course, applies to our regular employees. We hire temporary men for our summer season, but they are hired only for the season.[8]

Employment and cyclical setbacks in production are related in still another way. A decline in business forces management to seek ways to reduce production costs, especially labor costs. A downturn in sales becomes a signal for checking payrolls. Marginal workers and workers whose services are not vital for production are laid off. The rise in unemployment permits management to tighten control over the efficiency of individual workers. At the same time, management improves its methods of production to meet increasing business competition. Such measures tend to cause a relatively greater cut in employment than in production.

In severe depressions, losses in employment lag behind losses in production, but the reverse is true in a moderate setback. (See Table 26.)

7. *Ibid.*, pp. 212–13.
8. *Ibid.*, pp. 218–20.

TABLE 25

MOST COMPANIES LAY OFF IN THE DULL SEASON BUT MANUFACTURING FIRMS USUALLY SHARE THE WORK

Question: If during the dull season of the year there isn't enough work to go around, what does your company do about employment?

Response	Total	Manufacturing Companies	Nonmanufacturing Companies
Number of respondents	87	47	40
Measure to adjust employment:			
Layoff	33	14	19
Work sharing	22	19	3
Vacation, leaves, etc.	11	4	7
Shift to maintenance or other work	3	2	1
Firm has no dull season	18	8	10

Source: W. S. Woytinsky and Associates, *Labor and Management Look at Collective Bargaining*, Twentieth Century Fund, New York, 1949, p. 217.

TABLE 26

DEPRESSION LOSSES IN PRODUCTION AND EMPLOYMENT IN MANUFACTURING INDUSTRIES, 1920–1938

Period and Manufacturing Group	Percentage Change in Production	Percentage Change in Employment of Production Workers
Average for all five periods		
All manufacturing	−20	−17
Durable goods	−30	−22
Nondurable goods	−13	−13
1920–1921		
All manufacturing	−24	−23
1923–1924		
All manufacturing	− 6	− 7
Durable goods	− 8	− 7
Nondurable goods	− 4	− 6
1926–1927		
All manufacturing	− 1	− 2
Durable goods	− 6	− 6
Nondurable goods	+ 5	+ 3
1929–1932		
All manufacturing	−48	−38
Durable goods	−69	−50
Nondurable goods	−25	−25
1937–1938		
All manufacturing	−23	−17
Durable goods	−36	−25
Nondurable goods	−10	− 7

Source: Computed from employment indexes of the Bureau of Labor Statistics and production indexes of the Federal Reserve Board. Only annual indexes were taken into consideration.

NATIONAL INCOME

Although cyclical variations in national income are closely correlated with the ups and downs in manufacturing production, there are appreciable differences in both the timing and the amplitude of the cycle in the different sectors of the national economy. These differences become particularly conspicuous when annual totals or averages are used for production and national income. Indeed, in a moderately severe setback, a time lag of four or six months can affect annual totals to such an extent that the index of annual industrial production will indicate a decline while that of national income indicates a rise.

Depressions before 1929

In comparison with the heavy cyclical losses in manufacturing production, the reaction in national income (adjusted to prices, Martin's series) before 1929 was rather mild. In 1904, for example, when production declined from the preceding year by 5 per cent, national income showed no loss. In 1908, when production dropped 18 per cent, current national income declined only 2 per cent and national income adjusted to prices did not decline at all. In the two subsequent decades cyclical setbacks in production and national income varied in magnitude as shown in Table 27.

TABLE 27

PERCENTAGE LOSSES IN MANUFACTURING PRODUCTION AND NATIONAL INCOME, SELECTED PERIODS, 1910–1924

Period	Manufacturing Production	Current National Income	National Income Adjusted to Prices
1910–1911	5	a	a
1913–1914	6	1	3
1916–1919	14	0	0
1920–1921	20	17	4
1923–1924	5	0	0

a. Less than 1.

Source: For manufacturing production, see Appendix Table 4; for national income, Appendix Table 5. In the last column, national income is adjusted to the consumers' price index.

Recent Depressions

The disparity between the amplitude of cyclical variations in manufacturing production and in adjusted national income before 1929 contrasts with the experience of the great depression of the 1930's, when manufacturing production and national income changed in the same direction and at practically the same rate. This is shown in Table 28.

TABLE 28

INDEXES OF MANUFACTURING PRODUCTION AND NATIONAL INCOME, 1930–1934 COMPARED WITH 1929

(*1929 = 100*)

Year	Manufacturing Production	Current National Income	National Income Adjusted to Prices
1930.........	85	86	88
1931.........	72	67	76
1932.........	54	48	60
1933.........	63	45	60
1934.........	69	56	71

Source: For manufacturing production, see Appendix Table 3. In the last column, national income (Department of Commerce) is adjusted to the consumers' price index.

Allowing for the margin of error in the respective indexes, it appears that from 1929 to 1933–1934 adjusted national income and manufacturing production fell at about the same rate. This pattern, however, was not duplicated in the three more recent economic setbacks. In 1938 the index of manufacturing production fell 21.4 per cent (from 103 to 81); from 1943 to 1946, 29 per cent (from 225 to 160); and from October 1948 to July 1949, 17 per cent (from 202 to 168).[9] The first setback was accompanied by a loss of 7 per cent in adjusted national income, the second by a loss of 6 per cent, the third by a loss of 2 per cent.

Thus losses in production and national income were related in about the same way in recent cyclical setbacks as before the great depression. All in all, the developments after the 1930's confirm the conclusion drawn from the experience of earlier business cycles. Appreciable losses in manufacturing production, especially in the production of durable and capital goods, do not necessarily imply a proportionate contraction of all economic activities as reflected in the flow of national income. It is true that a setback in production is associated with layoffs in manufacturing industries, losses in earnings of factory workers and in profits, decline in the volume of transportation and trade, and so forth. But factories employ only 20 to 25 per cent of the labor force of the nation. Thus a 20 per cent cut in employment in manufacturing industries directly affects not more than 4 to 5 per cent of the working population. Such a setback in manufacturing is not necessarily followed by immediate and proportionate layoffs in trade and other services. Theoretically, it can start a deflationary spiral, but the records show that in nine out of ten business cycles the revival began before such a spiral was set in action.

Despite the interdependence of manufacturing, building construction, agriculture, trade, transportation and so on, each field of economic activity is largely controlled by particular factors

9. Seasonally adjusted index of the Federal Reserve Board; 1935–1939 average = 100.

and is to some extent autonomous in its reaction to changes in business conditions. The characteristic feature of the depression of the 1930's was the coincidence of exceptionally unfavorable factors in all the principal sectors of the economy—manufacturing, agriculture, construction, finance. The characteristic of the current postwar expansion is the coincidence of favorable factors in all these fields. Not all depressions will follow the pattern of the 1930's nor will all spells of prosperity duplicate the pattern of the early phase of postwar expansion.

Summarizing the findings of the National Bureau of Economic Research, Arthur F. Burns pointed out that:

> Although every business cycle is a unique historical episode, the characteristic features of business cycles have been substantially uniform in the long run. . . . If . . . business cycles actually have undergone secular or structural or rhythmical changes, such changes have not impressed themselves very clearly on statistical records and must be small in comparison with the rather haphazard variation of successive business cycles.[10]

The Course of Economic Progress

The course of economic progress in the United States in the past century can be roughly portrayed by a curve rising at a rate of approximately 4 per cent a year or 48 per cent a decade — the average rate of growth of national income adjusted to prices. (See Figure 23, trend line A.) In terms of adjusted per capita income, the long-range trend since 1879 can be portrayed by a curve rising at an annual rate of approximately 2 per cent. (See Figure 23, trend line B.)

These are, however, very rough approximations. They can be improved if the smooth trend lines that characterize the average rate of progress are replaced by wavy lines, with a succession of advances and setbacks. Such hypothetical lines should not necessarily follow the chronology of particular business cycles. Nor should they forecast the timing and range of future cyclical ups and downs. Rather, they serve to picture the general pattern of progress, in which the long-range upward trend is overlapped by cyclical fluctuations. The range of fluctuations for national income will hardly

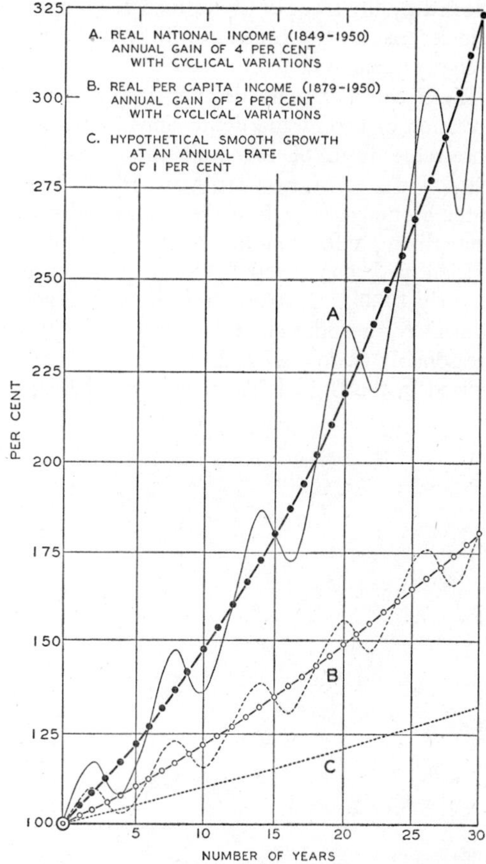

Figure 23. Patterns of Economic Growth

exceed 8 per cent. The duration of each cycle can be set tentatively at five or six years, as in Figure 23. Many observers may prefer to set a shorter span, perhaps four years or less, as suggested by the National Bureau of Economic Research. Such a change, however, would not appreciably affect the over-all picture.

A comparison of the long-range trend in real national income in the United States with the amplitude of cyclical variations makes one doubt whether the cyclical setbacks have seriously retarded the economic growth of this nation. There is, in fact, no evidence that the average annual rate of progress would have been considerably greater than 4 per cent for real national income and 2 per cent for real per capita income without cyclical ups and downs. If these fluctuations were ironed out at the expense of the speed of progress in the expanding phase of each business cycle, the average rate of long-range growth of the economic system — as

10. Arthur F. Burns, *Stepping Stones toward the Future,* Twenty-seventh Annual Report of the National Bureau of Economic Research, New York, 1947, pp. 9–10.

reflected by the real per capita income — might be lower than that recorded over the past seventy or eighty years.

These considerations do not imply that a succession of booms and depressions is the only conceivable form of economic progress. The destructive effect of excessive cyclical fluctuations on the economic growth of the nation and their demoralizing effect on the people have been sufficiently demonstrated by the experience of the early 1930's. The responsibility of the government for keeping cyclical fluctuations within a reasonably narrow range has been widely recognized in the United States, as in other democratic countries. But it is an open question whether such a responsibility of the government calls for drastic measures each time that business conditions begin to deviate in either direction from the hypothetical trend. If certain indexes of economic activity deviate upward from the imaginary trend line, their advance is likely to be checked in the next phase of readjustment. If kept within reasonable limits, such cyclical ups and downs can serve economic growth. They are likely to occur in the present phase of economic progress in this country, and a long-range wage policy must take into account the typical succession of fat and lean years.

Chapter 7

PRODUCTIVITY AND WAGES *

The relationship between productivity and wages is the focal point of much controversy. Some of it results from real differences in basic philosophy, but a large part from simple misunderstanding. When stripped of confusing issues and placed in appropriate perspective, the wage-productivity relationship may be seen, not as a center of discord, but as an area in which most groups have a common interest.

The Concept of Productivity

Much effort has been expended, most of it fruitlessly, on attempts to give quantitative significance to such abstract notions as "worker," "management" or "capital" productivity, meaning in each case the change in production that can be attributed exclusively to one or another of these factors. It is highly doubtful whether any greater measure of success is ever to be anticipated. Suppose that, in such a simple case as that of two groups of workers engaged in an identical process, one group produces more in an hour than the other. This may suggest that the more productive group is working harder ("labor" contribution), or that it has better supervision ("management" contribution). Without additional information it will be impossible to choose objectively between these alternatives, and even with more data it may not be possible to make an unqualified statement since, in fact, both may be contributing factors.

Because of these difficulties, workers in the field have mainly adopted a more direct approach. Productivity in its most general sense is defined as the ratio between production, *measured in some specified units,* and any selected input factor, *also measured in specified units.*[1] Once such a specific definition is adopted, the factors that will influence the productivity ratio or be influenced by it are irrevocably fixed. There is no choice in the matter. For example, labor productivity (output in terms of labor input) may be affected by technological developments, the rate of operations, the competitive balance between producing units, the regularity of materials supply, the effectiveness of management, the skill of the work force, the state of labor relations, and other factors, including in many cases the weather. The effect of changes in labor productivity on other economic variables is nearly as pervasive.

From the definition above, it is clear that productivity may be defined in terms of any of the factors used in production. Thus many special measures of productivity are used in particular situations. For example, kilowatt-hours produced in terms of coal input, measured by either weight or thermal content, are a useful measure of materials productivity for the electric-power-generating industry. To the motorist, mileage per gallon of gasoline is an important productivity measure, which he knows will be influenced by his equipment, fuel, road conditions, and his driving habits. General interest, however, usually centers on labor productivity — the output achieved per unit of labor input as measured in terms of employment or man-hours worked. When the term "productivity" is used without other qualification, labor productivity is ordinarily meant, and this usage will be adopted in the following text.

There are several reasons for a special concern with labor productivity. Perhaps most important, labor productivity is the link between the physical aspects of an economy and the use of an economy's ultimate resource — human labor. On the one side we have production,

* By W. Duane Evans, Chief, Division of Interindustry Economics, Bureau of Labor Statistics. The opinions expressed in this chapter are those of the author, and not necessarily those of the agency with which he is associated.

1. It will be noted that productivity defined in this sense (sometimes referred to as "average" productivity) is quite distinct from "marginal" productivity as used in some types of economic analysis. In theory, a change in production might accompany the use of an additional (small) unit increment of some factor of production, with the use of all other factors remaining the same. The ratio between these hypothetical quantities is defined as the marginal productivity of the factor under the given conditions. Aside from its advantages for theoretical analysis, the concept of marginal productivity has limited practical application because of the virtual impossibility of giving it quantitative content in particular circumstances.

which is designed to meet and satisfy human needs and desires; on the other we have the real price that in the final analysis is paid for production, the sacrifice of human time and effort. As the connection between these quantities, labor productivity is a key and central fact for any economic system.

Measurement of Production

Although productivity can be made a fairly clean-cut and specific concept, many difficulties may arise in attempting to measure it. The question of defining production, for example, may be troublesome even though only a single product is covered.

Alternative yardsticks for measuring production are available in many instances. The choice between them may be arbitrary; or it may be fixed by the type of problem being considered, but it will not be set simply by specifying that a "physical" measure be employed. In metal mining, for example, production might be measured in terms of the tonnage of ore removed or in terms of the metal content of the ore. The two indexes would differ as richness of the ore varied and might indicate quite different trends in output per man-hour. This actually occurred during the recent war period, when steady production and some increase in mechanization raised the rate of ore produced per man-hour to new peaks but the exploitation of low-grade ore bodies made necessary by urgent demands for metal caused a fall in metal produced per man-hour.

Neither of these competing measures of productivity in metal mining is more "correct" in the abstract than the other. One might be preferable to the other in analyzing certain problems. Both of them taken together provide more information than either separately.

Another difficulty in measuring production, even where only a single product is involved, is that the yardstick may stretch or shrink. Quite generally, quality tends to improve, or at least to change, but seldom is the change measured or measurable. Quality change is usually ignored in the preparation of production indexes, including those used in measuring productivity.[2]

Some of the most difficult problems arise when productivity is measured over large and complex areas of industry. A single over-all index of production is usually desired, but most industries produce a number of products that normally shift in relative importance over a period of time. Compilation of a single production index covering many products thus must involve the use of some technique to equate the different kinds of production both at the same time and over different periods of time. A choice must be made among the available techniques.

Even after a particular kind of weighting system is selected, the problem of a basis for comparison remains. For example, if weights reflecting conditions in a given year are used to establish a production measure, additional and equally valid measures may be prepared using different weights for other years. It is generally true, therefore, that a completely unambiguous productivity measure can normally be prepared only when a single product is being considered. Analysis of more than one product will almost always involve a choice of measures. Accordingly, quantitative statements regarding productivity in major sections of the economy are highly abstract; they must be treated with considerable care if they are to be used with reasonable consistency.

Measurement of Input of Labor

Indexes of labor input used in measuring productivity also may be less definite than would at first appear. For one thing, it is necessary to define the groups of persons whose labor is to be related to production. The industry indexes most generally available cover only "production workers" or "wage earners," and so exclude clerks and other salaried workers; design, engineering and research personnel; sales and advertising staffs; supervisors, executives, and others. These excluded groups account for a considerable — and perhaps an increasing — proportion of the total human time spent in productive activity. This limitation to particular groups and the possible biases it introduces must be considered in interpreting indexes of productivity.

Questions also arise in accounting for time

2. This limitation is not always as critical as it might appear. For example, the real increase in productivity during some period may be understated to the extent that quality has improved. At the same time, the real purchasing power of wages may be understated to the extent that quality improvements have not been reflected in price indexes. For purposes of such a comparison, the two biases tend to be compensating.

spent in productive activity. Most of the available measures refer to time paid for — which includes travel time, waiting time, call-in pay and vacation pay — rather than to time actually worked. The difference is perhaps not large and introduces only a small trend bias, but it is growing larger.

The conventional indexes of man-hours treat all labor hours the same, regardless of differences in pay or skill. In pointing this out, the intention is not to suggest that this procedure is inappropriate, but rather to call attention to one of the properties of the usual basis of measurement.

Measurement of Productivity

The measurement of productivity presupposes, of course, that data on both output and labor input are available for the industrial areas to be considered. In many instances, although the information may be reasonably satisfactory for indicating trends in output and labor input, a small margin of error in either may be sufficient to invalidate their use together to estimate changes in productivity.

Another difficulty is the requirement that production and labor data be comparable. Quite frequently, production data are on a "wherever-produced" basis, whereas employment data are recorded on an establishment basis. A tendency for an industry to manufacture new or unrelated products, or to manufacture components that previously were purchased, might destroy comparability and invalidate productivity measures.

Productivity is an economic concept of great value where the consumption or use of some input factor is consistently required to achieve a result definable in quantitative terms. However, it has little meaning or is of limited value in areas of economic activity where a satisfactory measure or definition of output is difficult to establish. For example, employment in retail trade can be measured within reasonable limits but it is difficult to devise a reasonably satisfactory measure of "production" for this activity. Similar problems occur in attempting to measure the physical volume of construction activity. In government or in community services, the notion of productivity may become even more nebulous.

In all economy-wide measures of production and productivity, the questions raised above are, in one way or another, implicitly answered by the measurement method adopted. The rather arbitrary way in which the results are sometimes achieved does not invalidate them as useful, and perhaps invaluable, measures. Nevertheless, these limitations must be given consideration in interpreting broad coverage measures and their relationships through time.

Despite the difficulties involved in establishing quantitative measures of productivity change, many studies of productivity have been made because of the broad usefulness of the results. The United States Bureau of Labor Statistics has made occasional productivity studies since the last century, and has regularly issued indexes and studies covering many mining, manufacturing, utilities and transportation industries since 1941. Historical information on changes in productivity was also made available through the WPA National Research Project, which published indexes of output per man-hour for many industries over the period 1919 to about 1935, together with numerous associated studies and analyses. The National Bureau of Economic Research has compiled careful and valuable historical analyses of productivity trends in major industries. Many universities and other research agencies continue to contribute to knowledge in this field.[3]

Total Wage Payments and National Productivity

Measurement of Gross National Product

To investigate the relationship between wages and productivity on a national scale, it is first necessary to agree on a specific measure of national production. The measure most commonly used is the gross national product (usually abbreviated to GNP), as defined by the Department of Commerce. Although it is subject to many of the limitations and qualifications indicated previously, it probably constitutes the most useful and satisfactory comprehensive index of national economic activity.

The gross national product may be considered

3. A résumé of current sources of quantitative information on productivity is contained in "Major Sources of Productivity Information," Bureau of Labor Statistics, June 1949 (mimeographed).

A discussion of technical and conceptual problems involved in productivity measurement may be found in "A Review of the Bureau of Labor Statistics Indexes of Output per Man-Hour, Part I," Bureau of Labor Statistics, 1947 (mimeographed).

a measure of the total production of goods and services available either for consumption or for future productive use, or it may also be considered as the total of payments made to individuals or other economic entities and representing claims against goods and services produced. Whether considered from the product side or the payment side, the gross national product is the same. In a sense, then, the gross national product is the result of a double-entry bookkeeping system for the entire economy, with a credit item balancing every debit. It illustrates the fact that, with minor qualifications, consumption and production must be equal, and that whenever goods are produced, an equivalent claim against them is likewise created within the economy.

We now set up the following relationship:

$$P = E \times \frac{H}{E} \times \frac{P}{H}$$

in which P stands for the gross national product, E for total employment, and H for the total number of man-hours worked. It will be noted that this equation constitutes what some might call a truism and what the mathematician calls an identity, in that it must hold regardless of the values assigned to the symbols.

We observe, then, that the total national product may be obtained by multiplying three factors. The first is total employment, and the gross national product will be expected to increase or decline with employment. The second factor, total man-hours divided by total employment, represents the average number of man-hours expended per employed worker in the time period being considered. The third factor, total production divided by total hours worked, is a measure of national productivity.

Considered from the income side, one of the largest elements in the gross national product is wage payments. The left-hand side of the equation set down above may then be broken into two parts—one representing wages (W), the other representing all other payments on the income side of the gross national product (O). We now have

$$W + O = E \times \frac{H}{E} \times \frac{P}{H}$$

In this form, the relationship of national productivity to wage payments is clear. With no change in employment or working hours, an increase in national productivity on the right side of the equation will both permit and make necessary an equal increase on the left side. The increase may be absorbed wholly by an increase in wage payments or by an increase in the other payments (which include salaries, interest, profits and rents), or it may be divided between the two. Similarly, a decline in national productivity will affect either wage payments or other payments or both.

There are thus a limited number of ways in which real national wage payments can be increased. These include a reduction in payments to other sections of the economy in favor of wages (on the left side of the equation), an increase in the number of persons working in the economy (a possibility that is limited during periods of prosperity but clearly important when unemployment is high), an increase in average working hours (also a limited possibility) and, finally, an increase in national productivity.

To digress for a moment, let us modify the first equation presented above by dividing both sides by the size of the population. The left side is then converted into gross national product per capita, which is a reasonable measure of the average material standard of living in the economy. The first term on the right-hand side of the equation becomes total workers divided by population, or the proportion of the population which is employed. We thus have, for any economy, the standard of living as the product of three factors: percentage employed, average work schedules and productivity.

Unequivocal figures covering, say, the past fifty years are not available for gross national product per capita (deflated to account for price fluctuations). However, the various studies that have been made agree generally in placing the rate of increase at about 2 per cent a year, equivalent to a doubling every thirty-five years. This increase in material living standards in the United States has been due almost entirely to a steady increase in output per man-hour. Over the last half century average working hours have tended to decline. In the period since 1910 the ratio of employment to population has remained relatively constant at about 40 per cent, except during depression years, when employment declined sharply, and during the war years, when an abnormal increase in employment was recorded. Productivity increase has, then, been the main source of the higher living standards in the United States—standards that have tended to double with each generation.

To return to the second equation presented above, it is obviously desirable to examine the relationship between wage payments and the other forms of payment included in the gross national product. Unfortunately, figures on wage payments are not available separately. Information is available, however, on wage and salary payments combined. Furthermore, total salary payments are known to be substantially smaller than total wage payments, and in many cases the distinction between wage and salary payments is somewhat arbitrary. Wage payments may be defined as compensation paid to individuals not working on their own account and not paid in salary form. For many forms of salary payment, especially in the lower-income occupations, the distinction between wages and salaries is rather artificial and the two forms of compensation tend to move in very much the same fashion.

Wages and Salaries as Percentage of GNP

Total wage and salary payments in private industry are shown as a percentage of private gross national product in Table 29 for the years 1919–1948. The comparison is confined to the private segment of the economy (with government excluded) because of the arbitrary way in which it is necessary to define the government contribution to the gross national product.

The proportion of wage and salary payments to gross national product has been astonishingly stable over this period. After 1920 there were only a few scattered years in which the proportion fell below 49 per cent or exceeded 51 per cent. The figures show very little evidence of a trend in one direction or another or of any significant dependence on the levels of economic activity prevailing in the different years.

Attempts to explain the remarkable consistency of this ratio on theoretical grounds have not been wholly successful or convincing. It is perhaps better to accept this consistency as an observed phenomenon, and to conjecture that a substantial change in the ratio (considering its constancy during both boom and bust periods) could occur only after major changes in the general economic structure.

The data presented in Table 29 leave a very important question unanswered. Has the proportion of the population depending on wage and salary payments increased or declined in relation to the proportion depending on the other forms of payment recorded in the gross national product? Even if sufficient information were available to indicate the answer to this question, it is doubtful if it could be answered in clean-cut fashion, since many persons in the United States derive significant portions of their income from both direct compensation and other sources of income.

TABLE 29

COMPENSATION OF PRIVATE EMPLOYEES AS PERCENTAGE OF PRIVATE GROSS NATIONAL PRODUCT, 1919–1948

Year	Per Cent	Year	Per Cent	Year	Per Cent
1919....	47.5	1929....	48.9	1939....	49.4
1920....	50.8	1930....	51.1	1940....	48.7
1921....	49.5	1931....	51.8	1941....	48.2
1922....	50.1	1932....	52.2	1942....	48.8
1923....	51.0	1933....	50.5	1943....	50.3
1924....	47.1	1934....	49.4	1944....	49.8
1925....	49.2	1935....	48.9	1945....	49.7
1926....	49.5	1936....	48.1	1946....	51.2
1927....	46.1	1937....	50.8	1947....	49.7
1928....	50.5	1938....	50.0	1948....	49.1

Source: Department of Commerce (unrevised data).

Ratio of Wages to Value Added by Manufacture

The relation of wage payments to other payments may be examined, however, for a very important sector of the economy — manufacturing. For the years covered by the Census of Manufactures, total wage payments in manufacturing may be expressed as a percentage of "value added by manufacture." (See Table 30.) Value added by manufacture represents the manufacturer's return for goods produced, minus payments for purchased materials, components and energy. In the aggregate, value added by manufacture is very nearly equivalent to the contribution of the manufacturing industries to the gross national product.

Despite appreciable year-to-year variations, the ratio of wages to value added by manufacture shows no clear trend and no immediate relationship to volume. Between 1899 and 1919 the ratio remained approximately constant, near 40 per cent. In 1921, when manufacturing volume was low, it rose to 43 per cent, the highest proportion recorded. After 1921 there was an irregular decline, with low percentages reported in 1929 and 1933 — the first a peak year, the second a depression low. In 1935 and 1937 the ratio returned to about 40 per cent, a figure

TABLE 30

WAGE PAYMENTS AND VALUE ADDED BY MANUFACTURE, ALL MANUFACTURING INDUSTRIES, 1899–1947

Year	Total Wage Payments, in Billions	Value Added by Manufacture, in Billions	Wages as Percentage of Value Added by Manufacture
1899	$1.893	$4.647	40.7
1904	2.441	6.019	40.6
1909	3.206	8.162	39.3
1914	3.709	9.238	40.1
1919	9.611	23.735	40.5
1921	7.451	17.253	43.2
1923	10.149	24.569	41.3
1925	9.980	25.668	38.9
1927	10.099	26.325	38.4
1929	10.885	30.591	35.6
1931	6.689	18.601	36.0
1933	4.940	14.008	35.3
1935	7.311	18.553	39.4
1937	10.113	25.174	40.2
1939	9.090	24.683	36.8
1947	30.243	74.432	40.6

Source: Census of Manufactures.

again reached in 1947 after a drop to 37 per cent in 1939.

A partial explanation for these odd fluctuations is furnished by the data presented in Figures 24 and 25. It appears that in some of the years during this period an increase in output per man-hour in manufacturing contributed to a reduction in manufacturing costs, but this was not equally reflected in price changes, as shown by the varying movements of output per man-hour and real average hourly earnings in manufacturing in Figure 25. As a result the relative importance of wages to value added by manufacture declined between 1921 and 1933.

CHANNELS FOR DISTRIBUTION OF PRODUCTIVITY GAINS

Before proceeding further with the question of wages and productivity, it may be helpful to examine their relationship in a single plant. To bring this into concrete terms, a hypothetical distribution of manufacturing costs per unit in a single imaginary enterprise is presented in Table 31. It is assumed that total costs amount to $10 per unit produced. The materials cost is $4, the labor cost is $3, and the sum of all other costs, including costs of administration, supervision, planning, research, advertising, sales, accounting, procurement, engineering and so on, as well as profit, is set at $3.

Where an item required in manufacture can be specified, the contribution of the item to cost per unit produced can be separated into the quantity required per unit and the price paid for it. For example, in our imaginary plant four pounds of some material are required per unit produced. At 50 cents a pound, this ma-

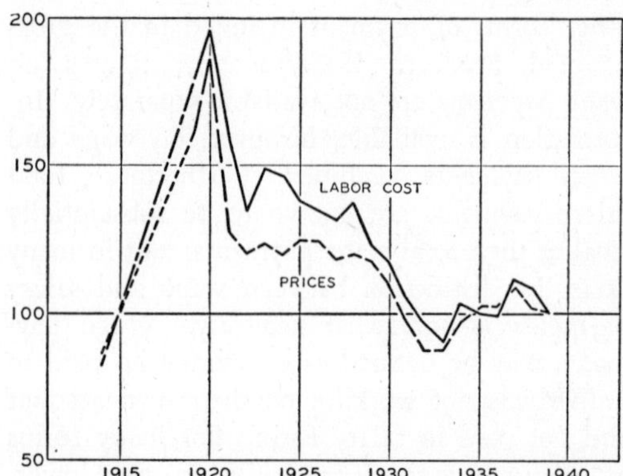

FIGURE 24. INDEXES OF UNIT LABOR COST AND PRICES OF MANUFACTURED PRODUCTS, 1914–1939

(*1939 = 100*)

Source: Indexes computed by Bureau of Labor Statistics.

The index of unit labor cost is obtained by dividing an index of total payrolls in all manufacturing industry by an index of the volume of manufacturing production. Prices are represented in this figure by the Bureau of Labor Statistics index for manufactured goods.

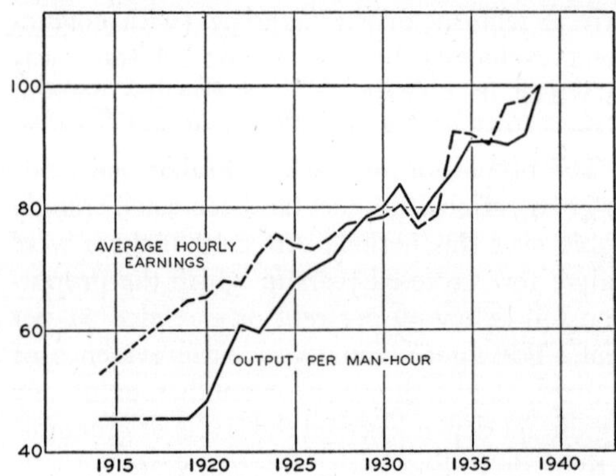

FIGURE 25. INDEXES OF REAL HOURLY EARNINGS AND OUTPUT PER MAN-HOUR IN MANUFACTURING INDUSTRIES, 1914–1939

(*1939 = 100*)

Source: Indexes computed by Bureau of Labor Statistics.

The index of real hourly earnings shows the aggregate payroll of all manufacturing industries divided by the number of man-hours worked and adjusted to consumer prices. The index of output per man-hour is derived from the index of manufacturing production divided by the number of man-hours worked. The relationship between these two indexes is the same as between the volume of manufacturing production and total real earnings of factory workers.

TABLE 31

HYPOTHETICAL DISTRIBUTION OF UNIT MANUFACTURING COSTS FOR A SINGLE PRODUCT

Item	Quantity per Unit	Price	Detailed Unit Costs	Total Unit Costs
Materials — A	4 lbs.	$.50 per lb.	$2.00	
— B	2 sq. ft.	.40 per sq. ft.	.80	$4.00
— Other	....	....	1.20	
Labor				
Direct	2 hours	.90 per hr.	1.80	3.00
Indirect	1 hour	1.20 per hr.	1.20	
Other costs and profit	....	....	3.00	3.00
Total cost	....	....	....	$10.00

terial adds $2 to the total unit cost. This quantity and price breakdown can also be applied to labor. It is assumed that three hours of direct and indirect labor at an average cost of $1 an hour are required per unit produced. The first factor represents productivity; that is, in this plant one third of a unit will be produced per man-hour. The second factor is, of course, the average rate of wage payment — in this case $1 an hour. The two together determine the unit labor cost and in part total manufacturing costs. The example illustrates the way in which wages and productivity enter the cost structure of a plant making a homogeneous product.

Suppose now that labor productivity increases substantially in the imaginary firm, while all other cost factors remain the same. In this case, unit labor cost will drop proportionately. If, for example, productivity doubles, unit labor cost will be cut in half, from $3 to $1.50.

What can be done with this reduction in costs? Normally there will be only three avenues of distribution. The saving may be used to increase wages, to increase profits, or to lower prices, or it may find an outlet in some combination of these three.

Relationship to Wages

Suppose that the increase in productivity is balanced by an increase in wages, so that labor costs remain unchanged. If the wages paid to the workers employed by the imaginary enterprise were previously equal to those paid for similar work in other firms in the same locality, a disbalance in the wage structure will be created; that is, unless there are balancing changes in other plants, the new wage levels will be substantially higher than wages elsewhere in the same area.

Initially, it may be possible to achieve a wage position in a given plant somewhat above the general level. The mobility of labor is imperfect, and various institutional factors may help to set the plant apart. For example, a requirement of long training to hold the type of job involved, or strong membership restrictions on the part of a union, may encourage the establishment of a differential wage structure. Some firms pay somewhat more than the going wage level in order to minimize labor turnover and assure a better selection of workers. However, it is unlikely that the process will continue after the establishment of an initial differential. For one thing, the operators of the business will object to paying substantially more than a competitive wage for work of a given complexity. Beyond this, unless the firm enjoys a monopoly position, competitive influences may limit the extent to which the single firm has freedom of action. In summary, substantial advances in productivity may permit the creation of a differential in wages between a particular firm and others in the same industry or area, but a widening of the differential through continuing advances in productivity is hardly to be expected.

Relationship to Profits

Let us examine now the possibility of funneling cost savings achieved through productivity advance into increased profits. It is clear that here as well as in the case of wages an advantage in productivity can be translated into a differential over competing firms. As is also true of wages, however, there is a limit to the differential that can be maintained under competitive conditions. If the firm does not enjoy a monopoly with respect to the product, it may also be assumed that it does not enjoy a monopoly with respect to the means for technological change, so that other firms may be expected to duplicate sooner or later the productivity advances made by the first firm. If competitive conditions prevail, an aggrandizement of profits is not likely. Even where a near-monopoly position is encountered, the concentration of savings achieved through higher productivity in the profits column will probably result eventually in competing enterprises being formed or in a demand for public regulation.

In earlier societies, profits were regarded almost exclusively as a payment for enterprise or for a risk of capital. In a technologically advancing society, profits have come to have an additional function. Firms enjoying a favorable profit position because of technological leadership and high productivity have made increasing use of part of their profits for research into methods for maintaining their position. At the same time, profits have become an important source of funds for capital expenditures.

Relationship to Prices

The third avenue for distributing savings growing out of increased productivity is in the form of price reductions. As indicated above, beyond the establishment of limited differentials with respect to wages and profits, the economies from productivity increase are likely to seek this third outlet. We should expect, therefore, that where extraordinary advances in the technology of manufacture of a particular product occur, a substantial portion of the saving in labor costs will be transferred to the buying public in the form of lower prices. (Some or all of the change may, of course, take the form of an improvement in quality, which is equivalent to a reduction in real price.) This may simultaneously broaden the market for the product and to some extent have a second-order favorable influence on wages, profits, productivity and prices.

Nothing has yet been said about the increases in overhead costs that may accompany increases in productivity. There is a very common notion that little or no net economy may be achieved, because substantial productivity increases are usually the result of changes in technology, which usually require increased capital expenditures for new equipment. This point of view is certainly valid under some circumstances. However, there is some evidence that this has not been generally true in manufacturing industries. Furthermore, there are instances where technical change may bring about a reduction in unit capital charges as well as unit labor costs. For example, a new metalworking machine may cost more than the machine it replaces but because of improved design may have a substantially greater output per hour of operation. As a result, both labor and capital charges per unit produced may fall.

Labor Costs and Prices

This discussion has been concerned primarily with single firms. As the area of study is broadened to include a number of firms, some of which sell to others, unit labor costs become more important in the total cost picture, since increases or decreases in unit labor costs in one firm may influence the costs of materials in other establishments purchasing part of the first firm's output. When all manufacturing industries are considered together, unit labor cost seems to have been the principal element determining price movements. (See Figure 24.) During the entire period from 1914 through 1939, the trend in prices of manufactured goods very closely paralleled the trend in unit labor costs. Both more than doubled between 1914 and 1920, and both declined substantially in the following two years. Between 1922 and 1933 the series did not coincide, but their general trends were similar.

A considerable degree of similarity between price and labor cost movements should, of course, be expected, since labor costs are a very large element in total costs. Furthermore, other elements in the cost picture may be strongly influenced by the movements of wages, which in turn influence labor costs. It is surprising, nevertheless, to find these two quite independent and imperfect statistical series agreeing so closely over such a long period.

In such broad economic segments as manufacturing, prices may be determined very largely by labor costs, and so in part by wages. Real wages — what wages will buy — are, in turn, partly determined by price levels for manufactured goods. Thus prices influence real wages in two ways — first, as manufactured goods are purchased by the wage earner and, second, as price changes in manufactured goods influence the prices of other items purchased by wage earners. We might therefore expect to find a relationship between output per man-hour of workers in manufacturing and real wages such as the fairly high level of agreement shown in Figure 25. The two series show considerable discrepancies in some periods but over longer periods of time a balance has generally been reached again.

We should expect closer agreement between the series shown in Figure 24 than between those shown in Figure 25. The first deal exclusively with economic magnitudes in manufacturing, while the second bring in external influences — in particular, the price levels for goods and services produced outside manufacturing as these affect the real content of the wage dollar.

The general relationship between real earnings and output per man-hour may be summed up as follows: In a single firm there is no necessary requirement that wage and productivity trends be similar. Productivity may remain constant and wages rise, or the reverse may be true. In a major segment of the economy, such as manufacturing, we may expect a high degree of correspondence between movements in real hourly wages and output per man-hour. Discrepancies may occur, but closer analysis will usually reveal that they involve redistribution of income, either in favor of or at the expense of other sections of the economy. For the economy as a whole, the correlation between real wages and productivity is almost complete. Wages may rise or fall somewhat in relation to other forms of income payment, but such shifts are likely to be small.

General Wage-Price-Productivity Relationship

The data previously presented indicate that in the past wage and nonwage costs have tended to move together for the economy as a whole, and they strongly suggest that this will continue in the future, barring radical changes in the basic economic structure. Accepting this thesis, the interrelationships of general wage, price and productivity movements are sharply limited to three main possibilities: (1) If money wage levels increase on the average somewhat more rapidly than productivity, unit labor costs and, in turn, general price levels may be expected to rise. (2) If wage and productivity movements correspond, unit labor costs and average prices will tend to remain more or less constant. This very definitely does not imply a constant price level for all commodities but suggests that prices will fall if productivity increases are above average, and that the converse will also be true. (3) If money wages lag behind increases in productivity, a generally declining price level will result.

Wage and price policies cannot be considered independently. It is clear that wage movements will depend on price policy, or, alternatively, that price movements will be determined by wage policies.

Falling prices tend to discourage present purchasing and have a generally depressing influence on economic activity. A price decline is regarded with uneasiness by those concerned with keeping employment and production levels high. Falling prices tend to encourage saving for the future at the expense of immediate consumption and so may exaggerate savings beyond investment needs. They offer a windfall profit to persons holding monetary obligations.

Rising prices, in contrast, encourage a high level of current consumption and tend to discourage savings. In this way, a rising price level may foster inadequate replacement and improvement of productive equipment. Rising prices represent a steady discount or hidden tax on all obligations expressed in monetary terms. Annuitants, insurance beneficiaries and bondholders are immediately affected, and as a result, people may be discouraged from assuming obligations of this character.

A generally constant level of prices is free of most of the defects mentioned above and favors forward planning by both industry and consumers. Although opinion is not unanimous on this point, perhaps a comfortable majority believe that a generally stable level of prices is likely to contribute best to the health of the economy.

Few economists would deny that under special circumstances either rising or falling general price levels may be beneficial. For example, many feel that the higher postwar price (and wage) levels were a necessary part of postwar readjustment, since otherwise it would have been difficult to support the federal debt accumulated during World War II. Others feel that the spur of a small but steady rise in price may be needed to maintain production and employment at high levels. Nevertheless, although a modification in policy might be necessary to meet special circumstances, a majority would probably favor a relatively stable price level as a long-run objective.

Various reasons have been advanced in favor of a particular price policy that, if adopted, would in turn require a particular wage policy. We could examine the question in reverse to see if there are strong reasons for adopting a particular wage policy that in turn would determine the movements of prices. But we can see no advantage in posing the question in this fashion. Real wages, in the aggregate, will be determined, as we have seen, by productivity and by the distribution of income among the various claimant groups. The general pattern of distribution seems deeply rooted in the structure of the economy — so firmly that it has hardly been altered by changes from prosperity to depression and from peace to war. It is clear, then, that broad wage movements that do not correspond with changes in productivity are only changes in money wages. Real wages, which alone are of importance to the individual, are not likely to be substantially affected.[4]

Effect of Economic and Political Pressures

The upshot of these arguments is the positing, as a desirable objective, of a situation in which average wage levels keep pace with average changes in productivity. This would lead to a situation in which prices tended to decline in the more progressive industries and perhaps increase in those that lagged. Of course, we cannot expect such an ideal result in a busy and changing world, with constant readjustment of uneasy political-economic balances. However, it represents a target point in an obscure area.

Irrespective of theories or particular policies, it is true that wage movements that are inconsistent with productivity changes will inevitably influence price levels. Some economic relationships are at least partially responsive to policy decisions or political pressures, but others are not. With minor qualifications, no more can be consumed within an economy than is produced. To a limited extent, economic or political pressures may alter the distribution of goods among various economic groups. But to the extent that the initial distribution resulted from natural forces operating within a stable economic structure, the mechanism can be tampered with only with risk to continuing economic health. Beyond the limited shifts permitted within the existing structure, the source of all real improvements in compensation for each group, and for all groups together, must be increased productivity, in the future as it has been in the past.

The separate groups within the economy are like roped mountain climbers ascending a slope. All must have some freedom of movement independent of the others, but each climber's movements must be limited by the position of the group as a whole.

Wage changes in any given plant or industry, considering the broad sweep, must in general follow the pattern of the general wage structure. Even in cases of near-monopoly, productivity increases are not likely to be used continuously to create a wage structure far out of line with prevailing levels. It is equally unthinkable that wages should lag in a plant or an industry simply because productivity change has failed to keep up with the general improvement. Only by increasing wage rates, even though this requires price rises, can such a firm or industry maintain its labor force.[5]

But while this general movement must be maintained, there is no similar restriction on the wages to be paid individuals or on relative wage levels in different plants or industries. Since the wage structure is constantly changing, inequities and disbalances will appear and need to be corrected. Wage levels will not, however, rise of themselves. They will change only as the result of many thousands of separate bargains and agreements, reached daily under widely varying conditions. In this chaotic type of market, it is almost inevitable that increases beyond the average will occur almost haphazardly to lead the way.

Industry Wage and Productivity Relationships

The preceding discussion, concerned largely with necessary interrelationships between broad movements of wages and prices, has nevertheless indicated that in particular industries there is much greater possibility of independent move-

4. We are, of course, speaking of the individual's true economic interest, not of his interest as he imagines it to be. It would be difficult to convince many individuals that under some circumstances an increase in monetary earnings might result in no net benefit.

5. It may be noted, of course, that just as certain plants or unions have been able to maintain restrictions that permit a higher than average wage level, there are other economic restrictions that in the past have favored the continuation of a substandard wage level. Where a class of workers has been offered only limited opportunities for employment, because of social or other barriers, a low wage level has been perpetuated in some instances for long periods of time.

ment. To what extent, then, may individual industries escape the bonds of economic (and arithmetic) law that circumscribe the economy at large? Data for a fairly large number of manufacturing industries or groups of industries are available on changes in productivity and wages over a considerable number of years. (See Appendix Table 20.) An examination of these data may help to distinguish between facts and fancies in the productivity field.

A low absolute level of wages is commonly believed to discourage the search for methods of increasing productivity, and a relatively high wage level to encourage the installation of labor-saving equipment, which leads to larger increases in productivity. This notion may be checked by comparing changes in output per man-hour in various industries from 1923 to 1939 with hourly earnings in the same industries in 1923. (See Figure 26.) The years 1923 and 1939 are well suited for a comparison of this kind since neither represents a peak of business activity or a depression period. The chart clearly shows little or no correlation between earnings in 1923 and subsequent changes in output per man-hour.

A related notion is that large increases in productivity will tend to create high wage levels, or that small increases in productivity will subsequently be associated with low wage levels. A comparison of changes in output per man-hour in manufacturing industries between 1923 and 1939 with their average hourly earnings in 1939 shows little or no correlation between changes in productivity and subsequent wage levels. (See Figure 27.)

Despite the popular notion that such a relationship does or should exist, there is little reason to expect any substantial correlation between productivity movements and wage levels. As a matter of fact, an inverse movement might occur under certain circumstances. An industry facing a declining market because of competition might strongly resist increases in wage levels but at the same time have a strong incentive toward increasing its productivity and thus cutting costs. Something of this sort apparently occurred between 1923 and 1939 in the cigar industry. During this period cigarettes supplanted cigars in public favor, and the market for cigars declined. At the same time, the industry largely converted from hand to machine production of cigars, and productivity levels increased accordingly. At the other end of the scale, an industry with a relatively favorable market for its products might find it possible to pay high wages and at the same time be under limited pressure to improve its productivity.

A somewhat different picture appears when percentage changes in average hourly earnings are plotted against percentage changes in output per man-hour. (See Figure 28.) Although the correlation between the two is not particularly high, it is nevertheless significant. If a few extreme instances are omitted, the degree of relationship is considerably improved. Thus we can conclude that percentage changes in earnings are more likely to be related to changes in productivity than are the absolute levels of earnings either before or after the productivity change.

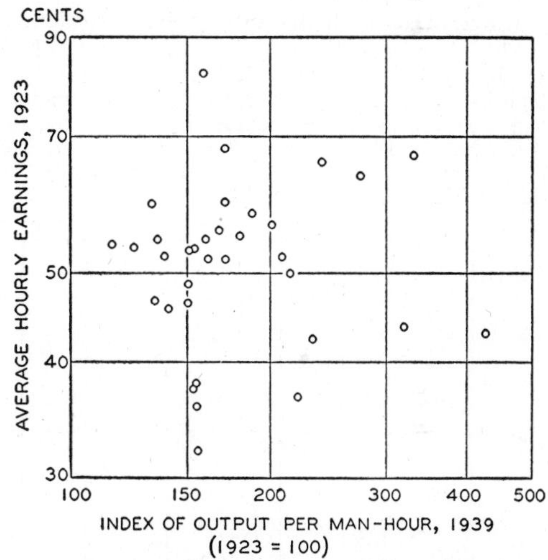

FIGURE 26. AVERAGE HOURLY EARNINGS IN 1923 AND INDEX OF OUTPUT PER MAN-HOUR IN 1939 COMPARED WITH 1923, IN 34 MANUFACTURING INDUSTRIES

Source: Data from Bureau of Labor Statistics.

Each dot on this chart represents one of 34 manufacturing industries, plotted to show average hourly wages in 1923 and output per man-hour in 1939 as a percentage of the corresponding figure for 1923. For example, the dot in the second cell from the left at the top of the chart represents newspapers and other periodical publishing, in which hourly earnings averaged 82.1 cents in 1923 and output per man-hour increased 58.2 per cent from 1923 to 1939. The dot at the extreme right represents the rayon industry, in which average hourly earnings were 43.2 cents in 1923 while output per man-hour in 1939 was 425.5 as compared with 100 in 1923.

If the rate of increase in productivity were directly related to wage rates, the dots would be distributed in an area stretching from the bottom left corner to the top right corner of the chart.

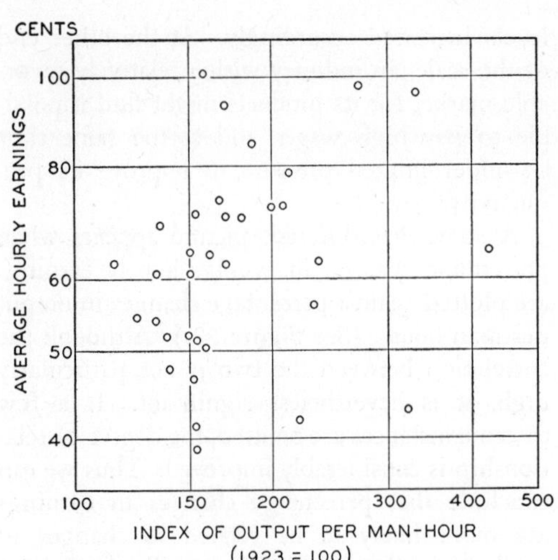

FIGURE 27. AVERAGE HOURLY EARNINGS IN 1939 AND INDEX OF OUTPUT PER MAN-HOUR IN 1939 COMPARED WITH 1923, IN 34 MANUFACTURING INDUSTRIES

Source: Data from Bureau of Labor Statistics.

This chart is of the same type as Figure 26. If average hourly earnings in 1939 were particularly high in the industries in which output per man-hour had been increasing most rapidly and vice versa, the dots representing single industries would be clustered in an area stretching from the bottom left corner to the top right corner of the chart.

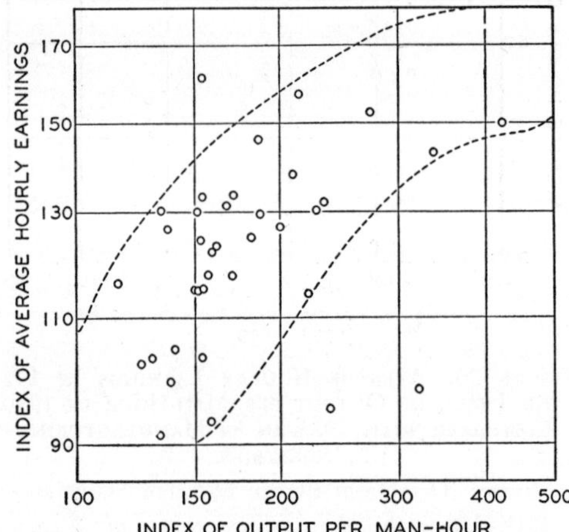

FIGURE 28. INDEXES OF AVERAGE HOURLY EARNINGS IN 1939 AND OUTPUT PER MAN-HOUR IN 1939 COMPARED WITH 1923, IN 37 MANUFACTURING INDUSTRIES

(*1923 = 100*)

Source: Data from Bureau of Labor Statistics.

The correlation between relative changes in average hourly earnings and output per man-hour from 1923 to 1939 is checked here in the same way as in Figures 26 and 27, but with a different result. Percentage changes in wage levels are more closely associated with productivity changes than are absolute wage levels at either the beginning or the end of the period. The freehand broken lines suggest the approximate limits of the area in which all but three dots are located.

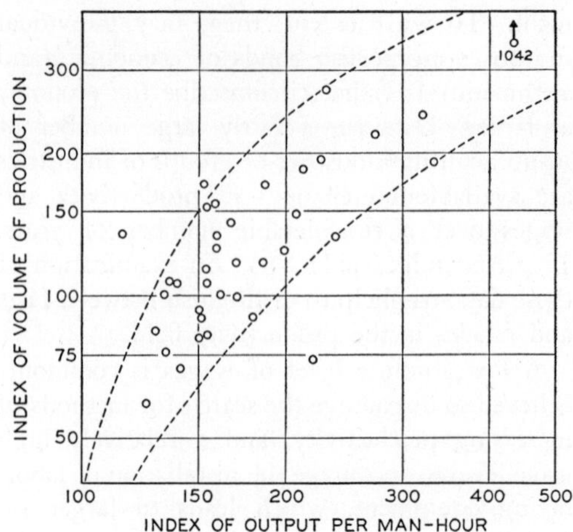

FIGURE 29. INDEXES OF VOLUME OF PRODUCTION AND OUTPUT PER MAN-HOUR IN 1939 COMPARED WITH 1923, IN 37 MANUFACTURING INDUSTRIES

(*1923 = 100*)

Source: Data from Bureau of Labor Statistics.

The clustering of the dots indicates a fairly close correlation between the two factors that determine the location of each dot — the change in volume of production and change in output per man-hour between 1923 and 1939. The freehand broken lines suggest the approximate limits of the area in which all but three dots are clustered. This area is appreciably narrower than in Figure 28.

Effect of Production Changes

A part of the explanation for this is suggested by the data presented in Figure 29, which shows changes in production between 1923 and 1939 in relation to changes in output per man-hour. Here a higher degree of correlation is exhibited than in the three previous charts.[6]

The data presented in Figures 28 and 29 suggest a possible mechanism that has operated to affect the relationship between wage and productivity movements. Where industries have greatly increased production levels, it is virtually certain that existing plants have been greatly expanded or that new plants have been built. This generally means more modern equipment and possible improvements in manufacturing techniques. Expansion of production indicates a favorable market for the industry's products,

6. The relationship between production and productivity changes shown in this figure should not be confused with what is called the capacity utilization factor. At any given time a firm or an industry tends to record a somewhat higher level of output per man-hour if it is operating at a high rather than a low level of production in relation to capacity. For manufacturing industries generally there is reason to expect that the rates of capacity utilization were not too dissimilar in 1923 and 1939.

and this in turn may have made funds available both for research on means of improving technology and for changes in techniques or equipment. It is not surprising, therefore, to find a degree of association between changes in production and productivity.

At the same time, where production levels are rising it may be necessary to attract additional workers to the industry, and this favors higher wage levels. New techniques of manufacture may lead to new occupations. The very fact that the occupational structure of an industry is unsettled will facilitate upward adjustment in wage levels. Furthermore, with widening markets and rising productivity, profit margins year after year may be somewhat larger than anticipated, since pricing policy is usually based on current or past experience rather than on expected developments. Taken together, these conditions create a climate favorable to upward revisions in wages. To some extent, such upward adjustments can be anticipated whether or not previous wage levels were relatively high or low.

The situation in an industry where the total production level shows little change or actually declines is likely to be quite different. Since existing capacity will seem adequate, there will normally be less incentive to invest capital in new equipment or processes that may increase productivity. Few new plants with more modern equipment will be constructed. Research in new techniques may lag.[7] On the wage side, an established rate structure in a set group of plants may inhibit the gradual and partially hidden upward adjustment in wages that may occur if the occupational structure changes. Finally, limited profit margins may create greater resistance to wage adjustments.

The intercorrelations of productivity, production and wage movements tend to support these conclusions. The correlation between wages and productivity in the thirty-seven industries, with constant production levels, is so small as to be hardly significant. The correlation between wage changes and changes in production levels is somewhat higher though still small. The correlation between changes in production levels and productivity changes, with wages held constant, remains high.[8]

In summary, the absolute level of wages in an industry seems to have little relation to subsequent changes in productivity, and productivity changes, in turn, seem to have little relation to subsequent wage levels. Among industries with substantial increases in production, however, there are likely to be increases in productivity and, to a lesser extent, in wages, and these will occur whether the previous wage level was relatively high or low. Other things being equal, then, industries of this class are most likely to be the wage leaders, that is, the ones in which wage advances presage or cause a general upward movement in the wage structure.

Claims on Productivity Benefits

Increases or decreases in productivity have often been used as reasons for granting or refusing wage adjustments in particular industries. But does a particular class or group, because of an unusual contribution, have a special claim or right to benefits from productivity advances?

The mainsprings of advance in productivity have been claimed to reside in labor, in management or in capital — often by proponents of a scheme for a redistribution of the fruits of productivity gains in favor of one or another of these groups. An examination of the question, however, yields little evidence to support any class theory of origins of technological change.

Technological Advances

The real foundation of greater productivity is in the steady accumulation of technical knowl-

7. These statements may seem to be contradicted by the extensive mechanization of the cigar industry that occurred after the cigar market began to decline. However, the program of industrial research that led to the development of the cigar machine was started about 1895 and was completed by 1917, before the decline. Also, the decline in cigar production in part represented price competition with other forms of tobacco, and attempts to reduce costs were important in retaining a share of the market.

The behavior of the cigar industry nevertheless suggests that with a larger body of data one might find a general tendency for productivity improvement to be least among industries where production levels remain approximately constant over long periods of time. Some of the reasons for expecting large increases in productivity where production levels advance sharply are given in the text. The experience of the cigar industry suggests that at least in some instances vigorous competition for a declining market might also produce increases in productivity, although these would be limited by reluctance to invest new capital in a declining industry. Among industries with a reasonably constant production level, none of the forces described above would operate with the same effect and productivity increases might lag behind industries on either side.

8. The respective coefficients of partial correlation are 0.11, 0.21 and 0.75.

edge. During the past century there has been a very rapid growth in technical information about how to apply mechanical energy to reshape natural resources to fit them better for human use. Today's library of technical information is for the most part a social property. It does not belong to any particular group or, for that matter, to any one nation.

Only within the past hundred years has more than slight use been made of mechanical energy. In earlier times, manufactured goods were normally produced by hand and the energy used in production was supplied by human beings. Today most of the energy requirements for production are supplied from mechanical sources. The worker today is much less a source of energy and much more a director of the use of mechanical energy.

In 1850, human workers in the United States supplied an estimated 2.7 billion horsepower-hours of energy while all mechanical sources combined provided 1.0 billion.[9] Work animals, used primarily in transportation and farming, outweighed both human and mechanical sources with 13.9 billion horsepower-hours. By 1940, human workers provided 10.5 billion horsepower-hours, but the amount supplied from mechanical sources had grown to 260.4 billion. The energy supplied by work animals had increased only modestly, to 18.5 billion horsepower-hours.

We see from these figures that in 1850 the mechanical supplement to human energy used in production amounted to only a little more than a third of the human total but by 1940 it was twenty-five times greater. This basic alteration in the technological structure of production is a key factor in the enormous growth of production and productivity in the United States during this period.

The extremely close relationship between ability to apply mechanical energy and ability to increase production, productivity and living standards is illustrated in Figure 30. The real national income of the United States increased 16.5 times between 1850 and 1940. During this same period total energy consumption increased 16.4 times.

The process whereby an increasing amount of mechanical energy is used to extend and make

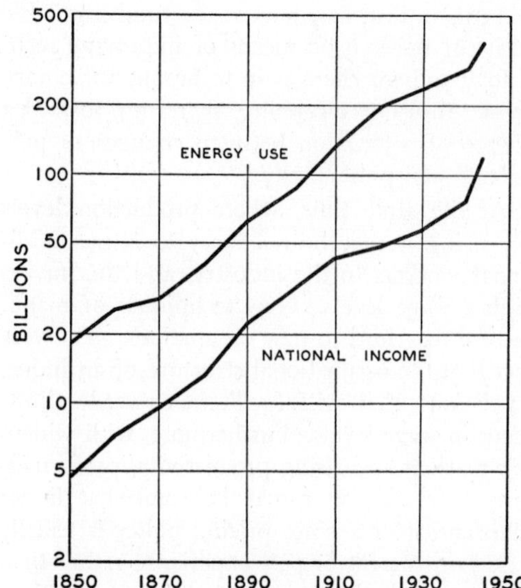

FIGURE 30. TOTAL ENERGY CONSUMPTION AND TOTAL NATIONAL INCOME, 1850 TO 1944
(*Energy Consumption in Billions of Horsepower-Hours; National Income in Billions of 1940 Dollars*)

Source: Based on J. Frederic Dewhurst and Associates, *America's Needs and Resources,* Twentieth Century Fund, New York, 1947.

The data have been plotted on a ratio scale, so that the same percentage change is represented by the same horizontal distance anywhere in the chart. The lines show that, in general, increases in real national income have been accompanied by nearly proportional increases in the use of energy in the United States over the past century.

more fruitful the available supply of human labor shows no signs of approaching a limit. The first machines made to harness and apply mechanical energy were relatively crude. Early designs tended to be wasteful of both human and mechanical energy and usually required considerable human control. More recently, the function of control has been relegated to mechanical devices to an increasing extent. One of the most important aspects of current technological development is the use of instruments and devices, especially of an electronic nature, for control purposes.

Interrelation of Technological Changes

Specific changes in technology have occurred within a vast web of constantly increasing complexity. New materials, products, techniques and types of equipment have been produced in a steady stream, and developments in one field have frequently had unforeseen, far-reaching

9. Estimates from J. Frederic Dewhurst and Associates, *America's Needs and Resources,* Twentieth Century Fund, New York, 1947.

effects in others. For example, our present systems of transportation are dependent in no small measure on radical improvements in communications. Also, much of the present structure of marketing and production could not have come into being except as a result of developments in transportation. A vast number of essentially new industries have been created within the life span of the last generation. Probably most workers in the United States today are using equipment or processes or are engaged in the manufacture of products that were virtually unknown or were mere curiosities before 1900.

It is beyond the scope of this discussion to trace out any particular series of developments in technology or to classify the types of technological changes. It is sufficient for the present purpose to observe the interdependent character of modern technology. Each new advance is built on a foundation of earlier knowledge erected by the common efforts of all classes and all groups. No one person or group can lay any valid exclusive claim to these advances.

Other Contributing Factors

There have been many other contributing factors — for example, a wider knowledge and application of managerial techniques, which permits greater production with the same or less expenditure of human effort or time. This, however, is marginal. No genius of management can achieve the same results with obsolete techniques and equipment as can be produced by even moderately competent direction in a modern plant. Doubtless, the flint-chippers of the Stone Age gave thought to improving methods, but the attainment of modern living standards had to await the advent of modern technology.

The average worker today is undoubtedly better trained, better educated and healthier than workers in earlier periods, and so is better fitted to contribute to our economic life. However, this improvement is a consequence of economic environment, which in turn is the product of current levels of productivity.

The relationship between high productivity and mass production is another interesting factor. High levels of productivity, creating high levels of national income, have helped to make mass markets possible. These have enhanced the opportunities for large-scale manufacture, which has had its effect on productivity. In this country it is possible to use highly economical manufacturing techniques that would be wholly unpractical for small-scale operation. Standardization of materials and parts and specialization in manufacture, which together contribute substantially to high productivity, are themselves outgrowths of earlier technological development.

Distribution of Benefits

With this discussion in mind, we may again ask whether, because of its unusual contributions, any one class has a special claim to the benefits or fruits of increasing productivity. In general the answer is clearly in the negative. Among the working group, for example, it is rather doubtful whether the average worker is called on for greater mental or physical effort today than at the beginning of the century. In fact, many of the developments of modern technology have been concerned with reducing the demands on physical energy. Others have been directed at eliminating the need for continued mental concentration or for skills that can be acquired only over long periods of time. The general question can be reduced to an absurdity by inquiring whether workers have been called on for three times or five times as great a personal contribution in those industries where productivity has increased in these ratios.

We may also inquire whether management as a class should receive special consideration in a similar situation. It is, of course, a proper function of management personnel to maintain the establishments for which they are responsible in a state consistent with advances in technology. A management that permitted its facilities to become hopelessly obsolete would be considered derelict in its duty. Management as a class, therefore, should not be entitled to special treatment simply because it does its proper job.

A very similar argument can be made with respect to capital. Capital is invested in business enterprise with the anticipation of a return. It is expected that in a free economy the average rate of return will be sufficient to attract the required amount of capital. No very satisfactory argument can be advanced for any special benefit (beyond added payment for possible unusual risk) that should accrue to the individuals who make capital available, simply because this capital is used to implement progressively newer productive methods.

There is therefore little support for the notion that labor, capital or management, as groups, should receive special benefits because of increases in productivity. Indeed, the consequences of accepting any such thesis might well be disastrous. The probable result of funneling the increment in purchasing power made possible by rising productivity into the hands of any single group would be to create, in time, a dangerous instability and probable collapse of the economy.

No attempt will be made here to define the particular distribution of the gains of increasing productivity that would contribute best to economic stability and continued health. The actual distribution is, of course, controlled by the myriad sales, bargains and agreements concluded daily throughout the country. These decisions are, and should be, reached primarily in terms of the interests of the various bargainers as they see them. It is the very essence of a free economy that internal balances should be achieved in this way. The effort should be, not to constrain the bargainers, but rather to provide them with a broader appreciation of where their real interests lie.

To look at the question in a little different way, most people would agree that the return to the individual should bear some relationship to that individual's action or contribution. The return may be considered as a reward for past performance or as an incentive for continued good performance. In a sense, then, some of the conclusions stated above might seem to conflict with basic American thought.

The conflict is more apparent than real. The preceding discussion has been in terms of benefits to classes, not in terms of benefits to individuals or other economic units in relation to their performance. It is expected that the more efficient worker will in some way receive extra compensation for superior performance. Where piece rates or other wage incentive systems are used, there is, of course, a direct relationship between the worker's production and his earnings. Even in other instances, the superior worker will usually receive preferment in some way. He is most likely to receive promotion, a bonus or some other form of material or nonmaterial compensation.

The same principle holds for the firm. It is to be expected that a company that is more efficient than competing firms will be able to hold or expand its markets and show a somewhat more favorable profit margin. Everyone economically dependent on such a firm may expect to benefit. The workers have greater job security than employees of less efficient enterprises and greater chances for above-average wages. Stockholders should receive larger dividends, and management should also benefit by job security, better salaries and other rewards for successful performance.

Although there is little evidence that any particular group is primarily responsible for rises in productivity and so entitled to most of its fruits, there is clear evidence that individual workers, managers and investors by their actions, ability and vision can contribute to high productivity. Furthermore, we may expect that those making extra or unusual contributions to higher productivity will on the average receive extra benefits in return. A general acceptance of the justice and propriety of this notion has, in part, determined the kind of economic system we have.

WAGES AND RESTRICTIONS ON PRODUCTIVITY

Discussions of productivity sometimes arouse emotional responses that make it difficult to remain objective. A principal source of emotional bias is, of course, to be found in the various interconnections among productivity, wages, profits and prices. A defensive reaction to vague or imperfectly defined concepts that nevertheless may affect personal welfare is quite natural, and productivity is frequently used as an argument for a change in the relative economic positions of different groups.

The issue of productivity is often raised during wage negotiations, but seldom in a way that has an immediate or cogent bearing on the essential issues. A notable exception to this general rule is found in the two-year General Motors–United Automobile Workers contract of 1948, which stated that, irrespective of other developments, three cents an hour would be added to the wages of workers each year. This figure agrees approximately with the annual percentage gain in average productivity in the United States (about 2 per cent a year), and it is consistent with the broad principles of wage-productivity balance previously discussed. A five-year contract embodying the same principle was signed by the same parties in 1950. This agreement may contribute substantially to the gradual development of economically logical wage policies in the United States.

The introduction of productivity notions into wage discussions frequently leads to charges that one or another group is failing to make its appropriate contribution to national production. This is most often heard in connection with workers, when it is alleged that for one reason or another output is restricted.

There are instances where restriction of output is fully documented, in the sense that it is embodied in collective bargaining agreements. It is then frequently attacked by management as "featherbedding" and defended by workers' representatives as a necessary protection against exploitation of the workers through a speed-up, deterioration of working conditions, or otherwise. In most such instances it is extremely difficult to reach an objective evaluation of the opposing arguments. Because the issue is to be decided in a context of collective bargaining, there is usually some element of both truth and weakness in the arguments advanced by each side.

Quite aside from protections against exploitation that are written into contracts or are established customs in certain lines of industry, there are undoubtedly many instances of restriction of output by workers. These practices are usually found in three prototype situations — all related to feelings of insecurity on the part of the worker. The first is that where employment is likely to be or has been irregular. In such cases workers have a strong incentive to stretch out the work in order to extend the period of employment. Among highly developed crafts, the same objective is sometimes achieved by rigidly limiting the number of persons who may enter the occupation. The second situation is where workers fear insecurity in the wage structure, especially if past experience has indicated that a speed-up may be instituted. Workers may also establish a fixed work pace as a partial protection against the concealed speed-up that may take place, for example, where jobs are reorganized under a poorly planned and frequently revised incentive wage payment system. The third case is where workers feel insecure in their relationship with their employer. In a large company with poor relationships the workers may first be unwilling to perform any extra work (feeling it will accrue only to the benefit of the company), and this may easily change later into direct restriction of output. One of the major dangers of adopting such restrictions is that the practice tends to become institutionalized; it may persist for long periods after the original cause has vanished. This is well illustrated by the experience of some European countries, where output restriction, practiced as a patriotic duty under Nazi rule, tended to linger after the Nazis were driven out.

The practice of output restriction by a limited group of workers may not reduce their actual earnings. Under some circumstances small groups may even increase their earnings. Of course, output restriction by any group tends to reduce total potential national production and in this way reduce the average material living standard (and real wages) for the population as a whole, but this fact is not likely to carry much weight with the group that has found output restriction a successful means for increasing income. However, restriction of output, if practiced on a broad enough scale, will reduce not only general living standards but also very probably the real earnings of the groups immediately involved. The economy at large has little to fear from sporadic or occasional output restriction by workers, but the spread of the practice could disorganize and demoralize the national economic life.

"Technological Unemployment"

Workers sometimes restrict output by resisting technological or managerial innovations. They fear loss of their jobs, or "technological unemployment." The result for the economy is much the same as that from more direct limitations on production.

Technological displacement causes little uneasiness in periods of prosperity, but the chorus of protests rises with unemployment. During the 1930's, a congressional subcommittee offered a unanimous opinion "that mechanical and other laborsaving devices are the chief cause of the growing number of unemployed." The ratio between those who hail our continuing technical progress and those who deplore the advancing encroachment of the machine is an excellent index of the current position in the business cycle.

Technological change, the most important

element in rising productivity, almost necessarily implies in a free economy some loss in employment and earnings. Society accepts this injury to a limited number of individuals as a price exacted for greater benefits expected for the group as a whole. The harmful effects on the displaced worker can be ameliorated by preplanning of changes with proper consideration of the human factors involved, efforts at prompt placement of the displaced, separation benefits and, as a last resort, unemployment compensation.

The amount of technological unemployment cannot be measured, for many of the consequences of change are indirect or remote. There is reason to believe, however, that its extent on the average is small in relation to unemployment arising from other imbalances within the economy. But in some instances the type of unemployment caused by technical change may be peculiarly agonizing — in particular, where a slowly acquired skill is rendered obsolete and a worker, perhaps middle-aged, faces a lack of demand for his special abilities.

In any case, there is abundant evidence that the cure for high levels of unemployment is not technological stagnation, and that steady technical progress and reasonably high levels of employment are quite compatible. The alternatives to the limited unemployment and loss of earnings demanded by technological change in a free economy would appear to be a most unpalatable form of rigid state control or permanent economic stagnation.

The practice of restricting output is not confined to workers. Management may defer technological improvements for fear future market changes might make the investment unprofitable. Such failures to achieve potential increases in productivity and production have the same dubious justification and harmful consequences as restriction of output by workers. Some balance between prospective risk and return must be established in the economy, but excessive fear of undertaking a risk of capital may limit potential economic growth as directly as excessive fear of unemployment. No matter what group practices it, restriction of output because of fear of the future is detrimental to the continued growth and health of the economy.

GENERAL WAGE AND PRODUCTIVITY TRENDS

In general conclusion, the relative rates of return to individuals, whether in the form of wages or other compensation, will be governed to some extent by individual contributions to national productivity. At the same time, compensation for groups is limited by the necessity for a general system of compensation that is relatively consistent from company to company or industry to industry. Thus the wage trend in a particular industry is ordinarily related only remotely to productivity trends in the same industry. Broad classes of compensation will almost necessarily be controlled by the general rate of improvement in productivity for the entire economy. The material living standards of the United States cannot exceed the ability of the people to produce goods for consumption.

We need only look outside our borders to receive direct and graphic confirmation of the necessary interdependence between real wages and productivity. Great Britain, at one time the industrial leader of the world, has gradually fallen behind the United States, and British productivity today is believed to be substantially below levels in this country.[10] Real wages in Great Britain are also substantially and necessarily lower.

Differences in real wages between countries are sometimes obscured by arbitrary exchange rates and differences in prices, but they may be revealed through translation into the universal unit, human labor. The London *Economist* estimates (in its issue of July 9, 1949) that, after allowance for personal taxes, the average British wage earner must work 4½ weeks to purchase the cheapest British-made radio, 7 weeks for the cheapest man's suit, 55 weeks for the cheapest automobile. The sharp contrast with the United States is obvious.

Yet British productivity, while low by American standards, is higher than in most other countries. The Statistical Office of the United Nations estimates that per capita income in the United States during 1947 amounted to $1,400. In fourteen other countries it ranged between $400 and $900. In other areas containing well over half the world's population, it was less, and in many cases much less, than $100. To a very great extent, these low incomes and living standards are an accurate and necessary reflection of low productivity.

10. For a detailed and interesting discussion see L. Rostas, *Comparative Productivity in British and American Industry,* Occasional Paper No. 13, National Institute of Economic and Social Research, Cambridge University Press, Cambridge, 1948.

An elaborate comparison of the purchasing power of an hour's work in the United States and eighteen other countries — limited to food — has been made by the Bureau of Labor Statistics.[11] Only in Australia will an hour's work purchase more food than in the United States. The other seventeen countries range below, with Soviet Russia — where four or five times as much working time is needed to pay for the same food purchase — appearing near the bottom of the list. If nonfood items were included, the comparisons would undoubtedly be even more favorable to the United States.

11. Irving B. Kravis, "Work Time Required to Buy Food," *Monthly Labor Review,* November 1949.

Differences in real living standards among the nations of the world are a dominant international economic problem. A large part of the foreign policy of the United States has been directly concerned with narrowing the gaps between areas of abundance and areas of scarcity. This is a significant objective of the Marshall Plan (and such subsidiary organizations as the Anglo-American Council on Productivity), as well as of Point Four and other technical assistance programs.

As the key to a higher standard of living and higher real wages, productivity becomes increasingly the central economic problem of mankind.

CHAPTER 8

OUTLOOK FOR WAGES *

THE LONG-RANGE TRENDS in production, national income and wages described in preceding chapters cast light on the probable future developments. For several reasons, however, these trends should not be extrapolated precisely into the future. First, some of the trends are not very clear; second, the rate of economic growth has varied widely from decade to decade in the past and is likely to vary in the future; third, future development will be determined by the interplay of various forces, some of them similar to those that prevailed in the past, others essentially new, still others unknown as yet and unpredictable. No attempt will be made in this chapter to forecast trends in real wages in the United States. Its purpose is to establish the probable background of coming wage negotiations and the range of problems that the parties in collective bargaining will face.

THE NEW SETTING OF WAGE DETERMINATION

The unprecedented strength of labor unions is the salient feature of the new setting of wage determination. From 3.6 million in 1928, union membership increased to 8.3 million in 1938 and approximately 15.5 million in 1948.[1] The fact that union membership has doubled in each of the past two decades does not necessarily imply that it will double again by 1960. Unionization may progress as unevenly in the future as in the past. After having more than doubled between 1910 and 1920, union membership suffered a severe setback and did not make appreciable progress until 1937, when the drive for organization of unskilled labor was launched. A similar interruption in the growth of unions may occur again, or their growth may possibly slow down as unions move toward industries and areas that have been outside their influence.

On the other hand, in contrast to the experience after World War I, unions maintained their membership in the difficult time of reconversion after World War II and have made substantial subsequent gains. It is sound, therefore, to account labor unions a steadily growing force, even if their rate of growth in the coming decade or two cannot be predicted.

Progress of Collective Bargaining

The progress of unionization implies a gradual expansion of the scope of collective bargaining and union agreements. More than 100,000 contracts, determining labor conditions of 15 million workers, are now in force.[2] Indirectly, they affect the wages of many workers in nonunionized industries. With the growing strength of unions, it is quite possible that direct or indirect control of labor conditions by collective bargaining will expand over the whole labor market.

Collective bargaining and union agreements are, of course, not new. Adam Smith considered wage determination by "workmen combinations" a normal process. There is a substantial difference, however, between a situation in which union influence is limited to certain industries and occupations and one in which powerful centralized organizations control the entire supply of labor in the nation.

An important feature of the new situation is the growing variety of matters covered by union contracts.[3] Wages, as the main item of labor cost for the employer and the main source of income for the employee, remain the main issue in collective bargaining. But in the day-to-day relations of labor and management, other issues — regulation of work hours, safety provisions, vacations, welfare of workers, pensions for the aged, hiring and layoffs, promotion and so on — are increasingly significant.

Progress of Labor Law

Changes in labor law, partly due to the growing political strength of labor and partly reflecting the progress in our democratic institutions, are another important feature of the new setting of wage determination.

---

* By W. S. Woytinsky.

1. See Chapter 18, Table 68, and Appendix Table 53.

2. See p. 247.

3. See Chapter 20.

Labor laws and union agreements often overlap. The law not only protects collective bargaining and the right of a worker to belong to a union,[4] but also prescribes minimum wages and maximum hours of work, establishes safety rules, specifies conveniences for workers at the place of work, provides old-age pensions, and so on. In many fields labor laws and union agreements supplement one another. Agreements between unions and large firms usually precede legislative action. But after the law has established a pattern for a broad sector of the economy, unions try to improve it, as in the recent drive for pension agreements. An alternative develops: certain problems will either be regulated for all industries by law or be treated piecemeal in collective bargaining. For management the dilemma is whether to fight out the issue with the union, establishment by establishment and industry by industry, or to join forces with the union and demand legislative action. The union, for its part, has to choose how to distribute its strength between negotiations with employers and political activity.

Thus new elements enter into the picture of wage determination. The scope of problems expands, and direct labor-management negotiation merges with political activity by both parties. More often than not, labor and management appear in the political arena as proponents of opposite interests; but in some situations they pull in the same direction despite their political differences.

These developments have changed the setting of wage determination. Labor unions have begun to think of a long-range wage policy as integrated with their general policy. They have outgrown the period of "guerrilla warfare" in which expediency could determine their approach to each wage dispute. To make full use of their strength, unions must have a clear idea of the pattern of wage determination they consider most desirable. And management, no less than labor, feels a need for a definite policy to guide it in wage disputes.

The two parties will probably be far apart on the principles of wage policy as well as on the application of such principles in particular cases, and neither party will be able to impose its will on the other. It is likely that in the future, as in the past, their differences will be settled by compromise, within the framework of economic realities, and it will help them considerably if they can agree on these realities.

4. See Chapter 10.

The Determinants of Wages

In a general way, the level and the structure of wages in an economic system are determined by four sets of factors:

(1) the size of the aggregate output of goods and services — the real national income — which is the common source of wages, profits and other incomes
(2) the relative share of employees' compensation in this aggregate
(3) the system of wage differentials, by occupation, industry, geographic area, size of community and firm, personal characteristics of workers, and so on
(4) the price and cost-of-living structure, which determines in dollars and cents each individual's share in the aggregate income of the community.

Outlook for Real National Income

The probable future growth of the real national income can be estimated on the basis of long-range trends in the past. Several measurements may be used:

volume of production in different industries
volume of production per worker or per man-hour
national income adjusted to prices
adjusted income per capita of population
adjusted income per man-hour of work

Each measurement has advantages and shortcomings. The long-range trend in volume of production has the advantage of avoiding the bias resulting from adjustment of money values to changing prices. The measurement of real national income, on the other hand, has the advantage of covering all economic activities. The measurement of output or real national income on a man-hour basis makes it possible to isolate technological progress from other factors.

The various measurements mentioned in the preceding chapters indicate a wide range of average annual rates of growth and show considerable variation in these rates from decade to decade. (See Table 32.) In manufacturing industries, output per man-hour increased 2.07 per cent a year in the period 1870–1950. The annual advance in aggregate real national income averaged 4.5 per cent in 1869–1909, 2.3 per cent in 1909–1929, 4.0 per cent in 1929–1950.

The question arises whether an estimate of the probable rate of growth in the coming decade or two should rely on past trends in aggregate national income or in output per man-hour.

Present Situation

The United States economy is now in a phase of transition from peacetime postwar expansion to a new emergency pattern. The nation completed the reconversion to a peacetime economy, demobilized its armed forces and industry, and passed through the stages of postwar inflation and primary postwar adjustment, both in a very mild form. The low point of the readjustment setback was probably reached in the summer of 1949; after that the nation entered a new phase of economic growth, analogous, in some respects, to the period after 1921. But this development has been interrupted by the outbreak of the Korean war and the inauguration of a rearmament and defense program incompatible with a peacetime business-as-usual economy.

In this phase an accelerated growth of production can be expected, but it may be combined with deceleration in the rise of consumption and real disposable income per capita. Despite this temporary retardation in the rise of the consumption level, technology is likely to advance rapidly as a result of intensified scientific research and the accumulation of new methods and new ideas in the realm of metallurgy, chemistry, electronics, motive power and so on. On the other hand, the coming decade will be

TABLE 32

AVERAGE ANNUAL PERCENTAGE RATE OF GROWTH IN PRODUCTION, EMPLOYMENT AND OUTPUT PER WORKER, ACCORDING TO VARIOUS MEASUREMENTS

Item	Average Annual Percentage Rate of Growth
Production, 1860–1914 (Frickey)[a]	
All industrial and commercial production	5.38
Manufacturing	4.95
Durable goods	5.90
Nondurable goods	4.50
Transportation and communication	5.82
Production of finished goods, 1879–1939 (Shaw)[b]	
All finished goods	3.2
Consumers' perishable and semidurable goods	2.9
Consumers' durable goods	4.7
Producers' durable goods	3.6
Production of goods and services, 1899–1939 (Fabricant-Stigler)[c]	
Total output	2.7
Employment	0.7
Output per worker	2.0
Output in six industries, 1899–1940 (Stigler)[d]	
Agriculture	1.1
Mining	3.3
Manufacturing	3.3
Electric light and power	10.7
Gas	4.9
Steam railroads	2.2
Output per worker, 1899–1940 (Stigler)[d]	
Agriculture	1.6
Mining	3.6
Manufacturing	1.7
Electric light and power	4.7
Gas	2.1
Steam railroads	1.9
Manufacturing, 1870–1950 (Woytinsky)[e]	
Total output	4.05
Factory employment (production workers)	2.46
Output per man-hour of work of production workers	2.07
Output per man-year of work of production workers	1.55
Output per man-hour of work of all factory workers	1.86
Output per man-year of work of all factory workers	1.40
National income adjusted to prices[f]	
1869–1909 (Martin)	4.5
1909–1929 (Martin)	2.3
1929–1950 (Department of Commerce)	4.0
Per capita income adjusted to prices[f]	
1869–1909 (Martin)	2.3
1909–1929 (Martin)	0.8
1929–1949 (Department of Commerce)	2.0
1879–1950 (Woytinsky)	2.0
Hourly wages adjusted to prices (Bowden)[g]	
1840–1865	0.5
1865–1890	2.2
1890–1914	0.6
1914–1929	1.9
1929–1947	2.3
1890–1947	1.5

a. See Chapter 3, Figures 3 and 4 and Table 6. Cf. Appendix Table 2.
b. See Chapter 3, Table 9.
c. See p. 30.
d. See Chapter 3, Figure 5. Computed by the present writer from figures reproduced in Appendix Table 3.
e. See p. 32. The trend of total output computed from the combined index of manufacturing production shown in Appendix Table 4.
f. For Martin's figures see p. 36 and Appendix Table 5. For Department of Commerce figures see pp. 38–39 and Table 15. For the present writer's estimate (1879–1950) see p. 39.
g. See Chapter 5. Computed from figures in Tables 19 and 21.

marked by comparatively slow growth of the labor force, as a result of low birth rates in the 1930's and restriction of immigration. All in all, an average annual rate of increase of 3.5 to 4 per cent for aggregate national income adjusted to prices, or 2.5 to 3 per cent for real income per man-hour, is within the realm of probability.

The gap of one per cent between the two rates corresponds roughly to the annual increase in the input of labor in terms of man-hours. It reflects the growth of population of working age (a little less than one per cent in the coming decade or two); a moderate immigration; the increasing participation of women in gainful work; improvement in health, and so on. It also takes into account the higher ages at which boys and girls begin work and the reduction in weekly hours of work. The combined effect of all these factors on the total number of man-hours worked cannot be estimated precisely. The actual input of labor will, of course, vary from year to year with changes in business conditions, but the average increment will probably not be far from one per cent a year.

Similarly, the estimate of a 2.5 to 3 per cent annual advance in real income per man-hour is a rough generalization. Reflecting past experience in the growth of the over-all productivity of labor in the United States, it also allows for accelerated progress and is, therefore, on the optimistic side. The allowance for acceleration is not very important, however. Hourly wages adjusted to prices increased at an average annual rate of 2.3 per cent between 1929 and 1947. The postulated rate of 2.5 to 3 per cent would mean that labor productivity is expected to increase by approximately a third in a decade and double in twenty-five or thirty years. Because of the probable reduction in weekly hours of work, output per man-year of work (or per full-time employee, as estimated by the Department of Commerce) would advance at a somewhat lower rate. Assuming that one third of the annual gain in productivity is used for increasing leisure and two thirds for raising the material standard of living in the nation, the average rate of increase in real income per man-year would amount to 1.7 to 2 per cent a year or 18 to 22 per cent a decade, while the normal work week would be cut by five hours a decade.

Share of Wages

The ratio of wages to national income showed no consistent trend in the past two decades. Employees' share in private national income[5] was 55.5 per cent in 1929, 70.3 per cent in 1932, 59.1 per cent in 1948 and 60.3 in 1950. (See Appendix Table 13.)

It seems sound to assume that in coming years, likewise, the relative share of employees in national income will increase in lean years and decline in fat years. The amplitude of variations in the ratio of wages to national income will depend, as in the past, on the amplitude of cyclical fluctuations in business. Assuming a boom-and-bust economy, as in the 1920's and 1930's, the ratio of compensation of employees to national income might range between 60 per cent and more than 70 per cent; in the event of smoother economic progress, the range will probably be 60 to 65 per cent.

A gradual increase in the relative share of wages and salaries in national income is not impossible. It would be in line with progress in industrialization and urbanization, with reduction of the relative share of fixed income as a result of the general rise of prices, and so on.

This is, however, a slow process. It is fairly certain that the rise in the ratio of all wages to total national income during 1943–1945 and its decline during 1946–1948 were related to the mobilization of the economic system and its reconversion to peacetime conditions. The origin of variations after 1948 is less clear. A rise in the share of employees in national income in the period of the armament boom can be anticipated, but it will probably be followed by a new setback after the return of the economic system to more normal peacetime conditions.

Furthermore, a closer examination of the structure of national income by distributive shares shows how narrow is the range of possible changes in the percentages going to the major factors of production.

In 1947, for example, employees' compensation totaled $128 billion, income of unincorporated enterprises (businesses, professions and farming) amounted to $35.4 billion, rental income of persons and net interest accounted for $10.6 billion, and $24.7 billion went to corporations. Of the last amount, $11.9 billion was taken by the government in taxes, so that corporations netted $12.8 billion. In 1948 the share of employees increased to $140.2 billion

5. Private national income amounts to total income minus salaries of government employees.

and that of corporations, after taxes, to $18.7 billion.[6]

One may assume that the struggle over the distribution of national income is restricted essentially to the contest between employees and corporations. Their combined part of the social dividend was $140.8 billion in 1947 and $158.9 billion in 1948, of which wages and salaries represented 90.9 per cent in 1947 and 88.2 per cent in 1948. Whatever the cause of this shift, 3 per cent of $158.9 billion amounts to about $4.8 billion — a substantial objective for a contest between labor and management. From a long-range outlook, however, a range of ±3 per cent in the share of employees in the joint dividend allocated to wages and corporate profits is of minor significance. The difference, in fact, is roughly equivalent to the average annual increment in national income. If an increase in the ratio of wages to profits is accompanied by curtailment in capital formation and investment and results in a leveling off of the growth of real output per man-hour, the increased ratio will not improve workers' well-being.

It is therefore sound to assume that compensation of employees will keep pace with total national income, with the ratio of wages to national income rising in depressions and wars and falling back in peace and prosperity. In other words, in the coming decade or two the total real compensation of employees can be expected to increase 3.5 to 4 per cent a year while real earnings per man-hour are advancing 2.5 to 3 per cent a year.

This estimate is subject to the same reservation as the long-range trend in national income: it shows the probable upper limit of annual gains. The upward adjustment it introduces into the trends of the past is, however, rather moderate, as is shown by comparing it with the actual rise in real income per full-time employee in the 1929–1950 period.

Average annual earnings per full-time employee rose from $1,421 in 1929 to $3,024 in 1950, a gain of 113 per cent in twenty-one years. Nearly half this apparent gain, however, was due to the rise in prices. Adjusted to the cost of living, the rise was approximately 52 per cent in twenty-one years, an average rate of about 2 per cent a year. When the reduction in hours of work is taken into account, and the index of weekly hours of work in manufacturing industries is applied to the whole economy, it is found that real earnings per man-hour rose in this period at an average annual rate of 2.7 per cent.[7] (See Figure 31.) When the average annual growth of real earnings per man-hour is estimated at 3 per cent for coming years, the cumulative upward deviation of this hypothetical trend from the actual trend in 1929–1950 (Figure 31) is 0.3 per cent each year, or slightly more than 3 per cent in a decade.

Wage Differentials

The aggregate compensation of employees, as a distributive share in national income, includes not only all wages and salaries but also supplementary income of employees, such as employers' contributions to social insurance and private pension and welfare funds, compensation for injuries, directors' fees and so on. It includes payments varying widely in type and size. Actual earnings of each group of workers are determined by their position in the occupational pyramid, which depends, in turn, on their occupational skill, regularity of employment, and many other factors. The system of employment and wage differentials [8] is, therefore, vital for the well-being of each group of workers — as vital, indeed, as the aggregate share of labor in national income.

Patterns of employment change as time goes on, but their general trend is not clear and nothing positive can be said about the outlook. Certain types of wage differentials have recently tended to narrow, while others have not changed appreciably. Since the total amount of goods and services at the disposal of workers is determined by the volume and patterns of production and is only indirectly affected by changes in wage rates, the real objective in fixing these rates is to determine the relative share of the respective groups of workers in the aggregate compensation of employees. If the wages of a certain group advance appreciably faster than

6. Appendix Table 12. The net income of corporations does not include the book gains resulting from the rise of prices of inventories. Similarly, book losses caused by the fall of prices of inventories are not subtracted.

7. This estimate does not pretend to be final. By changing dates and method one arrives at other rates, which are as defensible as this one. It appears, however, that all plausible estimates vary within a reasonably narrow range.

8. The related problems are examined in detail in Parts III and IV of this report.

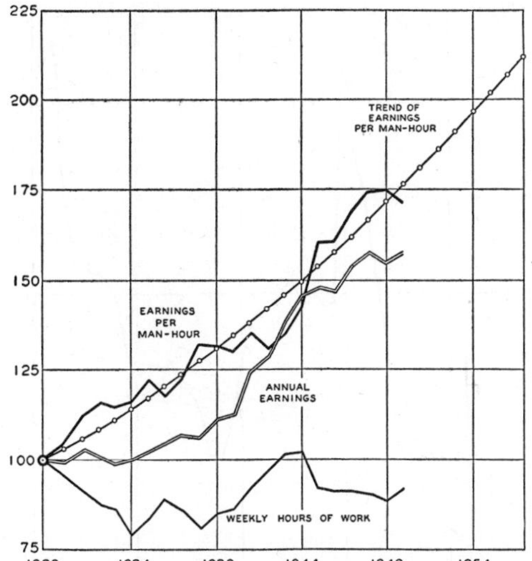

FIGURE 31. INDEXES OF EARNINGS PER FULL-TIME EMPLOYEE ADJUSTED TO CONSUMERS' PRICES AND OF WEEKLY HOURS OF WORK, 1929–1950

(1929 = 100)

Source: Computed from national income statistics of the Department of Commerce.

the average, this group will be better off than other employees. If wage rates in an occupation or an industry lag behind the average, that occupation or industry will deteriorate in economic and social status.

The structure of wage differentials in the United States may appear chaotic and arbitrary. Management tries to improve it — at least within some concerns — by systematic job evaluation.[9] Unions try to narrow the range of remuneration within a given job classification, to reduce differences between skilled and unskilled occupations, and to iron out regional differences in wage rates. It is not clear whether or not such efforts of both parties have tended to make the system of wage differentials more intelligible. Since there is no universally accepted yardstick for determining the logic and fairness of particular wage rates, the structure of wages cannot be said to be either logical or fair. It is controlled essentially by the interplay of the forces of supply and demand in different sections of the labor market. The function of labor-management negotiations is simply to test these forces.

From the broad economic point of view, a trend toward equalization of wage rates is sound in certain situations and harmful in others. It is sound when the wage differential rests on tradition and prejudice, as in occupational discrimination against women and Negroes. It can be harmful when the differential is based on differences in skill and in the economic value of the services rendered by workers.

The system of wage differentials serves many important purposes. It controls the geographical redistribution of the labor force and capital in the nation, encourages training for jobs that require skill and knowledge, and is vital for the selection of workers. Since conditions in the different sectors of the labor market are continually changing, periodic adjustment of wage rates is vital for the smooth operation of the whole economy. If the existing wage differentials were replaced by a system of rigid rates for all industries, occupations and areas, the labor market would lose the flexibility required in a dynamic, expanding economy. Indeed, a system of scientifically graded and centrally operated wage rates presumes an economic organization fundamentally different from that in the United States, with other incentives, other methods of economic planning and management, and other patterns of labor-management relations.

To sum up, fundamental changes in the structure of wages in the next decade or two are not very probable. Apart from the elimination of certain obsolete differentials and the narrowing of certain spreads, the system of wage differentials is likely to retain its present features. This implies that a vast field will remain for adjustment and manipulation of particular wage rates, independent of long-range changes in average levels of earnings.

Outlook for Prices

There is no way to compare the general levels of prices precisely over a long period. Certain prices, especially the prices of food and services, are several times higher than they were fifty years ago; others, especially the prices of articles in mass production, have been consistently declining. The problem of determining the weighted average of the divergent movements is solved, in a general way, by using a chain of price indexes linked to one another. Such indexes, stretching back to the middle and even to the beginning of the nineteenth century, reveal price changes of different origin and character — short-range fluctuations related to the business cycle; longer waves, each embracing several cycles; and sporadic inflationary out-

9. See Chapter 35.

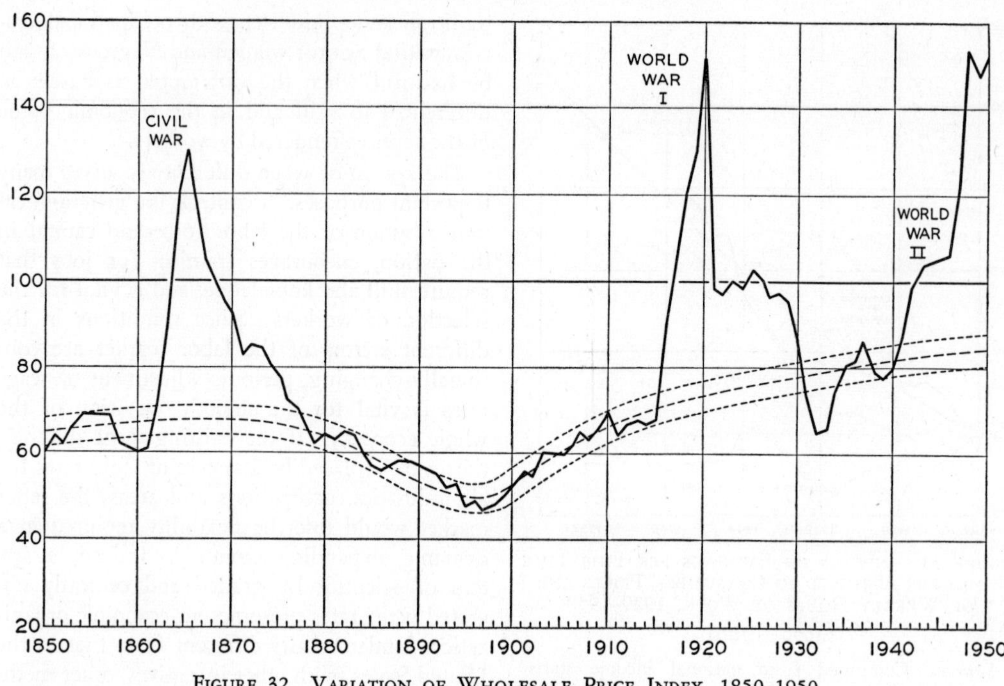

FIGURE 32. VARIATION OF WHOLESALE PRICE INDEX, 1850–1950

(1926 = 100)

Source: Bureau of Employment Security.

bursts, usually related to war. (See Figure 32.) We are now in the phase of price adjustment after one such outburst, but there is no way of telling how long this adjustment will last and where it will stop.

The trend of wholesale prices, with a deviation margin of five points in either direction, plotted in Figure 32 is fairly clear for the period from 1880 to 1914 but less certain for the subsequent thirty-five years. The slight upward trend suggested by the chart rests on a comparison of price levels before the outbreak of World War I with those in the late 1930's. This is, however, a shaky basis for far-reaching conclusions. A downward trend in prices seems to have prevailed from the end of the Civil War until the middle of the 1890's and an upward trend during the more recent period. But the more recent trend is too uncertain to permit extrapolation. The outlook for prices should rely, rather, on an analysis of the economic forces that are likely to prevail in the postwar economy.

As a rule, prices are more likely to rise than to decline in a period of rapid economic expansion. But articles that have been overpriced in comparison with other commodities are likely to fall in price. Thus prices of farm products will probably go down after the restoration of world agricultural production. Ultimately, however, their level in relation to industrial prices will be determined by price-support policy, and it is very unlikely that they will be permitted to slip far below parity.

Prices and Wages

The further movement of prices in this country will depend largely on the trend in wages. In fact, if there can be some doubt about the impact of a change in wage rates on the cost of production, its effect on consumer purchasing power is obvious. If the rise in total wages and salaries lags behind the rise in output, part of the goods and services designed for mass consumption will remain unsold unless producers cut their prices. If the amount of wages and salaries outruns the growth of national output, prices will rise.

This simple relationship between prices and wages is bound to frustrate any attempt of labor to offset the pinch of the rising cost of living by raising wage rates. The unrest among rank-and-file union members may compel union leaders to support continual adjustment of wage rates to the rise in the cost of living.[10] Moreover, under certain conditions such a policy does not do much harm to the economic system. In so far as an inflationary adjustment of prices is desirable, the race of wages and prices may even serve a useful purpose.[11]

But the ideas of fighting rising prices by raising wage rates and of increasing real earnings by giving people more money at a time of rising prices are fallacious. A cost-of-living bonus can work only when it is awarded to a group of workers so small that the addition to their earnings does not appreciably change the total purchasing power of the community. In this event, the bonus exercises no influence on the general level of prices, and the position of those who receive it improves both absolutely and in relation to the rest of the community. The principle of a cost-of-living bonus is therefore sound when it is applied to a particular group of workers whose wages have lagged behind the rise in prices and in the wages of the great majority of the working population. It does not make sense as a basis for a nation-wide wage policy.

Wages usually lag behind prices when prices are rising rapidly or falling sharply. If, however, wages cannot catch up with prices, prices are readily adjusted even to drastic changes in wage rates.

Furthermore, changes in the general level of wages and prices do not necessarily affect the relative shares in the distribution of national income. In the nation as a whole, a rise in wage rates cannot increase labor's share during an inflationary whirlwind. Similarly, a cut in wages cannot increase aggregate profits of corporations during a severe depression. The trend in money wages affects the level of real earnings of workers not by itself but indirectly, through its impact on prices and the volume of production.

In a general way the trend in prices is controlled by the relationship between wages and production. If wage rates lag behind the increase in production per man-hour, prices go down; if wage rates inch up, keeping pace with over-all labor productivity, the over-all price index fluctuates in a narrow range; if wage rates increase faster than the productivity of labor, prices go up. These truisms are often forgotten in the heat of wage negotiations.

Desirable Trend in Prices

Few people will find kind words for an inflationary or deflationary spiral of prices. The choice is between gradual advance in prices, gradual decline and stability. A gradual decline in prices can keep wages stable and give consumers the fruits of technological progress. This trend, however, would have serious disadvantages. It would result in a continuous growth in fixed income (based mostly on property rights) in comparison with current earnings; it would increase the burden of debts, compelling the debtor to repay his loan in money with a greater real value than that in which the original loan was given; it would increase the risk of investment; it would make long-range planning in business hazardous. In brief, falling prices are not only characteristic of periods of depression; they also are likely to provoke economic stagnation.

The choice is therefore between stability of prices and a gradual rise. The two patterns differ subtly.

Price stability does not imply a complete rigidity in the price structure, but only a rough balance between divergent movements of prices so that the purchasing power of the consumer's dollar fluctuates within a narrow margin. Such a situation seems to be most favorable for long-range investment and planning, most equitable for debtors and creditors, and most likely to ensure the necessary flexibility of wages and to provide a sound background for the settlement of labor-management controversies. This has been the price policy of the United States since the middle of the eighteenth century. Sumner Slichter writes:

> It may be taken for granted that the people of the United States are content to let the results of technological progress continue to be distributed mainly in the form of higher money wages rather than in the form of lower prices to consumers. This is what has happened during the last century or more and it has evoked no serious protest.[12]

The same advantages are inherent in a situation in which the price index is slowly inching

10. Cf. W. S. Woytinsky and Associates, *Labor and Management Look at Collective Bargaining,* Twentieth Century Fund, New York, 1949.

11. It has been pointed out that an inflationary rise of prices after a major war serves to reduce the burden of public debt accumulated during the war in relation to national income.

12. Sumner H. Slichter, in "Comments on the Steel Report," *Review of Economics and Statistics,* November 1949, pp. 287–88.

up, say one per cent a year, as it has since the last decade of the nineteenth century.

Since the trend in prices can be controlled by a combination of wage policy with appropriate monetary and fiscal measures, it can be assumed that in coming years — aside from unpredictable events — the price level will not be permitted either to sink or to rise by leaps and bounds. The general objective of economic policy will probably be to let prices fluctuate within a comparatively narrow range, but few people will be alarmed if such fluctuations result in a gradual advance of the price index.

The Main Wage Determinants

Under the assumptions made above, the main determinants of wages for the next decade or two can be summarized as follows:

The volume of production and real national income will probably increase at an average of approximately 3.5 to 4 per cent a year.

Real national income per man-hour of work is likely to advance at an average rate of approximately 2.5 to 3 per cent a year, varying from year to year with business conditions.

The relative share of wages and salaries in national income (the wage-to-national-income ratio) will likewise vary with the business cycle, rising in its descending slope and declining in the phase of expansion, but will hardly change appreciably in the long run.

The growth of average real hourly earnings will parallel that of real national income per man-hour of work, gaining approximately 2.5 to 3 per cent a year.

No fundamental change is expected in the wage structure, although some particular differentials in wage rates will be narrowed or eliminated as time goes on. Wage rates will about keep pace with the productivity of labor, though appreciable fluctuations in the relative position of wages in particular occupations and industries and minor discrepancies in the advance of wage rates and of productivity are possible. Whenever such a discrepancy develops, it will be reflected in changes in prices; but so long as the discrepancy between the trends in wage rates and productivity is small, shifts in the price level are not likely to be large.

Outlook for Wage Negotiation

Like all projections, our estimates of future wage determinants rest on thin ice. Serious objections can be raised, for instance, against the assumption of a continuous rise of production per man-hour and real hourly wages at a rate of 2.5 to 3 per cent a year. As has been pointed out, this assumption is based on experience in the past, with allowance for a slight acceleration in the speed of technological progress. It is offered here not as a forecast but as a working hypothesis that can be conveniently used by labor and management in wage negotiations.

In practice, particular wage rates will be fixed and revised by particular contracts. Each case will be negotiated separately and settled as the parties to the negotiation decide. Economic realities, however, are stronger than the president of the strongest union or the directors of the richest corporation. The ability of even very powerful personalities to influence the trend in wages is indeed limited.

They can, of course, change the relative position of a particular group of workers in the wage scale. Such changes will be made time and again as long as the competitive labor market exists.

Successful union drives can also change the general level of money wages — for example, raise them each year at an arbitrary rate in a succession of "rounds" as in 1946–1948. But two items are outside the scope of collective bargaining: the real social dividend, in terms of goods and services, and the ratio of wages to national income. Labor leaders often describe their wage policy as a deliberate attempt to change the pattern of distribution of the social product between labor and capital. So far as this has been their policy, it has not been very successful. After having learned from experience how futile are their efforts to increase the share of labor in national income, labor unions will be compelled to develop a more realistic long-range wage policy that would take into account both the growing strength of labor and the increasing complexity of the economic system. The purpose of such a policy would be, not to maximize the earnings of a particular group of workers, but to maximize the total real compensation of employees by maximizing the total real national income.

Approaching the problem from this broad point of view, most people will agree that the best wage policy is one that promises the greatest stability of prices without prejudice to their flexibility and leaves open the possibility of a gradual and slow eventual rise of prices but excludes the danger of a race between wages and prices. Such a policy can be based on the principle of an annual rise in the average level of wages by approximately 3 per cent.

This idea is not new. Slichter has recently recommended it:

> The rise in output per man-hour will set the approximate rate at which real wages can be increased over a considerable period of time. Output per man-hour is likely to increase faster than in the past when it rose about 2 per cent a year, because industrial research by business and government is growing by leaps and bounds. Output per man-hour, however, is hardly likely to grow by much over 3 per cent a year in the long run. Hence the rate at which real wages can be increased will be in the neighborhood of 3 per cent per year.
>
> An increase of 3 per cent in real hourly earnings per year may seem small, but 3 per cent for 20 years is nearly 81 per cent.
>
> It is high time that all groups in the community realize that real wages are tied to productivity and that collective bargaining cannot raise real wages faster than output per man-hour.[13]

Basis of Negotiation

It is a question whether wage negotiation should start with the general principle of tying wage rates to the productivity of labor. Such an approach would involve several controversial issues: How measure labor productivity? How has productivity changed since the expiring contract was signed? Who is to blame for slowness of progress?

The principle of productivity will be of help in wage negotiations only if it is accepted in an indisputable form, as a tentatively established formula of normal growth. Without precluding adjustment of particular wage rates, such a formula would establish a point around which such adjustments should be clustered. Acceptance of this principle by both parties would change the psychological climate of collective bargaining.

Arguments relating to the productivity of labor would be increasingly focused on progress in the over-all efficiency of the economic system rather than on output per man-hour in a particular industry or an individual establishment.

The cost-of-living-and-price argument would be eliminated as unsound, since an inflationary rise in the cost of living cannot be stopped by a rise of wage rates and a deflationary spiral cannot be stopped by a cut in wages.

13. *Loc. cit.*, p. 288.

The argument of the wage position of a particular group of workers in relation to other workers would be recognized as sound and pertinent.

The capacity-to-pay argument would be accepted within the scope of the preceding argument, as a factor supporting or limiting it.

To sum up, the principle that wage rates should keep pace with the growth in the productivity of labor does not imply an award of a special bonus in addition to the "package" claimed by unions. It provides, rather, a yardstick for measuring the package.

Wage Rates and the Business Cycle

Assuming that in the long run wage rates rise an average of approximately 3 per cent a year, how will the rise be distributed during a period of appreciable fluctuation in business conditions?

The answer will be worked out by the forces of demand and supply. Economic realities will prevail, as always, over the intentions of the parties concerned. Raises in money rates will be concentrated in good years and partly offset by rising prices, and in bad times real hourly earnings will be shored up by price declines, without any rise in money wages.

Duration of Union Agreements

An understanding of labor and management on the general principles of wage determination would probably enable them to sign contracts for at least two or three years. The prevailing practice of annual contracts is time-consuming and expensive for both parties. By introducing an element of uncertainty and instability into industrial relations and spreading unrest, continual negotiations accompanied by threats of work stoppage and mutual accusations and counter-accusations are detrimental to the growth of production. Ultimately they lower the real earnings of workers and the profits of employers. Both union leaders and business executives realize the advantages of longer contracts, but unions are reluctant to commit their members to any fixed wage rates for more than a year.[14] Short-run contracts insure them against a sudden rise in living costs or a considerable gain by a rival union.

Annual contracts would become obsolete if

14. See Chapter 20, Tables 82 and 83.

each union could anticipate a definite, more or less smooth trend in the cost of living and the general level of wages in the nation. A three-year contract providing for a gradual raise of wage rates is more advantageous for both labor and management than a succession of three rounds of bargaining resulting in an equivalent aggregate raise. Long-run contracts involve a risk, however, and few unions will negotiate and sign such agreements unless the new practice is supported by central federations.

For management, settlement of a wage problem for two or three years ahead has a considerable advantage over annual negotiations. A graduated 10 per cent raise during a three-year period might prove preferable to three wage rounds, each involving a 3 per cent raise.

Impact on Prices

Although the outlook for wage negotiation described above starts with the desirability of preventing a race between prices and wages, it does not guarantee perfect stability of the price level. If a 3 per cent annual raise is accepted as a general pattern, and changes in particular wage rates are considered as adjustments within this general trend, upward adjustments in wage rates are likely to prevail over cuts. Thus, a planned gradual rise of wages by 3 per cent a year would result in an actual average increase of more than 3 per cent.

There is no solution to this dilemma. To be acceptable to labor, the general rise of wages should be proportionate to the growth of productivity. To meet its purposes the wage system must be sufficiently flexible and a considerable margin must be left for adjustment of particular wage rates. And if such adjustments are admitted, they are likely to raise the general level of wages.

There should be no illusion as to the effect of such a development. If wage rates rise faster than the productivity of labor, the difference in speed never increases the relative share of labor in the national product but can result only in a rise in prices. This conclusion, however, does not invalidate the idea of a gradual rise of the wage level at a definite rate. As has been pointed out, a moderate advance in prices — say one per cent a year — is not dangerous. This has been the general trend in prices since the 1890's (see Figure 32), and it may prove to be as favorable to economic expansion as perfect stability of the price index. Moreover, if the described pattern of development of wage rates and the practice of signing longer contracts improve labor-management relations and reduce industrial unrest, the rise in the productivity of labor could exceed the postulated rate of 2.5 to 3 per cent a year and the rate of advance in prices would be less than the average rise of wage rates minus 2.5 to 3 per cent.

Wages and Workers' Living Standards

The standard of living of workers is determined by the amount of goods and services they can buy or obtain free of charge. However, the "free" community services they receive (education, public health services, recreational facilities, social security and so on) are necessarily taken from the same source as the goods and services they buy directly, from the aggregate national product. Any improvement in the standard of living of workers depends, therefore, on the growth of production, both over-all and in relation to types of goods and services. It is doubtful whether a rise in wage rates can increase real wages at the expense of profits, but it is fairly certain that, in the distribution of real national product among different groups of population, luxury articles compete with articles of mass consumption. And it is certain that an increase in the productivity of labor, as well as all other factors bolstering total production, adds to the share of national output allocated to labor. Ultimately labor gets its share in the fruits of technological progress, even if the introduction of new techniques and laborsaving devices results in the displacement of workers and a spell of technological unemployment in certain areas and occupations.

Inversely, progress in the standard of living of workers and in their real earnings is being slowed down by all factors that interfere with technological progress and with increased productivity. Among such factors are not only restrictive practices of corporations and unions but also policies designed to eliminate the economic pressures that control the distribution of labor and capital among industries and geographical areas. For example, the policy of concentrating public spending in the areas where the rate of unemployment is considerably higher than the average for the nation can be detrimental to the real earnings of workers, although it may appeal to union leaders and employers in these areas. If the local unemployment is caused by the fact that the area is losing ground in competition with other areas and local industries are shifting to new sites, an attempt to stop such a shift amounts to interference with the economic growth of the nation. Similarly, the excessive emphasis on full employment as a goal of economic policy can create a psychological climate unfavorable to technological progress and improvement in the standard of living of the population.

With reservations for exceptional situations that may require exceptional measures, the problem of wages and the standard of living of workers can be reduced to a few authentic equations:

Rising real wages = increasing productivity of labor
Increasing productivity of labor = technological progress
Technological progress = laborsaving devices, displacement of labor by machines, shifts in capital and labor force, continual challenges of economic pressure met by appropriate response

Unions' Role in Wage Determination

Agreement between labor and management on the desirability of a definite trend in wages would not mean permanent industrial peace. In fact, it would not exclude clashes of interest and work stoppages.

The competitive market requires two conflicting forces to determine prices. Similarly, a free labor market cannot operate unless management and labor are pulling in opposite directions. A sound determination of wage rates would be impossible if management were ready to meet any request of unions or if unions were ready to accept any offer of management. Even if labor and management agree on the general principles of wage policy, they will differ on questions of everyday industrial relations. More specifically, the function of unions in wage determination is largely to disagree with management and to claim more than they can get.

Agreement between unions and management on the principles of wage policy does not rule out a militant position of unions in applying this principle to particular situations. The prosecutor and the defense attorney are both servants of justice, but they argue against each other and their dispute before the court is to permit the jury to arrive at a fair decision. In union-management disputes there usually is no court to decide on the merits of the arguments of the two parties and they themselves reach a decision by taking into account not only the arguments of the opposite party but also the reactions of public opinion, the prospects of a work stoppage, and so on.

This is obviously an imperfect and eventually an expensive method for settling industrial disputes. But the existing economic system provides no satisfactory substitute. How could a flexible system of wages be maintained if the determination of wage rates were not left to the play of the forces of supply and demand represented by unions and business management? And how could the parties be brought to an agreement unless, in the absence of agreement, they had to bear the onerous consequences of the discord?

These fundamentals of wage determination are deeply rooted in the nature of the competitive economy. Despite the radical changes in the economic and institutional setting of the labor market, these fundamentals are now essentially the same as they were at the time of Adam Smith, when modern economic science was founded.

PART II

THE INSTITUTIONAL SETTING

Chapter 9

THE INSTITUTIONAL SETTING OF THE LABOR MARKET *

THE INSTITUTIONAL SETTING of the labor market can be described as the system of laws, administrative practices and usage that define the scope and procedure of labor-management negotiation and establish certain rights and obligations of both parties that by force of law or usage cease to be the subject of free agreement between them.

This system of regulation of labor-management relations in the United States has changed greatly in the past twenty years. Some of the changes originated as emergency measures during the depression of the 1930's. But before the depression was over, new emergencies developed — first the threat of war and then all-out war — and the labor market regulations introduced during the depression became the foundation of our war economy.

Now, after a long period of emergencies and dislocations, the United States economy has entered a phase of organic growth similar to that of the 1920's, with all the potentialities and dangers characteristic of a postwar — and now a new war-emergency — expansion. But it entered this period with a system of labor laws and regulations strikingly different from those on the books after World War I.

The recent changes are not limited to any one field of labor problems. The whole system of labor legislation has been reshaped. This chapter summarizes the developments in five broad fields:

(1) The scope and philosophy of our labor laws as public intervention in labor-management relations
(2) Protection of special groups of workers
(3) Labor welfare
(4) Collective bargaining
(5) Labor disputes and arbitration

In the other chapters of Part II the changes in the institutional setting of the labor market are discussed in detail.

The Labor Laws

The change in the basic attitude of the state toward labor-management relations has been the most spectacular and far-reaching change in the institutional setting of the labor market.

Labor unions, which the law and the government had reluctantly tolerated as private associations of doubtful public usefulness, have become the legal spokesmen not only for their members but also, under certain conditions, for all of the nation's wage earners. Collective bargaining has become the normal procedure for determining wage rates.

The first steps toward this end were taken in the Railway Labor Act of 1926 and the Norris-LaGuardia Anti-Injunction Act of 1932. Then, in 1935, the National Labor Relations Act, commonly known as the Wagner Act, radically changed the role of labor unions. This law was hailed by labor unions as their Magna Carta Libertatis and decried by management as one-sided and biased.

The Labor-Management Relations Act of 1947, commonly called the Taft-Hartley Act, modified many parts of the Wagner Act but left the principle of collective bargaining intact and indisputable. This act plays a historic role in recognizing that in our economic system individual wage agreement must yield to collective agreement.

Another far-reaching change in the legal setting of labor relations was marked by the Fair Labor Standards Act of 1938, frequently called the Wage-Hour Act. Starting from the old principle of federal supervision over production of goods shipped in interstate commerce, this act assigned to the federal government a new responsibility — supervision over labor standards in a wide sector of the economy. This new interpretation of the federal government's role, although contrary to tradition, was sustained by the courts.

In combination with recent legislation controlling labor-management relations, the Labor

* By W. S. Woytinsky.

Standards Act has created essentially new premises for the determination of wages: the state not only invites labor and management to negotiate in good faith and to search for agreement, but also declares that the conditions on which they agree must meet certain minimum standards.

Protection of Special Groups of Workers

Any law protecting a special group of workers, or establishing conditions for their employment, necessarily restricts the scope of matters open for settlement through labor-management agreements. Such restriction tends to go further than the law directly provides. For example, a law providing that women can be employed only on premises that meet definite standards of safety and hygiene tends to establish such standards as minimum working conditions for all workers. Once established, these standards cease to be subject to labor-management negotiation and agreement. Three types of protective measures are examined in this part of the report: regulation of child labor (Chapter 11), regulation of women's work (Chapter 12) and veterans programs (Chapter 13).

Protective legislation in the United States has followed essentially the same trends as in other industrial countries. Our early advances were slow, but more progress has been made in the last fifteen years than in the preceding century.

Children and Women

The first timid attempts to establish legal protection for working children and women in this country were made more than a century ago. As early as 1842, Massachusetts had established a maximum 10-hour day for children under 12 years of age. In 1845 that state explored, but rejected, the possibility of similar regulation of work by women. Fifty years later the principle that state laws must protect working children and women received wide public acceptance. However, the state laws serving this purpose were utterly inadequate and only a few of them were enforceable. Not until the turn of the century did effective laws providing a maximum of 8 hours of work and a weekly day of rest for women appear on the books of a few of the most progressive states.

The movement toward regulation of child labor and protection of working women gained momentum after World War I. In the 1930's it entered a new phase, largely under the impact of the industrial codes of the National Industrial Recovery Administration, which tried to protect each state against unfair competition of other states. Temporary relaxation of the regulations applying to the labor of children and women during World War II did not reverse the trend. In the course of its social, legal and technological development, our economy has practically eradicated employment of children, reduced to insignificance the amount of industrial homework by women, and established strict and enforceable conditions for such work.

This development has affected the whole labor market. The pressure of reserves of cheap and tractable female and child labor has been checked, and regulations originally intended to protect women and children, the weak and defenseless, have been gradually extended to all workers. Though the equal-rights constitutional amendment remains a controversial issue, recognition has been given to the principle of equal rights in the sense that protection accorded to working women has become the minimum standard for men.

Veterans

Current programs for veterans differ strikingly from what was done for veterans after World War I. "Individual responsibility" was the gospel in 1918–1919, but during and after World War II the nation felt a keen responsibility for the welfare of returning servicemen. Even before the outbreak of the war the groundwork for reinstating veterans as civilians was laid in the Selective Training and Service Act of 1940. Later legislation amended but did not greatly alter the act. The ambitious program of retraining, education, grants and loans developed in the "G.I. Bill of Rights" has enabled millions of young men released from the armed forces to return to work with new skills and new faith in their country.

Aside from their immediate effect in the period of transition from war to peace, the laws that give protection to veterans and the diversified activities of the Veterans Administration are bound to have lasting results. Through these laws the federal government awards special protection to nearly half of all male workers and in some age classes to a much larger percentage. This is a new and potentially very significant element in the institutional setting of the labor market.

The philosophy behind the veterans program is that the nation owes a debt to those who were exposed to privations and dangers during the war. But once such a philosophy has taken root in a democratic society, similar protection is likely to be extended to other groups of the population.

Labor Welfare

Institutions designed to promote the welfare of workers include social security plans and measures to protect the safety of workers on the job and their health at work and at home. Apart from serving their direct purposes, these measures have a threefold effect on labor conditions: they impose definite obligations on management, ensure definite rights of workers, and influence the scope of labor-management negotiations and agreements by solving questions that would otherwise require settlement through union agreements.

The welfare program has not yet reached full development. Although federal and state laws, combined with privately sponsored programs in the field of labor welfare, have greatly increased the security of the individual worker, they are generally considered an unfinished job; revision of federal laws has been strongly advocated by the present Administration, expansion is on the agenda of state legislatures, and labor unions are making a great effort to supplement governmental programs by collective agreements.

Four groups of labor welfare problems are examined in subsequent chapters: social security proper, including old-age and survivors insurance, unemployment insurance and public assistance (Chapter 14); training and job placement as activities closely related to unemployment insurance and largely administered by the same agencies (Chapter 15); protection of health and safety of workers on the job (Chapter 16); and various forms of insurance against sickness and disability for workers and their families (Chapter 17).

Social Security

Social security legislation is still a controversial issue. But the controversy now centers about expansion of the program; the principles embodied in the Social Security Act of 1935 and supplemented in 1939 and 1950 seem to be universally accepted.

Until recently, the United States was far behind other industrial countries in social insurance. It even lacked insurance for permanent disability such as Bismarck introduced in Germany seventy years ago. The antiquated laws pertaining to compensation for work injuries served better to protect employers against workers' claims than to compensate workers for injuries suffered in the course of their work. Not until the turn of the century did a few states pass laws providing for compulsory insurance against industrial accidents, and for the next decade the constitutionality of these laws was under fire. The first statute on workmen's compensation to pass the test of constitutionality and go into continuing operation was adopted in 1911.

Until the 1930's the United States had little or no interest in providing the type of social security that was developed in Great Britain, Germany and other industrialized countries. This attitude probably resulted from the country's rapid industrial growth and relative wealth, its shifting and heterogeneous population, the tradition of "rugged individualism." Moreover the craft unions, the only articulate spokesmen of labor, were opposed to the idea of social insurance sponsored and controlled by the government.

The great depression acted as a powerful catalyst on public opinion. It made people realize that the absence of social security legislation was an unfortunate gap in our institutions. The Social Security Act of 1935 marked a turning point in the attitude of labor and the general public. The act was amended in 1939 and again in 1950. Disability insurance is also attracting growing public attention.

The significance of the social security program cannot be measured merely by the benefits and pensions paid out to unemployed and retired persons and survivors of deceased workers. More important is the fact that this program has lessened the pressure of insecurity on workers, especially the superannuated and the unemployed. Thanks to unemployment insurance, a worker who loses his job no longer feels compelled to take any work offered him, but has time to look for a suitable job. This change undoubtedly strengthens workers' independence.

At least in the short run, it does not make the task of management easier. The new situation, however, conforms to the general trend toward democratization of our industrial system and more effective use of our labor force.

Social security legislation has made workers conscious of what these laws fail to give to them. This may be the immediate cause of labor's increased interest in health insurance, in the form of both cash sickness benefits and prepaid medical care.

Training and Job Placement

The government has been moderately interested in training and job placement since 1917, when the federal Vocational Education Act was passed. However, the program made little progress before the 1930's. Training and placement remained essentially the personal concern and responsibility of the individual worker. Then, during the great depression, the government launched a large-scale training program for young workers who could not get the customary on-the-job training. During World War II it extended this activity to meet the urgent demand for skilled labor in munitions factories, and since the war a similar program has been carried out for veterans.

The Wagner-Peyser Act of 1933, by providing for a network of public employment offices, made government responsible for bringing workers and jobs together. During the first five years these offices did little more than refer job-seekers to relief projects. Their role became more important after 1938 when they were incorporated into the federal-state program of unemployment insurance. Their work was further increased during the war when the U.S. Employment Service was transferred to the War Manpower Commission.

In the postwar period of "more-than-full" employment, the Employment Service has not attracted much attention, but it has consolidated its position as a public job placement agency and become a device for directing the flow of demand and supply in the labor market.

Safety on the Job

The record of industrial accidents in this country is far from satisfactory. Though a few big corporations have almost eliminated accidents, progress in some industries, especially in small establishments, has been slow. Protection of the safety and health of workers has recently become a subject of heated discussion in labor unions, newspapers, the Congress and state legislatures.

Preventive regulations in force in most states do not meet the national standards recommended by experts. Work conditions prohibited as unsafe in one state may be permitted in another. Provisions for workmen's compensation are as unsatisfactory and chaotic as health and safety regulations. The laws vary widely from state to state; there is still greater variation in the practices of insurance companies, the actual carriers of this form of insurance.

Labor unions consider the existing protective and remedial laws inadequate and try to strengthen protective measures for their members' safety and health by collective bargaining. Often, however, their demands impinge on matters traditionally within the jurisdiction of management. When unions demand a larger crew on a job or a slower speed of work, it is sometimes difficult to decide where legitimate protection of the workers' safety and health ends and "featherbedding" begins. The question usually boils down to whether or not a certain measure is actually necessary for work safety. Figure 33 illustrates such an instance. It reproduces in facsimile two newspaper advertisements, one published by management and the other by a labor union, in a dispute about the number of men who should be employed on a diesel locomotive. The exchange of arguments fails to prove conclusively which party is right, but it typifies arguments used by the two sides in similar disputes.

Insurance against Sickness and Disability

The problem of insurance for workers against the losses and costs of sickness and disability has entered a critical phase. In recent years people in all walks of life have become conscious of the advantages of the insurance method of budgeting their outlays for medical services and the economic losses incurred because of sickness. The Blue Cross, Blue Shield and other plans have mushroomed over much of the nation. Programs for cash benefits during sickness have been enacted in Rhode Island, California, New Jersey and New York, and similar bills have been introduced in the legislatures of many other states. The President has recommended extension of the federal social security program to cover both wage losses during temporary and permanent disability and medical care costs, and labor unions are trying to supplement government-sponsored and voluntary health insurance programs by industrial welfare plans.

Despite considerable progress in recent years, we are still at the beginning of the road. Few employees have adequate insurance against losses from sickness and expenses for medical care. Many have partial protection but most have no insurance at all.

There are no universally accepted standards of medical care and disability insurance, and even the principle of compulsory prepayment of medical expenses is opposed by the organized medical profession. The drive for insurance against the costs of sickness and disability nevertheless is gaining momentum. Provision of cash sickness benefits for insured workers in some states has increased pressure for similar measures in other states and in the nation as a whole. The introduction of welfare plans in some enterprises and industries has also increased the pressure of other workers for similar arrangements. The success of voluntary plans for prepayment of medical and hospital costs has strengthened the movement.

Collective Bargaining

Three developments characterize recent trends in the field of labor-management negotiations: the growth of labor unions, the expanding scope of collective bargaining, and the steadily rising importance of collective agreements. The labor market has become the scene of action of powerful unions. Wages for hundreds of thousands of workers, sometimes for practically a whole industry, are bargained across a table. Union agreements determine — directly or indirectly — labor conditions for the greater part of the working population. These developments are discussed in Chapters 18–20.

Labor Unions

Some of the unions now in existence in the United States were founded nearly a century ago. The American Federation of Labor is approaching the venerable age of seventy. In recent years, however, unions have changed conspicuously in type and scope.

Until recently, labor unions represented skilled crafts almost exclusively. Except for a brief period during and immediately after World War I, union membership fluctuated narrowly, between 2 and 4 million. Rapid expansion began with the start of industrial mass organization in 1937. During World War II, unionization advanced by great strides, until by 1944, unions had more than 14 million members. The greatest gains were made in the basic industries. In contrast to the short-lived expansion during World War I, the unions not only maintained their strength after the end of the second world war but made new progress. By 1948–1949 the number of union members was probably between 14 and 16 million, almost five times more than in the 1920's.

This rapid growth has been accompanied by changes in the composition of unions, their economic and political strength, and their role in wage determination. Though the crafts maintain their leading position in some old unions, the center of gravity has moved toward large industrial unions, in the CIO, the AFL and among the unaffiliated or independent unions.

The new position of unions in this country is often said to represent a form of monopolistic control over the labor force. The structure of our labor unions, however, lacks the essential features of a monopoly: strict centralization and ability to make decisions at the center and to enforce them. In their wage policy the national unions are independent of the central organizations, the AFL and the CIO; locals are largely independent of their national headquarters. The structure of particular unions, their statutes, traditions, strategy, vary greatly. In many industries, often in the same locality, CIO and AFL unions compete for the right to represent this or that group of workers in collective bargaining. Bitter jurisdictional disputes often develop between unions affiliated with the same central organization. All these features are in striking contradiction to the connotations of "monopoly."

Without being an absolute monopoly, however, labor unions have become a powerful factor in our political life and their weight is felt in the daily operations of the labor market.

Collective Bargaining

Like labor unions, collective bargaining is not a new phenomenon on the American scene. But the scale on which it is now practiced is new. About 100,000 union-management con-

A. Management Appeals to Public Opinion

LEADERS OF FIREMEN'S UNION

NEEDLESS EXTRA ENGINE CREW

Regular Engineer

Regular Fireman

LEADERS OF ENGINEERS' UNION

This is a diesel *...a modern locomotive that means better service to you.*

Leaders of two unions think it's a feather-bed *...a "make work" grab that means less service to you.*

● Leaders of unions representing railroad engineers and firemen seek to force railroads to add extra, needless men on diesel locomotives. This is sheer waste—a "make-work" program which would mean fewer improvements and higher costs—for YOU!

Railroads use modern diesel locomotives because they are one of the means of giving faster, better service to you.

Two men compose the crew of a diesel. They occupy a clean, comfortable cab at the front. The engineer handles the throttle. The fireman sits and watches the track ahead. With no coal to shovel, he has practically nothing else to do.

No Benefit To You

Now the leaders of the Brotherhood of Locomotive Engineers and the Brotherhood of Locomotive Firemen and Enginemen want to use the diesel locomotive as a means of forcing a feather-bedding scheme on the railroads. The extra men they propose to add to the diesel crews are not needed. There is no work for them.

The union leaders are fighting among themselves about which union should furnish these extra, needless men. The Brotherhood of Locomotive Engineers have even threatened a strike. You may not be interested in this dispute of these two unions, but you would be vitally concerned if these groups succeed in putting through this feather-bedding scheme, because it would mean a slowing up of the improvement program of the railroads—of which the diesel is the outstanding symbol.

Diesel crews are among the highest paid railroad employes—real aristocrats of labor! Their pay is high by any standard. Granting of these demands, therefore, would mean that the railroads would be paying out millions in unearned wages to those in the very highest pay brackets.

We'd Like To Spend This Money On You

You know how much the diesel has meant to you in increased speed, comfort and convenience. The railroads have many more of them on order for even greater improvement in service to you. But needless drains of money, such as this present demand of the unions for needless men on diesels, reduce the ability of the railroads to spend money on better service for you.

Proud as the railroads are of the diesel, it is only a small part of their improvement program. Since the War, literally billions of dollars have been spent on improvement of tracks and stations, on new passenger and freight cars, as well as on diesel locomotives, and on the many other less conspicuous details of railroading that contribute to improved service.

Feather-Bedding Means Less Service To You

But brazen feather-bedding schemes like the one now proposed would, if successful, divert large sums of money from our present improvement programs. Even worse, they make improvements like the diesel worthless, by making the cost of their operation prohibitive.

These demands are against YOUR interests—as well as those of the railroads. They are schemes to "make work". Neither you nor the railroads should be forced to pay such a penalty for progress.

That's why the railroads are resisting these "make work" demands to the last ditch—and why they are telling you about them.

We are publishing this and other advertisements to talk with you at first hand about matters which are important to everybody.

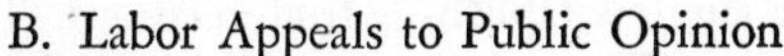

B. Labor Appeals to Public Opinion

FIREMAN-HELPER

An engineer alone in his cab when sudden illness strikes . . . a signal missed because his fireman-helper had left to attend a Diesel unit behind . . . such is the story behind many a great disaster. This may not happen often. But once is too much!

His Helper wasn't there!

ENGINEER

FROM CAB TO REAR UNIT 75 YDS.

Disaster a Split Second Away! 400 People Hurtling to Destruction at 100 Miles an Hour—because the Engineer was All Alone!

A HIGH-POWERED DIESEL train hurtling through the stormy night! You are all comfortable inside, but up ahead are two men responsible for the safety of that train. These men are the engineer and his fireman-helper.

A modern Diesel locomotive has four Diesel units, linked together in series, each one delivering terrific power. All of the delicate mechanism of the Diesel engine is contained behind the engineer in these four units. It is susceptible to fire and explosive hazards. These four units need constant attention. But, today, on most high-powered Diesel trains the only person available for this job is the fireman-helper. *And he is needed up in front.*

He's needed up in front with the engineer because, on a train traveling at 100 miles an hour, no man knows when an emergency may strike. Disaster after disaster has happened because the fireman-helper had left his post in the cab to do an engineer's job on one or another of the Diesel units behind.

The Brotherhood of Locomotive Engineers has urged on the railroads of the country the necessity of adding to all Diesel locomotives an additional engineer qualified to supervise, adjust and make necessary running repairs. The railroads have replied that they would prefer to save the money and let the fireman-helper do the job. Disaster after disaster has shown that money saved this way is saved at the risk of human lives.

It's in the Record

Here is an excerpt from the report of an emergency board appointed from the National Railway Labor Panel:

> ". . . the organizations point to three recent disastrous wrecks—one of them virtually a holocaust—on one road within the last two years. In each instance the fireman was not in the cab at the time of the wreck. In its report concerning one of these wrecks, the Interstate Commerce Commission called particular attention to the fact that under the existing operating practice the fireman was away from the control cab 85 per cent of his time . . .
>
> "At high speeds, with signals rapidly fleeting by, with the fireman away from the cab 15 to 20 minutes at a time, if anything should happen to the engineer adverse signals might go entirely unobserved. . . . It is operation under adverse conditions and in emergencies that requires the utmost care, and it would appear that safety requires that trains be manned for the possibility of adverse conditions"

If that doesn't mean that the fireman is needed in the cab with an additional engineer to supervise and make necessary running repairs in the engine room, what does?

About those "Feather-Beds"

The railroads have characterized this proposal as "feather-bedding." Anyone who has supervised and kept in good running repair 4500 horsepower for hundreds of miles will tell you that it's no "feather-bed."

The simple truth is that there's an important job to be done by an additional engineer on a modern high-powered Diesel locomotive. And at the same time it's essential that the fireman-helper should be released to do his own indispensable job in the front cab.

Two Railroads Already Agree

It so happens that two great Eastern railroads seem to be already in agreement with us about this necessity. Today these two railroads assign an employee other than a fireman to supervise and adjust the engine room machinery en route, thereby leaving the engineer and fireman to perform their important duties in the cab. We are glad that these two railroads feel that the small extra cost is far better than a gamble with human lives. Our plea is that every railroad in the country should feel the same.

We say that there is something more important than talking about "feather-beds", and making light of possible disaster. We say that the public safety, as well as the future of high-speed railroad travel, calls for an adequate number of men to handle the Diesel monsters that speed crack trains across the country.

This Advertisement is Published in the Public Interest by the

BROTHERHOOD OF LOCOMOTIVE ENGINEERS

FIGURE 33. MANAGEMENT AND LABOR APPEAL TO PUBLIC OPINION

Source: Evening Star, Washington, D. C., February 1 and 7, 1949.

These two newspaper advertisements illustrate the procedure used by management and labor in disputes. In this instance the issue arose from technological changes not foreseen in the existing contract. Both parties are trying to win the support of public opinion. Management accuses the union of "featherbedding" at the expense of consumers. In its rebuttal, the union justifies its stand on the ground of safety and accuses management of neglecting the public's welfare.

tracts are negotiated each year, some of them for a handful of workmen in a single establishment, others for whole industries. The recent fight around the Wagner and the Taft-Hartley Acts was tempered by acceptance of collective bargaining as the foundation for determining wages and labor conditions in the United States.

Two features are of paramount significance for the new setting of the labor market: the extreme diversity of collective bargaining procedures and the lack of firmly crystallized opinions on related problems, among both labor leaders and business executives. A survey made by the Twentieth Century Fund in connection with the present study has shown that within each camp there are widely divergent and often conflicting opinions on the desirable scope of negotiations, forms of representation, extent of arbitration, and so forth. There is no firmly established employer or employee view on collective bargaining. As a method of determining labor conditions, collective bargaining has outgrown the old mold and has not yet found its new form.[1]

Union Agreements

About 15 million workers are directly covered by existing union contracts, but these agreements indirectly determine wages and working conditions for an additional 20 to 25 million.

Union agreements have tended to cover an increasing number of questions. The trend has been toward extending the coverage of agreements not only to union members but to all employees eligible for membership and, at the same time, toward elaborating clauses to protect "union security." The checkoff of union dues has become standard practice in recent years, and was more firmly established when millions of workers signed individual checkoff assignments in compliance with the Taft-Hartley Act. Another important change in the content of union agreements has been increasing inclusion of provisions for arbitrating grievances and of clauses outlawing strikes and lockouts for the duration of the contract.

Generally speaking, the trend in union agreements is toward formalizing relations between labor and management, clarifying their respective rights and responsibilities, and transforming common usage into a written code of industrial relations. The cumulative effect of these changes has been to establish a new pattern of labor-management relations. It is questionable whether actual "industrial democracy" has resulted, but a union agreement today is a written constitution that establishes a system of rights for employees and their union and restricts the powers of management.

Labor Disputes and Arbitration

The test of the new institutional setting of wage determination is its effect on work stoppages, especially in industries of vital importance to the nation. Work stoppages are discussed in Chapter 21, while Chapter 22 deals with the settlement of grievances and labor disputes by arbitration.

Work Stoppages

The first test came in the period of industrial demobilization after World War II, and at first glance its results do not appear very encouraging. In 1946 there were almost 5,000 work stoppages, involving 4.6 million workers and 116 million man-days of work. Public opinion rebelled not only at the number of strikes but also at their size: 750,000 workers were involved in the famous dispute in the steel industry; 340,000 miners were on strike in April and 335,000 in November 1946. Work stoppages on the railroads and in the communication industry were also extensive. The wave of strikes receded as rapidly as it rose, however. In retrospect the disturbances of 1946 appear to have been caused by the shift from a war to a peacetime economy, rather than by the new setting of the labor market. In fact, the labor-management conflicts of 1946 were of the same character and had essentially the same cause as the strikes after World War I.

The number of strikers per thousand industrial workers was lower in 1946 than in 1919, and after the first clash, the percentage of workers involved in strikes dropped in 1947–1950 to about the same level as in 1921. The social and political repercussions of labor stoppages were fundamentally different in the two periods. The labor-management clashes after World War I were characterized by extreme bitterness, acts of violence and a spirit of despair. After World War II there was practically no violence; most conflicts were fought out within the frame-

1. See W. S. Woytinsky and Associates, *Labor and Management Look at Collective Bargaining,* Twentieth Century Fund, New York, 1949.

work of established rules and apparently did not leave much bitterness on either side.

The loss caused by the postwar work stoppages to the nation and especially to the workers — 1.43 per cent of all working time in 1946 — was high. But no industrial country has made the shift from wartime regulations to a peacetime competitive economy without friction and waste, and our experience compares favorably with that of other nations.

On the other hand, the relative lull in work stoppages in 1947–1950 does not prove that the new framework of the labor market holds no danger to industrial peace. In these years many unions obtained wage gains without strikes. Some business executives interviewed in the course of the Fund's labor-management survey said they could avoid work stoppages in their industry only by making concessions to unions. They were ready to make concessions because the sellers' market enabled them to pass the cost on to consumers. The final test of the effect of the new setting on labor stoppages is still to come.

Arbitration of Labor Disputes

Day-to-day arbitration of grievances under existing contracts has become a feature of modern labor-management relations. Arbitration procedures and techniques are not yet crystallized. Different industries use different methods, and opinions on what matters should be subject to arbitration differ widely among labor and business representatives. However, both parties have accepted the principle of arbitration as the alternative to strikes and lockouts in the event of a deadlocked dispute under an existing contract. Without coercive legislation and by mutual agreement, labor and management have practically outlawed work stoppages resulting from disputes over the interpretation of contract terms. Since, in many instances, a contract can be interpreted in a very broad sense, the technique of arbitration is widely used for regulating relations that are not spelled out in the existing agreement.

The success with which arbitration has been used to settle disputes under existing contracts explains the increasing public interest in the possibility of using the same technique for negotiating new contracts. Arbitration seems to be a way to shorten the tedious procedure of collective bargaining, to prevent work stoppages and, most important of all, to eliminate strikes and lockouts in industries that vitally affect the public interest. A closer analysis reveals, however, that labor arbitration is no panacea for industrial unrest.

All in all, labor unions now tend to favor arbitration of new contracts more than does management, but for both parties this is a matter of expediency rather than of principle. Management distrusts the impartiality of arbitrators; unions believe that they will usually get at least a part of their claims. A change in economic and political conditions might reverse these attitudes.

Recent experience shows that successful arbitration of labor disputes depends on the attitude of the two parties — on their sincere desire to reach a settlement. Arbitration cannot eliminate hatred and mutual suspicion, which sometimes are the real cause of a deadlock in collective bargaining. Under such conditions, the arbitrator's award would lead only to a precarious truce, rather than to peace.

Impact of Recent Trends

The antecedents of recent changes in the setting of the labor market lie far back in the history of the United States. Some of these trends began to develop more than a century ago, gained momentum gradually, and then made rapid advances in the past two decades. In some cases new federal laws have blazed the trail for state legislation; in others, the states have taken the initiative. Some features of the new setting of the labor market have resulted from clashes between the administrative, legislative and judicial branches of government or between the federal government and the states.

Far from reflecting any internally consistent philosophy, the new regulations often conflict with one another. They are sometimes described as the trappings of a paternalistic welfare state, as opposed to the rugged individualism of the past. But this charge has a closer relation to the relief program of the early 1930's than to the recent trends in social security, collective bargaining, union agreements, and so on. These trends are probably better described as a shift from individual to collective responsibility. If the recent changes in labor market regulations and labor-management relations are looked at in this way, they are closely related to the general trends in social organization and political institutions in all industrialized countries.

Wage Negotiations in the New Setting

Whatever may be their long-run impact on the economic system — and therefore on the real earnings of workers and on profits — there is little doubt that the new patterns of wage determination, collective bargaining and grievance settlements mean new tasks for management and labor unions. When unions bargained for a small minority of the working force, each penny increase in wage rates meant one penny more for each union member. There was no danger that a raise might bring a proportionate rise in the cost of living. Under present conditions, however, the nation-wide rounds of wage raises threaten to increase arbitrarily the amount of money in the hands of consumers and to lead to a general rise in prices.

Paradoxically, a comparatively weak union in the past could obtain an increase in real wages for its members more readily than a larger union can today. In the future a still more powerful union will be even less successful. To illustrate, let us assume a much higher degree of unionization of workers and centralization of unions and business than actually exists — a Big National Union representing the entire labor force and a Council of Big Business that fixes all prices. Suppose that the Union demands that all wage rates be doubled. The Council can reject the demand and challenge the Union. But suppose it accedes to the demand, doubles all wage rates and simultaneously doubles all prices (thereby proportionately widening the margin of profit). Though considerable dislocation in the financial structure of the economy would result, the real earnings of workers would not change. Basically the same thing happens if we assume a more realistic situation — for example, a series of consecutive raises in various industries of, say, 10 to 20 per cent. Thus, the procedure of attempting to raise real earnings by demanding higher pay, the procedure that has been the traditional weapon of workingmen's combinations since their inception, becomes less effective when labor unions become strong enough to control the nation's labor force.

The transition from old to new labor market conditions is slow and gradual. Unions continue to demand higher wages for their members, not only because that is what the members expect from them but also because that is precisely their function in the economic system. In fact, smooth operation of the labor market presumes that management tries to reduce labor costs while unions do their utmost to increase the workers' share in the social dividend. Just as other prices are established through the continual clash between buyers and sellers, so labor and management *must* pull in opposite directions in wage negotiations. But sooner or later a point is reached beyond which the pulling alone, even in the right direction and with growing strength, promises no real advantage to labor.

Economic Background

Labor and management leaders today are facing each other in an institutional setting very different from the one in which they served apprenticeship. Until a new behavior pattern is developed, both parties may be expected to use tactical methods that have become antiquated. Both labor and management must appraise the new situation in light of economic trends and the economic outlook.[2] The crucial question is whether ours is a mature, stagnating economy or a dynamic and expanding system.

In a stagnating economy the struggle for better living conditions for workers is a question of distribution. If wages and profits are to be carved out of a pie that remains the same or tends to become smaller, wages cannot be raised except by trimming profits; conversely, profits can be increased only by keeping wages low.

In an expanding economy, on the other hand, wages and profits move in the same direction. The gain to each comes from increased productivity. Though there is a broad field of controversy on how these gains should be distributed, labor and management have a common interest in solving the fundamental economic problems. Under these conditions, strong unions should not be regarded as a threat to business, nor should powerful companies be objects of suspicion and fear to unions.

How labor and management approach their problems depends largely on their economic philosophy and on their appraisal of the present phase of our economic history.

The analysis of economic trends in the first

2. See Chapter 1.

part of this report suggests that our economic system is vigorous and dynamic, with tremendous flexibility and an almost infinite capacity to expand. It suggests also that since the last war our economy has entered a period of particularly rapid growth. Reconciliation of the interests of labor and management in such a system and in such a period requires a clear recognition of their common goal: to promote economic expansion and technical progress in the nation.

An expanding economy has still another important implication: Growth seldom means exact reproduction of an old pattern at an increasing rate. More frequently, progress is accompanied by changes in the structure of the growing system and in the relationships among its parts. With economic progress, the social pattern of the nation is bound to change.

The recent trends in the institutional setting of the labor market indicate the probable direction of future changes. Discussion of daily labor-management problems in coming years is likely to take place against an economic background of increasing production and rising standards of living and in an institutional setting characterized by a growing recognition of the principle of collective responsibility.

CHAPTER 10

LABOR LAW IN THE UNITED STATES *

AMERICAN LABOR LAW is diffused. There is no single code of laws or centralized administration. Legal regulations and administrative agencies are as pluralistic as the American political state, wherein governmental authority is divided and distributed among geographic divisions and among the executive, legislative, administrative and judicial branches. (See Table 33.)

Through the balances and counterbalances in American labor law, neither employers nor unions enjoy a dominant position. Although in our economy the employer's position is generally superior, workers improved their position in recent years with the aid of friendly Administration and Congress. Then public opinion, sensitive to overpowering growth, brought about new legislation to restrict union power. In combination with the legal tradition of individual liberty and the capacity of a vigorous people to disobey civil regulations without destroying the sense of authority, American labor law is intended to encourage cooperation between labor and management rather than prescribe the terms and conditions of employment relations.

Law draws on custom, and custom gives it stability. The force of law may confirm and strengthen existing practices or lead to their modification. When legislation alters or suppresses an established way of doing things, the law, too, is changed as the practices are altered. The complex and dispersed character of American labor law is illustrated by a case study in Appendix Note 2.

Our system of labor laws comprises laws and administrative and judicial agencies on three government levels: federal, federal-state and state. Some functions are reserved to a fourth level: county and municipal governments.

Federal statutes regulate (1) labor-management relations, (2) labor standards and (3) part of the social security program initiated in 1935. Important in the first area are the Labor-Management Act of 1947, the Norris-LaGuardia Anti-Injunction Act of 1932 and the Railway Labor Act of 1926; in the second, the Fair Labor Standards Act of 1938 and the Public Contracts Act of 1936; in the third, federal old-age and survivors insurance. Federal-state cooperation forms the basis of another part of the social security program: unemployment insurance and employment service. State legislation partly overlaps federal laws, as in state labor relations and anti-injunction acts, but also has very important fields of its own: protection of health and safety, regulation of wage payments, and workmen's compensation. Local or municipal bodies license certain trades — craftsmen in the building trades, for example — and local police regulations affect such matters as picketing and the distribution of union leaflets. (See Table 33.)

FEDERAL LAWS ON LABOR RELATIONS

From 1935 to 1947, federal statutory regulation of relations between labor and management was embodied in the National Labor Relations Act (the Wagner Act), which was amended by the Labor-Management Relations Act of 1947 (the Taft-Hartley Act). The new act and the controversy about its revision can best be understood through a review of the legal philosophy of the original statute and of its place in the American scheme of government, which will also bring into focus the other federal laws regulating labor relations, the Norris-LaGuardia Anti-Injunction Act and the Railway Labor Act.

The National Labor Relations Act

The National Labor Relations Act of 1935 came into being principally because previous legal regulations had not sufficiently protected collective bargaining as a method of regulating wages, hours and working conditions. The rights of workers to form unions of their own choosing and to bargain collectively with their employers were uncertain; though accepted in theory by the courts, they were often contested and sometimes denied altogether by judicial decree in particular cases.

* By Joseph Kovner, Attorney, Washington, D.C.

The act gave positive legal protection to these rights. It prohibits employers from interfering with exercise of these rights by coercion or intimidation, or by discharging an employee because of union activity, or by forming unions dominated, controlled or aided by the employer. It requires employers to bargain collectively in good faith with the representative freely chosen by a majority of the employees in a bargaining unit. To settle any questions of representation, the National Labor Relations Board decides the unit — craft, plant or area — and, after election or other proof, certifies the union that has been chosen by the majority in the unit. This certified representative is then legally entitled to represent all the employees in the unit for purposes of collective bargaining.

The act is enforced by the National Labor Relations Board, which investigates alleged violations, and, upon the finding of a violation, after notice and hearing, issues orders requiring the employer to cease his violations and to remedy past violations by dissolving employer-dominated unions, rehiring employees discharged for union activity and paying back pay to such discharged employees.

Importance of the Judiciary

To understand the legal origin of the National Labor Relations Act, the place of the judiciary in American government must be appreciated. The judiciary is a potent branch of the American government. The courts, especially the United States Supreme Court, construe the law. They interpret the Constitution and statutes and set forth the common law, the customs, usage and legal principles that govern relations for which there is no constitutional or statutory rule of law.

It is this third function especially that has been used in judicial regulation of employer-employee relations. Until the Clayton Act of 1914 no federal statute specifically regulated private industrial relations. Labor law in the United States was judge-made, and it was developed principally in lawsuits to enjoin unions from interfering with the legal rights of the public, employers, and nonunion employees.

Judicial Theories before NLRA

The judge-made law was based on prevailing legal ideas of individual contract in an economic system of free competition. Conduct not covered by contract was regulated by rules of tort, or wrongful injury done to another independent of a contract. Most judges held that the individual relations between an employer and an employee were primary; though they granted that employees had a right to combine into unions for their mutual interest, strikes or boycotts inflicting a tort or damage upon the public, employers or other employees were often held to be unjustified and therefore unlawful.[1] Employers could require employees to agree not to join a union, and any attempt to organize these employees was a wrongful attempt to induce breach of contract.[2] The gathering of union members on picket lines and in street meetings was held to be a violation of public order.[3] The attempt of unions to eliminate competition based on wages and other labor costs was considered in restraint of trade.[4]

These views were common among both state and federal judges. The federal courts secured jurisdiction over labor disputes by virtue of the Sherman Antitrust Act. This federal statute, enacted in 1890, prohibited *any* restraint of trade, and the Supreme Court held that it applied to labor unions. The assumption of federal jurisdiction was important because state judges, being elected locally for a term, are generally more responsive to local popular feeling than federal judges, who are appointed for life on good behavior. Employers seeking to enjoin strikes and boycotts often preferred to go to federal courts.[5]

Anti-Injunction Acts

The first federal labor legislation concerned with collective bargaining was aimed at freeing unions from judicial injunction. One of the major actions of the Woodrow Wilson Administration was to amend the antitrust laws by the Clayton Act (in 1914), exempting unions from the ban on illegal combinations and monopolies. The legislation also specified union actions that

1. See dissenting opinion of Mr. Justice Brandeis in *Duplex Printing Press Co.* v. *Deering,* 254 U.S. 443 (1921), at p. 479.
2. *Hitchman Coal and Coke Co.* v. *Mitchell,* 245 U.S. 229 (1917).
3. *American Foundries* v. *Tri-City Council,* 257 U.S. 184 (1921).
4. *Loewe* v. *Lawlor,* 208 U.S. 274 (1908).
5. Employers "eagerly sought" injunctions in federal courts according to Felix Frankfurter and Nathan Greene, *The Labor Injunction,* Macmillan, New York, 1930, pp. 13 and 14.

TABLE 33

Labor Laws in the United States Classified by Type and by Branch and Level of Government

Type of Law	Legislative Branch	Administrative Branch	Executive Branch	Judicial Branch
		Level: Federal Government		
Labor Relations	Labor-Management Relations Act of 1947 Regulates collective bargaining in industries affecting interstate commerce. Establishes Federal Mediation and Conciliation Service.	National Labor Relations Board Prosecute, through general counsel, and decide cases of unfair labor practices. Federal Mediation and Conciliation Service.	President Appoint chief officers (subject to Senate approval). Appoint emergency fact-finding boards. Secretary of Labor File reports. Attorney General Enforce criminal penalties. Secure 60-day injunctions.	Review NLRB orders. Grant temporary injunctions. Decide criminal violations. Jurisdiction over civil suits. Grant 60-day injunctions pending final conciliation.
Labor Relations	Railway Labor Act (1926, amm. 1934) Regulates collective bargaining in railroads and airlines.	National Mediation Board Certify representatives. Mediate disputes. National Railroad Adjustment Board Settle grievance disputes.	President Appoint Board and emergency fact-finding boards. Attorney General Prosecute violations of rights through federal district attorneys.	Enforce provisions for collective bargaining rights by injunction and criminal penalties. Exercise limited review of grievance adjustment decisions.
Labor Relations	Norris LaGuardia Anti-Injunction Act (1932) Limits judicial regulation of labor disputes.			Enforce limitations on their own power.
Labor Standards	Fair Labor Standards Act (1938) Minimum wages. Maximum hours. Child labor.		Secretary of Labor Administer provisions. Attorney General Prosecute criminal violations.	Enforce standards by injunction and criminal penalties. Decide civil suits for damages for failure to pay minimum wages.
Labor Standards	Public Contracts Act (1936) Labor standards.		Secretary of Labor Investigate and prosecute violations.	Enforce standards by civil suits.
Labor Welfare	Social Security Act (1935, amm. 1939 and 1950) Federal old-age and survivors insurance program.	Federal Security Agency.	President Appoint chief officers. Treasury Collect taxes.	Enforce tax liabilities. Review denial of benefits.
Labor Welfare	Railroad Retirement Act (1934, amm. 1938 and 1946) Old-age and survivors insurance, unemployment compensation, sickness disability compensation.	Railroad Retirement Board.	President Appoint Board. Treasury Collect taxes.	Enforce tax liabilities. Review denial of benefits.
Labor Welfare	Civil service legislation Pensions, sick leave and accident compensation for federal workers.	Civil Service Commission Supervise employment standards applied by federal agencies.	President Appoint Commission.	
Labor Welfare	Federal workmen's compensation laws: Railroad Employers' Liability Act (1908); Merchant Marine Act (1920); Longshoremen's and Harbor Workers' Act (1927, amm. 1938).	Federal Security Agency.		Decide suits for death and wrongful injuries. Decide suits for personal injuries. Review decisions of administrative agencies.

TABLE 33—CONTINUED

Type of Law	Legislative Branch	Administrative Branch	Executive Branch	Judicial Branch
	Level: Federal Government—Continued			
Other	Investigatory powers: standing and special committees.			
	Criminal statutes: Anti-Racketeering Act (1934, amm. 1946); Antitrust Act (1890, amm. 1914); Corrupt Political Practices Act (1947); Coercive Practices in Radio Act (1946); control of checkoff and welfare funds (1947).		Attorney General Prosecute violations through federal district attorneys.	Decide cases (defendants entitled to jury trial).
				Exercise constitutional power to decide controversies (judicial common law), to interpret statutes, to enforce Constitution.
	Level: Federal-State Cooperation			
Labor Welfare	Unemployment compensation: federal standards, state administration.	Federal Security Agency Supervise standards. State commissions Administer benefits. State tax collectors Collect taxes.	Governors Appoint officers (subject to approval by state senates).	
	Employment service: federal standards, state administration.	Federal Department of Labor. State departments of labor.		
	Level: State Government			
Labor Relations	Labor relations acts Conciliation service Anti-injunction laws	State boards.	Governors Appoint chief officers (subject to approval by state senates).	Review board orders against unfair labor practices.
Labor Standards	Minimum wages Maximum hours Health and safety regulations Wage payment	State commissions and departments of labor.		Review administration of standards. Decide criminal cases.
Labor Welfare	Workmen's compensation Regulation of employment agencies	State commissions.	County and state district attorneys Prosecute violations.	
Other	Criminal laws Restriction or prohibition of union membership as condition of employment. General.		County and state district attorneys Prosecute violations.	
	Level: Local Government (County and Municipal)			
	Municipal labor relations agencies Local licensing of crafts and trades Local ordinances against breach of peace	Local boards.	Mayors Appoint officers. City attorneys Prosecute violations. Mayors Appoint officers (subject to approval by city councils).	Local police courts decide criminal cases.

were to be immune from injunction. But the Supreme Court, using its power to interpret statutes, held that Congress had intended to exempt only lawful union actions and reserved it to the courts to determine what was lawful.[6] The federal courts continued to issue labor injunctions.

In 1932 the Norris-LaGuardia Anti-Injunction Act made it clear that the federal courts were no longer to issue injunctions against peaceful exercise of the rights to strike and picket. It was fully enforced by the United States Supreme Court,[7] and by 1940 federal labor injunctions were a rarity.

Although the Court interpreted the act broadly, extending it to every type of labor dispute and all forms of peaceful, not independently unlawful, union action, the Anti-Injunction Act was negative legislation, limited to the special purpose of ending judicial regulation of the exercise of economic pressure in the form of strikes and boycotts. It left an employer free to retaliate against union action in order to prevent unions from organizing his employees, and to eliminate or weaken them whenever possible. He could fire men for union activity, and he could form associations and direct or urge his employees to join them.

The Railway Labor Act

The Railway Labor Act of 1926, which preceded the Wagner Act by almost a decade, was passed to furnish positive protection of the right of railroad workers to organize and bargain collectively. Though limited to the railroad industry, this act was important not only in its own sphere but also as a precursor of the more general legislation. It was adopted before a general law because of the strength of the railroad unions and because of the public interest involved in labor disputes in the railroad industry. Furthermore, many railroad managers agreed with the unions that legislation protecting collective bargaining was essential to the orderly operation of the railroads.

The act specified the procedure for establishing collective bargaining relations but employed general language to prohibit interference with the rights of employees and employers to choose their representatives freely for the purpose of collective bargaining. The federal courts gave this general prohibition specific and stringent enforcement in 1930, when a district judge issued an injunction prohibiting a carrier from various forms of interference with the union of its employees and the Supreme Court upheld the decree.[8] These judicial decisions supporting collective bargaining in the railroad industry paved the road for the adoption and enforcement of the National Labor Relations Act.

Constitutionality of NLRA

The National Labor Relations Act raised two major legal questions at the outset: first, whether the federal government could limit the employer's rights in order to promote collective bargaining; and second, whether federal powers extend to employer-employee relations in manufacturing and other industry.

In upholding the constitutionality of the act, the Supreme Court confirmed the legal justification of collective bargaining—that the individual employee is helpless to bargain over terms and conditions of employment with his employer and that unions are essential to give employees equality in dealing with their employers.[9] This view superseded the old doctrine that each individual employee had equal right with the employer to freedom of contract.

The second question had to do with the power of Congress to regulate interstate commerce. Before 1937 the Supreme Court had consistently held this federal power to be limited to the regulation of the physical movement of goods and commercial exchanges from one state to another.[10] But in a decision written by Chief Justice Charles Evans Hughes, the Supreme Court abandoned precedent to meet the pressure of contemporary political and economic developments. The Court accepted the theory of the statute that labor relations in a locality affect interstate commerce, and that Congress can protect interstate commerce from harmful effects by regulating labor-management relations. Specifically, the theory of the statute was that the refusal of employers to accept collective bargain-

6. See *Duplex Printing Press Co.* v. *Deering,* previously cited.
7. *Lauf* v. *E. G. Skinner & Company,* 363 U.S. 323 (1938).
8. *Texas and New Orleans Railroad Co.* v. *Brotherhood of Railway and Steamship Clerks,* 281 U.S. 548 (1930).
9. *National Labor Relations Board* v. *Jones and Laughlin Steel Corp.,* 301 U.S. 1 (1937).
10. *Carter* v. *Carter Coal Co.,* 298 U.S. 238 (1936).

ing led to interruptions in the production of goods entering into interstate commerce.[11]

The decision worked a radical change in the American legal system. The doctrine that the federal power extends to relations affecting interstate commerce became a major premise of federal power, and thus broadened it embraces the entire economy. The doctrine now imposes at least one simple test: If an enterprise imports any substantial amount of its materials from another state, or if it sends any substantial part of its products to another state, or furnishes essential supplies or services to interstate businesses, it can be regulated by the federal government. Limitations on the extent of a federal regulation of commerce now depend on the discretion of Congress and the administrative agency enforcing a law.

NLRA and the Administrative Branch of Government

The National Labor Relations Act was involved in a third great change in the American legal system, the development of administrative agencies. The Constitution recognizes only three departments of government: executive, legislative and judicial. Administrative agencies were originally regarded as agents of the legislature, empowered to make detailed rules and regulations that had been delegated under a general statute. By 1930, however, it became apparent that administrative boards and commissions were applying the law to particular cases and thereby sharing not legislative, but judicial, functions. In 1937, when the National Labor Relations Act was declared constitutional, judicial alarm at this "new bureaucracy" had reached its peak.

The courts were jealous of their constitutional power to enforce laws in particular cases. An administrative agency, clearly, cannot constitutionally enforce its orders: it cannot fine violators or send them to jail. To secure enforcement, it has to obtain judicial approval of its order, usually from a federal circuit court of appeals; the court then issues a decree directing a person to obey the order as issued or as modified by the court, and disobedience becomes a contempt of court. The courts thus exercise a power of veto and review over the decisions of any administrative agency such as the National Labor Relations Board; they can either grant the agency wide discretion or reduce it to an advisory role. The struggle was over the determination of the facts. Legal questions were, it was to be assumed, for the courts to decide. The National Labor Relations Act declared that findings of fact by the Board should be conclusive if supported by the evidence; the Supreme Court accepted this principle and assigned to the Board the power to determine the facts. The result of this decision was to establish administrative agencies as a fourth department of government.

The Supreme Court refused to interrupt or intervene in the administrative procedures of the Board. It reserved the exercise of judicial power to the final act of reviewing any order of the Board before it becomes legally enforceable. The administrative agency, as the finder of facts, must grant a full and fair hearing to the interested parties; it must apply its law to the facts and it cannot exceed its statutory authority or invade constitutional rights. Within these limits, it has wide discretion.

NLRA and a Labor Code

The National Labor Relations Act was broadly worded and its concepts of collective bargaining relations were new to the courts. Interpretation of the statute posed a fourth fundamental issue: Would the courts construe it liberally to favor and encourage collective bargaining, or would they restrict it and limit its potential impact on employer power and individual relations? The courts chose in favor of the broad purposes of the act. Occasionally they enforced the change from individual to collective industrial relations by turning to the favorite judicial storehouse of wisdom — custom and usage.[12] The Board was resourceful in enforcing the statute, with judicial approval, to ensure full protection of the collective rights of employees,

11. The Jones and Laughlin Steel Corporation case, cited above, illustrates the general legal theory. The steel mill drew raw materials from various parts of the country and shipped its finished products to various areas. Suppliers and customers in turn bought and sold goods in interstate commerce. A strike over collective bargaining in the steel mill stopped the flow of supplies to the mill and of the finished product to its customers.

12. In *Order of Railway Telegraphers* v. *Railway Express Agency,* 321 U.S. 342 (1944), 346, the Court said: "Collective bargaining was not defined by the statute which provided for it, but it has generally been considered to absorb and give statutory approval to the philosophy of bargaining as worked out in the labor movement in the United States."

checking direct and indirect forms of employer interference with these rights. It developed a detailed code, containing many bans on employer actions and aids to unions.

Moreover, judicial interpretation of the statute resolved several legal problems of collective bargaining. The legal status of a collective bargaining agreement had been in doubt; the courts had not been able to assimilate its group relationships into common-law notions of contract and individual employer-employee relations. The Supreme Court ended these legal uncertainties by holding that under the National Labor Relations Act the terms of a collective bargaining agreement govern all the individual hirings of employees covered by the contract, and its terms cannot be waived or modified to the advantage or disadvantage of a single employee. Collective bargaining establishes the common rules of employment for a given group of employees.[13]

The Labor-Management Relations Act of 1947

Twelve years after the National Labor Relations Act was passed, Congress amended it to impose duties and restraints upon unions. The Supreme Court had made a limited but important move in that direction when it held that on principle a union cannot discriminate against the employees it represents but owes each one fair and nonhostile representation — specifically, that a white majority cannot deprive Negro members of the bargaining unit of their seniority rights.[14] But the Court had added that its power was confined to enforcement of the fundamental principle of fair play. It was for Congress to make specific regulations.

Employers opposed the original act in 1935 largely on the grounds that employer-employee relations ought not to be regulated by the federal government and that unions interfered with individual freedoms of employers and employees. The revision of the act, however, was based on a different policy. The Taft-Hartley Act further elaborates federal regulation of industrial relations, increasing the powers and the jurisdiction of the National Labor Relations Board. It is based essentially on the legal theories of the original Wagner Act and occupies the same place in the American scheme of government, but it contains a new element: control of the power of unions. Unions are prohibited from coercing employees in their choice of a union and from refusing to work for or handle goods of persons who deal with an employer involved in a labor dispute. It also makes more extensive use of direct judicial powers. The courts are authorized to issue temporary injunctions to restrain violations of the act, pending decision by the Board. Moreover, collective agreements are enforceable by suit in the federal courts. The Board not only may enjoin certain unlawful strikes and boycotts, but persons damaged by these unlawful strikes and boycotts may sue the union involved for damages in federal courts. The statute also invokes criminal penalties to regulate checkoff and joint union-employer welfare schemes.

The act also established the Federal Mediation and Conciliation Service. American law and policy is opposed to compulsory settlement of labor disputes generally; any legislation of this sort not limited to specific emergency situations would face serious constitutional objections. The statute therefore seeks to aid toward settlement of disputes by offering the services of conciliators and mediators. The law limits legal compulsion to a sixty-day stay on any strikes or lockouts or disputes affecting the national health and safety, and attempts to effect extraordinary mediation through a special fact-finding board and a poll of the employees. Mediation actions are functions of the executive branch of the government. The sixty-day injunction is to be granted automatically by the courts.

FEDERAL LAWS ON LABOR STANDARDS

The second major objective of federal labor laws is protection of standard working conditions.

Fair Labor Standards Act of 1938

The Fair Labor Standards Act of 1938 (the Wage-Hour Act) fixes standards of working conditions, of which there had been relatively little previous regulation by law. The chief standards in the act are (1) a minimum hourly wage rate (75 cents by 1949 amendment); (2) an overtime rate, for work in excess of 40 hours in any work week, calculated at one and a half times the regular rate; (3) a prohibition against the employment of child labor; and

13. *J. I. Case Co.* v. *NLRB,* 321 U.S. 332 (1944).
14. *Steele* v. *Louisville and Nashville Railroad Co.,* 323 U.S. 192 (1944).

(4) control, including prohibition, of industrial homework, by regulations of the administrator of the act. The act was the result of depression experience, which strengthened the feeling that the government must set minimum standards of labor conditions to protect public health and safety. Earlier federal legislation excluding goods produced with child labor from interstate commerce had been held invalid on the ground that it regulated local manufacturing and not interstate commerce and therefore was outside the scope of federal power.[15] Legislation fixing minimum wages and maximum hours had been held to be an invasion of freedom of contract.[16] The decision upholding the National Labor Relations Act weakened these precedents, and thus the way was open to declare the Fair Labor Standards Act constitutional.[17]

The legal basis of federal jurisdiction over employment conditions in the Wage-Hour Act is somewhat different from that in the Labor Relations Act. Its standards are applicable to employment in the production of any goods shipped in interstate commerce. Since these goods compete with similar goods moving in interstate commerce, Congress, it is held, is entitled to regulate labor conditions in the respective industries in order to prevent unfair methods of competition. As in the antitrust laws, this task implies discrimination between sound and harmful competition. It is assumed that competition that secures a cost advantage by low wages, long hours, exploitation of child labor and the like is harmful to the community and therefore unfair. Hence, the federal government is entitled to take measures against such competition. This theory was a skillful adaptation of the theory of the antitrust laws regulating restraint of trade and monopoly in interstate commerce.

The Wage-Hour Act is enforced directly through suits in court, brought either by the administrator or by aggrieved employees. The federal courts therefore have had the main responsibility for interpreting the standards. Because of a bitter, protracted legislative conflict within the Democratic Party, the statute was broadly worded, and it was feared at first that judges would narrow its meaning by interpretation. Some early decisions tended in that direction. The Supreme Court, however, has applied the act broadly, as when it held working hours to include travel and make-ready time,[18] a decision that made wages payable to many workers for time not previously included in paid hours. Several unions pressed the Court's ruling to extremes and brought suits claiming billions of dollars of back pay, until, in 1947, employers obtained amending legislation limiting their liability.

Public Contracts Act

The Public Contracts Act prescribes labor standards in the performance of work under government contract. It is a special regulation and has a special legal basis, namely, that Congress may fix the terms on which the executive branch will let contracts, and the courts will not review the exercise of executive discretion under the act.[19] The enforcement of the standards as part of a contract in a particular case is subject to judicial review.

FEDERAL LABOR WELFARE LAWS

The most important federal law in the field of labor welfare is the Social Security Act of 1935, amended in 1939 and 1950. It was preceded by the Railroad Retirement Act of 1934, which has similar objectives for railroad workers. The two systems of social security operate independently.

Old-Age and Survivors Insurance

The provisions of the Social Security Act for federal old-age and survivors insurance represent the third great piece of federal legislation affecting employment, ranking with the National Labor Relations Act and the Fair Labor Standards Act. In addition to the old-age program, the Social Security Act of 1935 established federal-state unemployment insurance and federal grants-in-aid to various state welfare programs, including aid, in cases of need, to the aged, the blind and families with dependent children.[20] Federal old-age insurance was converted into old-age and survivors insurance by the amendments of 1939 and its coverage was broadened in 1950. It is financed by a tax on

15. *Hammer* v. *Dagenhart,* 247 U.S. 251 (1918).
16. *Adkins* v. *Children's Hospital,* 261 U.S. 525 (1923).
17. *United States* v. *Darby,* 312 U.S. 100 (1941).
18. *Jewell Ridge Corp.* v. *Local No. 6167,* 325 U.S. 161 (1945).
19. *Perkins* v. *Lukens Steel Co.,* 310 U.S. 113 (1940).
20. For further information see Chapter 14.

employers' payrolls and on employee wages.

Since old-age benefit rights and amounts are based on a worker's record of covered employment and wages over his entire working life and since many workers move from state to state, a federal rather than a state system was considered necessary. The constitutionality of the Social Security Act was attacked on the grounds that public welfare is constitutionally as well as traditionally a matter of only state and local concern and that the federal government could not tax and spend for old-age pensions or unemployment compensation. The Supreme Court cast this proposition aside. The Constitution gives Congress power to tax and spend for the "general welfare" of the people. The concept of "general welfare" is not static, the Court asserted, but depends on contemporary judgments. "The purge of nation-wide calamity that began in 1929 has taught us many lessons," said the Court, and one of them is that federal action is necessary to save men and women from the "rigors of the poor house," whether because of unemployment or old age.[21]

The decision upholding the Social Security Act obviated a test of the constitutionality of the Railroad Retirement Act. Administration of these laws involves relatively few legal issues, except for occasional questions of coverage and benefits; the courts have consequently had little to do with them.

Federal Workmen's Compensation Laws

Railroad workers, longshoremen and seamen are special objects of federal labor legislation because their employment is in the physical handling of goods moving in interstate commerce and foreign commerce. Railroad workers were the first to be assured of compensation for injuries arising out of their employment. The first statute, in 1906, was held unconstitutional because it did not expressly except from its provisions railroads engaged only in intrastate commerce.[22] A carefully drafted second statute was quickly enacted, and this one was upheld, the Supreme Court pointing out that the safety of workers is obviously related to efficient transportation.[23] The statute changed the old common-law definition of an employer's liability for injuries arising in the course of employment, making him liable except where the accident is due solely to the employee's own carelessness. This change made recovery in suits at law likely for almost all accidents.

The law did not create any special commission, and claims not settled by the parties are tried in the courts. The statute permits railroad workers to sue not only in the federal courts but also in the more numerous, and hence more accessible, state courts.

The same procedure is used in the workmen's compensation act for seamen, but claims of longshoremen are heard in the first instance by an administrative commissioner. The longshoremen's act is patterned after state workmen's compensation legislation described later in this chapter.[24]

Other Federal Laws Significant for Labor

Congressional Investigations

The investigatory powers of Congress are unique and are practically unlimited by the executive or judicial branches. Their formal function is to help the legislature decide whether legislation is needed and, if so, what kind. They also serve other purposes, principally to bring facts or opinions to public notice.

Congressional hearings have played a dramatic role in labor legislation. The reports of industrial commissions in 1902 and again in 1916 provided moral support to unions long before labor relations acts afforded them statutory support. The findings of these reports have been used repeatedly to prove the persistent fundamental claims of the labor movement.[25]

Years of hearings before congressional committees preceded the 1947 revision of the National Labor Relations Act. The testimony at these hearings confirmed the public's impression that labor had abused its powers and made apparent the refusal of union leaders to offer any remedial measures.

The Criminal Law

Criminal statutes, since they are not effective for detailed regulation but rather serve to police the outer limits of allowable conduct, have been

21. *Helvering* v. *Davis,* 301 U.S. 619 (1937).
22. The Employers' Liability Cases, 207 U.S. 463 (1908).
23. Second Employers' Liability Cases, 223 U.S. 1 (1912).
24. For further information see Chapter 16.
25. See *NLRB* v. *Jones and Laughlin,* previously cited, p. 43.

of relatively little use in federal regulation of labor relations. Though the Railway Labor Act, for example, provides a criminal penalty for breach of collective bargaining rights, this penalty has rarely been invoked and the statute has been enforced mainly by the judicial power of injunction. Present-day administrative regulation of industrial relations is derived from the judicial civil injunction, rather than from criminal law.

Criminal penalties are, however, part of the enforcement scheme of the Wage-Hour Act, which uses them mainly as a threat to compel compliance by the many small employers affected by its provisions. Criminal penalties carry a threat that is not conveyed by the cease-and-desist orders of an administrative agency, which warns before it punishes.

Executive Powers

In addition to federal statutory regulation, independent executive and judicial powers are exercised over labor relations and employment conditions. Presidents have influenced critical labor disputes considerably. Grover Cleveland, for example, broke a railroad strike in 1894 by ordering federal troops into action to protect the mails and keep the trains running. Theodore Roosevelt mediated the 1902 anthracite coal strike and helped establish the coal miners' union. Harry S. Truman settled the steel strike of 1946. Such exercise of presidential power is formalized in the emergency boards established by the Railway Labor Act and the Labor-Management Relations Act of 1947.

In time of war, when presidential authority expands into the powers of Commander-in-Chief, presidential policies become decisive for labor relations. Both Wilson and Franklin D. Roosevelt favored the principles of collective bargaining; and the War Labor Boards of 1917 and 1942 decided disputes by applying these principles.

The Supreme Court and Constitutional Rights

Besides playing an important role in the development of statutory regulations of collective bargaining and employment, the Supreme Court has made independent contributions to the cause of labor in its decisions protecting the exercise of civil liberties in employment relations. Thus the Court has held peaceful picketing to be an exercise of the constitutional right of freedom of speech, which "in the circumstances of our times" it has also held to include the peaceful dissemination of information about labor disputes. It has set aside convictions under state and local laws forbidding picketing, directly or indirectly, as disorderly conduct [26]—though the constitutional protection afforded to picketing has been greatly restricted in later cases.

The right to picket is not an absolute freedom. Besides prohibiting violence and disorder, the Supreme Court has upheld bans by state legislatures and state courts on picketing in certain situations, for example, where a union has no members, or where it is in aid of a monopoly in violation of antitrust law.[27] In some cases the Court has held the distribution of leaflets to be an exercise of freedom of the press,[28] and union meetings to be constitutionally protected by the right of free assembly.[29]

These freedoms are also protected by federal criminal law penalizing state or local officials who deny people their constitutional rights. Local officials who halted the distribution of union leaflets at plant gates or prevented union meetings or peaceful picketing have been threatened with federal prosecution. Notice of the Supreme Court decisions has often been sufficient to end interference with union activities. These decisions served to break down the hostility of local authorities to the activities of union organizers in their communities.

FEDERAL-STATE COOPERATION

The federal government and the states cooperate on various welfare programs, unemployment insurance and employment services. Through grants-in-aid to states, the federal government helps finance various state welfare programs, such as assistance to needy aged persons, the needy blind and needy families with dependent children. This kind of pure subsidy is not new; federal aid in financing the building and maintenance of local highways and other improvements is as old as American politics.

---

26. *Thornhill* v. *Alabama,* 310 U.S. 88 (1940); *Carlson* v. *California,* 310 U.S. 106 (1940).
27. *Building Service Employees International Union, Local 262* v. *Gazzam,* 339 U.S. 532 (1950); *Giboney* v. *Empire Storage & Ice Co.,* 336 U.S. 490 (1949).
28. *Schneider* v. *Irvington,* 308 U.S. 147 (1939).
29. *Hague* v. *CIO,* 307 U.S. 496 (1939).

Unemployment Insurance

The Social Security Act imposes a federal tax on payrolls for unemployment insurance, but only a fraction of this tax is taken by the federal tax collector, the rest being offset by employers' payments under state unemployment insurance systems, provided the state systems conform to certain standards. In addition to allowing the tax offset, the federal government makes grants to states to pay the administrative costs of state unemployment compensation agencies. Every state now has an approved unemployment compensation law.[30] This federal-state program was held constitutional at the time the provisions for old-age insurance were upheld.[31]

Perhaps unemployment compensation could be more efficiently administered under federal auspices, but its state basis was a political compromise conciliating sentiment for such a measure with fear of increasing federal power. This fear was potent not only in states that reluctantly agreed to establish unemployment insurance under pressure of the federal tax but also in Wisconsin, the pioneer in unemployment insurance.

Employment Services

Federal grants-in-aid help to finance state employment services. While such services could best be maintained nationally, particularly in view of the interstate nature of the labor market, the states have held them to be part of the unemployment insurance program. During World War II, when labor mobility had to be channeled to meet war production needs, the President asked the state governors to "lend" the state employment services to the federal government for the emergency, and they did so. At the end of the war, after a brief skirmish on Capitol Hill, Congress passed a law directing the speedy return of the services to the states.[32]

State Laws

Labor Relations

Much of state government and state legislation is patterned on or similar to federal models, but there are important variations and some purely state measures. The first state labor relations acts, for example, were modeled after the federal legislation, as were the state anti-injunction laws. But while Congress resisted changes, the states moved toward prohibiting unfair labor practices by unions, Minnesota and Wisconsin being among the first to do so. The provisions of these state laws were forerunners of many amendments to the National Labor Relations Act.

The rapid increase in the size and strength of unions since 1940 has led to the outlawing of the requirement of union membership as a condition of employment in some eighteen states. In most of these states agriculture prevails over industry, and half of them are in the South. The Supreme Court upheld the power of the states to enact these laws,[33] rejecting union arguments that the laws were forbidden either by federal regulations of labor relations or by provisions of the Constitution. The Court has thus removed itself from the arena of dispute over legislative policies and left to the ballot box decisions on the wisdom of specific labor regulations. At the same time it has maintained an important area of state action.

Workmen's Compensation

The workmen's compensation laws, which exist in all states, establish insurance against work-connected accidents and, in some instances, disease. They have become an established and permanent part of our industrial code, but their adoption in the 1900's involved a radical change in legal doctrine.

Before these laws were enacted, an employer's liability for the costs of injuries suffered by his employees in the course of their employment was governed by judicial common law. The common-law rules were, significantly, classified under the legal category of master and servant. The employer was not liable for industrial injuries in most cases, because the employee assumed the common risks of employment. He was not liable for injury resulting from the carelessness of a fellow employee. He was liable only when he or one of his supervisory agents personally was at fault, and an employee's own carelessness could bar him from recovering any compensation for his injuries even though all the other conditions of employer liability were met. Litigation was frequent and lengthy; juries

30. See Chapter 14.
31. *Steward Machine Co.* v. *Davis,* 301 U.S. 548 (1937).
32. See Chapter 15.

33. *Lincoln Federal Labor Union* v. *Northwestern Iron and Metal Co.,* 335 U.S. 525 (1949).

would find for injured workmen regardless of the rules of liability, and employers would then appeal to have the jury verdicts set aside as contrary to law.

For the uneven and unjust distribution of costs under this system, workmen's compensation statutes substituted an insurance plan, under which the costs of specified industrial accidents were spread among groups of employers and were made a part of the costs of production. Compensation for a specified class of injuries was guaranteed, regardless of fault on the part of the employee, short of willful recklessness, and at the same time the benefit amounts were limited and fixed.

Though the statutes uprooted the old legal rule of no tort liability except for fault and substituted a system of insured absolute liability, the Supreme Court found the scheme so eminently practical that it easily upheld the laws.[34] Mr. Justice Holmes wryly observed that industrial accidents "probably will happen a good deal less often when the employer knows he must answer for them if they do." The Court justified state action by pointing to the social consequences of uncompensated industrial injuries: the health and safety of workers suffered, with risk of consequent poverty, vice and crime. These were legitimate objects of legal concern. A sense of moral responsibility combined with social reform to validate workmen's compensation laws.

These laws were the first to break down the old concepts of individual contract governing employment relations, replacing them by modern ideas of social insurance and collective responsibility. They were helpful precedents in the argument for insurance against the risks of unemployment.

Since one of the evils of the old system was lengthy and expensive litigation, workmen's compensation laws were placed under administrative commissions, lawyers' fees were regulated, and proceedings were simplified to factual presentations. The courts retained supervision through their power to settle questions of law. Thus, the workmen's compensation statutes paved the way for use of the administrative agency as a device for regulating economic affairs. They were used also as an argument for placing unemployment compensation on a state-unit basis. At the present time, the statutes in the forty-eight states present a varied picture; some states have hardly changed the laws since their first introduction, others have improved and extended the coverage and amount of benefits.[35]

Health and Safety Laws

In the same category as the workmen's compensation statutes are the state laws protecting the health and safety of workers, such as laws requiring safe machinery and ventilation or prohibiting child labor and night work by women. All these laws have essentially the same justification, that the state may regulate employment in order to protect the health, morals and safety of its inhabitants. This justification represents a moral idea — that the weak and helpless should be protected against superior forces and unfavorable circumstances.

The law has sometimes been ignorant of economic realities and been slow to recognize well-rooted economic changes; but it also has imposed moral ideas upon economic relations. The law is always moralistic, though the moral principles it applies may vary from time to time or may be in conflict with the current situation. From 1900 to 1936, when the Supreme Court and state courts nullified some protective labor legislation, they did so on moral principles of freedom of contract and individual self-help, but these principles tended to yield when catastrophes such as fires, explosions and economic depression altered the view of economic realities.

New York State, which has been a leader in protective labor legislation, was stirred to action in 1911 by the Triangle Shirt Waist disaster, in which more than a hundred women employees in a New York City loft, locked to keep out union organizers, jumped or burned to death when fire broke out. More recently, a major coal mine explosion left employers morally disarmed against union demands for federal safety inspection and a comprehensive welfare plan financed by a tax on coal.

Experience in the depression of the 1930's ushered in the final legal triumph of the moral principle of protecting the weak over the tradition of individual self-help and endurance of suffering. In the economic distress, even the strongest were helpless to remedy their misfor-

34. Arizona Employers' Liability Cases, 250 U.S. 400 (1919).

35. See Chapter 16.

tune. Thirty years of judicial resistance to protective state legislation had placed a heavy strain on the American system of government. The Supreme Court, often by a bare majority of five to four, had invalidated legislation supported by popular majorities. The Court, its critics pointed out, was exceeding its function as umpire of a federal-state, individual-rights system and imposing its own "economic predilections" upon the entire government. When the Supreme Court abandoned its previous values and accepted those of the New Deal, it did so by accepting the view that the welfare of the weaker and exploited classes in the community is a deserving and special object of legislation. In so doing it opened the door to state legislation of a protective nature. In 1939, the Fair Labor Standards Act was validated on this basis.[36]

Before that time, regulation of hours of work of minors and women was permitted, but regulation of men's hours only in dangerous occupations.[37] Minimum wages for women had been rejected by the Court even though proponents of such legislation argued that economic hardship often forced women into prostitution.[38] The depression proved that men and women, employees and employers, are demoralized when wages fall far below prevailing standards. American social and legal philosophy has always added a pragmatic element to its legal moralizing. Eliminating unsafe and substandard conditions, promoting equality in labor relations and ensuring economic security are, it is always urged, not only morally right, but also necessary to a prosperous economy.

Employment Agencies

Before the depression, state regulation of the fees of employment agencies had also been barred by Supreme Court decision, though it was argued that workers often had to pay exorbitant fees and sometimes were defrauded by being sent to nonexistent jobs.[39] Later the Court permitted licensing of employment agencies and prevention of excessive fees and fraudulent practices; and finally it allowed statutes directly to fix the maximum amount of fees.[40]

36. *United States* v. *Darby,* 312 U.S. 100 (1941).
37. *Muller* v. *Oregon,* 208 U.S. 412 (1908); *Holden* v. *Hardy,* 169 U.S. 366 (1898).
38. *Adkins* v. *Children's Hospital,* 261 U.S. 525 (1923).
39. *Ribnik* v. *McBride,* 277 U.S. 350 (1928).
40. *Olsen* v. *Nebraska,* 313 U.S. 236 (1941).

Experience during the depression encouraged the establishment of public employment services by the states, aided by a federal subsidy. No legal questions were raised, since the public services are entirely voluntary except for people who claim unemployment insurance benefits, who must register with the state employment service and take suitable jobs offered to them by the public service.[41]

State Criminal Laws

The anti-closed-shop statutes mentioned earlier are a recent application of criminal laws to labor relations. Criminal laws have been used most dramatically, from the days of the Haymarket bombing to the disorders in the 1946 strikes.

In the American scheme of government the states are the chief guardians of public order; cities and towns make minor police regulations and federal criminal law is restricted to special offenses. State criminal laws are enforced in the first instance by local police and county sheriffs, supplemented by a small highly trained state police force, used mainly for highway patrol. The state governor controls an emergency police force, the National Guard. He can send in troops to aid local police authorities or he may take over direct and complete control by declaring that an emergency exists and imposing martial law upon an area. Martial law supersedes civil law, including the basic right of habeas corpus, which limits criminal law to specific crimes and offenses and ensures the right to bail pending trial.

These emergency powers have been invoked in labor disputes when masses of workers have gathered to shut down plants and prevent others from taking their jobs. One reason why craft unions were more easily established in this country than industrial unions is that, in addition to other advantages their members possessed as skilled workmen, they acted together in small groups. Their picket lines did not create a general civil commotion, and local police authorities were likely to be sympathetic to local artisans. Moreover, their chief weapons were boycotts and refusal to work on nonunion goods or with nonunion employees. Thus, legal resistance to the spread of craft unions was centered in judicial regulation of boycotts, while the rise of mass industrial unions was checked by criminal laws.

41. See Chapter 15.

State criminal laws are outer limits, invoked most typically when differences between unions and employers break out into violent physical conflict. The ghost of violence haunts labor relations in an economic depression. It is likely to be at hand on the first introduction of collective bargaining in hitherto employer-controlled relations. But once this stage is passed, the criminal laws lose significance. They are not continually applied to regulate employment relations.

Local Labor Law

Local labor regulations are confined chiefly to licensing workers in certain occupations, such as building craftsmen and barbers, and — in the larger cities — to health and safety regulations. Local police regulations concerning breach of peace, disorderly conduct, littering of streets, parades and house-to-house solicitation have been of critical importance to the growth and spread of unions. The removal of these local restrictions by Supreme Court interpretation of the Constitution is a concrete and dramatic illustration of the importance of fundamental law in American life.

Once established, unions become lawful elements in the community, and they now are rarely troubled by local police regulations. Free local association lies at the base of the American social and legal system. National political parties are coalitions and combinations of local parties and interests. Economic problems require federal legislation, but senators and congressmen respond most sensitively to their local constituents. Equally responsive to local public opinion are local officials charged with the administration and enforcement of local laws and regulations.

The durability and permanence of relationships between employers and employees in this country are a product of the local association of employers and employees in other social relations, such as politics, religious devotions and fraternal societies. The ultimate guarantee of a democratic, limited government, as expressed in the *Federalist,* lies in the existence of "so many parts, interests and classes of citizens that the rights of individuals, or of the minorities, will be in little danger from interested combinations of the majority." [42]

It has often been thought that economic interests determine the character of a legal system. In many important respects, economic forces have molded American laws dealing with employment, wages, collective bargaining and collective agreements. The force of economic pressure is modified, however, as the law is fitted into the American scheme of government and shaped by the legal philosophy of American politics.

42. The *Federalist,* No. 21.

CHAPTER 11

REGULATION OF CHILD LABOR *

IN OUR SYSTEM of labor law, regulation of child labor is among the measures designed to protect the physical health and safety of workers and the common welfare. It is based essentially on the idea of protecting the weak. The virtual abolition of paid child labor resulting from legislation over more than a century is perhaps the most impressive evidence of economic and social progress in the United States.

In poorer countries, the unremitting labor of young and old, men, women and children, is the price of survival. As industrialization and modern technology make human labor more productive, a smaller part of the total population can supply a country's demands for goods and services, even though the variety and amount of goods demanded by the people is greatly increased.

An initial effect of the Industrial Revolution was to make it possible for unskilled workers, using simple machines, to perform work previously done by skilled craftsmen. Women and children, whose labor had been taken for granted in an agricultural and family-enterprise economy, thus were able to work in mills, factories and mines. The drop in child mortality helped further to ensure a plentiful supply of cheap, unskilled labor.

In industry, however, children lacked many of the safeguards they had when they worked at home as members of the family or under paternalistic relationships like that between apprentice and master. Indignation was soon aroused by the sight of young children at work in factories from dawn to dark. Their monotonous industrial tasks, moreover, unlike work on a farm or in a craft, had little value in teaching skills that would be useful in later life.

With the rise of industrialization and urbanization, formal education became more and more important to the individual and the nation. Laws requiring school attendance complemented legislation directly concerned with regulating or abolishing child labor. Later the declining birth rate helped direct attention to the importance of the quality of the nation's population. Apart from its humanitarian aspects, exploitation of children that endangered their physical and mental growth was seen to be socially wasteful. The availability of cheap and docile labor, furthermore, acted as a brake on the efforts of adult workers to improve their wages and working conditions. Labor unions early joined women's clubs and religious and civic organizations in opposing child labor. To some extent, the development of modern industrial technology has helped to eliminate children from the labor force. Modern machines are too complicated for a child to operate.

Regulation of child labor is essentially a function of the states and is supplemented by federal laws relating either to certain industries (the Public Contracts Act and the Sugar Act) or to the whole field of interstate commerce (the Fair Labor Standards Act).

STATE LAWS

In 1842 Massachusetts established a 10-hour working day as the maximum for children under 12 years of age, Connecticut for children under 14. But these states were far ahead of their time. Employment of young children in coal mines, steel mills, glass factories and textile mills for 12 or 13 hours a day remained a common practice in this country long after the middle of the nineteenth century.

At its first convention, in 1881, the American Federation of Labor asked that the states abolish employment of children under 14 years of age. In their efforts to improve child labor laws, labor unions and women's organizations were later aided by the National Consumers League, organized in 1899. The persistent and combined efforts of these organizations have led to remarkable progress in the scope and standards of child labor legislation at both the state and federal level.

In 1880 few states had laws regulating hours for children in factories. Only one state regulated hours for children in "any gainful occu-

* By Judith Grunfel, formerly Labor Economist, Bureau of Labor Statistics, U.S. Department of Labor.

pation." The maximum work day was fixed at from 10 to 12 hours; only one state had a maximum as low as 8 hours. By 1930 all but four states had child labor laws for manufacturing establishments, and about two thirds of the states had laws covering various nonmanufacturing occupations.

During the 1930's the states made considerable progress in child labor legislation. The "codes of fair competition" of the National Industrial Recovery Administration, established in 1933, prohibited child labor in industries engaged in interstate commerce, in most cases specifying a minimum age of 16 years. Although these regulations were nullified when the National Industrial Recovery Act was invalidated two years later, they greatly influenced state legislation. Labor unions, too, have urged state legislatures to strengthen laws against child labor. Finally, a growing appreciation of education and rising standards of vocational training contributed to progress in raising the legal age for beginning work.

Status of Legislation in 1940

Though protection of child workers advanced throughout the country in the 1930's, legal standards relating to minimum age, maximum hours, night work and hazardous occupations vary greatly from state to state and among occupations in the same state. Standards of enforcement also vary. The White House Conference on Children in a Democracy, held in 1940, declared:

> Uniformity of protection for all the children of America against the injuries of premature and unsuitable employment seems still far in the future. . . . Evidently, the protection afforded by state laws is very uneven.[1]

Employment in Factories

By the end of 1940, thirteen states had established a basic minimum age of 16 years for the employment of children. Only nine states, however, applied this standard to employment at any time in factories. Of the thirty states that fixed a minimum age of 14 for factory work, thirteen permitted employment at a lower age outside school hours or in certain types of establishments. In the states with a 14- or 15-year minimum age, the actual age limitations varied because of numerous exemptions.

Nonfactory Employment

Minimum-age standards for nonfactory employment were somewhat lower and varied even more than those for factory work, particularly with respect to vacation and out-of-school work.

In agriculture and domestic service there was little regulation of child labor except for indirect restriction through school attendance requirements. Street trades were not regulated in twenty-seven states, although larger cities in some states regulated them by municipal ordinance. Of the twenty-one states that had some legislation on this subject, eleven permitted boys under 12 years of age to engage in certain street trades.

Protection of Older Children

For protection of boys and girls of 16 and 17, state laws set different standards according to occupation, age and sex and made various exemptions. Six states did not limit their hours of work at all; twenty-one had hours regulations that applied to girls but left boys free to work any number of hours and at any time; twenty-three states had some legislative restriction on hours applying to both boys and girls, but in some of these the limit was as high as 10 hours a day.

Ten states prohibited night work, with varying degrees of inclusiveness, for both boys and girls aged 16 and 17. Twelve more had some regulations applying only to girls. The other twenty-six states had no limitations on night work for either boys or girls of this age, except in messenger service.

Recent Developments

Under the pressure of wartime demand for labor, the prewar trend toward improvement of child labor regulations was interrupted and standards were relaxed: Three times as many boys and girls aged 14 to 17 years were working in the spring of 1945 as in 1940. Many boys and girls, some of them under 14 years of age, were working long hours, at night, in hazardous occupations or under other unsuitable conditions.[2]

1. *White House Conference on Children in a Democracy,* January 18–20, 1940, Final Report, Publication No. 272, Children's Bureau, 1942, pp. 229–34.

2. *Why Child Labor Laws?,* Publication No. 96, Bureau of Labor Standards, 1948.

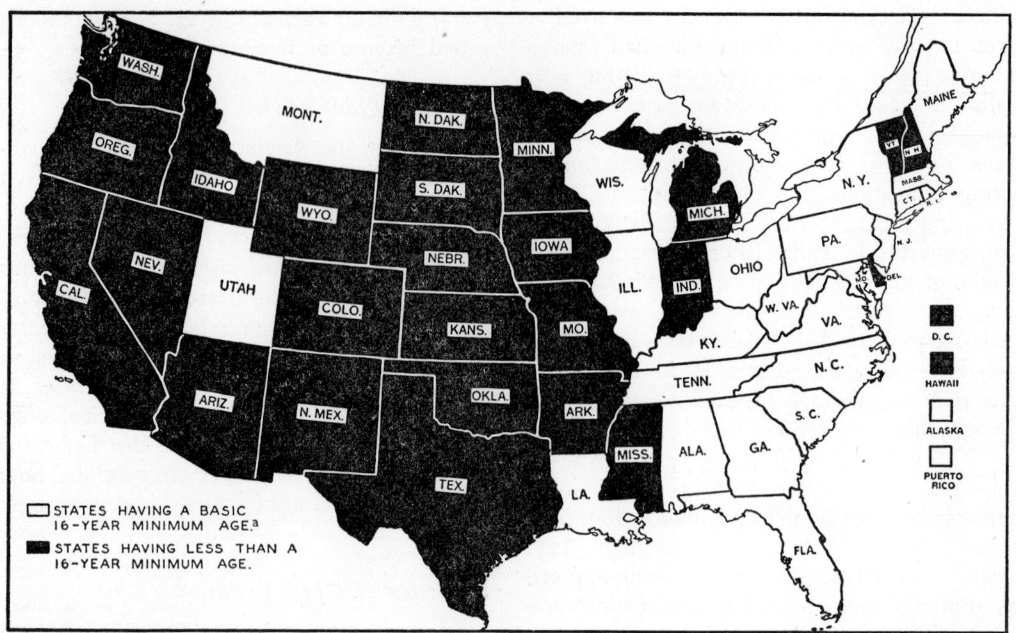

FIGURE 34. BASIC 16-YEAR MINIMUM AGE FOR EMPLOYMENT UNDER STATE CHILD LABOR LAWS, JULY 1950

a. States with this standard have a 16-year minimum age either for factory employment at any time or for all work during school hours, except, in some states, in agriculture or domestic service. A few states have both standards.

Source: Bureau of Labor Standards.

State laws regulating child labor vary in their provisions on the minimum age for employment during school hours and for factory employment in general. In the West, only Montana and Utah have established age 16 as a minimum for factory employment. In the East, this limit is enforced in almost all states, except Vermont, New Hampshire, Delaware and the District of Columbia.

Early in 1945, when many state legislatures were in session, the Children's Bureau initiated a drive to encourage the states to establish a 16-year minimum age for employment in any manufacturing or mechanical establishment at any time or in any gainful occupation during school hours. It also urged improvements in other child labor standards.

Simultaneously the annual conventions of the AFL and the CIO adopted resolutions urging states to set a minimum age of 16 years for employment. The National Child Labor Committee also supported the movement. Many bills were introduced in 1945, and child labor laws were actually improved in seven states — Illinois, Maine, New York, Connecticut, Rhode Island, California and Nebraska.[3]

By July 1950, twenty-three states had met the basic minimum standard of 16 years for employment, as compared with thirteen states at the end of 1940. Despite this noteworthy progress, more than half the states set a minimum age under 16 years for work during school hours or in manufacturing establishments. (See Figure 34.)

The general provision of a minimum age of employment in state legislation is usually accompanied by limitations and restrictions for certain industries and occupations, as illustrated by the New York State regulations, summarized in Table 34.

States vary widely in prohibition of night work, time allowed for meal periods, and limitation of hours of work added to hours in school. Although nearly all states have some provision prohibiting night work for children under age 16, half have practically no such provisions affecting either girls or boys of 16 and 17 years. (See Appendix Table 21.) About one third of the states limit hours of work added to hours in school for children under 16; and only four give this protection to those aged 16 to 17.

Surveys conducted by the New York State

3. Norene McDermott, "States Improve Child-Labor Standards," *The Child,* October 1945, pp. 60–62.

TABLE 34

NEW YORK STATE REGULATION OF HOURS OF EMPLOYMENT OF MINORS

Industry or Occupation	Employees Covered	Maximum Hours Daily	Maximum Hours Weekly	Days per Week	Daily Meal Period (*In Minutes*)	Prohibited Night Work
Factory	High school graduates 14 and 15	8	44	6	60	5 P.M. to 8 A.M.
	Male minors 16 and 17 [a]	8[b]	48	6	60	12 midnight to 6 A.M.
	Females 16 to 21 [c, d]	8[b]	48	6	60	9 P.M. to 6 A.M.
Mercantile and beauty parlors	Minors 14 and 15 [e]	8	44	6	45	6 P.M. to 8 A.M.
	Male minors 16 and 17 [f, g]	8[b]	48	6	45	12 midnight to 6 A.M.
	Females over 16 [d, h]	8[i, j]	48[j]	6[j, k]	45	10 P.M. to 7 A.M.[k]
Hotels and restaurants	Minors 14 and 15	8	44	6	45	6 P.M. to 8 A.M.
	Male minors 16 and 17	8[b]	48	6	45	12 midnight to 6 A.M.
	Females 16 to 21 [l]	8[b]	48	6	45	10 P.M. to 6 A.M.
Elevators	Females over 18	8	48	6	45	10 P.M. to 7 A.M.[m]
Telegraph or messenger service	Male minors 14 and 15	8	44	6	45	6 P.M. to 8 A.M.
	Male minors 16 and 17	8[n]	48[n]	6[n]	45	10 P.M. to 5 A.M.[o]
	Male minors 18 to 21	—	—	—	45	10 P.M. to 5 A.M.[o]
Street trades [p]	Male minors 12 to 17 [q]	—	—	—	—	7 P.M. to 6 A.M.[r]

a. Does not apply to male minors 16 to 18 in fruit and canning establishments between June 15 and October 15, except that such persons shall not be employed between 12 midnight and 6 A.M.

b. May be employed 10 hours in any one day in order to make a shorter work day or holiday in the week. In such case, the shorter work day may not be more than 4½ hours and the other four days may not be more than 9 hours each.

c. Females over 18 in fruit and canning establishments between June 15 and October 15 may work up to 10 hours in any day and up to 60 hours in any week. The Board of Standards and Appeals may adopt rules permitting these employees to work not more than 12 hours per day for 6 days or 66 hours per week between June 25 and August 5. Females over 18 employed in sauerkraut establishments between September 1 and December 1 may work up to 10 hours in any day and up to 60 hours in any week. The prohibition of night work is the same as for other factory employees.

d. These provisions do not apply to stenographers or other office workers (opinion of Attorney General).

e. These regulations also apply to employment of minors 14 to 16 employed in or in connection with any business office, apartment house, theater or other place of amusement, bowling alley, barber shop, shoe-polishing establishment or in the distribution or transmission of merchandise, articles or messages, or in the sale of articles.

f. These provisions also apply to the distribution or transmission of merchandise or articles but not to the delivery of newspapers.

g. The provisions on maximum hours, days per week and prohibited night hours do not apply in mercantile establishments or in the distribution or transmission of merchandise or articles from December 18 to December 24 inclusive, and on two additional days at any time of the year for purposes of stocktaking.

h. The provisions on maximum hours and days per week do not apply to mercantile establishments from December 18 to 24 inclusive, and for two periods each year for the purpose of taking inventory. The number of additional hours worked in each period may be six in a plant working 8 hours 6 days per week, or five in a plant scheduled to work 5½ days. The prohibition of night work after 10 P.M. remains in force.

i. Such persons may be employed 10 hours in any one day in order to make one or more shorter work days in that week; or they may be employed 10 hours on any one day of the week and 9 hours on any of four other days, provided that on the remaining day they work no more than 4½ hours and the total hours worked in the week do not exceed 48.

j. These provisions do not apply to females over 16 years of age employed in beauty shops in cities and villages having a population of less than 15,000.

k. These provisions do not apply to female writers or reporters employed in newspaper offices, or to duly licensed pharmacists.

l. These provisions do not apply to females employed solely as singers and performers or to females employed in resort or seasonal hotels and restaurants in cities or villages having a population of less than 15,000.

m. If elevator is used in connection with a business in which employment of women before 7 A.M. is not prohibited, the operators may begin work at 6 A.M.

n. Limitation on daily and weekly hours applies only to the delivery of articles and merchandise, not messages. Individuals covered may be employed 10 hours in any one day in order to make a shorter work day or holiday in the week.

o. These provisions apply only in cities.

p. Provisions of this section apply only to cities having a population of 20,000 or more, except that the Board of Education of cities having a population of more than 4,500 may elect to come under the law.

q. The education authorities in a city of 20,000 population or more have power to regulate further the work of boys less than 18 but may not lengthen the specified hours.

r. Children 14 and 15 employed in the distribution of newspapers, where they obtain the newspapers for delivery at the place they are produced and the establishment is engaged in interstate commerce, may not begin work before 7 A.M. if they are employed on school days in both the morning and afternoon. (Provision of the federal Fair Labor Standards Act of 1938.)

Source: "An Abstract of Laws Governing the Employment of Minors in New York State," Division of Women in Industry and Minimum Wage, Department of Labor, New York State, June 1943.

Department of Labor and Education showed that high school boys and girls often attempted to carry both a full-time school program and a full-time job, to the detriment of their health and education. The Brook-Coudert Law, enacted in New York State in 1945, limits the employment of boys and girls attending school to 3 hours a day and 23 hours a week at ages 14 and 15 and to 4 hours a day and 28 hours a week at age 16. The limitations apply to all types of employment except farm labor and the sale and distribution of newspapers.

Employment certificates or work permits, usually issued by local public school authorities, are considered a basic requisite for effective administration of child labor regulations. They facilitate enforcement of employment standards established by child labor legislation as well as of educational standards set by school attendance laws. Some states also require attendance of working children at continuation schools for a certain number of hours a week.[4]

Not only have child labor laws improved since the war, but enforcement methods also are becoming more effective. For instance, the educational and enforcement work of the New York State Department of Labor has resulted in a considerable drop in the number of children found illegally employed.[5]

Child Labor Standards

Since 1934, the annual National Conference on Labor Legislation has recommended basic standards for state child labor legislation. These recommendations, which reflect the best experience in state law, are widely accepted as desirable goals.

At the Fourteenth National Conference on Labor Legislation, held in December 1947, the Committee on Child Labor recommended the following standards:

Minimum age — A 16-year minimum age for all employment during school hours and for employment in manufacturing, mechanical and processing establishments at any time. A 14-year minimum age for other employment outside school hours and during vacations.

Maximum hours — A maximum 8-hour day, 40-hour week for minors under 18, with provision for a meal or rest period of at least 30 continuous minutes between the third and fifth hours after commencement of the working day. Combined hours of school and work not to exceed 8 hours a day for minors under 18 years of age.

Night work — Prohibition of night employment of children under 16 between 7 P.M. and 7 A.M., of minors 16 and 17 years of age between 10 P.M. and 7 A.M.

Hazardous occupations — Prohibition of employment of minors under 18 in hazardous occupations, with power given to the state department of labor to determine occupations hazardous for this age group.

Employment certificates — Requirement of employment certificates for minors up to 18 years of age, such certificates to be issued upon presentation of a statement from the employer of his intention to employ the minor, documentary proof of the minor's age, school record showing grade completed, and medical examination showing fitness for the job.

Required school attendance — Requirement of school attendance for all children up to 16 years of age, and for minors 16 and 17 unless they are employed or have completed high school.

Workmen's compensation — Provision for at least double compensation for injuries to minors illegally employed. Consideration of probable adult earnings in computing compensation for any minor permanently disabled or killed.

For effective administration, the committee stressed the importance of adequate penalties. It urged review of penalty provisions and, where necessary, amendment to make the penalty a real deterrent to violation of the law.

The committee expressed great concern over the lack of schooling and the poor living conditions of children who migrate from state to state for employment in industrialized agriculture. It recommended that employment of children in industrialized agriculture be regulated by state child labor laws and that a 16-year minimum age be established for such employment during school hours and a 14-year minimum for employment during vacations and outside school hours.

In presenting its program the committee said:

> The Committee [on Child Labor] believes that the time is at hand to go forward in enacting these standards into law in order to give all the children in the United States the opportunity for education and training, and for the better physical, mental and social development that good child-labor legislation helps to make possible. To this end it urges state labor commissioners and organized labor to take the initiative in mobilizing public opinion and in enlisting the cooperation of other citizen groups to work together to achieve these objectives.[6]

Recommended Standards and Existing Laws

The standards developed by the Fourteenth National Conference on Labor Legislation es-

4. For detailed information by state, see *State Child Labor Standards,* Bulletin No. 98, Bureau of Labor Standards, 1949.

5. *Annual Report of the Industrial Commissioner for 1946,* Legislative Document No. 74, New York State Department of Labor, 1947, p. 371.

6. *Résumé of the Proceedings of the Fourteenth National Conference on Labor Legislation,* December 9 and 10, 1947, Bulletin No. 92, Division of Labor Standards, 1948, pp. 42–44.

tablish the immediate goals for state legislation and show the direction in which this legislation is moving. Nearly every point of the program exists in the laws of some states, but most states are still far behind the program as a whole. The objective of the program is to unify protection of children throughout the nation by strengthening laws in all states along the lines established by the more progressive state legislatures.

Similar standards have been recommended by the International Association of Governmental Labor Officials for State Child Labor Legislation. The extent to which present laws meet these recommendations is shown in Table 35.

Federal Regulations

Apart from the Public Contracts Act of 1936 and the Sugar Act, which contain some provisions limiting child labor,[7] federal regulation of child labor is effected through the Fair Labor Standards Act of 1938. This law prohibits the shipment in interstate commerce or to any foreign country of goods produced in establishments in the United States in which "oppressive child labor" has been employed within thirty days of removal of the goods. "Oppressive child labor" is defined as the employment of minors under 16 years of age in any occupation covered by the act and the employment of minors between 16 and 18 years of age in occupations found and declared to be particularly hazardous by the Secretary of Labor. Children between 14 and 16 years of age may be employed in occupations other than manufacturing and mining if and to the extent that the Secretary of Labor determines that such employment does not interfere with their schooling or their health and well-being. Exemptions include children working (1) in agriculture outside of school hours, (2) as actors in motion pictures or theatrical productions, and (3) for their parents in occupations other than manufacturing or mining.

Where state and federal regulations overlap, the regulation imposing the higher standard prevails. All these provisions of the Fair Labor Standards Act are now enforced by the Wage and Hour and Public Contracts Divisions of the Department of Labor; until July 1946, administration of the child labor provisions was a function of the Children's Bureau, then in the Department of Labor.

What Has Been Done

Administration has followed four general lines: (1) setting standards, based on fact-finding, to define nonharmful work in which children 14 or 15 years of age may be employed as well as occupations particularly hazardous for minors of 16 or 17; (2) inspecting places of employment; (3) making age certificates available to help prevent violations; and (4) bringing injunction suits of criminal prosecution. Thus "administration has been geared to a nation-wide movement toward good labor standards for children, integrating both state and federal activities, and carrying them to a more effective conclusion than would be possible for either state or federal government alone." [8] Enforcement plans require cooperation of state and federal labor departments, since the act provides for the utilization of state labor law enforcement agencies and preserves all higher standards set by state laws.

Several hazardous-occupation orders, issued by the Secretary of Labor after special investigation and public hearings, have raised the minimum age for employment to 18 years in certain occupations.[9]

Experience of more than a decade with the Fair Labor Standards Act has proved the great social benefits of its child labor provisions. Two important loopholes have been found in the provisions of the act, however, which the Secretary of Labor, testifying before a House Education and Labor Subcommittee in 1947, pointed out should be plugged. One of these is in the

7. The Public Contracts Act of 1936 set a minimum age of 16 for boys and of 18 for girls in any work performed under contract for the federal government.

The Sugar Act of 1948, like that of 1937, contains certain provisions with which producers engaged in the production and harvesting of sugar beets or sugar cane must comply to obtain benefit payments. These provisions include a minimum age of 14 years for employment and a maximum 8-hour day for children between 14 and 16 years of age. Members of the immediate family of the legal owner of at least 40 per cent of the crop at the time the work is performed are exempted from these provisions.

8. Beatrice McConnell, "Five Years of Federal Control of Child Labor," *The Child,* December 1943, pp. 83–92.

9. For information on the occupations now covered by hazardous-occupation orders, see *A Guide to Child-Labor Provisions of the Fair Labor Standards Act,* Child Labor Bulletin No. 101, Wage and Hour and Public Contracts Divisions, Department of Labor, 1950.

TABLE 35

MAJOR STANDARDS RECOMMENDED BY THE INTERNATIONAL ASSOCIATION OF GOVERNMENTAL LABOR OFFICIALS FOR STATE CHILD LABOR LEGISLATION AND THE EXTENT TO WHICH EXISTING STATE CHILD LABOR LAWS MEET THESE STANDARDS

Topic	Recommended Standards	Extent to Which State Child Labor Laws Meet Recommended Standards
Minimum age	16 years, in any employment in a factory; 16 in any employment during school hours; 14 in nonfactory employment outside school hours.	23 states, Alaska and Puerto Rico approximate this standard in whole or in part (Ala., Conn., Fla., Ga., Ill., Ky., La., Maine, Md., Mass., Mont., N.J., N.Y., N.C., Ohio, Pa., R.I., S.C., Tenn., Utah, Va., W.Va., Wisc.)
Hazardous occupations	Minimum age 18 for employment in a considerable number of hazardous occupations.	Few, if any, states extend full protection in this respect to minors up to 18 years of age, though many state laws prohibit employment under 18 in a varying number of specified hazardous occupations.
	State administrative agency authorized to determine occupations hazardous for minors under 18.	21 states, the District of Columbia, Alaska, Hawaii and Puerto Rico have a state administrative agency with such authority (Ariz., Colo., Conn., Fla., Kans., La., Maine, Md., Mass., Mich., N.J., N.Y., N.C., N.Dak., Ohio, Oreg., Pa., Utah, Wash., W.Va., Wisc.)
Maximum daily hours	8-hour day for minors under 18 in any gainful occupation.	15 states, Alaska, the District of Columbia and Puerto Rico have an 8-hour day for minors of both sexes under 18 in most occupations (Calif., Ky., La., Mont., N.J., N.Y., N.Dak., Ohio, Oreg., Pa., Tenn., Utah, Va., Wash., Wisc.)
		7 other states have this standard for girls up to 18 (Ariz., Colo., Ill., Ind., Nev., N.Mex., Wyo.)
Maximum weekly hours	40-hour week for minors under 18 in any gainful occupation.	5 states (Ky., N.J., Tenn., Va., Wisc.), Alaska and Puerto Rico have a 40-hour week for minors under 18 in most occupations; 4 states (La., Oreg., Pa., Utah) a 44-hour week for such minors.
		7 other states (Ala., Fla., Ga., Md., N.C., R.I., W.Va.) and Hawaii have a 40-hour week for minors under 16 in most occupations, and 3 states (Miss., N.Mex., N.Y.,) a 44-hour week for such minors.
Work during specified night hours prohibited	13 [a] hours of night work prohibited for minors of both sexes under 16 in any gainful occupation.	10 states, Hawaii and Puerto Rico meet or exceed this standard, at least for most occupations (Iowa, Kans., N.J., N.Y., N.C., Ohio, Okla., Oreg., Utah, Va.)
		13 states and the District of Columbia prohibit 12 or 12½ hours of night work for minors under 16 (Ala., Ariz., Ill., Md., Mass. — 12½ hours; Minn., Mo., N.Mex., N.Dak., Pa., R.I., Tenn., Wyo.). The Alabama law prohibits such work for 12 night hours during the regular school term, and "after 7 P.M." at other times.
	8 [a] hours of night work prohibited for minors of both sexes between 16 and 18 in any gainful occupation.	13 states, the District of Columbia and Puerto Rico meet or exceed this standard, at least for most occupations (Ark., Calif., Conn., Fla., Kans., Ky., La., Mass., Mich., N.J., Ohio, Tenn., Wash.)
Employment certificates	Required for minors under 18 in any gainful occupation.	23 states, the District of Columbia, Hawaii and Puerto Rico require employment or age certificates for minors under 18 in most occupations (Calif., Conn., Fla., Ga., Ind., Ky., La., Md., Mass., Mich., Mont., Nev., N.J., N.Y., N.C., Ohio, Oreg., Pa., Utah, Va., Wash., Wisc., and where continuation schools are established, Okla.). One other state (Ala.) requires such certificates for minors under 17.

a. The numbers 13 and 8 refer to definition of "night work." A law prohibiting work for minors under 16 from 7 P.M. to 8 A.M. and for minors between 16 and 18 from 10 P.M. to 6 A.M. would meet the recommended standards.

Source: Bureau of Labor Standards, July 10, 1950.

wording of the act, which appears to allow employers to resort to the simple expedient of holding up interstate shipment of goods produced by children for thirty days. The other is the fact that the law does not cover employers engaged in interstate communication or transportation. Women's organizations, also, have urged that the statute be amended to forbid the employment of oppressive child labor by employers "engaged in commerce" as well as by employers engaged in "the production of goods for commerce."

CHAPTER 12

REGULATION OF WOMEN'S WORK *

LIKE CHILD LABOR LEGISLATION, regulation of the employment of women was undertaken for the national welfare. The immediate aim has been to protect the health of working women, who often combine the function of wage earner with that of mother. Unlike the child labor laws, which are directed toward curtailment and abolition of child labor, the purpose of the laws for women workers has been to improve their conditions of employment without prejudice to their opportunity to work.

The employment of women is regulated by an agglomeration of state laws enacted at different dates and in different circumstances, repeatedly changed and amended, and in many cases only loosely adjusted to one another. Some types of laws — like those requiring a weekly day of rest and those setting minimum wages — were later extended to cover male workers. The federal legislation on maximum hours and minimum wages for workers of both sexes engaged in interstate commerce was also developed from protective regulations for women workers. Since most women are engaged in intrastate fields of employment, however, state laws are still of primary importance in regulating their employment.

Development of State Laws

The main objectives of state laws protecting women workers are limitation of hours of work, requirement of a day of rest, prohibition of night work, and regulation of homework. Each of these types of regulation has a long history. Progress was slow before the turn of the century, and some of the most important regulations have become effective only in the past two decades.

Early Regulation of Hours

The first attempt to protect women workers by a state law was made in 1845, when the Lowell Female Labor Reform Association, a group of workers in Massachusetts textile mills, urged the state legislature to pass a law establishing a 10-hour maximum work day for women. According to their petitions, women had to work 13 to 14 hours a day under unhealthy conditions and thus were "hastening through pain, disease and privation, down to a premature grave." The special legislative committee appointed to consider the petitions carried out the first governmental investigation of labor conditions in the United States. It decided against the proposed legislation. The health of the operatives, the committee reported, was not being impaired by long hours of work, and the state could not reduce hours, because this would endanger its ability to compete with other states. Better conditions should be brought about, the committee pointed out, "by improvements in the arts and sciences, and in a higher appreciation of man's destiny, in a less love for money, and a more ardent love for social happiness and intellectual superiority." [1]

A few years later, in 1852, Ohio enacted a law establishing a 10-hour day for women workers. Minnesota passed a similar law in 1858 and the Territory of Dakota in 1863, and in 1874, Massachusetts followed their example. These laws, like those enacted at the same time for both men and women in several other states, had little effect on actual hours of work. No penalty was provided except when employers "compelled" women to work longer than 10 hours, and low hourly wage rates induced women to agree to work longer hours. Not until 1879 did amendments put teeth into the Massachusetts 10-hour law. It can be considered the first enforceable maximum-hour law for women.[2] The first enforceable 8-hour laws for women to have practical effect were enacted

* By Judith Grunfel, formerly Labor Economist, Bureau of Labor Statistics, U.S. Department of Labor.

1. Reported in *Women's Bureau Conference,* February 17–19, 1948, Bulletin No. 224, Women's Bureau, 1948, p. 28.

2. *State Labor Laws for Women with Wartime Modifications,* Bulletin No. 202-5, Women's Bureau, 1946, pp. 7–19.

much later, in 1911, in California and Washington.

The early laws applied exclusively to manufacturing and mechanical establishments. Extension of protective legislation to cover other industries became the next goal. Massachusetts extended coverage to mercantile establishments in 1883. Legislation in other states moved in the same direction. In 1905, Pennsylvania pioneered in passing a maximum-hour law applying to women in "any occupation." This term, however, did not imply universal coverage, for the law made many exceptions.

Day of Rest

California, in 1893, passed the first law requiring a weekly day of rest for women workers. Massachusetts enacted a similar law in 1909. Several states followed suit before World War I. The New York day-of-rest law in 1913 provided for adequate enforcement and applied to men as well as women. Even the most advanced laws of this type had serious limitations in occupational coverage.

Night Work

The first law prohibiting employment of women during night hours in excess of the scheduled work day was enacted by Massachusetts in 1890. It applied to manufacturing establishments and prohibited employment of women after 10 P.M. Only seventeen years later, overtime employment of women in textile mills in Massachusetts was eliminated, in effect, by a regulation prohibiting employment of women after 6 P.M.

Several other states passed laws prohibiting or regulating night work by women at about the same time. The first New York law for adult women, enacted in 1899, was declared unconstitutional in 1907. Six years later new night-work laws were promulgated in New York, covering manufacturing and mercantile establishments; night work by women was later prohibited in other industries, such as restaurants and street railways, and in other occupations, such as messenger service.

Among the states that do not prohibit night work by women, Connecticut, in 1909, was the first to pass a law regulating it.

Industrial Homework

Early legislation regulating homework was directed primarily toward protecting the health of consumers and homeworkers. The more recent laws combine this purpose with protection of labor standards in factories so as to eliminate the competition of homework. Some laws prohibit homework for factory employees; others permit it only where working conditions at home meet the legal minimum standards prescribed for factories.

The first state law to regulate homework, passed by New York in 1884, was declared unconstitutional. Subsequent New York laws emphasized supervision of sanitary conditions of work and obligated employers to obtain employment permits for homework from factory inspectors. Other states introduced licenses for employers or homeworkers. Some states outlawed the manufacture of certain goods under conditions detrimental to the public health. But these measures did not bring about appreciable improvements, for state labor departments were not adequately staffed to inspect licensed homework.

A decisive drive to prohibit homework was launched in the 1930's and found expression in some of the NRA codes and the "model bill" drafted in 1936 by a committee of state labor law administrators in cooperation with the U.S. Department of Labor. Several important industrial states — among them Massachusetts, New York, Pennsylvania and Rhode Island — enacted laws containing provisions similar to those in the "model bill." These states completely prohibit homework on certain commodities and empower state labor commissioners to prohibit it in any industry upon finding that the working conditions (1) are unsatisfactory from the point of view of the safety and health of the workers or (2) do not meet other factory standards. In reference to the second condition, the Women's Bureau points out that:

> Though health had long been a basis for regulation of homework, these states are the first to give formal recognition to the social importance of maintaining desirable working conditions standards in the factory by prevention of undercutting through cheaper manufacture made possible through exploitation of homeworkers.[3]

This observation illustrates the indirect effect of the state laws protecting women workers on labor conditions in general. According to the homework laws of New York, Massachusetts and Pennsylvania, the employer's permit and the homeworker's certificate are subject to revo-

3. *Ibid.*, p. 18.

cation for violation of the conditions under which each is issued. One of the conditions is that the daily hours may not exceed maximum legal factory hours in the state.

The New York State homework law, besides providing for strict control, requires "gradual elimination of industrial homework in order to safeguard the health and welfare of homeworkers and to protect factory workers and industries." The New York Industrial Commissioner is required to inspect the materials issued to the industrial homeworker and the houses in which the work is permitted. In addition to special orders restricting homework in four major industries, the Industrial Commissioner issued a general Homework Order, effective July 16, 1945, which restricts industrial homework in all other industries.[4]

Other state laws also reflect the trend toward a broader social outlook in protecting homeworkers. For instance, Oregon and Rhode Island have prohibited homework in connection with state minimum-wage orders on the ground that since there is no way to ensure payment of legal rates to homeworkers, prohibition of homework is essential to safeguard established minimum-wage rates.

Status of State Laws in 1940

In 1940, forty-three states and the District of Columbia had laws limiting daily and weekly work hours for women in one or more industries. The five states without such laws were Alabama, Florida, Indiana, Iowa and West Virginia.

State laws in effect in 1940 for the regulation of working conditions for women may be summarized as follows:

Maximum hours — Hours of work were limited to 8 or 8½ a day by the laws of nineteen states, to 9 hours in twenty states, and to 10 and more in a few states.

Day of rest — In twenty-three states, labor laws limited the number of days a woman might work in succession, usually to six days out of seven.

Night work — Sixteen states prohibited night work by women in certain industries or occupations.

Industrial homework — Twenty states had industrial homework laws or regulations. Some prohibited entirely the making or processing in homes of specified articles, including foods and beverages, drugs and poisons, surgical and sanitary supplies, toys, dolls, children's clothing and tobacco.

Occupational limitations — Twenty-six states had laws prohibiting or regulating employment of women in one or several specified occupations.

Seating laws — Practically all the states and the District of Columbia had laws requiring some kind of seating accommodations for women workers. Most of these laws provided that women employees be permitted to sit when not actively engaged in their duties; others that seats be used to the extent necessary to preserve health.

Wartime Developments

At a conference called by the Secretary of Labor in January 1942 and attended by state labor officials and representatives of federal departments responsible for defense production, the delegates agreed that the optimum hours for war work by either men or women were the 8-hour day, the 6-day and 48-hour week. They recommended that state departments permit employment in excess of such hours only for limited periods of time and after certain administrative requirements had been satisfied.[5] In the summer of 1942 the eight United States government agencies chiefly responsible for the war program[6] issued "Recommendations on Hours of Work for Maximum Production." This guide to government establishments, field representatives of procurement agencies, and contractors working on war production stressed among others the following important points:

> While a 40-hour week is generally accepted in peacetime there is a widespread and increasing agreement as a result of actual experience, both in this country and abroad, that for wartime production the 8-hour day and 48-hour week approximate the best working schedule for sustained efficiency in most industrial operations. While hours in excess of 48 per week have proved necessary in some instances due

4. *Abstract of Laws Governing the Employment of Women in New York State,* Department of Labor, State of New York, New York, 1948, p. 18.

5. "Statement of Federal War Policy with Reference to State Labor Laws," Department of Labor, January 27, 1942 (mimeographed).

6. War Department, Navy Department, Maritime Commission, Public Health Service, War Manpower Commission, War Production Board, Commerce Department, Labor Department.

to a limited supply of supervisory and skilled manpower, there has been some tendency to continue longer schedules after sufficient opportunity has been afforded to train additional key employees.

Plants which are now employing individual workers longer than 48 hours a week should carefully analyze their present situation with respect to output and time lost because of absenteeism, accident, illness and fatigue. They should reexamine the possibilities of training additional workers now, in order to lessen the need for excessive overtime during the long pull ahead.

Hours now worked in some plants are in excess of those which can be sustained without impairing the health and efficiency of workers and reducing the flow of production.

Referring to several states that had laws at the outbreak of the war setting 60 hours as a legal work week for women, the Women's Bureau said:

The unfavorable effect on production of such overlong hours has been so generally recognized that few employers presumably would wish to employ women, even under war conditions, for as many hours as these state laws permit in peacetime.[7]

During the three war years 1942–1944, twenty-four states and the District of Columbia modified some or all of their laws pertaining to standards for women to take account of the war emergency. Most of the states adopting wartime hours legislation did not provide for outright exemptions from basic standards for all employers but delegated power to the state labor official to grant administrative exceptions, or "permits," to individual employers or industries in special cases. Thus relaxation of standards, where really needed, was permitted for a limited period or for the duration of the war.

Present Regulations

Present state regulations concerning employment of women vary widely. In some states the law applies to a particular group of working women, in others to all women under 21 years of age or even to all women of any age or to all workers of both sexes. In many states some aspects of women's work are regulated by special laws for women, in others, by legislative and administrative acts covering labor conditions of both men and women. (See Appendix Table 22.)

Minimum-wage laws and orders of various types are on the books of twenty-six states and the District of Columbia. (See Appendix Table 23.) In five states — Arkansas, Massachusetts, Nevada, New Hampshire and South Dakota — the minimum-wage laws have statutory rates set by the legislature. The other minimum-wage laws fix no rate but authorize the state commissioner of labor to establish a minimum rate in a particular industry or occupation through wage board procedure. Minimum-wage orders are usually issued by wage boards composed of representatives of workers, employers and the public.

Extended coverage and a marked increase in the level of minimum wages have been achieved through new and revised wage orders issued since the end of World War II. Particular attention has been given to traditionally low-wage trade and service industries, such as laundries, dry-cleaning establishments, restaurants, department stores and other intrastate businesses in which considerable numbers of women are employed.

At the Women's Bureau Conference of State Minimum Wage Administrators in April 1950 the Secretary of Labor urged states having minimum-wage legislation to extend their wage orders to cover more occupations and provide higher rates, and encouraged the Women's Bureau to continue its efforts to promote minimum-wage legislation in states that do not have it.[8]

Standards of the Women's Bureau

The standards established by the Women's Bureau serve the same purpose as the child labor standards examined in Chapter 11. They establish the goals for state legislation, show the direction in which this legislation is moving, and try to promote protection of women by improving state laws along the lines established by the most progressive states.

In January 1950 most of the states were far behind the Bureau's standards. (See Table 36.) Five states had no limits on work hours, either daily or weekly. In half the states, the 8-hour day for women workers had no legal basis. The 9-hour day with a 50- or 54-hour week was the limit in eight states; the 10-hour day with a 50- to 60-hour week, in nine states. One state set a 54-hour weekly limit only. (See Figure 35.)

7. *State Labor Laws for Women,* p. 25.

8. *Report of Proceedings of the Women's Bureau Fifteenth Annual Conference of State Minimum Wage Administrators, Held in Washington, D.C., April 20–21, 1950,* Department of Labor, June 1950, p. 2.

TABLE 36

STATE LABOR LAWS FOR WOMEN IN JANUARY 1950 AS COMPARED WITH MINIMUM STANDARDS ESTABLISHED BY THE WOMEN'S BUREAU

Topic	Approved Standards	States
Maximum daily hours	8-hour day	24 states and the District of Columbia have set 8 hours a day and/or 48 hours a week or less in one or more industries. In 23 of the 24 states (Kansas is the exception), manufacturing establishments are covered by such standards. In Connecticut, daily hours may not exceed 8 in mercantile establishments or 9 in other employment, including manufacturing plants. The 8-48 hours law in Kansas applies to public-housekeeping occupations and telephone exchanges; in manufacturing establishments, the maximum is 9 hours a day, 49½ a week.
Maximum weekly hours	48, with overtime pay for hours worked over 40 up to 48	
Day of rest	One day of rest in every 7 consecutive days	22 states and the District of Columbia prohibit employment of women for more than 6 days a week in some or all industries. In two of these states, Colorado and Utah, the law does not apply to manufacturing establishments.
Meal periods	A lunch period of not less than 30 minutes if food is available on the premises; a longer period if food is not available	27 states and the District of Columbia have provided that meal periods varying from ⅓ hour to 1 hour must be allowed women in some or all industries. This provision applies to manufacturing in all but four of these states.
Rest periods	A rest period of at least 10 minutes in each 4-hour or half-day work period with no extension of daily hours	8 state laws provide such rest periods for employees in various industries.
Night work	Considerations of health and opportunity for normal social life make it desirable, in so far as possible, to eliminate night work	13 states prohibit night work for adult women in certain industries or occupations. In 4 other states, the laws regulate such employment by limiting the number of hours that may be worked at night. In 4 additional states, night-work prohibition applies only to persons under 21 years of age in messenger service. In one other state similar limitations apply only to girl messengers.
Prohibitory laws	Existing legislation prohibiting employment in specific occupations should be studied to determine the need for its continuance. Regulations to reduce the dangers of hazardous work are desirable rather than statutory prohibition of women's employment	17 states prohibit employment of women in mining; several states also prohibit employment in selling intoxicating beverages, or in some hazardous occupations.
Industrial homework	Enactment of legislation leading to elimination of industrial homework through prohibition in all industries, except for handicapped workers entitled to special certificates; or by authorizing the state labor commissioner to issue orders prohibiting homework in additional industries	21 states have industrial homework laws or regulations. In all but three, the law applies to "persons."
Minimum wage	Establishment of a statutory rate applicable immediately to women workers in all occupations in the state; provision for wage boards to raise the statutory rate in accordance with changes in the cost of living; provision for adequate enforcement	26 states and the District of Columbia have minimum-wage laws. Most of them are all-inclusive in their coverage of industries, with a few listed exemptions, usually domestic service and agriculture. The Maine law is the only one of limited scope, applying only to fish packing. In five states, the laws apply to men and women; in five states they apply to women only; in all others, to women and minors.
Equal pay		12 states have enacted statutes that prohibit discrimination in rate of pay because of sex. Two of these, Illinois and Michigan, cover only manufacturing.
Maternity	Leave of absence for a minimum specified period before and after childbirth with re-employment rights. Health legislation containing provision for adequate maternity benefits	6 states have laws prohibiting the employment of women before and after childbirth.

Source: "Summary of State Labor Laws for Women," Women's Bureau, January 1, 1950 (mimeographed).

MAXIMUM WEEKLY HOURS FOR WOMEN IN INDUSTRY a

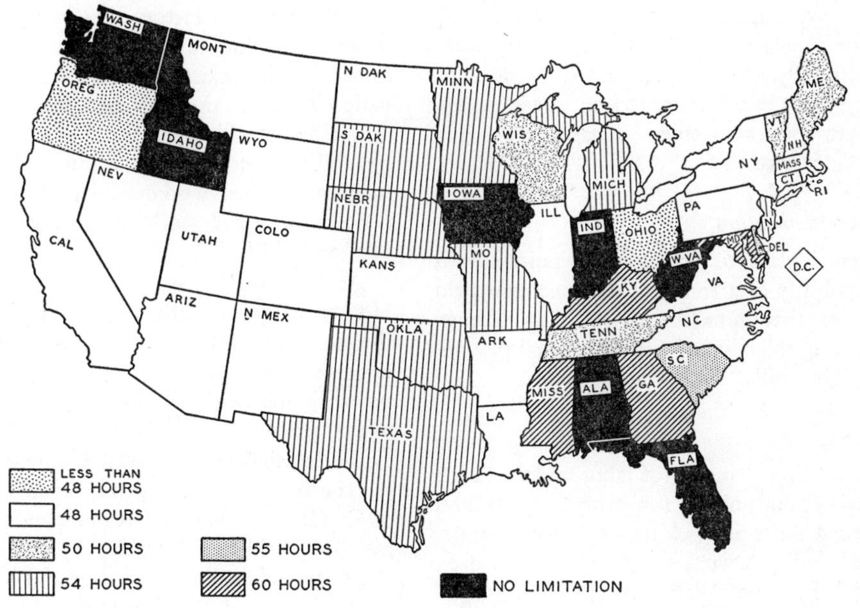

MAXIMUM DAILY HOURS FOR WOMEN IN INDUSTRY a

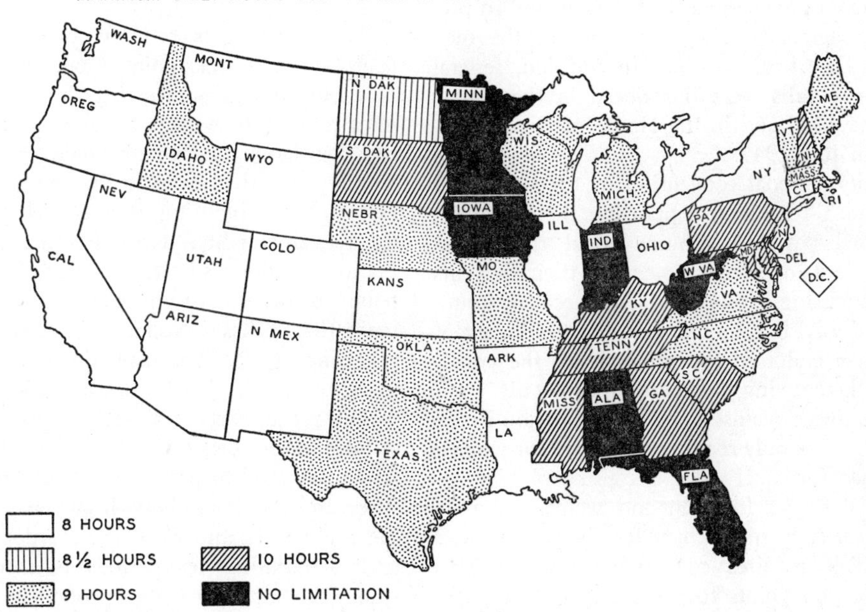

FIGURE 35. STATE LAWS ON EMPLOYMENT OF WOMEN, 1950

a. The standard shown here is that for the industry for which the shortest hours have been set by law.

Source: Women's Bureau.

Maximum weekly hours for women in industry in 1950 were set at 48 or less in most of the eastern industrial states (including New York, New Hampshire, Massachusetts, Connecticut, Pennsylvania), in Ohio and Illinois, in all the western states except Idaho and Washington, and in a few southern states. Nearly all these states limited the daily work of women to 8 hours. Five states (Iowa, Indiana, West Virginia, Alabama and Florida) had no maximum hours for women. Idaho and Washington limited daily hours but had no weekly maximum. Minnesota had a limit for weekly hours but none for daily hours. In Georgia, Mississippi, Montana and South Carolina the hours law indicated applied to men also.

More than half the states did not require a weekly day of rest; twenty-one had no requirement of a pause for a meal; twenty-two states were without minimum-wage laws. Most of the existing laws were restricted in coverage and failed to protect women in agriculture and domestic service.

Pending Legislation

Recent legislative developments point toward the possibility of arriving at some general principles for the protection of working women. This is the objective of pending equal-pay and equal-rights bills.

Equal Pay

The wartime demand for labor widened occupational opportunities for women, permitted them to acquire new skills, and demonstrated their efficiency in work formerly performed exclusively by men. Between 1942 and 1949, largely on the basis of this experience, ten states adopted equal-pay laws designed to ban the traditional underpayment of women and to prevent undercutting the wage rates of the men whom they had replaced.[9] In addition, federal equal-pay bills were introduced in the Senate in June 1945 and in the House of Representatives in July 1947.

At its national convention in 1946 the CIO adopted a resolution supporting the principles of equal pay and genuine equal rights that would not deprive women of their benefits under existing legislation. The Executive Council of the AFL in its report to the 1946 convention also endorsed the principle of the equal-pay bill, reserving judgment on its details.

The clause against wage discrimination in the 1947 bill not only requires equal pay for women and men for equal work, but also prohibits differential wages for men and women who do "work of comparable character, the performance of which requires comparable skills." This qualification points to a most important problem. For many women do not perform work "equal" with that of men, in the exact sense of this term, but do work that is comparable to the work of men and requires comparable, though not necessarily identical, skill. Even in manufacturing, it is not usual for men and women to do exactly the same kind of work. Rather, processes in which women workers have proved more satisfactory than men are for the most part being turned over to women. The same situation exists in the predominantly female clerical occupations and professions, such as nursing, teaching and social work. The equal-pay bills try to ban the traditional underpayment of women workers by replacing the old concept of *equal* work by one of *comparable* jobs and skills.

At hearings before a subcommittee of the House of Representatives in the spring of 1948, the equal-pay bill was supported by women's organizations and several unions but it was opposed by the National Association of Manufacturers, which accepted its principle but objected to the legislation. A special House subcommittee considered the Women's Equal Pay Act of 1949 (H.R. 1584) and recommended that the bill be considered favorably by the full Committee on Education and Labor and be reported to the House of Representatives for passage.[10]

Equal Rights

The equal-rights bill has provoked heated controversy. It was pointed out at the Women's Bureau Conference that the special problems relating to women require special protective legislation and that women can be more readily assured of equality by recognizing this fact than by ignoring it and seeking only a theoretical equality. On the other hand, the National Woman's Party has intensified its campaign for the equal-rights constitutional amendment that it has introduced in Congress each year since 1923. This amendment is designed to abolish all legal discrimination against women; the Party lists 1,101 discriminatory statutes in the forty-eight states, including legislation designed to protect women — minimum-wage and maximum-hour laws, laws prohibiting night work and work in hazardous occupations or requiring rest periods, lunchrooms and seats. According to the proponents of the amendment, these protective laws are designed to keep women out of certain types of work and out of the better-paid jobs, since true protective legislation ought to cover men as well as women. Among the most influential supporters of the equal-rights amendment are the

9. Only two states enacted such statutes after World War I.

10. *Women's Equal Pay Act of 1949,* Report of Special Subcommittee to the Committee on Education and Labor on H.R. 1584, 1950.

National Education Association, the General Federation of Women's Clubs and the National Federation of Business and Professional Women's Clubs.

In 1944 the amendment was endorsed in the platforms of both major political parties. In July 1946 it was voted on for the first time in the Senate and obtained a majority, though far from the necessary two thirds.

Opposing the amendment, labor unions emphasize the increasing need for protective legislation, which for all its benefits has not constituted a handicap to increasing employment of women. It is argued, also, that while the equal-rights amendment, if carried, would throw overboard a century of effort in securing state legislative protection for women, there is no assurance that any such protection will be extended to men in the near future. Moreover, opponents charge that "legal chaos would result from applying a rigid rule of equality to the rights, privileges and responsibilities of men and women." [11]

In February 1947 a bill was introduced in the House of Representatives (H.R. 2003) to establish a commission on the legal status of women in the United States and to declare a policy on distinctions based on sex, in law and administration. This bill declared that it shall be the "policy of the United States that in law and its administration no distinctions on the basis of sex shall be made except such as are reasonably justified by differences in physical structure, biological, or social functions." The bill is designed to secure the advantages of the equal-rights amendment while eliminating its threat to protective legislation for women workers.

The equal-rights amendment (S.J.Res. 25) was debated in the Senate on January 23, 24, and 25, 1950. On January 25, by a vote of 63 to 19, the Senate passed it, after inserting the provision that no "rights, benefits, or exemptions now or hereafter conferred on women" shall be impaired. No action on the measure has been taken in the House.

11. Margaret Perry Bruton, "Present-Day Thinking on the Women Question," *Annals of the American Academy of Political and Social Science*, May 1947, p. 12.

CHAPTER 13

VETERANS PROGRAMS *

MEN AND WOMEN who served in World War II and their dependents represent about one third of the population of the United States. Veterans programs therefore affect, directly or indirectly, the well-being of a large segment of the nation and an even larger part of its labor force. This chapter tells who the veterans are and describes the steps taken by government and private organizations to facilitate their return to civilian life and peacetime jobs.

WHO ARE THE VETERANS?

In the main, veterans [1] were, when they entered service, young, unmarried, of better than average education, with relatively little work experience, and with weak claims to — or even lack of interest in — the jobs they left. Uprooted, impressionable, and somewhat apprehensive of the "deal" they would get after discharge, they wove their new experiences into dreams of and plans for the future.

General Characteristics

An estimated 16.5 million persons served in the armed forces of the United States at some time between September 16, 1940, the beginning of the Selective Service System, and July 25, 1947, the end of the war from the standpoint of many veterans benefit programs. (See Table 37.) About three out of every ten males aged 20 years or over in 1947 and about two out of every three in the 20-to-34 age group had some service. Approximately 11.4 million of the 16.5 million participants served with the Army, 4.2 million with the Navy, 700,000 with the Marine Corps, and 200,000 with the Coast Guard. About 1.5 million, or 9 per cent of all participants, were officers. As of June 30, 1950, more than 15 million participants were in civilian life (i.e., "veterans") and more than 500,000 were still in service (i.e., "potential veterans"). Some 400,000 died in service; about half as many died by mid-1950, after their return to civilian life.

TABLE 37

NUMBER AND STATUS OF WORLD WAR II PARTICIPANTS AS OF JULY 25, 1947

Status	Number, in Thousands	Per Cent
Total	16,535	100.0
Living	16,051	97.1
In civilian life	14,479	87.6
In service	1,572	9.5
Died	484	2.9
In civilian life	75	0.4
In service	409	2.5

Source: Veterans Administration.

Women, numbering about 332,000, represented 2 per cent of all World War II participants. Negroes comprised 9 per cent of all male participants.

The median age of males entering the armed forces in enlisted grades from about the beginning of Selective Service to June 30, 1945 was 23.5 years. As of June 30, 1949, the average age of World War II veterans was 29.9 years; more than half (55 per cent) were in the age group 25 to 34. (See Table 38.)

The length of service of veterans between September 16, 1940 and July 25, 1947 averaged thirty months. About 37 per cent served three years or more; 11 per cent, four years or more. (See Figure 36.) Three fourths of all participants had overseas service, averaging eighteen months.

About 28 per cent of the males who entered the armed forces in enlisted grades before June 30, 1945 were married. By June 1946 the proportion of married veterans had increased to 52 per cent,[2] and by June 1950 to 75 per cent.[3]

* By Irving H. Siegel, Johns Hopkins University, with the assistance of Harry Hoffner, Veterans Administration, and Edgar Weinberg, Bureau of Labor Statistics.

1. The term "veterans," unless otherwise qualified, is used here to refer only to persons in civilian life who served in World War II. Unless otherwise credited, the statistics cited were developed by the Veterans Administration and the Selective Service System from records of the armed forces.

2. *Statistics Bulletin,* National Housing Agency, November 1946 (No. 7), p. 20.

3. Estimated by the Veterans Administration from Bureau of the Census data.

TABLE 38

Percentage Distribution of Living World War II Veterans, by Age, as of June 30, 1949 [a]

Age	Total	Men	Women
Total	100.00	100.00	100.00
Under 20 years	0.40	0.41	0.02
20–24	22.46	22.82	6.72
25–29	32.81	32.38	51.08
30–34	22.42	22.44	22.01
35–39	11.81	11.85	10.01
40–44	6.62	6.65	5.71
45–49	2.33	2.32	3.13
50–54	0.89	0.87	1.23
55–59	0.16	0.16	0.09 [b]
60–64	0.06	0.06	
65 years and over	0.04	0.04	
Average age, in years	29.9	29.9	30.5

a. Refers to veterans who were civilians after July 25, 1947.
b. 55 years and over.

Source: Veterans Administration.

In the main, the physical condition of veterans is above average. Persons with serious defects were generally kept out of the armed forces; in fact, 95 per cent of the men inducted through Selective Service were classified as available for general duty. Despite the complaints of the citizen-soldier become citizen again, he enjoyed a better diet and better medical care than he could usually afford in civilian life. Most of the 1.6 million World War II veterans receiving compensation for service-connected disabilities as of June 30, 1949 were employable. Three fourths of these veterans had disability ratings of 30 per cent or less. (See Table 39.)

As might be expected, the distribution of World War II veterans by geographic area is closely correlated with that of the total civilian population. Regional differences largely reflect the varying impact of Selective Service occupational deferment policies. According to estimates of the Census Bureau, about two out of every three male veterans were urban residents in April 1947.

Education and Employment Background

On the whole, World War II veterans are better educated than other males. Census figures for April 1947 indicate that 59 per cent of all male veterans completed one to four years of high school; an additional 16 per cent completed one or more years of college. (See Figure 37.) For other males aged 18 or over the comparable percentages are 31 and 11. The median for men entering service in the enlisted grades before June 30, 1945 was nine years of schooling; 57 per cent completed one to four

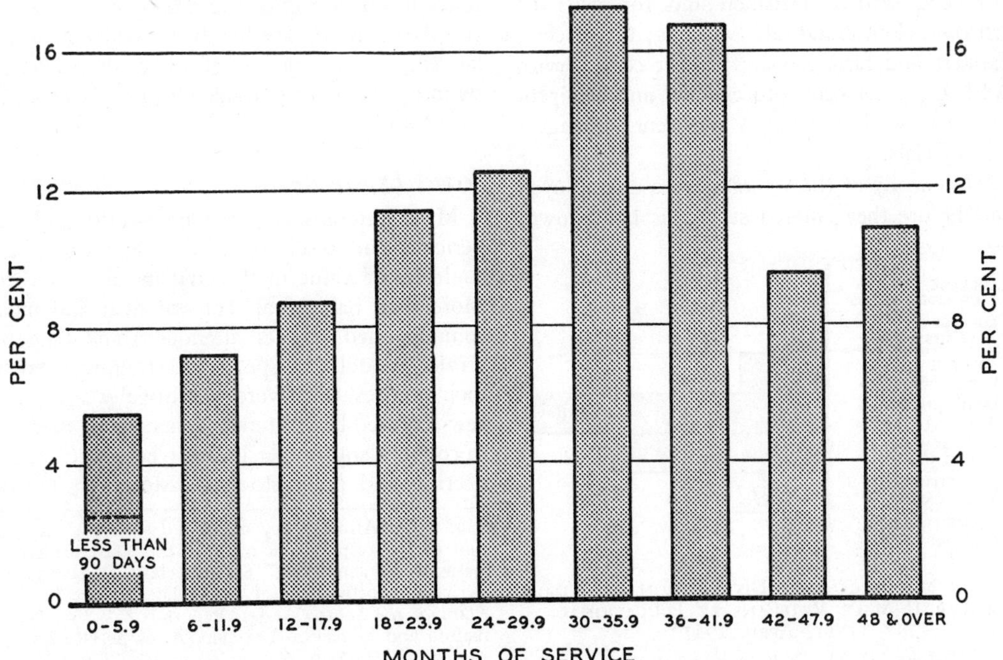

Figure 36. Percentage Distribution of World War II Veterans by Length of Service
Source: Veterans Administration.

TABLE 39

NUMBER AND PERCENTAGE DISTRIBUTION OF SERVICE-DISABLED WORLD WAR II VETERANS, BY TYPE AND DEGREE OF IMPAIRMENT, JUNE 30, 1949

Degree of Impairment	All Disabilities		Tuberculosis		Neuro-psychiatric Diseases		General Medical and Surgical Conditions	
	Number, in Thousands	Per Cent	Number, in Thousands	Per Cent	Number, in Thousands	Per Cent	Number, in Thousands	Per Cent
All veterans [a]	1,638	100	33	100	401	100	1,204	100
10–30 per cent	1,236	76	2	7	276	69	958	80
40–60	281	17	10	31	79	20	192	16
70–90	51	3	1	3	18	4	32	2
100	70	4	20	59	28	7	22	2

a. Includes only World War II veterans receiving compensation.

Source: Annual Report of the Administrator of Veteran Affairs, 1949, p. 173.

years of high school, and an additional 12 per cent had a year or more of college. According to the 1940 census, the male population aged 18 to 44 years had a median of eight years of schooling, and only 41 per cent had completed one to four years of high school.

The armed forces apparently tapped most of the broad occupational categories in proportion to their representation in the labor force. As a result of deferment policies and differences in age and other characteristics, however, relatively more operatives served than managers, officials, farmers and farm laborers. About 39 per cent of the men enlisted before June 30, 1945 had been operatives or laborers in civilian life; 14 per cent, skilled craftsmen and foremen; 12 per cent, clerical and sales workers; 11 per cent, farmers and farm laborers; 5 per cent, service workers; 4 per cent, professional and semiprofessional workers; and 3 per cent, managers and officials.

How many of the veterans were unemployed just before they entered service is not known.

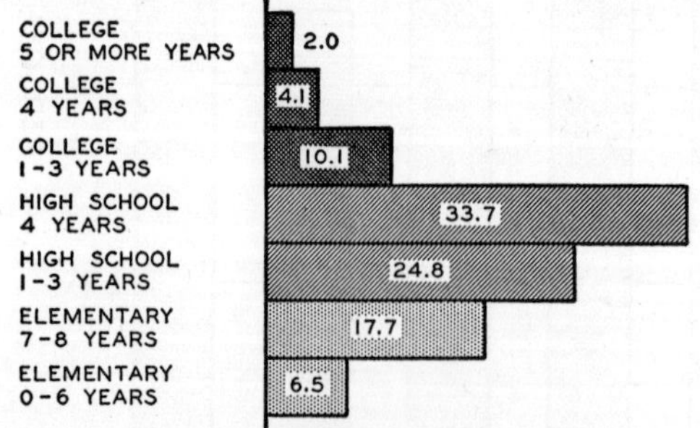

FIGURE 37. PERCENTAGE DISTRIBUTION OF WORLD WAR II MALE VETERANS BY EDUCATIONAL LEVEL, APRIL 1947 [a]

a. Highest school grade completed not reported for 1.1 per cent of World War II male veterans.

Source: Bureau of the Census.

Doubtless many unemployed persons and others with little work experience were included among the 8 per cent of men who entered enlisted grades from "nonclassifiable" occupations by June 30, 1945. Probably many jobless persons were also included among the 5 per cent classified as students.[4]

When the entire labor market experience of veterans is considered, it is clear that unemployment and wartime employment made up a good part of their preservice work histories. Because of the youth and the limited work experience of most veterans, they generally had only tenuous claims or little attachment to the jobs they left. Only a small minority had statutory re-employment rights and would care to exercise them. Relatively few had worked for their last employers long enough to acquire sufficient seniority credit to outrank older or "essential" workers exempted or deferred from service.

Service Experience

Many veterans acquired new skills and experience and received training in service that could be of value in the civilian labor market. More than half of all enlisted men and most commissioned officers attended some type of service school for specialized training. Some took courses that were vocationally useful, a few acquired basic literacy, others were assigned to colleges and universities for languages, engineering and other studies.[5] Moreover, practi-

4. In an Army survey made in 1944, only one per cent of the respondents reported their last preservice status as "unemployed" (or not classifiable) and 10 per cent reported themselves as students. See *Postwar Plans of the Soldier Series,* Report No. B-133, Information and Education Division, Army Service Forces, March 14, 1945, p. 6.

5. See Reports of Commission on Implications of Armed Services Educational Programs, American Council on Education, Washington, 1946–1948.

cally every military occupation has elements in common with one or more civilian occupations. According to an Army survey made in 1944, one sixth of the enlisted men and one fourth of the officers who had been employed before the war and planned a change in their civilian work said they learned their new jobs in service.[6]

Against the worth of such training must be set the opportunities lost through absence from a fluid labor market characterized by good wages, plentiful jobs and rapid upgrading; the deterioration of preservice skills not used in service; and the waste of special abilities through misassignment or underutilization.[7] Furthermore, the transferability of service-acquired skills is restricted in practice by insufficient demand (for example, Air Corps skills usable in commercial aviation); the tendency of employers to discount successful military experience of young men (especially officers) without significant civilian attainments; and institutional barriers such as apprenticeship and seniority requirements.

Postwar Plans

Surveys of the post-separation plans of servicemen, made by the Army in the summer and fall of 1944 and by the Navy in August-October 1945, revealed a widespread desire for change.[8] Many wished to reassert, through self-employment in business or farming, an independence trammeled by military discipline. Others hoped that a change of employer or occupation would give them greater satisfaction. Still others intended to improve their economic and social status through education.

The Army surveys, made while the provisions of the "G.I. Bill of Rights" were little known, revealed that 13 per cent of the men had "definite" plans for self-employment and another sizable group had only "tentative," vague, or even inconsistent plans. In contrast, only 8 per cent said they had been self-employed before service. Furthermore, about one fifth of the white enlisted men and three eighths of the enlisted Negroes definitely planning to enter a business had no previous experience in their projected fields of interest either as employees or in their own business.

According to the Navy surveys, which were made at the end of the shooting war, a large proportion of the male enlisted reserve personnel (26 per cent) and the male reserve officers (19 per cent) not intending to remain in service had plans for self-employment. Closer examination of the replies discloses, however, that more than one third of the enlisted personnel expressing interest in self-employment also had inconsistent plans to work as employees after separation, and another tenth were not employed full time before service. It also appears that more than one fifth of the officers had no experience in the lines they wished to enter.

The surveys suggested that fewer servicemen would return to farms, but they also revealed a considerable interest in farming on the part of veterans with little or no agricultural experience. Thus, 31 per cent of the white enlisted Army men expressed some interest in full-time or part-time farming, but only 8 per cent had definite plans for full-time work on farms. Most of the 8 per cent had at least a year of farming experience; two thirds had definite farms in mind. According to the Navy surveys, about 7 per cent of the enlisted personnel and one per cent of the officers intending to return to civilian life wished to operate farms or ranches, but only two fifths of these enlisted men and one fifth of these officers had previous agricultural experience.

Over three fourths of the Army men who had been employees before service still planned to work for others, but less than half of them planned to return to the same kind of work. More than half of the white enlisted men who had been agricultural, unskilled, semiskilled or sales employees wanted to do other work, to go to school, to be self-employed, or were undecided.

About nine out of ten Navy enlisted men planning to take a job after separation had been

6. *Postwar Plans of the Soldier Series,* Report No. B-133, p. 20.

7. Only 30 per cent of the scientists and engineers responding to a questionnaire indicated that their special abilities were utilized "in primary field and at proper level of competence [training and experience] throughout most of military service." *Scientists in Uniform, World War II,* Logistics Division, General Staff, U.S. Army, 1948, p. 11.

8. *Postwar Plans of the Soldier Series,* especially Reports No. B-129 (March 1, 1945), No. B-130 (January 15, 1945), No. B-131 (December 20, 1944) and No. B-133 (March 14, 1945); also *Report on a Survey of Reserve Officers' Postwar Plans* (January 10, 1946) and *Report on a Survey of Male Enlisted Reserve Personnel Postwar Plans* (January 24, 1946), Research Division, Bureau of Naval Personnel. A comprehensive analysis of the Army reports appears in S. A. Stouffer and others, *The American Soldier,* Princeton University Press, Princeton, 1949.

previously employed, but only half had preservice experience in the occupations they planned to enter. The same was true of Navy officers; for example, about 40 per cent of those wanting employment as managers or officials, 32 per cent of those wanting engineering jobs, and 23 per cent of those wanting to be auditors or accountants had their main preservice experience in other occupations.

Army and Navy personnel, especially the younger single men who had completed high school but not college, expressed keen interest in full-time schooling. About 11 per cent of the white enlisted Army men and 16 per cent of the Army officers had definite or tentative plans for full-time schooling; the corresponding percentages for Navy enlisted men and officers planning to leave the Navy were 19 and 26. Two thirds of the Army men with definite plans for full-time schooling were students before they entered service; about half of the Navy enlisted men and a third of the Navy officers planning to enter full-time courses worked full time before induction.

Employment Aid Programs

The new standard of social responsibility that developed between the two world wars[9] particularly benefited veterans. Plans for their readjustment were devised well in advance of demobilization and were far more comprehensive than those for veterans of any prior war.[10] Since employment is one of the main avenues of readjustment, it naturally was emphasized in aid programs.

Coordination of Programs

The numerous employment programs for veterans were, on the whole, only loosely coordinated. Two new federal bodies were established — the Retraining and Reemployment Administration and the Veterans Placement Service Board. Each state also established an agency to coordinate veterans programs. In many communities, business, labor, veterans', civic and other groups set up advisory centers — often with federal sponsorship (but not funds) — to provide information and service to veterans.

The Retraining and Reemployment Administration was established by Executive Order in February 1944 and incorporated into the new Office of War Mobilization and Reconversion created by act of Congress in October 1944.[11] This act reduced its broad powers under the Executive Order to coordinating the functions of all federal agencies (except the Veterans Administration, the administrator of which was also the first head of the new agency) concerned with retraining, re-employment, vocational education and vocational rehabilitation. The new agency was also authorized to "confer" with state and local officials in charge of similar programs. Perhaps the most important action of its three-year career was its "order" in May 1944 establishing in each state a Veterans Service Committee — representing the Selective Service System, the War Manpower Commission and the Veterans Administration — to cooperate with state agencies and to sponsor the creation of community "Veterans Information Service Centers" where required. Through its advisory council, composed of officials of most federal bodies administering programs in some way affecting veterans, the agency also sought to develop uniform government policy and to coordinate information on benefits. In 1946 it set up standards for on-the-job training, federal civil service employment and employment of the handicapped. Despite arduous efforts, it failed, however, to reconcile the conflicting viewpoints of labor, management, veterans' organizations and federal agencies on veterans' re-employment rights.

The Veterans Placement Service Board was created by the G.I. Bill of Rights in 1944 to "cooperate with and assist" the U.S. Employment Service in carrying out the "intent and purpose" of Congress "that there shall be an effective counseling and employment placement service for veterans and that, to this end, policies shall be promulgated and administered so as to provide for them the maximum of job opportunities in the field of gainful employment." This board — consisting of the Administrator of Veterans Affairs, as chairman, the Director of Selective Service and the Administrator of the Federal Security Agency (or whatever other agency had charge of the U.S. Em-

9. See Chapter 9.

10. See *Demobilization and Readjustment: Report of the Conference on Postwar Readjustment of Civilian and Military Personnel,* National Resources Planning Board, June 1943.

11. Public Law 458, 78th Cong. The Baruch-Hancock report, *War and Postwar Adjustment Policies* (February 15, 1944), was the blueprint for this agency as originally established.

ployment Service) — did its basic work before V-J Day, operating in effect as a subcommittee of the Retraining and Reemployment Administration's advisory council. One of its major actions, taken in August 1945, was to authorize priority for veterans in job referral by public employment offices.[12]

Re-employment

To the Selective Service System was assigned primary responsibility for carrying out the re-employment provisions of the Selective Training and Service Act of 1940.[13] The same law provided for legal assistance to veterans by federal district attorneys, conferred re-employment rights on federal civil service employees, and declared it to be the "sense of the Congress" that state employees "should be restored" to preservice positions.[14] The Veterans Preference Act of 1944,[15] administered by the Civil Service Commission, outlined a program for veterans that goes far beyond re-employment rights.

The Selective Training and Service Act of 1940 and related legislation [16] provided (1) that a qualified veteran who left a position "other than temporary" should be restored to his former position or one of "like seniority, status, and pay, unless the employer's circumstances have been so changed as to make it impossible or unreasonable to do so"; and (2) that a restored veteran should be considered as having been on furlough "without loss of seniority" and not be subject to discharge "without cause" within one year after restoration.

Despite their ambiguity, the re-employment provisions of the 1940 act were never substantively altered in later legislation. Officials of interested government agencies and spokesmen for labor and management groups refrained from pressing Congress for clarification, in the belief that any probable change would increase rather than relieve tension.[17] The original act proved unworkable largely because it was not designed for a drastic conversion to munitions production, a war lasting several years, a military force of millions, or service that turned out to be, on the average, much longer than one year. No administrative machinery was provided for adjudicating the inevitable disputes.[18] Though federal district attorneys and "re-employment committeemen" of local draft boards were fairly successful in obtaining amicable settlements, recourse to the courts was often necessary. Judicial processes finally settled two important points, in May 1946 and April 1947,[19] but the rights of many veterans had expired by the second date.

In May 1944 the Director of Selective Service issued Local Board Memorandum No. 190-A interpreting some of the difficult aspects of the re-employment provisions. The principle of absolute reinstatement and retention for one year set forth in this memorandum (dubbed "superseniority" by its opponents) was bitterly attacked by union leadership and by some employer groups.[20] The controversy raged for some time but, as re-employment friction proved much less serious than anticipated, it seemed to abate even before the first Supreme Court decision in 1946. This, and the 1947 decision, held, in effect, that re-employment rights were not absolute and had to be interpreted within the seniority framework: that these rights protected veterans (1) against dismissal without cause for one year, and (2) against loss of seniority, status and pay upon reinstatement.

12. Under the Reorganization Act of 1949 Congress abolished the Veterans Placement Service Board and transferred its functions to the Secretary of Labor.

13. Public Law 783, 76th Cong. Public Law 26, 80th Cong., approved March 31, 1947, transferred to the Secretary of Labor the re-employment functions of the Selective Service System; as a result, a Bureau of Veterans' Reemployment Rights was established in the Department of Labor.

14. Most states subsequently passed legislation conferring re-employment rights on such employees.

15. Public Law 359, 78th Cong., as amended.

16. Public Res. 96, 76th Cong., and Public Law 213, 77th Cong., as amended.

17. *Employer Responsibility for Veteran Reemployment,* Personnel Series No. 83, American Management Association, New York, 1944, pp. 46–50; and *Seniority and Reemployment of War Veterans,* Studies in Personnel Policy No. 65, National Industrial Conference Board, New York, 1944.

18. E. F. Scoles, "Veterans Reemployment — Statute and Decisions," *Iowa Law Review,* January 1946, p. 157. See also *Interpretative Bulletin and Legal Guide,* Bureau of Veterans' Reemployment Rights, January 1948.

19. *Fishgold* v. *Sullivan Drydock and Repair Corp.,* 328 U.S. 275, and *Whirls* v. *Trailmobile Co.,* 331 U.S. 40.

20. See, for example, the resolution of the Seventh Annual Convention of the CIO, the April 12, 1945 statement of the CIO Veterans Committee, and the report of the Executive Council of the AFL to the Sixty-sixth Convention. Also illuminating are T. F. Silvey, "Labor's Viewpoint on Veterans Reemployment," in *Employer Responsibility for Veteran Reemployment,* pp. 35–45, and B. B. Shishkin, "Organized Labor and the Veteran," *Annals of the American Academy of Political and Social Science,* March 1945, pp. 146–57.

Assessment of the Re-employment Problem

In retrospect, it appears that the re-employment problem failed to become critical mainly because of the high level of employment throughout the reconversion period and the availability of unemployment and self-employment allowances, education and training benefits, and business and farm loans. Other important factors were the common sense displayed by labor and management in working out difficulties at the plant level, the relatively small number of veterans who had re-employment rights, and the indifference of many veterans to their old jobs.[21] The Supreme Court decisions demonstrated the doubtful value of statutory job rights. If job opportunities are abundant, such rights are not needed; if jobs are scarce they cannot assure re-employment.

The legal debate tended to obscure the favorable attitude of workers toward the return of veterans. A survey of "representative" factory workers made by the Opinion Research Corporation in 1945 [22] showed rank-and-file acceptance of so-called "superseniority." Ninety-five per cent of the workers agreed with the idea that "a former employer must rehire a veteran at his old job or one just as good." In fact, 61 per cent favored displacement by veterans of other workers with greater seniority; an additional 10 per cent had no opinion. Furthermore, 57 per cent felt that veterans who had no jobs before the war should have some preference rather than "take their chances along with everybody else."

General Employment and Self-Employment

Besides assistance in re-employment, the federal and state governments provided various forms of aid to veterans in employment and self-employment. Nongovernment groups also provided employment help to veterans.

The G.I. Bill set up machinery in public employment offices specifically to aid veterans. It directed the U.S. Employment Service to assign a veterans employment representative to each state to execute the policies of the Veterans Placement Service Board, and to assign personnel in local offices to the counseling and placement of veterans. Such strengthening of the public employment service for veterans contrasted sharply with the failure to provide adequate facilities for veterans following World War I.[23]

The Civil Service Commission, under the Veterans Preference Act, extends preference to World War II veterans and certain relatives "in certification and appointment, in appointment, in reinstatement, and in retention in civilian positions in all establishments, agencies, bureaus, administrations, projects, and departments of the Government." At the state and local level of public employment, forty-four states and at least 559 cities of 10,000 or more inhabitants have given preference to veterans.[24]

Labor-management agreements accorded certain benefits to new as well as old veteran employees, but no important preferences. In a study made for the Veterans Administration, the Bureau of Labor Statistics found that, of 133 agreements negotiated after V-J Day, 111 dealt with the rights of employees entering or returning from service.[25] Temporary employees, who had no statutory re-employment rights, received essentially the same re-employment rights as permanent employees in 34 of the agreements but were specifically excluded in 20 others. In 12 agreements, veterans who were new employees had an opportunity to acquire seniority equal to their period of military service after they completed the regular probationary period, but such service was of no assistance in obtaining a job. In this connection, it is interesting that the Veterans of Foreign Wars joined with

21. According to an unpublished estimate of the Retraining and Reemployment Administration, as of August 1945 less than one fourth of all World War II participants had and would exercise re-employment rights. According to a popular earlier estimate, only 20 per cent had such rights (see, for example, *Employer Responsibility for Veteran Reemployment,* p. 7). According to the 1944 Army survey (*Postwar Plans of the Soldier Series,* Report No. B-129, pp. 18, 26), 25 per cent of all enlisted men who had been employees counted on returning to former employers and another 14 per cent considered return likely.

22. *Factory Management and Maintenance,* Opinion Research Corporation, New York, December 1945, pp. 91–92.

23. E. J. Howenstine, Jr., "Lessons of World War I," *Annals of the American Academy of Political and Social Science,* March 1945, p. 182; and M. F. Jessup, "Public Attitude toward Ex-Servicemen after World War I," *Monthly Labor Review,* December 1943, pp. 1060–73.

24. "State Veterans Legislation," *Research Studies,* Veterans Administration, July 31, 1946, pp. 1–4; and *Municipal Yearbook,* Chicago, 1947, pp. 127–28.

25. "Veterans' Rights and Union Agreements," Bureau of Labor Statistics, October 1946 (mimeographed). See also J. Silver and T. Atkins, "Reemployment of Veterans under Collective Bargaining," *Monthly Labor Review,* May 1947, pp. 801–15.

the AFL and the CIO in a statement of principles in July 1944 but withdrew when the unions insisted that seniority could be acquired only after veterans obtained jobs.[26]

Many firms made timely arrangements for accommodating veterans.[27] Some went beyond their legal obligations in reinstating former employees, established special veterans divisions in their personnel offices, gave preference whenever possible, and instituted training programs.

The Disabled

The special problems of disabled veterans have been universally recognized.[28] The federal government, the states, unions, management and civic organizations have all promoted programs to aid them. The federal government gives disabled veterans extra preference in employment, provides vocational rehabilitation and training for them, offers special assistance in placement through public employment offices, gives them unique opportunities to become farm operators, and has assumed leadership in national efforts in their behalf. The first full week of October was designated as "National Employ-the-Physically-Handicapped Week" in 1945,[29] and drives to stress the needs and the competence of disabled workers are held at that time each year.

In 1947 the President created a federal Interagency Committee on Employment of the Physically Handicapped to coordinate placement efforts in order to arrive at a continuing, year-round program. Most states have promoted employment of the disabled by enacting laws for "second-injury funds" or equivalent arrangements to protect employers against extra compensation costs in the event of total disablement of previously handicapped employees.[30] In 20 of the 133 labor-management agreements studied by the Bureau of Labor Statistics, special consideration was given to the disabled even though they had no statutory rights.

Assistance to the Self-Employed

Several government programs were designed to give practical assistance to the self-employed. Under the G.I. Bill, the federal government, through the Veterans Administration, guarantees or insures up to 50 per cent of the principal of private loans at 4 per cent interest or less made to eligible veterans for the purchase of business or farm property or equipment or for use as working capital. The maximum guaranteed or insured amount is $4,000 for real estate loans and $2,000 for non-real-estate loans. The government also pays to the lender, in behalf of the veteran, 4 per cent of the guaranteed or insured portion of the loan. For almost all veterans, this loan privilege will end by July 1957. The G.I. Bill also extends to veterans who meet certain standards of eligibility under the Bankhead-Jones Farm Tenant Act low-interest loans, administered by the Department of Agriculture, to purchase or improve farms or refinance farm indebtedness.

Federal allowances to farmers, businessmen and other self-employed persons, amounting to the difference between $100 a month and the veteran's net monthly earnings, were provided under the G.I. Bill for a maximum of 10.4 months, the period depending upon length of service. These benefits were paid through state unemployment compensation agencies by arrangement with the Veterans Administration; for almost all veterans, they expired in July 1949. Other federal agencies, including the Departments of Commerce and the Interior, the Office of Price Administration, and the War Assets Administration, have also provided aid to veterans in business or farming. State aids include loans, exemption from license and other fees, and protection of professional status without re-examination.[31]

26. Scoles, *op. cit.*, p. 167.

27. See, for example, E. W. Noland and E. W. Bakke, *Workers Wanted: A Study of Employers' Hiring Policies, Preferences and Practices in New Haven and Charlotte,* Yale Labor and Management Center Series, Harper, New York, 1949; *Employment of Veterans: Information for Employers,* U.S. Chamber of Commerce, February 1945; and T. P. Wakefield, "Re-employment Program of the International Harvester Company," *Annals of the American Academy of Political and Social Science,* March 1945, pp. 122–26.

28. See, for example, *Annals of the American Academy of Political and Social Science,* May 1945, devoted entirely to "The Disabled Veteran."

29. Public Law 176, 79th Cong. Studies have also been undertaken to facilitate the counseling, training and placement of the disabled. See, for example, *The Performance of Physically Impaired Workers in Manufacturing Industries,* Bulletin No. 923, Bureau of Labor Statistics, 1948, prepared for the Veterans Administration.

30. See Chapter 16.

31. *State Government,* Council of State Governments, December 1946; and *Research Studies,* Veterans Administration, July 31, 1946, pp. 1–4.

Education and Training

Extensive education and training benefits, administered by the Veterans Administration, were made available by the G.I. Bill and the Vocational Rehabilitation Act.[32] Both laws provide for tuition and other payments, for subsistence allowances to veterans and certain of their dependents, and for educational and vocational advice and guidance.[33]

Under the G.I. Bill, training must be started before July 1951 and may extend to four years, according to length of service. Included are institutional education, on-the-job training, and a combination of institutional education and on-farm training. The supervisory authority of the Veterans Administration is substantially restricted by the G.I. Bill provision that "no department, agency, or office of the United States . . . shall exercise any supervision or control, whatsoever, over any State educational agency, or State apprenticeship agency, or any educational or training institution."

On the other hand, the Veterans Administration has close control over courses pursued under the Vocational Rehabilitation Act, which is designed primarily "to restore employability lost by virtue of a handicap due to service-incurred disability." The objective here is job placement, and the Administrator of Veterans Affairs has "the power and the duty to prescribe" as well as to provide "suitable training."

Other educational training opportunities have been made available to veterans on both the federal and state levels. For example, veterans receive preference for foreign scholarships under a program administered by the Department of State. Many states offer scholarships and other student aid to resident veterans.

Unemployment Benefits

The G.I. Bill provides federal unemployment allowances of $20 a week, less wages in excess of $3, for a maximum of 52 weeks according to length of service. For most veterans, these benefits, administered by state employment security agencies under arrangements with the Veterans Administration, ended in July 1949. States have also aided jobless veterans by honoring preservice credits accumulated under state unemployment compensation systems.

TABLE 40

Estimated Number of World War II Veterans at End of Each Quarter, 1944–1950 [a]

(*In Thousands*)

Year	March	June	September	December
1944.....	—	1,601	1,725	1,976
1945.....	2,138	2,469	3,628	8,333
1946.....	11,274	12,687	13,373	13,928
1947.....	14,208	14,361	14,555	14,745
1948.....	14,870	14,914	14,973	15,058
1949.....	15,116	15,182	15,252	15,294
1950.....	15,346	15,386	15,404	15,276

a. Returns to civilian life of persons who served in the armed forces at any time between September 16, 1940 and July 25, 1947, adjusted to exclude veterans who died or re-enlisted.

Source: Veterans Administration.

Postwar Employment Experience

The record of readjustment after past wars indicates that "failure of civil employment" to absorb returning veterans "opens a rift, like those more dangerous cleavages between economic groups and races that frequently appear under postwar tensions." [34] But after World War II the economy did not fail; and the sense of separateness, which is latent or dominant in new veterans, did not become a more permanent characteristic. Despite incredibly swift demobilization, most veterans found jobs in a relatively short period. The quick transition helped servicemen to overcome their real and imagined disadvantages. Those who did not find suitable work immediately or who wanted to improve their earning capacity availed themselves of liberal government benefits for unemployment, education or training.

Demobilization

When V-J Day actually came, the intended schedule for demobilization was drastically revised.[35] Nevertheless, the economy showed remarkable capacity to accommodate the returning millions of veterans at the very time when millions of war workers were shifting back to peacetime industry. Before V-E Day and for a while thereafter, it was generally assumed that at least a year would elapse between the German

32. Public Law 16, 78th Cong., as amended.

33. As aids in the advice and guidance program, the Veterans Administration has issued *Occupational Outlook Information* (VA Manual M7-1), technical bulletins on education for the professions, etc.

34. Dixon Wecter, *When Johnny Comes Marching Home*, Houghton Mifflin, Boston, 1944, p. 17.

35. *Review of the Month*, Veterans Administration, November 30, 1945, p. 2; and *Statistical Summary*, Veterans Administration, November 30, 1948, pp. 122 and 124.

TABLE 41

EMPLOYMENT STATUS OF MALE WORLD WAR II VETERANS, NOVEMBER 1945 — NOVEMBER 1949

(*In Thousands*)

Status	November 1945	November 1946	November 1947	November 1948	November 1949
All male veterans [a]	5,600	13,030	14,127	14,395	14,581
In civilian labor force	3,830	11,380	12,760	13,287	13,593
Employed	3,310	10,680	12,247	12,850	12,810
In agriculture	300	770	884	855	944
In other pursuits	3,010	9,910	11,363	11,995	11,866
Unemployed	520	700	513	437	783
Not in civilian labor force	1,770	1,650	1,367	1,108	988
In school	170	1,100	1,035	836	720
Other	1,600	550	332	272	268

a. In continental United States and not in institutions.

Source: "Monthly Report on the Labor Force," Bureau of the Census. Cf. Appendix Table 24.

and the Japanese surrenders, and that only limited demobilization would take place in the interval. The Army plan announced several weeks after V-E Day envisaged the release of only 2 million soldiers between June 1945 and May 1946; the Navy expected to release only 325,000. Demobilization after V-J Day was also conceived as a gradual process that would require two or three years; the expected peak monthly separation rate was 750,000.

The actual tempo of demobilization after V-J Day was in sharp contrast to these plans. (See Table 40.) From V-J Day to the end of 1945 between 5 and 6 million persons were demobilized. In the last quarter of 1945 the actual separation rate was more than double the anticipated maximum of 750,000 a month. More than 10 million veterans returned to civilian life between V-J Day and June 30, 1946. The rate of separation tapered off soon thereafter; the World War II veteran population increased by only 1.7 million in the year ended June 30, 1947, and by fewer than 600,000 in the following year. At the end of 1950 the estimated number of veterans exceeded 15 million; about half a million others who had served in World War II were still in the armed forces.

Labor Force Participation [36]

Most returning veterans tried to fit into the patterns of civilian life as quickly as possible. Many complained of frustration, "the run-around" and "red tape" as they sought to get into particular jobs, businesses or schools. Some who were perplexed, disappointed or restless delayed making up their minds and remained for a while on the fringe of the labor force. A relatively small group came back vowing "to ride the gravy train." But with the help of time, governmental and other assistance, and the opportunities provided by favorable business conditions, almost all veterans have been reconverted into "civilians."

According to Census estimates, 68 per cent of the male World War II veterans were in the labor force in November 1945, 87 per cent a year later, and 93 per cent in November 1949. (See Table 41.) The proportion of veterans outside the labor force and in school [37] increased from 3 per cent in November 1945 to 8 per cent a year later, but the percentage then declined somewhat as veterans completed or discontinued their courses and entered the labor force. The residual group outside the labor force diminished sharply, from 29 per cent of the male veteran population in November 1945 to 4 per cent the following year and to less than 2 per cent by November 1949.

The proportion of all World War II veterans participating in the education and training and readjustment allowance programs rose to more than one fourth by early 1947, but declined thereafter to one sixth by the end of 1949.

In November 1945 only three out of five male

36. Throughout the remainder of this chapter, reference will be made without specific citation to material derived from the *Current Population Reports* of the Bureau of the Census, especially the "Monthly Report on the Labor Force." Cf. Appendix Tables 24 and 25.

The Census figures refer to less than the total World War II veteran population — that is, only to males in continental United States and not in institutions.

37. Census estimates of veterans outside the labor force and in school are considerably below Veterans Administration figures, which have no reference to labor force status.

veterans were employed. A year later the proportion was about five out of six, and in November 1949 about nine out of ten. In the span of four years, employment of veterans increased from 3.3 million to more than 12.8 million. In general these gains were not made by displacing any other group, although they were made possible in part by the withdrawal of women and youths from the labor market. Certainly the situation most feared — the widespread displacement of nonveterans by veterans — did not develop.

Nonagricultural Employment

In the first postwar year for which Census data are available (November 1945 — November 1946), the number of male veterans employed in nonagricultural pursuits increased threefold, reaching 9.9 million. By November 1949 close to 12 million were employed. The distribution of veterans by industry quickly approached the pattern for other male nonagricultural workers; a relatively large number of veterans, however, are employed in government.

More than one third of the veterans employed in nonagricultural industries are in manufacturing. Wholesale and retail trades account for a good part of the other two thirds. Despite general reductions in federal employment, the number of World War II veterans in civil service increased to 635,000, or about 35 per cent of the civil service total, by December 1949.

Although most veterans found employment, their initial job adjustments were often unsatisfactory. In manufacturing industries veterans had a higher quit rate than nonveterans in the early postwar period.[38] (See Table 42.)

U.S. Employment Service reports show that greater effort was required in placing veterans than others (that is, there were more referrals per placement). Surveys made several months later of Army veterans discharged in July and December 1945 showed that many had left jobs because they failed to advance above their prewar status and because they felt that employers gave inadequate consideration to their military experience in assigning them in terms of skill and pay levels.[39] A study made toward the end

TABLE 42

COMPARATIVE TURNOVER RATES FOR WORLD WAR II VETERANS AND OTHERS IN MANUFACTURING, DECEMBER 1945 — JUNE 1947

(*Per 100 Employees*)

Item	December 1945	June 1946	December 1946	June 1947
Quit rate				
Veterans	5.7	5.4	3.7	4.0
Other employees	3.7	3.6	2.7	2.8
Layoff rate				
Veterans	1.0	1.6	1.3	1.6
Other employees	2.0	1.7	1.4	1.6

Source: Bureau of Labor Statistics.

of 1946 found, however, that 83 per cent of veterans were "reasonably well satisfied" with their jobs; among Negro veterans only 65 per cent were satisfied, for they encountered traditional occupational barriers.[40] During the war Negro troops had been more optimistic than others about their prospects; a greater percentage of Negroes than of whites believed they would fare better after the war than they had before it.[41]

Wage and salary workers seeking reinstatement in their former jobs usually did not encounter difficulty, despite their frequent lack of clear-cut rights and the changes brought about by conversion and reconversion. There was some litigation, but most cases were settled out of court, sometimes for a cash consideration. Displacement of nonveterans occurred only occasionally — for example, in shipyards, aircraft plants, and certain federal agencies where wartime operations were drastically curtailed. Although many veterans were not interested in jobs with their former employers, competitive pressure forced some to reconsider. Older men, presumably those who had held better jobs, were more interested than younger men in returning to their old jobs.

On-the-Job Training

The G.I. Bill program for on-the-job training had assisted 1.5 million veterans by June 30, 1950. At that time about 200,000 were still in training; another 100,000 had probably interrupted their training temporarily. (See Appendix Table 26.) According to a survey of on-the-job training made by the Veterans Administration as of April 30, 1947, employment objectives in both the manual and the white-

38. E. J. Polinsky, "Veterans Return to the Nation's Factories," *Monthly Labor Review,* December 1946, pp. 924–34.

39. *Research Studies,* Veterans Administration, January 31, 1946, pp. 8–14, and May 31, 1946, pp. 6–10.

40. "The Fortune Survey," *Fortune,* December 1946, p. 5.

41. *Postwar Plans of the Soldier Series,* Report No. B-129, pp. 21–22.

collar fields were well represented. (See Table 43.) Veterans in apprenticeable trades comprised one fourth of all trainees. The course length averaged thirty-two months for all trainees.

The early program for on-the-job training was criticized on many counts. The states did not have adequate standards and facilities for approving and supervising training establishments. Training for dead-end and overcrowded occupations was common. Some employers used the program as a device for obtaining cheap labor. The absence of any income limitation permitted some relatively high-paid veterans to draw subsistence benefits as pseudo-trainees, while other trainees (especially those with dependents) complained of the inadequacy of the benefits.

Widespread criticism led to the enactment in August 1946 [42] of specific criteria to guide states in approving on-the-job training establishments; of "ceilings" on the amount of pay plus subsistence; and of a two-year, rather than a four-year, limit on training for other than apprenticeable trades. One important criterion was that there should be "reasonable certainty" that the job for which the veteran was training would be available to him at the end of training. By June 30, 1947, approval was accordingly withdrawn from 36 per cent of all reinspected establishments and subsistence allowances were reduced or discontinued for 47 per cent of the trainees. The new ceilings became unsatisfactory, however, when wages and living costs surged upward after price control was eliminated. Some bona fide trainees were forced out of the program and some veterans were discouraged from entering. In May 1948, amendatory legislation [43] raised the ceiling for trainees, increased subsistence allowances, and established new differentials for veterans with dependents. Despite these amendments, participation in the training program declined.

The special efforts to train and place the disabled met with some success, but there is still a dearth of opportunities for the seriously handicapped. By June 30, 1950 about a quarter of a million disabled veterans had taken some type of job training under the Vocational Rehabilitation Act. About 36,000 were still in training and the remainder had finished or discontinued their courses. Only about half of those who had terminated their training were considered rehabilitated. In the four years 1946–1949 the U.S. Employment Service had made about 494,000 placements, but 72,400 veterans were still listed in the active file at the end of this period.

42. Public Law 679, 79th Cong.
43. Public Law 512, 80th Cong.

TABLE 43

EMPLOYMENT OBJECTIVES OF VETERANS IN TRAINING ON THE JOB UNDER PUBLIC LAW 346, APRIL 30, 1947 [a]

Employment Objective	Number
Total	619,647
Mechanics and repairmen — motor vehicle and railroad	56,764
Farm managers and foremen	44,678
Mechanics and repairmen, not elsewhere classified	43,985
Managers and officials	39,131
Retail managers	32,196
Carpenters	23,379
Machine shop and related occupations	22,785
Clerks and kindred occupations	19,615
Salesmen, brokerage and commission firms	18,822
Agricultural occupations	17,732
Salespersons, not elsewhere classified	16,444
Linemen and servicemen	16,346
Electricians	15,850
Plumbers, gas and steam fitters	12,680
Tinsmiths, coppersmiths and sheetmetal workers	10,402
Butchers	9,609
Pressmen and plate printers, printing	9,213
Printing and publishing occupations, not elsewhere classified	8,618
Salesmen, insurance	7,430
Toolmakers, die sinkers and setters	6,538
Jewelry, watchmaking, gold and silversmiths	6,043
Cabinetmakers	5,647
Laundering, cleaning, dyeing and pressing	5,548
Brick and stone masons and tilesetters	4,953
Draftsmen	4,755
Engineering	4,656
Painters, construction and maintenance	4,656
Upholsterers	4,458
Compositors and typesetters	4,260
Bookkeepers and cashiers, except banks	3,863
Buyers and department heads, stores	3,665
Bakers	3,566
Shoemakers and repairmen, not in factory	3,566
Mortuary science	3,368
Airplane mechanics	3,269
General woodworking occupations	3,170
All other courses	116,600
Not stated	1,387

a. Based on one per cent sample.

Source: Vocational Education and Rehabilitation Information Bulletin, Veterans Administration, December 24, 1947.

Self-Employment

Veterans doubtless accounted for a good share of the new businesses started in 1946 and 1947 and for a good part of the increase of more than a million in self-employed males in nonagricultural enterprises during the four years ended November 1949. A study of business loans made in 1946 by the Federal Reserve Board [44] and inquiries at community centers and Department of Commerce field offices indicate that veterans were particularly attracted to retailing and service industries, which require relatively little experience and capital.

Despite the hazards faced by new firms, it appears from the low rate of business discontinuances and the small number of nonfarm claimants for self-employment allowances that veterans in business have made a good start. They have had to overcome such handicaps as limited capital, high costs and competition from established firms. Testimony in February 1946 before the House of Representatives Committee on Small Business, and complaints to community centers, suggest that veterans were also impeded by the practices of materials suppliers, who naturally favored "regular" prewar or wartime customers in the postwar period of shortages.[45]

Loans and self-employment allowances under the G.I. Bill were not extensively used for nonagricultural enterprise. By June 1950 the Veterans Administration had approved for guarantee or insurance only 121,000 business loans, averaging $3,094 in amount. Well over half of these loans had been made by mid-1947. Despite the government guarantee, lenders have been reluctant to make loans to relatively inexperienced veterans at low interest rates. Probably less than one fourth of the veterans who had filed claims for self-employment allowances by June 30, 1950 were engaged in nonagricultural activities.

Agricultural Employment

About 7 per cent of all employed veterans are engaged in agriculture. According to Census estimates, agricultural employment of veterans rose from 300,000 to 944,000 between November 1945 and November 1949. The seasonal peak has been in the neighborhood of one million in each year.

There is some evidence to suggest that many veterans who left farms to enter military service did not return to farm work upon demobilization. According to a study by the Department of Agriculture,[46] only 1.8 million veterans leaving the armed forces between September 1940 and January 1947 went to live on farms, whereas 2.4 million entered the armed forces from farms in the same period. A Census survey made in April 1947 showed that out of every twelve male World War II veterans under age 45 who headed households only one was engaged in a farm occupation; the proportion for other male household heads of similar age was one out of six. The Census Bureau attributes this difference not only to Selective Service policies in deferment of farm workers but also to the failure of veterans to return to farms after discharge.

Relatively few veterans have obtained farm loans, and those who did were presumably among the more prosperous. By June 25, 1950 the Veterans Administration had guaranteed or insured under the G.I. Bill only 57,000 farm loans, averaging about $3,800 each. One fifth of the loans were made in five West North Central farm states and averaged $3,100. Approximately 3 per cent of the loans, averaging about $6,000, were made in California, Arizona and Nevada. By June 30, 1950 only about 9,700 veterans had received direct farm ownership loans from the Department of Agriculture under the Bankhead-Jones Farm Tenant Act; [47] these loans averaged about $7,800.

The less prosperous veteran-farmers, normally ineligible for loans, have had to rely on self-employment allowances. Perhaps three fourths of the claims for self-employment allowances came from veteran-farmers. The proportion has been particularly large in the South. The predominantly agricultural South Atlantic and South Central states received about two thirds of the $591 million paid in self-employment allowances through June 1950. The same regions accounted for about three out of every five new initial claims for self-employment allowances and about three out of every four "exhaustions of entitlement." Mississippi alone obtained over 9 per cent of the total self-employment payments.

---

44. "Security Pledged on Member Bank Loans to Business," *Federal Reserve Bulletin,* June 1947, p. 676.
45. "Veterans in Small Business," *Research Studies,* Veterans Administration, December 31, 1946, p. 1.
46. "Farm Population Estimates: United States and Major Geographic Divisions, 1940–1947; States, 1940–1945," Bureau of Agricultural Economics, August 1947, p. 1.
47. Public Law 731, 79th Cong.

The institutional on-farm training program, unlike the other education and training programs under the G.I. Bill and the Vocational Rehabilitation Act, was still expanding in the summer of 1950. As late as December 1949, about one out of every three veterans in agriculture was participating. The number of participants rose from about 107,000 on January 31, 1947 to 362,000 by June 30, 1950. More than half of all trainees were in the southern states. It is very likely that the program has encouraged some veterans to undertake or to remain in uneconomic enterprises.[48]

Administration of the farm training program has involved many difficulties. Not until September 1947 was the Veterans Administration able to have written into law[49] some of the criteria it had established a year and a half earlier. These criteria defined the concept of a full-time course, set forth the subject of training, established minimum hours of instruction, and indicated size and other qualifying requirements for farms. According to these standards, the training course must include instruction in planning, production, marketing, farm mechanics, conservation of resources, food conservation, farm financing, farm management, and the keeping of farm and home accounts.

Unemployment Changes

Veterans as a group have experienced two major periods of unemployment since World War II: during the first half of 1946, when recently demobilized veterans sought jobs as civilians; and during late 1948 to early 1950, when business activity declined and veterans as well as other workers lost their jobs. The course of unemployment among veterans may be traced through two indicators: (1) the unemployment series of the Bureau of the Census (published in the "Monthly Report on the Labor Force") and (2) the number of continued claims for unemployment allowances (or the "insured unemployment" series derived therefrom), compiled by the Veterans Administration from reports of state employment security agencies.[50]

According to the Census series, which shows the number of veterans seeking work during the survey week of each month, unemployment rose to a peak of 1.2 million by the end of mass demobilization in March 1946 and then declined (except for seasonal variations) during 1947 and 1948. The improvement in the employment position of veterans is confirmed by comparison of unemployment rates for veterans and other male workers in the same age groups. In December 1945 the rate for veterans was 150 unemployed per thousand in the labor force; the rate for other men aged 20 to 44 years was 24 unemployed per thousand in the labor force. In November 1948 the two rates were much closer — 30 per thousand and 28 per thousand. The rate for the most important age group of the veteran population, 25 to 34 years, coincided for the first time with the rate for other men of comparable age in November 1948 — 24 per thousand.

According to the series for continued claims (or the derived series for "insured unemployment"), unemployment of veterans increased rapidly in the early months of demobilization and reached a high plateau of 1.6 to 1.8 million from March through August 1946.[51] (See Figure 38.)

When claims for unemployment allowances continued at a high level in the latter part of 1946, federal and state agencies decided to interpret the eligibility conditions more strictly. This change was prompted by the widespread condemnation of "52–20 clubs" and "rocking-chair brigades," by concern that veterans were exhausting their entitlement to unemployment

48. See, for example, *Veterans Employment News,* U.S. Employment Service, December 1946, pp. 20–22.

49. Public Law 377, 80th Cong.

50. See also "Continued Claims for Unemployment Allowances," *Research Studies,* Veterans Administration, May 31, 1946, pp. 1–5. The second series and its analogues for workers covered by programs established under the Social Security Act and the Railroad Retirement Act form the basis for estimates of "insured unemployment" issued by the Federal Security Agency.

51. During this period, the unemployment allowance figures were substantially higher than the Census estimates — in July 1946 almost twice as high. After mid-1947 the claims series was consistently below the Census series. These statistical differences underscore the difference between the concepts of unemployment used in the two series. A veteran claiming an unemployment benefit need not be "looking for work" but must simply be "able to work and available for suitable work" — the burden of looking for work, in effect, devolves upon the public employment office. Obviously, the amount of unemployment reflected by the claims concept depends on such factors as the strictness with which federal and state agencies interpret the conditions of eligibility, the number of weeks of entitlement remaining to the veteran, and the attitudes of veterans themselves toward claiming benefits, which sometimes equal or exceed the wages they could command if they deduct their "costs of going to work."

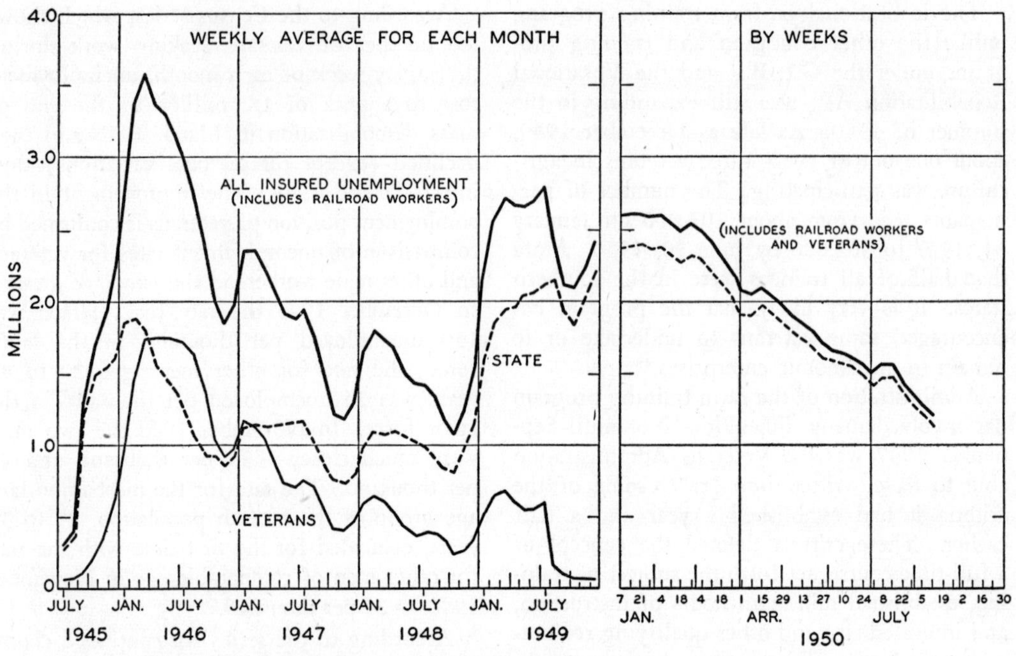

Figure 38. Insured Unemployment,[a] July 1945 to August 12, 1950

a. Includes insured partial and part-total unemployment.

Source: Federal Security Agency, based on data from Bureau of Employment Security, Railroad Retirement Board and Veterans Administration. Cf. Figure 67.

The statistics on insured unemployment represented by claims filed for unemployment benefits or waiting-period credit in this figure are based on weekly reports to the Bureau of Employment Security from state employment security agencies, the Veterans Administration and the Railroad Retirement Board. The data, therefore, include only weeks of unemployment covered by claims filed under the three unemployment benefit programs of these state and federal agencies. State-by-state figures are based on data from the state employment security agencies only. Initial claims are excluded from both the United States total and the state distribution, since in general they merely indicate the beginning of a period of unemployment.

These data are preliminary and subject to correction. Week-by-week comparisons should be made with caution, since the changes may be caused by operational as well as economic factors. Similarly, interstate comparisons may be affected by the differing eligibility factors among the states. Since the data are based on claims filed, they include some persons whose claims are subsequently disallowed.

Insured unemployment for a specified week represents weeks of unemployment experienced in that week for which waiting-period credit or benefits were claimed. Under the state and veterans programs "calendar-week" and "flexible-week" states differ in time lag between the period of unemployment and the date of filing claim. In states that use a fixed calendar week as the period for which benefits are paid and claims are filed, the filing of a continued claim during a particular calendar week generally represents insured unemployment during the preceding calendar week. In states that set a separate benefit week of seven consecutive days for each claimant depending upon when he filed his first claim, the filing of a continued claim during a particular calendar week represents, on the average, insured unemployment for the week ending about the middle of the same calendar week; in these states allowance for this half-week lag was made by taking the average of continued claims filed during a particular calendar week and during the preceding calendar week to represent insured unemployment during the preceding calendar week.

The coverage of these data and the definition underlying them differ significantly from those used in the Census Bureau's "Monthly Report on the Labor Force." The Census estimates are based on a monthly sample of the entire population and therefore include all unemployed workers, whether covered by unemployment benefit programs or not. The unemployed are defined by the Census Bureau as those not employed and looking for work. This definition of unemployment does not include several groups who might file claims under one of the unemployment benefit programs: (1) persons with jobs, but temporarily not working because of labor dispute, bad weather, temporary lay-offs, etc.; (2) persons employed only part of the week, or receiving substantially less than their usual earnings because of reduced hours; (3) persons unemployed at their regular job during the entire week, but who picked up a few hours of casual work. It appears also that some workers who were registered at public employment offices as available for employment and who did not take any other active steps to find a job were reported in the Census survey as not looking for work.

allowances in a period of relatively favorable employment conditions and sacrificing protection against possible future need, and by the increasing reluctance of employers to hire veterans who had drawn benefits for extended periods.[52] In August 1946 a program of re-interviewing veterans who had been on the rolls for twenty or more consecutive weeks was undertaken, and special attention was given to their needs. By early 1947 the rolls had declined considerably as veterans adapted themselves to the prevailing job and wage situation.

The second important period of unemployment among veterans began in November 1948 and continued until the spring of 1950. According to Census figures, the number of unemployed veterans more than doubled between November 1948 and March 1949, reaching 915,000, and increased to a million in July 1949 as veterans completing the school year entered the labor force. By February 1950 a peak of 1.1 million was reached. As business recovered in the spring of that year, unemployment among veterans declined and by June 1950 was down to 540,000.

Since veterans were probably lower on the seniority ladder than other males of comparable age, their unemployment rates were somewhat higher. As mentioned earlier, the rates for the two groups at ages 25–34 coincided in November 1948 — at 24 per thousand. From this point, the rates rose for both veterans and others, but more sharply for veterans: in February 1950, 69 per thousand veterans and 58 per thousand other males were unemployed. With recovery in the spring of 1950, unemployment declined sharply, and in June 1950 the veteran rate was lower than that for other males — 32 per thousand as against 46 per thousand.

The series on claims for unemployment allowances also reflected the second unemployment rise among veterans up to July 1949, the expiration date of the program for most veterans. Even before this virtual ending of the program, however, the reliability of the series as an indicator of the magnitude of unemployment was diminished by the rising number of "exhaustions of entitlement." During the week ended July 9, 1949, 585,000 continued claims were filed by veterans. In the same week the Census reported one million unemployed veterans.

The course of the continued claims series for veterans unemployment allowances differs significantly from the course of the corresponding series for workers covered by state unemployment compensation programs. Although the veteran population was much smaller than the working population covered by the state programs, the weekly continued claims filed by veterans actually surpassed the other total for almost a year, between March 1946 and February 1947. Both series reached comparable peaks early in 1946, but the veteran series declined more consistently thereafter and to a much lower level. In October 1948, for example, continued claims filed by veterans were less than one third the number filed under the state programs.

The extent to which veterans have relied on the unemployment allowance program may be seen from the fact that by June 30, 1950 almost 9 million filed at least one claim and more than 8.2 million had received a total of $3.2 billion in benefits. Thus, participating veterans received an average of $392 — more than nineteen weeks of assistance. By the same date more than 900,000 veterans had exhausted their entitlement.

Veterans in School

The G.I. Bill has had its most profound effects in the field of education, encouraging and subsidizing veterans who would not otherwise have been able to continue their schooling and introducing new goals for the nation's educational system.[53] Veterans responded as enthusiastically to the opportunities afforded them as the attitude surveys of the Army in 1944 and the Navy in 1945 had suggested they would. In April 1947, 21 per cent of veterans aged 20 to 24 and 8 per cent of those aged 25 to 29 were in school, as compared with 8 and 3 per cent of other males of comparable age.

From the inception of the program through June 1950 the federal government paid out more than $11.5 billion for veterans education and training. Most of the money was paid under the G.I. Bill, and most of it in behalf of veterans in school (rather than for on-the-job training).

52. See, for example, "Hidden Costs to Veterans of Unemployment Allowances," *Research Studies*, Veterans Administration, December 31, 1946, pp. 4–6.

53. See, for example, I. L. Kandel, *Impact of War upon American Education*, University of North Carolina Press, Chapel Hill, 1948, p. 278.

Although Census statistics are restricted to veterans in school who are outside the labor force, they show the essential movements of the entire veteran school population. In November 1945 only 170,000 male veterans, or less than one tenth of the total outside the labor force, were reported in school. Between the fall of 1946 and May 1948, however, the number in school exceeded a million and represented something like two thirds or three fourths of the total number of veterans outside the labor force. At the beginning of the 1946–1947 academic year, many veterans who had been resting or making plans while technically available for work evidently entered school and shifted from the unemployment allowance rolls to the subsistence rolls. This shift would also help to explain the reversal in the relationship of the insured unemployment and the Census unemployment series in 1946–1947.[54] The Census estimate of the veteran school population fell below 900,000 in the fall of 1948 and then rose to 971,000 in February 1949. In the next two semesters, however, enrollment fell below three quarters of a million.

If account is taken of all veterans in school without reference to whether or not they are in the labor force, the impact of education on the ultimate skill pattern of veterans is more evident. According to the U.S. Office of Education,[55] veterans accounted for nearly half of the total enrollment and two thirds of the male enrollment of higher educational institutions in the fall of 1947, and for about one third of the total and one half of the male enrollment in the fall of 1949. According to statistics of the Veterans Administration, by June 30, 1950 more than 5 million veterans had taken some type of school course — almost half at the college level or higher — under the G.I. Bill or the Vocational Rehabilitation Act. About 4.3 million of them had completed, discontinued or temporarily interrupted their courses; about one million were still in school.

A survey made by the Veterans Administration as of April 30, 1947 gives a picture of student veterans that confirms the impression of educators concerning their comparative maturity, seriousness, persistence and proficiency.[56] The average age of the G.I. Bill student was 26 years. About 32 per cent were married, and 77 per cent were taking full-time courses. About two fifths of those in colleges and universities had taken some college work before service. At the college level and above, where the length of courses averaged thirty months, veterans were concentrated in such fields as liberal arts, sciences, business administration, engineering, medicine and law. Below the college level, veterans were taking school training in crafts, trades, industrial arts, business and flying. (See Table 44.)

Like all the other readjustment programs, the education program has had its quota of difficulties. Various aspects have been criticized, such as the hopeless division of responsibility between federal and state agencies, the limited provisions for counseling,[57] the enrollment of veterans in avocational or recreational courses, and the multiplication of profit-making vocational schools offering lengthy courses of little worth. Laws enacted in 1948, 1949 and 1950[58] sought to curb some of these tendencies. Veterans, too, have had complaints — for example, about the quality of on-campus housing and the level of subsistence allowances in relation to living costs. Despite these difficulties, the program has afforded millions of veterans an opportunity normally restricted to persons with above-average financial resources or superior scholastic records.

54. See footnote 51, p. 151.

55. Circular No. 264, November 10, 1949.

56. *Vocational Education and Rehabilitation Information Bulletin,* December 24, 1947. See also R. Walters, "Statistics of Attendance in American Universities and Colleges, 1948," *School and Society,* December 18, 1948, pp. 419–30, and the results of a comprehensive study of the comparative scholastic achievements of veterans and nonveterans made by the Educational Testing Service.

57. See, for example, *New York Times,* May 26, 1947, February 1, 1948 and August 31, 1948.

58. Public Law 862, 80th Cong., restricted enrollment in recreational courses; Public Law 266, 81st Cong., required schools to be in operation on their own for at least a year before they could accept veterans under the G.I. Bill; and Public Law 610, 81st Cong., introduced stricter educational standards for profit schools and defined attendance requirements for full-time trade and technical courses. On January 2, 1951 the House Select Committee to Investigate the Educational and Training Program under the G.I. Bill issued a report (H.R. 3253, 81st Cong., 2d sess.) on "alleged abuses" and recommended the strengthening of "criteria for the approval of educational institutions" so that unethical practices might be restricted and higher standards enforced.

TABLE 44

PRINCIPAL COURSES OF VETERANS IN TRAINING IN SCHOOLS UNDER PUBLIC LAW 346, APRIL 30, 1947[a]

Principal Course	Total	Schools of Higher Learning	Other Schools
Total	1,825,118	1,125,999	699,119
Humanities	392,567	356,557	36,010
Engineering	229,084	171,885	57,199
Crafts, trades, and industrial courses	208,380	33,774	174,606
Business courses (other than business administration)	153,944	73,820	80,124
Business administration	146,403	125,446	20,957
Elementary and secondary school courses, not elsewhere classified	81,816	4,704	77,112
Flight training	81,494	2,412	79,082
Agriculture	69,518	30,035	39,483
Medicine and related courses	59,316	52,832	6,484
Education (preparation for teaching)	56,615	54,762	1,853
Physical and natural science	45,977	43,545	2,432
Art and design (other than fine arts)	42,032	8,685	33,347
Social studies	35,124	32,810	2,314
Law	33,233	31,843	1,390
Domestic and personal service	24,965	1,809	23,156
Music	22,338	14,233	8,105
Managerial (other than business administration)	12,810	4,704	8,106
Journalism	10,514	8,081	2,433
Entertainment and public speaking	9,760	3,740	6,020
Architecture	9,311	6,996	2,315
Theology	8,979	7,358	1,621
Forestry	6,152	6,152	0
Dancing	4,178	241	3,937
Social work	3,377	3,377	0
All other courses	20,637	6,393	14,244
Not stated	56,594	39,805	16,789

a. Based on a one per cent sample. Because of the small size of the sample, all figures less than 3,000 in the table are not considered to be reliable.

Source: Vocational Education and Rehabilitation Information Bulletin, Veterans Administration, December 24, 1947.

Chapter 14

SOCIAL SECURITY *

"Social security" is used in this chapter to mean government programs designed primarily to help individuals meet the loss of earnings or the increase in expenditure caused by birth, sickness, accident, disability, unemployment, old age and death. Such programs entail cash benefits, which can be of three kinds — social insurance, allowances and assistance.

The distinctions among these three types of benefits may be seen most readily in the conditions of eligibility that are characteristic of each. Eligibility for social insurance is determined by a record of previous work or contribution, usually by both. Eligibility for allowances is determined by the status of the individual, as in family allowances that are paid to all families where there are children irrespective of the employment or income of the head of the household. Eligibility for assistance is based on individual need and is determined by a means test.

The three types of benefits differ also in the way they are financed. Social insurance involves premiums paid by or on behalf of the covered worker, which either alone or in conjunction with a government contribution equal the total cost of benefits paid out. Allowances may call for separate financing, but there is no attempt as in insurance to relate the benefit of a particular worker to his individual contribution. Assistance is usually financed out of legislative appropriations, the size of the appropriation depending on the funds available and estimates of current need.

In the United States the main programs are a federal system of *old-age and survivors insurance;* a federal-state system of *unemployment insurance;* and *assistance* to the needy aged, needy dependent children, the needy blind and the needy permanently and totally disabled, administered by the states with the aid of federal grants. All three programs are incorporated in the Social Security Act of 1935 and subsequent amendments, the most recent those of August 28, 1950 and 1952. That act also provides for federal grants-in-aid to states for various health and welfare programs that supply services only, not cash benefits. Special federal programs cover railroad employees, veterans and federal employees. (See Appendix Table 27.) Apart from these programs, each state has its own system of workmen's compensation and several states pay cash benefits to insured industrial workers during sickness. Many states and localities also make provision for a general assistance or relief program.

These federal and state programs are supplemented by voluntary insurance for hospitalization and medical service [1] and by industrial welfare and pension plans either established by employers or based on union agreements.[2]

The concept of social security covers a large number of programs, some new, others old.

Beginnings of Social Security

The problem of economic security is as old as civilization. For centuries, individual has joined with individual in developing measures for protection against the economic consequences of the contingencies of life. The first such measures in our political and social tradition were directed toward the major cause of insecurity — physical violence — during the Anglo-Saxon settlement of England. Laws scheduling compensation for injuries sustained by one man at the hands of another date back to the seventh century. Life and limb, eye and ear, wounds and broken bones, each carried its specific indemnity to be paid by the aggressor. References in these laws point to the probable existence of brotherhoods or guilds, the members of which made themselves mutually responsible for the payment or collection of these indemnities.

* By Karl de Schweinitz, Professor of Social Welfare, University of California, Los Angeles, California, and Robert M. Ball, Assistant Director, Bureau of Old-Age and Survivors Insurance, Social Security Administration, Federal Security Agency. Opinions expressed here by Mr. Ball are not necessarily those of the agency with which he is associated.

1. See Chapter 17.
2. See Chapter 20.

Ordinances adopted in the tenth century indicate the establishment in London of a system similar to the vigilance committees that in the United States accompanied the development of the West. Men organized for mutual protection against thieves and maintained a common fund to reimburse the members for stolen property. Provision was also made for prayers for the dead.

The Guilds

The earliest extant charters of guilds in England belong to the first half of the eleventh century. They specify contributions to a common purse, mutual aid in time of need, participation in funeral ceremonies, the oath of brotherhood, and provide that, to quote the Thanes Gild at Cambridge, "all the society should ever support him who has the most right."

In the years after the Norman Conquest there came a great extension of associative effort. The businessmen of those days, combining the functions of importer, manufacturer and retailer, formed themselves into merchant guilds to advance their trade interests. These groups often also gave assistance to their members in time of need and on occasion engaged in general acts of charity. The craft guilds, which followed later as industry began to specialize, developed much further the security provisions of this type of mutual aid. Guilds of saddlers, weavers, armorers, shoemakers, carpenters and the like included, along with activities looking toward control of their respective trades, sick benefits, help to the needy of the fraternity, ceremonial feasts, prayers for the dead, and funeral processions.

Paralleling the growth of the merchant and craft guilds in the years after the Conquest was an extensive development of religious and social guilds. Social security was the central purpose of these guilds. Although they performed the ceremonies that were characteristic of all types of guilds, their principal benefits had to do with sickness and infirmity. Their mutual aid varied from definitely specified payments into and benefits from a common fund to general provisions like that of the Gild of the Holy Trinity:

> If any brother or sister of the gild becomes so feeble through old age or through any worldly mishap that he has not and cannot earn the means of livelihood, he shall have such help at the cost of the gild that he shall not need to beg his bread.[3]

The guilds were the associative effort of a rising middle class. Organizations of neighbors and entrepreneurs, they typically included neither landed proprietors and the upper ranks of the nobility, except occasionally as patrons, nor the very poor. While many of these societies specified the amounts of both contributory payments and benefits, individual need and the state of the treasury were qualifying factors. Mutual acquaintanceship helped solve the problem of eligibility for benefits, for the organizations usually were small, often having as few as twenty members. Everybody could know the personal and economic situation of everybody else. At the same time, the spirit of brotherhood, expressed in the association of neighbors and kin or through the fraternity of trade and craft, lent dignity to the status of beneficiary.

In 1389 the guilds had increased in number and influence to the point of causing Richard II to call for reports about their "beginning and continuance and governance." This order brought returns from more than five hundred of these organizations, at a time when the population of London is estimated to have been 35,000 and that of England 2.5 million. Two centuries later the guilds were no longer the source of mutual aid they had been for the five preceding centuries and more. In 1545 and 1547, following the expropriation of the abbeys in the previous decade, Henry VIII and Edward VI took over the property of the religious guilds. The trade and craft guilds began increasingly to be organizations of capitalists. They no longer served the working people as they had in the days when artisan and entrepreneur were one and the same person.

During and following the years when the action of government against monastery and religious guild was eliminating the charity of the one and the charity and mutual aid of the other, England found herself in a period of inflation and unemployment. In this situation and in the presence of mounting economic distress, Parliament was obliged to establish measures to prevent starvation. In a series of legislative enactments between 1536 and 1601, England developed the system of local relief

3. Joshua Toulmin Smith (Ed.), *English Gilds,* Trübner, London, 1870, p. 234.

through overseers of the poor that, down to the twentieth century and in the United States as well as in Britain, represented the only public program aimed at economic need. Relief was administered through a means test so applied as to keep the individual on a very low standard of living and in a constant state of uncertainty.

Private Insurance

While this system of income maintenance was being developed for the lowest-paid and least secure groups in the community, an entrepreneur-organized insurance was evolving as a source of profit to the insurer and of investment to the person insured. Even in the sixteenth century, commercial insurance of maritime ventures was an ancient device. Schemes for annuities and death payments were promoted, increasing rapidly through the seventeenth and eighteenth centuries, many of them so highly speculative that they were spoken of as wager insurance. The problem of forecasting the duration of life and the chances of death attracted some of the best minds of the time, and their efforts led to the beginning of actuarial science.

With the start of the Equitable Assurance Society of London in 1762, the first company of its kind to carry through to the present time, the foundations of modern life insurance were laid. This insurance came to be based on a careful selection of risks and a forecast of life expectancy. At first employed by the upper income groups, it gradually attracted increasing numbers of wage earners.

Friendly Societies

The basic provision for working people, however, was not a profit-oriented insurance but a revival of the principle of mutual aid through associative effort. What came to be known as friendly societies were organized. The beginnings of the movement are obscure, but these societies were starting to be a feature of British life before the end of the seventeenth century. They were formed by neighbors, men and women, who usually met at the local alehouse and combined social intercourse with an arrangement to provide against sickness and death, through weekly benefits of a specified amount and lump-sum payments to the survivors of the insured person. Like their predecessors, the guilds, the friendly societies were small. Even as recently as the beginning of the present century, half of them had fewer than a hundred members.[4]

Some of the friendly societies developed a secular ritualism and a national organization with local lodges. They were the origin of the fraternal orders that were introduced in the United States early in the nineteenth century. They also played an important part in the labor movement. Trade unions were suspect in England when they first appeared in the second quarter of the seventeenth century. In 1799 and 1800, Parliament forbade, under severe penalties, any man to "enter into any combination to obtain an advance of wages or to stop work." [5] Until the repeal of these laws in 1824, mutual-benefit activities provided a device through which workers could come together. Strategy as well as protection against the vicissitudes of life became a reason for what might well have been called labor-friendly societies. Some of these organizations established out-of-work benefits as well as sick benefits without distinguishing too clearly between what would be available in time of unemployment and in time of strike.

Even after labor no longer needed this disguise, many unions included insurance among their activities. Emphasis upon this type of program increased after the failure of efforts toward universal suffrage, which occupied the energies of working people from the repeal of the combination laws until the collapse of Chartism in 1848. The 1850's and 1860's saw a rise in mutual-benefit provisions, and when the labor movement became a national institution with the organization of the Trades Union Congress in 1868, union-operated schemes of sickness, unemployment and death benefits were not uncommon.

By the end of the past century people in England were increasingly engaged in associative effort to ensure their economic security, scarcely a county being without its friendly society. There was also a growing use of accident, life and annuity insurance. Most of the population, however, had inadequate protection or none at all. The lengthening span of life and the hazards of industrialization were increasing the need for the maintenance of income in old

4. William H. Beveridge, *Voluntary Action; A Report on Methods of Social Advance,* Allen and Unwin, London, 1948, p. 24.

5. 39 George 3d, c. 81, 1799, and 40 George 3d, c. 106, 1800 (the combination laws).

age and during periods of unemployment or of disability following work-connected and other injuries. The poor law, with its harsh means test, was unacceptable as a measure of security — if, indeed, a system intended to keep the individual barely alive and in a constant state of uncertainty could be called security. Something more than the existing provisions in private enterprise, mutual aid and governmental action was wanted. There came a mounting demand for a more nearly adequate program, one that would serve all the people.

Social Insurance in Germany

This demand was quickened by developments in Germany. Here as in England there had been a history of guild and friendly society, but whereas in British manufacture, associational activities had been largely confined to master craftsmen, in Germany journeymen also had been organized. The mutual aid of these employees was directed to financial provision in time of sickness and death and during the search for employment. Their societies were sponsored and supervised by the employers. The journeymen paid all the cost of the benefits, but the employers, in overseeing the operation of the insurance fund, assumed a kind of formal responsibility that did not exist in England.

Extensive organization for mutual aid was a special characteristic of the mining industry. The societies were voluntary and independent of employer supervision, but as early as the sixteenth century, mining ordinances defined amounts of compensation for accidents and sickness. The employers avoided any legal responsibility but gave the miners permission to sell the leftovers from the mining operations and apply the proceeds to the common fund.

The democratic movement that swept Europe in the 1840's had its effect upon insurance established in Germany by or for workers. In 1845, membership in their societies was made compulsory for the less skilled employees, and in 1854, employers in certain industries were obliged to contribute half the payments to the mutual-aid funds. The employer could also be required to advance the employee's share of the fund, charging it against the next payment of wages. From this time on, the state took an increasingly active part in the promotion and regulation of guild and friendly society and of the whole movement for the economic security of labor.

State Responsibility

Government provision for the relief of need became a matter of public policy in the eighteenth century. Frederick the Great (1740–1786) liked to think of himself as king of the poor. Laws enacted in Prussia during his reign set forth "the duty of the state to provide for the sustenance and support of those of its citizens who cannot . . . procure subsistence themselves."

The English poor law of a century earlier had undertaken to supply relief to people unable to work and employment for the able-bodied, but it included no such express statement of responsibility as in Prussia. In England the theory that the individual has a right to assistance when in need developed after the enactment of the poor law and was, in part at least, deduced from the fact that the statute existed. On the other hand, Germany, in emphasizing the authority of the state, saw that authority as carrying with it a definite obligation. Fichte, writing at the turn of the eighteenth century, held that the state should not be negative, merely exercising a police function, but that it should be filled with Christian concern, especially for the weaker members. The state is to help make men contented, wealthy and strong in body and mind.

Bismarck subscribed to this philosophy. At the same time he saw its application as a way of combating the rising socialist movement in the second half of the nineteenth century. He initiated the legislation that led to the first system of social insurance. Sickness insurance was adopted in 1883, the employee paying two thirds and the employer one third of the cost of the benefits. The friendly societies were used as administrative agents. Industrial accident insurance came in 1884, the employer paying the cost. In 1889 invalidity and old-age insurance was enacted, with contributions from the employer, the employee and the state.

The German legislation stimulated British thinking. In 1897 the British Parliament passed its first workmen's compensation law. In 1908 the newly elected Liberal government established a system of noncontributory old-age pensions with determination of eligibility through a modified means test. There was considerable study of the German program of sickness and disability insurance; Lloyd George, then Chancellor of the Exchequer, went to the continent for this purpose. England adopted its national health insurance law in 1911, like Germany utilizing its friendly societies for administration. At the same time, it led the way in unemployment insurance by setting up the first nation-wide system for this purpose.

Social Security in the United States

The Bismarck program was inaugurated at a time when German education and science had great prestige in the United States. The new legislation attracted the attention of scholars and a few government officials. John Graham Brooks made a brilliant report on the new system to the U.S. Commissioner of Labor in 1893. Other studies followed, but they aroused no general interest in this country.

We had had no such history of associational effort as prepared Germany and England for the adoption of social insurance. The fraternal orders that represented the extension of the friendly societies in the United States had no comparable influence on us, nor had the co-operative movement taken great hold on public opinion. Our emphasis had been on insurance through commercial companies, and so far as wage earners were concerned, this insurance consisted largely of payments designed to cover funeral expenses.

Workmen's compensation was the one exception to this indifference. At the beginning of the twentieth century, insurance for this purpose was already carried by many corporations. To extend this principle to a governmental program involved no such departure as was entailed in the adoption of a general social insurance program. The workmen's compensation movement had considerable civic backing, notably that of President Theodore Roosevelt. Under his leadership, a system was enacted in 1908 for federal employees, who were not protected by the liability laws of the states. State legislation began in 1902, but the first statute to be declared constitutional and to go into continuing operation was enacted in 1911. The movement then spread rapidly among the states.

This fact and the British health insurance program of that same year added to our interest in social insurance. A handful of social scientists, social workers and progressive employers urged unemployment insurance, but for two decades there was no legislative progress. The public generally and labor, except for a few individual unions, were still imbued with the idea that each person would make his own arrangements for meeting the contingencies of life.

Maintenance of Income

The impact of the great depression, following the experience of 1921–1922 and 1914–1915, changed the course of thinking in the United States. The distress of the depression brought government into the field of income maintenance on a scale never before conceived. Within two years of the overwhelming onset of unemployment in the fall of 1930, philanthropy, local public relief and state-administered assistance had proved to be inadequate. The federal government was forced to act. The Federal Emergency Relief Administration was followed by the Works Progress Administration. The people now looked to the federal government for measures that would enable them to deal with the problem of maintaining income. In 1932 the American Federation of Labor called for unemployment insurance. In 1934 came the Townsend movement for old-age pensions, the first demand of the middle class for social security.

The Social Security Act itself represented the work and planning of President Franklin Delano Roosevelt, who, when Governor of New York, had advocated unemployment insurance and old-age assistance; of a few men in the Senate and the House; a few federal and state officials; and certain interested authorities in the universities, in social work and in business. The insistence that something be done was general. The law that emerged was the result of the interplay of administrative leadership, technical recommendations and legislative compromise.

From this act, which became law on August 14, 1935, our system of social security derived its name. Its two insurance titles and its three titles of public assistance laid the foundation of that system. Its cornerstone is formed by the two insurance provisions: Title II, setting up a national administration of old-age insurance, to which in 1939 was added survivors insurance, and Title III, which promoted, through a federal tax offset, unemployment insurance operated by the states under federally prescribed standards of administration supported by federal approval of administrative expenditures. Although expenditures under these two programs have not been so large as under public assistance and the Veterans Administration (see Appendix Tables 27 and 38), they constitute the nucleus of our system of social insurance.[6]

Old-age and survivors insurance, the only one of the three programs that is wholly federal, is administered by the Bureau of Old-Age and Survivors Insurance in the Social Security Administration, a part of the Federal Security Agency. Federal responsibility for public assistance is in the Bureau of Public Assistance in the Social Security Administration, and that for unemployment insurance is in the Bureau of Employment Security of the Department of Labor.

Old-Age and Survivors Insurance

Federal old-age and survivors insurance covered 35.3 million persons in June 1950, or close to 60 per cent of the total paid employment of 60 million. (See Table 45.) The largest industrial groups excluded from coverage at that time were self-employed persons, including farmers, and persons in public employment, including federal civilian and military personnel and employees of state and local government. Domestic and farm workers were excluded, as were railroad employees, who are covered by a special program. Effective as of January 1, 1951, the Social Security Act amendments of 1950 added to this coverage most of the urban self-employed, regular agricultural and household workers, certain groups of public employees and persons working for nonprofit organizations, and a few smaller groups. In June 1950 the number in these groups was about 9.2 million. As of January 1951, when the new coverage went into effect, perhaps 45 million persons were under the program. Of those still excluded, nearly 7 million were protected under other government programs. Not counting those who work in self-employment on a part-time basis and earn relatively little in the course of a year, public retirement programs in the United States now cover all but about 10 per cent of paid employment.

Because of the movement of workers in and out of the labor force, and continual shifts between covered and noncovered industries and between employment and unemployment, the total number of persons who have wage credits is considerably larger than the number of workers in covered industry at any given time. The Bureau of Old-Age and Survivors Insurance has estimated that a total of 82.4 million persons had wage credits under the old-age and survivors insurance program by the beginning of 1951, 60 million with sufficient credits to give them some protection under the program.

6. For particulars on the operations of the Veterans Administration, see Chapter 13; for programs for sickness benefits, Chapter 17.

TABLE 45

Estimated Paid Employment by Status of Coverage by Federal Old-Age and Survivors Insurance, June 1950

(*In Thousands*)

Industrial Group	Number of Persons
Total paid employment	60,000 [a]
Covered before 1950 amendments	35,300
Mining and manufacturing	15,600
Contract construction	2,400
Public utilities	2,400
Trade, finance, insurance, real estate	11,000
Service industries	3,600
Other industries and occupations	300
Not covered before amendments	24,700 [a, b]
Covered by 1950 amendments	9,200 [a, b]
Nonfarm self-employed	4,650 [b]
Agricultural wage workers	850
Household workers	1,000
Civilian employees of the federal government	250
Employees of state and local governments	1,450
Employees of nonprofit institutions	600
Not covered by 1950 amendments	15,500
Covered by other government programs	6,800
Members of the armed forces	1,300
Civilian employees of the federal government	1,500
Employees of state and local governments	2,400
Railroad workers	1,600
Not covered by other government programs	8,700
Nonfarm self-employed	1,500 [c]
Agricultural wage workers	1,200
Agricultural self-employed	4,700 [c]
Household workers	1,100
Clergymen and members of religious orders	200

a. Excludes 150,000 American citizens employed by American firms outside the United States and 400,000 workers in Puerto Rico and the Virgin Islands.

b. Includes 400,000 workers covered by change in the definition of "employee."

c. Includes 1,000,000 individuals whose net earnings from self-employment are less than $400 a year.

Source: Bureau of Old-Age and Survivors Insurance.

BENEFITS

Old-age and survivors insurance, under the Social Security Act, provides for the payment of nine types of benefits, as follows:

1. The old-age insurance benefit, payable to the retired worker at age 65. The amounts of all other benefits are related to this old-age insurance benefit.
2. The wife's benefit, equal to one half of the old-age insurance benefit and payable to the wife of a retired worker if she is 65 or if she has a child of the worker in her care.
3. The husband's benefit, equal to one half of the old-age insurance benefit and payable at age 65 to the dependent husband of a retired worker.
4. The widow's benefit, equal to three fourths of the old-age insurance benefit and payable at age 65 to the widow of a deceased worker.
5. The widower's benefit, equal to three fourths of the old-age insurance benefit and payable at age 65 to the dependent widower of a deceased worker.
6. The child's benefit, equal to one half of the old-age insurance benefit and payable to the child under 18 of the retired worker; three fourths to the child of a deceased worker unless there is more than one child, in which case the benefit is one half of the old-age insurance benefit for each child under 18 plus an additional one fourth of the old-age insurance benefit divided equally among the children under 18.
7. The mother's benefit, amounting to three fourths of the old-age insurance benefit and payable to the widow or divorced wife of a deceased worker if she has a child of the worker in her care. (A divorced wife must have been receiving at least one half of her support from the worker pursuant to agreement or court order.)
8. The parent's benefit, amounting to three fourths of the old-age insurance benefit and payable to the dependent parents of a deceased worker at age 65, if the worker left no widow, widower, or child eligible for monthly benefits.
9. The lump-sum death payment, amounting to three times the old-age insurance benefit and payable on the death of any insured worker.

Computing Benefits

The amount of the old-age insurance benefit is determined as a percentage of the worker's "average monthly wage." As a result of the 1950 amendments to the Social Security Act, there are two different methods of computing this benefit amount. The first method is primarily designed for persons who were already on the rolls before the amendments were passed and those who retire or die in the near future. The benefits are computed essentially as they were under the old law and the amount so derived is raised in accordance with a conversion table printed in the law. This computation may also be used for many persons who can qualify for benefit computation under the second method, described below, if it will produce a higher benefit amount.

The second method of computation is based on wages and self-employment income paid after 1950. It may be applied in any case where an insured worker has at least six "quarters of coverage" after 1950 (that is, about a year and a half in covered work). It must be used if the computation is based on the record of a worker who had at least six quarters of coverage after 1950, and attained age 22 after that year. The formula for the old-age insurance benefit under this method is 50 per cent of the first $100 of the average monthly wage, plus 15 per cent of the remainder up to a total wage of $300.

The average monthly wage is computed by dividing (1) the total wages and self-employment income — not exceeding $3,600 a year — the worker has received after 1950 (or after the quarter before he attains age 22, if later and if it produces a higher benefit) and before the time his benefits are computed by (2) the number of months elapsing in this period. Thus periods of time spent outside covered employment from 1950 on operate to lower the average monthly wage and consequently the benefits payable to the worker or his family.

The minimum monthly benefit payable to a retired worker is $20. For persons whose average monthly wage is $35 or more, the minimum benefit is $25. The maximum payable to a family on the wage record of one person is $150 or 80 per cent of his average monthly wage, whichever is less, except that the maximum will not be applied to reduce the family total below $40. Benefits are not payable for any months in which a beneficiary under age 75 earns more than $50 in covered employment, but no suspensions on account of earnings are made after the beneficiary reaches age 75. When the benefits of an old-age insurance beneficiary are suspended, the benefits of all dependents are suspended as well. With the coverage of nonfarm self-employment in 1951, benefits are also suspended for one or more months of any year in which a person under age 75 engages substantially in such self-employment if his net earnings from it average more than $50 a month.

Growth of the Program

The number of beneficiaries has increased from year to year since the inauguration of the program. At the end of June 1950 about 2.9 million persons were receiving benefits under the program. (See Table 46.) There was also a slow increase in the average amount of benefits of all types up to 1950. (See Appendix Table 28.) In the months following the enactment of the amendments of 1950, benefit amounts increased sharply. The number of beneficiaries also rose because of the liberalized eligibility provisions.

Some indication of the effect of the increase in benefit amounts resulting from the 1950 amendments may be found in the changes in amounts payable to various types of family units. The average benefit paid to a retired man and his wife aged 65 or over was $41.40 in December 1949 and $76.40 in September 1950; to families consisting of a widow and one child, $36.50 in December 1949 and $79.80 in September 1950; to families consisting of a widow and two children, $50.40 in December 1949 and $94.00 in September 1950.

TABLE 46

NUMBER OF BENEFICIARIES OF OASI AND AVERAGE BENEFITS, END OF JUNE 1950

Type of Benefit	Number	Average Benefits
Total	2,930,357	—
Primary	1,384,823	$26.30
Wife's	419,123	13.93
Child's	665,351	13.27
Widow's	290,307	20.94
Widow's current	156,664	21.21
Parent's	14,089	13.84

Source: Bureau of Old-Age and Survivors Insurance. See also Appendix Tables 28 and 29.

ELIGIBILITY

Eligibility for benefits under old-age and survivors insurance is based on the proportion of time the worker spends in employment covered under the program out of the whole period during which it is reasonable to expect he might have been so employed. A worker is "fully insured," [7] and he and his survivors are entitled to most types of benefits, if he has been in covered employment for roughly half the period between the end of 1950 or the time he attained age 21 and the time his benefits are computed, with a minimum of a year and a half, or if he has approximately ten full years of covered employment. If he does not meet this requirement, his survivors are nevertheless eligible for certain types of benefits — mother's, child's and the lump-sum — if he is "currently insured" [8] at death, that is, if he has worked in covered employment for roughly half the three years immediately before his death.

Benefits for a dependent husband or widower, however, may be paid only if the woman on whose wage record they are based was *both* fully and currently insured at the time of her entitlement to old-age insurance benefits or her death.

FINANCING

The present old-age and survivors insurance program as amended in 1950 is financed by contributions from covered employers and employees. At present, employers deduct from the wages of their employees one and a half per cent of all wages up to $3,600 a year, and add to it their own contribution of one and a half per cent. The contributions are turned over each quarter to the Bureau of Internal Revenue,

7. To be "fully insured" a worker must have at least one "quarter of coverage" for every two calendar quarters elapsing after 1950 (or after the quarter in which he attains age 21, if later) up to the quarter in which he attains age 65 or dies, if earlier. (A "quarter of coverage" is a calendar quarter in which a person was paid $50 or more in covered wages or credited with at least $100 of self-employment income.) There is a minimum requirement of six quarters of coverage, but in no case are more than forty such quarters required. Quarters of coverage earned before 1951 count toward meeting the required total.

8. To be "currently insured," a worker must have six "quarters of coverage" within a period consisting of the quarter in which he dies or becomes entitled to old-age insurance benefits and the twelve quarters immediately preceding.

together with a list of employees' names, account numbers and wages in the quarter. The self-employed who are covered under the program report their earnings and make their social security contribution (equal to two and a quarter per cent of their income up to $3,600) once each year when they file their federal income tax returns.

The wages and self-employment income are posted on individual records by the Social Security Administration and are used in determining eligibility for benefits and benefit amounts. The contributions are deposited in the Federal Old-Age and Survivors Insurance Trust Fund and are used to pay the benefits and administrative expenses of the program. That portion of the fund which is not required for current disbursements is invested in interest-bearing United States government securities.

The 1950 amendments provide for periodic increases in the contribution rates as follows (in per cent):

	Employer	Employee	Self-Employed
1951–1953	1.5	1.5	2.25
1954–1959	2.0	2.0	3.0
1960–1964	2.5	2.5	3.75
1965–1969	3.0	3.0	4.5
1970 and thereafter...	3.25	3.25	4.88

This schedule of rates is designed to make the system self-supporting and to eliminate any need for support from general revenues. With these rates there will continue to be an excess of income over outgo for many years, resulting in further growth of the reserve, which amounted to $13.7 billion at the end of 1950. When the program matures, the system is designed to meet benefit costs and administrative expenses through a combination of contribution income and earnings on this reserve.

Expenditures under old-age and survivors insurance are relatively low in the early years of the program, largely because those already old find it difficult to meet the earnings requirements. As the program matures, a larger and larger proportion of those attaining age 65 are eligible for benefits. Then, too, the proportion of aged in the total population is growing. Benefit payments increased each year under the 1939 amendments to the Social Security Act and will continue to increase during the next half century of operation under the 1950 amendments. In 1940, the first year in which monthly benefits were paid, benefit payments amounted to $35 million, or 0.1 per cent of covered payrolls; in 1949 the comparable figures were $667 million and 0.8 per cent. As a result of the program liberalizations enacted in 1950, expenditures are expected to increase sharply in 1951, amounting to slightly more than $2 billion, or 1.9 per cent of payrolls.[9] Thereafter the increase will be gradual, and for the year 2000, according to the estimate used by Congress in arriving at the contribution schedule, expenditures will be over $11 billion and almost 8 per cent of payrolls.

Unemployment Insurance

Each of the fifty-one states and territories has a system of unemployment insurance that pays weekly benefits to unemployed workers during weeks when they are willing to work and available for work but are unable to find the kind of work that is suitable for them. All systems together handled in 1949 more than 17 million initial claims to benefits and paid compensation for more than 86 million weeks of unemployment. (See Appendix Table 30.)

THE FEDERAL-STATE PROGRAM

The fifty-one systems of unemployment insurance were initiated and their continuance was assured by the Social Security Act. Under this act a 3 per cent federal tax is levied on the first $3,000 paid in wages by employers of eight or more persons in industry or business. However, if an employer subject to this tax pays a contribution to a state unemployment insurance system that has been approved as meeting the standards set down in the federal act, then he may "offset" the tax paid to the state against all but 10 per cent of his federal tax. Thus, in the absence of such an approved system in a given state the employer would have to pay the full 3 per cent tax to the federal government. Since the federal act does not provide benefits, unemployed workers in such a state, moreover, would not receive any compensation. All states, therefore, quickly passed approved systems, and employers have been paying to the federal government only 10 per cent of the 3 per cent tax, or 0.3 per cent of covered payrolls. Although

9. "Actuarial Cost Estimates for the Old-Age and Survivors Insurance System as Modified by the Social Security Act Amendments of 1950," July 27, 1950, prepared for the use of the Committee on Ways and Means by Robert J. Myers, Actuary to the Committee.

these federal funds are not earmarked, they have generally been considered to be for the payment of the administrative expenses of the program, for which the federal government makes grants to the states.

Under the present act, employers can offset against the federal tax all but the 0.3 per cent of covered payrolls even though they pay a rate of less than 2.7 per cent to the state, if that lower state rate is based on experience rating. Experience rating, which is in effect in all states in one form or another, is the term given to various methods of relating the tax rate of a particular employer to his unemployment record. Because of the reduction allowed for experience rating, the effective state tax rate for the country as a whole during 1949 was approximately 1.3 per cent of covered payrolls, while the federal government collected an additional 0.3 per cent. (See Appendix Table 31.)

Conditions Federally Imposed

As a condition of allowing employers in a state the offset against the federal tax, the federal law requires that the state shall: (1) make its unemployment insurance payments through a public employment office (the Secretary of Labor may approve other state agencies for this purpose, but in practice he has not); (2) turn over its receipts from state unemployment taxes to the federal government for credit to the state's account in an unemployment trust fund managed by the federal treasury;[10] (3) allow workers to refuse new jobs without having their benefits withheld if the job vacancy was due directly to a labor dispute, or if taking the job requires workers to refrain from joining or to resign from a labor union of their own choosing or to join a company-dominated union, or if the pay and other conditions of work of the job offered are substantially less favorable than those generally prevailing for similar work in the locality. Federal approval of a state law may be revoked if it is found that a state law ceases to conform with these provisions.

Additional federal requirements, largely administrative, are set up as a condition of the payment of federal grants to the states for administrative expenses.[11] Federal grants may be withheld if, in practice, it is found that a state does not comply with these conditions.

The states, however, determine entirely under their own laws the amounts of benefits, their duration, the conditions of eligibility under which they are paid, and, in general, the conditions under which they may be withheld.

The fifty-one systems of unemployment insurance in the United States differ widely in size and many other characteristics. During August 1950, South Dakota and North Dakota paid benefits to weekly averages of 275 and 330 persons, while New York and California compensated weekly averages of 228,298 and 105,475. In five states and Alaska, fewer than 60,000 persons were employed in covered industry in an average month during 1949; in another five, more than 2 million. A system may have three field offices or well over a hundred, many thousand employees or a hundred. Benefit disbursements in the fiscal year 1950 ranged from $1,168,000 in South Dakota to nearly $371 million in New York, and administrative expenses in the fiscal year 1950 from $397,000 in Delaware to more than $24 million in New York. Ten states have 63 per cent of the covered workers in the whole country, while at the other end of the scale ten states cover only 2 per cent.

COVERAGE

Although the federal act applies only to services for employers of at least eight employees in each of twenty different weeks within the calendar year, only twenty-one state laws followed this federal exclusion at the end of 1950. Six states included services for employers without regard to number of employees, length of employment, or size of payroll, and eleven

10. These funds may be withdrawn only for the payment of unemployment insurance benefits, except that in 1946 the law was amended to allow withdrawals for disability benefits up to an amount equal to receipts from employee taxes. Nine states in all have had employee taxes at some time since the beginning of the program.

11. (1) The states must provide for methods of administration that are reasonably calculated to ensure full payment of unemployment compensation when due, including a merit system for the selection of employees, and administrative funds may be refused any state that in a substantial number of cases denies unemployment insurance to persons entitled to it under state law. (2) The states must provide a fair hearing for anyone whose claim to benefits is denied. (3) They must make such reports as are required by the federal government. (4) The states must furnish information to the Railroad Retirement Board and afford reasonable cooperation to all United States agencies administering any unemployment insurance law.

others covered services for employers of one or more in certain circumstances. The remaining thirteen jurisdictions have various size-of-firm restrictions. (See Appendix Table 32 for comparable data for the year 1949.)

The other coverage provisions in the federal act are substantially the same as those of old-age and survivors insurance before the 1950 amendments to the Social Security Act. All the states include at least employment covered by the federal act; generally they do not cover employment it excludes. In New York State practically all state employees have unemployment insurance protection, and eight states cover some state employees. Hawaii covers all employees of nonprofit institutions except clergymen and members of religious orders. A few other states cover some nonprofit employees excluded by the federal act.

Household workers in private homes are included in New York if four or more are employed by the same employer for at least fifteen days in the calendar year. The federal definition of agricultural labor, which is very broad and includes large groups of workers employed under substantially industrial conditions in such activities as packing and processing of agricultural products, is followed verbatim by thirty-two states and in substance by three others. The term "agricultural labor" is not defined in the statutes of the other sixteen jurisdictions, and they include by regulation many of the borderline workers excluded by the federal act.

In an average week in July 1949–June 1950 there were about 47.8 million paid employees, of whom 30.8 million, or nearly two thirds, were covered by federal-state unemployment insurance programs and an additional 1.5 million by unemployment insurance provisions of the Railroad Retirement Act. (See Table 47.)

TABLE 47

LABOR FORCE, BY STATUS OF COVERAGE BY UNEMPLOYMENT INSURANCE IN AN AVERAGE WEEK OF THE YEARS ENDED JUNE 30, 1948 AND 1950

(*In Millions*)

Group	Number of Persons 1948	1950
Total labor force	62.0	64.1
Unemployed	2.1	3.7
Employed	59.9	60.4
Self-employed and unpaid family workers	12.8	12.6
Farm operators and unpaid family workers	6.3	6.0
Urban self-employed and unpaid family workers	6.5	6.6
Paid employees	47.1	47.8
Covered by unemployment insurance	32.9	32.3
Federal-state programs	31.3	30.8
Federal program for railroad workers	1.6	1.5
Not covered by unemployment insurance	14.2	15.4
Agricultural workers	1.7	1.6
Household workers	1.7	1.9
Employees of nonprofit organizations	0.9	1.2
Employees in small nonagricultural establishments	3.4	3.5
Public employment	6.5	7.2
Civilian employees of the federal government	1.7	1.8
Members of the armed forces	1.3	1.4
Employees of state and local governments	3.5	3.9

Sources: Data on labor force, unemployed and total employed from "Monthly Report on the Labor Force," Bureau of the Census; employment covered by unemployment insurance estimated by the Bureau of Employment Security; employment not covered by unemployment insurance from Bureau of the Census, adjusted by Bureau of Old-Age and Survivors Insurance and Bureau of Employment Security.

BENEFITS

The amount of benefits to which a worker is entitled is always related in some way to the rate at which the worker earned wages in covered employment. Most laws aim at replacement of from 50 to 60 per cent of previous wages for workers whose benefits are below the maximum. Eleven states pay an additional weekly allowance for dependents.

In the early laws the weekly benefit rate was usually defined as a percentage of the "full-time weekly wage," but this approach proved difficult administratively and most laws now try to get at the same objective presumptively, expressing the benefit rate as a fraction of the highest quarterly earnings in the base period. Eight states relate the weekly rate not to high-quarter earnings but to total base period earnings, and two relate it to average earnings during weeks of actual employment.

Limits on Benefits

Although the intent of the high-quarter-wages and the total-base-period-wages approach is to vary benefits according to the earnings of the worker, this goal is not realized in a large percentage of cases because of the operation of the maximums in the state laws. During 1949, 60 per cent of all weeks of total unemployment compensated were at the maximum. (See Appendix Table 33.) The maximum weekly benefit amounts allowed by state laws range from $15 to $26 for single workers;[12] in those few states with allowances for dependents the maximums may be considerably higher, rising in Massachusetts, which has no dollar maximum, to average weekly earnings during specified periods. (See Appendix Table 34.)

The effect of the maximums is to reduce greatly the percentage of wage replacement for the higher-paid workers. Thus, with a $25 maximum benefit, a $50-a-week worker would get a 50 per cent replacement but a $75-a-week worker would get only a 33⅓ per cent replacement.

The minimum provisions have the opposite effect. A worker whose benefit rate is raised by the minimum receives a higher percentage of his highest-quarter earnings than the formula provides for. All but four states have minimums of $5 or more for single workers; eight states have minimums of $10 a week; one, of $15 a week. In 1949, however, a little less than 2 per cent of the weeks of total unemployment compensated were at the minimum rate specified in the state law.

Most weekly payments are for amounts considerably above the minimums. During 1949, 87 per cent of all weekly payments for total unemployment were $15 or more, and the average payment was about $20.50. Less than 3 per cent of these payments were below $10; 70 per cent were $20 or more; and 30 per cent were $25 or more. (See Appendix Table 33.)

The duration of benefits also varies greatly from state to state. Fifteen states have a uniform duration — that is, the maximum number of weeks for which benefits are payable is the same for everyone. Among these fifteen states, the uniform number of weeks for which benefits are payable ranges from twelve weeks in one state to twenty-six in another. In the remaining states, the number of weeks for which benefits are payable varies according to the total wages earned or the weeks of employment during the base period. In the states with variable duration the maximum ranges from sixteen to twenty-six weeks and the minimum duration from more than one week to fifteen weeks. (See Appendix Table 35.)

12. In Kansas the maximum varies. For claims filed between January 1 and December 31, 1950, the maximum is $27.

ELIGIBILITY

The eligibility requirements in unemployment insurance are of two types: (1) those that test the worker's previous attachment to covered employment, by requiring either a certain period of work in covered employment or covered wages of a certain amount, and (2) those designed to determine the willingness, the ability and the availability of the claimant for work.

It is estimated that in 1949 more than 44 million workers had some covered employment but only 36 million had enough to entitle them to benefits in the event of unemployment. The criteria used in determining whether there has been sufficient attachment to the covered labor force to justify the payment of benefits differ widely from state to state. Wisconsin, Michigan and Ohio use a direct measure of time worked, requiring that the claimant shall have worked in each of at least fourteen weeks in a year; Utah requires nineteen weeks. Most states measure attachment indirectly by requiring earnings during a one-year qualifying period equal to a certain multiple of the weekly benefit amount, most frequently thirty. These states accompany this formula by a requirement of minimum annual earnings in the one-year qualifying period and sometimes also require that a minimum amount must have been earned during the quarter of highest earnings. This criterion ordinarily assumes employment in more than one calendar quarter with a specified distribution of earnings between the high quarter and the rest of the year. Nineteen states have a simpler requirement, namely, that a minimum amount, varying from $100 to $600, must have been earned in the one-year qualifying period; this is supplemented occasionally by a requirement of some earnings in at least two calendar quarters. (See Appendix Table 34.)

All states require that a worker file a claim and register for work with the employment service as a test of his availability, but they differ on such questions as whether he must seek work actively on his own initiative (twenty-two states now have this requirement) or whether it is sufficient for him to apply for jobs to which the employment service refers him. The states also differ in the interpretation of their laws as to what shall be considered availability for and ability to work. The states are placing increased emphasis on intensive periodic reinterviews with claimants in order to ascertain their continued availability for work.

DISQUALIFICATIONS

Disqualifications for benefits, contained in all state laws, are an attempt to determine whether the claimant genuinely desires to work and to compensate only unemployment that is not the worker's own fault. A worker may be disqualified for three main causes: refusal of suitable work without good cause, discharge for misconduct, and voluntary leaving without good cause. (See Appendix Table 36 for state provisions.) All states also disqualify, at least for a limited period, workers whose unemployment is directly due to a labor dispute in their work place.

The eligibility conditions relate to a continuing current situation; that is, to be eligible for benefits a person must be able to work, willing to work and available for work throughout the period for which he is drawing benefits. Disqualifications, on the other hand, are related to a specific act that usually results in disqualification for benefits for a given period or, under some laws, in some sort of penalty such as reduction or cancellation of benefit rights.

FINANCING

In financing unemployment insurance the most significant fact is the relationship of the program to the business cycle. The problem is to have income approximate outgo over a relatively brief period such as might ordinarily encompass a single cycle.

The Advisory Council on Social Security, in its report to the Senate Finance Committee at the close of 1948, estimated that the benefit costs of a considerably liberalized program would average between 1.7 and 2.0 per cent of covered payrolls over the next ten years. The costs for the individual states would, of course, depend on the incidence of unemployment. On the basis of past benefit experience the Advisory Council showed a range in costs for the individual states of from 0.8–0.9 to 2.5–2.9. (See Appendix Table 37.)

These estimates were based on two economic assumptions, one of a business cycle with from 2 to 5 million unemployed and one of a cycle with 2 to 10 million unemployed. Even more pessimistic prospects, however, do not increase costs greatly; according to the Council, a cycle with unemployment going as high as 13 million would increase costs by only 5 to 10 per cent. This is true because in a severe depression an increasing proportion of the unemployed are not entitled to the insurance benefit, since they will have exhausted their rights and will find it difficult to earn eligibility for new benefits. Thus the fact that unemployment insurance is insurance against only relatively short-term unemployment limits the uncertainty in estimating costs and makes it possible to finance the system on an insurance premium basis.

Income from taxes over the past ten years has greatly exceeded benefit costs, so that very large reserve funds have been built up in most states. The total reserve for the country as a whole was $6.7 billion on June 30, 1950. Since in unemployment insurance there is no reason for the reserves to be more than a contingency amount, it would be desirable for many states over the next ten-year cycle to set contribution rates below the cost of benefits and to utilize a portion of the excess reserves for benefit payments.

IMPACT OF UNEMPLOYMENT INSURANCE

The ultimate justification of social security is the welfare of the individual. Unemployment insurance, however, has a usefulness that goes beyond the payment of benefits to individuals. It is also a device for cushioning the contraction of consumption in periods of declining employment. This effect tends to smooth the cyclical ups and downs in business activity. Unemployment insurance is particularly useful for this purpose because it functions automatically.[13] It is not necessary to get agreement on the need for measures to combat the deflationary effects of a depression; a going system of unemployment insurance pays out cash at the time when it will do the most good, automatically, at the very beginning of a downward trend in employment.

Unemployment insurance would be most effective in preventing unemployment from affecting the purchasing power of workers if it were to provide benefits equal to their wage losses. But if benefits were equal to full-time wages, workers would have little or no economic incentive to prefer work to benefits. For this reason, unemployment insurance will always

13. Sumner H. Slichter, *The American Economy: Its Problems and Prospects,* Knopf, New York, 1948, pp. 107–12.

have to replace less than the income lost through unemployment. The goal might well be the one stated by the Advisory Council on Social Security to the Senate Finance Committee: "Unemployment insurance payments should be as high a proportion of wage loss caused by unemployment as is practicable without inducing people to prefer idleness to work."

It is obviously quite impossible to tell with any degree of accuracy at what point benefits are so high as to induce people to prefer idleness to work. Presumably, therefore, the statement contemplates that benefits should be placed at a level that would not serve as an inducement to idleness for the great majority of persons under the program.

Several factors have an important bearing on the question of incentives and level of benefits.

1. The offer of benefits is for a limited time only. When good jobs are difficult to get a worker would be unusually shortsighted to prefer benefits for a maximum of twenty to twenty-six weeks followed by a possible period of unemployment without benefits to a steady job, even for a weekly wage not much higher than his unemployment benefits.
2. Realistically, in considering incentives, benefits should be related to the net income from work rather than the gross wage. The expenses of working — transportation, additional clothes, income tax and so on — may average from 5 to 10 per cent of earnings.
3. The most significant factor in considering incentives is the relationship of the benefit rate to the individual worker's earning capacity and standard of living. Incentives are not primarily concerned with the relationship of the benefit to some generalized standard of living such as a "subsistence standard" or a "health and decency standard," but to what a particular worker has come to consider his own standard and what he can command in the labor market. A worker who has regularly earned wages less than sufficient for the subsistence needs of his family has less economic incentive to work if the benefit paid is enough for subsistence than does an $80-a-week worker who is offered a $40-a-week benefit.
4. It is likely that benefits for lower-paid workers can be somewhat higher in proportion to earnings than those for higher-paid workers without affecting incentives. Practically all income of lower-paid workers goes for absolute necessities, and a difference of 20 to 25 per cent between benefits and wage income may be crucial in providing the necessities in the family budget. To the $75- or $80-a-week worker, 20 or 25 per cent of his weekly wage may not be crucial.
5. The same general reasoning applies to workers with dependents as compared with those without dependents. There is less leeway in the budget of the family man than in that of a single man who earns the same amount; preference for a job as against benefits can probably be preserved for a family man on a smaller differential between benefits and earnings than for a single man.

From the standpoint of incentives, benefits can probably be considerably higher in dollar amounts for those who earn more, but higher in proportion to previous earnings for lower-paid wage earners and those with dependents.

To function effectively as a device for cushioning the contraction of consumption in a period of unemployment, unemployment insurance benefits need to be considerably liberalized, particularly at the maximum. Duration also needs to be extended in many states, and coverage should be more inclusive. It is probable that in the country as a whole unemployment insurance now compensates for not more than 15 to 20 per cent of all income loss resulting from unemployment and probably for only about 30 per cent of the loss suffered by persons eligible for benefits.

The effectiveness of unemployment insurance as a method of reducing the ups and downs of business is also limited by the experience-rating plans now in effect in all states. These plans differ widely in their sensitivity to changes in general employment conditions, but they all to a greater or lesser degree tend to cause an increase in tax rates at the very time that business is least able to afford increasing costs. The situation would be greatly improved if unemployment insurance taxes were put on a flat basis so that the same percentage of payrolls would be collected in bad times as in good. An even better device from the standpoint of fiscal policy would be to relate the tax rate to the volume of employment in such a way that the tax would rise when employment was good and fall as unemployment increased.

Public Assistance

The responsibility for public assistance programs in the United States is shared by local, state and federal governments.

With the passage of the Social Security Act in 1935, the federal government assumed substantial responsibility on a continuing basis for public assistance to the needy aged, blind, and dependent children. The Social Security Act amendments of 1950 added a new category, aid to permanently and totally disabled persons, effective as of October 1, 1950, and also authorized the federal government to share in assistance payments for the mother or other relative caring for dependent children. Before the 1950 amendments, the federal government could not share in the cost of medical care for recipients of assistance unless an amount for such care was included in the payment to the recipient himself. By the terms of the new amendments, however, the federal government may now share in payments made directly to doctors or others who have furnished the recipient with medical care.

For the four special categories of assistance, the federal government pays one half the cost of administration; it also supplies somewhat more than half of the assistance payments, on the basis of formulas specified in the law. Several changes have been made in these formulas since 1935, the latest occurring in 1948 and 1952. The formula for aid to permanently and totally disabled persons was made in 1948 the same as the one established for old-age assistance and aid to the blind. In these three categories, the formula determining the federal share is three fourths of the first $20 of the average monthly payments in a state plus half the remainder, within individual maximums of $50. In aid to dependent children the federal share is three fourths of the first $12 of the average payment plus half the remainder, within maximums of $27 for an adult caring for the children, $27 for the first child in the family, and $18 for each additional child.[14] Except for the emergency programs in the early 1930's no federal funds have been made available for general assistance.

14. The 1950 amendments extended federal participation in all public assistance categories to Puerto Rico and the Virgin Islands, but on a more limited basis.

State Administration

Although the federal government has been providing considerably more than half the money for the categories of assistance included in the Social Security Act, administration of the program remains a state responsibility. The Social Security Act sets up certain broad standards to which the states must conform as a condition of receiving federal funds, but the states have considerable latitude in determining who shall be eligible for assistance and how much they shall receive. Consequently, there is a wide range in the proportion of persons receiving assistance in the several states. The range in the amount of the average payment (see Appendix Table 38) not only indicates differences in the need to be met and ability to meet the need, but also reflects the wide state diversity in standards and policies.

Some states base the assistance grant on a detailed budget of what a particular person needs and, subtracting all he himself has, pay the difference. In states with insufficient appropriations, grants may be consistently only a fraction of this "budgetary deficiency." In old-age assistance, a few states do not use a detailed budget in arriving at the grant but subtract any income the recipient may have from a flat figure assumed to be the minimum needed by all aged persons. Except for the aid-to-the-blind category, states are required to take into account all income and resources of the individual in determining eligibility for and amount of payment. The federal law, however, does not require that a recipient be completely destitute, and thus a person may be found eligible even though he owns certain minimum amounts of real and personal property. The 1950 amendments made it mandatory (as of July 1, 1952) for states to disregard the first $50 of earned income of a blind recipient.

Safeguards

Regardless of state differences, all approved programs must provide for certain safeguards of the rights of individuals. These safeguards, set down in federal law, clearly distinguish the spirit of the public assistance program of the Social Security Act from the older poor-law philosophy of punishment and reformation; general assistance, which remains outside the Social Security Act, is still administered within many states in the spirit of the poor law. Federal leadership, moreover, has been influential in getting increasingly more objective and uniform administration of assistance, so that the right of needy persons to aid has become clearer.

The safeguards in the federal act include the right of every person who wishes to make application for assistance to be given the opportunity to do so; the right to a fair hearing if a person's claim for assistance is denied or is not acted upon with reasonable promptness; the right to confidential treatment of information given by an applicant or recipient; the right to receive a cash payment without restriction on its use; and the right of participation in the state plan regardless of the part of the state in which a person may live. The federal act also places restrictions on the residence and old-age requirements a state may impose; prohibits any citizenship requirement that excludes a citizen of the United States; requires efficient and proper administration, including the selection of personnel on a merit basis; and makes certain other administrative and financial requirements.

Trends in Social Security

Social security in the United States is still evolving in concept, organization and administration. Although more than a decade and a half has passed since the Social Security Act became law, we have yet to arrive at an established and settled pattern. We have gone far enough, however, to acquire characteristics of our own with resemblances to and differences from the basic measures of other nations.

Universalization

The United States, like other countries, shows a tendency toward universalizing social security in terms of the people covered and the risks against which they are protected. Universalization in the sense of the inclusion of all income groups was established in the original legislation. Persons may qualify for old-age and survivors insurance and for unemployment insurance no matter how large their earnings have been. People quite generally, even persons far from the lower income groups, want to be included in old-age and survivors insurance and count on these benefits in making their plans for retirement and other eventualities.

Amendments to the original Social Security Act have substantially broadened it, both by adding new categories — to the old-age insurance program, survivors insurance, and to the public assistance program, the permanently and totally disabled — and by bringing new groups into old-age insurance and public assistance.[15] In unemployment insurance, individual states have included occupations and the smaller establishments excluded by the federal act.

Four states have established cash sickness benefits for insured workers. The federal program of railroad retirement has been amended to include unemployment insurance, sickness and disability. Medical care insurance is a hotly debated subject, but all parties to the argument agree that sufficient facilities should be established to make these services universally accessible. Permanent and total disability insurance was voted by the House of Representatives in 1950 but failed to pass the Senate.

Structure of Contributions and Benefits

The principle of contributions from the insured individual was incorporated in the original legislation for old-age and survivors insur-

15. The 1952 amendments to the Social Security Act increased old-age and survivors insurance benefits, beginning with the month of September 1952. The new benefit formula provides a monthly benefit for the retired worker equal to 55 per cent of the first $100 of the average monthly wage plus 15 per cent of the next $200. This formula will provide an average benefit of about $65 for the man retiring in the near future, and when both man and wife are entitled the combined benefits will probably average slightly more than $100. The benefits of about 4.5 million people already on the benefit rolls were also increased, those for the retired worker by 12½ per cent or $5, whichever was the larger. The average benefit for September 1952 for retired workers on the roll was increased to about $48. The "retirement test" was raised from $50 to $75 and maximum benefits for a family were raised from $150 to $168.75.

The federal share in the matching formula for public assistance was also changed. The federal government now pays for aid to dependent children four fifths of the first $15 of average payment plus one half of the remainder, with maximums of $30 for an adult caring for the children, $30 for the first child and $21 for each additional child. For the other assistance categories the federal government pays four fifths of the first $25 of the average payment and one half of the balance up to a maximum of $55 monthly for an individual.

ance. In unemployment insurance, nine states have required employee contributions at one time or another. Only two now have this provision, but there is some demand for reintroduction of employee contributions. For old-age and survivors insurance, the contributory principle has general support. For both programs the concept of prior work as a condition of eligibility for benefits and of wages as the basis for determining benefits is strongly supported. A wage-connected program clearly differentiates itself from the means test and makes plain what has been called the individual's proprietary right to his insurance.

In the United States both contributions and benefits are geared to earnings. Both old-age and survivors insurance and unemployment insurance reflect wage differentials. In old-age and survivors insurance lower-paid workers receive the largest percentage of their wages in benefits. Thus the man who earns more receives more, but the man who earns least receives the largest percentage of what he earns.[16]

Financing

Social insurance in the United States, unlike the British and most other systems, has not included a government contribution. Unemployment insurance has no need for support from general taxes. It is possible, however, that in the long run a government contribution will be introduced in old-age and survivors insurance. A level premium rate for the present system that would cover the cost of benefits for those with a working lifetime under the program would be about 2 per cent of wages up to $3,600 for the employee and 2 per cent for the employer. Yet, unless the present method of financing is revised, workers and their employers will eventually be paying at the combined rate of 6½ per cent. This is because the cost of paying full-rate benefits to workers already old at the beginning of the system and able to pay only a fraction of the cost of their annuities has been included in the general contribution rate. The Committee on Economic Security recommended in 1935 that this cost should be borne by a government contribution out of general taxation, and the Advisory Council of 1948 recommended that at least the major part of this cost be borne in this way.

Insurance or Assistance?

The pioneers of 1935 saw social security as essentially a system of social insurance, and this has been the goal of the program. The framers of the original act, however, incorporated three titles on public assistance, designed to provide for persons who were not eligible for any or adequate insurance, for example, the aged who were no longer in the labor market or persons who were in excluded occupations or had not earned enough in covered jobs to qualify for any or adequate benefits. The hope then, as now, was that the insurance program would soon be extended to everybody and that the number of persons receiving assistance would be kept to a minimum.

The number of recipients of old-age assistance has declined recently. It was steadily increasing before World War II, dropped slightly during the war, and rose again after the middle of 1945. The first postwar decrease occurred in October 1950, mainly as a result of the sharp increase in the number of aged persons becoming eligible for benefits under old-age and survivors insurance following the enactment of the 1950 amendments to the Social Security Act. In 1950 the number of aged persons receiving old-age and survivors insurance benefits exceeded, for the first time, the number of recipients of old-age assistance. (See Figure 39.)

Although public assistance represents an improvement over the poor law, it still carries the liabilities of the means test, inevitably a difficult personal experience for prospective and actual recipients. The fact that the best administrators of assistance are also the most vigorous advocates of social insurance shows how deeply those who understand the means test appreciate the depressing restrictions it places upon the individual. Granted that there will always be a number of persons in need who will not receive insurance benefits or who, though receiving insurance, will require supplementary assistance, the $2 billion in federal and state funds paid for assistance in 1950 may be said, in general, to evidence gaps in our insurance program.

16. Although typical of most social insurance systems, this benefit structure differs sharply from the British system. In England, insurance is contributory and work-connected, but both contributions and benefits are flat amounts.

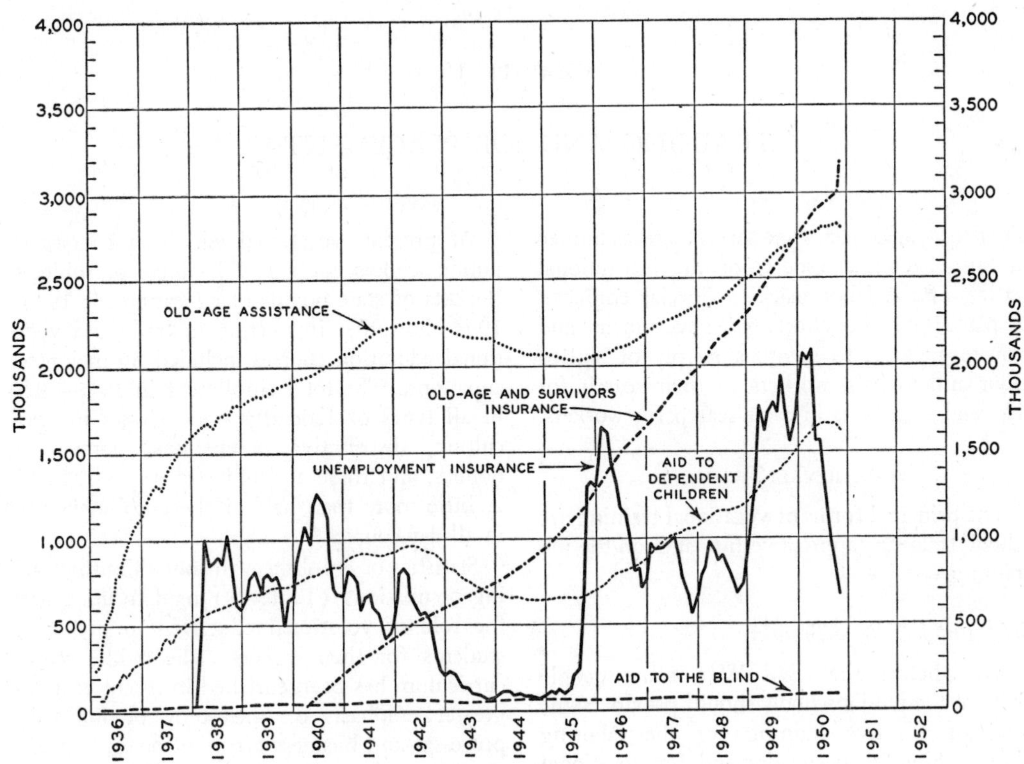

FIGURE 39. SOCIAL INSURANCE BENEFICIARIES AND PUBLIC ASSISTANCE RECIPIENTS UNDER THE SOCIAL SECURITY ACT, FEBRUARY 1936–OCTOBER 1950

Sources: For data through June 1947, Annual Report of the Federal Security Agency, 1947, p. 17; other data from *Social Security Bulletin* and Bureau of Old-Age and Survivors Insurance.

CONCLUSION

The program of social security that was inaugurated in 1935 is one of the most constructive expressions of the change that has taken place in the attitude of the state toward the citizen, especially the worker. During most of the years in which our democratic free-enterprise society has been emerging, the function of government has been essentially negative, its aim being to police. Today, however, social security forms a large segment of the services offered to the individual to aid him in developing a satisfactory way of life for himself. The state thus becomes a form of social utility, a facility that men can use in solving such problems as that of maintaining an income when work is interrupted by old age or unemployment. In the past man has often achieved security at the price of freedom and freedom at the price of security. Democracy in its new function has embarked on an experiment aimed to make both security and freedom possible.

CHAPTER 15

TRAINING AND JOB PLACEMENT *

TRAINING AND JOB PLACEMENT are examined in this chapter as aspects of the institutional setting of the labor market. Special emphasis is placed on the efforts of government and private agencies to secure a supply of skilled labor and to help workers in their search for jobs and employers in their search for workers.

VOCATIONAL TRAINING

The principal forms of vocational training are school training, apprenticeship and on-the-job training.

School and College Training

Even before the Civil War, some people thought the public schools should provide some kind of effective training for the laboring classes. Since then the demand for vocational education in the public schools has increased. Only limited progress has been made, however, because the schools, in keeping with tradition, have continued to emphasize the classics and college entrance requirements. Some effort has been made to supplement the customary curriculum with "applied sciences," practical mathematics, drawing courses, and commercial and shop training. In 1914, 23 technical high schools were listed in the Report of the Federal Commissioner of Education. Most of these were in the larger cities, where diversified industries made a large demand on the schools for trained workers.

In 1917, Congress passed the Vocational Education Act (the Smith-Hughes Act), which provides federal aid to states in establishing and expanding vocational training. Since then the program of vocational education has slowly advanced. By 1937, total expenditures of local, state and federal government for vocational education in schools amounted to $30 million, or 0.9 per cent of the total outlay for public education.[1]

At present, vocational education courses in public schools cover a wide range of subjects. Reports of state boards of education for 1943–1944 show that instruction in trade and vocational education courses included 89 major occupations. The total enrollment in 1948–1949 in all types of federally aided classes in agriculture, distributive occupations, home economics, and trade and industry was 3,094,646. A little more than half of the enrollment was in all-day courses.[2]

Statistics of enrollment in courses in the leading occupations (Table 48) tend to understate the role of vocational education in preparing students for their careers. The public school curriculum has been enriched in recent years by greater emphasis on the study of industrial processes and business organization and on employment opportunities in various fields of work. In addition, many schools now provide vocational counseling to help students appraise their qualifications and interests in the light of occupational requirements and opportunities. Some of the benefits accrue indirectly through the students' ability to make better and quicker vocational adjustments, rather than through their direct preparation for specific jobs. In fact, most of the students start in unskilled jobs, and there is only a loose relationship between their expressed interests and their subsequent occupational distribution in the labor force.

In recent years vocational education has been receiving attention in both junior and senior colleges. The courses, which vary from one institution to another, are generally designed to develop practical knowledge of principles and competence in specific skills in various occupational fields. The typical course requires two years' study and frequently is tailored to meet the needs of employed workers seeking advancement.

---

* By Collis Stocking.

1. Quoted in Arthur Beverly Mays, *Concept of Vocational Education in the Thinking of the General Educator, 1845–1945,* College of Education, University of Illinois, Urbana, 1946, p. 91.

2. *Digest of Annual Reports of State Boards of Vocational Education,* Office of Education, Federal Security Agency, Washington, 1949, p. 2.

TABLE 48

ENROLLMENT IN PRINCIPAL TRADE AND VOCATIONAL EDUCATION COURSES, 1943–1944

Occupation	Enrollment
Public service	75,575
Machinist	58,270
Office occupations	33,084
Auto mechanic	32,665
Electrician	24,494
Carpenter and other woodworking occupations	19,871
Dressmaker	15,022
Draftsman	13,061
Foreman	11,784
Printer	11,340
Nurse	9,558
Radio repairman	9,452
Cosmetologist	9,090

Source: Vocational Education in the Years Ahead, Office of Education, Federal Security Agency, 1945, p. 254.

Opportunities for engineering and technical training for those few with the means and ability for such advanced work preceded vocational training in the public schools by fifty years or more. Rensselaer Polytechnic Institute granted degrees in civil engineering as early as 1835. Before 1862, when federal land grants stimulated the states to establish agricultural and technical colleges, five important scientific institutions had been established in this country.

The Office of Education recently made a survey of 1,259 institutions granting the bachelor's or more advanced degrees in 1948–1949. It found that out of a total of 366,634 bachelor's or first professional degrees granted in that school year, 61,624 were in business and commerce, 43,604 in engineering, 37,765 in education, and 14,366 in law. Out of 56,120 advanced degrees, education headed the list with 14,509, followed by engineering with 5,007 and business and economics with 3,926.[3]

Apprenticeship

The apprenticeship system, through which skills are taught to apprentices by master craftsmen, has never made much progress in this country. Rapid adoption of industrial techniques in factories made the all-around master craftsman relatively unimportant. Labor unions were slow in gaining recognition and were not strong enough to exercise much influence in determining who should or should not be permitted to enter a particular trade. The responsibility for providing such training as was necessary fell chiefly to the employer except in the crafts least affected by factory-system organization.

Apprenticeship training has created many problems between workers and employers. The number of journeymen employed places a limit upon the number of apprentices; for if there were too many apprentices, the journeymen would run the risk of lower wages or reduced opportunity for employment. Fearing that their position might be jeopardized, journeymen have often shirked teaching apprentices all the secrets of the trade. The employer has frequently been reluctant to go to the expense of rotating apprentices among different jobs because he could not be sure they would remain with him after becoming journeymen.

Nor has apprenticeship always been attractive to the apprentice. As crafts have been split up, apprentices have still been compelled to serve the customary years in training, at very low wages, although less time is now required to learn the skills. Often it has been impossible to recruit the number of apprentices agreed upon by unions and employers.

Efforts to Revive the System

During the depression of the 1930's practically all apprenticeship training was discontinued. In 1937 an effort was made to revive it through the Apprenticeship Training Act. This law authorized the Secretary of Labor to set up standards to guide industry in employing and training apprentices, to bring management and labor together to work out plans for the training of apprentices, to appoint such national committees as were needed, and to promote general acceptance of the standards and procedures agreed upon.

The Secretary established the Apprentice Training Service and the Federal Committee on Apprenticeship, made up of representatives of management, labor and interested government agencies. This committee adopted the principle that the training of apprentices should be jointly developed by and mutually satisfactory to employers and employees. Basic standards were accordingly formulated. These required, among other provisions, that apprentices be protected by a written agreement registered with a state apprenticeship council or with the Federal Committee where no state council exists. Since the passage of the act, slightly more than

3. Office of Education, Circular 262, November 1949.

half the states have established apprenticeship councils. Most of these states have also enacted legislation governing apprenticeship training.

Apprenticeable Occupations

The Federal Committee decided that only those occupations should be apprenticeable that involve skills requiring 4,000 or more hours to learn. Under its program, schedules of work processes to be learned must be established and provision must be made for progressively increasing the scale of wages until apprentice wages average approximately 50 per cent of the journeymen's rate.

Apprenticeable occupations must be ones that have customarily been learned in a practical way through training on the job and involve development of skills sufficiently broad to be applicable in similar occupations throughout industry. Occupations in selling and retailing, and similar occupations in the distribution field, managerial occupations and clerical occupations are for the most part excluded. More than a hundred basic trades have been approved, and several hundred specific occupations are included in the apprenticeable list.

Apprenticeship training has many vestigial features, and the training time for some occupations bears little relation to actual training needs. For example, apprentice time for the "top-hat" job of tool and die maker in a machine shop is four to five years, and the same time is required for so simple a job as that of mailer in the printing and publishing business.[4]

Training during the Depression

During the depression, because of the collapse of apprenticeship training, the government had to undertake the rehabilitation and training of youth through such programs as the Civilian Conservation Corps and the National Youth Administration.

In seven years the CCC enrolled nearly 2.5 million youths and organized them in resident camps. Each camp normally housed about 200 enrollees. The CCC program provided work experience in reforestation; soil conservation; bridge and road building; and lodge, cabin and dam construction. It also provided special training in mechanical trades, communications, surveying and mapping, drafting, blueprint reading, carpentry, electrical wiring, and many other occupations and pursuits. Millions of other youths were trained by the NYA in its job shops throughout the country, where it taught the principal operations and uses of machines and tools used in machine shops and sheet metal working shops; in welding, forge and foundry work; and in electrical equipment and radio manufacturing.

Defense and War Experience

Both NYA training and vocational training in public schools were given a big fillip in 1940 when Congress appropriated $15 million for training in occupations essential to national defense. Between 1940 and 1945 Congress made available a total of nearly $327 million for training defense and war production workers in industrial occupations and trades and $63 million for training in agriculture through the rural and food production training programs.

At first the training was governed largely by the facilities available and the interest of individual training officers, rather than by defense needs. Later programs were better adapted to the needs of the trainee who went directly into war work. After we entered the war, however, it was possible for totally inexperienced youths to find employment at relatively high wages and to be trained on the job. Indeed, because of the rigidity of union-fixed wages as compared with wages paid in the new war industries, many young, inexperienced war workers soon could earn more than their master-craftsmen fathers working in old-established industries.

On-the-job training expanded greatly during the war. The demand for skilled labor was so urgent that it could not be met by the apprenticeship system with its long years of training. Jobs were broken down so that workers with a few weeks' training could perform the simpli-

4. The requirements for mailer according to the U.S. Employment Service Dictionary of Occupational Titles (revised edition) are: "Mailer — Printing and Publishing — Mailing Room Clerk: Performs any one or a combination of the following duties concerned with mailing or dispatching newspapers, periodicals, envelopes and cartons or other bulk printed matter: addresses bundles and individual copies by hand or machine, or stamps, tags, or labels them with other identifying information. Inserts, takes from escalators, sacks, bundles, wraps and ties printed matter. Stacks bundles for shipment and loads and unloads bundles onto and from trucks and conveyors. Sorts and routes bundles, operates stencil machines, and files and corrects stencils. Counts and keeps record of number of bundles or individual copies handled."

fied, single-skill tasks. Supervisory training was especially emphasized so that skilled workers might be used more effectively.

Only in this way were we able to achieve the phenomenal production record of World War II. In no industry did we have enough skilled workers, by normal standards, to meet requirements. For example, in the beginning there were simply not enough skilled workers to carry out the construction schedule, yet it was achieved in record time as "hammer-and-saw men," "lumber butchers" and "Jacks-of-all-trades" functioned under the watchful direction of master craftsmen.

It was said that anyone who innocently entered a hardware store to purchase a few nails to patch up a back porch or repair a chicken coop was recruited on the spot and immediately transported to a job site as a carpenter. The story is apocryphal, of course, but it illustrates the extent to which unskilled workers were quickly integrated into our labor force. Inexperienced factory workers would sometimes quit after a few weeks' work and find employment in another plant at a grade or two above the beginner's rate. The fact that the embryonic craftsman was not without recognition save in his own plant was among the causes of the enormous turnover in employment.

The Postwar Period

Since World War II, government subsidies under the Servicemen's Readjustment Act of 1944 have reinvigorated apprentice training. The ex-serviceman who enters into an apprentice contract is entitled to receive payments from the federal government to supplement his apprentice wage while he is in training. According to the records of the Apprentice Training Service (since 1948, the Bureau of Apprenticeship), 236,515 registered apprentices (veterans and others) were in training in June 1949. Two thirds of them were concentrated in ten occupations. The apprentices constituted only a small fraction of the total employed in these occupations as reported in the 1940 census. (See Table 49.)

The government allowance to veterans has tended to divert attention from the facts that the apprenticeship term for some occupations far exceeds the time necessary to learn the skills and that, in many instances, not enough credit is allowed for experience or skills acquired before indenture. The subsidy has not overcome, and in some instances has intensified, the controversy between labor and management over the number of apprentices necessary to assure an "adequate" supply of craftsmen in the future.

TABLE 49

REGISTERED APPRENTICES IN TEN MAJOR OCCUPATIONS, JUNE 1949

Occupation	Years of Training	Number of Apprentices	Number of Persons in the Occupation, 1940 Census
All occupations	—	236,515	—
Ten major occupations	—	151,762	3,013,936
Carpenter	4	39,450	766,213
Auto mechanic . .	3–4	29,062	441,845
Electrician	4–5	19,563	227,102
Plumber and fitter	4–5	21,274	210,815
Machinist	4	9,751	521,093
Toolmaker	4–7	6,291	96,885
Painter	3	6,480	442,659
Tinsmith	4	10,124	91,595
Cabinetmaker . . .	3–4	5,226	58,837
Meat cutter	3	4,541	156,892
Other occupations . .	—	84,753	—

Source: Bureau of Apprenticeship.

Veterans Training [5]

The Servicemen's Readjustment Act of 1944 sharply stimulated vocational education and training. In addition to providing for rehabilitation of the disabled, the act entitles persons whose education or training was delayed or interrupted by service in the armed forces, or who desire a refresher or retraining course, to receive further education or training at government expense. The amount of training or education depends on the time spent in service, and in most cases is set at two years. Schools and institutions providing training are entitled to regular tuition fees not to exceed $500 annually for each registrant under the act. Establishments offering on-the-job training are not entitled to tuition for the trainees. Originally an ex-serviceman with no dependents was entitled to a subsistence allowance of $50 a month, an ex-serviceman with dependents to $75 a month; these amounts have been raised, first to $65 and $90, respectively, and later to $75 and $105 for student veterans with one dependent and $120 for those with more than one dependent.

At the beginning of the program, no basic standards governed the activities in which train-

5. Cf. Chapter 13.

ing could be given or the curricula to be offered. Consequently, allowances to veterans for on-the-job training were frequently used merely to subsidize low wages in occupations requiring little training.[6]

Schooling for Veterans

Training in educational institutions raised many similar problems. New institutions were established and old ones were rapidly expanded to collect the tuition fees that the government allowed for training ex-servicemen. Ex-servicemen were persuaded to enroll for training in already overcrowded fields. Sometimes "schools" offered training on a "cafeteria" basis in social dancing, elocution and public speaking, photography, elementary music and so forth.

According to the law, no federal department or agency could exercise any supervision or control whatsoever over any state educational agency or state apprenticeship agency, or any educational or training institution that trained veterans under the government's program. The Administrator of Veterans Affairs therefore gave the governors of the states major responsibility for selecting and approving training projects.

Early in 1946, however, the Veterans Administration issued a circular on the supervision of veterans enrolled for training purposes. The field managers were directed to supervise veterans enrolled in schools and in on-the-job training to the extent necessary to protect the interests of the government and the veterans. Shortly afterward the Retraining and Reemployment Administration, working through an intergovernmental committee, developed "Recommended Criteria for Approval of Establishments Offering Non-Agricultural On-the-Job Training for Veterans." Some of these criteria were later included in the act passed in the same year (Public Law 679), which prevented a veteran from drawing full subsistence allowances while engaged in employment in which training was only incidental or in which wages were so high as to scarcely justify a subsidy. The act limited the total amount a trainee could receive in wages plus allowances to $175 a month for trainees without dependents and to $200 for trainees with dependents. Since this was less than the apprentice wage scale in some occupations, the law was changed in 1948 to allow $210 for trainees without dependents, $270 for trainees with one dependent, and $290 for trainees with more than one dependent.

In January 1950 nearly 2.4 million persons were enrolled in the various types of training subsidized under the Vocational Rehabilitation Act and the Servicemen's Readjustment Act. (See Table 50.)

Job Placement

Approximately 1,750,000 persons, mostly boys and girls graduated from school, enter the labor market each year. These new entrants have a wide variety of experience and ability. A few have the necessary educational qualifications to fill technical and professional jobs. Practically all possess the minimum educational qualifications for more than two thirds of the occupations found in our economy, but few are qualified to fill semiskilled occupations, since these qualifications can be acquired only on the job.

Theoretically, each new entrant will be looking for work that he is qualified for and that will equip him for progressively more responsible, more challenging and better-paying employment suitable for an adult career. He has probably discussed his future many times with his parents and his chums; perhaps he has even taken a guidance course in school. His father may have asked the foreman in the plant where he works to consider his son for a job. Maybe an uncle, a friend or some chance acquaintance knows of a job. Perhaps the job-seeker finds an opportunity in the help-wanted section of a newspaper. Maybe he just starts out making the rounds of establishments in the community without the benefit of "leads." Or maybe he goes to his local public employment service or to a private agency.

In some instances the new entrant will embark on a work career that will not change, except through promotion, during the rest of his life. More likely, however, because of plant shutdowns or because of his personal dissatisfaction and the urge to "get ahead," a worker will be looking for a job many times during his life, will have many employers, and more than

6. A few ex-servicemen who were already well established vocationally before they entered military service returned to their old, well-paid positions and claimed subsistence allowances, declaring themselves in training for the presidency of the company for which they worked.

TABLE 50

ENROLLMENT IN TRAINING SUBSIDIZED UNDER VOCATIONAL REHABILITATION ACT AND SERVICEMEN'S READJUSTMENT ACT, JANUARY 1950

Type of Training	Enrollment
Total	2,397,429
Institutions of higher learning	842,241
On-the-farm training	343,507
On-the-job training	306,362
Others (high schools, industrial schools, etc.)	905,319

Source: Monthly Progress Report, Veterans Administration.

once will use the services of employment agencies. The big difference between finding the first and subsequent jobs is that along the line a worker gains skill and experience that he can try to sell to each new prospective employer.

Private Employment Agencies

Most workers obtain their jobs through friends or neighbors or through chance information, without the help of employment agencies. However, a vast number of agencies specialize in finding jobs for workers and workers for jobs. Among the most important are labor agents and contractors, private employment services, employer and union employment services, and public employment services.

Labor Agents and Contractors

With the tremendous increase in demand for labor in the second half of the nineteenth century, labor agents began to appear. Their sole business was to comb foreign countries and centers of population in this country to procure workers for railroad and other construction projects and basic industries. A crimp was put in the foreign search for workers in 1885 when the federal government prohibited the importation of contract labor; but stories of the opportunities in the new world, supported by letters from relatives and friends already in this country, stimulated a more or less continuous flow of immigrants. Along the eastern seaboard and wherever newly arrived immigrants congregated, labor agents continued to carry on a thriving business.

Since its beginning, the labor agent business has taken many different forms. Sometimes an establishment in need of workers employs agents to recruit them, sometimes it contracts with an independent labor agent and agrees to pay a specified sum for acceptable workers delivered to the job site. Fees vary widely and may be charged to both employers and employees or, in some instances, to employees only. The agent may merely recruit and deliver the labor or he may subsequently provide a commissary service at the job site. In some cases, as in seasonal agricultural work, the agent may contract with the employer to furnish a labor force to do a specified job, such as harvesting a crop, and the wages for the whole group may be paid to the labor contractor, who in turn pays the workers at a lower wage rate.

The business of labor agents, or "labor scouts," as they are sometimes called, boomed during World War I. Frequently they operated as labor pirates and enticed men from their current employment with promises of better jobs. After collecting a crew of workers for one employer, they sometimes sold the crew to a second employer who was willing to outbid the first. Sometimes, not satisfied with the substantial fee received from one employer, they would immediately transfer the crew to another employer in a different locality and collect again for the same workers. Labor pirating became so extensive that the federal government established the United States Employment Service and required employers of a hundred workers or more to hire all "common" labor through it.

During the depression of the 1930's, certain segments of the labor agent business prospered. Millions of industrial workers, as well as farm owners and tenants, were uprooted from their customary pursuits and engulfed by a tide of unemployment, privation and uncertainty.[7] Labor agents and labor contractors played an important role in the employment of agricultural workers along both the eastern and western seaboards, of beet-sugar workers in Michigan, Ohio and Wisconsin, and of railroad maintenance and construction workers throughout the country.

The contract system was originally developed in the employment of aliens in California agriculture. The House Select Committee appointed in 1940 "to inquire into the interstate migration of destitute citizens" found that though the use of alien immigrant labor in California agriculture had definitely decreased, in relation to the use of so-called white American labor,

7. Steinbeck dramatically portrayed the fate of some of these people in their search for employment in *The Grapes of Wrath.*

nevertheless, the contract system was much more prevalent throughout California agriculture than was commonly supposed. The committee investigators reported that some one hundred and fifty licensed labor contractors and a larger number of unlicensed contractors were operating in that state, and many also in Arizona, Oregon, Washington, Idaho and Utah.

Certain contractors, the investigators found, employed as few as six to twelve or fifteen workers, some as many as five or six hundred. According to the committee, employers generally avail themselves of the contract system in order to escape responsibility for workmen's compensation insurance and for maintenance of labor camps and adequate housing, and to reduce the expenses of recruitment, transportation and supervision. The system leads to abuse, not only in the form of excessive recruitment of workers, which keeps wage rates down, but also in excessive deductions by the contractors from the workers' meager earnings.

Recruitment of railroad maintenance and construction workers through labor agents is a long-established custom. Commissary agents also recruit workers through advertising and recruitment agents at an agreed fee for each worker. Sometimes the agent charges the worker an additional fee for getting him a job. The workers are generally housed in company facilities, with the commissary furnishing board, which is paid for by deductions from the workers' earnings.

Because of their varying operations and the ease with which labor agents may start business, no statistics on their activities are available; but we know they figure prominently in some fields of employment. In many others they are anachronistic hangers-on from a day when the employment market was unorganized. When something happens to disturb the customary employment process — a depression, a shortage of labor — labor agents reappear in force. They have been used at times to recruit labor for strikebreaking purposes and for activities that could not be manned in any other way.

The comments of the Chairman of the House Select Committee throw some light on the importance of the labor agent in our enocomy. Testifying in 1941, he said:

> Out of the voluminous testimony taken by the committee, in more than 20,000 miles of travel throughout the country, emerges a distressing picture of fraud and abuse in the recruitment of labor by numerous unscrupulous private employment agencies and labor contractors. The committee learned of the deliberate spread of misinformation, with regard to employment, by those labor agents and labor contractors who prey on the defenseless migrant. It was informed of excessive fees, paid by workers for employment, out of all proportion to the wages earned. It obtained proof of exorbitant registration charges and of workers being sent to nonexistent jobs only to be left stranded and at the mercy of the community. Many witnesses told of agencies inducing the discharge of workers solely for the sake of collecting additional fees, and even splitting these fees with some of the very employers of the discharged workers.
>
> The committee found that not only the worker but frequently the employer as well is victimized. Employers have no guaranty, after paying fees to obtain labor, that the labor agent will not take away the crew and sell them to other employers at a higher price.
>
> Witnesses described commissaries and store camps, set up by labor contractors, charging oppressive prices to workers compelled frequently to patronize them. They told of camps and lodging houses, unsanitary and dangerous to health, run by contractors greedy for additional profits.
>
> These uncontrolled practices include the importation of workers from distant points to many communities where local labor is not fully employed. The labor market is glutted, wage and hour standards are depressed, and community facilities are overburdened. A severe burden is placed on the community to which the unfortunate migrant is misdirected.[8]

Private Employment Services

To most persons trying to find a job, private employment services or agencies are far more important than labor agents and contractors, to which private employment services are in a sense successors. The nature and the scope of the business conducted by these private agencies vary so widely, however, that it is difficult to classify them. Few agencies today specialize in recruiting and placing unskilled workers as such, although many are organized on an industrial basis and may deal with all types of workers in an industry. Some of the more important occupational groups in which the private employment services specialize are domestic servants, restaurant and hotel workers, skilled and semiskilled workers, factory workers, commercial and clerical workers, school teachers, technicians and engineers, and actors, radio artists and musicians.

---

8. Hearings before the Subcommittee of the Committee on Labor, 77th Cong., on H.R. 5510, A Bill to Regulate Private Employment Agencies Engaged in Interstate Commerce, House of Representatives, 1941, p. 14.

Private employment agencies thrive because the labor market has become very complex; a large number of establishments do the hiring for a wide variety of occupations requiring a broad range of labor skills and abilities. The private agencies become thoroughly familiar with the jobs in which they specialize and with the industrial processes and the practices of individual employing establishments. They learn to recognize quickly the job requirements and the qualifications necessary for filling them. They frequently try to give highly personalized service to both employer and worker. For some jobs this may include investigation of the character and personality of the applicant. Occasionally they help applicants assess their experience and recommend the work they should pursue. Theatrical or motion-picture agencies may establish a continuing artist-manager relation that goes far beyond what is popularly regarded as the business of a private employment service. Generally, however, the efficiency of private services depends primarily on their understanding of the particular segment of the labor market in which they operate and their good relations with employers who have jobs to offer.

Most private services are financed solely by fees paid by the applicants they place. The fee is generally a percentage of the first week's or first month's pay. Some agencies charge workers a small registration fee to discourage aimless job-shoppers.

There are an estimated 3,000 to 4,000 private agencies in this country. Although accurate figures on their volume of business are lacking, they no doubt make millions of placements each year.[9]

Private agencies often organize themselves into trade associations. While the purposes of these associations vary, most of them try to stamp out agency abuses. In their standards or codes of ethics, they agree to avoid misrepresenting wages and conditions of employment, referring workers without employer authorization, splitting fees with foremen or other employer officials, and recruiting workers for strikebreaking purposes.

Because of abuses and because of the belief that "a man should not have to pay for the right to work," private services have been under constant attack. Labor unions, attempting to increase their share in the placement business, have regarded private agencies as competitors. In 1919 the American Federation of Labor stated in its reconstruction program:

> Essentials in industry and commerce are employees and employer, labor and capital. No one questions the right of organized capital to supply capital to employers. No one should question the right of organized labor to furnish workers. Private employment agencies abridge this right of organized labor. . . . Private employment agencies operated for profit should not be permitted to exist.[10]

Forty-two states, Alaska, Hawaii and the District of Columbia have laws dealing with private employment services. Most of the laws merely require private employment services to obtain a license and post a bond. Little attempt was made to regulate fees after 1928, when the United States Supreme Court held unconstitutional a New Jersey statute that attempted to grant licenses only to agencies keeping their fees below a designated figure. In 1941, however, the Court reversed itself and held that a private employment agency is "vitally affected with public interest" and subject to state regulation of its fees.[11]

Though private employment services have lacked champions, their right to exist has been treated sympathetically by the courts. When the state of Washington passed a measure forbidding employment agencies to charge fees for finding employment or telling a person where employment might be found, the Supreme Court of the United States said:

> Certainly there is no profession, possibly no business which does not offer peculiar opportunities for reprehensible practices; and as to every one of them no doubt some can be found quite ready and earnest to maintain that its suppression would be in the public interest. Skillfully directed agitation might also bring about apparent condemnation of any one of them by the public. Happily for all, the fundamental guaranties of the Constitution cannot be freely submerged if and whenever some ostensible justification is advanced and the police power invoked.[12]

In 1941 Congress considered but did not pass federal legislation to regulate private employment agencies engaged in interstate commerce. In the international forum of the International Labor Office, the representatives of this

9. It is estimated that in New York City alone they make more than a million placements annually.

10. Hearings, previously cited, p. 195.
11. *Olsen* v. *Nebraska,* 313 U.S. 236 (1941).
12. *Adams* v. *Tanner,* 244 U.S. 590 (1917).

country have opposed prohibition of private employment agencies.[13]

Employer and Union Employment Services

Another form of private employment service is maintained by employers themselves. Typical are the offices maintained by local chapters of the Metal Trades Association, with which members list all their job openings and to which they direct all their laid-off workers. Employers feel that in this way they can keep experienced workers in the industry and, within limits, stabilize employment. In so far as they keep their workers off unemployment insurance rolls, employers reduce their payroll taxes, out of which unemployment insurance benefits are paid.

Unions, too, have consistently tried to extend their influence over employment markets by controlling the channels through which workers obtain jobs. Many union contracts require the employer to obtain workers through the union. The recruiting activities of some unions have been very important, and some craft unions have customarily supplied a substantial percentage of the workers required in their field. The maritime unions have been singularly successful. The future of union activity in this field has been rendered somewhat uncertain, however, by the provisions of the Taft-Hartley Act prohibiting discrimination in hiring on the basis of union membership.

Some welfare associations also maintain private employment agencies as a service to the people with whom they deal. Some of these emphasize vocational and employment counseling and play an important role in helping their applicants make a better vocational adjustment.

The Public Employment Service

The need for some public facility for bringing workers and jobs together was recognized as early as 1907, when, in order to relieve congestion in ports of entry, the Information Division of the Immigration Service in the Department of Labor was authorized to supply immigrants with information on employment opportunities. In 1913 it began to supply information to all unemployed workers. When labor shortages developed during World War I, the Information Division was reconstituted as the United States Employment Service. After the war, this agency passed out of existence for all practical purposes, although some of the state and municipal exchanges continued to operate independently.

The depression of the 1930's brought persistent unemployment on an unprecedented scale. In 1933, after spending billions of dollars in emergency relief and public works programs, the federal government took the first step in its long-range attack on the problems of employment and unemployment by enacting the Wagner-Peyser Act. This act established a federal-state system of public employment offices to organize the employment markets and to bring workers and jobs together.

The public employment offices were to be administered by the states. Federal responsibilities were to be vested in the U.S. Employment Service, established in the Department of Labor. The Service was directed: to assist the states in coordinating the public employment offices throughout the country and to increase their usefulness by developing and prescribing mini-

13. In 1933 the International Labor Office adopted a convention providing for the abolition of all private employment agencies within three years. Because of the harshness of the convention, it was adopted by only six nations, not including the United States. In 1938 an amendment to the convention was offered, providing that private agencies should be abolished "within a limited period of time determined by competent authority" instead of "within three years." The United States, in commenting on this proposal, observed:

"Aside from the fact that the economic and social practices of this country and this Government would not tolerate the abolition of fee-charging agencies which operate for profit, a serious question is raised with respect to the practical implications of such a prohibition.

"Fee-charging agencies which operate for profit, as well as those which do not, fill a real need in many segments of our industry, furnishing the kind of specialized personal service which is beyond the scope of a public employment service system. Furthermore, if the free public employment service in this country is to discharge the responsibilities assigned in its creation, it must continue to be free not only in the sense of making no monetary charge for its services, but also in the sense that workers and employers may use it or other private employment agencies without limitation on their freedom of choice." *Employment Service Organization,* Report IV-2, International Labor Office, Geneva, 1946, p. 43.

When the United States decided to abstain from recommending amendments to the convention because its eventual ratification by this country was doubtful, the management representatives introduced an amendment substituting "control" of private agencies for "abolition," and the amendment was carried over the opposition of labor. Subsequently, when the amended convention returned from the drafting committee, labor mustered enough votes to defeat it.

mum standards of efficiency; to assist them in meeting problems peculiar to their localities; to promote uniformity in administrative and statistical procedures; to furnish and publish information about opportunities for employment and other information of value in the operation of the system; to maintain a farm placement service, a veterans employment service and a system for clearing labor among the several states.

The administrative costs of these offices were to be financed jointly by federal and state governments on a fifty-fifty basis. Pending the enactment of necessary state legislation and appropriation of state funds, a federal re-employment service was established and financed with emergency funds.

Two years later the federal government took the second step in its attack on employment problems with the passage of the Social Security Act, which provided for state unemployment insurance programs.

The establishment of a nation-wide network of public employment offices and the state unemployment insurance programs stems directly from these two pieces of legislation. The earlier efforts of the states to establish employment service and unemployment insurance programs had been almost completely ineffective. A few states and municipalities tried to operate public employment services, but no coordinated national system had existed since the liquidation of the U.S. Employment Service after World War I. Only two states had enacted unemployment insurance laws.

During its first five years, the public employment service was engaged primarily in referring unemployed workers to relief and public projects. Its facilities had to be expanded in 1938 when the states began to pay unemployment compensation benefits and to require claimants to register for work with the public employment offices as a condition of eligibility. Since it was unemployment insurance that made this expansion necessary, the federal government paid the entire cost, raising its share of the administrative costs of the programs of employment service and unemployment compensation to more than 95 per cent of the total. The registering of claimants brought millions of workers into local offices for the first time and encouraged the offices to go after the business of industrial and commercial employers.

War Experience

In the beginning, the U.S. Employment Service placed a great deal of emphasis on improving placement techniques and procedures. Among other things, the Dictionary of Occupational Titles was developed and, when introduced in 1939, enabled the Service for the first time to classify workers uniformly according to their skills and experience and to relate their qualifications to employers' specifications.

As soon as the national defense program was launched in 1940, the Employment Service began to gear its methods and procedures to the requirements of an expanding defense economy. Occupations in which shortages were expected were analyzed and grouped into related or interrelated "families." Complicated jobs were broken down into component parts that could be handled by a worker trained in a single skill. The Employment Service both determined and provided information on "demand occupations" as an aid to training authorities in meeting war production needs. As soon as munitions production got under way, the distribution of the various occupations in different activities was analyzed by the Service, and occupational composition patterns were prepared for the guidance of new contractors.

The Employment Service also began making local-area labor market analyses, which included detailed information obtained from employers on current and anticipated labor needs in the various occupations. It obtained information on supply from union locals and other community sources and supplemented it with estimates of the number of new entrants who could be brought into the labor market under the stimulus of wartime needs. It then classified activities as "essential" or "less essential" according to their relative importance to the war effort, and made estimates of the number of workers in less important activities who could be expected to transfer to war or essential civilian production. In short, the Employment Service obtained and analyzed all the information on labor market developments and prospects in each important labor market area. Each month it analyzed labor market conditions in important industrial areas and, in collaboration with procurement authorities, developed procedures for allocating contracts and locating new facilities to take advantage of the manpower resources of each community.

In 1939 the U.S. Employment Service had been transferred to the Social Security Board in the Federal Security Administration and its administration had been combined with unemployment insurance. As a result of the war emergency, the administration of the employment service was separated from unemployment insurance, and in 1942 the entire system, including state administrative offices, was put under federal control. Later in the same year, the Service was transferred to the War Manpower Commission. Here it immediately became the agency for carrying out the war-manpower programs in all production centers.

The basic elements of this program included the use of management-labor committees as advisory and appeals bodies; the requirement of hiring exclusively through the local employment office or through channels approved by it; the issuance of statements of availability permitting workers to transfer from one essential job to another; a system of priority for placing workers where they were most needed; and the establishment of ceilings to limit the number of workers a plant could employ.

Current Activity

Shortly after the Japanese surrender, the U.S. Employment Service was again transferred to the Department of Labor, where it remained until June 30, 1948, when it was returned to the reconstituted Bureau of Employment Security in the Federal Security Agency. In August 1949, as a part of this Bureau, it was for the third time transferred to the Department of Labor.

The farm labor program, which was carried on in the Department of Agriculture during the war years, was returned to the U.S. Employment Service on January 1, 1948.

Employment service depends on the staff and facilities of the 1,756 local offices and 2,365 part-time or itinerant offices administered directly by the state agencies affiliated with the U.S. Employment Service. In 1949, 171.7 million calls were made upon the employment offices for job placement, job information, job counseling and other services connected with the payment of unemployment benefits. Some 8.4 million persons filed job applications; employment counseling interviews numbered 900,000 and employer service calls 2.4 million. There were 17.1 million job referrals, resulting in 13.5 million placements in practically every type of employment and industry.

The Employment Service maintains a system of clearance for all types of workers among the several states, giving particular attention to workers with skills not available in the community in which there is demand for them and to professional and technical workers whose employment opportunities are in the national labor market.

The U.S. Employment Service has conducted a vast amount of occupational research work and made great progress in defining and describing the more than twenty-five thousand occupations found in our economy. It has devised a number of specific occupational, aptitude and oral trade tests for selecting qualified workers in accordance with employers' specifications. Since the war the Employment Service has supplied the states with a general aptitude test battery, by means of which local-office personnel can get a more complete picture of an applicant's qualifications and interests. (See Appendix Note 3.)

Since their return to state administration, the public employment offices have been financed wholly by the federal government.

The Employment Office cooperates with other departments of the government and maintains, in accordance with statutory requirements, a national advisory council composed of representatives of management, labor and the public to analyze employment problems and make recommendations to the Bureau of Employment Security on the public employment service system and its activities in facilitating employment adjustments.

Special Public Employment Agencies

Functions similar to those entrusted to the U.S. Employment Service are performed for certain groups of workers by two special types of agencies: the railroad employment service and the civil service employment offices.

The railroad employment service was established in 1938, when the Railroad Unemployment Insurance Act removed railroad employees from coverage under state unemployment compensation laws. Railroad workers file claims for unemployment benefits in depots, in offices of the carriers, and in railroad employment offices in those cities where regional offices of the Railroad Retirement Board exist.

Many of the jobs in state and federal government are filled on a merit basis. Every state and the federal government maintain some sort of employment office for examining and classifying workers for referral to government agencies. With the increase in public service employees in the past two decades, these offices have grown in importance.

CHAPTER 16

PROTECTION AGAINST WORK INJURIES *

NEARLY 2 MILLION PERSONS — 3 per cent of the working population — suffered work-connected injuries in 1949; 15,000 injuries terminated fatally and 79,400 resulted in permanent partial disability. Most of the injuries, almost 95 per cent, caused temporary disability. About 75 per cent of the injured were employees, the rest self-employed persons.[1] (See Table 51.)

In terms of working time lost in 1949 these injuries represented about 39 million man-days, or 130,000 man-years of work. The amount of time lost because of these accidents, especially those causing death or permanent injury, is, of course, not restricted to the calendar year in which they happened. The estimated total time loss for injuries that occurred in 1949 was 204 million man-days, or nearly 700,000 man-years of work, equivalent to $2 billion in wages.[2] Of this total, perhaps a little over one half represents time loss by workers subject to the federal and state workmen's compensation laws.[3]

Public measures to protect workers from industrial injuries and their consequences are of two types: (1) safety laws and various state regulations that aim to prevent work injuries and occupational diseases, and (2) the system of workmen's compensation and rehabilitation laws designed to ameliorate such injuries by providing for medical care and cash compensation.

The number of work injuries in the United States each year and the number of man-days of work lost because of them have not changed greatly in recent years. Despite progress in some industries and some companies, our average injury rate does not compare very favorably with other industrial countries.

Frequency of Work Injuries

Bureau of Labor Statistics estimates of the number of work injuries and their distribution by industry and by type are available from 1936 on.[4] (See Table 52 and Appendix Table 39.) Work injuries in manufacturing industries increased during World War II as many inexperienced workers entered industrial employment and safety measures were relaxed; in 1943 there were almost four times as many factory accidents as in 1938.

Annual estimates of work injuries are available for manufacturing industries beginning with 1926. (See Table 53.) For all injuries (most of which result in temporary total disability) the general trend has been downward, except for short-term rises due to changes in business conditions and a conspicuous rise during the war. The number of injuries causing death and permanent total disability fluctuated widely from year to year before 1935 and then declined. Injuries resulting in permanent partial disability did not begin to decline until after 1937. Since then, except in the war years, they have fallen off sharply.

The frequency rate for work injuries varies widely from industry to industry, depending not only on differences in industrial hazards but also on preventive measures taken by industrial establishments. (See Appendix Table 40.) In large establishments where concerted efforts have been made to reduce injuries, accident rates are comparatively low; in small establishments and in certain industries, notably agriculture, rates are particularly high. It is esti-

* By Barkev S. Sanders, Federal Security Agency, Social Security Administration; Lecturer on Health Economics at the American University and on Health Statistics and Labor Economics at the Catholic University of America, Washington, D.C. Opinions expressed here are those of the author and not necessarily those of the agency with which he is associated.

1. The proportion of individuals suffering two or more disabling injuries during the year is so small that for all practical purposes the number of injured individuals can be taken as equal to the number of injuries reported.

2. *Handbook of Labor Statistics,* 1947 edition, Bulletin No. 916, Bureau of Labor Statistics, 1948, p. 163, and *Monthly Labor Review,* March 1950.

3. See Table 56 for estimate of the wage loss in 1948 among workers subject to workmen's compensation laws.

4. Comparison of the Bureau of Labor Statistics figures on injuries to workers subject to workmen's compensation laws with those reported by the National Council on Compensation Insurance suggests that the BLS figures are too low, particularly those for temporary disability, and that the average duration is too short.

TABLE 51

DISABLING INJURIES, BY INDUSTRY, 1949

(In Thousands)

Industry	All Disabilities		Fatalities		Permanent Total Disabilities		Permanent Partial Disabilities		Temporary Total Disabilities	
	Total [a]	To Employees	Total [a]	To Employees	Total [a]	To Employees	Total [a]	To Employees	Total [a]	To Employees
All groups	1,870.0	1,409.0	15.0	10.7	1.6	1.2	79.4	61.1	1,774.0	1,336.0
Agriculture	340.0	60.0	4.3	1.1	.4	.1	15.2	3.6	320.1	55.2
Mining and quarrying	70.0	65.0	1.0	.9	.1	.1	3.0	2.8	65.9	61.2
Construction	183.0	142.0	2.1	1.7	.3	.2	7.3	5.7	173.3	134.4
Manufacturing	381.0	374.0	2.3	2.2	.2	.2	19.2	19.0	359.3	352.6
Public utilities	27.0	27.0	.4	.4	[b]	[b]	.6	.6	26.0	26.0
Trade	329.0	263.0	1.5	1.2	.1	.1	7.9	6.3	319.5	255.4
Railroads	46.0	46.0	.5	.5	.2	.2	3.2	3.2	42.1	42.1
Miscellaneous transportation	126.0	105.0	.8	.7	.1	.1	6.0	5.0	119.1	99.2
Services, government and miscellaneous industries	368.0	327.0	2.1	2.0	.2	.2	17.0	14.9	348.7	309.9

a. Includes wage and salary workers (except domestics) and self-employed persons.
b. Fewer than 50.

Source: Monthly Labor Review, March 1950, p. 266.

TABLE 52

INDUSTRIAL INJURIES, BY TYPE OF DISABILITY, 1936–1949

(In Thousands)

Year	All Workers: All Injuries	All Workers: Fatal and Permanent Total Disability [a]	All Workers: Permanent Partial Disability	All Workers: Temporary Disability	Employees: All Injuries	Employees: Fatal and Permanent Total Disability [a]	Employees: Permanent Partial Disability	Employees: Temporary Disability
1936	—	—	—	—	1,407	16.2	66	1,325
1937	1,838	19.8	126	1,692	1,663	18.0	112	1,534
1938	1,375	16.6	99	1,260	1,237	15.1	85	1,136
1939	1,604	16.4	109	1,478	1,430	15.0	95	1,321
1940	1,890	18.1	90	1,782	1,697	16.6	81	1,600
1941	2,180	19.2	101	2,060	1,983	17.5	92	1,874
1942	2,268	19.9	101	2,147	1,835	14.8	81	1,739
1943	2,414	20.1	108	2,286	1,961	14.8	87	1,860
1944	2,230	17.6	94	2,118	1,802	12.6	76	1,714
1945	2,020	17.8	88	1,914	1,601	12.8	70	1,518
1946	2,056	18.3	92	1,945	1,615	13.1	73	1,529
1947	2,059	18.8	90	1,950	1,635	13.7	72	1,549
1948	2,020	17.8	88	1,915	1,552	13.1	68	1,471
1949	1,870	16.6	79	1,774	1,409	11.9	61	1,336

a. In 1936–1938, permanent total disability included in permanent partial disability.

Source: Annual estimates of the Bureau of Labor Statistics published in the *Monthly Labor Review.*

TABLE 53

INDEXES OF FREQUENCY RATES OF WORK INJURIES IN MANUFACTURING INDUSTRIES, 1926–1949 [a]

(*1926 = 100*) [b]

Year	Injuries per Million Hours Worked [c]	All Injuries	Death and Permanent Total	Permanent Partial	Temporary Total
1926...	24.2	100.0	100.0	100.0	100.0
1927...	22.6	93.6	107.1	96.3	93.3
1928...	22.5	93.2	107.1	104.6	92.5
1929...	24.0	99.2	92.9	109.2	98.7
1930...	23.1	95.5	107.1	111.0	94.6
1931...	18.9	78.0	92.9	102.8	76.5
1932...	19.6	80.9	107.1	113.8	78.9
1933...	19.3	91.8	85.7	110.1	90.8
1934...	20.2	93.6	107.1	128.4	91.6
1935...	17.9	88.1	92.9	121.1	86.2
1936...	16.6	85.7	85.7	114.7	84.1
1937...	17.8	85.8	85.7	122.0	83.7
1938...	15.1	71.7	71.4	78.9	68.1
1939...	14.9	73.4	71.4	80.7	73.9
1940...	15.3	75.3	71.4	84.8	75.6
1941...	18.1	85.8	80.3	93.7	86.3
1942...	19.9	93.5	70.7	83.4	94.1
1943...	20.0	94.4	70.7	83.4	95.0
1944...	18.4	88.3	62.8	75.3	89.7
1945...	18.6	81.9	62.8	72.3	83.0
1946...	19.9	84.3	60.1	77.9	85.3
1947...	18.8	78.4	51.7	70.1	79.3
1948...	17.2	69.8	51.7	67.3	70.6
1949...	15.0	61.2	44.3	61.9	61.6

a. Before 1936 the Bureau of Labor Statistics surveys were limited to wage earners in thirty industry classifications. Since 1936 all employees in all types of manufacturing are included.

b. Before 1937 the index numbers represent the change in the frequency rate of the entire reporting sample for each year as related to the base year, 1926. Beginning with 1937, the indexes have been computed by chain-link methods, using the percentage of change in the frequency rates for identical establishments in each pair of successive years. Index changes, therefore, do not necessarily correspond to the changes in the all-manufacturing frequency rates shown in the table.

c. Before 1936, unweighted; since 1936, weighted averages.

Sources: Handbook of Labor Statistics, 1947 edition, Bulletin No. 916, Bureau of Labor Statistics, 1948, p. 165; *Monthly Labor Review,* 1949, 1950.

mated that 70 per cent of all industrial injuries occur to employees of smaller firms.

In industry as a whole, the decline in the rate of accidents is not too impressive. But this statement does not mean that state safety laws and the efforts of individual employers and private insurance carriers have had little effect. Without these efforts, the accident rate, instead of declining, probably would have increased as a result of changes in industrial processes. It is also certain that the progressive broadening of the scope and coverage of workmen's compensation [5] has resulted in more complete reporting of industrial injuries, thus masking some of the improvement.

5. See pp. 193 ff.

Long-Range Trend

Some industries for which reasonably reliable long-range statistics are available show a decisive decline in injury rates, particularly for fatal injuries. These include coal mining, mineral mining, quarrying and coke ovens, for which fields the Bureau of Mines has compiled accident rate data since 1910. (See Appendix Table 41.) In coal mining, fatal injuries declined from 2.0 per million man-hours, a fairly usual rate before 1930, to 0.9 per million man-hours in 1949; nonfatal injuries, from more than 90 per million man-hours in 1930 to an average of 58 per million in 1949.

The experience in mineral mines between 1931 and 1947 shows similar trends for both fatal and nonfatal injuries. The rate of injuries in quarrying and related industries has likewise declined by one third to one half between the early 1920's and the present time. Progress has been even more marked in coke ovens, where the frequency rate of injuries is less than half that of twenty or twenty-five years ago.

Injury rates for workers on steam railroads, compiled by the Interstate Commerce Commission, showed a downward trend up to World War II, a temporary rise, and then a new drop after the war. (See Appendix Table 42.) For fatal injuries, the decline, in round numbers, was from 0.4 deaths per million man-hours in 1922 and 1923 to less than 0.2 in 1949. Injuries causing disability lasting three days or longer declined from about 31 per million man-hours in 1923 to 7 in 1938–1940, rose to more than 12 in 1943–1945, and fell back to about 7 in 1949.

Accident Prevention

Since 1923 the National Safety Council has published reports of industrial injuries from certain employers. An analysis of these reports for 1930–1946 shows a definite downward trend in both frequency and severity of work-connected injuries.[6] A later report shows a sharp decrease in 1948 as against earlier years.[7]

Employers who have gone all out to promote safety among their workers have achieved impressive results. (See Figure 40.) Impressive also is the accident prevention work of the Navy, which cut injury rates from 20.3 per million

6. *Accident Facts,* 1947 edition, National Safety Council, Chicago, pp. 26 and 36.

7. *Ibid.,* 1949 edition, pp. 25 and 35.

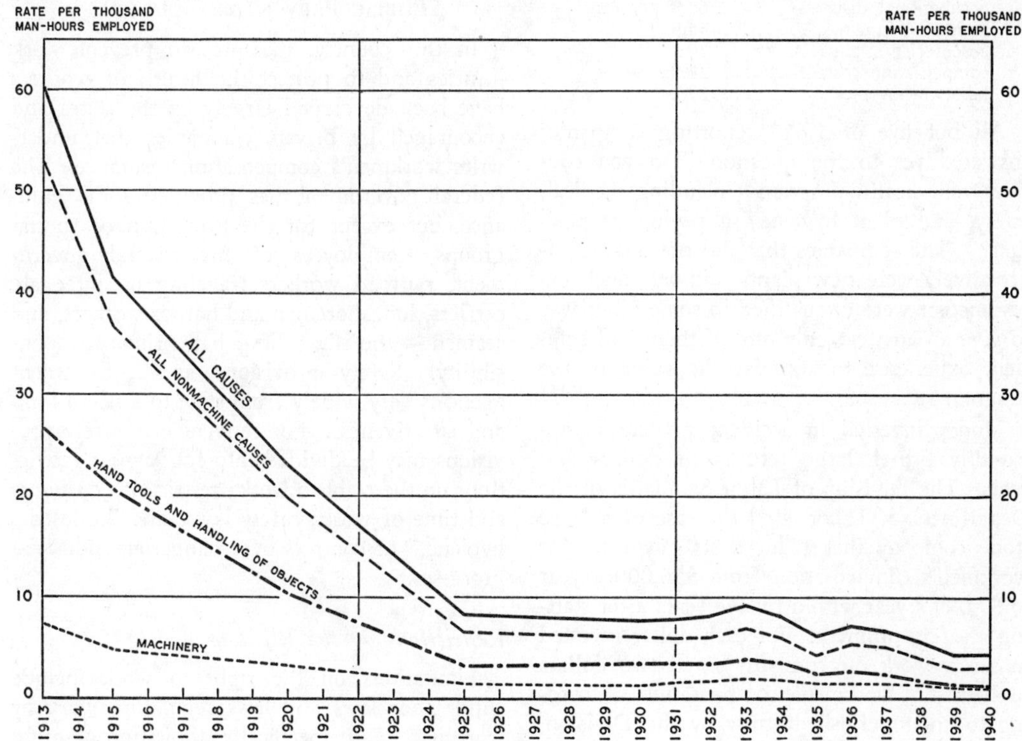

FIGURE 40. RATES OF DISABLING INJURIES IN A SELECTED GROUP OF IRON AND STEEL ESTABLISHMENTS, BY CAUSE OF INJURY, 1913–1940

Source: Compiled from publications of the Bureau of Labor Statistics.

This chart illustrates the results achieved by a group of employers in the iron and steel industry who have gone all out to promote safety among their workers.

man-hours in 1926 to 5.17 in 1935 and reduced time loss from 2.09 days to 0.62 days per worker.[8] More recent Navy experience indicates a still further reduction in time loss — 0.48 days per worker per year in 1948.

Each year the National Safety Council publishes a list of industrial establishments with outstanding safety records in each industry. In 1950 these establishments, 36 in all, had in the aggregate 244 million man-hours, or 122,000 man-years, of work without any accidental injury. In comparison with the injury and severity rates in each industry, based on the 1950 experience of more than 6,000 establishments reporting to the National Safety Council, the 36 outstanding establishments in 1950 averted 2,088 accidental injuries. This meant a saving of 190,000 man-days, or 764 man-years, of productive work.[9] (See Appendix Table 43.) The actual saving of productive man-days by these establishments was even greater in terms of the average injury and severity rates in the various industries for the country at large, since the 6,000 or so establishments reporting to the National Safety Council had injury and severity rates that were appreciably lower than the averages in the corresponding industries for the nation at large. Many lives and millions of man-days could, of course, be saved each year if all establishments throughout the nation did as much as the 36 outstanding establishments to prevent work injuries.

In a study of the experience of 2,064 plants providing medical services to their employees, the National Association of Manufacturers listed the following savings: [10]

8. Marshall Dawson, *Problems of Workmen's Compensation Administration,* Bulletin No. 672, Bureau of Labor Statistics, 1940, p. 148; Bernhard J. Stern, *Medicine in Industry,* Studies of the New York Academy of Medicine Committee on Medicine and the Changing Order, Commonwealth Fund, New York, 1946, pp. 110–12.

9. *Accident Facts,* 1951 edition, pp. 35, 36 and 41.

10. *Health on the Production Front* (January 1944) and *Industrial Health Practice* (1941), p. 14, National Association of Manufacturers, New York. For

occupational diseases ...... 62.8 per cent
accident frequency 44.9
absenteeism 29.7
compensation costs 28.8
labor turnover 27.3

All but five of 1,625 reporting companies answered yes to the question "Do you consider your health program (including medical, safety, and plant hygiene) a paying proposition?" The companies that did not answer affirmatively were new plants without much experience or were unqualified in some other way to give an answer; only one of them had sufficient experience to appraise the value of the program.

Money invested in accident prevention apparently brings large returns in dollars and cents. The Division of Labor Standards of the Department of Labor cited the case of a large stone company that reduced its payments for workmen's compensation from $56,000 a year to $7,000 a year within twelve years after starting a safety program. For each dollar invested in safety work the company saved two dollars in the cost of workmen's compensation. According to an unpublished study by the Division, a group of manufacturers estimated they saved $1.60 in workmen's compensation costs for every dollar invested in safety.[11] Moreover, the monetary losses suffered by employers from industrial injuries average five times workmen's compensation costs.

International Comparisons

Where international comparisons can be made, they indicate a higher injury rate for the United States than for other leading industrial countries. For instance, in a comparison of average accident rates in coal mining in 1934, fatal injuries per thousand men employed full time varied as follows: 4.26 in the United States, 2.23 in Germany, 1.34 in Great Britain, 1.16 in Belgium, and 1.03 in France. Without careful comparison of the methods of production and safety measures in this country and abroad, however, it is difficult to assess these records.[12]

similar findings, see Dean K. Brundage, "An Estimate of the Monetary Value to Industry of Plant Medical and Safety Services," *Public Health Reports,* August 21, 1936, pp. 1145–59.

11. *Safety Subjects,* Bulletin No. 67, Division of Labor Standards, 1944.

12. John R. Commons and John B. Andrews, *Principles of Labor Legislation,* 4th edition, Harper, New York, 1936, pp. 208–09.

Public Preventive Measures

In this country, measures to prevent work injuries and to protect the health of workers have been developed largely by the states and encouraged by private companies that underwrite workmen's compensation insurance. The federal government has provided some guidance, but except for the protection of special groups — employees of the federal government, railroad workers traveling on interstate carriers, longshoremen and harbor workers, and seamen — the states have had primary responsibility. Safety provisions and enforcement agencies vary widely from state to state in kind and effectiveness. For convenience, safety provisions may be divided into four types: restrictions on the right to work; restrictions on hours and time of work; safety laws; and "industrial hygiene," or controls over dangerous industrial processes.

Restrictions on the Right to Work

Limitations on the right to work include child labor laws and laws regulating work by women — more specifically, limitation of night work, restrictions related to pregnancy, and prohibition of work in certain industries.[13] Although devised primarily for the well-being and safety of special groups — minors and women — these laws have helped indirectly to reduce hazards for all workers.

Other laws that could be classified in this category bar persons with certain diseases or propensity to disease from certain industries — for example, state laws requiring physical examinations for workers in the compressed-air and lead trades. Ohio, Pennsylvania, New Jersey and certain other states require monthly examination of workers in manufacturing of the more dangerous salts of lead — white lead, red lead, arsenate of lead, and so on. In New Jersey such examinations are required for workers engaged in the manufacture of pottery, tiles or porcelain-enameled sanitary wares in which lead is used.[14] Some states bar persons with certain diseases from getting work or continuing work in bakeshops, creameries or other food establishments. Such laws are primarily intended to protect the public. Public safety is also the primary objective of laws requiring that railroad

13. See Chapters 11 and 12.

14. See Commons and Andrews, *op. cit.,* pp. 189–92.

workers be free from certain defects and diseases, like color blindness and defective vision, and of federal regulation of air traffic and licensing of pilots.[15]

Restrictions on Hours and Time of Work

Prevention of work injuries is not the main purpose of legislation limiting the time and hours of work. These laws were first passed to protect women and children, then were gradually extended to include other workers. There is no doubt, however, that the fatigue resulting from long hours of work increases industrial hazards; limitation of hours of work has implications for the safety and health of all workers.[16]

Safety Laws

Every state in the Union has industrial safety laws. Some of the laws are general requirements to assure a safe place of work. Some pertain to special industries, like mine inspection laws, navigation laws and laws for certain other groups. Safety laws set minimum standards for commercial and industrial buildings relating to working space requirements and ventilation and sanitary conditions. They require protection against such obvious hazards as unguarded openings, shafts and elevator wells. They prescribe fire precautions, including accessible and suitable fire exits, call for the use of guards and other protective devices on dangerous machines and special clothing or other accessories in certain occupations or processes.

Some safety laws go beyond minimum requirements and prescribe conditions of work that are not only safe but reasonably comfortable. Laws of this sort may call for suitable temperature ranges; proper ventilation; proper lighting; first-aid facilities; reduction of noise, vibration, obnoxious odors and other nuisances. They may require sanitary drinking fountains, lavatories, separate rest rooms for men and women, or other facilities to assure reasonable comfort and encourage sound personal hygiene habits among workers.

In general, safety laws are enforced by state labor departments; in some instances, municipal agencies enforce municipal building and safety codes. In many states, all industrial safety laws are administered by one state agency, corresponding to a state labor department. Some states have separate agencies for miners and mine inspection and, in a few cases, for agricultural workers.[17]

In addition to making unscheduled visits to plants in response to complaints or on invitation, some state agencies try to make routine examinations of all plants once a year. In other states almost all plant visits are made in response to complaints or requests.

The early safety laws specified minimum standards. More recent laws are quite general and allow the administrator to work out the standards and detailed regulations. Sometimes the law may guide the administrator by referring directly to some public or quasi-public organization that has developed accepted standards. The administrator at his discretion may make compliance with such standards obligatory.[18]

Factory inspection laws, designed originally for the protection of workers in the plant, were in time extended to include pieceworkers in the home. This type of legislation began in Massachusetts in 1891 with the passage of "an Act to prevent the manufacture and sale of clothing made in unhealthy places." It has since spread to other groups of workers and to other states.[19]

Safety Laws for Miners

Paralleling the safety and health laws for factory workers are safety laws for miners in all states in which mining is important. Some states entrust enforcement of these laws to the labor department, others to a special agency. In most states, even where there is no separate administrative agency for mine safety, there are specialized mine inspectors with considerable authority. Some even have authority to order a work stoppage in cases of failure to comply with important provisions of the safety code.

15. *Ibid.*
16. *Hours of Work and Output* (H. Doc. 318, 80th Cong.), Bulletin No. 917, Bureau of Labor Statistics, 1947, pp. 37–40.

17. John B. Andrews, *Labor Laws in Action,* Harper, New York, 1938, Appendix, pp. 230–34.
18. Among organizations that have developed widely accepted standards of industrial safety are: the American Standards Association, the National Conservation Bureau, the National Fire Protection Association, the Underwriters Laboratories, the American Society of Mechanical Engineers, the American Society of Heating and Ventilating Engineers, the Illuminating Engineering Society, the National Safety Council. Commons and Andrews, *op. cit.,* pp. 206–08.
19. *Loc. cit.*

Safety standards in mines have been improved considerably through the work of the federal Bureau of Mines, established by an act of Congress in 1910 to make studies and recommend standards to promote the health of miners. In 1941 a new act authorized federal mine inspectors to inspect mines and recommend necessary safety measures to the operators. A federal mine safety code was developed as a necessary corollary of this activity. In 1946, when the Department of the Interior took over the operation of coal mines, the federal code for coal mines was made a part of the agreement between the union and the government.[20] Since that time, contracts between the United Mine Workers and the operators have incorporated the provisions of the federal code. The provisions of the code are enforced by safety committees organized by the union membership in each mine.

Workers in Transportation

Because the federal government has certain powers over interstate commerce, workers in transportation are protected through federal as well as state safety legislation. Moreover, protection of transportation workers cannot be separated from provisions for the safety of the public.

Safety in water transportation, especially navigation on the high seas, is regulated mainly by federal statutes. There are a few state regulations, such as laws requiring inspection of boilers and signal lights, but by and large seamen have looked to the federal government for protection. As early as 1798 Congress recognized the need of special protection for this group of workers and enacted a law that led to the establishment of marine hospitals for the care of seamen. In modern terms, the original federal law provided for compulsory health insurance, financed by contributions deducted from the seamen's wages. The act has since been amended many times. The federal government continues to provide medical care through marine hospitals administered by the United States Public Health Service of the Federal Security Agency, but the program is now financed entirely from general revenue.[21]

Both the federal and state governments have passed extensive safety regulations concerning railroads and streetcars. Some state laws preceded federal regulation. When the Interstate Commerce Commission was established in 1887, its initial purpose was to regulate rates; it had no powers over safety. Not until 1893 did federal laws require all roads engaged in interstate traffic to equip their cars and locomotives with approved automatic couplers and to provide other safeguards. Finally, in 1910, an act of Congress, in addition to making new safety provisions, gave the Interstate Commerce Commission power, after proper hearings, to "designate the number, dimensions, location, and manner of application of appliances." Any failure to comply with the Commission's requirements was made equivalent to refusal to comply with the act. The act also gave the Commission authority to investigate all collisions, derailments and other accidents. Funds were provided to the Commission to make tests and establish standards, to make boiler inspections and to enforce other safety measures.

States protect railroad employees and the public by regulating the height of bridges and other overhead structures, providing for maintenance of proper clearance around tracks, blocking of frogs and switches, and so on. State safety requirements also include sheds to protect track workers from inclement weather and caboose cars equipped for employees traveling with freight or stock trains. Where there have been conflicts between state and federal regulations, the courts have almost always given precedence to federal laws.

Street and interurban railway employees are protected by state and local laws. A number of states have passed full-crew laws and other safety measures. These laws have often been contested on the ground that they deal with matters of interstate commerce subject to federal control. The courts have held uniformly that where Congress has not legislated, the states are entirely free to do so. In most states the enforcement of protective regulations for railway work-

20. *Federal Mine Safety Code for Bituminous Coal and Lignite Mines of the United States* (1946) and *Safety Standards of Anthracite Mines* (Information Circular No. 7449, February 1948), Department of the Interior.

21. Bernhard J. Stern, *Medical Services by Government; Local, State and Federal,* Studies of the New York Academy of Medicine Committee on Medicine and the Changing Order, Commonwealth Fund, New York, 1946, pp. 146–53.

ers has been entrusted to railway or public utility commissions created primarily to supervise or regulate rates.[22]

Industrial Hygiene

As industrial processes became more and more complex, the early factory inspection laws proved inadequate to safeguard the health of workers. To develop standards of industrial hygiene and assure their observance, forty-five states, eleven municipalities and two territories have turned to their health departments.[23] The Public Health Service of the Federal Security Agency has stimulated this development through its Division of Industrial Hygiene. At least thirty-three states have developed specific codes and regulations containing provisions relating to industrial hygiene. (See Table 54.)

One of the most important provisions in many codes is concerned with the maximum allowable concentration (MAC) value of specific toxic substances. About sixty harmful substances are enumerated in the various codes; there are, however, wide differences in substances subject to control and in the maximum allowable limit for some of them. (See Appendix Table 44.) Theodore C. Waters, Chairman of the Legal Committee of the Industrial Hygiene Foundation, has said of these codes:

> I think it may be fairly stated that many of these codes, while well intentioned, were adopted without full consideration of the various problems of industry to which they would apply. In many instances they establish arbitrary standards of permissible concentrations of toxic dust, fumes and gases and say to industry, "Thou shalt not permit concentration exceeding a stated limit." In most instances the codes do not attempt to advise industry of the ways and means to accomplish compliance. . . . It is unfortunate that there is not greater uniformity in the State Codes presently effective.[24]

At its convention in Chicago in 1950, the American Conference of Governmental Industrial Hygienists, recognizing the importance of safety from toxic substances, developed maximum allowable standards for gases, other toxic agents and radiation. The list of toxic agents it has established is far more inclusive than that in any of the existing state codes, and the maximum allowable limits are also in many instances lower than those in existing state and municipal codes. (See Appendix Table 45.) The Conference is promoting the adoption of uniform standards conforming to its recommendations.

The government discourages or prohibits the use of certain highly toxic substances in industry when substitutes can be used. The imposition of a federal tax to prevent the use of poisonous phosphorous in the manufacture of matches is the earliest and most outstanding example of this kind of restriction.[25]

Workmen's Compensation

Our present system of workmen's compensation consists of fifty-four separate state and federal laws developed through a long-drawn-out process. In almost all states the scope of workmen's compensation laws has been extended in the past two or three decades to cover more workers and types of injury and to provide greater benefits.[26] Progress has been slower in some states than in others, and workmen's compensation laws today are very diverse.

Although workmen's compensation is classified here as a remedial measure, unquestionably such programs may serve indirectly to prevent industrial injuries. The practice of basing workmen's compensation premiums on the actual accident experience of each employer where a reliable index is available over a five-year period is believed to have stimulated preventive efforts. In fact, some writers declare that the greater incidence of accidents in smaller plants, in comparison with larger ones, is due entirely to this factor. They argue that in larger plants insurance carriers advise management on safety matters and that management sees the advantages of a safety program in reducing premiums. No

22. Commons and Andrews, *op. cit.,* pp. 212–19.

23. Two states, New York and Massachusetts, have placed specific industrial hygiene responsibilities on the state labor department. Illinois has assigned specific responsibilities to the labor department, while broad powers are assigned to the health department. Only Delaware and Nevada are not conducting any activity in the field of industrial hygiene. J. J. Bloomfield, "Codes for the Prevention and Control of Occupational Diseases," *Health in Industry,* Transactions Bulletin No. 8, Industrial Hygiene Foundation of America, 1947 (brought up to date by Mr. Bloomfield).

24. Theodore C. Waters, "Legal Developments Respecting Occupational Health," *Health in Industry,* Transactions Bulletin No. 8, Industrial Hygiene Foundation, pp. 65–70. See also Stern, *Medicine in Industry.*

25. Commons and Andrews, *op. cit.,* pp. 159–60 and 194.

26. Arthur Hallam Reede, *Adequacy of Workmen's Compensation,* Harvard University Press, Cambridge, 1947.

TABLE 54

SUMMARY OF SUBJECTS COVERED IN STATE INDUSTRIAL HYGIENE CODES, AS OF JULY 1947

Jurisdiction	Maximum Allowable Limit of Toxic Substances: Legal Limit	Maximum Allowable Limit of Toxic Substances: Guide Only	Sanitation	Ventilation	House-keeping	Illumi-nation	Temperature, Humidity, Air Movement	Personal Protective Equipment	Pressure	Radiant Energy	Noise	Skin Contact
Alabama	—	X	X	—	—	—	—	—	—	—	—	—
Arkansas	—	X	X	X	X	X	—	—	X	—	—	—
California [a]	—	X	X	X	X	X	—	X	—	—	—	—
Colorado	X	—	X	—	—	—	—	—	—	—	—	—
Connecticut	X	—	X	X	X	X	X	—	—	—	—	—
District of Columbia	—	X	X	X	X	X	X	—	—	—	—	—
Florida	X	—	X	X	X	X	X	X	X	X	X	X
Idaho	—	X	—	X	—	—	—	—	—	—	—	—
Illinois	—	X	X	X	X	X	X	X	X	X	—	—
Indiana	—	X	X	—	—	—	—	—	—	—	—	—
Kentucky	X	—	—	—	—	—	—	—	—	—	—	—
Maine	—	X	X	—	—	—	—	—	—	—	—	—
Maryland [b]	X	—	—	—	—	—	—	—	—	—	—	—
Massachusetts	X	—	X	X	X	X	—	X	X	X	—	—
Michigan [c]	X	—	X	X	—	—	—	—	—	—	—	—
Minnesota	X	—	X	X	X	X	X	X	X	—	X	—
Mississippi	X	—	X	X	X	X	X	X	—	—	—	—
Missouri [d]	—	X	X	X	X	—	X	—	—	—	—	X
New Jersey [e]	—	—	—	—	—	—	—	—	—	—	—	—
New York	—	X	X	X	X	X	—	X	X	X	—	—
North Carolina	—	X	X	X	X	X	X	—	—	—	—	—
Ohio [f]	X	—	X	X	X	—	—	X	—	—	—	—
Oregon	X	—	X	X	X	—	—	X	—	—	—	—
Pennsylvania	—	X	X	X	X	X	X	—	X	—	—	—
Rhode Island	—	X	X	—	—	X	X	—	—	—	—	—
South Carolina	X	—	X	X	—	X	X	—	—	—	—	—
Tennessee	—	X	X	—	—	—	—	—	—	—	—	—
Texas	—	X	X	—	—	—	—	—	—	—	—	—
Vermont	—	X	X	X	—	—	X	—	—	—	—	—
Virginia	—	X	X	X	X	—	—	—	—	—	—	—
Washington	X	—	X	X	X	—	—	X	X	—	—	—
Wisconsin	X	—	X	X	X	—	—	X	—	—	—	—
Hawaii [g]	X	X	X	X	X	X	X	X	—	—	X	X

a. Similar code provisions for Los Angeles city and county.
b. Baltimore city has its own code.
c. Detroit has its own code.
d. St. Louis and Kansas City have their own codes.
e. A code was enacted in New Jersey in 1948 — provisions not known.
f. Cleveland assigns certain powers to the city health department though it has no separate code.
g. Code also covers infectious material.

Source: Prepared by the Division of Industrial Hygiene of the Public Health Service, Federal Security Agency.

such economies can be demonstrated in the smaller plants.[27]

Beginnings of the System

Until the middle of the nineteenth century, employers were required, under common law, to provide a safe place of work and safe tools. Injury due to an employer's negligence was actionable as a tort. But the employer had many ways of escaping his liability. First, under the "fellow-servant" doctrine, the employer, even though negligent, was not liable if the injury was caused by a fellow worker. Contributory negligence on the part of the injured employee represented another defense. The employer could also deny his liability by maintaining that the injured employee had "assumed" the risk. The injured worker was said to have "assumed" the risk if he had continued on his job despite his knowledge that the employer was neglecting to correct a work hazard. This rule held good even when the employee's injury resulted from violation of a safety law by the employer. Because of these loopholes, workers could rarely recover damages for injuries suffered in the course of employment.

A gradual modification of these common-law rules began in some states shortly after the middle of the nineteenth century. Georgia led the way in 1856. Iowa followed by abrogating the fellow-servant rule for railroad accidents. New statutory provisions enabled survivors to sue for damages in fatal accident cases — whereas, under common law, the right to recover damages ended with the death of the injured employee. Other statutes either abrogated or limited common-law rules concerning "assumed" risk and contributory negligence. Meanwhile the common law itself was undergoing changes as judges gradually accepted the more humane attitudes of the legislatures.[28]

The Principle of Workmen's Compensation

While interest in the United States was centered on legislative modification of employer's liability, industrial countries in Europe adopted an entirely new principle of distributing the losses resulting from industrial accidents — the principle of workmen's compensation. According to this concept, the employer's liability for an accident does not depend on a question of negligence or fault. The basic idea behind workmen's compensation is that industrial injuries are part of the cost of production and that an injured worker should be compensated by the employer who, in turn, should shift the cost to the consumer by adding it to the selling price of the product.[29]

After the turn of the century the United States also broke away from the idea of negligence and fault and adopted the principle of workmen's compensation. The first law of this type was passed by Maryland in 1902. It was restricted to a small group of industries and was later declared unconstitutional. The oldest workmen's compensation law still in effect (later extended and completely overhauled) was passed in 1908 for federal employees. State laws followed in rapid succession; ten acts were approved in 1911, three in 1912, eight in 1913. The pace slackened when three state laws were declared unconstitutional. It was resumed, however, after the Supreme Court upheld three different types of acts in 1917.[30] Today all the forty-eight states and all territories have workmen's compensation laws.[31] Federal statutes provide protection to federal employees, to private employees in the District of Columbia, and to longshoremen and harbor workers.

Coverage

None of the state workmen's compensation laws cover all employees. Compensation laws are either compulsory or elective: twenty-eight of them require every employer within the scope of the law to accept it; in twenty-six, employers have the option to accept or reject the act. If an employer subject to the act rejects it, however, he cannot plead the customary common-

27. *Safety Subjects,* 1944, pp. 9–13 and 15.

28. Harry Weiss, "Employers' Liability and Workmen's Compensation," Chapter 6 in *History of Labor in the United States, 1896–1932,* by Don D. Lescohier and Elizabeth Brandeis, Macmillan, New York, 1935, Vol. III, pp. 564–610; Samuel B. Horovitz, *Injury and Death under Workmen's Compensation Laws,* Wright and Potter, Boston, 1944, pp. 2–10. See also New York Commission on Employer's Liability and Other Matters, First Report, 1910, pp. 29–31, and James Willard Hurst, *The Growth of American Law: The Law Makers,* Little, Brown, Boston, 1950.

29. Germany led in the enactment of workmen's compensation legislation when, in 1884, it passed such a law as part of the social legislation program designed by Bismarck to counteract the growth of socialism. Other European countries rapidly followed suit. Austria enacted a workmen's compensation law in 1887, Hungary in 1891, Norway in 1894, Finland in 1895, Great Britain in 1897. Weiss, *op. cit.,* p. 570.

30. Horovitz, *op. cit.,* pp. 11–72.

31. In several states, including New York, the state constitution was modified in order to ensure the constitutionality of the laws.

law defenses. Under some types of elective laws, acceptance of the act by employers or employees is presumed unless specific notice of rejection is filed. Twenty laws make this presumption, but under the other six elective laws, the employer must accept the law in writing. Some laws are partly elective and partly compulsory. Some elective laws and two compulsory laws permit the employee to reject coverage.

No workmen's compensation law covers unpaid family workers; and almost all the laws exclude domestic workers either expressly or through an elective provision. This is true also of farm workers; where there is no provision expressly excluding them, other provisions achieve the same end. Almost all the laws exclude casual workers.

The state laws exclude interstate railroad workers, merchant seamen, longshoremen and harbor workers, and federal employees. Longshoremen, harbor workers and federal employees are covered by federal law. Merchant seamen are not covered. They have opposed workmen's compensation (which is favored by most of their employers), believing they fare better under the Jones Act and related legislation, under which they can sue the employer for damages.[32] Interstate railroad workers have an employer liability law, which they prefer to a workmen's compensation law since it gives them the right to sue.

Besides making specific exclusions, twelve state laws limit coverage to "hazardous" or "extrahazardous" employments; such employments are listed in some acts, and the list is not always inclusive. This limitation was an expedient adopted in the early days of workmen's compensation when it was feared that the law might be declared unconstitutional unless it could be shown to be a necessary exercise of the police power of the state. In some states the limitation materially restricts the coverage of the law.

In thirty states and two territories, employers who have less than a certain number of employees are exempted from coverage, but most of the acts permit voluntary acceptance on the part of such employers. Under some laws, the numerical exemption does not apply to all employments.

32. *Workmen's Compensation and the Protection of Seamen,* Bulletin No. 869, Bureau of Labor Statistics, 1946.

Most public employees and all federal workers are protected against work-connected injuries. In thirty-seven states the laws governing state and local employees are compulsory for all or for some specified groups. In the remaining eleven states coverage of state and local employees is elective in some instances and in part voluntary or permissive.

Many states exclude from coverage employees of charitable organizations. Sometimes certain occupations or special classes of workers — for example, higher-paid workers, clerical workers and teachers — are excluded, sometimes whole industries. (See Appendix Table 46.)

A recent publication of the Department of Labor estimates that probably not more than 50 per cent of all gainfully employed workers are actually protected by workmen's compensation.[33] Arthur H. Reede has estimated that workmen's compensation laws covered 27 million workers in 1940 and 35 million in 1945. His procedure would lead to an estimate of nearly 39 million for 1948.[34]

These estimates are too high, however, for they take no account of employers (and, in some instances, employees) who "elect out." This group rejecting coverage must be large, although how large it is, is not known.[35] Another group of unknown size included in the estimates above consists of workers who are not protected because their employers fail to insure them, though legally required to do so.[36] A third group of workers likewise included in these estimates are covered only in theory since they cannot collect compensation for an injury because the insurer is insolvent at the time. When allowance is made for all these groups, the actual coverage is perhaps close to 34 million, or about 73 per cent of all wage and salary workers.

33. *State Workmen's Compensation Laws as of October 1, 1948,* Bulletin No. 99, Bureau of Labor Standards, 1948, p. 4.

34. Reede, *op. cit.,* pp. 17 and 380.

35. J. D. Williams, Chairman of the Industrial Commission in Minnesota, said in 1938 that "electing out" in Minnesota had increased to such an extent during the depression that practically one third of the employers were outside the act. The act was changed from elective to compulsory coverage. Dawson, *op. cit.,* p. 19.

36. In 1933–1934 a study in Pennsylvania found 9,692 delinquent employers. *Pennsylvania Labor and Industry in Depression,* Special Bulletin No. 39, Pennsylvania Department of Labor and Industry, Harrisburg, 1934.

Compensable Injuries

Workmen's compensation laws are limited to certain accidents and occupational diseases. In most states, injuries due to a worker's intoxication, willful misconduct or gross negligence are excluded from compensation. Compensable injury is usually defined as injury "arising out of and in the course of employment." Most early laws covered only "accidental" injuries.[37] Some laws omit the word "accidental" but specifically exclude occupational diseases. Under several laws, however, the terms "injury" and "personal injury" have come to include occupational diseases by definition or court interpretation.[38] At the end of 1949, forty-one states, the District of Columbia, Alaska, Hawaii and Puerto Rico had specific provisions for occupational diseases. The federal law also makes specific provisions for federal employees and longshoremen and harbor workers. Twenty-eight laws provide full coverage for these diseases and the remaining eighteen list compensable diseases, ranging from injury or death by gas in Kentucky to a list of forty-six specific conditions and diseases in Virginia. Seven states[39] have no provision of occupational diseases. In the nation as a whole, occupational diseases are estimated to account for 2 per cent of workmen's compensation claims and for 4 per cent of the costs.[40]

Few states publish information on the compensation costs for occupational diseases as distinct from other occupational injuries.[41]

Insurance Carriers

To assure benefit payments when due, a covered employer is required to obtain insurance or, under many laws, to give proof of his ability to provide self-insurance. In seven states[42] — all of which enacted workmen's compensation laws before 1919 — and Puerto Rico, employers are required to insure their risks with the state fund only; some of these states permit self-insurance. These states do not allow commercial insurance in workmen's compensation cases and are known as "exclusive" states. In eleven states[43] employers may choose to insure with the state fund or a commercial insurance company. In all other states employers, unless allowed self-insurance, must insure with a commercial insurance company.

Benefit Provisions

The law specifies the amount of compensation payable to an injured worker, usually a percentage of his wage, limited by a weekly maximum, an aggregate maximum and often a weekly minimum.[44] The duration of benefit payments may also be limited. These specifications and the method of payment vary with the type of injury — fatal injury, permanent total disability, permanent partial and temporary total disability. In some states the rate of compensation is higher for married workers and it is sometimes based on the number of dependent children. There are also provisions for medical benefits to the injured worker.

---

37. Stern, *Medical Services by Government; Local, State and Federal,* p. 31.

38. For a thorough discussion of the legal meaning of words and phrases such as "personal injury," "accident," "arising out of," "in the course of," "of the employment," and how these concepts have been broadened in time, see Samuel B. Horovitz, "Current Trends in Basic Principles of Workmen's Compensation," *Rocky Mountain Law Review,* February 1948, pp. 117–80.

39. Alabama, Kansas, Louisiana, Mississippi, Oklahoma, Vermont and Wyoming.

40. Eighth Report of the Department of Labor and Industries, Calendar Years 1940 and 1941, Washington State, p. 10.

41. The director of the Wisconsin Workmen's Compensation Department, speaking in 1937 at a meeting of the International Association of Industrial Accident Boards and Commissions, said that over a period of seventeen years the cost of occupational disease (95 per cent of which was silicosis) represented 2.5 per cent of the payments for workmen's compensation benefits in the state. The highest relative cost was 7.3 per cent of the total in 1935.

At the 1943 meeting of the IAIABC, the chairman of the Wisconsin Industrial Commission said that in 1937 occupational diseases accounted for 3 per cent of the entire cost of workmen's compensation; in 1938, 3.2 per cent; in 1939, 3.5 per cent; in 1940 and 1941, 3.4 per cent; and in 1942, 4.1 per cent. In Pennsylvania, compensation for occupational diseases in 1946 represented 7.4 per cent of the total. *Annual Accident Report, 1946,* Pennsylvania Department of Labor and Industry, Harrisburg, 1947.

In Illinois the costs of occupational diseases for the period 1935 through 1945 ranged from 1.1 per cent to 2.2 per cent of the total cost of workmen's compensation. Figures for the state of Washington fall short of 2 per cent of the amount spent for occupational injuries. In New York State, cash compensation cases for occupational diseases constituted 3.3 per cent of the cases terminated in 1946; benefit payments to these cases represented 3.4 per cent of the total. *Compensated Cases Closed in 1946,* Research and Statistics Bulletin No. 3, New York State Workmen's Compensation Board, 1947.

42. Nevada, North Dakota, Ohio, Oregon, Washington, West Virginia and Wyoming.

43. Arizona, California, Colorado, Idaho, Maryland, Michigan, Montana, New York, Oklahoma, Pennsylvania and Utah.

44. Arizona and Alaska are the only jurisdictions that do not have a weekly maximum.

State laws show wide differences, especially in their day-to-day application. One source of variation is lack of uniformity in the method of determining the average weekly wage, basic to all cash benefits.

Death Benefits

All states except Oklahoma provide death benefits, but methods of compensation vary widely. (See Appendix Table 47.) The laws of Arizona, Minnesota, Nevada, New York, North Dakota, Oregon, Washington, West Virginia, Wyoming and the District of Columbia and Hawaii, and the federal laws for civil employees and longshoremen, provide for benefit payments to widows for life or until remarriage,[45] and to children until they reach a specified age. Other acts limit either the period of payment or the total amount payable or both. Time limitations in thirty-three states range from 240 to 600 weeks; in some instances, the limitation is waived for children until they reach a specified age. In Massachusetts, payments to widows continue in periods in which they are not self-supporting. Maximum amounts specified for a widow and children range from $3,500 to $20,000. Six states have only a monetary maximum.

In most of the compensation laws the death benefit is a given percentage of the average weekly wage of the deceased worker; the exceptions are Kansas, Massachusetts, Oregon, Washington, West Virginia, Wyoming, Alaska and Puerto Rico, where flat pensions are paid. In some states, the percentage varies with marital status of the deceased and number of dependent children. The benefits are limited by a weekly maximum and usually also by a weekly minimum. The weekly maximum payment for a widow and children ranges from $15.60 to $153.85, and the weekly minimum from $3.00 to $19.00. Where actual weekly earnings are less than the minimum, many laws limit the amount of compensation to actual earnings.[46]

Permanent Total Disability Benefits

In eighteen states and the District of Columbia, and also under the federal legislation, benefits for permanent total disability are payable for life. In all other jurisdictions these benefits are limited as to time and/or total amount. Time limits range from 260 to 1,000 weeks and maximum total amounts from $3,000 to $14,000. The federal act for civil employees and the laws of Arizona, Nevada, Washington and Hawaii provide additional benefits if an attendant is required. In practice, payments for attendants have been limited almost exclusively to blind beneficiaries. In some states benefit amounts are higher for married workers, with supplementary benefits for dependent children.[47]

Permanent Partial Disability Benefits

Permanent partial disabilities are classified as specific, or "schedule," injuries (such as loss or loss of use of a member) and "nonschedule" injuries, or those of a more general nature (such as disability caused by injury to the head or back). Compensation for schedule injuries is usually paid for a specified number of weeks, but under the laws of Alaska, Washington and Wyoming the payments are fixed sums, and in California they are based on degree of disability in terms of the age and occupation of the injured worker. Payments for nonschedule disabilities are determined by extent of loss in earning power.

In thirty-three states, the District of Columbia, Alaska, Hawaii and Puerto Rico, and under the federal longshoremen's act, compensation for permanent partial disability is paid in addition to any payable for temporary total disability. In the other fifteen states, the temporary total benefit payments are deducted from the maximums allowed for permanent partial disability. Additional benefits for dependent children are granted in nine states and Alaska.

Some jurisdictions allow supplementary payments for disfigurement, usually of the face. Arizona, Minnesota, Mississippi, New York, Ohio, West Virginia, Wisconsin, the District of Columbia and the longshoremen's act provide additional benefits for vocational rehabilitation, usually for maintenance during training. For schedule injuries, the laws of forty-six states, the District of Columbia, Hawaii and Puerto Rico, and the longshoremen's act, specify fixed payments for a certain number of weeks

45. Some states pay widows a lump sum upon remarriage, usually equivalent to their periodic payments for the two preceding years.

46. *State Workmen's Compensation Laws as of July 1, 1950,* Bulletin No. 125, Bureau of Labor Standards.

47. *Ibid.,* p. 25.

for a given injury. Although there is some advantage to the worker in knowing what he is entitled to, fixed amounts make compensation less flexible; therefore, compensation for nonschedule disabilities is, as a rule, greater than for schedule injuries.[48]

Temporary Total Disability Benefits

Since only temporary disability is involved in most compensation cases, they usually end with the recovery of the injured person and his return to the labor force. Unlike the practice in other countries, temporary disability under our workmen's compensation laws is not restricted to the first six months of compensable disability, but may be continued for many years until the administrative agency decides the disability is permanent. It may then reclassify the case as permanent. Only a few cases of disability, therefore, are recorded as permanent total disability from their onset. (See Table 51.)

Temporary total disability benefits are usually determined on the basis of the injured worker's average weekly wage, subject, as a rule, to a weekly maximum and a minimum. In addition, most laws provide for a maximum duration of benefit payments and some for a maximum total amount. Thirteen states and Alaska pay larger disability benefits to workers with dependent children. (See Appendix Table 48.)

Waiting Period for Cash Compensation

All the laws except that of Oregon provide that cash compensation shall not be paid for a specified period of time, usually seven days, immediately following the injury. The purposes of this waiting period are to minimize the danger of fraudulent claims and to exclude minor injuries. The costs of insuring such injuries are out of proportion to the benefits that would be disbursed, and it is assumed that the expenses of minor injuries can be borne by the worker.[49] Most of the laws provide that if the disability continues for a certain number of weeks, compensation payments shall be retroactive to the date when the disability began. (See Appendix Table 49.)

Medical Benefits

All workmen's compensation laws specify that medical service shall be given to injured workers. In the early laws the provision for medical care was narrowly circumscribed and sometimes absent. More recently the limits on the duration of and the expenditure for medical care have been made broader or removed entirely. Over a period of years expenditures for medical care have progressively increased as compared with outlays for cash benefits. Unlike cash benefits, medical benefits are granted without a waiting period. (See Appendix Table 50.) Besides providing for medical services, forty-five laws require the employer to furnish artificial limbs and other appliances when needed. Except in Oklahoma, provisions are made for burial benefits. In five states burial benefits are paid only when there are no surviving dependents.[50]

Special Provisions

In a few states, a handicapped worker may, by a special contract, waive his right to compensation in the event of subsequent injury. This provision is supposed to facilitate the employment of handicapped workers. In most jurisdictions (forty-six) this problem is met through "second-injury" funds or equivalent arrangements. If a handicapped worker is injured, the employer compensates him to the extent of his second injury. Supplementary benefits are paid from the second-injury fund so that the total amount is commensurate with the extent of the worker's disability resulting from the current as well as earlier injuries.

Some state laws compensate workers who are injured while working outside their state of residence, others exclude this type of case, still others make no provision for it.

All compensation laws protect legally employed minors in covered employment. Seventeen laws[51] provide extra compensation for injury to minors who are illegally employed. Under twenty-nine acts compensation is paid to illegally employed minors on the same basis as that to legally employed minors. Seven laws[52] do not cover minors illegally employed. Some states impose a fine on the employer of an illegally employed minor, to be paid into the state fund. Two states allow the right of suit

48. *Ibid.,* p. 25.
49. Reede, *op. cit.,* p. 30.
50. *Ibid.,* p. 38.
51. Alabama, Florida, Illinois, Indiana, Maryland, Massachusetts, Michigan, Mississippi, Missouri, New Hampshire, New Jersey, New York, Pennsylvania, Rhode Island, Utah, Wisconsin and Puerto Rico.
52. Delaware, Nebraska, Oklahoma, South Dakota, Tennessee, Vermont and West Virginia.

in such cases in addition to workmen's compensation benefits.

A number of laws use increase in liability or decrease in benefits as punitive measures. In Wisconsin, for instance, if an employer's negligence causes injury, the injured worker is entitled to 15 per cent additional benefit, while negligence of the worker reduces his compensation by 15 per cent of the scheduled amount.

Certain states bar nonresident alien dependents of deceased workers from compensation;[53] others have discriminatory provisions. The constitutionality of such laws is subject to doubt with respect to the nationals of the thirteen countries with which the United States has treaties for reciprocal treatment of injured workers.

Claims Administration

Workmen's compensation laws have not been completely successful in mitigating costly and protracted litigation, although this was one reason for their adoption. In five states[54] the compensation acts are administered directly through the courts. New Hampshire combines court and agency administration. All the other laws entrust administration to a commission, but provide for final appeal to the courts, sometimes starting with the lower courts. Most acts limit court review to matters of law, others include matters of fact and law.[55]

Some states with administrative commissions employ direct settlement, as in Wisconsin. Payment is made in uncontested cases by the employer or the insurance carrier, under the supervision of the industrial commission to see that the compensation conforms to the law. In checking these settlements, the commission relies principally on the reports of employers and insurance carriers. Employers are required to report every compensable injury case and must file a subsequent report when the benefit payments are stopped. In addition, the commission establishes direct contact with the injured worker. When a case is contested, usually at the injured person's initiative, an examiner or a member of the commission holds hearings at the county seat and makes a decision. The decision may be appealed to the commission and ultimately to the courts.

In other jurisdictions settlement is by agreement, as in Pennsylvania. The employer and the employee reach an agreement and submit it to the state board for approval. Without vigilant supervision by the board, the injured worker is hardly in a position to defend his interest. When agreement cannot be reached, a claim is filed and a referee is appointed to hear and decide the case. Either party may appeal the referee's decision to the board and, further, to the courts.

Still other states follow the hearings system, most extensively developed in New York. There, every report of injury is investigated, and when the claim is compensable, a hearing is scheduled and an award fixed. In many cases this system, while it gives the worker the best guarantee of getting his due, appears too cumbersome and costly.

Cost and Benefit Payments

Complete and accurate information is not available on the amount industry spends for workmen's compensation, the amount paid to injured workers, the number of compensable injuries, or the number of beneficiaries. On the basis of available information, the author estimates that industry spent a total of $1.014 billion for compensation of work-connected injuries in 1948. The 1949 figures cannot be much different.

The Social Security Administration of the Federal Security Agency, relying on the available piecemeal information, has estimated the amount of benefit payments under workmen's compensation laws since 1939. The amount and distribution of these payments by type of benefit and insurance carrier are shown in Table 55.[56] These estimates indicate a progressive decline in the proportion of medical benefits as compared with disability payments. This is a reversal of the long-range trends shown by Reede and others.[57]

53. *State Workmen's Compensation Laws as of July 1, 1950*, pp. 45–47.

54. Alabama, Louisiana, New Mexico, Tennessee and Wyoming.

55. Ontario and certain other Canadian provinces have found it more expeditious and efficient to entrust workmen's compensation enforcement in all phases to an independent commission, without the right of appeal to the courts. *Discussion of Industrial Accidents and Diseases, 1946*, Convention of the International Association of Industrial Accident Boards and Commissions, Portland, Oregon, Bulletin No. 87, Bureau of Labor Statistics, 1947; and Dawson, *op. cit.*

56. *Social Security Bulletin*, Social Security Administration, January 1942, pp. 6–14; and December 1948, pp. 15–16.

57. Reede, *op. cit.*, pp. 270–73.

TABLE 55

ESTIMATED ANNUAL AMOUNT OF BENEFIT PAYMENTS UNDER WORKMEN'S COMPENSATION LAWS AND PERCENTAGE DISTRIBUTION BY TYPE OF BENEFIT AND INSURANCE CARRIER, 1939–1948

Year	Benefits, in Millions	Percentage Distribution by Type of Benefit			Percentage Distribution by Type of Insurance Carrier		
		Medical	Disability	Survivors	Commercial	Govern-mental	Self-Insured
1939	$235	36	51	13	52	29	19
1940	256	37	50	13	53	28	19
1941	291	34	53	13	55	26	19
1942	330	33	56	11	57	25	18
1943	356	31	58	11	60	23	17
1944	387	31	59	10	61	22	17
1945	411	31	59	10	61	22	17
1946	435	32	58	10	62	22	16
1947	487	33	58	9	62	22	16
1948	537	33	58	9	62	23	15

Source: Social Security Bulletin, Social Security Administration.

Relation of Benefit Payments to Wage Loss

The proportion of wage loss compensated by benefits paid for different types of injury varies widely among the states. In North Carolina in 1940, for example, estimated benefits paid in fatal cases represented 19.6 per cent of the estimated annual wage loss; in permanent total cases, 24.2 per cent; in permanent partial cases, 24.4 per cent; and in temporary total cases, 47.7 per cent. The average for all types of injuries was 26.4 per cent. Comparable percentages in Massachusetts in 1935 were: 14.8 per cent for fatalities, 75.4 per cent for permanent total disability, 32.4 per cent for major permanent, 39.2 per cent for minor permanent, and 54.9 per cent for temporary total disability. The average for all types of cases was 34.6 per cent.[58]

For workers subject to workmen's compensation in the United States as a whole in 1948, the proportion of wage loss compensated by benefit payments was probably 30 per cent for all injuries, 10 per cent for fatal injuries, and 44 per cent for all types of disabling injuries.[59] If payments are related to the estimated wage loss of all injured workers, whether or not they were covered by workmen's compensation laws, payments for injuries represented 22 per cent of the loss in wages in 1948, 7 per cent of the loss from fatal injuries, and 32 per cent of the loss from all types of disability. (See Table 56.)

Relation of Benefit Payments to Employers' Contributions

Benefits disbursed under workmen's compensation systems in 1940 amounted to less than 61 per cent of the premiums paid by employers. At one extreme, injured workers received in benefits 95 per cent of the contributions paid on their behalf under the federal employees' program, while under private insurance, beneficiaries received less than 50 per cent. (See Table 57.)

There has always been great disparity between the ratios of benefits to contributions under governmental and commercial plans. This disparity was observed in 1918[60] and in the 1930's and still exists. The relationship of benefits to premiums in 1948 for various broad types of insurance has been estimated by the author as follows:

	Benefit Disburse-ments, in Millions	*Premiums, in Millions*	*Benefits as Percentage of Premiums*
Total	$539.0	$1,014.2	53.1
Self-insurance	80.2	84.5	95.0
Competitive state fund	47.7	91.6	52.1
Exclusive state fund	76.4	87.6	87.2
Private insurance	334.7	750.5	44.6

Some authorities attribute the high cost of private insurance to the fact that the commercial companies render services that the state funds do not provide.[61] Undoubtedly this argu-

58. *Ibid.,* pp. 207 and 212.

59. These estimates are based on Department of Labor statistics of work injuries. If higher injury rates are assumed, as suggested by the experience of the National Council on Compensation Insurance, the percentages would decline to 26 for all injuries, 7 for fatal injuries, and 35 for all types of disability.

60. Carl Hookstadt, *Comparison of Workmen's Compensation Insurance and Administration,* Bulletin No. 301, Bureau of Labor Statistics, 1922, pp. 21 and 8.

61. David McCahan, *State Insurance in the United States,* University of Pennsylvania Press, Philadelphia, 1929.

TABLE 56

WORKMEN'S COMPENSATION BENEFITS IN RELATION TO ESTIMATED WAGE LOSS FROM INDUSTRIAL INJURIES INCURRED BY ALL EMPLOYEES AND BY EMPLOYEES SUBJECT TO WORKMEN'S COMPENSATION LAWS, 1948 [a]

Type of Injury	Number of Injuries, in Thousands: All Employees	Number of Injuries, in Thousands: Employees Subject to Workmen's Compensation Act	Loss of Time, in Thousands of Years: All Employees	Loss of Time, in Thousands of Years: Employees Subject to Workmen's Compensation Act
All injuries	1,552.1	1,133	571	417
Fatal	11.7	9	234	171
Permanent total	1.4	1	27	20
Permanent partial	68.1	50	221	161
Temporary total	1,470.9	1,074	89	65

Type of Injury	Wage Loss, in Millions: All Employees	Wage Loss, in Millions: Employees Subject to Workmen's Compensation Act	Cash Benefits, in Millions	Benefits as Percentage of Wage Loss: All Employees	Benefits as Percentage of Wage Loss: Subject Employees
All injuries	$1,670.7	$1,220.1	$363.3	21.7	29.8
Fatal	684.7	500.3	50.1	7.3	10.0
Permanent total	79.0	58.5	313.2 (permanent total, permanent partial and temporary total combined)	31.8	43.5
Permanent partial	646.6	471.1			
Temporary total	260.4	190.2			

a. These estimates by the author are based on the work injury statistics reported by the Bureau of Labor Statistics. Statistics on compensated cases available from the National Council on Compensation Insurance are higher and show longer average duration per case than the BLS.

TABLE 57

WORKMEN'S COMPENSATION BENEFITS IN RELATION TO ESTIMATED EMPLOYERS' CONTRIBUTIONS, BY INSURANCE CARRIER, 1940

Insurance Carrier	Benefits, in Millions	Contributions, in Millions	Benefits as Percentage of Contributions
Total	$255.8	$420.3	60.9
Carrying own risk	62.8	66.1	95.0
Federal government	13.0	13.7	94.9
Other	49.8	52.4	95.0
State insurance	59.5	84.4	70.5
Competitive funds	28.2	44.7	63.1
Exclusive funds	31.3	39.7	78.8
Private insurance	133.5	269.8	49.5
Stock companies	84.3	166.8	50.5
Mutual companies	46.5	96.9	48.0
Other companies	2.8	6.0	46.4

Source: Arthur Hallam Reede, *Adequacy of Workmen's Compensation,* Harvard University Press, Cambridge, 1947, p. 247.

ment has some merit when the performance of the average state fund is compared with that of outstanding private companies. It is uncertain, however, whether the services rendered by the average commercial carrier are perceptibly better than those of the average state fund. For example, allegations concerning the value of the safety work of private insurance companies do not withstand critical scrutiny.[62] As Marshall Dawson points out:

> The crux of the problem of private insurance arrangements is . . . their relatively high operating cost. As offsetting advantages, some insurance carriers provide superior service in preventing accidents and in furnishing or supervising medical aid to injured workers, with resulting savings to employers through a plan known as experience rating. An examination of the items of overhead expense of the private companies does not, however, disclose that any of them had spent more than a few cents on the premium dollar for safety activities, while on the other hand the stock companies have usually spent 17½ cents on the insurance dollar for acquisition cost of production of business.[63]

The experience of private insurance companies registered in New York State as compared with the state insurance fund points up the higher expense ratios of private carriers, especially stock companies. In the five-year periods 1934–1938 and 1939–1943 the costs of acquiring business took from 16 to 18 per cent of the premium income of stock companies and

62. Frank Lang, *Workmen's Compensation Insurance Monopoly or Free Competition,* Division of Research, Association of Casualty and Surety Executives, Irwin, Chicago, 1947, pp. 207–09.

63. Dawson, *op. cit.,* p. 23.

TABLE 58

AMOUNT OF PREMIUMS AND PERCENTAGE DISTRIBUTION OF DISBURSEMENTS UNDER WORKMEN'S COMPENSATION BY COMPANIES IN NEW YORK STATE AND BY THE NEW YORK STATE INSURANCE FUND, 1934–1938 AND 1939–1943

Item	Stock Companies		Mutual Companies		State Insurance Fund	
	1934–1938	1939–1943	1934–1938	1939–1943	1934–1938	1939–1943
	Amount, in Millions					
Premiums	$604	$880	$278	$551	$83	$116
	Percentage Distribution of Disbursements					
Total	100.0	100.0	100.0	100.0	100.0	100.0
Benefits	56.3	57.6	56.1	56.7	79.2	77.3
Expenses:						
Acquisitions	17.6	16.4	4.6	4.9	0.7	0.7
Administration	9.1	8.6	5.6	5.6	5.5	6.3
Claim adjustment	9.1	8.5	7.1	7.1	9.5	8.6
Inspection and Rating Bureau	2.4	2.2	2.7	2.8	2.4	2.1
Taxes and fees	3.3	3.4	2.2	2.4	0.4	0.4
Net gain	2.2	3.3	21.6	20.5	2.3	4.5

Source: Adapted from Eighty-fifth Annual Report of the Superintendent of Insurance, State of New York, 1943, Vol. III.

their general administration costs another 9 per cent, as compared with 5 and 6 per cent respectively under the mutual funds. (See Table 58.) Stock companies carry more of the smaller employers than mutual companies, which fact partly explains their higher expense ratios.[64] The net gain of the stock companies going to the stockholders is 2 or 3 per cent. For mutual companies 20 to 22 per cent of the premium payment is returned to the employer in the form of dividends or is counted toward his next year's payment. In contrast, less than one per cent of the costs of the New York State fund are for acquisitions and about 6 per cent for general administration. The percentage of earned premium spent for inspection and the rating bureau — which includes all expenditures for safety — is about the same for all three, less than 3 per cent. Furthermore, premiums charged by the New York State fund are less than the manual rates used by stock and mutual companies.

64. Reede, *op. cit.*

The experience of New York and other states leaves no doubt that claim services and accident prevention can be greatly improved under a state-administered program based on sound legislation and expert administration, with higher benefits to injured workers and their families and/or lower costs to the employer than are possible for commercial insurance.

The premiums paid by an employer for workmen's compensation are only part of the cost to him of injuries suffered by his employees. A study published in 1930 in the *Monthly Labor Review* showed that work accidents indirectly cost the employer four dollars for every dollar of direct cost paid for workmen's compensation.[65] The National Safety Council has estimated the total loss to employers and workers from work injuries in 1949 at $2.6 billion, of which the wage loss was estimated at $750 million.[66]

65. H. W. Heinrich, "Costs of Industrial Accidents to the State, the Employer, and the Man," *Monthly Labor Review,* November 1930, pp. 1116–24.

66. *Accident Facts,* 1950 edition, p. 13.

CHAPTER 17

HEALTH INSURANCE FOR WORKERS AND THEIR FAMILIES *

NINETY-FIVE PER CENT of the health hazards of workers are considered to be of nonoccupational origin. The well-being of workers and their families, therefore, depends largely on the quality, quantity and timeliness of the preventive and curative medical services available to them and on the continuance of income when illness cuts off earnings. When such protection is not available, workers strive to meet these needs through collective bargaining. The picture of the institutional setting of the labor market would be incomplete, therefore, without consideration of existing arrangements to help workers meet sickness costs and losses to themselves and their families.

Because no one can predict when he will be sick or disabled or how long and serious his incapacity will be, the individual worker and his family cannot adequately budget these costs. The difficulties of such budgeting have increased progressively with advances in medicine and the resulting specialization of medical services, including new diagnostic techniques, which have made medical care more costly and yet more indispensable because it can accomplish more.

The desire to protect health and to guard against loss of wages in sickness through some form of pooling of risks is neither new nor peculiar to this country.[1] In all periods and all parts of the world, organized groups have tried to moderate the economic impact of illness and disability. In the United States, such efforts have been made sporadically since the establishment of the nation. Abroad, some forty countries, including almost all the industrial nations, have governmentally sponsored programs for meeting medical care costs of workers and their dependents and replacing part of the wage loss caused by disability. In the United States, voluntary commercial and nonprofit health insurance plans have grown rapidly in recent years. Since the inauguration of the social security program, many bills for health and sickness insurance have been introduced in Congress and in state legislatures.

The Costs of Ill Health

In a broad sense, the costs of ill health to the individual and the nation as a whole are incalculable. Only the medical costs that employees incur for the care of themselves and their dependents and the wage losses they suffer, primarily through temporary total disability of nonoccupational origin, are measurable.

The most recent data indicate that in the United States the average worker loses 7.5 work days a year through temporary total nonoccupational disability, that is, disability lasting not more than six months.[2] In the absence of any compensation during illness, this loss in working time is equivalent to 3 per cent of annual earnings. Applying this rate to the total wages and salaries of the nation, exclusive of the armed forces, the total wage loss in 1949 would have been more than $3.6 billion, after deduction of sick-leave pay given to salaried employees and certain groups of wage earners. An additional $7 billion or more is lost by some 3 million potential workers as a result of total disability lasting longer than six months. The loss from partial disability is probably at least as great as the loss from total disability, or at least $10 billion. Thus the total wage loss attributable to total and partial disability in 1949 probably exceeded $21 billion (exclusive of the earnings losses of the self-employed).

Various studies of consumer expenditures indicate that the medical care costs paid directly

* By Barkev S. Sanders, Federal Security Agency, Social Security Administration; Lecturer on Health Economics at the American University and on Health Statistics and Labor Economics at the Catholic University of America, Washington, D.C. The opinions expressed here are those of the author and not necessarily of the agency with which he is associated.

1. Cf. Chapter 14.

2. Frank S. McElroy and Alexander Moros, "Illness Absenteeism in Manufacturing Plants, 1947," *Monthly Labor Review*, September 1948, pp. 235–39; William M. Gafafer (Ed.), "Absenteeism," *Manual of Industrial Hygiene and Medical Service in War Industries*, Saunders, Philadelphia, 1943, pp. 430–66.

by families average about 4 to 5 per cent of consumers' expendable income.[3] More recent studies come closer to 5 per cent. If an average rate of 4.5 per cent is applied to the national total of wages and salaries (exclusive of military pay and the earnings of the self-employed), expenditures of worker families for medical care would total $5.9 billion for 1949, or $210 per household. On the assumption of a 5 per cent rate, these amounts would be nearly $6.6 billion for the total and $233 per household.

For a worker's family experiencing illness, however, these totals and averages have no meaning unless there is a pooling of losses and resources. Many workers have no significant wage loss through sickness in a given year, while some lose all potential earnings. Many families spend only small amounts for medical care in a given year, but a few have to mortgage their future earnings in their attempt to save a member of the family.

A frequently quoted study by the Committee on the Costs of Medical Care showed that 58 per cent of all families paid 18 per cent of the medical care bill of the year; 32 per cent paid 41 per cent; and the least fortunate 10 per cent paid the remaining 41 per cent.[4] The unpredictability and uneven incidence of the costs of illness led the representatives of the seventeen national organizations who participated in the National Health Assembly in Washington in May 1948 to conclude that:

> The principle of contributory health insurance should be the basic method of financing medical care for the large majority of the American people in order to remove the burden of unpredictable sickness costs, abolish the economic barrier to adequate medical services and avoid the indignities of a "means test." [5]

3. Bureau of Labor Statistics: *City Family Expenditures and Savings in 1944,* December 9, 1945; *Family Spending and Saving in Wartime,* 1945; *Family Income, Expenditures and Savings in 1945,* Bulletin No. 956; *Survey of Prices Paid by Families in 1946,* L.S. 49–3497; Helen M. Humes, "Family Income and Expenditures in 1947," *Monthly Labor Review,* April 1949. *Civilian Spending and Saving, 1941 and 1942,* Office of Price Administration, 1943. According to the Department of Commerce (*Survey of Current Business,* July 1950), expenditures of consumers for medical care amounted to 4.2 per cent of total disposable income in 1949. This estimate appears too low, however.

4. *National Health Program,* Hearings before a Subcommittee of the Committee on Labor and Public Welfare, U.S. Senate, 80th Cong., 1st sess., on S. 545 and S. 1320, Part 3, July 9, 10 and 11, 1947, p. 1488.

5. Oscar R. Ewing, *The Nation's Health,* A Ten-Year Program, A Report to the President, Federal Security Agency, 1948, p. 62; *America's Health,* A Report to the Nation by the National Health Assembly, Harper, New York, 1949, p. 221.

Protection against Costs and Losses

In the United States there has been a slow but progressive growth of public provision for the diagnosis and care of certain chronic diseases, such as tuberculosis, mental disease, venereal disease, cancer and heart disease. Broader provisions, varying widely in adequacy in different areas, are made for medical care of the indigent and, often, the medically indigent. Although workers, like others, share in the benefits of these public measures, they can hardly be regarded as part of the institutional setting of the labor market. The further discussion is limited to measures largely participated in by wage and salary workers.

Insurance protection against sickness costs and losses is provided by commercial insurance, nonprofit voluntary plans (such as Blue Cross for prepayment of hospital care and Blue Shield for medical care), industrial plans and governmental programs. The various plans are not coordinated with one another. Almost all have been growing rapidly in recent years, but the total protection they provide to workers and their families falls far short of meeting demands or needs. This fact explains both the rapid growth of all forms of health insurance and the efforts of labor unions to supplement them by union and employee-employer welfare plans, as well as organized labor's demand for governmentally sponsored health insurance.

In 1949, employees received $950 to $960 million in medical services or indemnity for medical costs from all organized risk-bearing and other programs (commercial insurance, nonprofit prepayment plans, programs of industrial establishments and government agencies the benefits of which flow primarily to workers). This total represents about 15 per cent of the medical care costs of employees and their dependents. For wage loss from temporary disability, total payments from all sources in 1949 amounted to $255 to $265 million, about 7 per cent of the wage loss (exclusive of sick leave, which is deducted from the total in estimating losses). Benefit payments for permanent total disability totaled $390 to $400 million. More than two thirds of the payments for permanent disability and nearly one third of the payments for temporary disability and medical care were supplied from governmental sources, the rest by commercial insurance, nonprofit prepayment plans and industrial plans. (For details see Appendix Table 51.)

Commercial Insurance

In the United States some four hundred insurance carriers offer thousands of different types of contracts designed to provide protection against the costs and losses of illness, including both wage loss and medical care. Commercial insurance is not restricted to employees; it has been estimated that 10 to 15 per cent of the policies are held by the self-employed.

In general, health and accident policies provide protection for a limited period of time, usually thirteen or twenty-six weeks, occasionally fifty-two weeks and rarely for longer periods of wage loss, and sometimes indemnity for certain medical costs. These contracts as a rule exclude risks covered under workmen's compensation laws. Permanent-disability contracts in general have no such time limitation. Most health and accident contracts have a waiting period during which the insured is not indemnified for wage loss. For individual policies, and to a much lesser extent for group policies, the risks are graded according to the occupation of the insured.

In individual insurance, the health status, age, sex and color of the insured determine insurability and the premium rate. In group insurance, higher premium rates are charged for groups with a high percentage of females and persons of non-Caucasian races. All individual health and accident policies have an age limit, sometimes as low as 50 years, usually 55 or 60, sometimes 65 or even 70. In group insurance, benefit provisions for the aged are usually restricted.

Individual Policies

The following types of policies are sold to individuals:

Commercial. These are policies with relatively comprehensive coverage against wage loss caused by disability. They often carry supplementary provisions for indemnity of the costs of hospitalization, surgery and, occasionally, physicians' services. As a rule, these policies provide a considerable lump-sum payment in the event of accidental death or dismemberment. Only select and preferred risks are eligible to purchase this type of policy. Premium payments are usually annual.

Semicommercial. These policies are more restricted in the scope and extent of protection. They may be purchased by insurable individuals in all insurable occupations.

Noncancelable. These policies equal or exceed commercial policies in breadth of coverage and extent of indemnity. They differ from commercial policies in that the carrier cannot cancel the contract; the option to continue the contract up to the designated age of 50, 55 or 60 is vested solely in the insured. This type of policy developed rapidly after World War I, but sales came to a virtual standstill after 1930.

Monthly Premium. These policies, designed for manual workers, are more limited than the commercial. They may provide a small lump-sum payment for accidental death or dismemberment.

Weekly Premium Industrial. These are policies for low-paid manual workers. They provide minimum protection against wage loss and often a small lump-sum payment ($200–$1,000) for accidental death or dismemberment.

Limited. These are policies covering only specified accidents and/or diseases. They include travel ticket policies (the precursor of health and accident insurance), newspaper policies designed primarily to increase circulation, automobile accident policies, policies against catastrophic diseases like polio, and so on.

Franchise. These are individual policies, like the others described so far, but are sold to employees with the consent of their employer. In addition to weekly benefits, they may provide indemnity for various medical costs and lump-sum payment for accidental death or dismemberment.

Hospitalization. These policies are individual contracts to indemnify the costs of hospital care. They may include indemnity for surgical costs and even for other medical attendance. Hospital indemnity consists of fixed daily payments for a specified maximum number of days. The per diem indemnity is increased by a specified factor to allow for certain usual incidental costs.

Permanent Disability. Life insurance companies began underwriting insurance against permanent disability at the end of the past century. The early arrangements consisted of a provision waiving premiums in periods of

TABLE 59

NUMBER OF INDEMNITY POLICIES PROVIDING PAYMENTS AGAINST WAGE LOSS AND NUMBER OF POLICYHOLDERS, DECEMBER 31, 1949

(*In Thousands*)

Type of Policy	Policies in Force	Policyholders with Accident and Health Protection
Total	28,320	21,666
Individual policies	18,060	11,406
Accident only	4,345	209
Health only	278	
Health and accident combined	13,437	11,197
Group certificates	10,260	10,260

Source: A. L. Kirkpatrick, "The Extent of the Health Coverage of Insurance Companies," *American Economic Security,* August–September 1950, pp. 34–37.

TABLE 60

ESTIMATED NUMBER OF POLICIES PROVIDING INDEMNITY AGAINST MEDICAL COSTS AND ACCIDENTAL DEATH AND DISMEMBERMENT, DECEMBER 31, 1949

(*In Thousands*)

Risk	Total	Type of Policy: Group Certificates	Type of Policy: Individual Policies
Hospital expense	32,426	17,697	14,729
Subscriber	17,050	8,500	8,550
Dependent	15,376	9,197	6,179
Surgical expense	24,905	15,590	9,315
Subscriber	13,755	8,396	5,359
Dependent	11,150	7,194	3,956
Medical expense	5,086	2,736	2,350
Subscriber	3,273	1,712	1,561
Dependent	1,813	1,024	789
Accidental death or dismemberment	12,769	6,669	6,100[a]

a. Estimated, assuming 5 per cent of individual premium income is paid for protection against accidental death and dismemberment.

Sources: Group Insurance and Group Annuity Coverage — Continental United States Business — 1948 and 1949, all Life, Accident and Health, and Casualty Insurance Companies, estimated by the Life Insurance Association of America from data contributed by 227 United States and Canadian companies; A. L. Kirkpatrick, "The Extent of the Health Coverage of Insurance Companies," *American Economic Security,* August–September 1950, pp. 34–37.

disability. This provision developed into payment of monthly benefits of $10 or even $15 for each $1,000 of life insurance. Inadequate rate structure, careless underwriting brought about by competition, and the depression caused heavy losses to the companies, however. Since 1932 most companies have restricted their underwriting of this risk to the waiving of premiums during disability. Some cautious revival of permanent-disability business has taken place since. Permanent-disability policies have a waiting period of three to six months; that is, a disability, even though total and permanent, is not compensated until at least three or, more usually, six months have elapsed.

Group Policies

In addition to the policies sold to individuals, commercial insurance companies write accident and health policies for groups of workers. In group policies, the master policy is usually issued to the employer or the union as the contracting party, and individual certificates, indicating the provisions of the contract, to the members of the group. These policies are not sold to groups of fewer than 25 persons, and most companies do not deal with groups smaller than 50; in 1949 the average group contract covered about 190 persons.[6] To guard against adverse selection, at least 75 per cent of the group must participate. A group policy may provide weekly indemnity and indemnity for hospitalization, surgery and other medical services to workers and their dependents. Frequently it also provides a lump-sum payment for accidental death or dismemberment.[7]

Extent of Protection

According to the United States Chamber of Commerce, more than 28 million indemnity policies providing payments against wage loss were in force at the end of 1949. It is estimated that at that time nearly 22 million policyholders had one or more policies for weekly indemnity.[8] (See Table 59.)

The same study reports more than 32 million individual policies and group certificates with hospital indemnity for subscribers and dependents; 25 million policies or certificates for surgical indemnity; about 5 million for other medical care costs. (See Table 60.)

Total benefit payments of commercial insur-

6. This numerical limitation has been removed in the states with cash sickness insurance where insurance companies are allowed to participate under the state plan. As a result, the average number of workers covered per master policy is declining.

7. Ralph H. Blanchard, *Survey of Accident and Health Insurance,* Bulletins No. 1, 2, 3, Bureau Memorandum 62, 1945, Bureau of Research and Statistics, Social Security Board, Federal Security Agency; Edwin J. Faulkner, *Accident-and-Health Insurance,* McGraw-Hill, New York, 1940, pp. 45–46, 81–182, 293–300; Joseph B. Maclean, *Life Insurance,* 6th edition, McGraw-Hill, New York, 1945, Chapter 14.

8. A. L. Kirkpatrick, "The Extent of the Health Coverage of Insurance Companies," *American Economic Security,* August–September 1950, pp. 34–37.

TABLE 61

ESTIMATED LOSSES FROM ILLNESS AND NONINDUSTRIAL INJURIES FOR THE ENTIRE POPULATION AND FOR WAGE AND SALARY WORKERS, COMPARED WITH ESTIMATES OF INDEMNIFICATION OF THESE LOSSES THROUGH COMMERCIAL INSURANCE, 1949

(*Dollar Figures in Millions*)

	Losses		Benefit Payments		Percentage of Loss Indemnified		Percentage of Loss Recouped by the Insured [a]
Risk	Entire Population	Wage and Salary Workers	Entire Population	Wage and Salary Workers	Entire Population	Wage and Salary Workers	
Total	$24,922 [b]	$18,400 [b]	$617 [c]	$523	2.5	2.8	—
Total medical expenditures	9,372 [d]	6,500	276	221	2.9	3.4	31
Hospital	1,800	1,400	174	139	9.7	9.9	38
Surgical	1,450	1,050	91	73	6.3	7.0	36
All other medical	6,122	4,050	11	9	0.2	0.2	6 [e]
Earnings loss	15,550 [e]	11,900	341	302	2.2	2.5	—
Temporary disability	4,250 [f]	3,600	211	190	5.0	5.3	10
Permanent disability	9,500	7,000	102 [g]	90	1.1	1.3	[h]
Accidental death and dismemberment	1,800 [i]	1,300 [j]	28 [k]	22	1.6	1.7	[h]

a. Coverage is based on the estimates by the Survey Committee of the Health Insurance Council for the end of 1948 and 1949 (*A Survey of Accident and Health Coverage in the United States,* August 1949 and August 1950). Figures used are the mid-points.
b. Includes a small fraction of losses incidental to accidental death and dismemberment.
c. Includes $539 million paid through accident and health insurance contracts and $78 million paid under life insurance contracts as cash benefits for permanent total disability.
d. Based on the assumption that consumers spend 5 per cent of their disposable income for medical care.
e. Exclusive of partial disability, except for a negligible fraction included with accidental death and dismemberment.
f. Has been reduced by $400 million assumed to represent continued payment of wages as sick leave.
g. Exclusive of waiver of premiums under life insurance contracts.
h. Estimate of coverage not given.
i. *Accident Facts,* 1950 edition, p. 13.
j. Does not include payments made under life insurance policies.
k. Includes miscellaneous other benefits not included elsewhere.

Source: Estimated losses based on family expenditure data and expendable income for 1950, earnings losses based on studies of time loss from disability and average earnings in 1949, indemnities based on *Spectator Casualty Insurance by States,* 1950 edition, The Spectator, Philadelphia, p. 238.

ance carriers in 1949 were $617 million of which $539 million [9] was paid through accident and health insurance contracts and the remainder, $78 million, through life insurance contracts. Of the $539 million, $276 million was for specific medical care costs, $235 million for weekly indemnity (that is, payment for disability regarded primarily as temporary), and the remainder of $28 million for accidental death and dismemberment and other payments under limited policies. Of the medical indemnities paid out, wage and salary workers probably received 80 per cent of the total — $221 million. Probably 90 per cent of the $235 million paid for weekly indemnity, or about $211 million, went to wage and salary workers. Of this amount, $190 million was paid for temporary disability. For wage and salary workers, insurance indemnities in 1949 represented 3 to 4 per cent of their total outlay for medical care. Payments for weekly indemnity represented 5 to 6 per cent of the wage loss caused by temporary disability.[10] (See Table 61.)

The protection provided against permanent total disability is largely through disability clauses in life insurance contracts. In 1949, benefit payments for such disability under life insurance contracts amounted to $78 million; this figure suggests that 2.5 to 3 million workers may have had such insurance protection.

Limitations

Undoubtedly commercial insurance has helped millions of workers during disability. It has developed the concept and technique of spreading medical risks and will have a continuing role in the future. It has many limitations, however. It is not inclusive — it discriminates against persons of advanced age, those with serious handicaps, those in occupations hazardous to health. Many individual policies may not

9. *Spectator Casualty Insurance by States,* 1950 edition, The Spectator, Philadelphia, p. 238.

10. Possibly 7 to 10 per cent of the payments for weekly indemnity were paid for disabilities past the temporary period of twenty-six weeks, and may be regarded as payments for long-term or permanent disability.

be renewed after the policyholder reaches age 55 or 60. It is costly — in 1948, for instance, holders of accident and health policies (including weekly indemnities and indemnities against medical care costs) collectively paid $1.84 in premiums for each $1.00 of benefit collected. For individual insurance the relationship of premiums to benefits was $2.43 to $1.00; for group insurance, $1.37 to $1.00.[11] These relationships remain relatively constant from year to year. The operation of private insurance is such that the workers least able to pay, on the average, pay more for equivalent benefits than those in better economic circumstances. This is just the opposite of what social insurance aims to achieve.

Nonprofit Voluntary Prepayment Plans

The nonprofit plans considered here are all limited to meeting medical care costs, not wage loss from disability. Like commercial insurance, these plans are not designed exclusively for wage workers, but a very large portion of the participants, about 80 per cent, are wage workers and their dependents.

At the end of 1949 nearly 35 million persons, or almost a quarter of the total population, had substantial protection against the costs of short-term hospitalization. The plans, on the average, paid 65 to 70 per cent of the hospital bill. In addition, some 14 million persons, about 9 per cent of the population, had some protection against surgical costs. Of this number, about half had limited protection against certain additional costs — usually physician's fees for hospital treatment of nonsurgical complaints. The total contribution of the 14 million with surgical and related coverage was at an annual rate of $98 million, of which $86 million was returned in benefits to the participants — not all of whom, of course, were workers or their dependents.[12]

Until the last four or five years, the trend in hospital insurance plans had been toward broader coverage of hospital services, while medical care plans administered by medical societies have tended to narrow the scope of medical services. Although existing plans indemnify workers for only a small fraction — about 5 per cent — of their aggregate expenditures for medical care, they deserve close attention as a new approach to the problem of meeting the economic risk of sickness. These voluntary plans return a much larger fraction of the contribution to the participants than do commercial insurance carriers.

Hospital Care (Blue Cross)

Hospital care plans, by and large, are organized and controlled by the hospitals. The American Hospital Association has been a leader in the development and expansion of such arrangements, which are known as Blue Cross plans.

Prepayment of hospital care has been practiced in many communities for many decades, but the beginning of Blue Cross plans is conventionally set at 1929. In that year the teachers in Dallas, Texas, made an agreement with the Baylor University Hospital to be eligible for as much as three weeks of hospital care a year, with all incidental costs, for a fee of $3 a semester, $6 a year. The first general arrangement for meeting hospital care by prepayment was in Sacramento, California, in 1932.

Faced with large and growing deficits, hospitals saw prepayment plans as a possible means of stabilizing income. In 1933 the American Hospital Association favored the plans; in 1937 it established the Hospital Service Plan Commission and authorized it to recommend approval of nonprofit hospital plans meeting certain standards. The early plans were developed without special legislation, but in New York it was necessary to pass a special enabling act. Most states subsequently passed similar acts for nonprofit voluntary hospitalization and/or medical care plans. These associations are considered charitable and benevolent organizations and are exempted from federal, state and local taxes other than taxes on real and personal property.[13]

The growth of Blue Cross plans has been phenomenal. (See Table 62.) In many states

11. Derived by the author from premiums collected, losses paid and expenses incurred given in the *Spectator* publications. In 1949, premium collections against benefits of $539 million disbursed by accident and health insurance companies were $862 million. *Spectator Casualty Insurance by States,* 1950 edition, p. 238.

12. *National Health Program, 1949,* Hearings before a Subcommittee on Labor and Public Welfare, U.S. Senate, 81st Cong., 1st sess., pp. 375–405. The 1948 figures have been brought up to date for 1949.

13. Unlike employees of other charitable organizations, the employees of these organizations are mandatorily subject to the federal and state social security laws.

TABLE 62

NUMBER OF BLUE CROSS PLANS AND NUMBER OF PARTICIPANTS, AS OF FIRST OF THE YEAR, 1933–1951

Year	Number of Plans	Participants, in Thousands
1933	1	2
1934	6	12
1935	10	54
1936	17	214
1937	26	608
1938	38	1,365
1939	49	2,874
1940	59	4,410
1941	65	6,012
1942	66	8,399
1943	74	10,215
1944	73	12,659
1945	75	15,748
1946	80	18,881
1947	81	24,250
1948	83	28,143
1949	84	30,498
1950	84	33,381
1951	84	37,300

Source: Based on data of the Blue Cross Commission. Since the approval program of the American Hospital Association was not instituted until 1937, the plans enumerated before that date include some that subsequently did not meet its standards for approval.

these plans cover a significant fraction of the population. (See Appendix Table 52.)

There are a number of nonprofit hospital plans that have not been approved as Blue Cross plans. The present membership of these is about half a million. A number of Blue Shield surgical and medical care plans provide hospitalization benefits as well; participants at the end of 1949 numbered about 950,000.[14]

Enrollment Policies

Enrollment in Blue Cross plans has generally been on a group basis. Almost all plans enroll groups of ten or more; some, groups of three or more. For groups of ten or less, enrollment must be 100 per cent; for groups of ten to twenty-five, it may be 90 to 50 per cent; and lower percentages are allowed in still larger groups. Employed persons subscribe, but the coverage generally includes dependents—spouse and children under 18 or 19. All plans permit persons who leave a group to continue membership by paying to the plan directly. Some plans do not extend this privilege to those aged 65 and over.

In recent years the plans have given increasing attention to individual enrollment. At present 66 of the 84 plans provide for it. Individual enrollment at first proved financially disastrous for underwriters, but recent experience, in which the underwriting is surrounded with various safeguards, has been satisfactory. Premium charges for the individually enrolled are generally somewhat higher, for comparable accommodations, than for those enrolled in groups.

Most plans have no age limit for group subscribers. The usual method of collecting subscriptions from employed groups is through wage deduction.

Scope of Services

The Blue Cross plans provide predominantly hospital service. Originally these plans paid the full hospital bill for the period of hospitalization specified in the contract if the patient used no better accommodation than that specified in the contract and if he did not have any of the excluded services. Recently a number of plans, instead of providing services, have indemnified the patients up to a specified amount. Of the 84 plans in existence in 1949, 52 provided service contracts, the rest indemnities. Even some of the 52 with service contracts had alternative contracts providing indemnity instead of service.

The basic services provided are hospital room and board, general nursing care, use of operating and delivery rooms, specified laboratory services, and routine medication and dressings. Most plans provide additional special services. All provide some obstetrical care in connection with family contracts, usually after a period of eight to twelve months subsequent to enrollment.

Benefit provisions vary widely from plan to plan. There are four distinct patterns. (1) Some plans specify the number of days of hospital service or indemnity in the contract. In 1949, 26 of the plans were of this type. The maximum period of benefits specified varied from 21 to 150 days per condition requiring hospitalization. At least one plan varied the maximum, allowing a longer period for those under age 65 and a much shorter one for those aged 65 or over; and other patterns may be

14. Several organizations that provide hospital care do not bear the label Blue Cross. There are other plans, many of them affiliated in one form or another with Blue Cross, providing service or indemnity for other medical needs. Louis S. Reed, *Blue Cross and Medical Service Plans,* U.S. Public Health Service, Federal Security Agency, 1947, p. 36. *Voluntary Prepayment Medical Care Plans, 1950,* Council on Medical Service, American Medical Association.

found among the 26 plans, since some of them have alternative contracts. (2) Some plans offer a flat benefit for a specified number of days and partial or reduced benefits for an extended period of days afterward. In 1949, 37 plans were in this class. Their basic benefit duration varied from a maximum of 21 days to 70 days, most of them having 21 or 30 days. The additional days with reduced benefits ranged from 31 days to an indefinite period, during which time the patient was allowed either 50 per cent of the regular daily benefit or a specified dollar amount per day. (3) The third type is one in which the days of benefit allowed in a year increase with the second, third or even the fourth year of membership, remaining uniform thereafter. In all 4 plans in this class the maximum benefit in the first year was 21 days; this increased to 30 or 31 days for persons with additional years of membership. (4) Finally, some plans have variable maximums depending on years of membership and also have a period of extended benefits at reduced rates; such plans numbered 17. The maximum for the initial year was, with one exception, 21 days; this increased for second-year members and, in some plans, for those in the third and fourth year. These plans paid reduced benefits for another thirty, sixty or more days.[15]

Originally, almost all plans excluded care for pre-existing conditions, mental disease, tuberculosis, quarantinable diseases, venereal diseases, alcoholism, drug addiction, self-inflicted injuries and congenital defects. Now, with few exceptions, plans have abandoned one or more of these restrictions. Most plans will not provide care for the sole purpose of obtaining a diagnosis. All deny service for cases in which care is available through workmen's compensation or governmental facilities.

Persons who choose hospital facilities better than those specified in the contract have to pay for them but receive an indemnity that is somewhat less than the amount the plan would have had to pay for the services specified in the contract. Of the 52 service plans, 29 provide semiprivate accommodation only, 11 provide ward accommodation only, and the other 12 a combination of two accommodations — usually semiprivate and ward, although a few cover private accommodations also. All plans pay a smaller amount for care in a nonmember hospital than that paid to member hospitals. Some plans have reciprocal agreements extending the same services to participants of certain other plans as they do to their own.

For some years the Blue Cross Commission tried to develop a nation-wide plan for the convenience of employers with nation-wide operations. This became a reality in connection with the collective bargaining provisions in the steel industry. A number of local Blue Cross plans are operating as agents for nation-wide coverage.

The nation-wide plan provides uniform benefits in all areas where there are Blue Cross member hospitals. Such a contract offered by the Blue Cross Plan of Pittsburgh has the following provisions: service benefits for a maximum period of 70 days for each period of confinement, semiprivate accommodations with supplementary services including general nursing care, use of operating room, anesthesia when administered by a salaried employee, casts and splints, surgical dressings, laboratory examinations, basal metabolism tests, X-ray examinations, electrocardiograph, physiotherapy, hydrotherapy, oxygen when provided by the hospital, drugs and medicines. When the patient elects a private room he gets $6 a day as indemnity. Maternity care is covered for 10 days; it is available for all initial members, but for those who marry or are hired subsequently it will be available only after 9 months' membership. The contract provides emergency care and a daily rate of $7.50 in nonmember hospitals, with higher daily amounts for very short periods of confinement.[16]

Subscription Rates

With benefit provisions differing so greatly, monthly subscription rates are sure to vary also. Irrespective of accommodation or scope of services provided, the monthly subscription rates in 1949 for a single subscriber ranged from $0.70 to $2.10, averaging $1.25; for husband and wife, from $1.30 to $3.00, averaging $2.50; for a family, from $1.60 to $4.60, with an average of $2.90.[17]

15. *Blue Cross Guide,* Blue Cross Commission, November 1949.

16. "A Master Plan of Blue Cross Hospitalization for the Employees of Blank Steel Corporation." See also "Insurance Benefits Plan, Group Life Insurance Accident and Sickness Insurance Surgical Reimbursement and Hospitalization Benefits," American Chain and Cable Company, March 1, 1950.

17. *Blue Cross Plans for Hospital Care,* Blue Cross Commission, 1950, p. 6, and correspondence with the Blue Cross Commission.

Besides the regular subscription, some plans have an enrollment fee, usually $1.00, paid once. The rates are often lower for group enrollees than for individual enrollees. With the recent sharp rise in hospital charges, many plans, instead of raising subscription fees, have reduced benefits, sometimes shifting to cash indemnity in lieu of service.

Member Hospitals and Their Utilization

Over 80 per cent of the 4,500 general hospitals are member hospitals. Few tuberculosis and mental hospitals are members. The enabling acts of nearly half the states place some restriction on the hospitals that can participate in Blue Cross. Some require that the hospital be approved by some recognized agency. Besides legal requirements, some plans have their own criteria of acceptability.

In 1949, Blue Cross participants utilized hospitals as follows: admissions per member, 0.118; days per admission, 7.55; days per participant, 0.880. Comparable figures for the general population (exclusive of mental and tuberculosis hospitals) were: admissions per person, 0.111; days per admission, 10.6; days per person, 1.18.[18]

There is no doubt but that Blue Cross participants seek and obtain hospital care more freely than they would if they did not have the protection of the plan. Largely because of favorable selection of participants, however, their average utilization of hospital care is less than the per capita rate for the general population. This difference cannot be explained by the exclusion of long-term hospitalization and of hospitalization for pre-existing conditions, and it is the more impressive because an overwhelming majority of Blue Cross membership is from urban areas, where hospital utilization is two to three times greater than in rural areas.

Income and Expenditure

The total subscription income of Blue Cross plans in 1949 was $358 million, of which $303 million was paid to hospitals for service, $32 million was used for administration, and the remainder was for reserves.[19] The hospital payment averaged $9.50 per participant. Taking into consideration the utilization per participant in 1949, this would represent a per diem cost of about $10.80.

Payments to hospitals under plans providing service benefits are determined by negotiations between the plan and the hospitals. There are three basic methods of payment: a flat per diem rate uniform for all hospitals or groups of hospitals, used by about a third of the Blue Cross plans; regular charges, used by more than a fourth of the plans; the hospital's cost of operation, used by relatively few plans. Various combinations of the three methods are also in use. When flat rates are paid, per diem payments are almost always higher for shorter cases.

Extent of Protection

According to the few studies available, the Blue Cross meets from 50 to 90 per cent of the hospital charges incurred by its participants. In a study of fourteen plans, Reed [20] found that even for those who use the accommodation specified in their contract, the Blue Cross plans pay only 80 to 97 per cent of the hospital bill. In 1949, when the Blue Cross payment was about $10.80 per diem, the average patient-day expenditure of general hospitals (both long-term and short-term), including state and local hospitals, was $12.70. The per diem expenditure of nongovernmental hospitals was $14.65, and that of short-term nongovernmental hospitals was $15.14. In 1949 Blue Cross paid, on the average, about two thirds of the general hospital care costs of all its participants.[21] Compared with commercial insurance, Blue Cross and similar nonprofit plans return to the public a much larger fraction of the premium dollar. In 1949 premiums per dollar of benefit amounted to $1.18.

18. Figures on Blue Cross utilization were secured through correspondence with the Blue Cross Commission; figures for the general population are derived from the "Hospital" volume of the *Journal of the American Medical Association* (Vol. 143, No. 1), May 6, 1950.

19. These figures are somewhat lower than the official figures, which include certain surgical and other benefits provided by a few Blue Cross plans.

20. Reed, *op. cit.*

21. A study in the District of Columbia of patients admitted to general and allied hospitals in November and December of 1949 and January of 1950, for short-term hospitalization, showed that those with group hospitalization recouped on the average 84 per cent of the hospital costs and those with hospitalization and other medical services 91 per cent. The average hospital cost for the first group was $124.30, for the second $120.80, while the average for those without any protection was $144.20. *Journal of the American Medical Association,* November 4, 1950.

MEDICAL CARE

These nonprofit voluntary plans, like the others that have been considered so far, derive the overwhelming majority of their participants from employed workers and their dependents.

In 1930 there were in various parts of the country at least 150 group clinics with prepayment features. These early plans, some of which still exist, have had little influence on recent developments. Medical care prepayment plans began to flourish in 1939–1940 and gained impetus in 1943 after the House of Delegates of the American Medical Association established a Council on Medical Service and Public Relations to promote them. Standards for acceptance were developed, and approved plans were awarded the Blue Shield insignia. There is considerable collaboration between Blue Shield and Blue Cross. In many areas Blue Cross administers the medical care plan.

Types of Plans

Recent development has been, with few exceptions, in plans approved by medical societies. The first plans of this type, organized in Washington and Oregon in the second decade of this century, provided service benefits of a wide scope similar to those offered by consumer-organized plans and group clinics. The newer medical society plans are narrower in scope; they often make provision for cash indemnity only and sometimes are nothing more than approval of commercial indemnity policies. Their object is to meet part of the costs of medical care in catastrophic illness rather than to ensure timely service and preventive care.

A recent compilation by the AMA Council on Medical Service describes 78 voluntary prepayment medical care plans in some detail.[22] These are only a fraction of the total, but they include most of the membership and are typical of the plans that are increasing in membership. Seventy-two of the 78 are approved by medical societies and the AMA Council; that is, they are Blue Shield plans.

The AMA summary shows that in 7 plans commercial insurance contracts provide the enrollment and benefits. Nearly half the membership of one other plan is through commercial carriers. The total membership of the 7, all of them Blue Shield plans, was 640,000 at the end of 1949. The remaining 71 nonprofit voluntary plans had 13.9 million members, of whom nearly 13.2 million were in the 65 Blue Shield plans. Most of the medical society plans are state-wide, but some states have more than one plan. Only Georgia, Maryland and South Carolina had no medical society plans at the end of 1949. In South Carolina a plan has since been organized, and the other two state medical societies expect to have plans soon.

Some plans are organized under the state enabling acts for prepayment hospital and medical care plans; others, under general insurance laws, as nonprofit organizations, even though underwriting may be done through commercial carriers; some are partnerships. Only 6 of the 78 plans described by the AMA were established before 1940; 25 were established between 1940 and 1944 and 45 since 1945 (for 2 plans the date of establishment is not given). In all medical society plans physicians constitute the majority of the governing body; some plans have no other representation in this body.

Types of Contracts

Contracts differ in benefits and coverage. Only 6 of the 78 plans provide service benefits exclusively; 38 provide service benefits to subscribers below a specified income level and cash indemnity to others; and 34 provide indemnity only. Some of the 38 plans in the second group have only one income limit for the family; others have different limits for single and married persons; still others take actual family size into consideration. The income limit for the individual subscriber varies from $1,500 to $5,000, with the largest cluster at about $2,500; for families, the range is from $2,400 to $6,500, with the greatest concentration near $3,000. Sometimes when hospitalized patients use private accommodations, physicians charge more than the prepayment contract provides, regardless of the patient's annual income.

With one exception, the plans restrict enrollment to employed persons; usually dependents are included at the option of the subscriber, sometimes under narrower benefit provisions. Most plans enroll only groups; ten or more is the usual size, but some accept smaller groups. When the group is very small, all or a very large proportion must enroll; for larger groups the requirement may be as low as 40 per cent.

22. Kirkpatrick, *op. cit.; Voluntary Prepayment Medical Care Plans, 1950,* Council on Medical Service, American Medical Association.

Plans that do not provide hospital care require membership in a hospital plan as a prerequisite.

Although in a broad sense no plan provides complete medical care, the types of services offered cover a wide range.

Of the 78 plans studied, 20 provide only surgical services or indemnity for such services. Where the contract with the subscriber assures service, the physician is paid on the basis of an agreed fee schedule, with no additional charges. Where the insured is entitled to indemnity, the physician usually charges more than the amount in the fee schedule on which the indemnity is based.

Thirty-five plans provide medical attendance in the hospital as well as surgery. The number of visits and the fee per visit are specified in the contract.

Nine plans, in addition to surgical services and physicians' services in the hospital, provide limited physicians' services at home and in the office. Generally the first two or three visits are excluded from coverage and there are limits on total number and on frequency in a given period of time as well as on charges per visit.

Besides the three types — surgical, surgical-medical in hospital only, surgical-medical both in and outside of hospital — there are 14 plans providing surgical benefits plus certain medical care options as riders to the contract. (Cf. Table 63.) Almost all medical care plans provide limited payments for various laboratory and other auxiliary services incidental to surgical and nonsurgical care given by the physician.

All plans exclude workmen's compensation cases and cases for which care may be obtained from the government. Excluded also are plastic surgery and, as a rule, appliances and drugs. Care for pre-existing conditions is excluded or provided only after a protracted waiting period. Almost all plans have a waiting period for all types of elective surgery. When maternity care is included, there is almost invariably a waiting period, generally ten months. Maternity care may be included only in family contracts or contracts including both husband and wife.

Contributions

In the last two or three years the variation in the medical care plans has been increasing. The charges under these plans have also tended to become highly variable. Charges differ according to type of contract; scope of services provided; number, sex and certain other characteristics of the individuals covered; group or individual enrollment; monthly, quarterly or annual payment of premiums; and sometimes other circumstances. Because of these many variables, summary is difficult. Nevertheless, an attempt has been made, in Table 64, to approximate the most usual charges and to indicate the range of variation for the principal types of surgical and other medical care contracts.

OTHER PREPAYMENT PLANS

A study by the Social Security Board in 1945 gives information on 205 prepayment medical care plans (by and large nonprofit) in the continental United States. A report by the

TABLE 63

DISTRIBUTION OF 71 NONPROFIT PREPAYMENT PLANS [a] AND THEIR PARTICIPANTS [b] BY TYPE OF CONTRACT AND SERVICES PROVIDED, DECEMBER 31, 1949

	Number of Plans				Number of Participants			
Services Provided	Total	Service	Service and Indemnity	Indemnity	Total	Service	Service and Indemnity	Indemnity
Total	71	6	38	27	13,943,916	613,274	8,943,493	4,387,149
Surgical only	19	2	8	9	1,750,350	93,496	580,415 [b]	1,076,439
Surgical and medical (in hospital)	32	—	20 [c]	12	4,927,831	—	3,280,645 [c]	1,647,186
Surgical and medical	8	4	4	—	908,132	519,778 [d]	388,354	—
Surgical with various options for other medical coverage	12	—	6	6	6,357,603	—	4,694,079	1,663,524

a. Excludes 7 medical-society-approved plans in which enrollment and coverage is through commercial carriers. Includes 6 nonprofit plans that have no medical society approval.
b. Excludes 32,480 members — part of the membership of one plan covered by commercial carriers.
c. Includes one plan for which enrollment began January 1, 1950.
d. Excludes 80,723 dependents who are entitled only to medical, surgical and hospital services at fees lower than those that prevail for nonmembers.

Source: Voluntary Prepayment Medical Care Plans, 1950, Council on Medical Services, American Medical Association.

TABLE 64

ESTIMATED MONTHLY CHARGES FOR DIFFERENT TYPES OF CONTRACTS UNDER BLUE SHIELD AND RELATED NONPROFIT PLANS, BY CLASS OF PARTICIPANT, 1949

Class of Participant	Surgical Only		Surgical and Medical in Hospital		Surgical and Medical at Home, Office and Hospital [a]	
	Modal Value	Range	Modal Value	Range	Modal Value	Range
Subscriber	$ .80	$ .40–1.35	$1.20	$ .60–3.45	$2.90	$1.50–5.00
Subscriber (male)	.75	.40–1.17	[b]	[b]	2.40	1.25–2.50
Subscriber (female)	1.15	.60–1.58	[b]	[b]	3.00	1.75–5.00
Subscriber and spouse (without maternity)	1.60	1.20–2.60	2.00	1.70–2.80	[b]	[b]
Subscriber and spouse (with maternity)	2.00	2.50–2.70	3.00	1.75–6.00	5.00	3.20–8.64
Family (without maternity)	2.00	1.60–2.30	2.60	2.10–3.84	[b]	[b]
Family (with maternity)	2.60	1.75–3.10	3.15	2.00–7.50	7.00	3.00–12.96

a. Some plans in this group include hospitalization as well.

b. Not enough quotations of monthly charges.

Source: Compiled and adjusted by the author.

American Medical Association, published in 1948, gives information for 69 prepayment plans, 28 of which were not included in the publication of the Social Security Board.[23] A current study by the Division of Research and Statistics of the Social Security Administration indicates an appreciable proportion of these 233 prepayment plans are no longer in operation. These types of plans are apparently being displaced by Blue Cross, Blue Shield and commercial accident and health insurance contracts. Besides, some of the plans are among the 78 described in the latest (1950) AMA publication on voluntary prepayment plans.

Twenty-five of those plans that may still be in operation had a total coverage of about a quarter of a million, with a per capita contribution of roughly $25 to $30 a year. Of these participants, nearly 20 per cent were from rural areas. An additional 14 plans were group clinics of one type or another. The participants in these clinics also approximated a quarter of a million. If we were considering only the membership not covered by some other program providing medical benefits, perhaps the number would not exceed 400,000.

INDUSTRIAL PREPAYMENT PLANS

It is estimated that as of June 1950 more than 7 million workers were covered by health and welfare provisions of collective agreements.[24] A large part of this coverage was through commercial insurance and voluntary prepayment plans already considered, notably Blue Cross and Blue Shield. Some of these workers, however, were in "industrial" plans — programs administered directly by management or unions or by the two jointly. Not all industrial plans rest on collective agreements, though that is the trend. There are three types of industrial plans: medical service; cash sickness benefits; and permanent disability benefits — often referred to as pension plans.

MEDICAL SERVICE

Among workers in some industries remote from population centers — mining, logging, railroading — and in certain cotton mill villages, prepayment for hospital and medical services was widespread as early as the past century. It is estimated that plans of this type now cover some 2.5 to 3 million workers and their dependents lacking other forms of insurance protection against the costs of medical care.

Coal Mining

The 1947 medical survey of the bituminous coal industry by the Coal Mines Administration [25] found the "checkoff" practice for medical care widespread. In the sample studied, 60 per cent of the mines and 73 per cent of the miners had prepayment medical care plans; in 136 mines both prepaid medical care and hospitalization were available, usually separately; 19 mines had a medical care plan but not hos-

23. Margaret C. Klem, *Prepayment Medical Care Organizations,* Bureau Memorandum No. 55, Bureau of Research and Statistics, Social Security Board, 1945; *Report on the Study of Consumer-Managed Prepayment Health Plans,* Council on Medical Service, American Medical Association, August 20, 1948.

24. Estimated by the Bureau of Labor Statistics.

25. *A Medical Survey of the Bituminous Coal Industry,* Coal Mines Administration, Department of the Interior, 1947.

pitalization. In addition 36 mines had hospitalization only.

Medical care plans included the miner and his dependents and were financed almost exclusively by deductions from wages. The monthly deductions (not including hospitalization) ranged from $0.75 to $3.00 for an unmarried person, from $1.20 to $3.00 for persons with dependents. In a few instances the deduction was the same for all participants regardless of dependents, and in some the services to dependents were more circumscribed than those available to the worker. The plans often had no clear-cut contract. Almost all excluded treatment for venereal diseases, self-inflicted injuries, injuries incurred in the course of crime, pre-existing conditions, chronic diseases and maternity services. Simple medicines were dispensed without extra cost, but for others there were additional charges. As a rule, there was no choice of physician.

Prepayment plans for hospital care existed in 172 mines (66 per cent), and about two thirds of the miners in the sample participated in such plans. Prepayment included hospital bed and board, floor nursing, routine medication, use of operating rooms, diagnostic X-rays and chemical laboratory examinations. The monthly deduction for these services ranged from $0.50 to $4.80 for single persons, from $0.75 to $4.80 for persons with dependents. When hospital charges were combined with medical costs, the range was from $0.75 to $5.80 for single persons and from $1.00 to $6.80 for persons with dependents. For both medical care and hospitalization there was little or no rational relationship between the scope of services available and the contributions.

Maternity provisions in nearly a fourth of the hospital plans covered normal delivery without extra charge. Most of the plans provided X-ray and radium therapy. There were no services for mental diseases, tuberculosis, contagious diseases, venereal diseases, alcoholism, self-inflicted injuries, or injuries related to intoxication or crime. Workmen's compensation cases were, of course, excluded. New members had to serve a waiting period before they were eligible for service in case of disease but not accidents. There was a waiting period also for maternity and elective surgery. The maximum period of hospital care varied from 20 to 120 days.

In the 172 mines with hospital plans, there were 197 plans. Of these, 122 were administered by hospitals, 26 by nonprofit associations (including Blue Cross), 16 by unions, 14 by commercial carriers, 9 by physicians, 9 by employers, and one by a commission.

The sample covered by the study represented 15 per cent of all the bituminous coal mines with an annual production of 50,000 tons or more. Its findings are in agreement with an earlier study made in 1930–1931 by the National Bureau of Economic Research,[26] which included industries other than coal mining. The two surveys suggest that some 60 per cent of the miners, perhaps 500,000, belonged to prepayment plans providing medical care, hospitalization or both. Assuming that each miner had three dependents, the total coverage would be 2 million — perhaps about 1.7 million with prepaid medical care, some without hospitalization, and about that many with hospitalization, but some without medical care. Excluding coverage by Blue Cross, Blue Shield and similar plans already considered, as well as by commercial carriers, the nonduplicated count would be about 1.2 million.

Railroads

A study of work injuries in the railroad industry by the Railroad Retirement Board in 1938–1940 contains the following comments:

> To a large extent the medical care is furnished by the employers directly through their hospital and medical departments. . . . Hospital associations furnish the other principal source of medical care. These are part of the employee welfare plans. Financed by dues from the employees and contributions by the employers, they undertake to provide medical care not only for work injuries but for all medical requirements of the employee.[27]

The report indicated that the employees regarded the services as satisfactory. Total present coverage may be from 700,000 to 800,000 or 40 to 50 per cent of all railroad employees. Only a few plans extend services to dependents.

Other Industries

The study by the National Bureau of Economic Research showed prepayment plans to

26. Pierce Williams, *The Purchase of Medical Care through Fixed Periodic Payment,* National Bureau of Economic Research, New York, 1932.

27. *Work Injuries in the Railroad Industry, 1938–1940,* U.S. Railroad Retirement Board, Chicago, Illinois, Vol. I, pp. 177–80.

be concentrated in certain industries — coal mining, railroads, logging, and cotton mills in the South; instances in other industries were rare. The study by the Social Security Board in 1945 and the AMA report of 1948 [28] lead to an estimate of 103 industrial prepayment plans, excluding those known to have been discontinued. Of the total, 19 covered railroad employees and one coal miners. The participants in the remaining 83 industrial plans numbered about 900,000.

This estimate includes the well-known Union Health Center of the International Ladies' Garment Workers, the United Auto Workers Clinic in Detroit, and similar union-sponsored organizations, some of which give ambulatory care only, supplemented in some instances by indemnity for hospital care or hospital services through Blue Cross. Included also are such organizations as the Labor Health Institute of St. Louis, which comes nearest to meeting almost all the medical care needs of workers and their dependents. The count includes plans developed by management, such as Consolidated Edison's, the Kaiser Permanente Health Plan, the Endicott Johnson plan for employees and their dependents, and all similar plans.

The estimated total cost of industrial prepayment plans, including those of mines and railroads, is between $75 and $85 million a year.

CASH SICKNESS BENEFITS

Some industrial prepayment plans are supplemented by arrangements to pay cash benefits for wage loss through disability; but coverage of the same group of workers by both plans under direct industrial management is infrequent. Plans for cash disability benefits operated by management or unions or jointly provide protection to 2 to 2.5 million workers. Benefits paid in 1949 totaled perhaps $110 to $160 million. The payment exclusive of sick leave probably falls short of $15 million.

Sick Leave and Other Employer-Administered Plans

In lieu of insurance, some employers have developed a policy of continuing to pay wages to disabled workers for a relatively short period of time. In some cases such arrangements are included in union contracts. How many workers have this form of protection is not known. In a recent compilation by a group of commercial insurance representatives the number was estimated at a little more than 4.5 million.[29]

This estimate is based on the ratio of coverage by group insurance in four local studies. These studies, in Massachusetts, New Jersey, New York and Washington,[30] were all conducted by questionnaires sent out to employers when there was active consideration of legislation for a state cash sickness program, to which employers were opposed. The estimates are probably exaggerated. From a careful check of the surveys, and fragmentary data available from a score or more studies made by the Bureau of Labor Statistics, this writer believes that perhaps only 2 million, and at most 2.5 million, workers have any appreciable protection against wage loss through sick-leave plans or management-administered sickness insurance plans.[31] If account were taken of the duplication of coverage with commercial insurance, the

---

28. Klem, *op. cit.; Report on the Study of Consumer-Managed Prepayment Health Plans.*

29. *A Survey of Accident and Health Coverage in the United States,* August 1950, prepared by the Survey Committee of the Health and Insurance Council.

30. *Report on Sickness Benefits,* State Advisory Council, Division of Employment Security, Commonwealth of Massachusetts, Boston, December 4, 1946; *Cash Sickness Benefits,* Fourth Report of the State Commission on Postwar Economic Welfare, Trenton, New Jersey, April 9, 1946, p. 8; *Compulsory Sickness Compensation of New York State,* National Industrial Conference Board, New York, 1947, p. 120; *Disability Compensation Study,* Office of Unemployment Compensation and Placement, Olympia, Washington, December 1, 1946, pp. 12, 14 and 22.

31. *Supplementary Wage Practices in American Industry, 1945–1946,* Bulletin No. 939, Bureau of Labor Statistics. This report stated: "Formal plans for paid sick leave for plant workers were found in less than 3 per cent of the manufacturing establishments studied, although more than 8 per cent granted sick leave to office workers. . . . Sick leave was granted more frequently in the nonmanufacturing industries studied than in manufacturing." More intensive studies in Buffalo, New York (Bulletin No. 991), show that among office workers and especially among plant workers health insurance (through commercial carriers) is much more prevalent than sick leave. This is also indicated in Philadelphia, Pennsylvania (Bulletin No. 1008). In Denver, Colorado (Bulletin No. 985), on the other hand, a higher proportion of office workers had sick leave, and the proportion of plant workers with sick leave almost equaled the proportion with health insurance. See also Bulletins 986 through 990, 992, 995, 997 and 999; also earlier studies of this type, such as those in Bulletins numbered 960–1, 960–3 and 960–4, published in 1949. Also indicative of the probable extent of sick-leave plans are the Bureau's industry-wide studies of wage structure, for example, in Airframes, Life Insurance, Petroleum Refining.

nonduplicated count might fall short of 1.5 million. Benefits disbursed under such plans in 1949 may have amounted to $100 to $150 million.

Mutual-Benefit Associations

The coverage of sickness benefit plans carried by mutual-benefit associations [32] is likewise unknown. This type of insurance has been declining in the past two decades. Formerly, for example, it included railroad workers, who are now protected primarily by the amended Railroad Unemployment Insurance Act. The present coverage is only about a few hundred thousand persons, perhaps no more than 500,000 — a smaller number, of course, if we were considering only workers with no other type of protection against wage loss caused by sickness. The aggregate benefit disbursements under these plans in 1949 may have amounted to $4 or $5 million.

Union and Employer-Employee Plans

The number covered by union and employer-employee plans can be judged roughly from recorded disbursements. The AFL, which has almost all such plans, reported total benefit payments of $1.0 million as early as 1934. Since then there has been no extension of this type of coverage. In fact, in recent years, under collective bargaining, there has been a tendency for exclusively employer-financed plans, with commercial insurance carriers, to replace union-financed and union-managed plans. Recent AFL annual reports indicate larger disbursements in comparison with 1934. The figure given for 1946, for instance, is $4.3 million; for 1948, $6.1 million; and for 1949, $7.3 million.[33] These amounts, however, definitely include employer contributions under collective agreements providing along with sickness benefits other forms of insurance. As a rough estimate, the nonduplicated coverage may not exceed a quarter of a million, with a total disbursement of $3 to $4 million in 1949 under all such plans.

PAYMENTS FOR PERMANENT DISABILITY

Several employers and some AFL international unions and locals provide benefits for permanent total disability. Benefits disbursed under these plans aggregate perhaps $15 or $20 million. Of this amount the United Mine Workers account for about half. The benefit disbursement by the AFL unions was about $1.4 million in 1949.[34] Since then, largely as a direct consequence of the steel strike in 1949, provisions for benefits for permanent total disability for employees with at least fifteen years of service have been included in collective agreements in many industries.[35] As these new plans approach maturity the annual benefits paid for permanent total disability will be more than double what they were in 1949.

GOVERNMENTAL PLANS

Governmental plans for health protection in its broadest sense include a number of programs for medical care at the federal or state level, as well as payments of cash benefits for wage loss incurred through sickness or permanent total disability.

Federal medical care programs apply to veterans, to certain employed groups such as merchant seamen, coast guard personnel and their dependents, and to certain others (exclusive of the men in the armed forces). Medical services are extended to construction workers of the Tennessee Valley Authority and emergency medical care is given to certain federal employees in Washington, D.C., and in some other centers. In this class may also be included expenditures for medical restoration under the federal-state program for vocational rehabilitation. In 1949, total federal expenditures under these programs were of the general magnitude of $600 to $650 million.

Medical expenditures by state and local agencies — other than for indigents and health examinations and limited services to school children — include emergency services provided by

32. Associations of employees, usually in a single plant, which among other common interests provide death and sickness benefits to their members. These are financed by regular dues and/or periodic assessments.

33. *Bulletin of the Metal Trades Department,* American Federation of Labor, Washington, May 1948; Report of the Executive Council of the American Federation of Labor to the Sixty-eighth Convention, St. Paul, Minnesota, October 3, 1949, pp. 25–29; and Report of the Executive Council of the American Federation of Labor to the Sixty-ninth Convention, Houston, Texas, September 18, 1950, pp. 80–84.

34. *Report of the Proceedings of the Sixty-ninth Convention of the American Federation of Labor,* held at Houston, Texas, September 1950, pp. 142–46.

35. Joseph Zisman, "Permanent and Total Disability Benefit Provisions in Industrial Pension Plans," *Social Security Bulletin,* January 1, 1951.

a few states and some municipalities to their employees; hospitalization benefits paid to covered workers under the cash sickness insurance plan in California, which came into operation in 1950; the compulsory health insurance program for San Francisco and the payments by New York City to the Health Insurance Plan of Greater New York on behalf of the city employees in the plan; and, finally, expenditures for medical restoration by states and localities under vocational rehabilitation. In 1949 all the expenditures under these various programs may have amounted to $15 or $20 million.

Under federal programs for cash benefits as partial replacement of wages fall such programs as veterans benefits for non-service-connected disabilities; disability benefits to railroad employees under the Railroad Retirement Act, paid for jointly by employers and employees; and payment for permanent total disability for customary work, available to federal employees with five years or more of service. In this category also are payments for disabling sickness to railroad employees under the Railroad Unemployment Insurance Act, financed by employer contributions, and sick-leave payments to regular federal employees. In 1949, expenditures under these programs aggregated $450 to $460 million.

State and local programs of the benefits-for-wage-loss type include provisions for permanent disability that certain state and local governments have made for their own employees. They also include compulsory cash sickness programs in Rhode Island, California, New Jersey and New York for time loss caused by disability, applying to all workers subject to the state unemployment compensation laws. Expenditures under these different programs, exclusive of those already covered under private insurance plans, totaled $175 to $180 million in 1949.

FEDERALLY PROVIDED MEDICAL CARE

Seamen

Congress enacted a law in 1798 to provide medical services to merchant seamen, the cost to be met by a tax of 20 cents a month on seamen's wages. This was the beginning of the marine hospitals and the Public Health Service. In 1884 the tax was discontinued, and since 1905 the program has been financed by direct congressional appropriation. In 1949, medical services to seamen cost about $11 million; nearly 900,000 hospital days were provided to about 130,000 seamen entitled to these services.

Other medical care beneficiaries of the Public Health Service include the medical corps and certain other Public Health Service employees and their dependents, coast guard personnel and their dependents, and certain other groups. The hospital days used by these other groups in 1949 exceeded a million, and the costs amounted to about $13 million.[36]

Veterans

Since by far most veterans are employees, the medical care and disability benefits to veterans deserve brief mention. At the end of 1949, living veterans of all wars numbered 19 million; of these, 15.3 million were veterans of World War II. During 1949, veterans received 39.5 million days of care in VA and other hospitals at Veterans Administration expense. Admissions during the year totaled almost 588,000. On December 31, 1949, approximately 102,000 veterans were in hospitals, almost 68,000 of them for non-service-connected conditions. Veterans receive hospital service for non-service-connected conditions only if beds are available in a veterans hospital and if the veterans state that they cannot pay for the service.

During 1949, in addition to hospital care, the medical program provided almost 6.3 million out-patient examinations (to 2.4 million veterans), more than 5.3 million treatments (to 1.9 million veterans), 551,000 dental examinations, 452,000 dental treatments, and about 2.5 million prosthetic and sensory aids and appliances. The number of examinations and treatments is not the same as the number of *individuals* examined and treated, since a single veteran may be examined and treated for more than one condition or for the same condition on several occasions. Almost 17,000 veterans were receiving domiciliary care at the end of the year. Total VA expenditures during 1949 under the medical program amounted to about $581 million, of which $470 million was for

36. Data specially compiled for the author by the Public Health Service. See also Annual Report of the Federal Security Agency, 1949 and 1950, Public Health Service, especially p. 80, Table 7, in 1949 report.

hospitalization, the only care given to veterans for non-service-connected conditions.[37]

CASH SICKNESS BENEFITS

The most important federal plan for cash sickness benefits is that for railroad workers. Of greater potential importance are the state plans for workers covered by the state unemployment insurance system; besides the four that are already in operation, others are under consideration by state legislatures and special commissions.

Federal Railroad Plan

Sickness insurance benefits to railroad workers under the amended railroad unemployment compensation act became payable in July 1947. The benefits are financed from the unemployment tax paid by railroad employers. Eligibility and benefits are determined on the basis of earnings in covered employment in the base year. All workers with earnings of $150 in the base year are eligible for benefits during the benefit year for a maximum period of twenty-six weeks. The daily benefit amount is $1.75 to $5.00. After the initial waiting period and the first benefit week, payments are fortnightly, with ten compensable days in each two-week period.

Separate benefits are provided for maternity cases among covered workers for as long as 115 days. The rate of payment per day is the same for maternity as for sickness, but payments are made for each day, instead of for ten days out of fourteen. Moreover, during the first fourteen days in the maternity period and the fourteen days immediately after delivery, daily benefits are increased by 50 per cent.

Benefits are paid for all types of disability, but if the claimant is entitled to payment from his employer or a third party, the fund is empowered to recover an amount equal to damages or the benefits paid, whichever is the smaller.

During the first benefit year, ended June 1948, the number of claims paid was 154,000, total benefit payments exceeded $29 million, and the number of weekly benefit payments was about 1.6 million. The number of employees with qualifying wages eligible for benefits was 2.3 million. During the second benefit year, ended in June 1949, total benefit payments were well over $31 million, with 115,200 claimants. The number of eligible workers was 2.1 million. In the calendar year 1949, total benefit disbursements were $30.1 million, including maternity benefits.[38]

State Plans for Workers

Rhode Island, California, New Jersey and New York, as already mentioned, have cash sickness insurance for workers subject to the state unemployment insurance laws. Legislation for similar programs was introduced in 1948–1949 but not passed in Connecticut, Illinois, Maryland, Massachusetts, Michigan, Montana, New Mexico, Ohio, Pennsylvania and Wisconsin.

Rhode Island. Cash sickness legislation was enacted in Rhode Island in May 1942. The contributions are paid to a single state fund and benefits are received from this fund. The benefits are financed by a contribution of one per cent of covered wages up to a maximum of $3,000 in a year.

The plan now pays weekly benefits ranging from $10 to $25, based on high-quarter earnings. Benefits are paid for a maximum period varying from five to twenty-six weeks in any benefit year, which under the present law is initiated with the filing of a valid claim for cash sickness benefits or for unemployment insurance benefits. The maximum duration of payments is determined by the total taxable earnings in the base period and the taxable earnings in the quarter of highest earning.

Workers with taxable earnings of $100 or more are eligible for benefits. A waiting period of one week is required for the first spell of sickness in a benefit year. There are certain limitations on benefit payments for cases covered by workmen's compensation and for pregnancies.

At present 6 per cent of the contributions are available for administration. Contributions in 1948 amounted to $4.4 million, benefit disbursements to $4.3 million, administrative costs to $0.2 million. The estimated number of workers protected under the plan was about 300,000; of beneficiaries, about 34,000; of

37. Veterans Administration. See Annual Report of the Veterans Administration, 1949, 1950.

38. Annual Report, 1948, 1949, Railroad Retirement Board; also, *The Labor Market and Employment Security,* Bureau of Employment Security, October 1950, p. 23.

weekly benefits paid, 257,000. In 1949, total benefit disbursements were $5.4 million. The disbursements for 1950 would be somewhat higher.[39]

California. In 1946, California amended its unemployment insurance law to provide cash benefits in periods of disability to workers covered by unemployment insurance. Benefits are financed by a one per cent contribution by employees on taxable wages up to $3,000 in a year. Workers with taxable earnings thirty times the weekly benefit amount or one and one third times high-quarter earnings, whichever is the lesser, but not less than $300, are eligible for benefits.

Weekly benefit amounts range from $10 to $25, depending on taxable earnings in the high quarter of the base year. The benefit rate is one twentieth of high-quarter earnings, within the range indicated. The maximum duration of benefits ranges from twelve to twenty-six weeks in a benefit year, the same as for unemployment. The benefit year begins when a valid claim is filed for unemployment or sickness benefits. There is a waiting period of seven days with each spell of sickness (unless the interval is less than fourteen days). Workmen's compensation cases, pregnancy cases and persons who have been outside of the labor force for three months or more prior to their disability are not compensated.

A private plan may substitute for state coverage if it meets the standards fixed by the statute. Workers covered by approved private plans are relieved from contributing to the state fund.

Benefits to unemployed workers and to qualified workers no longer in covered employment are paid from a separate fund, financed from the interest on total employee contributions to unemployment insurance in 1944, 1945 and before December 1, 1946. When a deficit occurs in this fund, assessments are to be made on the state fund and on private plans proportionate to covered taxable payroll at the time, up to a maximum of .03 per cent. The liability of private plans to pay benefits continues for two weeks after a worker's separation from the plan.

Administrative costs allowed to the state plan are 5 per cent of contributions. The added cost in supervising private plans is charged to these plans, but is not to exceed .02 per cent of the taxable payroll.

In January 1949, private plans covered 823,000 workers; in January 1950, 1,176,000. The estimated coverage under the state unemployment compensation program for 1949 is about 2.4 million. Private coverage is still increasing.[40]

An amendment in 1949 provides hospital indemnity of $8 for each day of hospitalization for a maximum period of twelve days in a benefit year. Payment of these benefits began in 1950.

In 1948, contributions to the state fund totaled $46 million; benefit payments by the state, $22 million; and administrative costs, $2 million, including the cost involved in supervising private plans. The corresponding figures for 1947 were: contributions, $51.5 million; benefit payments, $17.7 million; administration, $1.8 million. In 1948, compensable cases numbered about 111,000; weeks compensated, more than one million. In 1949, benefit disbursements by the state amounted to $23.2 million, for more than a million weeks of compensable disability.[41]

New Jersey. The New Jersey plan became effective in June 1948, and benefit payments began in January 1949. The coverage is the same as for unemployment insurance. New Jersey, like California, allows the participation of private plans, but without many of the safeguards found in the California law.

To be eligible, a worker must have covered

39. *The Labor Market and Employment Security,* pp. 21–26.

40. There are indications that private plans take care of the better risks, from the point of view of the insurance carrier: (1) workers under private plans have higher average base period earnings; (2) the number of female claimants is four fifths as large as that of male claimants in the state plan, and only two fifths in the private plans; (3) the average claim duration of state cases is 10.3 weeks, while that of private coverage is 6 weeks; (4) in 1947, duration per claim averaged 8.9 weeks for males and 9.2 for females in the state plan, 3.8 and 4.8 in the private plans; (5) in 1948, 27 per cent of the state claimants, and only 8 per cent of the private, had their benefit year previously established by an unemployment claim; (6) a much higher proportion of state benefit payments than of private are for heart disease, cancer and other chronic conditions; (7) the proportion of claimants over age 50 is much higher in the state coverage than in the private; (8) in 1947, 25 per cent of the state claimants, and only 5.1 of the private, exhausted their benefits. California Department of Employment, Report 1031, No. 1, Research and Statistics, February 2, 1949.

41. *The Labor Market and Employment Security.*

earnings totaling thirty times his weekly benefit amount. The weekly benefit amount is one twenty-second of his high-quarter earnings in the base year, with a minimum of $10 and a maximum of $26. (Before July 1950 these limits were $9 and $22.) Workmen's compensation cases and pregnancy cases are not compensated.

To provide for unemployed workers who become disabled, a separate account is set up. Into this account is paid the interest from $50 million.[42] In case of deficit in this account, an additional tax, not to exceed .02 per cent of the taxable payroll, may be imposed on the state plan and private plans. Special limitations surround benefit payments from this account, including a maximum combined duration for unemployment and sickness benefits of 150 per cent of the duration allowed under either.

Private plans established before January 1, 1949 need not meet the standards set for approved plans until the contract under which they were set up expires. In January 1949, private plans covered 787,000 workers; at the same time in 1950 the number was 856,000 and in October of that year it exceeded 889,000. The labor force subject to the state unemployment compensation act in 1949 was about 1.25 million; 1.8 million had sufficient covered earnings to qualify.

The state plan for employed workers is financed by a tax of .75 per cent on covered wages for employees and .25 per cent for employers.[43] The employer tax is subject to experience rating and may vary between .10 and .75 per cent of covered payroll, depending on the experience of the employer and the level of the reserves.

Administrative costs are paid from a separate account, into which is paid 6 per cent of the contributions collected. In addition, private plans are assessed for costs incurred in their supervision; the assessment is not to exceed .02 per cent of taxable payroll.

Total benefit disbursements by the state during 1949, the first year of operation, were $3.4 million, paying for about 161,000 compensable weeks. Benefit disbursements for the first nine months of 1950 were $3.7 million — $2.9 million to employed workers and about $0.9 million to unemployed workers.[44]

New York. Administration of the cash sickness insurance program in New York differs from that in the other three states in being carried out by the state's workmen's compensation agency, rather than its unemployment agency. The coverage is different from that of unemployment; maritime and state employees included in unemployment insurance are not covered for sickness. Separate provisions are made for paying benefits to employed workers who become disabled and for those who are unemployed when they become disabled. There is a special fund for paying unemployed workers, and it is to be replenished, when necessary, by assessments on the state and private plans participating. Two classes of unemployed workers may qualify for sickness benefits: (1) those who qualify for unemployment benefits but are disabled, and (2) those who, though not qualifying for unemployment benefits, had earnings of $13 or more in twenty weeks out of the thirty preceding the last day worked in covered employment. No benefits may be paid for any week of disability occurring more than twenty-six weeks after the last covered employment.

Employers subject to the act are required to insure their employees with a private carrier, with the state fund or through self-insurance. The weekly benefit amount is 50 per cent of average weekly earnings, with a minimum of $10 or the actual earnings if they were less, and a maximum of $26. Benefits are paid for a maximum period of thirteen weeks in a fifty-two-week period. The program for employed workers is financed by employee contributions of 0.5 per cent of earnings, not to exceed 30 cents a week, and an additional contribution by the employer if needed. There is a waiting period of seven days with each period of illness. Private plans may have provisions less generous than the above if they were in existence at the beginning of the program and the original contract has not terminated, or if the agreement is made under collective bargaining. Benefit payments began after July 1, 1950.[45]

42. The amount that the state withdrew for this purpose from the unemployment trust fund.

43. The employee continues to pay .25 per cent of taxable wages to the state unemployment insurance fund.

44. *The Labor Market and Employment Security,* cited earlier; see also *Summary of New Jersey Disability Insurance Activities,* Division of Employment Security, Department of Labor and Industry, State of New Jersey.

45. *The Labor Market and Employment Security;* see also Comparison of Temporary Disability Insurance Laws, December 1, 1949, Unemployment Insur-

PROVISIONS FOR SICK LEAVE

The federal government and many state and local governments have sick-leave provisions for their employees. A study of sick and annual leave for federal workers[46] showed that in September 1947, 1,703,540 employees in the executive branch of the government, or about 80 per cent, were subject to sick-leave regulations. Fifteen days of sick leave are allowed in a year; the unused leave may be accumulated, up to a maximum of sixty days. Sick leave taken in the first nine months of 1947 averaged 5.9 days per employee and was estimated to have cost the government $110 million in salaries. For 1949, costs may have been $150 million.

No comparable data are available for state and local employees. It has been estimated that 65 to 75 per cent of state employees have some sick-leave provisions. *The Municipal Year Book*[47] shows that among employees of cities with 10,000 or more inhabitants, 63 per cent are in communities that have sick-leave provisions for all their employees and 14 per cent in communities that have provisions for some of their employees. Sick-leave provisions are probably less common for employees of smaller cities and counties. All in all, some 2.2 million state and local employees are entitled to sick leave. Some of the provisions are very limited — three days, for example — while some are very liberal; some permit accumulation of unused leave from year to year. Often a teacher on sick leave must pay the salary of a substitute. Sick-leave payments to state and local employees may be about $125 million.

PERMANENT DISABILITY BENEFITS

The federal government and many state and local governments provide disability benefits for employees who become incapacitated for life or for protracted periods of time through nonoccupational diseases or injuries. Almost all the disability programs of this type require a long period of prior service, seldom less than five years and frequently fifteen years or even longer. Moreover, under many programs the benefit formula is based on the number of years of service, so that even if those who have not been in service for as much as fifteen or twenty years get benefits, these benefits are of little significance. It is therefore not possible to estimate even roughly the number of persons actually protected or the extent of the protection. Only the number of beneficiaries and the amount of their benefits are known.

At the end of 1949 there were 39,100 beneficiaries among federal civilian employees, and their benefits during the year amounted to $35.3 million. The estimated number of beneficiaries among state and local government employees for the fiscal year 1949 was 29,000; and the benefits totaled $22 million. Railroad employees under the Railroad Retirement Act are now entitled to disability benefits if they are less than 60 years of age, are totally and permanently disabled, and have had ten years of railroad employment. If disability is in connection with current work and the claimant has not attained age 60, he must have twenty years of railroad employment to be entitled to benefits. In 1949 there were 70,000 such beneficiaries, whose payments totaled $72 million.[48]

These figures are dwarfed by disability benefit payments to veterans. In December 1949, 2.3 million veterans were receiving compensation or pensions for disability: 1.9 million for partial and 375,000 for total disability (about 55,000 were receiving pensions for age). Among those receiving benefits for total disability were approximately 262,000 to whom the payments were made on account of non-service-connected disabilities. Benefit payments in 1949 totaled about $1,459 million. Payments for non-service-connected disability were $161 million. In addition, some 15,000 United States Government Life Insurance and National Service Life policies with disability riders were drawing disability benefits at the end of 1949. Such payments totaled about $10 million.[49]

REHABILITATION

Active planning for vocational rehabilitation took place during and after World War I. In 1918, Congress enacted a program for vocational rehabilitation of disabled servicemen.

ance Program Letter No. 186, Bureau of Employment Security, January 17, 1950.

46. *Sick and Annual Leave,* Report of the Committee on Appropriations, U.S. Senate, on Sick and Annual Leave in the Executive Branch, 80th Cong., 2d sess., S. Doc. 126.

47. *The Municipal Year Book, 1947,* International City Managers' Association, Chicago, 1947, pp. 134–60.

48. *Social Security Bulletin,* Annual Statistical Supplement, 1949, September 1950, p. 27.

49. Veterans Administration.

Two years later it enacted legislation providing federal grants to the states for rehabilitation of vocationally handicapped civilians. This law continued with minor modifications until 1943, when its scope and financial basis were greatly enlarged.[50] At present the Office of Vocational Rehabilitation is one of the component agencies of the Federal Security Agency.

The present federal-state cooperative program covers all the states and territories. State agencies select the cases for rehabilitation and arrange for services. The federal task includes the establishment of standards for the services, technical assistance to the states, and approval of state plans. Both the physically and the mentally handicapped are eligible for rehabilitation services. Administrative costs, including the costs of vocational guidance and placement, are met by federal grants. The costs of medical treatment, vocational training and similar services are shared equally by the state and federal governments. The cost of rehabilitating war-disabled civilians is met entirely by federal moneys.

It has been estimated that at least 1.5 million persons are in need of rehabilitation and that about 250,000 persons a year suffer injuries or disease requiring rehabilitation. In the fiscal year 1948, state-federal vocational rehabilitation services reached 191,062 persons; of these, 53,131 were successfully rehabilitated, and 117,794 cases continued their rehabilitation into the fiscal year 1949. The corresponding figures for the fiscal years 1949 and 1950, respectively, were: cases served, 216,999 and 225,724; cases carried over, 133,715 and 140,941; and cases in which the rehabilitation was completed, the individuals having been placed in suitable gainful work, 58,020 and 59,597.[51]

In the fiscal year 1948 the increase in the annual earnings of rehabilitated persons over their earnings as a group at the time they applied for rehabilitation was three times the combined federal-state expenditures for rehabilitation. The author has estimated the increased earnings of these 53,131 persons over their anticipated lifetime as $1.6 billion — sixty-six times the amount spent for rehabilitation in the fiscal year 1948. Further speculative arithmetic to evaluate the significance of these increased earnings from the taxpayer's standpoint also yields impressive results. If the federal income tax (at 1949 rates) that is likely to be levied on these increased earnings is computed and to it is added the estimated total loss in taxes that would have followed if these 53,131 cases and their dependents had remained largely dependent on friends or relatives, the savings to taxpayers would be almost twenty times the tax funds spent for rehabilitation in 1948. Such a comparison would be still more impressive if present increased tax rates were used.

There can be no doubt that rehabilitation pays.

50. Mary E. Macdonald, *Federal Grants for Vocational Rehabilitation,* University of Chicago Press, Chicago, 1944.

51. Annual Reports of the Office of Vocational Rehabilitation, Federal Security Agency, for 1948, 1949 and 1950.

Chapter 18

LABOR UNIONS *

In the past decade and a half, labor unions have grown so rapidly that an understanding of the nature, objectives and development of unions is now prerequisite to a discussion of wage policies. Certain features of the structure and behavior of unions are so deeply rooted in their past that an understanding of their current strategy and tactics is hardly possible without reference to their history.

The formation of unions of workingmen for their mutual protection in this country antedates the Declaration of Independence. In 1789, separate craft organizations, although short-lived and confined to local areas, were active in several cities. After great effort, labor unions were able to greet the start of the twentieth century with a million members. By 1904 they had pushed their membership up to 2 million. Three decades and one war later, union membership stood at only 2.8 million; less than 10 per cent of the country's nonfarm employees were organized, and collective bargaining was unknown in much of the nation's basic industry.

American labor unions have developed in depth and breadth only in the past decade and a half. A significant change in governmental attitude, the second world war and a tremendous expansion of the nation's industrial activity, all gave impetus to a fivefold increase in union membership. In 1950 roughly one out of every three nonfarm employees — or a total of some 14 to 16 million men and women in all phases of industrial activity and in all sections of the country — belonged to unions.

Acceptance of Unions

The history of labor unions in this country is largely a struggle for survival — a struggle carried on for many years against employer opposition, governmental opposition or indifference, legal obstacles and workers' apathy. Although the last law affecting management-labor relations has not been written and the final judicial attitude has not yet been reached, it is sound to say that labor unions have won their struggle for survival and have been accepted as a permanent institution in the country's legal framework. The acceptance is still grudging. As one writer puts it, "Business enterprise is the dominant institution of economic life, while the union is not yet *fully* recognized as legitimate." [1] Nevertheless, organized labor has moved from its traditional position outside the community to a position in the community.

Unions, which now count among their members a large section of the "public," are accepted in the "public mind." [2] The decades of struggle for survival, however, have left deep traces in the thinking and feeling of union leaders and rank-and-file members, even in the language they use. The problems of union security, of the closed shop versus the union shop, do not make much sense when divorced from the history of the labor movement in this country.

The importance of labor unions goes beyond their role in collective bargaining. With their large membership, unions now have a dual impact on the labor market — directly, as a party to collective bargaining, and indirectly, as one of the strongest political pressure groups.

Present-Day Character

The American trade union considers itself an integral part of the economic system of capitalism; it accepts that system and is designed to operate within it. In the course of the labor-management survey made by the Twentieth Century Fund,[3] the president of one international union was asked whether he would favor

* By Thomas C. Fichandler.

1. Arthur M. Ross, "The Trade Union as a Wage-Fixing Institution," *American Economic Review*, September 1947, p. 575. Italics supplied.

2. "The American public is firmly convinced that unions are a means to an end, and should by no means be done away with. They are committed to the principle of labor unions." Elmo Roper, "Public Attitude toward Labor Unions," *Labor and Nation*, October 1945, p. 37.

3. W. S. Woytinsky and Associates, *Labor and Management Look at Collective Bargaining*, Twentieth Century Fund, New York, 1949.

requesting employers not to raise prices following a wage increase. He answered, "No, that would be a definite restriction of free enterprise, which is the keystone of our economic system. We'll steer clear of that." Another replied to the same question: "That's an invasion of free enterprise; it's not justified." Although union leaders and members certainly would not be unanimous in their opinions, this view probably comes closer than any other simple formulation to expressing the basic economic philosophy of American unions today.

The present character of the American labor movement is largely a result of today's economic climate. Concentration on essentially nonpolitical "business unionism" and efforts to bring about gradual reforms and improvements within the existing social order can be expected to continue while employment remains high. As in the past, however, economic storms may change the course of organized labor in the United States. H. A. Millis and R. E. Montgomery have described the effects of economic changes on union policies as follows:

> Pragmatism, concentration of effort upon immediate "business" objectives, recognition of the unions, and improvement in working conditions, rather than espousal of all-embracing "uplift" programs, have generally been characteristic — although of course by no means the sole characteristics — of periods of rising prices and enlivened business activity. When, on the other hand, prices have been falling, business depressed, and employers able "to bring labor to its senses," the tactics and aims of "pure and simple" trade unionism have more often been looked upon with a degree of skepticism, and labor has been more disposed to harken to the plea of those promising, if only they are listened to and followed, fundamental reconstruction of the social order and an economic hereafter from which the trials and hardships of the present would be permanently excluded.[4]

Important to an understanding of the attitudes of organized labor today is the fact that, through long tradition, unions have been conditioned to consider themselves as the spokesmen of underdogs and have retained this attitude despite labor's rise up the economic and social ladder. It manifests itself in general union objectives as well as in their immediate goals and their approach to wage determination.

GENERAL OBJECTIVES

The formal and ultimate objective of a union is to gain for its members the greatest possible economic benefits. Like most other institutions, it also has a less formal, and frequently more immediate, objective — its own survival and growth. The two objectives are generally consistent, but there are occasions when both cannot be served. It is not hard to see that when a choice must be made union officials and members often put union strength first.

Another union goal is to establish the employee's right to meet management on an equal footing to decide the conditions of his employment. Management has been surprised more than once to find that a unilateral decision granting a substantial wage increase failed to prevent union organization of employees. A union's charge that an employer refuses to bargain in good faith may cover a multitude of sins, but it evokes a warm response from the union rank and file against the "high and mighty" employer. The protection a strong union can give its members against arbitrary firings, job changes or wage-scale adjustments by management does more than secure their economic welfare. It fulfills an important desire for independence and dignity through recognition that the worker has earned a right to his job that will not be disregarded lightly.

Sumner H. Slichter, in defining collective bargaining, says it has two principal aspects. He calls it a method of price making, and "a method of introducing civil rights into industry, that is, of requiring that management be conducted by rule rather than by arbitrary decision." [5] In bargaining collectively, unions have sought to enforce employees' industrial civil rights by establishing formal grievance procedures designed to eliminate arbitrary and discriminatory actions so far as possible. The unions' day-to-day work in pursuing this objective often is considered to have a greater impact than wage bargaining on management-labor relations.

IMMEDIATE GOALS

Even when struggling for a wage increase, a new law or the repeal of an existing law, most union leaders speak in terms of a defensive, rather than an offensive, campaign. They recognize the success of an offensive strategy after the campaign is over, but keep themselves and

4. H. A. Millis and R. E. Montgomery, *Organized Labor,* McGraw-Hill, New York, 1945, p. 6.

5. Sumner H. Slichter, *Union Policies and Industrial Management,* Brookings Institution, Washington, 1941, p. 1.

their union on the defensive while the struggle is going on. Asked what they considered the biggest problems facing their unions in the spring of 1948, more than half the union leaders questioned mentioned the Taft-Hartley Act, and one out of three named wages and hours. (See Table 65.) They explained that the drives for repeal of the Taft-Hartley Act and for higher wages had the same powerful incentive — the desire to regain lost ground.

The past gains can be real or imaginary — such as the allegedly high real earnings during the war — but the unions are convinced that they are fighting to rectify an injustice inflicted on their members. The wage question, said the *CIO Economic Outlook,* "is very simple. It is a question of whether, once the people have attained a decided improvement in real earnings, as they did in 1945, they should ever turn the clock back. Should the men, women, and children who have begun eating fresh fruit and vegetables, milk and meat go back to a diet of cornbread and peas? . . . The CIO says 'NO.' "[6]

Taft-Hartley Repeal

In the Fund's labor-management survey, 26 union leaders, representing 6.6 million members, singled out the Taft-Hartley Act as the labor movement's biggest problem. "The . . . Taft-Hartley law," said one leader, "is a slave law. Every problem we have today stems from the Taft-Hartley law." In somewhat more restrained words, the same theme was reiterated time and again.

The union leaders saw the Taft-Hartley Act as a threat to the strength and the very existence of their organizations. Although few mentioned specifically the implications of a weakened labor movement for wages and workers' economic welfare, those fears were in the back of everyone's mind.

Higher Wages

Although repeal of the Taft-Hartley Act was clearly the number one political-legislative objective of unions, the leaders emphasized wage increases as their primary economic goal for the next few years. Of the 51 union leaders queried, 46, representing unions with 10.8 million members, said higher wages would be among their unions' most important collective bargaining objectives if high and stable employment levels continued during the next five years. (See Table 66.) To most union leaders this is a regular, continuing objective, a function that unions must always perform.

6. *CIO Economic Outlook,* June 1948, p. 2.

TABLE 65

UNION LEADERS PICK TAFT-HARTLEY ACT AS BIGGEST PROBLEM FACING THEIR UNIONS IN 1948

Question: What would you say are the biggest problems facing your union today?

Response	Number of Unions	Union Members: Number, in Thousands	Union Members: Percentage of Total
Number of respondents	51	11,213	100.0
Taft-Hartley Act	26	6,585	58.7
Wages and hours	13	4,064	36.2
Organization	11	1,541	13.7
Political problems	8	1,950	17.4
Political organization of labor	4	755	6.7
Curbing inflation; peace	4	1,195	10.7
Welfare and pension plans	5	2,624	23.4
Unemployment	3	325	2.9
Other	10	1,608	14.3
None	4	618	5.5

Source: Unpublished data collected by W. S. Woytinsky and Associates for *Labor and Management Look at Collective Bargaining,* Twentieth Century Fund, New York, 1949.

Welfare and Pension Plans

Welfare and pension plans were second in importance to wage increases as a collective bargaining objective. During the war years, because of the temporary freezing of wages, much of the union drive for improved standards was channeled into "fringe" adjustments, among which welfare and pension plans proved the most popular. Twenty-eight leaders of unions, with 8 million members, gave welfare and pension plans as one of their unions' most important collective bargaining goals.

Four more leaders said this would become a major objective later. "It has captured the imagination of our people. Their whole aim is for security," explained the president of one large industrial union. "It looks like our people are starting to get conscious of the welfare fund idea," remarked another union official. "It was up in our last agreements and will come up stronger and stronger because of all the publicity it's gotten through John L. Lewis." A third declared: "We are now coming into a period where unions are showing more interest in benefit plans. Previously we've advised our

TABLE 66

UNION LEADERS (IN 1948) SAY HIGHER WAGES, WELFARE AND PENSION PLANS WILL BE THEIR MOST IMPORTANT COLLECTIVE BARGAINING OBJECTIVES DURING NEXT FIVE YEARS IF HIGH AND STABLE EMPLOYMENT LEVELS CONTINUE

Question: Assuming that high and stable levels of employment continue during the next five years, what do you think will be your union's most important collective bargaining objective?

Response	Number of Unions	Union Members: Number, in Thousands	Union Members: Percentage of Total
Number of respondents	51	11,213	100.0
Main objectives [a]			
Higher wages	46	10,802	96.3
Welfare and pension plans	28	7,950	70.9
Union security	20	3,293	29.4
Reduction in hours	18	3,893	34.7
Guaranteed annual wage	9	2,912	26.0
Better working conditions	6	963	8.6
Vacations and premium pay	4	1,021	9.1
Other	4	465	4.1
Nothing specific	3	141	1.3

a. In addition to the main objectives, secondary objectives were given as follows: union security — 3 unions, with 1.1 million members; reduction in hours — 4 unions, 345,000 members; welfare and pension plans — 4 unions, 295,000 members; and guaranteed annual wage — 9 unions, 1.8 million members.

Source: W. S. Woytinsky and Associates, *Labor and Management Look at Collective Bargaining,* Twentieth Century Fund, New York, 1949, p. 249.

unions to shun such plans, but since last August when the plan was instituted, covering retirement programs for 14,000 people, we find our workers very anxious to have such benefits." [7]

Other Goals

Union security and reduction in hours of work ranked third and fourth among the collective bargaining goals. The slogan of union security, under existing conditions, was tied to the Taft-Hartley Act and included efforts to adjust union practices to the provisions of the law until it was repealed or amended.

Reduction in hours of work (but with the same take-home pay) was singled out as an immediate, burning issue only by the railroad labor leaders, who pointed out that the railroad worker, once in the van, had fallen behind other workers. The railroad unions were ready to drive for a basic "40-hour week with 48 hours take-home pay, including time and a half and double time. We've got to get in step both on the work week and our wage setup." Unions in other industries, while listing reduction in hours as a specific objective, indicated that little pressure would be put behind this request so long as the demand for labor remained high.

These are the primary objectives. There will be others, such as guaranteed-annual-wage plans, paid vacations, overtime and holiday pay, and improved working conditions and facilities. The survey suggests, however, that union leaders were somewhat uncertain about plans to guarantee annual wages. Many appeared to have a wait-and-see attitude; others who mentioned a guaranteed-annual-wage plan as a specific objective appeared to feel that it was something they ought to favor.

Objectives in 1949–1950

Contract negotiations during 1949 and 1950 indicated much the same union objectives as the 1948 survey had revealed. During 1949, however, when the cost-of-living index was dropping, unions placed major emphasis on pension and social insurance provisions. In that year the CIO Steelworkers negotiated comprehensive pension and insurance plans covering a large part of their membership; the CIO Auto Workers and the Ford Motor Company agreed on a health and welfare plan; and many other unions — including the AFL Teamsters, the Bakery Workers and the Hatters, the independent Machinists and the CIO Rubber Workers — pressed for such provisions.

In 1950, when prices started upward again, the unions felt they could justify wage increase demands more easily. Consequently, wage increases joined pension and insurance plans as their major immediate objectives.

UNIONS AS INSTITUTIONS

Unions, like other social organizations, have developed a series of activities designed to give them status and prestige in the eyes of their members and to establish them as accepted insti-

7. The drive for welfare and pension plans established through collective bargaining is not likely to spread to all industries. The railroad unions, for example, look to Congress for their welfare and pension provisions. Unions in the construction trades consider welfare and pension clauses in collective agreements unpractical because of the brief employer-employee relationship typical of the industry. Unions in the trade and service industries indicated little interest in these plans, largely because of the high rate of turnover among their members. The CIO unions were much more interested than the others in pushing for welfare and pension plans.

tutions in the community. As such, they have also developed their own institutional objectives, which may be distinguished from other more general goals and may occasionally conflict with them. These institutional objectives and activities have strong influence on union policies.

Union Security and Wages

The fact that today's union is an institution — and, more specifically, a political institution — has an important bearing on its wage policies. A trade-union leader will not pursue a wage policy he cannot get his members to accept. The size of a wage demand may depend almost entirely on the wage scales negotiated by a competing union. In certain circumstances, a costly strike may be called over a difference of two cents an hour to prove the leadership's militancy and to strengthen its hand against a competing faction in the union. Or union officers may be willing to take less than they could get from a particular firm in order to maintain uniformity of wage scales for their members and thus ensure "peace within the family."

The leadership of a union has many pressures to reconcile. It has to consider the union as an organization and to protect its own future. The union, says Ross, is "a political agency representing the sellers of labor, led by officials who stand in an essentially political relationship with the rank and file, the employers, the other organizational levels of the union, the rest of the labor movement and the government." [8]

The union's institutional objectives, of course, need not be in conflict with the formal objective of promoting its members' economic welfare. And when there is a conflict, the decision to sacrifice an immediate wage gain in favor of strengthening the organization may be considered as merely a tactical step to increase the likelihood of ultimate economic gain. To the union member, the survival and growth of his union is represented as the surest guarantee of his long-run economic welfare. The "ultimate" and the "long-run," however, are far in the future, and in the meantime wages will be affected by the union's short-run institutional needs. Because of the importance and permanence of labor unions in our economic structure, wage policies designed to encourage high levels of employment and production appear more likely to succeed when they coincide with unions' needs as institutions. Ross says that "there is no point in exhorting unions to behave in a manner incompatible with their survival or growth; if we want them to follow a certain course of action, we must make it consistent with their institutional aims." [9]

To raise wage rates is the immediate goal of unions, as it was when Adam Smith wrote of workingmen who "combine of their own accord to raise the price of their labor." [10] But the policies of unions are too complex to be reduced to a one-dimensional formula. They are determined by many considerations, which are not necessarily the same in all industries or all parts of the country. These considerations may change as time goes on and may also differ from the economic arguments the union presents to support its claims. They are so complicated that "little is known about the determinants of union wage policies." [11]

Welfare Activities

From the beginning, union members have looked to their unions for more than wage increases and improvement of working conditions. Financial aid in the form of loans and death benefits was an important function of the earliest unions. Union dances, picnics and athletic leagues have provided much-appreciated social and recreational outlets for members and their families. These long-established activities provide greater security for members, attract new members, and hold and increase the loyalty of old members.

Union welfare programs have included producers' and consumers' cooperatives, credit unions and labor banks, and insurance and benefit programs. In recent years, however, the unions have concentrated their welfare activities almost entirely in the field of insurance and benefit programs.[12] These programs have passed

8. Arthur M. Ross, "The Dynamics of Wage Determination under Collective Bargaining," *American Economic Review,* December 1947, p. 793.

9. Ross, "The Trade Union as a Wage-Fixing Institution," p. 588.

10. Cf. Chapter 1.

11. Sumner H. Slichter, "Wage-Price Policy and Employment," *American Economic Review,* May 1946, p. 305.

12. Rising price levels appear to have increased somewhat union interest in credit unions and consumer cooperatives. The AFL executive council report to the 1947 convention states: "Today the importance of consumer cooperatives and credit unions

through several cycles of popularity. They were the *raison d'être* of the mutual-aid societies that initiated the labor movement, but by the end of World War I they were on the decline. Unions returned to them with increased interest during the 1930's when, in organizing the mass-production industries, they found that company unions held workers through welfare and recreational programs. In order to induce workers to leave company unions, trade unions had to offer similar programs.

Financing Welfare Plans

The early welfare activities were entirely union-financed, but during the 1930's and 1940's unions began to press, through collective bargaining, for partial financing by employers. The World War II "Little Steel Formula," which limited wage increases but left the way open for fringe adjustments, stimulated the recent rapid growth in the number and extent of employer-financed health and welfare plans. At present some of the benefit programs are union-financed and some are supported partially or wholly by employers.

Death allotments, occasionally supplemented or replaced by group insurance plans, are the most common form of union-financed benefit activity. Many unions pay benefits in sickness, unemployment, disability and old age, and some maintain homes for their aged and disabled members. Seventy-three AFL unions reported that they had paid out $68.5 million in benefits to their members during 1948, divided as follows: death benefits, $20.2 million; sick benefits, $6.1 million; unemployment benefits, $1.1 million; old-age benefits, $11.8 million; disability benefits, $1.7 million; and miscellaneous benefits, $27.5 million.[13]

Welfare plans established through collective bargaining and at least partially financed by employers have emphasized benefits for sickness and nonoccupational accidents, hospital and medical care and, recently, retirement. In 1945 about 600,000 workers were covered by some type of health benefit plan negotiated by employer and union; three years later, about 3 million workers were so protected,[14] and by mid-1950 more than 7 million were covered by health, welfare or pension plans under collective bargaining.[15] Most of these plans are entirely employer-financed; they may be administered by the union, by the union and management jointly, or by a private insurance company.

As long as union membership was limited mainly to relatively well-paid skilled craftsmen, the unions could handle the financing of their limited retirement, disability and death-benefit plans. When the craft unions began to open their ranks to less skilled workers, they created a special nonbeneficial membership class for them. Such members pay less in dues than the beneficial "Class A" members and are not entitled to the union's old-age and disability pensions. Wide-scale organization of unskilled and semiskilled workers, who had been made social security conscious by the great depression and the social security legislation that followed, forced unions to expand their benefit programs and to get employers to finance at least part of the expansion. Essentially, unions have concentrated on winning benefits supplementary to the government's social security program and on filling in the major gap in the government's program — health and disability benefits.

For some years a number of unions, particularly the International Ladies' Garment Workers' Union (AFL) and the Amalgamated Clothing Workers (CIO), have incorporated fairly complete welfare plans in their collective agreements, but the recent establishment of a comprehensive security system for workers in our most hazardous industry — coal mining — has given new life to the entire movement for union-negotiated welfare plans. The United Mine Workers of America negotiated contracts in 1946 setting up three welfare funds for the protection of about 450,000 miners in 3,000 mines in 23 states.[16] Some 375,000 bituminous coal miners were covered by a welfare and re-

in meeting current problems of high prices and reduced consumer buying has become obvious to many of our local unions. Many of these unions have gone forward with educational campaigns and some have reached the point of organizing credit unions and cooperatives." *Report of the Proceedings of the Sixty-sixth Convention,* American Federation of Labor, Washington, 1947, p. 206.

13. *Report of the Proceedings of the Sixty-eighth Convention,* American Federation of Labor, Washington, 1949, pp. 100–04. Twenty-eight internationals paid no benefits, and the remaining unions did not report.

14. *Labor Information Bulletin,* Department of Labor, August 1948, p. 1.

15. *Employee Benefit Plans under Collective Bargaining, Mid-1950,* Bulletin No. 1017, Bureau of Labor Statistics, 1951, p. 1.

16. *Union Health and Welfare Plans,* Bulletin No. 900, Bureau of Labor Statistics, 1947, p. 3.

tirement fund, financed by a tax on employers for each ton of coal produced, and a medical and hospital fund, financed by a wage check-off. About 75,000 anthracite miners were covered by another welfare and retirement fund similar to that negotiated for bituminous miners. Collective agreements signed in 1948 set the employer contribution to the welfare and retirement funds at 20 cents a ton of coal; in 1949 it was raised to 30 cents.

Despite the status unions gain in the eyes of their members and the public from such large financial operations, most of them would prefer to leave this field to the government. The railroad unions for a long time have concentrated on plans for governmental protection of their members and, according to the Fund's opinion survey, six out of seven union leaders preferred comprehensive governmental plans to union-negotiated plans. In the absence of such governmental action, however, the unions are sure to negotiate more and better plans. And once a union wins such a plan for its members and begins to administer it jointly with management, the union is hardly likely to give up what amounts to a new direct way of servicing (and holding) its members.

Educational Activities

The educational activities of unions are as old as trade unionism itself. These activities began with the training of apprentices, which the skilled craft unions regarded as one of their major functions. Unions undertook this activity partly to ensure maintenance of craft standards, partly to control entrance to the trade and labor supply, and partly because employers were hesitant to spend money to train apprentices who might be hired by their competitors.

Unions are proud of their apprenticeship programs. The Brotherhood of Painters, Decorators and Paperhangers, for example, holds annual contests to demonstrate its apprentices' skills. Unions also conduct refresher courses to polish up rusty skills and give workers opportunity for improvement. The Printing Pressmen and Assistants' Union runs a full-fledged technical school where members can learn the latest techniques and prepare themselves for better jobs.[17]

Unions have also cooperated in the development of vocational schools. They make allowance in their apprenticeship programs for apprentices to attend the schools part time to obtain the necessary formal off-the-job training, and they give financial support to vocational schools. The United Hatters, Cap and Millinery Workers International Union, for example, has financed scholarships at the Central High School of Needle Trades in New York City.

Apprenticeship and vocational training programs are designed to develop better workers. Activities designed to make better union members are usually classified as "workers' education." They include the study of economic and social problems, the philosophy and activities of organized labor, and specialized courses to prepare workers for union leadership. Such training is given in lectures or movies at local meetings, night classes at local union halls or public school buildings, regular schools financed by union donations in addition to student fees, special institutes, lectures or training conferences, or extension services at universities.

Interest in workers' education has been greater in recent years than ever before. In 1947, for example, the International Union of United Automobile, Aircraft and Agricultural Implement Workers of America (CIO) ran schools in seven states and in Ontario, Canada, attended by 2,500 workers during the summer; week-end conferences and institutes attended by 18,000 workers; and individual courses completed by 33,000 workers during the year. The International Ladies' Garment Workers' Union (AFL) registered nearly 9,000 members in 306 classes and groups during the year. The Textile Workers Union of America (CIO) held seven one-week institutes in the summer of 1947, with an enrollment of 342 students; and the United Steelworkers of America (CIO) enrolled 1,475 workers in classes held for one- or two-week periods in universities all over the country.[18]

In cooperation with unions, many universities and colleges[19] include workers' education

17. See Florence Peterson, *American Labor Unions*, Harper, New York, 1945, p. 163.

18. Arthur A. Elder, "Note on the Progress of Workers' Education in 1947," *Monthly Labor Review*, April 1948, pp. 406–08.

19. Cornell University, Rhode Island State College, Roosevelt College (Chicago), the University of California, University of Chicago, University of Illinois, University of Michigan and others. The Secretary of Labor listed sixty universities and colleges as furnishing some form of workers' education in 1948 and

in their extension services or as part of a program of industrial relations. Voluntary organizations, such as the American Labor Education Service, and the AFL's Workers Education Bureau disseminate information and conduct conferences. A number of resident summer schools train union members for leadership positions. These schools are independent of the unions, but the unions cooperate closely with them, frequently supplying board members and scholarships. Harvard University has a resident training program for union leadership to which unions send experienced members for a year's study.

Labor Press

The labor press is in itself an established institution. Unions regularly publish monthly or weekly some five hundred papers and journals. The AFL has a monthly magazine, the *American Federationist,* a monthly economic review, *Labor's Monthly Survey,* and a *Weekly News Service.* The CIO publishes a weekly paper, the *CIO News,* and a monthly, *CIO Economic Outlook. Labor* is the official weekly paper of the "Fifteen Recognized Standard Railroad Labor Organizations." Almost all international unions have regular publications, mostly on a monthly basis. Many local unions issue their own papers and practically every city and county central organization publishes a paper for the members of its affiliated unions. In addition to these regular publications, countless special-purpose pamphlets are prepared by union education, research and publicity departments and by local-union committees.

Public Relations

Unions have always considered their educational programs as vital links between the union and its members and between the union and the general public. The recent rapid growth of union membership has increased the importance of this aspect of union work. The millions of new members, organized quickly, require considerable union education before they can be completely assimilated. Similarly, the public, which quickly accepted the new, enlarged labor movement as an accomplished fact, requires considerable education before it will accept that fact as a good thing. To reach their new members, unions have expanded their education departments and programs. This expansion, added to the already widespread educational activities described above, represents a comprehensive, far-reaching program that is likely to win and retain the loyalty of union members.

The public relations programs of unions have no such firm foundation on which to build, and their past attempts to reach the general public have been on a smaller scale and much less effective than their efforts to reach their own members. Spurred by the passage of the Taft-Hartley Act, unions intensified their efforts to win public favor. One move in this direction is perhaps the most impressive proof that organized labor has "arrived" as a truly American institution. On June 15, 1948, President William Green announced that the AFL had appointed a New York advertising agency "to execute the Federation's new and comprehensive public relations program." [20] This development followed a trend established by various unions, among them the American Federation of Musicians, the United Mine Workers of America, the International Union of United Automobile Workers of America (AFL) and the International Hod Carriers', Building and Common Laborers' Union of America (AFL), which have retained professional public relations firms to present their case to the American people.

History of Growth

The following pages outline some of the more salient developments in the labor movement in the United States, specifically, those necessary for understanding the origin of the two giant organizations that now dominate the movement — the American Federation of Labor and the Congress of Industrial Organizations.

Trade-union growth in this country has been marked by sudden upsurges in membership followed generally by equally rapid declines. Before the present century, union expansion was particularly short-lived. Although the first unions were organized strictly on a temporary basis to win a specific goal, attempts were made very early to establish permanent organizations. These disappeared, however, almost as quickly

seven more with proposed programs. Hearings on H.R. 1980, Labor Extension Act of 1949, Committee on Education and Labor, House of Representatives, 1949, p. 48.

20. *American Federationist,* July 1948, p. 15.

as the temporary organizations. Not until the late 1890's, after many false starts, was the foundation of the present-day labor movement made secure. Even with this solid foundation, however, union membership fluctuated widely.

UNIONISM BEFORE 1897

The long list of forerunners of modern labor unions begins with charitable and beneficial societies of craftsmen in colonial times and local unions of wage earners at the time of the Revolutionary War. It includes unions of craftsmen and factory workers, together with the first city centrals and the first national trade unions in the late 1830's. As early as the 1850's, local unions in a number of trades formed national organizations, some of which exist today. Time and again, unions rose in prosperous years and disappeared in years of depression. (See Table 67.)

The first large labor organization to appear on the American scene was the Noble Order of the Knights of Labor, the direct antecedent of the American Federation of Labor. The Knights of Labor started in 1869 as one of the many secret orders designed to circumvent lockouts and blacklists. It abandoned secrecy in the 1880's and in a few years attracted great numbers of workers, farmers, professional persons and even employers. Its goal was to replace the wage system by a cooperative society, but its immediate objectives included higher wages, shorter hours of work, and abolition of child labor. By the end of 1886, the Order had 700,000 members. A year later its membership had dropped to 500,000; by 1890, to less than 100,000.[21]

The rapid growth of the Knights of Labor showed the need for mass organization of workers in the United States. Its rapid decline was proof that heterogeneous groups with rather nebulous aspirations could not be united in a centralized national organization. The American Federation of Labor emerged from the recognition of these facts.

The AFL traces its beginnings to the Federation of Organized Trade and Labor Unions, which was founded in 1881 as a league of autonomous affiliates. This federation was primarily a legislative organization, and its affiliates had about 45,000 members in 1881.[22] The AFL started with an estimated membership of 138,000 in 1886.[23] It added economic functions to the legislative functions of its predecessor and concentrated on winning skilled workers to its banners.

21. Selig Perlman, "Upheaval and Reorganisation (since 1876)," in John R. Commons and Associates, *History of Labor in the United States,* Macmillan, New York, 1921, Vol. II, pp. 344 and 482.

TABLE 67

ESTIMATED MEMBERSHIP OF LABOR UNIONS, SELECTED YEARS, 1836–1897

(*In Thousands*)

Year	Number of Members
1836	300
1869	170
1872	300
1878	50
1883	200
1885	300
1886	1,000
1890	400
1897	440

Sources: For 1836, Edward B. Mittleman, "Trade Unionism (1833–1839)," in John R. Commons and Associates, *History of Labor in the United States,* Macmillan, New York, 1921, Vol. I, p. 351; for 1869–1878, John B. Andrews, "Nationalisation (1860–1877)," in *ibid.,* Vol. II, pp. 47 and 177; for 1883–1886, Selig Perlman, "Upheaval and Reorganisation (since 1876)," in *ibid.,* Vol. II, pp. 312 and 398; for 1890, Richard A. Lester, *Economics of Labor,* Macmillan, New York, 1941, p. 549; and for 1897, *Brief History of the American Labor Movement,* Bureau of Labor Statistics, October 1947, p. 18.

UNIONISM SINCE 1897

The depression of 1893–1896 proved that labor unions in the United States were at last solidly and permanently established. For the first time, they weathered a major economic setback without loss of membership. During that entire period, and despite several defeats in contests with management, they retained close to 400,000 members. In 1897, when the modern period of unionism in the United States began, some 440,000 workers held union cards.[24] (See Table 68 and Figure 41.)

22. Alfred L. Bernheim and Dorothy Van Doren (Eds.), *Labor and the Government,* Twentieth Century Fund, New York, 1935, p. 152.

23. *Brief History of the American Labor Movement,* Bureau of Labor Statistics, October 1947, p. 6.

24. Membership figures for the years 1897–1946 are from *ibid.,* pp. 17–19; the figures through 1934 are based largely on those compiled by Leo Wolman. The membership figures are for all unions with headquarters in the United States and therefore include members in locals outside continental United States, primarily in Canada. According to the Thirty-eighth Annual Report on Labour Organization in Canada, Canadian Department of Labor, 675,044 Canadian workers were members of "international" unions in 1948.

TABLE 68

MEMBERSHIP OF LABOR UNIONS, 1897–1947 [a]

(In Thousands)

Year	Number of Members	Year	Number of Members
1897	440	1923	3,629
1898	467	1924	3,549
1899	550		
		1925	3,566
1900	791	1926	3,592
1901	1,058	1927	3,600
1902	1,335	1928	3,567
1903	1,824	1929	3,625
1904	2,067		
		1930	3,632
1905	1,918	1931	3,562
1906	1,892	1932	3,226
1907	2,077	1933	2,857
1908	2,092	1934	3,249
1909	1,965		
1910	2,116	1935	3,728
1911	2,318	1936	4,164
1912	2,405	1937	7,218
1913	2,661	1938	8,265
1914	2,647	1939	8,980
1915	2,560	1940	8,944
1916	2,722	1941	10,489
1917	2,976	1942	10,762
1918	3,368	1943	13,642
1919	4,046	1944	14,621
1920	5,034	1945	14,796
1921	4,722	1946	14,974
1922	3,950	1947	15,414

a. Specific estimates for later years are not available. The membership figures are for all unions with headquarters in the United States and therefore include members in locals outside continental United States, primarily in Canada. According to the Thirty-eighth Annual Report on Labour Organization in Canada, Canadian Department of Labor, 675,044 Canadian workers were members of "international" unions in 1948.

Source: Appendix Table 53.

Organization of Craftsmen: 1897–1904

Starting from this base, the unions made their first great advance during the prosperity and the industrial expansion of 1897–1904. In seven years the number of affiliated national unions increased from 58 to 120, and membership in all labor unions expanded from less than half a million to a little more than 2 million. Relatively little further gain was added to this initial burst of organization during the next thirty years.

Consolidation of Craft Unions: 1905–1915

The membership gains made during this early period were never lost, however, despite adverse factors that in earlier times had decimated the ranks. As had happened after the spectacular growth of the Knights of Labor, employer opposition stiffened after 1904. Courts, furthermore, continued to be unfriendly to labor, and business recessions occurred periodically. Nevertheless, union membership never fell appreciably below the 1904 level.

Although the unfavorable developments after 1904 failed to reduce union membership, they did retard its growth. During the next eleven years, unions added only half a million members; by 1915 they had enrolled only 2.6 million.

Union structure and policy were among the many factors that contributed to the long period of relative stagnation.[25] The unions of this period were predominantly organizations of workers in the same or related crafts.[26] Their organizing efforts were limited largely to the higher-skilled workers. When labor unions reached a membership of 2 million in 1904, their organizing potentials had almost been fulfilled.[27] The period from 1897 to 1904 may be viewed as the time when the American skilled worker was permanently won over to trade unionism. Not until many years later, when conditions favored the inclusion of the relatively unskilled mass-production workers, could another major advance be made.

Wartime Advance and Postwar Setback: 1916–1923

Conditions during and immediately after World War I were unusually favorable for union growth. Labor shortages, which increased union bargaining power, and favorable public policy enabled them to double their size in five years — from 2.6 million members in 1915 to 5.0 million in 1920. The gains in membership, however, were largely made within existing unions, in relatively few industries and occupations. About a dozen new unions sprang up during this period, but altogether they garnered only 350,000 of the 2.4 million new union members. Moreover, the Amalgamated Clothing Workers, which accounted for half the gains of these new unions, was the outgrowth of an established union, organized in 1914 by a group of

25. Leo Wolman, *Ebb and Flow in Trade Unionism,* National Bureau of Economic Research, New York, 1936, pp. 38–39.

26. An important exception was the United Mine Workers, an industrial union with about 12 per cent of total union membership during most of this period.

27. Millis and Montgomery, *op. cit.,* p. 83, footnote 1.

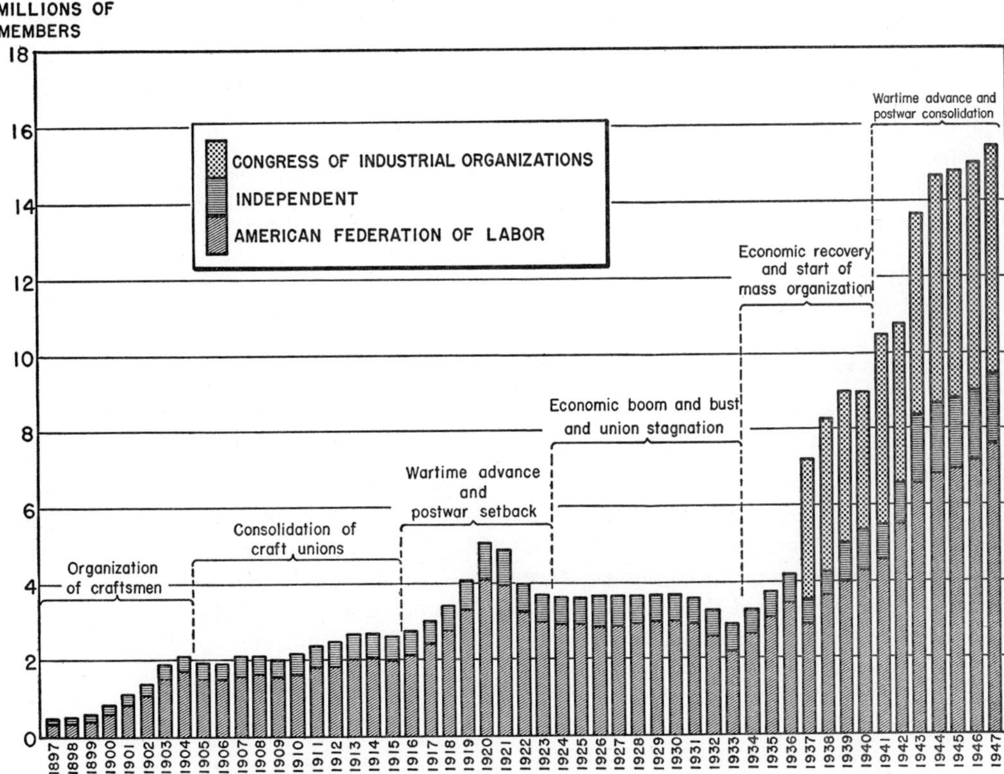

FIGURE 41. UNION MEMBERSHIP, BY AFFILIATION, 1897–1947

Source: Appendix Table 53.

In the first third of this century, union membership ranged between 2 and 4 million workers, almost all in the skilled crafts. Since unionization of the great mass-production industries began in 1937, the AFL, as well as the CIO, have organized millions of unskilled and semiskilled workers. Membership as shown here is for all unions with headquarters in the United States and therefore includes members in locals outside continental United States.

workers who seceded from the older United Garment Workers. Building and transportation unions and unions in the metals, machinery, shipbuilding and clothing industries accounted for three fourths of the 1915–1920 membership gains. At the end of the period, the craft unions had a higher percentage of the total membership than at the start.[28]

The unions of 1920 were in a sense merely the unions of 1915, war-inflated. When employment in war plants and shipyards contracted, union membership declined rapidly. Unions in the metals, machinery and shipbuilding industries, which had added 635,000 members between 1915 and 1920, lost 602,000 members in the next three years. Setbacks such as these, plus the losses inflicted by the depression of 1920–1921 and the growing pressure of employers through the open-shop drive, left union membership in 1923 at 3.6 million, a million above the prewar membership.

Union Stagnation: 1924–1933

During the prosperous 1920's little progress was made in increasing union membership, despite the rise in employment. The lack of growth was due partly to the very high rate of replacement of old industries by new and the almost complete concentration of prosperity in those sections of the economy least penetrated by trade unionism in the past. Other causes were: (1) the aggressive labor policy of many large firms — outright opposition to unionism plus positive steps such as profit sharing, group insurance and similar devices of "welfare capitalism" designed to win labor's loyalty; (2) more general application of mass-production tech-

28. Roughly estimated at 78 per cent in 1920, as compared with 75 per cent in 1915. See Wolman, *op. cit.*, p. 92.

niques and the resulting declining demand for craftsmen, who comprised by far the greater part of union membership; (3) technological unemployment, which created a labor surplus during good times, a surplus made up of the strongest union element, skilled workers; (4) the decline of such union strongholds as the textile and bituminous coal industries to the status of "sick" industries, and the movement of large parts of these industries from union to nonunion regions; and lastly (5) the unsuitability of the dominant craft-type of union organization for the job of unionizing the growing mass-production industries.[29] Two other important considerations should be added to this list: the rise in workers' real earnings and the unfavorable position of unions in the courts.[30]

When the great depression began in 1929, unions had 3.6 million members. During the next four years of severe unemployment they lost more than one fifth of their membership; at the depth of the depression in 1933 they had only 2.8 million members. This loss, however, seems small in comparison with the severity of unemployment. The comparatively strong resistance of unions to such bad times suggests that by 1929 the labor movement had just about reached the hard core of basic craft unionism staked out at the turn of the century. In the first three decades of the century almost everything in the country had either changed radically or grown prodigiously; the labor movement in 1930, however, might well have carried the label "Built in 1900."

Beginning of Mass Organization: 1934–1940

The prolonged mass unemployment of the early 1930's led to a revaluation of the role of labor unions in the United States economy. Union organizers, whose arguments had fallen so flat a short while before, began to find sympathetic listeners when they stressed the need for a new type of industrial relations in a modern industrial society. As Wolman says:

> Already in 1933, as a reaction against considerable reductions in wages and the widespread violation of labor standards and in response to new and vigorous organizing campaigns, several groups had gathered a considerable number of new members. . . . From 1932 to 1933 . . . unions in the mining, leather, shoe and clothing industries and in the public service gained 280,000 [members].[31]

The government that was voted into power at the depth of the depression considered the growth of unions and collective bargaining an important element in its program of economic recovery. The new labor policy found immediate expression in Section 7a of the National Industrial Recovery Act of 1933, which required that every code of fair competition include the provision that employees had the right to organize and bargain collectively through representatives of their own choosing without interference, restraint or coercion on the part of employers. In the National Labor Relations Act of 1935, the Wagner Act, the government reaffirmed this right and provided more effective means to protect it. The government's new labor policies "transformed the labor code of the United States from one of the most restrictive among the industrially advanced nations to one of the most liberal . . ." [32]

Emergence of the CIO

This new public policy helped bring about a fundamental change in union philosophy and strategy. Though the AFL had developed predominantly as a federation of craft unions limited largely to skilled workers, elements within the Federation had long urged organization along industrial lines, covering workers at all levels of skill. They found new ammunition in the low level of union membership in the early 1930's and the new vistas opened by the government's favorable attitude toward union expansion. When the first real opportunity to unionize the mass-production industries presented itself under the NRA in 1934, they pressed for recognition of industrial unionism as the proper form of organization for these industries.

The AFL side-stepped the issue at its 1934 convention and proceeded to organize many of these workers into temporary, directly affiliated federal unions.[33] The industrial unionists, however, grew increasingly critical of the dominant craft-union group and blamed the policies of that group for the Federation's failure to take full advantage of opportunities for organizing

29. *Ibid.*, pp. 35–39.

30. Millis and Montgomery, *op. cit.*, pp. 153 and 160.

31. Wolman, *op. cit.*, p. 42.

32. Millis and Montgomery, *op. cit.*, p. 192.

33. The number of such unions increased from 673 in 1933 to 1,788 in 1934. *Ibid.*, p. 205.

in the mass-production industries. The dissenters brought the issue to a head at the 1935 convention by presenting a resolution favoring organization along industrial and plant lines. The convention rejected industrial unionism and endorsed, in its stead, a policy of leaving production employees in the industrial unions but "protecting ultimately" jurisdictional rights of the craft unions.

A month later, in November 1935, the officers of eight AFL unions, with about 940,000 members,[34] established a Committee for Industrial Organization to organize "the unorganized workers in mass production and other industries upon an industrial basis." Two other AFL unions soon joined the committee, and all ten were suspended from the AFL in August 1936 on the charge of organizing a rival union movement. When the temporary Committee for Industrial Organization became the permanent Congress of Industrial Organizations in 1938, it had 32 international affiliates and 9 organizing committees; its membership of 4 million exceeded that of the AFL by about 400,000.

The formation of the CIO brought the great mass of industrial workers effectively within the organizing range of the American labor movement. New unions were founded and old ones expanded. In the ensuing competition for new members, AFL unions have more than kept pace with the CIO unions.

By 1934, when economic recovery began, the third great membership advance of the century was under way. In the first three years of this advance, membership increased steadily to a total of 4.2 million. Then, between 1936 and 1937, with the newly organized Committee for Industrial Organization in the lead, organized labor added 3 million members to its rolls, more than in any other year of its history. With this 73 per cent rise, union membership reached a new high of 7.2 million, more than 2 million above the previous peak in 1920. The 1937–1938 recession retarded organization, and by 1940 it had come to a virtual standstill, with union membership at 8.9 million.

Wartime Advance and Postwar Consolidation: 1941–1949

Conversion to a war economy, with labor shortages and cost-plus contracts, brought wage gains and a renewal of labor's upward climb. When the United States entered the war in 1941, unemployment stood at about 4 million and union membership at 10 to 11 million. Unemployment virtually disappeared in the next two years and, as war production rose to its peak in 1943, union membership shot up to 13.6 million. Between 1942 and 1943, unions enrolled more new members (2.9 million) than in any other single year except during the hectic organizing days of 1936–1937.

Unions had many appealing arguments to offer prospective members during the war years. They could promise — and deliver — wage increases. They offered their services in improving working conditions, which had deteriorated in the feverish rush to expand production. They supplied the workers' desire for greater participation in the war effort through labor-management committees and union-organized community activities. The unions could claim direct participation, at the highest government levels, in planning and administering the war production program. The appointment of official representatives of organized labor to positions of authority in the Office of Production Management and later in the War Production Board and the War Manpower Commission gave unions considerable prestige in the eyes of the workers they sought to enroll.

During the war three factors contributed to the unions' ability to offer economic gains to attract new members. One was the general shortage of labor. A second was the readiness of employers to grant wage increases within the limits of the government's wartime wage policy — wage increases they could easily pass on to the ultimate consumer, the government, in the form of an added cost item under their cost-plus contracts. The third was the War Labor Board's machinery for controlling wages. This machinery put a premium on forceful presentation of wage demands, and the need to substantiate requests for wage increases made technical assistance important. Unorganized workers could easily be made to see the advantages of having union officials, qualified by years of experience, prepare their case for a wage increase and present it before the War Labor Board.

As during World War I, the greatest union gains were made in the basic war industries — in shipyards and in aircraft and automotive plants, which absorbed the greatest numbers of

34. *Ibid.*, p. 210.

war production workers. The International Union of United Automobile Workers (CIO), which began the war with 600,000 members, in 1943 became the first union in the history of American labor to pass the million mark. The United Steelworkers of America (CIO), whose membership averaged 400,000 in 1941, reached an all-time high of 973,000 in June 1945. The International Association of Machinists (independent) more than tripled its membership during the war, from 200,000 to about 670,000. The AFL Boilermakers skyrocketed from about 40,000 members to almost 400,000 members, and the CIO Marine and Shipbuilding Workers from approximately 50,000 to 250,000 members. Unions in the construction trades also expanded rapidly. The AFL Carpenters raised their membership from about 300,000 in 1940 to almost 900,000 in 1943, and the AFL Hod Carriers from under 200,000 in 1940 to more than 400,000 in 1942.[35]

Membership began to decline from the wartime peak in the Hod Carriers' union after 1942 and in the others in the following year or two. In contrast to the situation after World War I, however, these losses were compensated for by steady growth in other unions. Total membership continued to rise in each successive year, reaching 14.6 million in 1944, 14.8 million in 1945, and 15.4 million in 1947.[36] Moreover, despite the readjustments necessitated by reconversion to peacetime production, the larger war-expanded unions retained most of their gains. The CIO Auto Workers, although suffering large losses when war plants shut down, again approached their wartime peak of just under a million members in 1949. In the same year, the CIO Steelworkers reported 960,000 members, the AFL Carpenters about 735,000, the Machinists just under 600,000, and the AFL Teamsters were over the one million line, laying claim to the title of largest union.[37]

Reaction to the tremendous growth of unions and to postwar labor-management disputes took concrete form in the Labor-Management Relations (Taft-Hartley) Act of 1947. Labor leaders, seeing the act as a threat to the security of their unions, redoubled their organizing efforts and embarked on a major political campaign to secure its repeal. Largely as a result of this campaign, unions played a more effective role in the 1948 national elections than in any previous election. Although the act placed obstacles in the way of organizing, union membership seems to have remained at about the 1947 level.

Character of Recent Gains

The union expansion that began in the 1930's and continued through the war (see Figure 42) is explained by the coincidence of many developments. Among the more important were: new trends in public policy and in the attitude of government; labor's strengthened bargaining position as a result of economic recovery and the wartime boom; aggressive competitive membership drives among semiskilled and unskilled workers by both the AFL and the CIO; and the new spirit among rank-and-file workers.

The encouragement that governmental policy gave to union organization through the National Recovery Administration and then the National Labor Relations Act ranks high among the factors contributing to recent union growth. Of greater importance, however, has been the workers' spontaneous drive toward unionization. "In many nonunion industries and regions," says Peterson, "the urge to organize emanated from the workers themselves, with union organizers in many instances unable to keep up with the demands made upon them." [38]

The rapid growth of company unions under the NRA provides additional evidence of the workers' readiness for organization, a readiness of which employers apparently were well aware. The first company union was launched in 1898; by 1932 such plans covered 1,263,194 workers.[39] In the next three years, after Section 7a

35. Figures for Marine and Shipbuilding Workers taken from Harry A. Millis, *How Collective Bargaining Works,* Twentieth Century Fund, New York, 1942, p. 963, and Peterson, *op. cit.,* p. 325. Other figures supplied by individual unions.

36. Union membership for 1948 and 1949 is estimated at 14 to 16 million by the Department of Labor. Although a firm figure for those years is not available, the Secretary of Labor has used 15.5 million on several occasions. Estimates of total union membership are subject to a substantial margin of error for all years, but particularly for the past few years, when the CIO was expelling a number of its unions and when the propaganda aspect of membership "figures" was important.

37. *Directory of Labor Unions in the United States, 1950,* Bulletin No. 980, Bureau of Labor Statistics, 1950.

38. Peterson, *op. cit.,* p. 24.

39. *Collective Bargaining through Employee Representation,* National Industrial Conference Board, New York, p. 16; quoted in Bernheim and Van Doren, *op. cit.,* p. 77.

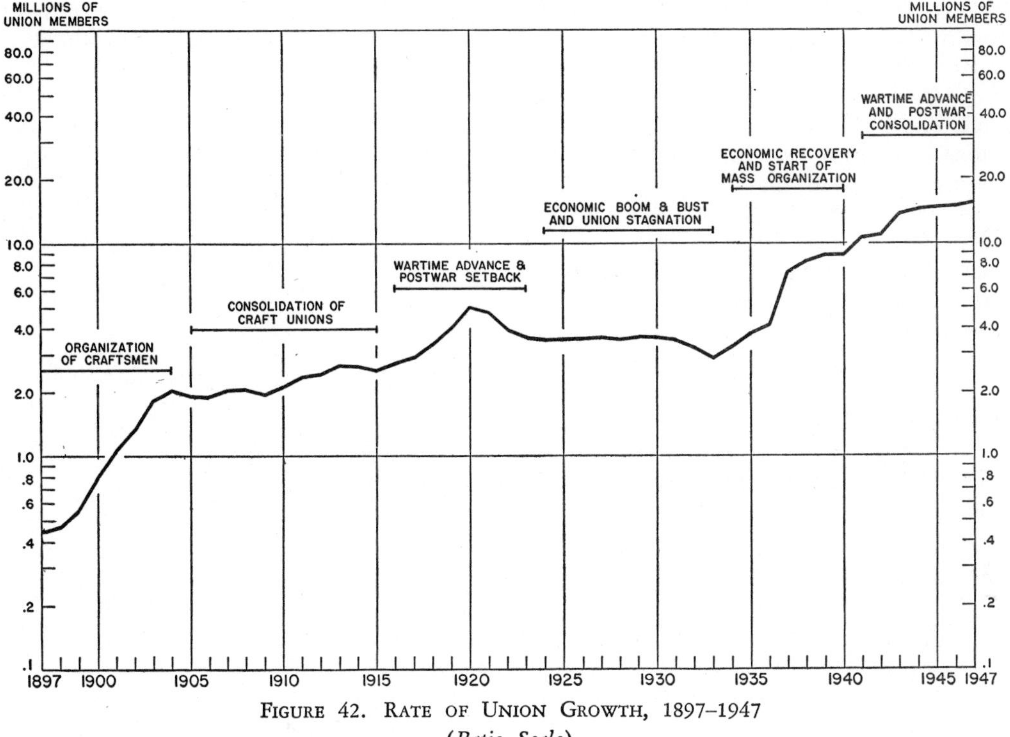

FIGURE 42. RATE OF UNION GROWTH, 1897–1947
(*Ratio Scale*)

Source: Appendix Table 53.

Unions made their most rapid organizing strides at the turn of the century, when they organized the skilled crafts, and in recent years, when they unionized the mass-production industries.

had guaranteed workers the right to organize for collective bargaining, management doubled the coverage of company unions, increasing the number of employees covered to about 2.5 million.[40] Employers, legally restrained from refusing to bargain collectively, and correctly assessing their employees' desire for unionization, pushed company unionism "primarily as insurance against advent of the trade union." [41]

The desire of workers to organize was demonstrated again in the union shop elections held under the Taft-Hartley Act. In 17,476 such elections held between October 1947 and June 1948, 94 per cent of the 1.6 million workers involved voted in favor of requiring union membership as a condition of employment.[42]

DETERMINANTS OF UNION GROWTH

The growth pattern of labor unions in the United States was accurately described more than sixty years ago as one that "may be compared to the incoming tide. Each wave advances a little further than the previous one . . ." [43] Since that time, union membership has advanced and receded in wavelike movements apparently superimposed on a fundamental, long-run upward trend.

Certain generalizations about the causes of this pattern of growth may be made on the basis of past experience. The rise in union membership has been intimately connected with the nation's industrial development. The short-run wavelike fluctuations around the long-run rising tide of union membership result from many factors, among which three stand out: the business cycle, the attitude of government, and internal union structure and policies.

Business Cycles

Union membership generally has fluctuated with the business cycle, rising during business upswings and falling with economic setbacks.

40. *Ibid.,* p. 79.
41. Millis and Montgomery, *op. cit.,* p. 840.
42. Based on data supplied by the National Labor Relations Board, Information Division.

43. Richard T. Ely, *The Labor Movement in America* (1886), p. 90; quoted in Millis and Montgomery, *op. cit.,* p. 79.

For the most part the labor movement in this country has been concerned with the limited objectives of "business unionism." Except on rare occasions, improved wages and working conditions, rather than fundamental economic and social reforms, have been its aims. Unions have realized these aims most readily during business upswings, when, because of labor shortages and good profit prospects, they have been able to win concessions from employers. Wage earners, concerned primarily with the gap between prices and wages, have turned to the unions in large numbers during such periods.

During prosperous times, unions have also grown by the addition of new employees in regions where the unions were already well established. Conversely, in the downturn of the cycle, labor surpluses and poor prospects for profits have reduced the unions' ability to protect the wage earner and he has turned elsewhere for assistance. Moreover, the union member who lost his job soon became an ex-member.

There have been several important exceptions to this general rule, however. The first occurred during the depression of 1884–1886, when workers joined the Knights of Labor in great numbers and, as a result, union membership expanded more rapidly than at any other time on record. But the objectives of the Knights were not those of business unionism. During a period of widespread unemployment, when the economic system was stalling badly, the Order's reformist program had wide appeal to workers.

The second exception was the period of the prosperous 1920's, when unions made no progress despite rapid industrial expansion. The many reasons [44] for this lack of progress included the following conditions: the usual incentive toward organization was lacking during this period since wages advanced more than the cost of living; also, the unions ran into strong, united employer opposition and were unable to point to many concessions won through their efforts.

The third exception was the continued membership increase during the extremely sharp recession of 1937–1938. This economic setback coincided with the great splurge of organizing activity that followed the Supreme Court's affirmation of the constitutionality of the Wagner Act in 1937.

With these exceptions, business ups and downs have been a major reason for the wavelike fluctuations of union membership.

Governmental Attitudes

Changing governmental policies have alternately retarded and accelerated union growth. The government's adoption of a friendly attitude toward labor during World War I aided union growth. A change in this attitude and renewed use of broad injunctive powers against unions — against the miners in 1919 and the railway shopmen in 1922, for example — and adverse court rulings played a part in weakening unions in the 1920's. The Norris-LaGuardia Act, the NRA and the Wagner Act marked another shift in governmental policies in the direction of protecting the right of workers to organize. In this period of the 1930's and in the favorable atmosphere of World War II, when the government treated unions as partners in the war effort, unions had their greatest expansion.

The last three union advances — during World War I, the 1930's and World War II — were stimulated both by friendly governmental policy and by rising employment. During 1920–1921 and 1929–1932, unions were weakened by the unfriendly attitude of government and by business downswings. On the other hand, the absence of friendly governmental policies helped counterbalance the expansive force of the economic upswing after 1921.

Union Structure and Policies

Union structure and policies also have affected the growth and composition of union membership. When the skilled craftsman dominated the industrial scene, the AFL established itself as his spokesman. As the occupational composition of the labor force changed, the AFL began to lose its dynamic strength. It failed in its attempt to organize steelworkers in 1919 and the automobile industry in 1927. Both were multi-union campaigns, and both failed because of lack of cooperation among the separate craft unions involved.[45] In the 1930's the CIO industrial drives brought heavy industry into the union fold and the AFL unions, dropping their craft exclusiveness, proceeded to organize unskilled and semiskilled workers

44. See Wolman, *op. cit.,* p. 31.

45. Lester, *op. cit.,* pp. 558–59.

along with the skilled. Membership figures quickly reflected this change in the organization principles of the union movement.

Union Structure

The basic organizational unit of the American labor union is the international.[46] Internationals may range in size from a hundred to a million members and in coverage from a single craft or a small area to an entire industry, but all are autonomous bodies that give up little of their freedom when they are affiliated with a federation. Most of the 209 internationals, accounting for about 85 per cent of total union membership, are affiliated with the American Federation of Labor or the Congress of Industrial Organizations. (See Table 69.) The unaffiliated ("independent") unions frequently combine among themselves and with affiliated unions for special campaigns; some are banded together in loose federations.

The internationals were subdivided into more than 70,000 local unions at the end of 1949. The local union is the place where the worker and his union come into direct contact and where, at membership meetings, individual members may influence union affairs. Locals have considerably less autonomy than internationals. Although the extent of local freedom varies from union to union, the basic policies and procedures of the local must conform to those of the international. The local's freedom lies mainly in applying basic policies in day-to-day operations. A few local unions for which there are no appropriate internationals are affiliated directly with the AFL and the CIO, and those bodies function as their internationals.

AFL and CIO Structure Compared

In formal organizational structure the AFL and the CIO are very much alike. (See Figure 43.) What structural differences there are may be traced to the fact that the typical AFL union is primarily a craft or multicraft union, while the typical CIO union is primarily an industrial

46. The term "international" customarily includes both national unions — those whose coverage is limited to the United States and its territories and possessions — and international unions — those centered in the United States but with members in foreign countries. For the most part, international unions have foreign membership only in Canada. See Appendix Table 54 for a complete list of internationals with their affiliation and membership.

TABLE 69

National and International Unions with Specified Number of Members, by Affiliation, December 1949

Membership	Total	Affiliated with AFL	Affiliated with CIO [a]	Independent [b]
Total	209	107	39	63
Under 1,000	22	10	—	12
1,000–4,999	31	12	1	18
5,000–9,999	22	7	4	11
10,000–24,999	26	17	4	5
25,000–49,999	35	18	9	8
50,000–99,999	36	21	13	2
100,000–199,999	16	13	2	1
200,000–299,999	7	3	2	2
300,000–399,999	3	1	2	—
400,000–499,999	3	3	—	—
500,000 and over	6	2	2	2
Unknown	2	—	—	2

a. Includes nine unions expelled by the CIO executive board during 1950 and excludes one international chartered early in 1950.

b. Excludes eight unions expelled by the CIO during 1950 (two of the nine expelled have merged).

Source: Based on *Directory of Labor Unions in the United States, 1950,* Bulletin No. 980, Bureau of Labor Statistics, 1950, Table 1, p. 3.

or semi-industrial union. As a result, the AFL has had to devote much more attention than the CIO to machinery for solving jurisdictional conflicts and for coordinating the activities of related craft unions in collective bargaining.

The AFL constitution provides for protection of the jurisdictional rights of its affiliates, and the AFL undertakes to define those rights carefully. It has set up its departments largely to help resolve jurisdictional conflicts between affiliates and has established local trades councils to bring related crafts together in dealing with employers.

The CIO constitution, on the other hand, makes no mention of jurisdictional rights as such, and the CIO leaves it pretty much to the internationals to stake out their own jurisdictions.[47] Although its constitution provides for

47. Some jurisdictional questions already have arisen (between the International Union of United Automobile, Aircraft and Agricultural Implement Workers of America and the United Farm Equipment and Metal Workers of America, for example) and more are likely in the future if the internationals continue to grow in size and number and the number of unorganized workers declines. The 1948 convention of the CIO authorized the executive board to investigate affiliates that had "failed to make substantial progress in organizing the unorganized" and to take "appropriate action" to bring about effective organization of the workers "within the jurisdiction of these affiliates." Immediately after the convention, the executive board ordered the United Farm Equipment and Metal Workers of America to merge with the United Automobile, Aircraft and Agricultural Imple-

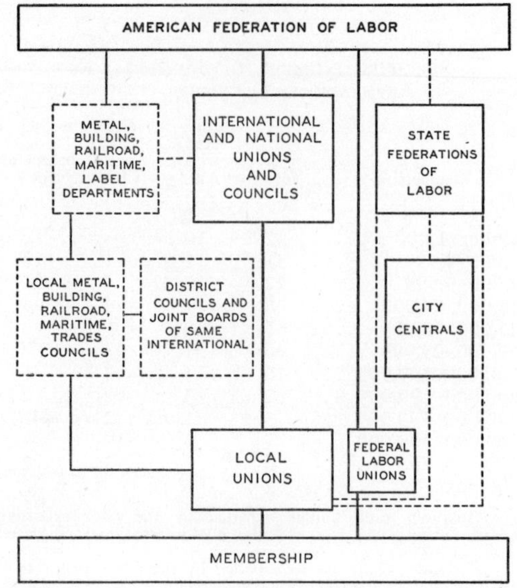

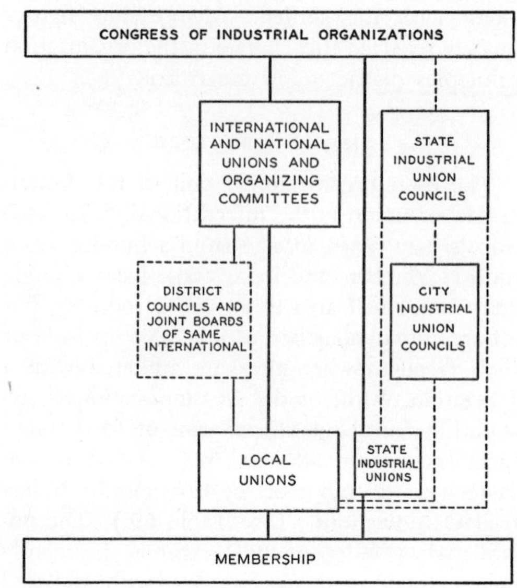

FIGURE 43. STRUCTURE OF THE AFL AND THE CIO

Source: Florence Peterson, *American Labor Unions,* Harper, New York, 1945, p. 40.

The AFL and the CIO have parallel organizational structures. The main difference arises from the AFL's need to coordinate the work of separate craft unions in the same industry.

the establishment of departments, the CIO never has set up any; nor has it felt the need to create local trades councils, since its industrially organized unions can bargain with an employer for all his employees.

The international affiliates look to the AFL and the CIO to carry out certain major functions: (1) to act as a policy-forming body and to advance such policies before all branches of government; (2) to further union organization by setting up federal labor unions in fields outside the jurisdiction of existing internationals and by assisting and coordinating international organizing campaigns; (3) to define the jurisdictional rights of internationals and to protect them against encroachment; (4) to influence public opinion in favor of organized labor; (5) to coordinate the use of labor's economic weapons, such as the union label; (6) to organize and provide support to affiliated unions involved in industrial disputes; and (7) to stimulate participation in electoral campaigns in order to help elect candidates friendly to labor.

ment Workers of America within sixty days; the Farm Equipment union refused, however, and subsequently merged with the United Electrical, Radio and Machine Workers of America, which was expelled from the CIO at the 1949 convention.

THE AMERICAN FEDERATION OF LABOR

The American Federation of Labor, with more than 8 million members at the end of 1949, is the larger of the two federated labor organizations in the United States. From the small group of unions that came together in 1881 for mutual aid and protection, the AFL has developed into a complex organization linking 107 internationals, 5 organizing councils and some 40,000 locals and coordinating their activities on international, national, state and local levels.

The AFL is organized primarily on an occupational basis. Its main unions, for the most part, cover workers in related occupations, wherever employed. Nevertheless, even the oldest craft-type unions make use of the industrial form of organization where necessary — for example, the United Brotherhood of Carpenters and Joiners of America in logging camps and in furniture factories and the International Brotherhood of Electrical Workers in plants manufacturing electrical equipment.

The Federation

The Federation itself is a rather loose organization of autonomous, self-governing internationals, which may withdraw from the parent body at will. The Federation speaks for its affiliates on matters of common interest, provides leadership and settles their jurisdictional disputes; but the basic power of the organization resides in the internationals, and the Federation has only the powers they grant it.

Annual conventions and, between conventions, a fifteen-man executive council govern the AFL, defining the specific activities to be carried on. The executive council consists of the president, the secretary-treasurer and thirteen vice-presidents. There are only two full-time elected officials, the president and the secretary-treasurer. With the aid of an appointed staff, which includes lawyers, economists, writers and organizers, they carry on the day-to-day operations.

The number of delegates that international affiliates send to the annual convention is based on membership — one delegate for unions with fewer than 4,000 members, two for those with 4,000 or more, three for those with 8,000 or more, four for those with 16,000 or more, five for those with 32,000 or more, and so on. City centrals, state federations, departments, federal labor unions and directly affiliated local unions and fraternal organizations (the British Trades Union Congress and the Canadian Trades and Labour Congress) are each entitled to one delegate.

Voting is normally by show of hands, but on closely contested issues or upon demand of one tenth of the delegates, a roll-call vote is used. In such cases, each international delegate and each directly affiliated local-union delegate has one vote for every hundred members or fraction thereof he represents; each of the remaining delegates has but one vote. Thus, on either type of vote, but particularly on important issues, the vote of the internationals outweighs by far the votes of all other groups. At the 1949 convention, for example, the internationals had 62 per cent of the delegates and 99 per cent of the votes. (See Table 70.)

Powers of the Federation

The executive council, consisting of the president, the secretary-treasurer and thirteen additional members, is elected at the convention. The president and the secretary-treasurer devote full time to the Federation, but the other council members, who generally are chosen from among the presidents of internationals, continue as international officers. The internationals thus effectively control the council as well as the convention.

TABLE 70

Representation at 1949 Convention of American Federation of Labor

Group	Number of Unions	Number of Delegates	Number of Votes
Total	335	624	70,852
Internationals	93	385	70,207
Local trade and federal labor unions	58	54	461
Central labor unions	132	132	132
State branches	45	45	45
Departments	4	4	4
Fraternal organizations	3	4	3

Source: Report of the Proceedings of the Sixty-eighth Convention, American Federation of Labor, Washington, 1949, p. xxviii.

The Federation is financed largely from a monthly per capita tax of 3 cents a member on the fully paid-up membership of each international and 37 cents a member on the membership of directly affiliated local trade unions and federal labor unions. It also receives 25 per cent of the total initiation fees of the directly affiliated local unions. Each city central and state federation pays $10 a year to the Federation. Additional revenue may be raised in the form of special assessments by the convention or the executive council.

The AFL has acquired its 107 international affiliates in two ways: it has granted charters to independent internationals upon their application, and it has created internationals by combining groups of its own federal labor unions. A union seeking to affiliate generally is granted a charter if its jurisdictional claims do not conflict with any affiliated international and if its aims and characteristics are consistent with the Federation's basic principles. The Federation, in keeping with its role as agent of the internationals, has little power over its affiliates except its power to expel them. It can urge, but cannot compel, them to do anything.

Coordination of Activities

In addition to the over-all coordination provided by the conventions and the executive council, the American Federation of Labor has established departments, which internationals with closely related interests are urged to join. Four departments have been set up to serve as media through which internationals can settle their jurisdictional conflicts and can work together in collective bargaining, in organizing and in protecting their common interests before government bodies. These are the Building and Construction Trades Department, the Metal Trades Department, the Railway Employees' Department and the Maritime Trades Department. A fifth, the Union Label Trades Department, functions somewhat differently from the others; its major aim is to spread union organization by educating consumers to use only union-made goods. The departments hold their own conventions and are financed by initiation fees and per capita taxes paid by each affiliated international. Some AFL internationals have affiliated with more than one department, but many remain entirely unaffiliated.

The primary interest of each international is to improve the wages and working conditions of its own members. But all internationals are interested in improving the lot of all workers by legislation, in educating the public on labor issues, in promoting better educational facilities for workers, and similar matters. The AFL itself coordinates the internationals and focuses their united strength on these issues nationally. It carries out these functions at the state and local levels through state federations of labor and city centrals, which coordinate the efforts of the local unions of the separate internationals. These state and city organizations are delegate bodies that are financed by per capita taxes paid by affiliated locals; locals are not required to affiliate, but most do.

The state federations are concerned largely with educational and legislative matters and political affairs within each state. The city central (which may be called a trades and labor assembly, trades and labor council, central labor council or central labor union) also does educational, legislative and political work. City centrals also assist their affiliated locals in collective bargaining, serving as information centers and supporting the locals with funds and manpower during industrial disputes.

To secure united action in collective bargaining and uniform conditions within the same industry in a city or area, the AFL and its internationals provide two further means of interlocal cooperation: combinations of locals of different internationals with jurisdiction over related crafts in the same industry (called trades councils) and combinations of locals of the same international (called joint boards, city trades councils or district trades councils). Most internationals have joint boards where there are three or more locals in an area, and most require their locals to join the councils in their areas.

Federal Labor Unions

Although most local unions are part of the AFL through their internationals, about 1,200 locals are directly affiliated with the AFL. These locals, known as local trade or federal labor unions, are usually in areas over which none of the affiliated internationals have jurisdiction.[48] They are the means by which the AFL, using its staff of 196 paid and 1,592 volunteer national organizers, spreads union organization into new fields. The AFL serves as the international for these unions, advising them and assisting them financially out of the special defense fund set aside from their per capita payments to the AFL. Whenever feasible, the AFL transfers these locals to existing internationals or combines them into a newly chartered international. Before becoming a chartered international, a group of locals may be combined into an organizing council, an intermediate organizational form with semiautonomous status. In 1950 the AFL had six such councils.

The Internationals

The AFL's international affiliates range in size from the 55-member International Association of Siderographers to the million-member International Brotherhood of Teamsters, Chauffeurs, Warehousemen and Helpers of America. They range from single-craft unions, such as the Diamond Workers' Protective Union, to unions covering all occupations in several industries, such as the Bakery and Confectionery Workers' International Union. Intermediate are multicraft amalgamations, such as the Bricklayers, Masons and Plasterers International Union and the Brotherhood of Painters, Decorators and Paperhangers, and industry-wide unions, such as the International Ladies' Garment Workers' Union and the United Textile Workers of America. The oldest AFL affiliate, the International Typographical Union, traces its beginnings back to 1852; the Railway Patrol-

48. On August 31, 1949 there were 1,182 local trade and federal labor unions, with an average membership of 201,019 for the fiscal year ended June 30, 1949. *Report of the Proceedings of the Sixty-eighth Convention,* p. 84.

men's International Union was chartered in 1949. Nearly half of all AFL members are now organized in half a dozen internationals.[49]

THE CONGRESS OF INDUSTRIAL ORGANIZATIONS

The Congress of Industrial Organizations, which in the years immediately following its formation reported a higher membership than the AFL, is now believed to have fewer than 4 million members.[50] Like the AFL, from which it sprang, the CIO is a complex structure coordinating the activities of 31 internationals, 2 organizing committees and some 10,000 local unions. In organization and in their constitutional provisions, the two federations have many more similarities than differences.

The relationship between the CIO and its international affiliates is much the same as in the AFL. Although the fact that the CIO is primarily a federation of industrial unions and the AFL is organized basically along occupational lines still represents an organizational difference of great importance, its importance has diminished somewhat in recent years as the AFL has moved toward industrial forms during its large-scale membership drives. The main CIO unions are younger and less wealthy than their AFL counterparts.

The Congress

Delegates to the annual convention of the CIO are chosen according to the same principles as in the AFL, with minor variations. Each international and organizing committee with fewer than 5,000 members has two delegates; with more than 5,000 members, three delegates; more than 10,000, four delegates; more than 25,000, five delegates; more than 50,000, six delegates; more than 75,000, seven delegates; and more than 100,000, eight delegates for the first 100,000 members plus one more for each additional 50,000 or major fraction thereof. Each local industrial union (locals directly affiliated with the CIO) and each industrial union council (city and state) has one delegate. On roll-call votes — which may be demanded by delegates representing 30 per cent of the total membership — internationals, organizing committees and local industrial unions have votes in proportion to their membership, but industrial union councils have only one vote apiece.

The CIO's executive board is larger than the AFL's, since it includes a president, vice-presidents and one board member from each international and organizing committee.[51] Whereas each member of the AFL executive council has one vote, each CIO executive board member, on roll-call votes, has votes in proportion to the membership of his international, and no officer may vote except the president, who votes only in case of a tie. Consequently, the CIO executive board may be controlled more easily by a few large unions; by the same token, actions of the AFL council are more likely to be determined by the representatives of a small percentage of the total membership.

Since the CIO vice-presidents generally hold the presidency or another important office in one of the internationals, the day-to-day administration of the CIO, like that of the AFL, is largely in the hands of its president and its secretary-treasurer. They are assisted by a staff of labor union officials.

The CIO obtains its revenue primarily from a monthly per capita tax of 10 cents a member payable by each international and organizing committee and $1 a month payable by each local industrial union. It also receives half the local industrial union's initiation fees, a $25 affiliation fee from each affiliate, and $25 annually from each industrial union council.

The CIO's organizing committees, as the name implies, have been the means for developing many of its internationals. Some affiliates have come to the CIO as complete organizations already set up; others have been formed by grouping directly affiliated local unions; but some of the largest internationals — the United Steelworkers of America and the Textile Workers Union, for example — grew out of organizing committees set up and financed by the CIO and its affiliates to organize the big mass-production industries. In 1951 the CIO had two organizing committees — the Government and Civic Employees' and the Insurance and Allied Workers' Organizing Committees. These committees, like the AFL's national councils, have semiautonomous status. Unlike the AFL coun-

49. For a brief sketch of these unions see Appendix Note 4.

50. Expulsions during 1949 and 1950 cut its membership by an unknown amount below the 6 million claimed in 1948.

51. In 1950, for example, it had 44 members.

cils, however, they have the same convention and executive board representation as full-fledged internationals.

Paralleling the AFL's state federations and city centrals are the CIO's state and city industrial union councils. The CIO internationals also coordinate the activities of their own locals through district councils and joint boards. In its directly affiliated local industrial unions, the CIO accommodates workers in industries and areas not covered by one of its internationals or organizing committees. These units are directly comparable to the AFL's federal labor unions, which, in contrast to directly affiliated local trade unions, are organized along industrial lines.

The Internationals

The CIO's affiliates are as varied as the AFL's. Some of its internationals antedate the CIO by many years: the International Union of United Brewery, Flour, Cereal, Soft Drink and Distillery Workers of America traces its origins back to 1881, the Amalgamated Lithographers of America back to 1882. The American Radio Association, on the other hand, was organized in 1948. The United Steelworkers of America has almost a million members, the American Radio Association only 1,600. The CIO comprises single-craft unions (the National Marine Engineers' Beneficial Association), multicraft unions (the Barbers and Beauty Culturists Union of America), industrial unions (the United Steelworkers of America) and multi-industry unions (the International Union of Electrical, Radio and Machine Workers). However, the CIO's main unions tend to cluster, even more than those of the AFL, around a common type, as is indicated by the structure of the six largest unions, which account for about three fourths of the CIO's total membership.[52]

INDEPENDENT UNIONS

About 2 million workers belong to the 71 internationals not affiliated with either of the two federations. Included among these independents are the "Big Four" railroad brotherhoods, the International Association of Machinists, the United Mine Workers of America, and unions in many other miscellaneous occupations and industries.[53]

Several groups of independent unions have formed loose confederations. The largest of these is probably the Confederated Unions of America, which describes itself as a national federation of independent unions and claims 70 affiliates with more than 100,000 members.[54]

52. See Appendix Note 4.
53. See Appendix Note 4.
54. *Directory of Labor Unions in the United States, 1950,* p. 1.

CHAPTER 19

COLLECTIVE BARGAINING *

COLLECTIVE BARGAINING has sunk its roots deep into the American economy; it is now "a firmly established institution of industrial relations in the United States." [1] About 100,000 separate contracts,[2] most of which are renegotiated every year, now determine the wages and other conditions of employment of some 15 million workers in the United States.[3] Moreover, they indirectly affect the wage patterns and general working conditions of many million other workers and thus have a pervasive impact on the nation's economy.

In 1946, collective bargaining determined the wages and working conditions of almost half the workers considered eligible for union-agreement coverage; [4] agreements covered 69 per cent of all manufacturing production workers.[5] In many industries — in the manufacture of agricultural equipment, in breweries, in leather tanning, in rubber and sugar production, among airline pilots and coal miners, actors and railroadmen — between 80 and 100 per cent of the wage earners worked under union agreements. In some of the nation's basic industries wages and working conditions were almost completely determined by collective bargaining. These industries included automobiles and parts, shipbuilding, steel, coal and metal mining, construction, railroading and trucking. The Bureau of Labor Statistics found no manufacturing industry in which less than 20 per cent of the employees were covered by union agreements. (See Appendix Table 55.)

THE BARGAINING UNIT

Individual bargaining necessarily takes place between an employee and his employer. Under collective bargaining, however, there are several possible combinations: between one union and one employer, between a group of unions and an employer, between one union and a group of employers, between a group of unions and a group of employers, and so on. These bargaining groups generally are organized along industrial or occupational lines and may cover part or all of the industry or occupation in a city or region or over the entire nation.

The size of the bargaining unit has an important effect on the structure of wages, working conditions and industrial relations. Small bargaining units are certain to mean more diversity in contract provisions than big units; standardization of wages and working conditions in an area or an industry generally has followed area-wide or industry-wide bargaining. Larger bargaining units increase the importance of avoiding breakdowns in industrial relations. An industrial dispute between a local union and one employer may have slight influence on the rest of the economy, but a dispute between the United Mine Workers and the bituminous coal industry can paralyze the nation's entire economy.

The size and the type of bargaining unit are determined by many factors — among them the character of the market for the industry's product or service, the relative strength of the unions and the employers, and the internal structure and degree of centralized control in the industry and the union.

Union Attitudes

As a rule, unions have pressed for larger units and management has preferred smaller

* By Thomas C. Fichandler.

1. *Brief History of the American Labor Movement,* Bureau of Labor Statistics, October 1947, p. 13.

2. "Size of Labor Unions in the United States," *Monthly Labor Review,* July 1950, p. 113.

3. This estimate excludes union members in unorganized plants and many in government employment, where written collective agreements are not common; it includes nonmembers in bargaining units covered by written agreements.

4. ". . . 48 per cent of the 31 million [workers] engaged in occupations in which the unions have been organizing and endeavouring to obtain written agreements. . . . This estimate of 31 million includes all wage and salary workers except those in executive, managerial, and some professional positions, but excludes all self-employed, domestic workers, agricultural wage workers on farms employing less than six persons, Federal and State Government employees, teachers, and elected or appointed officials in local governments." *Extent of Collective Bargaining and Union Recognition, 1946,* Bulletin No. 909, Bureau of Labor Statistics, 1947, p. 1.

5. *Ibid.*

TABLE 71

UNIONS PREFER MULTI-EMPLOYER CONTRACTS

Question: Sometimes collective bargaining agreements cover a single plant or employer, employers in a limited area, or a large part of an entire industry. If you had your choice, which type of coverage would you choose for your union's agreements?

Response	Number of Unions	Union Members: Number, in Thousands	Union Members: Percentage of Total
Number of respondents..	49	11,251	100.0
Coverage desired:			
Single plant	4	374	3.3
Single employer	9	1,023	9.1
Group of employers...	27	7,242	64.3
Reason:			
Elimination of wage competition ...	9	2,711	24.1
Simplicity	4	1,215	10.8
Other	14	3,316	29.4
No preference	9	2,612	23.2

Source: W. S. Woytinsky and Associates, *Labor and Management Look at Collective Bargaining,* Twentieth Century Fund, New York, 1949, p. 3.

ones. Of the union leaders questioned during the Twentieth Century Fund's survey [6] more than half (27 out of 49) preferred to bargain with groups of employers. (See Table 71.) These leaders saw in large bargaining units an opportunity to reduce competitive pressure on wages and to strengthen their own bargaining position. Some favored multi-employer agreements for the sake of simplicity, and others saw them as a way to avoid penalizing friendly employers.[7]

One union leader questioned during the survey remarked that industry-wide bargaining was "necessary because of the competitive situation. If you stabilize the wage bill in the industry as a whole," he said, "you remove the incentive for operators to reduce wages for competitive purposes . . ." Another said that his union definitely preferred to deal with groups of employers, because "you establish uniformity of standards in the area. You eliminate disparities of standards between firms. You even eliminate causing a disadvantage to a firm which may be willing to deal with a union."

Management Attitudes

In contrast to the attitude of union leaders, most of the business executives interviewed preferred negotiations covering only their own companies. More than half the management representatives questioned (45 out of 87) favored such a procedure because it gives them greater freedom of action and more flexibility. (See Table 72.) A typical reply was: "By negotiating alone we're able to consider factors that apply to us as an individual company."

Both employers and union leaders, however, differed among themselves on this point. Some unions preferred the tactical advantage to be gained from "whipsawing" employers. One of the 13 union officials favoring single-plant or single-employer bargaining took the extreme position that "We think this is guerrilla war. Advance where you can, retreat where you must — but don't allow them to get you lined up on one long front. We want to keep employers apart." Similarly, for tactical reasons, some employers preferred to present a united front to the unions. One management representative, speaking of negotiating through an association, argued that such an approach "would make it impossible for unions to whipsaw one employer against another . . . The present plan of action by the union is, of course, to go after the [firm] with the weakest case, get a whopping big settlement, and then try to use that as a pattern . . ."

Employers who have substantial labor costs and who are in highly competitive markets frequently are ready to forgo some of their individual freedom for the advantages of market-wide bargaining and wage standardization. One manager remarked, "If we ever tried to negotiate individually it would be murder. And we'd ruin ourselves and everyone else in the industry. Thank God we have an association." Another felt that "Industry-wide bargaining is the best for our industry. And I believe it's best and fairest for most industries, provided all groups are properly represented. It's the only way the little fellow can have an equal chance with the big fellow. The big manufacturer could afford to give concessions that would cut the little man's throat."

INDIVIDUAL EMPLOYER

Despite the trend toward wider collective bargaining units, and despite union preference for widening the coverage of collective bargaining, negotiations between a single company and its employees' local union are more frequent than any other type. Nearly 11 of the 15 mil-

6. W. S. Woytinsky and Associates, *Labor and Management Look at Collective Bargaining,* Twentieth Century Fund, New York, 1949.

7. These respondents might well be classified with those aiming to eliminate wage competition, since they could avoid penalizing friendly employers only by standardizing wage rates.

TABLE 72

SINGLE-COMPANY BARGAINING MORE POPULAR WITH BUSINESSMEN THAN GROUP NEGOTIATION

Questions: How does your company negotiate wage contracts — by itself alone, or jointly with some or all of the firms in your industry? *Which way is best?*

Response	Total	Manufacturing Companies	Nonmanufacturing Companies
Number of respondents	87	47	40
Preferred method of bargaining:			
By a single company	45	32	13
Through local employers' association or committee	24	8	16
Industry-wide	9	3	6
Depends on circumstances	7	2	5
No preference	2	2	—

Source: W. S. Woytinsky and Associates, *Labor and Management Look at Collective Bargaining,* Twentieth Century Fund, New York, 1949, p. 13.

lion workers covered by collective agreements were in single-employer bargaining units early in 1947.[8]

Where there is only one union among a company's employees (or where one of several has been certified by a government body as the employees' bargaining agent), negotiations and the collective agreement are between the employer and the local union. A local union frequently includes employees of more than one company; in such a case it will sign the agreement on behalf of its members in the particular company. Where employees are organized in separate craft unions, an employer may deal either separately with each craft, signing separate agreements, or jointly with all the craft unions, signing either a joint agreement or separate agreements.

In companies with more than one plant, workers in each plant may be represented by separate locals of the same union or by different unions.

In the first case, officers of the international union or a department of the international may negotiate for all the locals, but some unions insist on plant-by-plant negotiations because, as one union spokesman put it, "the top guys . . . are too far removed from the plant level to be able to give wise decisions." Some managers, also, prefer single-plant negotiations, since, in the words of one representative, "it gets down to the grass roots of human justice to both employer and employee."

Even when negotiations are company-wide, many questions are usually left for final settlement between the plant management and the local union. The company-wide discussions may define the union's status, the general wage adjustment, grievance and arbitration procedures, and leave to local negotiations such questions as individual wage rates, vacations and seniority rules. Consequently, separate plant-by-plant bargaining may actually result in no greater disparities than company-wide negotiations, particularly since the same basic policies of the company and the international union color all the negotiations.

When a multi-plant company bargains with a different union for each of its plants, there is little chance of joint negotiations. If the firm comprises more than one industry, there will probably be more differences than similarities among the plants, and joint negotiations would be of little value. If the separate plants are engaged in the same line of work, the different unions probably are competing and would prefer not to enter joint negotiations.

GROUPS OF EMPLOYERS

Early in 1947 more than 4 million workers, about equally divided between manufacturing and nonmanufacturing industries, were covered by agreements with groups of employers.[9] The proportion of workers covered by multi-employer agreements varied considerably from industry to industry, reaching 80 per cent or more in clothing manufacturing, coal mining, the laundry and cleaning and dyeing industry, among longshoremen, in the maritime trades, and in shipbuilding and boatbuilding. (See Appendix Table 56.)

Multi-employer bargaining units include employers in the same or very closely related industries in local areas, in broader regional areas, and in nation-wide or nearly nation-wide groups. Local bargaining groups are much the most common type, and many union leaders who prefer wider bargaining areas are not yet sure they are feasible. (See Appendix Table 57.)

Local-Area Basis

Local-area bargaining groups are most prevalent in industries characterized by many small establishments. Some of these industries serve a national market, but most have predominantly

8. *Collective Bargaining with Associations and Groups of Employers,* Bulletin No. 897, Bureau of Labor Statistics, 1947, p. 2.

9. *Ibid.*

local markets. City-wide bargaining is common in the needle trades, which serve a national market, and in baking, brewing, building construction, cleaning and dyeing, printing and publishing, restaurants, trucking and similar industries. Employers in this type of bargaining generally are represented by an association. A recent estimate puts the total number of local or city employer associations dealing with unions at about five thousand.[10]

Union-association bargaining may result in a single collective agreement binding on all association members or an agreement binding only on the members who ratify it. In other cases, the union and the association may merely work out a master agreement and each employer may sign a separate contract with the union. The employer associations may be formal organizations with regular officers to whom the unions can look for enforcement of the contract provisions. Or informal associations may be set up solely for the bargaining period. In these cases, the employers generally select some of their number to bargain for all, and enforcement of the contract terms is left largely to the union.

Local-area bargaining is also carried on by groups of employers and groups of craft unions. Local building trades councils negotiate agreements with employers' associations covering general industrial relations for all crafts.[11] The craft unions in book and job printing have cooperated in collective bargaining through their local councils, whose major function is to control the allied printing trades label.[12]

Regional Basis

Regional bargaining follows much the same pattern as local-group bargaining but is much less frequent. It is prevalent on the west coast. An outstanding example is the bargaining relationship that has existed since 1934 between the Pacific Coast Association of Pulp and Paper Manufacturers and two AFL unions. Eighteen individual companies with thirty-two mills deal through the association with the International Brotherhood of Pulp, Sulphite and Paper Mill Workers and the International Brotherhood of Paper Makers. Representatives of management and labor from all these mills meet annually to negotiate over "almost every conceivable phase of employer-employee relations." [13] Similarly, most of the west coast shipbuilding and boatbuilding industry is covered by a master agreement with the AFL Metal Trades Department; the Pacific Coast fishing industry deals with unions through several employer associations; collective bargaining in canning and preserving on the west coast is largely on an association basis.

Bargaining on a regional basis is also practiced by the maritime workers, who usually bargain with employer associations representing shipping operators on a given coast; the International Brotherhood of Teamsters, which deals with employer associations covering interstate trucking; and the Federation of Hosiery Workers, which bargains with the northern section of the industry through the Full-Fashioned Hosiery Manufacturers Association.

Industry-Wide Basis

Industry-wide bargaining, although much discussed, was limited until recently largely to the pottery, glass, wallpaper, elevator-manufacturing and men's clothing industries. The bargaining procedure in anthracite mining frequently is cited as an outstanding example of formal, complete industry-wide bargaining. Technically this is true, but the entire industry is concentrated in one rather small area, so it is certainly a special case of industry-wide bargaining. The United Mine Workers, however, recently did bring industry-wide bargaining to the important bituminous-coal-mining industry, which, like most other industries, is spread over many sections of the country. In 1945 the mine operators and the union signed the National Bituminous Coal Wage Agreement, which covered all of the industry organized by the United Mine Workers. Subsequent negotiations have been carried on nationally and have culminated in the signing of a single agreement. The railroad industry also recently moved to industry-wide bargaining, at least on major issues.

Not only the railroads but also the many railroad unions have joined together for bargain-

10. *Ibid.*, p. 13.
11. William Haber, "Building Construction," Chapter 4 in Harry A. Millis, *How Collective Bargaining Works,* Twentieth Century Fund, New York, 1942, pp. 207–08.
12. Emily Clark Brown, "Book and Job Printing," Chapter 3 in *ibid.*, pp. 139–40.

13. Clark Kerr and Roger Randall, *Crown Zellerbach and the Pacific Coast Pulp and Paper Industry,* Case Study No. 1, Committee on the Causes of Industrial Peace, National Planning Association, Washington, September 1948, p. 4.

ing purposes. During the fall of 1948, for example, the unions negotiated in two groups; one group included sixteen "nonoperating" unions[14] and the other the five "operating" unions. The operating group met with the carriers at the same time but split into two subgroups — the Brotherhood of Locomotive Engineers, the Brotherhood of Locomotive Firemen and Enginemen, and the Switchmen's Union of North America meeting with one committee that represented all the carriers, and the Order of Railway Conductors and the Brotherhood of Railroad Trainmen negotiating with another committee of carriers. Though negotiations have been on a national scale, the railroad unions have continued to sign separate agreements with each company or system; each operating union generally has signed a separate agreement with each system and the nonoperating unions joint agreements with each system. The railroad unions, although bargaining jointly with all companies, insist on separate agreements with each company, apparently out of a desire to continue a well-established tradition.

Considerable difference of opinion exists among unions on the question of industry-wide bargaining. In the Fund survey the 39 union leaders who had a definite opinion on the subject split 19 in favor and 20 opposed to industry-wide bargaining. (See Table 73.) Elimination of wage competition was the most common reason advanced in its favor, and differences in local conditions dominated the adverse arguments.

Unifying Influences

Nation-wide bargaining is limited at present to a relatively few industries. Results similar to those derived from nation-wide bargaining, however, are obtained in industries that formally adhere to the individual-employer unit, through the unifying influence of the union's national offices and through the leadership that major companies exercise in their industry. The degree of national-office control over local collective bargaining varies quite a bit from union to union. Considerably more national control exists, for example, in the newer CIO unions, which, in a sense, were organized from the top down, than in the older AFL national unions, which grew out of the amalgamation of established local unions. Also, more central control is exercised in unions such as the United Steelworkers of America, where the industry markets its product nationally.[15]

National-office participation in local bargaining necessarily brings the separate agreements closer to an industry pattern. The national officials, whose policies generally represent a compromise between different sections of the union, modify extreme local requests and help to bring the newer, weaker locals up to the level of the others.

Management representatives interviewed in the course of the labor-management survey ex-

TABLE 73

UNIONS EVENLY DIVIDED FOR AND AGAINST INDUSTRY-WIDE BARGAINING

Question: How about contracts covering a whole industry?

Response	Number of Unions	Union Members: Number, in Thousands	Union Members: Percentage of Total
Number of respondents	45	10,292	100.0
Position on industry-wide bargaining:			
Favor	19	4,828	46.9
Reason:			
Elimination of wage competition	5	1,285	12.5
Other	14	3,543	34.4
Oppose	20	4,124	40.1
Reason:			
Differences in local conditions	13	2,388	23.2
Other	7	1,736	16.9
No preference	6	1,340	13.0

Source: W. S. Woytinsky and Associates, *Labor and Management Look at Collective Bargaining,* Twentieth Century Fund, New York, 1949, p. 5.

14. Besides unions composed almost wholly of railroad workers, like the Brotherhood of Maintenance of Way Employees and the Brotherhood of Railway Carmen, these included the International Association of Machinists, the International Brotherhood of Boilermakers, Iron Shipbuilders and Helpers of America, and other unions with a relatively small part of their membership working on the railroads.

15. "Although the United Steelworkers negotiate on a company-wide basis, *the general* policy to be pursued in the separate company-wide negotiations is decided upon at the regular union convention, or at a special wage parley in which the various geographical units of the organization are adequately represented. . . . In the case of the United Automobile Workers (CIO), on the other hand, who also negotiate on a company-wide basis, the demands are formulated at separate conferences of workers from each of the separate companies. It must be noted, however, that the policies of these separate conferences are almost identical in most instances. This becomes particularly evident when one realizes that a 'wage leadership' policy prevails in the industry." Joseph Shister, "The Locus of Union Control in Collective Bargaining," *Quarterly Journal of Economics,* August 1946, p. 531.

pressed a strong preference for dealing with local, rather than national, union leaders. Despite the view held by a number of students of management-labor relations that national representatives are in a better position to accept reasonable compromises than local officers,[16] 52 of the 88 management representatives said they preferred to bargain with local-union officers. (See Table 74.) Only 20 favored dealing with national representatives, 7 said it depended on the pattern of organization, and 9 had no preference.

The following statements in support of bargaining with local officers are typical:

> By all means [I prefer] the local officers. They are familiar with the problems and are much better able to represent the workers and also know the company's problems and are responsible for them. There has been a great difference when the international officers came into the picture. We are much more likely to settle with local men. The international officers use a standard formula which does not apply in our case.

> We prefer the local officers — no question about that. The international officers cannot know the problems as well; their personnel is not big enough and their interests are too scattered. On the occasions when they do come in, they can't contribute much.

Leadership Principle

The principle of leadership by the largest producer in an industry has long been recognized in collective bargaining. Students of industrial relations have classified labor-management relations into three major types: generating, satellite and semi-isolated.[17]

The relations between General Motors and the United Auto Workers and between United States Steel and the United Steelworkers of America are cited as examples of the generating type. The relations between the Studebaker Corporation and Local 5 of the Auto Workers and between the Jones and Laughlin Steel Corporation and the United Steelworkers are given as examples of the satellite type. The generating type of negotiations provides a settlement pattern, particularly on wages, whose impact is

TABLE 74

MOST EXECUTIVES PREFER TO BARGAIN WITH LOCAL-UNION OFFICERS

Question: In cases where you could choose, would you prefer to bargain with the local-union officers in each plant or area, or would you rather negotiate with national-union officers?

Response	Total	Manufacturing Companies	Nonmanufacturing Companies
Number of respondents	88	47	41
Bargaining representative preferred:			
Local officers	52	24	28
National officers	20	12	8
Local and national officers for different types of agreement	7	4	3
No preference	9	7	2

Source: W. S. Woytinsky and Associates, *Labor and Management Look at Collective Bargaining,* Twentieth Century Fund, New York, 1949, p. 27.

felt throughout the industry. The stimulus that flows through management channels is reinforced by the union national office, which normally participates in negotiations at the "lead center" in cases of so-called "wage leadership," and subsequently influences local negotiations.

THE PROCESS

The process of collective bargaining, in a narrow sense, may be considered to start when unions and management convene for discussions and to conclude when the discussions end in a signed agreement or an industrial dispute. The more inclusive concept used in this study views collective bargaining as a more or less continuous activity beginning well in advance of negotiations and running through the stages of preventing industrial disputes — conciliation and arbitration — to the grievance procedures established for administration of agreements.[18]

NEGOTIATIONS

Unions can do three things in preparing for negotiations: (1) find out what the members want; (2) unify the membership behind a single set of demands; (3) try to win the public's support and sympathy.

Finding out what the members want may be done through special meetings or conferences, at regular conventions or even by circulating questionnaires. Conferences at which demands

16. ". . . local officers are usually less willing and able to exercise discretion than are national representatives." Sumner H. Slichter, *The Challange of Industrial Relations,* Cornell University Press, Ithaca, 1947, p. 133.

17. Frederick H. Harbison, Robert K. Burns and Robert Dubin, "Toward a Theory of Labor-Management Relations," in Richard A. Lester and Joseph Shister (Eds.), *Insights into Labor Issues,* Macmillan, New York, 1948.

18. Neil W. Chamberlain, "Grievance Proceedings and Collective Bargaining," in *ibid.*

are formulated, especially if they are large conferences, serve also to unify the membership behind the demands. The participants get a proprietary feeling toward the program they have helped to hammer out. Also, the discussions are an important phase of the educational campaign, which usually aims at convincing the members of the justness and reasonableness of the union's proposals. This theme is usually developed further in the union's regular publications and in special pamphlets and leaflets.

Of more recent vintage are unions' ventures into public relations. It is now commonplace for unions to use newspaper advertisements and radio programs and to disseminate research reports in an effort to educate the public about negotiations and to win its sympathy.

Management reaches its employees through regular "house organs" or special reports and appeals to the general public through newspaper and magazine advertisements. These publicity activities are carried on both by individual companies and, on a continuing basis, by employer associations like the United States Chamber of Commerce and the National Association of Manufacturers.

The journalistic appeal for public favor, which continues right through the negotiating stage, is made for the most part when collective bargaining is on a nation-wide scale or involves large industrial concerns. Most negotiations, however, are conducted with little fanfare and do not come to public notice. It is difficult to say which approach is more conducive to peaceful labor-management relations. Public statements on widely different positions may make it difficult for the two parties to compromise without loss of prestige. On the other hand, the appeal for public support, though weighted with emotional arguments, introduces facts, figures and even reason into a situation that might otherwise be decided solely by strength.

General Procedure

Negotiating procedure is relatively simple. The exact form depends on the level at which negotiations take place. Negotiations between a local union and a small company are usually carried on by the union committee and the employer, who may be assisted by his lawyer. The union committee, often a specially selected group, almost always includes the local officers. Sometimes the local president appoints the negotiating committee. If the local has a business agent, he is always included, and he generally plays an important part in the negotiations. When several locals of the same union are involved, the officers of the joint board or district council negotiate.

An international representative may advise the local negotiators and may participate in the bargaining, especially with larger employers. In the generating type of collective bargaining the national officers may conduct the negotiations. If the employer is a member of an association, its representatives may advise him or carry on the negotiations for him.

In negotiations between a local union and a single plant of a large corporation, the union's bargaining approach is the same as when it deals with a small company. On the management side, however, negotiations may be handled entirely by the plant manager, who may have the assistance of the company's industrial relations director, or his decisions may be subject to central-office approval. Occasionally the corporation's central office will handle all negotiations with the union.

In regional bargaining, if the membership of a national union is concentrated in one region, the national officers handle negotiations. Otherwise, a national-union representative usually has major responsibility. In both cases, the locals involved usually participate through their officers in formulating the demands to be presented to management and in ratifying the collective agreement. In regional bargaining, employers negotiate through their association, delegating the actual bargaining to the association's officers or a specially appointed committee of employers.

Industry-wide bargaining is carried on much as is regional bargaining, except that the national office of the union always takes a leading role in the negotiations. In both regional and national bargaining, negotiating committees representing different sections of the union decide on the exact form of the demands to be presented. These committees, because of their unwieldy size, generally select subcommittees to meet with management representatives. The subcommittees, in practice, make the final bargaining decisions.

Despite the hierarchic structure of union bargaining, the membership retains considerable control. In bargaining by the local union, the negotiating committee is constantly under the

TABLE 75

UNION WAGE AIMS IN 1947–1948 BASED CHIEFLY ON COST-OF-LIVING CHANGES

Question: In the last year or two your union undoubtedly had to decide what to do about wages. What factors did you or your locals consider in deciding how much of a wage adjustment to seek?

Response	All Factors			Most Important Factors		
		Union Members			Union Members	
	Number of Unions	Number, in Thousands	Per Cent	Number of Unions	Number, in Thousands	Per Cent
Number of respondents	52	11,523	100.0	52	11,523	100.0
Factors considered in setting wage goals:						
Cost-of-living changes	50	11,408	99.0	43	9,704	84.2
Comparison with other localities	34	8,112	70.4	1	200	1.7
Comparison with other occupations or industries	29	6,056	52.6	4	560	4.9
Comparison with other unions	26	5,061	43.9	—	—	—
Profits	25	5,253	45.6	3	1,137	9.9
Productivity	18	4,367	37.9	5	2,340	20.3
Standard of living	14	1,919	16.7	13	1,847	16.0
Other	3	950	8.2	2	640	5.6

Source: W. S. Woytinsky and Associates, *Labor and Management Look at Collective Bargaining,* Twentieth Century Fund, New York, 1949, p. 73.

eye of the members. It frequently must report back on the course of developments, and almost always the agreement it signs must be ratified by the membership. As bargaining moves out to broader units and up through the union structure, the membership has less and less direct control, although in some unions (the National Maritime Union, for example) even agreements covering large sections of the industry must be approved by a membership vote. Even where direct rank-and-file control is absent, the membership generally retains ultimate control.[19]

The formal procedures of negotiation are, of course, surrounded by many less obvious techniques. The "smoke-filled" room is not unknown in collective bargaining. Informal discussions at which union and management representatives "feel out" one another are common. Such discussions need not lead to a formal agreement, but they may provide both sides with sufficient information to enable them later to reach an acceptable formal compromise.

Recent Wage Bargaining

Although collective bargaining today covers many matters, its primary emphasis is still on wage rates. How unions decide what wage adjustment to seek and how management determines its counteroffer are of basic importance to the entire bargaining process.

In the Fund's labor-management survey, national union leaders were asked: "In the last year or two your union undoubtedly had to decide what to do about wages. What factors did you or your locals consider in deciding how much of a wage adjustment to seek?" In view of the trend of prices after the end of the war, it is not surprising that 43 out of 52 respondents mentioned cost-of-living changes among the most important factors considered in setting their wage goals; all but two said such changes played some part in determining their goals. (See Table 75.)

The replies indicated, however, that in periods of relative price stability the dominant considerations are wage rates for similar jobs in other localities, wage rates for workers in related occupations and industries, gains of other unions, and profits. Even at the time of the survey, when prices were rising, about half the union leaders questioned considered one or more of these factors.

One respondent put it this way:

> There are many factors. Old man High Cost of Living is very largely the determining factor, but wages in comparable industries and occupations also are significant . . . We try also to take profits into consideration. Very frequently the company shows us its books. There's no profit in our bankrupting an employer if he's trying to run a sound business.

Thirteen union leaders emphasized the need for a continuing standard-of-living approach. As one stated it,

> The need for guaranteeing every worker an adequate standard of living is the main, overriding factor. Other subsidiary factors are the cost of living, productivity, profits.

19. Shister, "The Locus of Union Control in Collective Bargaining," p. 545.

TABLE 76

LIVING COSTS, INDUSTRY AND AREA RATES ARE MAJOR FACTORS IN MANAGEMENT'S WAGE PROPOSALS IN 1947–1948

Question: In your last negotiation, when you made definite wage offers how did you arrive at your proposal — what factors did you consider?

Response	Total	Manufacturing Companies	Nonmanufacturing Companies
Number of respondents	88	47	41
Factor considered in developing proposal:			
Changes in cost of living	80	44	36
Wages, etc., of other firms in the industry	40	21	19
Wages, etc., of other firms in the area	39	23	16
Increases won by certain big unions	28	16	12
Earnings position of the company	25	11	14
Effect on price of product	20	12	8
Strength of union or a strike threat	12	4	8
Changes in productivity	6	4	2

Source: W. S. Woytinsky and Associates, *Labor and Management Look at Collective Bargaining,* Twentieth Century Fund, New York, 1949, p. 84.

Management made even more use than the unions of cost-of-living changes during wage negotiations immediately before the survey. Eighty of the 88 management representatives listed changes in the cost of living among the main factors considered by the company in determining its wage offer to the union. (See Table 76.) Next in importance in their minds were wages and related factors in other firms in the industry (40 respondents) or in the area (39 respondents). Twenty-eight said their offers were influenced by increases won by certain big unions, and 25 referred to the company's earnings position.

Automatic Tie to Cost of Living

For different reasons, both union leaders and management representatives rejected an automatic tie between wages and changes in the cost of living. Of 51 union leaders asked, only 4 favored such an automatic relationship and 2 had no opinion. (See Table 77.) The remaining 45 opposed it, largely on the ground that workers needed more than a cost-of-living adjustment if they were to advance their standard of living.

"I don't like it," said one labor leader. "When you predicate a wage increase on the cost of living, it presumes the prior wage was equitable." Another argued that "It means freezing at a certain level. Where would we have been if we had done that years ago? Our earnings are still below par."

TABLE 77

UNIONS OPPOSE LINKING WAGE RATES TO COST OF LIVING IN 1948

Question: It has been suggested that when the cost of living rises, wage increases of the same amount should follow automatically. What do you think of that?

Response	Number of Unions	Union Members: Number, in Thousands	Union Members: Percentage of Total
Number of respondents	51	11,383	100.0
Attitude toward automatic increase:			
Favor [a]	4	663	5.8
Oppose	45	10,118	88.9
Reason:			
Increase insufficient	21	3,949	34.7
Argument may be turned against workers	7	1,673	14.7
Increase insufficient and argument may be turned against workers	6	1,722	15.1
Other and no reason given	11	2,774	24.4
No opinion	2	602	5.3

a. Two of these four unions, with 206,000 members, would oppose wage decreases based on a decline in the cost of living; both consider that to be the time to correct the relationship between wages, prices and profits.

Source: W. S. Woytinsky and Associates, *Labor and Management Look at Collective Bargaining,* Twentieth Century Fund, New York, 1949, p. 105.

Sixty-nine management representatives turned thumbs down on the idea, while 12 favored it and 6 were uncertain. (See Table 78.) Several management representatives used the favorite

TABLE 78

MANAGEMENT OPPOSES LINKING WAGE RATE TO COST OF LIVING IN 1948

Question: What do you think of automatic wage adjustments tied to cost of living?

Response	Total	Manufacturing Companies	Nonmanufacturing Companies
Number of respondents	87	47	40
Attitude toward automatic adjustment to cost of living:			
Favor	12	5	7
Oppose	69	41	28
Uncertain	6	1	5

Source: W. S. Woytinsky and Associates, *Labor and Management Look at Collective Bargaining,* Twentieth Century Fund, New York, 1949, p. 111.

union argument for opposing the scheme: that it makes no allowance for increasing living standards. Most often, however, they argued either that such a device would strengthen the inflationary spiral or that it could not work because the unions would never accept downward wage adjustments when the cost-of-living index dropped. Typical comments were:

> I don't see how you can ever stop the spiral of inflation when the cost of living goes up. I'm much opposed to any escalator arrangement. It's like a dog chasing its tail.

> Theoretically, it sounds very good, but the unions generally are not responsive unless they have annual improvement given them. Also, there is a serious doubt that the unions would abide by an arrangement calling for a reduction in rates.

Underlying management's opposition to such an automatic plan was the fear of being tied to any long-run, inflexible arrangement. The management representatives preferred to let the so-called market factors have greater play. The Fund's survey indicated that both management and unions preferred to leave the wage question open to collective bargaining at frequent intervals and to avoid rigid formulas. "Wage problems can be handled better by explaining the situation to the union and negotiating," remarked a severe critic of the General Motors plan.

Determining Living Costs

Although unions and management were in apparent agreement on the factors to be considered, they differed widely on how to use these factors. It is hardly likely that the union found a ready basis of agreement with the company whose representative expressed the following extreme position: "We certainly considered cost-of-living changes — in a negative way. We didn't want to increase wage rates, since a raise of wages would increase the cost of living unduly."

But even when management was ready to use cost-of-living changes in the same way as the union, to measure needed adjustments in wages, they came out with different answers. The discrepancy generally arose because management insisted on comparing wages and cost-of-living changes since 1941, whereas the unions insisted on comparing changes since 1945. Similarly, both unions and management generally agreed that company profits had to be considered. How profits are to be measured and what constitutes a "reasonable" rate of profit are, however, questions on which agreement is not readily reached.

The widespread agreement on factors to be considered and the willingness of both sides to present their arguments in relation to these factors have meant avoidance of direct, head-on clashes in wage bargaining. The clash of interests is softened also by the cushion of formalized machinery that is being built up around negotiations. Such machinery is necessary to permit both sides to air their views and present their economic arguments, their formulas and statistics. Agreement that such factors are relevant, moreover, gives the conciliator more material with which to work and gives greater appeal to arbitration as a method for resolving differences between the two parties.

PREVENTION OF WORK STOPPAGES

Most collective bargaining negotiations reach the agreement stage with little public notice. Some, after threatening to break down, move on to a peaceful conclusion. Occasionally, skilled conciliation [20] is all that prevents negotiations from degenerating into work stoppages.

Conciliation

In providing conciliation services, government — local, state and federal — tries to prevent stoppages of production and the resultant losses to workers, employers and the general public.

Conciliation is essentially a voluntary [21] affair, the purpose of which is to help the negotiators reach an agreement. It is not a substitute for collective bargaining but an integral part of it and has two objectives: to maximize successful collective bargaining and to maintain the maximum industrial peace.[22]

Conciliation may be requested by either or both parties involved in collective bargaining,

20. "Conciliation" is used here to include mediation. The two terms are sometimes used to indicate a difference in the part played by the third party; i.e., conciliation is limited to the bringing together of the parties, and mediation includes guiding the bargaining process along certain lines.

21. Under the Taft-Hartley Act, the Federal Mediation and Conciliation Service may force the parties to continue negotiations, but it cannot force them to reach an agreement.

22. W. Ellison Chalmers, "The Conciliation Process," *Industrial and Labor Relations Review,* April 1948, p. 341.

or in certain cases the government may intercede on its own initiative.[23] The conciliator's job is to help the parties break the impasse in their negotiations: to help them "clarify their own objectives, to re-evaluate them in the light of the facts, to understand the objectives and problems of the other, and to reach a situation in which they can realistically make their own choice of alternatives." [24]

The success of conciliation depends on the confidence of the parties in the conciliator and on the willingness of the two parties to reach agreement. Figures of the Federal Mediation and Conciliation Service show that these basic attitudes are present in a surprisingly high percentage of cases and that conciliation is a highly successful tool in collective bargaining. In the fiscal year 1948–1949, for instance, the Conciliation Service was involved in some fifteen thousand disagreements between union and management and succeeded in getting the disputants to agree in almost 90 per cent of the cases.[25] An additional 2.5 per cent of the cases were terminated by mutual consent, and 3 per cent involved the jurisdiction of the National Labor Relations Board or were referred to an impartial arbitrator. In only 5 per cent of the cases did the Service withdraw without making progress toward a peaceful settlement.

Federal Conciliation Services

Expansion of collective bargaining into the fields of wage incentives, job evaluation, welfare and pension plans, and other issues of equal complexity, as well as general acceptance of collective bargaining, have increased the need for highly competent conciliation services. The federal government in 1950 had two independent agencies, the National Mediation Board and the Federal Mediation and Conciliation Service, to assist in the negotiation or renegotiation of collective agreements. The National Mediation Board was set up in 1934 under amendments to the Railway Labor Act to handle railroad disputes. The Federal Mediation and Conciliation Service was set up under the Labor-Management Relations Act in 1947 as the successor to the United States Conciliation Service, which was established in 1913 under the act creating the Department of Labor; it functions in interstate commerce, excluding the railroads.

Besides these federal agencies, there are many state conciliation services, some of which (Massachusetts and New York) date back to 1886.[26] In the Taft-Hartley Act Congress specifically admonished the Federal Conciliation Service to leave problems of primarily local concern to such state or local agencies.[27]

Arbitration during Contract Negotiations

If conciliation fails, the next step in preventing work stoppages is voluntary arbitration.[28] The use of arbitration to interpret existing agreements is fairly widespread. Its use in the negotiation of new agreements is more controversial.

The Fund's survey of collective bargaining indicates that unions are more disposed than management to use arbitration during negotiations. Three out of five of the union leaders questioned generally favored arbitration at such times, while one in five expressed general opposition. (See Table 79.) Moreover, 11 of the 50 union leaders questioned would be willing to submit any question to arbitration, and an additional 13 would withhold only questions concerning union recognition, security and internal government. Only 3 union officials said they would never arbitrate any issue, and only 4 would limit arbitration to minor issues.

Typical union comments concerning the conditions under which they would recommend arbitration during contract negotiations were:

A flat offer of arbitration of unsettled issues.

We always go to arbitration.

We are strictly for arbitration.

Arbitration is one of our main principles. We'll arbitrate anything except union security. If our demands are fair, we'll get a fair decision from an impartial arbitrator. We believe in arbitration.

On the other hand, management appears to think that the union can't lose in arbitration, that the arbitrator is bound to grant it some part of its demands as a consideration for stop-

23. Sections 203(b) and 204(a)(3) of the Labor-Management Relations Act, 1947 (Public Law 101, 80th Cong.).
24. Chalmers, *op. cit.*, p. 342.
25. Second Annual Report of the Federal Mediation and Conciliation Service, 1949, pp. 20–22.

26. See Florence Peterson, *Survey of Labor Economics*, Harper, New York, 1947, p. 571.
27. Section 203(b).
28. Cf. Chapter 22.

TABLE 79

UNION LEADERS TEND TO FAVOR ARBITRATION OF DISPUTES ARISING FROM CONTRACT NEGOTIATIONS

Questions: Let's assume that in negotiating to renew a contract you were unable to reach an agreement with management. Under what conditions, if any, would you recommend arbitration of the dispute? Are there any issues you would never wish to submit to arbitration?

Response	Number of Unions	Union Members: Number, in Thousands	Union Members: Per Cent
Number of respondents	50	11,073	100.0
Favor arbitration in general [a]	32	7,115	64.3
On all issues	11	1,623	14.7
On all issues except:			
Union recognition, security, internal government	13	3,107	28.1
Wages	3	965	8.7
Other	9	3,177	28.7
Oppose arbitration in general [b]	11	2,115	19.1
And would arbitrate only minor issues	4	1,570	14.2
And would never arbitrate any issue	3	211	1.9
No opinion	7	1,843	16.6

a. Because some persons excluded more than one issue, the sum of the items is greater than the total.
b. Because some persons did no more than express general opposition, the sum of the items is smaller than the total.

Source: W. S. Woytinsky and Associates, *Labor and Management Look at Collective Bargaining,* Twentieth Century Fund, New York, 1949, p. 54.

ping or forgoing a strike. The following is a typical management comment:

The union asks for a 10 cent increase. The company simply cannot pay any more than it is paying. But they argue and fuss around and the issue finally goes to arbitration and the decision comes down that the employer must pay 5 cents. As we see it, arbitration is simply an assurance that the union will win some wage increase.

Two thirds of the management representatives expressed general opposition to voluntary arbitration. (See Table 80.) Of the 87 respondents, 30 said they would never arbitrate any issue, 10 that they would be willing to submit only minor issues. One respondent summed up the general position of management when he said:

Arbitration has no place whatever in settling matters of wages, hours and other working conditions. These should always be settled through collective bargaining. The only time for arbitration is for the proper interpretation of a contract.

A typical minority management position was:

We've been living with it for many years and we think it is good. We use arbitration all the while and we think it is a fair way to settle disputes.

TABLE 80

MANAGEMENT MEN VOTE TWO TO ONE AGAINST ARBITRATION OF CONTRACT NEGOTIATIONS

Questions: Under what conditions do you favor voluntary arbitration through an umpire? Are there any specific issues you consider not appropriate for arbitration?

Response	Total	Manufacturing Companies	Non-manufacturing Companies
Number of respondents	87	47	40
Favor arbitration in general [a]	28	12	16
On all issues	12	3	9
On all issues except:			
Wages	5	5	—
Pensions, other welfare provisions	4	2	2
Other (relations with customers, production standards, working conditions, disciplinary discharges, etc.)	8	3	5
Oppose arbitration in general [a]	57	34	23
And would not arbitrate:			
Wages	13	8	5
Pensions, other welfare provisions	4	2	2
Other (relations with customers, production standards, working conditions, disciplinary discharges, etc.)	9	3	6
And would arbitrate only minor issues	10	5	5
And would never arbitrate any issue	30	21	9
No opinion	2	1	1

a. Because some persons excluded more than one issue, the sum of the items is greater than the total.

Source: W. S. Woytinsky and Associates, *Labor and Management Look at Collective Bargaining,* Twentieth Century Fund, New York, 1949, p. 62.

Management objected especially to arbitration of wage disputes, because of its fear that the arbitrator may impose excessive wage costs. One employer representative said:

I heard a man say that arbitration was the best-known legal way of letting someone spend your money for you. It's not their money, so what do they care?

Both the unions and the employers who objected to arbitration did so on the common ground that they can settle their disputes better than any outsider can. Thus a manager said: "I don't favor arbitration at all. I don't believe in letting outsiders set policies." A union spokesman agreed: "We see no sense in putting our problems in the hands of men who know nothing about us or our work."

The attitude of a union or an employer is likely to depend on who won the last award in arbitration. When an arbitrator refused to grant the Boston typographical union a wage increase in 1921 and scolded the workers for wanting phonographs and silk stockings, the union swore off arbitration, and it has not used it since.

An employer who said he flatly opposed arbitration began his comments with: "We've been beaten around so badly on arbitration we groan every time we hear the word." And another of the same view said: "I think arbitration should be used only as a last resort. . . . You are liable to get a decision which will be very costly. One time we arbitrated a contract settlement. It is very dangerous."

A union representative summed up the pragmatic approach of both sides:

> We don't generally like to submit new contracts or renewal contracts to arbitration. We use arbitration for the settlement of arguments during the contract term, and interpretation of what is meant by what is in the contract. We feel that arbitration on new contracts would tend to stagnate collective bargaining. We would recommend arbitration depending upon, first, the seriousness of the dispute and, second, the importance of the union's demands to its people. I say this because we often ask for things in negotiations which we do not think are too important, but we put them in so that when the employer resists we can withdraw on those as a gesture of cooperation. Third, it would depend on whether we were in a position to strike and on the over-all economic picture and the consideration we must give to the timeliness of strike action.

Fact-Finding Boards

If conciliation fails and arbitration is rejected, it has been suggested that government "fact-finding" boards be established in important disputes. Fact-finding boards are badly named, for in addition to determining the facts they often make recommendations for settlement of disputes. They have, however, no power except the support of public opinion to get labor and management to accept their recommendations.

These boards are direct descendants of the Railway Labor Act's "emergency" boards, which may be used as a last resort in disputes threatening "substantially to interrupt interstate commerce to a degree such as to deprive any section of the country of essential transportation service." The National Mediation Board is required to "investigate and report respecting such dispute."

Following this pattern, President Truman created a number of fact-finding boards to aid in settling important controversies that developed outside the transportation industry during the difficult transition days after World War II. These boards were the government's peacetime substitute for the National War Labor Board. Initially, the government intended to use them to keep wage settlements within reconversion wage-price policy designed to bridge the gap between wartime wage controls and normal, uncontrolled peacetime wage determination. It was hoped that later they would become an established device for settling major disputes in industries not covered by the Railway Labor Act.

Both management and labor have opposed the principle of compulsory fact-finding boards. The board members, unlike arbitrators, are not selected by the disputants, and both union and management consequently regard them as outsiders. The Labor-Management Relations Act of 1947 provided for presidential appointment of boards of inquiry in disputes that "imperil the national health and safety." These boards, however, were empowered merely to describe the facts of the situation and were prohibited from making recommendations.

All the devices used to prevent work stoppages are also used to end stoppages once they have begun. In the fiscal year 1946–1947, the U.S. Conciliation Service brought about agreement between the parties in almost nine out of ten of the work stoppages in which it was involved.[29]

ADMINISTRATION OF AGREEMENTS

With the signing of a collective agreement, the more spectacular phase of collective bargaining ends. At the same time, an equally important phase begins — the day-to-day administration of the agreement. Whether the agreement is a short statement of principles or a lengthy compendium of detailed clauses, it must be applied to the ever-changing conditions of the work place. Inevitably, situations arise that its provisions do not cover fully; in other instances, the two interested parties interpret its provisions somewhat differently.

29. Thirty-fifth Annual Report of the Secretary of Labor, Appendix Table C, p. 73.

When one party takes exception to an act or a decision of the other, "grievances" arise. The procedure for settling such disputes is known as the "grievance procedure." Formal grievance procedures vary in details, but usually they consist of a series of steps that move the dispute to successively higher management and union levels until it is settled. Most agreements provide for use of arbitration as a last step before resort to strikes or lockouts.

Grievance Procedures

Since in day-to-day operations it is the foremen who carry out the working arrangements established by management, most disputes start as employee grievances against foremen. The four stages (including arbitration) in handling such grievances are:

1. *Initial Presentation.* Most frequently the employee, his union representative or both together present the grievance to the foreman. The union representative at this stage may be either the shop steward or committeeman, the grievance committee or, occasionally, the union business agent. The Bureau of Labor Statistics found this to be the first step in the grievance procedure in 58 of 101 plants surveyed during 1944–1945.[30] According to one estimate, as many as 85 per cent of all grievances are settled at this stage in many industries.[31]

2. *Intermediate Steps.* There may be from one to five appeal steps between initial presentation and final appeal to top management. Two or three intermediate steps are most common. The Bureau of Labor Statistics found that to be the practice in slightly more than two thirds of the plants it studied.[32] There are many variations in the handling of the appeal at this stage. Most frequently, however, the employee is represented by a grievance committee consisting of plant employees. Business agents generally participate after the second step, and international representatives do not come in until next to the last step. Management usually is represented by someone with the rank of plant manager.

3. *Final Step before Arbitration.* In 70 per cent of the cases studied by the Bureau of Labor Statistics, international-union representatives represent the employee at the final appeal stage, and in a like percentage of cases company officials represent management.[33] In the larger companies, the union representatives at this stage may be top international officers, and the company representative, the president or general manager. In small companies, the local business agent generally handles the final appeal.

4. *Arbitration.* Most collective agreements provide for arbitration as the last step in the grievance procedure. The arbitration machinery, however, is separate from grievance or adjustment machinery as such, since it is used to settle not only grievances but also other disputes arising under a collective agreement.

Union shop stewards, grievance committees and business agents have a dual role in administering the collective agreement. They not only handle grievances brought to them by employees but also actively "police the contract" to see that no contract violations are committed. Frequently the company, or occasionally the union, pays them for time spent in handling grievances.[34]

The attitude of the participants is far more important for the successful administration of collective agreements than the formal grievance procedure. Unless each side approaches the adjustment of differences in a reasonable, cooperative spirit, with mutual respect, the best grievance procedure is of no avail.

Arbitration under Collective Agreements

Most collective agreements provide for submitting to arbitration unsettled differences that arise during the life of the agreement. Submittal may be voluntary or obligatory. Usually a request from one party is sufficient to refer a disputed issue to arbitration. Sometimes, however, both must agree; as a result, the party seeking a change (most frequently

30. "Grievance Procedure under Collective Bargaining," *Monthly Labor Review,* August 1946, p. 4. Most of the plants studied had more than a thousand workers in the bargaining unit; some had between 750 and a thousand.

31. S. T. Williamson and Herbert Harris, *Trends in Collective Bargaining,* Twentieth Century Fund, New York, 1945, p. 121.

32. "Grievance Procedure under Collective Bargaining," p. 179.

33. International-union representatives and company officials apparently meet in less than 70 per cent of the cases, since "there is no definite pairing of management personnel with union representatives." *Ibid.,* p. 181.

34. In four out of five plants surveyed by the Bureau of Labor Statistics, management compensated union representatives for time spent in handling grievances during working hours. *Ibid.,* p. 184.

the union) often is forced to accept the other's decision or resort to economic force.

Arbitration machinery may be permanent or it may be set up on a temporary emergency basis to handle particular disputes. It may take any of a great variety of specific forms, the most common of which is the bipartisan board with an impartial chairman chosen by the board.

The government, in the person of federal and state conciliation services, is being called on more and more to supply arbitrators. The U.S. Conciliation Service, for example, appointed 1,008 arbitrators in the fiscal year 1946–1947, as compared with 192 in the fiscal year 1940–1941.[35]

The government imposes compulsory arbitration only in the railroad industry, where, under the Railway Labor Act, the National Railroad Adjustment Board handles disputes arising under collective agreements. In a sense, since the Board consists of an equal number of permanent representatives of carriers and the railway unions, its function is as much negotiation as arbitration. When the Board cannot agree, it calls in a referee, who makes the award.

Legal Status

Collective bargaining in the United States has passed through several distinct changes in public policy.[36] The early repression period was followed by a toleration period and then by a period of encouragement; the most recent stage in the history of collective bargaining is still unfolding.

Repression Period

In the early 1800's American courts used the common-law "conspiracy doctrine" to declare illegal workingmen's attempts to bargain collectively. The premises of this doctrine were that collective action is more powerful and hence more dangerous than individual action and that if a number of people combine for an unlawful purpose the very act of combination is unlawful. Exactly what was an unlawful purpose was never clearly defined, so the application of the doctrine was highly confusing.

In the earliest cases, the courts ruled that the mere combination of workmen to raise their wages was illegal.[37] In some cases they ruled the collective action unlawful if it was aimed at benefiting the "conspirators" at the expense of others, and in some cases a conspiracy was found to exist only if the means used were considered "too arbitrary or coercive."

Despite the *Commonwealth* vs. *Hunt* decision of 1842, in which the Massachusetts Supreme Court declared that a strike for the closed shop was lawful, the attitude that there was something unlawful about combinations of workers remained dominant until the 1860's. At that period, several industrial states expressly legalized combinations aimed at improving wages and working conditions, and in the years that followed, the popularity of the conspiracy doctrine declined. By about 1890, criminal prosecutions for conspiracy had yielded largely to injunctions as a means for handling labor-management relations.

Toleration Period

Although the efforts of workers to engage in collective bargaining were no longer considered a criminal conspiracy, legal concepts strongly favored individual bargaining during the "toleration period." The government was supposed to act as an umpire with a "hands-off" attitude, intervening only to protect established rights. As outstanding students of labor legislation have remarked, the practical effect of this attitude was protection of employers against workers.[38] Lined up against unions and collective bargaining during this period were two potent legal concepts — the doctrines of restraint of trade and of the rights of liberty and property.

Restraint-of-Trade Doctrine

The restraint-of-trade doctrine rested on the right of every individual to dispose of his own property or labor as he pleases, free from the dictation of others. Earlier the courts generally had held that the objective of restraint of trade was itself wrongful and transformed a lawful combination into a criminal conspiracy. Gradually the courts began to consider whether the unions used "coercion" and whether the re-

---

35. Thirty-fifth Annual Report of the Secretary of Labor, p. 70.

36. John R. Commons and John B. Andrews, *Principles of Labor Legislation,* 4th edition, Harper, New York, 1936, pp. 374–75.

37. John R. Commons (Ed.), *Documentary History of American Industrial Society,* 10 vols., Clark, Cleveland, 1910, Vols. III and IV.

38. Commons and Andrews, *op. cit.,* p. 375.

straint was "unreasonable." With such vague concepts, however, judges had considerable latitude in hampering the growth of collective bargaining. Application to labor unions of the Sherman Antitrust Act of 1890, which formalized the restraint-of-trade doctrine, further restricted union activities. The courts banned many strikes and found boycotts illegal. In essence, decisions under this act "meant that even peaceful persuasion and peaceful assembly were illegal if they resulted in curtailment of trade and impairment of the 'good will' of business."[39]

Labor fought to win exemption from the antitrust laws. When the Clayton Act was passed in 1914, labor thought it had succeeded. This act said that antitrust laws should not be construed as forbidding the existence of labor organizations or the carrying out of their legitimate objectives. Nevertheless, the courts held that its enactment made no significant change in existing legal interpretations. Hence, "there were at least as many successful prosecutions of workingmen . . . after its passage as before."[40]

Rights of Liberty and Property

The doctrine of the rights of liberty and property was a powerful double-barred deterrent to collective bargaining. One bar was the theory that the law must treat workers and employers with formal "equality"; as long as a worker was free to quit for any or no reason, the employer must be free to fire him for any or no reason. Thus employers could fight unions and collective bargaining with "yellow-dog" contracts, black lists, company unionism and similar weapons.

The second bar was the view that the right to engage in business is a property. Acceptance of this concept required government to protect not only the employer's physical plant but also his access to commodity and labor markets. The courts thus were able to issue injunctions protecting the employer against actual or potential injury to his "property," that is, his right to do business. Labor had no equivalent "property right" entitling it to seek injunctive relief against employer actions.

Employers were able to get injunctions with relative ease. During the half century of "government by injunction" (1883–1932), federal and state courts issued more than two thousand injunctions; only about 10 per cent of those requested were denied.[41] Some injunctions were broad enough to prevent any effective organized effort against an employer; others were so vague that no one knew in advance what was or was not permitted under their terms.

The unions had looked to the Clayton Act for relief, but in 1921 the decision of the Supreme Court in *Truax* v. *Corrigan* made it clear that the Clayton Act did not prevent injunctions in labor disputes. Use of them was intensified in the following decade. Not until after the passage of the Norris-LaGuardia Act, in 1932, did the era of injunctions come to an end and the period of governmental encouragement of collective bargaining begin.

Early Governmental Support

The government had veered toward support of collective bargaining on several occasions during this period. At the height of World War I, the War Labor Board and other government agencies recognized labor's right to organize and to bargain collectively through their own representatives; the War Labor Board supported this right with its statement that workers were not to be discharged for trade-union membership. At the end of the war, however, this support was withdrawn, and collective bargaining, without government protection, shriveled under the withering "open-shop" drive of the 1920's.

In 1926, Congress passed the Railway Labor Act, explicitly giving railroad workers freedom to select their own collective bargaining representatives. In 1932 the Norris-LaGuardia Act declared collective bargaining to be good public policy, strictly limited the courts in their use of injunctions in industrial disputes, and made the anti-union "yellow-dog" contracts unenforceable in federal courts. A number of states followed the example of the federal government and enacted similar laws. But despite these advances, full acceptance of collective bargaining and active governmental support was still to come.

Encouragement Period

Collective bargaining won full governmental support in 1935, when Congress passed the Na-

39. Peterson, *op. cit.*, p. 591.
40. Commons and Andrews, *op. cit.*, p. 386.
41. Peterson, *op. cit.*, pp. 597–98.

tional Labor Relations (Wagner) Act, and full legal acceptance in 1937, when the Supreme Court declared that act constitutional. This legislation was preceded by the short-lived Section 7a of the National Industrial Recovery Act of 1933. Section 7a represented an attempt to spread to other industries the collective bargaining protection given to the railroads by the Railway Labor Act. After the NRA was declared unconstitutional in 1935, much of Section 7a, as well as the experience under it, was included in the Wagner Act.

Wagner Act

The Wagner Act gave to all employees in interstate commerce the right to organize, to bargain collectively through their own representatives, and to engage in supporting activities. To protect these rights, it forbade specific "unfair labor practices" by employers, among them interference with the right of workers to organize and carry on union activities, company unionism, discrimination in employment practices designed to affect union membership, and refusal to bargain collectively.

The act created its own special administrative agency, the National Labor Relations Board, to enforce its provisions. For the first time, the law of collective bargaining was to be enforced by an agency of government favorable to its development instead of by the police and the courts. In twelve years of operation, the NLRB dissolved 1,700 employer-controlled labor unions. In addition, it effected the reinstatement of more than 300,000 workers found to have been fired or demoted because of union activity. Moreover, the act gave workers an opportunity, through the secret ballot, to express their choice of bargaining agent without coercion. Between 1935 and 1947 the NLRB conducted nearly 37,000 elections, in which 84 per cent of the 9.1 million eligible workers participated in selecting their collective bargaining representatives.[42]

The period of positive governmental encouragement of collective bargaining continued during World War II. The War Labor Board strengthened the NLRB's powers and gave it added authority to force employers to bargain with unions. As a result of the War Labor Board's control over wages, perhaps the most significant gain was the expansion of collective bargaining into domains previously reserved for management's unilateral decisions. The War Labor Board brought into union-management discussions, and eventually into collective agreements, such topics as job evaluation, merit increases, dismissal pay, vacation pay, and health and welfare plans.

Recent Trends

At the very time that collective bargaining was establishing its permanence with the federal government's support, the states began to pass laws restricting the rights of unions.

After the war, Congress accepted the interpretation that the wave of labor-management disputes during reconversion showed an abuse of power by labor unions and passed the Labor-Management Relations, or Taft-Hartley, Act of 1947. This act met the desires of influential groups of employers and was vehemently opposed by labor unions. The new act reaffirmed the principle of the Wagner Act that it is the policy of the United States to encourage the "practice and procedure of collective bargaining." But it proposed to limit the scope of collective bargaining and to prevent unions from using certain economic weapons in their disputes with employers.

Control of Closed and Union Shop

Few provisions of the Taft-Hartley Act provoked more resentment and resistance on the part of labor unions than those outlawing the closed shop and controlling the union shop.[43] Closed-shop or union-shop provisions were both prevalent in collective agreements long before the advent of the Wagner Act. In recent years they had spread to many new industries. By 1946 half the 14.8 million workers covered by collective agreements worked under such conditions — 4.8 million in closed shops and 2.6 million in union shops.[44] Labor unions are used to considering closed and union shops as means of protecting union security. Actually, to maintain a closed shop or a union shop im-

42. Twelfth Annual Report of the National Labor Relations Board, 1947, p. 5.

43. A "closed shop" is a place of employment where, by agreement between employer and union, only members of the union in good standing may be employed. A "union shop" differs from a "closed shop" in that nonmembers may be hired but must join the union within a specified period and remain members in good standing thereafter.

44. *Extent of Collective Bargaining and Union Recognition, 1946,* previously cited, p. 3.

plies more than mere recognition of a union as representing the labor force in an establishment; it means entrusting the union with control over the labor force, which is presumably indispensable for making it responsible for the signed agreement.

The Taft-Hartley Act completely forbade the closed shop and instituted a complex procedure to be followed in negotiating for a union shop. First, at least 30 per cent of the employees in the bargaining unit had to petition the National Labor Relations Board for a union-shop election. If the union had complied with the registration and reporting requirements of the act and if a majority of all employees (counting those who did not vote because of illness or absence or for other reasons) voted for the union shop, the union could begin to bargain for it with the employer. Moreover, where the Taft-Hartley Act was more restrictive in this matter than state laws, the Taft-Hartley provisions were to apply; where state laws were more severe, they were to prevail. Toward the end of 1947 there were "no less than 20 states with such laws." [45]

Other Limitations

The Taft-Hartley Act also introduced limitations on health and welfare plans. It defined the beneficiaries, the scope and the form of welfare funds and prohibited certain types of welfare plans.

An avowed purpose of the Taft-Hartley Act was to bring about equality between management and labor. To accomplish this end, it restricted certain activities of unions. Some of these limitations — for example, the prohibition of strikes and boycotts in jurisdictional strikes — did not meet much opposition from unions; others were assailed by unions as attempts to deprive them of vital economic weapons. The outlawing of secondary boycotts was criticized as forcing workers to handle work that had been contracted out to their employer by an employer engaged in a dispute with another local of their union.

Even more important, in the opinion of some people, were a series of provisions that under certain conditions could endanger the very existence of labor unions. Under the act picketing could be restrained by injunction; employers could petition for a collective bargaining election; strikers could be held ineligible to vote, while their replacements could vote; and, if the balloting resulted in a "no-union" vote, the government would have to certify and enforce it.

Thus, without directly attacking the principle of collective bargaining or the idea that government should encourage it, and while recognizing labor's right to organize for collective bargaining, the Labor-Management Relations Act of 1947 has reintroduced

> . . . many pre-1930 restrictive notions, and has added restrictions advanced by groups which have traditionally been opposed in principle to the process of collective bargaining. At the very least, virtually every major debatable or debated issue in the area of labor-management relations has been resolved against labor . . .[46]

The years during which the Taft-Hartley Act has set the course for our labor-management relations are still too few to permit major generalizations about its impact. Moreover, the courts are still deliberating over the application of many of the act's provisions. But it is already clear that while the act has clipped the unions' wings somewhat, it has not succeeded in eliminating industrial unrest. Major work stoppages in autos, coal, steel and transportation since the passage of the act make this clear. The proportion of working time lost through stoppages in 1949 — 0.59 per cent — was exceeded in only one year, 1946, during the twenty-four years for which such data are available.

It is also clear that the unions are having a difficult time organizing. Union membership rolls have not risen, and may have dropped, since 1947, and the southern membership drives of the AFL and CIO have proved far from successful. What part of this organizing failure is attributable to the Taft-Hartley Act, what part to internal union problems, and what part to the resistance of the remaining unorganized workers to union overtures, is impossible to say.

45. Edwin E. Witte, "Labor-Management Relations under the Taft-Hartley Act," *Harvard Business Review,* Autumn 1947, p. 563.

46. Nathan P. Feinsinger and Edwin E. Witte, "Labor, Legislation, and the Role of Government," *Monthly Labor Review,* July 1950, p. 57.

CHAPTER 20

UNION AGREEMENTS *

SUCCESSFUL COLLECTIVE BARGAINING normally ends in the signing of an agreement between union and management. The agreement usually indicates which employees the union is entitled to represent and sets forth the length of time the agreement is to remain in force and the steps to be taken for its extension or renegotiation. It stipulates wages, hours, working conditions and seniority rights, grievance procedures, and the role of arbitration in settling disputes arising under the agreement. Besides these basic general provisions, individual agreements may cover at least some of the following subjects: vacations, employee benefits (sick leave, health and welfare plans), strikes and lockouts, management and union rights.

Union-management agreements are often called collective bargaining contracts. Unlike the usual business contract, however, the collective bargaining contract is not an agreement between a buyer and a seller of a commodity, in which the seller agrees to supply and the buyer to take a given quantity of a commodity at a specified price, time and place. Nor is it like the contract between an employer and an individual employee wherein the latter is hired to work for a certain period under specified conditions. In a collective bargaining contract, the employer does not commit himself, as a rule, to hire any particular number of workers; [1] he agrees merely to hire those he needs under certain conditions. The union, similarly, is not a seller or supplier of labor and generally makes no commitment to supply the labor needs of the employer.[2] Breach of contract normally is followed by a court suit for damages; the typical aftermath of a breach of a collective agreement is a strike or a lockout.

The collective bargaining agreement falls somewhere between a contract and a treaty. Its contractual aspects are exemplified by specific pledges in the agreement to do or to refrain from doing certain things. One of these is the union's pledge not to strike and management's pledge not to lock out for the duration of the agreement. When such a pledge is broken, the courts generally uphold damage suits against the offending party.

Although the courts are increasingly inclined to view collective agreements as contracts, the typical agreement is similar in some respects to a treaty. Labor and management are in the position of potential antagonists with conflicting interests who nevertheless must agree to work together on some terms. Behind their negotiations stalks the ever-present danger of temporary disagreement and industrial warfare. To prevent such warfare — or to end a conflict that is under way — both recognize the need for signing an agreement defining their respective rights and the basis of their cooperation toward common goals. Like treaties between nations, the agreements contain statements of intent to cooperate, procedures to be followed in ironing out difficulties, and escape clauses freeing one party if the other breaks the agreement. Also, the parties rely largely on common interest or the threat of force (economic), rather than on law, to guarantee adherence to the terms of the agreement.

The analogy may be carried one step further. Just as the prohibitive social cost of warfare between nations has led to international courts and the United Nations, so the cost of industrial warfare has led to the use of mediators, fact-finding boards and arbitrators to settle disputes arising under existing collective agreements. Thus, while collective agreements resemble treaties, treaties themselves have begun to be enforced as contracts. As the law of collective agreements continues to grow and their treaty aspects become increasingly subject to arbitration, collective agreements will move more and more in the direction of full-fledged business

* By Thomas C. Fichandler.

1. In a few exceptional cases, employers do guarantee a certain amount of annual earnings or employment for a specified number of employees.

2. Under closed-shop provisions or when a union maintains hiring halls, the union normally supplies the employer's labor needs. The purpose of such arrangements, however, is to achieve hiring preference for union members, and no breach of contract is involved if the union cannot supply all the workers needed.

contracts. This development appears to be the inevitable result of the expanded coverage of agreements and their growing influence on the nation's economic life.

Types of Agreements

Union agreements for the most part are written documents. Under the National Labor Relations Act and the Labor-Management Relations Act, once union and management have agreed on the terms of a contract, they are required to sign a written agreement if either party so desires. Oral agreements may exist in establishments not covered by federal labor laws, and written agreements may be supplemented by oral understandings when either party wishes to keep certain features confidential. Such understandings were used by the automobile and the steel unions during their mass organizing drives when they dealt with employers who, fearful of reprisals from among the employer fraternity, would grant concessions to the union only if they were unwritten and confidential. Only oral agreements were used in the men's clothing industry in Philadelphia for many years,[3] and almost 9 per cent of all agreements in Massachusetts in 1916 were unwritten.[4]

Agreements may be short, general statements that depend on day-to-day administration and union-management accommodation to fill in the details. Such "administrative" agreements are less common than the so-called "legislative" agreements. Legislative agreements spell out the mutually acceptable terms in great detail, running at times to more than a hundred printed pages. Some agreements are the handiwork of a single set of negotiations. Others are the result of negotiations spanning many years; an example of this type is the present much-amended bituminous coal agreement, which was first adopted in 1941 and was added to and changed in almost every year thereafter.

Trends in Content: 1939–1945

The collective agreement may be looked at as a temporary resting point in the changing relationship between labor and management. Each negotiation brings changes, some reflecting purely temporary influences, others the long-run evolution of labor-management relations.

Both types of changes are revealed by contract modifications made during World War II, although most of the changes coincide with persistent, long-run trends toward a greater voice for labor in determining working conditions.

Contract Coverage and Union Security

In 1939 none of a sample of contracts analyzed by the National Industrial Conference Board provided for maintenance of membership[5] as the way of preserving the union's security; in a 1945 sample, 43 per cent of the contracts included such provisions. (See Table 81.)[6] Maintenance of membership was a compromise device suggested by the War Labor Board and accepted by unions and management as a wartime expedient. For the long run, most unions undoubtedly will press for some form of the union shop or the closed shop,[7] if legal. Accompanying the spread of provisions for maintenance of membership was a slight, temporary decline in the proportion of contracts with closed-shop or union-shop provisions — from 30 to 25 per cent. On the other hand, a wartime trend that is likely to continue was the reduction from 70 per cent in 1939 to 32 per

3. See S. T. Williamson and Herbert Harris, *Trends in Collective Bargaining,* Twentieth Century Fund, New York, 1945, p. 50.

4. *Collective Agreements between Employers and Labor Organizations in Massachusetts, 1916,* Labor Bulletin No. 121 (Part III of the Annual Report on Statistics of Labor for 1917), Massachusetts Bureau of Statistics, Boston, 1917, p. 12.

5. Maintenance-of-membership clauses require all members of the union on a certain date to continue in good standing for the term of the agreement, but do not require new employees to join. Many provide an escape period during which members may resign.

6. The 1939 sample consisted of 114 contracts, 52 with AFL unions, 55 with CIO unions and 7 with independent unions; the 1945 sample consisted of 212 contracts, 95 with AFL unions, 94 with CIO unions and 23 with independent unions. Many different industries, types of business and locations are represented in both samples. Cf. Harold F. Browne, "A Comparison of Union Agreements," *Conference Board Management Record,* July 1939, pp. 101–09 and Abraham A. Desser, "Trends in Collective Bargaining and Union Contracts," *Conference Board Reports,* Studies in Personnel Policy No. 71, National Industrial Conference Board, New York, December 1945, pp. 3–14. The percentages used here and in the following pages reflect the number of contracts in which the particular provision is specified; a particular provision may be used in actual practice even though the contract fails to mention it. These percentages are therefore more reliable as indicators of trends in labor-management practices than as measures of their prevalence. They are, of course, good measures of the prevalence of contract provisions.

7. In a union shop, anyone may be hired, but employees who are retained must join the union after a certain period. In a closed shop, only union members may be hired.

TABLE 81

PERCENTAGE OF UNION CONTRACTS WITH SPECIFIED PROVISIONS, 1939 AND 1945

Contract Provision	Percentage of Contracts 1939	1945
Contract coverage		
Agreement covers:		
Only union members	27	3
All eligible employees	73	97
Employees ineligible for membership:		
Supervisory employees	50	64
Salaried employees	48	61
Union security		
Type of shop:		
No union security	70	32
Maintenance of membership	—	43
Closed or union shop	30	25
Preferential hiring	16	6
Checkoff	6	42
Rights and responsibilities		
Union:		
Union members not to coerce or solicit membership on company time	40	49
Strikes prohibited	38	78
Transaction of union business permitted on company property	10	16
Management:		
Company not to discriminate against union or interfere with employees' right to join	55	80
Lockouts prohibited	38	78
Company responsible for industrial health and safety of employees	40	49
Functions reserved to management:		
Employment	33	49
Promotion	4	36
Transfer	29	41
Suspension	29	41
Discharge	38	45
Layoff	29	42
Wages		
Minimum wage established	37	63
Wage scale or rates specified	21	38
Wage increases provided	6	32
Hours		
Regular working hours per day:		
Less than 8 hours	5	2
8 hours	74	78
More than 8 hours	2	2
Regular working hours per week:		
Less than 40 hours	4	3
40 hours	60	73
More than 40 hours	15	2
Days per week:		
5 days	62	45
6 days	10	3
Call-in pay		
Time payable when no work available:		
Less than 4 hours	27	28
4 hours or more	11	42
Vacations		
Vacations with pay	60	80
Grievance procedures		
Union representative allowed time off:		
With pay	8	31
Without pay	29	15
Arbitration:		
Provided	75	81
Award binding on both parties	65	75
Expenses shared jointly	50	54

Source: Based on analysis of 114 contracts in 1939 and 212 contracts in 1945 by the National Industrial Conference Board. Cf. Harold F. Browne, "A Comparison of Union Agreements," *Conference Board Management Record,* July 1939, pp. 101–09, and Abraham A. Desser, "Trends in Collective Bargaining and Union Contracts," *Conference Board Reports,* Studies in Personnel Policy No. 71, National Industrial Conference Board, New York, December 1945, pp. 3–14. Cf. also Appendix Table 58.

cent in 1945 in the percentage of contracts with no union security provisions.

Another development that is unlikely to be upset was the virtual elimination of contracts limited in coverage solely to union members. The Wagner Act authorized the union selected by a majority of the employees in a designated bargaining unit to bargain for all employees in the unit. As a result of this provision and increased union strength, the proportion of limited-coverage contracts dropped from 27 to 3 per cent between 1939 and 1945. The Taft-Hartley Act left this principle largely untouched and there is little chance of a swing back to contracts covering only union members.

The spread of checkoff [8] provisions was very rapid. The inclusion of checkoff clauses rose from 6 per cent to 42 per cent of all contracts during the war.

Rights and Responsibilities

Developments in the area of union and management rights and responsibilities have

8. Checkoff clauses provide for the employer to deduct union dues from the employee's pay and turn them over to the union; deduction of initiation fees and other union levies may also be provided.

been among the most significant. Clauses banning strikes and lockouts appeared in 78 per cent of the 1945 contracts as against only 38 per cent of the 1939 contracts. This development shows that the parties to collective bargaining are readier than before to recognize the binding nature of their agreements. Many of the no-strike, no-lockout clauses are, of course, conditional pledges, but even they tend to emphasize the contractual aspects of collective agreements.

Between 1939 and 1945 many companies appear to have won certain rights they did not have before the war. For example, only one third of the 1939 contracts recognized employment of workers as solely a function of management, while half the 1945 contracts analyzed reserved this right to management. Promotion was recognized as a management function in only 4 per cent of the contracts in 1939 and in 36 per cent in 1945. Management's right to transfer, suspend and lay off workers was spelled out in less than 30 per cent of the 1939 contracts and in more than 40 per cent of the later agreements.

These increases in the number of clauses reserving certain functions to management do not, however, represent a growth in management's powers. Earlier many of these so-called management prerogatives were not challenged by the unions; consequently, they went unmentioned in union-management agreements. As unions began to push for a greater voice in the determination of policies affecting their members, management reacted by seeking formal recognition of its established rights.

Wages and Hours

The proportion of contracts establishing a minimum wage rose from 37 to 63 per cent after the concept of a minimum wage was accepted in federal law in the Fair Labor Standards Act of 1938. Though the example of this law encouraged unions to seek minimum-wage clauses, some union negotiators undoubtedly felt such clauses superfluous in light of the legal minimum established.

A jump from 6 to 32 per cent in the provisions for wage increases was largely the result of the behavior of prices during the late 1930's and the early 1940's; the Bureau of Labor Statistics consumers' price index remained almost level in the late 1930's but rose almost 30 per cent in the early 1940's.[9]

The movement for a shorter basic work week continued even during the war, and a basic work week of more than 40 hours was rarely found in collective agreements in 1945.

Vacations with Pay

The number of contracts providing vacations with pay increased during the war. Agreements with such clauses rose from 60 to 80 per cent when unions and employers resorted to "fringe" adjustments approved by the War Labor Board instead of wage increases. This was merely a wartime acceleration of a well-established trend in collective agreements. Before the early 1930's, vacations with pay were usually limited to white-collar workers. Since that time, paid vacations for production workers have become more and more common.

Employee Benefits

In addition to vacations with pay, several other types of employee benefits began to appear in union agreements by 1945. These included health and welfare plans and paid holidays for production workers as well as white-collar workers. Life insurance, old-age and disability pensions, sickness insurance and similar benefits, which for a long time had been either the sole concern of the union or had been provided unilaterally by the employer, became part of collective agreements.

Grievance Procedures

The increase in the proportion of companies agreeing to pay union representatives for time spent on grievance work reflects management's growing recognition of the constructive role the union can play in day-to-day plant operations. From only 8 per cent in 1939, the proportion of contracts with such provisions jumped to 31 per cent in 1945.

The grievance procedure was further strengthened by an increase from 75 to 81 per cent in the relative frequency of clauses providing for arbitration of grievance disputes and an increase from 65 to 75 per cent in the proportion of contracts making the arbitration award binding.

9. *Historical Statistics of the United States, 1789–1945,* Department of Commerce, 1949, p. 236.

Trends in Wage Clauses

Despite the importance and even temporary dominance of other issues, the central question in collective bargaining is the amount that labor is to be paid for its services. At one time this question was handled simply (and completely) by a wage clause in the agreement. Today it is affected by clauses on vacation or holiday pay, health and welfare programs, overtime schedules and related provisions, as well as by the basic wage-rate clause. All these provisions have real monetary value to employees, all add to the employer's "wage bill" in a broad sense, all are, therefore, indirect or supplemental wage provisions. Contracts that now include such provisions were entirely devoid of them not long ago. Typical of these trends are the bituminous coal and the American Woolen Company agreements examined more closely in Appendix Note 5.

CONTENT, 1948

Union agreements in effect in 1948 reflected the results of a momentous period in the history of collective bargaining. Rapid unionization in the 1930's spread the basic features developed in long-standing collective bargaining relationships to the thousands of contracts negotiated between unions and employers new to the bargaining table. At the same time the growing power of unions and their advance into new industrial fields brought contract innovations. Many new features initiated under the pressure of wartime controls prevented collective bargaining from developing in its customary channels. While these new concepts were being consolidated in the early postwar years, state and federal laws virtually eliminated some of the oldest contract fixtures.

Probably no two of the tens of thousands of contracts in effect in 1948 were identical in all respects. They did, however, follow well-defined patterns. Of 100 contracts on file with the Bureau of Labor Statistics at the end of 1947, for example, the majority ran for a year or less. (See Figure 44.) Almost all had clauses providing for time rather than piece rates as the method of wage payment. Hardly any failed to provide for some type of grievance procedure. On the other hand, less than a third of the 100 contracts examined had clauses covering health, welfare and retirement plans, and only 5 mentioned bonus plans.

It is possible to single out the major types of contract provisions and, on the basis of a recent survey by the Bureau of National Affairs,[10] to indicate their prevalence.[11] The frequency figures mentioned below reflect only specific references contained in the contracts analyzed; agreements often fail to mention a practice that is actually in effect.

Some of the many clauses in union agreements relate primarily to the basic framework for collective bargaining. These are the provisions that determine the union's status in the eyes of the employer (union security and check-off), duration of contract, the conditions under which the collective bargaining relationship may be broken off (strikes and lockouts), and specific rights reserved to management and to the union.

Union Security

The clauses referring to union membership requirements were more affected by the Labor-Management Relations Act of 1947 than any other contract provisions. Since the closed shop was virtually outlawed by this federal law and by many state laws, it almost disappeared as a provision in agreements negotiated between September 1947 and July 1948; only 5 per cent of the agreements still required the employment of union members solely. These closed-shop agreements were chiefly in retail trade and construction, covering intrastate operations not affected by the federal act, but the legality of some of them was questionable.

Union-shop clauses, under which anyone may be hired but all who are retained must join the union after a certain period, appeared in about 30 per cent of all contracts included in the

10. *Basic Patterns in Collective Bargaining Contracts,* Bureau of National Affairs, Washington, 1948. All figures in the following pages on the frequency of contract clauses are taken from this study. Because of the limitations of the sample and difficulties in classifying many contract clauses, all percentages are only estimates. The estimates are based on "detailed analysis of a broad sampling of agreements, supplemented and tempered by experienced examination of the many thousands of contracts received annually by the staff of *Collective Bargaining Negotiations and Contracts.* Three fourths of the contracts surveyed are in manufacturing industries, a fourth in nonmanufacturing. All were signed during the period between September 1947 [after the Taft-Hartley Act became fully effective] and July 1948" (p. 15:25).

11. See Appendix Table 58 for a statistical summary of the prevalence of various provisions in agreements signed between September 1947 and July 1948.

FIGURE 44

CONTENT OF 100 SELECTED UNION AGREEMENTS ON FILE WITH UNITED STATES DEPARTMENT OF LABOR, DECEMBER 1948[a]

No.	Union and Company			Contract Expiration Date	General Provisions — Duration of Agreement: 1 year or less	Between 1 and 2 years	2 years or more	Employer Unit: Single plant	Single company, multi-plant	Multi-company	Coverage: Single craft or group of crafts	All prod. workers or all except crafts	All workers except selected groups	Union Security: Union or closed shop	Membership maintenance	Sole bargaining	Check-off: Dues	Initiation fees	Other assessments	Work Stoppages: Unqualified "no-strike or lockout" clause	Union responsibility limited	Some stoppages allowed	Other	Wages and Hours — Wage Payment Method: Time rates	Piece rates	Incentive pay	Individual Adjustment: Merit increases	Premium pay for hazardous work	Automatic service increase	Adjustments under Contract: Reopening any time or at certain times	Reopening under certain conditions	Cost of Living: Upward	Downward, with limit or floor	Hours of Work and Payment for Overtime: Less than 8-hr. day, 40-hr. week	Overtime after: 8-hour day	40-hour week	Overtime Rates: Time and a half	Double time	Graduated rate after certain period	Overtime outside designated hours
No.				1	2	3	4	5	6	7	8	9	10	11	12	13	14	15	16	17	18	19	20	21	22	23	24	25	26	27	28	29	30	31	32	33	34	35	36	37
1	Appliance	Ind.	Coleman	7–49		X			X				X			X	X					X		X		X	X		X								X			X
2	Auto Workers	AFL	Harley-Davidson	4–49	X			X				X		X						X				X	X	X														
3	Auto Workers	CIO	Briggs	7–50			X		X			X			X								X	X			X			X										
4	Auto Workers	CIO	Budd	6–50			X	X					X			X	X							X	X	X			X	X										
5	Auto Workers	CIO	Caterpillar Tractor	7–50			X	X					X			X	X	X	X		X			X						X					X		X			
6	Auto Workers	CIO	Ex-Cell-O	5–49	X				X			X			X		X	X	X	X				X													X		X	
7	Auto Workers	CIO	Ford	7–49	X				X			X			b		X				X			X											X	X	X			
8	Auto Workers	CIO	General Motors	5–50			X		X				X			X	X	X	X			X		X		X						X	X							
9	Auto Workers	CIO	Lamson & Sessions	7–50			X		X			X				X	X	X	X				X			X				X					X		X			
10	Auto Workers	CIO	No. Amer. Aviation	8–49	X				X				X		X		X	X	X		X			X																
11	Bakery Workers	AFL	Hershey Chocolate	12–50		X			X			c																				X	X		d					
12	Boilermakers	AFL	Calif. Metal Trades Assn.	3–49	X					X	X			X								X		X											X	X		X		
13	Building Service	AFL	Bldg. Mgrs.' Assn., Chicago	6–49	X					X	X				e					X				X																
14	Chemical Workers	AFL	Genl. Aniline & Film	6–49	X			X					X		X		X	X	X	X				X					X			X	X		X	X	X			X
15	Chemical Workers	AFL	Lever Bros.	3–49	X				X			X		X			X				X			X											X	X	X			
16	Clothing Workers	CIO	Clothiers' Exch., Rochester	4–52			X			X		X					X	X	X	X				X	X						X									
17	Communications Workers	Ind.	Chesapeake & Potomac Tel.	5–51			X		X		X					X	X							X			X		X	g										
18	Electrical Workers	CIO	Chapman Valve	7–49	X			X				X				X	X						X	X		X	X										X		X	
19	Electrical Workers	CIO	Elec. Storage & Battery	5–50			X		X			X			X		X	X				X		X	X			X		X							X		X	
20	Electrical Workers	CIO	Emerson Electric	7–50			X		X				X	X			X	X	X	X				X	X	X									X	X	X			
21	Electrical Workers	CIO	Maytag	5–49	X			X				X				X	X	X		X				X		X	X										X		X	
22	Electrical Workers	CIO	Monroe Calculating Mach.	3–49	X			X					X			X	X			X				X		X	X		X						X	X	X			
23	Electrical Workers	CIO	Sylvania Electric	5–50			X		X				h		i		X	X				X		X			X			X							X		X	
24	Electrical Workers	CIO	Thos. A. Edison	3–49	X				X			X				X	X					X		X											X	X	X			
25	Electrical Workers	CIO	United Shoe Mach.	6–49	X			X				X				X	X	X						X	X												X		X	
26	Farm Equipment Workers	CIO	Oliver Corp.	5–49	X			X				X				X	X					X		X	X	X				X					X	X	X			
27	Federal Labor Union	AFL	American Can	4–50			X	X				X			X		X	X		X				X						X					X	X	X			
28	Federal Labor Union	AFL	Gt. Western Sugar	7–49	X				X				X	X			X	X		X				X																
29	Food Workers	CIO	Amer. Tobacco	7–49	X			X					X			X	X				X			X	X		X			X					X	X	X			
30	Food Workers	CIO	Planters Nut & Chocolate	4–49	X			X				X				X	X	X	X		X			X	X										X	X	X			
31	Garment (Ladies) Workers	AFL	Phila. Waist & Dress Mfrs. Assn.	1–49			X			X		X		X			X	X	X			X			X						X	X	X							
32	Gas, Coke & Chemical	CIO	National Lead	3–50			X	X				X		X			X	X				X		X				X		X					X	X	X	X		
33	Gas, Coke & Chemical	CIO	Parke-Davis	4–49	X				X			X		X			X				X			X											X	X	X			
34	Glass & Ceramic	CIO	Pittsburgh Plate Glass	4–49	X				X			X		X			X	X	X		X			X		X				X				X	X	X	X			
35	Granite Cutters	AFL	Elberton Granite	6–50			X			X		X		X							X			X						X					X	X	X			
36	Hod Carriers	AFL	Master Bldrs.[k]	4–49	X					X	X			X						X				X											X		X			
37	Hosiery Workers	Ind.	Guild Hosiery Conference	8–49			X			X		X		X			X					X									X				X	X	X			
38	Hotel & Restaurant	AFL	Wash. State Restaurant Assn.	5–49	X					X	X			X										X											X		X			
39	International Affiliate[l]	CIO	Amer. Smelting & Refining	6–49	X			X				X			X		X							X											X	X	X			
40	Laundry Workers	AFL	Clng. & Dyeing Inst., Port., Ore.	2–49	X					X		X		X								X		X																
41	Longshoremen	AFL	Galveston Maritime Assn.	8–49	X					X	X			X						X				X	X															
42	Longshoremen	AFL	Port of N.Y. Harbor Carriers	3–49			X			X	X			X								X		X																
43	Marine & Shipbuilding	CIO	Todd Shipyards	6–50			X	X				X		X			X	X		X				X	X		X								X	X		X		
44	Marine Engineers	CIO	Columbia Basin River Operators	8–50			X			X	X			X						X				X																
45	Masters, Mates & Pilots	AFL	Columbia Basin River Operators	8–50			X			X	X			X						X				X																
46	Meat Cutters	AFL	Swift	8–49	X				X			X				X	X	X				X								X					X	X	X			
47	Metal Trades Dept.	AFL	Anaconda Copper	6–50			X	X			X			X						X										X					X	X	X			
48	Metal Trades Dept.	AFL	Pacific Coast Shipbldrs.	6–49			X			X	X									X				X						X								X		
49	Mine, Mill & Smelter	CIO	Amer. Smelting & Refining	6–49	X			X				X				X	X						X	X											X	X	X			
50	Mine, Mill & Smelter	CIO	Anaconda Copper	6–50			X	X				X		X			X	X	X			X		X	X					X					X	X	X			
51	Mine, Mill & Smelter	CIO	Phelps-Dodge	7–50			X	X				X				X	X					X		X						X					X	X	X			
52	Mine, Mill & Smelter	CIO	Phelps-Dodge Refining	6–50			X	X				X				X	X	X				X		X	X					X					X	X	X			
53	Mine Workers	Ind.	Bituminous Coal Operators	6–49		m				X		X		X			X	X	X					X	X															
54	Mine Workers (Dist. 50)	Ind.	Newport Industries	5–49		X			X			X				X	X	X					X							X					X	X	X			
55	Mine Workers (Dist. 50)	Ind.	Sherwin-Williams	6–49	X			X				X				X	X	X	X		X			X	X										X		X			
56	Molders	AFL	Chic. Foundrymen's Assn.	4–49	X					X		X		X				X						X											X	X	X			
57	Molders	AFL	Cleve. Foundries (12 cos.)	4–49			X			X	X			X								X		X						X							X		X	
58	Newspaper Guild	CIO	N.Y. Times	12–49		X		X				o			X		X						X	X					X		X			X	X	X	X			
No.				1	2	3	4	5	6	7	8	9	10	11	12	13	14	15	16	17	18	19	20	21	22	23	24	25	26	27	28	29	30	31	32	33	34	35	36	37

FIGURE 44—Continued

CONTENT OF 100 SELECTED UNION AGREEMENTS ON FILE WITH UNITED STATES DEPARTMENT OF LABOR, DECEMBER 1948 [a]

Fringe Issues

40 Number of Paid Holidays: 5 but less than 8	41 8 but less than 11	42 11 or more	43 Paid Vacations, Uniform Plan: 1 week or less	44 Between 1 and 2 weeks	45 More than 2 weeks	46 Graduated Plan: 2 weeks maximum	47 More than 2 weeks maximum	48 Other	49 Paid Sick Leave, Pay Rate: Full pay	50 Partial pay	51 Duration: Entire period	52 Specified period	53 Other	54 Health, Welfare and Retirement Plans, Coverage: Retirement	55 Life and/or dismemberment	56 Accident and sickness cash	57 Hospitalization and/or surgical	58 Medical care benefits	59 Other	60 Financing: Employer contributions	61 Employee contributions	62 Bonus Plans	No.
X						X																X	1
X						X																	2
								X	X		X												3
X						X										X				X			4
X					X																		5
						X																	6
X						X																	7
X								X															8
X						X																	9
X				X					X			X											10
								X											X				11
						X																	12
X						X																	13
X							X						X										14
	X						X		X			X		X	X	X				X			15
X								X						X	X	X	X	X		X			16
		X					X		X			X		X	X								17
X						X																X	18
X							X			X		X			X	X	X			X			19
X							X								X	X	X	X		X	X		20
						X																	21
	X					X																	22
X							X																23
	X						X																24
X							X																25
X						X																	26
X							X																27
				X																			28
X						X				X		X							X				29
			X																				30
X								X											X	X			31
X						X				X		X											32
							X																33
						X									X	X	X		c	X			34
			X																				35
																							36
X							X									X	X	X		X			37
						X																	38
X						X																	39
						X																	40
																							41
			X																				42
					X																		43
						X			X			X											44
						X			X			X											45
	X						X			X		X											46
X						X											X	X		X	X		47
						X																	48
X							X																49
X						X											X	X		X	X		50
X						X																	51
X						X																	52
		X						X						X	X	X	X	X	X	X	X		53
X						X																n	54
X						X							X										55
X						X																	56
X						X																	57
X							X						X		X								58

Seniority; Grievances and Arbitration

63 Seniority Unit Covered: Within craft or occupation only	64 Department-wide	65 Plant-wide	66 Company-wide	67 Other	68 Seniority Recognition: Layoffs	69 Promotions	70 Rehiring	71 Other	72 Employees with Special Seniority: Union stewards and/or officials	73 Specified skilled employees	74 Handicapped and disabled employees	75 Disabled veterans	76 Other	77 Grievance Procedure: Grievance representation established	78 Procedure outlined	79 Written notice required at some point	80 Arbitrator's Jurisdiction, Issues: Interpretation of contract clauses	81 New issues arising under contract	82 Other	83 Limitations: Not to add or change contract terms	84 Not to set general wage level	85 Not to decide prod.-standards disputes	86 Other	87 Arbitration Machinery and Costs, Type: Single arbitrator	88 Bipartisan board	89 Permanence: Permanent	90 Temporary	91 Financing: Paid for jointly	92 Paid for by loser	93 Other	94 Outside Machinery Used in Disputes: Federal conciliation machinery	95 State machinery	96 Arbitrator Appointed by: Labor Dept.; or chosen from fed. panel	97 State or city agency	98 Private agency	99 Other agency	100 Other	No.
			X					X		X				X	X	X																						1
			X					X	X					X	X	X																	X					2
			X		X	X	X		X					X	X	X				X	X	X		X			X	X										3
		X			X	X	X		X					X	X	X								X			X	X							X			4
	X				X	X	X		X					X	X	X	X			X				X			X	X			X							5
				X			X		X	X			X	X	X	X	X			X	X	X		X			X		X						X			6
				X			X		X					X	X	X	X			X	X	X	X	X		X		X										7
				X			X		X					X	X	X	X			X		X		X		X		X										8
	X				X	X	X		X					X	X	X	X							X			X	X			X							9
		X					X		X					X	X	X	X			X			X	X		X	X										X	10
																																					11
X							X							X			X			X										X								12
X								X						X																X							X	13
		X						X	X					X	X	X	X								X		X	X							X				14
				f				f					f	X	X	X	X			X			X							X			X					15
														X						X				X		X		X										16
		X			X	X	X							X	X	X	X			X			X	X			X	X							X			17
		X			X	X	X		X					X	X										X		X	X					X					18
				X	X	X	X		X					X	X	X	X			X					X		X	X								X		19
X					X	X		X	X					X	X				X					X			X	X										20
				X	X	X								X	X	X	X				X		X		X		X	X				X						21
	X				X	X	X		X					X	X	X	X								X		X	X							X			22
		X			X	X	X		X					X	X	X	X			X					X		X	X								X		23
				X	X	X	X					X		X	X	X	X													X							X	24
		X					X		X					X	X	X	X													X	X							25
		X					X		X					X	X	X	X			X	X				X		X	X									X	26
		X			X		X		X					X	X		X			X				X			X	X						X				27
		X					X							X	X	X			X						X		X	X			X							28
	X						X		X					X	X	X	X			j										X			X					29
	X							X	X	X			X	X	X	X			X						X		X	X						X				30
														X	X				X											X								31
				X				X						X	X	X									X		X	X									X	32
				X				X	X	X				X	X	X	X			X	X			X			X	X							X			33
				X	X	X	X							X	X	X		X					X							X							X	34
																																					35
														X	X															X								36
														X	X		X			X	X			X			X	X									X	37
														X	X		X	X						X			X	X									X	38
	X				X	X	X							X	X	X									X		X	X									X	39
														X	X																						40
														X	X		X													X								41
														X	X	X														X								42
	X							X						X	X	X	X			X					X		X	X						X				43
														X	X	X	X													X			X					44
														X	X	X	X													X			X					45
				X				X			X			X	X	X	X					X								X								46
								X						X	X																							47
														X	X	X	X			X					X		X	X									X	48
				X	X	X	X		X					X	X	X	X						X	X			X	X							X			49
														X	X		X				X			X				X			X							50
	X				X	X	X					X		X	X	X	X			X				X		X		X							X			51
				X	X	X	X		X					X	X	X		X						X			X	X									X	52
				X				X					X	X	X				X				X							X							X	53
				X				X			X			X	X								X		X		X	X										54
				X				X						X	X	X	X								X		X	X							X			55
		X					X		X					X	X	X																						56
														X																								57
				X	X									X			X						X							X							X	58

FIGURE 44—CONTINUED

CONTENT OF 100 SELECTED UNION AGREEMENTS ON FILE WITH UNITED STATES DEPARTMENT OF LABOR, DECEMBER 1948[a]

No.	Union and Company		Contract Expiration Date	General Provisions																			Wages and Hours																
				Duration of Agreement			Employer Unit			Coverage			Union Security			Check-off			Work Stoppages				Wage Payment Method			Individual Adjustment			Adjustments under Contract				Hours of Work and Payment for Overtime						
																															Cost of Living			Overtime after:		Overtime Rates			
				1 year or less	Between 1 and 2 years	2 years or more	Single plant	Single company, multi-plant	Multi-company	Single craft or group of crafts	All prod. workers or all except crafts	All workers except selected groups	Union or closed shop	Membership maintenance	Sole bargaining	Dues	Initiation fees	Other assessments	Unqualified "no-strike or lockout" clause	Union responsibility limited	Some stoppages allowed	Other	Time rates	Piece rates	Incentive pay	Merit increases	Premium pay for hazardous work	Automatic service increase	Reopening any time or at certain times	Reopening under certain conditions	Upward	Downward, with limit or floor	Less than 8-hr. day, 40-hr. week	8-hour day	40-hour week	Time and a half	Double time	Graduated rate after certain period	Overtime outside designated hours
No.			1	2	3	4	5	6	7	8	9	10	11	12	13	14	15	16	17	18	19	20	21	22	23	24	25	26	27	28	29	30	31	32	33	34	35	36	37
59	Oil Workers ... CIO	Pan Amer. Petro. & Trans.	6–50			X	X				X				X	X			X				X											X	X	X			
60	Oil Workers ... CIO	Sinclair	6–49	X				X				X			X	X			X				X											X	X	X			
61	Packinghouse Workers ... CIO	Amer. Sugar Refining	11–48	X			X				X				X	X	X			X			X											X	X	X			
62	Painters ... AFL	Ind. Area Pac. Coast States	12–48	X					X	X			X								X		X													X			X
63	Papermakers[p] ... AFL	St. Regis Paper Co. & Toggart	4–49	X					X		X			X					X															X	X	X			
64	Paperworkers ... CIO	W. Va. Pulp & Paper	8–49	X				X			X					X				X									X					X	X	X			
65	Petroleum, Central States ... Ind.	Standard Oil of Indiana	10–49	X			X				X				X				X				X						X										
66	Photo-Engravers ... AFL	Photo-Engrs. Bd. of Trade, N.Y.	10–49		X				X	X					X				X				X						X							X		X	
67	Pulp, Sulphite & Paper ... AFL	Brown Company	6–49	X			X				X		X			X			X																				
68	Pulp, Sulphite & Paper[q] ... AFL	Consolidated Water Power & Paper	4–49	X				X					X							X			X						X					X	X	X			
69	Pulp, Sulphite & Paper ... AFL	Paper Box Credit Bureau	8–50			X			X			X	X						X				X	X	X	X				X				X	X	X			
70	Retail Clerks ... AFL	Food Employers' Coun., L.A.	5–50			X			X	S			X									X	X					X			X								
71	Retail Clerks ... AFL	Retail Food Ind.,[t] Seattle	3–49	X					X	X			X										X											X	X	X			X
72	Rubber Workers ... CIO	Dayton Rubber	5–49	X			X					X		X		X	X	X		X			X	X	X				X					X	X	X			
73	Rubber Workers ... CIO	Dunlop Tire & Rubber	9–49		X		X				X		X			X						X		X										X	X	X			
74	Rubber Workers ... CIO	Gates Rubber	6–49	X				X			X				X	X	X	X			X		X	X	X									X	X	X			
75	Rubber Workers ... CIO	Mundet Cork	6–49	X				X			X		X			X			X				X		X				X							X		X	
76	Rubber Workers ... CIO	U.S. Rubber	6–50		u			X			X				X	X					X		X	X	X				X					X	X	X			
77	Seafarers ... AFL	Atlantic & Gulf Ship Oper. Assn.	9–50			X			X	X				v					X				X																
78	Seafarers ... AFL	Columbia River Basin Oper.	8–51			X			X			w	X						X				X																
79	Steelworkers ... CIO	A. C. Mahon	3–49	X				X			X				X	X			X				X											X	X	X			
80	Steelworkers ... CIO	Alcoa	4–49			X		X			X			X		X	X				X		X		X				X					X	X	X			
81	Steelworkers ... CIO	Bethlehem Steel	4–50			X		X				X		X		X	X	X			X		X		X				X					X	X	X			
82	Steelworkers ... CIO	Central Iron & Steel	4–49		X		X				x			X		X	X	X	X				X		X				X					X	X	X			
83	Steelworkers ... CIO	Chain Belt	4–50			X		X			X				X				X				X	X	X				X							X		X	
84	Steelworkers ... CIO	Jones & Laughlin	4–50			X		X				X		X		X	X	X			X		X		X				X					X	X	X			
85	Steelworkers ... CIO	Republic Steel	4–50			X		X				X		X		X	X	X			X		X	X	X				X					X	X	X			
86	Steelworkers ... CIO	U.S. Steel (Carnegie-Ill.)	4–50			X		X				X		X		X	X	X			X		X		X				X					X	X	X			
87	Steelworkers ... CIO	Wickwire Bros.	6–49	X			X					X	X		X	X	X			X			X			X		X						X	X	X			
88	Steelworkers ... CIO	Youngstown Sheet & Tube	4–50			X		X				X		X		X	X	X			X		X	X	X				X					X	X	X			
89	Street Railway ... AFL	Capital Transit	6–49	X			X					X	X			X	X	X				X	X											X	X	X			
90	Teamsters ... AFL	Private Carriers of Seattle	3–49	X					X	X			X								X		X											X	X	X			
91	Textile Workers ... AFL	Keasbey & Mattison	5–49	X			X					X	X			X				X			X	X										X	X	X			
92	Textile Workers ... CIO	Mt. Vernon-Woodbury Mills	8–49	X			X				X			X		X	X			X			X						X										
93	Textile Workers ... CIO	Pacific Mills	7–49	X			X				X				X	X				X			X	X					X										
94	Textile Workers ... CIO	Rock Hill Prtg. & Finishing	3–50		X		X					X		X		X				X	X		X						X										
95	Textile Workers ... CIO	Woodside Cotton Mills	3–49	X			X				X				X	X				X			X	X					X										
96	Typographical ... AFL	Publishers' Assn., N.Y.	9–49	X					X	X			X								X		X																
97	Transport Workers ... CIO	Phila. Transit	2–49	X			X				X		X			X			X				X					X											
98	Woodworkers ... CIO	Columbia Basin Loggers Assn.	3–49	X					X			X	X			X					X		X	X					X					X	X	X			
99	Woodworkers ... CIO	Columbia Basin Sawmills	3–49	X					X			X	X			X					X		X	X					X										
100	Woodworkers ... CIO	Minn. & Ontario Paper	4–50			X	X				X		X									X	X						X					X	X	X			
No.			1	2	3	4	5	6	7	8	9	10	11	12	13	14	15	16	17	18	19	20	21	22	23	24	25	26	27	28	29	30	31	32	33	34	35	36	37

a. An attempt was made to select a list of 100 agreements that (1) contained at least one from most of the larger internationals and (2) covered the largest possible number of worke however, the table does not include some important agreements, which were submitted to the Labor Department with the proviso that they be kept confidential, and others whose coverage co not be determined. The Labor Department file as a rule does not include agreements of unions not covered by the Labor-Management Relations Act of 1947. Agreements negotiated by railroad unions, for example, are excluded.

b. After July 1948, union security determined within framework of existing legislation.

c. Coverage of agreement not specified.

d. Overtime provisions apply to watchmen only: time and one half after 8-hour day or 40-hour week.

e. Union members must be replaced by union members or prospective union members.

f. Subject to local negotiations for the various plants.

g. Each party to agreement may reopen question of wages twice during life of agreement.

h. As specified by the National Labor Relations Board.

i. Union security provision became inoperative on May 6, 1948 as a result of the Labor-Management Relations Act of 1947. It is to go into effect again automatically to the extent permi by law on fifteen days' notice by the union.

j. Except as such power is conferred on arbiter by specific provision of the agreement.

FIGURE 44—CONTINUED

CONTENT OF 100 SELECTED UNION AGREEMENTS ON FILE WITH UNITED STATES DEPARTMENT OF LABOR, DECEMBER 1948 [a]

Fringe Issues

No.	Less than 5	5 but less than 8	8 but less than 11	11 or more	1 week or less	Between 1 and 2 weeks	More than 2 weeks	2 weeks maximum	More than 2 weeks maximum	Other	Full pay	Partial pay	Entire period	Specified period	Other	Retirement	Life and/or dismemberment	Accident and sickness cash	Hospitalization and/or surgical	Medical care benefits	Other	Employer contributions	Employee contributions	Bonus Plans
	Number of Paid Holidays				Paid Vacations						Paid Sick Leave					Health, Welfare and Retirement Plans								
					Uniform Plan			Graduated Plan			Pay Rate		Duration			Coverage						Financing		
	9	40	41	42	43	44	45	46	47	48	49	50	51	52	53	54	55	56	57	58	59	60	61	62
59		X							X									X						
60		X							X						X									
61		X							X															
62					X																			
63								X									X					X		
64								X								X								X
65		X								X														
66			X							X											X	X	X	
67								X													X			
68								X																
69			X					X									X	X	X			X		
70						X																		
71		X						X																
72		X						X							X									
73		X							X								X							
74		X						X																
75		X							X						X									
76		X							X							X								
77								X																
78								X			X			X										
79										X														X
80										X							X	X	X			X		
81									X															
82									X															
83								X																
84									X															
85									X															
86									X															
87								X																
88									X															
89		X							X		X			X		X						X	X	
90		X						X																
91		X						X																
92										X							X		X					
93								X									X		X			X		
94								X													X	X		
95		X						X																
96		X					X																	
97		X							X			X		X		X								
98								X																
99								X																
100										X	X			X										
No.	9	40	41	42	43	44	45	46	47	48	49	50	51	52	53	54	55	56	57	58	59	60	61	62

Seniority

No.	Within craft or occupation only	Department-wide	Plant-wide	Company-wide	Other	Layoffs	Promotions	Rehiring	Other	Union stewards and/or officials	Specified skilled employees	Handicapped and disabled employees	Disabled veterans	Other
	Seniority Unit Covered					Seniority Recognition				Employees with Special Seniority				
	63	64	65	66	67	68	69	70	71	72	73	74	75	76
59					X	X	X	X						
60					X				X					
61					X	X	X	X		X				
62	X							X						
63					X	X	X	X						
64					X				X					
65					X				X			X		
66														
67					X	X	X	X						
68					X	X	X	X						
69					X			X						
70	X					X								
71														
72					X	X	X							
73					X				X	X				
74					X				X	X		X		
75					X	X	X	X		X		X		
76					X									
77														
78														
79					X	X	X	X		X		X		
80		X				X	X	X		X		X		
81					X	X	X	X		X		X	X	
82					X	X	X	X		X				
83			X			X	X	X		X				
84					X	X	X	X						X
85					X	X	X	X		X			X	
86					X	X	X	X		X			X	
87		X				X	X	X						
88		X				X	X	X		X			X	
89					X					X				
90														
91		X							X	X			X	
92		X						X		X				
93		X						X		X				
94		X						X		X				
95		X						X						
96					X				X					
97					X	X	X	X		X				
98					X	X								
99		X				X	X	X						
100		X							X					
No.	63	64	65	66	67	68	69	70	71	72	73	74	75	76

Grievances and Arbitration

No.	Grievance representation established	Procedure outlined	Written notice required at some point	Interpretation of contract clauses	New issues arising under contract	Other	Not to add or change contract terms	Not to set general wage level	Not to decide prod.-standards disputes	Other	Single arbitrator	Bipartisan board	Permanent	Temporary	Paid for jointly	Paid for by loser	Other	Federal conciliation machinery	State machinery	Labor Dept.; or chosen from fed. panel	State or city agency	Private agency	Other agency	Other
	Grievance Procedure			Arbitrator's Jurisdiction							Arbitration Machinery and Costs							Outside Machinery Used in Disputes						
				Issues			Limitations				Type		Permanence		Financing					Arbitrator Appointed by:				
	77	78	79	80	81	82	83	84	85	86	87	88	89	90	91	92	93	94	95	96	97	98	99	100
59	X	X	X	X							X			X	X			X						
60	X	X	X			X											X	X						
61	X	X	X	X						X		X		X	X									X
62	X	X																						
63	X	X		X													X							X
64	X	X	X	X						X	X			X	X							X		
65	X	X	X	X	X					X							X			X				
66	X	X		X													X						X	
67	X	X		X						X							X							
68	X	X		X			r	X									X			X				
69	X	X		X													X		X					
70	X	X										X		X	X						X			
71	X	X		X	X												X							
72	X	X	X	X			X				X			X	X					X				
73	X	X	X																					
74	X	X	X	X				X				X		X	X									X
75	X	X		X			X					X		X	X						X			
76	X	X	X			X	X	X			X			X	X									
77	X	X		X								X	X			X								X
78	X	X	X	X													X			X				
79	X	X	X	X			X	X		X	X			X	X							X		
80	X	X	X	X			X					X	X		X									
81	X	X	X	X			X				X			X	X									
82	X	X	X	X			X				X			X	X							X		
83	X	X	X	X			X					X		X	X					X				
84	X	X	X	X			X			X		X	X		X									
85	X	X	X	X			X				X			X	X									
86	X	X	X	X			X					X	X		X									
87	X	X	X	X	X						X			X	X					X				
88	X	X	X	X			X				X			X	X					X				
89	X	X	X		X							X		X	X									
90	X																X							
91	X	X	X	X								X		X	X							X		
92	X	X	X	X			X				X			X	X									X
93	X	X	X	X			X				X			X	X									X
94	X	X	X	X			X	X			X			X	X			X				X		
95	X	X	X	X			X	X			X			X	X							X		
96	X	X	X	X						X							X							X
97	X	X	X	X			X			X		X		X	X							X		
98	X	X	X																					
99	X	X		X													X							X
100	X	X															X			X				
No.	77	78	79	80	81	82	83	84	85	86	87	88	89	90	91	92	93	94	95	96	97	98	99	100

k. Master Builders, Mason Contractors, Stone Mason Contractors, Excavators, and Concrete Construction Association.
l. Local that withdrew from Mine, Mill and Smelter Workers and is temporarily affiliated directly with CIO
m. Either party may terminate agreement earlier on thirty days' notice.
n. Company agrees not to discontinue practice of paying monthly bonus at Pensacola plant.
o. All in specified departments, except specified groups.
p. Also Carpenters (AFL), Electrical (AFL), Firemen (AFL), Machinists (ind.) and Pulp (AFL).
q. As specified by the National Labor Relations Board.
r. Except by mutual consent of union and company involved.
s. Clerical workers only.
t. Retail Food Ind. and Retail Grocers Assn., Seattle, Washington.
u. Specified in local supplements.
v. Preferential hiring.
w. All unlicensed seamen and enumerated crafts.
x. As specified by the National Labor Relations Board, plus specified categories.

sample. Attainment of a union shop under the Taft-Hartley Act depended on a favorable vote by more than half the employees in the bargaining unit as determined by the National Labor Relations Board. About a sixth of the union-shop clauses provided for a modified union shop in which certain employees were exempt from the membership requirement.

Maintenance-of-membership clauses appeared in 15 per cent of the agreements sampled. These clauses, the result of a wartime compromise, require all members to continue in the union but do not require newly hired workers to join the union. They usually provide an escape period during which members may resign.

Some of the remaining half of the contracts contained other security provisions: preferential-hiring clauses whereby the employer gives union members preference in filling vacancies and, sometimes, preferred status in layoffs; clauses under which the employer, by implication, sanctions union membership; clauses naming the union as the sole bargaining agency, either for its members or for all employees. Under special conditions, these provisions sometimes give the union the same degree of security as some of the broader security clauses. Preferential hiring through a "rotary" hiring hall in the maritime and longshore industries, for example, results practically in a closed shop.

In 1948, union-shop clauses replaced many closed-shop clauses, because of legal compulsion, and many membership-maintenance clauses, because of union insistence. The great amount of uncertainty surrounding the postwar labor legislation left many contracts without clear security clauses. During this period, many unions that did not comply with the requirements of the Taft-Hartley Act contented themselves with obtaining checkoff rights.[12]

Three fourths of the contracts, covering nearly nine out of every ten employees,[13] included clauses whereby the employer deducts union dues from the employee's pay and turns them over to the union. In almost every case, these checkoff clauses provided that the employees must first authorize the deduction in writing. About two in every five checkoff clauses also included deduction of initiation fees; about one in five, deduction of assessments; almost one in twenty, deduction of fines and other union levies. Checkoff provisions may be combined with almost any of the basic union-security clauses — with the closed or union shop, maintenance of membership and other clauses.

Duration of Contract

Union-management contracts are usually signed for a one-year period. Three fourths of the sample agreements signed between September 1947 and July 1948 were for a year or less; 15 per cent ran for two years or more; and the remaining 10 per cent ran for a period between one and two years.

The popularity of short-term contracts, however, appears to be on the wane. The Twentieth Century Fund's survey of union and management attitudes,[14] conducted during the first half of 1948, when most of the above-mentioned contracts were signed, revealed a general preference for longer contracts. The favorable attitude toward longer contracts was much more pronounced among businessmen than among union leaders.

Sixty-four of the 88 management representatives favored contracts for a period of two or more years, 11 preferred one-year agreements, and 13 had no preference. (See Table 82.) Among the 50 international union officials interviewed, 17 favored contracts running for two years or more, 15 preferred one-year contracts, 5 wanted an indefinite period for their contracts, and 13 had no preference. (See Table 83.) In most cases, however, neither union nor management representatives considered duration of the agreement a vital issue.

Many union leaders who preferred one-year contracts said that under more stable circumstances they would advocate contracts for longer periods. In the words of one union official:

> I'd choose a one-year contract, first, because of the unsettled conditions and, second, because of the Taft-Hartley Act, which prohibits us from negotiating a closed-shop agreement. We expect that law to be

12. One year later the Bureau of Labor Statistics found union-shop provisions in 50 per cent of a sample of 2,159 agreements, membership-maintenance clauses in 21 per cent, and sole bargaining rights for all employees in the bargaining unit in 29 per cent. See "Union Security Provisions in Agreements, 1949–50," *Monthly Labor Review*, August 1950, p. 224.

13. The Bureau of Labor Statistics survey of 1949–1950 contracts found checkoff provisions in about two thirds of its sample of 2,159 agreements. *Ibid.*, p. 226.

14. W. S. Woytinsky and Associates, *Labor and Management Look at Collective Bargaining,* Twentieth Century Fund, New York, 1949.

TABLE 82

COMPANIES (IN 1948) PREFER TWO-YEAR CONTRACT TO GIVE STABILITY, SAVE NEGOTIATING TIME

Question: For a wage contract which goes into effect this summer or fall, would you prefer a two-year contract with annual wage reopening or a straight one-year contract? Why?

Response	Total	Manufacturing Companies	Non-manufacturing Companies
Number of respondents	88	47	41
Length of contract preferred:			
One-year	11	3	8
Two-year	52	28	24
Longer than two years	12	8	4
Reason for preference:			
Gives greater stability	25	12	13
Saves time in negotiations	23	14	9
Avoids fringe demands	11	6	5
Causes less disturbance to employee morale	2	—	2
No preference	13	8	5

Source: W. S. Woytinsky and Associates, *Labor and Management Look at Collective Bargaining,* Twentieth Century Fund, New York, 1949, p. 46.

modified. But if conditions were stable, two years would make it better for the employer, the employees and the international union. It is a lot of work and headache for all three to have to negotiate every year.

Both union and management representatives gave greater stability of labor-management relations and reduction in negotiating time as their two main reasons for favoring long-term contracts. One businessman stated the case for the longer contract as follows:

I would prefer a two-year contract with one annual reopening. It would save us a lot of labor and the difficulty of negotiating and preparing for negotiating every several months. We also would like to have as much stability as possible, which we don't have when we are in negotiations or faced with them.

Most of the union officials and many of the businessmen favoring long-term contracts insisted on including a wage-reopening clause. Some union leaders wanted the privilege of reopening other "economic" issues as well.

Strikes and Lockouts

The signing of an agreement generally indicates labor's and management's intention to work together under the accepted terms for the duration of the contract. Most agreements attempt to fortify this intention with specific preventives against work stoppages. Fully 80 per cent of the selected agreements negotiated between September 1947 and July 1948 contained specific clauses banning or limiting the use of work stoppages during the life of the agreement.

TABLE 83

UNION LEADERS (IN 1948) SPLIT ON LENGTH OF CONTRACT DESIRED

Question: If you were negotiating an agreement now and you had your choice of a one-year or two-year contract, which would you choose? Why?

Response	Number of Unions	Union Members: Number, in Thousands	Union Members: Percentage of Total
Total	50	10,602	100.0
Length of contract preferred:			
One-year	15	2,549	24.0
Two-year or longer[a]	17	3,769	35.5
Indefinite period	5	721	6.8
Reason for preference:			
Stabilization of industrial relations	5	1,285	12.1
Deteriorating conditions in the industry	2	452	4.3
Miscellaneous reasons	10	2,032	19.2
No preference	13	3,563	33.6

a. Fourteen unions, with 2,779,000 members, preferred two-year or longer contracts only if wage-reopening clauses were included.

Source: W. S. Woytinsky and Associates, *Labor and Management Look at Collective Bargaining,* Twentieth Century Fund, New York, 1949, p. 38.

Half the contracts in the sample contained clauses banning strikes and lockouts for the life of the agreement. Another 5 per cent banned all work stoppages except when such action was necessary to enforce the agreement or to secure compliance with an arbitration award or when wage renegotiations were deadlocked.

In another 25 per cent of the contracts, the union agreed not to strike until the disputed issue had passed through the full grievance procedure. If the dispute was then subject to arbitration, the pledge against work stoppages remained in force. In some of these contracts, the arbitration clause was so broad that the pledge to refrain from work stoppages in arbitrable disputes amounted to an unconditional ban on strikes and lockouts.

Largely because a union is merely a representative and not a seller of labor, and therefore cannot guarantee that its members will always be available for work, agreements include clauses limiting union liability in the event of a strike. Such a provision appeared in more than half the contracts in the sample signed between September 1947 and July 1948, for the most part in contracts that had no-strike clauses. More than 70 per cent of the anti-liability clauses said that the union could not be held liable for any strike it did not authorize or aid. Almost three fourths of the limited-liability clauses were coupled with clauses requiring the union to take steps to halt the strike. In most cases if the union failed to take the prescribed steps, it then became liable for the work stoppage.

Management and Union Rights

Although the collective bargaining agreement as a whole may be considered as a description of union rights, it sometimes contains clauses listing specific employer privileges. Management rights generally consist of all those not specifically granted to employees under the terms of the contract or by established usage. In the past, employers have preferred not to refer specifically to management rights in the contract. Many still take that position, largely through fear that any statement or listing of management prerogatives in the contract may be taken as inclusive and may consequently restrict, rather than maintain, management rights. Contract provisions on union and management rights therefore are not reliable indicators of the fields of activity reserved to the two parties to collective bargaining.

About 60 per cent of the contracts analyzed included clauses designating the rights reserved to management. About a fourth of these clauses were merely general statements reserving to management all prerogatives not specifically abridged by the agreement. The other three fourths included specific listings covering items such as the right to direct the working force (hiring, firing and so forth) and the right to control business and production matters (production methods, materials used and so forth). Less than a third of all the contracts referred to company rules, but most of these gave the company the right to add new rules or to revise old ones. Only a few required union approval of proposed additions or changes.

Among the rights won by unions were safety provisions, some type of which was included in more than half the agreements. Some of these clauses merely provided for setting up joint safety committees or specified that the company would consider union safety recommendations; others pledged the company to furnish protective clothing and safety equipment or to maintain first-aid equipment and personnel. Sixty per cent of the contracts gave unions the right to use company bulletin boards; 10 per cent outlawed discrimination because of race, creed, color, national origin or sex. In 40 per cent of the contracts management agreed not to discriminate against employees because of union activities, and in 15 per cent the union pledged itself not to intimidate or coerce employees because of nonmembership in the union.

Wages and Hours

The general wage scale and the basic hourly schedule, though still the heart of the collective bargaining agreement, take up very little space in the average agreement. Supplementary wage practices and indirect controls on hours are spelled out in far greater detail. Detailed wage-rate schedules for individual jobs sometimes are included, usually as a supplement or an appendix to the basic agreement. Such schedules are too closely related to particular circumstances in the industry or the establishment involved to have general significance.

Wages

The general wage adjustment agreed on during negotiations usually appears as a simple statement that the company agrees to increase wages X cents an hour or Y per cent effective on a certain date for all employees covered by the agreement. There are many variations, including special provisions for piece rates and other incentive payments and differentials for separate classes of workers. Once the general wage scale is set it usually remains unchanged for a year.

Of the selected contracts signed between September 1947 and July 1948, 70 per cent did not permit renegotiation of wages within a year. In 10 per cent of the contracts, reopening of the wage question was permitted at any time. Most of the remaining 20 per cent permitted renegotiation only at specified periods; a few, however, required specific changes in economic conditions, such as a stated change in living costs, before the wage question could be reopened. Less than 3 per cent of the contracts provided for an automatic wage adjustment.[15]

15. Since the start of the Korean war in 1950 and the consequent intensification of the defense program, interest in automatic cost-of-living clauses has grown. During the July-September 1950 quarter alone, the number of workers covered by such escalator clauses

Most of these related wages to changes in the cost of living, and some guaranteed wage adjustments similar to those made by leading firms in the industry.

Nearly four of every five contracts guaranteed a minimum payment to employees reporting for work at the regular time or called back to work, whether or not work was available for them. About a third of these clauses, however, exonerated the company from payment if the lack of work was beyond the company's control, and about a fifth exonerated the company if the worker refused reasonable substitute work. As a rule, the minimum guarantee was equivalent to four hours' pay. Such clauses are designed to compensate employees for the time lost and the expense and inconvenience involved and to penalize management for inefficient planning.

Almost half the contracts protected the worker's wage rate in a temporary transfer to a lower-rated job. If the transfer was made for the company's convenience, the worker was guaranteed his regular rate of pay. About one in six of these clauses, however, permitted the company to reduce the worker's rate of pay to that of the new job after a certain time limit. Transfer to a higher-rated job, on the other hand, brought with it the higher rate of pay in nearly 40 per cent of all contracts, most frequently as soon as the transfer was made.

Few union contracts specifically banned incentive-wage plans; more often the widespread union opposition to such procedures was implicit in the absence of incentive clauses in the contract. Agreements providing for such plans generally did no more than indicate the union's role in setting or protecting standards. Usually this was limited to appeal against unsatisfactory rates set unilaterally by management.

Hours and Overtime

The 8-hour day and 40-hour week, although in practice the standard American work schedule, was provided for in less than half the sample of agreements signed between September 1947 and July 1948. About two thirds of the contracts designated a basic 8-hour day, but less than half specified a 40-hour work week. Some 5 to 10 per cent of the contracts called for a work day shorter than 8 hours and a work week shorter than 40 hours; between 1 and 5 per cent called for a longer work day, and 10 to 15 per cent for a longer work week. Many contracts made no reference to the basic work schedule; about a fourth omitted mention of the length of the work day and more than a third made no reference to the length of the work week.

Overtime clauses made it clear, however, that the 8-hour day, 40-hour week was observed as the basic schedule in most instances. Eighty per cent of the agreements provided for payment of overtime premium rates after 8 hours of work a day, and between 65 and 70 per cent after 40 hours of work a week. Moreover, overtime premiums after 40 hours a week were payable in many instances where the contract made no mention of the fact because, in all likelihood, the Fair Labor Standards Act applied.

Week-end work was discouraged by provision for premium pay rates on Saturday in 35 to 40 per cent of the contracts and on Sunday in 55 to 60 per cent. The proportion of workers protected by these provisions was much greater than would appear from the frequency of such clauses. About two out of every three workers were covered by the Saturday overtime provisions, and almost three out of four by the Sunday provisions. About a fifth of the contracts applied the 5-day-week principle to employees who normally work on week ends by requiring premium rates for work on the sixth and seventh consecutive days. Pay for Saturday or sixth-day work was almost always at the rate of time and a half; double-time pay for Sunday or seventh-day work was only slightly less general.

As compensation for night work, two thirds of the agreements established a shift differential. In most cases all employees on a late shift were paid a few cents more an hour than for the same work on the day shift. In about one out of three contracts third-shift workers received an additional bonus over second-shift workers. Absence of shift-differential clauses reflected in many cases merely the fact that the establishment covered by the contract operated on a one-shift basis.

Fringe Issues

Distinct from basic wage and hour clauses are the so-called fringe provisions, covering vacations, holidays and employee benefits.

rose from an estimated 500,000 to 800,000. See *Cost-of-Living Adjustments in Collective Bargaining,* Bureau of Labor Statistics, September 1950, p. 1.

Vacations

Most of the selected contracts negotiated between September 1947 and July 1948 provided for paid vacations. The few exceptions occurred where workers change employers frequently, as in the maritime and construction industries. Some contracts allowed vacation pay without time off. Such arrangements appeared in some automobile and machinery plants with heavy production backlogs and in some seasonal industries in which the workers preferred to work as long as possible.

Almost all contracts — about 85 per cent — related the amount of vacation time to the employee's length of service. About 10 per cent gave a uniform vacation to all employees. Less than one third allowed vacations for workers with less than a year's service, but nearly all contracts gave vacations after the first year. The vacation period most commonly designated was one week; almost 80 per cent of the contracts allowed one week after a year's service, slightly more than half granted only one week after two years' service, and almost half, after three years' service. A two-week vacation was not as common as one week until after four years' service, but almost 90 per cent of the contracts provided a two-week vacation period for workers with five years' service.

In 70 per cent of the contracts, vacation time was paid at the regular hourly rate. Some contracts even called for inclusion of the shift premium and average overtime earnings in the vacation pay. Between 15 and 20 per cent of the contracts related the vacation pay rate to the amount of time worked during the preceding year — normally as 2 per cent of annual earnings each week. A few contracts paid a uniform flat sum to all employees.[16]

Holidays

Collective bargaining agreements reflect the importance attached to holidays in this country. Ninety-five per cent of the contracts analyzed included clauses relating to holidays, and almost three out of four provided for the observance of some or all recognized holidays without loss of pay.

Between 60 and 65 per cent of all contracts recognized six holidays — usually New Year's Day, Memorial Day, Independence Day, Labor Day, Thanksgiving Day and Christmas. About 25 per cent recognized seven or more; about 5 per cent, fewer than six. Paid holidays, however, were fewer in number. Only 40 to 45 per cent of the contracts provided six paid holidays; only 15 to 20 per cent, more than six. In contracts in such basic industries as iron and steel, glass and clay products, and trucking, paid holidays were still relatively rare.

About 90 per cent of all contracts examined provided premium pay for holiday work. Double time was the most common premium rate; double-time or higher premium rates were provided in all but a few of the contracts that granted pay for unworked holidays. In contracts with unpaid holidays, on the other hand, a slight majority called for time and a half for holiday work, and the remainder for double time.[17]

Employee Benefits

Employee benefit provisions appeared in about 45 per cent of the agreements, but comprehensive programs providing substantial benefits for a wide range of disabilities were still the exception.

Absence of benefit clauses does not always mean that the employee has no such protection. Many unions and companies have initiated and operated benefit plans entirely outside the sphere of collective bargaining. Gradually, however, the unions are bringing more and more of these plans into collective bargaining discussions, where they become the springboard for more comprehensive programs.

Two types of employee benefit programs may be distinguished — sick-leave plans and health and welfare plans. About one agreement in five provided paid sick leave, most granting full pay. The amount of leave varied from less than one week a year to an indefinite period. A few clauses required short waiting periods — one, two or three days — without pay.

Slightly less than a third of all contracts contained health and welfare clauses. Between 15 and 20 per cent provided for life insurance, and

16. An analysis of 1,473 agreements in effect in late 1948 or early 1949 by the Bureau of Labor Statistics shows substantially the same pattern of vacation provisions. See "Paid Vacations under Collective Agreements, 1949," *Monthly Labor Review,* November 1949, pp. 518–22.

17. The same general pattern of holiday provisions was found in a Bureau of Labor Statistics survey of 2,316 agreements in effect in 1950. See *Labor-Management Contract Provisions, 1949–50,* Bulletin No. 1022, 1951, pp. 33–36.

the same proportion gave hospitalization protection. A slightly smaller number, between 10 and 15 per cent, provided benefits for nonoccupational sickness and accident,[18] and 10 to 15 per cent covered surgical expenses. About one contract in ten covered all these risks in a single comprehensive program. Benefits for death and loss of limb, maternity and occupational disability appeared in less than 10 per cent of the contracts. Only about 5 per cent mentioned old-age pension plans.[19]

Most health and welfare plans were to be financed solely by the employer. Only one benefit clause in six mentioned employee contributions toward meeting the program's cost.[20]

Hiring

Although collective bargaining negotiations generally emphasize the wage question, many agreements also define the worker's relationship to his job through clauses on hiring, discharge and layoff practices and promotion policies.

Almost every contract provided that after a layoff workers would be rehired in the reverse order of their separation from the "seniority unit." [21] In addition, some 10 per cent specifically guaranteed laid-off workers preference over new employees for jobs in seniority units other than their own.

Failure to return to work when recalled after a layoff meant loss of seniority and rehiring rights according to about two thirds of the contracts. Slightly more than half the contracts took away seniority and rehiring rights after a layoff lasting more than a specified period, usually after one year.

Discharge

Clauses designed to protect employees against arbitrary discharge were included in about 75 per cent of the contracts. Some of these cited justifications for discharge, others guaranteed appeal procedures, and some even provided separation pay. About half the contracts laid down a blanket rule that there should be no discharge except for "just cause." Another 10 per cent included lists of specific offenses warranting discharge, such as drunkenness, incompetence, insubordination and violation of company rules. Further grounds for discharge were included in company rules and, in many contracts, under the terms of the union-security provisions.

Most clauses on procedure for appeal from discharge emphasized speed — early filing and expeditious handling of the appeal. Half the contracts noted that appeals must be filed within a specified period, usually two to five days, and in 15 per cent the usual grievance procedure was shortened or a separate, briefer procedure was provided. About 40 per cent of all the contracts analyzed provided a guarantee of retroactive pay for time lost and of reinstatement of employees whose discharge was reversed.

A small proportion of contracts — about 10 per cent — granted special payments to discharged workers.[22] Separation pay on discharge has two purposes: to help the worker between jobs and to minimize discharges for trivial reasons. Generally such payments did not apply when a person was discharged for a serious offense, although a few contracts made no exceptions. The amount of separation pay varied greatly, from pay for only a week or two to as much as two weeks' pay for each year of service.

Layoff

Procedures to be followed in laying off workers were defined in all but a few contracts.

18. A Bureau of Labor Statistics analysis of 2,148 agreements covering more than 3.5 million workers during 1949 showed some type of nonoccupational sickness or accident benefit plan in three out of every ten agreements; the employer paid all costs in four out of five plans. See "Sickness and Accident Benefits in Union Agreements, 1949," *Monthly Labor Review,* June 1950, p. 637.

19. Since 1948, however, there has been a widespread movement toward establishing new health, welfare and pension programs or bringing existing ones under the scope of collective bargaining. In mid-1950, more than 7 million workers were covered by health and welfare plans and 5.1 million by pension plans under collective bargaining agreements. See *Employee Benefit Plans under Collective Bargaining,* Bulletin No. 1017, Bureau of Labor Statistics, 1951, Table 4, p. 4.

20. In mid-1950 about a third of the workers under health and welfare plans and about a fifth of those under pension plans contributed to the cost of the program. *Ibid.,* Table 5, p. 5.

21. The unit (department, plant, occupation and so forth) within which the employee's seniority is determined. Unless it is provided that employees in a unit affected by a layoff are to displace others with less seniority in other units, those with lowest seniority in the affected unit are laid off.

22. The Bureau of Labor Statistics found that 8 per cent of a sample of more than 2,100 contracts in effect during 1949 provided separation allowances for workers losing their jobs through no fault of their own. See "Dismissal-Pay Provisions in Union Agreements, 1949," *Monthly Labor Review,* April 1950, p. 384.

Most of these clauses were concerned with advance notice of layoff, and with the role of seniority in laying off workers.

Eighty per cent of the contracts called for advance notice of a layoff to either the union or the employees involved or both, and a fifth of these provided pay instead of notice. Advance notice gives the union a chance to propose methods of reducing the work force with the least possible hardship to individuals and gives the individual an opportunity to plan ahead. Very few contracts — about one in twenty — granted layoff pay to employees separated for a temporary period.

About 25 per cent of the contracts attempted to equalize the hardships of layoffs for long-service employees through the use of work sharing. Half of these called for work sharing among regular employees after all temporary employees had been separated, and half called for sharing among long-service employees after all short-service employees had been laid off. Short-service employees were usually defined as employees with less than a year's service, but some contracts included those with two, five or even ten years' service.

Contracts specifying work sharing placed two types of limits on it: more than half, a limit on the reduction in the work week, and a few a limit on the length of time work sharing could continue. Most clauses limiting reduction in the work week set a floor of 32 hours; if such a reduction should prove insufficient to take care of the decreased demand for labor, layoffs were to account for the rest. Clauses limiting the duration of sharing usually required a return to the normal work week after four weeks, followed by any layoffs that were necessary.

Seniority played some role in the layoff procedure in more than 90 per cent of the contracts analyzed. In almost three quarters of the contracts, the layoff clauses provided for separation of employees strictly according to seniority, those with the shortest length of service being the first to go. In a few contracts such other factors as skill and reliability were considered along with seniority. In some 15 to 20 per cent, seniority became a consideration only if two or more employees were considered equal in all other respects.

Promotion

In 35 to 40 per cent of the agreements negotiated between September 1947 and July 1948, selection of employees for promotion was to be based on length of service. An almost equal number — 30 to 35 per cent — provided that seniority should be used only if other factors were equal. More than a fourth of all contracts made no reference to promotion procedures.

The union's role in selection for promotion was limited almost entirely to review of the company's choice and appeal, if desired, through the regular grievance procedure. Between 5 and 10 per cent of the agreements specified that the company must consult the union before making the selection.

As a means of ensuring that no qualified employee would be overlooked when a better job opened up, about 35 per cent of the contracts provided for posting of vacancies. Interested employees were supposed to submit their bids for the vacant positions, generally within five days of the announcement. In addition, some 10 per cent of the agreements guaranteed preference to all company employees over outsiders for vacancies in other seniority units.

Grievance and Arbitration Procedures [23]

Almost all the selected agreements signed between September 1947 and July 1948 contained detailed grievance procedures, and nine out of ten provided for arbitration of unsettled grievances.

About three fourths of all contracts guaranteed an aggrieved employee the right to be represented by his union in initiating the complaint. Between 40 and 45 per cent provided that the union representative — generally the shop steward — should present the grievance at the first step in the procedure. The other 30 to 35 per cent called for presentation by the employee — if he desired, with the aid of the union and in the presence of union representatives; only 10 to 15 per cent insisted that the employee initiate the grievance procedure alone. At this first step, the management representative designated to receive the complaint was almost always the complainant's immediate supervisor.

At later steps in the procedure, the representation patterns outlined in the contracts varied considerably, depending largely on the structure of the union and company involved. The typical contract called for a union committee com-

23. For a more comprehensive analysis of labor arbitration problems, see Chapter 22.

posed of employees in the particular plant or establishment to present the employee's case at the intermediate stage. It reserved international-union representatives for the final steps. Generally, management was to be represented at the intermediate stages by industrial relations officers or personnel officers and at the final stages by top production or executive officials.

The advantages in prompt handling of grievances were recognized by both management and union. Primarily at management's insistence, a fourth of all contracts set a time limit — most often fifteen days or less — between the occurrence of the grievance and its initial presentation. Half the contracts required settlement or a company answer within a definite time after the grievance had been presented at each stage in the procedure.

Two out of five contracts recognized the union's role in handling grievances for its members to the extent of providing pay for at least part of the time union representatives spent on grievance work. Almost 25 per cent granted pay for all such time. On the other hand, almost 5 per cent of the agreements specifically ruled out company payment for grievance time and another 5 per cent required that grievance work be handled outside regular hours except in emergencies. About half the contracts made no reference to grievance time.

Arbitration of Grievances

Contract requirements for arbitration were limited almost entirely to questions arising out of the grievance procedure. Only one or 2 per cent agreed in advance to arbitrate deadlocks arising during negotiations for a new agreement and some 5 per cent, mostly in the textile industry, to arbitrate differences during wage reopenings. Almost 90 per cent of the contracts, however, provided for arbitration of unsettled grievances.[24] Less than 5 per cent required both parties to agree to submit the issue to arbitration; in all the others arbitration could be requested by either party.

In 85 per cent of the agreements arbitrators were to be chosen specially for each case; only 5 per cent provided for permanent arbitrators. Permanent arbitration procedures, however, appeared in contracts of a number of large companies or associations and covered, therefore, about 40 per cent of the workers. Choice of temporary arbitrators was to be by mutual agreement according to 65 per cent of the contracts; in three fourths of these, if the two parties could not agree, then an impartial agency, usually the Federal Mediation and Conciliation Service or the American Arbitration Association, was then to select the arbitrator. Twenty per cent of the agreements provided for immediate selection of the arbitrator by an impartial agency.

Half the contracts called for arbitration boards, generally consisting of three members; 40 per cent provided for a single arbitrator. Most agreements that mentioned cost divided it equally between the two parties. A few put all or a major portion of the cost on management or on the loser of the appeal.[25]

24. The Bureau of Labor Statistics found arbitration clauses in 83 per cent of a sample of 1,482 agreements in effect during 1949. See "Arbitration Provisions in Union Agreements in 1949," *Monthly Labor Review,* February 1950, p. 160.

25. The Bureau of Labor Statistics study revealed that the most popular single form of arbitration in 1949 contracts was the temporary board, which was provided in 52 per cent of the sampled agreements with arbitration clauses. *Ibid.,* p. 163.

CHAPTER 21

WORK STOPPAGES *

INDUSTRIAL RELATIONS involve the continual reconciliation of conflicting aims and interests. In by far most cases, management and labor are able to reconcile their differences and negotiate a mutually satisfactory basis of cooperation through collective bargaining. Most disputes are ironed out through grievance procedures, through mediation by third parties, or by arbitration. Occasionally all these methods fail, and normal labor-management relations are temporarily disrupted by a work stoppage.

The impact of a work stoppage — whether a strike called by the union or a lockout ordered by management — on labor-management relations, on wages and on working conditions is far greater than statistics on the frequency of stoppages would indicate. The terms on which one stoppage is settled often set the pattern for many other agreements.

Labor formally initiates most work stoppages. In a strict sense, therefore, strikes are much more numerous than lockouts. The distinction between the two, however, is highly artificial. If management desires to cut wages against employee opposition, it need not resort to a lockout to enforce its decision. It merely announces the cut and lets labor decide whether to accept the cut or call a strike. Similarly, when management rejects labor's demand for a wage increase, labor is put in the position of deciding between accepting management's refusal and striking. In short, because of the different positions of labor and management in initiating changes in wages and working conditions, a work stoppage is usually precipitated by a labor union although either party can be responsible for the deadlock in negotiations underlying the final break. Frequently, when referring to the same stoppage, the worker talks about a lockout and the employer about a strike.

Work stoppages that are clearly strikes include jurisdictional strikes, strikes resulting from disputes between rival unions or rival factions within the same union, and sympathy strikes in which management is not a party to the dispute.[1]

Work stoppages are not an unmitigated evil: a work stoppage or the threat of one may be the means of testing the market, of enforcing the "law of supply and demand." William Graham Sumner has stressed this positive aspect of strikes:

> Supply and demand does not mean that the social forces will operate of themselves; the law, as laid down, assumes that every party will struggle to the utmost for its interests . . . Buyers and sellers, borrowers and lenders, landlords and tenants, employers and employees, and all other parties to contracts, must be expected to develop their interests fully in the competition and struggle of life. . . . The other social interests are in the constant habit of testing the market, in order to get all they can out of it. A strike, rationally begun and rationally conducted, only does the same thing for the wage-earning interest.[2]

On the basis of the circumstances in which they occur, four types of strikes have been distinguished: depression strikes, prosperity strikes, organization strikes and sympathy strikes.

Depression Strikes

Depression strikes are usually desperation strikes. Under the pressure of declining profits and with an ample labor supply guaranteed by rising unemployment, management often demands from its employees greater production at lower pay. A final wage cut usually provides the spark, and the strike is on. Few such strikes have ended in victory for labor. But because depression strikes, even among organized workers, so often are spontaneous explosions, no history of failure appears likely to prevent them. The stronger, better-organized unions believe

* By Thomas C. Fichandler.

1. In some of these strikes, particularly those between rival unions, the employer is not always a passive bystander. He may, for example, encourage rival unionism in his establishment or have chosen to deal with one union though most of his employees prefer the other.

2. William Graham Sumner, "Strikes," in Maurice R. Davie, *Sumner Today,* Yale University Press, New Haven, 1940, p. 63 (reprinted in E. Wight Bakke and Clark Kerr, *Unions, Management and the Public,* Harcourt, Brace, New York, 1948, pp. 408–09).

they have a chance to succeed where unions of the past have failed.

Depression strikes have often been provoked by management as a means to weaken labor unions. An employer who has few orders on file can afford to bide his time until the union is exhausted.

Prosperity Strikes

Rising prices, which generally accompany a business upswing, provide labor unions with a strong argument in support of a wage raise; moreover, as orders pile up management hastens to improve its wage offers, especially since it can pass on increased costs in the form of higher prices. Prosperity strikes also usually coincide with growing strength of unions — increased membership and greater financial resources.

Prosperity strikes also include *organizing strikes* — work stoppages designed to establish a union and to win some measure of union security. Rarely, however, are strikes called solely for this purpose. Wage increases, better working conditions and similar demands almost always accompany the request for employer recognition of the union as bargaining agent.

Organization Strikes

The organization strike — as distinct from the organizing strike — is a work stoppage directed, not against the employer, but against another union. This includes jurisdictional and rival-union strikes. The *jurisdictional* strike is a conflict between two unions belonging to the same federation, both of which claim the same group of workers as part of their organizing sphere. The *rival-union* strike usually is a conflict between unions that do not belong to one federation but have similar trade jurisdictions.

Most jurisdictional strikes have occurred when changes in work methods, tools or materials have removed distinctions that formerly separated one craft from another. As steel replaced wood, for example, metalworking unions claimed jurisdiction over some jobs that the carpenters' union had claimed for years. Disputes of this sort, which could not be resolved within the federation to which the rival unions belonged, have caused work stoppages. In such disputes the employer is caught in the middle; if he signs with one union, he is in trouble with the other.

No one has a kind word for jurisdictional strikes. In recent years several states have enacted laws controlling them; the Taft-Hartley Act made it an unfair labor practice for a union to engage in a jurisdictional strike.

AFL unions, CIO unions and unaffiliated unions have used the strike as a weapon in competing with one another to become the bargaining agent for a group of workers. When the employer chooses to recognize one union while most of his employees prefer the other, the strike is aimed directly at him as well as at the rival union. Before the Wagner Act, a strike was often the only way a majority union could force the employer to recognize it in place of a minority union.

The election procedure under the Wagner Act for establishing the collective bargaining agent removed much of the justification for rival-union strikes, except in areas not covered by the act. The Taft-Hartley Act outlawed strikes aimed at forcing an employer to deal with a union that the National Labor Relations Board had not certified as the proper bargaining agent. The importance of organizational strikes has diminished greatly in recent years. Since 1942, jurisdictional and rival-union strikes together have comprised less than 6 per cent of all work stoppages resulting from labor-management disputes each year.[3]

Sympathy Strikes

The sympathy strike, like the organization strike, generally is not directed against the employer whose plant is struck. It is intended to give indirect aid to workers on strike in another part of the industry or trade. When a sympathy strike crosses industry lines and involves all or most of the workers in a community or a broader geographic area, it is termed a general strike. In both forms, the sympathy strike aims at broadening the group pressure on the employer to whom the demands have been made.

Neither the one-industry sympathy strike nor the general sympathy strike is common in the United States. The former has never accounted for as much as one per cent of all work stoppages in any year, and less than half a dozen general strikes have been recorded in the history of the country.[4]

---

3. Appendix Table 59.

4. Florence Peterson, *Survey of Labor Economics*, Harper, New York, 1947, p. 578. The general strike may take on a political goal rather than a specific

Issues in Work Stoppages

The issues over which work stoppages occur may be classified into broad groups: (1) differences between employer and employees over wages, hours and related questions, such as welfare and pension plans; (2) disputes over the bargaining agent, union recognition and union security; (3) questions concerning the conditions of work — job security, unsolved grievances and so forth; and (4) conflicts between rival unions and rival factions within a union.

Except for the period from 1934 to 1941, wages and hours have been the major strike issue in practically every year since 1881.[5] The question of union recognition and security — which usually was second to wages and hours — became the most frequent cause of work stoppages when the unions unleashed their mass organizing drive under the stimulus of economic recovery and the protection of the Wagner Act. The pattern changed when the United States entered World War II. Work stoppages on account of union organization questions declined sharply, from about 50 per cent to only 10 to 15 per cent of the total. (See Figure 45.) The wage issue again became the most important, followed closely by working conditions. Employee dissatisfaction with working arrangements, which in peacetime probably would have been handled by normal grievance procedures, exploded under wartime pressures into many short-lived strikes. Although such stoppages have declined from their wartime peak, they have continued since the end of the war at a slightly higher rate than stoppages relating primarily to union recognition and security.

In 1950, wages together with related "fringe" benefits were the primary issue in more than half the work stoppages, accounting for over four fifths of strike idleness. Pensions and social insurance, which had replaced wages as the primary postwar strike issue in 1949 (although the two were often combined), succumbed to the rising price level and yielded first place to wages in 1950.[6]

Few 1950 stoppages were concerned with wage cuts or with demands for a shorter work week. Working conditions, primarily questions of job security and internal shop conditions and policies, accounted for about a fifth of all stoppages and for nearly a third of all the workers involved. Union organization was the primary issue in only 13 per cent of all stoppages and accounted for only about 3 per cent of all the workers participating; union recognition, rather than attempts to strengthen established bargaining positions, was the primary issue in most of these stoppages. In another 6 per cent of the work stoppages, the issues of union organization and wages and hours were equally important.

Although work stoppages may be classified according to major issue, they rarely result from a single cause. Behind the typical stoppage are dissatisfactions that have accumulated over a long time. Employer-union controversies, internal union politics, workers' economic needs and their grievances against foremen — several or all of these, as well as other factors, may be present. The immediate issue bringing on the stoppage may be less important than others that may never be discussed openly. Figures on strike issues, such as those shown in Appendix Table 59, can give only a broad picture of the causes of work stoppages.[7]

History of Work Stoppages

The first recorded work stoppage in the United States took place in 1776 — the year the nation struck out for its independence — when painters in New York City "turned out" for higher wages. Since then the number of workers involved in work stoppages has risen gradually over the years, but not so much as the total labor force and far less than union membership. Fluctuations in the number of strikes and lockouts and in the number of workers involved have generally followed the business cycle. Major strike waves have occurred during organizing drives, during wars and, especially, in periods of postwar readjustment.

---

economic objective. In that form, it is a revolutionary general strike aimed primarily at demonstrating labor power, fusing labor solidarity and affecting governmental policies. Such work stoppages are rare and none has occurred in the United States.

5. See Florence Peterson, *Strikes in the United States, 1880–1936,* Bulletin No. 651, Bureau of Labor Statistics, 1938, Table 8, p. 23; Table 18, p. 39; and Table 28, p. 61. See also Appendix Table 59.

6. See Ann J. Herlihy, "Work Stoppages during 1950," *Monthly Labor Review,* May 1951, Table 3, p. 520.

7. The Bureau of Labor Statistics has classified work stoppages by major issue for the years 1881–1905 and since 1914; it warns, however, that its classification can be considered only approximate because of the great difficulty of determining the primary issue in a normally very complex situation. See Peterson, *Strikes in the United States, 1880–1936,* pp. 166–67.

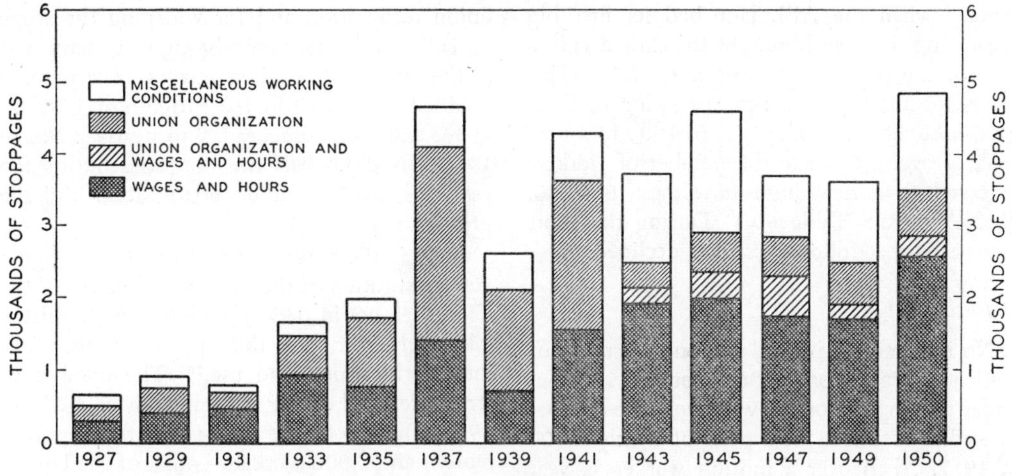

FIGURE 45. MAJOR ISSUES INVOLVED IN WORK STOPPAGES, 1927–1950

Source: Bureau of Labor Statistics. Cf. Appendix Table 59.

Wages and hours have been the most frequent major issue in work stoppages in almost all years except the late 1930's, when union organization was the primary issue in most stoppages.

The following pages outline the history of work stoppages only since 1881, within the life span of the AFL.[8]

1881 to 1905

The general trend in work stoppages was upward when the AFL appeared on the scene of the labor movement in the United States. From about 500 a year during 1881–1885, the number rose to more than 1,500 as business recovered from the depression of 1883–1885. (See Figure 46.) These were mostly strikes for higher wages, but they included many strikes arising from the drive for the 8-hour day. Among the stoppages in 1886 were the strike involving the famous Chicago Haymarket riot and the strikes on the Missouri Pacific railroad system.

Despite rising business activity from 1887 to

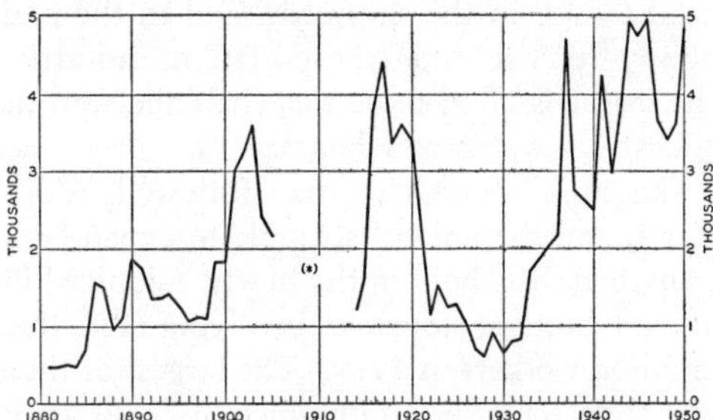

FIGURE 46. NUMBER OF WORK STOPPAGES, 1881–1950

* Data not available.

Source: Appendix Table 60.

The number of stoppages has risen over the years; peaks have coincided with periods of rising prices. union organization, wars and reconversion.

1889, the cost of living dropped and the number of work stoppages declined, falling below 1,000 in 1888. Renewal of the drive for the 8-hour day brought stoppages to almost 2,000 in 1890. From that level they declined to slightly more than 1,000 a year during the depression of 1893–1898. In 1894 almost 700,000 workers participated in stoppages, more than in any earlier year. Many of these were involved in coal-mining disputes and in the famous Pullman strike.[9]

Strikes increased sharply at the turn of the

8. For a more complete history of stoppages through 1940, see Florence Peterson, "Review of Strikes from 1915 to 1940," in *Handbook of Labor Statistics,* 1941 edition, Bulletin No. 694, Bureau of Labor Statistics, Vol. I, pp. 329 ff., and Peterson, *Strikes in the United States, 1880–1936;* for later years, see the following bulletins of the Bureau of Labor Statistics: *Strikes in 1941* (No. 711, 1942), *Strikes in 1942* (No. 741, 1943), *Strikes in 1943* (No. 782, 1944), *Strikes and Lockouts in 1944* (No. 833, 1945), *Work Stoppages Caused by Labor-Management Disputes in 1945* (No. 878, 1946), *Work Stoppages Caused by Labor-Management Disputes in 1946* (No. 918, 1948), *Work Stoppages Caused by Labor-Management Disputes in 1947* (No. 935, 1948), *Work Stoppages Caused by Labor-Management Disputes in 1948* (No. 963, 1949), *Analysis of Work Stoppages during 1949* (No. 1003, 1950).

9. President Cleveland intervened in this strike through the use of federal troops, over the protest of the Governor of Illinois, and the federal courts issued many injunctions requested by the Department of Justice.

century when the AFL launched its first big organizing drive and brought the skilled craftsmen of the country into the union fold. This drive, together with an upward swing of business, brought work stoppages in 1903 to a new peak of over 3,600 and the number of workers involved to a new high of almost 800,000. (See Appendix Table 60.) During the short depression that followed, strikes declined.

1914 to 1941

No information is available on the course of work stoppages from 1906 through 1913, but under the impetus of the war boom the number of strikes rose to a new peak of nearly 4,500 in 1917. Well over a million workers a year participated in the wartime stoppages, but, largely through the efforts of government labor boards, the strikes usually were short. Many of these strikes were in the building and the metal trades, in the shipyards, and in the coal, copper, lumber and transportation industries. The major issue in more than half the wartime strikes was wages and hours.

The rapid price rise that followed World War I, and the unions' struggle to expand and strengthen their hold in the newly unionized industries, brought stoppages involving more than 4 million workers in 1919. The largest of these were the steel strike — in which 367,000 workers were out in an unsuccessful attempt to win union recognition — and the bituminous coal strike — in which some 425,000 workers sought cost-of-living wage increases.

The number of strikes declined in the depression of 1920–1921 and continued to decline, through good times and bad, until 1933. The usual upsurge of stoppages during prosperity failed to materialize during the 1920's mainly because prices remained relatively stable while wages rose slightly.

The depression years 1929–1932 set the stage for profound economic, political and social changes. When economic recovery began, workers were ready to join unions in order to regain the wage losses suffered during the depression and to improve their working conditions. The NRA labor codes and the National Labor Relations Act of 1935 encouraged this development. Responding to these favorable conditions, the unions began mass organizing drives extending, for the first time, into all the country's basic industries. Pressure for higher wages, for union recognition and for widening the scope of collective agreements brought a sharp rise in the number of work stoppages. The number doubled, from 840 in 1932 to almost 1,700 in 1933, and then rose steadily to nearly 2,200 in 1936. In about half the stoppages during the years 1934–1936, union organization was the primary issue.

In 1937 the Supreme Court ruled the Wagner Act constitutional; the competitive drives of the CIO (set up in 1936) and the AFL shifted into high gear, and the sit-down strike came into fairly widespread use.[10] The number of strikes reached a new all-time high of 4,740 in 1937. But most were small; only two involved more than 50,000 workers — that of the United Steelworkers (CIO) against a group of steel corporations,[11] in which 92,000 workers participated, and that of the United Auto Workers (CIO) against the Chrysler Corporation, with 63,000 participating. Union organization was the main issue in almost three out of every five stoppages in 1937.

The 1937–1938 recession brought the usual decline in strikes, and stoppages ran at slightly more than 2,500 a year until the start of the defense boom. Under the spur of rising living costs and a growing demand for labor, the unions resumed their drive for higher wages and union recognition in 1941. The number of stoppages that year jumped to more than 4,000, involving well over 2 million workers.[12]

World War II

The number of stoppages declined during the first year of our direct participation in World War II, but rose to almost 5,000 a year by the end of the war. As in World War I, government labor agencies did much to keep the stoppages brief; the average duration in 1943 and 1944 was under six days. Few wartime strikes were authorized by national (or international) unions, and when local stoppages took place

10. One stoppage in ten during 1937 was a sit-down strike. Peterson, "Review of Strikes from 1915 to 1940," *Handbook of Labor Statistics,* Vol. 1, p. 338.

11. Independent steel companies (the Republic Steel Corporation, the Youngstown Sheet and Tube Company, the Inland Steel Company) and the Bethlehem Steel Corporation.

12. About 700,000 of this total were coal miners, who engaged in a series of stoppages during the year. Many workers were involved in several stoppages and thus are included in the count more than once.

union leaders generally cooperated with government agencies to bring them to a speedy end.

The most frequent issue in wartime strikes was wages, as prices continued a slow but steady upward climb. Relatively few stoppages were concerned with union organization, since the unions agreed to accept government decisions on their demands for recognition and union security. Many related to internal shop problems, aggravated by wartime tensions. Between December 8, 1941 and August 14, 1945 there were 14,731 work stoppages, most of them brief.[13]

Mining, rubber products, and the automobile and automobile equipment industry were the fields most seriously affected by work stoppages during the war. In 1943, and again in 1945, nearly 90 per cent of all the miners were out at some time during the year. In 1943 some 360,000 miners were out for an average of twenty days, and the industry lost more than 4 per cent of total working time. The 1945 strikes caused a loss of nearly 3 per cent of working time in the mining industry. The rubber products industry had almost half of its workers out during 1943 and considerably more before V-J Day in 1945; the industry lost more than 2.5 per cent of total working time that year, a large part before August. More than a fourth of the auto industry's workers were involved in strikes during 1943, and more than half during 1944. The proportion exceeded three fourths in 1945, but a large part of the total number involved were out after the end of the war. Toward the end of 1943 some 134,000 steelworkers were involved in a three-day stoppage in ten states. In all, there were 51 wartime stoppages involving 10,000 or more workers.

Among the industries that weathered the war with very little loss of time through stoppages were the apparel, the chemical, the construction and the printing and publishing industries. (See Appendix Tables 61 and 62.)

After 1945

V-J Day ushered in the most active period of strikes and lockouts in the history of the country. For almost four years, basic collective bargaining issues — wages and union security — had been settled within a government-determined pattern. When the government withdrew from the picture, pressing questions arose: Where would the postwar wage levels be stabilized? What type of union security patterns would be established? How many of "management's prerogatives" would be subject to collective bargaining? Management and labor had different views on these subjects. Settlement of the differences could hardly be expected without friction.

Although the number of stoppages was not much above wartime levels, remaining below the 5,000-a-year mark, the number of workers involved reached a new peak of 4.6 million in 1946. Moreover, almost 1.5 per cent of all potential working time was lost during the year.

During reconversion, the impact of work interruptions continued to be greatest in the mining industry, where stoppages, predominantly in the coal fields, caused a loss of more than 10 per cent of the industry's potential working time in 1946. (See Appendix Table 61.) The auto industry lost nearly 8 per cent of working time and the electrical machinery industry more than 7 per cent. Idleness also reached significant proportions in iron and steel (5.8 per cent), nonelectrical machinery (4.5 per cent) and nonferrous metals (3.9 per cent).

During the war, transportation, communication and other public utilities had experienced very few stoppages. In 1946, however, that industry group lost almost one per cent of working time, mainly through a series of stoppages in water transportation.

Early in 1946, at the height of the strikes in steel, electrical machinery, automobiles and meat packing, about 1.6 million workers were idle. Many reconversion stoppages, unlike those occurring during the war, ran for a long time. (See Table 84.)

Immediately after the end of hostilities, the unions sought wage increases to make up for the reduction in "take-home" pay when overtime, with its premium rates, disappeared. Later, when price control was relaxed and then abandoned, they sought to keep up with the rising cost of living. Although the number of stoppages declined after the initial shock of reconversion, the unions' desire to raise wages in line with rising prices during 1947 and most of 1948 and their drive for welfare and pension plans in 1949 kept the volume of stoppages between 3,000 and 4,000 a year. The sharp upturn in prices during 1950 was accompanied

13. *Work Stoppages Caused by Labor-Management Disputes in 1945,* p. 6.

TABLE 84

MAJOR RECONVERSION WORK STOPPAGES, 1945–1946

Business and Location	Union Involved	Beginning Date	Approximate Duration, in Days	Approximate Number of Workers Involved, in Thousands
		1945		
Bituminous coal mines, 8 states	United Clerical, Technical, and Supervisory Employees, District 50, United Mine Workers (ind.)	Sept. 21	30	209
Libby-Owens-Ford Glass Co. and Pittsburgh Plate Glass Co., 7 states	Federation of Glass, Ceramic, and Silica Sand Workers (CIO)	Oct. 16	102	13
Machine shops, shipyards, etc., San Francisco Bay area, Calif.	Machinists (AFL) and United Steelworkers (CIO)	Oct. 29	140	37
Textile mills, Conn., Me., Mass., N.H., R.I.	Textile Workers Union (CIO)	Nov. 1	133	18
Midwest Truck Operators Association, 21 states	Brotherhood of Teamsters (AFL)	Nov. 12	81	10
General Motors Corp., 11 states	United Automobile Workers (CIO)	Nov. 21	[a]	200
		1946		
Western Electric Co., New Jersey and New York	National Federation of Telephone Workers (ind.)	Jan. 3	65	24
Electrical manufacturing: General Motors, General Electric and Westinghouse plants	United Electrical Workers (CIO)	Jan. 15	[b]	174
Meat-packing industry, several states	Packinghouse Workers (CIO) and Amalgamated Meat Cutters (AFL)	Jan. 16	19	93
Steel, industry-wide	United Steelworkers of America (CIO)	Jan. 21	[c]	750
International Harvester Co., 4 states	United Farm Equipment and Metal Workers (CIO)	Jan. 21	86	29
Allis-Chalmers, 7 plants in 6 states	United Automobile Workers (CIO), United Farm Equipment and Metal Workers (CIO), United Electrical Workers (CIO) and CIO Industrial Union, 1424	Mar. 14	[d]	25
Bituminous coal mines, industry-wide	United Mine Workers (AFL after Jan. 1946)	Apr. 1	59	340
Maritime industry, unlicensed personnel — Atlantic, Gulf and Pacific Coast ports	Seafarers' International Union (AFL), National Maritime Union (CIO), Marine Cooks and Stewards (CIO) and Marine Firemen, Oilers, Watertenders and Wipers Association (ind.), supported by other AFL unions	Sept. 5	17	132
Maritime industry, licensed personnel — Atlantic, Gulf and Pacific Coast ports; longshoremen on Pacific Coast	Marine Engineers' Beneficial Association (CIO), Masters, Mates and Pilots (AFL), International Longshoremen's and Warehousemen's Union (CIO)	Oct. 1	[e]	142
Bituminous coal mines, industry-wide	United Mine Workers (AFL)	Nov. 21	17	335

a. About 4 months.
b. Settled in sections, running from about 1 to 4 months.
c. Settled in sections, running from about 1 to 3 months.
d. Settled in sections, running from about 5 to 11 months.
e. Settled in sections, running from about 3 to 8 weeks.

Source: Appendix Table 62.

by an increase in strike activity, and by the end of the year 4,843 stoppages had taken place. This number was almost as high as the 1946 postwar peak, but the number of workers involved and the man-days of idleness were well below 1946 levels.

The industries most affected by stoppages in the second postwar year were mining; transportation, communication and other public utilities; and transportation equipment. Each of these industry groups lost more than one per cent of potential working time through work stoppages. (See Table 85.)

The largest stoppage of 1947, the nation's first major telephone strike, involved about 370,000 workers. Another, involving almost as many workers, occurred in the bituminous coal mines when the government, which had seized the mines during the 1946 strike, returned them to private ownership. About 50,000 shipyard workers, mostly in Atlantic and Gulf Coast yards, participated in the year's longest strike.

In 1948 the bituminous mines were shut down again, this time for forty days, in a dispute over the method of handling the miners' pension funds. About 75,000 Chrysler auto workers were out for two weeks on the issue of wages, and some 28,000 west coast maritime workers on wage and other issues.

The year 1949 saw three complete coal stoppages and a partial stoppage in the form of a union-enforced three-day work week. The largest single stoppage, however, was the basic steel strike, involving 500,000 workers in twenty-nine states. Although a wage increase was one of the union demands, the major issue was a

TABLE 85

PERCENTAGE OF AVAILABLE WORKING TIME [a] LOST THROUGH WORK STOPPAGES, SELECTED INDUSTRY GROUPS, 1947–1950

Industry Group [b]	1947	1948	1949	1950
All industries	0.41	0.37	0.59	0.44
Manufacturing				
Primary metal industries	0.35	0.33	4.74	0.41
Fabricated metal products, except ordnance, machinery, transportation equipment			0.52	0.45
Ordnance and accessories			0.16	0.11
Electrical machinery, equipment and supplies	0.37	0.25	0.20	0.73
Machinery, except electrical	0.85	0.59	0.89	1.40
Transportation equipment	1.18	0.89	0.78	2.88
Lumber and wood products, except furniture	0.36	0.18	0.41	0.38
Furniture and fixtures			0.22	0.38
Stone, clay and glass products	0.46	0.27	0.10	0.55
Textile mill products	0.28	0.19	0.15	0.23
Apparel and other finished products made from fabrics and similar materials	0.06	0.08	0.07	0.08
Leather and leather products	0.21	0.19	0.55	0.17
Food and kindred products	0.19	1.27	0.42	0.19
Tobacco manufactures	0.78	0.02	0.06	0.16
Paper and allied products	0.17	0.12	0.44	0.33
Printing, publishing and allied industries	0.14	0.46	0.12	0.14
Chemicals and allied products	0.27	0.31	0.23	0.50
Products of petroleum and coal	0.67	1.54	0.15	1.39
Rubber products	0.69	0.90	1.30	0.66
Professional, scientific and controlling instruments, photographic and optical goods; watches and clocks	0.40	0.37	0.20	0.27
Miscellaneous manufacturing industries			0.17	0.22
Nonmanufacturing				
Mining	1.12	4.51	8.39	4.37
Construction	0.66	0.29	0.53	0.44
Trade	0.05	0.03	0.07	0.04
Transportation, communication and other public utilities	1.19	0.34	0.25	0.25

a. Estimated working time computed by multiplying the average number of employed workers each year by the average number of days worked per employee in that year. Employed workers as used here refers to all workers except those in occupations and professions in which there is little if any union organization or in which strikes rarely, if ever, occur. In most industries, it includes all wage and salary workers except those in executive, managerial or high supervisory positions or those performing professional work the character of which makes union organization or group action impracticable. It excludes all self-employed persons, domestic workers, agricultural wage workers on farms employing fewer than six, all federal and state government employees, and officials (both elected and appointed) in local governments.

b. Classification by industry not directly comparable with classification in Appendix Table 61.

Sources: The following publications of the Bureau of Labor Statistics: *Work Stoppages Caused by Labor-Management Disputes in 1947,* Bulletin No. 935, Table 3, p. 7; *Work Stoppages Caused by Labor-Management Disputes in 1948,* Bulletin No. 963, Table 4, p. 8; "Analysis of Work Stoppages during 1949," *Monthly Labor Review,* May 1950, Table 4, p. 504; "Work Stoppages in 1950," April 18, 1951, mimeographed.

pension and social insurance plan, upon which agreement finally was reached.

The major stoppages during 1950 were the coal stoppage that began in September 1949 and ran intermittently until March 1950 and a 102-day dispute between the CIO Automobile Workers and the Chrysler Corporation, involving 95,000 workers. The coal and auto disputes accounted for about 40 per cent of the man-days lost during the year through work stoppages. A major nation-wide strike threat by the Brotherhood of Railroad Trainmen and the Order of Railway Conductors was averted only by the federal government's seizure of all major railroad lines. Government "operation" of the railroads, which was still in effect at the end of the year, left unresolved basic disagreements between the railroads and the unions on questions of a shorter work week, pay raises and changes in operating rules.

The coal settlement included a substantial wage increase and a 50 per cent increase in employers' payments into the miners' welfare and retirement fund. The auto strike, which arose from differences over the form and administration of pensions and social insurance, concluded with agreement on a $100-a-month, jointly administered pension plan.

Two Postwar Periods Compared

The strike situation after the recent war bore many similarities to that immediately after World War I. More strikes occurred and more workers were involved after World War II than after World War I: in 1919, 4.2 million workers participated in 3,630 stoppages; in 1946, 4.6 million workers were involved in 4,985 stoppages. If these figures are adjusted for the change in the size of the working force, however, they suggest that one in every five workers was involved in stoppages in 1919 and one in seven in 1946.

Economic conditions during both periods were also somewhat similar. In both, stoppages developed primarily out of disputes over wages in relation to the rising cost of living. The major stoppages in both periods occurred in the same industries — steel, bituminous coal mining, and transportation and communication. On the other hand, there was a fundamental difference in the way the stoppages were conducted. For all the newspaper headlines, the 1946 stoppages were almost completely free of the violence that marked the strike wave in 1919. The contrast between the major stoppages of the two periods, the 1919 and 1946 steel strikes, is significant:

> *1919.* Mounted police, whom the strikers called "Cossacks," rode down strikers in the streets. In western Pennsylvania no union meetings were permitted; in Ohio pickets were clubbed and sent home. In Gary, Indiana, the United States Army took charge. In Duquesne, where Philip Murray and William Z. Foster tried to talk to the strikers, the mayor declaimed his classic: "If Jesus Christ himself came to Duquesne, he wouldn't be allowed to make a speech."
>
> *1946.* Peaceful picketing and no interference with civil rights. In New Kensington and two other towns, the mayors deputized union members, not company guards, as special police to keep law and order.
>
> *1919.* Picket lines and town squares were areas of open warfare between state police, deputized company guards, and the strikers.
>
> *1946.* Picket lines were "token" and pickets bored. Their sole active duty was to examine passes of union maintenance men and supervisors entering or leaving the mills.[14]

The public's great concern over the wave of stoppages after World War II arose partly from fear of union bigness and power. To many people, unions and strikes are synonymous. Their explanation of the postwar strike wave is simple: with a 15-million-member union movement, one must expect great numbers of strikes. Largely overlooked was the fact that though union membership almost quadrupled between 1919 and 1946, the proportion of employed workers involved in stoppages was lower after World War II than after World War I. Even more significant was the drop in the ratio of strikers to total union membership. (See Figure 47.) In 1919, to take the extreme case, the number of workers involved in stoppages exceeded the number of union members, whereas in 1946 it amounted to less than a third of total union membership. (See Table 86.)

Trends in Stoppages

There appears to be a definite relationship between the frequency of work stoppages and changes in business conditions; also, a marked seasonal fluctuation. Less clear is the long-run trend in the volume of stoppages.

---

14. Charles R. Walker, "Steel: A Retrospect," *Survey Graphic,* April 1946, quoted in Case Study No. 1, Committee on Causes of Industrial Peace under Collective Bargaining, National Planning Association, Washington, 1946, pp. ix–x.

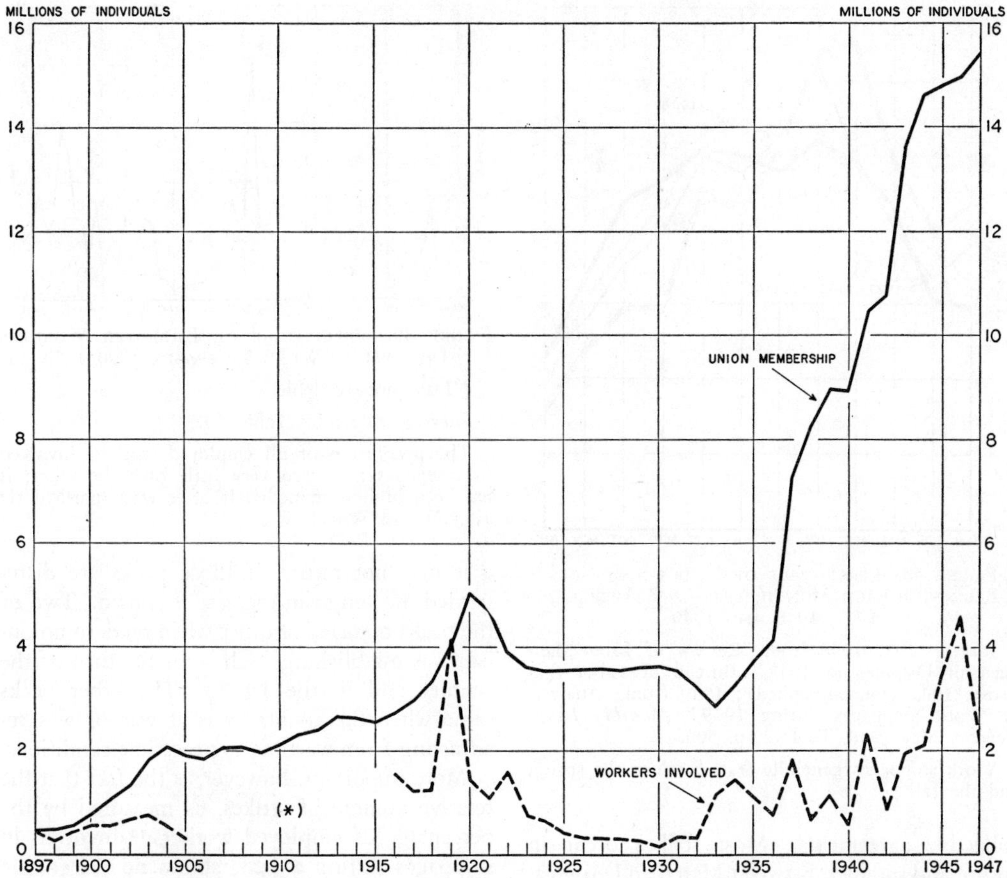

FIGURE 47. WORKERS INVOLVED IN WORK STOPPAGES AND UNION MEMBERSHIP, 1897–1947

* Data not available.

Sources: Appendix Tables 53 and 60.

The number of workers involved in stoppages has increased much less than the growth of union membership. The number of workers involved in strikes exceeded union membership after World War I, but represented only a fraction of the union membership after World War II.

TABLE 86

UNION MEMBERSHIP AND WORKERS INVOLVED IN WORK STOPPAGES AFTER TWO WORLD WARS

Year	Union Membership, in Millions	Workers Involved in Stoppages: Number, in Millions	Percentage of Employed Workers	Percentage of Union Membership
After World War I				
1919...	4.0	4.2	20.8	105.0
1920...	5.0	1.5	7.2	30.0
1921...	4.7	1.1	6.4	23.4
After World War II				
1946...	15.0	4.6	14.5	30.7
1947...	15.4	2.2	6.5	14.3
1948...	14.0–16.0	2.0	5.5	12.5–14.3

Sources: Appendix Tables 53 and 60.

Seasonal Movement

Stoppages generally reach their numerical peak during the spring and summer and decline sharply after August to a low point in December. (See Figure 48.)

The middle of the year appears to have been chosen as bargaining time as far back as the 1850's. Students of labor history point out that in the past, in the absence of set wage agreements, workers frequently struck in the spring for higher wages and again in the fall to prevent wage cuts.[15] Today, bargaining on terms of work also takes place mostly between spring and fall, depending on the expiration date of

15. John R. Commons and Associates, *History of Labor in the United States,* Macmillan, New York, 1921, Vol. I, p. 576.

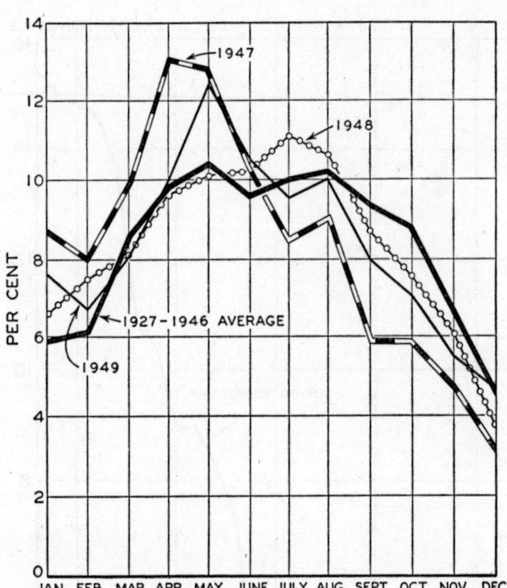

FIGURE 48. PERCENTAGE OF YEAR'S STOPPAGES BEGINNING EACH MONTH, 1927–1946 AVERAGE, 1947, 1948 AND 1949

Source: 1927–1948 from "Review of Labor-Management Disputes in 1948," Bureau of Labor Statistics, 1949 (mimeographed); 1949 from "Analysis of Work Stoppages during 1949," *Monthly Labor Review,* May 1950, Table 2, p. 500.

Work stoppages generally start between the spring and the fall.

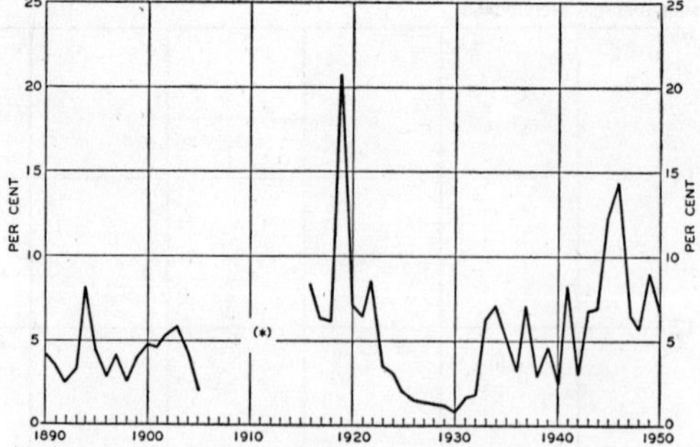

FIGURE 49. PERCENTAGE OF EMPLOYED WORKERS INVOLVED IN WORK STOPPAGES, 1890–1950

* Data not available.

Source: Appendix Table 60.

The proportion of all employed workers involved in stoppages has risen very little over the years; it has been highest immediately after wars, particularly after World War I.

collective agreements. Most strikes occur in spring and summer, between March and August, when, for example, 88 per cent of the contracts analyzed in Appendix Table 58 are renegotiated. During the rest of the year, when the agreements are in force, stoppages occur at a lower rate.

Long-Run Trend

The general increase that has taken place over the years in the number of stoppages does not mean much. The successive peaks in the number of strikes coincided with special events that may not recur. If those peaks are disregarded, no long-run increase is shown. Two of the peaks occurred at times when modern unionism was establishing itself — at the turn of the century and in the 1930's. The other peaks came when the country was at war or was readjusting from wartime to peacetime conditions.

More important, however, is the fact that the relative volume of strikes, as measured by the percentage of employed workers[16] involved in stoppages during a year, shows no discernible upward trend. Between 1890 and 1905 the ratio fluctuated around 4 per cent. (See Figure 49.) After a sharp rise immediately following World War I, it ran below 2 per cent a year for eight years (1925–1932) and then fluctuated around 5 per cent a year until the end of World War II. After another rise following World War II, the ratio moved back toward the 5 per cent level, and in 1950 it just about equaled the 1917 rate.

16. See Table 85, footnote a.

Chapter 22

LABOR ARBITRATION *

Arbitration is a method of settling labor-management disputes that substitutes the judgment of a third party for the force of strikes and lockouts. It is an institution of collective bargaining. There is no place for arbitration when the employer fixes the terms and conditions of employment without effective challenge by the employees, when a powerful union can set the terms upon which its members will offer their services to employers, or when, as in time of war, the government prescribes wages, hours and other working conditions.

Arbitration is founded upon the essential idea of collective bargaining: that individual employment relationships shall be governed by common rules or terms and conditions, formulated and administered by joint action of the employer and the organized body of employees. When the arbitrator makes a decision that is binding on employees, union and employer, either interpreting an existing rule or laying down a new rule, his powers rest on the consent of the union and the employer to submit to his judgment.

Labor arbitration takes many forms and serves a variety of purposes. Distinction should be made between arbitration over a new contract and arbitration over an existing contract. Generally speaking, in arbitrating an existing contract the arbitrator is interpreting existing rules, while in arbitrating a new agreement he is making a rule. Arbitration of disputed terms of an existing agreement is an everyday business of collective bargaining. Arbitration of new agreements is, by contrast, an occasional matter. Only a few industries, notably transportation and the building trades, have standing arbitration boards and procedures for handling disputes over the negotiation of new agreements.

The character of arbitration is determined by the state of the agreement between the parties and by their will to agree. When an agreement is incomplete, the arbitrator must interpret its meaning and make a rule. When, despite an elaborate agreement, the parties distrust each other, the arbitration of the terms is legalistic and adds to the barriers between them. By contrast, where collective bargaining is fully established, the infrequent differences over new terms can be easily settled by an arbitrator, who has only a narrow gap to close. The arbitration of a new rule may be simply an adaptation of an existing rule. If the parties wish to agree but for some reason cannot find the rule to reconcile their differences, or need a third party to absorb the heat engendered during their dispute, the arbitrator's decision can bridge a seemingly wide gap.

Arbitration rarely brings about great changes or radical adjustments. The art of arbitration is to decide the dispute by some existing rule or common principle or by applying a standard prevailing in comparable cases or, in wage disputes especially, by compromising offers and counteroffers. The skill of arbitration is to win the parties' assent to the decision, for in any case they must carry it out.

History of Labor Arbitration

Arbitration always has behind it the pressure of public and private interests. The private interest of unions and employers is aroused when they know that they cannot win a strike or lockout easily, whereupon they prudently seek to avoid foreseeable losses. Public interest suffers immediately from even brief interruptions of vital services, and this stimulates the development of arbitration in industries providing such services. Arbitration grows, on the one hand, out of negotiation of agreements and adjustment of disputes by joint boards of employer and union representatives; on the public's side, it is rooted in government mediation and conciliation agencies.

Early arbitration intermingled disputes over grievances and general wage rates. With the spread of collective bargaining, arbitration of disputes over existing agreements made steady progress and provided a firm underpinning for collective bargaining. Arbitration of new agree-

* By Joseph Kovner, Attorney, Washington, D.C.

ments, however, has been beset by recurrent breakdowns and mounting tensions.

Labor arbitration in the United States began in the late 1880's.[1] It was first practiced in the building and printing trades, where the early growth of strong craft unions induced employers to arbitrate differences, and in interstate steam railroads and urban street railways, where public need for uninterrupted service induced both parties to find substitutes for work stoppages.

As early as 1887, following bitter strikes and lockouts, local societies of masons and bricklayers agreed with the masters that disputes over new job rates should be settled without recourse to strikes or lockouts by a joint board with an umpire to settle board deadlocks.[2] This basic scheme of a joint board and an umpire or referee, which followed British practice, is a current pattern in the building industry, particularly in well-organized urban centers.[3]

The rise of national unions accelerated the use of joint boards and arbitration by umpires. National-union officers proved their worth by avoiding strikes hurtful to the membership and the union treasury. In many craft unions, the constitution directs locals to establish joint boards and, upon direction by national officers, to submit disputes to arbitration.[4]

In 1888 the New York State Board of Arbitration and Mediation, a typical state mediation agency of that period, reported that street railway service had been interrupted by a number of strikes in the preceding year and recommended that wages and other working conditions in the industry be regulated by law and work stoppages forbidden.[5] The national union of street railway employees thereupon made arbitration of all disputes the cornerstone of its policy, obviating the need for legislation.[6]

In the same year Congress set up arbitration panels to which labor disputes could be referred voluntarily, intended chiefly for use in railroad labor disputes. The parties to railroad disputes made no use of these panels, however, though they frequently agreed to use private arbitrators. In the next forty-five years Congress repeatedly attempted to fix by law the patterns of arbitration for railroad unions and management.

Only the legislation adopted in 1926 and perfected in 1934 proved workable.[7] It established a joint board of adjustment with jurisdiction over all disputes concerning existing rules, to which cases can be brought for final decision by either party and which, in the event of disagreement, refers the issues to a referee. It established a permanent board of mediation authorized to determine finally questions of representation and, in addition, to conciliate disputes over new rules. It also established special "emergency" mediation boards, acting under presidential appointment, to settle, by mediation and by public report, disputes over new agreements when a strike vote threatens to interrupt railroad service. This legislation followed the practices developed by the railroad unions and managers who accepted collective bargaining. Before it was adopted the constitutions of the railroad unions spelled out in detail the procedures for handling grievances and taking strike votes.

In 1902, President Theodore Roosevelt obtained agreement from the anthracite operators and the United Mine Workers to arbitrate the issues of a strike that had shut down the mines for nearly a year.[8] The operators had refused to recognize the union or to deal with it in any way. The arbitration commission settled the strike by ordering the establishment of a permanent system for the arbitration of grievances, consisting of a joint board of union and employer representatives and an umpire to be named by a designated federal judge. The

1. John A. Lapp, *Labor Arbitration,* National Foremen's Institute, New York, 1942, p. 5. There were sporadic cases before that time, for example, an anthracite arbitration in 1871. Arthur E. Suffern, *Conciliation and Arbitration in the Coal Industry of America,* Houghton Mifflin, Boston, 1915, p. 209.

2. Josephine S. Lowell, *Industrial Arbitration and Conciliation,* Putnam's, New York, 1893, pp. 81–110.

3. Harry A. Millis, *How Collective Bargaining Works,* Twentieth Century Fund, New York, 1942, p. 220; R. E. Montgomery, *Industrial Relations in the Chicago Building Trades,* University of Chicago Press, Chicago, 1927, p. 85; Sidney and Beatrice Webb, *Industrial Democracy,* Longmans, Green, London, 1902, Vol. I, Chapter 3.

4. For one example, see the constitution of the Brotherhood of Painters, Decorators and Paperhangers of America (1947), pp. 17–18.

5. Second Annual Report, 1888, New York State Board of Arbitration and Mediation, Troy Press, Albany, pp. 10–12.

6. E. P. Schmidt, *Industrial Relations in Urban Transportation,* University of Minnesota Press, Minneapolis, 1937.

7. Railway Labor Act of 1926 as amended in 1934, 45 U.S. Code, Secs. 151–64. Lloyd G. Reynolds, *Labor and National Defense,* Twentieth Century Fund, New York, 1941, Chapter 8; and Lloyd Garrison, "The Railroad Adjustment Board," *Yale Law Journal,* February 1937, p. 567.

8. Millis, *op. cit.,* Chapter 6; Suffern, *op. cit.,* pp. 251–56.

decisions of board and umpire were made binding on the parties, and work stoppages were prohibited. This machinery was patterned on the grievance arbitration system already operating in the soft-coal industry, particularly in Illinois, where the miners' union was first organized. It introduced the formal institutions of collective bargaining: union organization, the establishment of fixed rules, and their administration by joint employer-union action.

The board has functioned continuously since 1903, making improvements from time to time. Despite economic crises and serious wage disputes, it has produced a code of work rules applying uniformly to the entire hard-coal industry, with less and less recourse to the umpire.

This method of instituting and maintaining collective bargaining has become a fundamental principle of our national labor policy. Louis D. Brandeis used it to bring about peaceful bargaining in the men's clothing industry in 1910. It was used in the 1936-1937 organizing drives of the CIO; machinery for handling grievances accompanied recognition of the union.

Some of the first agreements in new union-employer relations provided for a grievance procedure but did not name an umpire for unsettled disputes, a defect that gave rise to many complaints. The National War Labor Board insisted, without exception, on complete machinery to settle all grievance disputes, and under its pressure or by direct orders, permanent umpires were established by U.S. Steel and the United Steelworkers union, by the Chrysler Corporation and the United Auto Workers, and others. By 1944 at least three out of every four collective agreements provided for arbitration of grievance disputes, and such agreements covered 83 per cent of all workers under collective bargaining.[9]

In some collective bargaining relationships resort to the umpire is rare. The Studebaker Corporation in its relations with the United Auto Workers since 1936 and the pottery industry since 1900, for example, have functioned without need for arbitration.

Current Problems

Current problems of arbitration of *existing agreements* are primarily those of coverage, techniques and extension. Should the arbitration machinery set forth in the agreement cover all sorts of disputes or only those concerning the meaning of the terms of the agreement? Is this type of arbitration best carried out by strict interpretation of existing rules, in which precedent plays a large part, or should the arbitrator attempt to mediate a dispute before he has to decide it, putting rules and precedents aside in favor of compromise solution of each dispute? Should this type of arbitration be extended to all collective bargaining agreements through the creation of public arbitration tribunals, to which either party may go for a final decision when the agreement does not itself provide the machinery of arbitration?

The problems of arbitration of disputes over *new agreements* are quite different. Some students of the subject have attempted to find a set of principles by which these disputes can be settled, but no one has yet succeeded in devising a code that has won common assent — except in so far as common practices provide a guide to the arbitration of a particular case. Although recurrent crises in labor relations always start up agitation for compulsory arbitration of new disputes, labor, management and experienced observers have opposed it.[10]

Arbitration of Existing Contracts

Legal Status

The specific rules of industrial employment — wages, hours, piece rates, seniority, layoffs, discharges, apprenticeship and so on — are for the most part the product of private agreements and arbitration of these agreements, rather than of public law and judicial decisions. Both the collective bargaining agreement and the arbitration process were until recently in a legal twilight even when they were in wide use. The collective agreement was treated as a nullity, a mere memorandum of terms alterable in each individual hiring transaction. Arbitration by private third parties was once regarded as a trespass upon the jurisdiction of the courts.

Statutes have clarified the legal ambiguities. Labor relations acts conferring exclusive bargaining rights on the union chosen by free majority vote have confirmed the force of the

9. For War Labor Board experience, see *Termination Report,* National War Labor Board, Washington, 1948, Vol. I, Chapter 9; and *Arbitration Provisions in Union Agreements,* Bulletin No. 780, Bureau of Labor Statistics, 1944.

10. *Law and Contemporary Problems,* Duke University Press, Durham, Spring 1947 issue, devoted to a discussion of settlement of labor disputes.

collective agreement.[11] Most states now provide for the enforcement of agreements to arbitrate and arbitration awards, either under a general arbitration statute or through special legislation for labor cases. The Taft-Hartley Act made collective bargaining agreements enforceable at law and authorized the federal courts to entertain damage suits for their breach. Many unions and employers, however, preferred to follow common usage and enforce their agreements by arbitration rather than by lawsuits. The collective bargaining relationship is a continuous one, and parties who must remain in a continuing relationship settle their differences out of court.

Jurisdiction over Persons

An arbitration award clearly binds the union and the employer who are parties to the contract, but its compulsion upon individual employees has met with some practical and legal problems. The refusal of a group of workers to abide by an award creates trouble. Fines, layoffs or discharges have been used to discipline the offenders or their ringleaders. But nonmembers and members whose claims are rejected or opposed by the union — as when in seniority disputes the union asserts a seniority right in favor of one person or group as against another — create jurisdictional problems.

The railroad unions, since they grew without benefit of the closed shop, treated grievance representation as a benefit of membership, exclusively controlled by the majority union. The statutory adjustment board of the Railway Labor Act operated on this basis, hearing only grievances brought by unions or employers. But the courts have ruled that a nonmember or a member whose claim is not favored by the union cannot be bound by an arbitration decision unless he is given notice and an opportunity to participate in hearings before the arbitrator.[12] In 1946 the Supreme Court ruled that even a member must authorize the union to represent him in arbitration; but the Court added that this authorization could be given through the union by-laws, to which each member is presumed to agree, or through handling by the union in the regular way, in which notice and assent were either actually given or could be presumed to be given.[13] Thus, the courts have emphasized the judicial nature of arbitration by conditioning its binding effect on the principles of due process: notice and hearing.

Scope of Subject Matter

The jurisdiction over subject matter in arbitration of existing agreements is flexible and depends on the scope of the agreement between the parties. The main types of coverage are: (1) all disputes arising during the life of the agreement; (2) all disputes except those relating to specified subjects; (3) only disputes over the meaning of the terms of the agreement.[14] Most agreements that do not confine the arbitration strictly to the terms of the agreement make some reservations in other areas. Management tends to favor a strict clause.[15] Even when the agreement is loosely worded, both union and employer assume that each has policies that are not subject to arbitration. Furthermore, unless the parties have agreed that the arbitrator may make a new rule, he cannot satisfactorily adjust a grievance if there is no rule to guide him. The real distinction is whether arbitration is to cover only the rules set forth in the agreement or to include job rules established by custom or usage.

The attempt to confine arbitration to the contract rules in the early stages of a relationship results either in unsettled grievances that cause work stoppages or in elaborate agreements that lead to dispute over the meaning of words. The restriction of arbitrable job rules to those specifically mentioned in the agreement is generally unworkable. Since the purpose of the agreement is to prevent work stoppages, this objective ought to be accomplished so far as possible. Any job rule within the area of common understanding between employees and employer can be arbitrated. As a practical matter, it is impossible to set down all job rules in writing. When shaped by experience rather than formal contract, arbitration covers the rules stated in the agreement and other similar rules,

11. *J. I. Case Co.* v. *National Labor Relations Board,* 321 U.S. 332 (1944).

12. *Nord* v. *Griffin,* 86 Fed. *2d* 481.

13. *Elgin-Joliet and Eastern Railway Co.* v. *Burley,* 325 U.S. 710 (1944); second opinion on rehearing, 327 U.S. 661 (1946).

14. *Collective Bargaining Contracts,* Bureau of National Affairs, Washington, 1941; *Arbitration Provisions in Union Agreements,* Bulletin No. 780, Bureau of Labor Statistics, 1944; Elias Lieberman, *The Collective Labor Agreement,* Harper, New York, 1939.

15. John Aspley and Eugene Whitemore, *Handbook of Industrial Relations,* 3d edition, Dartnell, Chicago, 1948.

for both have a common origin in bargaining and usage.

The Railway Labor Act, seeking a general statutory formula based on actual practice, applies the adjustment procedure to "any dispute growing out of grievances or out of the interpretation of agreements," leaving the term "grievance" to common understanding as meaning the application of any job rule or specified wage rate.[16] The award that settled the 1902 anthracite strike by establishing a board of arbitration did not specify the rules to be arbitrated; the parties knew or soon learned that arbitration best applied to customary job rules or fixed rates, including disputes as to whether a rule was in effect by custom or usage. The agreement between the steelworkers and Carnegie-Illinois refers to differences over the meaning and application of the agreement and any "local trouble," that is, disputes over local plant rules not set forth in the master agreement. The New York milk industry's agreement with teamsters provides for arbitration of the terms of the agreement and any matters "germane" to it.[17]

In industries with piece rates or changing job rates, the parties soon learn, as the Webbs pointed out,[18] that quick, cheap adjustments are essential and are best reached by price and rate experts of the union and the employer, rather than by arbitration. Thus, many contracts of the International Ladies' Garment Workers' Union provide that disputes shall be arbitrated by special adjustors or referees rather than by the general arbitrator, and some exclude arbitration altogether.[19]

Arbitration Techniques

The arbitration technique often depends on the attitudes of the parties toward each other. Even when a union has substantially identical contracts with two companies, the relation between the company and the union may compel the umpire in one situation to take a narrowly legalistic course in arbitration, while in the other, aided by the parties' confidence in each other, he may help them work out a constructive course and genuinely reconcile their differences to their mutual advantage.

Public Arbitration Tribunals

At the 1946 convention of the United Steelworkers of America, several delegates from small locals without recourse to a full-time umpire requested the national organization to share with the locals, by special subsidy, the expenses of occasional arbitration or, where possible, to establish a regular agency with joint funds. They complained that all too often they had been left with unsettled grievances because arbitration was too expensive for them.

The small locals were seeking relief for a common complaint. Labor arbitration is often expensive because the parties must bear all the costs, including the fees of the arbitrator and a stenographer and rental of a hearing room. The failure of arbitration hurts employees more than employers, because most grievances are complaints against an action of the employer, who generally has the initiative in the conduct of the business. He discharges a worker, or transfers one to a lower-rated job, or promotes one to a senior position. If the grievance against his action is not upheld, his action remains in effect. Since the costs of arbitration are a greater burden on a union than on an employer, he may, without malice, prolong the hearing and thus increase its cost. The local may then be for some time without funds for another arbitration. The steelworkers' convention, which denied the small locals a subsidy, advised the delegates to improve their voluntary adjustment techniques and, when necessary, to levy special assessments for important arbitration cases.[20]

Another remedy would be to establish a system of public arbitration tribunals, as William M. Leiserson has suggested.[21] The jurisdiction of such tribunals over subject matter would depend on the parties' agreement; jurisdiction over persons would be limited to those bound by the agreement. Public tribunals would not in any way displace or review private arbitration, whether by a standing umpire or by an occasional one named in the contract or selected

16. 45 U.S. Code, Sec. 153 (i).

17. For these and other examples, see *Proceedings of Conference on Labor Arbitration,* Labor Relations Council of the Wharton School of Finance and Commerce, University of Pennsylvania, Philadelphia, November 1948; Millis, *op. cit.;* Lapp, *op. cit.;* and Lieberman, *op. cit.*

18. *Op. cit.,* p. 237.

19. Kurt Braun, *Union-Management Co-operation; Experience in the Clothing Industry,* Brookings Institution, Washington, 1947, pp. 116–25.

20. *Proceedings of 1946 Convention,* United Steelworkers of America, pp. 108–15.

21. William M. Leiserson, "For a New Labor Law — A Basic Analysis," *New York Times Magazine,* February 6, 1949, p. 7.

in the course of a particular dispute. Appeal to a public arbitration tribunal could not be made until all the steps set forth in the contract, from shop steward and foreman to top joint board, had been exhausted.

The arbitration tribunals would be special courts, because arbitration of existing labor contracts is a special subject. Public arbitrators would be selected by public authorities. This would not be an innovation, for many collective agreements have provided for the selection of umpires by judges, by Labor Department officers or by public-spirited bodies such as the American Arbitration Association. A public arbitration system would be modeled on the best private arbitration practice and thereby improve both; its corps of experienced, secure arbitrators would strengthen the profession of private arbitrator; it would help to create a common law of job rules and collective bargaining relations.

Arbitration of New Agreements

Legal Status

An agreement to arbitrate a dispute over new terms of employment is lawful, and the arbitrator's award is enforceable, on the same principles as apply in arbitration of existing contracts.[22] An agreement to arbitrate a new contract, however, not only must name the arbitrator or provide clearly for his designation, as in the case of existing contracts, but also must specify clearly the dispute to be submitted to arbitration. Hence, the parties usually execute a detailed agreement submitting a particular dispute even if they have a prior general understanding to do so.

The reason for this additional requirement is apparent. The court is only enforcing an agreement of the parties; if it is to order a balking party to arbitrate, it must be able to determine from the agreement not only *how* but *what* they were to submit. Furthermore, one of the tests of the legality of an award is whether the arbitrator acted within the jurisdiction conferred upon him, and thus the agreement to arbitrate must specify what was submitted to him for decision. In a grievance arbitration, the existing contract supplies this information. The statutes that promote voluntary arbitration by describing specific procedures for a binding agreement are especially applicable to agreements for the arbitration of new terms of employment.

Attitudes of Unions and Management

The problems of arbitrating new agreements are like the problems of negotiating any agreement. Bargaining over wage rates and other conditions of employment is conducted with much higgling and haggling. The parties do not reveal their ultimate positions. To add to the arbitrator's difficulties, the parties themselves often do not know exactly what they will finally settle for; they await the trial of negotiations to find out. In any case, unions ask for more than they expect to get, and employers offer less than they will concede under pressure.

On the whole, unions are more disposed than management to use arbitration as a way out of bargaining deadlocks. Union leaders questioned in the Twentieth Century Fund's survey[23] — made at a time when wages were rising — were more inclined than management to favor arbitration of disputes over new contracts.[24] While the attitudes on arbitration of new agreements were pragmatic and determined by individual experience, almost all the persons interviewed said that of course they arbitrated disputes over the meaning of existing contracts.

Membership Attitudes

By custom and often by union laws, union negotiators must submit an agreement for membership approval before it becomes binding. This is a hard test of leadership. The union officer must know what sort of agreement will be acceptable to the membership — he will not stay in office if he guesses wrong too often.

An arbitrator's award is not subject to this procedure, and by its nature cannot be. The arbitration process must, however, take into account the assent of union members to new terms. In case of a deadlock in negotiations the submission to arbitration must often be authorized by the membership. Even when arbitration of new terms is a regular practice, it has to be authorized in each case, since the members must choose between the employer's last offer and arbitration; the possibility of a strike hovers in

22. C. M. Updegraff and W. P. McCoy, *Arbitration of Labor Disputes,* Commerce Clearing House, New York, 1946.

23. W. S. Woytinsky and Associates, *Labor and Management Look at Collective Bargaining,* Twentieth Century Fund, New York, 1949.

24. See Chapter 19, especially Tables 79 and 80.

the background. In the railroad industry, submission to final mediation, which is akin to arbitration, follows from a strike vote. As a matter of tactics, union negotiators will not weaken their hand by obtaining premature authorization to arbitrate.

Agreement to arbitrate renewal of contracts amounts, in effect, to a standing authorization to the union officers, and they must exercise this authority with great skill. Indeed, the pressure on union representatives is greater than that on management. Union representatives often suggest to the arbitrator that certain demands must be met or they cannot remain in office, and it is part of the skill of an arbitrator to distinguish between the union's serious objectives and its make-weight demands.

In 1946 the Ford Division of the Auto Workers Union rejected a pension plan their negotiators had won; the union officers were defeated in the next election, and the members lost what appeared to be a good bargain, but work did not stop. By contrast, refusal of the membership to accept an arbitration award creates a crisis. The Landis decision nearly wrecked collective bargaining in the building trades.[25] The New York Pressmen's Union was forced by its national officers to accept a 1922 award reducing union standards, but the resentment was so great that pressroom operations were disrupted until the award was changed.[26] A bitter and violent internal dispute in the United Mine Workers followed a decision of the Fuel Administrator in 1919 decreeing continuance of wartime penalty rates for illegal work stoppages. The men would have accepted the ruling from their own officers but were enraged by the imposition of a penalty upon them by a third party, a stranger to their troubles.[27]

In grievance arbitration the problem of individual assent is met to some extent by the requirement that the person concerned be given notice and the right to independent representation at the hearing if his claim is not being prosecuted by the union officers. In contrast, arbitration of new rules is like the legislative process; conduct of the proceedings is entirely in the hands of the official representatives.

25. Montgomery, *op. cit.*
26. Sylvia Kopald, *Rebellion in Labor Unions,* Boni and Liveright, New York, 1924, Chapter 8.
27. *Ibid.,* Chapter 2, especially pp. 77–78.

Submission to Arbitration

In 1915 the Boston local of the Street Carmen's Union lost an important arbitration case and thereupon became bitterly opposed to the principle of arbitration, demanding that the national union abandon it. The national president advised the local to lay down specific rules of arbitration in advance in the future so that it would be bound by the decision only in so far as the arbitrator followed the rules.[28] Management always favors strict submission, especially in wage disputes. Under the Railway Labor Act an agreement to arbitrate, besides designating the members of a board, must: "state specifically the questions to be submitted to the said Board for decision, and that in its award or awards the said Board shall confine itself strictly to decisions so specifically submitted to it." [29] The 1945 National Labor-Management Conference urged voluntary arbitration but specified that "the parties should agree on the precise issues, the terms of the arbitration submission, and the principles or factors by which the arbitrator shall be governed." [30]

Techniques

The procedures for arbitrating new agreements are different from those for arbitrating contract disputes. In the hosiery industry, grievance disputes are referred to a permanent umpire; while the three-year contracts provide for annual wage reopenings subject to arbitration as follows: wage disputes are submitted to a special board composed of a union and an employer representative; if these representatives cannot agree, the umpire designates a third person, who may not, however, be himself. This separation is made to protect grievance arbitration — which must be stable and continual — from the heat of disputes over new terms.[31] This is the uniform pattern in arbitration of new terms. The same arbitrator

28. Schmidt, *Industrial Relations in Urban Transportation,* p. 196.
29. *The President's National Labor-Management Conference,* Bulletin No. 77, Division of Labor Standards, 1945, p. 43.
30. *Ibid.*
31. *Proceedings of Conference on Labor Arbitration,* Labor Relations Council of the Wharton School of Finance and Commerce, University of Pennsylvania, Philadelphia, November 1948, p. 56. The renewal of the master agreement itself is not subject to arbitration.

rarely sits in successive disputes between the same parties over new rules; one decision uses him up for that relationship at least, although certain persons noted for their experience and skill are frequently called on by different parties.

Although arbitration of new disputes is conducted through a hearing, there are practically no rules of evidence. The parties urge every consideration of expediency and policy they can think of. There are no general principles, for different factors influence each case. Ability to pay is relevant in most cases; but the employer must meet minimum standards, on the one hand, and the union, on the other, cannot expect wage rates in a particular plant, even an exceptionally profitable one, to exceed the prevailing rate. The lack of principles to guide the arbitrator, especially in wage disputes, bedevils the process and often prevents proper functioning.

A management consultant in urban transit says that neither unions nor employers can develop objective standards; it is up to the public, speaking through expert arbitrators. Whenever there is conflict between what the public and what the parties consider a fair wage, the arbitrator must conform to the "results of collective bargaining." [32] Public opinion is influential, but the public's idea of a fair wage must impress unions and management before it can affect arbitration.

Writing in 1890, the Webbs said:

> In the really crucial instances — the issues relating to the conclusion of a new agreement — habitual and voluntary recourse to an umpire may be expected, we think, only in the unlikely event of capitalists and workmen adopting identical assumptions as to the proper basis of wages.[33]

Today unions and employers are no closer to identical assumptions of a fair wage, but that does not mean their disputes are irreconcilable. It is enough that they agree on methods of resolving their differences. Collective bargaining and procedures for the peaceful settlement of disputes have been extended to more and more industries and employments. Both unions and management hold that compulsory arbitration is no solution, and they both believe they can settle their crucial differences through negotiation and compromise.[34]

32. *Ibid.*, pp. 41, 66.
33. Webb, *op. cit.*, p. 237.
34. *Partners in Production,* Twentieth Century Fund, New York, 1949.

Arbitration and Mediation

Just as it is argued that the grievance umpire should not judge but mediate, so it is argued that the arbitrator of new terms should try to mediate a dispute rather than decide it. It is fairly well agreed that he should try to mediate *before* he decides, unless the parties make it clear that they do not want any attempt at mediation. Mediation is closer to arbitration of new terms than it is to the adjustment of grievances. But arbitration procedures are formal, while mediation is informal. The arbitrator sits with both parties; the mediator is a go-between, meeting with one and then the other. The mediator's responsibility ends with his attempt to secure an agreement, but the arbitrator must decide the dispute if he fails to help the parties reach agreement.

Arbitration boards are frequently tripartite, made up of union and employer representatives and a third party. Such boards are rarely used in grievance adjustments, where the parties exhaust the procedures for joint action before they turn the dispute over to an umpire. Skilled arbitrators seek unanimous agreement from union and employer members of a tripartite board by trying out different solutions until they find one that meets with common accord.

Methods for Settling Labor Disputes

Various proposals have been made for dealing with labor disputes that seriously hurt the public: compulsory arbitration; prohibition of industry-wide strikes; temporary governmental seizure of industrial establishments; injunctions to require cooling-off periods; and fixed steps of collective bargaining, mediation and voluntary arbitration.

Compulsory Arbitration

Some experts who urge compulsory arbitration would apply it only to certain industries, others to any dispute the President might find to endanger national health or safety. In either case, it is suggested, the law should guarantee that the terms awarded workers under compulsory arbitration will compare favorably with those in other employment.

The objections to compulsory arbitration amount to this: that arbitration as a part of collective bargaining can work only when, on failure to reach an agreement, workers have the right to strike and management has the right to close down the enterprise. The possibility of a strike keeps collective bargaining alive and holds the results of arbitration close to those that would be reached by bargaining. The right to strike is a fundamental freedom, and it can be regulated only when it is available as a possible course of action. That is one reason why direct prohibition of strikes was avoided even in wartime.

Strikes for certain specific purposes, such as a jurisdictional strike between two unions, can be made unlawful. It is almost impossible, however, to write a law defining those strikes that must be prohibited because they endanger the state. If such a law names specific industries, it will either be limited to those where it is not needed because arbitration is already practiced or be extended to situations in which compulsory awards will not be obeyed. If it is left to the President to invoke compulsory arbitration, this discretion cannot be exercised unless the government is prepared to take over and operate an enterprise in the event of disobedience. The general guarantee of an award of favorable conditions cannot ensure acceptance of an award in a particular case.

Prohibition of Monopoly Strikes

Prohibition of monopoly, or industry-wide, strikes has been advocated on the grounds that excessive power is sure to be abused and that no private organization can safely be permitted to exercise complete control over the supply of any goods or services, certainly not important ones. Following the argument that a "natural" monopoly, as in transport or utilities, must be regulated, losing its freedom in return for its inherent advantages, and that when a monopoly is not inevitable or "natural," it should be prohibited, it is urged that industry-wide strikes should be enjoined by statute, upon suit by the government. This measure has the same legal basis as antitrust regulation of business. But enjoining business combinations has been no easy task, and enjoining unions presents even more difficulties. Collective bargaining tends to establish uniform working conditions, and it is impossible to define the point where this tendency becomes monopolistic: May the auto workers' union strike against one large producer at a time, or two?

Certain specific practices of unions having monopolies can be prohibited, but not the power to establish some uniform conditions of employment — and these are often the issue involved in great labor disputes with employers. Here, too, a government edict against strikes must face the chance of mass refusal to obey. While official strikes can be prevented by fines on the union treasury, legal penalties will not put great numbers of men to work against their will.

Governmental Seizure

Governmental seizure was used during World War II. Strikes and lockouts in private industry were not legally prohibited; instead, wartime morale was expected to ensure compliance with the decisions of wartime labor arbitration boards. Nevertheless, some strikes occurred, and some employers refused to obey the War Labor Board's orders. The President, without statutory aid, took possession of a struck aircraft plant; troops kept the plant open to persons willing to work while military officers supervised its management. Congress later wrote this seizure power into the War Labor Disputes Act,[35] which was invoked in coal strikes and other cases. By the end of the war it became necessary to back up seizure with court injunctions.[36] To stop a threatened national railroad strike in 1946, President Truman acted under a statute dating from World War I that made the railroads subject to seizure; he placed the railroads under military control and obtained a court order against any interference by strikers. In 1950, placing the railroads under governmental control was enough to end a strike.

The theory of this course of action is that, though strikes are legal in private employment and subject in large degree to constitutional protection, they are not lawful in public employment. Private employees become public employees when the government seizes a facility to provide goods and services essential to public health and safety. The government can take such action whenever a private enterprise that ordinarily supplies essential goods or services is unable to do so for any reason, including labor disputes. Once the government has taken possession, no one may interfere with its operations; it may change working conditions and it

35. 50 U.S. Code (Appendix), Secs. 1503–06.
36. *United States* v. *United Mine Workers of America,* 330 U.S. 258 (1947).

must guarantee the past rate of earnings to the owners. Possession is to be temporary, until the reason for governmental operation has ceased to exist — that is, until the parties have come to terms or accepted those set by the government during its possession.

Some urge that governmental seizure should be left as an emergency power, exercised by both the President and Congress if need be; others say that it should be enacted into law in order to enable the President to act quickly in emergencies.[37] This type of action is an ultimate power of government. It will be invoked whether or not a statute is in effect. The drafting of a statute, moreover, raises questions that can be decided only on a case-by-case basis. If the statute is general, it vests grave powers in the Executive that can hardly be checked by the courts or the legislature. If it is specific, it becomes a form of compulsory arbitration, enforcing jurisdiction and awards by governmental seizure. This is the kind of statute that several states — among them Indiana, New Jersey, Michigan, Wisconsin and Virginia — have recently adopted to prohibit strikes in public utilities. Court injunctions are necessary adjuncts.

The objective of seizure is not to prevent or stop strikes directly but to provide essential goods or services that have been cut off by a work stoppage. The government can undertake the minimum action required for this purpose in any given case. It may, for example, run freight trains with nonstrikers or use supervisory personnel to operate an electric or gas utility.[38] In the meantime, efforts can be made to settle the strike by negotiations between the disputing parties.

Mandatory Cooling-off Periods

The Taft-Hartley Act authorized the President to appoint an emergency fact-finding board in the event of actual or threatened strikes or lockouts adversely affecting the national health or safety. For eighty days thereafter, work stoppages are illegal and can be enjoined at the suit of the Attorney General of the United States. At the end of the period, the injunction is automatically dissolved, and the parties have full freedom of action. In 1948 the United Mine Workers struck in violation of an injunction issued under the act, but they ended the strike when heavily fined for contempt of court and threatened with more fines if the strike continued. Again in 1950, a national bituminous coal strike was enjoined, but after the District Court freed the union of contempt charges, the strike was settled on terms favorable to the union. In four other cases under the act, from 1947 to 1950, injunctions were obeyed, though in two, including a strike in an atomic-energy plant, strikes took place after the cooling-off period.

The provision for a cooling-off period has provoked great controversy. Unions opposed it altogether; employers favored it. Most experts agree to the theory that parties to important disputes should maintain the status quo for a fixed period while the government attempts mediation with all the prestige it can command. Some think, however, that this status quo should not be enforced by legal penalties. They favor the scheme of the Railway Labor Act, which provides that during this period neither party may change the existing conditions of employment, though it may suspend operations altogether.

Fixed Steps in Collective Bargaining

The maintenance of existing conditions pending negotiation of a new agreement is usually proposed in conjunction with other legally fixed steps in collective bargaining procedures.[39] Thus, it would be a legal duty of both unions and employers to bargain in good faith. Although the duty to bargain is a general concept that cannot be exactly defined, common tests are: not making changes in existing rules without notice and meetings with the other party; making offers and counteroffers on issues of wages, hours and other working conditions; willingness to put into writing any agreement that is reached. In addition, the procedures of

37. The first procedure has been recommended by the Labor Committee of the Twentieth Century Fund in "Strikes and Democratic Government" (1947).

38. The British Labor government did not outlaw a strike of longshoremen but used troops to unload food, medicines and other critical supplies.

39. See Leiserson, *op. cit.;* George Taylor, *Settlement of Industrial Disputes,* address at Industrial Relations Research Association, December 1948 (reprinted in *Congressional Record,* Appendix, p. 703, February 10, 1949); and testimony of Leiserson, Taylor, Davis, Feinsinger and others in Hearings before the Senate Committee on Education and Labor on S. 690, 81st Cong., 1st sess., 1949.

bargaining would be regularized by requiring formal notice to the other party and to the federal conciliation service of intent to change existing terms; by uniform arbitration procedures that may be invoked by joint consent; and, in important disputes, by the appointment of a presidential mediation board with power to subpoena witnesses and records and to make public recommendations for settlement if mediation fails to produce an agreement.

PART III

EMPLOYMENT AND UNEMPLOYMENT

Chapter 23

THE LABOR FORCE *

Many factors control the supply of labor: size of population, its age composition, the age at which boys and girls customarily leave school to enter work, the extent of employment of married women, the usual age of retirement from work, employment opportunities for marginal workers, and so on. The number of persons in the labor force varies also with the season and with business conditions. Statistics on the labor force are also largely affected by the method of enumeration and the definitions of "labor force," "workers" and other terms.

Some factors affect the size of various groups of workers differently. For example, with the progress of industrialization the proportion of young workers has declined as a result of longer school attendance and the higher age at which new workers enter jobs, while the proportion of female workers has increased. A depression brings additional workers into the labor market from families in which the customary breadwinner is out of a job,[1] but at the same time it squeezes out marginal workers who would have been employable under better business conditions.

To estimate future labor supply one must examine long-range trends in the size and composition of the labor force, recent changes in these trends under the impact of war, and short-term seasonal and cyclical factors.

Long-Range Trends

Size

The number of workers in the United States increased from 12.9 million in 1870 to 53.3 million in 1940 and to more than 60 million in 1949. Workers represented 30 per cent of the total population in 1870 and more than 41 per cent in 1950. The increase in the percentage of workers in the total population was due essentially to the change in the age composition of the population — the decline in the proportion of children and the rise in that of persons of working age. In 1940 only 25 per cent of the population were less than 15 years old, as compared with 31.8 per cent in 1920, 34.4 per cent in 1900, and 39.2 per cent in 1870.[2]

The proportion of gainful workers among persons aged 10 years and over increased from 44.4 per cent in 1870 to 50.2 per cent in 1900. Among persons aged 14 years and over the proportion of gainful workers then declined slightly, from 55.0 per cent in 1900 to 54.5 per cent in 1930. Using a new definition of the "labor force," the Census Bureau shows a further decline in that proportion in the next decade, from 53.2 per cent in 1930 to 52.7 in 1940.[3] The percentage then increased during World War II, reaching a peak in 1944. It declined thereafter but is still appreciably higher than in 1940. (See Table 87.)

---

* By W. S. Woytinsky.

1. W. S. Woytinsky, "Additional Workers and the Volume of Unemployment in the Depression," Committee on Social Security, Social Science Research Council, Washington, 1940 (mimeographed).

2. Sixteenth Census (1940), *Population,* Vol. II, Part 1, p. 26.

3. Through 1930, our censuses relied on the concept of "gainful workers," letting the respondent decide whether or not he was a gainful worker. In 1940 the definition was tightened, and only persons working or seeking work during the week before the enumeration were registered as belonging to the labor force. This change resulted in a sizable reduction in the reported labor force. It has been estimated that if the new definition had been used in the 1930 census, some 47.4 million persons would have been found in the labor force, as compared with the 48.6 million counted as "gainful workers."

The "Monthly Report on the Labor Force" published by the Bureau of the Census, although based on the definition of labor force used in the 1940 census, introduced some correction into the census data and arrived at somewhat higher figures. Annual averages of population and labor force derived from these reports are higher than would be suggested by projections of the census figures. For population, they are higher because they refer to the middle of the year, while the recent censuses have been taken in March-April, so that the annual averages exceed projections of the census figures by one fourth of the annual growth of population. For the labor force, annual averages are higher because of the seasonal rhythm of the labor force: the annual average number of persons in the labor force in a given year is usually appreciably higher than the number at the end of March in that year.

TABLE 87

POPULATION AND LABOR FORCE, 1870–1950

Year	Population, in Millions	Population of Working Age, in Millions	Gainful Workers or Labor Force: Number, in Millions	Gainful Workers or Labor Force: Percentage of Population of Working Age
A. According to Decennial Censuses				
		10 Years and Over	Gainful Workers	
1870.....	39.8	29.1	12.9	44.4
1880.....	50.2	36.8	17.4	47.3
1890.....	62.6	47.4	23.3	49.2
1900.....	76.0	57.9	29.1	50.2
1910.....	92.0	71.6	37.4	52.2
1920.....	105.7	82.7	42.4	51.3
1930.....	122.8	98.7	48.8	49.5
		14 Years and Over		
1900.....	76.0	51.4	28.3	55.0
1930.....	122.8	89.1	48.6	54.5
			In Labor Force	
1930.....	122.8	89.1	47.4	53.2
1940.....	131.7	101.1	53.3 [a]	52.7
B. According to Monthly Reports on the Labor Force				
		14 Years and Over	In Labor Force	
1940.....	132.0	100.2	56.0	55.9
1941.....	133.2	101.4	57.4	56.6
1942.....	134.7	102.5	60.2	58.8
1943.....	136.5	103.5	64.4	62.2
1944.....	138.1	104.5	65.9	63.1
1945.....	139.6	105.4	65.1	61.8
1946.....	141.3	106.4	60.8	57.2
1947.....	144.0	107.5	61.6	57.3
1948.....	146.5	108.5	62.7	57.8
1949.....	149.2	109.6	63.6	58.0
1950.....	150.7	110.8	64.6	58.3

a. Adjusted figure. The unadjusted figure is 52.8 million. (Cf. Table 132.)

Sources: Sixteenth Census (1940), *Population — Comparative Occupation Statistics for the United States, 1870 to 1940,* pp. 91, 13; *Current Population Reports,* Series P-50 and P-57, Bureau of the Census.

Sex and Age Composition

The main long-range trends in terms of age and sex groups are a decline in the relative number of children, young people and the aged who are in the labor force, and an increase in the relative number of women at work. (See Appendix Table 63.)

The decline in paid work by the young is not limited to children under 14 years. Since the turn of the century there has also been an appreciable decline in the proportion of workers among boys and girls aged 14 to 19; 45.2 per cent of this age group were gainful workers in 1900 and only 32.0 per cent in 1930. Using another classification, the 1940 census recorded that 29.2 per cent of this age group were in the labor force in the enumeration week (as compared with 31.4 per cent in 1930).[4] This trend reflects longer school attendance and the general tendency to enter the labor market at a later age. There are indications of the same trend in ages over 19 years. Of males 20 to 24 years old, 91.7 per cent were gainful workers in 1900 and 89.9 in 1930; 88.8 per cent belonged to the labor force in the enumeration week in 1930 and 87.1 per cent in the corresponding enumeration week in 1949. At the same time, the proportion of workers in the age class 25 to 44 years was slowly increasing and the proportion of nonworkers declining.

The apparent decline in paid work among the aged is due largely to the shift of population from rural to urban areas and from farming to nonagricultural pursuits. On the farm the head of the family is regarded as a gainful worker even when he can no longer work regularly in the fields; in urban areas a man has to withdraw from the labor force when his efficiency and ability drop below the standard required by employers. Moreover, many people now retire at an earlier age than was customary before the turn of the century. During the great depression early retirement — often to the relief rolls — was forced upon workers by the reluctance of employers to hire persons over 50 years old, often even those over 45. For a worker, it was said, "death begins at forty."

Many people explained the unfavorable trend in employment opportunities for older workers by the increasing strain of modern mechanized work. During the war, however, this explanation proved to be wrong, for hundreds of thousands of retired workers were called back to work and showed themselves able to meet all the work requirements of modern factories. When the emergency ended, many aged workers retired for good. The proportion of workers among persons aged 65 years and over is lower now than during the war but higher than in 1940. (See Table 88.) A shortage of skilled workers favors employment of older persons. Workers who reach the age of 65 on the job are protected against layoff to some extent by the principle of seniority. In many industries employers recognize this principle, even when

4. The proportion of boys and girls in the labor force increased during World War II (50.9 per cent in 1944), declined after its end, but remained much higher than in 1930 and 1940 (36.1 per cent in 1949). Many among them worked on a part-time basis.

TABLE 88

NUMBER AND PERCENTAGE OF WORKERS AMONG MEN AND WOMEN AGED 65 YEARS AND OVER, 1890–1950 [a]

Year	Men: Number, in Thousands	Men: Percentage of Age Group	Women: Number, in Thousands	Women: Percentage of Age Group
A. According to Decennial Censuses				
Gainful Workers Aged 65 Years and Over				
1890	911	73.8	98	8.3
1900	1,064	68.4	139	9.1
1910	1,266	63.7	174	8.9
1920	1,494	60.2	197	8.0
Persons in the Labor Force Aged 65 Years and Over				
1930	1,795	53.9	243	7.3
1940	1,910	43.3	310	6.7
B. According to Monthly Reports on the Labor Force [b]				
1941	2,134	47.6	350	7.4
1942	2,190	47.8	400	8.2
1943	2,320	49.8	490	9.8
1944	2,420	51.0	500	9.8
1945	2,460	50.7	490	9.3
1946	2,340	47.2	450	8.3
1947	2,376	47.4	445	8.1
1948	2,384	47.1	514	9.3
1949	2,454	46.1	556	9.6
1950	2,454	45.8	584	9.9

a. Only noninstitutional population (excluding the armed forces).
b. Annual average.

Sources: Sixteenth Census (1940), *Population — Comparative Occupation Statistics for the United States, 1870 to 1940,* p. 93; *Current Population Reports,* Series P-50 and P-57, Bureau of the Census. Cf. Appendix Table 63.

it has not been established formally by collective agreements.

The outlook for employment of older workers in the years ahead is not very clear. Improving health, better hygienic conditions in work places, and shorter working hours act against the trend toward earlier retirement. However, the development of social security programs and private pension plans and the growth of savings may increase the number of persons who withdraw from work at an age when they still have enough vigor to enjoy their later years.

The increase in the percentage of women in paid jobs is due to the increase in urbanization and in opportunities for women in modern industry, the decrease in the size of families, and the simplifying of housekeeping. (See Table 89.)

Except for the spectacular expansion of the labor force during World War II, the proportion of workers among males aged 14 and over has been slowly declining since the turn of the century, while the proportion of workers among

TABLE 89

TRENDS IN NUMBER AND PROPORTION OF WOMEN WORKERS, 1870–1940

Year	Gainful Workers or Persons in Labor Force, in Millions: Both Sexes	Women	Percentage of Women Workers: In Labor Force	In Female Population of Specified Age
Gainful Workers, 10 Years Old and Over				
1870	12.9	1.9	14.8	13.3
1880	17.4	2.6	15.2	14.7
1890	23.3	4.0	17.2	17.4
1900	29.1	5.3	18.3	18.8
Gainful Workers, 14 Years Old and Over				
1900	28.3	5.1	18.1	20.4
1910	37.3	7.8	20.9	25.2
1920	41.2	8.4	20.4	23.3
1930	48.6	10.7	22.0	24.3
Persons in Labor Force, 14 Years Old and Over				
1930	47.4	10.4	21.9	23.6
1940	53.3	13.1	24.4	25.7

Source: Janet M. Hooks, *Women's Occupations through Seven Decades,* Women's Bureau, 1947, p. 34.

women in the same age classes has increased. Until 1940 the two movements offset each other, so that the ratio of gainful workers to total population aged 14 and over remained fairly stable.

IMPACT OF WORLD WAR II

Mobilization

Military and industrial mobilization had more than a temporary effect on the size and composition of the labor force.

When Hitler invaded Poland in September 1939, the labor force of the United States contained about 57 million workers, of whom more than 8 million were unemployed and about 2 million were seasonal farm workers. For another year, ups and downs in the labor force followed the normal seasonal rhythm.[5] Then in successive waves, from late 1940 through mid-1945, the unemployed went back to work, men took up arms and women stepped into their jobs, young folks quit school to work, older people put off retirement or came back to work — with the result that the annual average working force grew from about 56 million in 1940 to about 65.9 million in 1944. The increase was almost evenly distributed between the sexes, the number of men in the labor force rising from 41.9 million in 1940 to 46.5 million in 1944, and the number of women from 14.2

5. See Chapter 24.

million to 19.4 million. (See Appendix Table 64.)

This tremendous influx of new workers was not sufficient, however, to offset the losses of the civilian labor force to the armed forces. The civilian labor force declined from 55.6 million in 1940 to 54.6 million in 1944 and 53.9 million in 1945, on a year-round basis. To put it more strikingly, the number of men in the civilian labor force declined from 41.5 million in 1940 to 35.5 million in 1944 and 34.8 million in 1945, while the number of women rose from 14.2 million in 1940 to 19.2 million in 1944.

The labor force (including members of the armed forces) reached its peak in the summer of 1944 and remained at a high level until the end of the war, with only the usual seasonal declines. (See Figure 50.) From August 1944 to August 1945 the number of men in the armed forces stayed at about 12 million and the number of working women at more then 19 million — 5 million more than before the war, without counting women who took only seasonal jobs.

Demobilization

After V-J Day the labor force fell from 66.5 million (including about 2 million seasonal workers) in August 1945 to 59.1 million in February 1946. In those six months the number of fighting men was cut from 12 million to 5.2 million, and the number of working women fell from 19.6 million to 16.1 million. Most of the returned soldiers sought jobs within a few weeks after discharge, but many made use of their opportunity to return to school under the G.I. Bill of Rights. Accordingly, the number of men under age 25 not in the labor force went up from 1.8 million in June 1945 to 3.6 million in June 1946. A similar increase among men aged 25 and over was likewise due partly to the return of veterans to school. (See Appendix Table 65.)

In January 1949 the labor force (including members of the armed forces) consisted of 61.5 million persons (44.6 million men and 16.9 million women) — 6.8 million more than in January 1941. The increase of 3 million men and 3.8 million women was due largely to the growth of population of working age, from 100.9 million to 109.1 million. If the additional population aged 14 years and over had joined the labor force in the same proportion as in 1941, the labor force would have been augmented by 4.4 million persons — 3.4 million men and a million women. The trend toward increased participation of women, even if it had not been accelerated by the war, might have brought an additional 600,000 to 800,000 women into the labor market. Thus the actual labor force in January 1949 was 1.6 to 1.8 million larger than might have been anticipated. All the surplus was in the number of working women; the number of male workers lagged slightly behind the prewar pattern because of the increase in college attendance. In short, demobilization did not restore the labor force to its prewar size and composition.

Besides the increased enrollment of young men in colleges and the greatly increased employment of women, the war years produced appreciable changes in the distribution of workers according to skill. Millions of men and women acquired new skills in military service and munitions factories, many receiving special training they could use later in their daily work. Particularly notable are Negro workers, who were barred from skilled jobs before the war and were upgraded during the war emergency. After V-J Day some Negroes lost their wartime jobs but others were firmly established in new positions.

Projections for 1950–1960

Apart from short-term deviations and the possible effects of a national emergency, the future growth of the labor force can be foreseen with a greater degree of certainty than the growth of total population. Since all those persons who will be of working age in 1960 were born before 1946, the labor force in 1950–1960 will not be affected by current and future fluctuations in the birth rate, which introduce the greatest element of uncertainty into projections for total population. Estimates of the future labor force depend essentially on the assumptions made as to the percentage of workers among persons in different sex and age classes of the population. Such assumptions can be derived from long-range trends, with allowance for the effects of the war.

The projections are affected also by the bench mark used. Figures comparable with the current (monthly) estimates of the labor force issued by the Bureau of the Census are somewhat

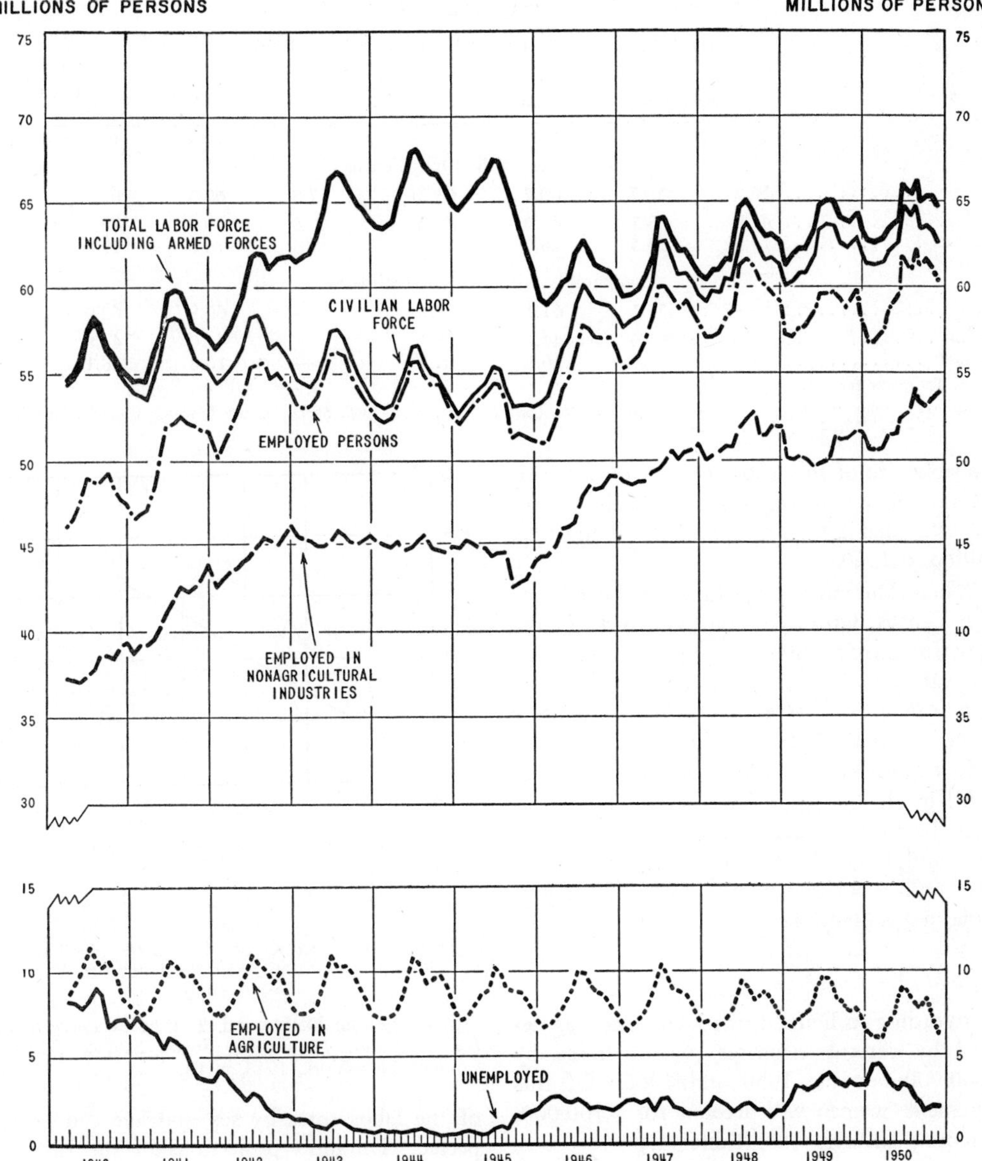

FIGURE 50. TRENDS IN THE LABOR FORCE, 1940–1950

Source: Bureau of the Census.

higher than those tied directly to the 1940 census. Nevertheless, estimates of the probable annual growth of the labor force from 1950 to 1960 vary within a comparatively narrow range.

Size

The widely used projections developed by John D. Durand suggest that, according to the prewar trend, the labor force as defined in the 1940 census would include 58.7 million persons in April 1950 and 63.2 million in April 1960. Because it is expected, however, that owing to the lasting effect of the war the figures will be appreciably larger, Durand adjusted his estimates to 60.3 million for April 1950 and 65.1 million for 1960. (See Table 90.)[6] The

6. Durand's "adjusted" figure for 1950 is almost identical with that suggested in *America's Needs and Resources* (60.0 million), but for 1960 he arrived at a slightly higher estimate (65.1 million, as compared with 63.4 million), the difference being essentially in the appraisal of the effect of the war on work habits. See J. Frederic Dewhurst and Associates,

TABLE 90

PROJECTIONS OF THE LABOR FORCE FOR 1945–1960 [a]

(In Millions)

Sex	Unadjusted Projections of Prewar Trends				Projections Adjusted for Effect of World War II			
	1945	1950	1955	1960	1945	1950	1955	1960
	Comparable with 1940 Census							
Total	56.2	58.7	60.7	63.2	57.8	60.3	62.4	65.1
Male	41.9	43.1	44.0	45.2	42.5	43.7	44.6	45.8
Female	14.3	15.5	16.7	18.0	15.3	16.6	17.8	19.3
	Comparable with Current Estimates							
Total	—	59.1	61.1	63.5	—	60.8	62.9	65.4
Male	—	43.4	44.2	45.3	—	44.0	44.8	45.9
Female	—	15.8	16.9	18.2	—	16.8	18.1	19.5

a. Estimates for April of each year.

Source: John D. Durand, *The Labor Force in the United States, 1890–1960,* Social Science Research Council, New York, 1948, pp. 251, 255, 257.

probable size of the labor force as recorded by the monthly reports of the Bureau of the Census was estimated at 60.8 million in 1950 and 65.4 million in 1960.

When Durand's projections are combined with Census Bureau data on the growth of the labor force from 1890 to 1945, it appears that the war caused a hump in the trend line of long-term growth (see Figure 51) amounting to about 7 to 8 million and will leave for 1950–1960 a residual increase of 2 or 3 per cent.

All in all, the labor force is expected to increase by approximately 400,000 a year between 1950 and 1955, about 500,000 a year between 1955 and 1960, and probably 600,000 a year between 1960 and 1965.

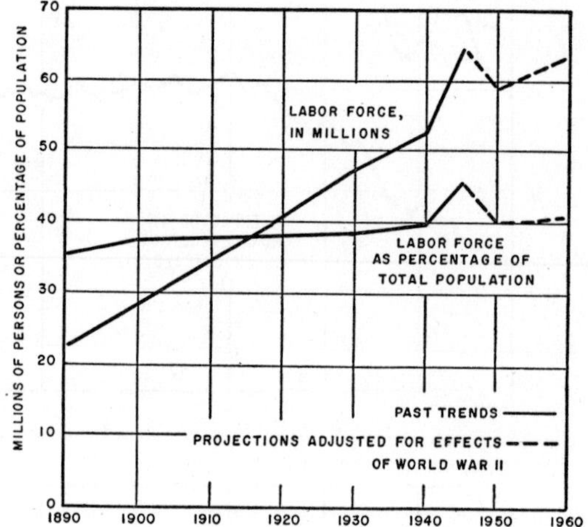

FIGURE 51. LONG-RANGE TREND OF THE LABOR FORCE, 1890–1940, AND PROJECTIONS FOR 1950–1960

Source: John D. Durand, *The Labor Force in the United States, 1890–1960,* Social Science Research Council, New York, 1948, p. 18.

Sex and Age Composition

According to Durand, the labor force, as defined by current estimates, will increase by 4,640,000 between 1950 and 1960. Of this increment, women will account for 2,700,000, or more than half. (See Table 91.)

The proportion of female workers in the labor force, Durand estimates, will rise from 25.4 per cent in 1940 to 29.8 per cent in 1960. This is consistent with the long-range trend.[7]

Because of appreciable variations in the birth rate in the past two or three decades and changing patterns of employment in different age and sex groups, definite changes in the composition of the labor force by sex and age can be expected. Durand's projections of the distribution of workers in 1950 and 1960 as compared with 1940 are shown in Table 92. The propor-

TABLE 91

ESTIMATED GROWTH OR DECLINE IN THE LABOR FORCE, BY SEX, 1940–1960 [a]

(In Thousands)

Period	Total	Men	Women
1940–1945	+11,110	+5,280	+5,830
1945–1950	— 3,930	—1,270	—2,660
1950–1955	+ 2,110	+ 850	+1,260
1955–1960	+ 2,530	+1,090	+1,440

a. Figures for April of each year.

Sources: For 1940 to 1950, see Appendix Table 64; for later years, see John D. Durand, *The Labor Force in the United States, 1890–1960,* Social Science Research Council, New York, 1948, p. 257 (projections adjusted for effects of World War II).

America's Needs and Resources, Twentieth Century Fund, New York, 1947, p. 571.

7. Cf. Table 89. The percentage of women in the labor force in April 1940 amounted to 24.4 according to the census enumeration but was set at 25.4 by the current monthly reports of the Bureau of the Census. (See Appendix Table 64.)

TABLE 92

ESTIMATED NUMBER OF PERSONS IN THE LABOR FORCE, BY SEX AND AGE, 1940, 1950 AND 1960[a]

(*In Thousands*)

Sex and Age	1940	1950	1960
Men, 14 years and over...	40,284	43,950	45,890
14–19............	2,619	2,020	2,030
20–24............	5,035	5,280	5,120
25–34............	10,076	11,170	11,030
35–44............	8,741	9,830	10,840
45–54............	7,381	7,990	8,860
55–64............	4,573	5,690	6,080
65 and over........	1,859	1,970	1,930
Women, 14 years and over.	13,015	16,800	19,500
14–19............	1,395	940	940
20–24............	2,688	3,090	3,150
25–34............	3,607	4,440	4,820
35–44............	2,500	3,720	4,410
45–54............	1,691	2,730	3,620
55–64............	859	1,490	2,090
65 and over........	275	390	470

a. Figures for April of each year.

Sources: For 1940, adjusted census figures; for 1950 and 1960, labor force figures based on comparable current estimates, adjusted for effect of the war, from John D. Durand, *The Labor Force in the United States, 1890–1960,* Social Science Research Council, New York, 1948, pp. 208–09 and 257.

tion of young workers shows a tendency to decline and the group aged from 45 to 64 to rise. In 1940 this age class represented less than 30 per cent of the male labor force and 20 per cent of the female. By 1960 it is expected to exceed 32 per cent of the male labor force and to approach 30 per cent of the female.

The prospect for aged persons is uncertain. Durand's projections suggest a decline in the proportion of workers aged 65 and over among men and an increase among women. Both tendencies seem in accord with past experience. It is largely a matter of judgment, however, what will happen during the next decade. It can be argued that if business conditions in the 1950's are as favorable as in the 1920's, many workers will be inclined to continue working after the age of 65 and many employers will be willing to use their services. Thus the proportion of workers among men over 65, instead of declining in accordance with the past trend, might be stabilized at about the 1930 level.

More specifically, the percentage of persons in the labor force among men aged 65 years and over, which declined from 53.9 in 1930 to as little as 43.3 in 1940 after a decade of mass unemployment (see Table 88), could be as much as 54 per cent in the 1950's. In this event, the number of aged men in the labor force would exceed 3.1 million in 1960.

On the other hand, it is possible that the number of young workers (aged 14 to 29) will be lower than Durand's projection suggests. The projection for the total labor force may prove accurate even if revisions of particular component items are necessary.

SHORT-TERM CHANGES

Many of the millions of persons in the work force remain solidly entrenched in jobs year in and year out or change jobs occasionally after only a brief interval of unemployment, never leaving the labor force. Others move in or out.

Even when jobs are most plentiful, approximately half the persons aged 14 and over are not in the labor force. At any given time about three out of four men aged 14 years and over and one out of four women of like age are at work or looking for a job, while one man out of four and three women out of four in such ages stay at home or are in school or otherwise out of the labor force. Some of those outside the labor force are workers, to be sure, in the sense that their labor in the home contributes to the well-being of their families, but they are not engaged in "gainful" work — work for pay or profit.

Even though a count in any week of the year would show 55 to 60 million nonworkers in the ages 14 years and over, several million of these drift in and out of the labor force.

Turnover among Workers

The entrance of young workers into the labor force and the withdrawal of the aged and disabled are major sources of change in the composition of the labor force. This turnover of generations accounts for some 2 million accessions to the labor force and for 1.5 million withdrawals each year. Withdrawals, re-entrances, and often re-withdrawals, of women whose work status changes with family responsibilities cause an additional turnover totaling a million or two.

Temporary disability is another source of shifts in the labor force. The number of persons compelled to withdraw from the labor market for a month or more runs to several million each year.

To these shifts are added the seasonal changes in the labor force.[8] Three million persons or more enter the farm labor force in the spring

8. See Chapter 24.

and withdraw in the autumn, a movement that goes in waves up and down the country as the seasons advance. Most temporary farm workers are members of farm families or other rural residents who leave the labor market — perhaps two or three times in a year — when the demand for work in the fields is no longer pressing. In summer, hundreds of thousands of students hunt farm and nonfarm jobs of all kinds, while many teachers leave the labor force for study or relaxation or stay in it to work in other fields. Seasonal workers are of all ages. Elderly persons and others with some regular income take jobs for short periods. Women, in particular, may return year after year to the same work in harvesting or in canneries or stores.

As a result of all these movements, the total number of persons who belong to the labor force at some time during a year may be 5 or 6 million greater than the total number of workers at the seasonal peak.

Turnover among Nonworkers

The possible number of temporary workers is only a fraction of the 50 million nonworkers. Some nonworkers — perhaps as many as 10 million — are permanently unemployable because of old age or physical handicap. Some are too young and will have no paid job during the year; of the 10 million persons aged 14 and over attending school, perhaps half belong to this group. Married women engaged in keeping their own homes are the largest group of nonworkers. Some of them can take a paid job occasionally, while others, because of family responsibilities or through choice, are unavailable for employment.

A very important group on the fringe of the regular labor force is made up of the 5 million farmers' wives who are not counted by the census as gainful workers, though their activities may add significantly to the real income of the family. Some of them appear in the farm labor force in the busy season. Some others take temporary jobs in canneries in fall or winter. As a group, however, they are not available for permanent paid jobs.

To sum up, approximately half the nonworkers are unemployable under any conditions. Of the other half, some work occasionally, for a few weeks or months in a year; others may take a job under exceptional conditions but are more likely to stay out of the labor market. Nonworkers who join the labor force at some time during a year may range between 10 and 12 million, in round numbers. The number of persons who are in the labor force during a large part of the year but not continuously (including those withdrawing because of death or disability) may reach 8 million.

Coverage by Old-Age and Survivors Insurance

The records of the federal system of old-age and survivors insurance give a measure of movement in and out of the labor force. In 1948 and 1949 the number of workers with wage credits under this program averaged 39.3 million and 38.4 million, respectively. (See Table 93.)

Wages were credited to 49.1 million different persons in 1948 and 47.2 million in 1949 — about 8 million more than the largest number of workers with wage credits in any single quarter in these years. Furthermore, not all workers with wage credits in a quarter were in the labor force throughout the quarter. The quarterly number includes new entrants, reentrants, persons who withdrew from the labor force during the quarter, persons only temporarily engaged in gainful work, and the like.

Of course, the ins and outs in employment covered by federal old-age and survivors insurance also include shifts between covered and noncovered industries and, to some extent, shifts between employment and unemployment. On the other hand, temporary workers in agriculture, many in domestic service, and others in all kinds of odd jobs are not covered by the records of old-age and survivors insurance. The

TABLE 93

WORKERS WITH WAGE CREDITS UNDER OASI, BY CALENDAR QUARTER, 1944–1949

(*In Millions*)

Calendar Quarter	1944	1945	1946	1947	1948	1949
Average	36.5	35.0	37.9	39.1	39.3	38.4
First	36.3	35.9	36.0	38.8	39.6	38.6
Second	36.9	35.9	38.1	39.8	40.2	39.5
Third	37.3	35.5	39.7	40.3	40.6	39.2
Fourth	35.6	32.7	37.9	37.4	36.8	36.1

Source: Quarterly Summary of Wages, Employment, and Benefit Data, Bureau of Old-Age and Survivors Insurance, August 1950, Table 2.

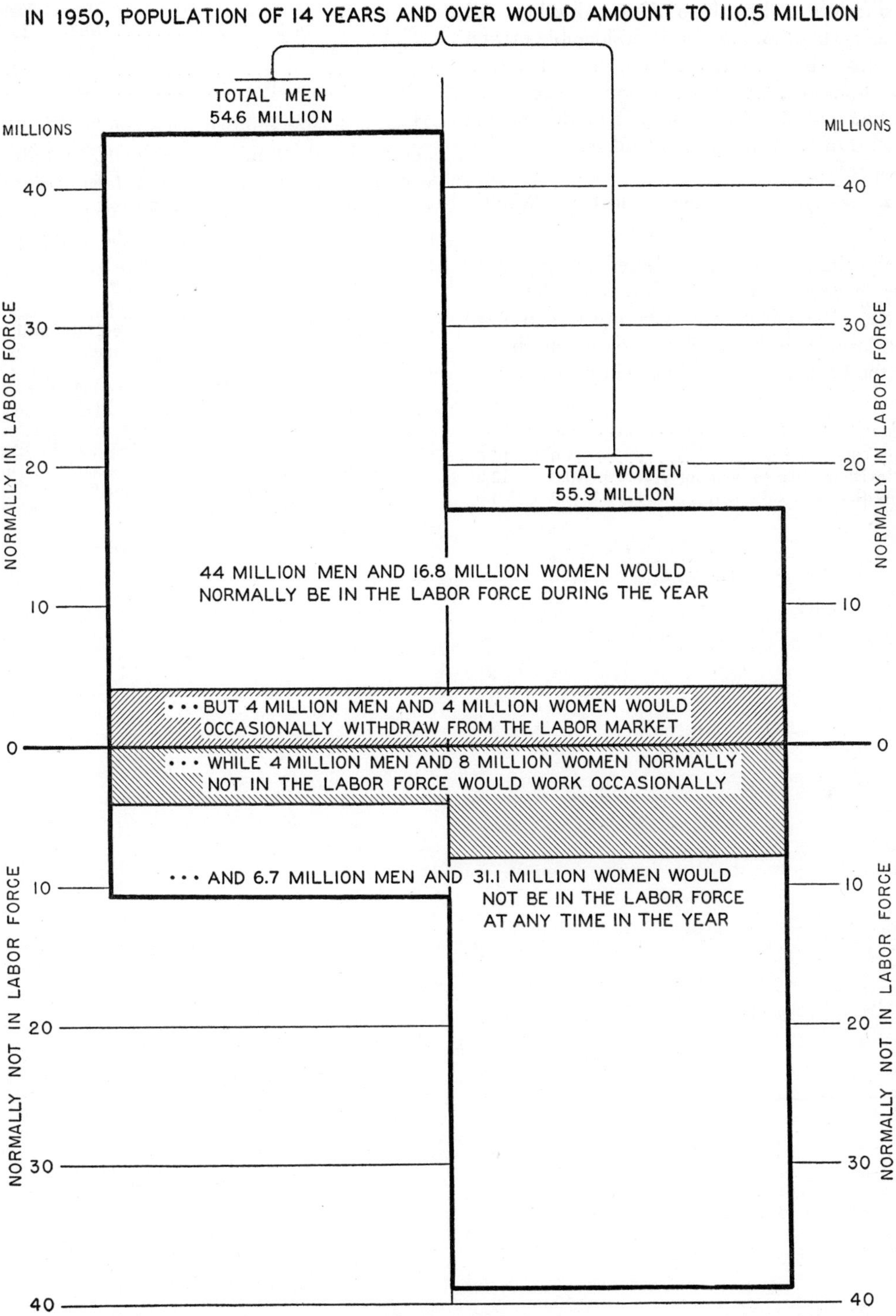

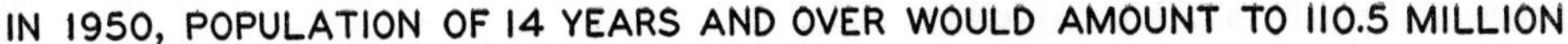

FIGURE 52. HYPOTHETICAL DISTRIBUTION OF POPULATION AGED 14 YEARS AND OVER, BY WORK STATUS, 1950

Source: See page 316. Cf. Figure 58.

two factors tend partly to offset each other. All in all, with allowance for a considerable margin of error, the magnitude of the ins and outs in industries covered by the program seems to be in line with our rough estimate of the shifting groups of workers and nonworkers.

Distribution of Population by Work Status, 1950

On the basis of these figures on long-range trends and short-range changes in the labor force, the population of working age in 1950 can be tentatively distributed by its attachment to the labor force as follows (in millions):

	Men	Women
Population over 14	54.6	55.9
Normally in labor force	44.0	16.8
In labor force throughout year	40.0	12.8
Withdraw occasionally	4.0	4.0
Normally not in labor force	10.7	39.1
Not in labor force at any time in year	6.7	31.1
Work occasionally	4.0	8.0

These estimates suggest that some 72.8 million persons in all, 48 million men and 24.8 million women, either worked or sought work during 1950, but that only 52.8 million, of whom 12.8 million were women, were in the labor force throughout the year.[9] (See Figure 52.)

9. The total number of persons either working or seeking work in 1950 as estimated here (72.8 million) is appreciably higher than the total number of those who worked for pay or profit in 1949, according to the Bureau of the Census (67,520,000) (*Current Population Reports,* Series P-50, No. 24). The main sources of the discrepancy are: (1) the labor force in 1950 was about 1.1 million larger than in 1949; (2) the present estimate makes a larger allowance for the group who work only occasionally.

Chapter 24

SEASONAL AND CYCLICAL VARIATIONS IN THE LABOR FORCE *

The long-term growth of the labor force — an average annual increment of 400,000 to 600,000 — is overlapped by seasonal and cyclical variations. The labor force does not increase at a uniform rate of 35,000 or 50,000 a month: its net gain or loss in a month may be more than twenty times this average monthly rate of growth. The biggest ups and downs are caused by seasonal influences, traceable to weather and custom; cyclical factors; and major upheavals, such as war.

Seasonal Changes in Size

Well-established customs increase the supply of labor in summer, when demand for labor is particularly great, and reduce it in winter. Young people enter the labor market after they graduate from school, usually in the spring. Many high school boys and girls and college students take temporary jobs in the summer. Farmers' wives take jobs in canneries in the summer and autumn. Retail trade, on the other hand, enrolls temporary employees for the Christmas rush.

Yet in the literature on seasonal variations in economic activities,[1] little attention has been paid to the rhythm in the size and composition of the labor force. Moreover, information on monthly changes has been available only since March 1940, through monthly reports prepared by the Bureau of the Census.[2] (See Appendix Table 64.)

A ten-year period would ordinarily be long enough to permit definite conclusions about the pattern of seasonal changes. Unfortunately, through the past ten years, seasonal factors have been largely overshadowed by the impact of war, mobilization, demobilization and the postwar boom, and it is unlikely that seasonal changes in coming years will parallel the average changes in the past decade. Moreover, in a study of the postwar labor market, the analysis should be restricted to the period after 1945, that is, to the years 1946–1950. Thus measurement of the seasonal component of changes in the labor force can be only rough and tentative.

The following computation of the typical seasonal rhythm in the labor force starts with the assumption that, apart from the seasonal factor and occasional ups and downs, the labor force rose and declined smoothly from January of one year to January of the next. The labor force computed on the basis of this assumption may be termed the hypothetical nonseasonal labor force for each month. Since the labor force is usually close to its low point in January, most of the figures recorded by the Census Bureau monthly reports are above this imaginary "nonseasonal" line.[3] Their average deviation from this line, after necessary smoothing, provides the measurement of the typical monthly increment over the nonseasonal hard core. (See Table 94; cf. Figure 53.)

The actual seasonal component of the labor force — measured as the deviation from the January-to-January trend — varies from year to year. Most outstanding are the variations in May and October, when the demand for labor in agriculture depends on changes in weather.[4]

In 1946–1950 the actual labor force deviated

* By W. S. Woytinsky.

1. See Benjamin J. Free, *Seasonal Employment in Agriculture,* Works Progress Administration, Washington, 1938; Simon Kuznets, *Seasonal Variations in Industry and Trade,* National Bureau of Economic Research, New York, 1933; W. S. Woytinsky, *Seasonal Variations in Employment in the United States,* Committee on Social Security, Social Science Research Council, Washington, 1939.

2. "Monthly Report on the Labor Force," *Current Population Reports,* Series P-57.

3. The "nonseasonal" line used in the following discussion is a freehand line fitted to the January data 1946–1951. When this nonseasonal line is raised to approximately half of the amplitude of seasonal variations in the labor force, the distance of the typical seasonal component of the labor force from this line shows the typical seasonal deviations of the labor force from the long-range trend. When the long-range changes are added to these deviations, typical seasonal deviations from the annual average can be ascertained. In Table 94, the long-range trend in the labor force is represented by a hypothetical increase of 50,000 a month.

4. The figures for the labor force recorded by the Bureau of the Census in these months also depend on minor shifts in the week in which the sample enumeration is taken.

TABLE 94

Typical Pattern of Seasonal Variation in the Civilian Labor Force, 1946–1950

(In Thousands)

Month	Deviation from January-January Trend	Deviation from Long-Range Trend	Deviation from Annual Average [a]
Annual average..	+ 1,620	0	0
January	0	— 1,620	— 1,895
February	+ 200	— 1,420	— 1,645
March	+ 400	— 1,220	— 1,395
April	+ 800	— 820	— 945
May	+ 1,300	— 320	— 395
June	+ 3,300	+ 1,680	+ 1,655
July	+ 3,500	+ 1,880	+ 1,905
August	+ 3,100	+ 1,480	+ 1,555
September	+ 2,150	+ 530	+ 655
October	+ 2,000	+ 380	+ 555
November	+ 1,800	+ 180	+ 405
December	+ 900	— 720	— 445

a. Seasonal variation of labor force combined with long-range increase at a rate of 50,000 a month.

Source: Derived from Appendix Table 64.

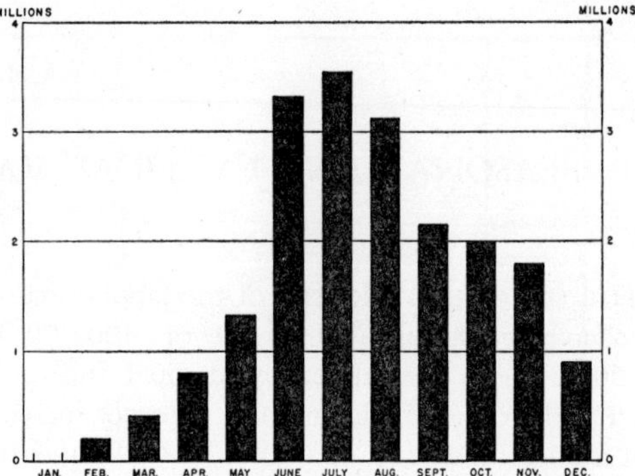

Figure 53. Typical Pattern of Seasonal Variation in the Labor Force, 1946–1950

(Deviation from January-to-January Trend Line)

Source: Table 94.

from the January-to-January trend as shown in Table 95. Except for changes in the timing of the summer expansion and the autumn contraction, the general pattern of the seasonal ups and downs was repeated each year: The low was usually in January-February, the high in June, July and August; the span from trough to peak was more than 4 million in 1946 and less than 3 million in 1950.

The rhythm of seasonal variation can be presented also in terms of upward or downward deviations from the year-round average, which is 1.6 million above the low point in January-February. (See Table 94, column 1.) To visualize the hypothetically "normal" flow of the labor force during a year, this seasonal rhythm should be related to the normal growth of the labor force, that is, the normal labor force in each month in relation to its size in the middle of the year. (Cf. Figure 54.) The labor force is closest to the annual average in May and November. The normal increment from January to July is close to 4 million; the contraction from July to the following January, about 3.5 million.

Seasonal Changes in Composition

Since the proportion of young people and women among seasonal workers is higher than the proportion among persons in gainful work throughout the year, the sex and age composition of the labor force changes with the season.

Proportion of Women

There is considerable difference in the timing of the entrance and withdrawal of male and female seasonal workers. (See Table 96; cf. Figure 55.)

TABLE 95

Deviation of the Actual Civilian Labor Force from the Nonseasonal Trend Line, 1946–1950

(In Thousands)

Month	1946	1947	1948	1949	1950
January	— 2,150	— 1,400	— 1,900	— 1,700	— 1,425
February	— 2,100	— 1,350	— 1,425	— 1,400	— 1,250
March	— 1,250	— 1,200	— 1,525	— 1,000	— 1,300
April	— 350	— 650	— 825	— 1,000	— 1,025
May	— 50	+ 350	— 950	+ 75	— 500
June	+ 1,400	+ 2,550	+ 2,050	+ 1,400	+ 1,400
July	+ 2,300	+ 2,300	+ 2,350	+ 1,725	+ 950
August	+ 1,650	+ 1,200	+ 1,650	+ 1,450	+ 1,400
September	+ 700	+ 150	+ 800	+ 500	+ 175
October	+ 350	+ 100	+ 125	+ 200	+ 650
November	+ 100	— 650	+ 25	+ 425	+ 875
December	— 600	— 1,400	— 375	— 475	+ 50

Source: Appendix Table 64.

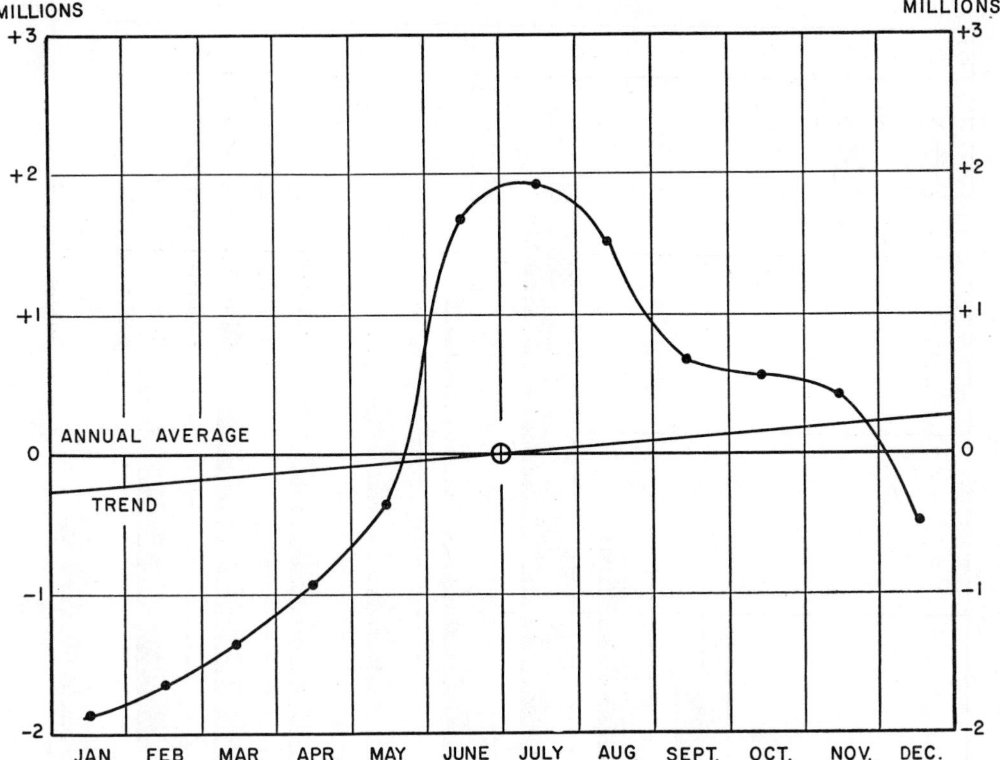

FIGURE 54. TYPICAL PATTERN OF DEVIATION OF THE LABOR FORCE FROM ANNUAL AVERAGE UNDER IMPACT OF THE TREND AND SEASON, 1946–1950

Source: Table 94.

Women who work seasonally may perform, in a year, the equivalent of 775,000 full years of work, or approximately 5 per cent of all the work performed by women. The comparable figures for seasonally working men are, roughly, 720,000 full years, or 1.5 per cent of the total performance of male workers. At the high point (June-July), manpower is 4 per cent above the winter low, while womanpower has risen 10 per cent.

TABLE 96

TYPICAL PATTERN OF SEASONAL VARIATION IN THE LABOR FORCE, BY SEX, 1946–1950

(Deviation from January-January Trend, in Thousands)

Month	Total	Men	Women
January	0	0	0
February	+ 200	+ 100	+ 100
March	+ 400	+ 200	+ 200
April	+ 800	+ 500	+ 300
May	+ 1,300	+ 600	+ 700
June	+ 3,300	+ 1,700	+ 1,600
July	+ 3,500	+ 2,150	+ 1,350
August	+ 3,100	+ 2,000	+ 1,100
September	+ 2,150	+ 1,000	+ 1,150
October	+ 2,000	+ 700	+ 1,300
November	+ 1,800	+ 550	+ 1,250
December	+ 900	+ 150	+ 750

Source: Derived from Appendix Table 64.

Age Distribution

Enrollment of young men in the armed forces and their return to civilian life after the war distorted the seasonal rhythm in the age composition of the labor force. Monthly reports of the Bureau of the Census show the general pattern of shifts of different age groups into and out of civilian work before, during and after the war (see Appendix Table 66), but the figures permit only tentative generalizations.

With this reservation, the following features in the composition of the temporary (seasonal) labor force during 1946–1950 deserve attention.

1. Almost all male seasonal workers are youths in the age groups 14–19 and 20–24 years. Seasonal increase in the number of working men of age 25 and over is almost negligible.

2. On the other hand, almost half the seasonal female workers are 25 years or over.

3. At the peak of seasonal work (in July)

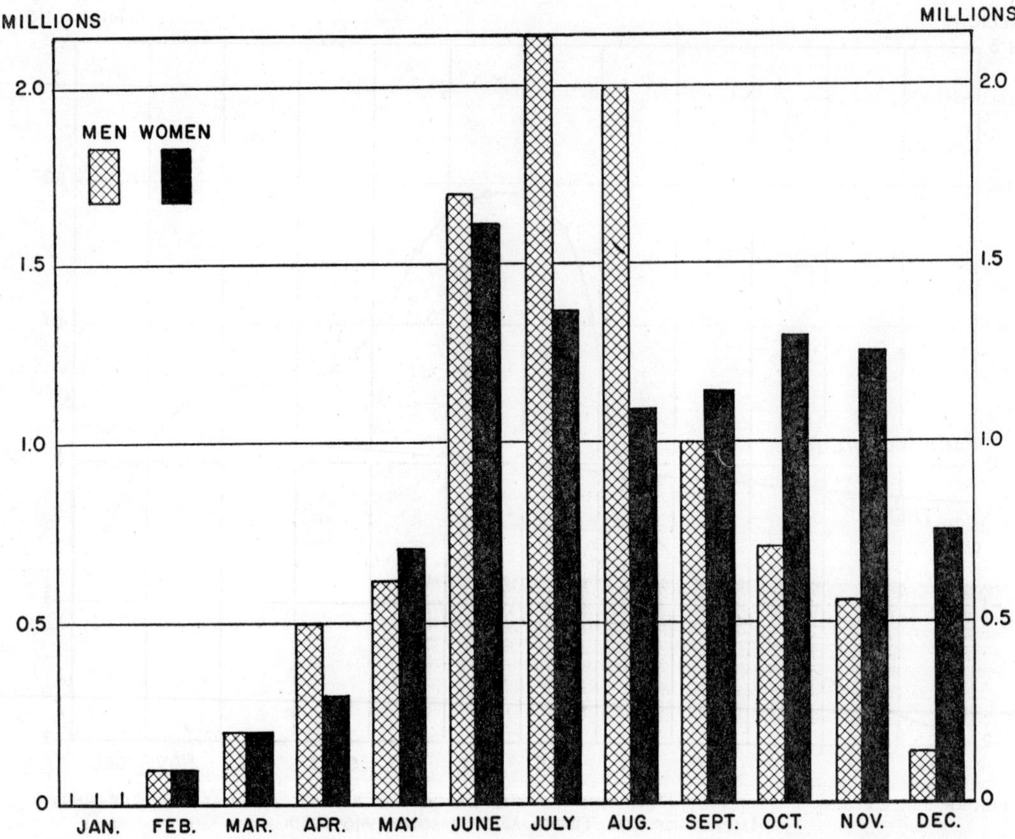

FIGURE 55. TYPICAL PATTERN OF SEASONAL VARIATION IN THE LABOR FORCE, BY SEX, 1946–1950
(*Deviation from January–January Trend Line*)

Source: Table 96.

school boys at work outnumber girls two to one.

4. The timing of entrance of boys and girls into the labor force is about the same, but there is some difference in the timing of their withdrawal: girls stay in seasonal work longer.

5. The timing of seasonal work of women aged 25 and over is strikingly different from the pattern for school girls and suggests two peaks, one in June and the other in November, with a trough between them.

TABLE 97

TYPICAL PATTERN OF DISTRIBUTION OF SEASONAL WORKERS, BY SEX AND AGE, 1946–1950

(*Excess of Workers in Specified Sex and Age Groups over January-to-January Trend Line, in Thousands*)

Month	Men			Women		
	Total	14–24 Years	25 Years and Over	Total	14–24 Years	25 Years and Over
January	0	0	0	0	0	0
February	100	50	50	100	25	75
March	200	125	75	200	50	150
April	500	350	150	300	75	225
May	600	425	175	700	150	550
June	1,700	1,150	450	1,600	750	850
July	2,150	1,650	500	1,350	800	550
August	2,000	1,600	400	1,100	650	450
September	1,000	625	375	1,150	600	550
October	700	375	325	1,300	500	800
November	550	300	250	1,250	250	1,000
December	150	100	50	750	200	550

Source: Derived from Appendix Table 66.

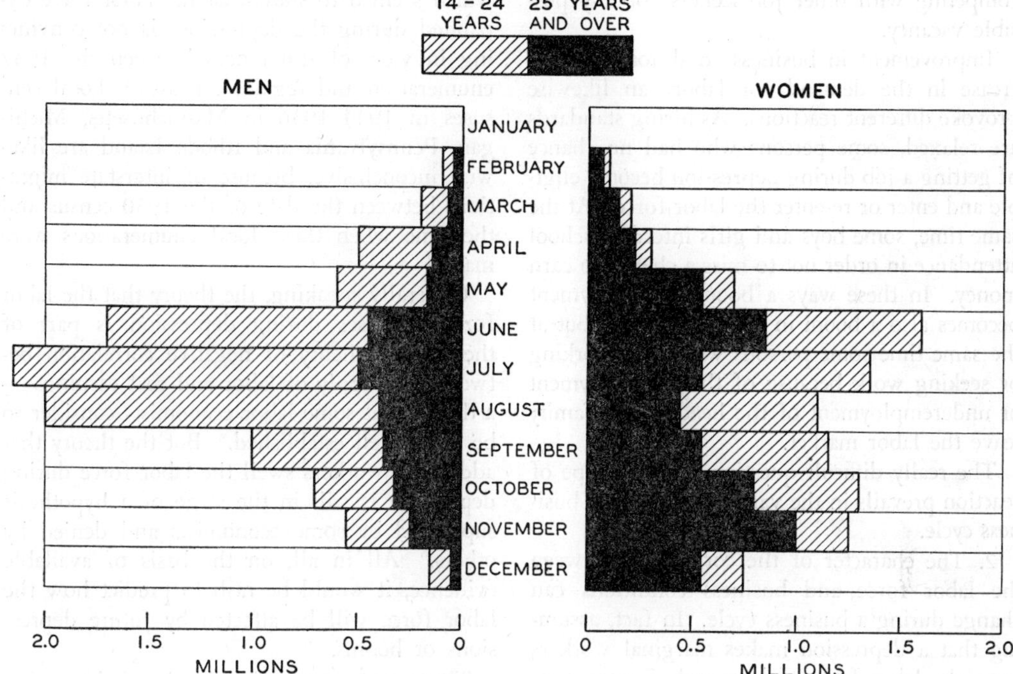

FIGURE 56. TYPICAL PATTERN OF DISTRIBUTION OF SEASONAL WORKERS, BY SEX AND AGE, 1946–1950

Source: Table 97.

The figures in Table 97, covering the period 1946–1950, show the typical surplus of people in the labor force in each month in comparison with the January-January trend, rather than the total number of seasonal workers in any particular month. It is fairly certain that at its seasonal low in winter the labor force includes some seasonal workers who will not be in the labor market in the summer. The number of seasonal workers in the labor force is therefore likely to be appreciably higher than shown in the table. (Cf. Figure 56.)

IMPACT OF THE BUSINESS CYCLE

How does the size of the labor force change with changing business conditions? Does a rise in unemployment increase or curtail the labor force? Does economic revival bring new workers into the labor market or encourage withdrawal of those who were seeking work during the depression?

These are open questions. Weighty arguments have been offered in support of opposite answers, and what seems to some observers an established fact is denied by others. The problem is confusing for two reasons.

1. Both improvement and deterioration of business conditions can act on persons on the fringe of the labor market in opposite ways — bringing some nonworkers into the labor force and encouraging withdrawal of some other marginal workers.

It is generally agreed that a long and severe depression tends to squeeze marginal workers out of the labor force. After losing their jobs and discovering that they are unwanted by employers, they gradually lose their attachment to the labor force. Some depend for support on public assistance, others on their relatives. First they lose hope, then spirit; the time comes when they lose their old skills and cease to belong to the active labor force.

A severe depression also postpones entrance of some workers into the labor force. When boys and girls have little or no chance to get jobs, some of them will stay in school a year or two longer.

A depression can also affect the labor force in the opposite direction. When the usual breadwinner is out of work, some members of his family who otherwise would not be in the labor force may be compelled to look for work, competing with other job-seekers for any possible vacancy.

Improvement in business conditions and increase in the demand for labor can likewise provoke different reactions. As hiring standards are relaxed, some persons who had no chance of getting a job during depression become eligible and enter or re-enter the labor force. At the same time, some boys and girls interrupt school attendance in order not to miss a chance to earn money. In these ways a boom in employment becomes also a boom in the labor force; but at the same time some persons who were working or seeking work because of the unemployment or underemployment of the head of the family leave the labor market.

The really difficult question is which type of reaction prevails in the various phases of a business cycle.

2. The character of the correlation between the labor force and business conditions can change during a business cycle. In fact, assuming that a depression makes marginal workers leave the labor force and compels former nonworkers to seek work, the two reactions are not necessarily proportionate to changes in economic activity. In either boom or depression, declines in the labor force can exceed gains under certain conditions; under other conditions gains prevail.

Since the problem is to determine the net balance of two opposite movements, it would seem logical to resolve it by the use of statistical records. Unfortunately, the empirical approach has failed to provide conclusive evidence on one side or the other.[5]

Comparison of the decennial censuses is inconclusive because of the effect of long-range factors. Comparison of the enumeration taken in 1937 with the censuses of 1930 and 1940, which seemed to show that the labor force expanded during the depression, is not convincing in view of differences between the 1937 enumeration and regular censuses.[6] Local censuses in 1934–1936 in Massachusetts, Michigan, Pennsylvania and Rhode Island are likewise inconclusive, because of interstate migrations between the date of the 1930 census and the time when these local enumerations were made.[7]

Generally speaking, the theory that the labor force increases during depression is part of the general theory of negative correlation between the supply of labor and real earnings — a theory that some labor economists consider to be fairly well established.[8] But the theory that additional workers swell the labor force during depression is still in the stage of a hypothesis supported by some economists and denied by others.[9] All in all, on the basis of available evidence, it would be rash to predict how the labor force will be affected by future depressions or booms.

Those who accept the theory of depression increase visualize the cyclical variations in the size of the labor force as pictured in Figure 57. Those who reject this theory would eliminate the hump of "additional workers" but would recognize the expansion of the labor force during a business boom.

The theory that the labor force increases both in a severe depression and in a boom implies that the proportion of the population outside the labor market is at a peak when business conditions are far from both extremes of boom and bust, that is, when economic pressure is not severe enough to force many additional workers into the labor market and the incentive of easy jobs with fancy pay is not great enough to

5. Paul H. Douglas (*The Theory of Wages,* Macmillan, New York, 1934) has shown that the percentage of gainful workers in various sex-age groups, as reported in the large cities of the United States by censuses in 1920 and 1930, is negatively correlated with prevailing real earnings. This correlation was further elaborated in an article by Douglas and E. M. Schoenberg ("The Relation in 1929 between Average Earnings in American Cities and Proportions Seeking Employment," *Journal of Political Economy,* February 1937), and confirmed by Clarence Long ("The Size of the Labor Force: Under Changing Incomes and Employment," National Bureau of Economic Research, mimeographed). All three authors, however, found only a static correlation, and Long stressed that there is no evidence that a similar correlation must exist between changes in business conditions and changes in the labor force.

6. John D. Durand, *The Labor Force in the United States, 1890–1900,* Social Science Research Council, New York, 1948, pp. 96–98.

7. W. S. Woytinsky, *Three Aspects of Labor Dynamics,* Committee on Social Security, Social Science Research Council, Washington, 1942, p. 115.

8. Richard A. Lester, *Economics of Labor,* Macmillan, New York, 1947, p. 104.

9. This theory has been developed by Woytinsky. See "Additional Workers and the Volume of Unemployment in the Depression," Committee on Social Security, Social Science Research Council, Washington, 1940 (mimeographed); *Three Aspects of Labor Dynamics;* and *Principles of Cost Estimates in Unemployment Insurance,* Federal Security Agency, 1948. Objections have been raised by Dan D. Humphrey ("Alleged Additional Workers in the Measurement of Unemployment," *Journal of Political Economy,* June 1940) and Clarence Long (*op. cit.*).

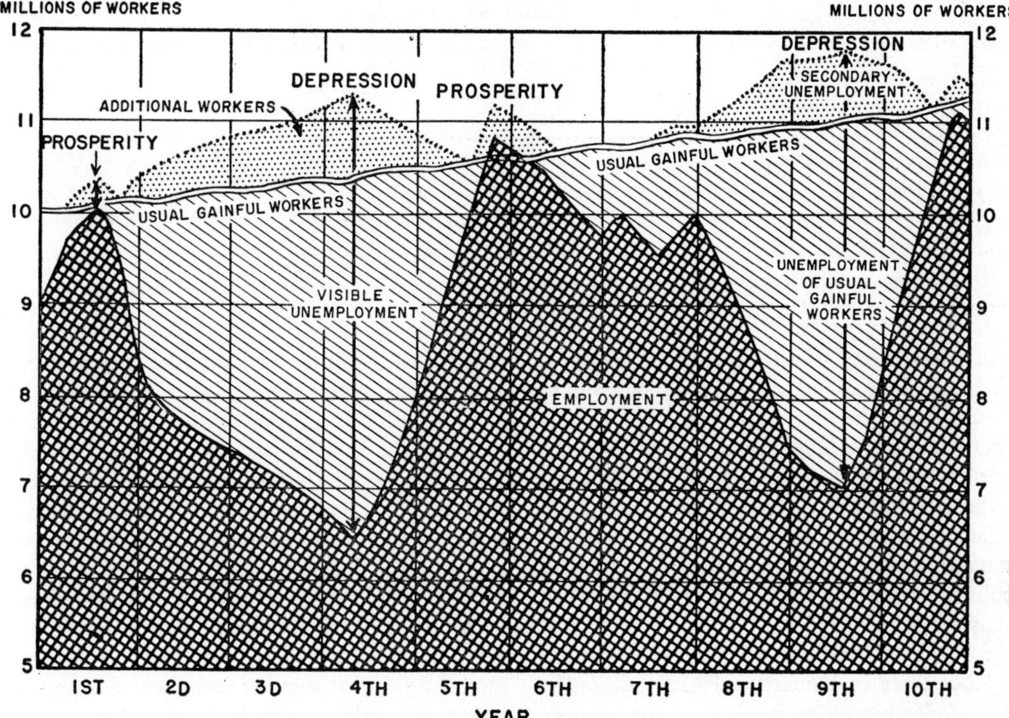

FIGURE 57. EXAMPLE OF VARIATIONS IN THE SIZE OF THE LABOR FORCE UNDER THE IMPACT OF BOOM AND DEPRESSION

(*Fictitious Numbers*)

Source: W. S. Woytinsky, "Additional Workers and the Volume of Unemployment in the Depression," Committee on Social Security, Social Science Research Council, Washington, 1940 (mimeographed).

induce boys and girls to desert classrooms for factories and shops. Such business conditions would be closest to "normalcy," in that they represent neither underemployment nor overemployment.

In other words, employment should be considered as adequate when the labor force is reduced to a minimum, so that the largest number of people can stay out of the labor market.[10] Like the theory that the labor force is expanded by additional workers during depression, this is a hypothesis rather than a universally accepted theory.

RECENT VARIATIONS

The increase in the labor force during the war came essentially from the same marginal groups of nonworkers that each year supply the economy with seasonal help. In fact, the composition of population *not* in the labor force was strikingly similar at the seasonal peak in the summer of 1941 and the seasonal low in the winter of 1944.[11] (See Table 98.) To interpret these data correctly, the growth of population and the long-range trend toward greater participation of women in gainful work should be

10. W. S. Woytinsky, *Studies in Income and Wealth,* Conference of Research in Income and Wealth, National Bureau of Economic Research, New York, Vol. X (1947), p. 111.

11. This similarity between the seasonal rush and the national emergency is not as clearly evident in the Census Bureau's monthly reports, because they do not show the sex and age composition of the total labor force, including the armed forces. They do show, however, the distribution of persons aged 14 years and over who are *not* in the labor force, and these data are sufficiently instructive.

The monthly reports on the labor force before October 1941 contain only a very summary age distribution of persons not in the labor force. For July 1941 the following data were published (in thousands):

	Men	Women
14 to 24 years......	2,530	7,590
25 to 54 years......	640	19,380
55 years and over...	2,870	8,490

("Labor Force, Employment, and Unemployment in the United States, 1940–1946," *Current Population Reports,* Series P-50.)

TABLE 98

PERSONS AGED 14 YEARS AND OVER NOT IN THE LABOR FORCE, BY SEX AND AGE, JULY 1941 AND JANUARY 1944

(In Thousands)

Date	Men			Women		
	Total	Under 25 Years	25 Years and Over	Total	Under 25 Years	25 Years and Over
July 1941 (seasonal peak)	6,040	2,530	3,510	35,460	7,590	27,870
January 1944 (seasonal low)	6,040	2,750	3,290	34,330	7,240	27,090

Source: "Labor Force, Employment and Unemployment in the United States, 1940–1946," *Current Population Reports,* Series P-50, No. 2, Bureau of the Census, September 1947, pp. 53, 56.

taken into account. It can be assumed, roughly, that the male nonworking population tends to increase one per cent each year, the female somewhat less. Under this assumption, the labor force in the winter of 1944–1945 included all the persons who in peacetime would have worked only in summer plus a few hundred thousand men and about a million women who would not ordinarily have been in gainful work in any season.

In 1941, 46.1 million persons were outside the labor force in January and 41.5 million in July. Under peacetime conditions, the number would probably have reached 47.5 million in January 1944 and 42.7 million in July. Actually, the figures were 40.4 million and 36.4 million, suggesting that about 6.5 to 7 million persons who would not have been in the labor force in peacetime were in uniform or in the civilian labor force in 1944. This is the extent to which labor reserves were mobilized at the peak of the war effort. Emergency mobilization brought into the labor force approximately 4–4.5 million persons who in peacetime would have worked for pay or profit only in summer, plus the hypothetical four-year increment of the nonworker group (approximately 1.3 million) plus a little more than a million persons who, under normal conditions, would not have joined the labor force in either winter or summer. Assuming that the wartime labor force (including the armed forces) contained in winter most of the people who in peacetime would have been available for work only in summer, the seasonal summer increment during the war years could be supplied only from groups that were not even on the fringe of the labor force in peacetime.

After the war, the distribution of the working and nonworking population by sex and age did not return to the prewar pattern; but the changes that remained after demobilization were minor indeed in comparison with the reshuffling of the population during the war emergency.

The effect of mobilization and demobilization on the labor force is best seen from the

TABLE 99

PERSONS AGED 14 YEARS AND OVER NOT IN THE LABOR FORCE, BY SEX AND AGE, 1940–1950 [a]

(In Thousands)

Sex and Age	1940	1941	1942	1943	1944	1945	1946	1947	1948	1949	1950
Total	44,240	43,920	40,950	38,830	38,040	41,870	45,600	45,540	45,690	45,950	45,700
Men	8,000	8,100	6,430	5,730	5,360	7,220	8,730	8,290	8,320	8,620	8,540
14–19	4,330 (14–24)	4,180	3,050	2,600	2,230	2,940	3,420	3,230	3,230	3,280	3,070
20–24		350	280	80	90	400	1,060	930	820	780	670
25–44	3,670 (25 and over)	240	160	180	220	750	680	600	610	680	660
45–64		900	700	600	670	890	1,010	950	1,030	1,180	1,160
65 and over		2,430	2,240	2,270	2,150	2,240	2,560	2,580	2,630	2,700	2,980
Women .	36,240	35,820	34,520	33,100	32,680	34,650	36,870	37,250	37,370	37,330	37,160
14–19	8,470 (14–24)	5,110	4,590	4,030	3,950	4,300	4,460	4,420	4,370	4,240	4,170
20–24		2,970	2,930	2,870	2,670	2,840	3,290	3,250	3,270	3,140	2,970
25–44	27,770 (25 and over)	13,520	13,070	12,470	12,470	13,080	14,030	14,120	14,260	14,380	14,270
45–64		9,930	9,630	9,380	9,170	9,760	10,180	10,420	10,300	10,320	10,300
65 and over		4,290	4,300	4,350	4,420	4,670	4,910	5,030	5,170	5,250	5,450

a. Figures for October of each year.

Sources: Appendix Table 65 and "Labor Force, Employment and Unemployment in the United States, 1940–1946," *Current Population Reports,* Series P-50, No. 2, Bureau of the Census, September 1947.

distribution of nonworkers by sex and age in the same month of each year. (See Table 99.) How, then, did the distributions in the peak year of mobilization and after demobilization compare with the levels that would have resulted from a "normal" rate of increase of one per cent a year? Assuming that under normal conditions all sex and age groups of nonworkers would have increased from 1941 to 1944 by 3 per cent and from 1941 to 1947 by 6 per cent, the nonworker groups in 1944 and 1947 showed losses or gains in comparison with 1941 as indicated in Table 100. Apart from the seasonal ebb and flow, up to October 1944 mobilization had brought into the labor force (including the armed forces) 3 million male and 4.2 million female nonworkers; demobilization returned 2.7 million men and 3.5 million women to nonworker status.

The labor force in 1947 had been increased, in comparison with 1941, by the growth of population and by the addition of approximately a million nonworkers. That figure, however, is deceptive as a measure of the effect of the war on the postwar labor force. The number of male nonworkers aged 20 to 44 had increased by 900,000, mainly as a result of enrollment of veterans in college. This factor was more than offset by a decline of 1.2 million in the number of male nonworkers under the age of 20. On the other hand, the number of women who were in the labor force in 1947 but would not have been there according to the 1941 pattern of work was probably much larger than 700,000, but this addition had been partly offset by the withdrawal of young mothers. All in all, the labor force in the fall of 1947 probably included 2.5 to 3 million persons who would not have been there according to the prewar pattern of work, but more than half this increase was offset by the temporary withdrawal of young mothers and student veterans.

TABLE 100

CHANGES IN NUMBER OF NONWORKERS AGED 14 YEARS AND OVER, 1941, 1944 AND 1947 [a]

(Deviation from Hypothetical Level Based on 1941 Pattern, in Thousands)

Sex and Age	1944 over 1941	1947 over 1944	1947 over 1941
Total	— 7,200	+ 6,180	— 1,020
Men	— 2,990	+ 2,700	— 290
14–19	— 2,080	+ 880	— 1,200
20–24	— 270	+ 830	+ 560
25–44	— 30	+ 380	+ 350
45–64	— 260	+ 260	0
65 and over	— 350	+ 350	0
Women	— 4,210	+ 3,490	— 720
14–19	— 1,310	+ 310	— 1,000
20–24	— 390	+ 490	+ 100
25–44	— 1,450	+ 1,240	— 210
45–64	— 1,060	+ 950	— 110
65 and over	0	+ 480	+ 480

a. Based on October figures for each year.

Source: Derived from Table 99 (see text at left).

DISTRIBUTION OF POPULATION BY LABOR FORCE STATUS

Patterns of mobilization of the labor force for seasonal and emergency work cast light on the structure of population according to actual or potential attachment to gainful work.

Fringes of the Labor Force

Seasonal increases in the labor force and its expansion during the war indicate that male reserves of labor are concentrated mainly in the youngest age classes, while female reserves are dispersed over all age groups. On the basis of this observation, the estimated population aged 14 and over in 1950 can be tentatively classified by attachment to the labor force, according to sex and age groups, as suggested in Table 101. (Cf. Figure 58.)

The concept of "continuous attachment to the labor force" used in this classification is by no means identical with employment or availability for work during all fifty-two weeks of the year. It allows for occasional interruptions of employment between jobs, spells of temporary disability, and the like. The table represents a hypothetical distribution of population in conformity with known changes in the labor force during the past decade. It does not suggest that the situation in 1950 conformed strictly to this experience.

Turnover of the Labor Force

The flow of applications for account numbers under the old-age and survivors insurance system provides corroborating evidence of the variations in the labor force described above.

Before amendment in 1950, the program covered approximately 75 per cent of all wage and salary workers, or 60 per cent of the total labor force. It did not include self-employment; work for federal, state and local governments; agriculture; certain types of non-profit organizations; or domestic service. Each

TABLE 101

HYPOTHETICAL DISTRIBUTION OF POPULATION AGED 14 YEARS AND OVER BY ATTACHMENT TO THE LABOR FORCE, SEX AND AGE, 1950

(*In Thousands*)

Sex and Age	Total Population	Normally in Labor Force [a] (Workers)		Normally *Not* in Labor Force (Nonworkers)	
		Continuously in Labor Force	Marginal Group	Marginal Group	Continuously *Not* in Labor Force
Total	110,560	52,750	8,000	12,000	37,810
Men	54,640	39,950	4,000	4,000	6,690
14–17	4,350	300	150	2,100	1,800
18–19	2,200	1,220	350	350	280
20–24	5,950	5,080	200	400	270
25–29	6,020	5,550	200	100	170
30–34	5,540	5,220	200	50	70
35–39	5,280	4,930	200	50	100
40–44	5,870	4,400	270	50	150
45–49	4,480	3,850	400	50	180
50–54	4,030	3,390	400	50	190
55–59	3,640	2,770	480	150	240
60–64	3,020	1,820	600	200	400
65 and over	5,260	1,420	550	450	2,840
Women	55,920	12,800	4,000	8,000	31,120
14–17	4,210	130	150	1,500	2,430
18–19	2,120	410	250	1,000	460
20–24	5,790	2,340	750	1,300	1,400
25–29	6,100	1,950	500	800	2,850
30–34	5,830	1,640	350	700	3,140
35–39	5,540	1,600	350	500	3,090
40–44	5,040	1,470	300	400	2,870
45–49	4,610	1,230	300	400	2,680
50–54	4,110	900	300	400	2,510
55–59	3,670	600	250	400	2,420
60–64	3,040	430	210	300	2,100
65 and over	5,860	100	290	300	5,170

a. "Labor force" comparable with the "Monthly Report on the Labor Force," *Current Population Reports,* Series P-57, Bureau of the Census.

Source: Computed on the basis of variations in the number and distribution of persons not in labor force, 1940–1949 (Appendix Table 65). For population figures see John D. Durand, *The Labor Force in the United States, 1890–1900,* Social Science Research Council, New York, 1948, p. 257.

person in a job covered by the program has an account number. Applications are also filed by many persons who are not yet employed in covered industries but intend to look for such employment. On the other hand, a person does not invalidate his account number by temporarily withdrawing from the labor force or by shifting to a noncovered job; theoretically, the account number identifies him throughout his life.

Applications for account numbers before 1950 reflect both entrance of new workers — young people and others formerly not in the labor force — and shifts to covered employment from noncovered jobs, such as those on farms or in government. They also include a certain number of duplications, but these do not affect the general picture.

The original registration for account numbers was completed in 1936–1937, when nearly 37 million accounts were established.[12] After declining in subsequent years, the flow of applications was between 5 and 6 million a year, probably representing more than 2 million new entrants and 3 to 3.5 million persons shifting from noncovered to covered employment. During World War II the number of applicants jumped to a high of 7.6 million in 1942. After the war it fell again, but even after twelve years of registration the yearly number was considerably higher than the total number of boys and girls entering the labor market each year after completing school. (See Appendix Tables 67 and 68.)

By the end of 1949 nearly 94 million accounts had been established. Excluding account holders who had withdrawn from gainful work because of old age, disability or death, there were approximately 81 million active accounts — more than two accounts per person currently employed in covered industries, and

12. W. S. Woytinsky, *Fluctuations in Employment Covered by the Federal Old-Age Insurance Program,* Bureau of Research and Statistics, Social Security Board, Federal Security Agency, August 1939.

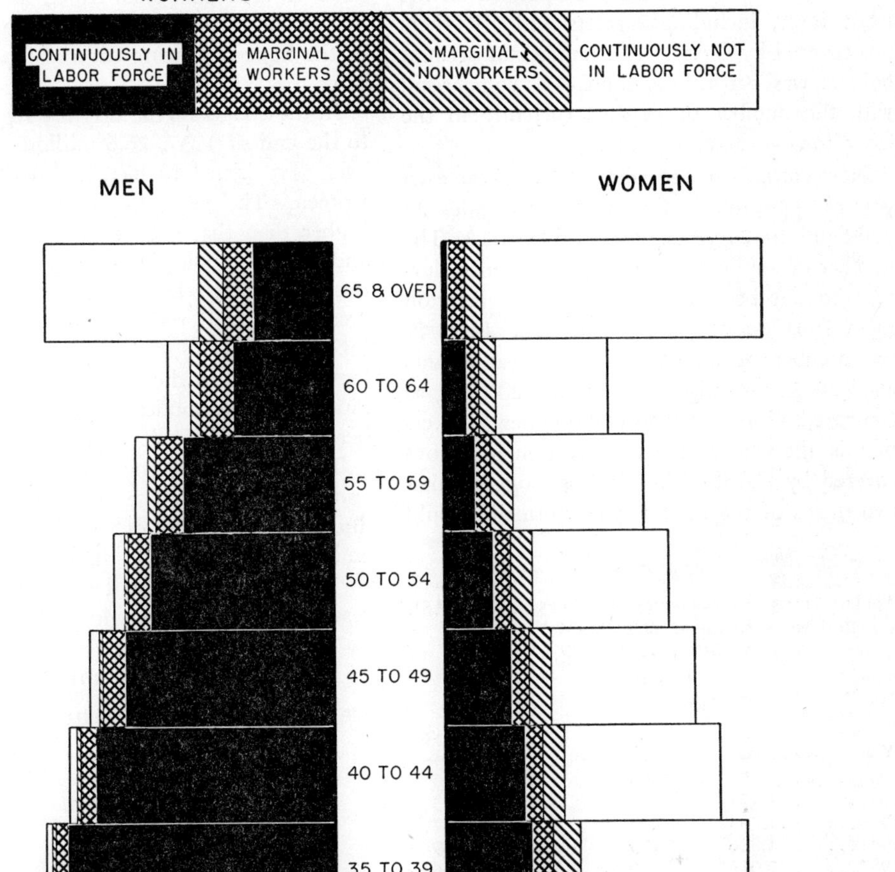

FIGURE 58. HYPOTHETICAL DISTRIBUTION OF POPULATION AGED 14 YEARS AND OVER BY ATTACHMENT TO THE LABOR FORCE, SEX AND AGE, 1950

Source: Table 101. Cf. Figure 52.

more than the total number of persons in the labor force, including farmers and all others not covered by OASI. The number of account holders was particularly high — in comparison with the number of persons currently in the labor force — among women.

New entrants to the labor force appear each year as applicants in the age groups under 20 years and 20–24 years. (See Table 102.) The number of applicants aged 20–24 declined during the war because of the heavy registration from 1941 on of youths under 20. In 1949 the number of accounts issued to applicants aged 20–24 was slightly more than 200,000, as compared with more than 600,000 new workers of this age who appear each year in industries covered by OASI. This contrast suggests that two thirds of the persons who normally would have entered the labor force at ages 20–24 worked or at least applied for account numbers in the hope of getting covered jobs during the war.

TABLE 102

APPLICATIONS FOR ACCOUNT NUMBERS UNDER OASI, IN UNDER-20-YEARS AND 20–24-YEAR AGE GROUPS, 1938–1949

(*In Thousands*)

Year	Men		Women	
	Under 20 Years	20–24 Years	Under 20 Years	20–24 Years
1938	877	668	588	435
1939	1,137	650	848	453
1940	1,264	499	873	367
1941	1,886	473	1,288	459
1942	2,013	226	1,707	486
1943	1,830	108	1,804	469
1944	1,213	97	1,232	292
1945	923	132	929	185
1946	747	236	853	147
1947	801	172	819	121
1948	912	123	858	115
1949	773	104	745	105

Source: Appendix Table 68.

In the course of the original registration, up to the end of 1937, 26.6 million account numbers were issued to men and 10.1 million to women. The ratio, five to two, is somewhat higher than that between the number of men and women employed at any given time in industries covered by the program but can be accepted as the ratio of individuals of both sexes who are employed — continuously or temporarily — in these industries during a year. Since that time, applications have varied in number as shown in Table 103.

The expansion of coverage of federal old-age and survivors insurance in 1950 has greatly reduced the possibility of shifts between covered and noncovered jobs. In the future, applications for account numbers will essentially reflect accessions of new workers into gainful work.

TABLE 103

APPLICATIONS FOR ACCOUNT NUMBERS UNDER OASI, BY SEX, 1939–1949

(*In Millions*)

Year	Men	Women
1939	3.5	2.4
1940	3.1	2.1
1941	3.7	3.0
1942	3.5	4.1
1943	2.8	4.5
1944	1.8	2.7
1945	1.5	1.8
1946	1.4	1.6
1947	1.3	1.4
1948	1.3	1.4
1949	1.1	1.2

Source: Appendix Table 68.

Chapter 25

DEMAND FOR LABOR *

The demand for labor in our economic system, as measured by the number of persons at work, varies from year to year and from month to month. Long-term changes are determined by the relationship between: (1) expansion and contraction of activities in various branches of the economy and (2) replacement of workers by laborsaving devices. Short-time fluctuations depend mainly on cyclical and seasonal factors.

Structure of Employment

The monthly labor force reports of the Bureau of the Census and the 1940 census count as employed all persons aged 14 and over who worked for remuneration or profit during the surveyed week or who were not at work but were holding a job. In addition to fully employed persons, the total includes part-time workers, those whose jobs were terminated during the week, and those who held a job but did not work because of temporary disability, layoff, industrial dispute and so on.

In 1946–1948, when unemployment was fluctuating around 2 million, the number of persons in these marginal groups was close to 10 million. The proportion of workers not fully employed is particularly high in agriculture. (See Table 104.)

The fact that 10 million "employed" persons worked less than 35 hours a week or did not work at all at a time when jobs were going begging, as in 1946–1948, proves that this marginal group cannot be regarded as indicative of hidden unemployment or underemployment. This group largely represents the normal turnover of labor due to temporary disability, vacations with pay, and interruptions of work or part-time work because of bad weather, industrial accidents, work stoppages and the like. It includes also persons who were available for work only part of a week and would not take full-time jobs.

Since 1940 the size of the group of persons who are employed but work less than 35 hours or are not at work in the survey week has fluctuated between 5.5 million and 12 million in nonagricultural industries and between 1 and 2.5 million on the farm.[1] It averaged 6.5 million in nonagricultural industries in 1940, declined slightly in 1943, at the peak of the war effort, increased to 7.7 million in 1945, when temporary marginal workers flooded the labor market, decreased in 1946, and has been growing steadily since then, in the period of more than full employment. The proportion of part-time workers is appreciably higher among women than among men. In December 1950, for example, nearly 34 per cent of employed women worked less than 35 hours a week, as compared with 17 per cent for employed men.[2]

It seems that the labor force now includes a much higher proportion of persons who are not available for full-time work. Apart from this, the proportion of part-time workers depends on the changing demand for labor, on the one hand, and the extent to which work sharing is practiced, on the other.

A sharp decline in labor demand is bound to increase the number of persons who work less than full time. At the depth of a severe and long depression, the practice of sharing the work can bring most employed industrial workers into the less-than-35-hours group. The statistical picture will be different, however, if, instead of reducing weekly hours of work, management and labor unions agree on some form of rotation of personnel.

Agricultural and Nonagricultural Employment

The agricultural and nonagricultural sectors of employment are not entirely independent. In fact, many farmers and farm laborers take nonagricultural work occasionally during the dull season in agriculture. In long-range trends and seasonal ups and downs in the demand for

* By W. S. Woytinsky.

1. Without counting weeks with legal holidays.
2. "Annual Report on the Labor Force, 1950," *Current Population Reports*, Series P-50, Bureau of the Census, 1951, p. 16.

TABLE 104

CIVILIAN LABOR FORCE, BY EMPLOYMENT STATUS AND HOURS WORKED IN MAY, 1946–1950

(In Millions)

Group	May 1946	May 1947	May 1948	May 1949	May 1950
Total civilian labor force	57.2	60.3	60.4	62.0	62.8
All employed persons	54.9	58.4	58.6	58.7	59.7
Worked 35 hours or more during week	44.8	48.2	48.6	48.5	49.0
Worked 1–34 hours or did not work	10.1	10.2	10.0	10.2	10.7
Employed in nonagricultural industries	46.0	49.4	50.8	49.7	51.7
Worked 35 hours or more during week	38.2	41.3	42.7	41.3	43.0
Worked 15–34 hours	4.8	4.8	4.9	5.1	5.1
Worked 1–14 hours	1.2	1.6	1.6	1.8	1.9
With a job but not at work	1.8	1.7	1.6	1.6	1.5
Employed in agriculture	8.9	9.0	7.9	9.0	8.1
Worked 35 hours or more during week	6.6	6.9	5.9	7.2	6.0
Worked 15–34 hours	1.9	1.7	1.5	1.5	1.6
Worked 1–14 hours	0.2	0.2	0.2	0.2	0.3
With a job but not at work	0.2	0.2	0.2	0.1	0.2
Unemployed	2.3	2.0	1.8	3.3	3.1

Sources: "Labor Force, Employment and Unemployment in the United States, 1940–1946," *Current Population Reports,* Series P-50, No. 2, Bureau of the Census, September 1947, and "Monthly Report on the Labor Force," *Current Population Reports,* Series P-57, Bureau of the Census.

labor, however, the agricultural and nonagricultural groups differ strikingly.[3]

Agricultural employment, as recorded by the monthly reports of the Bureau of the Census, averaged more than 9 million before the war, declined from 1942 to 1948, went up slightly in 1949 and declined again in 1950. The drop was particularly sharp in the number of persons employed at the seasonal peak, in June: from about 11.2 million in 1942 to 9.4 million in 1948, 9.7 million in 1949 and 9 million in 1950. The contraction of employment at the seasonal low point (January to March) was comparatively mild: from about 7.8 million in 1942 to 6.9 million in 1948, 7.1 million in 1949 and 6.4 million in 1950. (See Table 105.)

In contrast, the demand for labor in nonagricultural industries rose from an average of 38 million in March-December 1940 to an annual average of 45.4 million in 1943 and 45.0 million in 1944. After the end of the war and the termination of munitions contracts, civilian nonagricultural employment declined temporarily to 42.6 million in September 1945, but by the spring of 1946 it regained the wartime peak. It reached a new peak of 52.8 million in August 1948, dropped to a low of 49.8 million in May 1949, recovered again in the summer of the same year, advanced to 51.7 million in May 1950, and reached an all-time peak of 54.2 million in August 1950. In 1950 it was a third higher than in 1941.

3. For closer analysis of agricultural employment, see Chapter 30.

Self-Employment and Hired Labor

On a year-round basis, more than three fourths of all agricultural work is performed by farmers and members of their families and less than one fourth by hired labor. In nonagricultural pursuits, on the other hand, there are six or seven hired workers to each self-employed person or employer. (See Table 106.)

The number of independent nonagricultural jobs declined conspicuously during the war but has increased in recent years. From 5.15 million in 1943 and 5.12 million in 1944, the number of nonagricultural employers or self-employed rose to 6.6 million in 1949, an increase of 28 per cent, as against an 11 per cent increase in

TABLE 105

EMPLOYMENT IN AGRICULTURE, 1940–1950

(In Thousands)

Year	Annual Average	Low (January-March)	Peak (June)	Excess of Seasonal Peak over Seasonal Low
1940	9,540[a]	(8,500)	11,520	3,020
1941	9,100	7,770	10,780	3,010
1942	9,250	7,850	11,150	3,300
1943	9,080	7,750	10,970	3,220
1944	8,950	7,410	10,800	3,390
1945	8,580	7,590	10,220	2,630
1946	8,320	7,060	10,010	2,950
1947	8,270	6,890	10,380	3,490
1948	7,970	6,890	9,400	2,510
1949	8,030	7,050	9,700	2,650
1950	7,510	6,370	9,050	2,680

a. Estimated for 12 months.

Source: Appendix Table 69.

TABLE 106

NONAGRICULTURAL EMPLOYMENT, BY CLASS OF WORK, ANNUAL AVERAGE, 1940–1950

Year	Annual Average, in Thousands: Total	Self-Employed and Employers	Employees	Self-Employed and Employers as Percentage of Total
1940....	37,980	5,690	32,290	15.0
1941....	41,250	6,000	35,250	14.5
1942....	44,500	5,660	38,840	12.7
1943....	45,390	5,150	40,240	11.3
1944....	45,010	5,120	39,890	11.4
1945....	44,240	5,350	38,890	12.1
1946....	46,930	6,020	40,910	12.8
1947....	49,760	6,470	43,290	13.0
1948....	51,410	6,540	44,870	12.7
1949....	50,680	6,600	44,080	13.0
1950....	52,450	6,470	45,980	12.4

Source: Appendix Table 69.

the number of wage and salary workers. As compared with 1940, however, self-employed persons today represent a somewhat smaller percentage of nonagricultural workers. This relative decline is in line with the long-range trend, but it may be due at least partly to the change in business conditions.

During the depression of the 1930's many people who could not find employment tried to make a living by independent or quasi-independent work. The improved employment opportunities in 1947–1949 may have reduced the search for such work. Another factor contributing to the rise in the proportion of employees in the nonagricultural labor force has been the steady increase in the number of government employees (from 3.5 million in 1935 to 5.8 million in 1949).

Because of the exceptionally high level of employment, the proportion of independent jobs in 1948 was probably somewhat below the long-range trend, and it is likely to increase in the future after the postwar boom levels off.

The border line between self-employment and work for salary or wages is often not clear. A part-owner is often recorded as the salaried manager of an enterprise. Similarly, the leading stockholders in small corporations often hold salaried positions as directors and members of the board. Many professional workers work partly for salary, partly as self-employed businessmen. The distinction between independent and salaried jobs is particularly vague in work on a commission basis. It took the courts nearly a decade to decide whether private insurance agents are employees, and therefore covered by federal old-age and survivors insurance, or whether they are independent businessmen.

It is sound to assume, therefore, that during a year most self-employed persons and employers get part of their income in the form of salary or commission, while many persons classified as wage or salary workers have additional earnings from some kind of independent work. There are many border cases between the two groups and many persons keep shifting from one group to the other.

In the middle of 1950 (average for June and July) employment was distributed as follows (in millions): [4]

Total labor force	65.9
Armed forces	1.3
Civilian labor force	64.6
Employed	61.3
Agriculture	8.7
Nonagricultural pursuits	52.6
Self-employed and employers	6.7
Wage and salary workers	45.9
Unemployed	3.3

Nonagricultural Employment, by Industry

Under favorable business conditions, as during 1946–1950, wage and salary jobs in nonagricultural industries constitute about 75 per cent of all civilian employment. This percentage shrinks when business conditions decline. Layoffs of industrial wage workers usually begin in the initial phase of a recession, while commercial failures and the disappearance of independent jobs come much later. Moreover, a depression often calls into being many small quasi-independent pursuits such as peddling, neighborhood repair shops and the like.

Assuming a coming period of economic expansion, with only moderate cyclical ups and downs, the proportion of nonagricultural wage and salary workers in civilian employment is likely to fluctuate in the range 72–75 per cent, probably closer to the upper limit.

A little more than a third of all nonagricultural wage and salary jobs are provided by manufacturing industries; another third by transportation, communication, trade and finance; less than a third by all other industries and occupations combined, including government. (See Appendix Table 70.)

Manufacturing, the most important field for

4. *Survey of Current Business,* Weekly Supplement, August 11 and August 25, 1950.

employment of wage and salary workers, is also the sector of the labor market most sensitive to cyclical changes in business conditions. In the period 1929–1932, manufacturing laid off as many workers as all other industries combined; during the war boom it had the largest increase in employment; during the industrial demobilization it sharply reduced crews while other industries slowly but steadily increased their personnel. (See Table 107.)

Apart from these fluctuations, the share of manufacturing in nonagricultural employment has increased in the past two decades — from 32.7 per cent in 1929 to 33.9 per cent in 1950. The rise is probably due to the exceptional activity of the postwar economy. After the postwar boom levels off, the relative share of factories in employment may be stabilized at about 33 per cent, appreciably less than during the war, somewhat less than in 1950 but more than in 1929 and much more than in the 1930's.

The demand for labor in mining fluctuates within a comparatively narrow range. Because of technological trends in coal mining, the share of mining in total nonagricultural employment declined from more than 3 per cent in 1929–1930 to a little over 2 per cent in 1946–1950. The shortage of skilled labor and the reluctance of young workers to take jobs in mines have resulted in a spectacular rise in miners' earnings. The rise in labor cost has encouraged and accelerated the introduction of laborsaving devices. Temporarily, the labor problem has been solved, but with a decline in employment. Total employment in mining averaged 0.9 million in 1950, as compared with 1.0 million in 1929. During the same period, factory employment grew from 10.4 million to nearly 15 million. The number of miners per hundred factory workers declined from 9.5 in 1929 to 6.1 in 1950. It seems probable that this trend will continue.

Employment in contract construction is extremely sensitive to both the season and the business cycle. Moreover, cyclical ups and downs in building construction do not always follow the general business cycle exactly. Employment in the building trades may remain high during a depression of moderate severity. In fact, these trades suffered only minor losses in 1930 as compared with 1929 and in 1938 as compared with 1937. Because of the special rhythm of the building cycle, demand for labor in the building trades may decline at a time when other fields of economic activity are on the upswing, as occurred in 1928–1929.

TABLE 107

WAGE AND SALARY WORKERS IN MANUFACTURING AND OTHER NONAGRICULTURAL INDUSTRIES, ANNUAL AVERAGE, 1929–1950 [a]

(*In Millions*)

Year	Total	Manufacturing	Other Industries
1929	31.9	10.4	21.5
1930	30.0	9.3	20.7
1931	27.0	7.9	19.1
1932	23.8	6.7	17.1
1933	24.3	7.2	17.1
1934	27.5	8.4	19.1
1935	28.9	8.9	20.0
1936	31.9	9.6	22.3
1937	33.1	10.6	22.5
1938	31.5	9.1	22.4
1939	33.0	10.0	23.0
1940	34.8	10.9	23.9
1941	38.2	13.1	25.1
1942	40.7	15.3	25.4
1943	42.2	17.4	24.8
1944	41.5	17.0	24.5
1945	39.8	15.2	24.6
1946	41.4	14.5	26.9
1947	43.2	15.2	28.0
1948	44.3	15.3	29.0
1949	42.8	14.2	28.6
1950	44.3	15.0	29.3

a. Full-time employment equivalent, excluding armed forces, but including relief work.

Source: Appendix Table 70.

Transportation and public utilities employed 12.2 per cent of all nonagricultural wage and salary workers in 1929 and only 9 per cent in recent years. This decline is probably related to technological changes, especially the competition of cars and trucks with railroads.

In comparison with factory employment, the demand for labor in trade establishments is less sensitive to the business cycle and to technological changes. From 1929 to 1932, employment in wholesale and retail trade declined 23 per cent while employment in factories went down 36 per cent. In 1938, trade establishments laid off 2 per cent of their employees; the loss in factory employment was 14 per cent.

Employment in retail trade has been increased in the past two or three decades by services arising from automobile travel — filling stations, garages, roadside stands — and by recent trends in urbanization — the growth of urban population and its dispersion over large metropolitan areas, the development of satellite communities around a central city. As long as urban life continues to develop in this direction it does not seem very probable that progress in mechanization will substantially cut employment in trade establishments.

Service establishments employ 12 to 14 per cent of all nonagricultural workers. There has been no appreciable change in this percentage in recent years.

The share of government in nonagricultural employment increased from less than 10 per cent in 1929 to nearly 15 per cent in 1943–1944 and declined to 13.5 per cent in 1949.[5]

Employment in Manufacturing Industries

In economic analyses, manufacturing industries are often broadly divided into durable-goods industries and nondurable-goods industries. The demarcation is determined by the general characteristics of the respective industries rather than the actual durability of their products. The durable-goods group includes the iron and steel industry, machinery, electrical supplies, transportation equipment (including automobiles), nonferrous metals and their products, lumber and furniture, and stone, clay and glass products. Production of munitions and ordnance during the war was also listed in this group. The group of nondurable goods includes textiles and apparel, leather, the food industries, paper and allied products, printing and publishing, chemicals, rubber products and products of petroleum and coal.

From the point of view of employment, the chief difference between the two groups is that the demand for labor in durable-goods industries is more sensitive to changes in business conditions and less affected by seasonal fluctuations. In good times the durable-goods industries employ approximately half of all factory workers; in 1923–1926, for example, their share in factory employment averaged 49 per cent. The share of durable-goods industries in factory employment declines during depression; it fell to 38 per cent in 1932 and 1933. The war boom was primarily a boom in durable-goods industries. Since the industrial demobilization, the two groups of industries have shared about equally in employment. (See Table 108, Appendix Table 71 and Figure 59.)

Apart from the striking contrast in short-time fluctuations (both seasonal and cyclical),

TABLE 108

WAGE AND SALARY WORKERS EMPLOYED IN MANUFACTURE OF DURABLE AND NONDURABLE GOODS, ANNUAL AVERAGE, 1923–1949

(*In Thousands*)

Year	Total	Durable Goods	Nondurable Goods
1923	8,269	4,055	4,214
1924	7,678	3,755	3,923
1925	7,947	3,875	4,072
1926	8,097	3,993	4,104
1927	7,923	3,758	4,165
1928	7,937	3,804	4,133
1929	10,428	4,953	5,475
1930	9,309	4,197	5,112
1931	7,895	3,278	4,617
1932	6,678	2,546	4,132
1933	7,204	2,706	4,498
1934	8,364	3,366	4,998
1935	8,904	3,699	5,205
1936	9,645	4,198	5,447
1937	10,591	4,846	5,745
1938	9,131	3,815	5,316
1939	9,967	4,309	5,658
1940	10,882	5,025	5,857
1941	13,137	6,577	6,560
1942	15,284	8,376	6,908
1943	17,402	10,399	7,003
1944	17,050	10,225	6,825
1945	15,186	8,394	6,792
1946	14,491	7,233	7,258
1947	15,219	7,799	7,420
1948	15,288	7,779	7,509
1949	14,187	6,981	7,206

Sources: For 1923–1928, only production workers, as estimated by the Bureau of Labor Statistics (mimeographed release LS 49–1297); for 1929–1949, all factory workers, as given in national income estimates of the Department of Commerce. (Cf. Appendix Table 71.)

there is no consistent long-range trend in the relationship between these two divisions of factory employment. Moreover, the distinction between them is somewhat artificial. Some nondurable-goods industries supply parts and materials to durable-goods industries (rubber tires, paints, chemicals), while durable-goods industries provide parts and containers for the production of nondurable goods.

Assuming a long period of relative prosperity, it is probable that relative saturation of the demand for durable goods will develop while the demand for nondurables is still growing. In this event, of course, employment in the nondurable-goods group of manufactures would outrun employment in durable-goods industries.

Among the durable-goods industries, iron and steel mills rank first in the number of employed workers, machinery (except electrical) second and the automobile industry third. In good times the three groups together employ 25 per cent of all factory workers; in depres-

5. All data above refer to the number of full-time equivalent employees. See *Survey of Current Business,* National Income Supplement, 1951, pp. 180–81; cf. Appendix Table 70.

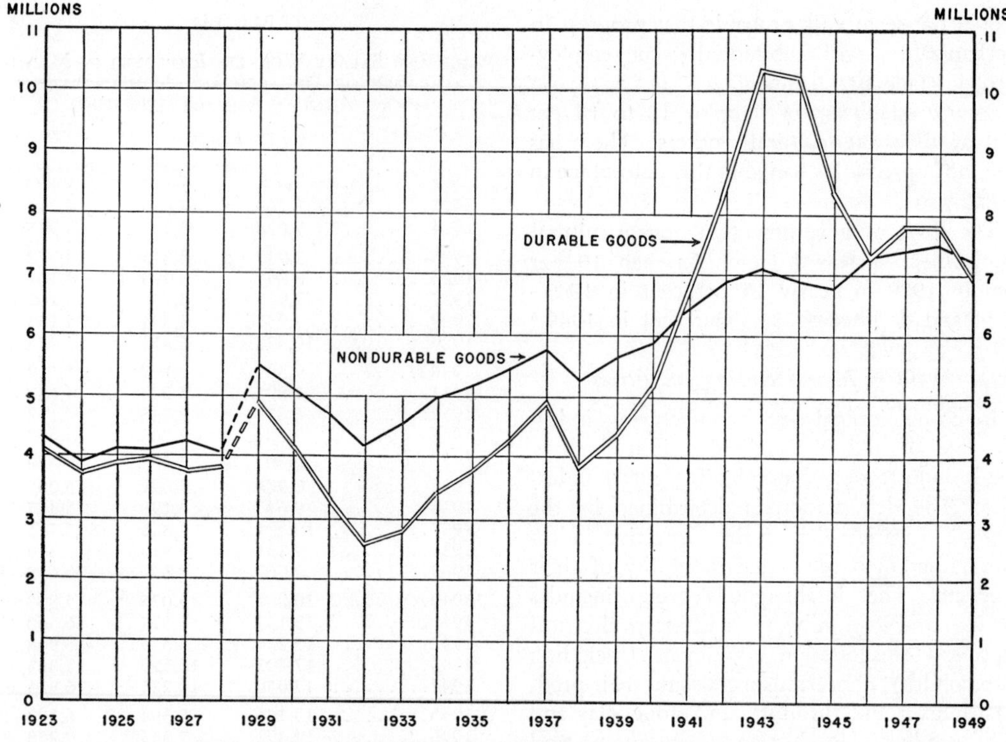

FIGURE 59. WAGE AND SALARY WORKERS EMPLOYED IN MANUFACTURE OF DURABLE AND NONDURABLE GOODS, ANNUAL AVERAGE, 1923–1949[a]

a. For 1923–1928, production workers; for 1929–1949, all factory workers.

Source: Table 108.

sion their share in factory employment may shrink to 10–12 per cent.

Transportation equipment (other than automobiles) includes railroad car, locomotive and airplane factories and shipbuilding. During the war it dwarfed all other industrial groups; by the autumn of 1943 it employed nearly 3.2 million workers. The crest of its expansion was passed in the winter of 1943–1944, after completion of the basic armament program. When Japan surrendered, the work force in these industries had already been halved.

Among the nondurable-goods industries, food products rank first in number of workers, textile industries second and apparel production third. All three groups include many small and middle-sized enterprises. In both good and bad times they account for a little less than half the total nondurable-goods employment.

Tobacco factories are remarkable for the steadiness of their operation. In no month from 1939 through 1948 did employment drop below 91,000 or rise above 111,000.

Since the end of the war, employment has been comparatively stable in several other industrial groups — for example, products of petroleum and coal, rubber, printing and publishing. In these industries, however, postwar employment has been much higher than prewar, and a sharp decline is fairly probable in the event of a cyclical setback in business conditions.

CYCLICAL AND SEASONAL VARIATIONS IN THE DEMAND FOR LABOR

Some of the variations in the demand for labor parallel changes in the supply of labor, like the changes that occurred during and after World War II or those that occur each spring in agriculture and each winter in retail trade. Other fluctuations in demand cause inverse fluctuations in unemployment. Variations in the demand for labor associated with the business cycle fall into the second class.

CYCLICAL VARIATIONS

The level of employment is closely related to the volume of business activity. So close is the apparent interrelation that the term "full employment" is often considered as synonymous with "prosperity." Yet sizable unemployment can develop without noticeable deterioration in business conditions, and a considerable decline in business is possible without noticeable increase in unemployment. The first situation may result from rapid technological changes and from concentrated efforts of industries to reduce their labor cost by stricter selection of workers, streamlining of work operations, layoffs of employees whose services are not absolutely necessary, and so on. Usually, such a management policy itself results from the pressure of deteriorating business conditions, but employment falls more sharply and recovers less rapidly than production. Typical of this pattern are changes in production and employment in manufacturing industries in 1920–1922, during the liquidation of the boom following World War I. (See Table 109.)

TABLE 109

INDEXES OF OUTPUT AND EMPLOYMENT IN SELECTED INDUSTRIES, 1921 AND 1922

(1920 = 100)

Industry	1921	1922
Manufacturing		
Output	80.1	102.9
Employment	76.6	85.2
Steam railroads		
Operation	76.4	81.3
Employment	82.1	80.0
Light and power		
Output	92.4	104.8
Employment	103.5	114.2

Sources: Manufacturing data adapted from George J. Stigler, *Trends in Output and Employment,* National Bureau of Economic Research, New York, 1947, pp. 57–58. Data for steam railroads and light and power from releases of the Bureau of Labor Statistics.

Although economically sound, this pattern of development is not very usual.[6] More frequently, declines in employment during an economic setback lag behind declines in output or volume of operation. In the brief depression of 1921, this happened in steam railroads and in production of electric power and light.

The practice of work sharing is chiefly responsible for differences in the trends in employment and output in the early phase of a depression. A factory can meet a slight contraction of sales by eliminating overtime work. If sales continue to drop and buyers refuse to pay the price demanded, management feels compelled to cut production and to take measures against further losses by reducing production costs. Usually this cost reduction is sought in the field of labor, and the goal is to reduce the input of labor in more than direct proportion to the decline in output. Temporary and marginal workers are laid off first, but sooner or later management must face the dilemma of cutting down the regular force or shifting to part-time work. In the early phase of a depression, the practice of work sharing may prevent layoffs even though fewer man-hours of work are available and despite speed-ups used by management as a means of reducing production costs.

On the whole, in good times the rise in employment tends to lag behind the rise in output, while in bad times employment usually declines less than output. This was the picture, for example, in manufacturing, production of electric light and power, and steam railroads from 1921 to 1929, from 1929 to 1932 and from 1932 to 1937. (See Table 110.)

Not all parts of the labor market are equally sensitive to the business cycle. Employment in trade, public utilities and service industries is more resistant to depression than that in manufacturing, mining and building construction. The government does not cut its rolls when private industries take a dive. Nor does agriculture, at least in the first stages of a depression.

The statement that employment declines less rapidly than production is true only for the early phase of a depression. A different relationship may develop during a long depression

TABLE 110

INDEXES OF CYCLICAL CHANGE IN OUTPUT AND EMPLOYMENT IN SELECTED INDUSTRIES, 1921–1937

(1929 = 100)

Industry	1921 (Low)	1929 (Peak)	1932 (Low)	1937 (Peak)
Manufacturing				
(a) Output	53.3	100.0	54.1	103.3
(b) Employment ..	77.0	100.0	62.6	102.1
Ratio of a to b.	69.2	100.0	86.4	101.2
Steam railroads				
(a) Operation	78.0	100.0	52.0	81.0
(b) Employment ..	101.0	100.0	62.0	68.0
Ratio of a to b.	77.2	100.0	84.0	119.1
Electric light and power				
(a) Output	36.3	100.0	92.7	136.3
(b) Employment ..	46.8	100.0	83.7	96.3
Ratio of a to b.	77.6	100.0	110.8	141.5

Source: George J. Stigler, *Trends in Output and Employment,* National Bureau of Economic Research, New York, 1947, pp. 57–58.

6. Wladimir Woytinksy, *Three Sources of Unemployment,* International Labor Office, Geneva, 1935.

or in protracted stagnation of production, even at a level that formerly seemed highly satisfactory. When the volume of production does not increase, long-range technological progress each year sets free a certain part of the employed labor force. Furthermore, when production remains stable, unemployment grows by each year's addition to the labor force. Both factors, combined with the influx of additional workers from families in which the usual breadwinner is unemployed, can result in heavy unemployment at a time when production is not much below the preceding peak.[7]

SEASONAL VARIATIONS

The seasonal rhythm of employment depends partly on weather conditions, partly on established practices in production. Agriculture and outdoor construction exemplify weather-controlled industries. The automobile industry, production of apparel, and retail trade are examples of industries in which seasonal fluctuations in employment are brought about by custom. But the two seasonality factors are not completely independent. Although weather conditions determine demand for labor in agriculture and building construction, the ways in which seasonal work is timed and the amount of labor needed to handle it depend largely on usage. Similarly, though customs determine seasonal ups and downs in the production of apparel, these customs in turn have their origin in the annual weather cycle.

Changing Patterns

The "seasonal" demand for labor is defined as a demand that appears each year at about the same time and in approximately the same volume, but the seasonal rhythm is not completely fixed.

Methods used in collecting monthly employment statistics accentuate the variability of seasonal ups and downs. The Bureau of the Census in its monthly surveys records the status of employment in surveyed households in a given week in the first half of each month. The Bureau of Labor Statistics registers changes in employment in identical industrial establishments for specified pay periods ending close to the middle of each month. Because both series identify the data by month, a shift in the date of the seasonal upturn or downturn by a few days or a week can appear in these statistical series as a change in the month in which the busy season begins or ends. On the other hand, changes occurring between the surveyed weeks are not recorded.

When seasonal fluctuations in employment are described in the form of a calendar[8] or by a set of indexes of seasonality,[9] allowance must be made for possible variations in the timing of the seasonal increase or decrease. Because of this flexibility of seasonal patterns, the Federal Reserve Board computes its seasonally adjusted series with the help of varying indexes of seasonality. The seasonal component of the monthly change of employment in each industry is estimated by the analyst with due regard to the behavior of the series in preceding years and immediately preceding months and all other useful information.

When the seasonal pattern of employment is computed according to strict mathematical rules, the resulting patterns are merely conventional averages that describe the typical behavior of a given statistical series in a given period of time. Such patterns, like many other statistical averages, are rapidly perishable goods: as time goes on, the seasonality of employment in an industry may change or disappear.

An industry may, for example, replace seasonal layoffs by temporary work sharing and keep all its employees on its payrolls, rotating

7. This pattern is illustrated by the following hypothetical model, in which the long-range growth in productivity of labor is set arbitrarily at 3 per cent a year and the growth of the labor force at 2 per cent in the first period of a depresssion and 1 per cent in later phases.

Year	Business Phase	Production	Labor Force: Total	Employed	Unemployed
1	Peak	100	100	95	5
2	Decline	85	102	87	15
3	Trough	70	104	74	30
4	Stagnation ..	72	105	73	32
5	Stagnation ..	75	106	72	34
6	Revival	85	107	77	30

These figures are purely illustrative. The essential point is that the same level of production (say 85 per cent of the preceding peak) may result in comparatively little unemployment at an early phase of depression and much greater unemployment a few years later.

8. W. S. Woytinsky, Calendar of the American Labor Market, in *Seasonal Variations in Employment in the United States,* Committee on Social Security, Social Science Research Council, Washington, 1939, pp. 100-11.

9. Aryness Joy and Thomas Woodlief, "The Use of Moving Averages in the Measurement of Seasonal Variations," *Journal of the American Statistical Association,* September 1928, pp. 241–52.

them during the dull season according to a plan established by agreement between management and labor unions. Such agreements are now in force in the textile industry and in coal mining. In agriculture, too, changes have occurred in the seasonal pattern of employment. In recent years, spurred on by the shortage of farm labor and the increase in wages of farm laborers, farmers have learned to use new equipment and machinery in such a way as to reduce their need for temporary hired labor.[10]

Generally, the span between seasonal troughs and peaks has been narrower in recent years than before the war, both absolutely and in relation to the average year-round demand for labor. It is not very clear, however, whether this marks a step toward greater stability of employment or is a temporary phenomenon due to the exceptional economic activity during the postwar boom. In some industries — coal mining, textiles, automobiles — seasonal fluctuations appear to have been reduced by management and labor unions. In others, however, temporary factors may have been responsible for ironing out seasonal ups and downs; for example, the high wages of farm laborers, as already pointed out, were responsible for cutting down seasonal employment in agriculture, while high prices in building construction have permitted contractors to continue some kinds of work in winter despite unfavorable weather conditions.

Prewar Seasonal Pattern

Before the war fairly regular seasonal variations in employment were discernible in agriculture, building construction, food industries, iron and steel, machinery, the automobile industry, textile mills, production of apparel, leather products, lumber mills, coal mining, steam railroads and railroad repair shops, wholesale and retail trade, service industries, and stone, clay and glass. Minor seasonal ups and downs occurred in other pursuits.[11]

The seasonal low point of employment was in January. Manufacturing industries usually hired workers in February, especially the automobile industry, clothing trades, leather and machinery. A rise in factory employment (approximately 160,000 new jobs) was partly offset by layoffs in trade (approximately 70,000 jobs terminated). In March and April, employment picked up in agriculture, manufacturing and construction, with only minor changes in other industries. In May and June, employment in manufacturing went down slightly (mainly in textiles, apparel, chemicals and automobile production), but in agriculture and building construction the demand for labor was rising.

The seasonal peak in agriculture and construction was reached in July-August. Farmers employed approximately 1,450,000 more hired hands in July than in January-February; building construction had approximately 1,125,000 seasonal jobs in good years and 675,000 seasonal jobs in bad years. In manufacturing and trade, on the other hand, employment declined in summer. On the whole, October was the peak month in employment, with a demand for hired labor more than 3 million above the seasonal low, not counting seasonal employment of family workers in agriculture (approximately 750,000) or independent nonagricultural jobs (perhaps an additional 300,000 to 500,000). If those two groups are included, employment in October was 4.1 to 4.3 million above that in January.[12] (See Table 111; cf. Figure 60.)

January did not mark the seasonal trough in all industries before the war. In that month, coal mines and textile mills worked at full capacity, and employment in trade was considerably above the seasonal trough (July-August) though below the annual average. All in all, some 420,000 seasonal workers held jobs in January, so that the number of seasonal workers fluctuated through a year between 420,000 and 4,550,000 or 4,750,000.

Postwar Seasonal Pattern

The postwar period is too short for generalization about the new pattern of seasonal demand for labor. The available data are not conclusive, because of unusual employment conditions in recent years — the rapidly rising demand for labor in 1946 (starting from the low point in January), the exceptionally high level of economic activity since 1947, several turning points in employment curves that were neither seasonal nor cyclical in their nature.

Clearly recognizable is the seasonal rhythm

10. This explains the narrowing span between the seasonal peak and trough of farm employment (Table 105). Cf. Chapter 30.

11. Joy and Woodlief, *op. cit.*, and Woytinsky, *Seasonal Variations in Employment in the United States.*

12. Woytinsky, *Seasonal Variations in Employment in the United States*, pp. 35–70 and 100–11.

TABLE 111

Pattern of Seasonal Variation in Employment, by Industry Division, before World War II

(Sum of Deviations from the Lowest Point in Single Industries in Each Group, in Thousands)

Item	Jan.	Feb.	Mar.	Apr.	May	June	July	Aug.	Sept.	Oct.	Nov.	Dec.
All hired labor [a]	420	510	860	1,460	1,975	2,600	2,950	3,040	3,400	3,440	2,600	1,910
All labor [b]	420	510	960	1,760	2,475	3,500	4,200	3,940	4,250	4,190	2,800	2,010
Agriculture												
Hired laborers	0	0	150	400	650	1,050	1,450	1,250	1,250	1,300	850	400
Family workers	0	0	100	300	500	900	1,250	900	850	750	200	100
Nonagricultural industries												
Total	420	510	710	1,060	1,325	1,550	1,500	1,790	2,150	2,140	1,750	1,510
Mining	66	65	57	36	42	35	24	35	57	70	76	75
Manufacturing	186	347	393	386	321	278	240	391	539	565	451	354
Transportation and utilities	7	2	14	45	81	97	119	124	119	115	74	21
Trade	133	66	88	163	182	176	29	20	200	305	324	628
Service industries	2	2	8	29	50	65	67	67	83	64	48	36
Building construction												
Bad years	0	0	75	225	375	525	600	675	675	600	450	225
Active years	0	0	125	375	625	875	1,000	1,125	1,125	1,000	750	375

a. Including adjustment for industries not classified separately and counting building construction as in active years.
b. Including family workers in agriculture.

Source: Appendix Table 72.

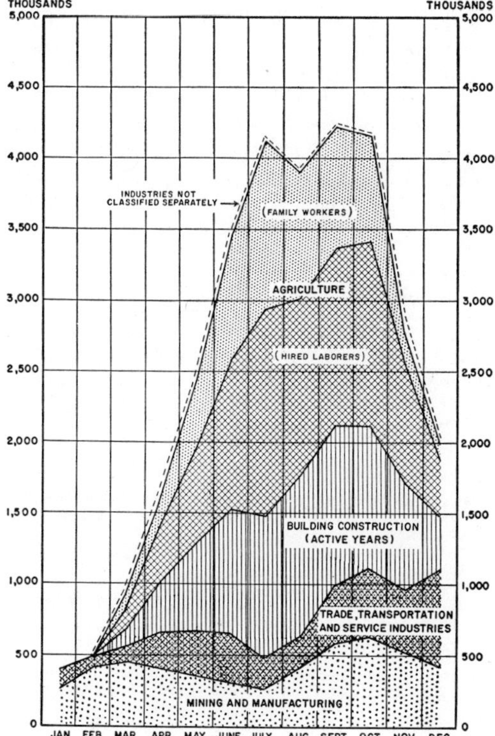

FIGURE 60. PATTERN OF SEASONAL VARIATION IN EMPLOYMENT BEFORE WORLD WAR II

(*Seasonal Increment in Comparison with the Seasonally Lowest Level in Each Industry during Year*)

Source: Table 111.

of agricultural employment, with the low point in January-February and the peak in June-July. The span between the two points is, however, less stable than it used to be before the war. The difference between the average number of persons employed in agriculture in June and July and that for the preceding January and February varied as follows: [13]

1944	3,365,000	1948	2,365,000
1945	2,720,000	1949	2,790,000
1946	3,160,000	1950	2,530,000
1947	3,510,000	1951	2,000,000
Average	3,190,000	Average	2,420,000

Employment in building construction reveals a seasonal pattern similar to that of the prewar years, but with a narrower span of variation, with the low point in February-March and the peak in August-September. (See Table 112.)

TABLE 112

EMPLOYMENT IN CONTRACT CONSTRUCTION, 1946–1950

(*In Thousands*)

Month	1946	1947	1948	1949	1950
January	1,085	1,527	1,871	2,016	1,919
February	1,101	1,502	1,731	1,926	1,861
March	1,203	1,534	1,805	1,947	1,907
April	1,356	1,619	1,933	2,036	2,076
May	1,438	1,685	2,052	2,137	2,245
June	1,532	1,768	2,173	2,205	2,414
July	1,627	1,847	2,219	2,271	2,532
August	1,713	1,894	2,253	2,340	2,629
September	1,747	1,904	2,239	2,341	2,626
October	1,753	1,896	2,197	2,313	2,631
November	1,713	1,854	2,161	2,244	2,571
December	1,644	1,788	2,078	2,088	2,403

Source: Monthly Labor Review, 1946–1951.

The seasonal component of employment in this industry can be estimated by comparing its employment figure in each month with that represented by a hypothetical trend curve drawn freehand and fitted to the January data for 1946 to 1951.[14] This method suggests the following pattern of seasonal variation, in terms of deviation from the nonseasonal level:

January	0	July	+ 280,000
February	— 80,000	August	+ 330,000
March	— 50,000	September	+ 320,000
April	+ 60,000	October	+ 270,000
May	+ 140,000	November	+ 230,000
June	+ 200,000	December	+ 90,000

The span of seasonal variation in building construction — between February and August — was somewhat more than 400,000, but it increased during the period of observation — from 320,000 in 1946 and 200,000 in 1947 to 600,000 in 1950.

Another major industry with a clear seasonal pattern is trade. (See Table 113.) During the first half of the calendar year demand for labor in this industry varies in a comparatively narrow range, layoffs in certain branches being offset by increasing employment in others. Employment begins to rise in August. Gains are slow at first but are accelerated in the fall, and in the Christmas rush trade establishments employ approximately 800,000 to a million more people than in the dull season, in February. Using the same method as that applied to employment data in building construction, the typical pattern of seasonal variation in employment

13. For 1944–1950 see Appendix Table 69; for 1951, *Monthly Labor Review,* December 1951.

14. Such a curve must rise in 1946–1948, decline in 1949 and rise steeply again in 1950.

in trade in 1946–1950 can be estimated as follows (in terms of deviation from January):

January	0	July	0
February	— 50,000	August	+ 25,000
March	— 25,000	September	+ 100,000
April	+ 50,000	October	+ 200,000
May	0	November	+ 400,000
June	+ 25,000	December	+ 900,000

Building construction and trade accounted for a large part of the visible seasonal fluctuations in nonagricultural employment in the past five or six years. To these massive fluctuations sizable seasonal ups and downs were added by the food industry (with a peak in August-September) and the apparel industry, and minor ups and downs by service industries, transportation and others.

In the food and apparel industries the seasonal deviations of employment from the trend line are similar to the prewar pattern but not identical with it. Seasonality in the demand for labor in the food industry has increased: the span between the low point and the peak was 210,000 before the war and 290,000 in 1946–1950. (See Table 114.) This change was probably accounted for by the spectacular growth of the highly seasonal canning industry.

The seasonal fluctuations in the food and apparel industries in 1946–1950 were so close to those in manufacturing as a whole that factory employment minus the food industry showed no clear seasonal variation.

All in all, seasonal employment was concentrated in the summer, from June to August — more so than before the war — with the trough in the first quarter of the year. The span between seasonal lull and high point was somewhat narrower in 1946–1950 than before the war. (See Table 115.)

TABLE 113

EMPLOYMENT IN TRADE ESTABLISHMENTS, 1946–1950

(In Thousands)

Month	1946	1947	1948	1949	1950
January	8,230	9,160	9,622	9,388	9,246
February	8,301	9,143	9,520	9,292	9,152
March	8,466	9,236	9,598	9,310	9,206
April	8,633	9,255	9,576	9,478	9,348
May	8,618	9,277	9,617	9,342	9,326
June	8,681	9,324	9,670	9,336	9,411
July	8,708	9,316	9,646	9,220	9,390
August	8,810	9,356	9,660	9,213	9,474
September	8,957	9,471	9,733	9,409	9,641
October	9,139	9,684	9,889	9,505	9,752
November	9,437	9,886	10,035	9,607	9,898
December	9,865	10,288	10,380	10,154	10,460

Source: Monthly Labor Review, 1946–1951.

TABLE 114

SEASONAL VARIATION IN EMPLOYMENT IN THE APPAREL AND FOOD INDUSTRIES, 1946–1950 COMPARED WITH PREWAR YEARS

(Deviation from January-January Trend, in Thousands)

Month	Apparel Industry 1946–1950 [a]	Apparel Industry Prewar	Food Industry 1946–1950	Food Industry Prewar
January	0	0	0	0
February	+ 30	+ 30	— 25	0
March	+ 30	+ 40	— 35	0
April	— 25	+ 30	— 50	0
May	— 55	0	— 30	0
June	— 50	— 10	+ 10	+ 40
July	— 80	— 30	+ 125	+ 90
August	0	0	+ 240	+ 160
September	+ 15	+ 20	+ 220	+ 210
October	+ 10	+ 20	+ 140	+ 140
November	0	0	+ 90	+ 70
December	0	0	+ 40	+ 30

a. Excluding 1949.

Sources: Figures for 1946–1950 computed from Appendix Table 71. Prewar figures derived from Appendix Table 72.

TABLE 115

PATTERN OF SEASONAL VARIATION IN EMPLOYMENT IN ALL INDUSTRIES, BEFORE WORLD WAR II AND IN 1946–1950

(Deviation from January-January Trend Line, Employees, Self-Employed and Family Workers, in Thousands) [a]

Month	1946–1950	Prewar
January	400	420
February	240	510
March	610	960
April	1,300	1,760
May	2,150	2,475
June	3,460	3,500
July	3,560	4,200
August	3,800	3,940
September	3,050	4,250
October	2,850	4,190
November	2,700	2,800
December	1,800	2,010

a. With allowance for seasonal employment in January of 420,000 before the war, as shown in Table 111; and an estimated 400,000 in 1946–1950.

Sources: Data for 1946–1950 computed, as explained in the text, from Appendix Table 69. Data for prewar years based on a more detailed analysis of employment in single industries (see Appendix Table 72 and Table 111).

Seasonal employment represented, roughly, 2,585,000 man-years of work before the war and 2,165,000 man-years in 1946–1950. In relation to all work performed (in terms of full-time man-years), seasonal work was equivalent to 6 per cent before the war and to 4 per cent in 1946–1950.

Seasonal fluctuations of unemployment reflect the interrelation between changes in the supply of labor and demand for it in agricultural and nonagricultural pursuits. Seasonal ups and downs in unemployment, however, are not very sharp in comparison with the seasonal turnover of labor. Typical of postwar labor market con-

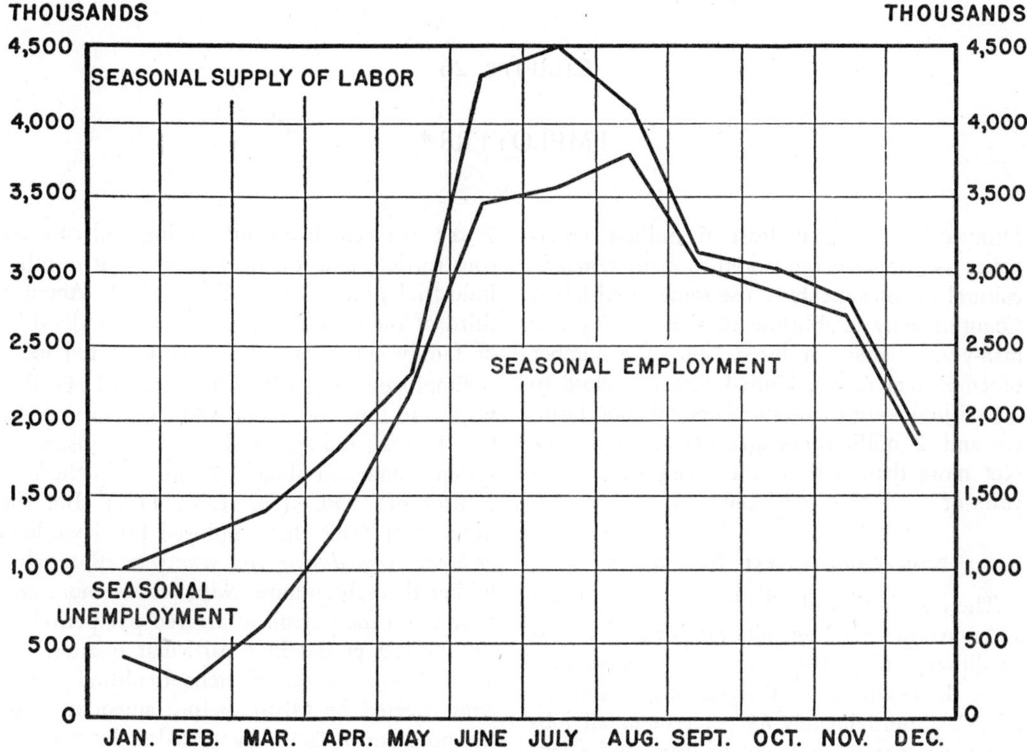

FIGURE 61. HYPOTHETICAL PATTERN OF SEASONAL VARIATION IN CIVILIAN LABOR FORCE AND EMPLOYMENT, 1946–1950

Both the seasonal supply of civilian labor and seasonal employment are estimated as average deviations from the nonseasonal level established by a freehand curve fitted to the January data for 1946–1951. For seasonal employment, deviations in single industries are taken into account (and employment in January has been determined in this way). For the curve of seasonal supply of labor it is assumed that some seasonal unemployment exists at any season and never falls below 100,000. This assumption has determined the location of the seasonal labor force in relation to the seasonal employment curve. Total unemployment consists at any given time of the seasonal and nonseasonal components. The first is tentatively indicated in this chart; the second is discussed in detail in Chapter 33.

ditions are two seasonal rises in unemployment, one in the winter — from the low point in November to the peak in February — the other in the summer, in July, after the close of school. The span between low point and peak varies from year to year. It averaged one million in 1946–1950. The summer peak was about as high as that in winter. (See Figure 61.) Although this seasonal rhythm is not very regular, it is noteworthy for the analysis of monthly changes in unemployment: an increase of unemployment by half a million is a very serious symptom of deteriorating business conditions if it occurs in spring or autumn but is less alarming when it coincides with the seasonal pattern.

The period of observation is too short for the described seasonal ups and downs in employment and unemployment to be considered as the new, postwar seasonal pattern. They are presented here for what they are — as tentative generalizations based on the available, admittedly insufficient information.

CHAPTER 26

EMPLOYERS *

DURING A YEAR, at least 6 million enterprises — 3 million farms and as many nonagricultural establishments — use some hired labor. Counting only establishments that employ one man-year or more of hired labor, the number of employers in the United States is close to 2.5 million — in round numbers, 500,000 farmers and 2 million nonagricultural employers. Not more than half of these employ 3 man-years or more of hired labor.

NONAGRICULTURAL INDUSTRIES

The distribution of jobs between agricultural and nonagricultural pursuits varies with business conditions and with the season. In prosperous years, the nonagricultural sector of the economy provides approximately 88 per cent of all jobs and more than 95 per cent of wage and salary jobs in winter, and 83 per cent of all jobs and 90 per cent of wage and salary jobs in summer. During a severe depression the share of nonagricultural pursuits may drop to 80 per cent of all jobs and somewhat more than 90 per cent of wage and salary jobs in winter, and 90 per cent of all jobs and 85 per cent of wage and salary jobs in summer.

Government agencies (federal, state and local, including public education and health services) employ about 10 per cent of the civilian labor force; private enterprises, 90 per cent.

Industrial Establishments

About 3 million nonagricultural business units were in operation in the United States during the depression of the 1930's and 3.3 million before the outbreak of World War II.[1] The number dropped to 2.8 million in 1943, increased rapidly after V-E Day, and was close to 4 million in 1947–1950. About half of all the business units are in retail and wholesale trade, approximately a fifth in service industries, 7 to 8 per cent in manufacturing and contract construction, and less than 15 per cent in other industrial groups. (See Table 116.) About a third of the operating businesses are individual or family enterprises that have no hired help.

Employers reporting payment of taxable wages to one or more workers covered by the federal old-age and survivors insurance system numbered about 2.7 million in the first quarter of 1950. (See Table 117.) But the number of firms that employed hired workers *at some time during the year* was appreciably higher than the number with one or more employees on the payroll in a given pay period — say the last period in a particular quarter. At a rough approximation, nonagricultural industries covered by OASI, before amendment of the program in 1950, comprised at least 3 million employing units, of which perhaps 2.4 million employed hired labor at any given time of the year. The insurance system included almost all private nonagricultural employers except railroads and nonprofit (religious, educational and charitable) organizations. Now, after amendment, the system includes practically all private commercial and industrial establishments.

"Employing Units" and "Employers"

In using OASI records a distinction should be made between "employers" and "units" reporting taxable wages.[2] Since an "employer" may represent either one or several reporting units, the number of reporting units is naturally larger than that of identified employers. Among concerns with a thousand employees or more, however, there are in some years more employers than reporting units, in others more reporting units than employers: on the one

* By W. S. Woytinsky (Nonagricultural Industries) and Louis J. Ducoff (Agriculture).

1. Not including the individual businesses of lawyers, physicians and other professional persons.

2. An "employer" is defined as a legal entity — a corporation, a partnership or an individual owner — for which a single tax return is filed. A "reporting unit" is an establishment or a group of establishments of the same firm (employer) engaged in the same activity and located in the same area, generally in the same county.

TABLE 116

OPERATING NONAGRICULTURAL BUSINESSES, 1935–1950 [a]

(*In Thousands*)

Year	All Non-agricultural Industries	Contract Construction	Manufacturing	Services	Trade: Retail	Trade: Wholesale	Other
1935	3,025	181	199	619	1,425	128	473
1939	3,307	207	215	636	1,589	144	517
1940	3,304	221	218	625	1,590	144	507
1941	3,341	241	225	631	1,591	144	509
1942	3,071	203	225	589	1,434	129	490
1943	2,836	147	228	548	1,318	114	481
1944	2,965	155	239	573	1,375	125	497
1945	3,369	198	273	727	1,494	167	509
1946	3,763	266	321	805	1,632	190	549
1947	3,944	304	330	847	1,698	200	565
1948	3,968	325	323	851	1,696	203	569
1949	3,942	332	293	851	1,690	204	570
1950	3,998	368	304	855	1,687	205	579

a. Data for the last quarter of the year.

Source: Survey of Current Business.

TABLE 117

NUMBER OF EMPLOYERS (FIRMS) REPORTING PAYMENT OF WAGES TAXABLE UNDER OASI, 1938–1950 [a]

(*In Thousands*)

Year	Number of Employers	Year	Number of Employers
1938	1,880	1945	2,001
1939	2,065	1946	2,280
1940	2,167	1947	2,487
1942	2,119	1948	2,590
1944	2,010	1949	2,620
		1950	2,700

a. For 1939, 1940 and 1942, third quarter; for other years, first quarter.

Source: Quarterly employer tabulations, Bureau of Old-Age and Survivors Insurance.

hand, several reporting units with fewer than a thousand employees each can be represented by one employer who reports more than a thousand workers; on the other hand, several reporting units with more than a thousand workers can be represented by a single employer. (See Table 118.)

Industrial Distribution of Employing Units

Two thirds of the employing units reporting to the old-age and survivors insurance system are concentrated in trade and services. Of the large concerns (those with 500 or more employees), two thirds are in manufacturing. (See Table 119 and Appendix Tables 73 and 74.)

Industries vary strikingly in the distribution of establishments by size. Large concerns are found in almost all industries, but in trade and services they are comparatively rare and the scene is dominated by small and middle-sized establishments, while in manufacturing and public utilities large concerns prevail.

Concentration of factory employment in large firms parallels the high concentration of production in a few leading concerns. As the Temporary National Economic Committee has reported, for articles representing 57 per cent of the total value of manufacturing production in the United States, the four largest producers of each individual product account for more than 50 per cent of the total national output of that product.[3]

In the first quarter of 1948, 15.2 million workers were employed by 271,107 manufacturing establishments (reporting units). About

TABLE 118

NUMBER OF ESTABLISHMENTS AND EMPLOYERS (FIRMS) REPORTING PAYMENT OF WAGES TAXABLE UNDER OASI, BY SIZE OF REPORTING UNIT, 1947 AND 1948 [a]

(*In Thousands*)

Size Class (Number of Employees)	1947 Establishments	1947 Employers (Firms)	1948 Establishments	1948 Employers (Firms)
Total	2,640.6	2,486.7	2,734.2	2,590.0
0	1,501.5	40.4	1,565.8	42.4
1–3		1,415.7		1,488.5
4–7	547.6	519.6	563.8	537.2
8–19	349.2	314.8	359.3	325.0
20–49	147.9	121.6	149.0	122.3
50–99	49.3	39.6	50.5	39.3
100–499	37.7	28.9	38.4	29.0
500–999	4.3	3.3	4.4	3.3
1,000 or more	2.9	3.0	3.0	2.9

a. First quarter.

Source: Quarterly employer tabulations, Bureau of Old-Age and Survivors Insurance.

3. *The Structure of the American Economy,* National Resources Committee, 1939, pp. 103 ff.; *The Structure of Industry,* Monograph No. 27, Temporary National Economic Committee, 1941, p. 275.

TABLE 119

NUMBER OF ESTABLISHMENTS REPORTING PAYMENT OF WAGES TAXABLE UNDER OASI, BY INDUSTRY DIVISION AND SIZE OF REPORTING UNIT, 1948 [a]

Industry Division	Total	Size of Reporting Unit (Number of Employees) 0–3	4–7	8–19	20–49	50–99	100–499	500–999	1,000 or More
Total	2,734,152	1,565,765	563,758	359,342	149,030	50,536	38,351	4,391	2,979
Agriculture	13,488	8,289	2,981	1,670	434	79	35	0	0
Mining	28,602	10,211	6,148	5,932	3,240	1,373	1,365	234	99
Contract construction	216,186	111,909	52,315	33,792	12,229	3,666	2,089	142	44
Manufacturing	271,107	73,397	52,894	59,425	40,922	19,558	20,076	2,788	2,047
Wholesale trade	248,066	113,358	57,563	47,501	20,608	5,937	2,883	161	55
Retail trade	944,009	558,622	224,364	113,425	34,345	8,325	4,253	388	287
Public utilities									
Transportation	87,274	44,785	18,151	13,512	6,427	2,387	1,709	182	121
Communication	8,868	2,814	1,927	1,763	1,110	481	552	103	118
Utilities	6,649	1,637	1,111	1,475	1,106	555	591	92	82
Finance	226,181	155,851	35,702	21,572	8,432	2,550	1,846	147	81
Services	631,668	444,903	102,355	56,113	19,632	5,534	2,933	153	45
Unclassified	52,054	39,989	8,247	3,162	545	91	19	1	0

a. First quarter.
Source: Appendix Table 73.

2,000 establishments accounted for more than a third of all factory employees. (See Table 120.) Concerns employing more than 10,000 workers represent from a fraction of one per cent of all employment, in printing and publishing, lumber, paper and allied products, and the apparel trades, to more than 75 per cent, in the manufacture of transportation equipment.

Concentration of employment in big manufacturing firms, especially in heavy industry, accounts to some extent for the role of these industries in setting the patterns of labor conditions for other industries. Labor disputes and collective negotiations in retail trade or service industries are often inconspicuous and of interest only to the workers and employers directly affected. Similar disputes and negotiations make the headlines and attain national significance when they occur in heavy industries and involve nationally and internationally known concerns.

TABLE 120

NUMBER OF MANUFACTURING ESTABLISHMENTS REPORTING PAYMENT OF WAGES TAXABLE UNDER OASI AND NUMBER OF THEIR EMPLOYEES, BY SIZE OF REPORTING UNIT, 1948 [a]

Size of Reporting Unit (Number of Employees)	Establishments Number	Per Cent	Employees Number	Per Cent
Total	271,107	100.0	15,198,057	100.0
0–3	73,397	27.1	132,066	0.9
4–7	52,894	19.5	280,113	1.8
8–19	59,425	21.9	740,557	4.9
20–49	40,922	15.1	1,274,744	8.4
50–99	19,558	7.2	1,359,890	8.9
100–499	20,076	7.4	4,181,769	27.5
500–999	2,788	1.0	1,920,772	12.6
1,000 or more	2,047	0.8	5,308,146	34.9

a. First quarter.
Source: Based on Appendix Tables 73 and 74.

In nonagricultural industries as a whole, the share of big concerns in employment is not so large as it is in manufacturing. In industries covered by OASI, small firms (employers with fewer than 100 employees) accounted for 43.0 per cent of all employment in 1948, middle-sized firms (those with 100–999 employees) for 22.5 per cent, and large concerns (1,000 or more employees) for 34.4 per cent. This distribution changed appreciably during the decade 1938–1948. The concentration of employment in large concerns increased during the war and reached its peak in 1945. (See Table 121.)

The increased concentration of employment during wartime was due to the expansion of heavy industries (munitions production) and the simultaneous contraction of service industries and trade. Since the end of the war the trend has been reversed. The number of small firms (with less than 100 employees) grew from less than 2 million in 1945 to 2.5 million in 1948 and the number of workers employed by this group of enterprises rose from 12.1 million to 15.4 million. At the same time employment in middle-sized concerns (with 100 to 999 employees) increased from 7.5 million to 8.1 million and employment in large firms (with 1,000 or more employees) declined from 13.2 million to 12.3 million.

Employment still is more highly concentrated,

TABLE 121

Percentage Distribution of Employers (Firms) Reporting to OASI and of Their Employees, by Size of Firm, 1938–1948 [a]

Size of Firm (Number of Employees)	Employers (Firms) 1938	1940	1945	1947	1948	Employees 1938	1940	1945	1947	1948
Total	100.0	100.0	100.0	100.0	100.0	100.0	100.0	100.0	100.0	100.0
0–3	61.8	58.5	59.9	58.5	59.2	7.8	6.6	5.9	6.8	7.0
4–7	19.4	20.7	20.2	20.9	20.7	7.8	7.2	6.3	7.6	7.6
8–19	10.9	12.0	11.7	12.7	12.6	10.1	9.6	8.4	10.6	10.7
20–99	6.4	7.1	6.7	6.5	6.2	19.8	19.3	16.3	17.9	17.7
100–999	1.4	1.6	1.4	1.3	1.2	27.3	27.2	22.9	23.0	22.5
1,000 or more	0.1	0.1	0.1	0.1	0.1	27.3	30.0	40.2	34.2	34.4

a. For 1940, third quarter; for other years, first quarter.

Source: Appendix Table 75.

however, than it was before the war. The share of small concerns has remained practically unchanged (42.7 per cent in 1940, 43.0 per cent in 1948), but that of middle-sized concerns has fallen (from 27.2 per cent to 22.5 per cent) and that of large firms has risen (from 30.0 per cent to 34.4 per cent). The long-range trend toward concentration of industrial employment — if such a trend exists — seems rather slow.

Agriculture

In 1945 — and the following two years — about half of all farms, or a little less than 3 million, hired some labor in the course of the year. However, most of the farmers reporting used hired labor for less than seventy-five days during the year, accounting for only a small percentage of the man-days of all hired labor in agriculture. (See Table 122.) Only 500,000 to 600,000 farms hired at least one man-year (250 man-days) of labor, but these farms accounted for almost 80 per cent of all the man-days of hired farm labor during 1945 and about 60,000 of the largest of them for more than a third of all the hired farm work.

TABLE 122

Percentage Distribution of Farms and of Hired Labor on Farms, by Man-Days of Hired Farm Labor, 1945

Economic Size of Farm (Man-Days of Hired Labor on Farms in 1945)	All Farms	Farms Using Some Hired Labor	Man-Days of Hired Labor
All farms	100	—	100
Farms using no hired labor	52	—	—
Farms using some hired labor	48	100	100
1–74 man-days	30	62	8
75–249	9	18	13
250–499	6	12	24
500–999	2	5	18
1,000 or more	1	3	37

Source: Wages and Wage Rates in Agriculture, Bureau of Agricultural Economics, July 1946, Table 3.

For more detailed information on the characteristics of the employing sector of agriculture, farms may be classified by "economic size," that is, by combined value of products, land and buildings.[4] For the United States as a whole, 8.7 per cent of all farms were in Classes I and II, the two top economic size classes, in 1945[5] and accounted for almost two thirds (63.1 per cent) of all cash wages paid to farm laborers. (See Table 123.) Their wage expenditures averaged $2,366, as compared with $132 per farm in all other size classes. (See Table 124.) The farms employing a substantial number of hired workers differed strikingly from other farms. They averaged nearly 1,000 acres in size and $36,530 in value in 1945, in contrast to an average size of 120 acres and value of $5,383 for all other farms. Their average investment in implements and machinery was about six times as great as that of other farms, while the average value of products sold was ten times as great.

Regional Variations

The distribution of farms by economic size and the proportion of the total cash wages paid by the two top classes vary widely from region

4. Louis J. Ducoff, *Wages of Agricultural Labor in the United States,* Technical Bulletin No. 895, Department of Agriculture, 1945; Louis J. Ducoff and Margaret Jarman Hagood, *Differentials in Productivity and in Farm Income of Agricultural Workers by Size of Enterprise and by Regions,* Bureau of Agricultural Economics, August 1944.

5. For most of these farms, the total value of products in 1944 was $8,000 or more. A few farms with somewhat lower value of products qualified for the two top classes because of high value of land and buildings.

TABLE 123

PERCENTAGE DISTRIBUTION OF FARMS, THEIR VALUE AND THEIR WAGE EXPENDITURES, BY ECONOMIC SIZE OF FARM, 1945

Economic Size of Farm [a]	Farms	Value of Products Sold in 1944	Value of Implements and Machinery	Value of Land and Buildings	Cash Wage Expenditures
All classes...	100.0	100.0	100.0	100.0	100.0
I	1.7	24.2	12.5	16.9	38.7
II	7.0	25.2	23.4	22.5	24.4
III	20.0	30.5	36.0	27.5	22.5
IV	28.4	15.4	18.8	17.9	9.6
V	10.3	0.9	2.4	3.3	0.9
VI	15.8	3.1	3.6	4.5	1.5
VII	16.8	0.7	3.3	7.4	2.3

a. The size classes are in descending order of economic size as measured by value of products and value of land and buildings and, for the lowest three classes, by an additional criterion of days spent in off-farm work by the farm operator. See pages 15–16 of the source for a more detailed description of the classifications.

Source: Sample Census of Agriculture, Special Report, Bureau of the Census, 1945.

to region. Nearly a fourth of the farms in the Pacific states were in the first two economic size classes in 1944, in contrast to less than 2 per cent in the East South Central group. Farms in these economic size classes accounted for 86 per cent of all farm wage expenditures in the Pacific states, and for more than half of all wages in every region except the East South Central. The lowest concentration of wage expenditures was in the North Central states: the average wage expenditure per farm in Classes I and II was only $963 in the West North Central and $1,203 in the East North Central states. At the other extreme, farms in these first two classes in the New England states averaged $3,997 and in the Pacific states, $5,468. (See Table 125.)

California ranks highest in amount of hired farm labor and in the concentration of this labor on large-scale farms. That state had only 2.3 per cent of the farms in the United States in 1944, but it had 16 per cent of the total cash wage expenditures for farm labor and 17 per cent of its farms were in the top economic size class. These Class I farms used much more hired labor than the national average for this class: almost 30 per cent of all wages paid on the country's Class I farms were paid in California.

TABLE 124

COMPARISON OF FARMS IN THE TWO TOP ECONOMIC SIZE CLASSES WITH OTHER FARMS, 1945

Item [a]	Unit	All Farms	Economic Size Classes I & II [b]	Economic Size Classes III-VII [b]
Number of farms..............................	Thousands	5,859	511	5,348
Average size of farms.........................	Acres	196	992	120
Average value of products sold...................	Dollars	2,788	15,765	1,548
Average value of implements or machinery..........	Dollars	899	3,707	631
Average value of land and buildings...............	Dollars	8,100	36,530	5,383
Average value of wage expenditures................	Dollars	327	2,366	132
Average number of persons living on farms..........	Number	4.10	5.74	3.94
Percentage reporting cash wages...................	Per Cent	48.4	88.2	44.6
Percentage reporting tractors......................	Per Cent	34.4	85.7	29.5
Percentage reporting motor trucks.................	Per Cent	22.4	63.1	18.5
Percentage reporting combines....................	Per Cent	6.0	28.7	3.8
Percentage reporting milking machines.............	Per Cent	6.2	20.1	4.9

a. Inventory items relate to January 1, 1945, production and expenditure items to the year 1944.
b. See Table 123, footnote a.

Source: Based on unpublished tabulations of the 1945 *Sample Census of Agriculture* made available through the courtesy of the Bureau of the Census.

TABLE 125

PERCENTAGE DISTRIBUTION OF FARMS AND THEIR WAGE EXPENDITURES, BY ECONOMIC SIZE OF FARM, AND THEIR AVERAGE WAGE EXPENDITURES, IN THE UNITED STATES AND EACH GEOGRAPHIC DIVISION, 1944

Geographic Division and Economic Size Class [a]	Percentage of Farms	Percentage of Wage Expenditures	Average Wage Expenditure: Per Farm	Average Wage Expenditure: Per Farm Reporting Cash Wages
United States, all farms	100.0	100.0	$ 327	$ 675
I & II	8.7	63.1	2,366	2,682
III-VII	91.3	36.9	132	296
New England, all farms	100.0	100.0	563	1,276
I & II	9.4	67.1	3,997	4,504
III-VII	90.6	32.9	205	519
Middle Atlantic, all farms	100.0	100.0	481	920
I & II	9.9	62.9	3,056	3,387
III-VII	90.1	37.1	198	411
East North Central, all farms	100.0	100.0	244	474
I & II	10.9	53.7	1,203	1,434
III-VII	89.1	46.3	127	267
West North Central, all farms	100.0	100.0	266	444
I & II	14.7	53.2	963	1,102
III-VII	85.3	46.8	146	264
South Atlantic, all farms	100.0	100.0	211	454
I & II	3.3	51.8	3,273	3,755
III-VII	96.7	48.2	105	233
East South Central, all farms	100.0	100.0	93	288
I & II	1.6	44.1	2,535	2,884
III-VII	98.4	55.9	53	169
West South Central, all farms	100.0	100.0	302	697
I & II	5.9	54.5	2,794	3,040
III-VII	94.1	45.5	146	362
Mountain, all farms	100.0	100.0	761	1,215
I & II	18.2	73.7	3,071	3,332
III-VII	81.8	26.3	245	437
Pacific, all farms	100.0	100.0	1,488	2,488
I & II	23.3	85.5	5,468	6,002
III-VII	76.7	14.5	281	559

a. See Table 123, footnote a.

Source: Based on unpublished tabulations of the 1945 *Sample Census of Agriculture* made available through the courtesy of the Bureau of the Census.

CHAPTER 27

THE AGE FACTOR IN EMPLOYMENT *

WORK OPPORTUNITIES vary with age. The proportion of the population in the labor force increases with age from 14 years to 25–34 years among men and to 20–24 years among women. It declines thereafter, slowly and gradually among men, more abruptly among women. The decline among men is caused primarily by the increasing proportion of temporarily or permanently disabled; among women, it is due chiefly to withdrawal from the labor force after marriage or childbirth. The composition of the labor force according to class of work and employment status also differs for different age groups.

THE AGE FACTOR IN EMPLOYMENT ACCORDING TO THE 1940 CENSUS

Proportion Employed at Wages or Salary

In 1940, when the Sixteenth Census was taken, most of the boys and nearly half the girls aged 14 to 17 enumerated as in the labor force were unpaid family workers or unemployed persons, including new workers seeking their first jobs. Less than 40 per cent of the boys and only slightly more than 50 per cent of the girls of this age group were actually employed as wage or salary workers during the enumeration week.

Among boys and girls in the age group 18 to 19 the proportion of unpaid family workers was lower, but this group also had a very high rate of unemployment, partly because of inexperienced workers seeking their first jobs. Only 50.5 per cent of the boys and 66.0 per cent of the girls actually had paid jobs in the census week. Regular employment rarely begins before age 20. (See Table 126.)

Distribution of the Labor Force by Class of Work

The composition of the labor force by class of work changes with age partly because of shifts between agriculture and nonagricultural pursuits and partly because of changes within nonagricultural pursuits from a hired status to work on one's own account. A young factory worker or miner obviously has slim chance of becoming a factory or mine owner in middle age, but such a change in class of work is not unusual in retail trade, repair services, building construction and the service industries.[1]

The proportion of employers and self-employed persons in the labor force in 1940 increased with age from 8.2 per cent for men and 1.8 per cent for women of 20–24 years to 37.4 per cent and 21.3 per cent, respectively, in the age class 60–64. After the age of 30 the proportion of employed wage and salary workers declines, slowly up to 44 years, more speedily thereafter. The main cause of this decline is the change in the distribution of the labor force by class of work as one moves from younger to older age classes.

Median Age in Various Occupations

The median age of employed persons in different occupational groups in 1940 varied from 20.1 years for male unpaid family workers in agriculture to 44.5 years for women in protective services. (See Table 127.) These contrasts in age at different occupational levels depend on the interplay of several factors. Most people begin work in jobs that require little training and do not involve great responsibility; they gradually advance to better positions. Some inherit a managerial or proprietary position at a fairly advanced age. Positions requiring considerable training are rarely reached before 25 to 29 years of age. Certain proprietary jobs can be held by elderly people who would be unable to continue more competitive work for wages or salary.

The figures show that occupational advancement is rather common over a working life-

* By W. S. Woytinsky. Statistics on old-age and survivors insurance were arranged for this chapter by Franz Huber, Bureau of Old-Age and Survivors Insurance, Baltimore, Maryland.

1. W. S. Woytinsky, *Labor in the United States — Basic Statistics for Social Security*, Committee on Social Security, Social Science Research Council, Washington, 1938, pp. 45 ff.

TABLE 126

PERCENTAGE DISTRIBUTION OF PERSONS IN THE LABOR FORCE, BY CLASS OF WORK AND EMPLOYMENT STATUS, MARCH 1940

	Men					Women				
			Employed					Employed		
Age in Years	Total	Unem-ployed [a]	Employ-ers and Self-Em-ployed	Unpaid Family Workers	Wage and Salary Workers	Total	Unem-ployed [a]	Employ-ers and Self-Em-ployed	Unpaid Family Workers	Wage and Salary Workers
Total	100.0	14.6	22.1	2.5	60.8	100.0	13.3	7.4	3.2	76.1
14–15	100.0	14.2	2.6	47.7	35.5	100.0	24.8	0.8	29.3	45.1
16–17	100.0	33.2	1.9	26.9	38.0	100.0	40.2	0.5	8.6	50.7
18–19	100.0	32.2	3.7	13.6	50.5	100.0	30.0	0.8	3.2	66.0
20–24	100.0	20.0	8.2	5.7	66.1	100.0	15.0	1.8	2.1	81.1
25–29	100.0	13.3	14.2	1.9	70.6	100.0	9.3	3.4	2.3	85.0
30–34	100.0	11.6	18.4	0.9	69.1	100.0	8.5	5.5	2.8	83.2
35–44	100.0	11.4	23.6	0.4	64.6	100.0	9.8	9.3	3.6	77.3
45–54	100.0	12.9	29.6	0.2	57.3	100.0	11.1	14.9	3.8	70.2
55–59	100.0	15.0	33.6	0.3	51.1	100.0	12.2	19.3	3.4	65.1
60–64	100.0	15.2	37.4	0.3	47.1	100.0	11.8	21.3	2.8	64.1
65–74	100.0	10.7	47.9	0.2	41.0	100.0	7.4	29.2	2.5	60.9
75 and over..	100.0	4.7	61.3	1.0	33.0	100.0	4.5	36.5	1.3	57.7

a. Seeking work or employed on public emergency work projects.

Source: Sixteenth Census (1940), *Population, The Labor Force (Sample Statistics), Employment and Personal Characteristics,* 1943, pp. 68–69.

time, from youth to mature age. They fail, however, to cast light on the upper reaches of age. A rather high percentage of old people (65 years and over) are listed as guards and watchmen, as boardinghouse keepers or as "laborers" without further specification. Such positions are hardly representative of the highest occupational level these people have ever attained. Many of them may have been compelled to take what they could get after failing strength and ability disqualified them for the better positions they once held.[2]

Median Age in Various Industries

Except for the well-known shifts of population between farming and urban pursuits, there is no evidence that workers move in large numbers from one industry to another as they become older. The occupational upgrading already described — from unskilled to semiskilled and skilled jobs, from manual work to supervisory positions, and from work for pay to work on one's own account — usually takes place within the same industry. The principle of seniority and the practice of promotion favor workers who stay with the same company and discourage shifts between industries. There are, however, striking contrasts in the age distribution of workers in various industries.

2. W. S. Woytinsky, *The Labor Supply in the United States,* 2d edition, Committee on Social Security, Social Science Research Council, Washington, 1937.

The median age of employed wage and salary workers reported in the 1940 census ranged, for men, from 27.3 years (workers in filling stations) to 45.6 years (in railroads); for women, from 23.5 years (in limited-price variety stores) to 42.2 years (in postal service). In most industries the median age of male workers was between 34 and 38 years; of female workers, between 28 and 32 years. (See Table 128.)

Because of the difference in the kind of work performed by men and women, the correlation between the median age of the two groups of

TABLE 127

MEDIAN AGES OF EMPLOYED PERSONS, BY OCCUPATIONAL GROUP AND SEX, 1940

Occupational Group	Men	Women
Agriculture		
Unpaid family workers......	20.1	25.4
Hired farm laborers........	30.6	29.0
Farmers	46.1	53.3
Nonagricultural pursuits		
Common laborers	34.1	28.7
Operatives	34.0	30.4
Craftsmen and foremen......	41.2	37.5
Proprietors	44.5	44.3
Service workers		
Domestic service	39.0	33.7
Other personal services......	38.7	36.0
Protective services	38.7	44.5
Clerical, sales and kindred workers	34.7	28.3
Professional and semiprofessional workers	32.8	31.7

Source: Sixteenth Census (1940), *Population, The Labor Force (Sample Statistics), Occupational Characteristics,* pp. 53–57.

TABLE 128

MEDIAN AGE OF EMPLOYED WAGE AND SALARY WORKERS, BY INDUSTRY AND SEX, 1940

Industry	Men	Women
Agriculture	29.9	29.3
Forestry and fishing	35.1	—
Mining		
Coal mining	37.3	32.2
Crude petroleum	36.8	31.6
Metal mining	36.1	—
Other mines and quarries	36.2	—
Construction, manufacturing		
Food	34.6	28.4
Tobacco	37.8	31.6
Textile mill products	33.5	30.1
Apparel	38.7	29.8
Lumber, furniture, etc.	34.2	28.9
Paper and allied products	35.2	28.9
Printing and publishing	34.1	30.6
Chemicals	34.9	28.2
Petroleum and coal products	37.6	31.4
Rubber	36.4	28.9
Leather	35.5	28.8
Stone, clay and glass products	36.2	27.9
Iron and steel	37.3	27.9
Nonferrous metals	36.0	27.6
Machinery	36.8	27.1
Transportation equipment		
Aircraft and parts	29.0	26.3
Automobiles	37.0	29.2
Ship and boat building	38.3	32.6
Railroad equipment	40.9	28.7
Other manufacturing industries	35.2	27.2
Transportation		
Air transportation	30.1	26.4
Railroads and railway express	45.6	41.3
Street railway and bus lines	41.0	37.8
Trucking service	32.6	28.6
Water transportation	39.8	34.0
Other transportation	35.9	30.2
Communication		
Telephone and telegraph	37.0	31.0
Radio broadcasting	32.1	27.3
Utilities		
Electricity, light and power	38.1	30.8
Gas	38.7	31.0
Water and sanitary service	45.2	37.1
Wholesale and retail trade		
Food and dairy products	29.4	27.6
General merchandise stores	32.5	28.5
Apparel	35.9	34.5
Furniture	34.8	29.3
Motor vehicles	36.1	28.4
Filling stations	27.3	28.2
Drug stores	28.3	25.1
Eating and drinking places	34.3	27.9
Hardware and farm implements	35.1	29.4
Lumber and building material	37.3	30.2
Other retail stores	33.9	29.4
Finance, insurance, etc.		
Banking	37.3	30.5
Insurance and real estate	41.0	31.3
Business and repair service		
Automobile repair service	32.7	28.6
Other business and repair service	34.4	29.1
Personal service		
Domestic service	40.2	33.0
Hotels and lodging places	36.2	37.3
Laundering, etc.	33.1	31.8
Amusement and related service		
Theaters and motion pictures	34.0	27.0
Other amusement and recreation	31.5	29.1
Professional and related service	37.3	32.7
Government		
Postal service	43.3	42.2
Civilian government, not elsewhere classified	41.8	33.1

Source: Sixteenth Census (1940), *Population, The Labor Force* (*Sample Statistics*), *Industrial Characteristics*, pp. 57–60.

workers is rather loose. In some industries the median age of men is nine to twelve years higher than that of women — for example, in the iron and steel industry, machinery manufacturing, railroad equipment, insurance and real estate. In the postal service the age of the two groups of workers is about the same. In a few fields of work the median age of employed women is higher than that of men, as in filling stations and hotels and lodging places.

There is no correlation between the median age of workers in different industries and longevity or life expectation in those industries. The age pattern of employment in an industry depends, rather, on hiring and promotion policies. In industries with firmly established seniority rules, such as railroads and postal service and other governmental service, middle-aged workers prevail. The median age of workers is particularly low in such relatively new and rapidly expanding industries as air transportation and radio broadcasting.

THE AGE FACTOR IN CONTINUITY OF WORK

Valuable information on the age factor in employment and, more particularly, in continuity of work and attachment to the job is provided by the records of old-age and survivors insurance.

The OASI Records

The method of determining eligibility for and the amount of benefits under the Social Security Act makes it necessary to record all taxable wages received by each worker covered by the law in all calendar quarters in which he received these wages. The records have been kept continuously, beginning with January 1,

1937, or the date at which the worker entered covered employment if that occurred later. They tell, in highly condensed form, the work history of scores of millions of persons.[3]

Before amendment in 1950, OASI covered only workers employed in private nonagricultural establishments, excluding railroads and public agencies; hence the records are restricted to only part of the economic system. They cover, however, approximately 60 per cent of all the work performed annually in the nation, about 70 per cent of all nonagricultural work, and a much larger part — as much as 95 per cent — of private nonagricultural work for wages or salary. Unlike other employment statistics, these records permit a cross-tabulation of employment and earnings data with such personal characteristics as sex, race and age.

Age of Workers Covered by OASI

On the whole, workers in covered employment under the original OASI program were somewhat younger than those in jobs excluded from coverage, most of whom were self-employed persons in agriculture, trade and service industries or were in public employment.

During the period January 1, 1937–December 31, 1949, about 86.4 million persons received wages in covered employment. Some were in covered jobs for only short periods, others in most or even all of the fifty-two calendar quarters. The number of different workers covered by OASI at some time in the calendar year increased from 32.9 million in 1937 to 49.5 million in 1950. (See Table 129.)

The entrance of millions of young workers into the armed forces and of emergency workers — mainly women — into civilian employment drastically changed the age distribution of workers under the program. During the war, the median age of male workers with previous wage credits went up and that of new entrants went down; the reverse happened after the war ended. (See Table 130.)

The number of aged workers covered by the system increased greatly during the war. The number of men aged 65 and over who received wage credits rose from 724,000 in 1941 to 1,259,000 in 1944; of women, from 78,000 to 183,000. Men aged 65 and over represented 2.5 per cent of covered male workers in 1941, 4.5 per cent in 1944, and 4.6 per cent in 1945; for women the proportion rose from 0.7 per cent to fully one per cent. After the war, the proportion of men aged 65 and over decreased slightly, while that of women continued to increase. (See Appendix Table 76.)

The relation of age to degree of attachment to the labor market, to a particular industry, and to a particular job is shown in the OASI records in the patterns of withdrawals from covered employment, number of quarters of covered employment per year, and frequency of change of employer and industry.

TABLE 129

WORKERS WITH WAGE CREDITS UNDER OASI, 1937–1950

(*In Millions*)

Year	During Year	For First Time in Each Year	Cumulative to End of Year: Unadjusted for Deaths	Cumulative to End of Year: Adjusted for Deaths (Living Workers)
1937	32.9	32.9	32.9	32.7
1938	31.8	4.0	36.9	36.5
1939	33.8	4.5	41.4	40.8
1940	35.4	4.4	45.8	44.9
1941	41.0	6.5	52.3	51.0
1942	46.4	7.9	60.2	58.5
1943	47.7	7.3	67.5	65.3
1944	46.3	4.7	72.2	69.5
1945	46.4	3.5	75.7	72.3
1946	48.8	3.1	78.8	74.8
1947	48.9	2.7	81.4	76.8
1948	49.1	2.7	84.1	78.7
1949	47.2	2.3	86.4	—
1950	49.5	—	—	—

Source: Bureau of Old-Age and Survivors Insurance.

3. For each year beginning with 1937, the Bureau of Old-Age and Survivors Insurance has tabulated sample data covering workers and wage credits during the specified year. The samples have varied in size from 100 per cent in 1937 and 1938 to one per cent in some recent years. Because of periodic revisions and corrections, there are some slight discrepancies in the totals in OASI tables released at different dates. Beginning with the period 1937–1940, the Bureau has tabulated data showing the work history of workers in covered employment since the system was inaugurated. The sample used in these tabulations has been confined to one per cent of all account number holders but will be enlarged to 2.5 per cent. The sample for both the annual and the continuous work history tabulations consists of records of persons who have certain specified digits in their social security account numbers. In the work history sample, the accounts of new workers, selected on the basis of the same digits in the social security account number, are added each year, but persons who die are not removed from the sample. *Social Security Yearbook,* Social Security Administration, 1945, pp. 2 ff.

For further discussion of wage statistics of old-age and survivors insurance, see Chapter 36. For a detailed description of the character and purpose of the continuous work history sample, see Jacob Perlman and Benjamin Mandel, "The Continuous Work History Sample under Old-Age and Survivors Insurance," *Social Security Bulletin,* February 1944.

TABLE 130

MEDIAN AGE OF WORKERS WITH WAGE CREDITS UNDER OASI, 1937–1947

Year	All Workers			Workers with Previous Wage Credits			New Entrants		
	Total	Men	Women	Total	Men	Women	Total	Men	Women
1937[a]	31.6	33.2	28.0	—	—	—	—	—	—
1938[a]	32.3	33.8	28.5	33.1	34.6	29.3	25.3	26.4	24.1
1939	32.4	33.9	28.7	—	—	—	—	—	—
1940	32.5	34.0	28.8	33.3	34.7	29.6	23.7	24.4	22.6
1941	32.2	33.7	28.6	33.5	34.9	29.8	22.7	22.9	22.4
1942	32.8	34.7	28.7	33.9	35.5	29.9	22.9	22.0	23.5
1943	33.9	36.8	29.1	35.1	37.7	29.9	22.6	19.1	24.7
1944	34.9	38.6	29.2	36.0	39.4	29.9	20.3	19.1	22.9
1945	34.9	38.2	29.0	35.9	39.0	30.1	19.9	19.5	21.0
1946	33.8	35.7	29.7	34.5	38.9	33.7	20.7	21.7	17.9
1947	34.0	35.6	30.4	34.6	36.2	31.2	19.6	19.5	19.6

a. Includes only workers through age 65; wages of workers over 65 were not taxable in 1937 and 1938.

Source: For 1937–1945, data for "All Workers" derived from Appendix Table 76; other data from Bureau of Old-Age and Survivors Insurance.

Withdrawals from Covered Employment

In recent years the number of persons in covered employment in one year who received no wage credits in the next year has never been less than 4 million; during the war it approached 9 million.

A fairly large proportion of the persons who withdraw from covered employment return to it after a year or more. The age and sex distribution of these persons gives some clue to the reasons for their withdrawal. For example, most of the men aged 18 to 35 who withdrew during the war presumably entered the armed forces; most women who withdraw between ages 20 and 30 or 35 presumably become housewives and mothers; and many other women who left in 1945 and 1946 were probably going back to their homes upon the return of their men from military service. After age 55 or 60 it is likely that an increasing proportion of the withdrawing workers have become handicapped by ill health, and beginning with 65 years most are probably retiring from the labor force altogether.

At every age, relatively more women than men leave covered employment. The percentage of men withdrawing is smallest between the ages of 25 and 54; of women, between the ages of 35 and 54. The percentage increases rapidly after age 60 for women and 65 for men. A large proportion of women withdraw between the ages of 20 and 29 years. (See Appendix Table 80.)

Quarters of Covered Employment per Year

The proportion of workers with wage credits in all four quarters of a year increases consistently from the youngest group (under 20 years) to 45–54 years and declines thereafter. Inversely, the percentages of three-quarter, two-quarter and one-quarter workers are comparatively high among the young and old workers and lower in the middle-aged groups. (See Appendix Table 78.) The group of young workers includes many new workers who enter the labor force after a quarter or more of the year has elapsed. Similarly, among the aged workers there are many who are on their way out of the labor market.

Workers between the ages of 35 and 59 who had wage credits in less than four quarters were fairly evenly distributed among one-, two- and three-quarter workers, although one-quarter workers were somewhat more numerous among women, while the generally greater employment stability among men was reflected in the larger proportion of men with three quarters in covered employment.[4] The age groups over 60 years, as would be expected, were not as steadily employed as the middle-aged groups. Among women, however, the difference was considerably less pronounced than among men, particularly in the group aged 65 and over, mainly because even in the age group 35 to 59 there is much less employment stability among women. (See Appendix Tables 77, 78 and 79.)

Change of Employer

Young workers tend to change employers much more frequently than others. (See Table

4. Although the number of quarters in covered employment does not show the number of months, weeks or days during which an employee worked in a covered job, it is the only measure of duration of employment in a given year that is available from these wage records.

TABLE 131

PERCENTAGE DISTRIBUTION OF WORKERS WITH WAGE CREDITS UNDER OASI, BY NUMBER OF EMPLOYERS, 1944

Age in 1944	Total	Number of Employers 1	2	3	4	5	6	7	8	9 or More
Men	100.0	65.5	18.5	7.6	3.6	1.9	1.1	0.6	0.4	0.7
Under 14	100.0	81.7	13.6	3.1	1.0[a]	0.4[a]	0.1[a]	0.1[a]	0	[a, b]
14–15	100.0	65.1	21.8	7.7	3.1	1.3	0.5[a]	0.2[a]	0.1[a]	0.2[a]
16–17	100.0	47.2	26.6	13.2	6.4	3.1	1.6	0.9	0.5	0.6
18–19	100.0	51.6	23.2	11.8	6.0	3.2	1.7	1.1	0.5	0.8
20	100.0	51.7	21.1	11.3	6.5	3.7	2.0	1.4	0.9	1.3
21–24	100.0	55.5	20.5	10.1	5.6	3.2	1.9	1.2	0.7	1.3
25 and over	100.0	68.5	17.4	6.7	3.2	1.6	1.0	0.6	0.4	0.7
Women	100.0	68.3	19.8	7.0	2.7	1.2	0.5	0.3	0.1	0.2
Under 14	100.0	86.0	9.8[a]	2.2[a]	1.2[a]	0.2[a]	0.5[a]	0	0	0.2[a]
14–15	100.0	74.3	18.5	4.7	1.6	0.4[a]	0.2[a]	0.1[a]	0.1[a]	[a, b]
16–17	100.0	57.9	25.8	9.8	3.7	1.5	0.7	0.3	0.2[a]	0.1[a]
18–19	100.0	53.7	26.8	11.1	4.5	1.9	0.9	0.5	0.2	0.3
20	100.0	59.4	23.2	9.5	4.0	2.0	0.9	0.4	0.3[a]	0.3[a]
21–24	100.0	63.6	21.6	8.4	3.5	1.5	0.7	0.4	0.2	0.2
25 and over	100.0	73.3	17.4	5.5	2.1	0.9	0.4	0.2	0.1	0.1

a. Fewer than 100 persons in sample. b. Less than 0.05 per cent.

Source: Appendix Table 81.

131.) Fairly high job stability among youngsters of 14 to 15 years, particularly among girls, may be due to the paternalistic character of early jobs and lack of courage or ability to change.

The highest rate of employer change is found between the ages of 16 and 19. Only slightly more than half of these young people stayed with one employer during 1944; one out of four changed employers once; one out of four changed twice or more; one in twenty changed at least four times. The relatively unstable job tenure of these young workers is typical of people who are trying out their abilities, beginning with whatever work they can get and actively seeking something better. Then, too, the turnover of young workers was particularly high in 1944 because the war economy offered inexperienced workers unusual opportunities for choice.[5]

By the time workers are 20 years old, they have a more stable attachment to an employer, though by this age men and women begin to differ. Relatively more 20-year-old women than men remained with one employer in 1944, and relatively more women changed jobs only once. At ages 21 to 24, employer changes were less frequent than at age 20. About three of every five workers aged 21 to 24 worked in one covered job throughout the year, and one out of five changed employers only once. (See Appendix Table 81.)

Among workers over 24 years of age, seven out of ten stayed with one employer. These workers had become a relatively stable element in the labor market. It may also be that the more mature age groups have less opportunity to change jobs.

Change of Industry

A worker who changes employers during a year may seek another job in the same industry or in another pursuit. These are two different types of mobility of labor. A change of employer in the same industry is usually accounted for either by the temporary character of the jobs in the industry — as in building construction, seasonal hotels and so on — or by the worker's dissatisfaction with his employer. A change of employer combined with a change of industry suggests either an industrial shift of the labor force or the desire of the individual worker to get another kind of work.

The records of OASI show that change through individual choice prevails. Six workers out of seven who had two employers during 1944 also changed industry. Simultaneous change of employer and industry is particularly common for workers under 25. Among workers aged 16 to 19 who changed employers once, 90 per cent also changed industry. (See Appendix Table 82.) A similar pattern prevailed in 1944 among workers who had more than one employer change during the year. One or more industry changes were relatively numerous be-

5. See pp. 384 ff.

tween 14 and 24 years of age, regardless of the number of employer changes, and relatively few among older workers.

The fact that change of employer is combined with change of industry more frequently among young persons than among older workers can be traced to experimentation on the part of younger workers, who are trying out their industrial and occupational aptitudes and preferences. Such mobility of labor is part of the normal and sound process of adjustment of the labor force to the available jobs.

Chapter 28

EMPLOYMENT OF WOMEN *

Women held about a fourth of all civilian jobs in the spring of 1940, when the Sixteenth Census was taken. They accounted for more than a third of all persons in civilian employment in 1945, when a fourth of the men who normally would have been in the labor force were in uniform. The proportion of women in the labor force dropped to less than 28 per cent early in 1947 but has risen again and is now close to 30 per cent. The rise from 1940 to 1950 reflects the long-range trend in women's employment, which can be expected to continue.

Prewar Employment Pattern

In 1940, women constituted a larger proportion of the labor force in cities than in rural areas and a larger proportion of wage and salary workers and unpaid family workers than of employers and persons working on their own account. (See Table 132.) The proportion of women among wage and salary workers in urban areas was slightly over 30 per cent in 1940 and is now close to 35 per cent, rising above this annual average in summer and declining in winter.

Marital Status of Working Women

About half of the women at work in 1940 were single, 35 per cent were married, and 15 per cent were widowed or divorced. (See Table 133.) The ratios changed when millions of wives of servicemen went to work. The number of "working married women with spouse absent," according to the census, increased during the war from less than a million to 4 or 5 million and contracted after the war.

Occupations of Working Women

Employment of women is heavily concentrated in certain types of work and certain industries. When occupations are classified in broad groups, women predominate in domestic service and form a considerable part (40 per cent or more) of the professional group and of clerical and kindred workers. Comparatively few are farmers or farm laborers, craftsmen or foremen, or are engaged in protective service. (See Table 134.) The low proportion of women among unpaid family workers on farms is due largely to the census practice of classifying farmers' wives as members of the labor force only if they work in the fields and excluding them if their activities are limited to the house and garden.

Industrial Distribution of Working Women

Women predominate in industries providing personal services — hotels and lodging places, laundries, beauty shops and so on — and in professional and related services, such as teaching and clerical work. Considerable numbers are employed in manufacturing, wholesale and retail trade, finance and insurance, communication, and amusement and recreation services. Women work less frequently in agriculture, mining, building trades, transport, and business and repair services. (See Table 135.)

Wartime Employment

The distribution of working women among occupations and industries changed drastically during the war. Women found many opportunities for work in automobile and airplane factories and shipyards, in jobs traditionally believed to require masculine strength and mechanical skill. Their highly satisfactory record in such jobs has had a lasting effect; after the reconversion of industry, the return of veterans, and the withdrawal of emergency workers from the labor force, the industrial and occupational distribution of working women did not revert precisely to the prewar pattern. Women have firmly established themselves in positions previously closed to them, and the line between men's work and women's has become less sharp. The records of old-age and survivors insurance

* By W. S. Woytinsky. Data relating to operation of old-age and survivors insurance were prepared by Franz Huber, Bureau of Old-Age and Survivors Insurance, Baltimore, Maryland.

TABLE 132

NUMBER AND PERCENTAGE OF WOMEN IN THE LABOR FORCE, BY CLASS OF WORK, 1940

Class of Work	Urban Areas: Number, in Thousands: All Workers	Urban Areas: Number, in Thousands: Women	Urban Areas: Women as Percentage of All Workers	Rural Areas: Number, in Thousands: All Workers	Rural Areas: Number, in Thousands: Women	Rural Areas: Women as Percentage of All Workers
Labor force	32,614	9,606	29.4	20,176	3,239	16.0
Experienced labor force	32,057	9,371	29.2	19,965	3,169	15.9
Employers and workers on own account	3,463	609	17.6	6,518	354	5.4
Unpaid family workers	199	144	72.3	1,266	284	22.4
Wage and salary workers	28,395	8,619	30.4	12,180	2,530	20.8

Source: Sixteenth Census (1940), *Population,* Vol. III, Part 1, p. 7.

TABLE 133

NUMBER AND PERCENTAGE DISTRIBUTION OF WOMEN IN THE LABOR FORCE, BY MARITAL STATUS, 1940

Marital Status	Urban Areas: Number, in Thousands	Urban Areas: Percentage	Rural Areas: Number, in Thousands	Rural Areas: Percentage
Total	9,606	100.0	3,239	100.0
Single	4,849	50.6	1,501	46.3
Married				
Spouse present	2,756	28.6	1,051	32.4
Spouse absent	580	6.0	174	5.4
Widowed or divorced	1,422	14.8	513	15.8

Source: Sixteenth Census (1940), *Population,* Vol. III, Part 1, p. 22.

show that more women now have jobs, and that those jobs are more widely dispersed over all fields of activity.

WOMEN IN EMPLOYMENT UNDER OASI (1937–1949)

The employment records of the federal old-age and survivors insurance system show changes in the number of women employed as wage and salary workers and in their distribution among industries, and significant differences in the employment status of male and female workers.

Proportion in Covered Employment

Because of the greater turnover of women in the labor force, they constitute a larger proportion of all workers with wage credits under OASI during the year than of workers employed at any given date. The proportion of women among workers with wage credits during the year fluctuated around 28 per cent in the period 1937–1939, rose rapidly during the war, and reached 39 per cent in 1944. By 1949 it had fallen to 32 per cent but was still well above each of the first five years of the program. (See Table 136.)

The increase in the absolute number of women in covered employment was even more spectacular: in 1944, 18.2 million women received wage credits; this was twice the number in

TABLE 134

NUMBER AND PERCENTAGE OF EMPLOYED WOMEN, BY OCCUPATIONAL GROUP, 1940

Occupational Group	Number, in Thousands: All Employed Workers	Number, in Thousands: Employed Women	Women as Percentage of Total
All occupations	45,166	11,138	24.7
Professional workers	2,882	1,370	47.5
Semiprofessional workers	463	99	21.4
Farmers	5,144	152	2.9
Proprietors, managers, and officials, except farmers	3,749	424	11.3
Clerical and kindred workers	7,518	3,157	42.0
Craftsmen, foremen, etc.	5,056	107	2.1
Operatives	8,252	2,046	24.8
Domestic service workers	2,111	1,969	93.3
Protective service workers	681	4	0.6
Other service workers	2,777	1,257	45.3
Unpaid family workers on farms	1,165	223	19.1
Hired farm laborers	1,925	97	5.0
Laborers, except farm and mine	3,064	98	3.1
Occupation not reported	379	134	35.4

Source: Sixteenth Census (1940), *Population,* Vol. III, Part 1, p. 10.

TABLE 135

NUMBER AND PERCENTAGE OF EMPLOYED WOMEN, BY INDUSTRY DIVISION, 1940

Industry Division	Number, in Thousands: All Employed Workers	Number, in Thousands: Employed Women	Women as Percentage of Total
All industries	45,166	11,138	24.7
Agriculture, forestry and fishing	8,475	487	5.7
Mining	913	11	1.2
Construction	2,056	34	1.7
Manufacturing	10,573	2,322	22.0
Transportation	2,178	78	3.6
Communication	393	211	53.5
Public utilities	542	57	10.5
Wholesale and retail trade	7,539	2,030	26.9
Finance, insurance and real estate	1,468	454	30.9
Business and repair services	864	77	8.9
Personal services	4,009	2,876	71.2
Amusement, recreation, etc.	395	79	20.0
Professional and related services	3,318	1,845	55.6
Government	1,753	339	19.3
Industry not reported	689	238	34.5

Source: Sixteenth Census (1940), *Population,* Vol. III, Part 1, pp. 180–81.

1937. In almost all industries the proportion of women increased during the war and declined when the wartime emergency was over, but not to the prewar level. In 1949 there were still 15.5 million women with wage credits.

The increase was most pronounced in trade, finance and, especially, in manufacturing, where the number of female workers grew from 3.6 million in 1939 to 8.1 million in 1944. This increase of 4.5 million women in manufacturing represented half the total increase in the number of women with wage credits under old-age and survivors insurance. (See Figure 62 and Appendix Table 83.) After the war, women in manufacturing industries decreased in number by some 2 million and in proportion from 37 to 31 per cent. In all other major industry divisions, except contract construction and wholesale trade, the number of women actually increased between 1944 and 1946.

TABLE 136

NUMBER AND PERCENTAGE OF WOMEN AMONG WORKERS WITH WAGE CREDITS UNDER OASI, 1937–1949

Year	Number, in Thousands	Percentage of All Workers
1937	9,093	27.6
1938	8,931	28.1
1939	9,391	27.8
1940	9,821	27.7
1941	11,606	28.3
1942	14,525	31.3
1943	17,532	36.8
1944	18,195	39.4
1945	17,567	37.9
1946	16,663	34.1
1947	16,167	33.1
1948[a]	16,100	32.8
1949[a]	15,500	32.3

a. Preliminary.

Source: Quarterly Summary of Wages, Employment and Benefit Data, Bureau of Old-Age and Survivors Insurance, Baltimore, August 1950, Table 3, and other data from the Bureau of Old-Age and Survivors Insurance.

Continuity of Employment

The relative continuity of employment of men and women is shown by the proportion of new entrants and withdrawals in the two groups and by the number of quarters of the year in which men and women receive wage credits.

New Entrants

Under normal conditions, the proportion of new entrants among working men and women is directly related to the average duration of the working life of the two groups. Since the average working life of men who take their first jobs in youth is approximately twice as long as that of women, the proportion of new entrants among women must be about twice that among men.

Actually the rates fluctuated widely as business conditions changed and were distorted by the exceptional conditions of the war economy. The proportion of new entrants among women with wage credits was particularly high during the war. It fell below the prewar level during 1945–1948 because most women who could have taken jobs in covered industries in those years had already done so during 1942–1943. (See Table 137.)

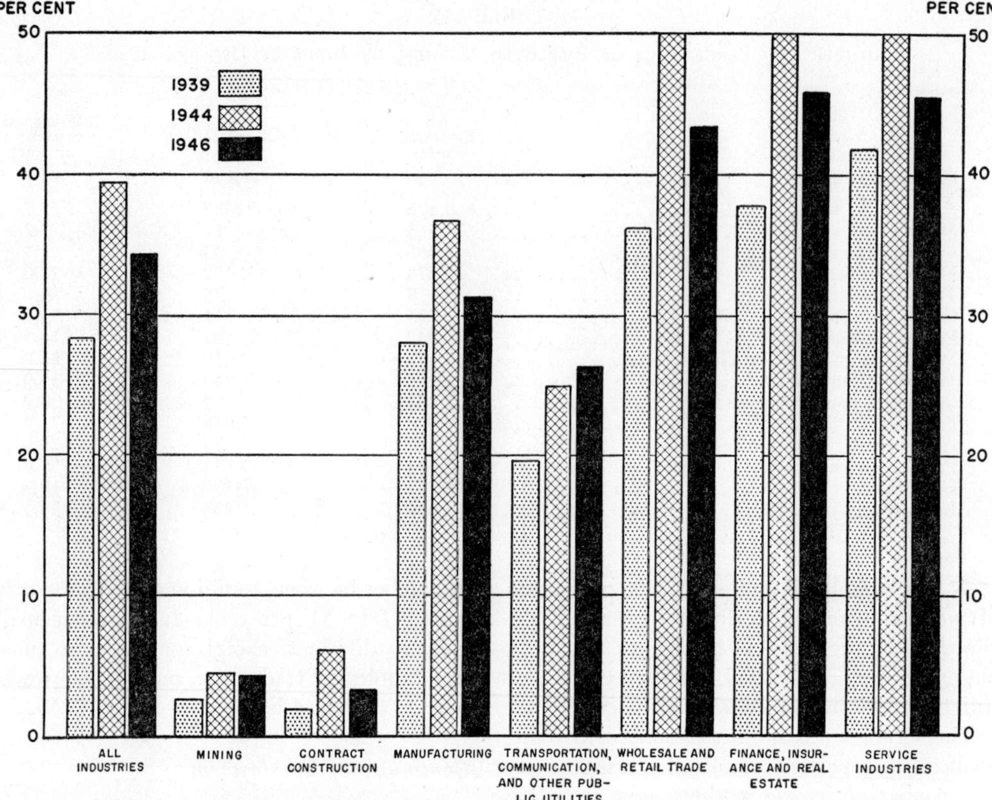

FIGURE 62. PERCENTAGE OF WOMEN AMONG WORKERS WITH WAGE CREDITS UNDER OASI, BY INDUSTRY DIVISION, 1939, 1944 AND 1946

Source: Appendix Table 83.

Withdrawals

The rate of withdrawal is measured by the proportion of persons with wage credits in a given year who did not have any wage credits in the following year. Thus withdrawal rates of 9.8 per cent for men and 15.4 per cent for women in 1940 show the proportion of men and women in covered employment in 1940 who were not in covered employment in 1941. (See Appendix Table 80.)

The rate of withdrawal among men increased during the war because of enrollment in the armed forces; among women, because of the rising mobility of female workers. (See Table 138.) Sex differences in mobility are more apparent in age groups in which few men joined the armed forces. In the age group 50–54 years the proportion of withdrawals was 40 to 50

TABLE 137

PERCENTAGE OF NEW ENTRANTS AMONG WORKERS WITH WAGE CREDITS UNDER OASI, BY SEX, 1940–1948

Year	Men	Women
1940	10.0	14.4
1941	14.2	15.9
1942	13.2	27.0
1943	10.4	24.9
1944	7.3	15.5
1945	5.8	11.0
1946	4.7	9.3
1947 [a]	4.1	8.1
1948 [a]	4.1	8.1

a. Preliminary.

Sources: For 1940, 1944 and 1947, Appendix Table 77; other data from Bureau of Old-Age and Survivors Insurance.

TABLE 138

PERCENTAGE RATES OF WITHDRAWAL FROM EMPLOYMENT COVERED BY OASI, BY SEX, 1940–1945 [a]

Year	Men	Women
1940	9.8	15.4
1941	11.3	16.9
1942	19.3	17.0
1943	18.5	18.7
1944	14.6	19.7
1945	14.9	23.8

a. Measured by percentage of persons with wage credits in a given year who did not have any covered employment in the following year.

Source: Appendix Table 80.

per cent less among men than among women. Among persons aged 40 to 54, one man in twelve and one woman in six was not in covered employment for two successive years. (See Table 139.)

Proportion of Four-Quarter Workers

In almost all industries the percentage of women is lower among workers with wage credits in all four calendar quarters than among workers with wage credits in less than four quarters. In manufacturing industries in 1946, for example, women represented 27.7 per cent of the four-quarter workers and 37.2 of the workers with less than four quarters in covered employment. (See Appendix Table 84.) In other words, the percentage of four-quarter workers is higher among men than among women. This disparity is largely due to the more rapid turnover of women in the labor force, particularly to the larger percentage of new entrants among women; but even when new entrants are excluded, men as a group have a larger proportion of four-quarter workers than women. (See Table 140.)

Number of Quarters in Covered Employment, 1937–1946

Over a period of years, women generally work for a shorter time than men, as measured by the number of calendar quarters in which they receive wage credits under OASI. Of all women in covered employment at some time during 1937–1946, only 4 per cent had wage credits in all forty quarters, as compared with 11.8 per cent of the men. Furthermore, 28.3 per cent of the women, as compared with 19.2 per cent of the men, had wage credits in less

TABLE 139

PERCENTAGE RATES OF WITHDRAWAL FROM EMPLOYMENT COVERED BY OASI, BY SEX AND AGE GROUPS, 1940–1945 [a]

Group	1940	1941	1942	1943	1944	1945
40–44 years						
Men	7.9	7.0	9.8	8.6	8.0	11.0
Women ...	12.8	12.4	14.0	17.7	18.3	21.8
45–49 years						
Men	8.1	6.6	8.6	9.2	8.6	11.5
Women ...	13.4	13.0	13.8	17.6	18.2	21.9
50–54 years						
Men	8.5	7.8	9.1	9.9	9.0	11.8
Women ...	13.6	13.7	15.0	19.1	18.7	22.0

a. Measured by percentage of persons with wage credits in a given year who did not have any covered employment in the following year.

Source: Appendix Table 80.

TABLE 140

PERCENTAGE OF FOUR-QUARTER WORKERS AMONG MEN AND WOMEN WITH WAGE CREDITS UNDER OASI, 1940–1948

	All Workers		Workers with Wage Credits in One or More Prior Years	
Year	Men	Women	Men	Women
1940......	66.2	58.1	65.2	60.6
1941......	65.1	53.4	70.4	63.9
1942......	61.4	48.6	64.0	59.3
1943......	63.3	49.4	67.1	59.1
1944......	66.6	52.9	69.5	59.2
1945......	60.9	51.7	64.0	56.5
1946......	61.1	50.7	63.5 [a]	55.0 [a]
1947......	68.7	54.4	69.5 [a]	56.1 [a]
1948 [a].....	71.8	57.1	—	—

a. Preliminary.

Source: Bureau of Old-Age and Survivors Insurance.

than five quarters during this decade. Nearly 78 per cent of all women, but only 59.3 per cent of all men, were in covered employment in half or less than half of the forty quarters. (See Appendix Table 85.)

Change of Employer

Women with wage credits under the OASI program change jobs less frequently than men. The percentage of workers with wage credits in 1944 who worked for only one employer was: among white men, 67 per cent; among white women, 69 per cent; among Negro men, 52 per cent; among Negro women, 60 per cent. Among workers who had more than one employer, almost two thirds of the white women, as compared with somewhat more than half of the white men, had only two employers. Proportionately twice as many white men as white women, and two and a half times as many Negro men as Negro women, worked for five or more employers. (See Appendix Table 81.)

One reason for fewer changes of employer among women is the relatively short duration of their covered employment during the year. Another is the high proportion of women in seasonal employment, where there is less opportunity and incentive to change employers. In addition, the pressure to obtain full-time, continuous employment is generally stronger on men, who are usually the main breadwinners for the family and therefore, when they lose one job, are more likely to take up other employment. Furthermore, women's job opportunities, although considerably better and more diversified than before the war, are still more restricted than those of men.

CHAPTER 29

EMPLOYMENT OF NEGROES *

NEGROES CONSTITUTE about one tenth of the population and the labor force of the United States. Nearly 95 per cent of all "nonwhite" workers are Negroes, the remaining 5 per cent consisting of native Indians, Chinese, Japanese and other minor groups. The problem of "nonwhite" workers is a problem of Mexican workers in Texas and Arizona; of Mexicans, Chinese and Japanese on the Pacific Coast; and, most seriously, of Negroes in the South, where that race represents nearly half the population and labor force in Mississippi and South Carolina and averages about a fourth in other states. Employment of Negroes is a less acute problem in the North, where they represent 4 per cent of the labor force, and is practically nonexistent in the West, where they constitute slightly more than one per cent.[1]

In statistics for the United States, Negroes are sometimes enumerated as such and sometimes counted with other "nonwhite" races.[2] In national totals and averages the two classifications give almost identical results. The following pages deal specifically with Negroes because of the particular significance of the problem of their employment and the considerable changes that have taken place in the patterns of their work and earnings in recent years.

* By W. S. Woytinsky. Data relating to the operation of old-age and survivors insurance were prepared by Franz Huber, Bureau of Old-Age and Survivors Insurance, Baltimore, Maryland.

1. Sixteenth Census (1940), *Population,* Vol. II, Part 1, p. 54.

2. According to the census, the "nonwhite" population in the South consists of 9.9 million Negroes and 103,000 persons of other races, most of them Indians. The proportion of Negroes in the "nonwhite" population in other parts of the United States is much lower. In the North there were 2.8 million Negroes and 123,000 other "nonwhite" persons, two thirds of them Indians; in the West, 170,000 Negroes, 157,000 Indians, 168,000 Chinese and Japanese and 39,000 Filipinos and others. In addition, there were registered at the end of 1940, 423,000 aliens born in Mexico, of whom 184,000 were in Texas, 146,000 in California, 28,000 in Arizona, and the rest dispersed over the country. Neither in the census nor in statistics of old-age and survivors insurance are Mexicans classified as "nonwhite," but their wages and their employment present similar problems.

PREWAR EMPLOYMENT PATTERN [3]

Negro Workers in Urban and Rural Areas

Despite their gradual shift from rural to urban areas, Negroes are still concentrated primarily on farms. (See Table 141.)

The urban-rural distribution of Negroes in the labor force corresponds roughly to that in the population. There are appreciable sex differences, however. In urban areas in 1940, Negroes accounted for 6.7 per cent of all employed male workers and 12 per cent of the female workers; the corresponding ratios for rural nonfarm areas were 7.2 per cent and 13.1 per cent, and on the farm, 13.8 per cent and 29.2 per cent. (See Table 142.)

The proportion of women among Negro workers is one and a half that among white workers. This difference is due mainly to the pressure of poverty in Negro families, but it also depends partly on the method of classification used by the census: relatively more Negro women than white are recorded as unpaid family workers.

Class of Work

In the South the distribution of nonwhite workers by broad classes of work — employers and workers on own account, unpaid family workers, wage and salary workers — differs only slightly from that of white workers. (See Table 143.) Much greater is the difference in

TABLE 141

PERCENTAGE OF NEGROES IN THE POPULATION, BY URBAN AND RURAL AREAS, 1910–1940

Area	1910	1920	1930	1940
Total	10.7	9.9	9.7	9.8
Urban areas	6.3	6.6	7.5	8.4
Rural nonfarm	—	9.0	8.5	7.8
Rural farm	—	16.3	15.5	14.9

Source: Sixteenth Census (1940), *Population,* Vol. II, Part 1.

3. W. S. Woytinsky, *Labor in the United States — Basic Statistics for Social Security,* Committee on Social Security, Social Science Research Council, Washington, 1938, pp. 36 ff.

TABLE 142

NUMBER AND PERCENTAGE OF NEGROES IN THE LABOR FORCE, BY CLASS OF WORK, 1940

	Both Sexes			Men			Women		
	Number, in Thousands		Negroes as Percentage of Total	Number, in Thousands		Negroes as Percentage of Total	Number, in Thousands		Negroes as Percentage of Total
Area and Class of Work	All Workers	Negro		All Workers	Negro		All Workers	Negro	
Labor force	52,789	5,389	10.2	39,944	3,582	9.0	12,845	1,807	14.1
Employed	45,166	4,479	9.9	34,028	2,937	8.6	11,138	1,542	13.8
Urban	27,593	2,303	8.3	19,278	1,303	6.7	8,314	999	12.0
Employers [a]	3,319	191	5.7	2,729	94	3.4	590	96	16.3
Family workers	196	5	2.5	53	2	4.0	143	4	2.8
Wage and salary workers [a]	24,079	2,107	8.7	16,496	1,208	7.3	7,582	899	11.9
Rural nonfarm	7,957	680	8.5	6,204	449	7.2	1,753	230	13.1
Employers [a]	1,281	54	4.2	1,111	31	2.8	170	23	13.5
Family workers	90	4	4.4	34	2	5.9	56	2	3.6
Wage and salary workers [a]	6,586	621	9.4	5,059	416	8.2	1,527	205	13.4
Rural farm	9,616	1,496	15.5	8,545	1,183	13.8	1,071	313	29.2
Employers [a]	5,158	661	12.8	4,979	609	12.2	179	51	28.5
Family workers	1,158	293	25.3	932	166	17.8	226	127	56.1
Wage and salary workers [a]	3,300	542	16.4	2,635	408	15.4	666	134	20.1

a. Employers includes workers on own account. Persons whose class of work was not reported are counted with wage and salary workers.

Source: Sixteenth Census (1940), *Population,* Vol. II, Part 1, pp. 44–46.

the distribution of Negro workers and other workers within these classes: Negroes working on their own account as farmers are often sharecroppers; Negro wage and salary workers usually hold the least attractive jobs and are often restricted to service occupations.

Occupational Distribution

Most Negro workers are farmers, farm laborers (hired or unpaid family workers), manual urban laborers or service workers. Of the 13.0 million men and 3.8 million women employed in these occupations in the 1940 census week, 2.4 million men and 1.4 million women were Negroes. Thus Negroes supplied nearly 25 per cent of the labor force in these occupational groups. In all other occupations the census enumerated 24.8 million employed workers, of whom only a million were Negroes.

TABLE 143

PERCENTAGE DISTRIBUTION OF NONWHITE WORKERS IN THE SOUTH, BY CLASS OF WORK, 1940 [a]

Class of Work	Men		Women	
	Total	Nonwhite	Total	Nonwhite
Total	100.0	100.0	100.0	100.0
Employers and workers on own account	31.0	27.3	10.9	11.8
Unpaid family workers	5.2	6.6	7.1	10.2
Wage and salary workers	63.8	66.1	82.0	78.0

a. Only "experienced" workers, excluding persons seeking the first job and those employed on public work projects.

Source: Sixteenth Census (1940), *Population,* Vol. III, Part 1, p. 17.

Nonwhite workers were practically excluded from clerical jobs, professional and semiprofessional work, protective services and skilled manual trades and in 1940 only a few had reached the position of factory operatives. (See Table 144.)

Industrial Distribution

The distribution of Negro workers among industries is governed essentially by their concentration in the South and the practice of assigning to them primarily heavy manual tasks and service jobs. Outside of the South, Negroes are employed mainly in industries that have such jobs to offer.

Negroes represent more than 20 per cent of the labor force in forestry and sawmills, tobacco manufacturing and service industries. In 1940 they also represented a sizable part of the total labor force in agriculture, water transportation, eating and drinking places. In mining, Negroes accounted for 6.0 per cent of the male workers and 2.1 per cent of the female workers in 1940; the corresponding rates in construction were 7.3 and 4.0 per cent; in all manufactures, 5.7 and 2.4 per cent; in communication, 1.5 and 0.2 per cent; in wholesale trade, 4.2 and 1.7 per cent; in retail trade, 6.0 and 3.4 per cent. (See Table 145.)

TABLE 144

NUMBER AND PERCENTAGE OF EMPLOYED NONWHITE WORKERS, BY OCCUPATIONAL GROUP, 1940[a]

Occupational Group	Men: Number, in Thousands: All Employed Workers	Men: Number, in Thousands: Nonwhite	Men: Nonwhite as Percentage of Total	Women: Number, in Thousands: All Employed Workers	Women: Number, in Thousands: Nonwhite	Women: Nonwhite as Percentage of Total
All occupations	34,102	3,081	9.0	11,279	1,572	13.9
Professional and semiprofessional workers	1,893	58	3.1	1,460	67	4.6
Farmers	4,997	656	13.3	164	50	30.4
Proprietors, managers, and officials, except farmers	3,327	50	1.5	427	12	2.8
Clerical and kindred workers	4,361	65	1.4	3,191	25	0.8
Craftsmen, foremen, etc	4,959	136	2.7	117	3	0.3
Operatives	6,196	376	6.1	2,067	104	5.0
Domestic service workers	146	90	61.6	1,961	912	46.5
Protective service workers	670	16	2.4	5	—	—
Other service workers	1,526	367	24.0	1,255	165	13.1
Unpaid family workers	927	175	18.9	220	130	59.1
Hired farm laborers	1,806	440	24.4	100	72	72.0
Laborers, except farm and mine	2,972	631	21.2	103	15	14.6
Occupation not reported	323	21	6.5	207	17	8.2

a. Based on a 5 per cent sample; the figures for all workers differ slightly from those derived from complete census returns.

Source: Sixteenth Census (1940), *Population, The Labor Force (Sample Statistics), Occupational Characteristics,* 1943, pp. 119–24.

IMPACT OF WORLD WAR II

As in the employment of women, the wartime labor shortage broadened the work opportunities of Negro workers. In 1941–1942 many Negroes were working in pursuits that became unimportant in the national emergency, when the labor force became the main obstacle to expansion of the munitions industry. Utilization of this labor force for defense was one of the tasks of industrial mobilization. After some hesitation and confusion, jobs were opened up to Negroes, who shifted from agriculture, domestic service and service industries to factories and eventually were upgraded occupationally. Frequently their employment in war industries meant migration from the Deep South northward and westward.

After the war, many of the jobs that Negroes held were abolished. Following seniority rules, munitions factories laid off first those workers who had been hired last, and in many cases these were Negroes.

Despite the disappointing experience after the war, the brief spell of enforced "fair labor practice" has greatly improved the employment status of Negro workers. In many industries unions have reversed their traditional policy of denying certain jobs to Negroes. In some industries a considerable number of Negro workers have joined unions. The proportion of Negroes among factory workers, especially among women, has remained not far below the peak it reached during the war.

NEGROES IN EMPLOYMENT UNDER OASI

Employment records of the old-age and survivors insurance system show both the progress in employment of Negro workers in recent years and the weakness of their position in the labor market in comparison with white workers.

Proportion in Covered Employment

Between 1941 and 1944 the proportion of Negroes among workers with wage credits in covered industries increased from 7.1 per cent to 9.7 per cent. For Negro male workers, the advance was from 8.2 per cent to 10.1 per cent, while the proportion of Negroes among women with wage credits more than doubled, from 4.0 per cent to 9.1 per cent. After the war, the proportion of Negroes among all men in covered employment declined slightly but remained far above prewar levels. The number and proportion of Negro women in covered employment continued to increase in 1945 and remained at a high level in 1946. (See Table 146.)

Industrial and Regional Distribution

Beginning with 1939, the OASI records show the gains in employment of Negroes in various industries. The greatest gains made during the war by Negro men were in manufacturing industries, while women found new opportunities not only in munitions factories but in nearly all industrial divisions. When white workers

TABLE 145

NUMBER AND PERCENTAGE OF EMPLOYED NONWHITE WORKERS, BY INDUSTRY DIVISION, 1940 [a]

Industry Division	Men: Number, in Thousands: All Employed Workers	Men: Number, in Thousands: Nonwhite	Men: Nonwhite as Percentage of Total	Women: Number, in Thousands: All Employed Workers	Women: Number, in Thousands: Nonwhite	Women: Nonwhite as Percentage of Total
All industries	34,102	3,081	9.0	11,279	1,572	13.9
Agriculture	7,858	1,287	16.4	498	253	50.8
Forestry and fishery	101	24	23.5	2	b	—
Mining	895	53	6.0	13	b	2.1
Construction	2,055	151	7.3	40	2	4.0
Manufacturing	8,251	468	5.7	2,350	56	2.4
Food and kindred products	896	49	5.4	202	9	4.6
Tobacco	50	12	24.2	60	12	20.1
Textile mill products	689	22	3.1	480	8	1.6
Apparel	265	7	2.7	525	13	2.5
Lumber	890	162	18.2	54	3	6.0
Paper and allied products	256	12	4.8	71	1	1.4
Printing and publishing	502	9	1.7	133	1	1.0
Chemicals	364	38	10.5	76	1	1.2
Petroleum and coal products	187	8	4.1	15	b	0.1
Rubber	123	3	2.7	35	b	0.3
Leather	230	3	1.5	140	b	0.3
Stone, clay and glass products	293	20	7.0	45	1	2.1
Iron and steel	1,173	67	5.7	94	1	1.2
Nonferrous metals	236	7	2.9	40	b	0.5
Machinery	908	8	0.9	165	b	0.1
Transportation equipment	816	30	3.7	64	b	0.7
Other manufactures	373	10	2.6	148	4	2.7
Transportation	2,095	174	8.3	81	3	3.5
Communication	183	3	1.5	210	b	0.2
Utilities	478	22	4.6	57	b	0.7
Wholesale trade	1,017	43	4.2	181	3	1.7
Retail trade	4,480	269	6.0	1,861	63	3.4
Banking and finance	334	6	1.9	150	1	0.7
Insurance and real estate	688	51	7.4	314	11	3.5
Business and repair services	792	49	6.2	79	1	1.7
Personal services	1,140	263	23.1	2,864	1,046	36.5
Amusement, recreation, etc.	317	29	9.1	83	5	6.1
Professional services	1,485	89	6.0	1,836	97	5.3
Government	1,408	51	3.6	350	9	2.7
Industry not reported	525	49	9.4	310	20	6.5

a. Based on a 5 per cent sample; the figures for all workers differ slightly from those derived from complete census returns.
b. Fewer than 500.

Source: Sixteenth Census (1940), *Population, The Labor Force* (*Sample Statistics*), *Industrial Characteristics,* 1943, pp. 9–12.

TABLE 146

NUMBER AND PERCENTAGE OF NEGROES AMONG WORKERS WITH WAGE CREDITS UNDER OASI, 1937–1946

Year	Both Sexes: Number, in Thousands	Both Sexes: Percentage of All Workers	Men: Number, in Thousands	Men: Percentage of All Men	Women: Number, in Thousands	Women: Percentage of All Women
1937	2,270	6.9	1,891	8.0	379	4.2
1938	2,295	7.2	1,890	8.2	405	4.5
1939	2,415	7.2	2,015	8.3	400	4.3
1940	2,478	7.0	2,083	8.1	395	4.0
1941	2,909	7.1	2,439	8.2	470	4.0
1942	3,894	8.4	3,046	9.5	848	5.8
1943	4,384	9.2	2,970	9.9	1,414	8.1
1944	4,489	9.7	2,831	10.1	1,658	9.1
1945	4,477	9.6	2,845	9.9	1,632	9.2
1946[a]	4,594	9.4	3,141	9.7	1,453	8.7

a. Data for all nonwhite workers.

Source: Bureau of Old-Age and Survivors Insurance.

abandoned their jobs for more attractive ones, employers replaced them with Negroes. (See Table 147 and Appendix Table 86.)

The improved opportunities of Negroes were closely related to the migration of Negro workers from the South toward industrialized areas in the North and the West. The geographic distribution of Negroes with wage credits in 1939 and 1944 bears this out. The share of the Pacific, the Middle Atlantic and the East North Central states advanced by strides, while that of the Southeast declined. (See Table 148.) In 1939, 53 per cent of all Negro workers with wage credits were in the Southeast; in 1944, only 40 per cent. Not only had there been a decline in each of the eleven states in this region, but also in the District of Columbia,

TABLE 147

NUMBER AND PERCENTAGE OF NEGROES AMONG WORKERS WITH WAGE CREDITS UNDER OASI, BY INDUSTRY DIVISION, 1939, 1944 AND 1946

Sex and Industry Division	1939 Number, in Thousands	1939 Percentage of All Workers	1944 Number, in Thousands	1944 Percentage of All Workers	1946 Number, in Thousands	1946 Percentage of All Workers
Men	2,015	8.3	2,831	10.1	3,141	9.7
Mining	61	5.9	65	6.3	64	5.8
Contract construction	223	11.5	220	12.7	314	12.1
Manufacturing	637	6.8	1,319	9.5	1,254	9.4
Transportation	107	10.9	184	12.4	187	11.4
Communication	4	2.1	3	2.4	7	2.6
Public utilities	18	3.8	15	4.7	20	4.6
Wholesale and retail trade [a]	415	8.9	600	10.6	654	9.3
Finance, insurance and real estate	73	7.4	69	8.5	89	8.1
Services	248	11.4	279	13.0	333	11.9
Not distributed	229	—	77	—	219	—
Women	400	4.3	1,658	9.1	1,453	8.7
Mining	1	4.0	2	3.7 [b]	2	4.1 [b]
Contract construction	1	2.6	11	9.9	4	4.5 [b]
Manufacturing	102	2.8	637	7.9	460	7.6
Transportation	2	3.4	15	7.9	9	5.9
Communication	1	0.3	4	1.1	7	1.2
Public utilities	1	0.9	2	2.0	2	2.1
Wholesale and retail trade [a]	99	3.6	479	8.1	417	7.3
Finance, insurance and real estate	20	4.3	55	6.5	51	5.6
Services	141	10.5	408	18.9	433	18.7
Not distributed	32	—	45	—	68	—

a. Excludes persons employed in wholesale and retail trade combined, not elsewhere classified.
b. Fewer than 100 persons in sample.

Source: Bureau of Old-Age and Survivors Insurance.

Note: For detailed breakdown by industry of Negro group as a whole, see Appendix Table 86.

TABLE 148

PERCENTAGE DISTRIBUTION OF NEGRO WORKERS WITH WAGE CREDITS UNDER OASI, BY GEOGRAPHIC REGION, 1939, 1944 AND 1946

Region [a]	1939 Men	1939 Women	1944 Men	1944 Women	1946 Men	1946 Women
All	100.0	100.0	100.0	100.0	100.0	100.0
South Atlantic	36.7	42.3	28.8	24.7	29.2	26.3
East South Central	16.5	10.0	14.1	10.0	13.1	9.4
West South Central	16.2	10.9	14.8	11.6	13.7	11.1
Total	69.4	63.2	57.7	46.3	56.0	46.8
Middle Atlantic	13.0	17.3	15.5	21.6	17.3	22.8
East North Central	11.8	13.1	16.6	19.6	17.5	18.4
Total	24.8	30.4	32.1	41.2	34.8	41.2
New England	1.1	1.2	1.2	1.6	1.4	1.8
West North Central	3.1	3.7	3.5	4.8	3.4	4.4
Mountain	0.4	0.4	0.3	0.3	0.4	0.5
Pacific	1.1	1.4	4.9	5.4	3.8	5.4
Total	5.7	6.7	9.9	12.1	9.0	12.1

a. For regional classification of states, the six socio-economic regions developed by Howard W. Odum and Harry E. Moore are used: Northeast — Connecticut, Delaware, District of Columbia, Maine, Maryland, Massachusetts, New Hampshire, New Jersey, New York, Pennsylvania, Rhode Island, Vermont, West Virginia; Middle states — Illinois, Indiana, Iowa, Michigan, Minnesota, Missouri, Ohio, Wisconsin; Northwest — Colorado, Idaho, Kansas, Montana, Nebraska, North Dakota, South Dakota, Utah, Wyoming; Far West — California, Nevada, Oregon, Washington; Southwest — Arizona, New Mexico, Oklahoma, Texas; Southeast — Alabama, Arkansas, Florida, Georgia, Kentucky, Louisiana, Mississippi, North Carolina, South Carolina, Tennessee, Virginia. (*American Regionalism,* Holt, New York, 1938, pp. 435–61.)

Source: Appendix Table 87.

West Virginia and Maryland. The decline in the Southeast is particularly significant because the proportion of all covered workers in this region, about 15 per cent of the national total, remained almost unchanged between 1939 and 1944.

The wartime changes in the demand for Negro labor, especially in manufacturing industries, at least doubled the proportion of Negroes among covered workers in fifteen states. As a group these states, all outside the Southeast, accounted for more than 26 per cent of all Negro workers in 1944, as against 15 per cent in 1939. While several were western states with relatively small populations (Oregon, Washington, Nevada, Idaho, Utah, Montana and Wyoming), the group also included such important industrial states as New York, Illinois, Connecticut, Massachusetts, Wisconsin and California. (See Appendix Table 88.)

Despite the over-all national increase, the proportion of Negroes among covered workers decreased in eleven states, mostly in the Southeast and the agricultural areas of the Northeast. In eight states — the remaining states of the Southeast region and several states bordering on it — the proportion increased, but at less than the national average rate. (See Figure 63.)

The number of states in which Negroes represented less than 5 per cent of all workers with wage credits declined from 33 in 1939 to 24 in 1944 and to 23 in 1946, reflecting the greater geographic dispersion of employment opportunities of Negroes. The sixteen states that had a more-than-average proportion of Negroes among workers with wage credits in 1939 accounted for 67 per cent of all covered workers that year but for only 53 and 52 per cent, respectively, in 1944 and 1946.

Continuity of Employment

Employment of Negroes in industries covered by old-age and survivors insurance is less stable and continuous than that of white workers in terms of the number of calendar quarters with wage credits and the number of changes of employer during a year.

For both men and women, the proportion of Negroes with wage credits in all four quarters of a year is lower than that of white persons and the proportion of one-quarter workers is higher. In 1946, for example, 16.1 per cent of Negro men with wage credits were in the one-

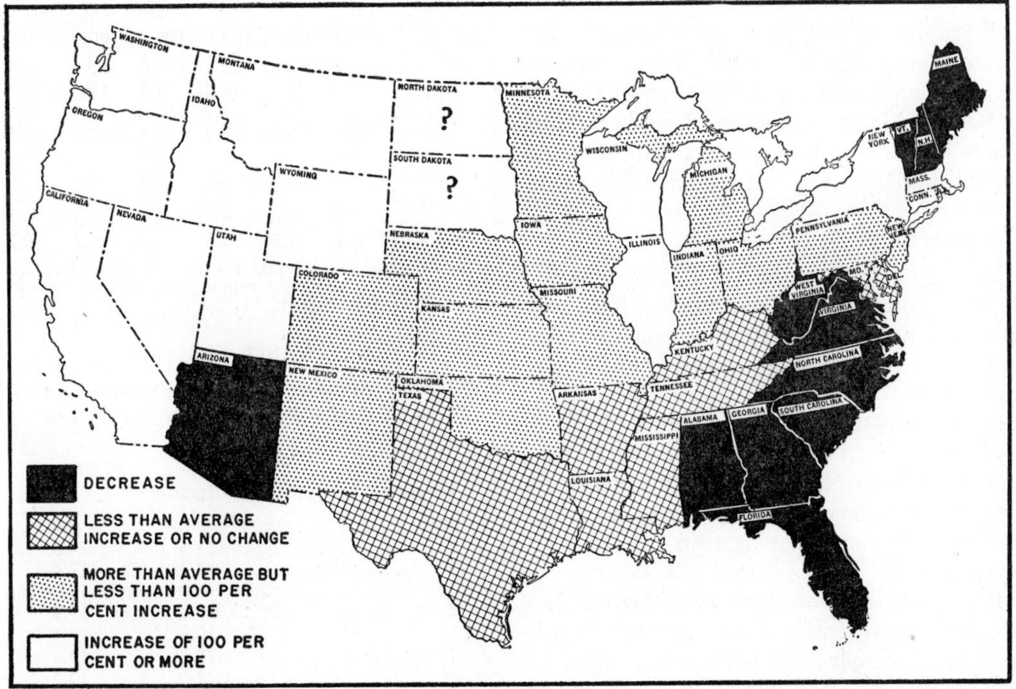

FIGURE 63. CHANGES IN PROPORTION OF NEGROES AMONG WORKERS WITH WAGE CREDITS UNDER OASI, 1939–1944

Source: Appendix Table 88.

TABLE 149

Percentage Distribution of White and of Negro Workers with Wage Credits under OASI, by Number of Quarters in Covered Employment, 1944 and 1946

Race and Sex	1944					1946				
	Total	Quarters Employed				Total	Quarters Employed			
		1	2	3	4		1	2	3	4
All workers										
White	100.0	13.6	12.5	12.8	61.0	100.0	14.2	13.9	14.7	57.1
Negro	100.0	18.9	17.0	15.9	48.2	100.0	19.2	17.3	16.7	46.9
Men										
White	100.0	12.0	10.4	10.0	67.6	100.0	12.4	12.5	13.2	62.0
Negro	100.0	15.3	13.6	13.1	58.0	100.0	16.1	15.0	15.1	53.9
Women										
White	100.0	15.9	15.3	14.2	54.6	100.0	17.4	16.2	14.4	52.0
Negro	100.0	24.8	22.1	16.8	36.2	100.0	25.2	21.5	16.3	37.0

Source: Bureau of Old-Age and Survivors Insurance. Cf. Appendix Table 89.

quarter group and 53.9 per cent in the four-quarter group, as compared with 12.4 per cent and 62.0 per cent for white male workers. (See Table 149.)

In 1944 and 1946, white men in covered employment averaged 3.3 quarters with credits each year, while Negro men averaged 3.1 quarters in 1944 and a little more than 3.0 quarters in 1946. White women averaged 3.1 quarters in 1944 and 3.0 quarters in 1946; Negro women, 2.6 quarters in each year. (See Appendix Table 89.)

Continuity of employment, as measured by number of quarters with wage credits, increases with age among both Negro and white workers, but in almost all age groups Negro workers have a somewhat lower average than white and represent a higher proportion of workers with credits in less than four quarters than of four-quarter workers. (See Appendix Table 90.)

Change of Employer

During 1944, 45 per cent of all Negro workers with wage credits, as compared with 32 per cent of white workers, changed employers at least once. Nearly 24 per cent of the Negro workers held three or more jobs during that year, as compared with less than 14 per cent of the white workers. (See Table 150.) The contrast between Negro and white workers in degree of attachment to employment is more strongly pronounced among men than among women.

Because of their weaker attachment to the job, Negroes constitute a comparatively small percentage of one-employer workers (8 per cent for both men and women in 1944) and a much higher percentage among multi-employer workers (22.8 per cent among men and 15.4 per cent among women who changed employers six times in 1944). (See Table 151.) Most striking is the high proportion of Negroes among male workers with more than four employers in the age groups under 25 years. (See Appendix Table 81.)

TABLE 150

Percentage Distribution of White and of Negro Workers with Wage Credits under OASI, by Number of Employers, 1944

Number of Employers	Both Sexes		Men		Women	
	White	Negro	White	Negro	White	Negro
Total	100.0	100.0	100.0	100.0	100.0	100.0
1	67.9	54.8	67.1	51.9	69.1	59.8
2	18.7	21.6	18.2	21.1	19.5	22.3
3	7.0	10.3	7.2	10.8	6.7	9.5
4	3.0	5.5	3.4	6.1	2.6	4.5
5	1.4	3.0	1.7	3.6	1.1	2.0
6	0.8	1.8	1.0	2.2	0.5	1.0
7	0.4	1.1	0.6	1.5	0.2	0.4
8	0.3	0.6	0.3	0.9	0.1	0.2
9 or more	0.4	1.3	0.6	1.9	0.2	0.2

Source: Handbook of Old-Age and Survivors Insurance Statistics, Social Security Administration, Federal Security Agency, Baltimore, 1944, p. 84.

TABLE 151

Percentage of Negroes among Workers with Wage Credits under OASI, by Number of Employers, 1944

Number of Employers	Men	Women
Total	10.1	9.1
1	8.0	8.0
2	11.5	10.3
3	14.3	12.4
4	16.9	14.9
5	19.4	15.9
6	20.8	17.6
7	22.8	15.4
8	22.6	15.5
9 or more	26.8	13.2

Source: Bureau of Old-Age and Survivors Insurance.

CHAPTER 30

EMPLOYMENT IN AGRICULTURE *

THE PATTERNS of employment in agriculture differ from those in nonagricultural pursuits because agriculture, alone of all industries, produces living things — plants and animals — and derives products directly from them. Agricultural production is being modified continually in amount and kind by the interplay of changing physical, biological, technological and economic factors. Soil types, climate, rainfall, pests and diseases, the development of new or improved varieties of crops and livestock, and prices and production costs affect production. The processes of growth impose a timetable of labor demands that a farmer cannot easily modify. Farmers are thus dependent upon more factors beyond their control than are nonagricultural entrepreneurs.

Agriculture also differs greatly from other industries in the United States in the number and dispersion of its establishments. The 5.4 million establishments that qualified in 1950 as "farms" by census definition were nearly twice the number in all other private pursuits combined. The fact that agriculture in the United States is essentially an industry of small-unit operations, carried on by millions of widely scattered, independent establishments, influences the volume of production, the degree of competition, and the existence of trade or labor organizations within the industry.

How farms are distributed among size groups is of prime importance for agricultural employment. The predominant organization of farms as family enterprises means that only about half of all farm operators hire any labor during the year, while the remainder rely wholly on their own and their families' labor. (See Table 122.) Many units classified as "farms," however, can hardly be considered as productive enterprises when judged directly by value of production or indirectly by land, equipment and other productive resources.

Workers and "Nonworkers"

The family enterprise nature of most of the farms in the United States affects the working conditions of the self-employed farmer and, to an even greater extent, those of unpaid family workers. The fact that the place of business is often also the home leads to informal work relationships, varying degrees of participation by family members, duality of status for some persons who work concurrently in paid and unpaid jobs, and interspersion of home or school duties with gainful work. Because of these conditions, it is difficult to differentiate unpaid family workers in agriculture from the unemployed on the one hand and from housewives, students and other categories of nonworkers on the other.[1]

During the winter, a housewife or a son of high school age may perform only a few chores, such as feeding chickens kept for home use or milking one cow. But as labor demands increase with the season, the same person may do more and more farm work until, at harvesttime, the unpaid family worker may be doing actual field work for 40 or more hours a week.

Because of the variety of chores and the unskilled nature of many types of farm work, people of almost all ages and degrees of physical capacity can be utilized in agriculture. When children do certain kinds of field work, especially in the South, their mothers may also work in the fields and still be near them. Housekeeping duties and care of children necessarily tend to make the farm work of most farm women part-time or marginal. Demarcation between workers and nonworkers on farms is also made difficult by the fact that chores and gardening, which might be considered as an extension or a part of "own home housework," are very similar to the work involved in producing livestock products and crops for the farm business. Separating cream and making butter, for ex-

---

* By Louis J. Ducoff, Bureau of Agricultural Economics, U.S. Department of Agriculture. Opinions expressed here are those of the author and not necessarily those of the agency with which he is associated.

1. Louis J. Ducoff and Gertrude Bancroft, "Experiment in the Measurement of Unpaid Family Labor in Agriculture," *Journal of the American Statistical Association,* June 1945, pp. 205–13.

TABLE 152

Farm Employment, Annual Average and Seasonal Peak and Low, by Geographic Division, 1950

Geographic Division	Annual Average		Seasonal Peak			Seasonal Low		
	Number, in Thousands	Percentage of Total	Month	Number, in Thousands	Percentage of Annual Average	Month	Number, in Thousands	Percentage of Annual Average
United States	10,351	100.0	Sept.	13,703	132.4	Dec.	6,782	65.5
New England	224	2.2	Sept.	273	121.9	Dec.	163	72.8
Middle Atlantic	612	5.9	Aug.	772	126.1	Dec.	453	74.0
East North Central	1,501	14.5	July	1,761	117.3	Jan.	1,164	77.5
West North Central	1,759	17.0	July	2,202	125.2	Dec. & Jan.	1,347	76.6
South Atlantic	2,118	20.5	Sept.	2,776	131.1	Dec.	1,159	54.7
East South Central	1,738	16.8	Oct.	2,865	164.8	Dec.	960	55.2
West South Central	1,470	14.2	Sept.	2,111	143.6	Dec.	878	59.6
Mountain	397	3.8	Sept.	546	137.5	Jan.	240	60.5
Pacific	532	5.1	Sept.	708	133.1	Jan.	367	69.0

Source: Bureau of Agricultural Economics.

ample, may be considered "home housework" if the family eats the cream and butter but "farm work" if the products are sold.

Along with seasonality go intermittent employment of operators and hired workers and unemployment or underemployment in slack months. In many special-crop areas the local supply of labor is inadequate to fill requirements during cultivating or harvesting peaks, and migratory farm workers fill the gap. On many types of fruit and vegetable farms, for example, the farm operator and his family can do all or almost all the work during most of the year, but in harvesttime dozens of hired workers may be employed for a few weeks.

The Farm Labor Force

Application of conventional labor force concepts to farm workers may give a far from complete picture. Agricultural operations in the main are geared to an annual cycle. For some purposes, therefore, concepts relating to work participation during an entire year may be profitably employed. For other purposes, the more conventional cross-section estimates of employment are more useful.[2]

Regional Distribution

Slightly more than half of all agricultural employment is in the three southern divisions of the United States. This regional concentration of agricultural manpower contrasts with the distribution of agricultural products that enter into commerce. In 1944, the last year

2. Two official statistical series on current agricultural employment are issued monthly in the United States. That of the Bureau of Agricultural Economics is based on reports from farmers relating to the number of persons employed on their farms during a recent week. This type of report from employers is similar to the reports obtained by the Bureau of Labor Statistics from nonagricultural establishments; the resulting employment statistics are identified as BAE series, based on *establishment reports.* The other official series on agricultural employment, issued by the Bureau of the Census, is based on a survey of households, in which some member of the household reports for a recent week the employment status, industry and occupation of each member of the household who is of working age. The resulting employment statistics are identified as the Census Bureau series, based on *individual reports,* population surveys or labor force surveys.

Although both series are based on reports for a current week, there are several differences in concepts: (1) the BAE series includes children under 14 years of age who are reported as working, while the Census series excludes them; (2) the BAE series includes persons who do a specified amount of farm work in the week even though they spend a major part of the week in nonagricultural work, while the Census classifies such persons as employed in nonagriculture; (3) the BAE series includes some duplication in the count of workers who work on more than one farm in a given week. Because of these and other differences, the BAE series runs two million or more higher than the Census series.

This chapter relies primarily on the BAE series for the geographical distribution of agricultural employment and for tracing long-time trends, since that series is available annually for the country as a whole back to 1909 and for major geographic divisions back to the 1920's, while the Census series is available only for the United States as a whole and only from 1940 on. For information on the composition of the farm labor force, such as age and sex distribution, the Census series is used.

See Louis J. Ducoff and Margaret Jarman Hagood, "Objectives, Uses and Types of Labor Force Data in Relation to Economic Policy," *Journal of the American Statistical Association,* September 1946, pp. 293–302; Charles Stewart and Loring Wood, "Employment Statistics in the Planning of a Full-Employment Program," *Journal of the American Statistical Association,* September 1946, pp. 313–21; Loring Wood, "Statistical Data on Employment and Unemployment from Sources Other than Labor Force Surveys," Appendix B in *Labor Force Definition and Measurement,* Bulletin No. 56, Social Science Research Council, New York, 1947.

TABLE 153

PATTERN OF SEASONAL VARIATION IN FARM EMPLOYMENT IN MAJOR REGIONS, 1950

(*Annual Average* = 100)

Type of Employment and Month	United States	North	South	West
Total employment				
January	70.6	77.2	66.4	65.3
February	80.4	84.1	78.9	72.8
March	90.6	91.6	91.6	80.1
April	102.6	102.0	104.1	97.1
May	111.3	107.1	114.7	111.2
June	113.0	117.2	108.6	119.6
July	112.5	121.6	103.5	123.8
August	116.0	116.6	113.1	129.8
September ..	132.4	115.6	144.9	135.0
October	118.8	103.9	131.2	113.3
November ..	86.4	86.5	86.8	83.0
December ..	65.5	76.8	56.3	68.7
Family workers				
January	78.8	83.7	74.6	80.1
February ...	87.2	90.1	84.5	88.9
March	94.9	96.6	93.6	93.4
April	108.3	106.9	109.2	110.4
May	113.8	109.3	117.9	110.2
June	106.8	111.4	102.6	109.5
July	101.9	111.2	93.5	107.7
August	106.5	107.6	105.5	106.5
September ..	122.5	107.3	136.1	114.0
October	115.5	101.4	128.3	107.2
November ..	90.7	91.4	90.4	88.4
December ..	73.3	83.2	63.9	83.0
Hired workers				
January	42.1	47.1	38.9	43.1
February ...	56.8	55.8	59.9	48.5
March	75.5	67.7	84.8	60.1
April	82.7	78.8	86.6	77.1
May	102.9	96.4	103.9	112.7
June	134.6	144.3	128.8	134.8
July	149.3	170.2	137.4	148.0
August	149.1	158.8	138.6	165.0
September ..	166.9	154.5	174.3	166.6
October	130.3	115.7	141.3	122.6
November ..	71.4	63.8	74.7	74.9
December ...	38.3	47.1	30.5	47.2

Source: Bureau of Agricultural Economics.

for which a Census Bureau record of production is available, the three southern divisions, utilizing 52 per cent of the manpower in agriculture, accounted for only 29 per cent of the value of farm products sold or traded. In areas outside of the South, higher investments in land and equipment per worker lead to higher average output. The heavy concentration of agricultural employment in the South also contrasts with the regional distribution of nonagricultural employment. In 1950 only 20 per cent of all employees in nonagricultural establishments were in the southern regions.

Seasonal Variation

According to the Bureau of Agricultural Economics statistical series, the number of persons employed on farms in the United States averaged 10.4 million in 1950 and varied seasonally from a low of 6.8 million in December to a high of 13.7 million in September. (See Tables 152 and 153.) The number of hired workers varied in a wider range than the number of family workers, and for both groups seasonality patterns differed from region to region.

Because peaks and lows occur at different times of the year in the various parts of the country, figures for the United States as a whole understate the amplitude of seasonal changes. Even so, the range from the low to the high month in 1950 was over two thirds the average annual number employed on farms. Employment in the peak month exceeded the low by over 100 per cent.

The seasonal swing is greatest in the South Central states, where the difference between the low and peak months is 98 per cent of the annual average. In these states the cotton harvest contributes to the high peak of employment. The smallest seasonal variations occur in the North Central, New England and the Middle Atlantic states, where the peak exceeds the low month by 50 to 70 per cent.

The seasonality of agricultural employment greatly affects the composition of the farm working force, the degree of utilization of labor, and the returns to agricultural workers.

Pronounced seasonality in the employment of unpaid family workers and hired workers accounts for most of the seasonal variation in farm employment. These two classes of workers make up approximately 42 per cent of the total average annual employment on farms. The monthly variation in the number of self-employed farm operators, who comprise the rest of the farm working force, is not very great; in 1949 and 1950 the number in the peak month exceeded that in the low month by around 17 per cent.[3] Hired farm workers in the peak month of 1950 were over four times as numerous as in the low month. The amount of variation differed greatly in the different geographic divisions. (See Table 153.)

Sex and Age of Workers

Although farm work is traditionally man's work, the farm working force includes many

3. "Annual Report on the Labor Force, 1950," *Current Population Reports,* Series P-50, No. 31, Bureau of the Census, 1951.

women. According to the Bureau of the Census, female workers made up 16.3 per cent of the average annual employment in 1950, and represented 22.5 per cent in June and 22.4 per cent in October, when many were employed at picking cotton.

Statistics on the age of farm workers are most meaningful when examined by class of worker. The self-employed in agriculture — the farm operators — have a higher median age than almost any other major occupational group.[4] In March 1940 the median age of employed male farmers and farm managers was 46.1 years, as compared with a median age of 38.3 for employed males in all occupations. In contrast, farm wage workers and unpaid family workers are below other occupational groups in age. In March 1940 the median age of employed male farm wage workers was 30.6. This date, however, is not a very satisfactory one for measuring the age of unpaid family workers because youths and children under 14 years of age make up such a substantial fraction of unpaid family workers in agriculture in the more active seasons of the year.

Part-Year Workers

Because of seasonal variations and high turnover, the number of different persons who engage in farm work at some time during the year is considerably larger than agricultural employment in terms of man-years. Estimates of the total number of persons who did some farm work in the year are available only for 1943.[5] Because the nation's manpower resources were mobilized for war at that time, these data do not fully represent the peacetime situation. They do, however, show the extreme fluidity of the farm labor force.

In 1943 only 8.2 million persons were employed on farms in January, but a total of 14.5 million persons did farm work at some time in the year. The size of the entire farm working force in the year exceeded the average for the year by 4.2 million and was even 2.6 million higher than the peak month's employment. Although various wartime programs in effect in 1943 were aimed at recruitment of nonfarm people to assist farmers at harvesttime, most of the workers who made up the seasonal expansion in agricultural employment were farm residents. Women, youths and older persons who did not remain in the labor force throughout the year contributed heavily to the seasonal increase.

In 1943, part-year workers substantially outnumbered workers engaged in farm work throughout the year. Only about 4.6 million of the 14.5 million total reported 2,500 or more hours worked on farms during the year. But these full-year workers accounted for about 60 per cent of all the days of farm work done in the year. Of the full-year workers, 4 million were farm operators and 600,000 were hired workers. The remaining 2 million farm operators included some who also did nonfarm work, older people farming on a semiretired basis, and operators whose farming activities did not require as much as 2,500 hours of work in the year.

Impact of Industrialization

The transition from an agrarian to a highly industrialized economy is reflected in the change in the proportion of the nation's workers engaged in agriculture. Farm workers made up 72 per cent of the total labor force in 1820, 53 per cent at the end of the Civil War, 27 per cent at the end of World War I, and about 14 per cent at the end of World War II.

Increase in Productivity

The condition basic to this shift has been rising productivity. In 1820 an agricultural worker produced, on the average, enough food and fiber to meet the needs of about four persons in addition to himself.[6] In 1950 the average farm worker in the United States produced enough for himself and twenty other Americans, besides contributing to exports.

Since 1820 the productivity of industrial workers has shown pronounced gains, accompanying industrialization, division of labor, and the development of specialized mass-production industries. As scientific and technological developments took place within the economy as a whole, agriculture shared in their results. After 1910 the absolute number of workers in agriculture — in contrast to nonagricultural industries — declined despite the continued increase in total population.

4. Cf. pp. 348–50.

5. *The Farm Working Force of 1943,* Bureau of Agricultural Economics, March 1944.

6. Carl C. Taylor and Associates, *Rural Life in the United States,* Knopf, New York, 1949, p. 246.

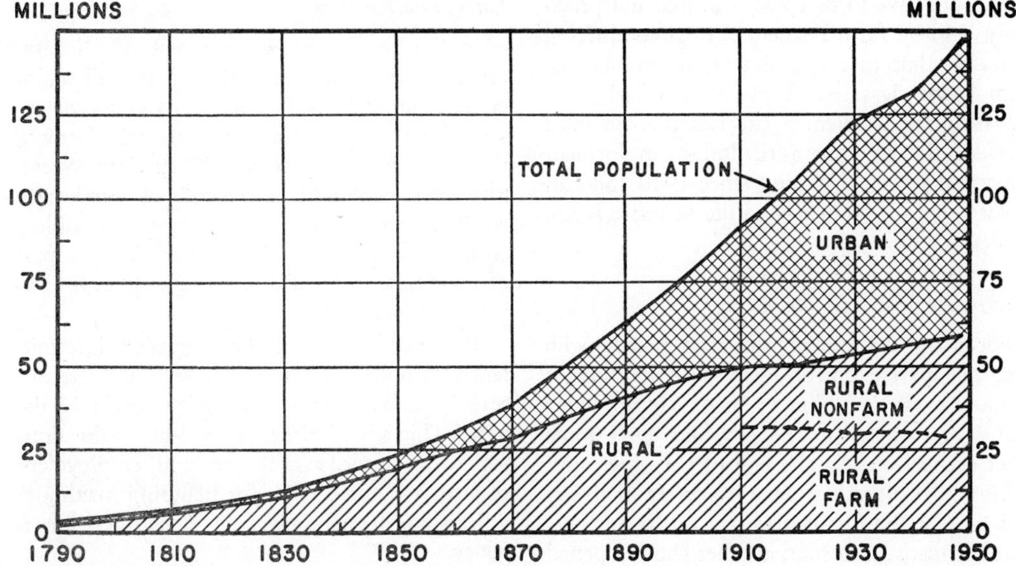

FIGURE 64. GROWTH OF POPULATION AND ITS DISTRIBUTION BETWEEN URBAN AND RURAL AREAS, 1790–1949

Source: Bureau of Agricultural Economics.

The total population of the United States increased from 4 million in 1790, when the first census was taken, to 149 million early in 1949. During the first eighty years after 1790, most of the population lived in rural areas. From 1870 to 1930, urban population increased rapidly—by 12 to 17 million each decade—because of a high rate of natural increase and because of immigration. The rate of increase in total population slowed down during the 1930's but picked up sharply after the middle of that decade. The urban population has grown in recent years at a more rapid rate than the rural—by 18 per cent from 1940 to 1949, in contrast to 7 per cent for the rural.

Population Shifts and Labor Supply

Rapid growth of cities has been a striking concomitant to industrialization in the United States. Migration from farms has contributed heavily to the increase of urban population. The rural population declined from 95 per cent of the total in 1790 to only 40 per cent in 1949. And slightly over two fifths of all rural dwellers now live on farms. (See Figure 64.)

Even though tens of millions of persons have shifted from farms to cities in the past century and a half, the farm population has generally offered an adequate supply of labor for agriculture. Birth rates on farms have been greatly in excess of death rates throughout the history of the United States. During the period 1905–1910 the net reproduction rate of the farm population was double that needed for population replacement, in contrast to the urban rate, which did not quite meet replacement needs. Between 1935 and 1940 — even though the depression accentuated the downward trend in birth rates and the net reproduction rate in urban areas was 30 per cent below replacement requirements — the rate in farm areas provided a 60 per cent increase each generation.

The high reproduction rates of farm people accounted for the maintenance of an adequate supply of farm workers in the past. The continued excess over replacement needs in recent decades has had a profound influence on employment and on return per worker in agriculture. It is fair to say that, because of the pressure of labor supply throughout the past century — except in periods of general labor scarcity during wars — farm workers have generally been at a disadvantage economically.

Even in 1940, after birth rates had been declining for decades, the number of farm boys aged 15 to 24 was one and two thirds the number needed to replace all the farm men 25 years old or over who would die or retire in the next ten years.[7] Thus two farm boys out of every

7. Conrad Taeuber, *Replacement Rates for Rural-Farm Males Aged 25–69 Years, by Counties, 1940–1950,* Bureau of Agricultural Economics, 1943.

five would have to find nonfarm jobs not previously held by farm residents. Regions differed markedly, but in no state was the number of farm youths less than replacement needs; aggravating the problem is the fact that, in most areas of the country, agricultural employment has actually been declining since 1940 and full replacement of workers who die or retire is not needed.

Alternative Work Opportunities

For many decades young farm people who were not needed on the farm had two choices: to move west and pioneer in developing new farms, or to move to the city and enter some other occupation. By the end of the nineteenth century agricultural areas were fairly well settled, so that the first course was no longer possible for many. But soon another choice opened up. The coming of the automobile and the increase in all-weather roads made it possible for farm residents to commute to nonfarm jobs in near-by towns or cities. By 1930, one in every seven workers living on farms was engaged in a nonagricultural occupation.

This situation continued despite the depression, and by 1940 the proportion had risen to one in five. The great demand for nonagricultural workers during World War II and the prosperous years following the war, along with the congested housing situation in many urban centers, accelerated the trend. By 1949, one out of every three employed workers living on farms was engaged in a nonagricultural occupation.[8]

This trend may greatly improve the economic position of farm workers. It may mean that the future supply of farm labor will respond more directly to agricultural labor requirements and that the widespread underemployment of agricultural workers in many regions of the country will diminish or disappear. To be sure, choice of work is limited by the centralization of industry in urban areas. But even in the less industrialized regions, trade and service establishments in the country and in small towns can provide employment for many farm residents.

Part-Time Farming

In the year 1949, 13 per cent of all farm operators reported nonfarm work as their major occupation and an additional 14 per cent reported some nonfarm work, though farming was their main occupation. When farm operators who spent part of the year at hired farm work on other operators' farms are added, almost two fifths of all farmers devoted part of their time to gainful work other than operating their own farms.

The number of persons engaged intermittently in nonagricultural industries and agriculture is probably much larger now than in the past. This situation has important implications for social security programs and employment services and, especially, for planning maximum utilization of manpower in a national emergency.

Technological Changes

Technological advance has been by far the most important factor in changing American agriculture during the past century. The most striking change has been the replacement of animal power by motor power and the accompanying shifts from hand to machine operations. Disease-resistant and higher-yielding varieties of plants and animals also have been developed and adopted. Scientific principles have been applied to farm management and cultural practices improved; soil conservation measures, fertilizers, pesticides and hormones have come into common use.

These advances have reduced the number of man-hours of labor required to produce a given amount of crops, livestock or livestock products. A recent analysis of the remarkable increase in man-hour productivity between World War I and World War II shows that if farmers in the United States had farmed in 1944 as they did during 1917–1921 — if they had used the same machines, tools and power units and had produced their crops and livestock in about the same proportions and at the same rates of yield — 9 billion, or 43 per cent, more man-hours of work than were actually used in 1944 would have been required to produce the agricultural output of that year.[9] The factors ac-

8. Bureau of the Census and Bureau of Agricultural Economics, Census-BAE Series, No. 14, January 1950.

9. Glen T. Barton, "Increased Productivity of the Farm Worker," *Industrial and Labor Relations Re-*

counting for this saving, in the order of importance, were: (1) increased mechanization, including decrease in the number of horses and mules (accounted for 48 per cent of the saving); (2) increased yields causing reduction of preharvest and harvest labor (accounted for 19 per cent); (3) increase in size of livestock enterprises and greater production per animal (13 per cent); (4) spreading overhead over a larger volume of production (7 per cent); (5) other factors (13 per cent).

Mechanization and Labor Requirements

During recent decades, mechanization has stood out as the prime factor in reducing agricultural labor requirements. The number of tractors on farms rose from a quarter of a million in 1920 to 1.6 million in 1940 and, despite wartime shortages, to 2.4 million by 1945. Greater availability of machinery after the war and high farm income led to a record increase in the next five years, bringing the number of tractors on farms to 3.8 million by 1950.[10] On the other hand, the number of horses and mules on farms was more than halved between 1920 and 1945,[11] and by 1950 horses and mules were only a little more than a fourth the number in 1920. (See Figure 65.)

In general, mechanization has been steady rather than spectacular, but there have been certain exceptions. The introduction of combines for harvesting wheat in the Great Plains effected a revolutionary change within ten or fifteen years. The size of the army of migrant workers who followed the harvest from Texas northward to or beyond the Canadian border about the time of World War I has been estimated at nearly a million. For some years now this type of agricultural employment has been virtually replaced by mechanized operations, largely carried out on a custom-work basis and involving not more than a tenth of the former number of workers.

A spectacular change now going on is the introduction of machines to harvest sugar beets. In California, 65 per cent of the 1947 harvest was mechanized, as compared with only a nominal percentage four or five years earlier. It is estimated that by 1950, 80 per cent of the sugar beet harvest was mechanized.[12] Other sugar-producing states have not yet mechanized the harvest to so great an extent, but strides are being made each year. Mechanization is also under way in the harvest of sugar cane, produced mainly in Louisiana.

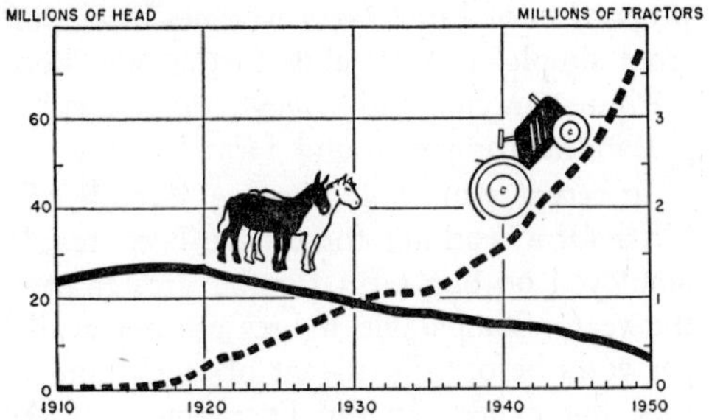

FIGURE 65. HORSES AND MULES AND TRACTORS ON FARMS, 1910–1950

Source: Bureau of Agricultural Economics.

Most farmers realize that their business has been going through drastic changes that will affect their prospective income. Men who still cradle wheat can see combines at work within a day's ride of their farms. The hoe has been replaced by multi-row corn planters and cultivators. These changes are well illustrated by the rapid increase in the number of tractors and the steady decline in the number of horses and mules.

Mechanization has affected not only the number of workers engaged in farm work but also the kind of work they do. Farm operators, who constitute a majority of farm workers, have probably felt most strongly the relief that machines give from the arduousness of farm work. The elimination of the care of workstock on mechanized farms also has probably shortened the length of the farm operator's work day. New skills and training are now required for successful farm operation. On crop farms, at least, skill with machinery now is more important than an elementary knowledge of veterinary medicine.

Machinery enables many a farm operator who once employed a year-round hired hand to get along without hired help except for seasonal workers at harvesttime. Thus, although a small

view, January 1948, pp. 264–82. See also M. R. Cooper, G. T. Barton and A. P. Brodell, *Progress of Farm Mechanization,* Miscellaneous Publication No. 630, Department of Agriculture, October 1947, p. 16.

10. *Outlook Chartbook, 1951,* Bureau of Agricultural Economics.

11. The cropland released from supplying feed for workstock between 1918, when horses and mules on farms reached their peak number, and 1945 was sufficient to produce food for approximately 25 million persons.

12. *1947 Beet Sugar Agricultural Survey,* Beet Sugar Development Foundation, Fort Collins, Colorado, August 1948, and unpublished data from a Bureau of Agricultural Economics study.

proportion of hired farm workers have shifted from simple manual labor to the operation of machines, mechanization has reduced work opportunities for year-round farm laborers.

In recent years only about a seventh of the hired farm working force have been regularly employed on one farm for the greater part of the year. Comparable figures are not available for years before the advent of trucks and tractors, but experts in the Department of Agriculture believe that the proportion of hired workers in the relatively high status group of regular workers was formerly much larger. As more and more harvest operations become mechanized, however, a great reduction can be expected in the casual employment of seasonal farm workers, as has happened in wheat harvesting.

The most dramatic development ahead is the potential mechanization of a substantial portion of cotton harvesting. Cotton picking occupies as much as a third of all the nation's hired farm workers in the fall;[13] a shift to mechanical pickers would greatly reduce not only the number of workers required in the cotton harvest but also the proportion of all hired farm workers doing hand labor.[14]

Crop Specialization

The long-time trend in agriculture has been away from subsistence farming and toward specialization in one or a few crops or types of livestock raised for sale. Extreme crop specialization was practiced in the South before the Civil War, of course, but even then most plantation managers tried to raise most of the food for the slaves and feed for the workstock. However, there is also a countertrend toward more diversified farming, a drive to "live at home" and get away from a single-cash-crop system.

The effects of specialization on agricultural employment are particularly noticeable in special-crop areas. Sharp seasonal demands for labor on the same or similar crops require more labor than the local residents can supply. Almost every state has areas that use migrant farm workers during at least part of the season, but the greatest concentration is probably on the east and west coasts.[15] Specialization of individual farms or whole regions in fruits, vegetables, cotton, sugar beets, sugar cane, tobacco and the like unquestionably has led to an increase in the seasonality and casual character of employment of hired farm workers.

Recent Trends in Employment

Aside from a gradual, long-term downward trend, agricultural employment has been rather stable since 1929. From a year of prosperity through the worst depression in the history of the country, through periods of extraordinary droughts and dust storms, through recovery, war, demobilization, to the highest level of peacetime prosperity on record, the average annual number of persons employed on farms has shown remarkably little variation. It varied around 11 million at the beginning of the period and had declined to about 10.4 million by 1950.

Agricultural employment held up during the great depression because farmers, unlike nonagricultural entrepreneurs, did not generally curtail production in the face of reduced demand. In fact, some farmers even expanded operations, trying to keep income up by selling more at lower prices.

What accounts for their behavior? In the first place, the many independent entrepreneurs in agriculture are, with some important exceptions, not organized, so that curtailment of production of a given farm commodity by one producer would have no perceptible effect on supply or price of the commodity. In the second place, at the present time four fifths of all agricultural labor is performed by farm operators and members of their families. In time of depression, most nonagricultural employers can reduce payrolls and other variable production costs by partial or complete shutdowns, letting the burden of unemployment fall on the workers or the public. But when a farm operator and members of his family find it difficult or impossible to get other work, continued work on the farm, even for greatly reduced returns, appears preferable to idleness and no return at all.

13. *Surveys of Wages and Wage Rates in Agriculture,* Report No. 19, Bureau of Agricultural Economics, July 1947, and unpublished data from the Bureau of Agricultural Economics.

14. *Study of Agricultural and Economic Problems of the Cotton Belt,* Hearings before the Special Subcommittee on Cotton of the Committee on Agriculture, House of Representatives, 1947, pp. 619–21.

15. *Preliminary Survey of Major Areas Requiring Outside Agricultural Labor,* Extension Farm Labor Circular No. 38, Department of Agriculture, September 1947.

Expansion of agricultural production during World War II brought opposite results in terms of farm employment. Technological advances permitted greater production per man-hour, while increased total production permitted fuller utilization of the farm working force, a substantial part of which had ordinarily been underemployed. In the depression years before the war, the piling up and inefficient use of manpower on the smaller and less adequately equipped farms largely obscured the effect of technological advances on farm employment. When defense activities led to rapid expansion in nonagricultural employment before our entry into World War II, the effects of the long depression began to fade out. The exodus from farms reached its peak in 1942, just after the United States entered the conflict, but losses in the farm population through migration and induction of farm men into the armed forces continued until the end of the war.

By January 1947 the return to farms of veterans, the high rate of natural increase of the farm population, and some net migration of civilians to farms after the war had led to recovery of nearly half the wartime loss in the farm population. During 1947, however, the farm population stabilized, and in January 1948 it was slightly smaller than a year earlier. Moreover, the proportion of farm residents holding nonfarm jobs was greater than before the war, so that agricultural employment increased between 1945 and 1947 by a much smaller proportion than the farm population — by only 3 per cent according to the Bureau of Agricultural Economics series. The wartime decrease between 1940 and 1945 had been 7 per cent; hence the combined effect of war and demobilization on over-all agricultural employment was a decrease of about 4 per cent.

Regional Differences

A phenomenal increase in output per farm worker occurred during the World War II years which brought the index of productivity of farm workers in 1945 to 31 per cent above that in the prewar year 1939. The record wartime gains in productivity are being maintained; the index for 1949 (on a 1939 base) was 12 points above the 1945 level. (See Table 154; cf. Figure 66.)

Farm labor is being used more efficiently throughout the country, but regions have differed somewhat in trends in farm employment, farm output, and output per worker since 1939. The rise in productivity, or output per farm worker, between 1939 and 1949 ranged from 28 per cent in the Middle Atlantic states to 61 per cent in the West South Central states. The regional pattern of productivity gains during the World War II years differed somewhat from those of the postwar period. The West North Central, the East South Central, and the Mountain states had the highest gains from 1939 to 1945, while the West South Central, the Pacific and the East North Central states showed the greatest increases from 1945 to 1949. All areas increased in productivity per worker from 1945 to 1949 except the West North Central states. In this division the index of output per worker remained about the same as it had been during 1945.

TABLE 154

INDEXES OF FARM EMPLOYMENT, OUTPUT AND OUTPUT PER WORKER, BY GEOGRAPHIC DIVISION, 1945 AND 1949

(1939 = 100)

Geographic Division	1945	1949
	Employment	
United States	93	92
New England	94	94
Middle Atlantic	96	95
East North Central	95	94
West North Central	96	95
South Atlantic	91	91
East South Central	87	86
West South Central	88	88
Mountain	97	97
Pacific	101	101
	Total Output	
United States	122	132
New England	118	124
Middle Atlantic	111	122
East North Central	117	129
West North Central	137	135
South Atlantic	115	121
East South Central	121	127
West South Central	107	142
Mountain	131	140
Pacific	120	135
	Output per Worker	
United States	131	143
New England	126	132
Middle Atlantic	116	128
East North Central	123	137
West North Central	143	142
South Atlantic	126	133
East South Central	139	148
West South Central	122	161
Mountain	135	144
Pacific	119	134

Source: Bureau of Agricultural Economics.

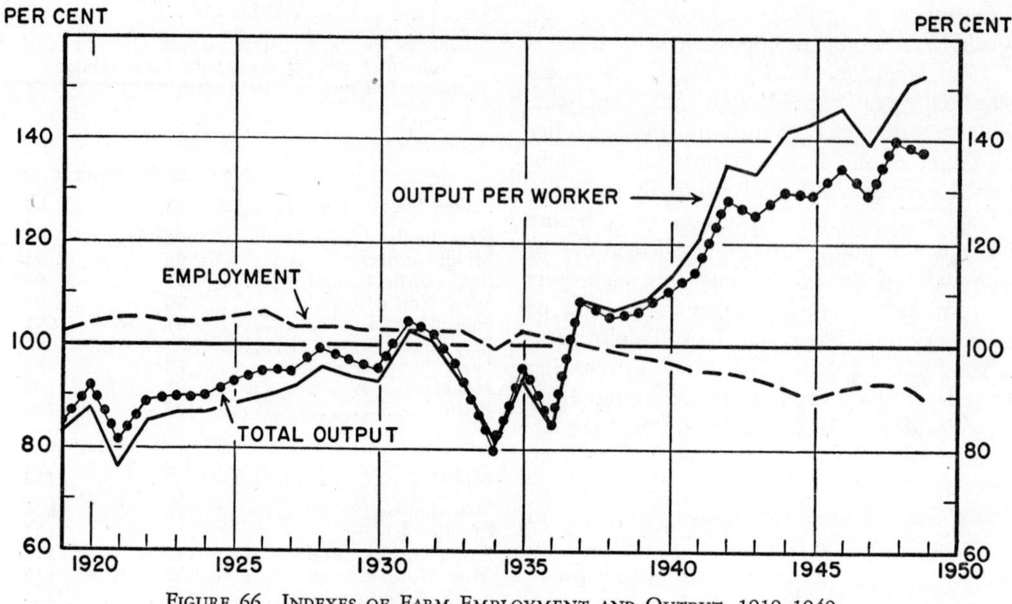

FIGURE 66. INDEXES OF FARM EMPLOYMENT AND OUTPUT, 1919–1949
(*Average for 1935–1939 = 100*)

Source: Bureau of Agricultural Economics.

Farm employment has been going down, farm output and output per worker up. The effects of these changes and favorable weather have been particularly noticeable since 1940. Along with mechanical aids, farmers are using more fertilizer, better animal husbandry, new plant varieties, better rotation and many conservation measures.

Composition of the Farm Labor Force

The agricultural working force did not change greatly in composition during the decade following 1929. The proportion of hired workers decreased slightly during the depth of the depression but increased after economic recovery set in. The principal change between 1929–1930 and 1939–1940 seems to have been the growing proportion of part-time farm operators and short-term hired workers. Also, because of drought, dust storms and displacement through mechanization, many white natives of Oklahoma, Arkansas and other states joined the streams of migratory farm workers in the west coast states, filling jobs that had previously been held mostly by minority groups — Mexicans, Filipinos, Japanese. Along the east coast, too, native white workers joined the stream of migrant workers, taking the place of Negroes or European-born immigrants.

Wartime Changes

Although the net decline in farm employment between 1940 and 1945 was only 7 per cent, the composition of the farm labor force changed markedly in that period. During the early war years, loss of manpower from farms caused grave public concern lest wartime goals for food production might not be attained. The great turnover in the farm working force was undoubtedly a very important cause of uneasiness in 1942, even though farm employment exceeded that of 1941 by a small amount. Moreover, many who left farms were experienced workers and young men, while women, boys, girls and older men prevailed among those who replaced them.

According to the Census Bureau series, the average annual number of women employed in agriculture nearly doubled between 1940 and 1943; in 1943, women constituted between a fourth and a fifth of agricultural employment. Figures on the employment of children are available only for July 1944, when a special survey showed 1.8 million children under 14 years of age at work on farms. When this number is added to the Census Bureau figures for farm workers aged 14 years and over, the number of persons working in agriculture was 12.4 million. Of that total, nearly 4.7 million, or 38 per cent, were women or children under 14 years of age.

These changes in age and sex composition were due, in the main, to replacement of young men who left to take nonfarm employment or to enter the armed forces by other members of the family and replacement of hired workers by unpaid family labor. Between 1940 and 1945 nearly four fifths of the decline in average annual hired employment was offset by the increase in the number of unpaid family workers.

In areas where migratory workers had been an important source of seasonal labor supply, reduction in their numbers owing to transportation difficulties and the availability of steady nonfarm jobs also changed the structure of the farm labor force. Farm placement agencies for directing and routing workers undoubtedly made for better utilization of those domestic migratory workers who continued to seek work in agriculture. Some domestic workers were also replaced by foreign workers brought into the country under a United States Department of Agriculture program. Since it was possible to route and transport such workers to areas where growers were willing to contract for their services, the 120,000-odd foreign workers imported in 1945 probably replaced a greater number of domestic migrants employed in prewar years. Prisoners of war also, but to a lesser extent than foreign laborers, took the place of migratory workers.

Programs to recruit special groups who had not normally done farm work brought other kinds of workers into the farm working force. Many nonfarm high school youths spent their summers on farms, and adults with nonfarm jobs often did farm work during vacations. Nevertheless, the available data indicate that farm residents formed the bulk of replacements for workers who left farms during World War II.

Early Postwar Period

Postwar changes have reversed the shifts in the agricultural working force that took place during the war. According to Census Bureau data, a net increase of 2 per cent in agricultural employment from the summer of 1945 to the summer of 1947 resulted from a 13 per cent increase in the number of employed men and a 26 per cent decrease in the number of women. Hired workers showed a net increase, unpaid family workers a net decrease. Veterans of World War II at work on farms in the summer of 1947 numbered 1.1 million, as compared with fewer than 300,000 in the summer of 1945.

Special studies of the Bureau of Agricultural Economics provide fairly detailed information on changes in the hired farm working force. The number of different persons who worked on farms for wages at some time during the year was almost the same in 1947 as in 1945, but in age, sex and number regularly employed the hired labor force had altered. Hired farm workers in 1947 included 42 per cent more young men between the ages of 16 and 35 than in 1945, and fewer women, boys and older men. The number of the more regularly employed hired hands — those with 150 days or more of farm wage work in the year — increased by 29 per cent between 1945 and 1947.

The Labor Market in Agriculture

Wage workers make up a good part of the farm labor force and outnumber family workers on the larger farms. In the course of a year, slightly more than 4 million different persons engage in farm work for wages.

Prewar Conditions

During the depression-ridden 1930's, workers shifted between agricultural and nonagricultural pursuits less frequently than now. In the main, the labor supply available for wage work on farms consisted of people who lived on farms or in rural areas. In the South and other nonindustrialized areas, nonagricultural employers offered little or no competition for this labor supply. And elsewhere large-scale unemployment meant that nonagricultural employers did not generally have to recruit workers from rural areas. People who did hired farm work were sometimes employed in the off season at nonfarm jobs, but usually at the lowest-paid, unskilled jobs. The general lack of competition from other employers was one of the reasons why the farm labor market tended to be a buyers' market.

The pressure of farm population operated in the same direction. As has already been pointed out, the number of young persons reaching working age on farms has always greatly exceeded the number needed for replacement. During the 1930's, when urban unemployment discouraged migration to cities, rural youths helped swell the supply of potential wage workers on farms.

The farm labor market of the 1930's was generally unorganized, and little in the way of placement services was available to farmers or workers. In areas not relying on migratory workers, this situation often meant that a reserve of local resident workers was idle for a great part of the year and employed only at seasonal peaks. Although few farmers may have deliberately planned to maintain such reserves, general economic conditions provided the reserve for them. Because the depression lasted so long, many farmers thought it "normal" for an ample reserve of farm labor to be on hand to work when needed and at virtually any wage offered.

The generally disadvantageous position of hired farm laborers in the 1930's, especially of seasonal workers, is well known. Their real wages over the decade averaged only 98 per cent as much as in 1910–1914, whereas the real hourly earnings of factory workers had nearly doubled. They shared in none of the benefits of the new social legislation that covered most nonagricultural employees: they were excluded from unemployment insurance and old-age insurance, from protection of their right to organize, and from minimum-wage and maximum-hour legislation. Thus the farm labor market was singularly unaffected by the general progress of labor in the 1930's, with the one exception of sugar-beet and sugar-cane workers, whose right to a "fair and reasonable" wage was recognized in the Sugar Act of 1937.

Wartime Changes

The great demand for labor that developed rapidly under the impact of the defense program and the war strongly affected the farm labor market. In many rural areas, farmers felt keenly the competition of other employers for the same labor. Many farm residents once unemployed or underemployed migrated or found nonfarm jobs within commuting distance. Surplus labor reserves diminished or vanished.

A nation-wide farm placement program was set up. Farm workers were imported from Mexico, Jamaica, the Bahama Islands and Canada to supplement the farm labor supply in some localities. Farm wage rates rose rapidly.

Postwar Situation

The high level of employment since reconversion has tended so far to maintain many of the wartime changes in the farm labor market. The hired farm working force, however, has returned more nearly to its prewar composition. A recent study provides details on an estimated 4.1 million persons who did farm wage work at some time during 1949.[16] Most of them were living on farms at the time of the survey. For every seven living on farms, about two were living in rural areas but not on farms and one was a city dweller. This was very similar to the distribution in 1945.

Almost a million hired farm workers were employed on farms for 150 days or more in 1949. Although they made up only 24 per cent of the entire hired farm working force, they accounted for 75 per cent of the total days of hired farm work. The average paid farm worker had only 90 days of hired farm work in the year, as compared with a 96-day average in 1945. Clearly, for the greater part of the year, most of the hired farm working force either were engaged in nonfarm work or in operation of their own farms or were out of the labor force.

Nearly 1.3 million workers reported hired farm labor as their major activity in 1949; 1 million of them did only farm work and 300,000 did some nonfarm work. Nearly 500,000 other farm wage workers reported nonfarm work as their main occupation. Thus nearly 800,000 persons who spent most of their time at gainful work held both farm and nonfarm jobs in 1949.

Workers engaged for part of the year in nonfarm wage jobs are the most important single source of seasonal hired labor on farms. Next in importance in 1949 were operators of small farms and sharecroppers whose own farming enterprises did not require all their time throughout the year and who occasionally took jobs on other farms. They numbered 683,000.

16. These 4.1 million workers were 14 years of age and over and lived in civilian households in December 1949. Children under 14 years of age, imported foreign workers, people in institutions, and certain other groups — an estimated total of 950,000 — were not included in the survey. They would bring the over-all number of farm wage workers in 1949 to 5.1 million. *The Hired Farm Working Force — 1948 and 1949,* Bureau of Agricultural Economics, November 1950.

In addition about 200,000 persons whose chief activity was unpaid farm work also worked on farms for wages at some time during 1949. The groups described reported that gainful work was their chief activity in 1949. Together they numbered nearly 2.7 million and represented 66 per cent of all farm wage workers, accounting for 88 per cent of the days of hired farm work.

The remaining 34 per cent of the 1949 farm wage workers were out of the labor force for the greater part of the year. Some 700,000 spent the time attending school; 570,000 women reported that for most of the year they were engaged in their own home housework; a miscellaneous group of 150,000 consisted mainly of older people who were available for work during only a small part of the year.

Hired Farm Workers

When most people think of a "typical" farm in the United States, they are likely to picture a good farm, probably in the corn belt, with one regular hired man employed the year around and some extra seasonal labor for a few weeks at harvesttime. Yet only about 10 per cent of our farms employ as much as one man-year of hired labor, and only 15 per cent of all hired farm workers are employed for the full year at farm wage work.

Moreover, only about one per cent of all farms use five or more man-years of hired labor during the year, and these farms employ 37 per cent of all year-round workers. An additional 27 per cent are on the 3 per cent of farms that use from two to five man-years. Thus only about a third of the year-round workers, or 5 per cent of all farm wage workers, are employed throughout the year on farms where their work is the main supplement to the work of the farm operator and his family.

The Regular Hired Man

Statistics are not available to document the trend in the number of regular hired men on farms. Descriptive literature, however, indicates that they once constituted a higher proportion of the hired farm working force than they do today. The rise in farm wage rates since 1939 may have led some farmers who formerly kept a year-round worker to hire help during only the more active part of the season. At the same time, greater availability of nonfarm work in the off season means that workers usually need not suffer unemployment during the winter. However, the shift from horsepower to tractors, trucks and motor-driven equipment has probably enabled many farmers to dispense with a regular hired man.

Year-round workers and other regular workers employed on one farm for more than half the year fare better than seasonal workers in several ways. Although their average hourly cash wages are lower, longer hours of work make their average weekly cash earnings higher. And regular workers, of course, do not lose days or weeks between jobs as do intermittent seasonal workers. In addition to cash wages, about three fourths of the regular workers receive a house or lodging without charge, in comparison with only one fourth of the seasonal workers, and they also receive other types of perquisites more frequently than seasonal workers.[17]

Nevertheless, the number of year-round workers appears to be declining and the "regular hired man" no longer typifies all hired farm workers.

Local Seasonal Workers

Most farm wage workers live in the neighborhood in which they work or near enough to return home each night, and are employed for short periods of a few weeks or months in the active season. These are about the only characteristics shared by the entire group.

The source of supply of such workers varies greatly in different parts of the country. In the East, near population centers, trucks take workers to farms from cities each morning and return them at night, on what is known as a day-haul basis. The same situation exists in the Mississippi Delta, where trucks carry cotton pickers daily between Memphis and farms some distance away. Urban residents, however, supply only a minor share of all seasonal farm wage workers.

Much more important are people living on farms, either on the employer's farm or near by. Some 13 per cent of all hired farm workers employed in a peak week of September 1948 were related by blood or marriage to the em-

17. Cf. pp. 486 ff.

ploying farm operator; a fourth of these were sons and daughters. Other farm operators and their families, and members of families headed by a farm laborer, are also important sources of seasonal labor.

Villages and towns in rural areas supply many wage workers to farms during the summer, including youths who attend school during the winter. In California there are a number of "farm labor" towns, inhabited almost wholly by families who work for wages on a succession of farms within commuting distance. They may get more than six months of employment during the year by working on first one farm and then another, approximating the migratory worker pattern. Most local seasonal workers on farms are more or less casually attached to the occupation, however, and spend the greater part of the year in some other occupation or activity.

Migratory Workers

Crop specialization and seasonality of demand for agricultural labor account for the employment of migratory farm workers. These workers have made up about a fifth of the hired farm working force in recent years.[18] The composition of the migrant labor force differs greatly from one special-crop area to another. More often than not, however, such workers come from groups that have failed to find regular employment because of race, nationality, or lack of education or occupational skills. Some travel in family groups, with wives and young children frequently working to augment the family earnings.

Economic forces affect the number of workers who, for want of a better alternative, leave their regular places of residence and, with or without families, seek work as migratory farm laborers. Most important have been the great depression, the droughts of the dust bowl area, and the displacement of farm workers by increased mechanization. In contrast, the manpower demands of a nation at war reduced the number of migrant workers available to farmers.

Migrants share many problems with local seasonal workers — intermittent employment; low wages; inadequate housing, medical care and educational facilities for children; low social status. In all these matters except wage rates, however, migrant workers are at a disadvantage as compared with local workers. The problems of migratory workers in agriculture have recently received attention from a Commission on Migratory Labor appointed by the President of the United States in 1950.

Special Groups

During World War II certain special groups of workers were used on farms. By 1945 as many as 130,000 German and Italian prisoners of war were employed. Growers paid the prevailing wage rates for this labor to the government, which credited the workers with 80 cents a day for their work. Although earnings were thus not an incentive to high output, experience with prisoners of war on farms was generally satisfactory.[19]

During the war, the United States government also entered into agreements with the governments of Mexico, Jamaica, the Bahamas and Barbados providing for importation of nationals of these countries on a temporary basis to work on farms and to do railroad maintenance work. The agreements stipulated that the workers were to receive transportation, prevailing wage rates, certain perquisites, and employment for not less than a specified percentage (usually 75 per cent) of the working days. The Department of Agriculture administered the program, assisted in placement activities by state and local offices of the Extension Service. At the beginning, growers often overstated their needs for labor, but later the allocation of the imported workers became more efficient.

After the war, the federal importation program was curtailed. But early in 1948, Mexico and the United States signed a new agreement, providing for the importation of Mexican nationals, with the employers bearing the expense of transportation. Importation of Mexicans and other foreign nationals is continuing on a substantial scale. Meanwhile, illegal entries of Mexican nationals into border states for farm work have increased greatly.

Veterans of World War II form a special group among the hired farm working force. In 1947–1949, half a million veterans worked on

18. This estimate and other material in this section are taken from Louis J. Ducoff, *Migratory Farm Workers in 1949,* Agriculture Information Bulletin No. 25, Department of Agriculture, 1950.

19. L. G. Sorden *et al., The Wisconsin Farm Labor Program, 1943–47,* Agricultural Extension Service, Madison, January 1948.

TABLE 155

PERCENTAGE DISTRIBUTION OF FARMS, OF VALUE OF PRODUCTS AND OF WORKERS, BY FARMS CLASSIFIED ACCORDING TO VALUE OF PRODUCTS, 1939

Farm Group by Value of Products	Percentage Distribution					Value of Products per Farm Worker
			Number of Workers			
	Farms	Value of Products	Total	Family Workers	Hired Workers	
All farms	100.0	100.0	100.0	100.0	100.0	$ 772
$1–$599	47.5	10.9	35.8	42.5	13.9	234
$600–$999	17.6	10.4	17.2	19.1	11.1	469
$1,000–$2,499	23.3	27.8	25.9	25.8	26.2	829
$2,500–$3,999	6.3	15.0	8.5	7.0	13.2	1,364
$4,000–$9,999	4.3	18.7	7.8	4.7	18.0	1,851
$10,000 or more	1.0	17.2	4.8	0.9	17.6	2,755

Source: Louis J. Ducoff and Margaret Jarman Hagood, *Differentials in Productivity and in Farm Income of Agricultural Workers by Size of Enterprise and by Regions,* Bureau of Agricultural Economics, 1944.

farms for wages at some time during the year, half of them reporting farm labor as their main occupation. In 1947, 47 per cent of the veterans reported earnings from nonfarm work, compared with only 27 per cent of nonveteran workers in the same age group.[20]

OUTLOOK FOR EMPLOYMENT

Forecasts of agricultural employment depend on assumptions about the general level of economic activity, progress in further mechanization and other technological advances in agricultural production, levels of agricultural production, and changes in the number of agricultural establishments and their distribution by size.

Within any reasonable range of expectations, during the next decade or two the number of workers engaged in agricultural occupations is likely to decrease. But the stability of agricultural employment in the past indicates that the decline will be rather gradual. Moreover, business cycles or other events may interrupt the trend, and a severe depression could temporarily reverse it. A general decline in the number of agricultural workers appears almost inevitable for some time, however, as technological progress in agricultural production enables fewer and fewer workers to produce increasing quantities of food and fibers.

The stability of agricultural employment is a composite effect of production and cost structures. Farms accounting for a very small part of agricultural production account as a group for a sizable share of agricultural employment. Employment on these farms is peculiarly insensitive to conditions that would cause more commercial farms to make changes in production and techniques, and hence in employment. The high ratio of fixed costs to variable costs in agriculture means that once a farm is geared to producing at a certain level it is difficult to curtail production. On the whole, agriculture has been much less flexible in decreasing production than in increasing production. This contributes toward year-to-year stability in agricultural employment.

Future agricultural employment will be determined primarily by the efficiency with which manpower is utilized and by changes in the supply of labor more or less permanently attached to agriculture. Output per worker varies widely according to region and, within each region, according to size of farm. In 1939, for example, the value of products per farm worker averaged $2,755 on farms with a total output value of $10,000 or more; it was less than $500 on farms with an annual output value of less than $1,000 — a group comprising more than 65 per cent of all farms. (See Table 155.)

If output per worker on a substantial proportion of the medium-sized farms were raised to the level of output on larger and more efficient farms, the same aggregate output could be obtained with much fewer workers. Such a development, however, would require reorganization of agricultural production, additional investment in capital and technological resources, and mass transferral of farm families to nonagricultural pursuits. Such changes usually take place very slowly, notwithstanding the significant advances made during World War II.

20. Based on sample surveys made at the end of each year by the Bureau of the Census for the Bureau of Agricultural Economics.

Future Employment

A realistic projection of future agricultural employment requires an extension of past trends with allowance for new influences. Because technological developments have been particularly important in influencing employment in recent years, trends in farm mechanization and output per worker will be key factors.

The Bureau of Agricultural Economics in a report on long-range agricultural policy prepared for the House Committee on Agriculture stated:

> Mechanization and other technological developments have been releasing farm workers for other work for many years, and by 1975 they may reduce the number of farm workers needed by another 15 to 20 per cent, despite a substantial increase in total farm output.[21]

A decrease of 20 per cent in farm employment by 1975, or of about 10 per cent by 1960, would mean that the average annual rate of decline would be slightly higher than between 1939 and 1947. If a high level of employment and prosperity is sustained, or if mechanical and technological advances now on the horizon become widely adopted, agricultural employment might decline even faster.

---

21. *Long-Range Agricultural Policy,* A Study of Selected Trends and Factors Relating to the Long-Range Prospect of American Agriculture, Committee on Agriculture, House of Representatives, prepared by the Bureau of Agricultural Economics, 1948.

Chapter 31

TURNOVER OF EMPLOYMENT *

In a dynamic economic system, employment is necessarily fluid. Births and deaths of business enterprises occur continually. Some businesses are expanding, others losing ground. Changes in techniques and in types of products often require changes in personnel. Just as management seeks a skillful and reliable staff, so workers shift from one job to another in search of more satisfactory working conditions. Turnover of employment is a process of distributing the square and round pegs among square and round holes, a process made particularly complicated and, at the same time, vitally important for the economic system by the continual changes in the shape and form of both the pegs and the holes.

Turnover of Enterprises

The turnover of businesses can be best measured by the ratio of the number of establishments that have been opened or closed to the number of operating concerns in a period when the total number of operating firms remains comparatively stable. Such was the situation in 1940 and 1941. There were 3,307,000 nonagricultural enterprises in this country in December 1939, 3,304,000 in December 1940, and 3,341,000 in December 1941,[1] so that the net change over the two years was only one per cent. During these years, however, 771,000 enterprises were discontinued and 805,000 new enterprises appeared on the scene. (See Table 156.) At the same time 490,000 firms were transferred to new proprietors. The turnover rate — including transfers — was nearly 20 per cent a year.

The rate of turnover is particularly high in building construction and the service industries, considerably lower in manufacturing and trade. In wholesale trade it is unexpectedly higher than in retail business.

Mortality is particularly high among young enterprises during their first year or two and declines with the increasing age of the concern. Among well-established firms, in a year of fairly favorable business conditions, 10 per cent, on the average, change hands and 4 to 5 per cent are dissolved or closed.

Labor Turnover

"Labor turnover" is defined by the Bureau of Labor Statistics as the movement of workers into and out of employment with individual firms. It covers accessions (new hirings and rehirings) and separations — voluntary (quits) and involuntary (discharges and layoffs) — as well as terminations of employment because of death, permanent disability, retirement on company pension, or entrance into the armed forces.

Monthly labor turnover rates are computed on the basis of reports from 6,800 manufacturing establishments (with 4.5 million employees), 500 mining establishments (245,000 employees) and public utility establishments (600,000 employees). These establishments, however, do not represent a typical cross section of all industries. Large establishments prevail in the sample, and industries with marked seasonal fluctuations in employment are excluded.[2] This selectiveness of the sample makes it tend to understate the over-all volume of labor turnover.[3]

Labor Turnover in Manufacturing Industries

Labor turnover rates in particular industries fluctuate widely from month to month. During the war, monthly accession and separation rates of more than 10 per cent were not unusual in munitions production, shipbuilding and aircraft industries. High turnover rates also characterize such industries as sawmills and meat packing. For all manufacturing industries as a group, 4

* By W. S. Woytinsky.

1. Table 116.

2. *Labor Turnover Reports,* Bureau of Labor Statistics (monthly mimeographed releases).

3. Labor turnover in large concerns that can readily transfer employees from one department to another is usually lower than in small firms. See W. S. Woytinsky, *Three Aspects of Labor Dynamics,* Committee on Social Security, Social Science Research Council, Washington, 1942, pp. 21–22.

TABLE 156

BUSINESS TURNOVER, 1940–1950

Year	Total	Manufacturing	Contract Construction	Trade: Retail	Trade: Wholesale	Service Industries	Other
			Number, in Thousands				
New Firms							
1940	357.2	27.2	54.0	107.2	17.2	91.2	60.4
1941	447.6	31.2	71.6	118.0	17.6	137.6	71.6
1942	334.8	29.2	56.0	71.6	8.4	109.6	60.4
1943	143.6	18.8	20.8	34.8	8.0	30.0	31.6
1944	272.8	24.4	21.6	110.4	18.8	56.0	41.6
1945	412.0	39.6	48.8	172.8	26.4	76.8	47.2
1946	615.6	60.0	80.8	262.0	37.2	116.4	58.8
1947	438.0	—	—	—	—	—	—
1948	338.0	31.6	62.8	104.4	24.8	72.4	42.0
1949	358.3	32.2	58.8	136.7	16.2	72.8	41.8
1950	397.4	42.9	71.4	139.5	17.2	73.5	52.8
Discontinued							
1940	360.4	23.6	40.0	106.4	17.2	102.4	70.8
1941	410.8	23.6	51.6	116.8	17.6	131.2	70.0
1942	604.4	29.6	94.0	228.8	22.8	150.8	78.4
1943	379.2	16.4	76.8	150.4	23.2	72.4	40.0
1944	143.6	12.4	13.6	53.2	7.6	39.2	25.6
1945	152.4	16.4	14.8	54.4	8.8	32.4	25.6
1946	182.0	17.6	24.0	61.2	11.6	38.4	27.6
1947	227.2	—	—	—	—	—	—
1948	273.6	31.6	36.0	93.2	20.4	54.4	37.6
1949	427.6	70.9	59.7	156.9	15.8	79.6	44.4
1950	357.9	43.1	42.5	148.9	14.9	70.9	37.6
			Percentage of Number at End of Preceding Year				
New Firms							
1940	10.8	12.7	26.1	6.7	11.9	14.3	11.7
1941	13.5	14.3	32.4	7.4	12.2	22.0	14.1
1942	10.0	13.0	23.2	4.5	5.8	17.4	12.0
1943	4.7	8.3	10.2	2.4	6.2	5.1	6.4
1944	9.6	10.7	14.7	8.4	16.5	10.2	8.6
1945	13.9	16.5	31.5	12.6	21.1	13.4	9.5
1946	18.3	22.0	40.8	17.5	22.3	16.0	11.6
1947	11.6	—	—	—	—	—	—
1948	8.6	9.6	20.7	6.1	12.4	8.5	7.4
1949	9.0	10.0	18.1	8.1	8.0	8.5	7.3
1950	10.0	14.2	21.0	8.3	8.5	8.6	9.3
Discontinued							
1940	10.9	11.0	19.3	6.7	12.0	16.1	13.7
1941	12.4	10.8	23.3	7.3	12.2	20.8	13.8
1942	18.1	13.1	39.0	14.3	15.8	23.9	15.4
1943	12.3	7.2	37.8	10.5	17.9	12.3	8.2
1944	5.1	5.4	9.2	4.0	6.7	7.2	5.3
1945	5.1	6.9	9.5	4.0	7.0	5.7	5.1
1946	5.4	6.4	12.1	4.1	6.9	5.3	5.4
1947	6.0	—	—	—	—	—	—
1948	6.9	9.6	11.8	5.5	10.2	6.4	6.7
1949	10.8	21.9	18.4	9.2	7.8	9.3	7.8
1950	9.1	14.3	12.5	8.9	7.3	8.3	6.6

Source: Survey of Current Business, 1947 Statistical Supplement, 1948, pp. 20–21, and other issues.

to 5 per cent a month seems to be the usual turnover rate in good years, and 3 to 4 per cent in a depression. (See Table 157.)

The number of both accessions and separations increases when employment is high and declines when the demand for labor is low. In 1932–1933 the monthly rate of accession was 4.3 per cent; of separation, 4.1 per cent — as compared with 5.9 per cent for accessions and 5.5 per cent for separations in 1946–1947.

The positive correlation between labor turnover and business conditions is due to two factors: (1) In good times there are more changes in production plans of individual firms; voluntary quits become more frequent when workers have a good chance of finding employment elsewhere. (2) The rate of voluntary quit is extremely sensitive to changes in business conditions; from less than one per cent a month, on the average, in 1931–1940, it shot up to more than 5 per cent in 1943–1945.

In bad times, when the chances of finding

TABLE 157

AVERAGE MONTHLY LABOR TURNOVER RATES IN MANUFACTURING INDUSTRIES, 1930–1950

(Per 100 Employees)

Year	Accessions	Separations: Total	Separations: Voluntary Quits	Separations: Other
1930	3.1	5.0	1.6	3.4
1931	3.2	4.0	0.9	3.1
1932	3.3	4.3	0.7	3.6
1933	5.3	3.8	0.9	2.9
1934	4.7	4.1	0.9	3.2
1935	4.2	3.6	0.9	2.7
1936	4.4	3.4	1.1	2.3
1937	3.6	4.4	1.2	3.2
1938	3.8	4.1	0.6	3.5
1939	4.1	3.1	0.8	2.3
1940	4.4	3.4	1.1	2.3
1941	5.4	3.9	2.0	1.9
1942	7.6	6.5	3.6	2.9
1943	7.5	7.3	5.2	2.1
1944	6.1	6.8	5.1	1.7
1945	6.3	8.3	5.0	3.3
1946	6.7	6.1	4.3	1.8
1947	5.1	4.8	3.4	1.4
1948	4.3	4.5	2.9	1.6
1949	3.5	4.2	1.6	2.6
1950	4.4	3.6	2.0	1.7

Source: Appendix Table 91.

an attractive job are thin and workers stick to their jobs, most separations are initiated by employers. When there are many openings and many workers quit in the hope of obtaining better jobs, the number of involuntary separations usually goes down.

Doubtless, excessive mobility of labor is detrimental to production, but it is not easy to determine where *excessive* turnover begins. A quit rate of 5 per cent a month (60 per cent on an annual basis) is obviously unsound, but a quit rate of less than one per cent suggests a labor force dominated by fear and suppressed industrial unrest.

Assuming favorable business conditions, with cyclical ups and downs, turnover rates in manufacturing industries in the years ahead will probably be somewhat lower than during 1942–1947 but higher than in the 1930's. Both accession and separation rates may be between 4 and 4.5 per cent a month, with the separation rate 0.1 per cent lower than the accession rate.

Total Labor Turnover

Only fragmentary information is available on labor turnover in nonmanufacturing industries. Accession and separation rates in mining are about the same as in manufacturing industries; in telephone and telegraph services, somewhat lower.[4] In government service, under normal peacetime conditions, turnover is particularly low; in contract construction, trade and service industries it is particularly high.

It is fairly certain, therefore, that for all nonagricultural establishments, including seasonal manufacturing concerns that lay off most or all their employees when the season is over, the average rates of accession and separation must be higher than in the large manufacturing firms reporting to the Bureau of Labor Statistics. Assuming that separation and accession rates in manufacturing average 4 to 4.5 per cent a month, the rates for all nonagricultural employment will hardly be below 5 per cent, without counting casual labor and domestic service. Assuming that 44 million wage and salary workers are employed by nonagricultural establishments through a year, there would be approximately 2.2 million job terminations a month, 27 million a year. If total nonagricultural employment increases 500,000 a year, the number of accessions must be as much higher, 27.5 million a year in round numbers. Separations then would include 10 million or more job terminations initiated by employers, and 17 million, or nearly 17 million, quits. The relationship between the two types of separation would be reversed in the event of a severe depression, as in 1932–1933.

Turnover Group in the Labor Force

The labor turnover rates issued by the Bureau of Labor Statistics are based on reports of individual concerns. If a worker shifts his job each month from one reporting firm to another, his movements are recorded as twelve separations and twelve accessions, and this is what they are from the point of view of labor management. From the viewpoint of the structure of the labor market, however, this measurement of labor turnover should be supplemented by an analysis of the incidence of separations and accessions in relation to the working population.

Turnover is not distributed at random over the whole labor force. Some workers remain with the same firm through many years and even decades, others shift frequently.[5] Even though there is no rigid demarcation between

4. *Labor Turnover Reports,* Bureau of Labor Statistics (monthly mimeographed releases).

5. Paul F. Brissenden and Emil Frankel, *Labor Turnover in Industry,* Macmillan, New York, 1922; Sumner H. Slichter, *Turnover of Factory Labor,* Appleton, New York, 1919.

TABLE 158

NUMBER OF WORKERS WITH UNEMPLOYMENT INSURANCE WAGE CREDITS AND AVERAGE NUMBER OF WORKERS EMPLOYED IN COVERED INDUSTRIES, 1940–1949

(*In Thousands*)

Year	Workers with Wage Credits	Average Employment
1940	31,900	23,096
1941	37,600	26,814
1942	43,000	29,349
1943	44,000	30,828
1944	43,000	30,044
1945	43,000	28,407
1946	45,500	30,235
1947	45,300	32,277
1948	45,600	33,088
1949	44,400	31,695

Source: Appendix Table 30.

the stable and the turnover groups, an attempt can be made to determine their relative size and to ascertain some characteristics of the people in these two sections of the labor force.

Scattered information provided by large manufacturing firms indicates that a rather small fraction of the labor force — say 10 or 12 per cent — is responsible for a very large part of the separations.[6] This observation, however, cannot be generalized and applied to all industrial establishments. It does not apply to building construction, where short-time jobs are customary and the floating group in the labor force is probably larger than the permanent personnel of the firms; it does not apply to retail trade and service industries; and it does not apply either to separations initiated by employers or to quits because of temporary disability, withdrawal from the labor force, and the like.

Assuming that the "normal" turnover rate of the labor force under fairly favorable business conditions is about 5 per cent monthly, the monthly rate of quit will be approximately 3 per cent and that of other separations 2 per cent. On the basis of experience (see Appendix Table 91) one per cent monthly appears to be the approximate minimum quit rate under the conditions most unfavorable for changes in jobs.[7]

On the other hand, some separations initiated by employers — for example, those when a plant is closed — can affect the stable group in the labor force to the same extent as the floating group, although in a partial layoff temporary workers are likely to lose jobs ahead of regular employees protected by the seniority rule. It seems likely that in the whole economic system, under favorable business conditions, not more than half of all separations are initiated by the floating group of workers.

All in all, as the records of social security prove, intermittent employment and shifts from job to job are more common in our economic system than steady work for the same employer throughout a year.

TABLE 159

NUMBER AND PERCENTAGE DISTRIBUTION OF WORKERS WITH WAGE CREDITS UNDER OASI, BY NUMBER OF QUARTERS IN COVERED EMPLOYMENT, 1938–1948

Year	Estimated Number of Workers, in Thousands	Percentage with Wage Credits in: One Quarter	Two Quarters	Three Quarters	Four Quarters
1938	31,822	14.1	11.7	11.4	62.9
1939	33,751	13.7	12.0	11.0	63.3
1940	35,393	13.5	11.6	11.0	64.0
1941	40,976	13.0	12.8	12.4	61.8
1942	46,363	15.5	14.0	13.1	57.4
1943	47,656	15.1	13.7	12.9	58.2
1944	46,296	14.0	12.8	12.0	61.2
1945	46,392	17.1	12.8	12.8	57.4
1946	48,845	14.8	14.0	13.3	57.8
1947	48,908	12.6	12.0	11.5	64.0
1948[a]	49,100	11.6	11.2	10.2	67.0

a. Preliminary.

Source: Bureau of Old-Age and Survivors Insurance.

CHANGES IN EMPLOYMENT STATUS

Workers and Man-Years of Work

Employers subject to state unemployment insurance laws are required to report the earnings of each person on their payrolls to the insurance agency. The state agency keeps records of each person to whom the reporting concern paid wages during each month. From these records, two figures can be established for each state: the number of workers in covered employment in the last pay period of each month and the number of *different* persons who have earned wages from reporting firms during some period of the year.

From these data, after some adjustment, the federal Bureau of Employment Security computes national totals for the number of different persons who had wage credits in covered industries during a year and the average number of workers employed in these industries during the year.[8] During the ten years 1940–1949 the

6. Woytinsky, *op. cit.,* pp. 23–28.

7. For factories not subject to seasonal fluctuations the rate is somewhat lower, but only once in the last two decades has it fallen below 0.7 per cent.

8. The last figure represents simply the average of the twelve monthly figures for all states, adjusted to eliminate duplications due to shifts of workers between states.

TABLE 160

PERCENTAGE OF FOUR-QUARTER WORKERS AMONG ALL WORKERS WITH WAGE CREDITS UNDER OASI, BY STATE, 1944

State	Per Cent	State	Per Cent	State	Per Cent
Connecticut	71.7	Missouri	57.8	Wyoming	50.0
Rhode Island	70.0	Minnesota	56.5	Montana	49.4
Massachusetts	69.4	Iowa	55.8	Colorado	49.2
New Jersey	68.5	Kentucky	54.7	Louisiana	49.2
Pennsylvania	68.3	South Carolina	54.7	Oklahoma	48.9
Michigan	66.0	Vermont	54.6	Texas	48.4
Illinois	65.5	Washington	54.0	Arizona	48.1
Ohio	65.4	Oregon	53.2	Utah	47.0
New Hampshire	65.3	Alabama	53.0	South Dakota	46.5
New York	64.8	Nebraska	53.0	Florida	45.9
Wisconsin	63.5	Virginia	52.9	North Dakota	44.9
West Virginia	63.4	North Carolina	52.3	Nevada	44.0
Maryland	61.9	California	51.9	Mississippi	41.3
Indiana	61.1	Tennessee	51.9	Arkansas	41.0
Delaware	60.8	Kansas	51.6	Idaho	40.4
Maine	58.2	Georgia	50.2	New Mexico	38.7

Source: Bureau of Old-Age and Survivors Insurance.

number of persons with wage credits was on the average 43 per cent larger than the number of workers currently employed by the same industries. (See Table 158.)

Quarters of Employment

The contention that not more than half the labor force is employed continuously through a year is confirmed by the records of the federal old-age and survivors insurance system showing the distribution of workers with wage credits by the number of calendar quarters in which they had covered employment. (See Table 159.)

In 1940, a year with fairly high unemployment and low labor turnover, 64 per cent of the workers covered by this program had wage credits in all four calendar quarters; 11.0 per cent, in three quarters; 11.6 per cent, in two quarters; and 13.5 per cent, in one quarter. During the war, partly because of the enrollment of workers in the armed forces and the influx of emergency workers, partly because of greater opportunity for employment and increased mobility of labor, the proportion of workers with four quarters in covered employment declined, falling to 57.4 per cent in 1945.

A four-quarter worker is not necessarily a twelve-month or a fifty-week worker. A person with occasional earnings in industries covered by the system is recorded as a four-quarter worker if he happens to have wage credits in four weeks, each of which is in a different quarter. The distribution of four-quarter workers by amount of covered earnings suggests that at least 20 per cent of them were not in covered employment throughout the year. With this correction, it appears that only from 40 to 50 per cent of the persons with wage credits in a given year are employed by the reporting establishments in all twelve months. This group, moreover, includes persons who changed jobs during the year or had only occasional employment in covered industries during a part of each month.

The distribution of workers by number of quarters of employment in industries covered by the federal insurance system varies with age, sex and race. The proportion of four-quarter workers is less than 40 per cent among workers under 25 years of age; it increases in middle age and declines among the aged.[9] Four-quarter employment is more usual, and one-quarter and two-quarter employment less frequent, among men than among women.[10] The pattern of employment of Negro males differs only slightly from that of white males, but there is a striking difference in the continuity of employment of Negro and white women. Among Negro women, the proportion of four-quarter workers is one third lower and that of one-quarter and two-quarter workers considerably higher than among white women.[11]

In agricultural states such as Mississippi, Arkansas, Idaho and New Mexico, the proportion of four-quarter workers is appreciably lower than in highly industrialized areas such as Connecticut, Rhode Island, Massachusetts, New Jersey and Pennsylvania. (See Table 160.)

9. Cf. p. 352, and Appendix Table 78.
10. Cf. p. 359, and Appendix Table 84.
11. Cf. pp. 365–66, especially Table 149; Appendix Table 89.

TABLE 161

PERCENTAGE DISTRIBUTION OF WORKERS WITH WAGE CREDITS UNDER OASI, BY PATTERN OF CHANGE OF JOB, 1939–1947

Pattern of Change of Job	1939	1940	1941	1942	1943	1944	1945	1946	1947
				Number, in Thousands					
Total	33,751	35,393	40,976	46,363	47,656	46,296	46,392	48,845	48,908
				Percentage Distribution					
Total	100.0	100.0	100.0	100.0	100.0	100.0	100.0	100.0	100.0
Single-employer	74.8	73.1	67.2	61.9	63.4	66.6	66.7	65.5	a
Multi-employer	25.2	26.9	32.8	38.1	36.6	33.4	33.3	34.5	a
Single-state	93.6	93.4	90.9	88.8	89.4	90.1	90.9	88.3	89.8
Single-employer	72.5	71.1	65.0	59.8	61.6	64.8	65.1	63.3	a
Multi-employer	21.1	22.3	25.9	29.0	27.8	25.3	25.8	25.0	a
Multi-state	6.4	6.6	9.1	11.2	10.6	9.9	9.1	11.7	10.2
Single-employer	2.3	2.0	2.2	2.1	1.8	1.8	1.5	2.1	a
Multi-employer	4.1	4.6	6.9	9.1	8.8	8.1	7.6	9.5	a

a. Not available.

Source: Bureau of Old-Age and Survivors Insurance.

Although it is not very clear to what extent this correlation is due to the shifts of workers between agriculture and covered industries, it suggests that continuity of industrial employment increases as one moves from less industrialized to more industrialized states.

Change of Employer

From a fourth to a third of the workers covered by OASI work for more than one employer during a year. The proportion of "multi-employer" workers declines in bad years and rises when jobs go begging. The proportion of covered workers employed during a year in more than one state (multi-state workers) varies in the same direction: from 6.4 per cent in 1939 it rose to 11.2 per cent in 1942 and declined to 9.1 per cent in 1945. (See Table 161.)

Multi-employer and multi-state workers do not represent the whole turnover group in the labor force. Many persons who shift during the year from covered to noncovered pursuits or are in the labor force for only part of the year are reported as single-employer workers in the OASI records. On the other hand, not all persons who change employers or move from one state to another during the year belong to the floating group on the fringe of the labor force. Some of them simply move from less attractive or temporary jobs to better permanent positions. Such shifts are probably most frequent among young workers. Mature workers who are in jobs that represent about the best they can expect from their abilities and background have little reason to change jobs and are the last to be laid off when a firm reduces its personnel.

Annual earnings of multi-employer workers lag slightly behind those of single-employer workers, but multi-state workers earn, on the

TABLE 162

AVERAGE ANNUAL WAGE CREDITS OF WORKERS UNDER OASI, BY PATTERN OF CHANGE OF JOB, 1939–1947 [a]

Pattern of Change of Job	1939	1940	1941	1942	1943	1944	1945	1946	1947
Total	$ 881	$ 926	$1,014	$1,127	$1,289	$1,369	$1,328	$1,394	$1,571
Single-employer	936	1,006	1,081	1,167	1,335	1,431	1,340	1,431	b
Multi-employer	720	711	871	1,063	1,208	1,244	1,283	1,280	b
Single-state	874	926	1,003	1,107	1,276	1,363	1,311	1,369	1,570
Single-employer	925	999	1,068	1,149	1,319	1,417	1,326	1,412	b
Multi-employer	700	694	838	1,021	1,179	1,225	1,276	1,261	b
Multi-state	981	926	1,106	1,284	1,399	1,423	1,415	1,452	1,572
Single-employer	1,269	1,243	1,459	1,670	1,879	1,949	1,940	1,998	b
Multi-employer	819	791	994	1,195	1,300	1,305	1,307	1,330	b

a. In 1939, all earnings; since 1940, only earnings up to $3,000 a year.
b. Not available.

Source: Bureau of Old-Age and Survivors Insurance.

TABLE 163

PERCENTAGE DISTRIBUTION OF WORKERS WITH WAGE CREDITS UNDER OASI, BY NUMBER OF EMPLOYERS, 1944

Number of Employers	Total	Sex: Men	Sex: Women	Race: White	Race: Negro
Total ...	100.0	100.0	100.0	100.0	100.0
1	66.6	65.5	68.3	67.9	54.8
2	19.1	18.5	19.8	18.7	21.6
3	7.4	7.6	7.0	7.0	10.3
4	3.3	3.6	2.7	3.0	5.5
5	1.6	1.9	1.2	1.4	3.0
6	0.9	1.1	0.5	0.8	1.8
7	0.5	0.6	0.3	0.4	1.1
8	0.3	0.4	0.1	0.3	0.6
9 or more.	0.5	0.7	0.2	0.4	1.3

Source: Bureau of Old-Age and Survivors Insurance.

TABLE 164

PERCENTAGE OF WORKERS UNDER 25 YEARS OF AGE AMONG PERSONS WITH WAGE CREDITS UNDER OASI, BY NUMBER OF EMPLOYERS, 1944 [a]

Number of Employers	Men	Women
1	16.4	33.9
2	24.7	45.8
3	29.2	51.1
4	30.7	53.1
5 or more..........	29.0	53.5

a. Only workers who shifted from one employer subject to the program to another such firm are recorded in these statistics as multi-employer workers. This group does not include persons who shifted between covered and non-covered pursuits or entered or left the labor market. Two-employer workers, as defined in the insurance data, have had one change of employer during the calendar year; three-employer workers, two changes, and so forth.

Source: Bureau of Old-Age and Survivors Insurance.

average, more than single-state workers (see Table 162); the latter difference is due partly to the fact that the single-state group is heavily loaded with persons who were in covered employment for only a short time during the year. The highest average annual earnings are recorded for multi-state, single-employer workers, that is, persons who are employed by concerns that operate several plants in different states. In attachment to the job, this is probably the most stable section of the labor force.

The proportion of multi-employer workers is higher among men than among women — in 1944, 34.5 per cent for men and 31.7 per cent for women. The same is true of multi-state workers, represented by 9.9 per cent of the men and 7.8 per cent of the women in 1945.

The group of multi-employer workers includes persons who worked for only two firms during the year and those who changed jobs many times. Persons who worked for three or more employers represented 16 per cent of the men and 12 per cent of the women in covered jobs in 1944. For both sexes, the ratio was 13.3 per cent among white workers and 23.6 per cent among Negroes. (See Table 163.)

The proportion of young persons is appreciably larger among multi-employer workers than among single-employer workers. (See Table 164 and Appendix Table 81.)

The distribution of workers by the number of employers for whom they worked during the year 1944 shows that there were about 650 changes of employer per 1,000 employees: 191 workers out of 1,000 had one change each; 74 had 2 changes each or a total of 148 changes; 33 had 3 changes each or a total of 99; 16 had 4 changes each or a total of 64; 9 accounted for 45 changes; 5 for 30 changes; 3 for 21 changes; and 5 for more than 40, say 50, changes. Nearly half of all changes were accounted for by the 71 workers (out of 1,000) who worked for 4 or more employers (that is, had 3 or more changes) during the year.[12] (See Table 165.) This indicates that about half the changes of employer within the coverage of OASI were concentrated in a comparatively small group of workers, while the other half were spread over a much larger group. Still broader is the section of the working force involved in other types of shifts in employment (ins and outs, shifts between agricultural and nonagricultural pursuits, and so forth).

TABLE 165

PERCENTAGE DISTRIBUTION OF WORKERS WITH WAGE CREDITS UNDER OASI AND OF CHANGES OF EMPLOYER, BY NUMBER OF EMPLOYERS EACH WORKER HAD IN 1944

Number of Employers	Distribution of Workers	Distribution of Changes
Total	100.0	100.0
1	66.6	0.0
2	19.1	29.5
3	7.4	22.8
4	3.3	15.3
5	1.6	9.9
6	0.9	6.9
7	0.5	4.6
8	0.3	3.2
9 or more.........	0.5	7.7

Source: Table 163.

Change of Industry

When a worker is laid off or quits voluntarily, does he look for a new job with another firm

12. This pattern of change of employer is characteristic of a period with exceptionally high turnover of the labor force. (Cf. Table 157.) Under normal conditions, the proportion of persons who work for three or more employers during one year is likely to be smaller than in 1944, and those who make fewer changes, larger.

in the same industry or does he seek an opening in another industry? In other words, how strong is a worker's attachment to an industry as compared with his attachment to an employer? [13]

Little is known about the pattern of shifts of workers from occupation to occupation and from industry to industry. There is evidence of a socio-occupational "ladder," that is, a gradual shift of workers from lower to higher positions, in agriculture as well as in industry.[14] Many farmers and farm laborers shift to urban pursuits in winter. It is evident also that extensive shifts of labor from one industry to another took place during the industrial mobilization for World War II and the demobilization. Only scattered data are available, however, on the pattern of change of industry as compared with change of employer.

On the one hand, it seems natural for a worker to look for a job in the field of his experience and training. On the other hand, when an industry reduces personnel, the laid-off workers must look for jobs elsewhere; likewise, a man who quits his job because of dissatisfaction with work conditions may be inclined to seek work in another industry.

In 1944 nearly a third of the workers covered by old-age and survivors insurance shifted between industries. (See Appendix Table 92.) Data for 1944 are not very typical, since they refer to a year of war economy. This year, however, was more typical of a full-employment economy than any other year from 1940 to 1946.

Among 46.3 million employees in covered employment in 1944, 33.4 per cent were recorded as multi-employer workers and 30 per cent as multi-industry workers, that is, as persons who worked during the year in more than one industrial branch.[15]

TABLE 166

PERCENTAGE OF MULTI-EMPLOYER AND MULTI-INDUSTRY WORKERS AMONG PERSONS WITH WAGE CREDITS UNDER OASI, BY INDUSTRY DIVISION, 1944 AND 1947

Industry Division in Which Worker Was Last Employed	Percentage of Multi-employer Workers		Percentage of Multi-industry Workers	
	1944	1947	1944	1947
All industries	33.4	a	30.0	26.2
Mining	31.6	a	23.1	22.3
Construction	56.9	a	51.6	49.6
Manufacturing	28.5	a	26.1	23.7
Transportation, communication and other public utilities	38.5	a	33.9	26.7
Trade	37.2	a	32.7	25.8
Finance, insurance, etc.	29.4	a	26.5	20.2
Service industries	39.8	a	34.7	21.7

a. Not available.

Source: Bureau of Old-Age and Survivors Insurance.

The proportion of multi-employer and multi-industry workers (following the classification in Appendix Table 92) varied from approximately 25 per cent in manufacturing, mining and finance to more than 50 per cent in construction. (See Table 166.) Even with reservation for the exceptional conditions of the wartime economy, experience in 1944 seems to show that a worker's attachment to his industry is not much stronger than his attachment to his particular employer.

CONTINUITY OF EMPLOYMENT

In 1950 some 73 million persons may have been engaged — at least temporarily — in work for remuneration or profit.[16] Some of these worked regularly — although not always continuously — year after year; others worked regularly one year and had only irregular employment in the following year; still others were always on the fringe of the labor force.

Perhaps the best over-all measurement of continuity of employment in our economic system is the distribution of the working population by work experience in terms of the number of years and quarters of work. Such a distribution of a very large sector of the population is provided by the continuous work history sample of OASI, for the period from 1937 through 1948. According to this source, less

13. Cf. pp. 353–54.

14. W. S. Woytinsky, *Labor in the United States — Basic Statistics for Social Security,* Committee on Social Security, Social Science Research Council, Washington, 1938, pp. 52 ff. Cf. Chapter 27.

15. In some cases workers may have worked in more than one industry without changing employers — when, for example, a concern operated plants in different industries or shifted to a new line of production. Other workers may have worked in different industries within the same industrial branch. The number of changes of industry branch depends partly on the method of classifying industrial establishments by branch: it declines if branches are set broadly so that they include a large number and a great variety of establishments. In this case a very broad — so-called two-digit — classification is used. A shift within such a branch (for example, from insurance business to banking, from a beauty shop to a hotel, from a shipyard to an automobile factory) is not counted as a change of industry.

16. See pp. 315–16.

than 10 per cent of the men and only 3 per cent of the women who had wage credits in covered industries at any time during these twelve years were employed — for even a day — in each of the forty-eight calendar quarters. The proportion of those employed in covered industries forty-five to forty-eight quarters was 15 per cent for men and 5 per cent for women; the proportion of those employed more than forty quarters was 19 per cent for men and just under 7 per cent for women. At the other extreme, 27 per cent of the men and 41 per cent of the women worked in covered industries eight quarters or less. (See Table 167.)

To some extent the small proportion of workers with wage credits in all elapsed calendar quarters is due to the fact that many workers employed in covered industries either had reached working age after 1937 or had retired from gainful work before the end of 1948. These members of the labor force are largely excluded if the analysis is narrowed down to those workers who were 45–64 years of age in 1948. In this group, 35 per cent of the men and 14 per cent of the women had wage credits for forty-one to forty-eight calendar quarters and 20 per cent of the men and 39 per cent of the women had credits for not more than eight quarters.

The median number of quarters of employment in covered industry was nineteen for all male workers, out of the possible forty-eight. For women the median was twelve quarters. For men who were 45–64 years old in 1948, the median was twenty-nine, and for women in the same age group, thirteen. The highest fourth of the workers, those with the greatest number of quarters with wage credits, worked for the following number of calendar quarters:

All men	36 or more
All women	22
Men aged 45–64 years.	46
Women aged 45–64 years. .	28

TABLE 167

Percentage Distribution, by Number of Quarters in Covered Employment, of Workers with Wage Credits under OASI at Some Time in 1937–1948

Quarters Employed	All Workers		Aged 45–64		Quarters Employed	All Workers		Aged 45–64	
	Men	Women	Men	Women		Men	Women	Men	Women
1–4. . . .	16.88	26.10	12.80	26.46	25–28. . . .	5.86	5.44	5.83	5.38
1.	5.72	8.63	4.16	9.57	25.	1.52	1.58	1.50	1.68
2.	4.35	7.17	3.20	7.18	26.	1.47	1.49	1.45	1.43
3.	3.60	5.53	2.90	5.30	27.	1.42	1.25	1.38	1.16
4.	3.21	4.77	2.54	4.41	28.	1.43	1.12	1.50	1.11
5–8. . . .	10.52	15.04	7.56	12.78	29–32. . . .	5.45	3.72	5.50	3.88
5.	2.77	4.17	2.11	3.71	29.	1.36	1.02	1.34	1.04
6.	2.71	3.93	1.92	3.30	30.	1.39	0.99	1.44	1.02
7.	2.53	3.55	1.81	2.89	31.	1.36	0.92	1.34	0.96
8.	2.51	3.39	1.72	2.88	32.	1.34	0.79	1.38	0.86
9–12. . . .	9.44	12.08	6.12	9.70	33–36. . . .	5.13	2.74	5.37	3.21
9.	2.41	3.27	1.62	2.69	33.	1.27	0.75	1.28	0.82
10.	2.39	3.10	1.51	2.43	34.	1.25	0.69	1.25	0.78
11.	2.32	2.94	1.50	2.37	35.	1.27	0.65	1.31	0.76
12.	2.32	2.77	1.49	2.21	36.	1.34	0.65	1.53	0.85
13–16. . . .	8.79	9.99	5.83	7.62	37–40. . . .	4.41	2.11	4.96	2.59
13.	2.27	2.67	1.46	2.09	37.	1.17	0.59	1.26	0.69
14.	2.23	2.53	1.53	1.96	38.	1.11	0.52	1.25	0.61
15.	2.15	2.42	1.42	1.78	39.	1.04	0.52	1.18	0.65
16.	2.14	2.37	1.42	1.79	40.	1.09	0.48	1.27	0.64
17–20. . . .	7.70	8.46	5.26	6.97	41–44. . . .	4.21	1.84	5.90	2.87
17.	2.02	2.23	1.32	1.78	41.	0.98	0.48	1.25	0.67
18.	1.97	2.18	1.32	1.73	42.	1.01	0.45	1.35	0.68
19.	1.89	2.06	1.30	1.75	43.	1.05	0.45	1.50	0.74
20.	1.82	1.99	1.32	1.71	44.	1.17	0.46	1.80	0.78
21–24. . . .	6.56	7.40	5.51	7.05	45–48. . . .	15.05	5.12	29.39	11.47
21.	1.73	1.98	1.34	1.72	45.	1.15	0.51	1.83	0.83
22.	1.64	1.95	1.33	1.85	46.	1.49	0.59	2.49	1.08
23.	1.61	1.82	1.41	1.72	47.	2.43	0.94	4.48	2.04
24.	1.58	1.65	1.43	1.76	48.	9.98	3.08	20.59	7.52

Source: Computed from *Handbook of Old-Age and Survivors Insurance Statistics,* Employment, Wages and Insurance Status of Workers in Covered Employment, 1948, Social Security Administration, Federal Security Agency, Baltimore, 1951, pp. 11–12.

At the other extreme, the lowest fourth, those with the least steady employment in covered industry, had wage credits in the following number of calendar quarters:

All men *	8 or less
All women *	4
Men aged 45–64 years	12
Women aged 45–64 years	4

* Includes young workers who were not in the labor force at the inauguration of the OASI program.

It is true that the period includes three years of heavy unemployment and four years of the war economy. Under more normal conditions, whatever our idea of normality, employment would probably be less irregular. It is true also that a quarter without employment in covered industry does not necessarily mean interruption in gainful work. The labor force includes farmers and farm laborers who work only temporarily in covered jobs, and persons who shift between private and public employment, wage work and self-employment, work in service industries and domestic service, and other pursuits excluded from the OASI system.

With allowance for all these, however, there is no doubt that continuous employment in nonagricultural establishments through many years, say a decade, is not the general rule for either men or women, but rather the exception.

Individual industries are not equally affected by the fluidity of the labor force, but the shifting of workers among industries makes it rather difficult to measure the relative stability of employment in each industry by means of the number of quarters in covered employment.

Chapter 32

UNEMPLOYMENT: ITS COMPOSITION AND MEASUREMENT *

Unemployment in the United States never fell below 400,000 during World War II. Despite the siphoning-off of 12 million men and women into the armed forces and the tremendous demand for labor, some people who were willing and able to work remained without jobs. The paradoxical situation of unemployment in the face of a national labor shortage was convincing evidence that some unemployment is inevitable in a modern industrial society.

Broadly speaking, unemployment may be attributed to two types of causes: changes in the day-to-day demand for and supply of labor, and changes in the general level of economic activity. Unemployment of the first type plays an important role in the operation of our economic system. The "unemployment problem," however, is essentially the problem of unemployment of the second type, that is, mass unemployment accompanying a drastic decline in the level of economic activity.[1]

The Concept of Unemployment

Perhaps the most widely accepted concept of unemployment in this country is that defining the unemployed as those who are *able and willing to work but unable to find suitable employment.* This definition does not, of course, make it possible automatically to classify everyone as either unemployed or not unemployed. It leaves wide open the problem of determining a person's ability and willingness to work and the type of employment suitable for him. It also leaves open the problem of classifying those who have some work but want more, seasonal workers in that fuzzy period between the "season" and the "off season," self-employed persons whose source of income is gradually drying up, and others. These, however, are essentially questions about the fringes of unemployment; the general concept provides a sufficiently clear basis for classifying the great bulk of the population by employment status.[2]

The Unemployed and the Nonworkers

The criterion of being both *able* and *willing* to work distinguishes the unemployed from nonworkers. Nonworkers are, by definition, persons outside the labor force. They include people engaged in keeping house or attending school, the retired and disabled, people in institutions, and others not engaged in economic pursuits. Close to the border line between workers and nonworkers, however, are some whom it is extremely difficult to distinguish from the unemployed. The inactive job-seekers, the so-called unemployables, the casual workers or floaters, the housewives or students who would take a job under certain restricted conditions, those who want only part-time work — no hard and fast line can be drawn to separate such groups into nonworkers and unemployed workers.

Whether a person is unemployable or unemployed frequently depends on economic and psychological circumstances. The marginal worker who has no chance of being hired during a depression may become a member of the labor force during a labor shortage. The casual worker suddenly finding himself in a lucrative, interesting job may decide to stay put. The housewife in search of part-time work may find the kind of full-time job that justifies hiring a full-time maid; or the student, for a similar reason, may switch from day to evening school.

Because of the fluidity of the labor market and the labor force, individuals frequently are in process of shifting from one status to another. The process may be so gradual that the person himself cannot tell when he moves over the border line. As time passes, for example, the

* By Thomas C. Fichandler.

1. See also Chapters 23, 24 and 25.

2. For a general discussion of problems in labor force classification see Louis J. Ducoff and Margaret Jarman Hagood, *Labor Force Definition and Measurement,* Bulletin No. 56, Social Science Research Council, New York, 1947, pp. 14 ff.

long-time unemployed have a smaller and smaller chance of regaining employment; eventually they may have no chance at all and, to all intents and purposes, cease to be part of the labor force. Some of the inactive job-seekers — people who are not actively seeking work, because they believe none is available for them — also fall into this category.

The almost imperceptible drift from one category to another makes measurement of the exact volume of unemployment extremely difficult, but it does not vitiate the general concept. In theory, at least, individuals do cross the border line between unemployment and nonworker status at some point, although the point itself shifts with changes in the economic climate.

The Unemployed and the Employed

Although most employed workers are easily distinguished from the unemployed, it is so difficult to classify some groups that there have been frequent suggestions for setting up a third labor force category intermediate between employment and unemployment. This category would include people who have jobs but are not at work, those who are employed less than full time, and some of the self-employed.

People with jobs but not at work make up a fairly heterogeneous group, with varying degrees of attachment to their jobs. At one extreme the group includes those who are not at work because they are on vacation or because their work has been interrupted by bad weather or some other factor and some who are not at work because of illness.[3] At the other extreme are new entrants into the labor force who are waiting to report to a job already promised. In between are laid-off workers with specific instructions to return to work after a short, definite period.

The main reason against viewing these borderline cases as unemployed workers is that they are not seeking work and therefore are not competing for available jobs. It might well be argued, however, that those who cannot work because of illness ought to be considered as neither employed nor unemployed, but as temporarily out of the labor force. It might also be argued that those temporarily laid off and waiting to return to their old jobs or to report to new jobs should be counted as unemployed since, temporarily at least, they do not participate in producing the nation's goods and services.

These proposed solutions raise their own problems, however. If a worker on vacation is not in the labor force, who would remain in the labor force on Sundays and holidays? If people temporarily disabled because of sickness are nonworkers, how classify employees entitled to sick leave and drawing salary during their disability? Such difficulties are likely to prevent hard and fast distinctions between employment and unemployment. A twilight zone, of people who for some purposes are best viewed as employed and for others as unemployed, appears inevitable.

The partially employed are people who work substantially fewer hours in a week than those on the normal, full-time schedule. There would be little point to considering as unemployed the part-time worker who is not available for full-time work. The situation for those who would like more work is less clear; they are in the ambiguous state of being both partially employed and partially unemployed at the same time. They can be thrown into one group or the other only on a fairly arbitrary basis.

Less important numerically than any of the other groups, but equally difficult to define, are the self-employed in periods when they have little or no earnings. The lawyer who has no clients or the storekeeper with no paying customers is almost always considered employed unless he has begun to seek other work. Since his shift from employment to unemployment is well-nigh impossible to spot before he takes this obvious step, a small amount of unemployment from this source is certain to go uncounted.

Despite all these difficulties, the concept of unemployment described above does separate out from the rest of the population most people who clearly want but do not have jobs.

Composition of Unemployment

During prosperity the unemployed fall into half a dozen separate categories. During depressions all these groups are dwarfed by the numbers of persons unemployed as a result of the decline in economic activity and demand for labor.

3. People who are without jobs and are not seeking work because of temporary illness are counted as unemployed by the Census Bureau. Most people disabled because of illness are considered nonworkers.

Unemployment in Prosperity

A major type of unemployment during prosperity is so-called transitional or turnover unemployment — brief unemployment occurring between jobs. Prosperity is a particularly good time, from the worker's point of view, to try to find a better job. Many take advantage of such a time to quit their jobs and shop around for higher-paying, more suitable work. In 1943, for example, quits accounted for more than two thirds of all the separations from jobs in manufacturing industries and were almost four times as frequent as layoffs.[4]

Business reorganizations, slumps in individual firms and industries, and even business failures occur in the best of times. Layoffs accompany these contractions, but expanding sections of the economy readily absorb the workers affected. When total unemployment runs around 3 million, transitional unemployment probably amounts to about half a million.

Labor Force Entrants

Under all economic conditions there are workers newly entering the labor force or re-entering the labor market after a considerable interruption due to sickness, military service or, in the case of women, family responsibilities. Some of these people go directly from a nonworker status to employment; many, however, enter or re-enter the labor force through unemployment. The boy or girl who leaves school to go to work generally must spend some weeks applying for jobs. Moreover, the new worker normally undergoes an adjustment period during which he shifts jobs at least once before settling down to steady employment. The volume of unemployment of these new entrants and re-entrants, and their unemployment in the initial adjustment period, varies with the season. It probably averages half a million a year, about the same as transitional unemployment.

Marginal Workers

Marginal workers provide another source of unemployment. These are the less adaptable, less efficient workers who are hired during severe labor shortages and let out when the need for labor slackens. The group includes many older workers whose attachment to the labor force has grown more and more tenuous and who are passing through unemployment on the way to nonworker status. It also includes handicapped workers, housewives and students who are available only for limited types of jobs or for certain hours of the day.

The amount of this type of unemployment varies widely with the season and with business conditions. It may shrink to almost zero in a period of exceptional labor shortage and expand to several million during a long and severe depression.

Seasonal Unemployment

Weather and custom give rise to seasonal unemployment — another type of unemployment that occurs in prosperity as well as in depression. Seasonal changes affect unemployment both directly and indirectly.[5]

Not all workers separated from seasonal employment suffer seasonal unemployment. There is considerable dovetailing of employment opportunities in different industries — some of it planned, but most merely fortuitous. Migratory workers, for example, move with the seasons, harvesting first one crop then another. The resort employee greets the summer in Maine and the winter in Florida.

Moreover, some seasonal unemployment is prevented by business planning. Some goods salable only during a limited season can be produced for stock the year around; some businesses have added lines or have expanded their markets to fill in the seasonal slack. Although more undoubtedly can be done in this direction, seasonal unemployment can hardly ever be completely eliminated — especially among workers normally attached to such industries as agriculture, construction and lumbering, where weather conditions largely determine the feasibility of work.

Technological Unemployment

Technological unemployment, the loss of jobs that accompanies the introduction of new machines and new methods of operation, is part of the cost of industrial progress. The relationship of technological progress and unemployment is sometimes immediately apparent. The growing use of diesel engines on railroads, for example, is raising the problem of technological unemployment for locomotive firemen and for

4. See p. 385.

5. See pp. 317–21 and pp. 336–41.

machinists, who were needed for frequent repairs to steam locomotives. The spread of self-service retail stores clearly tends to reduce the need for salesclerks.

Not all the replacement of men by machines is so obvious. For the most part, new machinery is introduced gradually and in expanding industries where the introduction of labor-saving devices appears to cause little or no unemployment. Often a firm that has introduced new machinery reduces its manpower without layoffs, simply by canceling jobs vacated in the course of normal turnover. Major technological changes may be introduced during a large-scale shutdown, when their impact on the demand for labor takes the form of reduced hirings rather than layoffs.

Changes in industrial methods that cost some workers their jobs may lead to an equal or a greater volume of new jobs for other workers. Inventions like the airplane, motion pictures and radio, while hurting some established industries, led to the development of vast new fields. Despite the salutary effect of such changes on the whole economy, they may inflict long spells of unemployment on displaced workers, particularly those with specialized skills and experience.

Technological unemployment, hard to distinguish and even harder to measure, occurs in all phases of the business cycle.

Irregular Employment

Even among regular workers who have the same jobs week after week, some unemployment arises from the irregularity of employment within the week. While clerical, supervisory and other salaried workers are usually hired on a weekly basis, most workers are paid by the hour or piece and rarely are guaranteed a minimum number of hours of work a week. When no work is available because of insufficient orders, changes in production plans, lack of materials or breakdown of machines, workers become partially unemployed even if they remain on the payroll of the firm.

This type of unemployment — often called underemployment — is more prevalent in hard times than during a general labor shortage. It is common in declining industries and regions from which the excess labor supply has not yet been drained, and especially in industries and occupations in which jobs are irregular and casual, such as longshoring and entertaining.

Unemployment in Depression

When business declines, another and more important source of unemployment is added to those present in good times — reduction in jobs. Unemployment from this source is called cyclical unemployment.

For unemployment to remain at prosperity levels, the number of jobs must grow enough each year to match the normal growth of the labor force. When the number falls during a business decline, unemployment rises by more than the drop in employment. During such periods, the entrance of new workers into the labor force appears to be partially discouraged by the shortage of jobs. Offsetting this, however, is the "forced" entrance of members of families in which the family head is unemployed. A very rough measure of the over-all development during the last depression is given by the American Federation of Labor, which has estimated that between 1929 and 1933, when about 11.3 million jobs disappeared, unemployment rose by 13.1 million.[6]

Although cyclical unemployment is all-pervasive, affecting every part of the nation's economy, its impact on different groups of industries is decidedly uneven. The industries that suffer most in a major depression are the so-called "heavy" industries; consumer and service industries fare relatively much better.[7]

The volume of cyclical unemployment depends entirely upon the severity of the depression. While unemployment in prosperity may be set at about 2 or 3 million, cyclical unemployment reached about 10 or 11 million, according to most estimates, at the depth of the depression of the 1930's.

These figures relate to total unemployment and do not take account of underemployment. Underemployment, present even during prosperous times, increases considerably in bad times when the work week is cut, work-sharing plans are introduced, and irregular employment is increased at the expense of regular employment.

Measurement of Unemployment

The current statistical measurement of unemployment in the United States began as recently as 1940. For the preceding decade we have

6. *American Federationist,* January 1936, pp. 66 and 71.

7. See pp. 331–36.

TABLE 168

ESTIMATED UNEMPLOYMENT, 1900–1929

Year	Number Unemployed, in Thousands	Percentage of Labor Force	Year	Number Unemployed, in Thousands	Percentage of Labor Force	Year	Number Unemployed, in Thousands	Percentage of Labor Force
1900......	1,647	5.7	1910......	553	1.5	1920......	558	1.3
1901......	1,721	5.7	1911......	1,571	4.1	1921......	4,754	11.2
1902......	500	1.6	1912......	920	2.4	1922......	2,917	6.8
1903......	1,523	4.8	1913......	1,018	2.6	1923......	749	1.7
1904......	1,430	4.4	1914......	2,214	5.6	1924......	2,034	4.6
1905......	621	1.8	1915......	2,355	5.9	1925......	817	1.8
1906......	— 143[a]	—	1916......	187	0.5	1926......	464	1.0
1907......	756	2.1	1917......	—1,933[a]	—	1927......	1,620	3.5
1908......	2,296	6.3	1918......	—3,099[a]	—	1928......	1,857	3.9
1909......	719	1.9	1919......	— 870[a]	—	1929......	429	0.9

a. Negative unemployment arises statistically from the fact that people not reckoned with as members of the labor force are drawn into the labor force during periods of increased labor demand.

Source: Conference Board Economic Record, National Industrial Conference Board, New York, March 1940, Table 1, p. 78.

only more or less controversial estimates based on employment statistics, the 1937 national census of unemployment, and a few local and state enumerations. Before 1930, censuses supplied only scattered data.

Unemployment Statistics before 1930

The decennial federal censuses of 1890, 1900 and 1910 collected data on the extent of unemployment of gainfully occupied persons during the previous year. These data were hardly reliable, because the respondents generally were unable to recall the facts accurately. Indeed, the replies to the 1910 unemployment query were so little regarded that they were not even tabulated.[8]

Several private agencies have published estimates of unemployment for early years. One of the best known is the series of the National Industrial Conference Board, prepared by subtracting estimated employment from the estimated number of gainful workers. Like all the early estimates, this series suffered, unavoidably, from lack of basic data and from questionable techniques. Since the unemployment estimates are derived from estimates of much larger magnitude — gainful workers and employment — a small error in these larger figures may yield a much greater relative error in the unemployment figures. (See Table 168.)

Estimates and Enumerations in the 1930's

The growth of unemployment into a critical national problem in the early 1930's brought a rush of enumerations and estimates. The first and most important enumeration during this period was the census of unemployment taken as part of the 1930 Census of Population. Although this census, unlike the earlier national canvasses, inquired into the individual's recent work history, its results were unsatisfactory.

It started with a count of persons who "usually work at a gainful occupation" but were not at work on the last regular working day before the census enumeration. People meeting this definition were divided into seven classes as follows: [9]

A. Out of a job, able to work and looking for a job.......	2,429,000
B. Having jobs but on layoff without pay, excluding those sick or voluntarily idle	759,000
C. Out of a job and unable to work	173,000
D. Having jobs but idle on account of sickness or disability	274,000
E. Out of a job and not looking for work	88,000
F. Having jobs but voluntarily idle without pay........	85,000
G. Having jobs and drawing pay, but not at work (on vacation, etc.)	82,000

The first two classes were defined as "unemployed." Although people in class B would not be considered as unemployed under the unemployment definition used by the Bureau of the Census in 1940 and in the "Monthly Re-

8. Florence Peterson, *Survey of Labor Economics,* Harper, New York, 1947, p. 135.

9. Fifteenth Census (1930), *Unemployment Bulletin, United States Summary, Unemployment Returns by Classes,* 1933, p. 84. Cf. W. S. Woytinsky, *Labor in the United States — Basic Statistics for Social Security,* Committee on Social Security, Social Science Research Council, Washington, 1938, pp. 148–49.

port on the Labor Force," it is generally agreed that the 1930 census understated the volume of unemployment. One sizable group of unemployed almost certainly missed were the new entrants into the labor force who had not had any work experience and in most cases were not considered as gainful workers.

A special census of unemployment, covering nineteen cities, was conducted in January 1931. The data from this source did not give national estimates directly, but they were used, together with the 1930 census figures, to derive new national unemployment estimates. Individual states undertook to count their own unemployed during this period — Massachusetts and Pennsylvania in 1934, Michigan in 1935, Rhode Island in 1936.

In 1937 the federal government conducted a voluntary registration of the unemployed by distributing postcards to every home and requesting the partially employed and the unemployed to fill them out and mail them in. Like all voluntary registrations, this gave highly unreliable results. Test checks in a few selected areas suggested a probable understatement of almost 30 per cent in the total unemployment figure. The checks were inconclusive, however, because business conditions changed rapidly between the time of the enumeration and the test checks.[10]

The inadequate 1930 census, the inaccurate 1937 registration, and the occasional state and city figures that appeared during the middle 1930's became the starting point for a series of unemployment estimates by various organizations and individuals. As a rule, the procedure was to start by adjusting the April 1930 unemployment figures and then to estimate the figures for other months by adding declines and subtracting increases in employment and by adding increases in the number of employables. Employment changes were estimated on the basis of Bureau of Labor Statistics indexes that were available for some industries only; where no indexes were available, the estimator had to use his judgment. Changes in the number of employables were derived from estimates of population changes or from the trends indicated by decennial censuses.[11]

10. Woytinsky, *op. cit.*, pp. 215–17.

11. Robert R. Nathan, "Estimates of Unemployment in the United States, 1929–1935," *International Labor Review,* January 1936, pp. 49–73.

TABLE 169

ESTIMATED UNEMPLOYMENT, 1929–1940

Year	Average Annual Number Unemployed, in Thousands	Percentage of Civilian Labor Force
1929	1,550	3.2
1930	4,340	8.7
1931	8,020	15.9
1932	12,060	23.6
1933	12,830	24.9
1934	11,340	21.7
1935	10,610	20.1
1936	9,030	16.9
1937	7,700	14.3
1938	10,390	19.0
1939	9,480	17.2
1940	8,120	14.6

Source: Handbook of Labor Statistics, 1947 edition, Bulletin No. 916, Bureau of Labor Statistics, 1948, Table A-12, p. 36.

With each estimator making his own adjustments and devising his own techniques, it is not surprising that estimates of unemployment during the decade before 1940 are inconsistent. For unemployment in the trough of the depression, for example, we can have our pick of estimates ranging from less than 12 million to more than 16 million. (See Appendix Table 93.) The only governmental estimates available for that time are those prepared by the Bureau of Labor Statistics. (See Table 169.)

Monthly Census Estimates

The 1940 census provided more accurate unemployment data than the earlier censuses. Also, the data were based on the new concept of "labor force," which the 1940 census substituted for the earlier concept of "gainful worker." The essential difference between the two approaches is in the time element. The gainful-worker concept had no definite time limit — a gainful worker was one who had either worked or sought work at some gainful occupation during an indefinite period of time and who believed, at the time of the enumeration, that work for pay or profit was his normal status. The labor force concept, on the other hand, relates to current activity. People are classified as in the labor force or out of it, as employed or unemployed, on the basis of what they were doing or what they considered to be their current status during the census week.[12] This

12. The week was chosen instead of the day because any particular day might be a holiday, a rest day, or otherwise atypical; the week was chosen instead of any longer period to avoid difficulties of forgetfulness and the necessity of determining how much work constituted employment. John D. Durand,

TABLE 170

ESTIMATED UNEMPLOYMENT, 1940–1950

Year	Average Annual Number Unemployed, in Thousands	Percentage of Civilian Labor Force
1940	8,120	14.6
1941	5,560	9.9
1942	2,660	4.7
1943	1,070	1.9
1944	670	1.2
1945	1,040	1.9
1946	2,270	3.9
1947	2,140	3.6
1948	2,060	3.4
1949	3,395	5.5
1950	3,142	5.0

Sources: Appendix Tables 64 and 94.

current-activity concept has been followed in the Census Bureau's "Monthly Report on the Labor Force," the present source of official monthly unemployment estimates.

These monthly estimates are derived from an enumeration of a scientifically selected sample of households. They are subject to a margin of error (the so-called sampling error) that can be determined mathematically and is insignificant in comparison with the errors in the earlier indirect estimates. At present, estimates are available only nationally and for a limited number of areas, but the same method can be used to develop estimates for any area desired, provided a sufficient number of households in that area are included in the sample.

According to these estimates, more than 8 million workers were unemployed on the average in 1940. Not until 1941, when the defense boom was under way, did unemployment really begin to decline significantly, and not until 1942, the first full war year, did it cease to be a problem. From then until the end of the war, the manpower problem was one of labor shortage, not of unemployment. With less than 2 million unemployed, the labor force lacked the elasticity needed to meet the rapid and varied changes in industrial activity. (See Table 170.)

Proper use of the monthly unemployment estimates requires a thorough understanding of exactly what they represent. The Bureau of the Census reports as unemployed those persons who did not work at all during the survey week and were looking for work or volunteered the information that they would have been looking for work except that (1) they were temporarily ill, (2) they expected to return to a job from which they had been laid off for an indefinite period, or (3) they believed no employment was available in their line of work or in the community.[13]

The Census estimates of unemployment have been criticized repeatedly as being too low because they are based on a too restrictive definition.[14] The groups most frequently suggested for inclusion with the unemployed are those on temporary layoff and those waiting to report to new positions.[15] There are strong arguments on both sides. On the one hand, classifying these groups as unemployed would violate the respondent's appraisal of his labor market status, since he apparently regards himself as having a job to which he is shortly to report. On the other hand, since an unemployment series ought to measure the labor force that is not utilized currently by the economic system, the unemployed should include those people who are involuntarily idle even though they have jobs.

The Census estimates have also been criticized for counting a sizable group of people as out of the labor force instead of as unemployed. These are persons who, although anxious for work, may not have sought it actively during the survey week. Unless such people volunteer information indicating they are really active job-

"Development of the Labor Force Concept, 1930–1940," in Louis J. Ducoff and Margaret Jarman Hagood, *Labor Force Definition and Measurement,* Bulletin No. 56, Social Science Research Council, New York, 1947, p. 89.

13. In accordance with this definition of unemployment and similar definitions of the labor force and employment, the Census Bureau publishes its estimates in the following form:

	August 6–12, 1950
Total noninstitutional population	110,924,000
Total labor force, including armed forces	66,204,000
Civilian labor force	64,867,000
Employed	62,367,000
At work	57,901,000
35 hours or more	50,005,000
15–34 hours	6,058,000
1–14 hours	1,840,000
With a job but not at work	4,469,000
Unemployed	2,500,000
Not in the labor force	44,718,000

See "Monthly Report on the Labor Force," *Current Population Reports,* Series P-57, No. 98, Bureau of the Census, September 8, 1950, p. 1.

14. Bruce Waybur and Russ Nixon, *National Unemployment Estimates,* United Electrical, Radio and Machine Workers of America (CIO), Washington, March 1949.

15. These groups, included in the "with a job but not at work" category, totaled 171,000 in the week of August 6–12, 1950.

seekers, they are assumed to have withdrawn from the labor force. Unquestionably, some unemployed are missed because the Census Bureau no longer (since July 1945) asks the so-called "inactive" job-seekers why they weren't looking for work during the survey week. It is felt, however, that such an inquiry would lead some people who actually are not in the labor force to rationalize their status in such a way that the enumerators would register them as unemployed workers, and that the resultant overstatement would be greater than the understatement resulting from the present approach.

A third criticism is that use of the week as the period for which employment status is determined results in some understatement of the volume of unemployment. Persons hired or fired during the survey week are counted as employed even if they had only one hour's work. Thus some short-run, turnover unemployment undoubtedly is missed by the Census series. Since approximately 100,000 jobs are terminated each day,[16] the total amount of turnover unemployment missed can run to half a million. It is a matter of opinion, however, whether these brief interruptions between jobs should be regarded as unemployment.

It is also argued that the underemployed should be viewed as unemployed. Many of those working less than 35 hours a week normally are on a reduced schedule and do not want more work. Some, however, do not have all the work they want. In the week of May 7–13, 1950, for example, the survey found an estimated 1.1 million persons who had worked less than 35 hours because of slack work, material shortages, job turnover and similar economic factors; another 1.1 million who had only part-time jobs wanted and could have accepted full-time employment.[17] The volume of underemployment should certainly be considered in evaluating the whole unemployment problem, but there are definite advantages to separating partial and total unemployment.

Although some of these problems are yet to be resolved, there is no doubt that the sampling approach of the "Monthly Report on the Labor Force" is the only feasible way to estimate unemployment on a current basis. Fortunately, the current surveys contain information that can be used for adjusting the official unemployment estimates to varying concepts and definitions of unemployment.

Unemployment Insurance Statistics

Data on claims filed for benefits under the state unemployment insurance programs, the veterans unemployment allowance program and the railroad unemployment insurance program provide a useful supplement to the unemployment estimates of the Bureau of the Census.[18] Two types of claims are important as unemployment indicators — initial claims and continued claims.

As a rule, a covered worker who becomes unemployed serves notice that he has lost his job by filing an initial claim, and then files a continued claim following each week (or other specified period) of unemployment. Theoretically, therefore, the number of initial claims

16. See p. 385.

17. "Full-Time and Part-Time Workers: May 1950," *Current Population Reports,* Series P-50, No. 26, Bureau of the Census, September 7, 1950, p. 1.

18. The Census unemployment estimates and the estimates of insured unemployment differ in coverage and in definition of unemployment. The coverage of the Census estimates is wider, but the estimates of insured unemployment include some people whom the Census series excludes, such as those with jobs but temporarily not working because of bad weather, temporary layoff or labor dispute, and those employed only part of the week. In addition, some claimants for unemployment benefits may not be considered as actively looking for work by the Census enumerators. Normally, the wider coverage of the Census series more than compensates for the difference in definition of unemployment, and the Census estimates of total unemployment generally exceed slightly the estimates of insured unemployment.

For a short period after the war, however, estimates of insured unemployment were higher than the Census estimates of total unemployment. More specifically, estimates of insured unemployment exceeded Census estimates for women and veterans. (See Loring Wood, "Statistical Data on Employment and Unemployment from Sources Other than Labor Force Surveys," in Ducoff and Hagood, *Labor Force Definition and Measurement,* p. 103.)

Many women who were drawn into employment during the war withdrew from work after their husbands were released from the armed forces. They filed claims for benefits but did not actively seek work. To the Census enumerator they were not unemployed, although in the eyes of unemployment insurance they were.

Similarly, the veterans readjustment allowance program envisaged a period during which the veteran would have an opportunity to look around for a good position rather than be forced to take the first one that came along. From the Census enumerator's viewpoint such a period represents temporary withdrawal from the labor force.

The inconsistencies between the two series immediately after the war highlight the difficulties of classifying the fluid, dynamic labor force into separate, distinct categories.

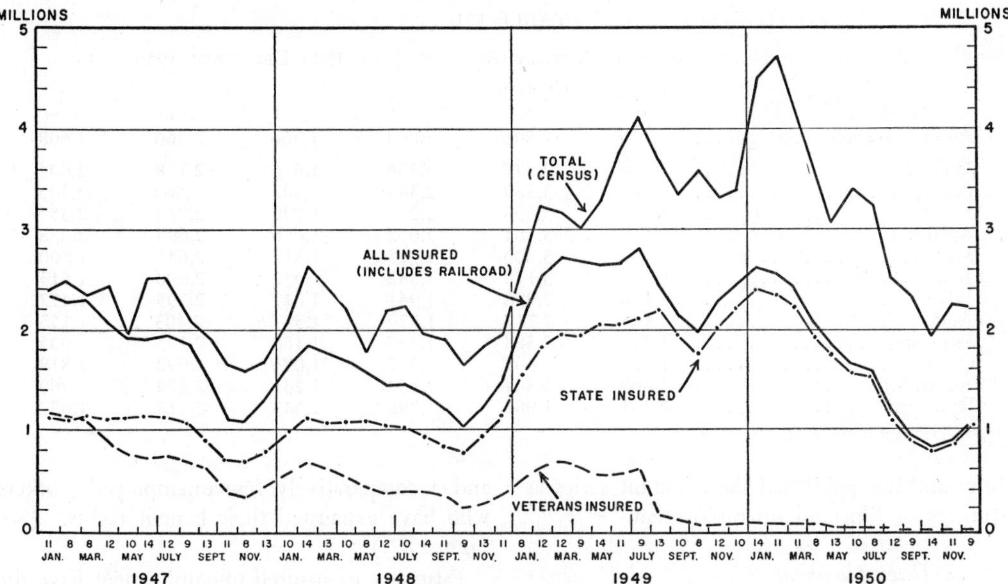

FIGURE 67. TOTAL AND INSURED UNEMPLOYMENT,[a] JANUARY 1947–DECEMBER 1950
(*Week Including the 8th of Each Month*)

a. The three insured unemployment series include partial and part-total unemployment.
Sources: Appendix Tables 94 and 95. Cf. Figure 39.

Total unemployment and insured unemployment followed the same general trends during 1947–1950, but the gap between the two series widened as the veterans program ran out, as more and more new workers entered the labor market, and as experienced workers remained unemployed for longer periods.

filed should indicate the emergence of new unemployment, while continued claims should reflect the volume of unemployment. The data are subject to certain limitations, however.

The unemployment insurance program does not cover agricultural workers, government workers, the self-employed, employees of nonprofit, religious and educational organizations, and, in many states, employees of small firms. New entrants as well as "additional" workers who enter the labor force during bad times are not eligible for benefits and do not file claims. Furthermore, not all workers in covered jobs meet the eligibility requirements of state laws, and claimants who remain out of work for long periods of time eventually exhaust their benefit rights and cease to file claims.

Data on claims, particularly initial claims, are affected by administrative factors. Not all states require the filing of an initial claim each time a worker begins a spell of unemployment. Many initial claims are filed by people already in the unemployed class when, owing to the passage of time, they move from one "benefit year"[19] into another. In some states, benefit years start on the same day for all claimants, so that anyone wishing to claim benefits in the new year, whether or not he is already unemployed, must file an initial claim. As a result, initial-claim statistics can be used as indicators of accessions to unemployment only if full attention is given to all the administrative niceties involved.

Continued-claims data, too, are distorted by administrative factors, though to a lesser degree. Ordinarily a worker must file a continued claim for each week of unemployment. In many states, and under the railroad program, one claim covers two weeks of unemployment. A timing problem arises from differences in the relationship between the date of filing a continued claim and the week of unemployment for which it is filed. To overcome both of these problems, the Bureau of Employment Security has adjusted the continued-claims series to eliminate the effects of time lag and biweekly

19. A twelve-month period set up for purposes of computing the claimant's benefit rights. A claimant is entitled to benefits in a benefit year (usually four calendar quarters) on the basis of his earnings during the base period (an earlier period of four calendar quarters).

TABLE 171

Insured Unemployment, Weekly Average, July 1945–December 1950

(*In Thousands*)

Month	1945	1946	1947	1948	1949	1950
Annual average	—	2,801	1,804	1,466	2,466	1,608
January	—	2,877	2,356	1,636	2,178	2,604
February	—	3,389	2,343	1,802	2,569	2,545
March	—	3,593	2,230	1,740	2,734	2,355
April	—	3,361	2,052	1,686	2,684	2,038
May	—	3,300	1,915	1,512	2,645	1,800
June	—	3,170	1,882	1,432	2,690	1,613
July	296	2,988	1,941	1,412	2,795	1,477
August	405	2,717	1,779	1,337	2,403	1,153
September	1,291	2,384	1,467	1,188	2,123	905
October	1,669	2,007	1,209	1,073	2,092	818
November	1,860	1,844	1,174	1,231	2,274	900
December	2,231	1,982	1,296	1,543	2,418	1,087

Source: Appendix Table 95.

filing, and has published the resultant series as estimates of "insured unemployment." [20]

Insured Unemployment

Insured unemployment may be defined as the unemployment of workers covered by any of the three programs during the period in which they remain eligible for benefits.[21] Except during and immediately after a major depression, when great numbers of the unemployed would not be protected by these programs, insured unemployment estimates should reflect a very large proportion of all unemployment. When employment is comparatively high, insured unemployment is an excellent indicator of economic trends, missing only the unemployment of new entrants and re-entrants into the labor market, the seasonal fluctuations in agricultural unemployment caught by the Census estimates, and a comparatively few unemployed workers who have exhausted their benefit rights. (See Figure 67.)

Estimates of insured unemployment have the great advantage of being readily available weekly on almost any geographic basis desired. They are, of course, more valuable for highly industrialized areas than for agricultural areas because of the difference in the proportion of workers covered by the programs.

These estimates, which are available from July 1945, reveal the rapid rise in unemployment immediately after the war. From less than 300,000 a week in July 1945, insured unemployment jumped to more than 3.5 million a week in March 1946. It dropped quickly from that peak and fluctuated between 1 and 2 million during most of 1947 and 1948. In the autumn of 1948 it began to rise, reaching a new peak, just below 3 million, in July 1949; since that time it has declined steadily, except for seasonal rises in the winters of 1949–1950 and 1950–1951. (See Table 171.)

20. Issued weekly in a mimeographed release, "Insured Unemployment during Week Ended ———."

21. Also included is their unemployment during the waiting period — usually one week at the start of a spell of unemployment.

CHAPTER 33

THE DISTRIBUTION OF UNEMPLOYMENT *

UNEMPLOYMENT IS NOT distributed evenly among the working population. It hits certain groups more than others, particularly during severe depressions, when some sections of the labor force become almost unemployable. But even during the high employment levels of recent years, when unemployment was too small to be nationally significant, it remained a real problem for some groups of people, certain limited areas and certain occupations.

Experience under unemployment insurance illustrates dramatically the uneven distribution of unemployment. The insurance records indicate that during the war and the early postwar years some persons suffered repeated spells of unemployment while the great majority of workers were regularly at work.

During 1943, for example, the total number of different persons filing claims for benefits equaled 4.2 per cent of average employment in industries covered by unemployment insurance. This figure would indicate that an employed person would have about four chances in a hundred of becoming unemployed once during the year. If the probability of losing a job were the same for all workers, whether or not they had been unemployed earlier in the year, the chance of becoming unemployed a second time for anyone who was rehired after a spell of unemployment would have to be less than four in a hundred — he necessarily would be exposed to the second job loss for less than a year.

Actually, however, 54.3 per cent of the persons who suffered unemployment during 1943 became unemployed more than once.[1] In other words, instead of less than 4 per cent, about half of the workers rehired after a spell of unemployment lost their jobs for the second time. Clearly, unemployment was concentrated in a comparatively small section of the labor force.

TABLE 172

PERCENTAGE OF RE-EMPLOYED WORKERS COVERED BY UNEMPLOYMENT INSURANCE WHO BECAME UNEMPLOYED AGAIN DURING THE YEAR, ASSUMED AND ACTUAL, 1943–1950

Year	Assuming Random Distribution of Unemployment [a]	Actual Experience [b]
1943	Less than 4.2	54.3
1944	" " 3.6	47.0
1945	" " 17.1	29.3
1946	" " 23.1	50.2
1947	" " 19.1	72.3
1948	" " 20.0	84.0
1949	" " 34.0	78.2
1950	" " 21.4	87.7

a. New claims filed as percentage of average annual covered employment. New claims are the first claims filed by a claimant during his benefit year.

b. Additional claims filed as percentage of new claims allowed. Additional claims are filed at the start of second or subsequent periods of unemployment during the claimant's benefit year. New claims allowed are those new claims for which sufficient wage credits are found to qualify the claimant for benefits.

Source: Based on data of the Bureau of Employment Security.

Almost the same pattern has been repeated every year since 1943. In each year the percentage of workers who became unemployed at least twice during the year has been much greater than it would have been if a random distribution is assumed. Only in 1945 and, to a lesser degree, 1946 was there any approach to randomness. In those years, however, the volume of one-time unemployment was exceptional because many workers were laid off dur-

* By Thomas C. Fichandler.

1. Computation of this and similar percentages is based on the assumption that all additional claims represent second periods of unemployment during the year. The ratio would be reduced to the extent that any such claims represented third or higher periods of unemployment. Such recurrent unemployment probably is small in volume, but to the extent that it does occur, it further illustrates the concentration of unemployment among relatively few workers.

In general, the ratio of additional claims filed to new claims allowed probably understates the rate of unemployment among re-employed workers over the long run, but may overstate it for a given year. The long-run understatement comes from the failure of some workers unemployed a second or third time during the year to file additional claims. The possibility of overstatement in a given year arises because claimants' benefit years do not necessarily coincide with the calendar year, and some additional claims filed during a given calendar year relate to new claims allowed during the preceding year. (Overstatement in one year usually means understatement in the preceding year.) The consistency with which this ratio exceeds the ratio of new claims to average employment year after year, however, is proof of the uneven distribution of unemployment. (For definitions of different types of claims, see footnotes to Table 172.)

TABLE 173

PERCENTAGE UNEMPLOYED AMONG GAINFUL WORKERS IN ALL OCCUPATIONS, IN NONAGRICULTURAL PURSUITS AND AMONG INDUSTRIAL WAGE AND SALARY WORKERS, BY SEX AND AGE, APRIL 1930

	All Occupations		Nonagricultural Pursuits		Nonagricultural Wage and Salary Workers	
Age Group	Men	Women	Men	Women	Men	Women
All ages, 10 years and over.	7.1	4.7	8.9	5.0	9.9	5.2
10–19	8.1	6.2	13.2	7.2	13.3	7.2
20–24	8.8	4.7	11.2	4.9	14.4	4.9
25–29	6.9	4.4	8.1	4.5	8.7	4.6
30–34	6.1	4.3	7.2	4.5	8.0	4.6
35–39	6.2	4.4	7.4	4.6	8.4	4.8
40–44	6.5	4.3	7.9	4.5	9.1	4.8
45–49	6.9	4.3	8.7	4.6	10.0	5.0
50–54	7.0	4.2	9.1	4.6	10.6	5.0
55–59	7.3	4.2	9.8	4.7	11.4	5.2
60–64	7.3	3.9	10.0	4.4	11.7	5.0
65 and over............	6.5	3.2	9.9	3.9	11.7	4.5

Sources: For all occupations, figures of the 1930 census (*Census of Unemployment,* Vol. II, 1933, p. 250); for nonagricultural pursuits and nonagricultural wage and salary workers, estimated rates from W. S. Woytinsky, *Three Aspects of Labor Dynamics,* Committee on Social Security, Social Science Research Council, Washington, 1942, p. 154.

ing the shift from wartime to peacetime production. (See Table 172.)

The differences in the incidence of unemployment among various groups of workers have serious implications. The greater the differences among groups of workers in their chance of becoming unemployed, the more complex is the problem of developing public policy designed to keep employment at a high level.

RELATION TO PERSONAL CHARACTERISTICS OF WORKERS

The rate of unemployment usually differs significantly by age and race but is very similar for male and female workers. The very young worker is more likely to be unemployed than are older members of the labor force; the nonwhite worker is jobless more frequently than the white worker. While women usually have a higher rate of unemployment than men, the difference is very slight and appears to be caused mainly by differences in the age distribution of the two groups.

Age Factor

The new entrant with no experience, and even the young worker who has worked for a short time, is generally less desirable from the employer's point of view than a seasoned member of the labor force. Young workers also lack seniority and, in layoffs based on that principle, are bound to be the first dropped and the last rehired. Moreover, the average young worker rarely finds his permanent industrial niche in his first or second job. It takes some time for him to find the job for which he is really suited, and, until he does, his chances of being fired or of quitting on his own initiative remain relatively high. He also is less likely to have responsibilities for family support. All these factors raise the rate of unemployment among young workers well above the rates for older workers.

Workers between 25 and 44 years of age usually have an appreciably lower rate of unemployment than the average worker. Above the 45-year mark the rate generally rises for each successive age group. Its upward trend is checked, however, by withdrawals of elderly workers who have lost their jobs and have little chance of finding a new one.

This pattern of unemployment according to age is much clearer among men than among women. Although the 1930 census failed to count new entrants into the labor force as unemployed, it shows a clear U-shaped curve of unemployment rates by age among male workers in nonagricultural pursuits, especially industrial wage and salary workers. (See Table 173.) The 1940 census showed a similar pattern, the only difference being that comparatively few persons who had reached 65 years of age were registered as unemployed. (See Table 174.) The same pattern appears in local censuses of unemployment in Philadelphia (1931, 1933 and 1938), Massachusetts (January 1934) and Pennsylvania (spring of 1934.)[2] It is also evident, though less clearly, in the

2. Richard A. Lester, *Economics of Labor,* Macmillan, New York, 1941, p. 375.

TABLE 174

PERCENTAGE UNEMPLOYED [a] AMONG PERSONS IN THE LABOR FORCE, BY SEX AND AGE, APRIL 1940

Age Group	Men	Women
All ages, 14 years and over...	14.8	13.3
16–17	33.3	40.8
18–19	32.6	30.1
20–24	20.3	15.0
25–34	12.6	8.9
35–44	11.6	9.8
45–54	13.1	11.1
55–59	15.1	12.1
60–64	15.4	11.4
65–74	10.7	6.9

a. Including persons on public emergency work.

Source: Sixteenth Census (1940), *Population,* Vol. III, Part 1, p. 19.

monthly labor force surveys of the Bureau of the Census.

All through the 1940's, except in 1946, the rate of unemployment was highest among very young workers; in 1946 it was highest in the group aged 20 to 24, which included many veterans without previous civilian work experience who were having some difficulty in finding satisfactory jobs. The relatively high unemployment rate for young workers has continued during good times and bad. In 1943, when 1.9 per cent of all workers were unemployed, 4.4 per cent of those under 20 had no jobs; in 1940, when the unemployment rate was 14.6 per cent for all workers, almost a third of the 14-to-19 age group were without work. (See Table 175.)

Between the early 1930's and the 1940's the rate of unemployment among workers who had reached age 65 dropped from above average to slightly below average. Three factors may have been responsible: changed business conditions, passage of the Social Security Act, and the new method of enumeration. During the mass unemployment of the early 1930's, older workers were unable to compete with those in the middle age brackets for the few available jobs and remained unemployed in large numbers; during the war and postwar years of high employment, opportunities for older workers were plentiful. Enactment of social security legislation, with its provisions for retirement at age 65, may have encouraged some unemployed older workers to withdraw from the labor force. The new Census Bureau approach emphasizes the individual's *current activity* in place of the older *usual activity;* older people, even if they regard their usual status to be that of a gainful worker, are likely more often than young people to feel themselves currently out of the labor force when a job ends.

TABLE 175

PERCENTAGE UNEMPLOYED AMONG PERSONS IN THE CIVILIAN LABOR FORCE, BY AGE, 1940–1950

Year	14 Years and Over	14–19 Years	20–24 Years	25–44 Years	45–64 Years	65 Years and Over
1940	14.6	31.4	18.8	11.3	13.4	8.8
1942	4.7	8.1	5.0	3.5	5.2	4.6
1943	1.9	4.4	2.3	1.3	1.6	2.5
1946	3.9	6.0	8.3	3.6	2.5	2.5
1947	3.6	8.3	6.5	2.8	2.4	2.4
1948	3.4	7.9	5.5	2.5	2.5	2.8
1949	5.5	11.7	8.7	4.4	4.2	4.6
1950	5.0	10.6	7.2	4.0	4.2	4.3

Source: Bureau of the Census. For distribution of the unemployed by sex and age, see Appendix Table 96.

TABLE 176

PERCENTAGE UNEMPLOYED AMONG PERSONS IN THE CIVILIAN LABOR FORCE, BY SEX, 1940–1950

Year	Total	Men	Women
1940	14.6	14.3	15.5
1941	9.9	9.5	11.2
1942	4.7	4.3	5.8
1943	1.9	1.5	2.7
1944	1.2	1.0	1.7
1945	1.9	1.8	2.2
1946	3.9	4.4	2.8
1947	3.6	3.7	3.2
1948	3.4	3.3	3.6
1949	5.5	5.5	5.4
1950	5.0	4.9	5.3

Source: Bureau of the Census. For distribution of the unemployed by sex and age, see Appendix Table 96.

Unemployment among Men and Women

Unemployment appears to be slightly more frequent among women than among men, as a rule. In the period 1940–1950 the rate of unemployment was higher for men only in 1946, 1947 and 1949. (See Table 176.) In 1949 the difference was small, and in 1946 and 1947 the unemployed were heavily weighted with young ex-servicemen. It would be incorrect to conclude that sex is a major determinant of risk of unemployment, for within a given age group unemployment is generally less severe among women than among men.

Of the forty possible comparisons of unemployment rates of men and women in the same age groups in Table 177, twenty-seven show a lower rate of unemployment among women. In 1940 and 1948 the rate for women was lower in three of the five age groups and in 1950 in four, yet it was higher for all women than for all men. This seeming paradox is explained by the higher proportion of young

TABLE 177

PERCENTAGE UNEMPLOYED AMONG PERSONS IN THE CIVILIAN LABOR FORCE, BY SEX AND AGE, 1940–1950

Sex and Year	14 Years and Over	14–19 Years	20–24 Years	25–44 Years	45–64 Years	65 Years and Over
Men						
1940..	14.3	32.8	18.1	11.1	13.4	10.0
1942..	4.3	7.2	4.3	2.9	5.2	5.0
1943..	1.5	4.0	2.5	0.8	1.4	2.6
1946..	4.4	7.1	11.6	4.1	2.6	2.6
1947..	3.7	9.1	7.9	2.8	2.5	2.5
1948..	3.3	8.2	6.3	2.3	2.5	3.0
1949..	5.5	12.0	9.8	4.3	4.4	4.8
1950..	4.9	10.8	7.7	3.7	4.2	4.6
Women						
1940..	15.5	27.8	19.9	11.8	13.3	2.1
1942..	5.8	9.7	5.9	5.0	5.3	2.5
1943..	2.7	4.8	2.2	2.3	2.3	2.0
1946..	2.8	4.6	1.5	2.3	2.0	2.2
1947..	3.2	7.1	4.0	2.6	2.1	1.8
1948..	3.6	7.3	4.2	3.1	2.6	1.9
1949..	5.4	11.1	6.7	4.8	3.6	3.6
1950..	5.3	10.3	6.3	4.7	4.1	3.1

Sources: Data for 1940 from Bureau of the Census; data for other years based on Appendix Table 96.

workers and new entrants among women workers than among men. In 1948, for example, 27.3 per cent of all women in the labor force were under 25 years of age, as compared with 17.9 per cent for men. Since the difference in unemployment rates is considerably greater between age groups than between the two sexes in the same age group, the heavier weighting of young age groups among women is sufficient to bring their average rate of unemployment above that for male workers.

Unemployment among White and Nonwhite Workers

The unemployment rate in the United States is consistently higher for nonwhite workers than for white workers. Fragmentary data for the last depression show rates for nonwhites well over double those for whites.[3] Even during labor shortages, as in the recent postwar years, the rate of unemployment among nonwhite workers was about one and a half times higher. (See Table 178.) The relationship between the rates for whites and nonwhites is approximately the same for both men and women.

Unemployment is higher among nonwhite than white workers in practically all sections of the country. In both March 1940 and April 1947 a larger proportion of nonwhite workers were unemployed in sixteen out of seventeen selected metropolitan districts, according to estimates of the Bureau of the Census. In 1940, unemployment of nonwhites was about twice as severe as for whites in most districts. In 1947, when unemployment was lower for both groups, the discrepancy between the rates was still greater; unemployment among nonwhites was more than three times that among whites in some metropolitan districts. (See Table 179.)

The nonwhite group is composed predomi-

3. Florence Peterson, *Survey of Labor Economics,* Harper, New York, 1947, p. 132.

TABLE 178

PERCENTAGE UNEMPLOYED AMONG PERSONS IN THE CIVILIAN LABOR FORCE, BY SEX AND COLOR, 1946–1950

Sex and Year	Total	White	Nonwhite
Both sexes			
1946..........	3.9	3.8	5.4
1947..........	3.6	3.3	5.4
1948..........	3.4	3.2	5.2
1949..........	5.5	5.2	8.2
1950..........	5.0	4.6	8.5
Men			
1946..........	4.4	4.2	6.1
1947..........	3.7	3.5	5.7
1948..........	3.3	3.1	5.1
1949..........	5.5	5.2	8.8
1950..........	4.9	4.5	8.9
Women			
1946..........	2.8	2.6	4.2
1947..........	3.2	3.0	4.7
1948..........	3.6	3.4	5.2
1949..........	5.4	5.2	7.2
1950..........	5.3	4.9	7.8

Source: Bureau of the Census.

TABLE 179

PERCENTAGE UNEMPLOYED AMONG PERSONS IN THE CIVILIAN LABOR FORCE, BY COLOR, SELECTED METROPOLITAN DISTRICTS, MARCH 1940 AND APRIL 1947

Metropolitan District	March 1940		April 1947	
	White	Nonwhite	White	Nonwhite
Atlanta, Georgia	10	16	2	4
Baltimore, Maryland	8	16	3	10
Birmingham, Alabama	12	20	4	5
Chicago, Illinois	13	35	2	7
Columbus, Ohio	11	27	2	5
Dallas, Texas	10	19	2	4
Detroit, Michigan	13	32	4	7
Memphis, Tennessee	10	19	4	7
New Orleans, Louisiana...	15	26	4	11
New York–northeastern New Jersey	16	26	7	12
New York division.....	17	26	8	13
New Jersey division.....	15	27	4	11
Norfolk–Portsmouth–Newport News, Virginia..	7	15	2	9
Philadelphia, Pennsylvania.	16	34	6	13
Pittsburgh, Pennsylvania ..	19	40	4	11
San Antonio, Texas.......	18	16	5	5
St. Louis, Missouri.......	13	33	3	10
Tulsa, Oklahoma	11	22	3	7
Washington, D.C.	7	17	2	6

Source: Bureau of the Census.

nantly of Negro workers, who are usually the last to be hired and the first to be fired. Outright discrimination against Negroes puts them at a competitive disadvantage even when they have the same skills and experience as white workers. Generally, however, Negroes come from lower-income families, have had less favorable educational opportunities, and have not been able to build up as extensive experience records as white workers. Even in the absence of discrimination, they are therefore more likely to remain without jobs than their white competitors. Customarily, also, a disproportionate number of jobs open to Negroes are in casual work, where unemployment is frequent; thus their employment turnover is much higher than that of white workers.

Rate of Unemployment in Various Areas, Industries and Occupations

The rate of unemployment in various sections of the country and in various industries and occupations is highly sensitive to changes in economic conditions, industrial and population shifts, technological changes and other factors.

The fragmentary data available do not permit generalizations concerning the distribution of unemployment by area and industry. They do prove, however, that considerable variation exists.

Unemployment in Various States

Unemployment insurance records for recent years indicate that the rate of unemployment in some states is from seven to ten times that in others. In 1947, for example, state-insured unemployment averaged 6.0 per cent of covered employment in California and 5.3 per cent in Washington, as compared with 0.8 per cent in South Dakota, Wisconsin and Wyoming. (See Table 180.) According to these figures, the Far West (California, Washington and Oregon) and the Northeast (Rhode Island, New York, New Jersey, Maine and Massachusetts) were experiencing sharper unemployment than any other sections of the country.

After the war the Pacific Coast states generally had the highest insured unemployment ratios of any states. (See Figure 68.) These states, more than any others, faced the problem of absorbing a tremendous population growth — the influx of war workers who decided to make the west coast their permanent home. The Pacific Coast states had the highest unemployment rates in relation to their labor force, but they also had the largest increases in employment over prewar years. Aside from this group, however, there has been little stability in the ranking of states.

Unemployment in Various Industries

Unemployment varies considerably from industry to industry. The average annual rate is

TABLE 180

Average Annual Insured Unemployment[a] as Percentage of Employment Covered by State Unemployment Insurance, by State, 1947

State and Rank	Per Cent	State and Rank	Per Cent	State and Rank	Per Cent
United States	3.2				
1. California	6.0	16. Alabama	3.0	33. Connecticut	2.0
2. Washington	5.3	17. West Virginia	3.0	34. South Carolina	1.9
3. Rhode Island	4.9	18. Arizona	2.8	35. Delaware	1.8
4. New York	4.8	19. Kentucky	2.8	36. District of Columbia	1.7
5. Tennessee	4.8	20. Louisiana	2.8	37. Virginia	1.6
6. New Jersey	4.5	21. Michigan	2.7	38. Minnesota	1.5
7. Maine	4.3	22. Mississippi	2.7	39. North Dakota	1.5
8. Massachusetts	4.0	23. Illinois	2.6	40. Indiana	1.4
9. Oregon	3.9	24. Pennsylvania	2.6	41. Texas	1.4
10. Oklahoma	3.8	25. Kansas	2.5	42. Iowa	1.3
11. Missouri	3.7	26. Georgia	2.4	43. Ohio	1.3
12. Florida	3.6	27. Vermont	2.3	44. Nebraska	1.2
13. Arkansas	3.3	28. Maryland	2.2	45. New Mexico	1.2
14. Nevada	3.2	29. Utah	2.2	46. Colorado	1.0
15. New Hampshire	3.2	30. Idaho	2.1	47. South Dakota	0.8
		31. Montana	2.1	48. Wisconsin	0.8
		32. North Carolina	2.1	49. Wyoming	0.8

a. Excludes veterans program and railroad unemployment insurance program; annual average derived from data for week including the 8th of each month.

Source: Bureau of Employment Security.

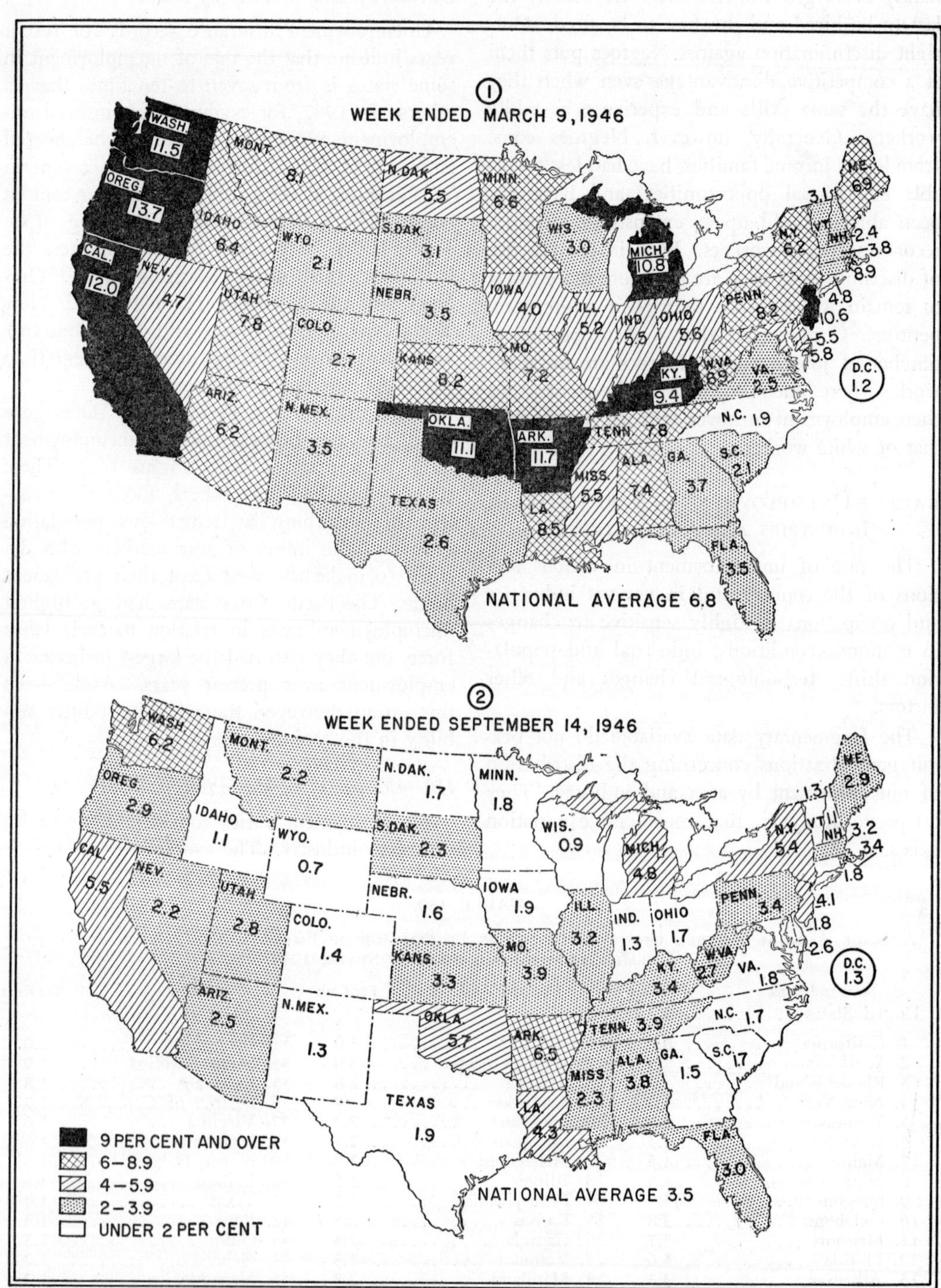

FIGURE 68. STATE INSURED UNEMPLOYMENT AS PERCENTAGE OF AVERAGE MONTHLY COVERED EMPLOYMENT, BY STATE, SELECTED WEEKS, 1946–1949

Continued on following pages

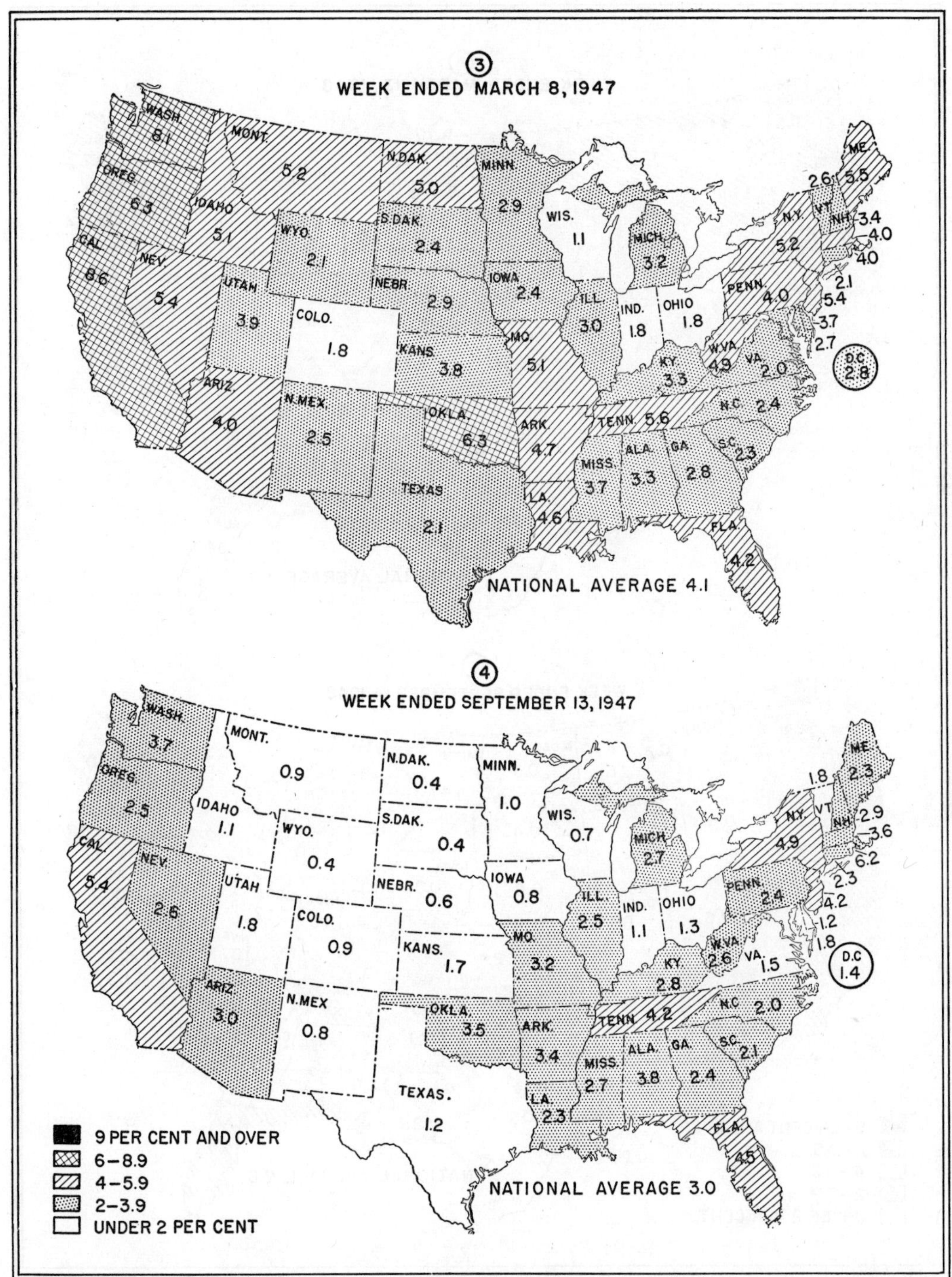

FIGURE 68.—*Continued*

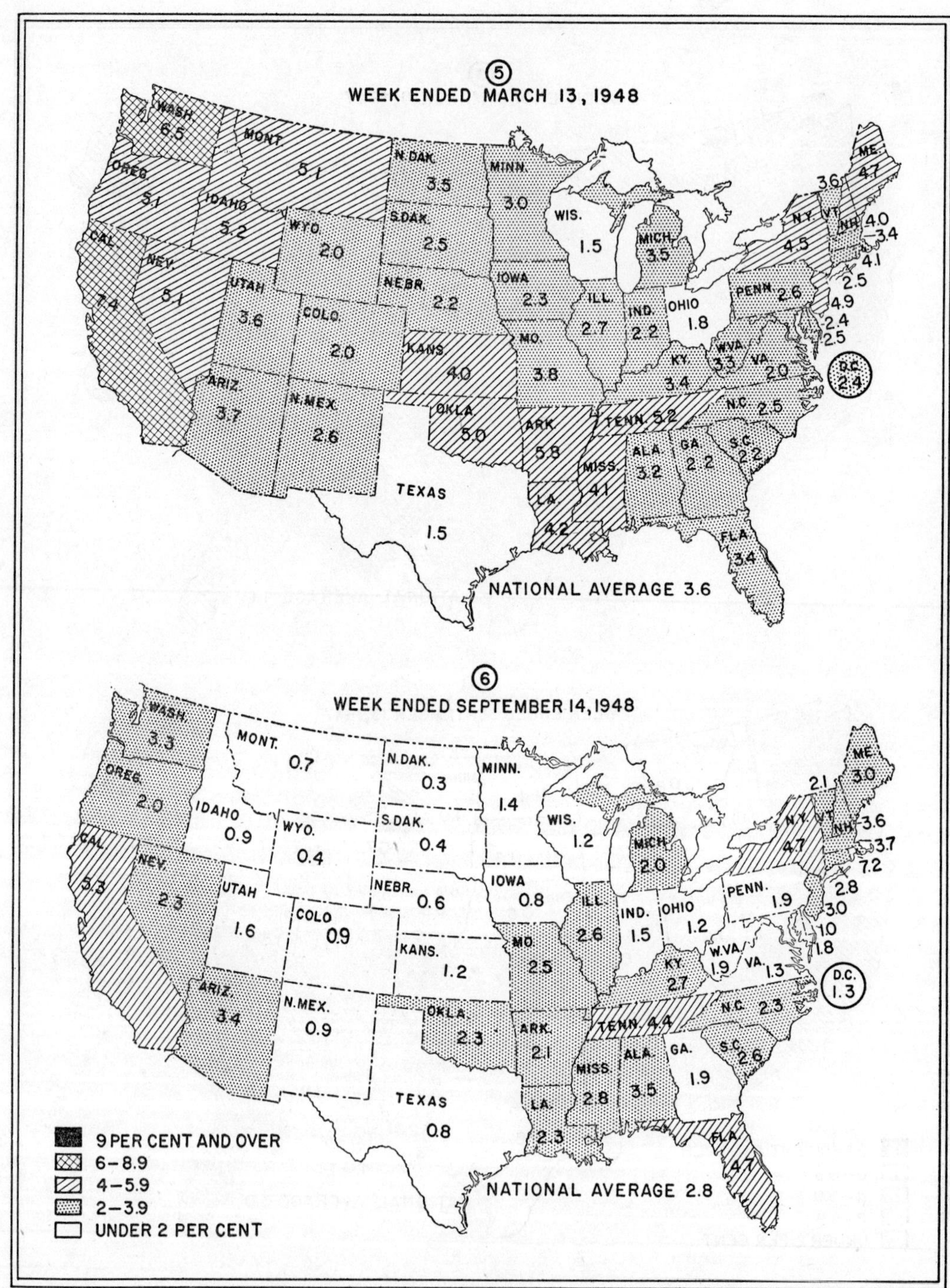

FIGURE 68.—*Continued*

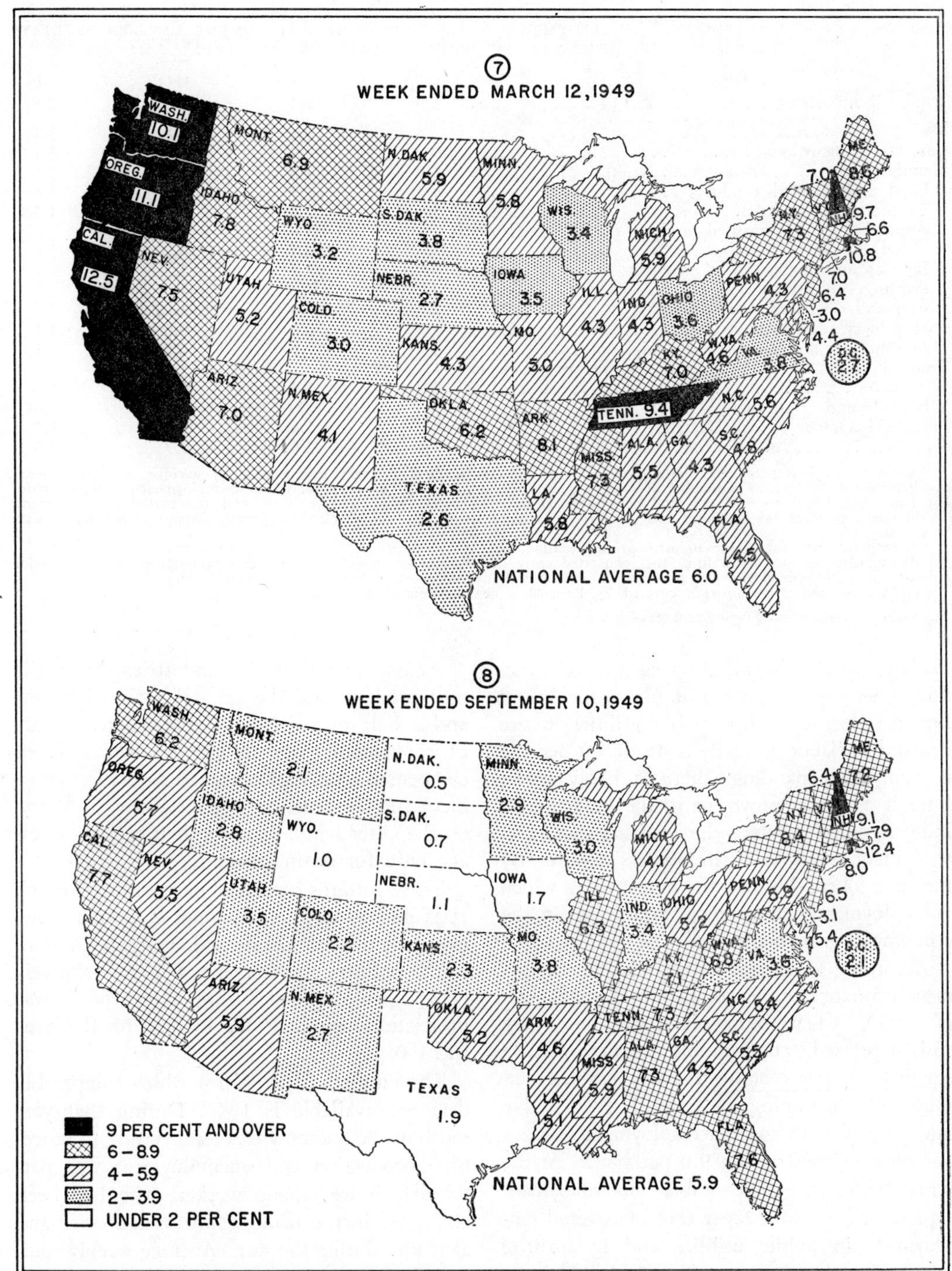

FIGURE 68. STATE INSURED UNEMPLOYMENT AS PERCENTAGE OF AVERAGE MONTHLY COVERED EMPLOYMENT, BY STATE, SELECTED WEEKS, 1946–1949

Source: Bureau of Employment Security. Average covered employment used for computation of percentage rates of unemployment in each state: for March and September 1946 and March 1947, the average in 1945; for September 1947 and March and September 1948, the average in 1946; for March 1949, the average in 1947; for September 1949, the average in 1948.

TABLE 181

AVERAGE ANNUAL COMPENSABLE UNEMPLOYMENT AS PERCENTAGE OF EMPLOYMENT COVERED BY STATE UNEMPLOYMENT INSURANCE, BY INDUSTRY, 1940–1942 AND 1946 [a]

Industry	1940 [b]	1941	1942	1946
Total, all industries	3.9	2.1	1.7	3.8
Mining	5.4	3.6	1.8	3.1
Contract construction	9.0	4.0	3.0	3.1
Manufacturing	3.9	1.8	1.7	5.5
Food and kindred products	4.1	2.7	2.0	3.6
Textile mill products	5.9	2.4	2.0	1.5
Apparel and other finished products made from fabrics and similar materials	7.7	4.4	4.2	3.8
Lumber and timber basic products	4.8	2.6	1.5	2.4
Printing, publishing and allied industries	2.7	1.7	1.6	1.3
Iron and steel and their products	2.4	0.8	1.0 [c]	4.4
Machinery, except electrical	1.5	0.6	0.6	4.1
Automobiles and automobile equipment	4.4	2.0	6.0 [d]	6.1
Transportation, communication and other public utilities [e]	2.2	1.4	1.1	1.7
Wholesale and retail trade	3.3	2.0	1.5	2.0
Finance, insurance and real estate	2.0	1.4	1.0	1.2
Services	3.9	2.6	1.7	2.3

a. Percentages computed by dividing the average weekly number of weeks compensated by average monthly covered employment for the year. The number of weeks compensated is the number of weeks for which unemployment benefits are paid. For 1940–1942, based on weeks of total unemployment only; for 1946, based on weeks of total and partial unemployment.

b. Based on data for 48 states and territories; excludes Kentucky, Maine and New Jersey, which did not report data by industry.

c. Includes data for major industry group — ordnance and accessories.

d. Includes data for some firms that converted early in 1942 to the manufacture of other products classified in major industry groups — ordnance and accessories and transportation equipment, except automobiles.

e. Excludes interstate railroads covered by Railroad Unemployment Insurance Act.

Source: Bureau of Employment Security.

likely to be high in industries such as construction, where operations are highly seasonal, and low in industries such as public utilities, where demand for labor normally is steady. When the economy is expanding, there is likely to be little if any unemployment in the heavy, basic industries that produce the machine tools and equipment essential to industrial growth. By the same token, those are the industries in which unemployment mounts most rapidly when the economy begins to contract.

According to records of the state unemployment insurance programs, in the average week of 1940, when economic conditions were still depressed, compensable unemployment [4] equaled 3.9 per cent of monthly covered employment. In mining the ratio of compensable unemployment to covered employment was 5.4 per cent, in construction 9.0 per cent.[5] At the other extreme, compensable unemployment represented 2.0 to 2.2 per cent of covered employment in public utilities and in finance, insurance and real estate. (See Table 181.)

4. Average weekly compensable unemployment equals total weeks for which unemployment insurance was paid during the year divided by 52.

5. Compensable unemployment is classified by industry on the basis of the claimant's industrial attachment when working.

Among manufacturing industries the textile mill products and the apparel groups had one and a half or twice their proportionate share of compensable unemployment. The ratio of compensable unemployment to covered employment for the nonelectrical machinery industry, on the other hand, was less than half the average ratio for all industries.

These patterns continued more or less through 1941 and 1942. An important exception, however, was the automobile and automobile equipment industry, which experienced relatively heavy unemployment during conversion to war production early in 1942. Its ratio for that year was 6.0 per cent.

The only other period for which comparable data are available is 1946. During that year much of the economy was reconverting to peacetime production and unemployment was particularly heavy among workers who had been employed in the manufacture of ordnance and airplanes during the war. Average weekly compensable unemployment of workers formerly employed in this industry group exceeded its average monthly covered employment. In the transportation equipment group (mainly shipbuilding and airplane production) compensable unemployment exceeded 40 per cent of current employment. Wholesale and retail trade, which normally accounts for its proportionate share of unemployment, had just about half its usual share in 1946.

Estimates based on Census data for all experienced workers — not merely those coming under the state unemployment insurance programs — show much the same variations in the rate of unemployment between industries as well as the quick change in the industrial distribution of unemployment that may accompany a shift in business conditions. (See Table 182.) In both 1948, a prosperous year, and 1949, when unemployment was on the rise, seasonal fluctuations accounted for much of the unemployment; in both years the rates were highest in the highly seasonal construction industry. But the decline in work opportunities during 1949 jumped the rates of unemployment in manufacturing and mining to more than double the 1948 rates. Although the rate of unemployment rose in all industries in 1949, since even seasonally unemployed workers could not find other jobs so easily, it remained relatively stable in agriculture and trade. Declining unemployment during 1950 shifted the distribution of unemployment back toward the 1948 pattern.

TABLE 182

Percentage Unemployed among Experienced Workers, by Industry Division and Class of Worker, 1948, 1949 and 1950[a]

Industry Division and Class of Worker	1948	1949	1950
All experienced workers	3.0	5.1	4.9
Agriculture, forestry and fishing			
Wage and salary workers	4.9	6.7	8.3
Self-employed workers	0.2	0.2	0.3
Unpaid family workers	0.3	0.3	0.3
Nonagricultural industries			
Wage and salary workers	3.7	6.2	5.4
Mining	2.3	8.0[b]	6.2
Construction	7.6	11.9	10.7
Manufacturing	3.5	7.2	5.6
Durable goods	3.4	7.4	5.2
Nondurable goods	3.6	6.9	6.0
Transportation, communication and other public utilities	3.0	5.2	4.1
Trade	4.3	5.8	5.8
Services	3.2	4.6	4.5
Government	2.0	2.9	2.8
Self-employed workers	1.0	1.6	1.8
Unpaid family workers	0.5	0.5	1.5

a. Unemployment rates for industry divisions represent the proportion of all civilian workers with a given industrial attachment who were unemployed. Industry refers to current job for the employed and to last full-time job for the unemployed. Excludes unemployed persons who never before had full-time civilian jobs.

b. October excluded in computing the rate for this industry; in October, during the coal mine work stoppage, a very large proportion of the miners were classified as unemployed because they were reported to be seeking substitute work. Inclusion of this group would have greatly exaggerated the typical situation during the rest of the year.

Source: "Annual Report on the Labor Force, 1950," *Current Population Reports,* Series P-50, No. 31, Bureau of the Census, March 9, 1951, Table I, p. 10.

Unemployment in Various Occupational Groups

Censuses of population show striking contrasts in the rate of unemployment by occupation — more specifically, by occupational level. In 1930, for example, the proportion of unemployed among unskilled and semiskilled workers was nearly three times as high as among professional persons and salaried employees. (See Table 183.)

Whether unemployment is high or low, laborers (primarily construction workers) lead all other occupational groups in extent of unemployment. Professional and semiprofessional workers, farmers and farm managers, and nonfarm proprietors, managers and officials, on the other hand, have the lowest rate of joblessness in all phases of the business cycle. (See Table 184.)

In March 1940, when 11.0 per cent of all experienced workers were without jobs, more than a third of all laborers (excluding those on farms or in mines) were unemployed. The rate of unemployment for this occupational group was more than twice that of its nearest competitor — craftsmen, foremen and kindred workers, among whom 15.1 per cent were jobless. Unemployment in professional and managerial ranks, ranging from 2.7 to 6.0 per cent, was only a fifth to a tenth as severe as among laborers.

In 1948, when business was good and only 3.0 per cent of all experienced workers were unemployed, 7.5 per cent of all nonfarm laborers were without jobs, as compared with less than 2 per cent of the professional workers, owners and managers. In 1949, unemployment among nonfarm laborers jumped to 12.6

TABLE 183

Percentage of Gainful Workers Unemployed among Nonagricultural Wage and Salary Workers, by Occupational Group, 1930

Occupational Group	Men	Women
Professional workers	4.4	2.4
Salaried employees	4.2	3.9
Skilled workers	11.0	5.4
Semiskilled workers	11.1	8.8
Unskilled workers	13.5	8.6

Sources: W. S. Woytinsky, *Labor in the United States — Basic Statistics for Social Security,* Committee on Social Security, Social Science Research Council, Washington, 1938, pp. 312–15; *idem, Three Aspects of Labor Dynamics,* Committee on Social Security, Social Science Research Council, Washington, 1942, p. 153.

TABLE 184

PERCENTAGE UNEMPLOYED, BY OCCUPATIONAL GROUP, MARCH 1940, AND ANNUAL AVERAGE IN 1948, 1949 AND 1950 [a]

Occupational Group	March 1940	Annual Average, 1948	Annual Average, 1949	Annual Average, 1950
All experienced workers [b]	11.0	3.0	5.1	4.9
Professional and semiprofessional workers	6.0	1.7	1.9	2.2
Farmers and farm managers	3.0	0.2	0.2	0.3
Proprietors, managers and officials, except farmers	2.7	1.0	1.5	1.6
Clerical and kindred workers	9.2	2.3	3.8	3.4
Salesmen and saleswomen	8.9	3.4	3.5	4.0
Craftsmen, foremen and kindred workers	15.1	2.9	5.9	5.6
Operatives and kindred workers	12.9	4.1	8.0	6.8
Domestic service workers	10.1	3.2	5.2	5.6
Service workers, except domestic	9.7	4.8	6.1	6.8
Farm laborers and foremen	12.5	2.3	3.9	5.0
Laborers, except farm and mine	33.6	7.5	12.6	11.7

a. Unemployment rates for occupational groups represent the proportion of all civilian workers with a given occupation who were unemployed. For the employed, occupation relates to the current job; for the unemployed, to their last full-time job; in 1940, persons on emergency relief work were also included with the unemployed and were classified according to their usual occupation. Occupation is currently tabulated only for the first month of each quarter, and the annual averages shown are weighted arithmetic means of the quarterly figures.

b. The unemployment rate for experienced workers is smaller than that for all civilian workers because it excludes "new workers," that is, unemployed persons who never before had full-time civilian jobs.

Sources: "Annual Report on the Labor Force, 1949," *Current Population Reports,* Series P-50, No. 19, Bureau of the Census, March 2, 1950, Table V, p. 8, and "Annual Report on the Labor Force, 1950," Series P-50, No. 31, March 9, 1951, Table H, p. 9.

per cent, while the rates for professional workers, owners and managers remained below 2 per cent, and 1950 repeated much the same pattern.

As a rule, the rate of unemployment is lowest among the self-employed and salaried workers, and highest among workers paid by the hour or day. For example, clerical and kindred workers, who are usually in the salaried class, were unemployed less frequently in the nonwar years of the 1940's than operatives and kindred workers, who usually work on an hourly or daily basis.

The combined effect of three adverse factors accounts for the relatively heavy rate of unemployment among nonfarm laborers. They lack specific skills; they are concentrated in the highly seasonal construction industry; and they are wage — as opposed to salaried — workers. The unemployment of the semiskilled operatives, who are essentially production workers, is related to the frictional and seasonal fluctuations of basic industry, where most of them work. The very low rate of unemployment among the self-employed is somewhat misleading, for many continue operating submarginal businesses instead of seeking other employment.

Within each of the major occupational groups listed in Table 184 the rate of unemployment varies considerably. Among male professional workers in 1940, for example, the rate was almost 40 per cent for actors but only 2.4 per cent for clergymen and 1.5 per cent for lawyers and judges. Among clerical and kindred workers it was less than one per cent for mail carriers and 11.5 per cent for messengers. Among craftsmen and skilled workers the ratio was 27.1 per cent for carpenters, 13.2 per cent for electricians, and only 3 per cent for factory foremen.[6]

DURATION OF UNEMPLOYMENT

Information on the number of workers without jobs gives only a one-dimensional picture of the impact of unemployment. A second important dimension is provided by data on the length of time people have been without work. Five million persons, each unemployed for two months, represent a different problem from 2 million unemployed for five months each. A short period of unemployment represents a loss in earnings to the worker and a temporary loss of productive work to society. Lengthy unemployment, however, puts a tremendous economic and psychological burden on those affected and may represent a permanent loss of productive skill because of long disuse.

If the unemployed were a completely homogeneous group, workers who lost their jobs would find new work in approximately the

6. *Statistical Abstract of the United States, 1949,* Bureau of the Census, 1949, Table 210, pp. 179 ff. Individuals on public emergency work counted as unemployed.

order in which they became unemployed. In that case, fewer people would be out of a job for 4 to 6 months than for 1 to 3 months; smaller still would be the number of people with 7 to 9 months and 10 to 12 months of unemployment, and so forth. Even with a fairly low monthly rate of reabsorption of the unemployed, the probability of a man's being unable to find a job during more than one year would be very slim.

The unemployed, however, are not a homogeneous group. Under conditions of mass unemployment, they definitely tend to separate into distinct classes. As widespread unemployment continues, more and more workers remain without jobs for very long periods. At different times during the 1930's, half or more of the unemployed had been without work for at least two years, according to surveys taken in a number of localities.[7]

In March 1940, when the Sixteenth Census was taken, 17.3 per cent of the unemployed for whom duration of unemployment was reported had been out of work for two years or more and 33.2 per cent for a year or more. (See Table 185.) The proportion of persons out of work for two years or more was particularly high (25 per cent or more of all the unemployed for whom duration of unemployment was reported) in coal mining, automobile manufacturing, manufacture of other transportation equipment, air transportation, railroads and banking. It was comparatively low in agriculture, the textile industries, water transportation, some branches of retail trade, and the service industries.[8]

Even in years when the economy was operating at very high levels, as in 1947 and 1948, some workers were without work for surprisingly long periods. On an average day in 1947, 7.5 per cent of the unemployed had been looking for work at least half a year; in 1948, 5.6 per cent were in the same situation. (See Table 186.)

Comparison of accession rates with unemployment in 1947 and 1948 suggests that if there were no differences among the unemployed, each separated worker would have had a 60 per cent chance of being re-employed dur-

7. Buffalo, New York; Bridgeport, Connecticut; Lincoln, Nebraska; Philadelphia, Pennsylvania; Massachusetts and Michigan. Lester, *op. cit.*, pp. 372–75.

8. Sixteenth Census (1940), *Population,* Vol. III, Part 1, pp. 283–84.

TABLE 185

PERCENTAGE DISTRIBUTION OF UNEMPLOYED PERSONS BY DURATION OF UNEMPLOYMENT, MARCH 30, 1940

Duration of Unemployment	Total	Men	Women
Noncumulated			
Total	100.0	100.0	100.0
Under 1 month	2.9	2.8	3.5
1 month	7.7	7.5	8.2
2 months	6.4	6.3	6.5
3 months	9.9	9.8	10.3
4 and 5 months	11.4	11.8	9.7
6–8 months	11.7	12.0	10.5
9–11 months	6.7	6.6	6.9
12–23 months	13.5	13.3	14.2
24–59 months	10.9	11.3	9.4
60 months or more	3.8	4.2	2.4
Not reported	15.2	14.3	18.5
Cumulated [a]			
Under 1 month	3.4	3.3	4.3
" 2 months	12.5	12.0	14.3
" 3 months	20.0	19.6	22.3
" 4 months	31.7	31.0	34.9
" 6 months	45.1	44.8	46.8
" 9 months	58.9	58.7	59.7
" 12 months	66.8	66.4	68.1
" 24 months	82.7	81.9	85.5
" 60 months	95.5	95.1	97.1
All reported	100.0	100.0	100.0

a. Excluding persons for whom duration of unemployment was not reported.

Source: Sixteenth Census (1940), *Population,* Vol. III, Part 1, pp. 14, 283 and 284.

TABLE 186

PERCENTAGE DISTRIBUTION OF UNEMPLOYED PERSONS BY DURATION OF UNEMPLOYMENT, ANNUAL AVERAGE, 1947–1950

Duration of Unemployment	1947	1948	1949	1950
Noncumulated				
Total	100.0	100.0	100.0	100.0
1 week or less	9.9	11.0	7.8	8.0
2 weeks	14.4	16.2	12.9	12.7
3 weeks	12.8	14.2	12.8	10.7
4 weeks	11.6	11.2	11.2	10.2
5–6 weeks	9.5	10.1	9.1	8.8
7–10 weeks	14.4	14.4	16.3	15.2
11–14 weeks	9.0	7.9	9.7	9.6
15–26 weeks	10.9	9.4	12.6	13.5
Over 26 weeks	7.7	5.6	7.6	11.4
Cumulated				
Under 2 weeks	9.9	11.0	7.8	8.0
" 3 weeks	24.3	27.2	20.7	20.7
" 3 weeks	37.1	41.4	33.5	31.4
" 5 weeks	48.7	52.6	44.7	41.6
" 7 weeks	58.2	62.7	53.8	50.4
" 11 weeks	72.6	77.1	70.1	65.6
" 15 weeks	81.6	85.0	79.8	75.2
26 weeks or less	92.5	94.4	92.4	88.7
Total	100.0	100.0	100.0	100.0

Sources: The following publications of the Bureau of the Census: *Current Population Reports:* "Annual Report on the Labor Force, 1948," Series P-50, No. 13, February 16, 1949, Table 12, p. 29; "Annual Report on the Labor Force, 1949," Series P-50, No. 19, March 2, 1950, Table 11, p. 22; "Annual Report on the Labor Force, 1950," Series P-50, No. 31, March 9, 1951, Table 11, p. 24.

ing the first month after separation, an 84 per cent chance of finding a job before the end of the second month, and a 94 per cent chance of returning to work before the end of the third month. Actually, the proportion of unemployed persons suffering comparatively long spells of unemployment was much higher than these average rates suggest.

The rise in unemployment during 1949 brought with it an increase in the length of unemployment. As is typical of a downswing in the business cycle, the contraction in job openings increased the average duration of unemployment from under nine weeks early in the year to over eleven weeks by the year's end.[9] The rise in unemployment duration continued into 1950, reaching a peak of over fourteen weeks in May. By the end of the year the drop in total unemployment had taken effect and the average was down to just over ten weeks.[10]

The debilitating effects of long unemployment eventually move many of the unemployed into the ranks of the unemployable. Students of the labor market have recognized the existence of two groups of unemployed at such times: the turnover unemployed, who have some chance of re-employment, and the hard-core unemployed, who have practically no chance of being re-employed under existing conditions.[11] The hard-core group is insignificant in prosperity, when it includes only a small group of marginal workers and some victims of technological unemployment,[12] but it increases in importance during a depression, especially when the slump lasts a year or longer. Under these conditions, when the labor force continues to grow, when labor turnover declines, and when most industries have practically no openings, most of the unemployed join the hard-core group.

9. "Annual Report on the Labor Force, 1949," *Current Population Reports,* Series P-50, No. 19, Bureau of the Census, March 2, 1950, Table 11, p. 22.

10. "Annual Report on the Labor Force, 1950," *Current Population Reports,* Series P-50, No. 31, Bureau of the Census, March 9, 1951, Table 11, p. 24.

11. W. S. Woytinsky, *Three Aspects of Labor Dynamics,* Committee on Social Security, Social Science Research Council, Washington, 1942, pp. 61 ff.

12. Cf. p. 396.

PART IV

WAGES AND EARNINGS

Chapter 34

THE FORMS OF WAGES *

THE TERM "WAGES" covers a variety of arrangements through which labor is compensated. The most important forms of wages are *basic wages,* which may be computed on the basis of either time or output, and *supplementary payments,* such as vacation pay, Christmas bonuses, shift differential pay, pensions and so on.[1] Relatively unimportant today are *payment in kind* and *tips.*[2]

BASIC WAGES: TIME PAYMENT

For the great majority of employees in this country, basic wages are computed on a time basis: so much an hour, a day, a week, a month or a year. For manual workers, rates are typically set by the hour or by the day; for white-collar and supervisory workers in private industry, by the week, the fortnight, the half month, the month or, less frequently, the year; for white-collar and supervisory workers in government, by the year. The length of the time period on which pay is based has often been regarded as some indication of the steadiness of employment, but in itself it has no necessary relation to job security. Hourly-paid workers with long seniority in industries that provide steady work may actually have more regular employment than some annually-paid white-collar workers.[3]

Payment on an hourly basis is probably somewhat more usual today than it was twenty years ago. Regulation of work hours and requirements of premium pay for overtime have made employers more conscious of the cost of "nonproductive" hours. Thus the 40-hour-week provisions of the Fair Labor Standards Act occasioned some transference of salaried workers, entitled to the overtime benefits, to hourly rates. It has also been common practice to transfer from the "salary roll" to the "hourly payroll" workers who have achieved collective bargaining rights, even when this change in status involves no change in overtime policy.

Time-Rate Systems

Time rates of both wages and salaries operate according to several systems. The most primitive — and it does not deserve to be called a "system" — is to pay different rates to different individuals without reference to any established method of fitting individuals into job categories. In contrast are the systems of job rates under which wage or salary scales are established for specific jobs, no matter who fills them, on the basis of job content rather than individual qualification.

Job-rate systems are of two basic types: the single- or flat-rate system and the rate-range system. Under the single-rate plan all workers in a classification are paid at the same wage or salary rate. In union contracts single rates are ordinarily designated as minimum rates to preserve the theoretical possibility of paying more to some or all workers — a situation that rarely occurs. Occasionally the so-called minimum rate may even be enforced as a maximum scale by agreement between management and union officials, in the effort to stabilize the labor force and restrict "labor pirating" by rival employers.

* By Philip Arnow, Bureau of Labor Statistics, U.S. Department of Labor. Opinions expressed here are those of the author and not necessarily of the agency with which he is associated.

1. Benefits provided by the government in such forms as unemployment compensation, old-age benefits, housing subsidies, veterans benefits and the like are normally excluded from the concept of "wages," although similar payments made by private employers are regarded as a part of wages. At this point the concept of wages becomes distinguishable from the concept of income only by virtue of the fact that wages, in whatever form paid or received, must be the product of an employer-employee relationship; income need not be.

2. For a somewhat different division, see the report of the International Labor Office, *Wages* (International Labor Conference, 31st session, San Francisco, 1948), Chapter 2, pp. 12–35.

3. Workers who are paid on an hourly or a daily basis (as well as those on an incentive basis where the incentive is computed on the basis of hourly or daily output) are usually referred to as "wage earners." Workers paid by the week or longer time interval are called "salary workers." This distinction has little meaning in the case of "salaried" workers whose salaries are reduced in short work weeks in proportion to the weekly or monthly salary.

Under the rate-range system, on the other hand, the individuals in a classification are paid at rates within the range between an established minimum and maximum.

The first system prevails for lower-skilled manual jobs, the second for manual jobs of greater skill and for most salaried jobs. The two systems may exist side by side in the same plant. Both are normally applicable to experienced workers; probationary and learner rates are usually lower than the flat rate or the minimum of the rate range. Where the probationary or learner period is of substantial duration under a flat-rate structure, it is often difficult to distinguish this type of system from a rate-range system.[4]

"Automatic Progression"

The existence and administration of rate ranges has long been a minor battleground in labor-management relations. Union officials, claiming that all workers in a single job classification are of substantially equal ability, and viewing a rate range as an opportunity for supervisory favoritism, have favored the single-rate structure. Management officials, pointing to wide differences of ability among workers and desiring to provide an incentive to improve performance, have favored the rate-range system with broad management power in its administration. Where management itself has instituted automatic systems of time progression from the bottom to the top of the range, as in the utilities, union officials have contended that the total time period, usually several years, is too long. During World War II, unions demanded elimination of ranges, or "automatic progression" from the minimum to the maximum of the range on a time basis not much longer than one year.

The result of these disputes was generally to preserve the status quo on the single-rate versus the rate-range issue. The National War Labor Board worked out two approaches to "automatic progression." The first was the policy of directing unions and management officials to agree on the criteria for intra-range increases, such as general ability, quality and quantity of performance. Once agreed on, these criteria were to be applied by management, subject to the union's right to appeal the decisions through the grievance procedure. A second approach, simpler in practice, was to make a portion of the wage-rate range automatic during a maximum period of about a year and to permit fairly free "merit" adjustments at the discretion of management over the rest of the range.[5]

Computing Working Time

The operation of a time-rate system requires definition of the period of time to which the wage rate is applicable. The period for which the worker is paid may or may not include all the time he actually spends on the job. Unions have generally urged that workers be paid for time spent in changing into work clothes, walking or riding on the employer's premises to the actual job site, and preparing tools or other equipment for the day's task, and in reversing these processes at the end of the day. While employers have agreed to such definitions of working time in many instances (sometimes by direction of the National War Labor Board or under the provisions of the Fair Labor Standards Act), they have pointed out that often they are paying workers for "nonproductive" time — for example, for the time that union stewards and other local officials spend on grievance matters or union business. As a result of changes in management practice, of collective bargaining settlements and of the enforcement of the overtime provisions of the Fair Labor Standards Act, the concept of compensable working time has been increasingly expanded.[6]

Basic Wages: Incentive Payments

About one fourth of all wage and salary earners in the country receive their basic wages through some form of incentive payment: piecework, bonus or commission.[7] Such is the common practice in several manufacturing indus-

4. For illustrations of collective bargaining provisions regarding wage schedules and their administration, see *General Wage Provisions,* Collective Bargaining Provisions Series, Bulletin No. 908.8, 1948, and *Wage Adjustment Plans,* Collective Bargaining Provisions Series, Bulletin No. 908.9, 1948, Bureau of Labor Statistics.

5. For a brief discussion of National War Labor Board experience with this problem, see the *Termination Report of the National War Labor Board,* 1948, Vol. I, pp. 274 ff.

6. For a discussion of one type of problem that has arisen in computing working time, see the Annual Report of the Administrator of the Wage and Hour and Public Contracts Divisions for 1948, pp. 61–71.

7. For statistics on the incidence of incentive plans among industrial workers, see the detailed industry wage survey reports of the Bureau of Labor Statistics.

tries — notably apparel, textiles, cigars, footwear, and some of the metalworking industries — where piecework or bonus payments are widespread; in the sales departments of retail and wholesale trade, where the commission method is common; and in the repair shops of the automotive-servicing industry. Practice is by no means uniform, however, even among plants making the same product. Among the major automobile producers, for example, Studebaker and Willys-Overland pay incentive wages to substantial proportions of their workers while the other well-known producers pay hourly rates.

No significant use of incentive pay is to be found in the transportation industries — railroads (except for certain mileage rates and shop incentives), steamship lines, local streetcar or bus systems, or local trucking; in any of the communications industries — radio, telephone, telegraph; or in the electric and gas utilities. In coal mining, where payment on the basis of tonnage produced once prevailed, the progress of mechanization has been accompanied by the substitution of day rates. Incentive payments have been virtually unknown in construction, banking, warehousing, the variety stores, the service trades, or in such manufacturing industries as baking, printing, tool-and-die production and chemicals. Incentive payments are not used in government-operated industrial establishments; in shipyards, for example, they have been banned by the federal law prohibiting the use of stopwatches. Few office workers are employed under incentive methods in any industry.

Requirements for an Incentive Plan

In order to establish an incentive plan it must be possible to measure output in homogeneous units. A further requirement is that there be a reasonable possibility that workers will maintain quality while increasing production. It is difficult, therefore, to work out appropriate incentives when workers are engaged on unpredictable assignments, when machines are so automatic that workers have no control over output, when a spur to production involves too many risks to the maintenance of quality or safety, or when methods of production and designs are changed frequently.

This is not to say that ingenious schemes cannot be worked out in difficult situations. In some establishments, incentives have been applied to assembly line operations where the speed of the line is controlled, to such "nonproduction" workers as sweepers, to the varied tasks of office workers, and even to fixed-speed operations where it is desired, not to increase production, but to maintain production at the very maximum or to improve quality.

When it has proved too difficult to work out direct incentives for particular groups of workers, incentive pay has frequently been based on the pay received by other groups. Thus maintenance and other nonproduction workers may be paid in relation to the incentive earnings of production workers. Bonuses for workers whose individual output cannot be measured directly are usually computed on a group basis, with each worker sharing equally or in proportion to his basic hourly rate.

In special and usually temporary circumstances, as in wartime production, plant-wide incentives have even been devised, based on over-all output in relation to man-hour expenditure.[8] Management and industrial engineers prefer, however, to use individual rather than group incentives wherever possible. The individual incentive is more direct and immediate, they feel, and offers less opportunity for internal friction.

A workable incentive-payment system involves more than the installation of an appropriate plan. Once installed, the plan must be maintained. The more difficult it is to devise an incentive-payment plan for a group of workers, the more difficult and costly will probably be its maintenance and its adjustment to changing conditions. Costs and engineering troubles have been obstacles to the further development of incentive methods in industry.

Types of Incentive Plans

The usual division of incentive-pay plans into three categories — piecework, bonus and commission — does not adequately reflect the great variety of specific plans that exist, frequently side by side in the same establishment. Even the simplest and most widespread of all the incentive plans, the piecework system, varies

8. See the *Termination Report of the National War Labor Board,* 1948, Vol. I, pp. 322 ff., and the opinion of the Board in the Grumman Aircraft Engineering Corporation case (No. 13–285, September 14, 1943).

widely from establishment to establishment in the method by which the piece rate is established, the existence or lack of a minimum-earnings guarantee, the method by which the guarantee is computed, the application of the piece price to the work of an individual or a group of workers. Under a simple piecework system, a single price is established for an entire finished piece of production, on the basis of experience, by the foreman or through collective bargaining. Substantially different are systems under which motion and time studies are made and past production records reviewed, or piece prices are established for each small segment of a finished article, or earnings are computed from many prices with a daily guarantee and a penalty for rejected production.

The variety among bonus systems is even greater. The pioneering ingenuity of Taylor, Halsey, Weir, Rowan, Gantt, Bedaux and others, together with the eclectic application of their systems by thousands of industrial engineers in the light of local problems, has produced almost as many different incentive plans as there are plants using incentive methods.

Standard Setting

One of the most important characteristics of any incentive method is the procedure by which the incentive-production standard is determined — whether the standard to be used for computing the price per piece, the standard task beyond which bonus will be paid, or time standards. As industrial processes have grown more complicated and work assignments have been further and further subdivided, the determination of standards has passed increasingly from the rough methods of personal estimating by an expert foreman to the procedures developed by industrial engineers. Careful study of methods, designed to establish the most efficient way of doing a job, is followed by repeated time studies of each element of movement that goes into a specific operation. After this measurement of the "objective factors" comes the elaborate process of "scientific" rate setting, which calls for evaluation of the "subjective factors," with due allowance for fatigue, time for changing tools, and so on.

One of the stated objectives of this procedure is to remove the setting of standards from the process of haggling over rates. A standard set by engineering methods, it is argued, reflects merely a standard level of production, unrelated to any specific wage rate. Whatever the general level of money wages, it can then be used as a base for determining an incentive rate and computing piece rates or bonus premium rates. The process of determining the money wage is entirely unrelated, except in one sense. It is generally held that an incentive plan may tend to aggravate existing inequities within a wage structure; it is urged, therefore, that internal alignment of basic hourly rates should precede their conversion to incentive rates.[9] In plants with incentive payments, production standards generally remain unchanged when there is a general increase in wage rates; piece prices and the premium bonus are merely recomputed. However, production standards can be tightened or loosened as a means of giving a wage increase or causing a wage reduction. This practice has also led to many wage disputes.

Most business executives agree that the basis for setting standards should be thoroughly explained to workers and trade-union officials. To some, this is purely salesmanship of a management plan; others believe that the basic principles of the plan can be covered by collective bargaining and spelled out in the contract, reserving to management the administration of the system and leaving to labor the established grievance procedure.[10]

Rewards for Increased Production

An equally significant characteristic of incentive plans is the extent to which they reward increased production. Under straight piecework, the worker is paid the same price for each unit of output no matter how many units he produces. Some bonus systems provide for extra pay above standard production in direct proportion to the additional output. In others, pay for output above the basic standard is less than proportionate to the increase in production. As nearly as can be ascertained, however, there has been a trend toward directly propor-

9. See Chapter 35 for a discussion of job evaluation.

10. For a fuller discussion of the attitudes of management and union engineers who have had extensive experience with the standard-setting problem, see Ralph Presgrave, *The Dynamics of Time Study,* 2d edition, McGraw-Hill, New York, 1945, and William Gomberg, *A Trade Union Analysis of Time Study,* Science Research Associates, New York, 1948.

tional, or point-for-point payment, under old as well as new plans.

Not all increases in production per worker under an incentive system are accounted for by the workers' individual efforts. Sometimes great increases are due to improvement of production methods or to an unusually long run in production of a particular item (as was the case with many standard types of footwear and apparel during World War II). Under such conditions, earnings can rise sharply while basic wage rates and incentive rates remain unchanged.

The problem of assigning the gain in earnings that results from such increased productivity can be approached in several ways. In some piecework industries it is common to permit most gains in productivity to accrue to the worker, but in most industries incentive rates are adjusted in such circumstances to re-establish the levels of earnings that prevailed before the changes occurred. Lump-sum bonuses are usually given to individual workers who have initiated improvements in methods of work that make possible a reduction of labor cost.

Guarantees of minimum earnings per hour, day or week under an incentive system protect the workers' interests in periods of intermittent work or machine breakdown, or when bottlenecks in production or shortages of materials are common. Either the base hourly rates payable for production at standard or a special set of "day rates" is used as the basis for computing the guarantees. Additional guarantees are usually provided for other special contingencies, such as experimental or repair work, or work on a new operation before an incentive rate is established; such guarantees are usually somewhere between the "day-rate" level and the normal level of incentive earnings. Some straight piecework plans have no guarantees at all.

Earnings under Incentive Plans

Job for job, incentive systems generally ensure higher earnings than time rates.[11] The difference varies from less than 10 per cent, when the incentive opportunity is relatively small, to more than 20 per cent. There are, of course, low-wage incentive plants in which earnings are below those prevailing in high-wage time-rate plants engaged in comparable work, and in some time-rate plants productive efficiency and expert supervision have made it possible to pay wages that compare favorably with those paid in establishments operating under incentive systems.

TABLE 187

UNIONS PREFER TIME PAYMENTS TO PIECE RATES

Questions: What type of wage system — time rates or piece rates — is most common among your membership? Which system do you think best?

Response	Total	Predominant Present Form of Wages: Time Rates	Piece Rates	Neither
Number of respondents	46	29	10	7
Attitude toward form of wages:				
Prefer time rates	32	26	4	2
Prefer piece rates	5	0	5	0
No opinion, or prefer another method	9	3	1	5

Source: W. S. Woytinsky and Associates, *Labor and Management Look at Collective Bargaining,* Twentieth Century Fund, New York, 1949, p. 158.

Union Attitudes toward Incentive Pay

Despite the immediate advantages that piecework and incentive plans promise to workers, these forms of payment have met with serious objections from labor unions. In many instances, union opposition is so strong that it prevents the spread of the incentive system; in others, the unions accept and even support the principle of piece payment provided piece rates are established in such a way as to eliminate the danger of speed-up practices and other abuses.

In the course of the canvass of views of labor and management leaders undertaken in connection with this survey,[12] union presidents were asked: "What type of wage system — time rates or piece rates — is most common among your membership? Which system do you think best?" Most of the respondents testified that time rates prevailed in their industries and that they considered this form of wages preferable to piece wages. (See Table 187.) The minority of union representatives expressed their preference for piece payment provided labor standards are protected.

There's no question but that piece work is best in our industry. It gives the worker the knowledge that

11. See p. 495.

12. W. S. Woytinsky and Associates, *Labor and Management Look at Collective Bargaining,* Twentieth Century Fund, New York, 1949.

TABLE 188

UNIONS WIDELY OPPOSE INCENTIVE-WAGE SYSTEMS

Questions: Do any of your members work under bonus or so-called incentive-wage systems? What do you think of such plans? What about group-production bonus plans?

Response	Incentive Systems of All Types			Group-Production Bonus		
		Union Members			Union Members	
	Number of Unions	Number, in Thousands	Percentage of Total	Number of Unions	Number, in Thousands	Percentage of Total
Number of respondents	51	11,423	100.0	42	8,465	100.0
Attitude toward incentive-wage systems:						
Favor	6	957	8.4	5	772	9.1
Favor conditionally	6	1,747	15.3	5	1,455	17.2
Oppose	33	6,444	56.4	26	4,546	53.7
Lead to exploitation, speed-up	12	3,754	32.9	5	1,127	13.3
Too complicated; lead to trouble	6	1,062	9.3	6	790	9.3
No reason given	15	1,628	14.3	15	2,629	31.1
No opinion	6	2,275	19.9	6	1,692	20.0

Source: W. S. Woytinsky and Associates, *Labor and Management Look at Collective Bargaining,* Twentieth Century Fund, New York, 1949, p. 165.

he doesn't have to be watched. It gives the employer exact knowledge of the cost. Our workers are reared in piecework, so there's no fear of speed-up.

I think for the good of the industry and the union the incentive system is the best, provided that it's operated with the consent of the union. The type of incentive plan we like is one that provides for human factors — rest periods and so on — where piece rates are not set so that you have to work every minute of the day to make the day's pay.

Much of the current trade-union opposition to piece payment stems from remembrance of abuses under the systems that existed fifteen or more years ago. Cumulative speed-up of machine and assembly line pace and the stretching out of work assignments to levels that tax human endurance, accompanied by rate cutting each time an advance in production results, are the usual charges leveled at the general idea of incentive payment. Added to these are the more general notions that competitive pitting of worker against worker may itself result in speed-up, and that workers, striving for maximum immediate earnings, will not always exercise reasonable self-interest in conserving their strength and health. Some union officials, however, accept the principle of piecework but are strongly opposed to "incentive" systems based on motion and time studies made by "efficiency" engineers or other systems that provide for rather complex methods of computing pay.

Despite prevailing union opposition, incentive plans are operated in some industries with the cooperation of local unions and to some extent with union supervision. Thus in the metal trades and in the automotive parts industry, international unions are decidedly opposed to incentive plans, but in many plants local unions accept them as a well-established institution.

A compromise between union opposition and management sponsorship of piece wages is sometimes worked out in a form known as "measured day work." Hourly rates are paid for production up to a certain level and an additional premium is paid when production reaches a stipulated higher point. This system may be applied on an individual or a group basis.

Bonus Plans

When voicing their opposition to "incentive" wage systems, most labor union leaders think of various bonus plans rather than of piece wages. In the aforementioned canvass of opinions, leaders of 51 unions were asked: "Do any of your members work under bonus or so-called incentive wage systems? What do you think of such plans? What about group-production bonus plans?" Only 6 respondents expressed themselves in favor of bonus plans without reservation; 6 approved them with explicit reservations, 33 were opposed and 6 had no opinion. (See Table 188.)

The reasons advanced against bonus plans are exemplified by the following answers:

An incentive plan is all right if it's fairly done. We are opposed to the incentive system, not because its idea is wrong, but because it offers so much chance for unfair manipulation. We've found that most employers use the incentive system to cut cost. They want to increase per man production and cut wages at the same time. And that is exploitation, pure and simple. If employers ever realize what incentive systems do to employer-employee relationships, they'd drop them. I guess these incentive rackets lead to more grievances than anything else. They pit the workers one against another until there's so much friction no one is the gainer and they all lose.

We don't like incentives, because they lead to grievances and to jealousy among the workers. In our industry, most of the plans are worked out on a group basis, but we still don't like them. However, they are not as bad as the individual bonus plans.

The way the incentive systems work is not good. We have to struggle along with them, but we're trying to tear them down. In every case, we feel incentives lead to discriminatory acts on the part of the employer, and they certainly lead to rackets. Group bonuses don't work any better than the individual plans.

The most emphatic views came from respondents who opposed incentives on the ground that the resulting speed-up injures the workers' health.

Incentive systems are aimed against the older workers. We know, and the employer knows, that people have a diminishing ability as they grow older. So if the incentive system gets working, first thing you know the employer will say that the older people can't keep up with the speed, and he'll want to fire them. And we feel that if a worker has worn himself out slaving for an employer, he deserves some consideration from that employer. So we won't let the incentive system get in. Group plans are less offensive than the individual type, but still we won't stand for them. We see no reason why the gambling by employers should have guaranteed returns.

It's my feeling that incentive plans are camouflaged forms of speed-up. No one has yet been able to measure what normal effort is. Yet all these plans attempt to do so. They're basically arbitrary; too much judgment is involved.

An incentive plan is bad no matter where or what it's in. It's bad all around—for the employer because every shortcut that can be devised will be used, whether it impairs the product or not. And for the employee, because it takes toll from his nervous system and tends to make him a careless, sloppy worker. And it creates friction among workers. Even on group production, we're against it.

Most of the union officials who have accepted incentive plans have given their approval to plans that have definite provisions to protect the interests of labor. Some have claimed full right to participate in rate setting as a bargaining process, no matter what standard-setting procedures management may use in arriving at the incentive rates it proposes. Others have been content to allow management the initial determination of incentive rates under agreed-upon standards, subject to the right of workers to protest through the grievance procedure. Still others have proposed that the initial rate-setting process be a joint enterprise of management and labor technicians. As a practical matter, however, few unions have developed sufficient technical staff to participate equally with management in setting standards. In fact, in many of the existing instances of cooperative rate setting, management itself has trained the union time-study stewards.

Management's position, that the necessities of continuous production will not allow haggling over incentive rates on new items of production before work can be started, has generally prevailed. Except in industries where the practice of direct bargaining on piece rates has been established over years of experience, management generally sets rates initially, subject to protest through grievance channels. In general, this was the procedure sanctioned by the National War Labor Board during World War II.

Supplementary Payments

The variety of supplementary benefits is great. All that can be done here is to list some of those most commonly found:

- vacation pay
- holiday pay
- call-in pay
- call-back pay
- night-shift bonus
- attendance bonus
- plant-neatness bonus
- sick-leave pay
- maternity-leave pay
- pension fund contributions
- medical and welfare fund contributions
- dismissal pay
- Christmas bonus
- year-end bonus
- paid lunch period
- profit sharing
- stock distribution or sale at below-market rates

The average money equivalent of such payments in all American industry is probably not much more than 10 per cent of total earnings, although rough estimates for some individual companies run to 25 per cent or more.[13] Supplementary payments have been extended since

13. For the only survey made in recent years, to the author's knowledge, see *The Hidden Payroll: Nonwage Labor Costs of Doing Business,* Economic Research Department of the Chamber of Commerce of the United States, Washington, 1949.

World War II, but all of the practices are of long standing. Some of them, such as shift differentials and payment for laundering uniforms, are peculiar to certain industries; others, like paid vacations, paid holidays and sick leave, have existed for years among certain groups of workers, especially salaried workers, and have been extended recently to many wage earners in various industries. However, in some industries — in the building trades, for example — paid vacations and holidays are still almost completely absent; lack of continuous employment with the same employer has made the administration of such plans difficult.

Historically, many labor unions have preferred increases in wage rates to equivalent supplementary payments when they have had a choice. Union leaders have often been lukewarm toward what they have described as paternalistic devices offered as alternatives to increases. But requests for paid vacations, paid holidays, shift differentials and other benefits have nevertheless been made, and welfare and security plans have gained in popularity in recent years. Some management officials have favored supplementary benefits as sound personnel devices; others have preferred wage adjustments as offering greater potential flexibility. For unions, the question whether to bargain for supplementary payments or straight wage increases has become less a matter of principle and more a matter of strategy. Usually the demand for supplementary benefits has increased when, as during World War II, other forms of wage increase have been limited.[14]

Many of the supplementary payments, notably Christmas bonuses, are normally made at the discretion of the employer, and cannot be counted on as a definite amount each year. In some industries, such as the brokerage trade, it is customary to pay rather sizable bonuses in prosperous years, often as a substitute for salary adjustments. With some exceptions, the greatest supplementary benefits — in dollars as well as in relation to basic wages — are found in industries where wage and salary rates are also relatively high.

Guaranteed Wages

Apart from the minimum daily earnings guaranteed to workers under incentive plans, some companies guarantee their employees a definite amount of earnings in a given period, ranging from a week to two years. Weekly guarantees exist in the meatpacking industry and in some distributive trades — in the latter, usually as minimum guarantees under commission sales plans. Guarantees computed on an annual basis have received considerable public attention in recent years. Such plans guarantee employment of varying amounts during a year (during two years in one case) to varying proportions of the force available for work. Such arrangements are few in number and affect substantially less than one per cent of the nation's nonagricultural labor force. They are generally regarded as successful industrial relations devices to assure employment security, often where such security exists in practice because of the steadiness of the volume of production but where the guarantee nevertheless has an important psychological value for the workers.[15]

14. See the expression of union and management attitudes in Woytinsky and Associates, *Labor and Management Look at Collective Bargaining,* Chapter 7.

15. See *Guaranteed Wage Plans in the United States,* Bulletin No. 925, Bureau of Labor Statistics, 1947, and *Guaranteed Wages,* Report to the President of the Advisory Board of the Office of War Mobilization and Reconversion, 1947.

Chapter 35

JOB EVALUATION *

Job evaluation is a formal procedure for determining wage differentials. The approach is a systematic appraisal of job requirements and job conditions — the skill, responsibility and physical effort demanded, and the favorability or unfavorability of working conditions. Money rates are usually determined by relating the selected evaluated jobs to rates of pay in the labor market and within the company.

The Evaluation Process

Administratively, jobs are first described, then evaluated, and finally wage rates are attached to them.[1]

Job Description

Some job descriptions go into considerably more detail than others, but the purpose is always to secure adequate information about the job. To facilitate the evaluation, the description usually includes both a general statement of duties and responsibilities and detailed information on each of the factors to be considered in evaluating the job. Some descriptions go so far as to indicate specifically the weight of each factor in the whole, and thus make the evaluation an almost automatic recording of the judgments of the persons writing the descriptions; but most descriptions leave evaluation mainly to the second administrative step.[2]

Job Evaluation

Evaluation usually begins with selected key jobs, and then the remaining jobs are evaluated — in a sense, interpolated — by reference to them. The key jobs are selected in such a way as to give adequate representation to different pay levels and types of work in the various divisions and departments of the company, and to include the most highly standardized jobs, which are the commonest in the labor market. Evaluation of the key jobs serves as a trial-and-error method of determining the relative weights to be assigned to the various factors. Evaluation of the key jobs also helps to fit the wages rates of the company into the prevailing structure of wages in the labor market.

Determination of Wage Rates

The final step of attaching wage rates to jobs goes beyond the considerations involved in evaluation. The general level of rates involves policy, and frequently bargaining; the grouping of jobs into labor grades or pay levels, also, is only loosely determined by evaluation. While the notion of a labor grade is a part of the procedure, the number of pay levels, and the consequent monetary increments from grade to grade, are based on the degree of simplicity desired in the wage structure, a meaningful promotional gradation, the relative emphasis desired on promotion as contrasted with transfer, and so on.

Job evaluation starts with the actual situation rather than preconceived notions, with an investigation of actual job requirements and conditions and with the wage differentials accepted as correct in key jobs. By an analysis of the correlation between the job requirements and conditions on the one hand and the wage differentials on the other, a wage structure is agreed upon as representing the relative worth of the jobs. While there is ample opportunity for difference of opinion as to whether or not this formal procedure is necessary or desirable in a particular case, at least it serves a definite purpose.

Purpose of Job Evaluation

The purpose of job evaluation is to create more nearly equitable, logical and consistent

* By E. R. Livernash, Director of Industrial Relations, J. F. McElvain Co., Nashua, New Hampshire.

1. See E. R. Livernash, *An Analysis of Job Evaluation Procedures* (unpublished doctoral dissertation, Harvard University, Cambridge, 1941).

2. Whether or not the true elements of skill can be adequately reduced to words is an open question. The better the raters' knowledge of the job, certainly, the better the evaluation.

relationships in wage rates. The underlying assumption is that wages that are "out of line" lower morale and productivity and generate wage grievances. Correction of wage inequities is the major objective.

Inequities arise from many sources. Decentralized control in a company may have led to a more liberal pay scale in one department than in another. Jobs almost identical in content may carry quite different wage rates. Job rates may have failed to reflect technological changes. A drastically simplified job, particularly one in which the simplification has come about gradually over the years, may still carry a high wage rate suited to the skill originally required. Certain wage rates may be high because they have become essentially personal rates, influenced by the exceptional ability or the long service of the incumbents. Grievances, formal and informal, may have exerted undue influence on certain rates. Or the original wage structure may have been quite haphazard, its high and low rates wholly inexplicable.

Job evaluation corrects inequities by establishing standards to show why one job is placed above another. Its purpose, to provide an objective approach to the problem of wage differentials, may be mixed with other intents, ranging from a desire to prevent unionization to a desire to provide a mechanism for joint union-management administration of wage policies.

Administrative Advantages

The idea of job evaluation is not new. In establishing and changing wage and salary rates, firms have always taken into consideration job content as well as wage rates paid in the community. Strictly speaking, many of the administrative improvements associated with job evaluation do not require a formal plan. Undoubtedly many firms have improved wage administration without such a plan or by a very simple informal procedure, but the usual vehicle of improved wage administration in recent years has been the formal plan.

The outstanding advantage of this method has been effective centralized control over the wage structure and wage changes. Classification of jobs by grades has converted the maze of wage rates into a logical system and provided a clear distinction between pay for the job and the personal rate of the individual worker as well as between promotion and transfer. Job analysis and description clarify job duties, make market comparisons more valid, and lay the groundwork for training and other personnel programs and practices. They also help the company in planning production and operating controls.

These advantages are very meaningful. The first step in a job evaluation program, for example, is to determine what jobs exist in the organization. After collecting information by questionnaire or interview as to what each worker is actually doing, job titles must be designated. Almost invariably, important discoveries are made at this stage of the work. Many common titles, such as "laborer," "machine operator" or "clerk," may cover widely different types of work. Other titles, like "machinist" or "secretary," while generally descriptive of the work performed, may include several clearly marked levels of skill. Different titles may carry different wage rates when the work is virtually identical, though perhaps performed in different departments. Other jobs may be confused as to exact requirements. Just what is an inspector supposed to do? Examples of this sort could be multiplied; they include the fancy title that boils down to very little — as, for example, the "fish culturist" who merely feeds the fish. An analysis of duties and responsibilities amounts to much more than a routine description of existing jobs; it also delimits jobs, clarifies and standardizes their requirements.

At the other end of the evaluation program — the classification of individuals in accordance with the job descriptions — actual work assignments are checked. Particularly when the same title has been broken down into subgrades, as "machinist A," "machinist B" and "machinist C," equitable payment is highly dependent upon correct classification.

These administrative advantages, although rightfully regarded as among the purposes of job evaluation, could be achieved without formal job classification. Some of the administrative advantages, however, are inseparable from an evaluation approach. The factual, analytical, three-step procedure of describing jobs, evaluating them and attaching rates to them provides the framework for a wage structure acceptable to management and labor. There is, indeed, a real difference between the basic acceptance by both parties of a job evaluation approach to the wage problem and a "horse-trading" procedure. Another important advantage of formal job evaluation is its use of "pooled" judgment. Job evaluation typically entails a rating committee, whose joint judgment is almost certainly sounder than that of any one individual, and a process of review and constructive criticism that comes as near as is possible to the goal of a correct placement of jobs.

Types of Procedures [3]

Job evaluation started as a simple program for classifying salaries and wages. Jobs were classified according to wage levels by analyzing duties and responsibilities but without naming or using specified job factors or characteristics. Frequently, general criteria were worked out to define the level of skill and responsibility to be recognized at each pay level. Civil service, both federal and state, uses this approach predominantly. Some companies strongly prefer it, particularly, but not exclusively, for salaried workers. For the most part, however, the trend is away from this informal kind of classification to "ranking" and "point" plans.

Ranking plans may or may not specify job factors. Their approach is simply to rank, through analysis of job content, all jobs from the lowest to the highest, usually within departments first and then among departments. Pay levels or grades of jobs are established in relation to the rates paid in the industry and the area for key jobs.

Point plans are by far the more common type today, though highly complicated point plans are not often found now. A reasonably simple point plan has become almost synonymous with the term "job evaluation." [4] Typical point plans include the following groups of factors: skill, responsibility, physical effort, working conditions.

3. See Charles W. Lytle, *Job Evaluation Methods,* Ronald Press, New York, 1946, Chapter 3.

4. Regardless of the numerical preponderance of fairly detailed point plans, a word of caution is in order. While there is a certain logic in going whole hog or none, evaluation is still in a process of evolution. The earlier, more informal plans have a refreshing simplicity, and may definitely be more consistent with important considerations that go beyond the scope of evaluation. The work of Lawshe, to be considered specifically later, certainly casts doubt upon some of the refinements in today's job evaluation plans. Unions are far from sold on these plans. The melting pot may produce a simpler procedure not too far removed from the early informal methods.

Skill may be subdivided into the requirements in training time, experience, education or knowledge and such other factors as manual dexterity, complexity of the job, initiative and ingenuity required, and so on. Training and experience are often consolidated as one factor. The time required for training and experience has proved a good measure of relative skill — not as a precise statistical measure, but to guide the raters' judgment. Knowledge required and manual dexterity are two quite distinct aspects of skill. Knowledge — or the education or judgment or ingenuity required to know what to do and how to do it — may be the major element of skill in one job, coordination or other elements of manual skill in another.

Responsibility may be broken down into responsibility for product, materials and equipment; it is often measured by the probability and potential amount of dollar loss, and the supervision received and exercised over others. Responsibility for the safety of others is also frequently considered. Responsibility, as found in ordinary factory jobs, is perhaps the most difficult of all the evaluation factors to define and apply if it really implies something different from skill. In salary plans the emphasis shifts to accuracy, errors, supervision received and given, and, perhaps, the complexity of the task and the ingenuity required.

Physical effort is judged in terms of the normal amount required in the job.

Working conditions are usually judged as a single factor, while hazard on the job is treated separately.

Point plans are of two types. In some plans the evaluation factors are weighted by assigning a point to each, and frequently by assigning points to the various degrees of each factor. In other plans no fixed weight is assigned to single characteristics of a job. The weighting of those factors necessary for final classification or ranking of jobs is worked out from scores developed for key jobs so that the agreed amount of cents per hour for each key job is distributed among the factors — skill, responsibility, working conditions and so on. Such a method is flexible, and two different applications of the plan might differ significantly in the relative weights given to each factor.[5]

5. For a detailed examination of this method of job evaluation, see E. J. Benge, S. L. H. Burk and E. N. Hay, *Manual of Job Evaluation,* Harper, New York, 1941, and other works of the same authors.

In practice, the two approaches are not far apart, particularly because skill and responsibility, taken together, usually account, at a conservative estimate, for 80 per cent of the points. Of most importance is the realization that weighting is a trial-and-error process. Weighting is tested with key jobs,[6] regardless of the plan used, and the great amount of overlap among factors minimizes the importance of the weighting technique.

Validity of Job Evaluations

Whether to use job evaluation and the scope of the use should be determined by broad considerations of the validity and limitations of the procedure. Experience in recent years appears to justify a double conclusion: first, common-sense consideration of the meaning of the factors applied in job classification should lead anyone to be reasonably humble in their use; second, with this reservation, plans are sufficiently reliable to narrow the area of controversy over wage rates for particular jobs within the existing wage system.

An analysis of jobs in terms of such factors as manual skill involved, complexity of the job, knowledge required, responsibility for product, responsibility for materials, responsibility for equipment, supervision received, physical effort required, mental effort required, favorable and unfavorable elements in working conditions, is adding apples and oranges and arriving at totals of unknown dimension. It is questionable whether the concept of favorable working conditions means quite the same thing to everyone and whether the physical effort required in a job can be measured. Assuming reasonable selection of workers and "normal" effort, a "heavy" job may be no more onerous than a "light" job. Recognizing the individual's ability to adapt his pace to his capacity, it is questionable whether any job can be said to "require" a definable amount of physical effort.

Mental effort is even less ascertainable. There is no way of measuring a highly standardized job requiring a high degree of manual dexterity but little knowledge in relation to one requiring low manual skill but considerable knowledge to deal with frequent variations in quality of materials. "Responsibility" is even less clear than other factors.

Consider, for example, two jobs in a shoe factory: "feeling for tacks" and "putting in laces." In the first job all the worker has to do is to hunt for tacks by feeling conscientiously inside each shoe. In the second the worker is required to place a lace in each shoe. Is one job more responsible than the other if the job duties are followed closely?

The work of C. H. Lawshe, Jr., and his associates bears out the common-sense conclusion that there is a great deal of overlap in the factors commonly used in job evaluation.[7] Although there is a temptation to generalize the relative importance of the various factors, a sounder approach is to remain open-minded with respect to the "best" factors in various situations but to emphasize the soundness of more simplified plans. Two or three skill factors may well be adequate.

David J. Chesler [8] found a close correlation among descriptions of standard jobs in companies using different job evaluation systems. His work, other studies and general observation lead to a rough conclusion that different plans and different raters are highly reliable within a range of plus or minus one labor grade. Considering the agreement of "pooled" judgment as contrasted with independent ratings, most jobs fall clearly within a specific labor grade. But for a significant number of jobs the range of opinion is likely to remain, on a common-sense basis, about plus or minus one labor grade.

6. This point is noted by Philip W. Jones in *Practical Job Evaluation,* Wiley, New York, 1948, pp. 126 and 138. An even more direct recognition of this test is to be found in Forrest H. Johnson and Associates, *Job Evaluation,* Wiley, New York, 1946, p. 36.

7. Lawshe and his colleagues worked with the National Metal Trades Plan, which has eleven factors: three related to skill (education, experience, initiative and ingenuity), four related to responsibility (for equipment or process, for materials or product, for the safety of others, for the work of others), two pertaining to effort (physical demand and mental or visual demand), and two associated with job conditions (working conditions and unavoidable hazards). By statistical techniques they isolated the three "best" factors in the application of this plan to three different plants and found that experience, unavoidable hazards and education were the "best" factors in the first plant; experience, initiative and ingenuity, and responsibility for the safety of others, in the second plant; and experience, unavoidable hazards, and initiative and ingenuity, in the third plant. C. H. Lawshe, Jr., "Toward Simplified Job Evaluation," *Personnel,* November 1945.

8. David J. Chesler, "Reliability and Comparability of Different Job Evaluation Systems," *Journal of Applied Psychology,* October 1948, p. 465.

Limitations of Job Evaluation

Whether or not job evaluation should be used as the only criterion of wage differentials is a difficult question.[9] While wage relationships are important determinants of morale, there should be some reservation in accepting "logical" appraisals of job content as a completely satisfactory goal. Economic forces and bargaining realities may develop inconsistencies that should be openly recognized in wage policy. A realistic rate structure is not static, and the desire for its logical perfection may become unrealistic at times.

There is a strong conservative tendency among workers to accept the status quo in wage differentials regardless of its origin and merits. Accepting wage grievances at face value, the remarkable fact is how seldom, not how frequently, the existing wage structure is questioned. The general distrust of job evaluation among trade-union leaders may be based largely on their unwillingness to admit far-reaching adjustments of wage differentials. In many instances union leaders have lost office, and unions have lost bargaining rights to rival unions, by agreeing to a job evaluation program.

Strong social relations are built up around existing wage differentials. One job may be regarded as better than another simply because it has always paid more. The question whether or not it is worth more may be of more importance to the analyst than to the workers. The prestige of a promotion secured after many years of waiting can be destroyed by a re-evaluation of jobs. The vividness with which workers recall changes made many years earlier and their persistence in seeking to restore the old relationships if the changes were to their disadvantage again emphasize the strength of custom. There seems to be little difference in the reaction of other groups of workers to a "logical" as contrasted with an "illogical" rate change.

For the individual, the most significant rate relationships are those within his small work group. The more distant the wage comparison — in level of wages, in work process or in geographical or departmental location — the less significant it is. This casts some doubt on the advantages of the job-content and average-market-relationship approach in job evaluation.

9. See Robert Tilove, "Functions and Limitations of Job Evaluation," *Personnel,* January 1946, p. 206.

Within certain limits, a wage structure can have inequities without giving rise to grievances, simply because the rates involved are in two different worlds from the workers' point of view. Job evaluation should perhaps be applied within closely related work groups to preserve existing relationships or to modify them, taking account of social factors beyond the scope of the evaluation. A promotional sequence might be preserved even at the expense of consistency. Two-way temporary transfers might be facilitated by a uniform wage rate. A dead-end job may warrant a premium for its lack of promotional opportunity. The social equality of two rival craft groups operating within the same department may be more important than the recognition of a small differential in skill. Considerations such as these can frequently be met by ungrading particular jobs; at times they may require out-and-out exceptions to the evaluation plan.

It is not always sufficient to adjust the structure of wage rates so that they meet market rates only on the average and for key jobs. Perhaps the job evaluation must meet most existing rates exactly, even if this course requires some departure from correct job placement. If several companies in the same industry are concentrated within a local labor market, it may be difficult for one of them to change the existing wage-rate relationships. If all of the companies are organized by the same union, the problem will be particularly difficult. A single company placing primary emphasis on job evaluation may face a situation in which the union will take a grievance position against all evaluated rates that are lower than market rates.

The less the necessity to meet specific market rates, the easier it is to avoid inconsistencies between market and evaluated rates. If a company is relatively isolated from its industry and if its general level of wages is above the average for the community, it can establish and change wage differentials without strong opposition from labor.

Even if the industry is geographically dispersed, however, a single union may make complete job evaluation difficult. A related, but distinct, problem is involved in dealing with more than one union in a particular plant. A high degree of craft consciousness within a union presents a similar problem. Variations in competitive cost position may also limit the

TABLE 189

UNIONS TEND TO OPPOSE JOB EVALUATION PLANS

Questions: What is your opinion of job evaluation plans? If such a plan were to be put into effect covering jobs of any of your members, would you want your union to participate with management in setting it up?

Response	Number of Unions	Union Members: Number, in Thousands	Union Members: Percentage of Total
Opinion of job evaluation:			
Number of respondents	47	10,844	100.0
Favor	10	2,052	18.9
Oppose	25	6,042	55.7
Arbitrary, rigid, mechanistic	6	2,224	20.5
Keeps wages down	6	921	8.5
Other or no reason given	13	2,897	26.7
No opinion	12	2,750	25.4
Attitude toward participation in setting up plans:			
Number of respondents	33	7,175	100.0
Want to participate	16	2,675	37.3
Do not want to participate	14	3,291	45.9
Do not know	3	1,209	16.8

Source: W. S. Woytinsky and Associates, *Labor and Management Look at Collective Bargaining,* Twentieth Century Fund, New York, 1949, p. 147.

application of job evaluation; in a company producing different types of products wage policy may of necessity depart from equal pay for equal work in order to maintain employment in less profitable lines.

A job evaluation plan reflects economic forces as they exist at the time the plan is installed. Maintaining sufficient flexibility to meet changes in these forces is difficult.

The strong tendency of workers to resist any change in the wage structure makes it important to move slowly in introducing a job evaluation plan. The insignificance of the more distant comparisons allows scope for recognizing economic factors and traditional differences without raising serious questions of inequity, but within smaller work groups evaluation may have to be seriously qualified.

UNION ATTITUDES TOWARD JOB EVALUATION

Suspicion is probably labor's most typical attitude toward job evaluation, but the attitudes of individual union leaders range from complete rejection to full acceptance.[10]

Opposition

In the course of the canvass of views of labor and management leaders carried out by the Twentieth Century Fund in connection with this survey,[11] union leaders were asked: "What is your opinion of job evaluation plans? If such a plan were to be put into effect covering jobs of any of your members, would you want your union to participate with management in setting it up?" Of the 47 responses to the first question, only 10 were in favor of job evaluation, 25 were opposed and 12 respondents had no opinion. (See Table 189.) Several of those opposed gave no reason, but others commented on the arbitrary, mechanical character of job evaluation plans and their depressing effect on middle-bracket wage rates.

The motives for complete rejection of job evaluation systems are exemplified by the following answers of the union presidents canvassed:[12]

> Job evaluation is nothing but scientific hogwash. Frequently the employer's interest in putting it in is to mystify the worker. You can't weigh and measure human beings as you do wheat or coal. The margins of error in evaluations are terrific and the results are no better than those based on just pure common sense.

> Job evaluation is an occult science, like astrology and phrenology — and it's just as useful. We won't discuss it with employers, and we won't arrange it. . . . We refuse to accept their job evaluation as a bargaining factor on the basis that you can't measure human efforts as you do machines.

> The job evaluation approach we've been faced with in bargaining negotiations has been simply a substi-

10. See William Gomberg, "Union Attitudes on the Application of Industrial Engineering Techniques to Collective Bargaining," *Personnel,* May 1948, p. 445; see also Solomon Barkin, "Wage Determination: Trick or Technique," *Labor and Nation,* June–July 1946.

11. W. S. Woytinsky and Associates, *Labor and Management Look at Collective Bargaining,* Twentieth Century Fund, New York, 1949.

12. *Ibid.,* p. 148.

tute for wage cutting. If we found a method of job evaluation that intelligently classified a job, we'd be for it. But, to date, we haven't seen anything where the motive behind the evaluation was the intelligent classification of jobs within an adequate level of wages.

Typical of the wariness of labor are the following complaints of another labor spokesman:

It's a good system if the evaluation is fair and the workers understand it as well as management. The reason it has such a black eye with unions is that industry is using a pseudo-scientific, highly technical type of evaluation. No one understands it — not management and not the workers. Management makes the points for each job fit what they want to pay for the job; they have the job rates predetermined before they start the evaluation.

The labor leaders who accepted job evaluation approved it on condition that labor has enough strength to exercise some control over work and pay standards.

We've had job evaluation since 1937. It's a necessary thing that makes sense. It helps the company and helps the worker. It gives some reason for differences in rates of pay. It takes differences out of the realm of unilateral judgment. . . .

There isn't a great deal of job evaluation in our industry. We're strongly for it, though, provided we can get the right standards of measurement. But if the companies do all the figuring, that's bad.

The negative attitude of the great majority of labor leaders toward job evaluation is probably due less to fear of its adverse effect on the level of earnings than to its impact on bargaining rights and union strength in the company. Undoubtedly job evaluation has been used by management to remove one reason for union organization by improving the wage structure. In this respect it is no different from other personnel practices. It has also been used as an appeal to authority. Some companies, though clearly a small minority, have taken the position that the evaluated placement of a job is not arbitrable. Keeping confidential some or all of the data used in an evaluation has also antagonized unions.

Finally, management has usually insisted that after final acceptance of a plan, it can be reviewed only if there has been a change in job content or if "mistakes" are discovered in the original evaluation. This position limits the scope of bargaining and is particularly repugnant to union leaders, since it implies that a job rate should be reduced if the job has been simplified through technological changes.

Reducing wage rates because of minor changes in job content gives rise to particularly strong controversy, and yet if minor changes are not considered separately, a succession of small changes may never be reflected in relative wage rates. Many job evaluation plans have been negotiated without a meeting of minds on this issue.

There may have been no meeting of minds, in fact, even on the broader issue of stability in the differential structure. The standoffish attitude of a labor union may mean the acceptance of job evaluation on a basis of pure expediency. If a plan promises a sufficient rise of average wages, job evaluation may be accepted in spite of its effect on wage differentials. In such circumstances the union's acceptance of the plan does not mean its agreement with management on the wage structure. Management may feel that differentials have been fixed for a long time and can be changed only in the event of a change in job content, while the union may consider the established scale of wages as a temporary arrangement and reserve the right to demand revisions in the placement of jobs.

In brief, many labor leaders feel that job evaluation threatens to reduce their freedom of action on behalf of union members. This explains sufficiently their distrust of the system unless they feel themselves strong enough to control it, at least partly.

The facts do not support the contention frequently voiced by union leaders that job evaluation is a device to cut wages. Unions can cite instances in which incentive standards are reviewed or installed with the net effect of reducing labor cost, but hardly cases of actual cuts in individual earnings. The installation of a job evaluation system requires too much administrative work and is too expensive to be used as a means for cutting wages. Indeed, this is not its purpose. So far, unions have been rather successful in obtaining a net increase in the course of installation of job evaluation, not only immediately — because of the provision that no worker will suffer a cut in wages but some can be upgraded — but also in the average level of new rates.

Participation

Where unions have accepted job evaluation, some have preferred direct participation in determining the ranking of individuals, and some

TABLE 190

IN MOST FIRMS THAT USE JOB EVALUATION WIDELY, UNIONS PARTICIPATE IN THE PLAN

Questions: Do you use job evaluation and standard-rate setting? In recent job analyses, did representatives of the union work with your engineers?

		Job Evaluation Used:					
		Widely		To a Limited Extent		Not at All	
Response	Total	Manufacturing Companies	Nonmanufacturing Companies	Manufacturing Companies	Nonmanufacturing Companies	Manufacturing Companies	Nonmanufacturing Companies
Number of respondents	88	19	8	15	14	13	19
Union's role in job evaluation:							
Participates	24	11	5	4	4	—	—
Opposes	8	—	1	1	1	3	2
Takes no part	56	8	2	10	9	10	17

Source: W. S. Woytinsky and Associates, *Labor and Management Look at Collective Bargaining,* Twentieth Century Fund, New York, 1949, p. 151.

have preferred not to assume responsibility for development of the plan. In the Fund's survey, union leaders with the second point of view represented a larger membership than those with the first point of view. The following answers reveal their motives:[13]

We would stay aloof so we could have a free hand in the adjustment of grievances.

We wouldn't go in on it at first. We'd see that the plan was explained to the workers, and we'd give it a fair trial. Then we'd go in on the negotiation of grievances, if there were any.

We encourage the unions to participate so far as actually studying the plan. We don't insist they enter into agreement on a lot of plans that are submitted. I don't think we would want to participate with management in setting one up, but it would depend entirely on what the plan amounted to.

We reserve for ourselves the right to question any job evaluation plan, using any yardstick we can prop up. In no way do we want to make ourselves a partner of the employer in setting up the evaluations. They are employers' tools, and acceptance of these plans by the union is merely the acceptance by the union of the employer's method of rating jobs.

Most of the business executives canvassed expressed the opinion that job evaluation plans cannot operate successfully against active opposition of labor unions, but they were divided on the desirability of direct participation by labor representatives in job analysis and the technical preparation of the plan. Of 27 companies that used job evaluation widely, 16 operated the plan with active participation of labor representatives and only one reported open opposition on the part of the union. Of 29 companies that used job evaluation to a limited extent, 8 had union participation. (See Table 190.)

13. *Ibid.*, p. 150.

While most employers considered the cooperation of union representatives with industrial engineers essential for the success of the plan, others believed that job evaluation is among the prerogatives of management and is no business of labor. Typical of the motives underlying this attitude is the following answer of a business executive:

The employees don't even know we have a job evaluation plan; they've never even seen the charts. I doubt if they would understand them if they did. Now and then they raise questions on specific wage rates, but it usually doesn't go as far as grievance procedure. Their questions arise from change of work load or change of job content. But that goes back to the old theory of management prerogative. We still retain the right to say what shall be produced in our mills and how we shall produce it.

In brief, whatever is said by both parties on the merits and faults of job evaluation, the main source of union-management controversy over this method of setting wage differentials is its impact on relative bargaining rights.

THE FUTURE OF JOB EVALUATION

Job evaluation has become well established in a large number of industries and companies. Some industries appear not to have made much use of the technique, and some companies in every industry prefer to avoid a formal plan; but most companies using job evaluation feel that a plan of some sort is superior to no plan.[14] While the period of most rapid spread of this

14. Helen Baker and John M. True, *The Operation of Job Evaluation Plans,* Princeton University Press, Princeton, New Jersey, 1947, p. 91.

procedure may well have passed, there seems reason to believe that the technique will remain and will gradually become more widely accepted and better understood.

Plans are likely to be simplified. There is an advantage in being able to demonstrate that all the important aspects of a job have received direct consideration, but the added accuracy is more superficial than real and tends to make the plan as a whole less comprehensible. If a plan is to be used democratically it must be easily understood by those affected. The use of a few simple and reliable factors best meets this requirement. Moreover, in the final consolidation of jobs, consideration should be given to traditional relationships, differences in promotional opportunity, group rivalries, transfer problems and other nonevaluation factors.

Recognition of such factors raises an important question. Why go to all the trouble of an evaluation if the door is to be opened to considerations of this sort? It is almost impossible, however, to maintain a rigid, logical wage structure without exceptions. More fundamentally, job content is probably not sufficiently valid to be used as a single criterion in setting wage rates. If the evaluation plan remains as the basis of discussion, with only well-supported exceptions, agreement upon it is the more likely to be lasting.

The most important issues of such an agreement are stability of the wage structure, adequate treatment of factors not covered by formal evaluation of jobs ("nonevaluation factors"), and adjustment of wages to technological changes.

Stability of Wage Structure

Any immediate gains from job evaluation in correcting inequities can be lost by continual reopening of the question of the ranking of individual jobs. Management frequently takes the point of view that the only basis for reconsidering the placement of a job is a change in its content. Unions take the stand that the placement of a job in the scale of wage rates can be questioned for any reason. There is a period of review before, and usually for a stated period after, the installation of the job evaluation plan when placement of all jobs may be freely questioned. It would seem desirable to have as thorough a review as possible before the installation and to limit the review period after installation. Thereafter, apart from changes in job content, the placement of a job should be reviewable for any reason but only at stated intervals. Without this possibility, the system may well prove to be too rigid to last.

It is of no fundamental importance whether existing market rates are considered as a primary factor in determining wages for individual jobs or whether the formal evaluation of jobs is regarded as the primary factor and existing rates are considered only in the process of assigning wage rates to certain key jobs. In either event, exceptions for nonevaluation considerations have to be based on specifically accepted reasons. Open recognition of such exceptions strengthens the system.

Acceptance of job evaluation necessitates labor-management agreement to revise wage rates whenever significant changes take place in job content. Some controversy in particular instances may be inevitable, but the policy of opposing any revision of existing rates can lead only to antagonism and internal friction between labor and management.

Management may sometimes expect too much from job evaluation and try to hold to a rigorous application of established rates. Unions may refuse at times to see any value in standards for wage differentials. With a simple evaluation approach involving an admitted area of judgment, and with a willingness and desire to maintain an agreed-upon structure recognizing reasonable exceptions and permitting periodical revision, both stability and flexibility may be maintained with a minimum of inequities.

CHAPTER 36

DISTRIBUTION OF WORKERS BY AMOUNT OF ANNUAL EARNINGS *

COLLECTIVE BARGAINING is usually focused on the wage rate, the amount stipulated for a time period or a piece of work, rather than on earnings, the money income of the employee. The worker's income depends on both the wage rate for his services and the continuity and regularity of his employment. Both factors, in turn, depend on many conditions: The wage rate is affected by the occupational skill, sex, race and age of the worker, the industry in which he is employed, the community in which he lives, and so on; the continuity of his employment is affected partly by business conditions and the general demand for labor, partly by his personal qualifications, health and propensities.

This chapter deals with the over-all distribution of workers by the amount of their annual earnings. Differentials in earnings and wages due to particular factors are examined in subsequent chapters.

STATISTICS ON WAGES AND EARNINGS

Wage statistics can be presented either in the form of average earnings in a specified period of time — for example, the hour, the week or the year — or as a distribution of workers by earnings interval — so many earning less than $10 a week, so many from $10 to $14.99, so many from $15 to $19.99, and so on. The two types of wage statistics supplement each other.

Average Earnings

Examples of the first type of wage statistics are the series of hourly and weekly earnings published by the Bureau of Labor Statistics and by the National Industrial Conference Board.[1]

Statistics of average annual earnings are available in two series — for all full-time employees, computed by the United States Department of Commerce as part of its survey of national income,[2] and for workers covered by the federal system of old-age and survivors insurance.[3] Both series comprise earnings of all classes of employees in all types of industries, except that the OASI series is necessarily limited to the industries covered by the program.[4]

---

* By W. S. Woytinsky.

1. *Handbook of Labor Statistics,* 1947 edition, Bulletin No. 916, Bureau of Labor Statistics, 1948, pp. 54–86; currently in the *Monthly Labor Review. The Economic Almanac for 1948,* National Industrial Conference Board, New York, 1947.

Both series are based on periodic reports of employers and are usually limited to industrial "production workers," excluding clerical, supervisory and professional personnel. Selected employers are requested to report how many production workers they had in a particular payroll period, how long this period was, and the amount of wages for the period. Then the aggregate payroll amount of each industry is computed and, by dividing it by the number of man-weeks or man-hours worked, the average weekly or hourly earnings of workers in each industry are determined.

2. *Survey of Current Business,* National Income Numbers.

3. *Handbook of Old-Age and Survivors Insurance Statistics,* Employment, Wages and Insurance Status of Workers in Covered Employment, Social Security Administration, Federal Security Agency, Baltimore. See also periodical releases of the Bureau of Old-Age and Survivors Insurance.

4. There is an important difference between the methods of computing average annual earnings and weekly or hourly earnings. Average annual earnings in an industry cannot be determined by prorating its wage total over all persons to whom payments are made. Such a ratio would be meaningless, since millions of persons who changed jobs or industries during the year would be counted several times. To reflect actual earnings in the various industries, average annual earnings must be computed in such a way that the amount of each industry's payroll is distributed among the estimated number of full-year workers or of persons attached to it, so that each worker is assigned to only one industry.

The average amount of annual earnings computed in the latter way is influenced by many factors: basic wage rates, overtime pay, bonus schemes; the extent of part-time work; the composition of the labor force by occupational level and skill; the proportion of women, inexperienced young workers and Negroes in the group, and so on. If new, unskilled workers are being added to the labor force, average earnings will probably fall. If the labor force is contracting and the less skilled, lower-paid workers are dismissed first, average earnings will rise. Changes in occupational distribution in establishments or whole industries and in the proportions of high-paid and low-paid workers may alsc affect average earnings even

Statistics of average annual or weekly earnings have the weakness of all statistical averages: When the range between the extremes is considerable — as, for example, between the salaries of executives and the wages of casual laborers — the averages become of doubtful significance. This shortcoming is partly eliminated in wage and earnings statistics that show the distribution of workers by level of earnings.

Earnings Distribution

Wage statistics of this type have been computed by the Bureau of Labor Statistics in its wages-and-hours surveys in various industries.[5] The Sixteenth Census used the same method in tabulations of wage income.[6] This is also the standard method in studies of consumer budgets. But never in the history of statistics, in this country or abroad, has this method been used as broadly as in the statistics of old-age and survivors insurance.[7]

when there is no change in the actual number of employees and their wage rates. See John T. Dunlop, *Wage Determination under Trade Unions,* Macmillan, New York, 1944.

5. Published in the *Monthly Labor Review.*

6. Sixteenth Census (1940), *Population, The Labor Force* (*Sample Statistics*), *Wage or Salary Income in 1939,* 1939.

7. Statistics of OASI, of both the average-earnings type and the frequency-distribution type, are based on quarterly employer reports showing the taxable wages of each employee, identified by name and social security account number. All other information on individual workers is obtained when the reported wages are posted to individual social security accounts. From these accounts, data can be obtained on the continuity of covered employment of each person, his changes of job, shifts from industry to industry, and so on. In brief, each account tells the work history of the individual. Since this history is of practical administrative significance only in combination with the worker's wage credits, many kinds of cross tabulations of earnings and other relevant factors are prepared and new tabulations are added from time to time to those carried on continuously. To reduce cost, statistics are based on a small sample, but the patterns of earnings shown for this sample are, for all practical purposes, as informative as if all accounts were processed.

As a by-product of an insurance program with limited coverage, earnings statistics of OASI have serious limitations. Before recent amendment of the program it covered 2.5 million private industrial establishments, but not agriculture, railroads, government, self-employment, domestic service, casual work, or nonprofit charitable and educational organizations. When a person works during a year both in covered and noncovered industries, only his earnings in covered industries are recorded.

Another shortcoming of these statistics is that, being based on quarterly reports, they permit no measurement of time worked in covered employment except in terms of calendar quarters. That an individual has four quarters with wage credits, however, does not necessarily mean twelve months of employment in covered industries, but can stand for anything from four weeks in such employment, each one in a different calendar quarter, to a year's continuous employment.

A third shortcoming is that, until recently, employers were not asked to report wages or salaries paid to an individual in excess of $3,000 during a calendar year. This limitation results in considerable distortion of the quarterly figures: salaries of high-paid executives ($12,000 or more a year, $3,000 a quarter) are reported only in the first quarter; salaries of many supervisory and professional workers ($6,000 to $12,000 a year) are reported in the first two quarters; and even the earnings of workers with annual salaries from $4,000 to $6,000 do not appear in all four calendar quarters.

TABLE 191

PERCENTAGE DISTRIBUTION OF WORKERS UNDER OASI, BY ANNUAL WAGE CREDITS, 1937–1948

Year	Less than $200	$200–$399	$400–$999	$1,000–$1,999	$2,000–$2,999	$3,000 and Over
1937..	21.7	10.5	29.2	28.7	6.8	3.1
1938..	25.0	11.4	29.2	25.3	6.2	2.9
1939..	23.6	10.9	28.7	27.2	6.5	3.1
1940..	22.7	10.7	28.1	27.7	7.5	3.4
1941..	21.1	10.5	25.5	27.8	10.4	4.6
1942..	20.7	10.5	22.3	25.2	13.6	7.7
1943..	19.1	9.8	18.9	23.7	16.0	12.5
1944..	17.9	8.9	17.4	23.6	16.7	15.5
1945..	18.7	9.8	17.4	24.0	16.3	13.7
1946..	16.0	9.1	17.7	25.6	18.1	13.3
1947..	13.4	7.9	15.7	23.4	20.4	19.2
1948..	12.3	7.0	14.4	21.1	20.6	24.8

Sources: Handbook of Old-Age and Survivors Insurance Statistics, Employment, Wages and Insurance Status of Workers in Covered Employment, Social Security Administration, Federal Security Agency, Baltimore, 1946, p. 125; *Statistical Abstract of the United States, 1950,* p. 234; *1951,* p. 232. Cf. Appendix Table 97, A.

ANNUAL EARNINGS OF WORKERS UNDER OASI

The distribution of workers by level of annual earnings in industries covered by the federal insurance program changes from year to year. When wages go up, the proportion of persons in the higher intervals increases. (See Appendix Table 97.)

All Workers with Wage Credits

Under the impact of the defense program and the war, the proportion of covered workers with annual wage credits of $2,000 or more rose from 10.9 per cent in 1940 to 30 per cent in 1945. (See Table 191.) These changes reflected the general rise in wages, the virtual disappearance of unemployment and part-time work, and the longer work week during the war. Contrary to this general trend, however, the proportion of workers in the lowest earnings groups (those with annual earnings under

$400) did not decline much: from 32.2 per cent in 1937 it went down only slightly, to 28.5 per cent in 1945.

After the end of the war the proportion of workers with annual wage credits of $2,000 or more continued to rise and reached 45.4 per cent in 1948, while the proportion of those with earnings under $400 declined sharply, falling to 19.3 per cent in 1948.

The stability of the proportion of persons with the lowest annual earnings under the OASI program in wartime appears still more striking when the change in the cost of living is taken into account. Because of the change in the purchasing power of the dollar, persons who were in the less-than-$600 earnings class in 1945 had real earnings roughly comparable to those who were in the less-than-$400 class in 1937. The percentage of such persons among all workers with wage credits not only did not diminish during the war, but rose from 32.2 per cent in 1937 to 35.4 in 1945. The percentage of male workers in this earnings class was 27.6 in 1937 and 30.3 in 1945; of female, 44.1 and 43.5.[8]

This pattern of change in the distribution of workers under the war economy was caused by the coincidence of two factors: On the one hand, the earnings of the great majority of workers went up, so that millions of persons shifted from lower to higher wage classes; on the other hand, the war increased the turnover in the labor force and opened occasional work opportunities to persons who would not be employable under peacetime conditions. This interpretation of the changes in earnings is confirmed by analysis of the distribution of workers who were in covered employment more or less steadily.

Four-Quarter Workers

"Four quarters in covered employment" does not necessarily mean continuous covered employment throughout the year. The group of workers with covered employment in each quarter of a given year includes, rather, some persons with irregular and occasional employment. Their proportion is not large, however.

In 1938 more than two thirds of the male workers with wage credits in four calendar quarters earned less than $1,600 and 18.3 per cent reported taxable wages of $2,000 or more. In 1945 only 21 per cent had annual earnings of less than $1,600 and two thirds earned $2,000 or more. (See Table 192.) To some extent, the general rise in earnings from 1938 to 1945 was due to the rise in the cost of living. This factor is eliminated if each $300 in 1945 is considered roughly equivalent to $200 in 1938. When male workers who had four quarters in covered employment in 1945 are distributed by wage brackets roughly equivalent in purchasing power to those in 1938, it is found that the proportion with annual wage credits under $1,200 in 1938 or under $1,800 in 1945 declined from 48.7 per cent to 25.9 per cent; the group with $1,200–$1,599 in 1938 or $1,800–$2,399 in 1945 remained almost unchanged (20.2 per cent and 18.7 per cent); and the proportion with $1,600 or more in 1938 or $2,400 or more in 1945 increased from 30.9 per cent to 55.4 per cent.

This comparison shows a substantial shift of workers with more or less regular employment from lower to higher intervals of real earnings.

Earnings and Continuity of Employment

Persons with continuous work usually earn more, month by month and week by week, than temporary workers. This correlation appears clearly in OASI wage statistics. Persons with covered employment in only one calendar quarter prevail in the group with wage credits under $200; persons with two and three quarters form the majority in the interval from $200 to $400; most workers in the interval from $400 to $600 have either two or three quarters in covered employment; four-quarter workers prevail in all intervals above $800. (See Table 193.)

In other terms, most of the four-quarter workers had wage credits of $2,000 or more in 1945

TABLE 192

PERCENTAGE DISTRIBUTION OF MALE WORKERS WITH FOUR CALENDAR QUARTERS OF WAGE CREDITS UNDER OASI, BY ANNUAL WAGE CREDITS, SELECTED YEARS, 1938–1948

Annual Wage Credits	1938	1945	1946	1947	1948
$ 1– 199	2.1	0.6	0.4	0.3	0.2
200– 399	4.4	1.4	1.0	0.8	0.6
400– 599	7.8	2.0	1.6	1.3	1.1
600– 799	10.4	2.4	2.0	1.7	1.5
800– 999	11.9	2.7	2.6	2.1	1.9
1,000–1,199	12.1	3.3	3.4	2.7	2.1
1,200–1,399	11.2	4.0	4.3	3.5	2.7
1,400–1,599	9.0	4.6	5.3	4.0	3.4
1,600–1,799	6.7	4.9	6.0	4.5	3.8
1,800–1,999	5.9	5.7	7.1	5.4	4.4
2,000–2,999	12.4	33.4	35.4	32.8	29.3
3,000 and over	5.9	35.0	31.0	40.8	48.9

Source: Appendix Table 97, B.

8. *Handbook of Old-Age and Survivors Insurance Statistics,* 1946, pp. 125–57.

and their typical wage credits amounted to $500 a quarter. Most of the three-quarter workers received $200–$999, with typical annual wage credits close to $600 and quarterly amounts of approximately $200. Most of the two-quarter workers received less than $400 and their typical annual wage credits were probably closer to $200 than $300, which gave them about $120 a quarter. Roughly, typical monthly wage credits amounted to $170 among four-quarter workers, $70 among three-quarter workers, and $40 among two-quarter workers; the prevailing amounts among workers with only one quarter were still lower.

Since 1945, wages of all four groups of workers have increased, but the general pattern of difference in their quarterly earnings has not changed.

The reported wages of many workers with less than four quarters in covered employment do not represent all their earnings in the year or the quarter. In fact, this group includes many farmers and farm laborers who take factory jobs during the dull season on the farm and many other persons who shift between covered and noncovered jobs. It also includes new entrants to covered employment; persons withdrawing from the labor market because of military service, superannuation and disability; persons unemployed during a part of the year; and all kinds of marginal workers. Of course, marginal workers can have wage credits in all four quarters of a year. The difference, however, is in the proportions: Occasional and temporary workers represent a fringe of the four-quarter group, but they predominate among persons with less than four quarters in covered jobs.

TABLE 193

Distribution of Workers under OASI by Amount of Wage Credits and Number of Quarters in Covered Employment, 1945

Annual Wage Credits	Total	Quarters Employed			
		1	2	3	4
	Percentage Distribution by Wage Credits				
Total......	100.0	100.0	100.0	100.0	100.0
$ 1– 199.	18.7	73.7	33.9	8.3	0.8
200– 399.	9.8	17.3	26.6	14.2	2.2
400– 599.	6.9	5.8	15.7	13.7	3.3
600– 799.	5.5	1.8	9.5	11.9	4.2
800– 999.	5.0	0.6	5.5	10.3	5.1
1,000–1,199.	5.1	0.3	3.3	8.6	6.3
1,200–1,399.	5.2	0.1	2.0	7.2	7.1
1,400–1,599.	5.0	0.1	1.2	6.1	7.3
1,600–1,799.	4.5	a	0.7	5.0	6.7
1,800–1,999.	4.2	a	0.5	4.2	6.5
2,000–2,999.	16.3	0.1	1.0	10.4	26.8
3,000	13.7	0.1	0.1	0.2	23.8
	Percentage Distribution by Number of Quarters in Covered Employment				
Total......	100.0	17.0	13.2	15.3	54.5
$ 1– 199.	100.0	67.0	23.9	6.8	2.2
200– 399.	100.0	30.0	35.9	22.2	12.0
400– 599.	100.0	14.1	29.9	30.3	25.7
600– 799.	100.0	5.6	22.2	32.5	39.9
800– 999.	100.0	2.0	14.0	30.4	53.7
1,000–1,199.	100.0	0.8	8.3	25.2	65.7
1,200–1,399.	100.0	0.4	5.0	21.2	73.4
1,400–1,599.	100.0	0.3	3.0	18.4	78.3
1,600–1,799.	100.0	0.2	2.1	16.9	80.8
1,800–1,999.	100.0	0.2	1.4	15.2	83.2
2,000–2,999.	100.0	0.1	0.8	9.7	89.4
3,000	100.0	0.1	0.1	0.3	99.5

a. Less than 0.05.

Source: Computed from *Handbook of Old-Age and Survivors Insurance Statistics,* Employment, Wages and Insurance Status of Workers in Covered Employment, Social Security Administration, Federal Security Agency, Baltimore, 1945, p. 93.

Decile Annual Earnings of Workers under OASI

Comparison of such distributions by wage credits as those shown in Table 193 becomes cumbersome and somewhat confusing when the contrasts between two distributions are not very great, and especially in periods marked by considerable variation in prices and in the purchasing power of the dollar.[9] The difficulties can be met by converting the distributions by earnings interval into sets of decile earnings.[10]

Computing Decile Wage Credits

The idea of describing the distribution of earnings in terms of deciles is very simple. Suppose we have a group of 100 workers with earnings ranging from $5 to $5,000 during a year and are not satisfied with the statement that the earnings of the group as a whole average $2,000. To learn more about the typical low, medium and high earnings in the group, the workers should be arrayed by the amount of their earnings, from $5 at the one extreme to $5,000 at the other. Then the whole distribution can be described by the earnings of the tenth, the twentieth, the thirtieth, the fortieth man, and so on, up to the ninetieth. These

9. When prices go up and the purchasing power represented by a dollar declines, each $200 interval becomes narrower and a direct comparison of the percentages of persons in identical dollar intervals becomes meaningless.

10. W. S. Woytinsky, *Earnings and Social Security in the United States,* Committee on Social Security, Social Science Research Council, Washington, 1943, pp. 2–6.

earnings represent, roughly, the deciles of the distribution. Moreover, similar computations can be made for a group of any size. Whatever its size, the group is divided into ten equal parts. Then the highest earnings in the first tenth will be the first decile, the highest earnings in the second tenth, the second decile, etc.

Two or more distributions showing the earnings of the tenth, twentieth, thirtieth, etc., workers in a group of 100 can be readily compared with one another, in the middle and at both ends of the distribution, eliminating only the extremes, which in this case are supposed to be not very typical or important. For practical purposes, a simple frequency distribution can be converted into a set of deciles by a graphic method as illustrated in Figure 69.

When this method is applied to wage statistics of OASI, which until recently did not report annual earnings in excess of $3,000, deciles beyond this limit can be estimated by extrapolation. Such extrapolated figures seem reasonably reliable as long as they are fairly close to $3,000 but become doubtful and of little value when they are much above $3,200.

Amount of Decile Annual Wage Credits

Wage credits of all groups of workers covered by federal old-age and survivors insurance have gone up since 1938, but the gains have been unevenly distributed among them. (See Appendix Table 98 and Figure 70.) The general trend in wages has been largely controlled by the rise of prices: the official consumers' price index rose by 38.5 per cent from 1938 to 1946. The purchasing power of a dollar in the hands of consumers was diminished also by deterioration in the quality of consumer goods, disappearance of many desired commodities from the market, and other factors. But even assuming that a dollar in the hands of moderate-income consumers in 1946 was equivalent to two thirds of a prewar dollar, impressive gains remain in the real purchasing power of workers at all points of the frequency distribution, and especially at its lower end.

The gains for four-quarter workers show the changes in real earnings of persons regularly employed in covered industries. In terms of current dollars, high-paid four-quarter workers got larger increases than those in the middle or lower part of the group. In terms of real earnings, however, after correction for the rise in living costs, gains at the seventh decile were not

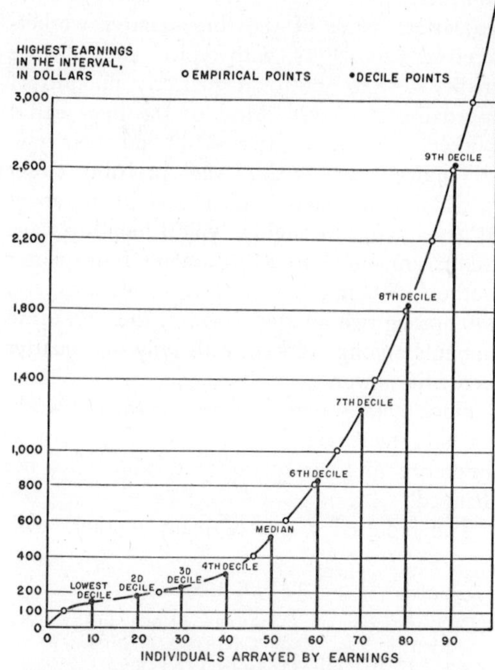

FIGURE 69. EXAMPLE OF FREEHAND GRAPHIC COMPUTATION OF DECILE EARNINGS FROM A PERCENTAGE DISTRIBUTION OF INDIVIDUALS BY EARNINGS INTERVAL

Computation of the decile earnings of a group of persons is based on their percentage distribution by earnings interval. In this case, for example, 3.5 per cent of the group have earnings of not more than $100; 25 per cent, not more than $200; 46 per cent, not more than $400; 53 per cent, not more than $600; 59.5 per cent, not more than $800; 64.5 per cent, not more than $1,000; 72 per cent, not more than $1,400; 79.5 per cent, not more than $1,800, and so on. These purely illustrative percentages have been plotted on the chart (open circles). Next, a freehand curve has been drawn through these points, and the points of its intersection with the vertical ordinates corresponding to 10, 20, 30 per cent and so on have been marked by black dots. The vertical ordinates of these points show the earnings of the tenth, twentieth, thirtieth, etc., persons out of the group of 100.

much larger than at the third decile. (See Table 194; cf. Figure 71.)

If the four-quarter workers in 1948 were the same persons as in 1938 and their relative ranking remained unchanged, one could conclude that, except for the lowest part of the group, say the lowest 25 per cent, wages were adjusted to the increased cost of living and, in addition, were raised for all workers, regardless of the amount of their prewar wages, by $345–$460. In relation to 1938 earnings, the largest raise was given to low-wage workers. After adjustment to the cost-of-living index, the earnings of the tenth and twentieth persons in a group

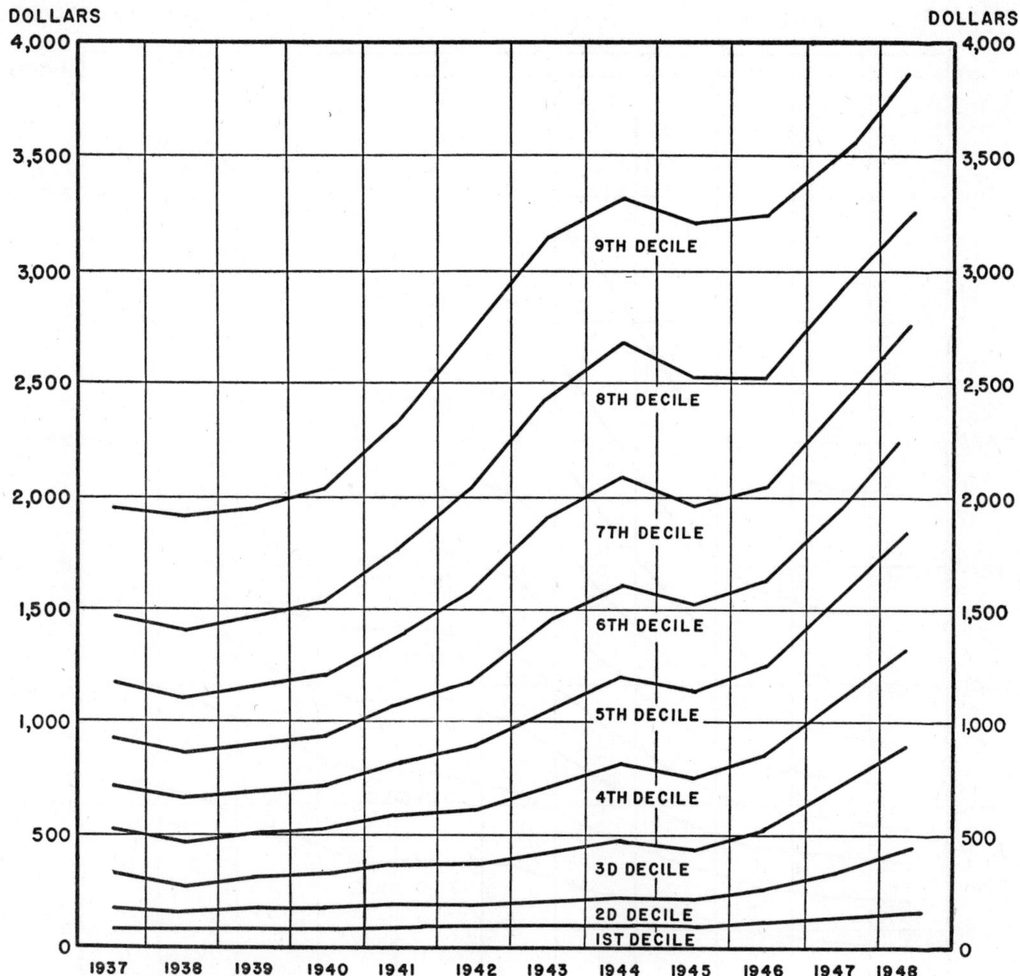

FIGURE 70. DECILE ANNUAL WAGE CREDITS OF ALL WORKERS UNDER OASI, 1937–1948

Source: Appendix Table 98.

Wages of both low-paid and high-paid workers covered by old-age and survivors insurance moved in the same direction from 1937 to 1948, although not necessarily at the same rate. A downward movement from 1937 to 1938 was followed by a slow rise from 1938 to 1940. The rise was accelerated under the impact of the defense program and the war to a peak in 1944. The next year brought a slight loss in annual wage credits at all points of the occupational scale. In 1946 the upward trend was resumed.

of 100 four-quarter workers increased by 55 and 48 per cent, respectively, while among high-paid workers the relative gain was much less: 37 per cent for the sixtieth person and 31 per cent for the seventieth in a group of 100.[11] (See Table 195.)

The relative gains of three-quarter and two-quarter workers were somewhat higher, but the general pattern was very similar: proportionally, persons near the upper end of the frequency distribution tagged behind those in the lower half. This disparity may be caused by the fact that recent years have brought not only a general rise in wage rates but also better work opportunities for unemployed and underemployed workers. Those in the upper earnings brackets, steadily employed before the war, had the advantages of rising wage rates, a longer work week and overtime premiums, while those who had been in the lower brackets before the war had the further advantage of more continuous work. There was also a general trend toward a narrowing of the gap between high and low wage rates.

11. Data for the eighth and ninth deciles in 1948 are not available.

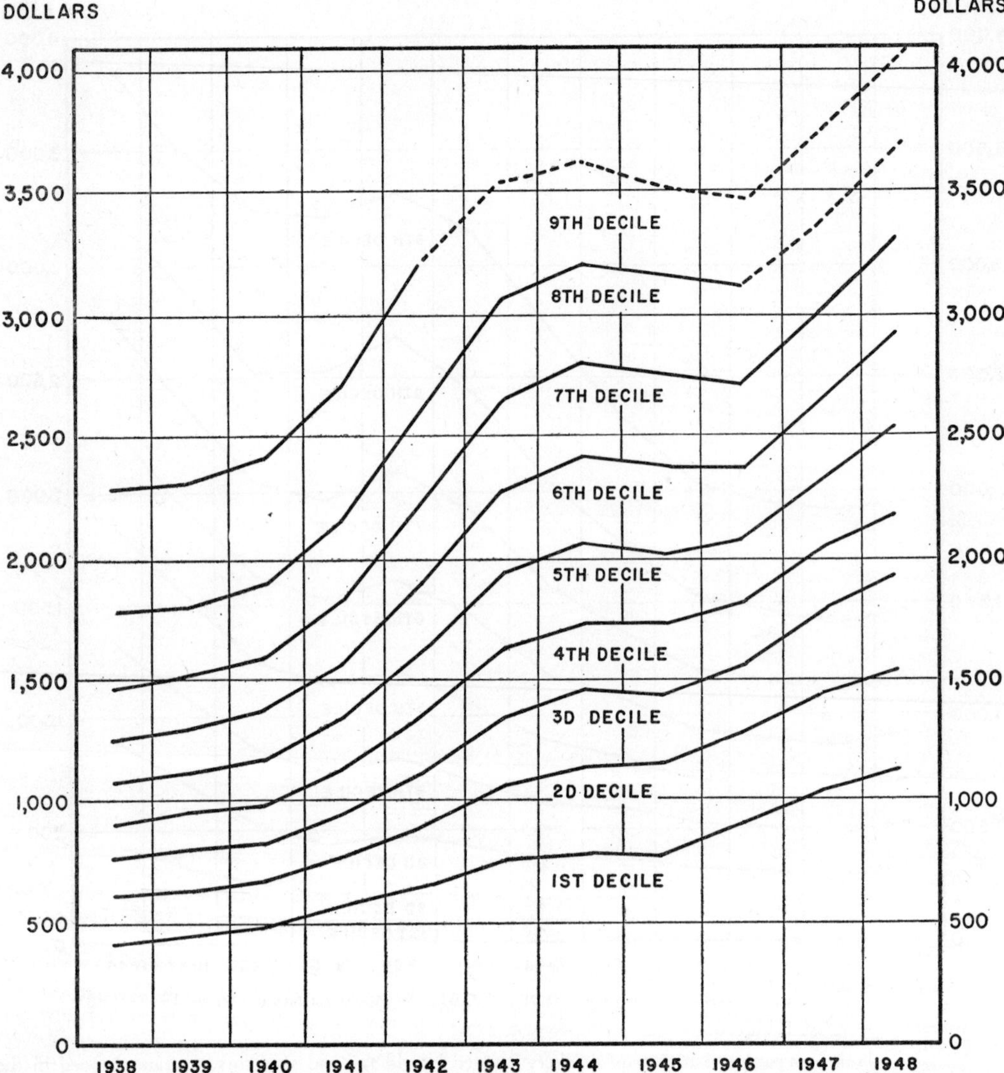

FIGURE 71. DECILE ANNUAL WAGE CREDITS OF WORKERS WITH FOUR QUARTERS IN EMPLOYMENT UNDER OASI, 1938–1948

Source: Appendix Table 98.

Annual wage credits of four-quarter workers increased at different and changing rates from 1938 to 1948. After the war, earnings of low-paid workers continued to rise, while those of high-paid workers suffered some losses during the immediate postwar period.

Changes in Inequality in Earnings

The differences in the rate of rise in earnings among different groups of workers narrowed the gap between low-paid and high-paid workers, as may be seen from the change in the ratios between decile earnings at the two ends of the frequency distribution, for example, the ratio of ninth-decile earnings to first-decile earnings, or of the eighth to the second decile, or of the seventh to the third decile. (See Table 196.) If wage credits at all points of the distribution were increasing or decreasing at the same rate, these "interdecile ratios" would have remained unchanged.

Analysis of the variation of such ratios leads to the following conclusions:

1. Interdecile ratios among four-quarter workers fluctuate within a comparatively narrow range, with a general downward tendency indicating a decline in the contrast between high and low annual earnings.

TABLE 194

GAINS IN DECILE ANNUAL WAGE CREDITS OF WORKERS WITH FOUR QUARTERS IN EMPLOYMENT UNDER OASI, 1938–1948

Decile	1938	1942	1946	1948
	Annual Wage Credits at Current Prices			
First	$ 420	$ 645	$ 890	$1,100
Second	610	895	1,270	1,525
Third	760	1,115	1,550	1,875
Fourth	905	1,350	1,810	2,200
Median	1,070	1,610	2,070	2,525
Sixth	1,250	1,895	2,360	2,900
Seventh	1,465	2,220	2,700	3,250
Eighth	1,775	2,620	3,110	—
Ninth	2,280	3,210	—	—
	Annual Wage Credits at 1938 Prices			
First	$ 420	$ 560	$ 645	$ 650
Second	610	775	920	900
Third	760	965	1,120	1,105
Fourth	905	1,170	1,310	1,295
Median	1,070	1,395	1,500	1,485
Sixth	1,250	1,640	1,710	1,710
Seventh	1,465	1,920	1,955	1,915
Eighth	1,775	2,265	2,250	—
Ninth	2,280	2,775	—	—

Source: Appendix Table 98.

TABLE 195

PERCENTAGE GAINS IN DECILE ANNUAL WAGE CREDITS OF WORKERS WITH FOUR QUARTERS IN EMPLOYMENT UNDER OASI, 1938–1948

Decile	Percentage Increase in Nominal Earnings, in Current Dollars	Percentage Increase in Real Earnings, at 1938 Prices
First	162	55
Second	150	48
Third	147	45
Fourth	143	43
Median	136	39
Sixth	132	37
Seventh	122	31

Source: Derived from Table 194.

2. Interdecile ratios among *all* workers are much higher than those among four-quarter workers, particularly at the extreme ends of the distribution (ratio of ninth to first decile and, to some extent, that of eighth to second). No general trend appeared toward a narrowing of the gap between high and low earnings among *all* workers. The interdecile ratios for this group increased during the war and declined after its end but were higher in 1946 than in 1937.[12]

12. For further discussion of recent trends in inequality of earnings see Chapter 44.

TABLE 196

INTERDECILE RATIOS OF ANNUAL WAGE CREDITS OF WORKERS UNDER OASI, 1937–1948

Year	9th to 1st Decile	8th to 2d Decile	7th to 3d Decile	6th to 4th Decile
	All Workers			
1937	24.4	8.5	3.5	1.8
1938	25.5	9.4	4.1	1.9
1939	22.9	8.6	3.8	1.8
1940	24.0	8.8	3.7	1.8
1941	24.6	9.3	3.8	1.8
1942	29.0	10.8	4.2	1.9
1943	30.1	11.7	4.5	2.0
1944	30.2	11.4	4.3	1.9
1945	30.6	11.5	4.5	2.0
1946	27.1	9.2	3.8	1.9
1947	23.3	8.4	3.5	1.8
1948	23.7	7.6	3.3	1.7
	Four-Quarter Workers			
1938	5.4	2.9	1.9	1.4
1939	5.2	2.9	1.9	1.4
1940	5.1	2.8	1.9	1.4
1941	4.8	2.8	1.9	1.4
1942	5.0	2.9	2.0	1.4
1943	—	2.9	2.0	1.4
1944	—	2.8	2.0	1.4
1945	—	2.7	1.9	1.4
1946	—	2.4	1.7	1.3
1947	—	—	1.7	1.3
1948	—	—	1.7	1.3

Source: Derived from Appendix Table 98.

Inequality in Earnings and Work Continuity

A comparison of the range of earnings and the interdecile ratios among all covered workers and among workers with an equal number of quarters of wage credits[13] indicates that the main source of contrasts in their earnings is the presence in the labor force of persons with irregular or brief employment. Among workers having the same number of months or weeks of wage credits there is undoubtedly much less disparity than among those with wage credits in four, three or two quarters. It is also likely that a survey of earnings in all pursuits would show less disparity than is found in the insurance statistics, which are restricted to earnings in industries that were covered by the OASI program before 1950.

13. Social Security Yearbook, Federal Security Agency, 1939, p. 59; 1941, p. 128; 1942, p. 114; 1943, p. 91; 1944, p. 63; 1945, p. 63.

Chapter 37

THE AGE FACTOR IN EARNINGS *

Earnings tend to vary with the age of the worker. The low earnings of young workers reflect not only their lack of skill and experience but also their higher rate of job turnover. At the other end of the age span, earnings tend to taper off somewhat because diminished speed and vitality lower the efficiency and employability of older people and disability increasingly deprives them of working days.

Earnings of skilled workers and manual laborers, men and women, white and Negro workers all show the same general age pattern. Among the various groups, however, the degree of variation of earnings with age differs appreciably. It is greater for men than women; it is greater for white men than for Negro men, but less for white women than for Negro women.

The relative spread in earnings between the highest and the lowest decile [1] is greatest in youth and is usually narrowest at 30 to 40 years of age. Differences between intermediate earnings levels — for example, the third and seventh deciles — usually reach their minimum at later ages.

Earnings Distribution

Wage statistics based on payrolls of reporting firms, such as statistics collected by the Bureau of Labor Statistics or the National Industrial Conference Board, provide no information on earnings differentials according to age.[2] Almost all we know about the changes of earnings with age is based on the experience of the old-age and survivors insurance system. These being the only available comprehensive data, the following observations are limited to the coverage of OASI; the term "earnings" as used in this chapter relates only to the taxable wages of the persons concerned as reported by their employers.

The insurance records show that the youngest workers are heavily concentrated in the lowest wage classes and that the proportion of workers in the lowest wage classes declines steadily up to the age group 45–54 years, beyond which it increases slightly. On the other hand, few young workers are recorded in the upper intervals, say from $2,000 up before the war, or from $3,000 up in recent years. The proportion of workers in the upper intervals increases with age to about 50 years and declines thereafter. (See Table 197.)

The concentration of young workers in the low wage intervals is largely due to the irregularity of their employment. To some extent, this is true also for older workers. After age 50, and especially after 65, the increasing proportion of workers in the lower intervals keeps pace with the decline in continuity of work.

Irregularity of employment is not the whole story, however, as is apparent from data on steadily employed workers. The same pattern of variation of earnings with age was observed in 1943 among four-quarter workers who had been in covered employment in preceding years. Most of the younger workers in this group received $400 to $1,200, and their most typical wage credits were close to $800. At ages 20 to 24, the greatest concentration was at $800–$1,600, with the typical amount close to the middle of this range. In the higher age classes — up to 55 years — the proportion of four-quarter workers who received less than $1,600 declined steadily, while the proportion of those with more than $2,000 increased. The inverse trend was characteristic of age classes beyond 55 years. (See Table 198.)

Decile Annual Earnings

The correlation between earnings and age appears still clearer when decile earnings are recorded for each age class.

---

* By W. S. Woytinsky. Data for this chapter were partly prepared by Dr. Elinor Pancoast, Goucher College.

1. See pp. 439–40.

2. Age is not recorded on payrolls, and the classification of workers by age in a wage survey would require a special investigation of each individual case. Such an inquiry, moreover, would be rather difficult, because very young and elderly workers are reluctant to tell their exact age to the employer or interviewer.

TABLE 197

PERCENTAGE DISTRIBUTION OF WORKERS IN SPECIFIED AGE GROUPS UNDER OASI BY ANNUAL WAGE CREDITS, 1939 AND 1944

1939

Wage Credits	All Ages	Age, in Years											
		Under 20	20–24	25–29	30–34	35–39	40–44	45–49	50–54	55–59	60–64	65–69	70 and Over
Total	100.0	100.0	100.0	100.0	100.0	100.0	100.0	100.0	100.0	100.0	100.0	100.0	100.0
$ 1– 199....	23.7	63.3	29.7	20.7	17.4	16.5	16.1	15.7	16.2	17.4	18.4	19.3	18.5
200– 399....	11.2	18.0	15.6	11.3	9.3	8.7	8.2	8.0	8.2	8.7	9.2	10.1	10.2
400– 799....	19.9	15.6	28.2	22.3	18.6	17.1	16.5	16.2	16.4	17.0	17.7	18.3	18.4
800–1,199....	16.4	2.8	18.4	20.8	18.0	16.0	15.2	15.3	15.9	16.7	17.4	18.2	19.0
1,200–1,599....	12.1	0.3	6.1	14.4	15.9	15.0	14.6	14.7	15.2	14.9	14.4	14.1	13.5
1,600–1,999....	7.3	—	1.5	6.6	10.2	11.0	11.0	11.1	10.5	9.5	8.7	7.4	6.4
2,000–2,399....	3.8	—	0.3	2.4	5.2	6.4	6.7	6.5	5.9	5.2	4.6	3.8	3.5
2,400–2,799....	2.0	—	0.1	0.8	2.4	3.5	3.9	4.0	3.6	3.1	2.7	2.3	2.4
2,800–2,999....	0.6	—	—	0.2	0.7	1.1	1.3	1.3	1.2	1.0	0.8	0.7	0.7
3,000	3.0	—	0.1	0.5	2.3	4.6	6.5	7.2	6.9	6.5	6.1	5.8	7.4

1944

Wage Credits	All Ages	Age, in Years			
		Under 25	25–44	45–64	65 and Over
Total	100.0	100.0	100.0	100.0	100.0
$ 1– 199.................	18.0	33.2	13.6	9.8	14.9
200– 399.................	8.9	15.4	6.9	5.5	7.6
400– 799.................	12.3	17.8	10.7	9.1	12.0
800–1,199.................	10.5	12.2	9.9	9.7	12.1
1,200–1,599.................	10.0	9.4	10.0	10.3	12.8
1,600–1,999.................	8.4	5.5	9.2	9.8	10.9
2,000–2,399.................	7.3	2.9	8.4	9.8	9.2
2,400–2,799.................	6.4	1.7	7.7	9.2	6.9
2,800–2,999.................	3.1	0.6	3.9	4.5	2.7
3,000	15.1	1.3	19.7	22.3	10.9

Note: Because of periodic revisions and corrections, there are some slight discrepancies in OASI tables released at different dates.

Source: Social Security Yearbook, Federal Security Agency, 1940, p. 135; 1945, p. 64.

All decile earnings of men rise steeply up to the age class 30–34 years, level off to a peak in the age group 40–44, then decline, slightly up to 50–54 years and more steeply after 55 years. At all levels of earnings, 60-year-old workers have about as much as those 35 years old, and workers aged 65 about as much as those 30 years old. (See Figure 72 and Appendix Tables 99 and 101.) The changes of decile earnings of women are less regular but follow a similar pattern. (See Appendix Table 100 and Chapter 38.)

Comparison of the decile earnings of all male workers who had wage credits in 1946 with those of four-quarter workers casts light on the combined effect on earnings of regularity of em-

TABLE 198

PERCENTAGE DISTRIBUTION, BY ANNUAL WAGE CREDITS, OF FOUR-QUARTER WORKERS IN SPECIFIED AGE GROUPS WHO HAD EARLIER WAGE CREDITS UNDER OASI, 1943

Wage Credits	Under 20 Years	20–24 Years	25–34 Years	35–44 Years	45–54 Years	55–64 Years	65 Years and Over
Total	100.0	100.0	100.0	100.0	100.0	100.0	100.0
$ 1– 199	3.7	0.6	0.3	0.4	0.4	0.6	1.8
200– 399	11.5	2.3	1.2	1.1	1.1	1.4	2.3
400– 799	29.7	11.8	6.2	5.1	5.0	5.5	8.0
800–1,199	28.7	24.0	11.9	10.0	10.0	11.2	14.6
1,200–1,599	15.6	23.6	14.4	12.1	11.6	13.4	17.6
1,600–1,999	6.2	14.4	13.8	12.3	12.4	14.1	15.4
2,000–2,399	2.5	9.1	12.3	12.7	13.1	13.9	12.4
2,400–2,799	1.1	5.6	11.5	12.1	12.0	12.7	8.7
2,800–2,999	0.3	2.1	5.3	5.6	5.5	4.7	3.2
3,000	0.5	6.5	23.0	28.5	28.7	22.5	15.9

Source: Bureau of Old-Age and Survivors Insurance.

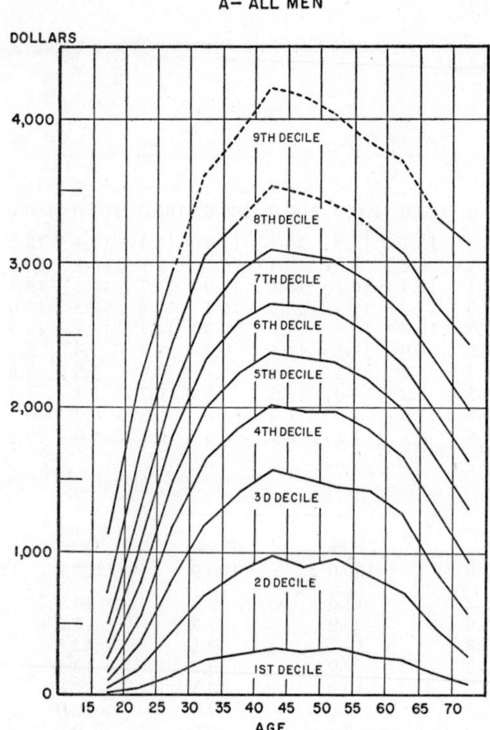

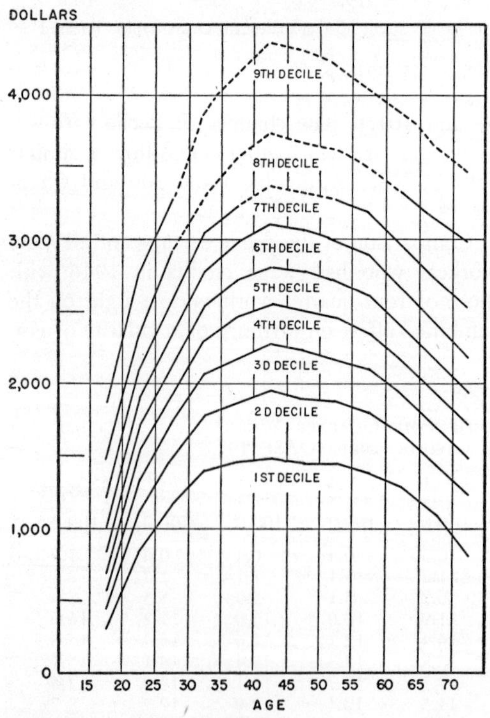

FIGURE 72. DECILE ANNUAL WAGE CREDITS OF MALE WORKERS UNDER OASI, BY AGE, 1946

Sources: Appendix Tables 99 and 101.

ployment and wage rates. In the three upper deciles at ages 35 to 54 wage credits are practically the same for all male workers (Figure 72, A) and for four-quarter men (Figure 72, B). Instability of employment (a high proportion of persons with wage credits in less than four quarters) affects earnings most among young and elderly workers, especially in the lower deciles.[3]

Earnings of Workers of Various Ages

The effect of age on earnings may change over a period of years. During the war, young and old workers made smaller gains in annual earnings than workers in the middle age groups. After the war, the relation of earnings to age was nearer the prewar pattern. (See Appendix Tables 99 and 100.)

This change of pattern may have been caused partly by changes in the composition of the labor force. Marginal workers flooded the wartime labor market. The proportion of persons with occasional and temporary employment and insignificant annual earnings was especially high among young and elderly workers. Therefore, earnings in these age classes did not increase at the same rate as the earnings of middle-aged workers, who generally were employed more regularly. During the reconversion, when many marginal workers withdrew from the labor market or were squeezed out of jobs, their disappearance from payrolls covered by OASI caused a noticeable rise in wage credits in the age groups under 20 and over 60 years.

Age Factor in Earnings of Men and Women

The general pattern of variation of wages with age is essentially the same among men and women: decile wages of both sexes usually increase up to 40–45 years and decline at more advanced ages. There is, however, an appreciable difference between men and women in the rate of change: decile earnings of men rise and decline more steeply than those of women. (Cf. Appendix Tables 99, 100 and 101.)

This difference is illustrated by the median wage credits of the two sexes in 1939, 1946 and 1948. In relation to the median for all age

3. In general, the decile curves in part B of Figure 72 show the effect of age on the earnings of regularly employed workers, while the analogous curves in part A show the combined effect of occupational promotion and demotion and changes in continuity of employment.

groups, median wage credits of young and old men are lower than those of women of the same age. Also, there were changes in the age-to-earnings relationship from 1939 to 1948: The decline in men's earnings after age 65 became sharper; the rise in women's earnings up to ages 45–49 became clearer. Both changes were probably due to changes in the composition of the labor force. (See Figure 73.)

At all ages, men earn more than women. The contrast increases as one moves from the youngest age groups up to 50 years. Later the difference narrows, but it does not disappear completely. The maximum difference is among low-paid workers (the lowest decile) in the age group 45–54; at these ages, wage credits of men are from three to five times as much as those of women. The ratio of men's to women's earnings usually declines after age 60, when the chances of interruption of employment because of poor health are about the same for both sexes.

Range of Earnings

A relationship between earnings and age appears not only in the level of earnings but also in the range of earnings of workers in different age classes.

The widest range in earnings of male workers is usually found in the ages under 25 and over 65, the age groups that include a large proportion of occasional workers with irregular employment. The narrowest range is at ages 30–44, the period of most regular work. The age relationship is not so apparent, however, when the extremes are eliminated. The ratio of the seventh to the third decile is fairly stable for all age classes from 30 to 65. It was somewhat narrower in 1946 than in 1939. (See Table 199.)

At all ages, the range of earnings is usually wider for women than for men, perhaps because of the large proportion of women who work only part of the year.

TABLE 199

Ratio of Seventh- to Third-Decile Annual Wage Credits of Male Workers under OASI, by Age, 1939 and 1946 [a]

Age Group	1939	1946
30–34 years	2.5	2.2
35–39	2.5	2.0
40–44	2.5	1.9
45–49	2.4	2.0
50–54	2.5	2.1
55–59	2.7	1.9
60–64	2.8	2.0

a. The seventh decile could not be computed for workers in age groups 30–59 in 1948. For the age group 60–64 the ratio was 2.0.

Source: Derived from Appendix Table 99.

Age Factor in Earnings of White and Negro Workers

Earnings of Negro men vary less with age than those of white men. A very young white man can expect a greater improvement in earnings in middle age and a greater decline in old age than a young Negro. Because of the high proportion of Negro workers with irregular employment, Negro men have a greater range of earnings than white men at every age interval except that of 15–19. (See Appendix Tables 102 and 103 and Table 200.)

Earnings of Negro women, on the other hand, generally vary more with age than those of white women. At all ages from 20 years on, the spread in earnings is generally greater for Negro women than for white women.

White workers earn more than Negroes at every age, but the contrast has declined since World War II. In the age group 40–44, for example, the median annual earnings of white men were 2.6 times as high as those of Negroes in 1937, as compared with a ratio of 1.8 to 1 in 1946. (See Table 201.) The greatest contrast between wage credits of white and Negro workers is in the low-paid pursuits (represented by the first decile), and here highly significant changes have taken place in recent years.[4]

The Earnings Cycle in the Life of a Worker

Differences in earnings among workers of different ages do not portray correctly the earnings cycle in the life of an individual worker. What they show are the earnings positions of workers of different ages in relation to wages prevailing at a given time. When the general level of wages rises, both young and old workers earn more but the general pattern of age differentials remains, though changing economic conditions may cause it to change in some detail. To visualize the probable typical cycle of earnings in the life of an individual worker, the pattern of age differentials in earnings should be related to the probable long-range trend in wages.

Assuming a continuous advance of per capita earnings at a rate of 10 per cent each five years, a young man starting his working life can ex-

4. See p. 453.

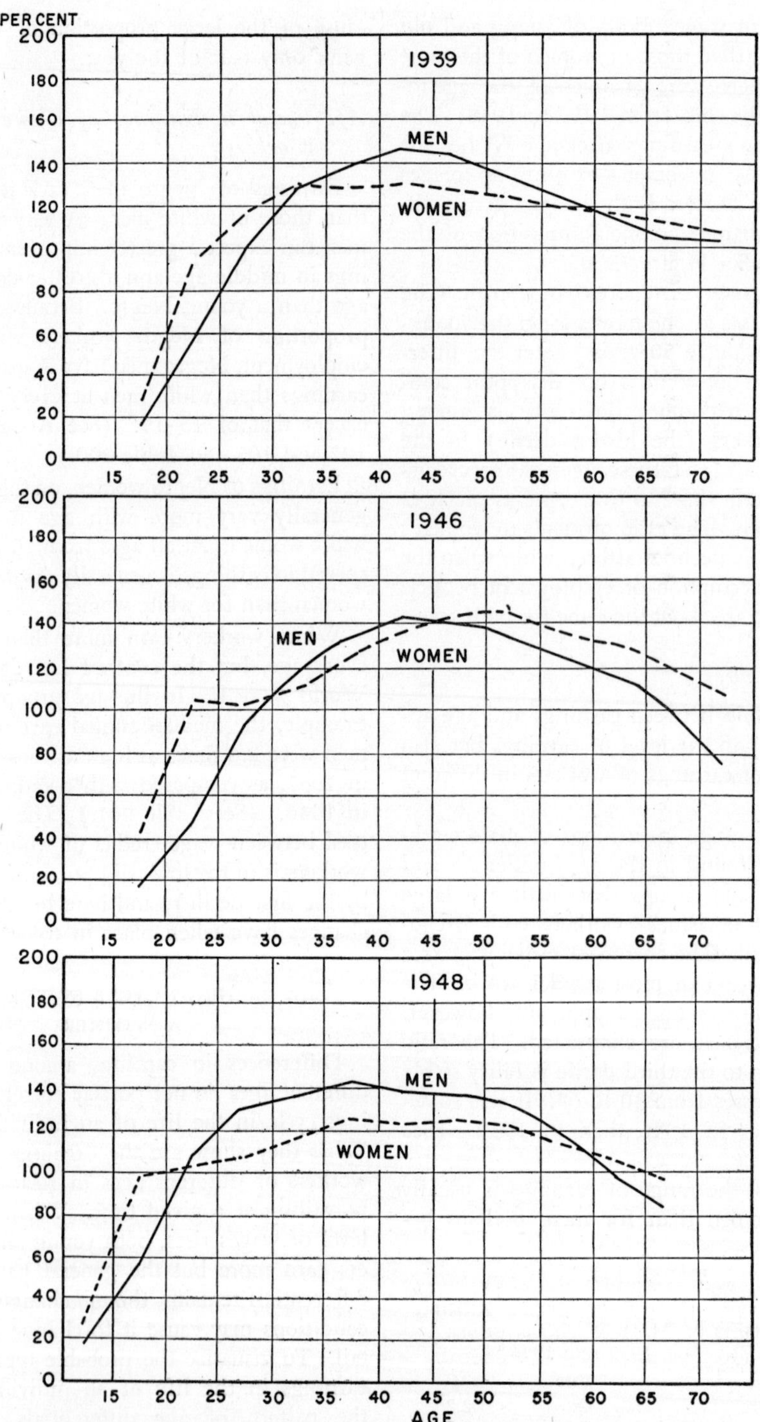

FIGURE 73. MEDIAN ANNUAL WAGE CREDITS OF MEN AND WOMEN IN SPECIFIED AGE CLASSES AS PERCENTAGE OF MEDIAN EARNINGS OF ALL MEN AND WOMEN UNDER OASI, 1939, 1946 AND 1948

Source: Derived from Appendix Tables 99 and 100.

TABLE 200

RANGE OF ANNUAL WAGE CREDITS OF WORKERS UNDER OASI, BY SEX, RACE AND AGE, 1937 AND 1946

	Men				Women			
	White		Negro		White		Negro	
Year and Age	Ratio of 9th to 1st Decile	Ratio of 7th to 3d Decile	Ratio of 9th to 1st Decile	Ratio of 7th to 3d Decile	Ratio of 9th to 1st Decile	Ratio of 7th to 3d Decile	Ratio of 9th to 1st Decile	Ratio of 7th to 3d Decile
1937								
All ages	23.0	2.9	46.0	4.8	34.0	3.6	63.0	5.6
15–19	49.0	4.3	47.9	4.3	53.3	5.2	42.0	3.0
20–24	20.8	2.9	48.0	4.6	26.3	3.1	56.5	6.3
25–29	12.4	2.1	38.0	4.1	23.2	2.8	47.7	4.2
30–34	12.1	2.1	33.4	3.5	24.2	2.9	34.0	3.9
35–39	14.1	2.2	32.0	3.5	25.3	2.9	34.5	4.0
40–44	15.0	2.1	33.5	3.6	23.5	2.8	35.0	4.1
45–49	15.7	2.2	37.7	3.7	23.2	2.8	34.5	4.2
50–54	16.5	2.2	36.8	3.9	24.9	2.7	40.0	4.7
55–59	19.3	2.4	41.0	4.1	26.6	2.8	44.3	4.8
60–64	20.8	2.5	47.2	4.2	25.4	2.8	54.6	5.0
65 and over	45.4	4.1	70.8	5.8	36.4	4.4	84.0	6.4
1946								
All ages	—	3.1	35.4	4.0	34.3	4.2	38.3	4.4
15–19	46.8	4.0	41.2	4.1	37.1	4.0	48.3	4.1
20–24	29.4	3.6	41.6	4.6	26.7	3.7	47.0	4.5
25–29	14.8	2.4	29.8	3.6	31.5	4.0	38.6	4.5
30–34	—	2.0	23.8	3.0	30.8	4.0	31.2	3.9
35–39	—	1.9	21.8	2.7	29.0	3.5	27.2	3.7
40–44	—	1.8	19.2	2.7	26.6	3.3	34.3	4.2
45–49	—	1.9	19.4	2.5	25.3	3.1	29.9	3.7
50–54	—	1.8	20.9	2.8	25.5	3.1	27.6	3.5
55–59	—	1.9	27.9	3.1	24.8	3.0	29.0	3.9
60–64	—	2.0	25.1	3.2	22.1	2.8	36.4	4.1
65–69	19.8	2.6	28.5	3.2	23.5	3.0	22.3	2.8
70 and over	30.3	3.4	45.9	5.1	30.0	3.8	36.3	3.9

Source: Derived from Appendix Table 102.

TABLE 201

RATIO BETWEEN SELECTED DECILE ANNUAL WAGE CREDITS OF WHITE AND NEGRO WORKERS UNDER OASI, BY AGE, 1937 AND 1946

	Men			Women		
Year and Age	First Decile	Median	Ninth Decile	First Decile	Median	Ninth Decile
1937						
All ages	4.0	3.0	2.0	3.5	2.9	1.9
15–19	2.1	2.6	2.2	2.4	2.6	3.0
20–24	4.3	3.6	1.9	3.5	4.0	1.6
25–29	5.6	3.0	1.8	3.3	3.1	1.6
30–34	5.4	2.8	2.0	2.8	2.5	2.0
35–39	4.8	2.7	2.1	2.8	2.4	2.0
40–44	4.8	2.7	2.1	3.0	2.4	2.0
45–49	5.3	2.6	2.2	3.0	2.5	2.0
50–54	4.9	2.6	2.2	3.2	2.7	2.0
55–59	4.7	2.6	2.2	3.3	2.8	2.0
60–64	4.8	2.6	2.1	4.2	3.1	1.9
65 and over	2.9	3.2	1.9	5.0	4.3	2.2
1946						
All ages	2.2	1.9	—	1.7	2.1	1.5
15–19	1.0	1.2	1.1	2.3	2.3	1.8
20–24	1.9	1.6	1.3	2.8	3.2	1.6
25–29	2.9	1.9	1.5	1.9	2.2	1.5
30–34	3.0	1.9	—	1.6	1.7	1.5
35–39	3.3	1.9	—	1.5	1.8	1.6
40–44	3.1	1.9	—	2.0	2.1	1.5
45–49	2.8	1.8	—	1.9	1.9	1.6
50–54	3.3	1.8	—	1.6	1.9	1.5
55–59	3.8	1.9	—	1.8	1.9	1.5
60–64	3.4	2.0	—	2.4	2.0	1.5
65–69	2.3	1.7	1.6	1.5	2.5	1.6
70 and over	2.6	2.4	1.7	1.8	2.0	1.4

Source: Derived from Appendix Table 102.

pect, over a period of twenty or thirty years, not only wage increases corresponding to the customary pattern of occupational promotion but also a share in the general growth of the social product. And for a man in his fifties the prospect that earnings will be curtailed with the approach of old age is offset to some extent by the general upward movement of wages.

Assuming that the pattern of age differentials in earnings remains the same, and that all earnings increase 2 per cent each year, or 20 per cent a decade, a man aged 20 to 24 — whether a

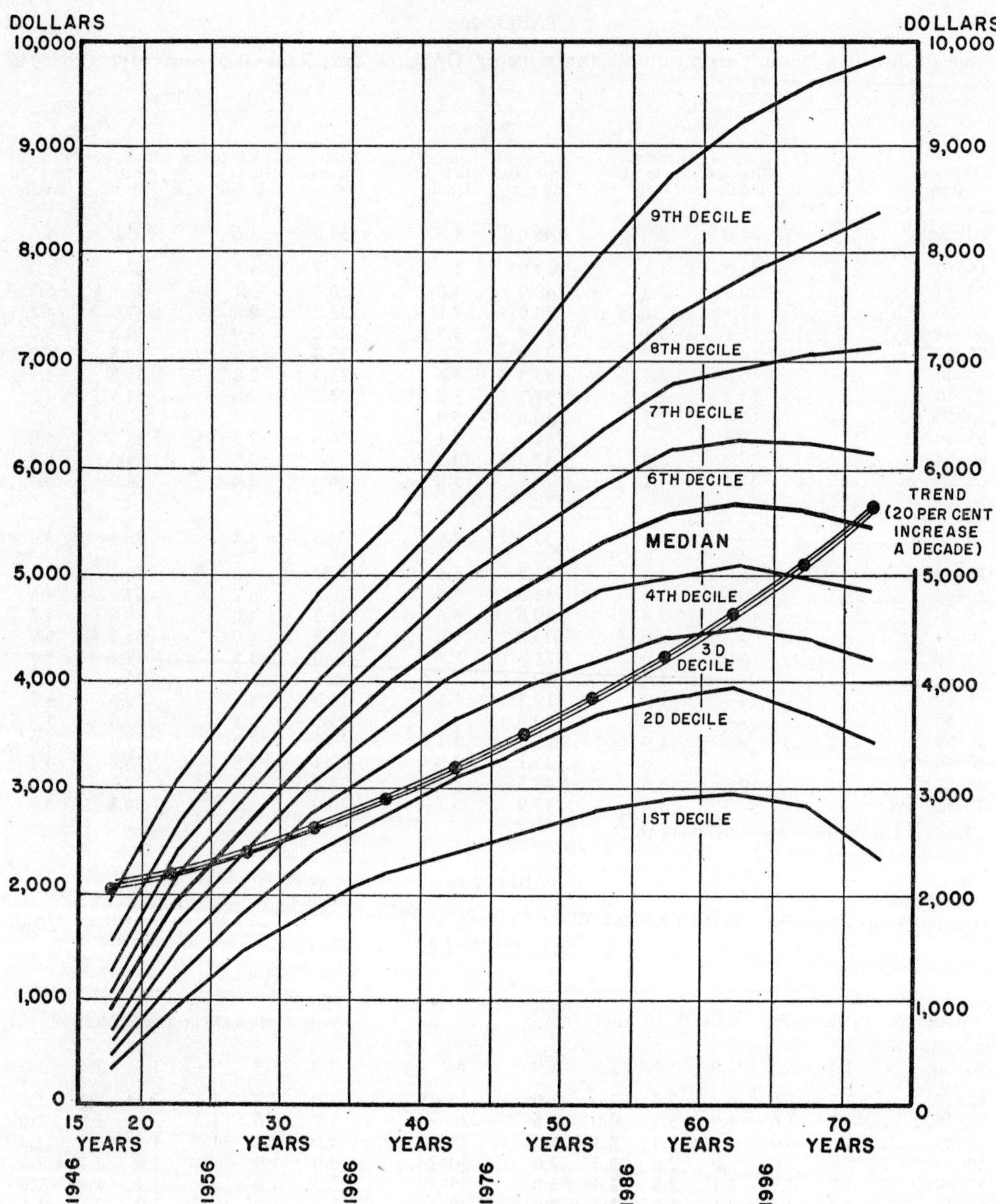

FIGURE 74. HYPOTHETICAL VARIATION OF ANNUAL EARNINGS OF A GENERATION OF MEN REGULARLY EMPLOYED IN INDUSTRIES COVERED BY OASI

The assumption of a continuous rise of wages at a rate of 20 per cent a decade (the hypothetical trend) is combined here with the pattern of wage differentials by age among four-quarter workers in 1946 as shown in part B of Figure 72. The decile earnings for the age class 15–20 years in 1946 are the same in both figures. The level of the trend line is irrelevant, since it serves only to show the relative long-range rise of wages.

low-paid manual laborer or a skilled white-collar worker — would have a very substantial increase in annual earnings before he reaches 55–59 years of age. His earnings are likely to decline thereafter if he is an unskilled laborer but will continue to rise as long as he stays in employment if he belongs to the upper third of the occupational pyramid. (See Figure 74.)

CHAPTER 38

EARNINGS BY SEX AND RACE *

GENERALLY SPEAKING, earnings of women have in recent years been half those of men, earnings of Negro men half those of white men, earnings of Negro women half those of white women. Outright discrimination in the sense of paying women lower rates for the same kind of work is not common practice.[1] Similarly, a company seldom has different wage rates for Negro and white workers employed side by side on identical or similar jobs. Sex and racial differences in remuneration rest essentially on differences in the work the different groups perform or in the work opportunities available to them.

Work Opportunities of Women

Restriction of the occupations open to women is due partly to custom, partly to the fact that, while men stay in the labor force throughout adult life, many women withdraw from work after marriage or after birth of the first child, and some women take paid work only temporarily as auxiliary earners in the family. Their lack of continuity of employment prevents many working women from acquiring skills and from obtaining seniority rights or promotion in a company. Another factor that affects the earnings of married women unfavorably is that they are less mobile, geographically and occupationally, than men.

This pattern in the participation of women in the labor force, rather than lack of physical strength and endurance, has determined the hiring practices of employers. The list of jobs assigned to men and women without discrimination is fairly short. The usual practice is to reserve certain positions for women and others for men. Although the range of occupations open to women has widened gradually from decade to decade, it still is narrow in comparison with the growing number of women seeking industrial employment. This fact has increased competition among women workers and has led to the widely accepted view that wage rates for jobs held by women are naturally lower than rates for jobs held by men.

Independently of wage rates, the annual earnings of women are restricted in comparison with those of men by the high proportion of women employed as casual, part-time and intermittent workers. As marginal workers, women are the first to be laid off. Furthermore, family and personal circumstances cause their turnover and absentee rates ordinarily to exceed men's.

Work Opportunities of Negroes

Similar circumstances are responsible for differences between earnings of white and Negro workers. Comparatively limited choice of occupations, geographical and industrial immobility, and irregular employment affect the earnings of Negroes unfavorably. To these factors are added differences in education and in customary standards of living. Very often Negroes are offered only those jobs that white workers would not take at the existing wage rate. In factories, Negro workers are usually denied promotion to positions that would involve supervision of the work of white workers.

Differences in the remuneration of men and women and of white and Negro workers appear more clearly in their annual earnings than in the rates of wages paid them for similar work.

DIFFERENTIALS IN ANNUAL EARNINGS

The effects of occupational distribution and continuity of employment on the earnings distribution of the different groups of workers are illustrated by the records of old-age and survivors insurance showing annual wage credits of male and female, white and Negro workers in 1945.[2] Taking the group as a whole, most workers were concentrated, in that year, in the

* By W. S. Woytinsky. Statistical data for this chapter were prepared by Dr. Elinor Pancoast, Goucher College.

1. Maurice Leven and K. R. Murphy, *The Income Structure of the United States,* Brookings Institution, Washington, 1938, p. 58.

2. The tabulation is based on a 3 per cent sample covering nearly 1.4 million persons.

TABLE 202

DISTRIBUTION OF WORKERS UNDER OASI BY SEX, RACE, NUMBER OF QUARTERS IN COVERED EMPLOYMENT AND AMOUNT OF WAGE CREDITS, 1945 (A 3 PER CENT SAMPLE)

(*In Thousands*)

		Four-Quarter Workers				Less-than-Four-Quarter Workers			
		Men		Women		Men		Women	
Wage Credits	Total	White	Negro	White	Negro	White	Negro	White	Negro
Total	1,364	448	44	236	16	316	40	233	32
$ 1– 199	254	2	—	3	—	117	18	97	17
200– 399	133	5	1	8	1	57	8	47	7
400– 599	95	8	2	13	2	36	4	28	3
600– 799	77	9	3	17	2	22	2	18	2
800– 999	71	10	3	22	3	15	2	14	1
1,000–1,199	71	12	4	28	2	13	1	10	1
1,200–1,399	72	15	4	31	2	11	1	9	—
1,400–1,599	69	18	4	30	1	9	1	5	—
1,600–1,799	62	20	4	25	1	8	1	2	—
1,800–1,999	58	25	4	19	—	7	—	2	—
2,000–2,199	52	28	3	14	—	4	—	1	—
2,200–2,399	47	30	3	9	—	5	—	—	—
2,400–2,599	44	32	2	6	—	4	—	—	—
2,600–2,799	41	32	2	4	—	3	—	—	—
2,800–2,999	39	32	1	2	—	3	—	—	—
3,000 and over....	178	169	3	5	—	1	—	—	—

Source: Bureau of Old-Age and Survivors Insurance.

lowest and the highest wage intervals — 35 per cent had wage credits amounting to less than $600 and almost 30 per cent over $2,000. (See Table 202.) Very different, however, were the distributions of the different sex and race groups. White men with four calendar quarters in covered employment were clearly concentrated in the upper wage intervals; most of them had wage credits of $2,600 or more. Negro men and white women with four quarters in covered employment were concentrated in the middle intervals; about half of them had credits from $1,000 to $2,000. Most of the four-quarter Negro women earned from $400 to $1,400.

Among workers with less than four quarters in covered employment, typical wage credits for the year were under $400 for white men, slightly over $200 for Negro men and white women, and less than $200 for Negro women. Moreover, a considerable minority of white men with less than four quarters were dispersed in the middle and upper intervals, up to $3,000 and over.

In brief, each sex and race group has its own pattern of distribution by level of earnings, but there is some similarity in the distribution of Negro men and white women.

Earnings of Men and Women

The rule of thumb that women usually earn half as much as men requires some qualification. Since the main source of difference in remuneration of the two sexes is that they are usually employed for different services, there is no point in comparing the hourly wage rates of men and women who happen to hold identical or similar jobs. The comparison should be focused, rather, on more or less similar groups of male and female workers, that is, on groups having the same number of quarters in covered employment and similarly placed in the scale of occupations — at the bottom, close to the middle, or at the top (lowest, middle and highest deciles [3]).

Such a comparison shows that the relative spread between earnings of men and women is broader among all workers with wage credits than among workers with the same number of quarters in covered employment. Close to the middle of the occupational ladder (median earnings) the ratio between earnings of men and women in 1946 was 2.2 among all workers and 1.6 among those with the same number of quarters in employment. (See Table 203.)

The ratio of median earnings of all male workers to those of all female workers increased during the war — from 1.9–2.0 in 1937–1939 to 2.5–2.6 in 1942–1944 — but declined to 2.2 in 1946. No such changes can be discerned in the four-quarters group or among those with three or two quarters in covered employment.

3. See pp. 439–40.

TABLE 203

RATIO BETWEEN SELECTED DECILE ANNUAL WAGE CREDITS OF MEN AND WOMEN UNDER OASI, BY NUMBER OF QUARTERS IN COVERED EMPLOYMENT, 1937–1946

	All Workers			Four-Quarter Workers			Three-Quarter Workers			Two-Quarter Workers		
Year	First Decile	Median	Ninth Decile	First Decile	Median	Ninth Decile	First Decile	Median	Ninth Decile	First Decile	Median	Ninth Decile
1937	2.1	2.0	1.9	—	—	—	—	—	—	—	—	—
1938	2.6	1.9	1.9	1.6	1.6	1.9	1.5	1.5	1.6	1.6	1.2	1.5
1939	2.6	1.9	1.9	1.5	1.7	1.8	1.3	1.5	1.7	1.4	1.3	1.5
1940	2.8	1.9	1.9	1.6	1.7	1.9	1.5	1.5	1.8	1.6	1.3	1.6
1941	2.8	2.2	2.0	1.6	1.8	2.0	1.6	1.5	1.8	1.5	1.4	1.7
1942	3.6	2.6	2.1	1.7	1.9	2.0	1.8	1.6	1.9	1.6	1.5	1.7
1943	2.2	2.5	1.9	1.8	1.9	—	1.4	1.6	1.7	1.6	1.4	1.6
1944	2.1	2.5	—	1.7	1.9	—	1.3	1.5	1.7	1.5	1.3	1.7
1945	1.7	2.1	—	1.8	1.8	—	1.1	1.5	1.5	1.6	1.4	1.7
1946	2.3	2.2	1.7	1.7	1.6	—	1.4	1.6	1.7	1.6	1.6	1.6

Source: Bureau of Old-Age and Survivors Insurance. Cf. Appendix Table 104.

Among workers with the same number of quarters of work, the ratios at all levels of the distribution fluctuated within a very narrow range, without a definite trend in either direction. This fact suggests that, despite the spectacular expansion of work opportunities for women and the increased proportion of women in covered employment, occupational discrimination against them still remains — relatively — as strong as before the war.

Earnings of White and Negro Workers

The earnings of Negroes are particularly low at the bottom of the occupational scale. In 1937 the wage credits of Negro men at the lower end of the distribution were only one fourth of those of white workers in similarly paid jobs; in the median jobs, Negroes had one third, and in the better jobs half, of the wage credits of white workers. (See Table 204.) The disparity in the earnings of the two groups was due largely to the difference in the stability of their covered employment: a sizable proportion of the Negro workers shifted between jobs covered by OASI and those that were excluded at that time — men between agriculture and urban pursuits, women between domestic service and industry.

TABLE 204

RATIO BETWEEN SELECTED DECILE ANNUAL WAGE CREDITS OF WHITE AND NEGRO WORKERS UNDER OASI, 1937, 1939, 1944 AND 1946

	Men			Women		
Year	First Decile	Median	Ninth Decile	First Decile	Median	Ninth Decile
1937	4.0	3.0	2.0	3.5	2.9	1.9
1939	3.7	3.0	2.1	3.5	2.5	1.7
1944	2.2	2.2	—	1.7	2.4	1.5
1946	2.2	1.9	—	1.7	2.1	1.5

Source: Derived from Appendix Table 102.

The contrast between the earnings of Negro and white workers declined during the war and did not increase after the war, when many Negroes lost the jobs to which they were admitted during the national emergency. In 1946 as in 1944, median earnings of Negro men under the insurance system amounted to 55 per cent of the median earnings of white men.

Range of Earnings

In the ten-year period 1937–1946, the range of earnings of men and women, as measured by the ratio between seventh and third deciles, fluctuated fairly narrowly: between 3.1 and 4.3 for all male workers; between 3.7 and 4.7 for all women; between 1.6 and 1.8 for four-quarter men; and between 1.5 and 1.6 for four-quarter women. (Table 205.) The ratio between ninth and first deciles was less stable.

For all workers, and especially for women, the range of earnings widened in the war years and then narrowed, probably because of changes in the extent of turnover of the labor force. The net change was significant only among men with four or three quarters in covered employment. For the middle 40 per cent of these groups, the ratios narrowed from 1.8 and 2.4, respectively, in 1938 to 1.6 and 2.1 in 1946. This trend may be related to the narrowing of the spread between wage rates of skilled and unskilled workers.[4]

In comparison with white workers, Negro workers, especially Negro women, have a very wide range of earnings. The gap between their highest and lowest earnings narrowed sharply as war and postwar conditions brought steadier

4. See pp. 470 ff.

TABLE 205

RANGE OF ANNUAL WAGE CREDITS OF MEN AND WOMEN UNDER OASI, BY NUMBER OF QUARTERS IN COVERED EMPLOYMENT, 1937–1946

Year	All Workers		Four-Quarter Workers		Three-Quarter Workers		Two-Quarter Workers	
	Ratio of 9th to 1st Decile	Ratio of 7th to 3d Decile	Ratio of 9th to 1st Decile	Ratio of 7th to 3d Decile	Ratio of 9th to 1st Decile	Ratio of 7th to 3d Decile	Ratio of 9th to 1st Decile	Ratio of 7th to 3d Decile
				Men				
1937	28.8	3.1	—	—	—	—	—	—
1938	32.6	3.7	5.1	1.8	12.0	2.4	15.0	2.7
1939	33.2	3.5	4.8	1.8	11.5	2.4	14.7	2.6
1940	32.3	3.3	4.6	1.7	9.9	2.3	14.6	2.7
1941	30.2	3.3	4.4	1.7	8.8	2.2	14.4	2.7
1942	33.8	3.5	4.2	1.7	8.1	2.3	14.6	2.8
1943	34.4	3.8	—	1.6	9.9	2.6	15.8	3.0
1944	—	3.5	—	1.6	10.2	2.6	18.3	3.2
1945	—	4.3	—	1.6	9.2	2.6	16.5	3.1
1946	26.4	3.2	—	1.6	6.8	2.1	13.1	2.6
				Women				
1937	31.7	3.7	—	—	—	—	—	—
1938	44.4	4.7	4.4	1.6	10.6	2.2	15.2	2.2
1939	45.2	4.5	3.9	1.6	9.1	2.1	13.2	2.3
1940	46.0	4.1	3.8	1.6	8.5	2.1	14.0	2.3
1941	40.8	4.1	3.5	1.5	7.8	2.0	12.6	2.3
1942	55.8	4.7	3.5	1.5	7.7	2.0	14.1	2.4
1943	38.8	4.3	3.8	1.6	7.8	2.1	15.5	2.5
1944	36.1	4.2	4.0	1.6	7.7	2.1	16.0	2.6
1945	34.5	4.0	3.7	1.6	7.2	2.2	14.8	2.6
1946	36.5	4.2	3.6	1.6	5.9	2.0	13.4	2.3

Source: Bureau of Old-Age and Survivors Insurance.

employment to low-paid workers; the narrowing was more marked for Negro women than for Negro men.

GEOGRAPHICAL DIFFERENTIALS

The relationship between earnings of men and women and between those of white workers and Negroes differs in various parts of the country and the patterns of difference have changed appreciably in recent years.

Earnings of Men and Women

In some states, earnings of women are low in relation to those of men for low-paid jobs and comparatively high for medium jobs or skilled trades; in other states the opposite is true. In California, in 1939, for example, women earned one third as much as men at the bottom of the occupational scale, approximately half in medium jobs, and somewhat more than half in high-paid positions. In New York, in the same year, women's wages were two thirds of men's in unskilled jobs and only half in the better-paid trades. In Missouri, the ratios were: nearly three fourths in unskilled jobs, more than half in the middle of the occupational scale, and less than half at the top. (See Appendix Table 105.)

The relationship between the earnings of women and men changed during the war, but not uniformly in all states or at all occupational levels. In 1946, in the country as a whole, the median earnings of women, in dollars and cents, were 15 per cent behind the median earnings of men in 1939. But in New England and the South Atlantic and East South Central states the median earnings of women were roughly equal to the prewar median earnings of men, while in the upper part of the occupational ladder women's earnings were in some cases (see, for example, the eighth decile) higher than the prewar wages of men. (See Appendix Table 105.)

Earnings of White and Negro Workers

In the United States as a whole, as has been stated, the earnings of Negroes are particularly low in comparison with those of white workers at the lower end of the distribution (the first decile). This tendency is far from universal, however. North Carolina and Louisiana are typical of states where the ratio of Negroes'

TABLE 206

DECILE ANNUAL WAGE CREDITS OF NEGROES AS PERCENTAGE OF THOSE OF WHITE WORKERS UNDER OASI, IN FOUR STATES, 1946

State	Men			Women		
	First Decile	Median	Ninth Decile	First Decile	Median	Ninth Decile
North Carolina	47.3	51.4	58.5	38.4	36.3	58.9
Louisiana	42.1	44.0	48.5	42.5	43.6	48.1
Tennessee	75.0	65.8	60.2	50.0	43.5	52.4
Arkansas	87.5	67.1	59.7	90.9	81.8	61.6

Source: Appendix Table 107.

earnings to those of white workers increases as one moves from low-paid to higher-paid occupations. Tennessee and Arkansas typify the opposite tendency. (See Table 206.)

Indeed, there is no universal pattern of relationship between Negro and white earnings at different occupational levels in different states. The statement that Negroes earn approximately half the customary earnings of white workers is correct for the nation as a whole and for medium occupations, but in some instances — for example, in coal mining and automobile factories — Negroes receive the same wages as white workers, and in others — for example, as service workers in offices — they earn less than one fourth of the prevailing wages of white workers.

The variety of patterns among states cannot be reduced to the contrast between South and North. In both regions, states differ in the level of earnings of Negro workers relative to those of white workers. In 1946, in Arkansas and Tennessee, Negro men at the median earned 67.1 and 65.8 per cent as much as white men, as compared with 44 per cent and 41.2 per cent in Louisiana and South Carolina. In New York and Pennsylvania the proportions were 56.5 and 69.5 per cent, as compared with 83.6 and 70.9 per cent in Michigan and Ohio. (See Appendix Table 107.)

While there is no clear geographic pattern of racial differentials in earnings, the trend in these differentials from 1939 to 1946 is clear. The spread between earnings of Negro and white men narrowed in nineteen states out of twenty for which comparable data were available.[5] The relationship between earnings of Negro and white women changed little, but in the nation as a whole the trend was toward reduction of racial contrasts. (See Table 207.)

5. These twenty states included all areas with a considerable proportion of Negroes in industrial employment.

TABLE 207

MEDIAN ANNUAL WAGE CREDITS OF NEGROES AS PERCENTAGE OF THOSE OF WHITE WORKERS UNDER OASI, IN SELECTED STATES, 1939 AND 1946

State [a]	Men		Women	
	1939	1946	1939	1946
South Carolina	31.7	41.2	22.9	32.1
Georgia	32.2	55.2	32.5	32.6
North Carolina	33.8	51.4	34.7	36.3
Louisiana	36.0	44.0	49.1	43.6
New Jersey	37.8	55.7	40.5	48.2
Maryland	38.2	55.2	28.2	41.1
Virginia	39.4	56.6	40.4	52.9
Florida	40.0	55.6	52.3	48.5
Missouri	41.3	58.7	57.2	42.0
District of Columbia	42.6	48.3	77.1	58.7
Texas	43.5	60.0	63.0	44.4
Mississippi	49.2	45.6	46.0	35.1
Alabama	50.0	64.8	47.0	39.8
Illinois	50.2	65.8	57.1	63.2
Ohio	50.6	70.9	59.2	46.2
Tennessee	50.8	65.8	40.9	43.5
New York	54.2	56.5	70.4	59.8
Arkansas	57.8	67.1	71.0	81.8
Pennsylvania	62.7	69.5	86.8	56.7
Michigan	65.2	83.6	64.4	51.1

a. States arrayed by ascending order of ratio between earnings of Negro and white male workers in 1939.

Source: Appendix Table 107.

INDUSTRIAL DIFFERENTIALS

Earnings of Men and Women

Nearly every industry has its own pattern of sex differentials in wages. Women's earnings compare most favorably with men's in contract construction, mining, transportation, communication and public utilities — all of which are industries that employ women mainly in clerical jobs. In the service industries, the ratio of women's earnings to men's is also high, particularly at the lowest part of the distribution. In manufacturing and retail trade — which together employ half of all men and two thirds of all women — women's earnings are particularly low in comparison with those of men. (See Table 208; cf. Appendix Table 112.)

In all industries except transportation, communication and other public utilities, and con-

TABLE 208

Decile Annual Wage Credits of Women as Percentage of Those of Men under OASI, by Industry Division, 1939, 1944 and 1946

Industry Division	1939			1944			1946		
	First Decile	Median	Ninth Decile	First Decile	Median	Ninth Decile	First Decile	Median	Ninth Decile
All Workers									
All industries	38.4	52.2	52.3	45.8	40.6	—	42.3	44.9	58.4
Mining	52.6	77.8	90.8	42.8	48.5	67.9	50.0	66.1	78.4
Contract construction	160.0	138.4	78.7	55.5	53.2	—	88.2	73.4	71.6
Manufacturing	37.5	48.5	47.4	45.9	44.7	—	37.5	52.0	59.9
Transportation, communication and other public utilities	160.0	76.2	64.8	83.3	58.0	—	85.7	67.8	—
Wholesale trade	40.0	48.0	42.9	63.6	51.0	—	46.8	54.3	—
Retail trade	37.7	38.7	50.2	40.0	39.4	44.9	41.1	38.8	50.0
Finance, insurance and real estate	86.3	67.5	47.0	56.4	52.1	—	49.0	56.4	—
Service industries	85.7	70.6	55.3	70.0	50.5	48.7	57.1	51.8	53.7
Four-Quarter Workers									
All industries	—	—	—	56.2	51.8	—	56.0	59.5	—
Mining	—	—	—	68.9	68.8	—	74.3	73.9	—
Contract construction	—	—	—	63.8	58.0	—	77.5	70.1	—
Manufacturing	—	—	—	60.5	53.7	—	62.1	61.8	—
Transportation, communication and other public utilities	—	—	—	69.6	58.5	—	74.6	68.5	—
Wholesale trade	—	—	—	69.4	55.6	—	61.0	63.4	—
Retail trade	—	—	—	63.9	51.8	—	57.7	54.8	—
Finance, insurance and real estate	—	—	—	73.4	53.0	—	70.8	56.7	—
Service industries	—	—	—	78.3	55.7	—	72.8	58.8	—

Source: Derived from Appendix Tables 110 and 111.

TABLE 209

Decile Annual Wage Credits of Negroes as Percentage of Those of White Workers under OASI, by Industry Division, 1946

Industry Division	Men			Women		
	First Decile	Median	Ninth Decile	First Decile	Median	Ninth Decile
All industries	44.8	51.4	—	58.3	46.5	65.0
Mining	60.6	83.9		—	—	—
Contract construction	65.0	51.4	62.7	—	—	—
Manufacturing	28.4	55.2	—	63.1	51.9	75.9
Transportation, communication and other public utilities	37.8	48.1	—	47.6	48.1	70.4
Wholesale trade	27.8	39.7	—	90.9	23.4	45.6
Retail trade	60.0	58.1	59.6	86.7	68.5	67.4
Finance, insurance and real estate	23.9	42.7	—	32.4	34.1	53.5
Service industries	114.2	58.7	61.5	93.3	51.6	58.6

Source: Bureau of Old-Age and Survivors Insurance.

tract construction, the spread between the earnings of the two sexes in 1946 was narrower among four-quarter workers than among all workers, but the ranking of industries was practically the same whether all workers or only those with covered employment in four quarters are considered.

In retail and wholesale trade the spread declined during the war; in manufacturing it increased.

Weekly earnings of women production workers in twenty-five manufacturing industries increased at a slower rate than those of men between 1939 and 1944, and rose faster from 1944 to 1946. Earnings of women in these industries in 1944 were only 57 per cent of those of men, as compared with 59 per cent in 1939 and 67 per cent in 1946.[6]

6. *The Economic Almanac for 1949,* National Industrial Conference Board, New York, 1948, p. 205.

Earnings of White and Negro Workers

Earnings of Negro workers are particularly low in comparison with those of white workers in those industries where Negroes are excluded from the jobs typical of the industry and are employed mainly in service jobs — as, for example, in wholesale trade, banks, insurance and real estate agencies. The contrast in earnings is less striking in those industries where Negroes and whites are employed in similar jobs, even though the racial groups may be segregated on the job. Mining, retail trade and services are typical of such industries. In manufacturing the relationship lies between these two extremes. (See Table 209.)

CHAPTER 39

INDUSTRIAL DIFFERENTIALS IN EARNINGS *

THE PATTERN OF EARNINGS in a particular industry can be described in terms of average hourly or weekly earnings; of annual earnings per person or per full-time worker; and of earnings of various groups of workers at different occupational levels. The last approach can be applied, theoretically, to annual, weekly and hourly earnings, but it is used here only in the analysis of annual earnings under the old-age and survivors insurance program.

The main difference between these approaches is in degree of emphasis on continuity of employment, which is minimized when comparisons are focused on hourly and weekly earnings and stressed in the examination of annual earnings, especially decile [1] earnings for industries and groups of workers.

AVERAGE WEEKLY AND HOURLY EARNINGS

Average weekly and hourly earnings in an industry are determined by many factors, among them the composition of the labor force in terms of sex, race, age, occupational level and skill; the location of the industry (whether in large cities or in rural areas, in high-wage or low-wage regions, and so on); the prevailing size of establishments; the trend of growth in the industry (whether it is an old and decaying branch of production or a growing one); current business conditions; the bargaining position and strength of labor unions. This list is not exhaustive nor does it pretend to enumerate the factors in the order of their significance.

Sometimes it is difficult to single out the principal cause of the relatively high or low level of wages in an industry. Tobacco manufacturing, for example, has lower average weekly and hourly earnings than any other industry in the United States. It is generally held that wages in this industry are low because plants are located in low-wage areas, close to tobacco plantations; because operations do not require much skill from workers; because tobacco factories employ many women and Negroes; and because most of the workers are not unionized. But nearly as low are average weekly and hourly earnings in the manufacture of apparel and other finished textile products, an industry that is concentrated in high-wage areas, requires considerable skill from workers and is as thoroughly unionized as any other industry in the nation.

Wage statistics of the Bureau of Labor Statistics show that, on the average, both hourly and weekly earnings of production workers more than doubled from 1939 to 1949 and continued to advance in 1950. But they reveal no appreciable trend toward a broadening or narrowing of industrial differentials in hourly earnings or in average weekly earnings. In 1939, average weekly earnings ranged from $16.84 (in tobacco and textiles) to $33.13 (in street railways and buses). In 1950 the range was from $41.08 (in tobacco) to $75.01 (in products of petroleum and coal). In both cases the lowest industry paid about half the wage prevailing in the highest industry. (See Table 210.) [2]

On the whole, the ranking of industries by average hourly and weekly earnings changed little from 1939 to 1950. The conspicuous exceptions are bituminous coal mining, on the one hand, and telephone service, on the other. In 1939, bituminous coal mining ranked close to the top (fourth) in hourly wages but was rather low (in the sixteenth place) in average weekly earnings. In 1950 it topped the list in hourly wages and was close to the top (third) in weekly earnings. The spectacular rise of wages in this industry was due to a combination of factors: improved business conditions and progress of mechanization in the coal industry, a shortage of skilled miners, a successful campaign on the part of the labor union, ability of management to pass on rising labor costs to consumers, and so on.

The telephone industry, which ranked fifth in hourly wages and fourth in weekly earnings

* By W. S. Woytinsky.

1. See pp. 439-40.

2. Mathematical analysis of the series shown in Table 210 indicates that the variations among industries were somewhat smaller in 1950 than in 1939, but the change was not very significant.

TABLE 210

AVERAGE WEEKLY AND HOURLY EARNINGS OF PRODUCTION WORKERS IN SELECTED INDUSTRIES, ANNUAL AVERAGE, 1939, 1949 AND 1950

Industry [a]	Weekly Earnings			Hourly Earnings		
	1939	1949	1950	1939	1949	1950
Tobacco manufactures	$16.84	$37.25	$41.08	$0.48	$1.00	$1.08
Textile mill products	16.84	44.83	48.95	0.46	1.19	1.24
Apparel manufactures	18.17	41.89	43.68	0.53	1.17	1.20
Lumber basic products	19.06	51.72	55.31	0.49	1.27	1.35
Leather manufactures	19.13	41.61	44.56	0.53	1.14	1.19
Furniture manufactures	19.95	49.48	53.67	0.52	1.23	1.28
Retail trade	21.17	45.93	47.63	0.54	1.14	1.18
Paper and allied products	23.72	55.96	61.14	0.59	1.34	1.41
Bituminous coal mining	23.88	63.28	70.35	0.89	1.94	2.01
Stone, clay and glass	23.94	54.45	59.20	0.64	1.37	1.44
Food and kindred products	24.43	53.58	56.07	0.61	1.29	1.35
Chemicals	25.59	58.63	62.67	0.65	1.43	1.51
Anthracite mining	25.67	56.78	63.24	0.92	1.88	1.97
Electrical machinery	27.09	56.96	60.83	0.70	1.44	1.48
Iron and steel [b]	27.52	60.78	67.24	0.74	1.59	1.65
Rubber manufactures	27.84	57.79	64.42	0.75	1.51	1.58
Machinery, except electrical	29.27	60.44	67.21	0.75	1.53	1.61
Wholesale trade	29.85	57.55	60.36	0.72	1.41	1.48
Telephone	31.94	51.78	54.38	0.82	1.35	1.40
Products of petroleum and coal	32.62	72.36	75.01	0.89	1.79	1.83
Automobiles and equipment	32.91	65.97	73.25	0.93	1.70	1.78
Local railways and bus lines	33.13	64.61	66.96	0.17	1.44	1.49

a. Industries arrayed by ascending order of weekly earnings in 1939.
b. In 1949 and 1950, primary metal industries.

Sources: Monthly Labor Review, June 1949, pp. 707–23, and October 1951, pp. 498–513; *Handbook of Labor Statistics,* 1947 edition, Bulletin No. 916, Bureau of Labor Statistics, 1948, pp. 52–86.

before the war, fell to the fourteenth and sixteenth positions, respectively, in 1950. The shift was caused by the change in the composition of the labor force in that industry — the increased proportion of women and new workers with little experience and without seniority rights.[3]

AVERAGE ANNUAL EARNINGS PER FULL-TIME EMPLOYEE

The figures on average annual earnings per full-time employee, by industry, currently published by the Department of Commerce reveal considerable shifts in the relative positions of industries from 1929 to 1939 and from 1939 to 1949–1950.[4]

Farm laborers have remained at the bottom of the list, but the gap between their earnings and those prevailing in manufacturing industries has narrowed. In 1929, annual earnings of farm laborers averaged $455, as compared with $1,543 in manufacturing; in 1950 workers engaged in farming averaged $1,365, as compared with an average of $3,303 earned by full-time employees in manufacturing industries. (See Table 211 and Appendix Table 108.)

Air transportation was a new industry in 1929 and paid the highest wages, but it lost its unique position after the war. Water transportation was among the low-wage industries in

3. In the Bell System the proportion of women increased from 60.1 per cent in 1939 to 64.7 per cent in 1949, while the proportion of workers with less than two years of service advanced among men from 3.4 to 13.4 per cent and among women from 8.3 to 25.2 per cent.

4. These data are not based on a direct statistical survey but represent an estimate based on current reports of old-age and survivors insurance, state unemployment insurance, and other agencies. Annual earnings per full-time employee as defined in these statistics do not represent the earnings for fifty-two normal weeks, but are computed by prorating the estimated wage bill of each industry over the estimated average number of workers employed by the industry through the year. (See Appendix Table 108.)

Conceptually, these averages are comparable with average weekly earnings as reported by the Bureau of Labor Statistics, with the difference that the annual data include not only production workers, as do the BLS figures, but also supervisory employees (above the level of foreman) and clerical staffs, routemen, salesmen and the like. Because of this difference in coverage, annual earnings per full-time employee as computed by the Department of Commerce are usually more than fifty-two times average weekly wages in the same industry as reported by the BLS.

Because of wider coverage (especially inclusion of farm laborers and domestic servants in private households), the range of industrial differentials in annual earnings (see Appendix Table 108) is broader than that in weekly earnings as reported by the BLS.

TABLE 211

AVERAGE ANNUAL EARNINGS PER FULL-TIME EMPLOYEE IN SELECTED INDUSTRIES, 1929, 1939, 1949 AND 1950

Industry [a]	1929	1939	1949	1950
Agriculture, forestry, etc.	$ 455	$ 403	$1,349	$1,365
Service in private households	701	520	1,409	1,414
Medical and other health services	925	907	1,995	2,107
Tobacco manufactures	979	916	2,089	2,258
Hotels, lodging places	1,098	958	1,950	1,991
Local utilities and public services	1,116	1,240	2,522	2,682
Textile mill products	1,155	960	2,565	2,767
Lumber basic products	1,172	956	2,296	2,519
Personal services	1,219	1,008	2,188	2,256
Water transportation	1,272	1,553	4,137	4,413
Amusement, except motion pictures	1,273	1,277	2,363	2,432
Bituminous coal mining	1,293	1,197	2,925	3,266
Highway freight transportation	1,298	1,521	3,557	3,812
Educational services	1,313	1,234	2,332	2,420
Leather manufactures	1,327	1,038	2,410	2,550
Highway passenger transportation	1,328	1,303	2,764	2,869
Apparel manufactures	1,361	1,025	2,383	2,492
Legal services	1,385	1,205	2,188	2,268
Telephone and telegraph	1,385	1,599	2,907	3,033
Furniture manufactures	1,398	1,138	2,651	2,846
Retail trade	1,409	1,224	2,686	2,807
Nonmetallic mining	1,413	1,171	3,021	3,245
Services allied to transportation	1,425	1,269	2,907	3,087
Public education	1,445	1,403	2,830	2,927
Food manufactures	1,503	1,372	2,926	3,071
Paper manufactures	1,514	1,414	3,230	3,474
Stone, clay and glass	1,557	1,359	3,014	3,263
Utilities: electric and gas	1,590	1,767	3,376	3,569
Rubber manufactures	1,597	1,548	3,225	3,528
Religious organizations	$1,610	$1,410	$2,163	$2,276
Metal mining	1,616	1,518	3,411	3,541
Commercial schools, etc.	1,650	1,529	3,270	3,462
Electrical machinery	1,655	1,601	3,247	3,369
Nonferrous metals	1,665	1,521	3,271	3,617
Chemicals	1,673	1,611	3,529	3,763
Contract construction	1,674	1,268	3,235	3,358
Local railways and bus lines	1,721	1,701	3,256	3,400
Anthracite mining	1,728	1,406	2,896	3,107
Iron and steel	1,740	1,549	3,390	3,628
Transportation equipment, except automobiles	1,747	1,667	3,600	3,753
Railroads	1,749	1,877	3,704	3,752
Automobiles and equipment	1,813	1,762	3,607	4,007
Repair services	1,814	1,603	3,465	3,627
Machinery, except electrical	1,827	1,681	3,478	3,757
Products of petroleum and coal	1,844	1,852	4,179	4,320
Federal civil service	1,924	1,842	3,335	3,552
Pipeline transportation	1,927	1,930	4,172	4,296
Printing and publishing	2,010	1,718	3,653	3,798
Crude petroleum and natural gas	2,019	1,684	3,735	3,834
Finance, insurance, etc.	2,090	1,761	3,083	3,279
Wholesale trade	2,164	1,773	3,671	3,900
Motion pictures	2,169	1,971	2,920	2,919
Business services	2,185	1,828	3,648	3,863
Engineering, professional services	2,314	1,973	3,922	4,144
Radio broadcasting and television	2,513	2,427	4,469	4,698
Air transportation	2,624	2,328	3,870	4,118

a. Industries arrayed by ascending order of earnings in 1929.

Source: Appendix Table 108.

the 1920's, but annual earnings of maritime workers more than tripled after the United States became a leading seafaring nation. Compare the rise in average earnings of air transportation workers from $2,624 in 1929 to $4,118 in 1950 with the rise in earnings of water transportation workers from $1,272 to $4,413 during the same period. In percentage terms, the average water transport worker earned 48.5 per cent of what his counterpart in air transportation earned in 1929, and 107 per cent in 1950.

Closer analysis of gains in earnings in various industries from 1929 to 1950 shows that a rise of 90 to 120 per cent was most usual for this period. Most manufacturing industries and several important nonmanufacturing industries (contract construction, retail trade, local railways, services allied to transportation) made about this gain. If gains of 120 per cent or more are described as "high" and those of less than 90 per cent are considered as "low," the group with "high" gains is found to include industries in which earnings were particularly low before the war (farming, water transportation, highway freight transportation, bituminous coal mining, tobacco manufactures, textile mills, medical and health services, and so on). On the other hand, the group with "low" gains includes many industries that had comparatively high earnings before the war (air transportation, radio broadcasting, engineering services, business services, motion pictures, wholesale trade, finance). (See Table 212.)

Apart from this general trend, the typical white-collar industries lagged behind manufacturing and manual labor.

Wide dispersion in the rate of advance in earnings — 35 per cent in motion pictures and 41 per cent in religious organizations to 247 per cent in water transportation and 200 per cent in farming — suggests that the general upward trend was overlapped by the effects of particular factors in individual industries, such as changes in relative supply of labor, business position and so on. As with changes in geographical differentials (Chapter 41), it is not very clear whether the drive of organized labor was a major factor in determining the rate of advance in earnings in each industry. The iron

TABLE 212

SELECTED INDUSTRIES CLASSIFIED BY PERCENTAGE GAINS IN AVERAGE ANNUAL EARNINGS PER FULL-TIME EMPLOYEE FROM 1929 TO 1950

High Gains (120 per cent or more)		Medium Gains (90 to 120 per cent)		Low Gains (Less than 90 per cent)	
Water transportation	247	Telephone and telegraph	119	Printing and publishing	89
Agriculture, forestry, etc.	200	Metal mining	119	Radio broadcasting and television	87
Highway freight transportation	194	Services allied to transportation	117	Personal services	85
Bituminous coal mining	153	Nonferrous metals	117	Federal civil service	85
Textile mill products	140	Highway passenger transportation	116	Educational services	84
Local utilities and public services	140	Railroads	115	Apparel manufactures	83
Products of petroleum and coal	134	Lumber basic products	115	Hotels, lodging places	81
Tobacco manufactures	131	Transportation equipment, except automobiles	115	Anthracite mining	80
Nonmetallic mining	130	Commercial schools, etc.	110	Wholesale trade	80
Paper manufactures	129	Stone, clay and glass	110	Engineering, professional services	79
Medical and other health services	128	Iron and steel	109	Business services	77
Chemicals	125	Machinery, other than electrical	106	Legal services	64
Utilities: electric and gas	124	Electrical machinery	104	Air transportation	57
Pipeline transportation	123	Food manufactures	104	Finance, insurance, etc.	57
Automobiles and equipment	121	Furniture manufactures	104	Religious organizations	41
Rubber manufactures	121	Public education	103	Motion pictures	35
		Service in private households	102		
		Contract construction	101		
		Repair services	100		
		Retail trade	99		
		Local railways and bus lines	98		
		Leather manufactures	92		
		Amusement, except motion pictures	91		
		Crude petroleum and natural gas	90		

Source: Derived from Table 211.

and steel industry, for example, obtained just the average increase. Bituminous coal miners have made impressive gains; but still larger, proportionally, were the gains of farm laborers and workers in water transportation. The earnings of workers in the automobile industry and in machinery and electrical machinery factories did not rise in the same proportion as those in tobacco manufactures and textile mills.[5]

Average Annual Earnings under OASI

Average annual earnings of workers in various industries, as reported by the Bureau of Old-Age and Survivors Insurance, differ substantially from the earnings per full-time employee in the same industries computed by the Department of Commerce. The industrial coverage of the insurance program is narrower; its wage records do not include earnings over $3,000 during a year; and its reports prorate the estimated total taxable wages over all persons who had wage credits in covered industries, while the Department of Commerce uses as divisor the estimated number of full-time employees (or full-time year-round jobs).[6]

The two sets of figures are very similar, however, in the ranking of industries by level of earnings. The great advantage of the OASI earnings statistics is that they identify the wage earners by sex and age, and in some series also by race.

In all industries, according to OASI records, women's earnings lag behind those of men. In 1945 the ratio of women's earnings to men's averaged 56 to 100 for all industries and 58 to 100 for manufacturing. (See Appendix Table 109.) In industries with a very small proportion of female workers — such as mining, construction, water transportation, railways and bus lines — average earnings of women compare favorably with those of men. In industries in which women constitute a large part of the work force, their earnings are as a rule substantially lower than those of male workers. Such is the case in apparel and leather manufactures, retail trade, hotels and lodging places, personal service industries, movies, educational services and so on.[7]

Differences in continuity of employment also contribute importantly to industrial disparity in the annual wage credits recorded by OASI. Moreover, a comparison of annual earnings per full-time employee with annual wage credits under the insurance program in the same industries (see Appendix Tables 108 and 109) shows that even annual earnings on a full-time basis are largely affected by continuity of employment. In industries with unstable employment and a shifting labor force, earnings on a full-time basis are conspicuously low in comparison with those in industries that have continuous and stable employment.[8] There is a double interdependence between industrial patterns of employment and earnings. In a high-wage industry, workers are more strongly attached to their jobs than in a low-wage industry. On the other hand, an industry employing a large proportion of casual laborers shifting from job to job has lower average wages than one in which an establishment is eager to have a permanent work force.

Decile Annual Earnings under OASI

The salient feature of industrial differentials in earnings is that the contrasts between high-wage and low-wage industries are more pronounced in the earnings of low-paid workers than at the top of the wage scale.

Industrial Patterns

In 1939, wage credits of low-paid male workers (the first decile) ranged among most indus-

5. Cf. pp. 500–01.

6. The Bureau of Old-Age and Survivors Insurance computes average annual earnings by industry on the basis of the wages credited to each person during the year. When all these wages were earned in a single industry, industrial classification presents no problem; but difficulty arises in the case of multi-industry workers. If the wages earned during a year by such workers are assigned to those industries in which they were actually earned, each multi-industry worker will be counted several times, each time with only a part of his annual earnings. Average earnings computed in this way will show, not the actual earnings of individuals, but average wage disbursements of the respective industries per person on their payrolls at any time during a year. It is therefore preferable, for analysis of industrial patterns in earnings, to count each employee only once and to assign him — with all his wage credits — to only one industry. In wage statistics of this type (without duplication in the number of multi-industry workers), people are classified by the last industry in which they were employed. This procedure is fairly rough but has the advantage of simplicity, and it is believed that the margin of error involved does not distort the general picture of industrial differentials in earnings.

7. Domestic service in private households is not in this list because it was not covered by OASI before amendment of the program in 1950.

8. W. S. Woytinsky, *Earnings and Social Security in the United States,* Committee on Social Security, Social Science Research Council, Washington, 1943, pp. 138–43.

TABLE 213

DECILE ANNUAL WAGE CREDITS OF MALE WORKERS UNDER OASI IN SELECTED INDUSTRIES, 1944

Decile	Food	Tobacco	Machinery	Auto-mobiles	Bitu-minous Coal Mining	Non-ferrous Metals	Apparel	Motion Pictures
First	$ 45	$ 165	$ 385	$ 380	$ 275	$ 325	$ 195	$ 35
Second	140	495	1,090	1,260	890	975	590	115
Third	310	890	1,890	2,070	1,485	1,650	1,115	225
Fourth	620	1,170	2,240	2,615	1,900	2,095	1,585	400
Median	1,100	1,460	2,620	2,930	2,235	2,425	2,030	720
Sixth	1,675	1,730	2,945	3,155	2,520	2,705	2,515	1,230
Seventh	2,170	1,910	3,220	—	2,760	2,985	2,925	2,100
Eighth	2,645	2,195	—	—	3,005	3,260	3,290	3,075
Ninth	3,165	3,045	—	—	—	—	—	—

Source: Appendix Table 110, C.

tries from $25 to more than $300, while the range at the median was from $315 to $1,670, and at a high occupational level (the eighth decile) from $920 to $3,220. In 1946 the range was from $40 to more than $600 for the lowest decile and from $385 to $2,555 for the median.[9] (See Appendix Table 110.)

The contrast between low-wage and high-wage industries is illustrated by a comparison of wage credits of male workers in food and tobacco manufactures, on the one hand, and machinery and automobile factories, on the other. Low-paid workers in food and tobacco plants earned about 25 per cent of the wages paid at the same occupational level in automobile and machinery factories; in the middle part of the distribution the proportion was close to 50 per cent; at high levels wage credits were practically the same in all four industries. (See Table 213; cf. Appendix Table 110.)

Moreover, the structure of wages varies from industry to industry. In some industries, prevailing earnings rise steeply from the low-paid jobs to the medium occupational level but increase little toward the top of the scale; in others, they are comparatively low up to the middle point of the distribution and rise thereafter. The first pattern is exemplified by the decile wage credits of male workers in bituminous coal mining and manufactures of nonferrous metals; the second, in apparel manufacture and the motion-picture industry.

Wartime Changes in Earnings

Among the factors responsible for changes in workers' earnings during the war, the most important was, of course, the shortage of labor. Since wage rates were frozen in many industries, earnings of individual workers were increased mainly by shifts to better jobs, upgrading, the longer work week, overtime pay, premiums and the like. At the same time, the influx of marginal workers into employment and the withdrawal of young men to the armed forces increased the proportion of persons with only brief employment in a year. Despite unprecedented work opportunities for all, part-time work and temporary employment were widespread during the war. These conditions account for the particular pattern of the wartime changes in the structure of earnings.

From 1939 to 1944, annual wage credits of male workers under OASI more than doubled in the middle part of the scale, but lagged behind this rate of gains for the low-paid and highest-paid workers. Gains in manufacturing industries resembled this over-all pattern, while in service industries earnings of the higher-paid workers — from the median up — increased more sharply than those of the lower-paid workers. (See Table 214.)

The pattern of increase in women's earnings was somewhat different. In all industries as a group, the greatest relative gains for women were recorded at both ends of the occupational ladder; in manufacturing and service industries, the largest gains were at the top.

Postwar Changes in Earnings

Reconversion from a wartime to a peacetime economy was marked by far-reaching changes in the structure of earnings, and these changes, combined with the rising cost of living, largely accounted for the feeling of uneasiness that prevailed in labor circles and found its expression in successive "rounds" for raises in pay.

9. Both in 1939 and 1946 industries at the extreme ends of the distribution are excluded. The highest deciles could not be computed for industries in which they were much in excess of $3,000.

The work week went back from an average of 45 hours to the customary 40 hours; veterans returned to the civilian labor force; many women withdrew from the labor market. Just as industrial mobilization was accompanied by upgrading and by shifts to more lucrative jobs, demobilization was marked by wholesale downgrading and the return of millions of workers to their prewar jobs. These factors tending to curtail per capita earnings were not offset by the general rise in hourly wage rates. In all manufacturing industries as a group, average hourly wage rates advanced 10 to 15 per cent from 1944 to 1946, but because of the shift of workers from high-wage jobs to less lucrative ones, average hourly earnings went up only 6.5 per cent, and because of shorter hours of work, average weekly earnings dropped 5 per cent.

The figures on annual wage credits under OASI show how these developments affected workers in various industries and in different parts of the frequency distribution.

Median annual wage credits of all men went down from $1,820 in 1944 to $1,670 in 1946, while the median for women rose from $740 to $750. Among four-quarter workers, the median for men declined from $2,595 to $2,435, while that for women increased from $1,345 to $1,450. (See Table 215.) These divergent shifts of the two sexes may have been caused by the changes in labor supply: while the supply of manpower was increased by the return of veterans, that of womanpower was curtailed by withdrawals of women from the labor market.

Gains and losses were very unevenly distributed among industries. For men, losses were concentrated in the industries directly hit by reconversion: mining, iron and steel, production of transportation equipment, electrical machinery and other machinery. On the other hand, men made gains in such manufacturing industries as food and tobacco, textiles, lumber basic products, furniture, paper, printing,

TABLE 214

DECILE ANNUAL WAGE CREDITS OF WORKERS UNDER OASI, IN ALL INDUSTRIES, MANUFACTURING AND SERVICES, 1939 AND 1944

	Men			Women		
Decile	1939	1944	1944 as Percentage of 1939	1939	1944	1944 as Percentage of 1939
All Industries						
First	$ 65	$ 120	185	$ 25	$ 55	220
Second	190	360	189	70	160	229
Third	385	775	201	160	295	184
Fourth	630	1,310	208	315	490	156
Median	870	1,820	209	455	740	163
Sixth	1,115	2,290	205	595	1,010	170
Seventh	1,370	2,740	200	735	1,255	171
Eighth	1,675	3,170	189	885	1,550	175
Ninth	2,160	—	—	1,130	1,990	176
Manufacturing						
First	120	185	154	45	85	189
Second	365	560	153	135	255	189
Third	620	1,130	182	280	470	168
Fourth	850	1,710	201	410	735	179
Median	1,070	2,200	206	520	985	189
Sixth	1,290	2,620	203	630	1,230	195
Seventh	1,490	2,980	200	745	1,480	199
Eighth	1,765	3,340	189	870	1,780	205
Ninth	2,235	—	—	1,060	2,185	206
Service Industries						
First	35	50	143	30	35	117
Second	110	150	136	95	110	116
Third	230	330	143	170	200	118
Fourth	390	615	158	290	325	112
Median	580	990	171	410	500	122
Sixth	800	1,445	181	550	720	131
Seventh	1,065	1,970	185	685	965	141
Eighth	1,400	2,580	184	830	1,255	151
Ninth	2,005	3,375	168	1,110	1,645	148

Source: Appendix Table 110, A–D.

TABLE 215

MEDIAN ANNUAL WAGE CREDITS OF WORKERS UNDER OASI, BY INDUSTRY, 1944 AND 1946

	All Workers				Four-Quarter Workers			
	Men		Women		Men		Women	
Industry	1944	1946	1944	1946	1944	1946	1944	1946
All industries	$1,820	$1,670	$ 740	$ 750	$2,595	$2,435	$1,345	$1,450
Mining	2,120	2,125	1,030	1,405	2,490	2,550	1,715	1,885
Contract construction	1,380	1,225	735	900	2,565	2,410	1,490	1,690
Manufacturing	2,200	1,910	985	995	2,790	2,480	1,500	1,535
Ordnance	2,430	2,135	1,210	1,285	2,925	2,665	1,740	1,715
Food	1,100	1,510	350	435	2,310	2,460	1,210	1,410
Tobacco	1,460	1,535	925	1,065	1,850	2,005	1,330	1,375
Textile mills	1,460	1,750	910	1,120	1,815	2,070	1,180	1,470
Apparel	2,030	1,890	940	920	2,650	2,925	1,270	1,420
Lumber	660	750	395	700	1,425	1,640	1,150	1,350
Furniture	1,320	1,430	650	765	1,955	2,045	1,250	1,405
Paper	1,915	2,040	850	990	2,395	2,510	1,290	1,490
Printing, etc.	2,320	2,345	870	1,025	2,845	3,135	1,340	1,565
Chemicals	2,160	2,150	1,050	1,265	2,680	2,630	1,560	1,730
Products of petroleum and coal	2,820	2,750	1,350	1,580	3,095	3,050	1,690	2,055
Rubber	2,435	2,390	1,150	1,315	3,015	2,775	1,680	1,770
Leather	1,785	1,805	870	1,035	2,180	2,235	1,210	1,390
Stone, clay, glass	1,690	1,705	900	1,085	2,255	2,270	1,360	1,550
Iron and steel [a]	2,520	2,330	1,210	1,310	2,835	2,400	1,665	1,750
Transportation equipment	2,900	2,065	1,610	1,280	—	2,590	2,255	1,915
Nonferrous metals	2,425	—	1,270	—	2,760	—	1,685	—
Electrical machinery	2,770	2,145	1,325	1,200	3,115	2,565	1,720	1,605
Machinery, except electrical	2,620	2,230	1,285	1,275	2,990	2,625	1,740	1,730
Automobiles	2,930	—	1,570	—	3,195	—	2,065	—
Transportation, communication and other utilities	1,930	1,945	1,120	1,320	2,510	2,610	1,470	1,790
Wholesale trade	1,830	1,915	935	1,040	2,605	2,655	1,450	1,685
Retail trade	925	1,145	365	445	1,880	2,095	975	1,150
Finance, etc.	2,070	2,080	1,080	1,175	2,630	2,800	1,395	1,590
Service industries	990	1,080	500	560	2,035	2,175	1,135	1,280

a. In 1946, primary metal industries.

Source: Appendix Tables 110, C–F, and 111.

leather, and stone, clay and glass. They gained also in transportation, communication and other utilities; wholesale and retail trade; finance; and service industries. In general, median earnings of men decreased during the reconversion in industries that were contracting and increased in those that were expanding. Median wage credits of women went down in transportation equipment and machinery factories, but rose in almost all other industries.

Essentially, changes in earnings at different occupational levels and in different industries have been controlled by economic forces — the supply of and demand for labor. These forces have dwarfed other factors, including the struggle of labor unions for raises in their respective industries.[10]

10. These statements do not offer a general dictum on the role of unions in determining wages. (See Chapter 43.) They refer strictly to the changes in industrial differentials in annual earnings from 1939 to 1944 and from 1944 to 1946.

Chapter 40

OCCUPATIONAL WAGE DIFFERENTIALS IN INDUSTRY *

Differences in the earnings of regularly employed workers result largely from occupational differentials in wage rates. This factor in the variation of earnings does not appear in the wage statistics examined in the preceding chapters, which are based on the industrial attachments and personal characteristics of workers without relation to the kind of work performed. As the central problem of job evaluation and one of the main issues in collective bargaining, grievance procedure and labor arbitration, the question of occupational differentials deserves closer examination.

Occupational differentials in wage rates are generally recognized as vital to the existing system of wages. Not only do they make possible compensation in accordance with skill, effort and working conditions, but they are necessary to ensure a sufficient supply of skilled and trained workers. In fact, certain jobs, especially in the professions, require considerable investment of time, effort and money in training. The present wage and salary system makes such investment attractive by the promise of future remuneration and prestige.

The question is: How wide should the occupational differentials in wage rates be to serve these purposes? This question cannot be resolved on the basis of theoretical considerations. In practice it is being resolved in the labor market by the trial-and-error method. The interplay of demand and supply ultimately determines the relative positions of different occupations and guides job evaluators as well as the wage negotiators of labor and management. Changes in demand and supply likewise determine the trend in occupational wage differentials.

Three broad groups of occupations are usually distinguished: skilled, semiskilled and unskilled. The semiskilled occupations are broken down into those involving mainly routine and repetitive tasks and those requiring considerable experience and specialized knowledge. The unskilled occupations are separated into those requiring arduous labor and those involving mainly lighter tasks. In this chapter these secondary breakdowns have been used only in analysis of the current situation; measurements of trends have been confined to the spread between skilled and unskilled rates.[1]

Current Differentials

Spread between Wages in Skilled and Unskilled Occupations

Wage rates of skilled workers in manufacturing industries were, on the average, about 55 per cent higher than those of unskilled in 1945–1947. Among semiskilled occupations, those requiring considerable ability paid, on the average, 35 per cent more than unskilled occupations, and those involving highly repetitive operations paid 15 per cent more. There was, of course, considerable variation within each group.

These variations can best be measured by expressing the usual wage rate in each skilled

* By Harry Ober, Bureau of Labor Statistics, U.S. Department of Labor. The author acknowledges the valuable assistance of Donald Helm of the same agency. Opinions expressed here are those of the author and not necessarily of the agency with which he is associated.

1. The wage data by occupation available for the past relate primarily to skilled trades and laborers. This is not a serious drawback, however, since the extremes of the occupational rate ladder define the limits within which all other rates are found. A narrowing of the spread between skilled and unskilled rates reflects a narrowing of differentials among all occupations.

Information on occupational wage differentials since 1945 is available from numerous wage studies made by the Bureau of Labor Statistics for manufacturing industries, gas and electric utilities, and building and printing trades. (*Wage Structure,* Bureau of Labor Statistics, Series 1 and 2, 1945–1949.) Data for earlier periods are not strictly comparable, but detailed occupational wage statistics on a fairly extensive basis were collected in connection with the 1940 census. (Sixteenth Census (1940), *Population — Comparative Occupation Statistics of the United States, 1870–1940.*) Useful data are also available from the studies of the National Industrial Conference Board covering the period since 1914. (N. Ada Benly, *Wages, Hours, and Employment in the United States, 1914–1936,* Studies, No. 229, National Industrial Conference Board, New York, 1936; *The Economic Almanac for 1948,* 1947.)

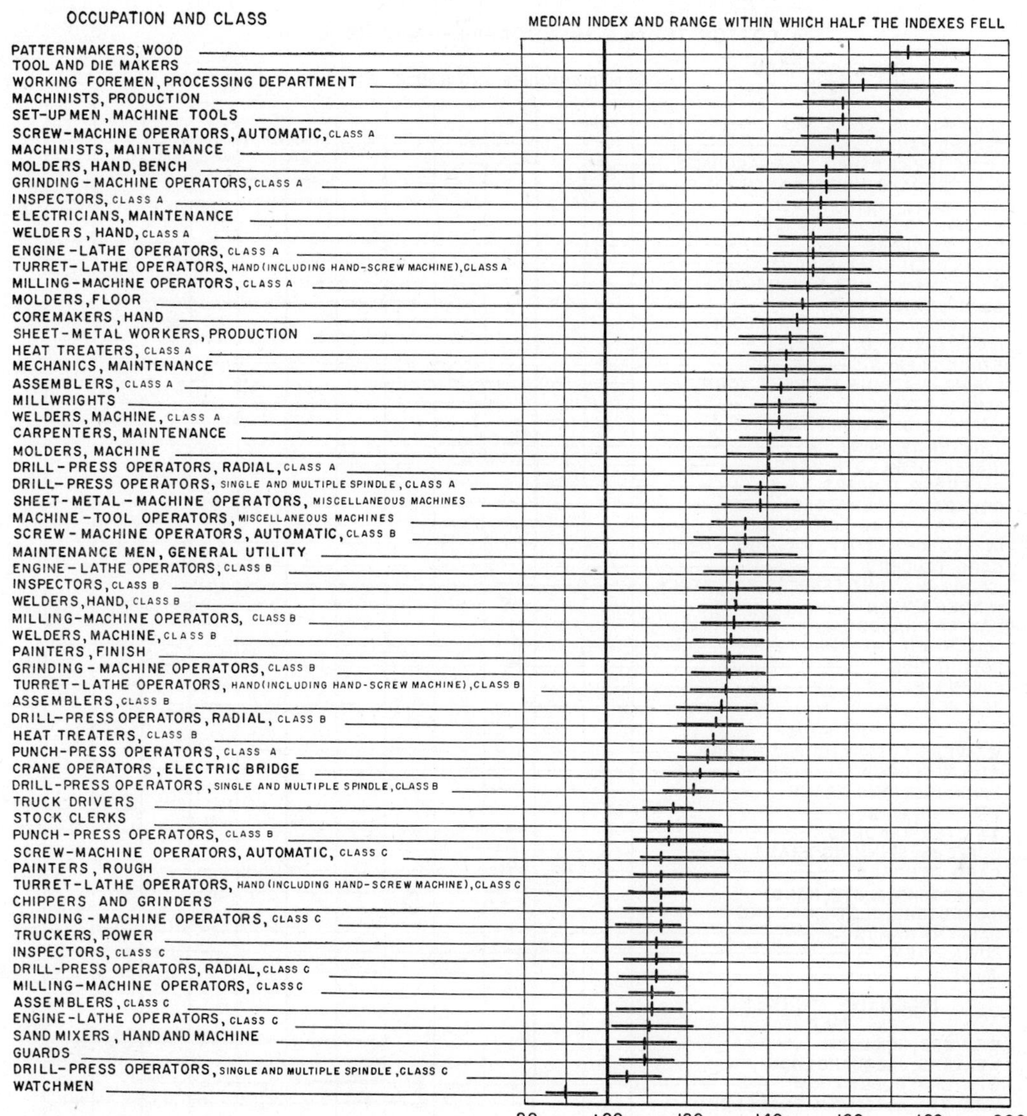

FIGURE 75. WAGE RATES OF MALE WORKERS IN KEY OCCUPATIONS IN MACHINERY INDUSTRIES AS PERCENTAGE OF WAGES OF JANITORS AND HAND TRUCKERS, JANUARY 1946

Source: Department of Labor.

Wage rates in selected occupations in machinery industries are expressed here as percentages of the wage rate for janitors and hand truckers (set at 100). Each horizontal bar represents the range of the middle half of such percentages recorded for the particular occupation. The short vertical line through each bar marks the ratio of the median wage in the occupation to the average wage of janitors and hand truckers, the median index.

Thus, for example, the median wage of wood patternmakers was 75 per cent above the average rate for janitors and hand truckers. The middle half of the wages in this occupation were from 170 to 190 per cent of the wage used as the basis of comparison.

and semiskilled occupation as a percentage of the usual rate for light unskilled work. Each individual wage rate can thus be represented by an index, with the unskilled wage rate set at 100.

In 1945–1947 the middle half of indexes so derived for skilled occupations ranged between 145 and 170; that is, one fourth of the indexes were less than 145 and one fourth were higher than 170. Half of the wages for the more diffi-

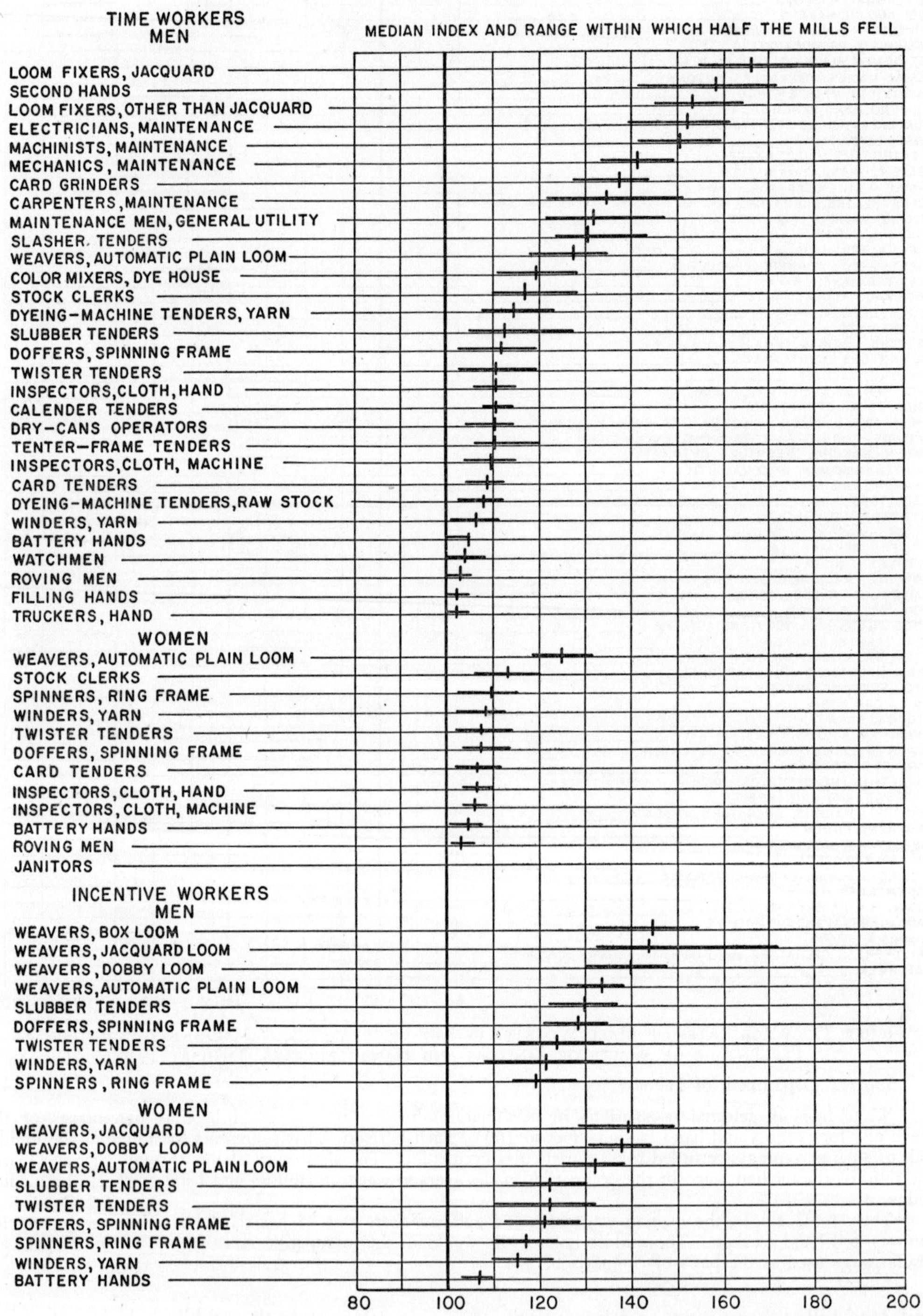

Figure 76 (*Continued on facing page*)

B. BAKERY INDUSTRY IN 85 CITIES, JULY 1945

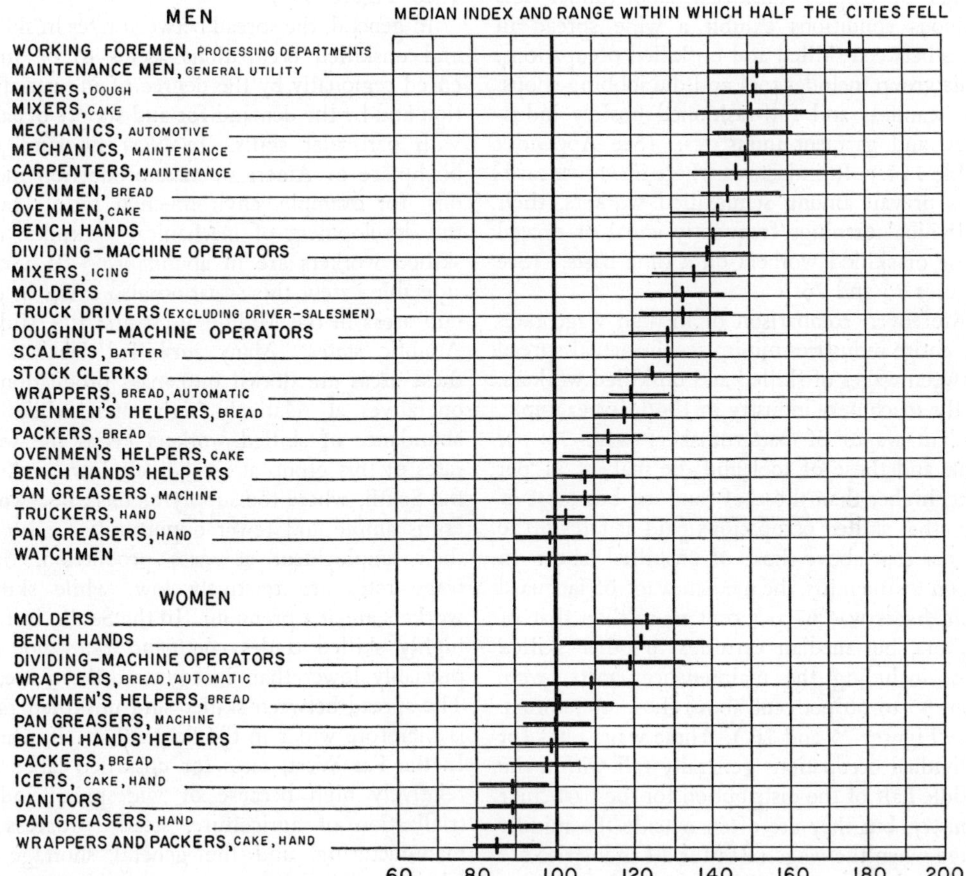

FIGURE 76. WAGE RATES IN SELECTED OCCUPATIONS AS PERCENTAGE OF WAGES OF MEN JANITORS

Source: Department of Labor.

This figure shows the median wage rates and the ranges of the middle half of wage rates of different occupations in two industries. The horizontal bars are used here in the same way as in Figure 75.

cult semiskilled jobs were 25 to 45 per cent higher than the wage for unskilled labor and half of the wages for the simpler semiskilled jobs were 10 to 25 per cent higher than this basic wage.[2] (See Appendix Table 113.) Wages in unskilled occupations vary within a comparatively narrow range: the rates paid for heavy tasks are only slightly higher than those paid for light tasks. The median index of wages for light unskilled jobs was 100 — or the same as the average for janitors and hand truckers, which generally are used as a base — and the middle half of the occupational indexes in this group varied from 95 to 105. Generally such occupations as watchman were found below the base occupational rates; and such occupations as hand trucker, above. The median index for unskilled tasks requiring heavy labor (and, also, the use of a variety of mechanical aids) was 15 per cent above the base, and the middle half of the indexes ranged from 105 to 120.

A comparison of skilled and unskilled occupations across industries shows that those industries employing unskilled labor under unpleasant and arduous conditions or requiring no unusually high skills have a narrow spread between skilled and unskilled rates (that is, skilled rates are less than 45 per cent higher than unskilled). Among such industries are mechanical rubber goods; soap and glycerin; leather tanning; copper alloying, rolling and drawing.

2. Harry Ober, "Occupational Wage Differentials, 1907–1947," *Monthly Labor Review,* August 1948, p. 128.

Industries that have rather high skill requirements or employ unskilled labor under less arduous conditions exhibit a wide spread in rates between skilled and unskilled occupations. This group includes tool and die jobbing shops, the seamless and full-fashioned hosiery industries, and garment industries. (See Appendix Table 114.) In industries where incentive earnings prevail among semiskilled workers, their individual earnings frequently equal or exceed those of skilled workers on a time basis. (See Figures 75 and 76.)

Moreover, comparison of median wage rates for entire industries minimizes the actual spread between wages of skilled and unskilled workers. In the machinery industry in 1946, for example, median wages of patternmakers were 75 per cent, and those of tool and die makers 71 per cent, higher than those of janitors, but most of the other skilled occupations paid at rates 50 to 60 per cent above those of unskilled labor. In cotton textile mills, the median wage of Jacquard loom fixers was 67 per cent more than that of janitors, but median earnings in other skilled jobs, including the maintenance crafts, were from 35 to 60 per cent above those of janitors. (See Figures 75 and 76.) These wage rates for individual occupations generally fall within the middle half of the distribution for the particular industry, but they are often outside the middle range when the wage rates for all industries are combined.

Regional Variations in Occupational Differentials

The spread between wage rates in skilled and unskilled occupations varies substantially from region to region. The widest range is found in the South, where the median wage index for skilled workers is 170 (1945–1947). The least spread is in the Far West (145 per cent). In the North Atlantic states and in the Middle West, the indexes for skilled occupations fall between these extremes (155 and 150 respectively). (See Appendix Table 115.)

Extreme regional variations are characteristic of industries that require highly skilled labor. In the machinery industries in 1945, for example, the index for tool and die makers was 300 in Norfolk, Virginia (as against 100 for janitors and hand truckers), 160–170 in most of the large cities of the Middle West and the North, and considerably less in such cities as Duluth, Minnesota, and Portland, Oregon. (See Figure 77.)

In general, the spread between rates in skilled and unskilled occupations seems to be influenced regionally by the degree of industrialization and by the demand for and supply of labor with particular skills. In New England, the birthplace of American mass-production methods, for example, environmental factors favor the development of mechanical aptitudes, and skilled workers are in abundance. To a considerable extent this situation also exists in certain areas in the Middle West and the Middle Atlantic states. Many unskilled laborers in these areas are drawn into mass production as operatives at relatively high rates, while the abundance of skilled workers keeps the wage rates of this group at a relatively low level. In the South, where the supply of unskilled workers is ample and fewer opportunities exist for their employment at mass production, their wage rates are relatively low, while skilled workers are at a premium. In the South, in fact, highly skilled trades command rates not appreciably lower than in some northern areas.[3] The spread between skilled and unskilled rates is therefore wider in the South than elsewhere. In the Far West, rates for unskilled labor are relatively high because of widespread industrialization of agriculture, steady progress in manufacturing, and the general shortage of labor in relation to resources.

TRENDS IN OCCUPATIONAL WAGE DIFFERENTIALS, 1907–1947

Manufacturing

In 1907 the wage rates of skilled factory workers were, on the average, about double those of unskilled, according to the available statistics. (See Appendix Table 115.) In 1947, in contrast, skilled rates were only one and a half times as high as unskilled. Thus, the spread was reduced by about half in forty years. The amount of reduction varied somewhat from region to region, but the differential narrowed in all parts of the country. Although the rate of change was not uniform throughout the period, the decline in the spread averaged about one per cent a year over the forty years.[4]

The timing of these changes in manufacturing industries suggests that cyclical fluctuations

3. Cf. pp. 477–78.
4. Ober, *op. cit.,* p. 130.

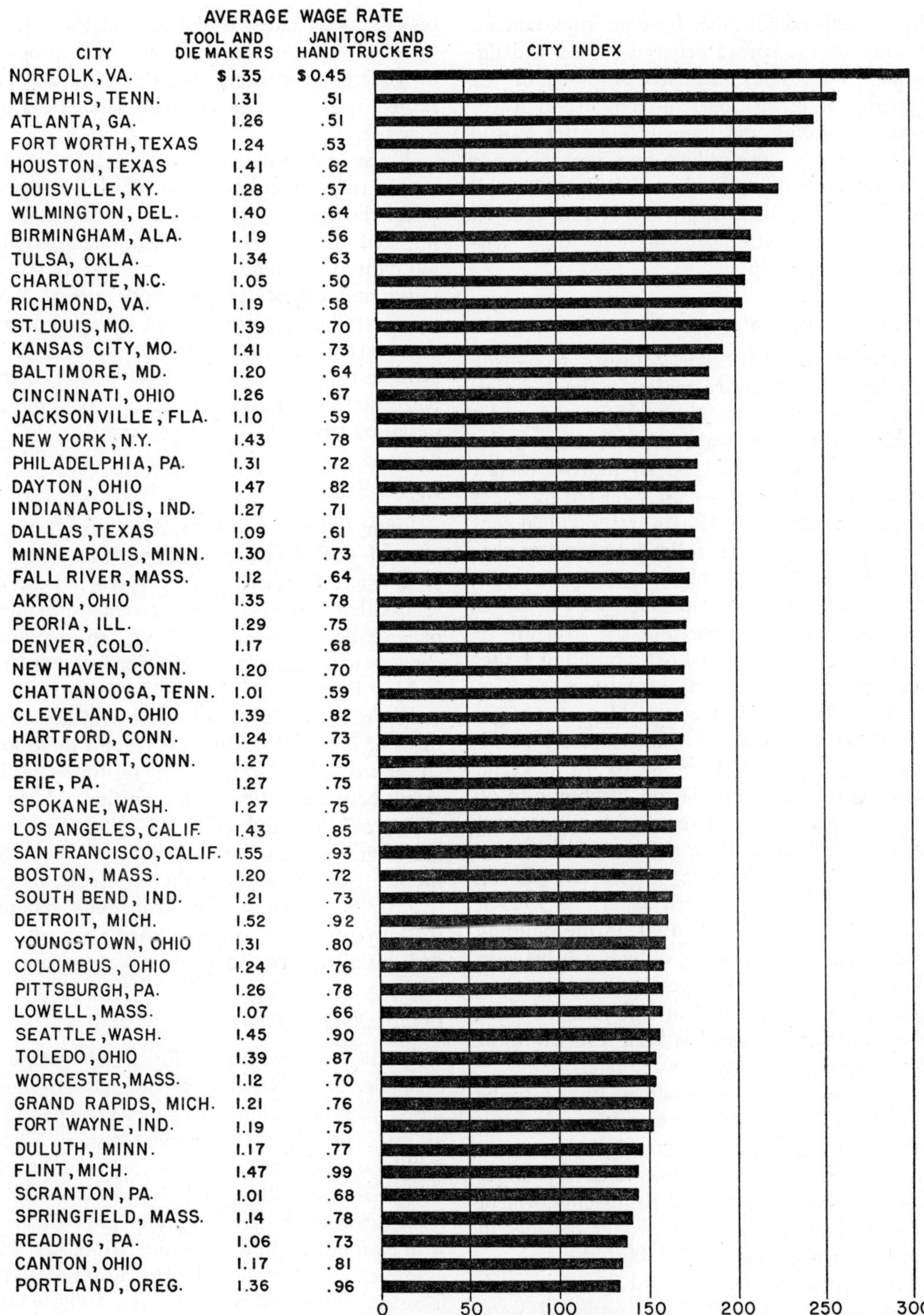

FIGURE 77. WAGE RATES OF MALE TOOL AND DIE MAKERS AS PERCENTAGE OF WAGES OF JANITORS AND HAND TRUCKERS, IN 54 CITIES, JANUARY 1945

Source: Department of Labor.

in the demand for labor have an important influence on the spread between skilled and unskilled wage rates. Apparently much of the leveling of occupational differentials in wages occurred during and immediately after World War I. Later, during the depression, the wage gap between skilled and unskilled labor widened again. During and since World War II, the trend has once again been toward a narrowing of the gap.

The Building Trades

The Bureau of Labor Statistics has made studies of union wage scales in the building trades annually since 1907.[5] (See Appendix Table 116.) Since wage rates in these trades are usually determined on an individual-craft basis, they are not very closely related to wages in other occupations. Moreover, individual contractors who specialize in limited phases of construction, such as plumbing or carpentry, are not interested in the occupational scale of wages in other trades. Despite this, the structure of wages and wage trends in the building trades are similar to those in manufacturing.

From 1907 to 1914 the spread between wages of skilled and unskilled workers in the building trades widened, from 85 to 99 per cent. After 1916 it began to narrow, dropping to 66 per cent in 1920; but it returned to 80 per cent by 1923 and remained at that level throughout the 1920's. In the late 1930's and during World War II it narrowed again; by 1947 it was at 43 per cent. All in all, in the building trades as in manufacturing, differentials between skilled and unskilled wages have narrowed in good years and widened in bad years; the net effect of these changes has been a lessening of occupational inequality in wage rates.

Wages of unskilled laborers appear to be more sensitive to cyclical fluctuations in business conditions than those of skilled workers. In fact, unskilled jobs show relatively larger wage increases in times of rising employment opportunities and relatively greater declines in depression years than skilled jobs.

The general tendency toward decreasing differentials between skilled and unskilled wage rates is not unexpected. Technological progress and the common use of mechanical devices have reduced the differences in requirements between jobs rated as skilled and those rated as unskilled. At the same time, the progress of general compulsory education has brought skilled workmen and common laborers closer together.

There has been more mechanization of unskilled tasks in industry than of skilled operations. Equipment for hoisting, loading, stacking and interprocess movement of materials; more careful planning of work; advance scheduling; and improvements in work methods have been introduced increasingly in unskilled operations. These changes not only have made it possible to compensate unskilled workers better but also have raised the social standing of unskilled labor.

Regional Trends

From October 1943 to April 1947, wage rates of skilled factory workers in the country as a whole increased 27.7 per cent; those of semiskilled workers, 34.5 per cent; and those of unskilled workers, 35.7 per cent. Similar changes took place in most regions, except that in New England and the Middle Atlantic states wages of unskilled labor increased less than those of semiskilled. In most regions there was an appreciable difference in relative rise in wages between skilled trades, on the one hand, and semiskilled and unskilled occupations, on the other, but there was little difference between the last two groups. For the most part, incentive pay in the semiskilled occupations accounts for inconsistencies between these occupations and unskilled labor in relative wage changes.[6]

Industrial Trends

In all industry groups for which data are available, occupational wage differentials show the same general trend. Changes in the spread of wage rates appear particularly sharp when skilled occupations are compared with semiskilled and unskilled, and the trends become less clear when the last two groups are compared with each other. In the machinery industry, for example, wages in unskilled occupations have increased about 400 per cent since 1907, while machinists' rates have increased only 300 per cent. In foundries, paper and pulp manufacturing, and iron and steel, the percentage increases for laborers have been substantially

5. *Union Wages and Hours; Building Trades,* Bulletin No. 930, July 1, 1946.

6. *Ibid.*

greater than those for skilled workers. In the building trades, union wages for laborers and helpers have increased more than fivefold, wages for the skilled trades less than fourfold.

TRENDS IN CENTS-PER-HOUR DIFFERENTIALS

The differences in cents per hour between wages in skilled and unskilled occupations do not move in the same direction as do the relative differences. In the building trades, cents-per-hour differences in union wage rates increased gradually from 1907 to 1918 and more rapidly through World War I and the immediate postwar years, when percentage differences were narrowing. From 1938 to 1947, when all wages increased and differences between skilled and unskilled rates in cents per hour remained practically unchanged, the relative spread between these rates declined rapidly. (See Appendix Table 116 and Figure 78.)

In 1937–1947, cents-per-hour differences between wages in skilled and unskilled occupations in seventeen manufacturing industries increased; at the beginning of this period the differential averaged 30 cents an hour, at the end 43 cents. There was also a considerable increase in the dispersion of differences: the middle half of the differences ranged from 25 to 35 cents an hour in 1937–1940, as against 32 to 57 cents in 1945–1947. But percentage differences were narrowing rapidly during this period. Thus, while in the building trades differences in cents per hour were stable, in manufacturing they increased — at a time when percentage differences narrowed substantially in both industrial groups.[7]

Changes in occupational wage differentials often result from changes in the general level of wages. Three basic types of wage changes that have taken place in recent years have had different effects on percentage and cents-per-hour differentials: (1) when uniform cents-per-hour increases were granted to all workers, percentage differences between skilled and unskilled occupations declined while cents-per-hour differences remained the same; (2) when uniform percentage increases were granted, cents-per-hour differences increased but percentage differences remained the same; (3) when skilled rates were increased more than unskilled

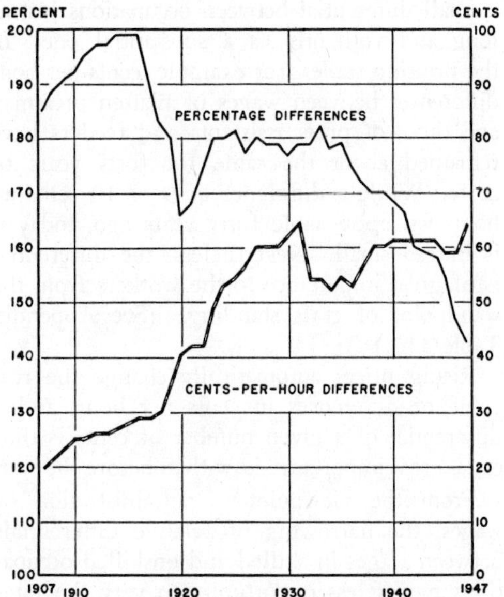

FIGURE 78. DIFFERENTIALS BETWEEN WAGES OF JOURNEYMEN AND LABORERS IN THE BUILDING TRADES, 1907–1947

Source: Department of Labor.

in terms of cents per hour but not sufficiently to equal the percentage increase for the unskilled, percentage differences narrowed while cents-per-hour differences increased. Naturally, decreases in wage levels had opposite effects.

During the early part of World War II (until about October 1942, when controls on wages were tightened), general wage changes in terms of cents per hour prevailed; from 1942 to V-J Day, general wage changes were rigidly controlled, and most changes in wages affected only parts of establishments or industries or particular occupations; during the postwar years general wage changes were resumed. At no time, however, have general wage changes been granted wholly in terms of percentages or cents per hour. Some industries and establishments have given increases in cents per hour, some have given uniform percentage increases, and some, general increases in cents per hour during one period and in percentage terms during another. The net result for manufacturing as a whole has been to narrow percentage differences and increase differences in cents per hour.

To the worker in a particular occupation, wage differentials mean additional income for more arduous or more skilled performance. Differentials also indicate differences in craft or trade prestige. Sometimes workers will guard

7. Trends similar to those in manufacturing appear in the printing trades from 1907 to 1946. (See Appendix Table 117.)

a small differential between occupations just as long and vigilantly as a substantial one. In the printing trades, for example, cents-per-hour differences between wages of platten pressmen and those of press assistants and feeders have remained about the same for forty years or more. While a difference of 9 or 10 cents an hour was appreciable forty years ago, today it is indeed small. Nevertheless, the differential is of great importance to the workers from the standpoint of craft standing. (See Appendix Table 117.)

Rising prices automatically change the real value of differences in cents per hour, and a differential of a given number of cents is thus of less real importance now than before the war.

From the viewpoint of administration of wages, the narrowing of relative differentials between wages in skilled and unskilled occupations means less opportunity to vary the rates of pay among occupations that become increasingly specialized and differentiated. In fact, the average spread of 55 per cent between skilled and unskilled manufacturing occupations in 1945–1947 provides room for only a fairly limited number of meaningful wage levels. In order to have significance, differentials in cents per hour doubtless have to be greater now than before the war.

Logically, the trend toward equality in wages of unskilled and skilled workers should simplify the wage structure. Many establishments have actually reduced the number of labor grades in recent years. The problem of maintaining a meaningful scale of wage rates within a narrowing range has probably contributed to the development of formal plans of job evaluation.[8]

Occupational Wage Differentials and Composition of the Labor Force

In analyzing occupational differentials in wages, it is important also to evaluate recent changes in the composition of the labor force by occupational level. No data on number of workers strictly comparable to the wage data used in this chapter are available, but the censuses from 1910 to 1940 indicate that semiskilled pursuits have constituted an increasing proportion of the labor force — 14.7 per cent of the total in 1910 and 21 per cent in 1940. The proportion of the labor force in skilled and unskilled occupations, on the other hand, has been going down since 1920. (See Appendix Table 118.) These trends have continued since 1940.[9]

The decline in the proportion of workers described and recorded by the censuses as "skilled" should not be interpreted as a decline in the skill level of American labor. As has been indicated, certain elements of skill in terms of dexterity of movement and manipulation of equipment have become pervasive among semiskilled workers, and the specialized craftsmen of former years have been replaced by highly efficient and adaptable operatives classified as "semiskilled."

The increase in the proportion of semiskilled occupations may affect occupational wage differentials in two ways. If the proportional growth is primarily at the repetitive, mass-production level, the effect on wage differentials is minor, since wages in these occupations differ little from those in the more arduous unskilled jobs. To the extent that the shift involves a greater proportional increase among the top grades of the semiskilled occupations, however, the differentials between these and the skilled jobs disappear, since there is substantial overlapping in the requirements of skilled and higher semiskilled occupations. The high level of employment throughout the war and since has stimulated a shift in the upward direction.

In general, the level of employment is one of the chief factors affecting wage differentials. The narrowing of differentials among rates paid for various skills in recent years has been due largely to the fact that these were years of prosperity. If the years ahead are marked by a high level of employment, they will probably bring a further movement toward greater uniformity of wage rates.

8. Cf. Chapter 35, *passim.*

9. Harold Goldstein, "The Changing Occupational Structure," *Monthly Labor Review,* December 1947, pp. 654–59.

CHAPTER 41

GEOGRAPHICAL DIFFERENTIALS IN EARNINGS *

REGIONAL AND STATE DIFFERENTIALS, like other differentials in wages and prices, are controlled by the interplay of supply and demand. The extent of such differentials is inversely correlated with the geographical mobility of industries and the labor force — that is, with the ability of industries to move toward areas where labor is relatively cheap and the ability of workers to move toward places where pay is relatively high. Wages of farm laborers are, therefore, more variable from region to region than earnings of industrial workers. For a similar reason, regional differentials are less among skilled workers than among common laborers and, in a more general way, less among high-paid than among low-paid workers.

Geographical differentials in wages of industrial workers are closely correlated with the level of economic well-being in different parts of the nation as reflected in per capita income. To some extent per capita income in an area is affected by locally prevailing industrial wages; but there is also an inverse correlation: in relatively poor, primarily agricultural states, the surplus of rural population flowing cityward exercises a continuous downward pressure on earnings in urban pursuits. Generally, earnings in regions from which people are emigrating are lower than those in areas of immigration.

The trend in state differentials in per capita income and earnings has changed several times in opposite directions in the past two decades. The gap between poor and rich areas widened in the early phase of the depression of the 1930's, narrowed with the progress of recovery, widened again at the beginning of the war, and has narrowed once more in recent years.

State differentials in earnings are probably affected more by differences in the composition of the labor force than by local differences in wage rates paid for the same work to workers of similar skill and similar personal characteristics.

* By W. S. Woytinsky.

PER CAPITA INCOME

Despite the general trend toward a leveling off of regional differences in wages, per capita income varies widely from state to state. In 1950 the range was from $698 in Mississippi to $1,909 in Delaware and $1,986 in the District of Columbia.[1] (See Figure 79.)

Average per capita income in the United States as a whole fell from $680 in 1929 to $368 in 1933, rose to $561 in 1937, fell back to $509 in 1938, and has risen steadily since that year with only a slight setback in 1949. Under the impact of the defense program, expanding industrial production, government spending and rising agricultural prices, per capita income has risen in all parts of the country. Proportionally, the largest gains have been in comparatively poor, primarily agricultural regions. The gap between rich and poor states has therefore narrowed.

This trend is shown clearly by the changing relationship between unweighted average per capita income in the five richest and five poorest states in each year. In 1932–1933, per capita income in the first group of states was more than four times that in the second group; in 1945–1950 the relationship was 2.2 to 1. (See Table 216.) With due allowance for the rough method of comparison and the unequal significance of the states included each year in either group, it appears that the relative difference between the "have" and the "have-not" areas has been cut by approximately half. The main factor in this development has been the

1. The figures on per capita income by state and region computed annually by the Department of Commerce are not intended to measure the actual average earnings of employees. They are derived by prorating the total income received by persons in a given area among the estimated number of residents of that area. The total income includes not only wages and salaries but also proprietors' incomes, dividends, interest, pensions, relief payments, all kinds of allowances, and so forth. The divisor includes all residents, whether workers or nonworkers. The ratio is intended to represent the relative level of well-being in the different parts of the nation; annual changes indicate regional and state differences in economic gains and losses.

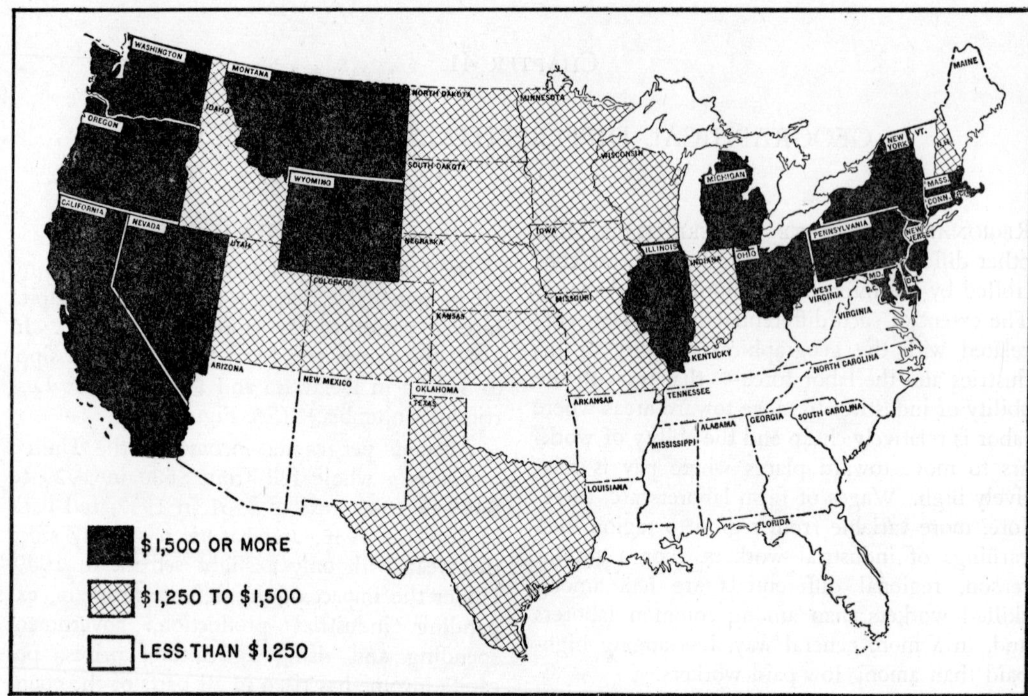

FIGURE 79. PER CAPITA INCOME PAYMENTS BY STATE, 1950

Source: Survey of Current Business, August 1951.

TABLE 216

PER CAPITA INCOME IN THE UNITED STATES AND AVERAGE FOR THE FIVE RICHEST AND FIVE POOREST STATES, 1929–1950

Year	United States	Five States with the Highest Per Capita Income (A)	Five States with the Lowest Per Capita Income (B)	Ratio of A to B
1929	$ 680	$1,027	$297	3.46
1930	596	963	231	4.17
1931	500	849	183	4.64
1932	380	687	155	4.43
1933	368	636	152	4.18
1934	420	678	195	3.48
1935	460	738	210	3.51
1936	531	829	247	3.36
1937	561	873	252	3.46
1938	509	808	241	3.35
1939	539	854	253	3.37
1940	575	907	263	3.45
1941	693	1,148	340	3.38
1942	876	1,281	463	2.77
1943	1,059	1,453	637	2.28
1944	1,160	1,515	626	2.42
1945	1,191	1,516	691	2.19
1946	1,211	1,617	705	2.29
1947	1,293	1,696	767	2.21
1948	1,383	1,768	861	2.05
1949	1,320	1,702	765	2.22
1950	1,436	1,880	820	2.29

Sources: Survey of Current Business, August 1951, p. 18. Cf. W. S. Woytinsky, *Earnings and Social Security in the United States,* Committee on Social Security, Social Science Research Council, Washington, 1943.

change in the position of agriculture in the national economy, as changes in the structure of prices have brought prosperity to farmers.

The improvement in the economic position of agricultural areas is dramatized by a comparison of per capita income in the District of Columbia and North Dakota. Per capita income in the District rose from $926 in 1932 to $1,473 in 1947; the corresponding figures for North Dakota were $181 and $1,582.[2] At the depth of the depression, Washingtonians earned five times as much as North Dakotans; in 1947, North Dakotans were better off than Washingtonians and not far behind New Yorkers. No less significant, though less spectacular, were the gains in Tennessee, Alabama and Texas.

The same leveling off of regional contrasts is revealed by a comparison of per capita income in major geographic regions with the average for the United States as a whole. In 1929, per capita income in the Southeast was 51 per cent of the average for the nation; in 1950, 67 per cent. In the Middle East, per capita income was 36 per cent above the na-

2. In 1950, per capita income in the District of Columbia rose to $1,986 and that in North Dakota went down to $1,298.

tional average in 1929 and only 17 per cent above the average in 1950. (See Figure 80.)

Although the recent narrowing of regional and state differentials in income has been due mainly to the improved position of farmers, that improvement has had a far-reaching effect on the structure of industrial earnings. To the extent that rural areas supply cities with unskilled labor, earnings of farmers and farm laborers tend to establish a floor for wages of industrial workers: when earnings of farm laborers rise, the gap between high-wage and low-wage states necessarily narrows.

Earnings in Various Industries

While the prevailing wages of industrial workers in a state are correlated with per capita income, this correlation is not very close, especially in the middle part of the distribution. Too many factors enter into the picture to permit any generalization other than the general statement that high wages prevail in rich areas, low wages in poor ones.

In states with low per capita income (see Figure 79), earnings of industrial workers, as represented by average wage credits reported under the old-age and survivors insurance program, are far below the average for the country as a whole. But earnings of industrial workers are low also in such high-income frontier states as Nevada and Montana, and in the District of Columbia, where per capita income is high but most workers are employed by the government and are not covered by the program. On the other hand, Michigan, far from the top in per capita income payments, is among the states with the highest average wage credits in jobs covered by OASI.

The pattern of regional and state differentials in earnings varies from industry to industry. Industries employing unskilled labor take advantage of the supply of cheap labor in primarily agricultural states, while industries that depend on skilled labor or need highly dependable and stable personnel must pay their workers about the same wages in the Deep South as in New York or Chicago. The manufacture of lumber basic products is typical of the first group of industries; printing and publishing, banks and trust companies, of the second. Workers in lumber manufacturing in the state of Mississippi earned in 1938 less than half the wages prevailing in the same industry in New

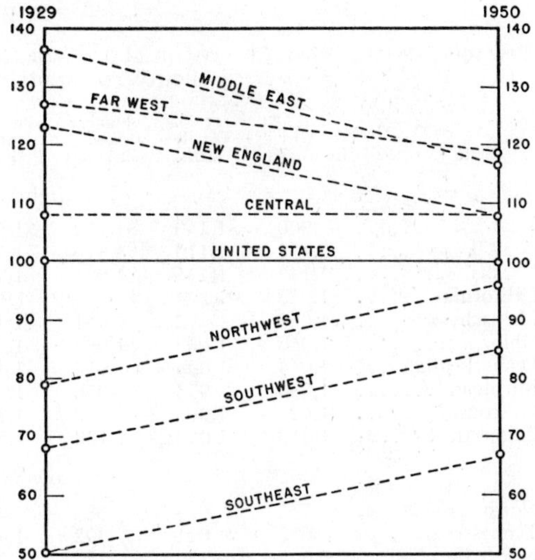

Figure 80. Per Capita Income in Each Region as Percentage of National Average, 1929 and 1950

Source: Survey of Current Business, August 1951. Cf. Table 238.

York, Connecticut or Ohio, while earnings of printers and bank employees were practically the same in all parts of the country. (See Table 217.)[3] Other industries fell between these extremes. The progress of industrialization in the South has been reflected in declining regional differentials in earnings.

Decile Annual Earnings under OASI[4]

As a rule, local differentials are far less pronounced among skilled and high-paid workers than among unskilled and casual laborers. This general pattern is illustrated by a comparison of decile annual wage credits in typical high-wage and low-wage states — as between Connecticut and Mississippi, New York and Arkansas, Pennsylvania and Alabama, California and Texas.

In 1939, white men in the middle of the scale (i.e., at the median) in Connecticut had 3.2 times as much wage credits as their counterparts in Mississippi; at the low end of the occupational ladder (the first and second deciles) the ratio was 7 to 1; at the upper end (the ninth decile), only 1.3 to 1. For white female

3. Table 217 shows average earnings by state and industry in 1938. No comparable data are available for more recent years.

4. Cf. pp. 437 ff.; for an explanation of deciles, see specifically, pp. 439–40.

TABLE 217

AVERAGE ANNUAL WAGE CREDITS OF MALE WORKERS UNDER OASI IN SELECTED INDUSTRIES IN TYPICAL HIGH-WAGE AND LOW-WAGE STATES, 1938

State	All Industries	Textile Mills	Lumber Basic Products	Printing and Publishing	Leather	Iron and Steel	Non-ferrous Metals	Machin-ery	Banks and Trust Companies
				High-Wage States					
New York	$1,200	$1,140	$1,102	$1,635	$1,083	$1,237	$1,282	$1,459	$1,611
New Jersey	1,158	1,119	1,326	1,558	1,041	1,242	1,373	1,450	1,505
Illinois	1,142	1,236	1,021	1,543	1,062	1,245	1,239	1,424	1,543
California	1,076	1,294	—	1,320	1,238	1,372	1,301	1,602	1,653
Massachusetts	1,062	892	951	1,482	1,000	1,248	1,224	1,370	1,567
Ohio	1,060	1,067	1,037	1,522	1,093	1,156	1,203	1,424	1,799
Pennsylvania	1,044	1,095	952	1,424	1,025	1,180	1,305	1,303	1,381
Michigan	1,030	953	856	1,427	1,114	1,170	1,180	1,380	1,674
Wisconsin	1,027	1,298	852	1,262	1,139	1,279	1,272	1,444	1,662
Connecticut	1,010	1,050	**1,128**	**1,527**	963	1,172	1,209	1,307	1,525
				Low-Wage States					
North Dakota	735	—	683	—	—	—	—	—	—
Tennessee	672	821	492	1,414	903	778	1,067	1,099	1,317
North Carolina	645	730	475	1,378	808	868	—	—	—
Alabama	628	641	421	1,362	—	975	—	—	1,410
Georgia	606	689	415	1,383	707	915	—	—	—
Florida	582	—	556	1,447	—	—	—	—	—
South Carolina	545	688	381	—	—	—	—	—	1,486
Arkansas	544	—	524	—	—	—	—	—	1,424
Mississippi	451	581	450	—	—	—	—	—	1,536

Source: Old-Age and Survivors Insurance Statistics, 1938, Federal Security Agency, 1940, pp. 48 ff.

workers, the ratios were 6.7 for the lowest decile, 2.6 for the median, 1.5 for the highest decile. Much the same contrasts held true between New York and Arkansas, Pennsylvania and Alabama, California and Texas. (See Table 218.) The differentials between the last two states in 1939 are typical. At the low end of the distribution, male and female workers in California earned 2.7 and 2.5 times as much as such workers in Texas; in the middle of the distribution, the ratios were 1.7 and 1.8, respectively; and at the upper end, only 1.1 and 1.3.

This pattern is so clear and regular that it may be described as the general tendency of geographical differentials in earnings: striking contrasts in earnings of common laborers or low-paid workers, smaller but significant differentials in the middle brackets, only slight disparity for high-paid workers.

Men and Women

The principal factor that holds down earnings in industrially undeveloped areas — the pressure of surplus rural population — affects unskilled trades chiefly, and the earnings of skilled and white-collar workers only indirectly. This is true for both men and women. State differentials in decile wage credits of men and women, as measured by ratios between high-wage and low-wage states, exhibit no clear and consistent pattern. In some cases the spread is wider for women, in others for men. Conclusions suggested by a dozen comparisons are vitiated by other comparisons.

White and Negro Workers

Interregional differences in decile earnings of Negro workers follow the general pattern.[5] Just as among whites, the greatest geographical difference is among the unskilled and the gap narrows toward the upper end of the occupational scale. There is, however, an appreciable difference in North-to-South ratios of earnings of Negro and white workers at different occupational levels: often the regional difference is weaker for Negroes than for whites in the lower part of the scale but somewhat higher in its upper part. The range between earnings in New York and Arkansas, for example, is greater for low-paid white workers than for low-paid Negro

5. Decile annual wage credits of Negro workers have been computed for twenty states in which a considerable number of Negroes are employed in jobs covered by OASI. These are eastern and central states, southern states from the Carolinas to Texas, and northern states from New York, New Jersey and Pennsylvania to Michigan.

TABLE 218

RATIOS BETWEEN DECILE ANNUAL WAGE CREDITS OF WHITE WORKERS UNDER OASI IN SELECTED HIGH-WAGE AND LOW-WAGE STATES, 1939 AND 1946

Decile	Ratio of Connecticut to Mississippi		Ratio of New York to Arkansas		Ratio of Pennsylvania to Alabama		Ratio of California to Texas	
	1939	1946	1939	1946	1939	1946	1939	1946
White Men								
First	7.0	5.3	5.8	5.9	2.9	2.8	2.7	1.9
Second	7.0	4.4	5.3	4.9	2.8	2.6	2.2	1.8
Third	6.0	3.9	4.8	4.7	2.4	2.6	2.3	1.8
Fourth	4.8	3.0	3.9	3.9	1.9	2.2	2.0	1.6
Median	3.2	2.3	3.0	3.0	1.7	1.7	1.7	1.5
Sixth	2.4	2.0	2.5	2.3	1.6	1.4	1.5	1.3
Seventh	1.9	1.7	2.2	2.0	1.4	1.3	1.3	1.2
Eighth	1.6	1.4	1.9	1.7	1.3	1.2	1.2	1.1
Ninth	1.3	—	1.7	—	1.2	1.1	1.1	—
White Women								
First	6.7	4.3	9.4	4.8	3.7	1.8	2.5	1.5
Second	4.7	3.0	4.9	4.0	2.3	1.6	1.9	1.5
Third	4.0	2.9	4.4	4.1	2.1	1.7	1.8	1.5
Fourth	3.4	2.8	3.8	3.9	1.8	1.7	1.8	1.5
Median	2.6	2.2	3.2	3.4	1.5	1.6	1.8	1.5
Sixth	2.1	1.8	2.7	2.6	1.3	1.4	1.7	1.4
Seventh	1.8	1.6	2.1	2.1	1.3	1.1	1.6	1.4
Eighth	1.6	1.5	1.9	1.9	1.2	1.1	1.4	1.3
Ninth	1.5	1.3	1.8	1.6	1.2	1.1	1.3	1.3

Source: Derived from Appendix Table 105.

TABLE 219

RATIOS BETWEEN DECILE ANNUAL WAGE CREDITS OF NEGRO WORKERS UNDER OASI IN SELECTED HIGH-WAGE AND LOW-WAGE STATES, 1939 AND 1946

Decile	Ratio of New York to Arkansas		Ratio of New Jersey to Mississippi		Ratio of Pennsylvania to Alabama		Ratio of Michigan to Florida	
	1939	1946	1939	1946	1939	1946	1939	1946
Negro Men								
First	4.2	3.3	3.7	3.8	2.7	2.5	8.0	5.3
Second	4.1	3.1	3.4	3.9	2.6	2.6	6.4	4.1
Third	3.6	3.2	2.8	3.7	2.5	2.4	4.9	3.8
Fourth	3.2	2.7	2.6	3.3	2.2	2.0	4.3	3.2
Median	2.8	2.5	2.5	2.9	2.1	1.8	3.8	2.8
Sixth	2.5	2.3	2.5	2.5	2.0	1.6	3.4	2.3
Seventh	2.3	2.0	2.3	2.1	1.9	1.4	3.1	1.9
Eighth	2.2	1.8	2.3	1.9	1.7	1.4	2.8	1.7
Ninth	2.2	1.7	2.3	1.8	1.5	1.3	2.5	1.6
Negro Women								
First	4.4	2.8	2.4	3.1	3.5	2.4	4.0	1.5
Second	2.7	2.7	1.6	3.0	2.5	2.3	3.0	1.6
Third	2.8	2.5	1.6	2.8	2.8	2.3	2.6	1.5
Fourth	3.2	2.7	1.7	2.6	2.9	2.3	2.5	1.6
Median	3.2	2.5	1.9	2.6	2.7	2.2	2.6	1.7
Sixth	3.0	2.4	1.9	2.6	2.4	2.2	2.6	2.0
Seventh	2.8	2.2	2.0	2.6	2.2	2.1	2.5	2.1
Eighth	2.6	2.0	2.0	2.3	1.9	1.8	2.3	2.0
Ninth	2.2	1.8	2.0	2.1	1.7	1.6	1.9	1.9

Source: Derived from Appendix Table 106.

TABLE 220

Decile Annual Wage Credits of White Workers under OASI in Middle Atlantic and West South Central States, 1939 and 1946

Decile	Middle Atlantic States		West South Central States		West South Central as Percentage of Middle Atlantic	
	1939	1946	1939	1946	1939	1946
			White Men			
First	$ 120	$ 235	$ 30	$ 70	25.0	29.8
Second	350	655	100	215	28.6	32.8
Third	625	1,190	180	435	28.8	36.6
Fourth	875	1,670	355	745	40.6	44.6
Median	1,105	2,040	580	1,175	52.5	57.6
Sixth	1,320	2,405	825	1,620	62.5	67.4
Seventh	1,560	2,790	1,140	2,120	73.1	76.0
Eighth	1,890	3,210	1,560	2,705	82.5	84.3
Ninth	2,480	—	2,030	3,320	81.9	—
			White Women			
First	65	85	10	35	15.4	41.2
Second	150	255	45	110	30.0	43.1
Third	280	465	85	190	30.4	40.9
Fourth	430	745	145	305	33.7	40.9
Median	565	1,025	230	470	40.7	45.9
Sixth	690	1,295	365	700	52.9	54.1
Seventh	810	1,540	525	990	64.8	64.3
Eighth	975	1,820	705	1,335	72.3	73.4
Ninth	1,250	2,220	970	1,790	77.6	80.6

Source: Appendix Table 105.

TABLE 221

Decile Annual Wage Credits of Negro Workers under OASI in Selected High-Wage and Low-Wage States, 1939 and 1946

Decile	High-Wage States: New York and Ohio[a]		Low-Wage States: Mississippi and Arkansas[a]		Low-Wage States as Percentage of High-Wage States	
	1939	1946	1939	1946	1939	1946
			Negro Men			
First	$ 45	$ 122	$ 10	$ 32	22.2	26.2
Second	132	367	30	100	22.7	27.2
Third	260	637	70	175	26.9	27.5
Fourth	412	995	125	295	30.3	29.6
Median	597	1,322	197	445	33.0	33.7
Sixth	782	1,670	280	647	35.8	38.7
Seventh	967	1,980	385	915	39.8	46.2
Eighth	1,162	2,262	482	1,202	41.5	53.1
Ninth	1,387	2,667	605	1,490	43.6	55.9
			Negro Women			
First	27	42	6	16	22.2	38.1
Second	75	125	28	50	37.3	40.0
Third	142	217	55	92	38.7	42.4
Fourth	252	355	87	147	34.5	41.4
Median	367	530	125	230	34.1	43.4
Sixth	485	750	170	325	35.1	43.3
Seventh	597	1,002	220	452	36.9	45.1
Eighth	695	1,220	280	620	40.3	50.8
Ninth	797	1,492	372	835	46.7	56.0

a. Unweighted averages for the two states.

Source: Appendix Table 106.

workers;[6] the difference levels off in the upper half of the distribution. (Cf. Tables 218 and 219.)

The fact that the best-paid Negro workers have appreciably higher earnings in the North than in the South indicates that in the North they have more opportunity to advance to better jobs. The striking regional contrasts in earnings of white common laborers may be accounted for by the competition of poorly paid Negro labor in the South.[7]

Recent Changes

From 1939 to 1946 the gap between earnings in high-wage and low-wage areas narrowed conspicuously in the lower and middle parts of the occupational scale. The change was less clear at the top of the ladder, particularly among women.

For white workers, these changes are illustrated by a comparison of decile annual wage credits under OASI in the Middle Atlantic states, as typical of high-wage areas, and the West South Central states, as representative of low-wage regions. (See Table 220.) Comparable data for Negroes are not available. Statistics for selected states indicate, however, that the tendency toward narrower regional differentials in wages was even stronger among Negro than among white workers. The most remarkable shift was toward greater similarity in wages of relatively high-paid Negro workers, as between the South (Mississippi and Arkansas) and the Northeast (New York and Ohio). (See Table 221.)

The tendency toward an ironing out of geographical differentials in earnings has been in conformity with the progress of industrialization in backward areas, especially in the South.

6. In 1946 the ratios between first-decile earnings in the two states were 5.9 for white men and 4.8 for white women, as compared with 3.3 and 2.8 for Negroes. The ratios for second-decile earnings were 4.9 and 4.0 for white male and female workers and 3.1 and 2.7 for Negroes. For the third deciles the corresponding ratios were 4.7 and 4.1 for white workers, as compared with 3.2 and 2.5 for Negroes, and so on.

7. Cf. Chapter 38, *passim*.

Chapter 42

WAGES IN AGRICULTURE *

The Patterns of employment and earnings in agriculture differ substantially from those prevailing in other industries. Some of the distinctive elements arise out of the seasonality of much of the work, the predominance in the work force of self-employed and unpaid family workers, the dispersion of hired labor among hundreds of thousands of small enterprises, the absence of unions and collective bargaining. Because of the differences in the factors affecting agricultural and industrial wages, farm wages present special problems and require special methods of investigation.

The Structure of Farm Wages

Farming in the United States includes many types of crops and livestock and consequently, in the course of a year, many types of operations. It is not surprising, therefore, that a great variety of forms of remuneration is found.

Types of Farm Wages

Hired farm workers may be paid on a time basis or at piece rates. Moreover, when the worker furnishes machinery, workstock or supplies, a combined remuneration for the items supplied and for labor may be paid, usually on a piece-rate basis. Such arrangements, known as "custom" rates, are frequent for threshing or combining wheat and other grains, spraying fruit trees and similar operations.

Except during the harvest season, time rates are more common than piece rates in every major region of the country, though the type of time rate predominating varies from region to region. In April 1948 the most common types of farm wages were: in the Northeast, weekly rates (received by 35 per cent of the hired workers); in the North Central states, monthly rates (36 per cent); in the South, daily rates (58 per cent); and in the West, hourly rates (44 per cent).[1] In September, however, because of harvest work, more workers in the country as a whole were employed at piece rates than at all types of time rates. The proportion of workers employed at piece rates varied from 25 per cent in the Northeast to 65 per cent in the South; in the West, piece rates and hourly rates were about equal in importance.

In addition to cash wages, farm operators supply some hired farm workers with goods and services without charge (perquisites).

Hourly and Daily Cash Wages

Hourly cash earnings of hired farm workers in the United States averaged 47 cents in April 1948 and 61 cents in September of that year. The increase was due almost wholly to the much larger proportion of short-time workers engaged for harvest work; hourly cash earnings of temporary workers are customarily higher than those of regular workers. The highest average hourly cash earnings were in the West, the lowest in the South. (See Table 222.)

For male hired farm workers employed in September 1948, hourly cash earnings over the country as a whole varied from less than 15 cents to over $1.00. Approximately one fourth were making less than 35 cents an hour, half

TABLE 222

Average Hourly and Daily Cash Earnings of Hired Farm Workers, by Region, April and September 1948

Region	Hourly Rate		Daily Rate	
	April 1948	September 1948	April 1948	September 1948
United States	$0.47	$0.61	$4.20	$5.30
Northeast	0.51	0.67	4.50	5.90
North Central	0.44	0.63	4.00	5.70
South	0.36	0.54	3.10	4.60
West	0.79	0.77	7.20	6.80

Source: Surveys of Wages and Wage Rates in Agriculture, Report No. 22, Bureau of Agricultural Economics, 1949.

* By Louis J. Ducoff, Bureau of Agricultural Economics, U.S. Department of Agriculture. Opinions expressed here are those of the author and not necessarily of the agency with which he is associated.

1. These figures, and others in this section for which no other source is cited, come from *Surveys of Wages and Wage Rates in Agriculture,* Bureau of Agricultural Economics, 1945–1949.

TABLE 223

PERCENTAGE DISTRIBUTION OF MALE HIRED FARM WORKERS IN EACH REGION BY AMOUNT OF DAILY CASH EARNINGS, SEPTEMBER 1948

Region	Under $3	$3–$7.99	$8 and Over
United States	21	66	13
Northeast	21	63	16
North Central	17	69	14
South	30	68	2
West	3	54	43

Source: Surveys of Wages and Wage Rates in Agriculture, Report No. 22, Bureau of Agricultural Economics, 1949.

were making between 35 and 75 cents, and one fourth made 75 cents or more. The middle half of the range, that part including 50 per cent of the workers, varied from 31–57 cents an hour in the South, at one extreme, to 65–99 cents in the West, at the other.

Daily cash earnings of all hired farm workers in the United States averaged $4.20 in April and $5.30 in September 1948 for a work day averaging slightly under 9 hours. In the West, daily earnings in September averaged $6.80; in the South, $4.60. Percentage distributions for male hired farm workers bear out the regional pattern. In every region the majority received $3 to $8 a day in September 1948, but the proportions receiving amounts outside this range differed widely from region to region. (See Table 223.)

Wages of Regular and Seasonal Workers

Seasonal workers are usually paid more per hour than regular workers. This is true in every region of the country and at all seasons of the year. For seasonal workers are employed during times of the year when the demand for labor is great; most of them are employed to do cultivating or harvesting jobs commanding higher rates; and they receive less in perquisites than regular workers. Seasonal workers averaged 65 cents in hourly cash earnings in September 1948, as compared with 48 cents for regular workers. (See Table 224.)

Hours of Work

On the average, seasonal farm workers are employed fewer days a week and fewer hours a day than regular workers. In April 1948, regular workers averaged 6.2 days or 57 hours a week; seasonal workers, 3.7 days or 32 hours. In September, a much busier month than April on most farms, each group averaged one hour longer a week. (See Table 225.) The average work week for all farm wage workers dropped from 42 hours in April to 37 hours in September,[2] even though both regular workers and seasonal workers averaged slightly longer hours per week in September than in April. The decrease in the average for all workers was due wholly to the increase in the proportion of seasonal workers in the hired farm working force in the fall of the year.

TABLE 224

AVERAGE HOURLY AND DAILY EARNINGS OF REGULAR AND SEASONAL HIRED FARM WORKERS, SEPTEMBER 1948

Region and Expected Duration of Employment	Hourly Earnings	Daily Earnings
United States		
Regular workers	$0.48	$4.50
300 days or more	0.47	4.50
150–299 days	0.50	4.60
Seasonal workers	0.65	5.60
75–149 days	0.55	4.90
Less than 75 days	0.55	4.60
Crew workers [a]	0.74	6.30
Northeast		
Regular workers	0.48	4.60
300 days or more	0.47	4.50
150–299 days	0.53	4.70
Seasonal workers	0.85	6.90
75–149 days	0.72	5.70
Less than 75 days	0.87	6.70
Crew workers [a]	0.87	7.60
North Central		
Regular workers	0.42	4.10
300 days or more	0.40	3.90
150–299 days	0.45	4.40
Seasonal workers	0.80	7.00
75–149 days	0.55	4.90
Less than 75 days	0.71	6.00
Crew workers [a]	0.97	8.60
South		
Regular workers	0.39	3.40
300 days or more	0.38	3.20
150–299 days	0.40	3.60
Seasonal workers	0.56	4.70
75–149 days	0.41	3.70
Less than 75 days	0.45	3.70
Crew workers [a]	0.68	5.80
West		
Regular workers	0.75	7.00
300 days or more	0.76	7.00
150–299 days	0.75	6.90
Seasonal workers	0.78	6.70
75–149 days	0.76	6.90
Less than 75 days	0.81	7.10
Crew workers [a]	0.72	5.90

a. Duration of employment was not ascertained for crew workers, but the great majority work for very short periods.

Source: Surveys of Wages and Wage Rates in Agriculture, Report No. 22, Bureau of Agricultural Economics, 1949.

2. As reported by employers for time worked on their farms. This kind of report slightly understates the total time spent at farm wage work during a week by individual workers, because some workers are employed on more than one farm in the same week.

TABLE 225

HOURS WORKED BY REGULAR AND SEASONAL HIRED FARM LABORERS DURING SPECIFIED WEEKS IN 1948

Region and Type of Worker	Time Worked on Reporting Farm					
	April 18–24, 1948			September 19–25, 1948		
	Hours per Day	Days per Week	Hours per Week	Hours per Day	Days per Week	Hours per Week
United States						
All workers	8.9	4.8	42	8.7	4.3	37
Regular workers	9.2	6.2	57	9.4	6.2	58
Seasonal workers	8.6	3.7	32	8.5	3.9	33
Northeast						
All workers	8.8	5.9	52	8.7	5.0	44
Regular workers	9.1	6.4	58	9.5	6.5	61
Seasonal workers	7.0	4.0	28	8.1	4.2	34
North Central						
All workers	9.2	5.5	51	9.1	4.8	44
Regular workers	9.6	6.5	63	9.8	6.5	63
Seasonal workers	8.3	4.1	34	8.7	4.0	35
South						
All workers	8.7	4.0	35	8.5	3.8	32
Regular workers	8.8	5.8	51	8.9	5.7	51
Seasonal workers	8.7	3.4	29	8.5	3.6	31
West						
All workers	9.1	5.6	51	8.8	5.4	48
Regular workers	9.4	6.1	57	9.2	6.3	58
Seasonal workers	8.8	5.1	45	8.7	5.1	45

Source: Surveys of Wages and Wage Rates in Agriculture, Report No. 22, Bureau of Agricultural Economics, 1949.

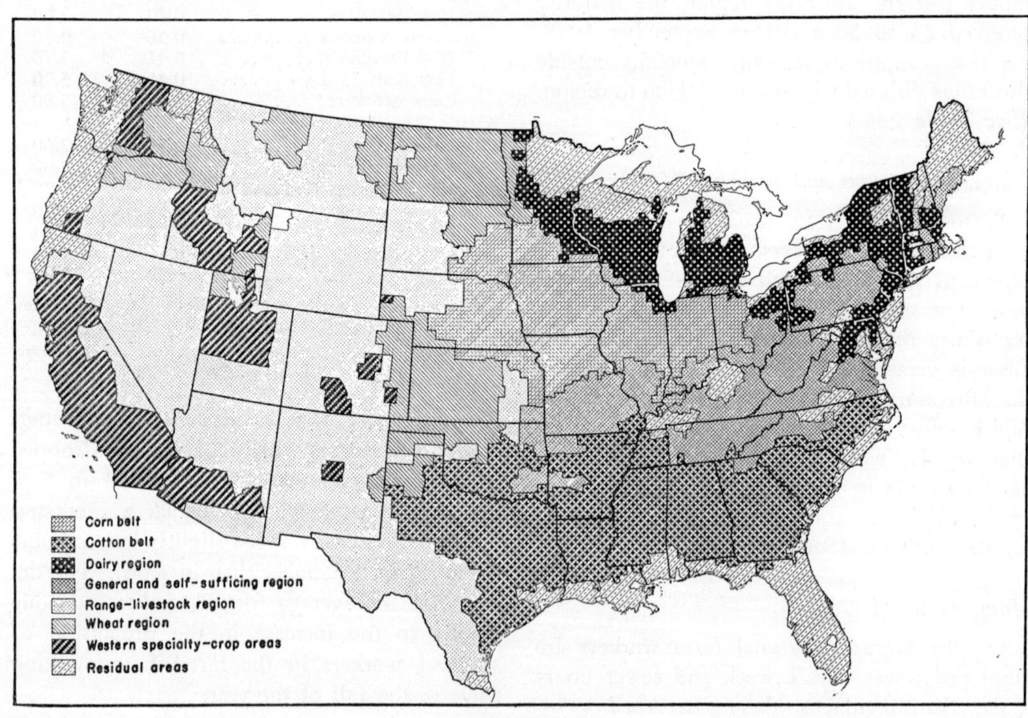

FIGURE 81. REGIONALIZED TYPES OF FARMING IN THE UNITED STATES (Special Adaptation, 1944)

Source: Bureau of Agricultural Economics.

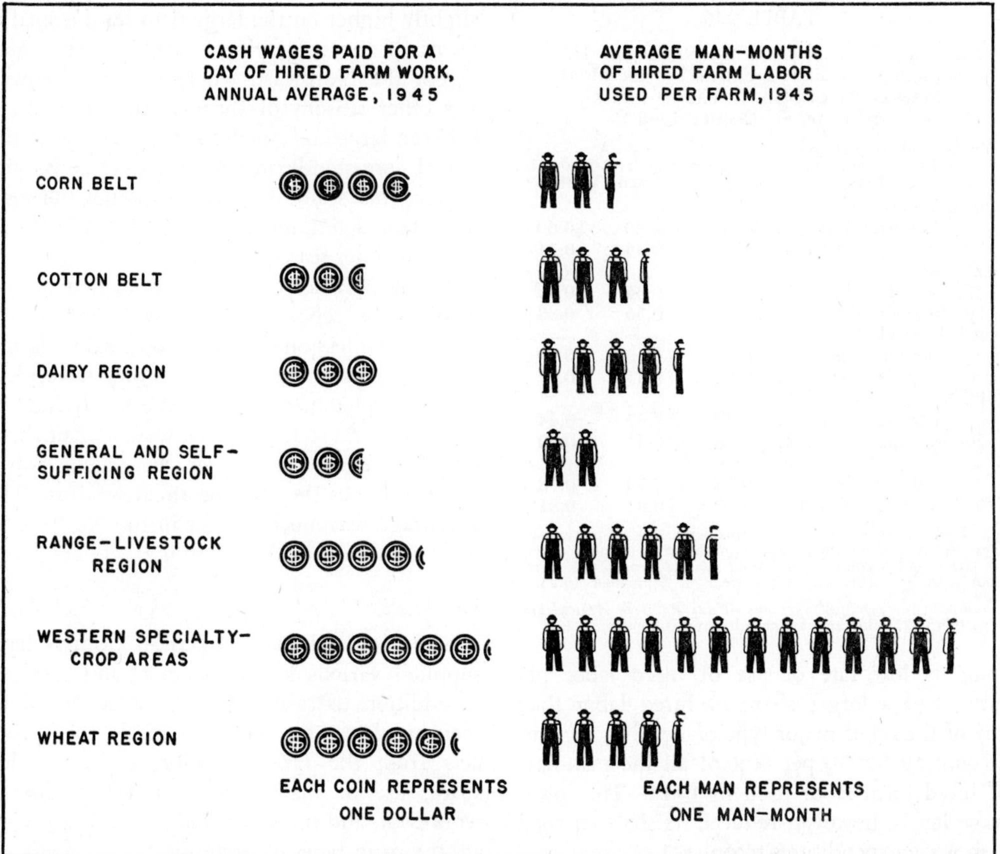

FIGURE 82. AVERAGE DAILY WAGES AND AVERAGE AMOUNTS OF LABOR HIRED IN MAJOR TYPE-OF-FARMING REGIONS, 1945

Source: Bureau of Agricultural Economics.

Hired labor is used most on farms in the western specialty-crop areas, where the highest wages are paid. At the other extreme is the general and self-sufficing region, where the least hired labor per farm is used and the lowest wages are paid.

Regional Variations by Type of Farming

In most farming areas, wage rates normally vary mildly with the season, rising as demands for farm labor increase and declining after the harvest season is over. Generally the highest rates in a year are paid at harvesttime, the period of peak labor demand.

Since different crops and areas reach their peak season at different times of the year, wage comparisons based on a cross-section week may not accurately reflect differences between regions in average wage levels throughout the year. From information on wages in selected weeks of 1945 and on the distribution of hired farm employment in the different parts of the year, estimates were developed of average cash wages paid for a day of hired farm labor in each of the eight major type-of-farming regions.

The western specialty-crop areas led all other areas of the country, with an average daily wage of $6.30 in 1945.[3] Next came the wheat region, with an average daily wage of $5.35. The range-livestock region followed, with an average of $4.35. (See Figures 81 and 82.)

Outside the West, wages were lower, and the average annual cash wage cost per farm was less than $400 in each region except a group of widely scattered specialized areas. Wages per day of hired labor were $3.95 in the corn belt, $3.05 in the northern dairy region, and only $2.55 in both the cotton belt and the general and self-sufficing region. The cotton belt, de-

3. Farms in these areas also led in the proportion using hired labor (72 per cent) and in the average amount of hired labor used on those farms that had hired labor (401 days).

TABLE 226

AVERAGE HOURLY CASH EARNINGS OF HIRED WORKERS ON FARMS USING 250 OR MORE MAN-DAYS OF HIRED LABOR DURING THE YEAR, SEPTEMBER 1948[a]

Region and Man-Days of Hired Labor Used in 1948	All Hired Workers	Regular Workers	Seasonal Workers[a]
United States			
250–499 man-days ...	$0.52	$0.40	$0.60
500 or more man-days.	0.70	0.55	0.71
Northeast			
250–499 man-days ...	0.62	0.36	0.95
500 or more man-days.	0.70	0.56	0.88
North Central			
250–499 man-days ...	0.43	0.38	0.59
500 or more man-days.	0.64	0.45	0.77
South			
250–499 man-days ...	0.49	0.37	0.44
500 or more man-days.	0.66	0.41	0.50
West			
250–499 man-days ...	0.67	0.59	0.78
500 or more man-days.	0.80	0.81	0.81

a. Excludes crew workers. Farms with 250 or more man-days of hired labor made up approximately 10 per cent of all farms and accounted for about 80 per cent of all hired labor used on farms. Data for week of September 19-25.

Source: Surveys of Wages and Wage Rates in Agriculture, Report No. 22, Bureau of Agricultural Economics, 1949.

spite its low rate of use of hired labor per farm, had a larger share of hired labor than any of the other major type-of-farming regions, accounting for 30 per cent ol all the man-days of hired farm labor used in 1945. The lower wage levels, however, reduced its share of total cash wage expenditures to only 21 per cent.

Differentials by Size of Farm

Hourly earnings of workers on large and smaller farms differ strikingly: regular workers on the smaller farms averaged 40 cents an hour and seasonal workers 60 cents in September 1948; the corresponding rates on large farms were 55 cents and 71 cents. For regular workers, the relative spread between rates on large and smaller farms is greatest in the Northeast and the West. Farms that used two or more man-years of hired labor in the year in these two regions paid their regular workers hourly cash wages 56 and 37 per cent higher, respectively, than farms using between one and two man-years. In the South the differential was only 11 per cent; in the North Central states, 18 per cent. (See Table 226.)

For seasonal hired workers, the difference between wages paid on large and on smaller farms is much less clear. Average hourly cash wages for seasonal workers (those whom the farmers expected to employ for less than 150 days in the year) in September 1948 were slightly higher on the large than on the smaller farms of the employing sector in each region except the Northeast, where they were lower. For other seasons of the year the differentials between large and smaller farms were not maintained consistently in the several regions, suggesting that scale of operations is not the most important determinant of differentials in wages of short-time, seasonal workers.

In the Northeast and the West, hourly cash earnings of regular and seasonal workers diverge much less on large than on smaller farms. In fact, on large western farms they were identical in September 1948. In the South and the North Central states seasonal workers had about the same relative advantage over regular workers on large as they had on smaller farms. The advantage was much greater in the North Central States than in the South.[4]

Perquisites

Since colonial days, American farmers have supplied various kinds of goods and services, in addition to cash wages, to some or all of their hired workers. Housing, meals, food products from the farm, laundry service, garden space, use of machinery, fuel, equipment or workstock, and transportation to and from work are the main types of perquisites.

A survey made by the Bureau of Agricultural Economics in May 1945 showed that approximately two thirds of all hired farm workers receive perquisites, but their value in comparison with cash wages is not so important as many people had thought.[5] In the United States as

4. Since most regions have one, two or three predominant types of farms, and since these vary by regions, only a few wage comparisons for the same type of farm can be made between regions on the basis of available sample data. In May 1945, daily cash wages on dairy farms were very little different in the Northeast and the North Central states — $2.55 as against $2.30. In the West, however, hired workers on dairy farms averaged $5.70 a day in the same week. Daily cash wages on corn farms in the North Central region were $4.05; in the South, only $2.50. In contrast, daily cash wages on wheat farms in the North Central region averaged $3.65 as compared with $3.50 in the South — but these southern wheat farms were mainly in the northern part of Texas and in Oklahoma, while the lowest wage areas are in the Southeast.

5. Barbara B. Reagan, "Perquisites Furnished Hired Farm Workers, United States and Major Regions, 1945," *Surveys of Wages and Wage Rates in Agriculture,* Report No. 18, Bureau of Agricultural Economics, 1946; Josiah C. Folsom, *Perquisites and Wages of Hired Farm Laborers,* Technical Bulletin No. 213, Department of Agriculture, 1931.

a whole the value of perquisites averaged $1.00 a day for regular workers and 40 cents for seasonal workers, as compared with cash wages of $3.40 and $3.75 respectively. (See Table 227 and Figure 83.)

Data on perquisites should be interpreted with an understanding of the make-up of the hired farm working force. By 1945 many farmers found themselves prosperous enough to give regular wages to members of their families who had previously worked without any regular remuneration. Thirteen per cent of all persons employed for wages on farms in May 1945 were related to the employing farmer by blood or marriage, and about half of these were sons or daughters. The perquisites of regular farm employees who were related to the employing farmer averaged $1.56 a day in value, as compared with $1.00 a day for nonfamily workers receiving perquisites.

Regional practices in furnishing perquisites vary greatly. The North Central region leads, with 89 per cent of its regular workers and 70 per cent of its seasonal workers on farms receiving perquisites in May 1945. In the West, where cash remuneration is highest, perquisites were of least importance and made up only 13 per cent of the total remuneration for regular farm workers and 4 per cent for seasonal workers.

TABLE 227

PERCENTAGE OF HIRED FARM WORKERS RECEIVING PERQUISITES AND AVERAGE DAILY VALUE OF WAGES AND PERQUISITES, MAY 20–26, 1945

Region and Type of Worker	Percentage of Workers Receiving Perquisites	Average Daily Value for All Workers [a]		
		Total Wages [b]	Cash Wages [b]	Perquisites
United States				
All workers	67	$4.20	$3.60	$0.60
Regular	80	4.40	3.40	1.00
Seasonal	59	4.15	3.75	0.40
Northeast				
All workers	65	4.70	3.75	0.95
Regular	76	4.45	3.30	1.15
Seasonal	39	5.45	5.10	0.35
North Central				
All workers	83	4.40	3.20	1.20
Regular	89	4.25	2.85	1.40
Seasonal	70	4.80	3.95	0.85
South				
All workers	67	3.00	2.55	0.45
Regular	79	3.45	2.75	0.70
Seasonal	64	2.85	2.50	0.35
West				
All workers	54	6.50	6.05	0.45
Regular	69	6.35	5.55	0.80
Seasonal	47	6.55	6.30	0.25

a. Excludes sharecroppers and tenants working as hired farm laborers on their landlords' farms, and custom workers.
b. Rounded to nearest 5 cents.

Source: Surveys of Wages and Wage Rates in Agriculture, Report No. 18, Bureau of Agricultural Economics, 1946, Tables 1, 4 and 9.

Transportation was the most common type of perquisite reported by southern employers of hired farm workers. In May 1945, southern employers provided about one fourth of their workers with transportation, mainly between their homes in near-by towns or elsewhere and the place of employment each morning and evening; this group also included some harvest workers in special-crop areas who were transported over longer distances at the beginning and end of the season. In other regions the transportation furnished included kinds that are more nearly bona fide perquisites — a ride to the nearest town at the week end or use of the employer's car or truck on specified occasions.

There are seasonal variations in the proportion of farm workers who receive perquisites, caused mainly by shifts in the relative importance of regular and seasonal workers, and variations in the different periods of the year in the relative importance of the particular types of farm food products furnished — for example, meat or fresh fruits and vegetables. The data on perquisites cited above, relating to May, come very close to approximating the average during the year.

WAGES IN AGRICULTURE AND INDUSTRY

In the past four decades farm wages in the United States have been consistently lower than wages in industry. It is not possible to make proper allowance for the degrees of skill required as between agricultural and industrial work, since there is no basis for classifying the hired farm working force into skill categories and no unanimity of opinion on the standards to be used in defining degrees of skill required for various farm jobs. Unquestionably, some groups of agricultural wage workers whose technical and practical knowledge of farming has been acquired through years of experience can be considered highly skilled workers by any reasonable standards. Although it is impossible to measure precisely the differences in skill between farm laborers and urban workers, nevertheless comparisons of farm and nonfarm wages reveal a contrast in favor of nonfarm workers

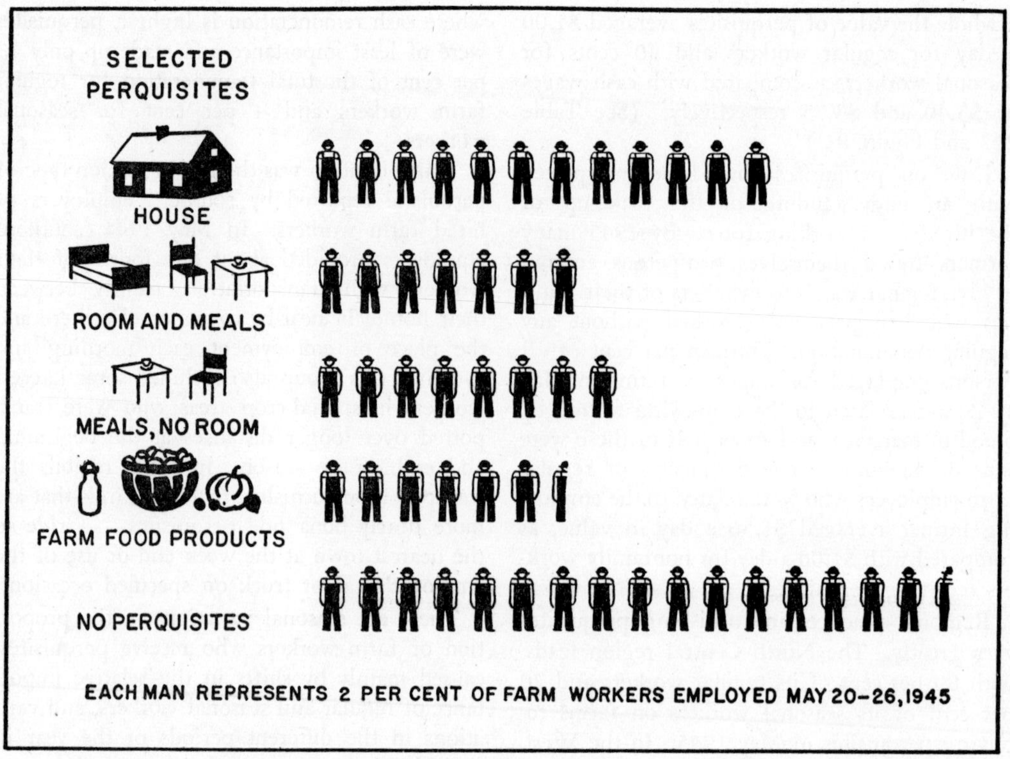

SELECTED PERQUISITES

HOUSE

ROOM AND MEALS

MEALS, NO ROOM

FARM FOOD PRODUCTS

NO PERQUISITES

EACH MAN REPRESENTS 2 PER CENT OF FARM WORKERS EMPLOYED MAY 20–26, 1945

FIGURE 83. PERCENTAGE OF HIRED FARM WORKERS RECEIVING PERQUISITES, MAY 1945
Source: Bureau of Agricultural Economics.

TABLE 228

AVERAGE HOURLY CASH EARNINGS OF FARM LABORERS, WORKERS IN MANUFACTURING INDUSTRIES, AND COMMON LABOR IN ROAD BUILDING, 1929–1948

Year	Average Hourly Earnings: Farm Laborers	Average Hourly Earnings: Workers in Manufacturing Industries	Average Hourly Earnings: Common Labor in Road Building	Hourly Earnings of Farm Workers as Percentage of Hourly Earnings of: Workers in Manufacturing Industries	Hourly Earnings of Farm Workers as Percentage of Hourly Earnings of: Common Labor in Road Building
1929	$0.239	$0.566	$0.39	42	61
1930	0.222	0.552	0.39	40	57
1931	0.173	0.515	0.36	34	48
1932	0.128	0.446	0.32	29	40
1933	0.113	0.442	0.38	26	30
1934	0.126	0.532	0.42	24	30
1935	0.137	0.550	0.41	25	33
1936	0.148	0.556	0.40	27	37
1937	0.168	0.624	0.40	27	42
1938	0.166	0.627	0.40	26	41
1939	0.164	0.633	0.42	26	39
1940	0.168	0.661	0.46	25	36
1941	0.205	0.724	0.48	28	43
1942	0.267	0.853	0.58	31	46
1943	0.351	0.961	0.71	37	49
1944	0.419	1.019	0.74	41	57
1945	0.466	1.023	0.78	46	60
1946	0.503	1.084	0.83	46	61
1947	0.543	1.221	0.91	44	60
1948	0.575	1.327	1.02	43	56

Sources: Earnings of farm laborers from Bureau of Agricultural Economics; earnings in manufacturing industries from Bureau of Labor Statistics; earnings of common labor in road building from Public Roads Administration.

greater than can be accounted for by any reasonable allowance for skill.

In 1929, hourly earnings of farm laborers averaged 42 per cent of hourly earnings of workers in manufacturing industries and 61 per cent of those of common labor in road building.[6] The depression forced farm wages down much more rapidly than nonfarm wages. By 1933, average hourly earnings of farm laborers were only 26 per cent of those of workers in manufacturing industries and 30 per cent of earnings of common labor in road building. There were minor fluctuations in later years of the 1930's, but all in all, farm wages maintained the same relationship with manufacturing wages during those years. In 1940, hourly earnings of hired farm workers were 25 per cent of factory workers' earnings and 36 per cent of those of road-building laborers. These ratios increased to 46 per cent and 60 per cent in the last year of World War II, and dropped to 43 per cent and 56 per cent by 1948. (See Table 228.)

Two factors largely account for the greater vulnerability of farm wages during depression. One is the pressure of the farm labor supply. For many decades, the high birth rates on farms have meant that the number of young persons who reach working age each year is much greater than is needed to replace older workers who die or retire. Migration from farms to cities slackens when urban unemployment is high, and an excess labor supply quickly accumulates on farms. In the early 1930's the farm population rose by nearly 2 million in the brief span of three years, and it took a decade before this excess was removed. Mechanization and other technological developments that have reduced labor requirements in agriculture have accentuated the effect of population growth on the farm labor supply. It is true that nonfarm wages were likewise under the pressure of unemployment during the depression, but this pressure apparently was less severe.

The low level of farm laborers' wages in the 1930's was due also to the fact that agriculture recovered from the depression later than most nonagricultural industries. Prices received by farmers were a third lower in 1940 than in 1929, whereas the index of wholesale prices of commodities other than farm products and foods was only 9 per cent below its 1929 level.

6. These averages relate to the United States as a whole, and are therefore affected to some extent by regional differentials. Low wage levels in the South, both in farm and nonfarm wages, have more influence on the national average of farm wages than of nonfarm wages, because the South has a greater share of the nation's farm than its nonfarm wage workers. The influence of the South, however, does not account for differentials as great as those cited.

TABLE 229

INDEXES OF FARM WAGES, 1930–1948

(1929 = 100)

Year	Unadjusted	Adjusted for Changes in Rural Living Costs[a]
1930	93	98
1931	72	90
1932	53	79
1933	47	70
1934	53	69
1935	57	73
1936	62	80
1937	70	87
1938	69	90
1939	68	90
1940	70	92
1941	86	104
1942	112	116
1943	147	137
1944	175	157
1945	194	167
1946	210	158
1947	227	142
1948	240	141

a. Adjusted by the index of prices paid by farmers for commodities used in living.

Sources: Bureau of Agricultural Economics; Louis J. Ducoff, *Wages of Agricultural Labor in the United States,* Technical Bulletin No. 895, Department of Agriculture, 1945.

TRENDS IN FARM WAGES

In 1933, farm wages were only 47 per cent of what they were in 1929. From this depression low point they rose gradually, with a slight setback in 1938 and 1939, but in 1940 they were still only 70 per cent of the 1929 average. (See Table 229.)

The rapid rise in farm wage rates during World War II was greatly accentuated by the fact that the rise started from a near-depression level. Even when expressed on a 1929 base, the index of farm wage rates showed very rapid gains each year through 1944, when it reached 175. Succeeding years saw further gains, but at a less rapid rate. By 1948 the index had reached 240. In 1949, farm wage rates began to weaken and fell slightly under the 1948 level. They began to move upward again after the outbreak of hostilities in Korea.

Changes in the farm wage rate index are less marked when adjustment is made for changes in rural living costs. On an adjusted basis, the

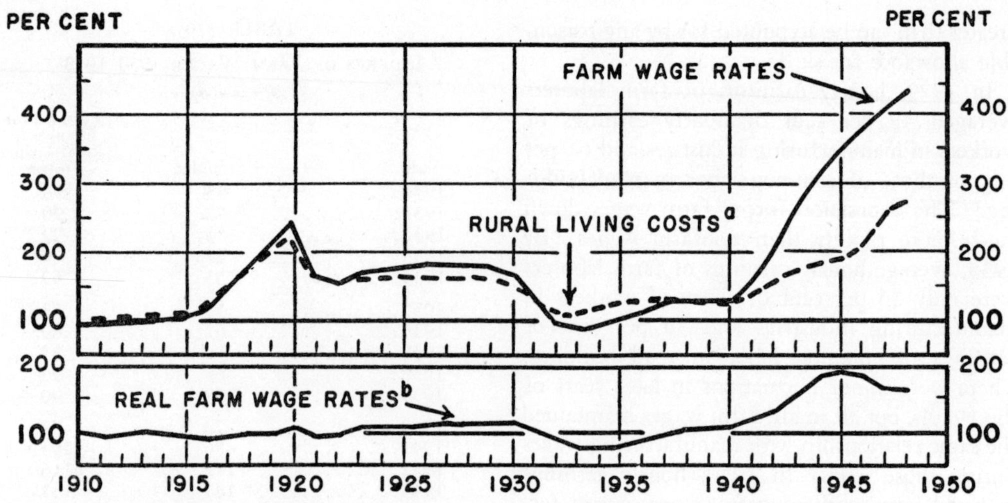

FIGURE 84. INDEXES OF NOMINAL AND REAL FARM WAGE RATES, 1910–1948
(1910–1914 = 100)

a. Prices paid by farmers for commodities used in living.
b. Wage rates divided by rural living costs.
Note: Data for 1948 are preliminary.

Source: Bureau of Agricultural Economics.

In dollars and cents, farm wage rates reached a record high in 1948. Despite the increases, however, gains in recent years have not held their own with increases in rural living costs. As a result, real farm wage rates have been falling since 1945.

low point was reached in 1934, when the index of real farm wage rates was 69, as against 100 in 1929. Effects of the depression still were evident in 1940, when the index was 92. The wartime rise reached a high point in 1945, when the index of real farm wage rates was 167. Since 1945, increases in rural living costs have outstripped further increases in money wages, and by 1948 the adjusted index of farm wage rates dropped to 141. (Cf. Figure 84.)

Regional Differentials

New England manifested the greatest stability in farm wages between 1929 and 1948. Without adjustment for changes in living costs, the low point of the farm wage index was 55 in 1933 (1929 = 100) and the high 195 in 1948. The Middle Atlantic states were the only other major geographic division in which the unadjusted index of farm wages in 1948 was no more than double the 1929 value. Farm wages in these industrialized areas had been among the highest in the country in 1929, matched only by those in the Pacific states, and farm wages in the Northeast are still higher than in any other part of the country except the Pacific states.

The four geographic divisions west of the Mississippi River all had somewhat higher than average net gains in farm wages between 1929 and 1948, with the 1948 index values ranging from 249 in the Mountain states to 255 in the West South Central. The greatest percentage rise in farm wages during the war was in the West North Central states, where wages had recovered less by 1940 than in other areas. In that region droughts and dust storms had accentuated the generally depressed economic conditions during the mid-1930's.

Apart from regional differences, the trends in agricultural wages in the past two decades have been affected by general business conditions in the United States, by the particular position of agriculture in our economy, and by the effects of the wartime economy.

Impact of World War II

At the outbreak of World War II, farm wages were very low in comparison with earnings in other pursuits. Farm-laborer families in rural areas received an average money income of $675 in 1941.[7] Approximately two thirds of

7. Louis J. Ducoff, *Wages of Agricultural Labor*

this income was derived from farm wage work and most of the rest from nonfarm work, plus a small amount from relief. These families averaged 1.66 persons working as farm laborers in 1941, so that the average amount of earnings from farm work per farm laborer was only $287. The money earnings of male workers from farm work in 1941 averaged $341, for an average thirty-five weeks worked.

The rapid rise of farm wages during the war was due mainly to the generally prosperous times experienced by farmers and the shortage of farm labor supply. At least three factors were operating, however, to keep farm wages from rising even faster than they did: importation of farm laborers from abroad, agricultural draft deferments and the program of farm wage regulation.

Wages undoubtedly would have gone higher in special-crop areas with acute labor needs if foreign workers had not been made available to the growers at what were determined to be "prevailing" wage rates. On the other hand, the agreements with foreign countries specified certain standards of housing, sanitation and medical care, and some growers may have carried these standards over to their local workers.

Agricultural deferments [8] tended likewise to slow down the rise of farm wages. The total number of agricultural deferments after the passage of the Tydings amendment to the Selective Service Act reached 1.7 million in March 1944, and went down to 1.3 million by the end of the war. What proportion of the deferees were hired farm workers is unknown. It seems reasonable, however, to suppose that the mobility of hired workers who had agricultural deferments — and hence their bargaining power — was curtailed. Such workers were less able to shop around for higher-paying farm jobs, since they ran a great risk of losing the deferment if they left the job for which they had been deferred.

On the other hand, the system of wartime wage controls tended to improve the wage position of farm workers in comparison with that of industrial workers. The program for stabilization of farm wages consisted of three parts: (1) setting a minimum level (the highest rate paid between January 1 and September 15, 1942) below which wages and salaries of agricultural laborers might not be reduced, (2) general control of agricultural wages and salaries at or above the level of $2,400 a year, and (3) setting specific maximum wage rates for particular crops and areas. The exemption of agricultural labor from the general stabilization order that "froze" nonagricultural wages as of September 15, 1942 was based on the following considerations, according to the Director of Economic Stabilization:

> That the general level of salaries and wages for agricultural labor is substandard, that a wide disparity now exists between salaries and wages in agriculture and in other essential war industries, and that the retention and recruitment of agricultural labor is of prime necessity in supplying the United Nations with needed foods and fibers.[9]

The ceiling of $2,400 a year was so high that it did not affect the great majority of hired farm workers. Later, $200 a month, or the equivalent thereof in shorter time units or in piece rates, was set as the level at which regulation should begin — in disregard of the fact that most hired farm workers get far less than twelve months of farm wage work in a year. The converted general ceiling affected many seasonal workers in addition to those whose wages were already governed by specific ceilings.

The specific wage ceilings for particular crops and areas probably had a greater effect on farm wages than the general wage regulation program. By the end of the war, specific wage ceilings had been set for particular crops and operations in various parts of seventeen states. Dr. William H. Metzler, who made a number of studies of the wage ceilings in California, has in general appraised the program favorably, although it did not work smoothly at first.[10]

Recent Developments and the Outlook

Farm wages continued to rise from the end of World War II until 1949, although not so fast as rural living costs. Of perhaps equal importance to the economic welfare of farm laborers has been the availability of supplementary nonfarm work in slack seasons. After declining slightly in 1949 and the first part of

in the United States, Technical Bulletin No. 895, Department of Agriculture, 1945.

8. *Agriculture Deferment,* Special Monograph No. 7, Selective Service System, 1947.

9. Federal Register, November 30, 1942, Vol. VII, p. 10024.

10. William H. Metzler, *Two Years of Farm Wage Stabilization in California,* Bureau of Agricultural Economics, Berkeley, California, 1946.

1950, farm wages began to move upward again following the outbreak of hostilities in Korea.

What developments are in prospect for farm wages in the near future? The upward trend observed in the last decade is likely to continue so long as conditions of high employment prevail. No significant departures from high employment levels appear in prospect in the immediate future in view of unsettled international conditions that necessitate large expenditures for the national defense. The differential between farm and nonfarm wages is less predictable. Thus far, no significant narrowing of the differential has taken place, as was the case in the early years of World War II, when the nation was recovering from a decade of depression. Continuation of full employment may prevent the widening of the differential, but substantial reduction may not occur until the farm labor market has assumed, to a much greater degree, characteristics of the industrial labor market, including the accepted practices of collective bargaining and equality of treatment under labor and other social legislation.

CHAPTER 43

UNION AND NONUNION WAGES *

WAGE RATES IN MANY INDUSTRIES are now determined wholly or largely through collective bargaining. There are practically no nonunion wages in such industries as coal mining, railroad transportation, local transit, automobile manufacture and basic steel. Some industries — electric light and power is an example — have comparatively small unorganized fringes. In still others, including cotton textiles, hosiery and many branches of metal fabrication, substantial union and nonunion segments are found. In many trade and service employments, the direct influence of unionism is comparatively small.

The level and structure of money wage rates in the United States are unquestionably strongly influenced by union wage actions. This fact has many implications for economic policy and for the course of economic development. The growth of labor organization has raised a host of controversial issues. It is suggested, for example, that "we may be faced with the danger of chronic inflation resulting from general wage increases which recurrently outrun the growth in productivity of the economy as a whole." [1] On the other hand, some support the view that strong unionism is not necessarily incompatible with high employment and stable prices.[2] To give another instance: the thesis has been advanced that unions take no account of the employment effects of their wage bargains.[3] This thesis is contrary to a substantial body of thought on the problem and has been challenged on the basis of recent research.[4]

Actually, experience in the United States with a broad and powerful labor movement has been rather brief. Moreover, union wage actions during the past decade have taken place largely within the framework of a basically inflationary situation. To a considerable extent, the postwar literature on wages has been conditioned by this fact. Definitive judgments on the economic consequences of large-scale union organization should be deferred until experience under more "normal" conditions has been accumulated. Even in the postwar period, union wage actions have exhibited surprising variety.[5]

The analysis that follows is not concerned, except at some points by indirection, with the broad issues of union economic power. An attempt is made (1) to review briefly some of the recent evidence on the relationship of wages in union and nonunion establishments within particular industries; (2) to point to union-nonunion differences in the prevalence of formal rate structures and in wage administration; and (3) to indicate the significance of wage differences for plant location.

UNION AND NONUNION WAGE LEVELS

The common assumption that wages for comparable work are always higher in union than in nonunion establishments is subject to a number of qualifications, as indicated below.

Differences on Nation-wide Industry Basis

On a nation-wide industry basis, union workers ordinarily do have higher average wage rates [6] than nonunion workers in the same occu-

---

* By H. M. Douty, Bureau of Labor Statistics, U.S. Department of Labor. Opinions expressed here are those of the author and not necessarily of the agency with which he is associated.

1. Emile Despres, Albert G. Hart, Milton Friedman, Paul A. Samuelson and Donald H. Wallace, "The Problem of Economic Instability," *American Economic Review,* September 1950, p. 535.

2. Walter A. Morton, "Trade Unionism, Full Employment and Inflation," *American Economic Review,* March 1950, pp. 13–39.

3. Arthur M. Ross, *Trade Union Wage Policy,* University of California Press, Berkeley, 1948, especially Chapter 4.

4. George P. Shultz and Charles A. Myers, "Union Wage Decisions and Employment," *American Economic Review,* June 1950, pp. 362–80.

5. This was true even in the immediate postwar years, when the "rounds" of wage adjustments lacked the uniformity often ascribed to them. See *Wage Movements: Changes in 1948 — War and Postwar Trends,* Industry Wage Studies, Series 3, Bureau of Labor Statistics, 1949. It was conspicuously true in 1949, when conditions were more stable, as demonstrated in the Bureau of Labor Statistics report, *Wage Developments through Collective Bargaining, 1949,* Industry Wage Studies, Series 3, 1950.

6. Unless otherwise qualified, the terms "wages," "wage rates" or "rates" as used in this chapter mean hourly rates for workers paid on a time basis or

pations. During 1946 and 1947, for example, the Bureau of Labor Statistics conducted occupational wage surveys in 32 manufacturing industries for which wages in union and nonunion establishments could be tabulated separately.[7] Average rates in union and nonunion establishments were shown for 902 selected occupations. In almost 87 per cent of these occupations, average rates in union establishments exceeded those in nonunion plants. In only one of the 32 industries did union workers in a majority of the selected occupations have lower average rates than nonunion workers.

Within individual industries, the size of the average wage difference between union and nonunion workers varied widely from occupation to occupation. In the leather (tanning, currying and finishing) industry, for example, information was shown for 39 occupations. In 29, union workers had an average wage advantage ranging from one cent to 36 cents an hour; the average advantage for nonunion workers in 10 occupations ranged from one cent to 32 cents.[8] In the cigar industry, the average union advantage varied from 2 cents to 27 cents an hour in 17 out of 24 occupations.[9] In ferrous foundries, the union advantage was 10 cents or more in 8 occupations and less than 10 cents in 11 occupations; in 3 occupations, the advantage (ranging from one cent to 7 cents) was with the nonunion workers.[10]

These figures suggest that, although a reasonably consistent wage advantage exists for union workers within given industries, there is little consistency in the size of the differential among occupations. Actually, however, the situation is much more complicated than this statement would indicate. An analysis of union-nonunion wage differences based on national data has limited significance in many situations.

Regional Differences

In studying the wage structure of an industry, it is frequently necessary to examine data by regional or even smaller areas of industry concentration. The general relationship of wages among broad economic regions has exhibited considerable stability over long periods of time.[11] When examined on a regional basis, the complexion of union-nonunion wage differences frequently changes.

The full-fashioned hosiery industry, for example, is found predominantly in the Middle Atlantic states and the Southeast. In 1946, about 45 per cent of all the workers in the industry were employed in union establishments; the proportion in the Middle Atlantic area was 63 per cent; in the Southeast, 18 per cent. In 35 of the 40 occupations for which union-nonunion comparisons were made, average wages were higher, on an industry-wide basis, for union than for nonunion workers. The average advantage of the union worker amounted to about 12 cents an hour. On a regional basis, however, the level of union wages was higher in only 23 occupations (out of 39 for which data could be shown) in the Middle Atlantic area, and in only 13 (out of 29) in the South.[12]

In three occupations in full-fashioned hosiery, chosen for illustrative purposes because they are highly important in terms of number of workers employed, the union advantage in the country as a whole amounted to 12 cents an hour or more, as Table 230 indicates. The union advantage within each of the regions was smaller, however, with a maximum difference

TABLE 230

STRAIGHT-TIME HOURLY EARNINGS OF UNION AND NONUNION WORKERS IN THE FULL-FASHIONED HOSIERY INDUSTRY, BY REGION AND SELECTED OCCUPATION, 1946

Region and Union Status	Knitters, Single Unit, and Backrack, Male	Seamers, Female	Toppers, Female
United States			
Union	$1.54	$0.90	$0.92
Nonunion	1.42	0.78	0.73
Middle Atlantic			
Union	1.63	0.93	0.94
Nonunion	1.61	0.92	0.91
Southeast			
Union	1.30	0.73	0.73
Nonunion	1.27	0.73	0.69

Source: Wage Structure, Series 2, Bulletin No. 32, Bureau of Labor Statistics, 1947, Table 10.

"earned" hourly rates (earnings exclusive of premium pay for overtime or late-shift work for a representative payroll period, divided by hours worked) for workers paid on an incentive basis.

7. *Wage Structure,* Series 2, Bulletin Nos. 27, 31–32, 35–38, 40–44, 46–52, 55, 57, 59–64, Bureau of Labor Statistics, 1947–1949. Data were tabulated for each industry on a national, regional and local-area basis. The locality tabulations generally were issued in the form of separate area releases.

8. *Ibid.,* Bulletin No. 57, Table 11.

9. *Ibid.,* Bulletin No. 27, Table 10.

10. *Ibid.,* Bulletin No. 49, Table 19.

11. See Joseph W. Bloch, "Regional Wage Differentials, 1907–46," *Monthly Labor Review,* April 1948, pp. 371–77. Of related interest is the study by Lily Mary David and Harry Ober, "Intercity Wage Differences, 1945–1946," *Monthly Labor Review,* June 1948, pp. 599–604.

12. *Wage Structure,* Series 2, Bulletin No. 32, Bureau of Labor Statistics, 1947, Table 10.

TABLE 231

AVERAGE HOURLY STRAIGHT-TIME EARNINGS OF UNION AND NONUNION WORKERS IN THE NONFERROUS FOUNDRY INDUSTRY, BY REGION AND SELECTED OCCUPATION, 1946

Region and Union Status	Coremakers, Hand	Molders, Machine	Shakeout Men	Chippers and Grinders
United States				
Union	$1.45	$1.53	$1.03	$1.11
Nonunion ..	1.37	1.50	0.96	1.02
Middle Atlantic				
Union	1.38	1.34	0.95	1.07
Nonunion ..	1.38	1.33	0.94	1.02
Great Lakes				
Union	1.50	1.56	1.08	1.17
Nonunion ..	1.42	1.55	0.99	1.03
Pacific				
Union	1.51	1.75	1.08	1.16
Nonunion ..	1.40	1.69	1.07	1.15

Source: Wage Structure, Series 2, Bulletin No. 49, Bureau of Labor Statistics, 1947, Table 20.

of 4 cents for toppers in the Southeast. Moreover, the level of union rates in the Southeast (and this holds generally for the great majority of the occupations for which this comparison can be made) was distinctly below the union level in the Middle Atlantic states.

For industries that have substantial segments in regions with different general levels of wages, the available evidence suggests that union-nonunion wage differences tend to be smaller on a regional (or smaller area) basis than on a national basis. Moreover, union wages in the lower-wage region are frequently below nonunion wages in the higher-wage region.

These tendencies, illustrated above with reference to full-fashioned hosiery, are plainly exhibited also in the nonferrous foundry industry. (See Table 231.) In each of four selected occupations [13] in this industry, the average wages of nonunion workers on the Pacific coast exceeded the average wages of union workers in the Middle Atlantic area; in comparison with union workers in the Great Lakes region, the average rates of nonunion workers on the Pacific coast were higher in one occupation and virtually identical in two. The wage differences were smaller in 7 of the 12 regional union-nonunion comparisons, and larger in 4, than the differences on a national basis for the same occupations. In one case, the two were identical.

Differences Related to Form of Wages

The tendency for union-nonunion wage differentials to narrow as comparisons are shifted from a national to a regional (or smaller area) basis may be counteracted by other factors associated with wage differences. These other factors may have a decisive effect on union-nonunion comparisons within an area, depending upon the incidence of unionization in the area.

Suppose that an industry has two groups of firms within a given area, one group using incentive methods of wage payment, the other paying time rates. Assume, further, that this is the only difference between them. If unionization is confined to the second group, average occupational rates for union workers will probably be below the average (earned) rates of the incentive workers in the nonunion group of plants. The differences may be substantial. Even greater differences may result, of course, if unionization is confined wholly or largely to the plants paying incentive rates. In either case, union-nonunion wage differences may be as great within the area as in the nation, or even greater.

In general, wages tend to be higher for incentive than for time workers in the same occupation.[14] In the four nonferrous foundry occupations already considered, the average hourly wages of incentive workers generally exceeded, often by a wide margin, the average rates of time workers. (See Table 232.) The two exceptions were union coremakers in the Middle Atlantic region and nonunion shakeout men in the Great Lakes region. Except in one occupation in one region, the average wages of union incentive workers exceeded the average wages of union time workers. Moreover, except in two instances, the average (earned) rates of nonunion incentive workers exceeded the rates of union workers paid on a time-rate basis, despite the fact that union workers paid on a time basis had higher average rates than nonunion time workers in every instance. Except for machine molders in the Middle Atlantic region and for coremakers, union incentive workers had higher average earnings than nonunion incentive workers.

The same types of wage relationships between union and nonunion time and incentive work-

13. The occupations again were selected to represent numerically important and stable occupations in the industry.

14. See *Effect of Incentive Payments on Hourly Earnings,* Bulletin No. 742, Bureau of Labor Statistics, 1943.

TABLE 232

Average Hourly Straight-Time Earnings of Time and Incentive Workers in Selected Occupations in the Nonferrous Foundry Industry, by Region [a] and Union Status, 1946

Occupation and Method of Wage Payment	United States		Middle Atlantic		Great Lakes	
	Union Foundries	Nonunion Foundries	Union Foundries	Nonunion Foundries	Union Foundries	Nonunion Foundries
Coremakers, hand	$1.45	$1.37	$1.38	$1.38	$1.50	$1.42
Time workers	1.42	1.29	1.39	1.29	1.44	1.29
Incentive workers	1.51	1.68	1.36	1.79	1.57	1.70
Molders, machine	1.53	1.50	1.34	1.33	1.56	1.55
Time workers	1.40	1.35	1.32	1.18	1.40	1.33
Incentive workers	1.68	1.65	1.39	1.48	1.77	1.65
Shakeout men	1.03	0.96	0.95	0.94	1.08	0.99
Time workers	1.00	0.96	0.94	0.92	1.02	1.01
Incentive workers	1.18	0.98	1.10	1.04	1.23	0.93
Chippers and grinders	1.11	1.02	1.07	1.02	1.17	1.03
Time workers	1.04	0.99	1.03	0.98	1.06	0.99
Incentive workers	1.31	1.22	1.20	1.17	1.35	1.26

a. Wages could not be tabulated separately for time and incentive workers in the Pacific region.

Source: Wage Structure, Series 2, Bulletin No. 49, Bureau of Labor Statistics, 1947, Table 28.

ers also may be derived from data for three important occupations in the machinery-manufacturing industry. (See Table 233.) Nonunion incentive workers had higher average wages than union time workers in each occupation on a national basis, and in seven of the nine regional comparisons. However, on a national basis, and in five regional comparisons, the average rates of union time workers exceeded those of nonunion time workers. Union incentive workers also had a wage advantage as compared with nonunion incentive workers in two of the three occupations nationally, and in six of the nine regional comparisons.

Differences Related to Size of Establishment and Size of Community

Several additional wage characteristics need to be noted briefly for the light they may throw on union-nonunion wage differences.

Wages tend to be higher in large establishments than in small.[15] To return again to the four nonferrous foundry occupations considered in Tables 231 and 232: on an industry basis, nonunion workers in each of these occupations in foundries employing 251 or more workers had higher average rates than union workers in small foundries (8 to 50 workers) or, with one exception, in medium-sized foundries (51 to 250 workers).[16] In establishments of comparable size, however, union workers had an average wage advantage in all except two instances.

Machinery manufacture provides further illustration. For this industry, data for 1946 are available by union status for establishments in four size groups.[17] The highest average wages among union workers were typically found in the largest establishments (501 or more workers). Among nonunion workers, the highest average wages appeared most frequently in the establishments with 251 to 500 workers. Average wages for nonunion workers in these establishments typically exceeded union wages in the groups of smaller union plants (8 to 50 and 51 to 250 workers). Within any given size group, union wages were higher than nonunion in most occupations, except in the Middle Atlantic area, where a nonunion advantage was found in several comparisons.

Wages in comparable occupations also tend to vary by size of community, being generally somewhat higher in large communities than in small. Unfortunately, data on union and nonunion wages in communities of different sizes have rarely been tabulated. It seems probable, however, that union rates will usually be higher than nonunion rates in communities of a given size; but nonunion workers in large communi-

15. For a general analysis of variations in earnings by size of establishment, see Jacob Perlman, *Hourly Earnings of Employees in Large and Small Enterprises,* Temporary National Economic Committee Monograph No. 14, 1940. See also the *Wage Structure* bulletins listed in footnote 7 and other bulletins in this series.

16. *Wage Structure,* Series 2, Bulletin No. 49, 1947, Table 26. A similar comparison is not possible on a regional basis in this industry. The data for large nonunion foundries were insufficient to warrant the presentation of regional averages.

17. *Ibid.,* Bulletin No. 51, Table 15.

TABLE 233

AVERAGE HOURLY STRAIGHT-TIME EARNINGS OF TIME AND INCENTIVE WORKERS IN SELECTED OCCUPATIONS IN THE MACHINERY INDUSTRY, BY REGION AND UNION STATUS, 1946

Occupation and Form of Wage Payment	United States		New England		Middle Atlantic		Great Lakes	
	Union Plants	Nonunion Plants	Union Plants	Nonunion Plants	Union Plants	Nonunion Plants	Union Plants	Nonunion Plants
Engine-lathe operators, Class A......	$1.45	$1.36	$1.34	$1.22	$1.48	$1.44	$1.47	$1.34
Time workers	1.40	1.34	1.15	1.17	1.35	1.39	1.44	1.33
Incentive workers	1.55	1.48	1.52	1.50	1.61	1.80	1.56	1.38
Milling-machine operators, Class A..	1.44	1.33	1.40	1.26	1.44	1.37	1.49	1.31
Time workers	1.39	1.30	1.15	1.18	1.33	1.32	1.48	1.28
Incentive workers	1.52	1.43	1.51	1.42	1.58	1.64	1.52	1.40
Turret-lathe operators, Class A......	1.42	1.34	1.36	1.30	1.44	1.42	1.45	1.34
Time workers	1.36	1.30	1.16	1.23	1.35	1.32	1.39	1.31
Incentive workers	1.49	1.49	1.44	1.42	1.50	1.68	1.53	1.42

Source: Wage Structure, Series 2, Bulletin No. 51, Bureau of Labor Statistics, 1948, Table 16.

ties will, in many instances, have a wage advantage over union workers in small communities.[18]

Over-All Comparison

It seems clear from the above analysis that not all union workers have higher wages than nonunion workers in comparable occupations. Nonunion workers in the North, for example, may have higher rates than union workers in the South. Even when the factor of regional differences is eliminated, organized workers appear to have no consistent advantage. Nonunion workers with incentive rates frequently have higher earnings than union time workers in comparable jobs. Similarly, the rates of nonunion workers in large establishments tend to be higher than those of union workers in small establishments. Nonunion workers in large cities probably tend to have higher wages than union workers in small towns.

Union wages, however, do tend to be higher than nonunion in comparable occupations in broadly comparable situations. That is, within a given industry in a reasonably homogeneous wage area, the earned pay of union incentive workers tends to be higher than that of nonunion incentive workers; the wages of union time-rate workers tend to be higher than those of nonunion, and so on. There are exceptions, of course, and the differences among occupations, and probably at different periods of time, tend to vary considerably.

The fact is that the American wage structure, which is extraordinarily complex, reflects the play of many forces. Although of increasing importance, unionism is only one factor in wage determination. Variations in regional and local-area labor market conditions, in methods of wage payment, in establishment size, in the technical efficiency of firms, and in company wage policies — these and other factors, in conjunction with union wage policy and union power, help determine the structure and the level of wages.

The specific influence of unionism is difficult to isolate; in any case, the extent and nature of this influence cannot be measured by union-nonunion wage relationships existing at any particular time. This matter is touched on in the concluding paragraphs of this chapter.

SOME OTHER ASPECTS OF UNION-NONUNION DIFFERENCES

The wage bargain has become increasingly complex. Although wage rates remain of basic importance, various forms of benefits supplemental to wages now enter into collective bargaining and into the calculations of nonunion employers. Paid vacations are widespread in both union and nonunion firms in manufacturing and in many nonmanufacturing industries. Premium pay for overtime, late-shift premiums, pay for holidays not worked, and insurance and pension plans of various types are among the supplements to basic wages that yield benefits to workers and represent cost to employers.[19] Data are not available to permit comparison, within specific industries, of the incidence of this cost in union and nonunion enterprises.

Wages are not only a matter of rates or earnings or supplemental benefits. The way in which wage structures are organized and ad-

18. There is partial confirmation for this statement in the studies of *union* rates by community conducted annually by the Bureau of Labor Statistics in five industries (construction, printing, local trucking, local transit, baking). The tendency for union rates in these industries to vary directly with community size is quite pronounced.

19. Cf. pp. 425–26.

ministered and the speed with which wages respond to changes in economic circumstances are also important.

Structure of Wages

Formal wage structures are more likely to be found in union than in nonunion establishments. A "formal" rate structure provides a recognized scale of rates, typically in writing, for at least the major occupations within an establishment.[20] The scale may consist of single rates or of rate ranges. The latter system usually includes a recognized procedure for advancing workers within the rate ranges. This procedure may relate to length of service or merit or to a combination of the two. In establishments with single rates, probationary or other special rates may exist: the rate for a given job, for example, may be $1.35, but a worker entering the occupation may have to serve a probationary period at a lower rate.

In contrast to formal rate structures are those in which markedly different rates may be paid to individual workers within a given occupation. In these situations, rates of pay are usually set by owners, managers or foremen on an individual basis, and wage increases or decreases are given in the same fashion. Formal rate structures were found in 75 per cent of the manufacturing establishments, numbering almost 16,000, in a comprehensive group of industries surveyed during 1945–1946 by the Bureau of Labor Statistics.[21] In office employment, on the other hand, individual wage determination is typical. Surveys of office workers in eleven large cities in 1948 indicated that "formal" [wage] structures are found primarily in very large establishments, or in those, relatively small in number, in which the office workers are covered by union agreements."[22]

Unions tend to insist on formal rate structures, partly to ensure equal pay for equal work and partly to facilitate the handling of wage grievances. Especially in large enterprises, formal rate structures possess many advantages for management, as wartime experience abundantly demonstrated.[23]

Administration of Wages

Somewhat related to the character of the rate structure is the question of union influence on the administration of wages. No wage structure administers itself. Many problems arise for decision on a day-to-day basis. In nonunion plants, wage administration is completely under the control of the employer. Employer action is limited, of course, by general considerations of worker efficiency and morale, and by the extent to which workers, as a matter of company policy, are consulted on administrative actions that affect their wage status.

In union plants, the union almost always exercises some measure of control over the day-to-day administration of the wage structure. Depending upon a number of factors, including the character of the industry and the strength and stability of the union, collective bargaining agreements indicate in greater or lesser degree how the practical problems of wage administration are to be met.[24] Disputes over the application of these provisions are subject, of course, to whatever type of grievance machinery is written into the contract.

What are some of the problems of wage administration? Piece rates and other incentive rates are usually fixed as to general level for the duration of a collective bargaining agreement; in unorganized plants with modern wage and personnel policies, the level of incentive rates is commonly considered fixed until a general revision of rates occurs. Particular rates may have to be altered, however, or new rates established, within the general framework of a stable system of rates.

It is generally conceded that technical changes affecting an operation may provide a valid occasion for revising an incentive rate. But how much of a technical change has to occur? And how shall the new rate be established? It may make considerable difference to the employees whether decisions on these points are arrived at unilaterally by the employer or on some kind of joint union-employer basis. Or suppose a

20. Such "formal" wage structure should not be confused with "formal" plans of job evaluation, examined in Chapter 35.

21. Lily Mary David, "Manufacturing Industries: Wage Rate Structures, 1945–1946," *Monthly Labor Review,* March 1948, pp. 281–82.

22. Kermit Mohn, *Salaries of Office Workers in Selected Large Cities,* Bulletin No. 943, Bureau of Labor Statistics, 1948, p. 3.

23. *The Termination Report,* National War Labor Board, 1948, Part I, Chapter 21.

24. *Union-Security Provisions in Collective Bargaining,* Bulletin No. 908, Bureau of Labor Statistics, 1947, especially Parts 3 and 8.

new product or a new operation is scheduled. How shall the incentive rates be set? In some industries — clothing, for example — new products or new styles require almost constant attention to the setting of piece rates. Or suppose a machine breaks down or the work does not flow evenly. How shall this down time or waiting time be compensated?

In any sizable establishment using wage incentives, hundreds of problems in the administration of the incentive system are likely to arise in the course of a year. Many of these problems may appear relatively insignificant, but they often have considerable importance to the workers directly involved and to management.

In nonunion plants, job evaluations are carried through by management or by engineering firms hired for the purpose. In union plants, the process may be conducted or supervised jointly.[25] Probably the most notable example of joint participation in the job evaluation process is provided by the United States Steel Corporation and the United Steelworkers of America (CIO).[26] Over a period of several years, the major meat-packing companies and the three unions functioning in the industry developed a bargained wage-rate structure that greatly reduced the complexity of the old structure and corrected many wage inequities.[27]

A host of other problems arise in the administration of wage structures. In plants using rate ranges, for example, a basic question is the way in which workers are advanced within the ranges for the several occupations or labor grades. Again, what policy shall be applied when workers are temporarily transferred from one occupation to another with a higher or lower rate of pay? Such apparently simple questions as how and when wages should be paid sometimes present problems. Should wages be paid in cash or by check? If by check, does the worker have to pay a service charge when he cashes his check? Are there convenient check-cashing facilities? How frequently should wages be paid?

Union influence on the administration of wages has probably been underestimated in comparison with the unions' role in pressing for general wage increases or resisting decreases. But this influence marks one of the great differences between union and nonunion establishments.

Flexibility of Wages

Management in nonunion firms does not have to bargain over changes in the general level of wage rates and has greater freedom, as we have seen, in the administration of wage structures. It is generally assumed, therefore, that nonunion wages are in some sense more flexible than union wages. For one thing, the general level of wages in union situations is usually stabilized for the duration of the contract. Moreover, unions tend strongly to resist reductions in wage rates, even under adverse economic conditions.

The difference between nonunion and union situations, however, appears at most to be one of degree. There is no clear-cut contrast between complete flexibility and complete rigidity. Wage rates tend generally to lag behind cyclical turns in business activity and employment.[28] This is true of nonunion as well as of union wages.

Collective bargaining undoubtedly tends to make wage rates more inflexible during downturns in economic activity. Even unions in strongly organized positions, however, have agreed to wage reductions.[29] In some cases, the maintenance of union rates in periods of depression has been more nominal than real.[30] Even in highly organized industries, substantial periods of wage stability can usually be discerned, corresponding to periods of stability in the industry or in the economy as a whole.

During upswings in business activity, especially when characterized by strong inflationary

25. Some unions prefer not to participate directly in the job evaluation process, thus retaining complete freedom to utilize the grievance machinery in cases of alleged misclassification.

26. Robert Tilove, "The Wage Rationalization Program in United States Steel," *Monthly Labor Review,* June 1947, pp. 967–82.

27. Edwin E. Witte, "Industrial Relations in Meat Packing," in Colston E. Warne (Ed.), *Labor in Postwar America* (*Yearbook of American Labor,* Vol. II), Chemical Publishing Company, New York, 1949, pp. 497 ff.

28. Daniel Creamer, *Behavior of Wage Rates during Business Cycles,* Occasional Paper No. 34, National Bureau of Economic Research, New York, 1950.

29. Richard A. Lester and Edward A. Robie, *Wages under National and Regional Collective Bargaining,* Princeton University Press, Princeton, 1946.

30. See William Haber, "Building Construction," in Harry A. Millis (Ed.), *How Collective Bargaining Works,* Twentieth Century Fund, New York, 1942, p. 210.

pressures, the contractual obligations of unions may tend to delay upward rate adjustments. In the period following World War II, added flexibility in many situations was achieved by provision for wage reopenings prior to contract expirations.[31] Wage escalator clauses based on changes in the Bureau of Labor Statistics consumers' price index have also increased considerably in recent years. On the other hand, long-term contracts with provision for stated yearly wage-rate increases add an element of inflexibility to the wage bargain.

Unionization and Plant Location

From time to time, the impact of unionization on wages and production costs is vividly demonstrated in the competition between the unionized and nonunionized sectors of an industry or in shifts of plants from unionized to nonunionized areas. Early in 1949 the Popular-Priced Dress Manufacturers Association objected to signing a new contract with the union (International Ladies' Garment Workers, AFL), even though no wage increase was involved. The association asserted that the union's failure to eliminate nonunion conditions in some parts of the industry confronted unionized employers with "unfair competition" that jeopardized their ability to stay in business. Approval of the contract by a majority of the members of the association was based on assurance by the union that an organizing campaign would be undertaken in nonunion shops in New York, Pennsylvania, Connecticut and Rhode Island.[32] This situation obviously points to the resumption of close cost competition in this industry after the boom conditions of the immediate postwar period.

Many shifts in the locational pattern of industries have grown, at least in part, out of the lower labor cost in the nonunionized sector. For example, in the 1920's the competition from nonunion coal fields in West Virginia, Kentucky and elsewhere, in face of the determination of the United Mine Workers to maintain the relatively high wage rates in the Jacksonville agreement, virtually wrecked the union.[33] In 1919, two thirds of the equipment of the full-fashioned hosiery industry was located in the Philadelphia area; about 90 per cent of the industry was unionized. Beginning in the 1920's, the industry began to spread into smaller Pennsylvania communities, to some localities in the Middle West, and into the South. Today, Philadelphia probably has 10 per cent of the equipment in the industry. The unionized portion of the industry sank to 25 per cent in 1931 and by 1949 was probably in the neighborhood of 50 per cent. Akron was once preeminent in the rubber tire and tube industry and is still the major center of tire manufacture. An official of the United Rubber Workers (CIO) has stated, however, that tire capacity outside Akron is now great enough to supply normal demands.[34]

The relative level of wage rates is only one of many factors that influence plant location. Wages (in terms of wage cost per unit of output) have some importance in all industries; they are critically important in industries in which the ratio of wages to other costs is relatively high and in which obstacles to plant mobility (such as large fixed capital) are not great. Union wage strategy, at least in the long run, is clearly affected by the possibility that union control will be weakened, and perhaps destroyed, through shifts in the location of an industry. Even in industries that are substantially organized, unions must take into account the relation between wages and location. New capital may flow, as it did in the full-fashioned hosiery industry in the 1920's, into areas of relatively low wage cost. Major locational shifts may render illusory gains in the unionized sector of an industry.

Impact of Unionization

The preceding discussion provides no answer to the question whether or to what extent unionism has improved, or can improve, the real wage position of workers as a class. Nor has it solved the limited question whether, over substantial periods of time, the wages of union workers (in unionized establishments or indus-

31. An unusual development during the late summer and fall of 1950 was the granting of substantial wage increases by important companies in the automobile and other industries before contracts expired or wage-reopening dates were reached. See *Monthly Report on Current Wage Developments,* Bureau of Labor Statistics, especially August–October 1950.

32. *New York Times,* February 2–4, 1949.

33. Waldo E. Fisher, "Bituminous Coal," in Millis, *op. cit.,* Chapter 5. In addition to wage rates, there were other economic factors in the union debacle.

34. *New York Times,* February 23, 1949.

tries) increase more rapidly than the wages of nonunion workers.[35]

It was suggested earlier that the impact of unionism on wages can be judged only imperfectly through an analysis of the patterns of wages in union and nonunion establishments. This point needs to be emphasized.

Unionism is a dynamic factor in the determination of labor conditions. Its influence is not confined to union members. It is partly for this reason that efforts to measure statistically the impact of unionization on wages are likely to prove exasperating. A wage increase granted by a nonunion firm may have been greatly influenced by wage increases secured in other firms by union action. Nonunion firms on occasion raise wages in anticipation of the outcome of collective bargaining negotiations involving other firms or to frustrate union organizing efforts. At least in part for this latter purpose, some nonunion firms adopt a policy of maintaining wages above levels in the industry and area.

Similarly, one of the limits to the freedom of nonunion firms to make downward wage adjustments during a depression is the relative stability of wages in unionized firms. It must also be remembered that, apart from bargaining over wage rates, unions are concerned with many other problems relating to working conditions that have a bearing on the welfare of workers and the costs of employers in industry, including nonunionized firms.

In substance, unionism is a social movement with wide ramifications. In the determination of wages as well as in other fields, unionism is likely to affect larger areas of economic and social relations than those directly subject to its influence.

35. This is a very difficult question to deal with statistically. According to Douglas, "The evidence seems to indicate that when labor organization becomes effective, it yields very appreciable results in its early stages, but that thereafter the rate of gain enjoyed by its members tends to slow down to a speed which does not appreciably exceed that of the nonunion industries." Paul H. Douglas, *Real Wages in the United States, 1890–1926,* Houghton Mifflin, Boston, 1930, p. 562. Unfortunately, Douglas, in his brief discussion of this matter, failed to relate his conclusions closely to the statistical data that he had developed in his great and pioneering investigation of wage movements. This perhaps explains why Ross, in his criticism of Douglas on this point, evidently misinterpreted the nature of the Douglas series on manufacturing. See Ross, *op. cit.,* Chapter 6. For an account of the derivation of the manufacturing wage series, see Douglas, *op. cit.,* Chapter 3.

CHAPTER 44

TRENDS IN WAGE DIFFERENTIALS *

IN THE LONG RUN, differences in wage rates and earnings are a part of general differences in income. The scale of remuneration for different types of ability and effort is determined by the interplay of many factors: the demand for and supply of labor meeting various specifications; competition among job-seekers for better positions and among employers for better workers; job evaluation and union pressures; customary preferences and discriminations of both workers and employers; the clash between the forces of tradition and economic and technological change. All these factors have left their mark on the existing wage differentials according to age, sex, race, area, industry and occupation. Their combined effect determines whether the wage structure moves toward equality or toward greater contrasts between the different groups of the working population.

The question of the general trend in wage differentials can be answered only by careful appraisal of the available statistical data, and the answer is necessarily restricted to the areas, industries, occupations and period covered by these data.

As Hugh Dalton pointed out:

> To determine whether, under modern conditions, inequality tends to increase or decrease, involves the enumeration of a large number of distinct and conflicting tendencies, and the weighing and balancing of them one against the other. . . . It is obvious that the result of this weighing and balancing may vary greatly both as between different communities at the same time, and as between different times in the same community. Conclusions pretending to much generality on this subject are to be mistrusted. Whether inequality is actually increasing or diminishing in a particular community during a particular period of time is, of course, a statistical question, which may be answered independently of general argument regarding economic cause and effect, provided, first, that the relevant income statistics are known, and, second, that a measure of inequality is agreed upon and applied to these statistics.[1]

Dalton's last point is particularly important. There is no single universally accepted device for measuring changes in inequality in earnings, and different measurements can point toward divergent conclusions. For example, the trend toward less inequality in the median earnings of two groups of workers does not preclude opposite trends in the lower and upper parts of the frequency distribution nor growing inequality of earnings within both groups. Similarly, the relationship between average per capita earnings in two industries or two states does not always change in the same direction as the relationship between median earnings in the same industries and areas. Within the same group of workers the contrast between the highest and lowest earnings can increase while the spread of prevailing earnings of the middle half of the group narrows, or vice versa. Moreover, the increasing contrast between the lowest and highest earnings does not necessarily exclude lessening inequality in the earnings of the majority of workers, say the middle 60 or 80 per cent.

To sum up, extreme caution is advisable in generalizations about trends in wage differentials, and a clear distinction should be made between observed changes and interpretation of such changes as milestones of development.

STABILITY OF THE INCOME AND WAGE STRUCTURE

Despite continual shifts in the relative positions of different groups of workers as to earnings and living conditions, the general structure of wages in a nation changes very slowly. Frequently an apparently significant shift toward equality proves to be temporary and is followed by a shift in the opposite direction.

Great Britain is an extreme example of such stability in wage structure. Almost half a century ago A. L. Bowley offered a very simple formula of the distribution of wages in Great Britain: If a typical group of 100 individuals are arrayed by their weekly wages, the man at

* By W. S. Woytinsky.

1. Hugh Dalton, *Some Aspects of the Inequality of Incomes in Modern Communities,* Dutton, New York, 1920, pp. 351–52.

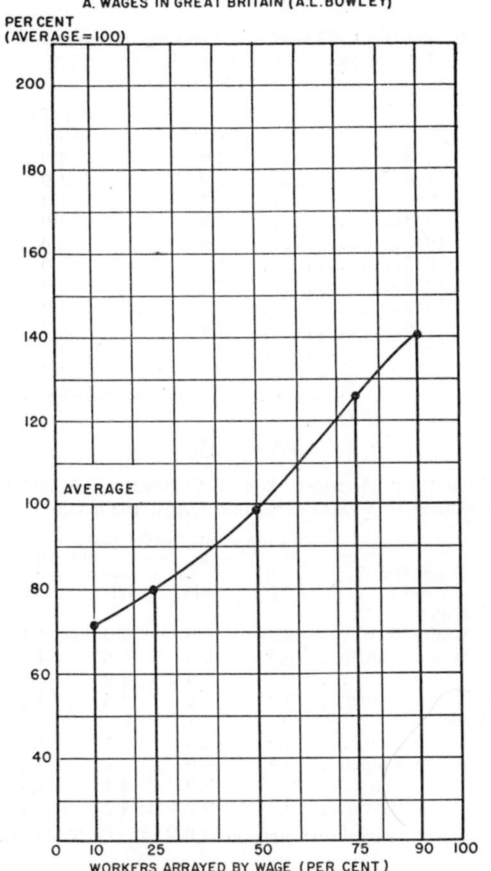

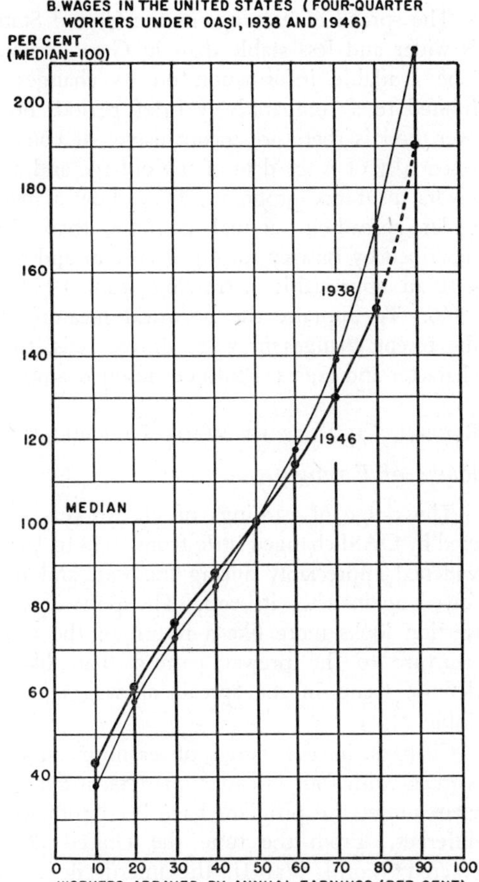

FIGURE 85. SPREAD OF WAGES IN GREAT BRITAIN AND THE UNITED STATES

A. L. Bowley's hypothetical model of the spread of wages in Great Britain (plot A) suggests that in the middle half of the occupational ladder the highest wage is approximately 56 per cent higher than the lowest wage. For the middle 80 per cent of the group (counting from the tenth to the ninetieth man out of a hundred) the highest wage is twice that of the lowest.

For the United States, annual earnings of four-quarter workers under old-age and survivors insurance are shown in plot B. The relative spread between low and high earnings narrowed from 1938 to 1946, but remained much broader than in Great Britain. In the middle half of the occupational ladder, the highest earnings in 1946 were twice the lowest earnings; for the middle 80 per cent, the ratio of highest to lowest earnings was about 4 to 1.

the middle (median) will have wages slightly below the average determined by dividing total earnings of the group by 100; the wage of the twenty-fifth man (first quartile) will amount to four fifths of the median and that of the seventy-fifth man (third quartile) to five fourths of the median; the wage of the tenth and ninetieth man (first and ninth deciles) will be nearly five sevenths and seven fifths of the median.[2] (See Figure 85.) Bowley commented on this formula as follows:

> A law of grouping will remain unchanged, if the proportionate demand for and supply of labor of various degrees of excess from normal skill do not vary; there is an impression among authorities that the tendency is to increase the demand for skilled labor, but this will only affect the law of grouping if this increase outpasses the increase of normal skill. At the least it may be granted that the change in grouping may be expected to be slow, and that this tentative law gives us some means of constructing the actual distribution of wages when we only know the median or average.[3]

Twenty years later another British economist found the same pattern of wage distribution in the United Kingdom in 1860, 1880 and 1914.[4]

2. A. L. Bowley, "Wages," *Encyclopaedia Britannica,* 10th edition, Vol. IX, 1902, p. 718.

3. *Ibid.*

4. W. A. Mackenzie, "Changes in the Standard of Living in the United Kingdom, 1860–1914," *Economics,* October 1921, p. 213.

The spread of earnings in the United States is wider and less stable than in Great Britain. The available information on its changes is limited to a comparatively brief period, however, and is therefore inconclusive. It consists essentially of wage data of the old-age and survivors insurance program. They show a much wider spread in annual earnings than that described by Bowley for Great Britain and suggest an appreciable narrowing from 1937 to 1946. To appraise the historical meaning of the recent changes in wage differentials, their character and causes should be closely examined.

Recent Changes in Wage Differentials

Range of Earnings

The range of earnings of all workers covered by OASI changed little from 1938 to 1941, widened appreciably during the war, and narrowed again after its end. The postwar contraction looks more like a return of the wage structure to the prewar pattern than like a definite trend in the spread of wages. (See Table 234.)

Changes in the range of earnings among workers with four calendar quarters in employment under the program have been somewhat different. From the time the United States entered World War II, the interdecile ratios of annual earnings of this group of workers declined steadily, and the gap between high and low wages in 1946–1948 was appreciably narrower than in 1938. (See Table 235.) There is no evidence to show whether these changes were temporary or whether they marked a definite trend.

Similarly inconclusive are the changes in the range of annual earnings for all covered workers classified by sex, race and age. A comparison of interdecile ratios for 1937 and 1946 indicates that the contrasts changed insignificantly for white men, increased slightly for white women, and decreased for Negro workers of both sexes. (See Table 236.)

TABLE 234

Interdecile Ratios of Annual Wage Credits of All Workers under OASI, 1938–1948

Year	8th to 2d Decile	7th to 3d Decile
1938	9.4	4.1
1939	8.6	3.8
1940	8.8	3.7
1941	9.3	3.8
1942	10.8	4.2
1943	11.7	4.5
1944	11.4	4.3
1945	11.5	4.5
1946	9.2	3.8
1947	8.4	3.5
1948	7.6	3.3

Source: Derived from Appendix Table 98. Cf. Table 196.

TABLE 235

Interdecile Ratios of Workers with Four Calendar Quarters in Employment under OASI, 1938–1948

Year	8th to 2d Decile	7th to 3d Decile
1938	2.9	1.9
1939	2.9	1.9
1940	2.8	1.9
1941	2.8	1.9
1942	2.9	2.0
1943	2.9	2.0
1944	2.8	2.0
1945	2.7	1.9
1946	2.4	1.7
1947	—	1.7
1948	—	1.7

Source: Derived from Appendix Table 98. Cf. Table 196.

TABLE 236

Range of Annual Wage Credits of Various Groups of Workers under OASI, 1937 and 1946

Race, Sex, Age	Ratio of 8th to 2d Decile		Ratio of 7th to 3d Decile	
	1937	1946	1937	1946
All ages				
White men	6.7	6.9	2.9	3.1
White women	8.5	9.0	3.6	4.2
Negro men	12.6	9.5	4.8	4.0
Negro women	15.0	9.6	5.6	4.4
Ages 25–29				
White men	3.9	4.8	2.1	2.4
White women	6.5	9.0	2.8	4.0
Negro men	9.0	7.9	4.1	3.6
Negro women	9.9	9.7	4.2	4.5

Source: Derived from Appendix Table 102. Cf. Table 200.

Relation of Earnings to Age

The patterns of differentials in earnings by age have changed since 1939, but the meaning of the changes is not very clear.[5] Probably most significant is the change in the variation of women's wages with age: Before the war, the highest annual earnings recorded for women were in the age group 30 to 44 years; in 1948 the peak was at ages 35 to 49. This shift may have been related to the broadening work opportunities for women. On the other hand, no particular significance should be attached to the fact that in covered industries the highest median earnings of women in 1948 were in a

5. See Chapter 37, especially Tables 199, 200 and 201.

TABLE 237

RATIO BETWEEN MEDIAN ANNUAL WAGE CREDITS OF WHITE AND NEGRO WORKERS UNDER OASI, 1937 AND 1946

Age	Men 1937	Men 1946	Women 1937	Women 1946
20–24 years	3.6	1.6	4.0	3.2
25–39	3.0	1.9	3.1	2.2
30–34	2.8	1.9	2.5	1.7
35–39	2.7	1.9	2.4	1.8
40–44	2.7	1.9	2.4	2.1
45–49	2.6	1.8	2.5	1.9
50–54	2.6	1.8	2.7	1.9
55–59	2.6	1.9	2.8	1.9

Source: Derived from Appendix Table 102. Cf. Table 201.

later age group than the highest median earnings of men. (See Appendix Tables 99–103; cf. Figure 73.)

Relation of Earnings to Race

The gap between earnings of Negro and white workers narrowed during the war and continued to narrow after its end. This held true for male and female workers under the OASI program, for all age groups and for all levels of wage credits. This conclusion is based on more than one set of observations.[6] Hundreds of tests, hundreds of checks can be made and all observations, with a very few exceptions, corroborate one another. There was a very sharp reduction in the customary ratio of earnings of white workers to those of Negro workers. The change is illustrated by a comparison of median annual wage credits of Negro and white workers by age in 1937 and 1946. (See Table 237.) All in all, the gap between median earnings of Negro and white workers narrowed by one third for men and one fourth for women. This trend continued after the war.

Earnings in Relation to Sex

The broadening of women's work opportunities has not changed appreciably the relationship between earnings of male and female workers. With minor fluctuations, the ratios in the total group of covered workers have remained fairly steady: 2 to 1 in the middle of the distribution, a little more than 2 to 1 at the lower end, slightly less than 2 to 1 at the top. Among four-quarter workers, the ratio between the median earnings of men and women was 1.6 to 1 in both 1938 and 1946; among three-quarter workers, it was 1.5 to 1 in 1938 and 1.6 to 1 in 1946.

In view of the far-reaching changes in the industrial and occupational distribution of working women and repeated drastic revisions of all wage rates, the stability of the relationship between the earnings of the two sexes may seem surprising. It seems to indicate that, all in all, the demand-supply relationship for female workers has changed in about the same way as that for male workers. Doubtless, women have gained access to jobs that were closed to them before the war. On the other hand, it seems fairly probable that some industries had a shortage of male workers after the war while the supply of female workers was abundant.

Moreover, the relationship between earnings of male and female workers appears stable only in terms of broad statistical averages. Divergent changes in the male-female ratio of earnings occurred among white and Negro workers, in the various geographic areas and in different industries. Among white workers, for example, the median wage credits of women in 1939 amounted to 40 per cent of those of men in the West (the West South Central, Mountain and Pacific states) and 60 per cent in the Southeast (the South Atlantic and East South Central states). In 1946 the ratio in the Southeast contracted to approximately 50 per cent, while that in the West remained as before the war. (See Appendix Table 105.)

Geographical Differentials

During the past two decades, and more particularly since the great depression, there has been a continuous trend toward equalization of incomes and wages among the different parts of the United States. Whatever may have been the specific causes of this development, its mainsprings have been the progress of industrialization in the backward, primarily agricultural areas and the rise of agricultural prices in comparison with those for manufactured goods.

The trend toward equality in per capita income among geographic regions is illustrated by a comparison of the ratio of state per capita income payments to the national average. In 1929, per capita income in 8 states was more than 30 per cent above the national average and in 10 states it was less than 60 per cent

6. Cf. pp. 453, 455 and 457.

TABLE 238

PER CAPITA INCOME IN EACH STATE AND REGION AS PERCENTAGE OF NATIONAL AVERAGE, 1929–1950

State and Region	1929	1940	1944	1945	1946	1948	1949	1950
Continental United States	100	100	100	100	100	100	100	100
New England	123	126	112	110	111	106	107	108
Connecticut	135	144	130	125	122	120	121	123
Maine	83	87	90	88	88	86	84	81
Massachusetts	132	133	112	112	114	106	109	111
New Hampshire	96	98	91	94	94	92	92	89
Rhode Island	125	125	114	111	110	105	106	109
Vermont	88	91	83	87	90	87	84	82
Middle East	136	131	118	120	119	116	117	117
Delaware	135	155	123	117	119	116	126	133
District of Columbia	175	189	114	118	117	116	131	138
Maryland	103	123	111	107	103	103	106	108
New Jersey	139	140	124	124	122	117	118	118
New York	165	150	132	138	137	131	131	130
Pennsylvania	113	109	105	106	106	104	104	106
West Virginia	68	69	70	73	74	79	75	73
Southeast	51	56	66	67	66	67	67	67
Alabama	45	47	61	61	59	60	58	58
Arkansas	45	44	56	60	63	63	59	57
Florida	71	81	87	88	85	78	83	84
Georgia	48	55	66	67	65	66	66	67
Kentucky	55	54	61	64	64	66	65	63
Louisiana	61	62	71	70	65	70	76	73
Mississippi	40	35	50	50	48	54	48	49
North Carolina	45	55	61	64	67	65	64	66
South Carolina	37	50	58	59	61	62	60	58
Tennessee	51	55	70	73	68	65	66	67
Virginia	62	78	80	79	76	77	79	81
Southwest	68	70	82	80	79	82	88	85
Arizona	84	81	83	85	81	85	86	86
New Mexico	56	62	69	72	72	76	81	77
Oklahoma	67	62	81	75	74	79	82	75
Texas	68	72	84	82	80	83	90	89
Central	106	105	105	105	106	110	107	108
Illinois	137	126	115	119	122	128	123	122
Indiana	86	94	100	101	97	102	99	101
Iowa	80	85	89	93	103	110	99	99
Michigan	110	113	115	106	105	107	108	110
Minnesota	83	89	84	90	96	98	94	93
Missouri	90	88	90	92	96	98	98	98
Ohio	110	112	113	111	107	109	108	110
Wisconsin	93	90	97	99	100	102	102	100
Northwest	79	79	95	96	97	103	96	96
Colorado	91	90	88	96	95	104	102	97
Idaho	76	77	89	92	98	95	92	90
Kansas	78	74	100	97	94	96	93	93
Montana	89	100	104	105	111	119	105	112
Nebraska	82	75	97	97	99	107	98	102
North Dakota	57	65	93	93	94	109	91	90
South Dakota	61	66	90	97	101	115	90	91
Utah	79	83	91	90	87	88	91	89
Wyoming	101	105	94	99	104	110	112	105
Far West	127	130	129	120	120	115	118	119
California	139	140	132	123	124	117	121	122
Nevada	120	143	119	125	134	122	126	131
Oregon	94	100	112	108	105	105	105	106
Washington	105	110	129	114	108	110	111	114

Source: Survey of Current Business, August 1951, p. 15. Cf. Figure 80.

of that average. In 1950 only Delaware, the District of Columbia, New York, and Nevada were at or above the 130 per cent mark, and only 4 states (Alabama, Arkansas, Mississippi and South Carolina) fell below the 60 per cent mark. In 1929, per capita income in 20 states fell within the range ± 20 per cent of the national average; the corresponding number in 1950 was 30. (See Table 238.)

In 1929 per capita income in typically rich states was 3.5 times that prevailing in poor states; in 1932–1933 the ratio was 4.3 to 1; in

1949, 2.2 to 1; in 1950, 2.3 to 1. (See Table 216.)

As impressive as these figures are, they do not prove that we are heading toward complete economic equality among states and regions. Local conditions vary too much to permit maintenance of such equality even if it were reached for a short time. It is fairly certain, however, that the trend toward equalization of per capita income in the different parts of the country has not reached its end. The industrialization of the South is gaining momentum; more attention is being given to the decentralization of industries vital for national defense; government and business are engaged in a policy of developing natural resources, including water power, in backward areas; support of agricultural prices has become a firmly established policy in the nation. All these factors tend further to narrow the gap between rich and poor states. This trend leads necessarily toward a leveling of state and regional differences in wage rates and earnings.

Considered against this background, changes in geographical differentials of annual earnings under the old-age and survivors insurance program become particularly significant. In all states decile annual wage credits of male workers — whether at the second decile, the median or the eighth decile — were substantially higher in 1946 than in 1939; nearly all the increases were between 70 per cent and 130 per cent. The various rates of gain, however, were not scattered at random over the map of the United States or over the levels of earnings in each state. The largest gains (those over 125 per cent) were heavily concentrated in the low-wage states and, within each state, at the lower end of the earnings distribution. The relatively smallest advances (those less than 75 per cent) were in the richest states and in the upper part of the distribution. (See Table 239.)

When the forty-eight states and the District of Columbia are distributed in four groups according to median earnings of male workers in 1939, the highest percentage gains are found in the poorest states and especially among low-paid workers (for example, at the second decile). At the lower end of the occupational scale in the poorest states the (unweighted) average gain in earnings from 1939 to 1946 was 130 per cent, while at the upper end of the distribution (eighth decile) in the richest states the average advance was only 73 per cent. (See Table 240.) Thus low-wage states have been catching up with high-wage areas and low-paid workers with those in higher brackets.

Industrial Differentials

Changes in industrial differentials in earnings have not been so clear or meaningful as those in geographical differentials. The trend is obscured by technological progress and changes in the structure of different industries and in their labor requirements. All in all, however, the contrasts between high-wage and low-wage industries have been greatly reduced since 1929.[7]

The most striking manifestation of this trend is the rise in wages in agriculture and water transportation. From 1929 to 1950, according to the national income statistics of the Department of Commerce, annual earnings per full-time worker tripled in agriculture and more than tripled in water transportation, while among iron and steel workers, automobile workers and workers in machinery factories gains ranged between 106 and 121 per cent. More than average gains were made also in manufacturing industries with conspicuously low wages in 1929, such as tobacco manufacturing and textile mills, and in bituminous coal mines. (See Tables 211 and 212.)

Industries with the highest earnings per full-time worker in 1929 had comparatively small gains in earnings, and those with the lowest, relatively large gains. Air transportation (with an increase of 57 per cent from 1929 to 1950), wholesale trade (80 per cent) and finance and insurance (57 per cent) are typical of high-earnings industries. Textile mills (with an increase of 140 per cent), tobacco factories (131 per cent), service in private households (102 per cent) and agriculture (200 per cent) are typical of industries with the lowest earnings in 1929. (See Table 241; cf. Tables 211 and 212.)

The changes were not wholly consistent in the middle of the range, but their general direction is clear. Typical white-collar industries that were at the top of the list in 1929 lagged behind manufacturing and mining. Agriculture, service industries and low-wage manufacturing industries moved up.

7. Cf. p. 461.

TABLE 239

SELECTED DECILE ANNUAL WAGE CREDITS OF MALE WORKERS UNDER OASI, BY STATE, 1939 AND 1946[a]

State[b]	Second Decile		Median		Eighth Decile	
	1939	1946	1939	1946	1939	1946
1. District of Columbia	$295	$385	$1,160	$1,915	$2,165	$3,375
2. Ohio	330	635	1,155	2,065	1,870	3,130
3. New Jersey	360	700	1,150	2,185	1,920	3,320
4. Michigan	310	665	1,150	2,135	1,845	3,195
5. Connecticut	420	810	1,135	2,160	1,755	3,340
6. New York	345	635	1,125	2,085	2,010	3,345
7. Illinois	330	565	1,125	2,110	1,915	3,290
8. Pennsylvania	345	655	1,060	1,970	1,710	2,965
9. Wisconsin	240	450	1,040	1,865	1,710	2,910
10. Massachusetts	335	605	1,030	1,980	1,750	3,035
11. Delaware	290	695	1,030	2,095	1,865	3,500
12. California	205	415	995	1,765	1,850	3,135
13. Washington	195	385	985	1,640	1,750	2,990
14. Maryland	290	550	980	1,845	1,745	3,055
15. Indiana	235	500	975	1,845	1,680	2,950
16. Rhode Island	335	570	940	1,930	1,540	2,990
17. Missouri	165	335	895	1,565	1,690	2,785
18. West Virginia	215	370	875	1,700	1,450	2,830
19. Oregon	160	405	875	1,630	1,580	2,890
20. Minnesota	140	305	855	1,535	1,650	2,705
21. New Hampshire	210	360	770	1,490	1,325	2,510
22. Wyoming	140	260	740	1,200	1,600	2,880
23. Nevada	165	290	730	1,280	1,575	2,930
24. Montana	125	255	730	1,220	1,590	2,645
25. Virginia	155	295	710	1,360	1,420	2,535
26. Utah	120	250	700	1,205	1,490	2,740
27. Iowa	110	270	695	1,320	1,420	2,500
28. Arizona	120	270	680	1,170	1,620	2,560
29. Colorado	130	230	680	1,200	1,490	2,560
30. Louisiana	125	290	665	1,270	1,565	2,795
31. Kentucky	120	235	660	1,255	1,355	2,470
32. North Carolina	165	290	650	1,215	1,170	2,185
33. South Carolina	150	290	630	1,320	1,065	2,250
34. Oklahoma	100	225	630	1,215	1,560	2,640
35. Tennessee	125	235	630	1,170	1,310	2,480
36. Maine	140	280	625	1,180	1,050	2,350
37. Vermont	115	370	625	1,440	1,260	2,360
38. Alabama	125	250	620	1,180	1,355	2,510
39. Georgia	120	235	605	1,140	1,280	2,450
40. Kansas	105	205	590	1,200	1,395	2,545
41. Nebraska	105	230	580	1,185	1,370	2,545
42. Texas	95	225	575	1,215	1,600	2,815
43. South Dakota	100	185	540	985	1,300	2,280
44. Florida	100	260	500	1,160	1,310	2,600
45. Idaho	90	240	470	1,220	1,350	2,700
46. New Mexico	90	160	455	810	1,325	2,255
47. North Dakota	55	140	390	895	1,250	2,390
48. Arkansas	65	130	380	700	1,055	1,920
49. Mississippi	60	185	355	920	1,110	2,340

a. For more recent years the eighth decile in high-wage states cannot be computed because of lack of information on earnings in excess of $3,000.

b. States arrayed by descending order of median earnings of male workers in 1939. It will be noticed that the ranking of states by second- and eighth-decile earnings differed slightly from their ranking by median earnings.

Source: Appendix Table 105.

TABLE 240

PERCENTAGE GAINS IN DECILE ANNUAL WAGE CREDITS OF MALE WORKERS UNDER OASI, 1939–1946 [a]

Group of States [b]	Second Decile	Median	Eighth Decile
Richest states (1–15)....	92	84	73
High-middle (16–25)....	94	83	80
Low-middle (26–35).....	106	87	81
Poorest states (36–49)...	130	110	90

a. Unweighted average for each group of states.
b. States arrayed as in Table 239.

Source: Derived from Table 239.

TABLE 241

PERCENTAGE INCREASES IN AVERAGE ANNUAL EARNINGS PER FULL-TIME EMPLOYEE IN HIGH-WAGE AND LOW-WAGE INDUSTRIES, 1929–1950

Industry	Percentage Increase
High-wage industries	
Air transportation	57
Radio broadcasting and television	87
Engineering, professional services	79
Business services	77
Motion pictures	35
Wholesale trade	80
Finance, insurance, etc.	57
Low-wage industries	
Water transportation	247
Lumber basic products	115
Textile mill products	140
Hotels, lodging places	81
Tobacco manufactures	131
Medical and other health services	128
Service in private households	102
Agriculture, forestry, etc.	200

Source: Derived from Tables 211 and 212.

The trend toward a leveling of industrial differentials in wages appears only in the ratios between wages in different industries, not in the absolute difference between dollar earnings in the industries. Unweighted average annual earnings per full-time employee for five typical high-wage industries were $2,280 in 1929 and $3,959 in 1950; for five typical low-wage industries, $1,101 and $2,417. The ratio between full-time earnings in the two groups went down from 2.07 in 1929 to 1.64 in 1950, while the dollar difference between average earnings in the two groups increased from $1,179 in 1929 to $1,542 in 1950.[8] (See Table 242.)

TABLE 242

ABSOLUTE AND PERCENTAGE INCREASES IN AVERAGE ANNUAL EARNINGS PER FULL-TIME EMPLOYEE IN FIVE TYPICAL HIGH-WAGE AND FIVE LOW-WAGE INDUSTRIES, 1929–1950

Industry	Average Annual Earnings 1929	1950	Percentage Increase
High-wage industries, average [a] for the group..	$2,280	$3,959	74
Air transportation	2,624	4,118	57
Radio broadcasting and television	2,513	4,698	87
Wholesale trade	2,164	3,900	80
Finance, insurance, etc..	2,090	3,279	57
Printing and publishing.	2,010	3,798	89
Low-wage industries, average [a] for the group...	1,101	2,417	120
Amusement, except motion pictures	1,273	2,432	91
Lumber basic products..	1,172	2,519	115
Textile mill products...	1,155	2,767	140
Tobacco manufactures ..	979	2,258	131
Medical and other health services	925	2,107	128
Excess of high-wage group.	1,179	1,542	—
Ratio of high-wage to low-wage group	2.07	1.64	—

a. Unweighted.

Source: Derived from Tables 211 and 212.

Wages in Agriculture

Because of the fundamental difference in the structure of wages in agriculture and industry, only a very rough comparison of trends in the two fields is possible.[9] According to the Department of Commerce, earnings of farm laborers — on a full-time basis — have increased greatly since 1929, in comparison with earnings of industrial workers. (See Appendix Table 108.) On the other hand, when hourly wages of farm laborers are compared with those of factory workers or common laborers in road building, the relative advance of farm laborers appears doubtful. (See Table 228.)

The apparent contradiction between the two observations is due partly to the difference in methods of measurement and partly to the basis of comparison. The Department of Commerce series measures annual earnings per full-time worker, regardless of the number of hours worked during a year. The comparison in Table 228 has to do with average hourly earnings.

8. A comparison of decile annual earnings of workers employed in industries under OASI (Appendix Table 110) in 1939 and 1946 fails to reflect the changes in industrial differentials shown by the surveys of the Department of Commerce. Several factors related to the insurance statistics may have obstructed the trend. First, wage statistics of the insurance system do not include earnings over $3,000 in a calendar year. Second, they cover a comparatively short period, 1939–1946. Third, annual earnings at all occupational levels in these statistics are heavily affected by changes in the rate of labor turnover, and the pattern of turnover in 1946 differed substantially from that in 1939. Fourth, the classification of industries in the insurance statistics was revised between the two dates.

9. Cf. Chapter 42.

The first method tends to cover all forms of wage payments, the second only straight cash wage rates. On the other hand, because of the narrowing of the spread between skilled and unskilled wages, wages of common laborers advanced more than those of craftsmen and white-collar workers. Therefore, if farm laborers' wages kept pace with those of low-paid industrial workers they advanced proportionately more than per capita earnings in industrial pursuits.

Occupational Differentials

The relative spread between wage rates of skilled and unskilled labor has been reduced by nearly half in the past forty years.[10] Median hourly wage rates of skilled factory workers were more than double those of unskilled laborers in 1907, 75 per cent higher in 1918–1919, and only about 50 per cent higher in 1945–1947. The trend in the building trades was similar, the only difference being that in this industry the relationship of skilled to unskilled wage rates remained fairly stable until the middle of the 1930's and then went down, the percentage decreasing from 179 in 1935 to 143 in 1947.

Any possible doubt about the meaning of this trend is dissipated by a comparison of occupational wage differentials in different parts of the country: The spread is wide in the comparatively backward areas and particularly narrow in the old stronghold of American industry, the Northeast and the Middle Atlantic states. The narrowing of the spread has kept pace with progress in industrialization and modern technology.

Craftsmanship flourishes in a static economy that gives the individual an opportunity to reach the highest degree of specialized skill in a limited field. The modern economy, however, is dynamic. Its methods of production are not rigid. The workers it requires — and shapes accordingly — may be assigned specialized functions but nonetheless must have generalized mechanical skill, resourcefulness, adaptability. This not only wipes out the demarcation between the skilled and unskilled worker but also blurs the difference between the manual worker and the engineer.

Thus the trend toward a leveling of occupational differentials in wages is intimately related to economic progress, and it is fairly probable that it will continue in coming years.

Wage Differentials and Economic Inequality

The preceding analysis of various types of wage differentials has shown that at least four kinds of disparity in earnings have been greatly reduced in recent years:

(1) Geographical differentials — the contrast between primarily agrarian, low-wage regions and industrialized, high-wage areas
(2) Industrial differentials — the contrast between low-wage and high-wage pursuits, particularly between agriculture and urban industries and between manual and white-collar workers
(3) Occupational differentials — the contrast between so-called skilled and unskilled labor
(4) Racial differentials — discrimination against Negro workers

These are highly meaningful developments in the structure of wages.

To what extent do they indicate a general trend toward equality in earnings and incomes or foreshadow such a trend?

One does not need to believe in Pareto's law of rigid distribution of income [11] to realize that the pattern of economic inequality in a society cannot change drastically in a short time unless the economic and social structure of that society undergoes a radical transformation. Changes in this field can be only slow and gradual. But such changes are possible. In fact, such changes are probably in progress, in one direction or the other, in every society at each stage of its development. The rhythm of such changes was described by Gustav Schmoller more than half a century ago:

> With economic progress, an increasing differentiation in individual incomes is as unavoidable as increasing social differentiation. In certain periods, however, contrasts in individual incomes become much more pronounced than differences in individual abilities, partly because of personal success or inheritance from one generation to another, partly as a result of

10. See p. 470 and Appendix Tables 115, 116 and 117.

11. Vilfredo Pareto, *Cours d'Economie Politique*, F. Rouge, Lausanne, 1897, pp. 320 ff.

ruthlessness, shrewdness, violence, and exploitation. Since none of these factors favors the same groups constantly, continuous growth of inequality in income is out of the question. The very fact that the highest and lowest layers of society often degenerate and decline more rapidly than the middle classes can result in increasing the importance of the last group. It may be expected that with moral progress and a growing sense of equity, violence will be checked and that the progress of general education will diminish inequality of opportunity and favor a more even distribution of income. In all probability, periods of growing inequality in income will be followed by periods in which contrasts will be partly ironed out. . . . The prevailing historic trend is neither a steadily growing inequality of incomes nor a steadily lessening inequality, but a temporarily progressive differentiation, followed by opposite movements which tend to reduce inequality.[12]

At the end of the nineteenth century the contrast between rich and poor in this country was probably on the increase. It is difficult to determine when this period ended and the trend toward economic equality began. It seems, however, that the general trend toward economic equality has been accelerated by the two world wars and the great depression. This tendency is probably reflected in the leveling of wage differentials discussed in the preceding pages.

There is a substantial difference, however, between the distribution of income among families or consumer units and the distribution of earnings among individuals. Persons with occasional and temporary employment and the smallest annual earnings are seldom the main breadwinners in a family; most of them are the second or third earners in the household. Their earnings widen the range of individual incomes tremendously but do not increase inequality in incomes of households. On the contrary, the temporary entrance into the labor market of an additional worker in the household often serves to offset losses caused by the temporary unemployment or disability of the usual breadwinner, or to meet extraordinary needs of the family. Therefore the wide spread in individual earnings due to instability of employment is not incompatible with the general trend toward greater equality in income. The narrowing of the spread in earnings of four-quarter workers under OASI may be related to this trend.

Distribution of Earnings and Human Ability

The long-range trend in wage differentials raises a question of the relationship between the distribution of earnings and human abilities. This is a very important point in wage discussion. Labor unions criticize the high salaries of executive officers of corporations; management opposes minimum-wage legislation as contrary to the spread of human abilities. As a rule, labor unions are inclined to minimize the contrasts, while business management stresses their significance.

The most striking disparity in the distribution of human abilities and of income is that human abilities are supposed to deviate from the average as frequently and as strongly in one direction as in the other, while incomes are distributed in such a way that the majority of people are concentrated in the lowest income brackets and a small minority have incomes many times higher than the average.[13] As A. C. Pigou puts it:

If we were to plot out the distribution of incomes in the form of a curve so drawn that the abscissae represent amounts of income, and the ordinates the number of people in receipt of these amounts, the curve would rise very quickly to its highest point and, thereafter, fall much less quickly. This would express in a picture the well-known fact that there are a very large number of people with incomes much below the average income, and, comparatively, a very small number with incomes above the average income. In short, the essential characteristic of current income distribution is that the great bulk of incomes are massed together near the lower end of the income scale. This fact is significant for the following reason. There is clear evidence that the physical characters of human beings — and considerable evidence that their mental characters — are distributed on an altogether different plan. When, for instance, a curve is plotted out for the heights of any large group of men, the resulting picture will not, as with incomes, have a humped and lop-sided appearance, but it will be a symmetrical curve shaped like a cocked-hat. It will, in short — to use a technical term — be the characteristic Gaussian curve, or curve of error, symmetrical about the mean in such wise that there is no massing near either end, but an equal number of people at every height as the distance from the mean in either direction is increased. Now, on the face of things, we should expect that, if, as there is reason to think, people's capacities are distributed on a plane

12. Gustav Schmoller, "Die Einkommensverteilung in Alter und Neuer Zeit," *Jahrbuch für Gesetzgebung, Verwaltung und Volkswirtschaft,* Viertes Heft, 1895, pp. 1076–77 and 1094.

13. H. L. Moore, *Laws of Wages, An Essay in Statistical Economics,* Macmillan, New York, 1911; F. C. Hicks, *The Theory of Wages,* Macmillan, London, 1902.

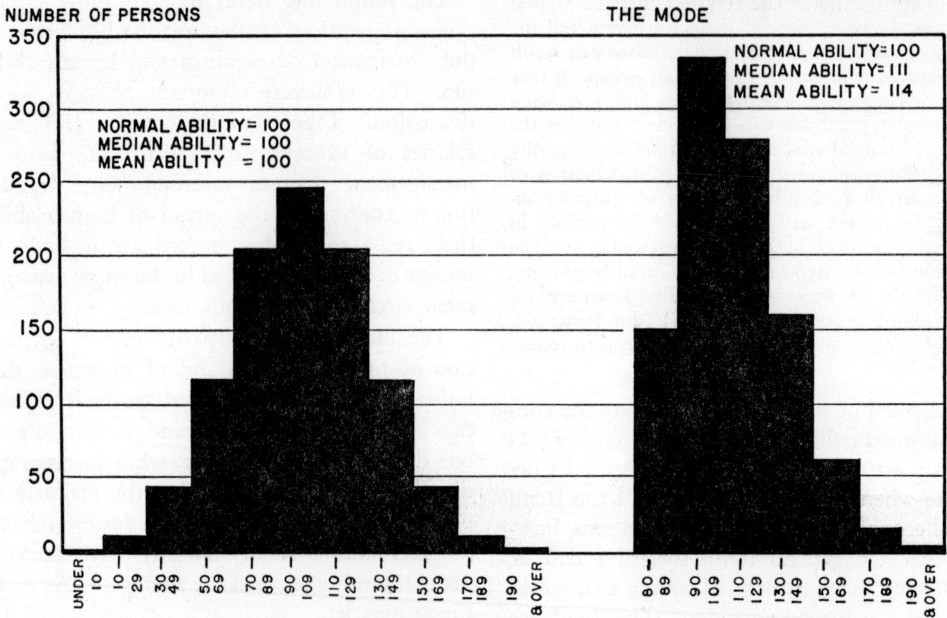

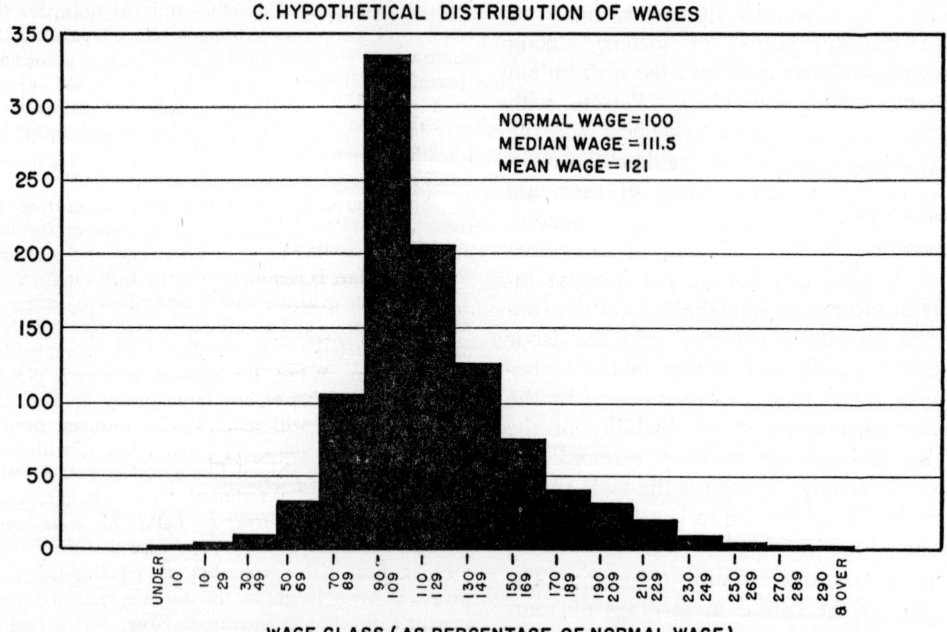

FIGURE 86. MODEL OF TYPICAL RELATIONSHIP BETWEEN THE DISTRIBUTION OF ABILITIES AND WAGES
(*Fictitious Distribution of 1,000 Individuals*)

Source: W. S. Woytinsky, *Earnings and Social Security in the United States,* Committee on Social Security, Social Science Research Council, Washington, 1943.

of this kind, their incomes will be distributed in the same way.[14]

This disparity between the two forms of distribution allows for more than one explanation. The disparity between labor incomes and property incomes is obviously due to the fact that the property factor is in no way correlated with ability,[15] while wage remuneration is more complicated, since it is based on the worker's performance. The shape of the wage and salary distribution is readily explained by the selective process that determines the chances of individual workers for employment, on the one hand, and the economic value of their services to the employer, on the other.

If the capacities of a group of workers were actually distributed in accordance with the Gaussian curve, the selective process is likely to prevent the distribution of their earnings from duplicating this curve. The value to an employer of a worker with personal ability 10, 20 or 30 per cent under the mode is likely to be less than 90, 80 or 70 per cent of the value of an average worker. In teamwork, his value may be zero and may even become negative if an inefficient worker diminishes the team's aggregate efficiency. Therefore, a worker whose capacity is considerably under the average has little chance of receiving wages proportionate even to his meager ability. More likely, he will either be eliminated completely from his occupation or will find only underpaid employment. On the other hand, from the angle of the employer, the value of a worker with personal capacity 10, 20 or 30 per cent above the mode may be greater than 110, 120 or 130 per cent of the average. Therefore, the number of employed workers with less than average ability is reduced and their pay rate cut more than in proportion to their ability, while the earnings of individuals with more than average ability are raised higher than in direct proportion to their capacities. Both developments contribute to a disparity between the mean and the modal wage: the modal (or normal) wage becomes less than the arithmetic mean, the great bulk of workers are massed around this point, and the Gaussian distribution of capacities results in an asymmetrical distribution of wages.[16]

The nonsymmetrical distribution of earnings is increased by provisions for minimum wages. Suppose, for example, that legislation or labor unions prevent wages from sinking to less than 50 per cent of the normal. In this event, workers with abilities that command such lower wages either will be dropped from employment or will obtain a raise, making the distribution of wages still more asymmetric.

The trend toward equality in earnings and the leveling of wage differentials thus by no means lead to symmetrical distribution of individual earnings around a "normal" rate. What is implied, rather, is an increasing concentration of the majority of workers within a comparatively narrow earnings interval close to the lower end of the frequency distribution. This does not preclude wide dispersion of the minority in higher earnings intervals in accordance with their ability, the economic value of their performance, their bargaining power and other factors.

---

14. A. C. Pigou, *The Economics of Welfare,* 4th edition, Macmillan, London, 1933, p. 650.
15. *Ibid.,* p. 651.
16. W. S. Woytinsky, *Earnings and Social Security in the United States,* Committee on Social Security, Social Science Research Council, Washington, 1943, pp. 81–82. See Figure 86.

REPORT OF THE COMMITTEE

The following chapter is the report of the Committee on Employment and Wages appointed by the Twentieth Century Fund. It was understood, in accordance with the Fund's regular procedure, that the Committee would not be bound by the research findings, and that the Committee's report, while it might refer to or draw upon them, would stand on its own feet independently of the findings.

At the Committee's request Professor Lloyd G. Reynolds, Chairman of the Department of Economics at Yale University, drafted a report for the Committee after extended conferences with its members to learn their views. Each member of the Committee was then invited to comment upon this report as he might wish, either on particular points or on the report as a whole. The extreme diversity of these comments is clear evidence that the subject is too complex to yield agreement from so large a committee.

These differences in opinion are expressed in footnotes at appropriate places in the report and in the form of more general comments appended to to the report. Messrs. Fisher, Zellerbach and Slichter submitted footnotes; Messrs. Garrison, Barkin, Bullis, Oliver, Stark and Teper submitted supplementary statements. However, these comments are but illustrative, and do not preclude the existence of other varying points of view that are not expressed. In the opinion of the Fund, the research findings, the Committee Report, and the comments made by the members of the Committee constitute a valuable aid to public thinking in a most difficult and important field.

Chapter 45

CONCLUSIONS AND RECOMMENDATIONS OF THE COMMITTEE

I. Wage Determination

Wage adjustments are the result of collective bargaining between unions and employers; of the forces that influence the wages of all workers, union and nonunion; of laws covering minimum wages; and of wage ceilings to curb inflation in periods of emergency.[1] The principles discussed in this report are applicable mainly to wage adjustment by collective bargaining; but they are also relevant to changes in nonunion wages and to governmental wage determinations.

The Complex Wage Structure

Recommendations can be realistic only if they take into consideration the fact that a complex wage structure already exists. The range of hourly wage payments extends from less than 50 cents to more than \$5.00.[2] Wages at a given time vary with skill, training and other elements involved in job classification, with regional differences, with the nature of the industry concerned, with the profitability of the enterprise, and with pressures on both sides of the wage bargain. Wage changes through time may be influenced not only by these factors, but by variations in the cost of living, changes in productivity, seasonal factors, demand and supply in the labor market as a whole and in its various sectors.

Wages even have different meanings to those concerned in their adjustment. The individual worker is inclined to regard them as the take-home pay in the wage envelope, affected as it may be by part-time or overtime work and by all deductions; the employer or accountant may regard them as the aggregate payroll, including all fringe benefits and deductions; the engineer may think of them as the cost of labor per unit of output; the economist may deal with them as real earnings, after taking account of changes in the purchasing power of money, or as the price of labor in reference to its supply and the demand for it, or as the share in the national income distributed to wage earners.[3] These and other views of wages affect the figures appropriate for discussion of a given wage level in different contexts, even though the same wage earners, receiving the same pay, are involved. As a practical matter, these differing conceptions of wages have an important effect on the outlook of union and management leaders in collective bargaining and on the content of wage agreements.

Methods of wage payment further complicate the picture. They extend all the way from a guaranteed annual wage[4] to payment by the

1. It seems to me more realistic to say that wages are determined by various economic, political and social forces which work themselves out in the labor markets of the economy. What wages will be paid will depend upon (1) the forces and conditions operating upon the demand and supply of labor and the goods and services that they produce; (2) federal and state laws, executive orders, and the pressure exerted by public officials or governmental agencies upon wage negotiations; and (3) the distribution of bargaining power between unions and employers in particular industries and in labor markets generally. Adjustments in wages are made through collective bargaining, unilateral action by employers, or federal and state governments.— Waldo E. Fisher

2. These two sentences seem to me to leave the wrong impression. There is no one wage structure but innumerable structures, which vary by industries, labor markets, regions, and even by companies. Certainly no one wage structure would contain the range stated in the second sentence. Furthermore, the range reported no doubt discloses the two extremes, but the significant range — the range within which the great body of rates fall — should also be given.— Waldo E. Fisher

3. Not only does the concept of wages vary with the different groups referred to above but the parties to the wage contract change their concept of wages from time to time, depending upon prevailing economic conditions and the bargaining strategy best suited to deal with those conditions. For example, when prices decline, labor's representatives in wage negotiations stress weekly earnings, and employers wage rates or hourly earnings. In periods of rising prices, the two parties reverse their positions. Again, when prices rise sharply labor emphasizes real wages, and when they decline, money weekly earnings.— Waldo E. Fisher

4. I do not consider a guaranteed annual wage a method of paying wages, but rather a measure for providing annual income or security of employment. The employer continues to pay a wage rate, a piece rate, or a weekly or monthly salary, but agrees to do so for a given number of weeks of designated hours or until funds set aside for this purpose are exhausted.— Waldo E. Fisher

hour, and from straight piecework to numerous forms of incentive payment or a combination of time- and piecework. These methods vary with managerial practice, with the nature of the operation, with the policies of unions, with the duration of agreements, with the tradition of the industry, and with the desires of the individual workers.

No Single Principle Possible

Because of these complications, no one simple principle can be applied uniformly to wage determinations. Wage determination must be a flexible process resorting to judgment and compromise, rather than the application of rigid yardsticks. The main principles involved can, however, be discussed. The principles considered here are applicable to general, across-the-board changes in a given company or industry. Space is inadequate to deal with the intricate problem of setting rates for individual jobs — though this problem may in concrete cases be associated with general changes.

Over a short period wage changes may be strongly influenced by all sorts of institutional pressures, personal motives of managers and union officials, or political events. In a longer run, however, economic forces (not immutable "natural laws") are likely to stand out more clearly. For example, the research report shows that, as a rule, industries with an unusually rapid growth in output and employment have in the past twenty years experienced larger increases in hourly earnings than others, as would be expected both from their need to attract workers and their profitability.[5] The growth of industry and of demand for labor in the South has been accompanied by a narrowing of wage differentials between South and North,[6] though legislation and the spread of collective bargaining have doubtless also contributed to this result. Wages of farm laborers, domestic servants and others in unskilled occupations rose during the 1940's much more rapidly than wages in general, probably because of the active demand for labor, which attracted the lower paid to more remunerative occupations.[7]

The Public Interest in Wage Determination

What difference does it make whether wage rates are set at one level rather than another? What kind of wage structure, and what kind of movement of wages over the course of time, are most nearly in accord with the general interest of the community? What factors condition the possible attainment of desired goals? Such questions may be considered in connection with common standards for determining what is fair and reasonable.

It should be emphasized that we are dealing here not so much with the actual process of wage determination as with the general arguments or criteria used in bargaining negotiations and in trying to explain or justify wage changes to the public. These are rationalizations rather than direct causes of wage changes.[8] Yet they are helpful both in classifying the ultimate forces behind wage movements and in developing standards by which a bystander can appraise the reasonableness of particular wage decisions and proposals.

While we consider these standard lines of argument worthy of analysis, we do not intend to take them more seriously than they deserve. In particular, we do not mean to imply that wage decisions either are or could be made on the basis of any one of the criteria discussed below, or any simple combination of these cri-

5. See pp. 458–65.
6. See pp. 475–81.
7. See pp. 466–74.

8. Are the "criteria" used in wage bargaining "rationalizations rather than direct causes of wage changes"? Employers and unions at the bargaining table, and government through its laws and the decisions of its wage-fixing agencies, may ignore them in establishing money wages, but they cannot set aside the impact of these criteria on real wages or the functioning of the economy. To illustrate, in the period 1919 to 1929, output per man per hour in manufacturing industries increased 72.6 per cent, but money wages were raised only 18.7 per cent and real wages rose only 20 per cent. Employers by failing to keep wages in line with productivity did not provide adequate payrolls and, therefore, an effective demand for their products. In the period 1939 to 1949, however, output per man-hour rose only about 9 per cent but money hourly earnings increased 109.6 per cent. Organized labor, with the help of World War II, a sympathetic federal administration, as well as inflation, was able to force wages far in excess of the increase in productivity, but much of that increase did not represent any gains in the workers' standard of living. Real wages rose only 30.2 per cent. The parties concerned with wage setting either had not learned or refused to be guided by the fact that during periods of inflation substantial wage increases feed inflation.

It is important for those who play an important role in wage determination to take these criteria seriously. Trends in productivity, ability to pay, cost of living, etc., are stubborn forces that affect real wages, employment opportunity, standards of living, and the functioning of our economy.— WALDO E. FISHER

teria. The pressures bearing on wage movements are so complex, and so highly variable from one situation to the next, that they will probably always defy any simple generalizations.

Increase of Output and Wages

In an expanding and progressive economy, one can expect that over the years national output will rise more rapidly than population, making possible a greater per capita consumption of goods and services and higher living standards. This has been the experience of the United States over the entire period for which we have statistical measurements. National output has increased much more rapidly than either population or man-hours worked. While this trend is sometimes described as "increasing productivity of labor," it is due to a complex interaction of factors: a higher level of skill and education among the gainfully employed population; probably a more rapid pace of work and more concentrated effort by workers;[9] larger supplies of capital and therefore of mechanical aids to production; a great variety of technical inventions and improvements; improved methods of management; fuller exploitation of natural resources; and a variety of other causes.

There is a presumption that this greater national output should be distributed broadly throughout the population and that the real income of virtually all Americans should rise decade after decade. This is not to say that all incomes need rise at the same rate. It may be desirable for some incomes to rise more rapidly than others in order to correct pre-existing inequities of income distribution. This leads into debatable problems that lie outside the scope of this report. Without getting into issues of equity, however, we can take it for granted that the real incomes of most wage and salary earners should rise rather steadily over the course of time.

The implications of this statement for wage and price behavior are not entirely clear. It has sometimes been argued that, as national output increases, money incomes should remain stable but the general price level should fall, thus making possible larger purchases of goods and services by everyone in the population. Another body of opinion maintains that, while this position may have some theoretical advantages, it also has serious disadvantages and cannot in any event be attained in practice. The preponderant view at present seems to be that we should aim over the long run at an approximately stable level of prices. This aim would require that money incomes rise at about the same rate as total national output, so that the rising output of goods and services could be taken off the market without serious disturbance of the price level.[10]

This general rule still provides no precise guide for the movement of particular wage rates. It does provide a general presumption that the average level of money wage rates should rise over the years and that, if the rate of wage increases is moderate, there need be no sustained rise in the price level.

There is strong historical support for this point of view. Over the past hundred years or so, money wage rates have risen much more than the general price level, thus raising workers' real wage rates and living standards. The rate of increase in real wage rates, moreover, seems to have coincided rather closely with the rate of increase in physical output per man-hour,[11] although our statistical measures of both items are imperfect. Workers' higher living standards have been made possible basically by the increasing productivity of the economy; and workers have been enabled to share in this greater productivity because wage rates have risen faster or fallen less rapidly than prices.

Labor's Share in Productivity Benefits

Attempts have sometimes been made to reduce this general principle to a formula for determining particular wage rates. It has been argued that if output per man-hour — taking

9. I feel that that is not necessarily factual. Performance is not variable to that extent.—HAROLD L. ZELLERBACH

10. I agree with the conclusion that stable prices are preferable to falling prices. I think that the report should point out, however, that the achievement of a stable price level would be an extraordinary accident. Certainly it would be remarkable if the relative bargaining power of unions and employers were such that unions could raise the average price of labor exactly as fast as but no faster than the engineers and managers raised output per man-hour. Indeed, if the community is successful in maintaining a high level of employment, a slow rise in the price level must be expected. The reason is that at high levels of employment, unions are in a strong enough bargaining position to push up the price of labor faster than the increase in output per man-hour.—SUMNER H. SLICHTER

11. See Figure 25, p. 68.

an average for the entire country — rises at a rate of X per cent a year, then particular wage rates in the system should also rise X per cent a year. While this reasoning is important, there are some difficulties in putting it into practice in wage determinations.

There are no very good measures of output per man-hour even for past years, and predictions for the future are bound to be still more uncertain. If money wages are raised at a predetermined rate, the outcome may be to undershoot or overshoot the mark. This problem is not too serious, however, for moderate discrepancies can be absorbed by movements of the general price level or minor shifts in the distribution of income. If wage rates rise 3 per cent in a particular year and it turns out that productivity rises only 2 per cent, this means that the price level will probably rise slightly.

This line of reasoning implies also that labor's per capita share in national income should remain constant relative to that of other economic groups. This may, of course, be regarded as a desirable simplification. Raising the price of labor in proportion to the rise in output per man-hour avoids any argument over labor's share in the national product. Raising the price of labor more than output per man-hour would require justification for an increase in labor's share of the national product; raising the price of labor less than output per man-hour would require justification for a shrinkage in labor's share.

If it is considered desirable that labor's share remain about the same, the money incomes of other groups in the economy — farmers, salaried people, business proprietors, bondholders, pensioners and so on — should rise as rapidly as wage rates. This would mean that if average wage rates were rising 3 per cent a year, all other types of income should rise at the same rate. This objective would not be easy to achieve. Certain types of income — notably pensions, rent and interest receipts, and some salaries — tend to lag considerably behind the rise in wages and other types of money income.

All wage rates in the economy should not advance at precisely the same rate over the course of time. There must be latitude for the correction of possible inequities in the wage structure, and to provide for long-run shifts in the quantities and types of labor required by each industry. Any target figure, such as 3 per cent a year, is simply a general average, which some industries will exceed and others will fail to attain.

Any such figure is also a long-run average over the course of decades, and need not necessarily be followed from year to year. It might not be desirable, for example, to try to push money wage rates up by 3 per cent during a year of general depression. An even larger increase than 3 per cent in *real* wages might occur if money wages were not reduced while a fall in prices was occurring.

These qualifications do not interfere seriously with the original proposition, which was that one should expect *real* wage rates to rise steadily over the course of time. Even in the decades before collective bargaining had attained its present strength, it was normal for money wage rates to rise in most years, and to rise at a faster rate than retail prices. In future years we should regard it as normal for money wage rates to rise in most companies most years, and for wage indexes gradually to pull farther and farther ahead of cost-of-living indexes. The only warning to be issued is that the average rate of wage increase in the economy as a whole should never be more than slightly out of line with the rate of increase in output per man-hour. It is the increase in productivity which is the basic source of higher living standards. Efforts to push up wage rates faster than productivity is rising will react mainly on the price level and may effect little if any gain in living standards.

Whether the amount of the annual "improvement factor" should be specified in cents per hour for several years in advance, as is done in the General Motors–United Automobile Workers agreement, is more debatable. This kind of clause may turn out to be much better adapted to some situations than to others. It may, for example, be best suited to industries with a better-than-average rate of technical progress and to periods, such as the present, in which most businesses can count on a high volume of production for several years ahead. Where conditions are favorable, this type of clause probably facilitates the writing of longer-term contracts, reduces the amount of year-to-year haggling over wages, and contributes to the general stability of industrial relations.

Changes in the Cost of Living

It has already been pointed out that, over the course of decades, the money wage level tends to pull farther and farther ahead of the retail price level, and that this is made possible basically by rising productivity. Over short periods of time, however, the movement of wage and price levels is very jerky and uneven.

During periods of falling prices, there is usually strong resistance to cuts in money wages. If wages fall at all, the drop is likely to be smaller and later than the drop in living costs. Periods of falling prices, therefore, are often marked by rather sharp increases in real wage rates.[12]

When retail prices are rising, workers and unions consider it reasonable that wages should at least keep pace with prices, and this view is shared by a considerable segment of management opinion. Since wage adjustments are made less frequently than retail price adjustments, however, there is some tendency for wages to lag behind in the race. Moreover, a general increase in money wages, by raising both the costs of production and the level of consumer demand, helps to set the stage for a new upsurge in the price level, which creates a new wage lag, and so on. It thus often proves quite difficult to keep wages fully abreast of prices, and real wages may decline. The more rapid the rate of price inflation, the more likely this is to happen.

This problem has led unions to take an active interest in cost-of-living escalator clauses, particularly during periods of sharp price inflation such as 1918–20, 1946–48 and 1950–51. During such periods unions hesitate to commit themselves and their members for a year in advance, and want protection either through an escalator clause or frequent wage reopenings.

The "Escalator Clause"

The escalator clause typically provides that wages shall be adjusted automatically at quarterly intervals in accordance with movements of the retail price index. Wage adjustments thus occur more frequently than under the traditional annual contract, though they do not necessarily add up to any more over the course of a year.

During periods of stable prices there is a tendency to lose interest in escalator clauses, and if prices fall for any extended period they are usually abandoned. It is difficult to convince workers that their wages should be cut repeatedly, even if living costs are falling. The cost-of-living escalator clause is thus not a device that can be applied continuously in the face of major changes in the economic climate. Its main usefulness is as a hedge for workers and union leaders during periods of strong inflation, usually associated with war or postwar reconversion.

Escalator clauses in union contracts are frequently criticized as contributing to "built-in inflation." It is argued that escalator clauses, by increasing the frequency, and possibly the size, of wage adjustments, help to maintain the upward momentum of an inflationary movement. There is considerable substance in this argument. A greater lag in wage adjustments would probably act as something of a brake on price inflation — though if the underlying inflationary forces were very strong this would be by no means sufficient to stop the movement. To use the wage lag as a brake, however, would mean reducing workers' real incomes in a manner that would be difficult to defend on grounds of equity.

It should be noted also that the wage escalator clause is one of several pricing devices in our economy which together contribute to automatic inflation whenever an excess of money demand occurs. These include the "parity" formula for agricultural price supports, the cost-plus pricing formulas used in many manufacturing industries, and the fixed percentage markups commonly used in retail trade.[13] While one may deplore the inflationary tendency of all these devices, it is questionable whether one can expect unions to give up their special form of price protection while other groups in the economy retain theirs.

12. These increases in real wage rates are frequently accompanied by layoffs and reduced working time and make it more difficult to remove the conditions and forces making for imbalance in the economy.— WALDO E. FISHER

13. I think it should be pointed out that cost-plus pricing formulas and fixed percentage mark-up are flexible arrangements and usually permit prices to fall in periods of depressed business but that the agriculture "parity" formula and wage escalator clauses tend to set floors below which prices and wages cannot fall when business slumps occur. The latter arrangements place roadblocks which interfere with the process of restoring equilibrium within the system.— WALDO E. FISHER

Some types of industry can live with a wage escalator clause much more easily than others. An industry in which prices are administered by a few large companies, and can be adjusted quickly to wage increases, is in the best position.[14] An industry whose prices are subject to legal regulation, on the other hand, may have more difficulty in adjusting to an escalator clause. Railroads, power companies, telephone companies and other public utilities are in this situation.

The Company's Ability to Pay

The company's ability to pay, i.e., its prospective earnings, plays an important part in wage negotiations. Future earnings usually cannot be estimated very precisely, however, because of the uncertainty of economic conditions. It is also difficult to get close agreement between union and management estimates, since the parties may start from different assumptions about the future.

Different companies in the same industry usually vary a good deal in efficiency and profits. Should the wage level of each company be set on the basis of its individual ability to pay, or should there be a standard level for all companies in an industry?

Under nonunion conditions, variations in ability to pay tend to be reflected in the wage structure, the more efficient and profitable companies paying somewhat higher wages than the less efficient. The relation between wage level and profitability runs both ways. High wages, by attracting superior workers and stimulating better performance on the job, may contribute to the profitability of the company.

The tendency of union policy is to establish uniform wage scales throughout a competitive area — the policy of "the standard rate." There are, however, numerous exceptions to this tendency. A company with low ability to pay is sometimes allowed a lower wage scale than its competitors, in order to keep it in operation and avoid forcing its employees to seek other work. The more profitable companies are sometimes charged above-average rates through subclassification of the industry on a geographical or product basis. It is also possible to impose heavier nonwage costs on companies able to bear them, while maintaining a uniform wage scale.

Adherence to uniform wage scales throughout an industry probably produces the more desirable results.[15] If a policy of graduating each company's wage level according to its ability to pay were followed, no management, no matter how efficient or enterprising, would be able to earn more than a certain rate of profit, since wage rates would be adjusted upward as fast as the company's earning power rose. Conversely, it would seem undesirable to lower wage rates as much as necessary to keep an inefficient enterprise in operation. Such a policy would penalize the more efficient managers, protect the inefficient, and yield widely differing wages to workers doing the same job in different companies. The policy of the standard rate, while requiring some modifications and adjustments here and there, seems preferable as a general principle.[16]

There is considerable variation in the wage-paying ability of different industries, just as there is variation among companies within the same industry. Young industries with rapidly rising output and a high rate of technical progress can stand a faster rate of wage increase than mature or declining industries. A more rapid increase often occurs in growing indus-

14. This is certainly misleading. It could easily give rise to the inference that monopolistic controls exist, in violation of the Federal Trade Commission and antitrust laws.— HAROLD L. ZELLERBACH

15. This is a controversial issue on which many people passionately disagree. While there are good reasons in support of such a concept, there are also factors to the contrary.— HAROLD L. ZELLERBACH

16. A standard-rate policy on an industry basis is definitely preferable to the policy of graduating each company's wage level to its profits. The latter policy would not only penalize competent management and help subsidize inefficient management, but it would create a wage structure which the union could not defend before its members. This does not mean, however, that a standard-rate policy for each industry is a desirable wage policy. The labor costs of firms in the same industry, particularly in extractive industries or in industries paying on a piece basis, vary substantially. Moreover, important differences prevail in the wages paid from market to market and region to region — witness the substantial differences in the wage levels of the north and south or the east and west.

An industry standard-rate policy, in many instances, would disrupt labor markets, make it impossible for some companies to attract needed workers, and require a wage level that would either force many marginal firms out of business or deny many workers as high a wage as the more profitable companies could afford to pay. A more realistic policy, from the union standpoint, would be to take wages out of competition in areas serving common markets (often regional or local) either by standard or variable time rates or by variable piece rates set at a level which will permit necessary marginal firms to continue to operate and then add nonwage costs on the companies in a better competitive position.— WALDO E. FISHER

tries, and is probably desirable, in moderation, in order to attract workers. Too much attention to the varying ability to pay of different industries, however, would produce the undesirable results just noted with respect to companies in the same industry. Progressive and expanding industries would be handicapped by very high wage rates; declining industries would be protected and subsidized by much lower rates; and there would be inequitable discrimination among workers in different types of industry.

Wage Comparisons with Other Companies

Comparison with wage levels in other companies is widely recognized as a valid and important factor in wage setting. The main difficulty is the wide variety of comparisons that can be made, each of which may lead to a different conclusion. What is the proper area of comparison? Should heaviest weight be given to other companies in the same industry, or other companies in the same area, or perhaps to "pattern-setting" industries such as steel, coal or automobiles? Assuming that this problem has been solved, just what should one compare in the various companies considered? Should one compare the size of the *increases* given in a particular year, or the actual *level* of wages in the various companies? If one wants to compare wage levels, should one use job rates, average hourly or weekly earnings, or plant minimum rates as the best indicator of wage level? There is no uniform answer to these questions. An actual wage determination is likely to involve preparing several types of comparison and then using judgment as to which are most relevant under the particular circumstances.

Comparison with other companies in the same industry assumes special importance under collective bargaining. A national trade union tends to work toward uniformity of wage scales throughout the area in which employers compete with one another, whether this be a locality, a region of the country, or the country as a whole. Many managements, particularly in industries that have been unionized for a long time, also favor the policy of wage standardization because it sets a definite wage floor under competition in the industry.

Comparison with other companies in the same geographical area is important mainly because of its repercussions on labor supply. A company cannot get too far below the wage level of other similar companies in its community and still hire the number and kinds of workers it wants.

Variation in the wage levels of different communities raises the problem whether a particular company shall conform to the wage level of its industry or to that of its geographical area. If it follows the industry, it may find itself too low or too high from an area standpoint. If it follows the area, wide variation of wage levels within the same industry creates competitive problems for the industry and may also cause internal difficulties for the union.

From the standpoint of the parties concerned this is one of many problems that have to be compromised in the course of wage negotiations. From the public standpoint, it raises the issue of what kind of geographical wage structure is desirable. Without attempting to answer this question, we would like to emphasize that any geographical wage structure that may develop will have important economic consequences.

Complete equalization of community wage levels throughout the country, for example, would probably have at least three effects. First, it would reduce the possibility of competitive undercutting of prices by companies located in low-wage areas. Second, it would alter the incentives to geographical migration of both capital and labor. Third, it would not achieve complete uniformity of *living standards* throughout the country, since living costs might still differ in different communities and regions.[17]

While we have emphasized the significance of industry and area comparisons, other types of comparison may also be important under collective bargaining. The increases won in a particular year by such unions as the Mine Workers, the Steelworkers and the Automobile Workers receive wide publicity throughout the country and tend to become "patterns" or "targets" for other unions as well. Where a single union em-

17. This discussion assumes that the equalization of community wage levels would somehow place employers on a more equal competitive basis and therefore reduce the tendency toward price cutting and migration of workers. Outlying fields must frequently have lower costs in order to compete in distant markets; old industrialized areas have more competent workers than new areas; availability and quality of raw materials vary from community to community; and in extractive industries geological conditions have varying impacts on costs. Equalization of community wage levels might well increase instead of decrease migration of capital and labor, price cutting and business failures in certain communities, industries and regions of the economy.— WALDO E. FISHER

braces several industries, it may seek the same minimum rate or the same general increase in all these industries. One may have "union-wide bargaining" rather than "industry-wide bargaining."

General Economic Considerations

The parties to wage negotiations often attach considerable weight to arguments concerning the effects of wage changes on the national economy. During the years 1945–48, for example, many unions argued that profits were unduly high and that since only a minor fraction of profits are spent for consumption, there was danger of insufficient consumer purchasing power. Wage increases, it was argued, would raise workers' incomes, reduce profits, increase consumer expenditures, and thus help maintain a high level of business activity and employment.

Employers frequently replied that profits (after taxes) had not risen as much since prewar days as had the general price level. Further, profits were needed and were actually being spent for new plant and equipment, and this kind of spending was doing as much as consumer spending to maintain high employment. The main effect of continued wage increases, employers contended, was simply to push up the price level without bringing any real benefit to workers or anyone else.

General economic arguments are, of course, much more pertinent in some situations than in others. A wage bargain between the associated dry cleaners of Peoria and a particular local union would not have much effect on the national economy. A bargain between United States Steel and the United Steelworkers, on the other hand, will have a substantial impact on national wage, price and employment levels. The parties to such a bargain ought to consider the probable consequences of their actions in the broadest terms.

Unfortunately, it is impossible to provide much factual foundation for such discussions. Economists are by no means agreed on the consequences of general changes in the money wage level. About all that can be said is that the effects are likely to be somewhere between the extreme pictures painted by union and management negotiators.

A general rise in money wages throughout the economy, at a time of full employment, will normally increase workers' purchasing power — that is, the quantity of goods and services workers are able to buy — provided output per man-hour is also rising. If wages rise more rapidly than productivity, however, there is likely to be some increase in the general price level. Increases in wages that outstrip productivity increases mean high costs of production and also increased demand for industry's products, so that on the usual bases for price setting some price increases are likely to result. These price increases will partly cancel out the effect of the wage increases, and the net increase in workers' purchasing power will be less than was originally expected. While purchasing power will rise, the rise will be less than unions sometimes contend; while prices will rise, this rise will be less than management sometimes predicts. Management is inclined to neglect the possibility of holding down price increases through improvements in productivity; unions are inclined to overplay productivity and to overlook the possibility of price increases.

If we were to examine any other issue, such as the effect of general wage increases on profit levels and the relation of profits to full employment, we would come out with a somewhat similar conclusion. The effects are highly uncertain, but it is likely that they lie somewhere between the more extreme union and management contentions. In the public interest, unions and managements should exercise due restraint in wage setting; they should avoid extreme claims of dire disaster or economic salvation resulting from wage decisions; and they should encourage careful study of these matters rather than assert that we already know all the answers.

RECOMMENDATIONS

The Behavior of Wage Rates

Because of the great complexity of the pressures bearing upon wages, it is undesirable to try to follow any rigid standards of wage determination. The essence of the wage-setting process is negotiation, compromise of conflicting pressures and interests, and adjustment of wage schedules to the numerous functions they must perform. This process cannot be replaced by any simple set of mechanical rules.[18]

---

18. There is, of course, no set of "mechanical rules," but those who negotiate wage levels have the moral obligation to give serious consideration (1) to economic forces and conditions and (2) to the

Over the long run the general level of wholesale and retail prices ought to be kept approximately stable. Attainment of this objective depends partly on government policies concerning money and credit, taxation and public expenditures. At the same time, union and management policies concerning wages and prices can make maintenance of price stability easier or more difficult.

If government does its part in preventing price inflation, it would be reasonable to expect unions to accept a moderate rate of increase in wages, i.e., a rate approximating the probable rate of increase in output per man-hour *for the economy as a whole.*[19] This does not mean that wage increases in a particular company or industry should be geared to the trend of productivity in that company or industry. It does mean that, over periods of a decade or so, the average rate of increase in all wage rates should be about the same as the average rate of increase of productivity in all sectors of the economy.

Acceptance of this principle implies the need for some method of avoiding undue hardship to groups in the economy whose incomes may lag behind the upward movement of wage rates. Unless it can be shown that these other types of income (salaries, pensions, rents, interest payments,[20] etc.) are currently too high relative to wages, equity would require that they be raised at about the same rate, so that all economic groups may share proportionately in the increasing national output. Over the past century, fixed-income groups have "gotten their own back" through periodic depressions, which forced prices and wages down. The public is increasingly unwilling to tolerate this method of economic readjustment and is increasingly insistent that full employment be maintained. This may necessitate new techniques for assuring that the incomes of different economic groups move upward in an equitable manner.

It will at best be very difficult to reconcile the objective of full employment with the objective of stable prices and a moderate rate of increase in money incomes. If each group in the economy insists upon exploiting to the full the "sellers' market" that arises under full employment, price stability may well prove unachievable. Union and management leaders should give increased attention to means of attaining price stability, an objective clearly beneficial to both groups as well as to the general public.

Turning from the general wage-price level to the detailed structure of wages, we note that it is normal for the wage levels of different industries to rise at somewhat different rates over the course of time. Work in some industries may be growing more skilled or difficult, while in others it may be growing simpler and easier. Some industries may be recruiting labor at a rapid rate, while in others employment may be declining. These elements and many others require flexibility in the relative movement of industry wage levels.

There has been a tendency in recent decades toward equalizing the wage levels of competing companies in the same industry. While this tendency may work some hardship in individual cases, it would seem to be generally desirable.[21]

impact of their decisions upon consumers, the public and the functioning of the economy.— WALDO E. FISHER

19. Do we wish the unions to limit their pressure for higher wages to such an extent that wages do not rise faster than output per man-hour? This question has interesting aspects. The rate at which output per man-hour rises seems to be affected by the amount of pressure from unions for higher wages. If unions demand higher wages so insistently that labor costs rise, an offsetting rise in prices is inevitable. But it will probably turn out to be true that the pressure for higher wages which makes labor costs rise also makes the managements try harder to increase output per man-hour and thus stimulates technological development. This is a result of the fact that the demand for a good profits record in terms of time and effort is what economists term an "inelastic demand." Incidentally, if this were not so, competition would discourage managerial efficiency rather than encourage it, since each competitor threatens the profits of his rivals. But since the demand for a good profits record on the part of management is normally an inelastic one, a threat to the profits of a concern usually leads the management to increase the time and effort spent on keeping up profits. Consequently, the country is likely to have a higher standard of living when the price of labor rises fast enough to force up labor costs slowly and to require a slowly rising price level. In any event I think that it is utopian to expect unions to refrain for any extended period from pushing up money wages as fast as their bargaining power permits.— SUMNER H. SLICHTER

20. I interpret "interest payments" as not meaning the rate of interest, at least not the rate of interest on new loans. In order to avoid injustice when the acceptance of new principles reduces the chance that prices will fall and increases the chance that they will rise, it would be necessary to raise interest payments on old loans, which would be equivalent to a rise in the rate of interest on old loans. No rise above the market rate of interest on new loans would be necessary because the rate on new loans would presumably discount the expected effect of wage movements on prices.—SUMNER H. SLICHTER

21. I cannot subscribe to this conclusion. One of the basic functions of wages is to direct the flow of workers into occupations, plants, labor markets and

It puts different companies on a fair competitive basis, it conforms with workers' standards of equity, it reduces the possibility of friction within the union, and it simplifies the negotiation and administration of collective agreements.

Other important tendencies in the wage structure during recent years have been: (1) a marked reduction, in most industries, of the percentage differential between the wage rates of skilled and unskilled workers; (2) some reduction of geographical inequalities in wage rates for the same type of labor. It would be unwise in this brief report to attempt any general appraisal of the desirability or undesirability of these two tendencies. There is, in fact, considerable disagreement between union and management officials, and even among academic economists, as to what constitutes a desirable occupational wage structure or a proper structure of geographical differentials. It is highly desirable that there be more study and discussion of these matters with a view to narrowing down the area of disagreement that exists at present.

While this policy statement has been concerned mainly with hourly wages rates and hourly earnings, weekly and annual earnings are of primary concern to the wage earner. Annual earnings are greatly influenced by regularity of employment; jobs in some companies and industries with high hourly rates yield rather low and variable annual incomes because of the irregularity of the work. This situation underlines the need for maximum effort to regularize employment and production in individual plants and industries. Many companies have already achieved a high degree of stability of employment, with profit to themselves and substantial benefit to their employees.

The Process of Wage Determination

Free collective bargaining has proved itself a flexible and effective method of determining wages.[22] It brings to bear the interests of the parties most directly affected, with a minimum of restraint and delay from outside sources.[23] In some cases collective bargaining may appear to have produced unduly high or low wage levels, and in others it has led to chronic interruptions of production. These defects do not, however, seem serious enough to justify departures from free collective bargaining except under conditions of national emergency.

The role of government under peacetime conditions should be limited primarily to setting minimum wage rates and other minimum standards of employment, which establish a floor under the terms arrived at through collective bargaining; to supplying information on wage rates, productivity, living costs and other matters so as to enable bargaining to proceed on a more informed basis; and to offering mediation and conciliation services in the event of continuing disagreement between the parties. When economic mobilization during periods of national emergency requires the institution of price and wage controls, the wage control system should recognize the complexity of the forces affecting wages and the importance of flexibility in handling particular cases.

While collective bargaining is an effective and useful method of determining wages, the bargaining process can be improved. It might arrive at wage rates that more accurately reflect the interests of all parties concerned (including consumers), and it might negotiate wage bargains with less friction, conflict, and interruption of production. Reasonable and peaceable wage bargains are likely to form part of a generally harmonious relationship between the parties. Anything that improves union-management relations in general is likely also to improve the process of wage determination.

---

regions which supply the greatest net social product. Standard wage rates interfere with that function and definitely hamper growing sections of the industry. See the more detailed analysis of the limitations of this suggested wage policy in my earlier footnote (number 16).—WALDO E. FISHER

22. Collective bargaining also has pretty important limitations. It is the best way of setting wages that is available in most situations, but it is not a completely ideal method.— SUMNER H. SLICHTER

Collective bargaining has not always been flexible and many times has been wasteful, time-consuming, and extremely costly to workers, industry and the public. Despite these limitations it is far superior to other known methods of wage determination.—WALDO E. FISHER

23. The principal limitation of collective bargaining is that it provides no way of representing the interests of the community as a whole in the kind of wage structure that is created by collective bargaining or in the movement of the wage level through time. The community has an important stake in both of these matters. Collective bargaining does not permit these important community interests to be effectively represented. Another important limitation is that collective bargaining sometimes simply fails to function because the representatives of one party or both are not willing to assume the unpleasant responsibility of making concessions.—SUMNER H. SLICHTER

Some of the most concrete and useful improvements in methods of wage setting will no doubt emerge from free experimentation by individual unions and managements. Without passing on the economic merits of the General Motors–United Automobile Workers agreement, for example, we believe that it shows promise of stabilizing relations between the parties over an extended period and avoiding year-to-year conflict over wage adjustments with the attendant risk of a work stoppage. It may be possible for other industries to move in the direction of longer-term wage agreements, either by this means or by other means. It is a great merit of collective bargaining that it stimulates grass-roots experimentation and initiative rather than mere conformity to principles laid down by some central authority.

There is need for continuing study by research groups of how wage rates are actually set, what are the economic consequences of present methods of wage determination, and what standards of public interest in wage matters can be established. The number of important observers doing basic research on these matters is still very small indeed. The immediate impact of research studies on actual methods of wage determination is likely to be slight. Over the long pull, however, they contribute powerfully to raising the level of public understanding on wage questions, which is a prerequisite to any intelligent national policy.

II. Employment Policies

Mobility

Development of satisfactory wage scales is only part of the problem of employment policy, the other part being the availability of adequate job opportunities. The well-being of workers does not depend solely on their rate of compensation but on their total present and future incomes, which, in turn, are dependent on the availability of work — access to job vacancies for the unemployed, steady work for those with jobs, and opportunity for advancement to better jobs over the course of time.

The pattern of employment in the American economy is subject to continuous flux and change. Technical developments, appearance of new products and obsolescence of old ones, failure of some businesses and expansion of others, regional shifts of industry, and other factors are continually eliminating jobs in some parts of the economy and opening up new jobs in others. These shifts oblige large numbers of workers to change jobs each year. In addition, many other workers change jobs voluntarily in the hope of improving their situation.

In years of peacetime prosperity, it is not unusual for the number of job changes to equal half the number of workers employed. During the war years 1942–45, the number of job changes each year was about as large as the total labor force.[24] The number of *individual workers* changing jobs during the year is of course considerably smaller, because some workers change jobs several times in a year and are thus counted several times in the total turnover. Even allowing for this overlapping, in a period of high employment 20 or 25 per cent of the labor force are likely to have different jobs at the end of the year from those they held at the beginning.[25]

This large-scale movement of labor is of major importance to the participants and the public. Management is interested in obtaining enough qualified employees to fulfill production requirements, and also wishes to match the capacities of each worker with the requirements of the job on which he is employed. Workers are interested in having an adequate total number of jobs available, steady work on these jobs, adequate information about vacancies and opportunity to move to better jobs, and a reduction in the hardships of involuntary movement and unemployment. The union has a stake in seeing that individual workers are protected against arbitrary layoff or discharge, that opportunities for advancement are distributed equitably among those who want them, and that fluctuations in the labor requirements of the company are handled so as to minimize the amount of hardship to employees.[26] The public also has an interest in the stability and efficiency of production, the proper matching of workers' abilities and interests against job requirements, and re-

24. See pp. 383 ff.

25. Not only do workers move from one job to another, but they leave the labor force and perhaps come back in again. The Monthly Labor Market Reports show that the movement in and out of the labor force is surprisingly large.— Sumner H. Slichter

26. I think that if this sentence read that the union has a stake in seeing that opportunities "for advancement are distributed equitably among those *qualified workers* who want them," it would be clearer.— Harold L. Zellerbach

duction of the personal hardship resulting from haphazard movement and unemployment.

While these interests may conflict at certain points, there is a large measure of overlap among them. This should make possible joint support of objectives and techniques beneficial to all. Specifically, we believe that the following policy objectives will command widespread support among informed students of employment, whether in unions, management or elsewhere.

A Steadily Increasing Demand for Labor

Maintenance of a steadily increasing, high level of production and employment is now generally accepted as a major goal of economic policy. We cannot discuss here the complex problems involved in attaining this objective and in reconciling it with other economic objectives, such as reasonable stability of prices. Many volumes have already been written on these problems, and many unsettled issues still remain.

We wish simply to emphasize that attainment of this objective is of critical importance for most of the other objectives discussed below. If economic depression is allowed to occur and continue, the most diligent search for work may prove fruitless, the most efficient public employment service will not be able to produce jobs for all those who want them, and the efforts of individual employers to regularize their operations and provide steady work will break down under the strain. Conversely, a high level of employment does more than anything else to create a general atmosphere of opportunity, to enable workers to move from poorer to better jobs, and to reduce the hardship of unemployment between jobs.

Employment Freedom for the Worker

Workers should be free, both legally and actually, to leave unsatisfactory jobs and seek better ones. Such freedom of movement is the only way of ensuring that the distribution of workers among jobs will take adequate account of individual aptitudes and preferences. It also helps ensure that employers will offer reasonably comparable terms of employment in order to attract and hold workers. In addition, free choice of jobs is basic to any democratic society.

If freedom of choice is to be fully effective, workers must have adequate information about job opportunities. A mechanism is necessary through which unemployed workers, or employed workers who are interested in changing jobs, can learn what vacancies exist at a particular time and what their characteristics are. It is not enough to know that "there are some jobs up at the X company." The worker applying for a job should have accurate advance information about the duties, skill and training requirements, working conditions, starting rate and rate range for the job, probable actual earnings (on piece-rate jobs), chances for advancement, probable permanence of the job, and many other matters. The employer will derive great benefit if applicants are given accurate job information in advance of hiring. A worker who accepts a job under a misapprehension is likely to leave it before long, and the result is added expense and trouble for the employer.

Adequate information about job opportunities is particularly important during the last years of school and the first years of employment. What a worker does between the ages of fifteen and twenty-five has a dominant influence on his later career. During this period he either gets or fails to get the specialized training necessary to enter a skilled, managerial or professional occupation. After he has married and acquired family responsibilities, it becomes much harder for him to make large changes in his occupational level.

During the years when it is still possible for them to make major strategic decisions, young people (and their parents) should be given a broad picture of the whole range of occupations in the United States. They should know what various occupations promise in monetary and other returns, and what training and ability they require. Some way should be found to finance the education of outstanding youngsters who wish to prepare for executive or professional work, but whose families are unable to bear the cost.[27]

Hiring Freedom for the Employer

The employer should be free to hire for or assign to a particular job the worker who he believes will be most proficient on that job, subject to reasonable protection of the rights of present employees, and subject to any legal re-

27. Would it not be better to endeavor to establish some medium whereby outstanding youngsters could be helped to finance themselves? A free education is not always possible but opportunities for self-help are innumerable.— HAROLD L. ZELLERBACH

quirements concerning discrimination in employment. He should have as much information as possible about alternative workers who may be available for employment. Pre-employment tests and other indicators of the worker's suitability for the job should be used wherever practicable. Effort spent on screening applicants and assigning them to suitable work yields benefits to workers as well as to the employer. A man hired by mistake or wrongly assigned will have to be laid off after a short time, with extra trouble and expense all around.

Role of the Public Employment Service

It is clearly important to the employment process that both workers and employers know what they are doing. If workers are poorly informed about job openings, and if employers have poor techniques for judging workers' capacities, one is bound to get a less satisfactory distribution of workers among jobs. Further, there will be much more waste motion in the labor market. A worker may have to experiment with several unsatisfactory jobs before finding one that suits him, and an employer may have to try out two or three candidates in each vacancy. The result will be heavier hiring and training costs for employers, longer periods of unemployment for workers, and a reduction of national output.

Rapid and efficient placement of workers in jobs can be facilitated through a well-managed public employment service. The public employment office provides a meeting place for labor demand and labor supply in an area, a point at which the requests coming in from employers can be matched against the skills of the unemployed workers available. The results should be better placement and quicker placement of workers than would otherwise occur. The benefits resulting from a public employment service depend on the skill with which the service is managed and on its acceptability to both workers and employers.

The public employment offices in each locality have to be linked together to provide something approaching a national labor market. In the United States, there are usually shortages of labor in some localities and surpluses in others. Word of vacancies in the areas of shortage should be passed back rapidly and accurately to workers in the areas of surplus. Adequate job information can do a great deal by itself to stimulate necessary geographical movements of labor.

While the present volume of placements through the employment service could be increased with benefit to all concerned, one should not expect that all or even most placements will be made in this way. Many workers will continue to feel that they can best further their job preferences by making an independent canvass of the market, and nothing should be done to discourage this kind of initiative. Most employers will also want to keep the way open for workers to apply to them directly, and to use a variety of recruitment methods. The function of the employment service is to facilitate and supplement, rather than to supplant, direct dealings between employers and workers.

Security of Tenure

Most workers, if not entirely satisfied with their present jobs, at any rate prefer to continue working at them. The desire for security of job tenure, for continued attachment to the same company, is strong in most workers. To a worker who has had five, ten, or more years of experience in one company and has accumulated pension and seniority rights as well as a network of personal associations, layoff or discharge is a major disaster. Long affiliation with a union also strengthens the desire to remain in the same location. This desire for security of tenure is natural and legitimate. It deserves to be given heavy weight in decisions about layoffs, discharges, transfers and other personnel shifts.

Steady Work for the Job-Holder

There are many workers who are perfectly secure in retaining their jobs but who get much less than a full year's work because of fluctuations in the employer's need for labor. This is one reason for the wide variation of annual earnings among workers in the same industry.[28]

Irregularity of employment is a serious hardship for the worker, for it not only reduces his annual income but also makes it difficult for him to plan ahead with any assurance. More regularized production and employment over the year, providing greater assurance of a steady income, would be welcome to most workers, and would in most cases save money for the employer as well. Labor unions also have a strong

28. See on this point pp. 336–41 and 438–39.

interest in regularizing employment, both through their concern for workers' welfare and through their need for union stability.

Problems Remaining under Full Employment

We have already emphasized the importance of taking steps to ensure that there will be enough jobs to employ everyone who is willing and able to work — the problem of maintaining "full employment." But even if there were assurance of 65 million jobs for 65 million people, there would remain the difficult task of matching the characteristics of individual workers and individual jobs in the best possible way, of achieving this matching with minimum delay and hardship, and — once satisfactory placement were achieved — of providing the worker with reasonable security of job tenure. Our policy suggestions are directed mainly toward these detailed problems.

The Community of Interest

On employment policy there is common interest among workers, unions and management. Measures that benefit labor are likely also to benefit management, and vice versa. One can, to be sure, find specific points at which interests appear to diverge — for example, the argument over seniority versus efficiency as a criterion in promotions. The parallel interests of the parties, however, are more numerous than the divergent. All parties stand to benefit from free and informed choice of jobs by workers, careful selection of workers by employers, security of job tenure after employment, and regularity of work on the job. Progress toward these objectives requires attention and foresight from union and management leaders as well as from government.

RECOMMENDATIONS

Management Policies

Management has primary responsibility in the recruitment, selection, transfer or promotion, and separation of employees, subject only to such rules as may be established by union agreement. Management policies therefore have a direct impact on the effectiveness of the labor market. In a number of ways management can contribute to the objectives already described, with results beneficial to itself as well as to workers and the public. It is understood that, in the case of companies operating under union agreement, most of the matters listed below can best be worked on in collaboration with the union organizations.

Employers can contribute to better operation of the labor market by: [29]

(1) Making maximum use of the public employment service, and taking a constructive interest in improving the efficiency of employment service operations.

(2) Considering all applicants for work on their merits, including applicants currently employed by other companies.

(3) Working, in cooperation with unions and public agencies, to eliminate hiring policies that discriminate among applicants on the basis of race, nationality or religion.

(4) Making careful efforts to test or estimate the capacities of individual applicants, to assign those who are hired to the jobs best suited for them, and to maintain adequate incentives during the first few months of employment, in order to reduce unnecessary and wasteful turnover among new employees.

(5) Maintaining a judicious balance in filling vacancies between promotion from within the company and recruitment from the outside.

(6) Making every effort to give security of job tenure to satisfactory employees who have completed the probationary period.

(7) Making a maximum effort to regularize production schedules and labor requirements over the year, thus providing as steady work as possible.

Union Policies

Unions become involved in the movement of

29. To the list presented here I would add that employers can contribute to better labor market operations by making a larger proportion of promotions on the basis of merit rather than on the basis of seniority. I think that employers have been somewhat lazy in the matter of promotions and have followed the course of least resistance. It is not easy always to tell which person is best entitled to promotion. If workers are to have proper incentives to develop themselves, employers need to take the trouble to check on the capabilities of different workers and to apply at least a "head and shoulders" test of merit. I mean by this that whenever a worker can be found who stands out definitely above the others, the next promotion should be on the basis of merit. I do not believe that it is necessary to make fine distinction, but I think that it is unfair to the community and unfair to the workers to make promotions on the basis of strict seniority. Many employers have yielded to the pressure for straight seniority promotions.— SUMNER H. SLICHTER

workers from job to job through a wide variety of rules governing admission to union membership, relation of union membership to job tenure, and the procedures to be used in making promotions, transfers, layoffs and discharges. Some of these rules are contained in the union's own constitution and by-laws, some in its agreements with employers. Care needs to be taken that these rules, while affording proper protection to employees, do not interfere with the free movement of workers to the places where they are most needed.

Unions can contribute to better operation of the labor market by:

(1) Providing union members with improved information about the labor market and about job opportunities.

(2) Encouraging members to make full use of the public employment service, and taking an active part in the improvement of employment service operations.

(3) Eliminating membership requirements that exclude Negroes, women, or other categories of workers from the union and may therefore exclude them from employment in the craft or industry.

(4) Working, through negotiation with management, toward contract rules that will promote security of job tenure, regularity of work, careful and fair hiring practices, adequate opportunity for promotion, and the other objectives already listed under "Management Policies."

(5) Working, in collaboration with employers, to stimulate the recruitment of new workers into expanding occupations or industries, and to encourage the exodus of workers from industries or occupations in which employment opportunities have permanently declined.

Government Policies

The contribution of government in this area cannot be made through direct control of or intervention in the hiring process, except to the limited extent necessary to prevent racial, religious or similar discrimination. Any other attempt to tell workers where they should work or employers whom they should hire is contrary to the spirit of free economic institutions and is likely also to detract from economic efficiency. The task of government is rather to create an environment within which the free choices of workers and employers can be made most effective.

Government can contribute to this end by:

(1) Developing better methods of forecasting the labor requirements of various occupations and industries for some period of time ahead, and disseminating this information through the employment service and other channels.

(2) Working, in conjunction with employers and unions, to ensure adequate training facilities for those who wish to enter skilled occupations.

(3) Extending and improving the facilities for vocational counseling in the public schools.

(4) Improving the personnel and procedures of the state employment services, and developing closer collaboration across state lines.

(5) Working, in conjunction with employers and unions, to eliminate discrimination in hiring on the basis of race, nationality, sex or religion.

(6) Eliminating legislation that restricts to an undesirable extent the free movement of labor from one occupation, industry or geographical area to another; for example, state laws forbidding anyone to recruit labor within the state for jobs in other states, and licensing laws for skilled occupations that are capable of being used simply to restrict the number of persons admitted to the occupation.

LLOYD K. GARRISON, *Chairman*
SOLOMON BARKIN
HARRY A. BULLIS
WALDO E. FISHER
E. L. OLIVER
SUMNER H. SLICHTER
LOUIS STARK
LAZARE TEPER
HAROLD L. ZELLERBACH

III. SUPPLEMENTARY STATEMENTS

MR. GARRISON'S STATEMENT

Productivity

I think the report exaggerates somewhat the value of obtaining and of using for collective bargaining purposes an annual figure of productivity for the country as a whole. Even if such a figure could be established with greater accuracy than is now the case, there would be difficulty in making practical use of the figure around the bargaining table. For one thing, unions representing the lowest-paid workers would naturally be unwilling to limit their demands to increases in terms of the national figure, because this figure, expressed as a percentage, would yield in cents per hour very little for the low-wage group. Again, the multiple factors entering into every collective wage contract — geographical factors, cost-of-living changes, the employer's financial situation, the history of bargaining in the unit, the pressures of competitive unionism, and so forth, would normally overshadow in importance any general productivity figure for the country as a whole. Indeed, I fear that for the most part the national figure would be of no more than academic interest in the rough and tumble of collective bargaining negotiations.

The report suggests that, assuming wage increases approximating the national productivity figure, other types of income (salaries, pensions, rents, interest payments, etc.) should be raised at about the same rate so that all economic groups could share proportionately in the increasing national output. However, unless we are to have a completely regulated economy, it is inevitable that these fixed forms of income will lag somewhat behind the national increases in productivity and behind wages and other flexible forms of distribution such as dividends and executives' compensation. For this very reason it might be politically and socially upsetting if wage increases should come to be standardized nationally at a productivity percentage figure, for then the sense of injustice which the other groups would feel would be much accentuated while at the same time the practical difficulties in the way of introducing flexibility into their payments would remain. These difficulties are obvious enough: imagine, for example, trying to introduce an annual productivity increment into bond interest or into the budgets of municipalities. The sense of injustice is of course present today and it has a real basis, but at least it is tempered by the fact that there is no national pattern of wage increases and that while some groups of workers come off spectacularly well, others remain stationary or lag behind. On the whole, it seems to me healthier in a free-enterprise economy to have something like the present crazy-quilt of wage adjustments than to move toward a uniform formula.

Profit-Sharing Plans

The report, like the research volume, does not go into the pros and cons of profit sharing as a form of employee compensation. I do not wish to exaggerate the importance of profit-sharing plans. They have not had a very good name in labor relations. They bloomed in the 1920's and largely died out in the great depression, when there were no profits to distribute. In recent years they have begun to gain ground, particularly when linked up with pension provisions. The causes of earlier failures have been examined and steps have been taken to meet them. My feeling is that pension plans deserve increased attention, not only in connection with pension arrangements but as a supplement to wage contracts.

In the case of ordinary profit sharing through current cash distributions, these plans have confronted some difficulties; e.g. (1) when given in the form of year-end or other widely spaced periodic distributions, they do not mean very much to the average worker in relation to his wage scale — they smack too much of "pie in the sky"; (2) profit-sharing commitments do not place the employer under any particular pressure to introduce operating economies or to expand sales or to make capital improvements. The inefficient employer who is not making much, if any, profits cannot expect to interest his workers in profit-sharing proposals.

The first of these two difficulties can be and has been met in some plans by building up a pool of profits to a point where distributions can be made concurrently with wage payments over, say, a year's period. The second difficulty might be met by combining profit-sharing arrangements with an annual "improvement" or productivity factor for the life of a long-term contract of the General Motors type. It seems to me that such a combination might turn out to be a fruitful one. The annual improvement factor would put the employer under salutary pressure to improve his methods while the profit-sharing provision would encourage the union and the management to work together on ways and means of encouraging output and cutting costs. The longer-term contract which the productivity provision presupposes would facilitate the making of joint plans along these lines.

I throw out these suggestions in the sketchiest form and without any attempt at a thorough analysis of the fields of exploration which they might open up.

The Role of the Government

I have the feeling that the interplay between governmental fiscal policies and wage levels is at once more complicated and more important than the report indicates. Most of us have a tendency to project the present into the future in thinking about wages; among other things we have a mental picture of full employment and production in which it should be possible to make wage bargains in a more or less reasonable way. Unfortunately, however, there may come a time when we are again faced with mass unemployment and great economic stresses and strains, and then all our hopes for a rational method of wage setting will, for the time being, go by the board. But the question goes deeper: it seems now to be a generally accepted fact of political life that no matter what party is in power at the time, the government cannot again afford to permit mass unemployment to exist in this country for any length of time. We simply cannot now foresee what measures the government may be forced to take if the feared contingency arises; but we do know that with each added year of unbalanced budgets and of prodigious military expenditures the task of government in converting from a wartime to a peacetime economy (if and when that day arrives) and maintaining full employment at the same time will probably necessitate a degree of governmental activity beyond anything which we have yet experienced. How far this activity in turn will cut across and modify, for better or worse, our present concepts of wage fixing, no one can now tell. I mention this subject, shrouded in uncertainties as it is, only because I think it well for us all to remember how fearfully complex our economic problems have become beneath the surface of full production and employment and how short-lived our present recommendations may be.

This thought leads me to a final suggestion. In the light of the tasks which may lie ahead, might it not be well for us now to try the experiment of bringing together into a continuing relationship the foremost leaders of industry and the foremost leaders of labor to consider their common economic problems in relation to each other and to the economy as a whole? We have had several experiences with labor-management conferences at the national level which have had useful though limited results. These conferences, however, have been episodic and transitory in character. It seems to me that the time has come when it would be worth while to create a standing conference which could meet periodically at stated intervals, with suitable staff assistance and with statistical and other help from the government, to explore and from time to time make recommendations regarding improved methods and procedures in collective bargaining and in wage fixing and to consider other relevant economic factors bearing upon the whole collective bargaining process — productivity and prices, the fiscal policies of the government, and so on. This is not the place to outline the details of such a proposal, and I mention it only because it seems to me that the more we try to come to grips with the matters discussed in this report, and particularly as we take into account the uncertain state of the future, the more it appears necessary that we should find some means of bringing the best brains of industry and labor together to contribute what they can to the improvement of their own relationships and to the general economic and social welfare of the country.

MR. BARKIN'S STATEMENT

The Committee Report properly affirms the widely accepted current guides for upward wage adjustment. In presenting them, the statement helps bring public evaluation of the issues in wage controversies abreast of the principles recognized in our industrial society. The general public will thereby be better prepared to understand the resolutions and regulations of such governmental agencies as the Wage Stabilization Board. The report, however, does not fully discuss several vital issues which must be dealt with; otherwise a wide gap will continue to exist in the analysis.

The very technical nature of the Committee's report tends to divert attention from the significant role which wages play in our society. Like other incomes, wages provide the leverage and incentive for worker participation in our society. They are the principal means by which he shares in our economic expansion. To the extent that his wages permit him to enjoy its advantages, he can identify himself with the community as a whole. Rising wages, particularly real wages, give workers a sense of participation. Since income is the primary measure of worth in our society, the upward movement of wages together with the concurrent leveling in the distribution of incomes helps greatly to democratize our society without reducing personal incentives. The lift in wage levels also supports other current forces for greater managerial and industrial advances. The experience of sharing in the growth of our society is further reinforced by the personal part played in securing these gains in income through collective bargaining agreements and organization of worker-management relationships. The collective bargaining process also adds a locus for the determination of wage rates other than the commodity market place or government. Human claims are added as determining considerations in the decisions of the business community.

I agree with the propositions (a) that a worker's real earnings should be protected against rising price levels (and I would prefer that this adjustment be automatic with the changes in the consumers' price index, however approximate this measure may be); (b) that workers should share systematically in the rise of our national per capita income; (c) that employers should pay no less than the union rate schedule for the industry or the locality, whichever is higher. But the above propositions do not constitute an adequate set of guides to the negotiation of wage levels in individual plants, companies or industries.

Guides to Negotiation of Wage Levels

First, inadequate attention is devoted to the importance of eliminating substandard wages. True enough, substandard wages were much more common before collective bargaining became widespread, but there are still vast areas of employment where rates are inadequate. The states have been most laggard in aligning themselves even with the 75 cents federal minimum, a standard which is widely recognized as obsolete in face of the rising costs of living and wage levels. Union progress in these lower-wage areas and industries has not been equal to the need.

The opponents of decent wages have helped to focus public attention on advances in union wage levels and in those of employees of unorganized plants which model themselves on the benefits gained by unions, thereby covering up low-wage employment. Legislative groups continue their resistance to efforts to modernize minimum-wage levels, and thereby perpetuate these pools of the underpaid. An exemption from federal controls for wages under $1.00 per hour is no substitute for a positive higher minimum-wage law.

The report deals most cavalierly with workers' rights to a higher proportion of the financial gains of the business enterprise. The need of workers for a larger share of income, which rarely assumes the form of a request for profit-sharing — not a proper answer to the need, has been a continuing one. When management and the public were less willing to recognize labor's rights to share the benefits of rising national productivity, this issue of labor's claim to a larger share of the income in our private economy was most vigorously argued. While current wage gains have tended to subordinate the issue, it has not been erased. If anything, the problem is likely to gain even greater prominence with the cutback in governmental expenditures on national security and the lowering of federal income tax rates and the consequent elimination of one of the great forces equalizing personal and corporate incomes. These changes will produce the demand that full employment and a comparable leveling of income be effected through the normal system of rewards in our private economy. Specifically, the argument will again be pushed that to create the vast volume of buying power necessary to absorb the products of our extensive new industrial capacity requires high wages, and reductions in profit margins and income payments to the higher income brackets. The national income must be more largely directed to the spending rather than the saving groups.

The Committee Report devotes too little attention to the obvious fact that no system of principles or guides for the consideration of wage changes can work in a vacuum. They must be related to the guides for the distribution of income and rewards to other claimants. To the extent that the community introduces points of reference for the consideration of wages, it should also define them for other income claimants. Wage rates help determine worker income and employer costs. But the worker's buying power is also dependent upon the prices he pays for goods and services. These prices are no longer set by elementary competitive forces. They are more generally the product of administrative business decisions. Price setters add, to the out-of-pocket expenses, charges which reflect managements' views on the proper return to the business and their policies on depreciation and capital replacement and other accounting conventions. No system of guides for wage determination can be stable or acceptable which does not take into account the practices, beliefs and behavior of other income claimants. To reach that goal and to provide mature guidance, the rules governing the behavior of each income claimant must be considered concurrently and in relation to one another.

It is true that we have no national institution for bargaining on the rightful principles to be followed in assigning income to the respective claimants. We depend primarily on bargaining in each distinct market, supplemented by governmental restraints. Such a system necessarily minimizes the public responsibility of the parties. It relies on the conflict of contending forces to attain the public good. The costs of such dispersed conflicts are the price we pay for the absence of such national agreement. In some areas competitive and conflicting groups and forces conspire together against other groups. Nor is the antitrust legislation conceived broadly enough to deal with these developments. These are the facts and they cannot be overlooked.

Wage policy must be visualized as being developed in this setting. It is therefore with considerable uneasiness that one reads the pleas in the Committee Report that the parties consider the broad economic consequence of policy or practice. These pleas reflect a yearning for more widespread responsible policy formulation by the private parties. But there are few direct rewards in our current business society for such conduct. Competitive business forces are not always effective. A mechanism must exist for encouraging such responsibility. It can probably come through a national bargain among the economic interests. Codes or guides for specific income claimants can only be hortatory while the groups pursue their independent courses. The most effective restraint on income claims exists with respect to wages, as employers tend to weigh wage requests in the light of their effect on their costs and returns. The other income claimants are freer to capitalize market situations when governmental controls are removed.

Employment Policies

As for the Committee's treatment of employment policies, it is essential to stress that an economy of full employment opens up jobs for all and thereby facilitates the process of finding the proper jobs for individuals. It is probable that the American people as a whole are now better adjusted, more optimistic and progressive-minded because of this high level of opportunities. The psychological benefits of this era are too frequently overlooked in defining the economic pros and cons.

Hitherto this period has seen little evidence of employment weaknesses in particular localities. Old and new activities were carried on concurrently to fill the vast voids created by the war, rising incomes and increases in families. But sick industries and regions are appearing. With the sharp changes in industrial structure resulting from alterations in mobilization plans and consumption habits, the problem of contracting industries or regions will become more important. Special machinery designed to aid these areas in the transition to expansion is essential. While our country boasts of a high rate of human mobility, it is hardly equal to the demands likely to be made by these changes. Nor would it be desirable to scrap the social investment in established communities. Reliance on spontaneous personal efforts is not enough. A more constructive program is to provide procedures for planning and aiding the economic resurgence of such declining areas. The vocational training and counseling services must be geared to this end.

A third fact overlooked in the Committee Report is that jobs must be made to fit people. Too much emphasis is ordinarily placed upon fitting people to jobs. The rapidly changing character of our work population, from the point of view of education, age, color, sex, urban experience, expectations and values as to job preference, demands extensive reconsideration of job characteristics and their design to fit the people.

A deliberate program of recasting jobs to allow for the employment of all the people also offers a constructive alternative to the currently criticized selective hiring policies of industry. The community must continue to demand that industry employ all persons who want employment, without discrimination. The line of unemployability must be moved back as far as possible. The larger the number of employed, the fewer the dependent and the better adjusted will the greatest number be. Current hiring policies are not so conceived. Only the force of an economy of full employment has produced some approximation of a nondiscriminatory hiring standard. It is vital that the adjustment be produced more deliberately. We are witnessing a mounting movement for assuring the employment of various marginal groups.

The Committee Report accepts the prevailing emphasis in management circles on the minor variations in productivity and qualifications among workers. This provides the rationale for highly selective hiring, placement and promotion policies. In contrast, unions and workers have taken the position that the main body of workers who have passed a probationary period of employment are generally equal, in value. They do not overlook the differences, but they believe that the range is small enough to be eliminated from consideration. In fact, differentiation would produce discrimination as it has in the past, and measures of these variations are so unreliable and deceptive that it would be unwise as well as unfair to depend upon them. The existence of extreme problem cases should not be used as a springboard for differentiation.

MR. BULLIS' STATEMENT

In considering the problem of wage determination, we should keep in mind the fact that the national total of wages represents labor's share in the national product. At a given level of production an increase in the share of labor means a decrease in the shares of others — owners, managers, farmers, and all who are in service occupations. This must be true, because the sum of the shares cannot exceed the total national product. However, the size of every share may be increased by increasing the total product, and it is such increase that makes it possible for wages to increase at a faster rate than prices. General increases in wages which in the aggregate exceed the increase in national production can only lead to price increases.

When wage determination occurs on a local basis, each employer determines how large a share of his sales dollar can go to his employees, and the effect of each agreement is not far-reaching. When wage determination is of regional or national scope, as it now is in many industries, the effects of wage agreements are far-flung and may set national patterns. The ultimate effect of setting wages on an industry-wide basis could conceivably be to squeeze the small and less efficient employers of labor out of business.

When there are inflationary pressures such as result from devaluation, deficit financing, and expansion of credit, it is only natural that labor should seek to protect itself by escalator clauses in wage agreements. Under such conditions labor is entitled to protection of its buying power. However, most escalator clauses are one-way streets, and to be of real economic value they should consider retreat equally as important as advance. In considering escalator clauses both industry and labor should remember that economic imbalance cannot be corrected by merely adjusting to its effects. Price inflation is the effect of an unbalanced situation, and adjusting wages to compensate does not effect a cure. It merely buys time to find and correct the cause.

It is important, therefore, that wage-rate structures be flexible and capable of adjustment to the needs of the economy so that full employment may continue and new jobs may be created for the additions to the labor force.

In my opinion, the entire increment of gain from increased productivity over long periods should not accrue to labor alone. In the long run the public should benefit by improved or cheaper products, and surely the investor who supplies the improved equipment is entitled to something. The distribution is generally accomplished through the operation of the free market.

It would be unfortunate if wages were pushed so high that prices could not follow without discouraging consumers. The effect would be to squeeze profits so that there would be no incentive for further investment in productive facilities. The results would be highly detrimental to the interests of labor and full employment.

I cannot subscribe to the idea that we may require new techniques to assure that incomes of different economic groups move forward in an equitable manner. This would presuppose full-scale economic planning and perhaps continuous inflation. Incomes of various groups would be controlled by politicians, and the groups wielding the greatest political power would be the gainers.

The primary objective in wage and employment policies of both employers and unions should be fairness to all concerned, including the public, which is the final judge and jury. In an atmosphere of fair play differences can be reconciled and production can go forward at rates needed to keep our economy and our society on an even keel.

MR. OLIVER'S STATEMENT

This comment should perhaps be divided into two sections, the first to point out parts of the report with which I am most in disagreement, the second — obligatory after the first — at least to sketch an approach from an angle thought to be preferable.

Preliminary to both of these, it must be kept clearly in mind that wage rates are set by human beings, not by economic forces, or by overall characteristics of something called "the economy," or in deference or response to conceptual creatures like "the upward momentum of an inflationary movement." Wages are always fixed in the short run, never in the long run; analyses based on "the long run," insofar as they imply that such perspectives determine wage rates, are worse than futile in handling real problems. No progress is made toward understanding wage fixing by opening the door, through the "long-run" hypotheses, for the importation into wage discussion of the trade jargon of professional economics.

The Long View vs. Realism

Most of my specific objections to the Committee Report arise out of the lapses into "long-run" economics. The impulse to pontification seems inseparable from economic theory. In this report (as almost invariably) that impulse results in the parading of manifest absurdities as though they were unquestionable verities. Thus: "It should be noted also that the wage escalator clause is one of several pricing devices in our economy which together contribute to automatic inflation whenever an excess of money demand occurs.". . . "Moreover, a general increase in money wages, by raising both the costs of production and the level of consumer demand, helps to set the stage for a new upsurge in the price level, which creates a new wage lag, and so on."

It must be recognized that these two statements are not only unjustified by anything in the factual background, but that they will be positively harmful if published with any seeming authority behind them.

The report has no single point of view (or any clear point of view) in its approach to the problems of wage determination. If it is used at all, one might fear that it would be quoted to actual wage-fixing bodies. Arbitration and related wage-setting processes are most common in the field of public utilities. The report goes uselessly afield to accept palpable error where it says: "Some types of industry can live with a wage escalator clause much more easily than others. . . . An industry whose prices are subject to legal regulation, on the other hand, may have more difficulty in adjusting to an escalator clause. Railroads, power companies, telephone companies and other public utilities are in this situation."

All railway workers are today covered by union agreements with escalator clauses. The agreements will come up for reconsideration in 1953 and 1954. No one can claim that the research underlying the Committee's report provides the slightest foundation for the general statement about escalator clauses in public utility industries; it flows from someone's economic theories. But those future railway wage disputes will be real, and serious to the workers and the country. The escalator clauses in question were good, the industry has had not the slightest difficulty in adjusting to them, and other public utilities have had similar experience. If the Committee Report influences anyone in future wage controversies in the public utility industry, it will have been definitely and unnecessarily harmful.

The Committee Report, to proceed to the second of the sections referred to in the opening paragraph of this comment, might very well have adopted exclusively the point of view of the public member of an arbitration or fact-finding board called upon to consider particular proposed wage increases. The actual processes by which wage proposals arise, and their prior and subsequent relationship to "productivity," might very well be the central subject of investigation in a report on employment and wages. What follows, though stated as "fact" and true in my judgment, would at least serve as working hypotheses for research, and — if verified — as the outline of the central part of a report on wage processes.

Aims of Workers and Employers

Working men and women try to get from their jobs the things they want. Those things, as found in actual trade union proposals and not deduced from any concept of "economic man," include better living conditions, more leisure, freedom from individual injustice and discrimination, changes in wage rates based on skill, experience, output, and other such elements, wage differentials for exceptionally difficult assignments, pensions, and an endless list of particular objectives.

The major single one of these objectives in the wage area is a higher living standard, with its negative corollary of no reduction in living standards. The desires for better living conditions originate in the immediate environment of the worker, in a consciousness of privation or in contact with some other person with higher income. The strength of the demand for improvement arises from the total environment, including characteristics of the work and the job. Unions, however imperfectly responsive to the total of individual worker desires, do reflect the nature and strength of those desires, in their proposals to employers and in their insistence on favorable action.

Employer response to union proposals for raising wage rates is likewise affected by what the employer wants in and from his establishment. Insofar as proposed wage changes will have immediate effect on unit labor costs, the employer gives consideration to many elements in his own business and its environment. Among these are questions of whether or not the apparent increase in cost can be avoided by management. The employer may consider the possibility of absorbing part of the increased cost, in lowered profit margins. Consideration may be given to passing along part of the apparent cost to consumers, and in that question will be involved the whole relationship of competing or associated businesses. The normal response of normally successful industry is a combination of these and other factors with variations in the importance of the several elements in the decision ultimately reached.

Both workers and employers have the paramount necessity of finding a basis upon which cooperation in production can continue. Over the bargaining table, or in the decision of an arbitrator, some compromise is worked out which will give some degree of satisfaction (at least as an alternative to a strike or lockout) to those concerned.

Chain of Causation

Whatever may be the factors which impel the individual employer to agree to some particular amount of wage increase, his unfailing response after the agreement is to seek ways to keep down labor cost per unit of output. Actual measurement of wages and labor cost by industries or (very roughly) for the country as a whole makes it clear that real wages have risen greatly, and not unsteadily, over any period of ten or twenty years in the last century, but that real labor costs have fallen. Experience suggests the reason for this observed pair of facts. Employers, increasingly intelligent and "scientific" in management, have constantly before them possibilities for reorganization of process, product, equipment, material, layout, etc. Decisions as to such changes rest primarily upon possible savings in cost, and especially on savings in labor cost. Changes which are inadvisable at one wage level become economical at a slightly higher level. Moreover, this slightly higher wage cost per man-hour need promise only a threshold saving, great enough to justify a technological change, without considering the total potential saving that may later flow from the change. Among the effects to be anticipated from higher wages, for example, is an increase in the efficiency of employees. But normally an employer will not make a particular technological change unless there is actually in sight enough saving to justify that change. Subsequent economies, that result from wage and process changes, will very frequently cut total other costs, as well as labor costs, per unit of output.

Rising real wages in one industry in any community broaden the demand by workers generally for better living standards. Employees in other establishments, in daily contact with workers whose wages have risen, want similar improvements for themselves. Their unions, their employers, and their productive processes go through the same cycle.

Wide variations in techniques in every American industry make it clear that the possibility of increased output per man-hour in the great majority of establishments is, at any one time, substantial. Those with lowest cost, also, are far from the peak of perfection in process or equipment. As machinery, buildings, power plants, and other physical equipment wear out or approach obsolescence, replacement by better installations becomes increasingly profitable with higher wage rates.

The chain of causation suggested by actual observation of wage changes thus is that improvements in living standards anywhere in the community, for whatever group and for whatever reason, stimulate the demand for improvement in successive groups of industrial workers. The strength of that demand will vary with facts as they appear to the particular group of employees. Employer resistance will vary with another set of facts. Neither of these sets of facts is reducible to generalizations, or even to segments of generalizations. Wages in fact do rise. Each such rise leads to proposals for other increases, in other occupations or industries. Technological change of various kinds offsets the increase in labor costs, and rising labor efficiency contributes to the total historical fact of rising real wages with falling real labor costs. Beyond the individual establishment, community-wide increases in real incomes result in broader markets for old, and added markets for new industrial products. Broader markets and greater sales in themselves lower unit costs of all kinds.

Wages rise with productivity; this is not a strange fact, because the real sequence is that productivity rises with real wages. The long-time agreement of real wage increases with labor productivity is not an accident or coincidence, nor does it flow from the limitation of wage increases by productivity increases. Rather does the correlation proceed from the natural fact that the almost limitless possibilities of increased industrial efficiency — in terms of output per man-hour — are increasingly realized as real hourly wage rates rise.

Living Standards Central

The most important characteristic of wage changes, then, is that they represent a response to a need or demand for rising living standards. The central standard for judging such a request, therefore, is whether or not the rate of proposed change in real wages is wise. The test must be, in large part, the general rise in the community or in the industry under consideration, in the present as well as in the past. Similar criteria may be applied to requests for changes in working conditions apart from the constantly necessary innovation. Within the general conclusion that industry normally can and should grant greater leisure, should improve work assignments, should provide orderly processes of promotion, etc., the current or normal improvement in industry generally provides the best criterion for testing any proposed change. Rising living standards and improving working conditions are the major objectives of industry, from the standpoint of the "community as a whole" which the arbitrator must consider, from the "human" standpoint, and from the standpoint of immediate industrial expansion and development.

Continuation of the rate of increase in real wages, either in individual industries or by communities or for the country as a whole, will impose no great strain upon employers in maintaining or reducing real labor costs per unit of output. Arbitrators, employers, government officials and any other agencies that may be concerned with fixing wages would be seriously mistaken in trying or expecting to influence the price level — of individual commodities or of all commodities — by changing or maintaining wage rates. If normal good judgment is used, and extreme wage fluctuations avoided, the effect on prices can be safely ignored.

MR. STARK'S STATEMENT

It seems to me that despite the progress in collective bargaining in recent years this function still partakes considerably of the characteristics bequeathed it from the jungle days. Collective bargaining is too often still a tug of war, with industry trying to hang on to profits and unions trying to squeeze as much as they can.

Certainly collective bargaining as at present practiced cannot be the last word. Use of economic force by unions is costly to the economy, as is the lockout or other employer retaliation. Is there not some possibility of creating machinery that will give labor a continuous interest in the day-to-day operations of a concern between collective bargaining sessions? Here and there, experiments in industrial establishments have demonstrated that methods of cooperation between men and management keep both sides on their toes, help decrease waste, improve products and further efficiency.

Increased Employee Participation

It seems to me that there is always room for further discussion on the problem of how great a participation by employees may produce maximum results and replace the type of industrial warfare that frequently marks collective bargaining today.

To achieve important results in this direction is no small responsibility, either for unions or for management. On their part unions would have to train workers to be cognizant of all phases of management and production, engineering, sales, prices, consumers' changing tastes and demands, and utilization of products. Needless to say, such a conception of the unionist's function is generally lacking today, both among unionists themselves and among employers. On its part management would have to be willing to discuss informally any subject that might be brought up by the employees without raising the "principle" of management prerogatives. Too often, fruitful discussions bog down when either side raises the barrier (often illusive) of "principle." It is virtually impossible to set down in writing all the matters involved in management prerogatives. Therefore employers need not hesitate to discuss informally upon request and without making commitments any subject that is brought up for the purpose of advancing common objectives of both groups.

This is neither an advocacy of syndicalism nor of codetermination. I would not have industry run by the workers nor management's responsibility vetoed by employee representatives, but I would invite the latter to contribute their ideas with the understanding that final responsibility for action depends solely upon management.

Advantages of Employee Participation

By participating more fully in day-to-day problems, employees, it seems to me, would be in a much better position to learn and understand and appreciate many problems which bear directly upon their employment, their continued usefulness, and their general relationship to the concern and the industry.

Increased participation by employees in discussions with management of joint and general problems would in the end tend to maximize efforts to regularize employment and would thus raise the low annual income of those who find that high hourly wages are no guarantee of improved living standards commensurate with these wage rates. I cannot help but feel that fuller participation by employees would bring out in greater detail that an important tendency in the wage structure during recent years has been a marked reduction in most industries of the percentage differential between wage rates of skilled and unskilled employees.

As the report points out, the "pressures bearing on wage movements are so complex, and so highly variable from one situation to the next, that they will probably always defy any simple generalizations." Because no such simple generalizations on wage movements can be made, it seems to me highly desirable to lead the way towards a more reasoned wage policy through the avenue of greater employee participation in the many problems faced by management.

If employees are to be able to take advantage of any invitation to participate more fully in the broader functions of industry, employees and unions will have to have a better grasp of technical processes, of economics, cost accounting, sociology, etc. The unionist himself may have little time to acquire this information, and therefore will be compelled more and more to turn to the technician. The latter's problem will be, as it already is in some unions, to decide whether he is a creature of the labor leaders who hire him, subordinating his viewpoint to theirs, or whether his role is that of a scientist who lays the facts before his principal and who sets down his observations and recommendations.

Undoubtedly there are many arguments that may be raised against fuller and freer participation by employees in discussion of management matters. Obviously business must be conducted on a quasi-authoritarian basis because of the psychological relationship between those who give orders and those who are expected to obey. Management feels an inherent superiority, believing that employees cannot, or perhaps will not, understand its problems and therefore will be unable to contribute to their solution. Employees, as recipients of orders, tend to feel themselves inferior, and this begets a feeling of frustration. Fuller participation in all discussions necessary for the carrying on of a business would tend to do away with this psychological handicap in dealings between management and workmen.

MR. TEPER'S STATEMENT

Wage Section of the Report

There can be little disagreement with the basic tenets of the report. It does highlight the complex character of our national wage structure, affected as it is by the diversity of wage payment methods; the variety of auxiliary or fringe wage provisions; the multiplicity of wage-setting formulas and their adaptation in practice; the character of wage determination, depending on whether it is carried out unilaterally by the employers, set up bilaterally by collective bargaining or established by governmental action, to say nothing of local custom, tradition and prejudices. The report also points up some of the arguments used in the course of the wage bargain and properly notes that over a period of time real wages must increase.

Importance of Time and Place

Because the wage system is complicated and because wage negotiations take place under different circumstances, it is difficult, if not impossible, to isolate the policies to be followed in specific wage negotiations from the circumstances in which they arise. The ultimate decisions regarding a specific wage problem are a function of the many interrelated influences which brought the existing wage structure into being, as well as of the dynamic changes which took place in economic, political, social and other spheres while the particular wage structure remained comparatively static. Certain economic factors facilitate agreement on higher rates of compensation to workers — improvements in productivity and industrial efficiency, ability of the industry or the firm either to absorb higher wage costs or to pass them on, heightened competition for labor brought about by changes in local or regional industrial patterns or in some other way, and so on.

Other factors may tend to retard such upward revisions — the inability of the firm or the industry to meet higher wages, declining prices or a reduced demand for the industry's products, excessive unemployment, competition from abroad or from other industries or areas, and so on. The relative bargaining strength of the parties, their outlook and evaluation of the future also play important roles. The modification of the particular wage structure resolves, in fact, a variety of tensions generated by the outlook and needs of the parties to the argument as well as by their relative militancy and economic strength. Under these circumstances, it is impossible to consider the ultimate effect of the specific wage adjustment as a proposition in the abstract.

Nor can one lay down a standard for what some would like to call a "responsible bargain." This evaluation must be left to the parties to the specific bargain, for they, better than anyone else, can evaluate the equities of the particular situation. On the other hand, if the lack of organization in a particular economic field or the marginal character of certain industrial or commercial undertakings is such as to drive wages to a level which provides a substandard level of existence to workers, the "responsible bargain" must be established through governmental intervention, even if, in some cases, it should result in temporary increases in the prices of specific products. Society cannot expect some segments of its population, at the cost of their own deprivation, to subsidize the rest. Nor can it afford to forget the minimum-wage standards, once established, and leave them at levels which general social advance or changing price levels render obsolete. The standards of adequacy, after all, have a meaning only for a specific time and place. They do not remain eternal, and as life becomes more bountiful for the great majority of our population the lower-paid group must be brought up as well. Thus, today, many of the minimum wages fixed by the states and the federal minimum under the Fair Labor Standards Act are definitely outdated and call for an upward revision. Unfortunately, the report overlooks this.

Furthermore, collective bargaining issues should not be limited by the rate of change in the productivity of our economy. Such a limitation could be argued only if wage earners continually represented a constant proportion of the total labor force and if the distribution of incomes, at any one time, could be shown to be fair and equitable. This, of course, is not the case. The very disparate character of the existing wage structures suggests the opposite, as does the fact that the prices of many goods and services are not determined by the forces of the market place but by the conscious actions of the sellers. Accordingly, when labor finds in a particular situation that goods are priced out of line with production costs, it feels free to base its arguments for a wage increase on the profitability of the particular firm or industry, i.e., on its ability to pay (just as employers, who view their profits as inadequate, argue their inability to meet higher wage costs). To limit wage increases by the rate of change in productivity, on the other hand, would call for a re-examination of the shares of other claimants upon the national income and the prescription of standards for them as well as for wage earners.

The report ignores the role played by wages in our society. While for workers, higher income constitutes a hope for a better standard of living, the pressure of wage increases forces industry to seek better tools and production techniques to counter the rise in labor costs. The pressure for higher wages thus spurs on technological innovations and raises productivity to new heights, benefiting society all around. Of course, in the final analysis, it will be the parties to collective bargaining who can best determine the equity of their particular bargain — all of them, after all, are interested in the survival of the employing enterprise and in the maintenance of employment and production.

Wage Controls

A few words may not be amiss about national wage policy during periods of emergency, when the nation, to prevent abnormal price increases and a general distortion of values, is forced to resort to economic controls as a rational substitute for the market forces. An equitable system of controls calls, of course, for sufficient flexibility to prevent the stifling of the economy; hence, the need for the review of specific ceiling prices and of whatever imbalances there may be in the wage structure. In addition, an equitable system of controls must be so devised as to prevent favoritism to any economic group.

This suggests that the level of controlled wages must be permitted to change with changes in the costs of living as well as with changes in the productivity of the economy. Adjustment of wages to the consumers' price index brings about a more stable relationship between wages and prices. (The correction is only partial at best, first because it is made after prices have advanced over a given period of time, secondly because the index fails to take account of some elements of increased costs to the worker, such as those brought about by increased income taxes or when the worker has to move to a higher-cost defense town.) Of course, once prices are comparatively stabilized, such wage movements come to an end as well. However, mere support of the purchasing power of the wage dollar fails to prevent a distortion in the relationship between the different factors of production. To the extent that productivity rises, even in the absence of a change in prices, the relative importance of labor's share in the proceeds of industry declines. Unless wage regulations do permit workers to claim their share in the gains of productivity, all of the benefits would accrue solely to the owners and management of industry.

Employment Section of the Report

It seems to me that the report dismisses much too lightly the general objectives of full employment. The maintenance of high levels of employment is the key problem of our generation. It must of necessity underlie all discussion of specific employment practices and policies. Many of the problems involved in searching for a job are minimized or eliminated when jobs are plentiful. Many of the dissatisfactions of individuals with their work do not have a chance to develop because the workers can find jobs that suit them.

On the other hand, the report puts too much weight on hiring freedom for the employer and overemphasizes the need for pre-employment testing of workers. This approach suggests keeping out of employment those whose handicaps may prevent top performance. Yet it is in the interest of all to provide employment for the largest possible number, provided they can perform reasonably well on the job. The report also fails to note that many of the tests in use are of very questionable value in judging ultimate performance. The ultimate test of sound employment policy must be fitting the job to the individual's capabilities, and not the reverse.

APPENDIX

APPENDIX NOTE 1 (CHAPTER 1)

WAGE THEORIES

W. S. WOYTINSKY

THE IRON LAW AND THE SUBSISTENCE-WAGE THEORY

The subsistence-wage theory prevailed in England early in the eighteenth century, near the beginning of the Industrial Revolution. Most economists then agreed that wages should provide workers with the subsistence minimum, but should not be permitted to rise above this level.

"Nothing but necessity will enforce labour." "Low wages make the lower classes of people do more work and become more careful and industrious." Such were the axioms of the preclassical theory of wages.[1] And this gloomy outlook fitted the times. Both in England and on the European continent wages were lower in the middle of the eighteenth century than ever before. In France, where the subsistence-wage theory was originally formulated by the Physiocrats, the peasants were so heavily taxed that few were appreciably above a state of starvation. Urban workers were not much better off. So the Physiocrats assumed, for the sake of simplicity, that there was a natural law according to which the wages of labor were kept at the subsistence limit.[2] When they said "subsistence" they meant, literally, just above starvation.

Adam Smith

At the time of Adam Smith — the second half of the eighteenth century — this theory already sounded obsolete. Working conditions in the new factories were deplorable: a work week of 84 hours was not unusual, and workers, recruited from poorhouses, were often treated like pack animals. Yet a large part of the working classes got wages sufficient to allow much more than mere existence, and the situation of the workers was improving. Thriving factories were beginning to compete with one another for trained workers; workers were learning to use "combinations" in the struggle for higher wages.

These new tendencies were in striking contrast to the subsistence-wage theory. Adam Smith took account of the new situation, and his wage theory was essentially focused on the new factor that permitted workers to improve their living conditions.

The economic optimism characteristic of the time of Smith proved short-lived. Of the period of the Napoleonic Wars, Alfred Marshall writes:

> Year by year the condition of the working classes in England became more gloomy. An astonishing series of bad harvests, a most exhausting war, and a change in the methods of industry that dislocated old ties, combined with an injudicious poor law to bring the working classes into the greatest misery they have ever suffered, at all events since the beginning of trustworthy records of English social history.[3]

Malthus

Malthus became the spokesman of capitalism in the darkest days of its history. For him the subsistence-wage theory was a natural law. Like the Physiocrats, he thought that workers were condemned to earn just enough for bare subsistence and to live on the verge of starvation. Wages, he declared, must be just sufficient to support the workers and the number of children per marriage necessary to maintain exactly the level of population, and can deviate only temporarily above or below this level according to the state of the real funds for the maintenance of labor.[4] He believed that ultimately the real wage is determined in such a way as to check and regulate increase in the laboring classes by checking and regulating their command over the means of subsistence.[5]

The remarkable feature of this wage theory is that it goes far beyond wage determination. This is, in fact, a theory of eternal misery based on the natural law of growth of population. It is not limited to the factory system or any other organization of production, but relates rather to real earnings, and primarily to the supply of food available to the poor — that is, to the great majority of the people, excluding only a thin layer of the privileged.

1. Lujo Brentano, *Hours and Wages in Relation to Production,* Sonnenschein, London, 1894, p. 3.
2. Alfred Marshall, *Principles of Economics,* 8th edition, Macmillan, London, 1920, p. 505.
3. *Ibid.,* p. 177.
4. T. R. Malthus, *An Essay on the Principle of Population,* reprinted from the last edition revised by the author, Ward, Lock and Co., London, 1890.
5. *Ibid.,* p. 363.

Ricardo

The Malthusian theory became the foundation of the wage theory of Ricardo, who claimed to have discovered "the laws by which wages are regulated and by which the happiness of far the greatest part of every community is governed." Ricardo distinguished between the "natural price" of labor and its "market price." The natural price of labor he defined as "that price which is necessary to enable the labourers, one with another, to subsist and to perpetuate their race, without either increase or diminution." [6] The market price of labor, he said, is the wage actually paid to workers. It deviates from the natural (subsistence) wage according to the play of demand and supply but has, like commodity prices, a tendency to conform to it. Yet in an improving society the market price of labor may for an indefinite period be constantly above its natural price.[7]

Ricardo concludes: "Like all other contracts, wages should be left to the fair and free competition of the market, and should never be controlled by the interference of the legislature." [8]

On closer inspection, Ricardo's conception of the "natural" price of labor proves to be much less rigid than it appears at first.

> It is not to be understood that the natural price of wages, estimated even in food and necessaries, is absolutely fixed and constant. It varies at different times in the same country, and very materially differs in different countries. It essentially depends on the habits and customs of the people. An English labourer would consider his wages under their natural rate, and too scanty to support a family, if they enabled him to purchase no other food than potatoes, and to live in no better habitation than a mud cabin; . . . Many of the conveniences now enjoyed in an English cottage, would have been thought luxuries at an early period of our history.[9]

Thus, as soon as Ricardo turns from the "natural" laws to the actual conditions in his country and in his time, his subsistence wage loses its mathematical austerity. In the last analysis, he considers only one law supreme: Government should not interfere with whatever wages are actually paid in the nation.

As time went on, the subsistence-wage theory as formulated by Ricardo became a part of official economic science. The vagueness of the concept "subsistence minimum" proved to be an advantage since it left a wide range of freedom for interpretation.

Lassalle

The famous German socialist Lassalle, announcing his "iron law of wages" as the foundation of the capitalist system, returned to the subsistence-wage theory in its original crude form, more in line with the terms used by the Physiocrats than with those used by Ricardo. Lassalle stated his "law" in 1863 in an open letter addressed to a labor committee campaigning for universal suffrage in Prussia. Along with other arguments, he used the following economic argument in support of the program: "This is the iron economic law that determines the wage of laborers under present conditions, under the play of supply and demand. The average wage is always limited to the level of subsistence which is required in a nation, according to its customs, for maintenance and reproduction." [10] He justified this law in the most orthodox way, as a true disciple of Malthus: Wages of workers cannot rise above the subsistence minimum because of the pressure of population. The only difference between Lassalle and the earlier supporters of the subsistence wage was that when speaking of "workers" he meant "factory workers" and, practically, the upper layers of factory workers whom he was addressing, while the earlier authors meant the "poor" of the nation.

Lassalle did not pretend to have discovered a new economic truth. On the contrary, he claimed that the iron law was universally recognized by liberal economists. He himself posed as a scholar who was revealing to the workers certain notions that were kept secret from them by their masters. But he was giving the old wage theory a new interpretation when he wrote to the members of the labor committee: "Gentlemen, you must bear this iron, gloomy law deep, deep in your souls and all your thinking should start from it. . . . To everybody who talks with you about the improvement in conditions of the laboring class, you should put, first of all, this question: Does he recognize this law or not?"

Lassalle's letter was not only brilliantly written but also perfectly timed. The labor movement in Prussia was carried along by the eco-

6. David Ricardo, *On the Principles of Political Economy and Taxation*, first American edition, Milligan, Georgetown, D.C., 1819, p. 67. This definition included explicitly the postulate of a stationary population, a postulate that was at variance with Smithian thinking.

7. *Ibid.*, pp. 68–69.

8. *Ibid.*, p. 81.

9. *Ibid.*, p. 71.

10. Ferdinand Lassalle, *Offenes Antwortschreiben an das Zentral Komittee zur Berufung eines Allgemeinen Deutschen Arbeiter-Kongresses zu Leipzig*, Ferdinand Lassalle's Gesamtwerke, Leipzig, 1899, p. 15.

nomic growth on which Bismarck was building his policy — the war against France and the assembly of German princedoms into a new empire under the emperor-king in Berlin. General suffrage was to become the symbol and vehicle of the Iron Reich engineered by the Iron Chancellor, and the "iron law" of Lassalle was designed to sell the idea of the political vote to workers.

To political opponents who accused him of having invented his "law," Lassalle answered by quoting the best authorities of the classical school who had preached the same doctrine.[11] All his quotations were correct, though he omitted mentioning that some of the authors had used different language. Slightly simplifying the classical theory — never distorting it — he dug out of its arsenal a wage theory that could be used through decades as a spiritual weapon against the capitalist system.

Lassalle knew, of course, that wages in a capitalist society can rise far above the subsistence minimum. He admitted casually that wages of German workers were rising, in his time, in somewhat the same proportion as profits of masters. He dismissed this situation, however, with the observation that in comparison with their masters, workers were as poor as ever, and were condemned to remain poor. One may note that with this correction the iron law loses the rigidity characteristic of iron. This was, however, irrelevant for the purpose which the law was intended to serve. It was not meant to be used as an argument against attempts of workers to raise wages but only to prove that these attempts would fail unless they were supplemented by political action.

In brief, what Lassalle discovered was not a new wage law but the possibility of using an old theory in a new way. The spectacular economic and political rise of workers in the first half of the twentieth century proved the fallacy of the subsistence-wage theory but did not put an end to its career. The theory is widely used now by the left opposition in labor unions as an argument against any hope of improving living conditions of workers within the existing economic system.

Wage Theory of Karl Marx

Apart from Lassalle's iron law, the growing bitterness of social clashes in the second half of the nineteenth century found expression in the surplus-value theory of Karl Marx. A survey of wage theories of that time would be incomplete without mention of this doctrine, although it is more a theory of profits than of wages. Karl Marx did not try to formulate a "law" of wages. In his *Capital* he neither accepts nor rejects the "iron law," but simply ignores it. The purpose of his treatise was to expose the origin of profit in a capitalist society; the section on wages is surprisingly brief, casual and superficial.

Apart from vehement denunciation of the American economist M. Carey, who had held that wages rise and fall in proportion to the productiveness of labor, this section contains a few illustrations of the general statement that "in comparison of the wages in different nations, we must take into account all the factors that determine changes in the . . . value of labour power; the price and the extent of the prime necessaries of life as naturally and historically developed, the cost of training the labourers, the part played by the labour of women and children, the productiveness of labour, its extensive and intensive magnitude."[12]

It contains hardly a word that would suggest a new theory of wages. Moreover, it may be argued that there is no place for a theory of wages in an economic philosophy based on the conception of capitalist profit as "booty pumped out of the labourer,"[13] or "surplus product embezzled by capitalists, because abstracted from labourers without return of an equivalent."[14] In fact, if profits represent the part of the product embezzled by capitalists, wages represent the part that capitalists have not succeeded in embezzling. Thus the theory of wages is fully included in the theory of capitalist profit: workers are always underpaid; their wages are always too low; fair or normal wages are a logical contradiction. Even if workers "can make some additions to their consumption-fund of clothes, furniture, etc., and can lay by small reserve-funds of money," this does not do away with the exploitation. "A rise in the price of labour, as a consequence of accumulation of capital, only means that the length and weight of the golden chain the wage worker has already forged for himself, allow of a relaxation of the tension of it."[15] "The rise of wages is confined within limits that not only leave intact the foundations of the capitalistic system, but

11. "Zur Arbeiterfrage," address to a worker meeting in Leipzig, April 16, 1863, Gesamtwerke, II Band, pp. 33–58.

12. *Capital: A Critical Analysis of Capitalist Production,* translated from the third German edition, Allen and Unwin, London, 1938 (reprint of 1889 edition), Vol. II, p. 571.
13. *Ibid.,* p. 607.
14. *Ibid.,* p. 624.
15. *Ibid.,* p. 631.

also secure its reproduction on a progressive scale." [16]

Essentially, Marx has reiterated the old subsistence-wage theory minus population law. His omission of the Malthusian explanation of the tendency of wages to fall to the bare subsistence minimum was an important improvement in the theory. The real contribution of Marx to wage theory was his analysis of those forces that tend to press wages to the subsistence limit.

According to Marx, the pivot upon which the law of demand and supply of labor works is not the growth of population but the cyclical oscillations in employment, the industrial reserve army that weigh down the active labor army in normal times and hold its pretensions in check during periods of overproduction and boom.[17] The analysis of the effect of the business cycle on wages is among the most penetrating sections of *Capital.*

Productivity Theory of Wages

In the United States, Paul H. Douglas is probably the best-known proponent of the productivity theory of wages. His theory starts with the general law of wages established by Marshall: An alert businessman distributes his outlay for wages and capital goods in such a way that the return of his last (marginal) expenditures for labor is proportionate to that of his other last outlays. The fact that wages are frequently determined by custom and pressure neither invalidates nor limits the principle of marginal productivity. Once wages are fixed, marginal productivity will determine the number of workers that will be employed.[18] Douglas did not, however, like some followers of the marginal-productivity theory, find in it a justification of the existing structure of wages.[19]

Continuing from the point where Marshall stopped, Douglas tried to find the mathematical law governing the distribution of the product between labor and capital. This problem led him to the question: To what extent is the growth of the product due to (1) an increase in employment of the labor force and (2) an increase in capital? The question could be expressed in mathematical terms by considering the volume of production as a "function" of two variables, labor and capital. As a working hypothesis Douglas assumed a definite type of function.[20] Then he tried to fit it to the available statistical data and found that of variations in the volume of product, one fourth or one third reflected changes in capital and three fourths or two thirds, changes in the employed labor force.[21] Available data revealed also that the processes of production were distributed, until 1922, in direct proportion to the hypothetical marginal productivity of labor and capital.[22]

Douglas believed also that there is a close negative correlation between the supply of labor and wages but no visible correlation between profits and the supply of capital,[23] and on this basis he applied the general mathematical margin theory to the theory of distribution.[24]

According to this theory (supported by an analysis of the relationship between value of production, employment and capital in various years and various industries in the United States, Australia, New Zealand, Canada and South Africa), there is a "substantial and indeed a surprising degree of agreement" between changes in production and those that would occur if the output depended approximately two thirds on labor and one third on capital.[25] There is also "an almost precise degree of agreement between the actual share received by labor and that which, according to the theory of marginal productivity, we would expect labor to obtain." The deviation of the actual relationship of value of output, employment and capital from the theoretically anticipated relationship can in most instances be explained, Douglas held, by imperfect or excessive competition and by expansion or contraction of demand.

These conclusions are open to criticism. They are based on data of manufacturing production in five countries, in different periods, and depend on the mathematical formulas used for their interpretation. The fitting of empirical data to theoretical formulas was obtained after

16. *Ibid.,* p. 634.
17. *Ibid.,* p. 654.
18. Paul H. Douglas, *The Theory of Wages,* Macmillan, New York, 1934, p. 66.
19. *Ibid.,* p. 67.
20. This hypothetical formula (supplied by Professor Charles W. Cobb) postulates that the product changes in direct proportion with some unknown potence of capital and in direct proportion with another, likewise unknown, potence of employed labor force, and that these potences are such that when capital and labor force change at the same rate, the product changes in direct proportion with them. See *The Theory of Wages,* p. 133.
21. *Ibid.,* pp. 133, 161, 169, 487.
22. *Ibid.,* p. 488.
23. *Ibid.,* p. 492.
24. *Ibid.,* pp. 493–94.
25. The formulas developed by Douglas and his associates are interpreted here in nontechnical terms for the benefit of readers who are not interested in the mathematical aspect of the theory. For a complete presentation of the theory see Paul H. Douglas, "Are There Laws of Production?," presidential address delivered at the sixtieth annual meeting of the American Economic Association, Chicago, December 29, 1947, *American Economic Review,* March 1948, pp. 1–41.

painstaking adjustment of statistics and formulas. Therefore, the relationships between the shares of labor and capital and their marginal productivities as established by Douglas cannot be generalized.

The mechanism of distribution in a dynamic society is too complicated to be expressed by an algebraic formula. "This is no door but only a little window that opens out upon a great world," Douglas has said of his theory. What this window shows is that the rate of sharing of the social dividend between labor and capital is likely to be related in some way to the marginal productivity of the two agents, even if this relationship cannot be expressed in simple mathematical terms.

APPENDIX NOTE 2 (CHAPTER 10)

LABOR LAW IN ACTION

JOSEPH KOVNER

THE COMPLEX, DISPERSED CHARACTER of American labor law, distributed among the different branches of government and enforced by federal, state and local authorities, defies logical analysis. It is full of life and movement. Any important union-employer relationship could be used to illustrate American labor law in action. The following story of the United Steelworkers of America and the "Little Steel" corporations was selected because it involved many of the important legal events of recent times and invoked a wide variety of legal concepts.

LITTLE STEEL STRIKE (1937)

In May 1937, a critical year for the labor movement in this country, the newly formed union of steelworkers called a strike at the plants of three of the Little Steel corporations, Republic, Inland, and Youngstown Sheet and Tube Company. The Little Steel strike call went to 80,000 workers in twenty plants, located in Pennsylvania, Ohio, Indiana and Illinois. With few exceptions, the men ceased work — many because they were ardent union members, others because they were ready to go along with strong action, and still others because they would not oppose a strong prevailing sentiment among their fellow workers.

Right to Strike and National Labor Relations Act

The legal right of the workers was clear. They could quit work in a body to bring economic pressure on their employers to accede to their demands so long as their demands did not involve unlawful claims.

In 1937, as today, the right to strike was protected by federal statutes, particularly by the National Labor Relations Act. This statute guaranteed the right of workers to organize and to engage in concerted action for their mutual aid. It also obligated the employer to bargain with the union chosen by the majority of his employees. The New Deal had been in power for four years; it had placed on the statute books the Social Security Act, the Public Contracts Act and the National Labor Relations Act. The last was the most important, and it was directly involved in the Little Steel strike. The major issue in that strike was the right to bargain collectively in the steel industry, the labor policies of which were models for other industries.

The Little Steel corporations not only refused to recognize or deal with the union; they also refused to recognize the force of the National Labor Relations Act, which they considered unconstitutional. They had competent legal advice that the United States Supreme Court would declare the statute invalid because it attempted to regulate local manufacturing activity and because it invaded the employer's freedom to hire and fire employees for any reason, including union membership. This belief dominated the employers' policies, even though in March 1937, two months before the strike was called, the Supreme Court had declared the act constitutional in a case involving another steel corporation, the Jones and Laughlin company.[1] But the Supreme Court decision was novel and surprising, not yet fully credible.

Background of the Strike

To the union, the decision upholding the National Labor Relations Act was proof that it was on the highroad of the times, and it was inspired to move forward aggressively. There was another reason for the strike. In March 1937, the United States Steel Corporation, the largest single steel concern, had signed an agreement with the United Steelworkers agreeing to deal with the union, for its members only, on certain specified matters — an action as surprising as the Supreme Court decision.

The union had concentrated its organizing efforts on U.S. Steel; it had poured money and men into a tireless campaign, expecting a bitter conflict before it would be recognized by the biggest industrial employer in the United States. The specter of the battle of Homestead between strikers and Pinkerton guards, in 1892, and of the lost strike in 1919 warned of a hard struggle ahead. But top management of "Big Steel," its operators and financiers, upset the gloomy predictions.

One of the factors in the 1937 change, pre-

1. *NLRB* v. *Jones and Laughlin Steel Corp.*, 301 U.S. 1 (1937).

saging the economic developments of the next decade, was the governmental and international demand for munitions and defense supplies. At that time, orders came largely from friendly foreign countries, particularly England, which had suddenly realized its need to refurbish its armaments. The managers and bankers of U.S. Steel were impressed with the damage that would be done to mighty international interests by any interruption of production caused by domestic labor disputes. It was also impressed by the landslide victory of the New Deal election of November 1936, in which the leaders of the steelworkers' union and their associates in the CIO had played a big part. It was clear that most steelworkers had voted for the New Deal. Convinced that they would vote for the union and support it in any conflict with the corporation, U.S. Steel signed a truce with the United Steelworkers.

Little Steel, however, refused to follow this example. A strike was inevitable. The union turned its ample bargaining resources and onrushing energies to the task of enrolling Little Steel employees. The union was confident of success as workers joined by the hundreds. Indeed, the strike was premature; it was called before the union had enrolled a clear majority of employees in all of the plants of the affected employers. The union hoped that the excitement of a strike movement would close its ranks. And the strike had that immediate effect.

Federal Intervention

The Little Steel strike was the major labor dispute of 1937. The federal government intervened and tried to mediate. The President appointed a special emergency "fact-finding" board to investigate the dispute and issue public recommendations for its settlement. This board had no legal powers, and the employers refused to accept its advice that they deal with the union. Thereupon the leaders of the steelworkers, and their fellow officials in the CIO, asked the President to withdraw government orders from the struck plants and to denounce the corporations. The President refused, calling down a "plague on both your houses."

Other federal agencies entered the strike situation. The Senate Civil Liberties Committee was investigating the use of violence and spies by employers in industrial disputes; the National Labor Relations Board was investigating the charges of unfair labor practices filed by the union against the steel corporations. But the main resolution of the strike shifted to the plants. The employers moved to resume operations and attract their employees back to work. The picket lines braced themselves to form a barricade at plant gates. Violence lay ahead.

State and Local Authorities

The issue at this point was no longer one of collective bargaining, but whether the plants would stay shut, encircled by pickets, or whether they would reopen, the pickets forced aside by legal authorities. The union argued that the laws against breach of peace should not be invoked against the workers' right to bargain collectively, that the local authorities should not help the employers violate the employees' fundamental rights by opening a way into the plants in the name of law and order. But the local laws against breach of peace and disorderly conduct were legally distinct and separate from collective bargaining rights. The union could not legally maintain that no one could go in or out of the plants until the strike was settled.

The strikers nevertheless had several practical advantages: At many plants, they included the energetic and aggressive workers; they had numbers on their side; they exercised their strength by massing at the plant gates. Before nonstriking employees could return to work, the picket lines would have to be removed altogether or reduced to a handful of watchers. As long as the strikers had the support of a majority of the employees, their picket lines held firm, especially where the strikers were a part of a sympathetic industrial community. As a practical matter, local authorities tended to respect prevailing sentiment. In a Michigan town where the union was a small minority, its pickets were swept aside.

Strike Violence

Each side tried to prove that the other was responsible for violence. In Chicago the union staged a mass parade on Memorial Day and the police, becoming panicky, fired into a crowd fleeing from tear gas and killed ten persons. The union gained martyrs to strengthen its cause; the strike went on and violence continued.

The Senate Civil Liberties Committee aided the union by showing the suppressed movies of the Chicago Memorial Day riot. The Senate Post Office Committee called upon employers to testify to illegal blockades by the strikers, which even stopped mail truck deliveries. The employers had taken movies of that action. The entire community in each strike locality was drawn into the conflict. Back-to-work movements competed for support with union appeals for the end of industrial tyranny.

The Strike Crisis

Ohio became the decisive battleground. Most of the plants of the chief anti-union corporation, Republic Steel, were located in that state. It sued in the state court at Warren, Ohio, for an injunction to open its gates and curb pickets. The state judge, torn by the conflict, issued an injunction restraining both sides from committing acts of violence and specifically limiting the pickets to twelve at each main gate and two elsewhere. The county sheriff, however, could not enforce the court order, and the union was prepared to disobey it. The order could be enforced only by the National Guard, and such a mobilization was the governor's prerogative.

The governor of Ohio was set upon by both sides; the union asked him to preserve order by keeping the plants shut, while the employers insisted that law and order entitled them to protection for free movement of goods and persons in and out of their plants. The governor at last made up his mind and ordered troops into the strike areas. They were received by cheering strikers, who expected that the troops would keep the plants closed. They did at first, but the governor decided to enforce the injunction order and the troops cleared the way to the plants. The union had lost. In Youngstown, the Bessemers blew once more, lighting the sky like huge victory bonfires.

The strike was not over, but it had lost its immediate momentum. Its prematurity now became apparent as new members broke away and drifted back into the plants. Local authorities, sensing the change, turned upon the union, backed by the troops of the National Guard. Picket lines were strictly limited, and free movement in and out of the plants was restored. In a desperate effort to meet force with greater violence, a handful of strikers tried to dynamite a plant. But they were caught in the act, and the union was defenseless before the charge that it was the violent party. Picket lines were abolished, strikers arrested by the hundreds, and union offices padlocked.

The union brought suit in the federal district court at Columbus, Ohio, seeking an injunction against state, county and city authorities, alleging that troops, sheriffs and police had invaded the civil liberties of union members. As the injunction proceedings dragged on, the number of workmen returning to their jobs increased, the troops were withdrawn, and a few pickets maintained the strike without any threat of violence. The union dropped the lawsuit. With one company, Inland Steel, the union settled the strike on the employer's offer of a nonexclusive contract; with another, Youngstown Sheet and Tube, it called off the strike without receiving any concessions from the company; it remained on strike at Republic Steel, but the strike was maintained by a handful of men, living on relief from the union and from local and federal public assistance.

End of the Strike

The fall and winter of 1937–1938 were hard times for the union. Production and employment were dropping sharply. Republic Steel treated the strikers as discharged employees and refused to rehire men whose places had been filled during the strike until vacancies occurred. It refused re-employment altogether to strike leaders and to those whom it believed guilty of violence. In Ohio, more than five hundred strikers had been formally charged and indicted for various offenses, ranging from disorderly conduct to felonious assault. The local prosecutors pressed for convictions.

But the union was not dead. It kept its organization alive. In many plants, key departments of skilled workers were staffed by union members, and they required superintendents and foremen to deal with them in practice, regardless of top company policy. In these plants, union shop leaders and company supervisors had to get along with one another, and often liked and respected one another. In local communities, bitterness abated. The prosecutors convicted the dynamiters and settled the other cases, collecting small fines in half of them and dismissing the rest.

Repercussions of the Strike

NLRB Proceedings

The federal labor laws became important again. At the outset of the strike, the union had filed charges of unfair labor practices with the National Labor Relations Board. It did so, however, more to publicize its case against Little Steel than to secure legal relief, on the theory that time-consuming administrative proceedings and court review would postpone benefits that a successful strike would quickly yield. When the strike was lost and local courts decided against workers for acts of violence, the union turned to federal authorities, accusing employers of breach of collective bargaining rights.

The agents of the National Labor Relations Board took over the case against the employers and the legal proceedings resulted in a victory for the union. The test was made in the case against Republic Steel. The order of the Board vindicating the union was upheld by the federal Court of Appeals and the Supreme Court.[2]

Although the union could not prove that it had a majority at the time the strike was called, the evidence showed that the company had never intended to bargain with the union and had provoked the strike by a deliberate policy of interference with its employees' rights. It was held that the union's offer to sign an agreement patterned after the U.S. Steel contract was an offer of industrial peace and that the employers in rejecting it left the union with no alternative but to wage economic war. The steel corporations, pointing to the records of local criminal courts and prosecutors, argued that the union was guilty of violence, but the federal statute protecting the right to collective bargaining was held to be independent of state and local criminal law. Indeed, the employers' argument strengthened the justification for the statute because it emphasized the fact that violence and conflict might have been avoided if employers and unions entered into collective bargaining peace treaties.

The decision reflected the public desire for peaceful industrial relations. The court allowed employers to refuse to rehire any strikers who had committed serious felonies during the strike. All other strikers were entitled to be rehired when they applied for their former jobs. If refused reinstatement, they were to receive pay for the wages they would have earned had they been reinstated in their former positions without loss of seniority. The back-pay awards were substantial. In addition, the employers were directed to cease all forms of interference with the union.

Government Contracts

The union was climbing back to the highroad. Business and employment levels rose; government orders increased. Under the Public Contracts Act requiring government contractors to pay "prevailing wages in the locality" as determined by the Secretary of Labor, the union instituted proceedings aimed at Little Steel. The union maintained that the Pittsburgh area, which produced over 90 per cent of basic iron and steel, fixed the prevailing wage for the industry. Most of the Little Steel plants were outside the Pittsburgh area, and some of them paid lower wage rates than those prevailing in Pittsburgh. There were other geographical wage variations. Little Steel companies insisted upon geographical differentials and argued for the rates prevailing in small localities. The Secretary of Labor established a scheme of four areas that resulted in lifting the wage rates paid on government contract work in a number of plants. Since a plant could not maintain separate wage rates for government contract work alone, these rates became the common scale. The proceedings thus brought about a wage increase for which the union could claim credit. The Little Steel corporations sued in federal court to set aside the Secretary of Labor's findings on the ground that the wage order abused the meaning of "locality," but the Supreme Court held that the terms and conditions under which the government let its contracts were none of the court's business.[3]

Resurgence of the Union

The United Steelworkers, now fully recovered from the shock and costs of the 1937 failures, accelerated its organizing campaign in Little Steel plants. It sent in crews of trained organizers, distributed leaflets and called meetings. It took full advantage of Supreme Court decisions protecting the exercise of civil liberties in everyday affairs. Protected by Labor Board decisions, union members in a plant, however small in number, took the offensive, seized upon grievances, passed out union buttons, and enrolled majorities in plant after plant.

By 1941, defense orders were mounting, the steel industry was at boom levels of production and could not possibly afford work stoppages. Employers accepted the legal rules and procedures of the federal labor relations law. Union majorities were duly certified by the National Labor Relations Board and the corporations signed agreements with the union, modeled after the current U.S. Steel contract. By this time, the union was recognized as the exclusive bargaining agent. A few companies held out until after Pearl Harbor, but the pattern was established, and in 1951 only one major steel producer had not signed a contract with the United Steelworkers.

Wartime Events

During the war years, labor relations were strictly governed. The federal government made extensive use of its moral and legal powers. The United Steelworkers, along with the rest of organized labor, agreed that it would not strike during the national emergency.

Since strikes and lockouts were forgone, a tribunal for the settlement of disputes was necessary. The President established the War

2. *Republic Steel Corp.* v. *NLRB,* 107 Fed. 2*d* 472, affirmed without review, 311 U.S. 7 (1940).

3. *Perkins* v. *Lukens Steel Co.,* 310 U.S. 113 (1940).

Labor Board by executive order. The War Labor Board provided unions with security through maintenance-of-membership arrangements under which workers were free to join or not to join a union but upon joining were bound to remain in good standing for the duration of the collective agreement. Wage increases were controlled and had to be approved by the War Labor Board. The formula regulating general wage increases in all employment was called the Little Steel Formula because it was reached in proceedings for a wage adjustment brought by the United Steelworkers for its members in the plants struck four years earlier.

During the war, the federal Fair Labor Standards Act (popularly called the Wage-Hour Act) had a special effect on wages. It fixed a standard work week of 40 hours, and required payment at the rate of one and a half times the "regular rate" for overtime work, that is, work in excess of 40 hours. The standard work week fixed by the Wage-Hour Act was originally intended to discourage overtime and thus spread work. During the war, national defense production required 48-hour operations. The government stipulated the longer work week in all contracts, and the result was a substantial automatic wage increase.

Postwar Events

In 1946, when the no-strike pledge was terminated and wage controls were lifted, the United Steelworkers went on strike for a wage increase. To impress the country with its fear that wage cuts would accompany the end of war production, the union called out all its members in basic steel plants and steel-fabricating plants as well; 750,000 persons ceased work. All but a few small employers made no attempt to operate their plants. There were no physical disorders; pickets were hardly needed. At some plants, managers supplied the pickets with hot coffee and doughnuts.

Although wage controls had been lifted, price controls were still in force, so that some measure of control over wage increases was still necessary. As a substitute for the War Labor Board, the President appointed emergency fact-finding boards, which had no power to end or halt strikes. The steel strike was settled by direct presidential mediation. The workers won a wage increase, and steel prices were raised.

In the second round of postwar wage increases, in 1947, steelworkers won another wage increase. Price controls had been lifted by this time; the industry raised its prices again. This time the United Steelworkers agreed to a two-year contract.

The United Steelworkers was not the only union that called strikes to win postwar wage adjustments. Great industry-wide strikes swept over the country in successive waves. Collective bargaining did not ensure industrial peace. The unions had grown under the protection of laws promoting collective bargaining. The steelworkers' union was now a powerful, established organization. It did not have the material resources of the major steel corporations, but it was the equal of many firms and could exercise superior pressure upon small producers, many of whom it forced to accept the pattern of its postwar wage increases without regard to their particular situation.

New Legislation

In the 1946 elections, the Democratic Party, favored by union leaders and members, lost heavily. A new majority now controlled congressional committees. They investigated labor union power as, in 1935, congressional committees had investigated employer power. Like the employers then, the union leaders insisted that no new legislation was needed, that there were no abuses that laws could correct. But prevailing political sentiment sought a new legal formula for industrial peace and a curb on union power.

The Taft-Hartley Act was passed over presidential veto in June 1947, amending the National Labor Relations Act in several respects. It restricts the requirement of union membership as a condition of employment and forbids jurisdictional strikes and secondary boycotts. The act has also established a statutory scheme of emergency fact-finding boards, supported by presidential authority, to secure sixty-day injunctions against strikes affecting the national health and welfare. It further requires union officers to submit affidavits affirming that they do not advocate the overthrow of the government by force or violence.

The new statute has had little effect on the United Steelworkers. As a token of their political opposition to the law, officers of the union at first refused to sign the required affidavits, for the period of its two-year agreements executed just before the law was passed. It complied in time to secure NLRB approval for the renewal of its union security agreements.

The steelworkers' union was affected by one provision of the Taft-Hartley Act. The law stipulates that collective agreements shall be legally enforceable and confers upon the federal district courts jurisdiction over suits for breach of these agreements. In 1948 the United Steelworkers was refused a wage increase at the current round of wage increases. It was bound by a two-year contract and could not strike without risking heavy damage suits under the new federal labor relations law. But other industries granted wage increases, and Big Steel yielded to the force of imitation and granted equivalent wage increases. This time, Little Steel, too, agreed to the pattern. In 1937, the law formed and enforced a pattern; in 1947, institutions established by law had their own momentum, even after the original law was changed to brake the movement it had favored.

In 1951, the union had won the endorsement of employers in the industry in elections to validate its union-shop contracts. Its affairs were being administered by experienced officers and plant committeemen. It confidently faced the prospect of negotiating wage increases and other improvements in working conditions under wage-price controls.

Appendix Note 3 (Chapter 15)

LOCAL EMPLOYMENT OFFICE PROCEDURES AND TESTS

Collis Stocking

To deal expeditiously with the vast number of job-seekers and employers, the local offices of the U.S. Employment Service follow uniform and objective methods and procedures. The completed application card and individual aptitude profile card reproduced in Figures 1 and 2 illustrate, step by step, how the local employment office deals with an individual applicant.

The applicant is asked to fill in the personal information — name, address, date of birth, and so on (Figure 1, page 1) — and to record his important civilian and military experience and training (Figure 1, page 2). The interviewer discusses the applicant's experience and training with him and makes note of any information that may be helpful in assisting him in finding suitable work. If the applicant is occupationally "set," that is, if he seems qualified by experience and some skill in an occupation, he will be immediately classified for referral to an employer on a suitable job. If the interview reveals that the applicant is occupationally unadjusted or has some work impediment, he will be introduced to a specialist in employment counseling. The counselor encourages him to discuss his aptitudes and ambitions, defines his employment problem, and helps him to develop a vocational plan. (See right half of page 4.)

Employers' job orders are recorded systematically and checked against the file of applicants to locate the best-qualified workers for a particular job opening. The applicants who have been selected are asked to call at the local employment office for referral to the job. On reporting, they are interviewed briefly concerning the job and receive an introduction card to the employer. The employer is requested to mail to the employment office a card attached to the introduction card indicating whether or not the applicant was hired and, if so, when he started work.

An Illustrative Case

The application card reproduced in Figure 1 shows the steps taken to register, test, classify, counsel and place on a suitable job a veteran who was not occupationally adjusted. Gregory Prince quit high school after two years because he stammered; he served three years in the Army and was now having trouble keeping a beginning trade job. The interviewer referred him to the counselor.

General aptitude tests showed that Prince was about normal in ability, with perhaps some superiority in form perception and finger dexterity. (Figure 2 and lower right section of page 1, Figure 1.) After the counselor helped him analyze his problem and develop a vocational plan (right half of page 4, Figure 1), the employment office's employer relations representative was asked to seek a job for him with a local utility that had a program for training gas meter repairmen. Prince was immediately referred to the local Vocational Rehabilitation office, which accepted him for corrective speech training. (Figure 1, page 3.) At the same time his problems were discussed with the utility company to be sure he would receive special consideration and training, and the company then hired him as an installer-helper. (Figure 1, page 3.)

Use of Tests

The interviewer may use oral trade questions to make sure that an applicant is not occupationally misclassified. These questions are few and carefully worded, developed out of experience in the trade to bring out knowledge of specific occupations and thus indicate the applicant's skills. The Employment Service so far has developed oral trade questions covering only some 240 occupations.

In the stenographic field, performance tests have been devised to measure skills in the use of the typewriter, taking dictation, spelling and other stenographic duties. The applicant performs the actual tasks through work sample exercises. These tests are used to measure the skills of both those who have had only training and those who have had experience as well.

For applicants who have selected a field of special interest but have had little or no work experience, the specific aptitude test battery is used. Test batteries are available for a wide range of occupations: adding machine operator, bus driver, chassis assembler, draftsman, electrical repairman, file clerk, gear inspector, hand worker, machine shop inspector, key punch operator, motorman, power presser, radio mechanic, stock clerk, watchmaker and so on.

FIGURE 1. UNITED STATES EMPLOYMENT SERVICE APPLICATION CARD (FACSIMILE)

Page 1

A B C D E F G H(60) I J 1 2 3 4 5 6 7 8 9

DO NOT WRITE BELOW THIS LINE

1. PRINT LAST NAME: Prince — FIRST: Gregory — MIDDLE:

5. SOCIAL SEC. NO.: 423 04 4212

2. NUMBER AND STREET ADDRESS, R. D. OR P. O. BOX NO.: 4216 Evergreen Avenue

4. TELEPHONE NO.:

3. CITY: Detroit — POSTAL ZONE: 7 — STATE: Michigan

6. DATE OF BIRTH: 7 15 25 (MO.) (DAY) (YEAR)

7. ☐ MARRIED ☐ DIVORCED ☒ SINGLE ☐ SEPARATED ☐ WIDOWED

8. HEIGHT: 5 10 (FT.) (IN.)

9. WEIGHT: 145 (POUNDS)

10. ☒ WHITE ☐ NEGRO ☐ OTHER

11. IF VETERAN, ENTER YOUR LAST MILITARY SERVICE

ENTRY ON ACTIVE SERVICE: Sept. 1943 (MO.) (DAY) (YEAR) — RELEASE FROM ACTIVE SERVICE: Aug. 23 1946 (MO.) (DAY) (YEAR) — SERIAL NO.: 42042124

12. IF NEEDED FOR WORK, DO YOU HAVE — TOOLS ☐ YES ☐ NO — AUTOMOBILE ☐ YES ☐ NO — LICENSE ☐ YES ☐ NO — TRUCK ☐ YES ☐ NO

13. IF UNION MEMBER, GIVE NUMBER, NAME AND AFFILIATION OF LOCAL

14. CIRCLE HIGHEST YEAR OF EDUCATION COMPLETED AND GIVE DEGREES RECEIVED

GRADE SCHOOL 1 2 3 4 5 6 7 8 — HIGH SCHOOL 1 (2) 3 4 — COLLEGE 1 2 3 4 5 6 7 — DEGREES

NAME SCHOOL AND LIST COURSES OR TRAINING (INCLUDING MILITARY) WHICH PREPARED YOU FOR WORK. GIVE LENGTH AND DATES ENDED.

Polk H.S. - Acad. Course - 2 yrs., June 1941
"B" Average - quit embarrassment speech impediment & need to learn. No subject particularly liked but "studies hard" particularly math.
AGF - Infantry Basic only
12/10/47 - Attending speech clinic some evenings

TURN TO INSIDE OF CARD

TITLES	CODES
Mech. or Metal Unit Assembler (including instrument repair)	4-X6.310
Floor Assembler Helper	9-65.64
Laborer (Uncrater)	9-65.45

SKILLS, KNOWLEDGE, ABILITIES	DATES
	11/2/47
	12/3/47

TEST RESULTS

12/3/47- B-1001, 14, 15, 16, 18, 20
G-V-N-S-P-Q-A-T-F-M
96-89-83-98-105-99-95-98-104-97

WILLING TO LEAVE CITY ☒ YES ☐ NO
WILLING TO LIVE AT WORK ☐ YES ☒ NO

USES-511 (9-46) — APPLICATION CARD — 16—54589-1 — DEPARTMENT OF LABOR UNITED STATES EMPLOYMENT SERVICE

Page 2 (Inside)

IMPORTANT CIVILIAN AND MILITARY EXPERIENCE

DESCRIBE YOUR LONGEST AND MOST IMPORTANT JOBS. BEGIN WITH YOUR MOST RECENT JOB

15. NAME EMPLOYER OR BRANCH OF MILITARY SERVICE: Edgewood Fabrication Co.
16. ADDRESS: 2132 - 30
17. EMPLOYER'S BUSINESS: Machine Shop
18. LENGTH OF JOB: 2 mos. — DATE ENDED: 10/47 — PAY: $140. mo.

19. NAME JOB AND DESCRIBE EXACTLY WHAT YOU DID AND HOW YOU DID IT: Helper - Assisted Floor Assembler in assembling varied machine products. Bucked-up riveting, did rough filing. (Enjoyed work but journeyman "didn't want to keep him.")

20. NAME EMPLOYER OR BRANCH OF MILITARY SERVICE: Navy Yard
21. ADDRESS:
22. EMPLOYER'S BUSINESS:
23. LENGTH OF JOB: 6 mos. — DATE ENDED: 3/47 — PAY: $165. mo.

24. NAME JOB AND DESCRIBE EXACTLY WHAT YOU DID AND HOW YOU DID IT: Laborer - Uncrated machinery using claw hammer and pinch bar. Assembled some parts of machinery by fastening bolts and screws. (L.O. reduction in force)

25. NAME EMPLOYER OR BRANCH OF MILITARY SERVICE: U. S. Army
26. ADDRESS:
27. EMPLOYER'S BUSINESS:
28. LENGTH OF JOB: 3 years — DATE ENDED: August '46 — PAY: --

29. NAME JOB AND DESCRIBE EXACTLY WHAT YOU DID AND HOW YOU DID IT: Rifleman - Heavy machine-gunner - in heavy weapons co.

30. NAME EMPLOYER OR BRANCH OF MILITARY SERVICE:
31. ADDRESS:
32. EMPLOYER'S BUSINESS:
33. LENGTH OF JOB: — DATE ENDED: — PAY:

34. NAME JOB AND DESCRIBE EXACTLY WHAT YOU DID AND HOW YOU DID IT:

35. NAME EMPLOYER OR BRANCH OF MILITARY SERVICE:
36. ADDRESS:
37. EMPLOYER'S BUSINESS:
38. LENGTH OF JOB: — DATE ENDED: — PAY:

39. NAME JOB AND DESCRIBE EXACTLY WHAT YOU DID AND HOW YOU DID IT:

FIGURE 1—*Continued*

Page 3 (Inside)

DO NOT WRITE BELOW THIS LINE

SUMMARY OF OTHER WORK EXPERIENCE Shoe-shine boy, pin-boy during school years

Carpenter's helper on construction job - inapt "not mechanically inclined" 3 weeks, 1947.

CALLED	REFERRED	EMPLOYER OR AGENCY	JOB TITLE OR PURPOSE	DUR.	PAY	RESULTS	REMARKS
	12/6/47	Vocat. Rehab.	Speech Training				Accepted
12/9MS	12/10/47	Detroit Gas & Elec.	Installer-Helper	R	$145 mo.	H	Employed

U. S. GOVERNMENT PRINTING OFFICE 16—54589-1

Page 4

DO NOT WRITE BELOW THIS LINE

SPECIAL INFORMATION Widowed mother, 7 children, money difficulties, family relations strained by his poor-earning ability.

Stammering of long duration began in elementary school. Worse since release from Army. Prefers to work alone. Likes mechanics but does not think himself mechanically inclined.

LEISURE-TIME ACTIVITIES Photography, has helped friend develop films.

EMPLOYMENT COUNSELING STATEMENT Problem: Applicant with speech defect, has worked mainly on elemental labor jobs, has lost several beginning trade jobs, although school record indicates higher level of abilities. Is work history a reflection of capacities or speech difficulty? Are mechanical interests supported by aptitude?

Plan: Seek employment in assembly & repair of small units, e.g. instruments (OAP-14). Of 5 OAP's, OAP-14 is highest aptitude level. Further field of work is Gas-Meter Repairman. ERR to solicit employer for entry job as repairman-trainee or installer-helper. Counselor attempt to instil confidence by discussing with applicant attractive jobs. Refer for speech retraining. 12/6/47. LHR

COMMENTS Rather tense, ill at ease. Should work alone or with one individual who is patient and sympathetic to speech defect until gains confidence.

INTERVIEWER L. H. Roberts

FIGURE 2. UNITED STATES EMPLOYMENT SERVICE APTITUDE TEST CARD (FACSIMILE)

COMMENTS: ____________________

Date 12/3/47 **INDIVIDUAL APTITUDE PROFILE** B- 1001

Part	Raw Score	G	V	N	S	P	Q	A	T	F	M
A	22					56					
B	70						99				
C	42							32			
D	17			63							
E	--										
F	29				57						
G	133								71		
H	16	13			41						
I	9	27		20							
J	16	56	89								
K	70							63	27		
L	29					49					
M	87										12
N	100										85
O	26									35	
P	33									69	
Aptitude Score		96	89	83	98	105	99	95	98	104	97

OCCUPATIONAL APTITUDE PATTERNS

0	1	2
3	4	5
6	7	8
9	10	11
12	13	**(14)**
(15)	**(16)**	17
(18)	19	**(20)**
21	22	23
24	25	26
27	28	29
30	31	32
33	34	35
36	37	38

16—51492-1 GPO

For applicants with no experience or no clear notion of which field of work they should enter, the general aptitude test battery is used. The Employment Service has determined minimum scores for twenty fields of work, representing approximately fifteen hundred occupations. The purpose of the test is to appraise ten aptitudes important for different types of jobs, coded as follows: G — intelligence, V — verbal ability, N — numerical ability, S — spatial ability, P — form perception, Q — clerical perception, A — aiming, T — motor speed, F — finger dexterity, and M — manual dexterity. (See Figure 2.)

There are fifteen tests in the battery, the raw scores for which are shown in the column on the left side of the Individual Aptitude Profile card. (Figure 2.) After the raw scores are converted into part scores for the ten aptitudes, the parts are added to give the total score for each aptitude. More than one test is required to measure most of the aptitudes. Prince scored 83 in numerical ability, 105 in form perception. These scores are recorded on his application card. (See right part of page 1, Figure 1.)

On the right side of the Individual Aptitude Profile card, five "occupational aptitude patterns" have been encircled. These represent fields of work in which Prince met the minimum-score requirements. Pattern 14, one of those in which Prince qualified, includes the following aptitudes: spatial ability, form perception, aiming (or eye-hand coordination) and finger dexterity. Occupations in the following fields involve this pattern of aptitudes: electrical unit assembling, mechanical or metal unit assembling (including instrument repair), and optical assembling. The counselor thus determines the fields of work in which Prince has the greatest chance of succeeding. Because of his deficiency in numerical aptitude, it would have been a mistake to refer him to work involving accounting, engineering, or clerical computing or recording.

The vocational plan developed for the applicant on the basis of test results and information concerning his experience and interest is indicated on the application card.

Appendix Note 4 (Chapter 18)

SUMMARY DESCRIPTION OF THE LARGEST LABOR UNIONS IN THE UNITED STATES[1]

Thomas C. Fichandler

A. *Largest Unions Affiliated with the AFL*

1. *International Brotherhood of Teamsters, Chauffeurs, Warehousemen and Helpers of America:* 1,103,000 members in 896 locals in the United States and Canada. Earliest branch organized in 1899 as the Team Drivers International Union. Trade jurisdiction includes teamsters, chauffeurs and helpers, stablemen; all who are employed on horses, harnesses, carriages or automobiles in and around stables or garages (other than mechanics); warehousemen; all classes of dairy employees, inside and outside; workers employed in ice cream plants; all other workers employed in the manufacture and distribution of milk and cheese and dairy products; all truck terminal employees. Collective agreements require the approval of the General President and the General Executive Board and wage provisions require the approval of the joint council concerned. Affiliated with the Building and Construction Trades Department. Organized along craft lines and along semi-industrial lines; some locals include only drivers, while in the dairy industry locals cover most of the inside workers and the deliverymen.

2. *United Brotherhood of Carpenters and Joiners of America:* 735,000 members in 2,786 locals in the United States and possessions, Panama, Mexico, Canada and Newfoundland. Earliest branch organized in 1881. Trade jurisdiction includes the milling, fashioning, joining, assembling, erecting, fastening or dismantling of all material of wood, hollow metal or fiber, or of products composed in part of wood, hollow metal or fiber; the laying of all cork and compo, all shingles; the erecting and dismantling of machinery and the manufacturing of all wood materials where the skill, knowledge and training of a carpenter are required, either through the operation of machine or hand tools. Includes carpenters and joiners; railroad carpenters; bench hands; stair builders; millwrights; furniture workers; shipwrights and boat builders; reed and rattan workers; ship carpenters, joiners and caulkers; cabinetmakers; boxmakers; bridge, dock and wharf carpenters; car builders; floor layers, underpinners and timbermen; pile drivers; shorers and house movers; loggers; lumber and sawmill workers; and all those engaged in the running of woodworking machinery or engaged as helpers to any of the above divisions or subdivisions or in the handling of material on any of the above divisions or subdivisions. Collective agreements are negotiated by the district council, or the local where no council exists, provided that trade demands must be approved by 55 per cent of the members affected; the General Executive Board has power to make agreements with employers that conform with the trade rules of the district. Affiliated with the Building and Construction Trades Department. Organized primarily along craft lines (in building construction) but also along industrial lines in logging and in furniture plants. Treasury had about $12 million in 1948.

3. *International Brotherhood of Electrical Workers:* 450,000 members in 1,493 locals in the United States and Canada. Organized in 1891. Trade jurisdiction includes the manufacture, assembling, construction, installation or erection, repair or maintenance of all materials, equipment, apparatus and appliances required in the production of electricity and its effects; the operation, inspection and supervision of primary electrical equipment, apparatus appliances or devices by which electricity is generated, utilized and controlled. Includes outside and inside electrical workers; voice, sound, vision, transmission and transference electrical workers; railroad and pullman electrical workers. Affiliated with Building and Construction Trades Department, Metal Trades Department and Railway Employees' Department. Organized primarily along craft lines (in outside construction work) but frequently along industrial lines in plants manufacturing electrical products and equipment.

4. *Hotel and Restaurant Employees and Bartenders International Union:* 400,000 members

1. Based largely on the descriptions in Florence Peterson, *Handbook of Labor Unions,* American Council on Public Affairs, Washington, 1944. Data on size of membership and number of locals from *Directory of Labor Unions in the United States, 1950,* Bulletin No. 980, Bureau of Labor Statistics, 1950. Data on wealth of internationals taken from tabulation of union leaders' replies to questionnaire appearing in *Life,* May 31, 1948, pp. 80–81.

in 700 locals in the United States and Canada. Organized and chartered in 1890 by amalgamation of several federal labor unions. Trade jurisdiction includes all persons employed in hotels, apartment hotels, clubs, restaurants, cafeterias, taverns, railroad dining and buffet cars, steamships, and other establishments engaged in similar capacities in the preparing and serving of food and beverages and in rendering service to the public. Collective agreements must be approved by the local joint executive board. Organized primarily along craft lines. Treasury had about $4 million in 1948.

5. *International Ladies' Garment Workers' Union:* 423,000 members in 489 locals in the United States and Canada. Organized in 1900. Trade jurisdiction includes all branches of the ladies' garment industry such as cloaks, suits, skirts, dresses, waists, wrappers, corsets, underwear, articles of children's wear, bathrobes, etc., and all work and processes connected with the production of such garments. Collective agreements are made by joint boards, district councils, local unions, or by the General Executive Board, depending on circumstances. Organized along industrial lines although some locals represent single crafts. Treasury had about $8.5 million in 1948.

6. *Brotherhood of Railway and Steamship Clerks, Freight Handlers, Express and Station Employes:* 350,000 members in 1,828 locals in the United States, Canada, Mexico and Newfoundland. Oldest branch organized in 1848. Trade jurisdiction includes clerks or other office employees, freight handlers, ticket sellers, baggagemen or other station employees, storehouse or storeroom employees, and express employees in the service of railroad, steamship, airline, express or other transportation companies. Collective agreements are negotiated by boards of adjustment in their respective jurisdictions. Organized along craft lines.

B. *Largest Unions Affiliated with the CIO*

1. *United Steelworkers of America:* 961,000 members in 2,000 locals in the United States and Canada. Organized by the CIO in 1936. Trade jurisdiction includes iron and steel manufacturing, processing and fabricating mills and factories. Collective agreements must be signed by the international officers, and the international union must be a party to all such agreements. Organized as an industrial union. Treasury had about $5 million in 1948.

2. *International Union of United Automobile, Aircraft and Agricultural Implement Workers of America:* 948,000 members in 1,031 locals in the United States and Canada. Organized originally as an AFL national council in 1934. Trade jurisdiction includes manufacture of parts (including tools, dies, etc.) and the assembly of these parts into farm, automobile, automotive, propelled products, aircraft and agricultural implements, including work of employees engaged in office work, sales, distribution and maintenance thereof, and such other branches of industry as the international executive board shall decide in accordance with the jurisdiction committee of the Congress of Industrial Organizations. Collective agreements require the approval of local members, the regional director and the international executive board. Organized as an industrial union covering several industries. Treasury had about $2 million in 1948.

3. *Amalgamated Clothing Workers of America:* 375,000 members in 572 locals in the United States and Canada. Oldest branch organized in 1914. Trade jurisdiction includes "workers employed in the trades and industries or branches thereof now within its jurisdiction and in such other trades and industries or branches thereof as the General Executive Board may from time to time designate." [2] Collective agreements are negotiated by union officials subject to ratification by the workers affected. Organized primarily along industrial lines. Treasury had about $6 million in 1948.

4. *Textile Workers Union of America:* 374,000 members in 752 locals in the United States, its territories and Canada. Oldest branch organized in 1901. Trade jurisdiction includes all workers employed in or about places of business engaged in processing by hand or machine, including dyeing, bleaching, printing and finishing of cotton, wool, silk, flax, jute, paper, and any other natural or synthetic materials in their original or altered state, to produce or manufacture batts, felts, yarns, cordage, threads, fabrics or other forms into textile or allied products, including but not limited to hosiery, knit goods, lace carpets, cordage, fabricated textile products and by-products of synthetic materials manufactured by textile or independent plants. Collective agreements are subject to the approval of the chairman of the executive council or the General President, and negotiations are subject to his supervision. Organized as an industrial union. Treasury had about $1.7 million in 1948.

5. *Communications Workers of America:* 240,000 members in 900 locals in the United States and Canada. Present organization traceable back to 1939, when National Federation

2. Union's constitution as quoted in Peterson, *Handbook of Trade Unions,* p. 88.

of Telephone Workers was organized as an independent union. Trade jurisdiction includes all communications workers, but actual membership is now limited to telephone workers (manufacturing and operating). Collective agreements are negotiated by the locals but must have the approval of the international executive board before being executed. Organized as an industrial union.

6. *United Rubber, Cork, Linoleum and Plastic Workers of America:* 150,000 members in 255 locals in the United States and Canada. Organized in 1935. Trade jurisdiction includes the rubber, plastic, linoleum and allied products industries. Collective agreements are negotiated by the locals, but in company-wide negotiations a tripartite agreement is used — between the company, the locals concerned and the international. Organized as an industrial union covering allied industries. Treasury had about $600,000 in 1948.

C. *Largest Independent Unions*

1. *Railroad Unions.* The railroad unions are the most important homogeneous group of independents. The "Big Four" railroad brotherhoods (Railroad Trainmen; Locomotive Firemen and Enginemen; Locomotive Engineers; Railway Conductors) were organized during or shortly after the Civil War and today account for about 430,000 members, representing by far the greater part of the total membership of the independent railroad unions. The independent railroad unions have maintained harmonious relations with both federations but have remained independent, largely because they felt their common interests would be submerged in a broader federation. The railroad unions have been singularly successful in winning favorable legislation: they won collective bargaining rights in the Railway Labor Act of 1926 for which other unions had to wait until 1935 and have social security legislation far more advanced than that for other workers.

The railroad unions are organized primarily on craft lines and therefore have found it necessary to cooperate closely in dealing with the industry. Besides cooperating on particular issues, the railroad unions have a formal mechanism for joint action, the Railway Labor Executives Association. This body, formed in 1926 to take advantage of the privileges of the Railway Labor Act, is a voluntary association of the chief executives of interested unions. In 1950 it had 21 members, including most of the AFL railroad unions, four independent unions and three maritime unions, one of which was the CIO Marine Engineers' Beneficial Association. Two of the "Big Four" brotherhoods (Railroad Trainmen and Locomotive Engineers) were not members.

2. *International Association of Machinists.* The largest independent union is a former AFL affiliate — the International Association of Machinists. The IAM, which traces its organization back to 1889, now has 582,000 members in 1,734 locals in the United States, its territories and possessions, Newfoundland and Canada. It is organized primarily along craft lines, and its constitution takes almost 2,000 words to describe the organization's trade jurisdiction. The IAM's quarrel with the AFL was over jurisdictional questions.[3] Negotiations for reaffiliation have failed, but as of mid-1950 the Machinists were considering reaffiliation.

3. *United Mine Workers of America.* The second largest independent union is the United Mine Workers of America, formerly affiliated with the AFL, then with the CIO, and again with the AFL until 1948. President John L. Lewis then notified AFL President William Green that "We disaffiliate." Organization of mine workers began in 1890 and the union now claims 600,000 members. It is organized as an industrial union with jurisdiction over all workers employed in and around coal mines, coal washeries, coal-processing plants, coke ovens, and in such other industries as may be designated and approved by the international executive board. In addition, through its catch-all District 50, the union has attempted to organize wherever opportunities presented themselves — among dairy farmers, railroad men, construction workers and elsewhere. The indiscriminate organizing of District 50 brought sharp jurisdictional squabbles with a number of AFL international unions.[4] The union, which was severely rocked by the 1929–1932 depression, is now one of the wealthiest in the country, with a treasury of approximately $50 million in 1948.

3. The IAM broke with the AFL in May 1943 over a jurisdictional dispute with the carpenters' union over who should represent workers in plants making wooden airplanes. See S. T. Williamson and Herbert Harris, *Trends in Collective Bargaining,* Twentieth Century Fund, New York, 1945, p. 19.

4. See *Report of the Proceedings of the Sixty-sixth Convention,* American Federation of Labor, Washington, 1947, pp. 567 ff.

Appendix Note 5 (Chapter 20)

RECENT TRENDS IN UNION AGREEMENTS: TWO CASE STUDIES

Thomas C. Fichandler

The trends in content and the elaboration of wage clauses in union agreements in the past ten or fifteen years are illustrated in the following pages by case studies of two contracts — one in the Appalachian bituminous coal industry, the other in the woolen industry. These contracts reveal the basic trends in collective contracts in this country although they are not exactly typical in detail of the development of all agreements. To a certain extent, the two series of agreements reviewed here give a more dynamic picture than contracts in other industries. In the past decade, the miners and the textile workers had first to catch up with advances made by other groups of workers. The well-organized crafts, for example, were able to obtain contract provisions for overtime and shift-premium pay long before the miners or the textile workers. On the other hand, the mine and textile contracts include features such as health and welfare benefits that are still relatively rare, though the trend toward the inclusion of such plans in collective agreements is unmistakable.

Bituminous Appalachian Agreement[1]

The agreement between the United Mine Workers and the bituminous mine operators that expired on June 30, 1949, covering the Appalachian area, included pay for overtime, travel time, holiday work and vacations, and provided for health and welfare programs. None of these subjects were mentioned in the 1933 contract.

The contract expiring in 1949 provided time-and-a-half rates for hours in excess of the regular work day or work week and for the sixth consecutive day of work, and double time for work on the seventh consecutive day. For inside day workers and inside tonnage- and piece-rate workers, the regular day was set at 8 hours and the regular week at 40 hours; for outside day workers, overtime started after a 7¼-hour day or a 36¼-hour week.

In 1933, when the first Appalachian agreement was concluded, it had no provision for overtime premium pay. When overtime premium rates were first provided in 1937, they covered only day workers; they were not extended to tonnage- and piece-rate workers until January 1943. Double-time pay for the seventh consecutive day of work was first provided in November of the same year. As with overtime work, the 1933 contract had no provision for premium pay for work on the second and third shifts. The 1945 contract, however, initiated payment of an additional 4 cents an hour for work on the second shift and 6 cents an hour for third-shift work.

In 1949 the time it took inside workers to get from outside the mine to their place of work was considered as regular working time and paid for accordingly. Such travel time was not compensated in 1933 and was first recognized in the contract signed in 1943. Time for lunch, which was also considered as regular working time under the contract expiring in 1949, was not paid for under the 1933 contract. When lunch time was first considered as regular working time in the 1945 contract, a quarter of an hour was recognized. This period was paid for at the regular hourly rate and was counted as part of the basic work day in determining when overtime began. The recognized lunch time was increased to a half hour in the 1947 contract.

Although some holidays were observed in the 1933 contract, there was no provision covering work performed on such days. Starting in 1943, however, the contracts provided for pay at time and a half for holiday work.

Paid vacations were not introduced into the contract until 1941, when employees with at least one year of service were granted a 10-day vacation and paid $20. By 1946 the amount of vacation pay had been raised to $100 and workers with less than a year's service received a prorated amount.

The most spectacular change in the bituminous coal agreement was the inclusion in 1946 of provisions for a welfare and retirement fund and a medical and hospital fund. The 1933 contract carried no provision for health and welfare benefits, but with the institution of these two funds the bituminous miners and their dependents or survivors acquired perhaps the

1. The discussion of this agreement is based on "Changes in Wages and Related Wage Practices Affecting Workers in Bituminous Coal Mines in the Appalachian Area, 1933 to 1948," *Monthly Labor Review,* March 1949, pp. 303–07.

most comprehensive protection of any industrial group in the United States against sickness, disability, death and retirement and for related purposes. The medical and hospital fund, which in 1947 was combined with the welfare and retirement fund, is financed from wage deductions. The welfare and retirement fund, however, is financed through operators' contributions. Originally these contributions were at the rate of 5 cents for each ton of coal produced for sale, but the contract expiring on June 30, 1949 called for a 20 cent contribution.

These supplemental wage provisions were not instituted at the expense of the bituminous miners' basic wage rates. On the contrary, between 1933 and 1944, straight-time hourly earnings provided in the contracts rose between 200 and 300 per cent, bringing miners from one of the lowest-paid to one of the best-paid industrial groups. The 1933 contract provided a straight-time hourly rate of $.595 for motormen, rock drillers and operators of rubber-tired shuttle cars — a relatively high-paid group of mine workers; their hourly rate of pay had risen to $1.78 in the contract expiring in 1949. A relatively low-paid group of mine workers — sand dryers, car cleaners and other able-bodied labor — received an even greater increase, from an hourly rate of $.450 in 1933 to $1.756 in 1949. Increases for tonnage- and piece-rate workers matched the increases for workers paid on a time-rate basis.

American Woolen Company Agreement [2]

The first written agreement between the American Woolen Company and the Textile Workers Union of America (CIO) was put into effect on February 1, 1939. The agreement signed in 1948 was in effect until February 1, 1950, subject to a six-month periodic reopening of the wage issue. The 1948–1950 agreement covered approximately 21,000 workers in 21 mills in 9 states.

The changes in wage and other clauses in this series of agreements have followed the same trend as in the bituminous coal agreements. These changes, however, have not been so sharp as in the coal agreements, primarily because the first agreement between the American Woolen Company and the Textile Workers was not signed until 1939, after the entire economy and organized labor had advanced considerably from the low point in 1933.

The 1939 American Woolen contract provided for premium pay for overtime and holiday work, but included no provision for pay for holidays not worked, for shift premiums, paid vacations, reporting time, down time, or health and welfare benefits. By 1948 all these were covered and the original provisions for overtime and holiday work were liberalized. As in the coal agreements, these changes were accompanied by a steady increase in the textile workers' basic wage rates.

The 1939 overtime provisions covered all production workers and certain specified classifications of nonproduction employees. The premium rate of time and a half was payable to all workers covered by the overtime provisions for Sunday work, to production workers for work in excess of 8 hours a day or 40 hours a week, and to specified nonproduction employees for work beyond 44 hours a week. The 1948 contract covered all employees without distinction and provided time and a half for work in excess of 8 hours a day or 40 hours a week and for work on Saturday, and double time for Sunday work.

The original agreement provided time and a half for work performed on seven specified holidays but no pay for holidays on which no work was done. The contract that went into effect in 1948 recognized the principle of paid holidays for the first time and established six holidays for which all workers were to receive their regular rate of pay. Work on these six paid holidays was compensated at time and a half in addition to the regular holiday pay; work on two nonpaid holidays was paid at time and a half.

Premium pay for work on late shifts was introduced in 1943, when the contract allowed 7 cents an hour for work on the third shift. The National War Labor Board awards in 1945 added a 4 cent allowance for work on the second shift.

The first provision for paid vacations was made in 1942, when workers with at least a year's service and 900 hours of work during the year received a one-week vacation with 40 hours' pay. Under the 1948 contract, employees who worked at least 900 hours during the preceding twelve months were entitled to paid vacations according to the following graduated schedule: one week's vacation and 40 hours' pay for those with one year but less than 3 years of service; one week's vacation and 60 hours' pay for those with 3 years but less than 5 years of service; 2 weeks' vacation and 80 hours' pay for those with at least 5 years of service. Both the 1942

2. The discussion of this agreement is based on Philip Arnow, Joseph W. Block and William C. Quant, "A Description of Changes in Wages and Related Wage Practices of the American Woolen Company, 1939–48," *Monthly Labor Review,* December 1948, pp. 584–88.

and the 1948 contracts made special provision for employees with less than 900 hours of working time in the preceding twelve months.

The 1939 agreement contained no clauses compensating employees who reported for work but were not provided with anything to do; pieceworkers who lost time because of a breakdown of machinery, a power failure or similar causes; or piece or incentive workers who suffered loss in earnings because of faulty material. The 1948 agreement, on the other hand, provided a minimum reporting-time allowance of four hours' pay, payment of down time to pieceworkers according to set schedules, and compensation for time lost by piece and incentive workers because of faulty material on the basis of the worker's average straight-time hourly earnings.

In 1945 a comprehensive health and welfare plan made its initial appearance in the collective bargaining agreements between the American Woolen Company and the Textile Workers Union. Under this plan the company financed group insurance providing weekly accident and sickness benefits, hospital expense benefits, medical expense benefits, surgical benefits, maternity benefits, and insurance against accidental death or dismemberment. The 1948 agreement added a $500 life insurance policy for each employee.

In addition to these so-called fringe issues, successive contracts have included general wage changes. The contract that became effective in February 1948 provided the ninth general wage increase since the original agreement was signed. Altogether, in the nine-year span, the increase in the basic hourly wage rate averaged about 75 cents. Along with these increases came the establishment of a minimum plant wage rate. The first such minimum was established by the 1941 contract — at 40 cents an hour. The 1948 agreement set the minimum at $1.05 an hour.

STATISTICAL TABLES

TABLE 1

Births, Deaths and Surplus of Births over Deaths per Thousand Population, 1915–1950 [a]

Year	Births	Deaths	Surplus of Births over Deaths	Year	Births	Deaths	Surplus of Births over Deaths
1915.........	25.0	13.2	11.8	1933.........	16.6	10.7	5.9
1916.........	24.9	13.8	11.1	1934.........	17.2	11.1	6.1
1917.........	24.5	14.0	10.5	1935.........	16.9	10.9	6.0
1918.........	24.7	18.1	6.6	1936.........	16.7	11.6	5.1
1919.........	22.4	12.9	9.5	1937.........	17.1	11.3	5.8
1920.........	23.7	13.0	10.7	1938.........	17.6	10.6	7.0
1921.........	24.2	11.5	12.7	1939.........	17.3	10.6	6.7
1922.........	22.3	11.7	10.6	1940.........	17.9	10.7	7.2
1923.........	22.1	12.1	10.0	1941.........	18.9	10.5	8.4
1924.........	22.3	11.6	10.7	1942.........	20.9	10.4	10.5
1925.........	21.3	11.7	9.6	1943.........	21.5	10.9	10.6
1926.........	20.5	12.1	8.4	1944.........	20.2	10.6	9.6
1927.........	20.5	11.3	9.2	1945.........	19.6	10.6	9.0
1928.........	19.7	12.0	7.7	1946.........	23.3	10.0	13.3
1929.........	18.8	11.9	6.9	1947.........	25.8	10.1	15.7
1930.........	18.9	11.3	7.6	1948.........	24.1	9.9	14.3
1931.........	18.0	11.1	6.9	1949.........	23.9	9.7	14.2
1932.........	17.4	10.9	6.5	1950.........	23.4	9.6	13.8

a. For 1915–1932, crude average rates for registration area; since 1933, crude average rates for all states. Since 1940, birth rates for total population including armed forces overseas, death rates for total population excluding armed forces overseas.

Source: Bureau of the Census, *Vital Statistics Rates in the United States, 1900–1940; Statistical Abstract, 1950,* p. 63; Bureau of the Census releases.

TABLE 2

Indexes of Production in the United States, 1860–1914

(1899 = 100)

	Unadjusted					Adjusted to Secular Trend		
	Manufacturing							
Year	Total	Durable	Non-durable	Transportation and Communication	Industrial and Commercial Production	Manufacturing, Total	Transportation and Communication	Industrial and Commercial Production
1860	16	13	18	10	13	106	93	99
1861	16	10	19	11	13	99	92	96
1862	15	10	17	12	13	87	93	90
1863	17	12	18	14	15	94	102	98
1864	18	13	19	15	17	98	106	102
1865	17	10	19	16	17	88	108	98
1866	21	15	24	16	19	104	101	102
1867	22	16	24	17	19	102	101	101
1868	23	17	25	18	20	102	98	100
1869	25	21	27	20	22	107	102	104
1870	25	20	28	21	23	101	104	102
1871	26	19	31	23	25	102	105	103
1872	31	27	34	25	28	114	107	110
1873	30	26	33	27	29	106	112	109
1874	29	24	33	28	28	98	106	102
1875	28	19	33	27	28	90	98	94
1876	28	18	34	27	28	86	94	90
1877	30	21	35	27	29	87	88	87
1878	32	23	37	28	30	88	86	87
1879	36	31	39	32	34	95	92	93
1880	42	38	46	36	39	106	98	102
1881	46	46	47	40	43	110	103	106
1882	49	49	50	44	46	111	106	109
1883	50	46	54	45	48	109	102	106
1884	47	38	54	46	47	97	99	98
1885	47	37	55	46	46	92	94	93
1886	57	51	61	51	54	106	99	103
1887	60	57	62	59	60	107	107	107
1888	62	56	65	60	61	104	104	104
1889	66	63	68	65	65	106	106	106
1890	71	71	71	70	71	110	108	109
1891	73	70	77	74	74	107	108	107
1892	79	77	80	78	78	110	107	108
1893	70	56	78	78	74	93	102	97
1894	68	51	77	74	71	86	91	88
1895	81	73	88	80	81	98	94	96
1896	78	63	82	80	77	85	88	86
1897	80	68	89	86	83	88	90	89
1898	91	86	93	92	92	95	91	93
1899	100	100	100	100	100	99	93	96
1900	100	94	102	106	103	95	94	94
1901	111	115	106	116	114	100	97	99
1902	127	138	118	126	126	109	99	104
1903	126	135	123	136	131	103	102	103
1904	121	121	123	138	129	94	98	96
1905	140	152	134	156	148	104	105	104
1906	152	169	138	172	162	108	110	109
1907	156	174	148	180	168	106	109	107
1908	127	123	137	164	144	82	94	88
1909	166	174	158	188	177	102	102	102
1910	172	190	160	200	186	101	103	102
1911	162	171	158	200	180	90	98	94
1912	194	214	174	220	206	103	102	102
1913	203	232	179	228	215	102	100	101
1914	192	208	181	220	206	93	92	92

Source: Edwin Frickey, *Production in the United States, 1860–1914,* Harvard University Press, Cambridge, 1947, pp. 54, 64, 117, 127, and 60, 119, 128.

TABLE 3

INDEXES OF PRODUCTION, EMPLOYMENT AND OUTPUT PER WORKER, 1870–1940

(1929 = 100)

		Production						Employment						Output per Worker						
No.	Year	Agriculture	Mining	Manufacturing	Electricity	Gas	Railroads	Agriculture	Mining	Manufacturing	Electricity	Gas	Railroads	Agriculture	Mining	Manufacturing	Electricity	Gas	Railroads	No.
1	1870.....	29.2	—	—	—	—	—	65	—	—	—	—	—	45	—	—	—	—	—	**1**
2	1880.....	43.8	8.8	—	—	—	—	81	—	—	—	—	—	54	—	—	—	—	—	**2**
3	1890.....	54.9	19.0	—	—	—	—	94	—	—	—	—	—	58	—	—	—	—	—	**3**
4	1899.....	69.4	25.7	27.5	—	15.8	31	—	—	53.5	—	—	55	—	—	51	—	—	57	**4**
5	1900.....	70.1	27.8	28.0	—	—	35	103	—	55.6	—	—	60	68	—	50	—	—	59	**5**
6	1901.....	68.7	29.3	31.6	—	22.7	37	—	—	58.3	—	—	63	—	—	54	—	—	58	**6**
7	1902.....	71.5	30.6	35.4	3.6	21.4	40	—	73.3	63.1	10.4	40.4	70	—	42	56	31	53	57	**7**
8	1903.....	72.2	34.9	36.3	—	24.0	44	—	—	65.2	—	—	78	—	—	55	—	—	56	**8**
9	1904.....	75.7	35.5	34.1	—	25.6	45	—	—	61.5	—	—	77	—	—	55	—	—	58	**9**
10	1905.....	75.0	39.6	40.7	—	26.7	48	—	—	68.4	—	—	82	—	—	58	—	—	59	**10**
11	1906.....	81.9	41.1	43.7	—	29.8	54	—	—	71.7	—	—	90	—	—	60	—	—	60	**11**
12	1907.....	76.4	44.5	44.2	7.5	32.8	60	—	—	74.9	16.3	53.9	99	—	—	58	42	61	60	**12**
13	1908.....	77.8	41.6	36.5	—	34.8	56	—	—	66.3	—	—	85	—	—	54	—	—	66	**13**
14	1909.....	77.1	47.3	43.4	—	37.7	56	110	—	74.3	—	—	89	70	—	58	—	—	63	**14**
15	1910.....	79.2	50.1	46.2	—	39.8	65	109	—	77.5	—	—	100	73	—	58	—	—	65	**15**
16	1911.....	81.2	49.4	44.2	—	41.8	65	109	—	77.5	—	—	99	74	—	57	—	—	56	**16**
17	1912.....	85.4	53.0	50.8	13.0	46.6	67	110	—	80.7	27.1	68.3	102	78	—	63	43	68	56	**17**
18	1913.....	82.6	55.8	54.4	13.6	48.5	75	110	—	81.3	—	—	109	75	—	66	—	—	68	**18**
19	1914.....	89.6	51.9	51.1	15.2	51.1	72	110	—	78.1	—	—	101	81	—	65	—	—	71	**19**
20	1915.....	89.2	56.6	59.9	16.6	52.3	69	111	—	81.8	—	—	92	80	—	73	—	—	75	**20**
21	1916.....	82.6	65.3	71.2	21.1	58.8	82	110	—	95.7	—	—	98	75	—	74	—	—	84	**21**
22	1917.....	86.1	68.9	70.6	24.5	64.7	96	109	—	102.1	36.1	77.4	106	79	—	69	62	83	90	**22**
23	1918.....	90.3	69.4	69.8	31.4	63.8	99	108	—	104.3	39.0	—	112	84	—	66	74	—	88	**23**
24	1919.....	86.8	60.2	61.0	36.0	67.2	93	107	—	100.5	41.1	79.4	116	81	—	61	80	85	81	**24**
25	1920.....	90.3	69.7	66.5	39.3	69.0	102	107	—	100.5	45.2	—	123	81	—	66	87	—	83	**25**
26	1921.....	81.9	57.1	53.3	36.3	62.9	78	107	—	77.0	46.8	—	101	84	—	69	77	—	77	**26**
27	1922.....	90.3	61.4	68.4	41.2	67.9	83	107	73.3	85.6	51.6	—	98	77	83	80	80	—	85	**27**
28	1923.....	91.7	84.6	76.9	50.0	73.7	98	106	—	97.9	66.9	—	112	84	—	79	75	—	87	**28**
29	1924.....	95.1	79.7	73.1	54.9	76.5	92	106	—	90.9	71.8	—	106	86	—	80	75	—	87	**29**
30	1925.....	95.8	82.5	81.9	63.5	77.8	97	105	—	93.6	73.6	91.7	105	90	—	87	81	85	92	**30**
31	1926.....	101.4	89.5	86.8	73.5	85.8	102	104	—	95.7	82.8	—	107	97	—	91	89	—	95	**31**
32	1927.....	97.9	91.8	87.1	81.7	90.4	98	103	—	93.6	85.9	—	105	95	—	93	95	—	93	**32**
33	1928.....	102.1	91.8	91.2	89.5	93.8	98	102	—	93.6	91.9	—	100	100	—	96	98	—	98	**33**
34	1929.....	100.0	100.0	100.0	100.0	100.0	100	100	100.0	100.0	100.0	100.0	100	100	100	100	100	100	100	**34**
35	1930.....	100.7	88.2	85.4	103.5	101.4	86	99	—	86.6	103.3	94.2	90	101	—	99	100	108	96	**35**
36	1931.....	104.2	73.5	72.0	101.9	98.9	69	98	—	73.3	96.1	89.4	76	106	—	99	106	117	90	**36**
37	1932.....	100.0	59.1	54.1	92.7	92.5	52	96	—	62.6	83.7	82.1	62	104	—	88	117	113	83	**37**
38	1933.....	97.2	64.0	62.6	92.8	88.4	55	95	—	69.0	78.5	85.6	59	102	—	91	119	103	93	**38**
39	1934.....	83.3	69.7	69.2	99.2	92.0	60	94	—	80.7	81.6	90.4	61	89	—	86	121	102	98	**39**
40	1935.....	92.4	75.3	82.7	108.2	95.5	63	92	58.8	85.6	83.7	91.3	60	100	128	96	130	105	105	**40**
41	1936.....	93.1	88.4	97.0	123.4	100.0	76	91	68.9	93.0	89.8	97.2	65	102	114	104	137	103	115	**41**
42	1937.....	106.2	99.5	103.3	136.3	103.7	81	90	71.9	102.1	96.3	97.4	68	118	139	101	142	106	119	**42**
43	1938.....	105.6	85.1	81.0	136.8	101.1	66	88	59.0	85.6	93.2	94.6	58	120	144	95	147	107	114	**43**
44	1939.....	110.4	94.1	102.7	151.6	106.3	75	87	60.6	94.1	92.7	95.3	60	126	155	109	163	112	125	**44**
45	1940.....	110.6	—	—	167.7	115.3	—	85	—	—	94.9	99.3	—	130	—	—	176	116	—	**45**

Sources: Solomon Fabricant, *Labor Savings in American Industry, 1899–1939,* Occasional Paper No. 23, National Bureau of Economic Research, New York, November 1945, pp. 43–50; George J. Stigler, *Trends in Output and Employment,* National Bureau of Economic Research, 1947, pp. 57–59. (Series for "output per worker" computed by the writer as reciprocal values of the original series for "employment per unit of output.")

TABLE 4

Index of Manufacturing Production, 1860–1950

(1899 = 100)

Year	Index	Year	Index	Year	Index	Year	Index	Year	Index	Year	Index
1860...	16	1875...	28	1890...	71	1905...	144	1920...	242	1935...	301
1861...	16	1876...	28	1891...	73	1906...	152	1921...	194	1936...	353
1862...	15	1877...	30	1892...	79	1907...	159	1922...	249	1937...	376
1863...	17	1878...	32	1893...	70	1908...	130	1923...	280	1938...	295
1864...	18	1879...	36	1894...	68	1909...	162	1924...	266	1939...	374
1865...	17	1880...	42	1895...	81	1910...	169	1925...	298	1940...	429
1866...	21	1881...	46	1896...	78	1911...	161	1926...	316	1941...	556
1867...	22	1882...	49	1897...	80	1912...	186	1927...	317	1942...	683
1868...	23	1883...	50	1898...	91	1913...	199	1928...	332	1943...	820
1869...	25	1884...	47	1899...	100	1914...	186	1929...	364	1944...	806
1870...	25	1885...	47	1900...	100	1915...	218	1930...	311	1945...	685
1871...	26	1886...	57	1901...	111	1916...	259	1931...	262	1946...	566
1872...	31	1887...	60	1902...	127	1917...	257	1932...	197	1947...	621
1873...	30	1888...	62	1903...	128	1918...	254	1933...	228	1948...	634
1874...	29	1889...	66	1904...	122	1919...	222	1934...	252	1949...	549
										1950...	627

Sources: For 1860–1899, Frickey's index (the same as in the first column in Table 2) from Edwin Frickey, ***Production in the United States, 1860–1914,*** Harvard University Press, Cambridge, 1947. For 1915–1939, Fabricant's index (see the third column in Table 3), recomputed on the basis 1899 = 100, from Solomon Fabricant, ***Labor Savings in American Industry, 1899–1939,*** Occasional Paper No. 23, National Bureau of Economic Research, New York, November 1945. For 1900–1914, an index combining the data of Frickey's and Fabricant's indexes for this period. From 1940–1950, the official index of manufacturing production recomputed on the basis 1899 = 100.

TABLE 5

NATIONAL INCOME IN CURRENT AND 1926 PRICES, 1799–1938

Year	National Income, in Millions: At Current Prices	Adjusted to Cost of Living	Adjusted to General Price Level	Per Capita National Income: At Current Prices	Adjusted to Cost of Living	Adjusted to General Price Level
1799	$ 677	$ 1,115	$ 1,092	$131	$216	$211
1809	915	1,441	1,423	130	204	202
1819	876	1,625	1,576	93	173	168
1829	975	2,057	2,083	78	164	166
1839	1,631	3,295	3,282	98	198	197
1849	2,420	5,319	5,450	107	235	241
1859	4,311	9,095	9,212	140	296	300
1869	6,827	8,995	8,843	180	237	233
1879	7,227	15,183	15,442	147	309	315
1889	10,701	23,675	23,780	173	383	385
1899	15,364	36,066	34,142	205	482	456
1909	26,456	52,596	48,102	292	580	530
1910	28,166	53,043	49,675	305	575	538
1911	28,104	52,927	50,096	300	565	535
1912	29,422	52,167	50,294	309	549	529
1913	31,450	56,872	53,761	326	589	557
1914	31,213	55,342	53,356	319	565	545
1915	32,533	57,176	54,042	327	576	544
1916	38,739	63,196	56,636	384	627	562
1917	46,376	65,595	57,043	454	642	558
1918	56,956	66,928	62,044	550	646	599
1919	62,945	65,093	62,199	599	620	592
1920	68,434	60,401	60,615	642	567	569
1921	56,689	57,787	59,485	524	534	550
1922	57,171	61,211	61,873	520	557	563
1923	65,662	68,469	68,044	589	614	610
1924	67,003	69,004	69,004	592	610	610
1925	70,051	70,474	70,474	610	614	614
1926	73,523	73,523	73,523	631	631	631
1927	73,966	75,630	73,966	626	640	626
1928	75,904	78,657	73,765	633	656	615
1929	79,498	82,810	75,929	654	681	625
1930	72,398	78,099	73,725	588	634	599
1931	60,203	72,013	68,647	485	580	553
1932	46,708	62,527	60,503	374	500	484
1933	44,713	62,274	59,301	356	495	472
1934	51,560	67,753	64,370	407	535	508
1935	56,254	71,028	66,337	441	557	520
1936	65,246	80,253	72,415	508	625	564
1937	69,419	81,766	73,693	537	633	570
1938	62,286	75,225	69,130	478	577	531

Source: Robert F. Martin, *National Income in the United States, 1799–1938,* National Industrial Conference Board, New York, 1939.

TABLE 6

PRIVATE PRODUCTION INCOME, BY INDUSTRIAL ORIGIN, 1799–1938

	Private Production Income		Percentage Distribution by Industry									
Year	In Millions, at Current Prices	Percentage of Total National Income	Agriculture	Mining	Light, Power, Gas	Manufacturing	Construction	Transportation, Communication	Trade	Services	Finance	Other
1799....	$668	98.7	39.5	0.1	[a]	4.8	7.9	24.0	5.2	9.6		8.8
1809....	901	98.5	34.0	0.2	[a]	6.1	8.0	26.2	4.6	12.2		8.8
1819....	855	97.6	34.4	0.2	[a]	7.5	6.8	20.6	6.4	15.4		8.7
1829....	947	97.1	34.7	0.3	[a]	10.3	7.0	15.1	6.4	17.2		8.9
1839....	1,577	96.7	34.6	0.3	0.1	10.3	6.0	17.6	8.6	14.1		8.6
1849....	2,326	96.1	31.7	0.7	0.1	12.5	5.7	17.1	8.4	15.3		8.5
1859....	4,098	95.1	30.8	1.1	0.1	12.1	4.5	16.9	12.1	14.0		8.4
1869....	6,288	92.1	24.1	1.6	0.4	15.9	6.2	11.4	16.5	15.4		8.5
1879....	6,617	91.6	20.7	2.3	0.5	14.5	5.4	13.5	17.6	16.6		8.8
1889....	9,578	89.5	15.8	2.4	0.5	21.1	6.6	12.0	18.8	14.0		8.7
1899....	13,836	90.1	21.2	3.0	0.4	19.6	4.7	11.0	18.6	12.6	1.4	7.3
1909....	24,033	90.8	22.1	3.6	0.7	20.1	4.8	11.0	17.9	10.6	2.0	7.2
1910....	25,569	90.8	21.8	3.7	0.7	21.3	4.4	11.2	17.6	10.0	2.1	7.3
1911....	25,385	90.3	20.6	3.7	0.8	21.5	4.4	11.6	17.9	9.9	2.3	7.2
1912....	26,559	90.3	21.4	3.9	0.8	22.6	4.6	11.7	16.7	8.9	2.5	7.0
1913....	28,391	90.3	19.6	4.2	0.8	22.6	4.6	11.5	17.9	9.5	2.4	7.0
1914....	27,954	89.6	19.7	3.6	0.9	21.5	3.5	11.6	19.7	10.1	2.4	6.9
1915....	29,114	89.5	20.3	3.5	0.9	22.0	3.4	11.5	19.5	9.7	2.5	6.7
1916....	35,032	90.4	20.2	4.1	0.9	25.0	3.1	10.6	17.8	8.7	2.3	7.4
1917....	42,014	90.6	22.8	4.2	0.8	25.8	2.5	10.2	16.6	8.0	2.0	7.1
1918....	49,520	86.9	23.4	4.1	0.8	26.4	2.3	10.9	15.8	7.7	1.9	6.6
1919....	55,539	88.2	22.9	3.4	0.8	25.8	2.9	11.0	16.5	8.0	2.2	6.4
1920....	60,995	89.1	17.3	4.3	0.8	27.6	3.6	12.3	16.5	8.9	2.4	6.3
1921....	48,763	86.0	15.5	4.1	1.0	24.1	3.5	12.9	17.5	11.1	3.3	7.0
1922....	49,036	85.8	14.4	3.8	1.2	25.1	4.3	12.7	18.0	10.9	3.4	6.3
1923....	57,213	87.1	13.8	4.6	1.2	26.7	4.9	11.9	17.0	10.4	3.3	6.2
1924....	58,178	86.8	14.7	3.9	1.5	25.1	4.9	11.7	17.1	11.1	3.5	6.4
1925....	60,949	87.0	14.8	3.7	1.5	25.3	5.0	11.4	17.1	11.1	3.7	6.3
1926....	63,857	86.9	13.5	4.0	1.6	25.3	4.9	11.3	17.0	11.8	3.8	6.7
1927....	63,942	86.4	13.4	3.6	1.7	25.5	4.8	11.3	16.7	11.9	4.1	6.8
1928....	65,653	86.5	13.3	3.2	1.9	25.8	5.0	10.9	16.6	12.1	4.4	6.8
1929....	68,872	86.6	12.7	3.3	2.0	26.2	4.7	10.8	16.6	12.2	4.6	6.8
1930....	61,968	85.6	10.9	3.1	2.5	25.8	4.7	11.3	17.2	12.7	4.8	7.1
1931....	50,066	83.2	8.9	2.6	3.0	24.7	3.9	12.1	18.3	13.8	5.4	7.4
1932....	37,132	79.5	8.2	2.5	3.6	23.0	2.5	12.9	18.8	14.6	5.9	8.0
1933....	35,074	78.4	10.8	2.6	3.3	24.0	2.2	12.7	17.5	14.0	5.2	7.8
1934....	40,205	78.0	11.6	2.9	2.8	26.0	2.3	11.9	17.0	13.4	4.4	7.5
1935....	44,037	78.3	12.5	2.8	2.6	26.6	2.4	11.6	16.6	13.7	3.8	7.3
1936....	49,852	76.4	12.8	3.0	2.4	28.4	2.9	11.2	15.5	13.4	3.2	7.3
1937....	54,959	79.2	12.3	3.2	2.3	30.3	3.3	10.8	15.3	13.0	3.0	6.6
1938....	47,468[b]	76.2	[c]	[c]	[c]	[c]	[c]	[c]	[c]	[c]	[c]	[c]

a. Less than 0.05. b. Preliminary. c. Not available.

Source: Robert F. Martin, *National Income in the United States, 1799–1938,* National Industrial Conference Board, New York, 1939.

TABLE 7

Private Production Income, by Distributive Shares, 1899–1937

Year	Percentage Distribution: Wages and Salaries	Percentage Distribution: Entre-preneurial Income	Percentage Distribution: Divi-dends	Percentage Distribution: Interest, Net Rent and Royal-ties	Wages and Salaries as Percentage of Total Income: Agri-culture	Min-ing	Manu-factur-ing	Con-struc-tion	Trans-porta-tion	Com-munica-tions	Trade	Services
1899.....	57.6	29.1	6.0	7.3	15.6	69.5	80.4	81.1	65.9	65.0	63.5	66.5
1900.....	58.2	28.2	6.4	7.1	17.3	75.9	78.9	81.0	66.3	68.7	64.0	66.5
1901.....	58.9	27.5	6.7	7.0	16.6	73.4	79.8	81.3	66.6	69.7	64.7	66.4
1902.....	59.6	26.7	6.9	6.8	17.7	75.1	79.6	81.3	67.1	67.8	65.7	66.4
1903.....	60.6	26.0	6.5	6.9	17.9	81.2	80.9	81.2	67.1	65.3	66.0	66.3
1904.....	60.4	26.6	6.0	7.0	19.3	78.9	82.2	81.4	67.2	65.3	66.6	66.4
1905.....	62.0	25.1	6.1	6.8	19.5	75.2	83.4	81.6	67.0	69.5	68.4	66.4
1906.....	62.0	24.6	6.8	6.6	20.5	70.9	83.0	81.5	67.2	70.6	69.7	66.3
1907.....	61.5	24.5	7.2	6.8	19.5	71.9	82.8	81.4	67.2	66.7	68.9	66.3
1908.....	58.4	27.1	7.1	7.5	18.8	73.3	81.2	81.2	65.4	66.2	66.4	66.3
1909.....	58.9	27.6	6.5	6.9	16.1	74.9	82.7	81.6	64.8	64.9	68.6	66.4
1910.....	59.1	26.9	7.1	6.8	15.3	74.7	82.7	81.5	65.2	66.9	68.7	66.2
1911.....	60.2	25.3	7.4	7.1	17.1	76.4	82.1	81.3	66.1	69.0	68.7	66.1
1912.....	60.2	25.6	7.3	6.9	15.8	75.5	82.8	81.6	67.1	68.8	68.9	66.0
1913.....	61.1	24.5	7.6	6.8	16.6	73.3	82.8	81.6	67.1	69.2	67.8	65.7
1914.....	60.7	24.9	7.3	7.1	16.3	74.6	82.6	81.6	66.7	68.3	68.4	65.7
1915.....	60.5	25.3	7.1	7.1	15.6	74.6	83.0	81.8	66.6	66.8	68.6	65.6
1916.....	59.5	24.7	9.5	6.4	14.0	65.6	80.6	81.7	68.4	69.3	68.9	65.5
1917.....	58.6	26.7	8.9	5.8	12.8	67.4	81.8	81.1	71.4	70.9	68.5	65.4
1918.....	60.4	27.2	7.1	5.2	12.5	73.7	84.7	80.9	78.2	72.6	68.2	65.5
1919.....	62.2	26.8	5.8	5.2	14.0	80.2	86.1	81.1	79.7	75.9	68.5	65.6
1920.....	68.0	21.7	5.1	5.3	19.3	83.4	86.6	84.8	83.6	79.8	67.2	65.8
1921.....	66.0	21.6	6.0	6.4	17.3	79.8	83.3	80.3	80.3	77.9	67.9	65.8
1922.....	67.7	20.7	5.4	6.3	18.1	80.5	84.3	78.7	78.2	78.1	70.5	65.8
1923.....	69.1	19.5	5.8	5.6	18.2	80.8	84.4	84.7	79.2	77.6	72.2	65.6
1924.....	67.4	20.9	5.9	5.8	16.6	78.5	84.1	83.8	78.1	77.1	71.5	65.5
1925.....	66.6	21.0	6.6	5.8	16.3	75.2	83.3	79.2	77.5	75.3	72.4	65.2
1926.....	67.7	19.7	7.0	5.6	17.7	76.3	82.9	86.7	77.9	75.5	72.7	65.1
1927.....	67.1	19.6	7.5	5.9	17.9	75.2	82.4	85.1	76.5	74.6	72.1	64.8
1928.....	66.6	19.6	7.9	6.0	17.7	73.9	81.2	84.5	76.7	75.7	72.0	64.8
1929.....	66.7	19.0	8.4	5.9	17.9	70.3	81.8	83.8	76.1	76.3	71.6	64.4
1930.....	66.7	18.2	9.1	6.0	19.6	72.3	79.3	81.5	74.3	74.0	73.4	63.1
1931.....	67.3	17.9	8.3	6.4	21.4	73.9	80.0	81.2	73.8	70.9	74.2	60.9
1932.....	67.2	18.1	7.1	7.6	20.4	70.8	82.2	78.1	72.4	68.0	75.1	59.8
1933.....	66.5	20.0	6.0	7.4	15.2	72.9	83.6	79.0	72.8	64.6	75.4	59.9
1934.....	67.2	20.2	6.2	6.4	13.2	73.1	84.2	83.1	72.7	65.8	77.1	60.7
1935.....	67.1	21.0	6.4	5.6	11.9	72.5	84.4	82.6	73.9	66.6	77.8	60.2
1936.....	66.5	21.2	7.7	4.6	12.0	69.7	80.8	81.9	75.7	71.3	78.5	58.7
1937.....	68.0	20.2	7.8	3.9	13.0	67.0	81.9	82.1	77.9	74.4	79.3	59.3

Source: Robert F. Martin, *National Income in the United States, 1799–1938,* National Industrial Conference Board, New York, 1939.

TABLE 8

National Income,[a] by Industrial Origin, 1919–1938

Year	Total	Agri- culture	Min- ing	Manu- factur- ing	Con- struc- tion	Trans- portation and Other Public Utilities	Trade	Finance	Serv- ices	Govern- ment	Miscel- laneous
					Amount, in Billions						
1919......	$65.9	$10.9	$1.8	$16.2	$2.0	$6.0	$10.2	$6.8	$6.1	$3.8	$2.2
1920......	76.4	9.1	2.3	19.8	2.6	7.4	11.5	7.4	6.8	7.0	2.4
1921......	60.3	5.5	1.7	12.6	2.0	6.3	9.5	7.8	6.7	6.2	2.0
1922......	61.5	5.9	1.3	13.1	2.3	6.2	8.6	8.3	7.4	6.1	2.3
1923......	72.9	6.7	2.0	16.8	3.3	7.1	10.1	8.8	8.3	7.0	2.7
1924......	73.4	7.1	1.7	15.6	3.7	7.1	9.8	9.6	8.6	7.3	2.8
1925......	77.8	7.9	1.8	16.8	4.0	7.6	10.2	9.8	9.3	7.4	3.1
1926......	82.8	7.5	2.2	18.1	4.3	7.9	11.5	9.8	10.1	8.1	3.2
1927......	81.4	7.5	1.9	17.2	4.1	7.8	10.6	10.3	10.3	8.5	3.3
1928......	83.4	7.3	1.6	17.9	4.0	8.0	11.0	10.9	10.7	8.3	3.7
1929......	87.8	7.7	1.8	19.8	4.1	8.5	11.4	10.9	11.3	8.9	3.5
1930......	77.6	5.8	1.4	16.3	3.5	7.7	11.0	9.7	10.4	8.9	2.9
1931......	60.3	4.0	0.83	11.0	2.2	6.5	9.0	7.9	8.8	7.4	2.6
1932......	42.6	2.8	0.48	6.3	1.1	4.9	6.3	5.9	6.5	6.2	2.1
1933......	41.8	3.6	0.48	6.6	0.71	4.7	5.2	5.2	5.8	7.5	2.0
1934......	49.5	4.7	0.83	9.0	0.83	4.8	7.0	5.1	6.8	8.2	2.3
1935......	54.4	5.4	0.92	11.4	1.0	5.2	7.4	5.7	7.4	7.5	2.6
1936......	62.7	6.1	1.2	14.2	1.6	5.8	8.5	6.0	8.3	8.2	2.9
1937......	70.1	6.3	1.4	15.9	1.8	6.1	9.0	6.6	9.1	10.7	3.2
1938......	64.9	5.5	1.1	12.6	1.7	5.5	9.3	6.5	8.9	10.8	3.0
					Percentage Distribution						
1919......	100.0	16.5	2.7	24.6	3.0	9.0	15.5	10.3	9.3	5.7	3.4
1920......	100.0	11.9	3.0	25.9	3.5	9.7	15.0	9.7	9.0	9.2	3.1
1921......	100.0	9.2	2.8	20.9	3.3	10.5	15.8	12.9	11.1	10.3	3.3
1922......	100.0	9.5	2.2	21.3	3.8	10.1	14.0	13.4	12.0	10.0	3.7
1923......	100.0	9.2	2.8	23.0	4.6	9.7	13.9	12.1	11.3	9.7	3.7
1924......	100.0	9.7	2.3	21.3	5.1	9.7	13.4	13.1	11.8	9.9	3.8
1925......	100.0	10.2	2.4	21.6	5.1	9.8	13.1	12.5	12.0	9.5	3.9
1926......	100.0	9.1	2.6	21.9	5.2	9.5	13.9	11.9	12.2	9.8	3.9
1927......	100.0	9.2	2.3	21.1	5.1	9.6	13.0	12.7	12.7	10.4	4.0
1928......	100.0	8.8	2.0	21.5	4.8	9.6	13.2	13.0	12.8	9.9	4.4
1929......	100.0	8.8	2.1	22.5	4.6	9.7	13.0	12.4	12.8	10.1	4.0
1930......	100.0	7.5	1.8	20.9	4.5	10.0	14.1	12.6	13.4	11.5	3.7
1931......	100.0	6.7	1.4	18.3	3.7	10.7	15.0	13.1	14.6	12.3	4.3
1932......	100.0	6.6	1.1	14.7	2.6	11.5	14.8	13.9	15.3	14.5	5.0
1933......	100.0	8.5	1.1	15.8	1.7	11.3	12.5	12.4	13.9	17.9	4.8
1934......	100.0	9.6	1.7	18.2	1.7	9.7	14.2	10.2	13.6	16.5	4.6
1935......	100.0	9.9	1.7	20.9	1.9	9.5	13.6	10.4	13.5	13.8	4.7
1936......	100.0	9.7	1.9	22.6	2.5	9.3	13.5	9.5	13.2	13.1	4.7
1937......	100.0	8.9	2.0	22.7	2.6	8.8	12.8	9.5	13.0	15.3	4.5
1938......	100.0	8.4	1.7	19.4	2.6	8.5	14.3	10.1	13.7	16.7	4.6

a. Unadjusted for disparity between depreciation and depletion charges at cost and reproduction prices, and gains and losses from sales of capital assets before 1929. Social security contributions of employers are omitted.

Source: Simon Kuznets, *National Income and Its Composition, 1919–1938*, National Bureau of Economic Research, New York, 1941, pp. 163–69.

TABLE 9

NATIONAL INCOME,[a] BY DISTRIBUTIVE SHARES, 1919–1938

Year	National Income	Wages and Salaries	Other Payments to Employees	Entrepreneurial: Withdrawals	Entrepreneurial: Savings	Rent	Dividends [b]	Interest	Corporate Net Savings	Government Net Savings
				Amount, in Billions						
1919....	$64.2	$36.7	$0.43	$11.8	$5.5	$4.0	$2.9	$3.2	$1.0	$—1.3
1920....	74.2	43.3	0.57	13.5	1.6	4.3	3.2	3.7	2.2	1.9
1921....	59.4	34.9	0.60	10.3	0.63	4.5	3.0	3.9	0.71	0.96
1922....	60.7	36.4	0.60	10.8	—0.09	4.9	3.0	4.0	0.23	0.85
1923....	71.6	42.7	0.62	11.3	1.2	5.2	3.8	4.2	0.97	1.6
1924....	72.1	42.7	0.62	11.9	0.87	5.6	3.8	4.4	0.42	1.7
1925....	76.0	44.4	0.61	12.5	1.6	5.5	4.4	4.6	0.83	1.6
1926....	81.6	47.4	0.62	12.5	2.1	5.1	4.7	4.7	2.3	2.2
1927....	80.1	47.8	0.65	12.6	1.1	5.1	5.1	4.9	0.56	2.3
1928....	81.7	48.7	0.66	12.9	0.91	4.9	5.5	5.3	0.92	1.9
1929....	87.2	51.5	0.69	13.4	1.1	4.9	6.3	5.6	1.5	2.2
1930....	77.3	47.0	0.73	12.8	—0.64	4.3	6.0	5.7	—0.67	2.1
1931....	60.3	39.6	0.88	11.2	—2.0	3.0	4.6	5.7	—3.1	0.34
1932....	42.9	30.7	0.98	9.7	—3.5	2.1	3.0	5.5	—4.8	—0.91
1933....	42.2	28.2	1.9	9.0	—2.4	2.1	2.5	5.0	—4.0	—0.11
1934....	49.5	32.1	2.8	9.1	—0.35	1.9	3.0	4.8	—3.3	—0.58
1935....	54.4	35.0	2.9	9.5	0.23	2.1	3.8	4.6	—2.1	—1.7
1936....	62.9	38.9	3.9	10.1	1.2	2.2	4.8	4.6	—0.71	—2.2
1937....	70.5	43.5	4.0	11.2	0.44	2.6	4.9	4.7	—1.4	0.50
1938....	65.5	39.7	4.7	11.1	0.27	2.6	3.5	4.6	—0.70	—0.18
				Percentage Distribution						
1919....	100.0	57.2	0.68	18.4	8.5	6.2	4.5	5.0	1.6	—2.0
1920....	100.0	58.4	0.77	18.2	2.1	5.8	4.3	4.9	3.0	2.6
1921....	100.0	58.8	1.0	17.3	1.1	7.5	5.0	6.5	1.2	1.6
1922....	100.0	60.0	0.99	17.8	—0.15	8.1	5.0	6.6	0.38	1.4
1923....	100.0	59.6	0.86	15.8	1.6	7.2	5.4	5.9	1.4	2.2
1924....	100.0	59.2	0.86	16.6	1.2	7.8	5.3	6.1	0.58	2.4
1925....	100.0	58.4	0.80	16.4	2.1	7.2	5.8	6.0	1.1	2.1
1926....	100.0	58.1	0.76	15.3	2.5	6.3	5.8	5.8	2.8	2.6
1927....	100.0	59.7	0.81	15.8	1.3	6.3	6.3	6.2	0.70	2.9
1928....	100.0	59.6	0.81	15.8	1.1	6.0	6.7	6.5	1.1	2.3
1929....	100.0	59.1	0.79	15.3	1.2	5.6	7.2	6.4	1.8	2.6
1930....	100.0	60.8	0.94	16.5	—0.83	5.5	7.8	7.4	— 0.86	2.7
1931....	100.0	65.6	1.5	18.6	—3.4	5.0	7.7	9.5	— 5.1	0.57
1932....	100.0	71.6	2.3	22.7	—8.1	4.9	7.0	12.8	—11.1	—2.1
1933....	100.0	66.8	4.4	21.4	—5.6	5.0	5.9	11.9	— 9.5	—0.27
1934....	100.0	64.8	5.6	18.4	—0.71	3.8	6.1	9.8	— 6.6	—1.2
1935....	100.0	64.3	5.4	17.5	0.43	3.9	6.9	8.5	— 3.9	—3.2
1936....	100.0	61.8	6.2	16.1	2.0	3.5	7.7	7.3	— 1.1	—3.5
1937....	100.0	61.7	5.7	15.9	0.62	3.7	7.0	6.7	— 2.0	0.70
1938....	100.0	60.6	7.1	16.9	0.41	3.9	5.3	7.0	— 1.1	—0.27

a. Includes social security contributions of employers and is adjusted for effects on the net savings of corporations and other business firms of (1) gains and losses from sales of capital assets, (2) inventory revaluations and (3) the use of cost rather than reproduction basis for depreciation charges.
b. Includes balance of international payments.

Source: Simon Kuznets, *National Income and Its Composition, 1919–1938,* National Bureau of Economic Research, New York, 1941, pp. 216–18.

TABLE 10

National income, by Industrial Origin, 1929–1950 [a]

(In Millions of Dollars)

No.		1929	1930	1931	1932	1933	1934	1935	1936
1	All industries, total	87,355	75,003	58,873	41,690	39,584	48,613	56,789	64,719
2	Agriculture, forestry and fishing	8,002	6,022	4,625	3,080	3,521	3,568	6,231	5,327
3	Mining	2,097	1,665	994	680	662	1,173	1,243	1,551
4	Metal mining	478	282	109	21	41	127	173	269
5	Anthracite mining	285	281	229	150	130	172	139	146
6	Bituminous and other soft coal mining	652	530	372	239	255	416	446	537
7	Crude petroleum and natural gas	486	383	176	220	195	390	404	487
8	Nonmetallic mining	196	189	108	50	41	68	81	112
9	Contract construction	3,691	3,088	2,139	1,030	735	1,034	1,257	1,918
10	Manufacturing	22,012	18,270	12,434	7,196	7,563	10,922	13,336	16,183
11	Food and kindred products	2,157	2,395	1,865	1,408	1,335	1,600	1,882	2,077
12	Tobacco manufactures	258	299	322	311	142	146	204	133
13	Textile mill products	1,797	1,404	1,147	713	697	1,100	1,200	1,356
14	Apparel and other finished fabric products	1,240	997	807	491	532	775	841	958
15	Lumber and timber basic products	850	613	281	118	122	263	327	447
16	Furniture and finished lumber products	678	508	372	211	183	284	342	442
17	Paper and allied products	563	503	388	270	290	419	463	502
18	Printing and publishing	1,580	1,490	1,213	880	790	925	1,037	1,161
19	Chemicals and allied products	1,136	1,035	827	557	690	725	810	959
20	Products of petroleum and coal	993	864	329	128	17	147	256	370
21	Rubber products	356	274	232	113	103	134	214	214
22	Leather and leather products	601	490	389	305	270	412	376	423
23	Stone, clay and glass products	799	611	439	123	208	329	409	573
24	Iron and steel and their products	2,978	2,212	1,109	410	682	1,085	1,478	2,061
25	Nonferrous metals and their products	767	640	415	197	155	385	469	561
26	Machinery (except electrical)	1,903	1,485	755	298	426	735	1,021	1,398
27	Electrical machinery	1,048	824	502	244	276	376	526	708
28	Transportation equipment, except automobiles	317	288	142	89	69	119	139	231
29	Automobiles and automobile equipment	1,394	842	561	168	384	649	935	1,153
30	Miscellaneous	597	496	339	162	192	314	407	456
31	Wholesale and retail trade	13,090	11,998	9,604	6,290	5,375	7,892	9,006	10,319
32	Wholesale trade	3,955	3,777	2,963	1,994	1,631	2,297	2,726	3,005
33	Retail trade and auto services	9,135	8,221	6,641	4,296	3,744	5,595	6,280	7,314
34	Finance, insurance and real estate	13,098	10,693	8,511	6,452	5,681	5,861	6,294	7,165
35	Transportation	6,562	5,513	4,285	3,133	2,958	3,326	3,612	4,168
36	Railroads	4,600	3,753	2,814	1,965	1,849	2,040	2,236	2,614
37	Local railways and bus lines	592	553	461	388	331	355	337	374
38	Highway passenger transportation	231	210	171	122	118	129	140	159
39	Highway freight transportation	482	458	413	357	356	399	451	502
40	Water transportation	267	216	172	127	153	178	200	243
41	Air transport (common carriers)	−3	−10	4	10	10	8	15	22
42	Pipeline transportation	130	105	81	56	47	104	107	106
43	Services allied to transportation	263	228	169	108	94	113	126	148
44	Communications and public utilities	2,878	2,787	2,625	2,281	2,000	2,195	2,285	2,478
45	Telephone and telegraph	1,130	1,097	991	794	692	740	779	841
46	Radio broadcasting	28	8	16	21	14	32	39	52
47	Utilities: electric and gas	1,640	1,606	1,562	1,404	1,237	1,359	1,405	1,522
48	Local public services, not elsewhere classified	80	76	56	62	57	64	62	63
49	Services	10,168	9,019	7,714	6,006	5,447	6,106	6,526	7,316
50	Hotels and lodging places	577	512	394	242	193	274	314	366
51	Personal services	1,220	1,148	985	766	667	749	819	915
52	Private households	3,117	2,246	1,734	1,321	1,177	1,301	1,382	1,591
53	Trade schools and employment agencies	49	43	29	16	15	22	28	34
54	Business services, not elsewhere classified	564	561	448	358	332	435	472	571
55	Misc. repair services and hand trades	284	274	249	205	175	186	199	210
56	Motion pictures	432	429	355	191	209	280	326	384
57	Recreation	371	328	263	176	152	192	205	243
58	Medical and health services	1,522	1,461	1,292	1,025	937	1,024	1,103	1,239
59	Legal services	689	683	701	591	561	600	624	647
60	Engineering and other professional services, not elsewhere classified	243	217	179	120	113	126	136	168
61	Educational services, not elsewhere classified	473	482	473	438	400	397	402	414
62	Religious organizations	355	356	341	314	289	285	284	288
63	Nonprofit organizations, not elsewhere classified	272	279	271	243	227	235	232	246
64	Government and government enterprises	5,114	5,336	5,447	5,171	5,349	6,295	6,747	8,130
65	Federal—general government	900	935	942	901	1,187	1,718	1,791	3,592
66	Federal—government enterprises	581	584	582	544	485	540	614	662
67	State and local—general government	3,456	3,630	3,737	3,565	3,531	3,884	4,178	3,696
68	State and local—government enterprises	177	187	186	161	146	153	164	180
69	Rest of the world [b]	643	612	495	371	293	241	252	164

[a] National income originating in each industry is the sum of factor costs incurred by the industry in production. Hence, it is the net value added to production by the industry, measured at factor costs. In the business sector of the economy, except government enterprises, it is equal to the excess of the market value of the industry's product and the subsidies it receives over the sum of the following costs: purchases of goods and services from other enterprises, indirect business tax and nontax liability, business transfer payments, and capital consumption charges. In the government and personal sectors of the economy, which do not produce for sale, and also in government enterprises, this value added in production (as measured in the present series) can be described only as factor costs incurred. "National income originating" is a more net concept of value added than that used by the Bureau of the Census in compiling the Census of Manufactures. "Value

TABLE 10—Continued

1937	1938	1939	1940	1941	1942	1943	1944	1945	1946	1947	1948	1949	1950	No.
73,627	67,375	72,532	81,347	103,834	137,119	169,686	183,838	182,691	180,286	198,688	223,469	216,716	238,963	1
7,249	6,003	6,120	6,599	8,880	12,875	14,561	14,830	15,642	18,251	19,424	21,829	17,033	17,657	2
1,941	1,483	1,601	1,903	2,341	2,599	2,757	2,950	2,789	3,071	4,350	5,445	4,589	5,038	3
458	274	348	445	513	592	507	417	349	324	557	686	610	703	4
137	113	126	138	165	190	211	238	219	286	302	343	267	283	5
603	457	503	628	809	989	1,130	1,271	1,204	1,241	1,827	2,112	1,551	1,793	6
604	536	497	543	654	583	671	800	795	925	1,293	1,870	1,709	1,790	7
139	103	127	149	200	245	238	224	222	295	371	434	452	469	8
2,017	1,930	2,254	2,593	4,370	6,625	5,551	4,375	4,571	6,651	8,550	10,551	10,564	12,204	9
19,304	14,997	17,936	22,368	32,897	45,239	58,104	60,456	51,918	48,905	59,459	67,215	63,157	74,075	10
2,400	2,255	2,280	2,483	2,683	3,619	4,334	4,992	5,009	5,573	5,822	6,637	6,599	6,635	11
195	223	298	291	215	184	191	289	243	332	370	429	467	528	12
1,597	1,093	1,259	1,511	2,036	2,831	3,001	2,956	2,973	4,015	4,687	5,229	4,120	4,592	13
982	910	1,016	1,109	1,429	1,872	2,308	2,598	2,726	3,242	3,242	3,441	3,285	3,297	14
561	428	491	595	887	1,081	1,146	1,158	1,067	1,433	1,914	2,204	1,733	2,220	15
508	423	508	551	765	866	935	1,029	1,052	1,378	1,535	1,762	1,608	1,881	16
562	573	555	660	1,034	1,123	1,254	1,352	1,336	1,709	2,234	2,377	2,192	2,656	17
1,246	1,132	1,206	1,247	1,359	1,428	1,724	2,045	2,250	2,724	3,073	3,277	3,366	3,563	18
1,165	1,005	1,205	1,489	1,941	2,761	3,355	3,399	3,250	3,337	3,846	4,383	4,444	5,026	19
595	507	458	686	833	1,198	1,502	1,360	1,326	1,679	2,488	3,632	2,959	3,391	20
292	204	279	319	485	587	877	991	919	1,090	1,125	1,083	989	1,002	21
459	401	423	456	614	767	842	865	898	1,071	1,113	1,213	1,088	1,133	22
649	502	662	757	1,072	1,168	1,193	1,137	1,147	1,561	1,851	2,154	2,092	2,691	23
2,586	1,592	2,259	3,057	5,048	6,897	9,099	9,081	7,376	5,588	7,647	8,713	7,783	10,377	24
702	440	594	793	1,201	1,476	1,939	1,942	1,659	1,748	1,934	2,079	1,954	2,203	25
1,759	1,247	1,492	2,181	3,850	5,459	6,037	6,000	5,191	4,829	6,324	7,115	6,324	7,352	26
908	659	850	1,136	1,915	2,481	3,353	3,732	3,047	2,391	3,432	3,661	3,484	4,790	27
332	264	397	813	2,276	6,223	12,103	12,494	7,732	1,703	1,548	1,874	1,912	2,010	28
1,298	700	1,188	1,602	2,364	2,015	1,337	1,413	1,120	1,920	3,557	4,132	4,949	6,653	29
508	439	516	632	890	1,203	1,574	1,623	1,597	1,582	1,617	1,820	1,809	2,075	30
11,938	11,652	12,126	13,748	15,903	19,055	22,361	25,137	27,999	34,137	37,324	42,192	41,707	43,269	31
3,693	3,507	3,558	4,108	4,708	5,618	6,209	6,995	7,598	9,512	10,850	12,611	12,287	12,254	32
8,245	8,145	8,568	9,640	11,195	13,437	16,152	18,142	20,401	24,625	26,474	29,581	29,420	31,015	33
7,943	8,026	8,216	8,489	9,523	11,052	12,237	13,088	13,278	14,696	15,666	17,780	18,439	20,251	34
4,530	3,961	4,543	4,915	6,188	8,462	10,672	11,197	10,495	10,182	11,481	12,641	11,918	13,236	35
2,797	2,368	2,735	2,934	3,779	5,550	6,998	6,954	6,034	5,472	6,311	7,161	6,426	7,199	36
371	332	338	321	321	428	545	571	574	601	599	565	580	559	37
174	166	177	202	257	450	628	676	688	785	773	794	745	736	38
564	569	642	702	907	1,082	1,215	1,305	1,383	1,673	1,946	2,240	2,296	2,794	39
292	206	280	337	436	428	596	858	991	828	876	830	782	790	40
26	30	44	57	77	112	151	177	192	217	240	302	342	367	41
129	121	131	130	145	117	130	147	132	128	152	196	199	207	42
177	169	196	232	266	295	409	509	501	478	584	553	548	584	43
2,713	2,713	2,863	3,039	3,313	3,659	3,952	4,100	4,283	4,850	5,157	5,939	6,652	7,245	44
923	948	1,008	1,022	1,135	1,368	1,557	1,676	1,772	1,987	2,085	2,471	2,695	2,980	45
64	64	75	90	106	107	139	177	187	207	228	252	265	311	46
1,662	1,639	1,716	1,860	2,002	2,113	2,178	2,167	2,240	2,569	2,748	3,109	3,573	3,832	47
64	62	64	67	70	71	78	80	84	87	96	107	119	122	48
8,049	7,728	8,080	8,637	9,709	10,870	11,993	13,268	14,135	16,614	18,345	19,821	20,395	22,009	49
431	412	436	471	520	610	815	914	1,005	1,180	1,177	1,215	1,211	1,225	50
1,058	977	1,001	1,129	1,320	1,500	1,768	1,931	2,065	2,452	2,555	2,573	2,509	2,594	51
1,829	1,633	1,761	1,933	2,076	2,030	1,982	2,220	2,445	2,591	3,070	3,369	3,624	4,272	52
41	33	35	38	62	136	186	147	84	112	144	169	189	211	53
605	596	637	656	753	804	897	1,053	1,205	1,481	1,665	1,896	1,890	2,052	54
225	236	238	235	389	505	628	683	548	614	754	817	779	813	55
430	420	428	435	497	634	810	871	905	1,116	1,028	904	908	874	56
293	256	278	298	338	348	386	453	540	721	712	723	731	741	57
1,308	1,313	1,365	1,444	1,587	1,816	1,998	2,315	2,450	2,900	3,363	3,746	3,956	4,314	58
680	666	692	719	763	804	822	892	974	1,165	1,280	1,457	1,497	1,583	59
179	194	210	240	333	508	391	373	409	554	631	756	766	856	60
434	446	452	460	471	479	515	539	580	690	839	983	1,053	1,119	61
295	300	303	304	300	307	320	341	354	373	405	439	478	511	62
241	246	244	275	300	389	475	536	571	605	722	774	804	844	63
7,795	8,548	8,550	8,796	10,479	16,445	27,239	34,211	37,423	22,647	18,529	19,609	21,804	23,434	64
3,036	3,529	3,444	3,537	5,046	10,836	21,255	27,905	30,614	14,741	9,356	8,922	9,979	10,783	65
675	698	716	741	788	870	1,027	1,083	1,153	1,404	1,426	1,618	1,790	1,891	66
3,889	4,121	4,185	4,280	4,368	4,443	4,621	4,883	5,296	6,080	7,262	8,517	9,445	10,143	67
195	200	205	238	277	296	336	340	360	422	485	552	590	617	68
148	334	243	260	231	238	259	226	158	282	403	447	458	545	69

added by manufacture" was obtained in the 1939 Census of Manufactures by deducting from the value of products only "the cost of materials, supplies, containers, fuel, purchased electric energy, and contract work."

[b] Income originating in the rest of the world. Profits received by domestic corporations from foreign branches are excluded from this line and included in the industry of the recipient corporation. Data required for their elimination are not available by industry.

Source: National Income Supplement to Survey of Current Business, July 1947, p. 26, and *Survey of Current Business,* National Income Supplement, 1951, p. 159.

TABLE 11

Percentage Distribution of National Income, by Industrial Origin, 1929–1950

Industry	1929	1930	1931	1932	1933	1934	1935	1936	1937	1938	1939
All industries, total	100.0	100.0	100.0	100.0	100.0	100.0	100.0	100.0	100.0	100.0	100.0
Agriculture, forestry and fishing	9.2	8.0	7.9	7.4	8.9	7.3	11.0	8.2	9.8	8.9	8.4
Mining	2.4	2.2	1.7	1.6	1.7	2.4	2.2	2.4	2.6	2.2	2.2
Contract construction	4.2	4.1	3.6	2.5	1.9	2.1	2.2	3.0	2.7	2.9	3.1
Manufacturing	25.2	24.4	21.1	17.3	19.1	22.5	23.5	25.0	26.2	22.3	24.7
Wholesale and retail trade	15.0	16.0	16.3	15.1	13.6	16.2	15.9	15.9	16.2	17.3	16.7
Finance, insurance and real estate	15.0	14.3	14.5	15.5	14.4	12.1	11.1	11.1	10.8	11.9	11.3
Transportation	7.5	7.4	7.3	7.5	7.5	6.8	6.4	6.4	6.2	5.9	6.3
Communications and public utilities	3.3	3.7	4.5	5.5	5.1	4.5	4.0	3.8	3.7	4.0	3.9
Services	11.6	12.0	13.1	14.4	13.8	12.6	11.5	11.3	10.9	11.5	11.1
Government and government enterprises	5.9	7.1	9.3	12.4	13.5	12.9	11.9	12.6	10.6	12.7	11.8
Rest of the world	0.7	0.8	0.8	0.9	0.7	0.5	0.4	0.3	0.2	0.5	0.3

TABLE 11—Continued

Industry	1940	1941	1942	1943	1944	1945	1946	1947	1948	1949	1950
All industries, total	100.0	100.0	100.0	100.0	100.0	100.0	100.0	100.0	100.0	100.0	100.0
Agriculture, forestry and fishing	8.1	8.6	9.4	8.6	8.1	8.6	10.1	9.8	9.8	7.9	7.4
Mining	2.3	2.3	1.9	1.6	1.6	1.5	1.7	2.2	2.4	2.1	2.1
Contract construction	3.2	4.2	4.8	3.3	2.4	2.5	3.7	4.3	4.7	4.9	5.1
Manufacturing	27.5	31.7	33.0	34.2	32.9	28.4	27.1	29.9	30.1	29.1	31.0
Wholesale and retail trade	16.9	15.3	13.9	13.2	13.7	15.3	18.9	18.8	18.9	19.2	18.1
Finance, insurance and real estate	10.4	9.2	8.0	7.2	7.1	7.3	8.2	7.9	8.0	8.5	8.5
Transportation	6.0	6.0	6.2	6.3	6.1	5.7	5.6	5.8	5.7	5.5	5.5
Communications and public utilities	3.7	3.2	2.7	2.3	2.2	2.3	2.7	2.6	2.7	3.1	3.0
Services	10.6	9.4	7.9	7.1	7.2	7.7	9.2	9.2	8.9	9.4	9.2
Government and government enterprises	10.8	10.1	12.0	16.1	18.6	20.5	12.6	9.3	8.8	10.1	9.8
Rest of the world	0.3	0.2	0.2	0.2	0.1	0.1	0.2	0.2	0.2	0.2	0.2

Source: Based on Table 10.

TABLE 12

National Income, by Distributive Shares, 1929–1950

(In Billions of Dollars)

Item	1929	1930	1931	1932	1933	1934	1935	1936	1937	1938	1939
National income	87.4	75.0	58.9	41.7	39.6	48.6	56.8	64.7	73.6	67.4	72.5
Compensation of employees	50.8	46.5	39.5	30.8	29.3	34.1	37.1	42.7	47.7	44.7	47.8
Wages and salaries	50.2	45.9	38.9	30.3	28.8	33.5	36.5	41.8	45.9	42.8	45.7
Private	45.2	40.7	33.6	25.3	23.7	27.4	30.0	33.9	38.4	34.6	37.5
Military	0.3	0.3	0.3	0.3	0.3	0.3	0.3	0.3	0.4	0.4	0.4
Government civilian	4.6	4.9	5.0	4.7	4.9	5.8	6.2	7.6	7.2	7.9	7.8
Supplementary payments [a]	0.6	0.6	0.6	0.5	0.5	0.5	0.6	0.9	1.7	1.9	2.1
Income of unincorporated enterprises	13.9	11.0	8.2	4.9	5.2	6.6	9.9	9.9	12.2	10.8	11.3
Business and professional [b]	8.3	7.0	5.3	3.2	2.9	4.3	5.0	6.1	6.6	6.3	6.8
Income	8.1	6.3	4.7	2.9	3.4	4.3	5.0	6.2	6.7	6.1	6.9
Inventory adjustment	0.1	0.8	0.6	0.3	—0.5	—0.1	—0.1	—0.1	0.0	0.2	—0.2
Farm	5.7	3.9	2.9	1.7	2.3	2.3	4.9	3.9	5.6	4.4	4.5
Rental income of persons	5.8	4.8	3.6	2.5	2.0	2.1	2.3	2.7	3.1	3.3	3.5
Corporate profits [b]	10.3	6.6	1.6	—2.0	—2.0	1.1	3.0	4.9	6.2	4.3	5.8
Profits before tax	9.8	3.3	—0.8	—3.0	0.2	1.7	3.2	5.7	6.2	3.3	6.5
Tax liability	1.4	0.8	0.5	0.4	0.5	0.7	1.0	1.4	1.5	1.0	1.5
Profits after tax	8.4	2.5	—1.3	—3.4	—0.4	1.0	2.3	4.3	4.7	2.3	5.0
Dividends	5.8	5.5	4.1	2.6	2.1	2.6	2.9	4.6	4.7	3.2	3.8
Undistributed profits	2.6	—3.0	—5.4	—6.0	—2.4	—1.6	—0.6	—0.3	0.0	—0.9	1.2
Inventory adjustment	0.5	3.3	2.4	1.0	—2.1	—0.6	—0.2	—0.7	0.0	1.0	—0.7
Net interest	6.5	6.2	5.9	5.4	5.0	4.8	4.5	4.5	4.4	4.3	4.2

TABLE 12—Continued

(In Billions of Dollars)

Item	1940	1941	1942	1943	1944	1945	1946	1947	1948	1949	1950
National income	81.3	103.8	137.1	169.7	183.8	182.7	180.3	198.7	223.5	216.7	239.0
Compensation of employees	51.8	64.3	84.9	109.2	121.2	123.0	117.1	128.0	140.2	139.9	153.3
Wages and salaries	49.6	61.7	81.9	105.6	116.9	117.7	111.2	122.1	134.4	133.4	145.8
Private	41.1	51.5	65.8	78.8	83.4	82.1	90.6	104.8	115.7	113.0	123.6
Military	0.6	1.9	6.3	14.4	20.6	22.6	8.0	4.1	4.0	4.2	5.1
Government civilian	7.9	8.3	9.8	12.4	12.8	13.0	12.7	13.2	14.7	16.1	17.1
Supplementary payments [a]	2.2	2.6	3.0	3.6	4.2	5.4	5.9	5.9	5.8	6.5	7.5
Income of unincorporated enterprises	12.7	16.5	23.0	26.7	29.0	31.2	35.4	35.4	39.8	33.9	36.0
Business and professional [b]	7.7	9.6	12.6	15.0	17.2	18.7	20.6	19.8	22.1	20.9	22.3
Income	7.8	10.2	12.9	15.1	17.2	18.8	22.4	21.3	22.5	20.3	23.8
Inventory adjustment	—0.1	—0.6	—0.4	—0.2	—0.1	—0.1	—1.8	—1.5	—0.4	0.6	—1.6
Farm	4.9	6.9	10.5	11.8	11.8	12.5	14.8	15.6	17.7	13.0	13.7
Rental income of persons	3.6	4.3	5.4	6.1	6.5	6.3	6.6	7.1	7.5	7.5	8.0
Corporate profits [b]	9.2	14.6	19.9	24.3	24.0	19.2	18.3	24.7	31.7	30.5	36.2
Profits before tax	9.3	17.2	21.1	25.1	24.3	19.7	23.5	30.5	33.8	28.3	41.4
Tax liability	2.9	7.8	11.7	14.4	13.5	11.2	9.6	11.9	13.0	11.0	18.6
Profits after tax	6.4	9.4	9.4	10.6	10.8	8.5	13.9	18.5	20.7	17.3	22.8
Dividends	4.0	4.5	4.3	4.5	4.7	4.7	5.8	6.6	7.3	7.6	9.2
Undistributed profits	2.4	4.9	5.1	6.2	6.1	3.8	8.1	12.0	13.5	9.8	13.6
Inventory adjustment	—0.1	—2.6	—1.2	—0.8	—0.3	—0.6	—5.2	—5.8	—2.1	2.1	—5.1
Net interest	4.1	4.1	3.9	3.4	3.1	3.0	2.9	3.5	4.3	4.9	5.4

a. Including employers' contributions to social insurance.
b. Including inventory valuation adjustment.

Source: Survey of Current Business, National Income Supplement, 1951, p. 150.

TABLE 13

PERCENTAGE DISTRIBUTION OF PRIVATE NATIONAL INCOME,[a] BY DISTRIBUTIVE SHARES, 1929–1950

Item	1929	1930	1931	1932	1933	1934	1935	1936	1937	1938	1939
Total private national income	100.0	100.0	100.0	100.0	100.0	100.0	100.0	100.0	100.0	100.0	100.0
Compensation of employees	55.5	59.1	63.7	70.3	70.0	65.6	60.7	61.0	60.6	61.5	61.4
Wages and salaries	55.0	58.5	62.9	69.3	69.1	64.8	59.9	59.8	58.4	58.8	58.6
Supplements to wages and salaries	.6	.7	.8	1.0	.9	.8	.7	1.2	2.2	2.8	2.7
Income of unincorporated enterprises	16.9	15.7	15.4	13.5	15.2	15.6	19.7	17.6	18.6	18.3	17.6
Business and professional[b]	10.0	10.1	10.0	8.8	8.5	10.1	10.0	10.7	10.1	10.8	10.6
Farm	6.9	5.6	5.4	4.7	6.7	5.5	9.7	6.8	8.5	7.5	7.0
Rental income of persons	7.1	6.9	6.8	6.9	5.9	5.0	4.6	4.7	4.8	5.6	5.4
Corporate profits and inventory valuation adjustment	12.5	9.4	3.1	−5.5	−5.8	2.6	6.0	8.7	9.4	7.3	9.0
Corporate profits before tax	11.9	4.7	−1.5	−8.3	.5	4.1	6.4	10.0	9.4	5.7	10.1
Corporate profits tax liability	1.7	1.2	.9	1.0	1.5	1.8	1.9	2.5	2.3	1.8	2.3
Corporate profits after tax	10.2	3.5	−2.4	−9.4	−1.1	2.3	4.5	7.6	7.1	3.9	7.8
Dividends	7.1	7.9	7.7	7.0	6.0	6.1	5.7	8.1	7.1	5.4	5.9
Undistributed profits	3.2	−4.4	−10.1	−16.4	−7.1	−3.8	−1.2	−.5	.0	−1.5	1.9
Inventory valuation adjustment	.6	4.7	4.5	2.9	−6.3	−1.5	−.5	−1.3	.0	1.6	−1.1
Net interest	8.0	8.9	11.1	14.9	14.6	11.2	9.1	7.9	6.6	7.3	6.6

TABLE 13—CONTINUED

Item	1940	1941	1942	1943	1944	1945	1946	1947	1948	1949	1950
Total private national income	100.0	100.0	100.0	100.0	100.0	100.0	100.0	100.0	100.0	100.0	100.0
Compensation of employees	59.3	57.6	56.7	57.5	58.1	58.9	59.9	60.8	59.1	60.6	60.3
Wages and salaries	56.7	55.2	54.5	55.3	55.8	56.5	57.5	58.2	56.7	58.0	57.4
Supplements to wages and salaries	2.6	2.4	2.2	2.2	2.3	2.4	2.4	2.6	2.4	2.6	2.9
Income of unincorporated enterprises	17.5	17.7	19.1	18.8	19.4	21.5	22.4	19.6	19.5	17.4	16.7
Business and professional[b]	10.6	10.2	10.4	10.5	11.5	12.9	13.1	11.0	10.8	10.7	10.3
Farm	6.8	7.4	8.7	8.3	7.9	8.6	9.4	8.7	8.7	6.7	6.4
Rental income of persons	5.0	4.6	4.5	4.3	4.3	4.3	4.2	3.9	3.7	3.9	3.7
Corporate profits and inventory valuation adjustment	12.6	15.7	16.5	17.0	16.1	13.2	11.6	13.7	15.6	15.6	16.8
Corporate profits before tax	12.9	18.5	17.5	17.6	16.3	13.6	14.9	16.9	16.6	14.5	19.2
Corporate profits tax liability	4.0	8.4	9.7	10.1	9.0	7.7	6.1	6.6	6.4	5.6	8.6
Corporate profits after tax	8.9	10.1	7.8	7.5	7.2	5.9	8.8	10.3	10.2	8.9	10.6
Dividends	5.6	4.8	3.6	3.2	3.1	3.2	3.7	3.6	3.6	3.9	4.3
Undistributed profits	3.3	5.3	4.3	4.3	4.1	2.6	5.1	6.7	6.6	5.0	6.3
Inventory valuation adjustment	−.2	−2.8	−1.0	−.5	−.2	−.4	−3.3	−3.2	−1.0	1.1	−2.4
Net interest	5.7	4.4	3.2	2.4	2.1	2.1	1.9	2.0	2.1	2.5	2.5

a. National income excluding compensation of government and government enterprise employees.
b. Including noncorporate inventory valuation adjustment.

Source: Survey of Current Business, National Income Supplement, 1951, p. 17.

TABLE 14

WAGES AND SALARIES AS PERCENTAGE OF INCOME ORIGINATING IN EACH INDUSTRY, 1929–1950

Industry	1929	1930	1931	1932	1933	1934	1935	1936	1937	1938	1939
All industries, total......	57.4	61.2	66.1	72.6	72.8	69.0	64.3	64.5	62.4	63.5	63.1
Agriculture, forestry and fishing	17.7	21.2	21.4	23.0	18.2	19.8	13.4	17.9	15.6	18.3	17.7
Mining	72.2	79.7	99.9	100.4	103.6	77.7	78.0	73.0	67.2	74.2	71.0
Contract construction	67.3	67.5	69.1	79.9	83.1	73.4	70.7	67.8	68.6	65.2	68.6
Manufacturing	73.1	75.8	86.9	106.7	103.5	88.3	81.2	76.7	75.5	78.9	75.7
Wholesale and retail trade.	71.0	72.2	78.7	93.8	98.2	77.4	73.5	70.0	68.4	68.6	69.0
Finance, insurance and real estate	21.3	24.5	27.7	31.1	32.1	32.6	31.3	29.9	29.0	27.8	27.8
Transportation	71.9	76.9	82.4	84.8	83.0	80.0	79.8	77.7	78.3	80.3	75.5
Communications and public utilities	52.8	55.4	53.6	52.2	53.0	51.9	52.2	52.2	53.0	53.2	51.3
Services	52.8	56.8	58.1	60.9	60.2	58.7	58.2	57.0	56.9	57.3	57.1

TABLE 14—CONTINUED

Industry	1940	1941	1942	1943	1944	1945	1946	1947	1948	1949	1950
All industries, total......	61.0	59.4	59.8	62.7	64.1	64.7	62.3	60.3	59.8	61.6	61.0
Agriculture, forestry and fishing	16.8	14.9	13.3	14.5	15.5	16.0	15.4	15.7	14.7	18.9	17.6
Mining	67.7	65.8	68.3	72.4	74.7	77.6	79.0	72.3	61.3	63.8	62.7
Contract construction	65.9	66.1	67.1	69.9	70.1	70.1	68.6	67.3	70.8	65.0	64.4
Manufacturing	69.7	66.0	68.5	71.0	71.5	73.6	75.8	69.3	69.1	69.3	66.8
Wholesale and retail trade.	65.5	64.9	60.0	55.5	54.6	55.1	59.6	60.6	57.1	61.4	63.4
Finance, insurance and real estate	27.8	26.2	23.7	22.3	21.7	22.5	26.3	26.0	28.7	27.1	27.4
Transportation	74.0	68.9	62.1	61.8	67.2	74.8	82.3	79.3	79.4	77.9	73.7
Communications and public utilities	50.8	50.7	48.6	48.2	48.6	51.1	57.1	60.8	64.1	60.7	58.1
Services	56.7	54.7	54.9	55.4	56.2	57.3	57.3	57.4	58.7	60.0	59.6

Source: For 1929–1947, based on *Survey of Current Business,* National Income Number, July 1947, pp. 26–27; for 1948–1950, on *Survey of Current Business,* National Income Supplement, 1951, pp. 159 and 161.

TABLE 15

Indexes of Wages and Prices, 1840–1890

(1860 = 100)

No.	Year	Nominal Wages: Hansen's Series [a]	Nominal Wages: Tucker's Series [b]	Nominal Wages: Aldrich Committee's Series [c]	Prices: Wholesale Prices [d]	Prices: "Cost of Living" [e]	Nominal Wages Adjusted by Wholesale Price Index [f]: Hansen's Series	Wholesale Price Index: Tucker's Series	Wholesale Price Index: Aldrich Committee's Series	Nominal Wages Adjusted by "Cost-of-Living" Index [g]: Hansen's Series	"Cost-of-Living" Index: Tucker's Series	"Cost-of-Living" Index: Aldrich Committee's Series	No.
1	1840	87.2	85.4	79.6	116.8	97.7	74.7	73.1	68.2	89.3	87.4	81.5	1
2	1841	87.2	82.9	83.7	115.8	98.1	75.3	71.6	72.3	88.9	84.5	85.3	2
3	1842	87.2	85.4	81.2	107.9	90.1	80.8	79.1	75.3	96.8	94.8	90.1	3
4	1843	85.1	82.9	79.4	101.5	84.3	83.8	81.7	78.2	100.9	98.3	94.2	4
5	1844	85.1	82.9	78.9	102.0	85.0	83.4	81.3	77.4	100.1	97.5	92.8	5
6	1845	87.2	85.4	82.0	102.8	88.2	84.8	83.1	79.8	98.9	96.8	93.0	6
7	1846	89.4	87.8	86.0	106.4	95.2	84.0	82.5	80.8	93.9	92.2	90.3	7
8	1847	89.4	87.8	87.4	106.9	95.2	83.6	82.1	81.8	93.9	92.2	91.8	8
9	1848	91.5	87.8	89.2	101.5	88.3	90.1	86.5	87.9	103.6	99.4	101.0	9
10	1849	91.5	87.8	88.9	98.7	83.5	92.7	89.0	90.1	109.6	105.1	106.5	10
11	1850	91.5	90.2	87.0	102.3	89.2	89.4	88.2	85.0	102.6	101.1	97.5	11
12	1851	89.4	90.2	87.9	105.9	98.6	84.4	85.2	83.0	90.7	91.5	89.1	12
13	1852	89.4	90.2	90.2	102.6	97.9	87.1	87.9	87.9	91.3	92.1	92.1	13
14	1853	91.5	92.7	90.7	109.0	105.0	83.9	85.0	83.2	87.1	88.3	86.4	14
15	1854	95.7	95.1	94.9	113.0	105.0	84.7	84.2	84.0	91.1	90.6	90.4	15
16	1855	97.9	97.6	96.6	113.1	109.2	86.6	86.3	85.4	89.7	89.4	88.5	16
17	1856	97.9	97.6	98.0	113.1	112.3	86.6	86.3	86.6	87.2	86.9	87.3	17
18	1857	100.0	100.0	100.1	112.5	114.0	88.9	88.9	89.0	87.7	87.7	87.8	18
19	1858	97.9	100.0	97.9	101.8	113.2	96.2	98.2	96.2	86.5	88.3	86.5	19
20	1859	97.9	100.0	98.8	100.2	102.9	97.7	99.8	98.6	95.1	97.2	96.0	20
21	1860	100.0	100.0	100.0	100.0	100.0	100.0	100.0	100.0	100.0	100.0	100.0	21
22	1861	100.0	100.0	101.6	100.7	103.0	99.3	99.3	100.9	97.1	97.1	98.6	22
23	1862	102.1	102.4	105.6	117.7	112.0	86.7	87.0	89.7	91.2	91.4	94.3	23
24	1863	117.0	117.1	121.0	148.6	129.0	78.7	78.8	81.4	90.7	90.8	93.8	24
25	1864	136.2	134.1	136.5	190.5	156.0	71.5	70.4	71.7	87.3	86.0	87.5	25
26	1865	153.2	148.8	152.7	216.7	168.0	70.7	68.7	70.5	91.2	88.6	90.9	26
27	1866	161.7	158.5	158.5	191.0	170.0	84.7	83.0	83.0	95.1	93.2	93.2	27
28	1867	166.0	163.4	167.0	172.2	168.0	96.4	94.9	97.0	98.8	97.3	99.4	28
29	1868	168.1	165.9	171.1	160.4	161.0	104.8	103.4	106.7	104.4	103.0	106.3	29
30	1869	176.6	173.2	173.7	153.5	156.0	115.0	112.8	113.2	113.2	111.0	111.3	30
31	1870	178.7	175.6	175.0	142.4	150.0	125.5	123.3	122.9	119.1	117.1	116.7	31
32	1871	183.0	175.6	174.2	136.0	147.0	134.6	129.1	128.1	124.4	119.5	118.5	32
33	1872	180.9	175.6	175.0	138.8	148.0	130.3	126.5	126.1	122.2	118.6	118.2	33
34	1873	180.9	175.6	173.9	137.4	145.0	131.7	127.8	126.6	124.8	121.1	119.9	34
35	1874	174.5	170.7	170.2	133.0	145.0	131.2	128.3	128.0	120.3	117.7	117.4	35

TABLE 15—CONTINUED

No.	Year	Nominal Wages: Hansen's Series [a]	Nominal Wages: Tucker's Series [b]	Nominal Wages: Aldrich Committee's Series [c]	Prices: Wholesale Prices [d]	Prices: "Cost of Living" [e]	Nominal Wages Adjusted by: Wholesale Price Index [f]: Hansen's Series	Wholesale Price Index [f]: Tucker's Series	Wholesale Price Index [f]: Aldrich Committee's Series	"Cost-of-Living" Index [g]: Hansen's Series	"Cost-of-Living" Index [g]: Tucker's Series	"Cost-of-Living" Index [g]: Aldrich Committee's Series	No.
36	1875	163.8	165.9	168.8	127.6	141.0	128.4	130.0	132.3	116.2	117.7	119.7	**36**
37	1876	157.4	161.0	161.8	118.2	133.0	133.2	136.2	136.9	118.3	121.1	121.7	**37**
38	1877	144.7	151.2	153.6	110.8	132.0	130.6	136.5	138.6	109.6	114.5	116.4	**38**
39	1878	142.6	146.3	150.5	101.3	132.0	140.8	144.4	148.6	108.0	110.8	114.0	**39**
40	1879	140.4	146.3	148.9	96.6	130.0	145.3	151.4	154.1	108.0	112.5	114.5	**40**
41	1880	140.4	146.3	152.8	106.9	132.0	131.3	136.9	142.9	106.4	110.8	115.8	**41**
42	1881	144.7	153.7	161.0	105.7	136.4	136.9	145.4	152.3	106.1	112.7	118.0	**42**
43	1882	148.9	156.1	163.4	108.5	137.3	137.2	143.9	150.6	108.4	113.7	119.0	**43**
44	1883	151.1	161.0	170.1	106.1	134.1	142.4	151.7	160.3	112.7	120.1	126.8	**44**
45	1884	151.1	158.5	165.7	99.3	129.1	152.2	159.6	166.9	117.0	122.8	128.4	**45**
46	1885	148.9	158.5	166.6	92.9	117.4	160.3	170.6	179.3	126.8	135.0	141.9	**46**
47	1886	148.9	158.5	168.1	92.0	117.5	161.8	172.3	182.7	126.7	134.9	143.1	**47**
48	1887	153.2	161.0	172.3	92.6	118.9	165.4	173.9	186.1	128.8	135.4	144.9	**48**
49	1888	155.3	163.4	173.7	94.3	121.1	164.7	173.3	184.2	128.2	134.9	143.4	**49**
50	1889	155.3	163.4	179.2	94.3	123.9	164.7	173.3	190.0	125.3	131.9	144.6	**50**
51	1890	157.4	168.3	185.0	92.3	117.9	170.5	182.3	200.4	133.5	142.7	156.9	**51**

Sources and Notes:

a. Alvin H. Hansen, "Factors Affecting the Trend of Real Wages," *American Economic Review,* March 1925, pp. 27–42. The index was designed to show the trend of daily wages and was derived primarily from *Report on Wholesale Prices, Wages and Transportation,* Senate Committee on Finance (Aldrich Committee), S.Rept. 1394, 52d Cong., 2d sess., Washington, 1893, Part I, p. 176. The Aldrich Committee's simple average of daily rates was used, with minor adjustments, especially as made for 1860 to 1880 by Wesley C. Mitchell (*Gold, Prices, and Wages under the Greenback Standard, 1860–1880,* University of California Press, Berkeley, 1908).

b. Rufus S. Tucker, "Real Wages under Laissez-Faire," *Barron's Weekly,* October 23, 1933, pp. 6–7. The Aldrich Committee's simple average of daily rates, converted to an hourly basis, was averaged with a composite index compiled by Carl Snyder. The Tucker index was adopted by Harold G. Moulton in his *Income and Economic Progress,* Brookings Institution, Washington, 1935, pp. 181–82.

c. The Aldrich Committee's index (constructed by R. P. Falkner) of daily wage rates adjusted by hours per day (Aldrich Committee Report, Part I, pp. 176–79). The wage rates of selected occupations were indexed by establishment; simple averages were made of the occupational indexes to obtain industry averages; and the industry averages were combined by use of census employment data to obtain a weighted general average. The wage quotations were obtained from records available in 1891, and the information for the earlier part of the period is fragmentary, but the general trend appears to be valid: the percentage change in the weighted day rate from 1849 to 1889 is the same as the percentage change in the average wage as derived from the Census of Manufactures for 1849 and 1889.

d. A series constructed by R. P. Falkner for the Aldrich Committee (the Committee Report, Part I, p. 93). The index is a simple average of the component series of wholesale commodity prices (January quotations).

e. For the years 1840–1860 and 1880–1890, this index is a wholesale price index derived by weighting commodity wholesale price quotations by estimates of consumption (the Aldrich Committee index, in the Committee Report, Part I, pp. 90–94). Commodities for which consumption estimates were not available were omitted, and such items as rent were not included. The index was designed by R. P. Falkner, who constructed it for the Aldrich Committee, as the best available approximation of a cost-of-living index. Its deficiencies as a cost-of-living index are especially serious in periods of rapid change, when wholesale prices are usually more elastic than retail prices. It is known that a serious divergence of the index from the trend of retail prices occurred in the period of extreme price change and economic dislocation during and after the Civil War. For that period, a detailed study of trends was made by Wesley C. Mitchell in his *Gold, Prices, and Wages.* Mitchell's index of the cost of living (p. 279) is used for 1860 to 1880, and the Aldrich Committee index for the period of comparatively stable prices from 1880 to 1890 is linked to the Mitchell index.

f. The index of wholesale prices has often been used to adjust various wage series. Such a series, however, has little claim to validity or significance and should in no sense be viewed as an index of "real wages." There is evidence of serious distortion as well as lack of comparability in both the price and wage series; and the wholesale price index, even if it is an adequate representation of the actual trend of wholesale prices, cannot be assumed to represent the trend of consumers' prices, especially of rents and services.

g. The wage indexes in these columns, as adjusted by the "cost-of-living" index (see note e), may be assumed to approximate much more nearly the trends of real wages than do the indexes given in the three preceding columns of wages adjusted by the wholesale price index. Even the indexes derived by use of the "cost-of-living" index, however, are significant chiefly as indicating the probable trends between periods of relative stability.

TABLE 16

INDEXES OF WAGES AND SALARIES, 1890–1947

(1926 = 100)

Year	Composite Wage [a]	Union Hourly Rates in the Building Trades [b]	Average Weekly Earnings of Wage Earners in Manufacturing [c]	Full-Time Equivalent Average Annual Earnings of Nonfarm Hired Workers [d]	Year	Composite Wage [a]	Union Hourly Rates in the Building Trades [b]	Average Weekly Earnings of Wage Earners in Manufacturing [c]	Full-Time Equivalent Average Annual Earnings of Nonfarm Hired Workers [d]
1890	29.6	22.8	34.2	37.8	1920	99.1	79.3	106.7	97.9
1891	29.9	22.8	34.5	37.9	1921	91.4	80.7	90.0	91.1
1892	30.2	23.2	34.8	38.3	1922	87.9	75.8	87.3	89.9
1893	30.3	23.2	32.8	37.4	1923	94.6	83.7	96.6	95.5
1894	29.6	22.8	30.1	35.4	1924	97.8	90.4	97.1	96.2
1895	29.5	22.8	32.5	36.6	1925	98.4	93.9	98.9	98.0
1896	29.9	23.0	31.7	36.3	1926	100.0	100.0	100.0	100.0
1897	29.8	23.2	31.8	36.3	1927	101.6	103.4	100.4	100.6
1898	30.2	23.2	32.1	36.6	1928	102.4	104.1	101.3	101.9
1899	30.9	24.1	33.2	37.4	1929	103.7	105.4	101.5	103.8
1900	32.0	25.1	34.0	38.1	1930	103.4	109.9	94.3	101.1
1901	33.0	26.2	35.6	39.1	1931	99.0	110.2	84.7	95.3
1902	34.3	27.6	36.9	39.8	1932	88.0	94.1	69.2	84.6
1903	35.8	29.3	37.9	41.3	1933	85.6	91.5	67.9	79.1
1904	36.1	29.7	37.2	41.2	1934	95.1	92.2	74.6	81.7
1905	36.7	30.4	38.5	42.0	1935	98.4	93.2	81.7	85.3
1906	38.2	32.0	39.5	42.9	1936	100.0	96.6	88.4	89.7
1907	39.5	33.2	40.7	44.6	1937	108.1	103.3	97.6	95.5
1908	39.2	35.3	37.0	42.6	1938	110.3	112.5	90.5	94.6
1909	39.6	37.0	40.4	44.5	1939	111.3	113.3	96.8	96.9
1910	40.4	38.5	43.5	46.3	1940	114.0	115.1	102.2	99.4
1911	41.2	39.1	41.9	45.8	1941	121.9	119.3	120.0	109.7
1912	42.4	40.0	42.9	47.7	1942	136.3	126.7	148.7	128.2
1913	45.6	40.9	45.1	49.6	1943	151.9	127.6	175.0	148.4
1914	46.0	41.8	44.7	47.3	1944	163.1	128.7	186.9	159.9
1915	46.4	42.1	46.0	49.3	1945	169.4	131.4	180.1	166.1
1916	50.0	43.5	51.8	55.8	1946	184.8	146.4	177.4	173.1
1917	56.5	46.2	61.4	64.6	1947	203.9	167.5	202.7	189.7
1918	69.6	51.3	78.4	74.8					
1919	81.7	58.8	89.6	85.2					

Sources and Notes:

a. For 1890 to 1913: a general index of average hourly earnings, representing substantially the general trend of basic wages and salaries (see p. 47), constructed by Paul H. Douglas (*Real Wages in the United States, 1890–1926,* Houghton Mifflin, Boston, 1930, p. 205). For 1913 to 1939: the composite index of wages constructed by the Federal Reserve Bank of New York; it is described as primarily an index of hourly earnings but includes farm wage rates and certain series of weekly or annual salaries. For 1939 to 1947: the composite index of wages and salaries (predominantly hourly earnings) constructed by the Federal Reserve Bank of New York, adjusted to include farm wage rates and linked to the 1913–1939 series. Both series make primary use of Bureau of Labor Statistics data, combined with data from several other sources.

b. The Bureau of Labor Statistics index, 1907–1947 (Bulletin No. 910, 1947, p. 2), to which is linked the Douglas index for 1890 to 1907 (*Real Wages in the United States,* p. 135).

c. For 1890 to 1913: the Douglas estimates of annual factory wages (*Real Wages in the United States,* p. 246), converted to a weekly basis. For 1914 to 1947: the Bureau of Labor Statistics series (Bulletin No. 852, 1945, p. 13, and mimeographed releases).

d. The series computed by Stanley Lebergott ("Earnings of Nonfarm Employees in the United States, 1890–1946," *Journal of the American Statistical Association,* March 1948, pp. 74–93), based on series prepared by Paul H. Douglas, the National Bureau of Economic Research and the Department of Commerce.

TABLE 17

Indexes of Wholesale Prices and Consumers' Prices, 1890–1947

(*1926 = 100*)

Year	Wholesale Prices [a]	Consumers' Prices [b]	Year	Wholesale Prices [a]	Consumers' Prices [b]
1890	56.2	42.4	1920	154.4	113.4
1891	55.8	41.2	1921	97.6	101.0
1892	52.2	41.6	1922	96.7	94.7
1893	53.4	40.8	1923	100.6	96.4
1894	47.9	39.6	1924	98.1	96.7
1895	48.8	39.6	1925	103.5	99.2
1896	46.5	40.4	1926	100.0	100.0
1897	46.6	40.8	1927	95.4	98.1
1898	48.5	40.8	1928	96.7	97.0
1899	52.2	41.6	1929	95.3	96.9
1900	56.1	43.3	1930	86.4	94.4
1901	55.3	44.1	1931	73.0	86.0
1902	58.9	45.3	1932	64.8	77.2
1903	59.6	47.3	1933	65.9	73.1
1904	59.7	46.9	1934	74.9	75.7
1905	60.1	46.9	1935	80.0	77.6
1906	61.8	49.0	1936	80.8	78.4
1907	65.2	51.4	1937	86.3	81.3
1908	62.9	49.4	1938	78.6	79.7
1909	67.6	49.4	1939	77.1	78.6
1910	70.4	52.2	1940	78.6	79.3
1911	64.9	53.9	1941	87.3	83.2
1912	69.1	54.3	1942	98.8	92.2
1913	69.8	55.9	1943	103.1	97.8
1914	68.1	56.8	1944	104.0	99.3
1915	69.5	57.4	1945	105.8	101.6
1916	85.5	61.6	1946	121.1	110.2
1917	117.5	72.5	1947	151.8	125.9
1918	131.3	85.0			
1919	138.6	97.9			

Sources and Notes:

a. Bureau of Labor Statistics index.

b. The Douglas series (*Real Wages in the United States, 1890–1926,* Houghton Mifflin, Boston, 1930, p. 41), linked to the Bureau of Labor Statistics series, 1913–1947, converted to the 1926 base. The Douglas series made use of the Bureau of Labor Statistics index of retail food prices (Bulletin No. 396, 1925) and various other sources.

TABLE 18

INDEXES OF WAGES AND SALARIES, ADJUSTED BY CONSUMERS' PRICE INDEX, 1890–1947

(1926 = 100)

Year	Composite Wage	Union Hourly Rates in the Building Trades	Average Weekly Earnings of Wage Earners in Manufacturing	Full-Time Equivalent Annual Earnings of Nonfarm Hired Workers
1890.....	69.8	53.8	80.7	89.2
1891.....	72.6	55.3	83.7	92.0
1892.....	72.6	55.8	83.7	92.1
1893.....	74.3	56.9	80.4	91.7
1894.....	74.7	57.6	76.0	89.4
1895.....	74.5	57.6	82.1	92.4
1896.....	74.0	56.9	78.5	89.9
1897.....	73.0	56.9	77.9	89.0
1898.....	74.0	56.9	78.7	89.7
1899.....	74.3	57.9	79.8	89.9
1900.....	73.9	58.0	78.5	88.0
1901.....	74.8	59.4	80.7	88.7
1902.....	75.7	60.9	81.5	87.9
1903.....	75.7	61.9	80.1	87.3
1904.....	77.0	63.3	79.3	87.8
1905.....	78.3	64.8	82.1	89.6
1906.....	78.0	65.3	80.6	87.6
1907.....	76.8	64.6	79.2	86.8
1908.....	79.4	71.5	74.9	86.2
1909.....	80.2	74.9	81.8	90.1
1910.....	77.4	73.8	83.3	88.7
1911.....	76.4	72.5	77.7	85.0
1912.....	78.1	73.7	79.0	87.8
1913.....	81.6	73.2	80.7	88.7
1914.....	81.0	73.6	78.7	83.3
1915.....	80.8	73.3	80.1	85.9
1916.....	81.2	70.6	84.1	90.6
1917.....	77.9	63.7	84.7	89.1
1918.....	81.9	60.4	92.2	88.0
1919.....	83.5	60.1	91.5	87.0
1920.....	87.4	69.9	94.1	86.3
1921.....	90.5	79.9	89.1	90.2
1922.....	92.8	80.0	92.2	94.9
1923.....	98.1	86.8	100.2	99.1
1924.....	101.1	93.5	100.4	99.5
1925.....	99.2	94.7	99.7	98.8
1926.....	100.0	100.0	100.0	100.0
1927.....	103.6	105.4	102.3	102.5
1928.....	105.6	107.3	104.4	105.1
1929.....	107.0	108.8	104.7	107.1
1930.....	109.5	116.4	100.0	107.1
1931.....	115.1	128.1	98.5	110.8
1932.....	114.0	121.9	89.6	109.6
1933.....	117.1	125.2	92.9	108.2
1934.....	125.6	121.8	98.5	107.9
1935.....	126.8	120.1	105.3	109.9
1936.....	127.6	123.2	112.8	114.4
1937.....	133.0	127.1	120.0	117.5
1938.....	138.4	141.2	113.6	118.7
1939.....	141.6	144.1	123.2	123.3
1940.....	143.8	145.1	128.9	125.3
1941.....	146.5	143.4	144.2	131.9
1942.....	147.8	137.4	161.3	139.0
1943.....	155.3	130.5	178.9	151.7
1944.....	164.2	129.6	188.2	161.0
1945.....	166.7	129.3	177.3	163.5
1946.....	167.7	132.8	161.0	157.1
1947.....	162.0	133.0	161.0	150.7

Source: Based on Tables 16 and 17.

TABLE 19

Average Hours per Week, 1890–1947

Year	Prevailing or Full-Time Weekly Hours: Manufacturing: Prevailing Hours (Census Data)[a]	Full-Time Hours[b]	Bituminous Coal Mining[c]	Steam Railroads[d]	Union Hours[e]: Building Trades	Book and Job Printing	Newspapers	Average Weekly Hours (Payroll Count of Employees)[f]: Manufacturing	Bituminous Coal Mining	Steam Railroads
1890	—	60.0	60.0	60	53.4	60.8	49.6	—	—	—
1899	59.6	59.1	52.7	60	—	—	—	—	—	—
1904	57.9	57.7	51.7	60	—	—	—	—	—	—
1907	—	—	—	—	47.6	54.1	45.7	—	—	—
1909	56.8	56.8	51.6	60	46.2	51.2	45.3	51.0	37.8	53.9
1914	55.1	55.2	51.8	60	45.1	51.0	45.0	49.4	35.2	54.1
1919	50.8	52.3	48.4	48	44.3	50.9	45.0	46.3	35.5	46.3
1921	50.3	50.7	48.2	48	44.1	45.1	44.8	—	—	43.4
1923	51.1	51.0	48.4	48	44.1	44.3	45.6	45.6	31.3	45.4
1929	50.6	49.6	48.5	48	43.3	44.2	44.6	44.2	38.4	44.4
1932	—	47.9	48.6	48	40.8	42.5	43.4	38.3	27.2	38.9
1939	—	—	—	—	38.3	39.6	37.9	37.7	27.1	43.4
1940	—	40.0	35.0	48	38.3	39.5	37.8	38.1	28.1	44.0
1941	—	—	—	—	—	—	—	40.6	31.1	45.6
1942	—	—	—	—	—	—	—	42.9	32.9	46.9
1943	—	—	—	—	—	—	—	44.9	36.6	48.7
1944	—	—	—	—	—	—	—	45.2	43.4	49.1
1945	—	—	—	—	—	—	—	43.4	42.3	48.5
1946	—	—	—	—	—	—	—	40.4	41.6	45.9
1947	—	—	—	—	—	—	—	40.3	40.6	46.3

Sources and Notes:

a. Computed from the frequency distributions in the censuses of manufactures by Leo Wolman (*Hours of Work in American Industry,* Bulletin No. 71, National Bureau of Economic Research, New York, 1938, p. 2).

b. Full-time weekly hours (essentially the same as the "prevailing" hours of the censuses of manufactures) were computed, for 1890 to 1923, largely from data collected by the Bureau of Labor and the Bureau of Labor Statistics, by Paul H. Douglas (*Real Wages in the United States, 1890–1926,* Houghton Mifflin, Boston, 1930, pp. 112–18). The remarkably close correspondence of the "prevailing" and the "full-time" averages, computed from completely independent sources, attests the substantial validity of both series. The 1929 and 1932 figures (included in Wolman's table) were computed by the National Industrial Conference Board. The 1940 figure of 40 hours is the standard straight-time week established by the Fair Labor Standards Act, which, after October 24, 1940, required premium pay for work in covered industries (including manufacturing) beyond 40 hours a week. At that time (1940) there was little overtime and the standard week closely approximated the average full-time week. At times, especially during the war, the regularly scheduled or full-time week has been considerably longer than the straight-time week.

c. Wolman, *Hours of Work,* p. 2, except the 1940 figure. Derived from Bureau of Mines data of hours of mine operation (*Minerals Yearbook*). A six-day week is assumed except for 1940; the five-day week with seven hours a day, had been adopted in 1933. Time is at the face of the mine or usual place of work, preceding the counting of travel time in the mine by underground employees as time at work. In 1947 the standard work week, including travel time, was raised to 40 hours.

d. Wolman, *Hours of Work,* p. 2, except for 1940. Computed by assuming a 10-hour day until 1917 and an 8-hour day later, with a 6-day week throughout. Wolman points out that there are important exceptions; e.g., many railroads had working agreements with groups of shop employees for the 8-hour day before its general adoption. The 8-hour basic day of road train and engine employees is not necessarily the time on duty. Some employees have arrangements for a 5½-day week.

e. Computed, for 1907 to 1940, from Bureau of Labor Statistics indexes (Bulletin No. 674, 1940, pp. 7, 30, and Bulletin No. 675, 1940, pp. 5, 26), using the 1939 absolutes. The indexes are computed on the basis of year-to-year changes in comparable coverages; the absolute figure for a current year is derived from all data reported for that year. The absolute averages as reported from year to year are therefore not exact measures of time-to-time comparisons, and the averages derived from the index numbers are necessarily approximate. The 1890 figures were computed from the Douglas series based on Bureau of Labor data (*Real Wages in the United States,* pp. 112, 136), by extrapolation back to 1890 of the Bureau of Labor Statistics indexes beginning in 1907.

f. Bureau of Labor Statistics series. In bituminous coal mining, beginning in 1944, hours include travel time in the mine by underground workers. Hours of railroad workers were computed from Interstate Commerce Commission reports. The employees are those reported on an hourly basis; the count of employees used is the number on payrolls during the month, averaged for the twelve months, and estimated, for earlier years, from the later ratio of the middle-of-the-month count to the count of those on payrolls during the month; the hours are hours paid for.

TABLE 20

INDEXES OF PRODUCTION, OUTPUT PER MAN-HOUR AND AVERAGE HOURLY EARNINGS IN SELECTED MANUFACTURING INDUSTRIES, 1919–1947

A = Index of Production
B = Index of Output per Man-Hour
C = Index of Average Hourly Earnings

(1939 = 100)

No.	Year	Agricultural Implements			Automobiles			Bread and Other Bakery Products			Cane Sugar Refining			Canning and Preserving			No.
		A	B	C	A	B	C	A	B	C	A	B	C	A	B	C	
1	1919	—	—	—	42.5	35.9	68.6	—	—	—	101.9	50.7	69.8	52.7	53.7	76.3	**1**
2	1920	140.1	37.2	—	48.1	39.1	79.4	—	—	—	105.6	55.0	83.2	—	—	—	**2**
3	1921	72.2	54.7	94.3	34.3	47.9	73.6	—	—	—	91.3	52.2	68.7	33.9	52.7	73.9	**3**
4	1922	47.0	31.5	—	54.1	51.6	67.8	—	—	—	131.2	66.5	67.6	—	—	—	**4**
5	1923	80.5	50.1	78.7	85.4	58.8	75.0	74.3	86.8	86.8	107.3	66.4	76.7	58.1	65.7	80.8	**5**
6	1924	73.4	58.6	81.6	76.5	59.6	76.5	81.6	94.2	88.6	116.4	75.2	78.3	56.6	72.2	81.0	**6**
7	1925	79.4	52.9	77.9	94.7	62.5	77.8	79.3	93.7	89.4	131.1	83.9	75.0	71.5	68.8	80.9	**7**
8	1926	112.0	66.4	81.3	100.1	66.1	75.1	85.8	98.6	90.1	132.2	86.9	72.6	77.3	71.2	—	**8**
9	1927	107.6	62.5	84.2	86.3	66.8	78.3	88.1	96.7	89.2	124.2	80.9	71.2	67.5	67.4	79.2	**9**
10	1928	123.2	60.7	86.5	110.2	70.6	79.2	91.7	95.0	88.5	121.1	82.9	72.3	81.1	72.4	—	**10**
11	1929	141.2	65.2	85.1	132.8	84.2	76.8	95.2	89.4	88.7	123.9	79.8	71.0	82.0	68.4	78.7	**11**
12	1930	109.7	77.4	86.7	86.5	89.2	73.4	92.2	90.6	91.7	121.8	81.6	72.5	87.4	76.5	80.8	**12**
13	1931	35.7	54.8	91.6	63.2	79.7	73.0	86.8	94.9	90.1	107.3	79.9	71.5	69.3	86.1	83.0	**13**
14	1932	—	—	—	39.8	69.3	73.3	80.4	95.5	82.8	97.3	85.3	70.3	50.6	85.0	79.7	**14**
15	1933	10.0	25.3	77.8	54.1	83.9	64.5	76.2	90.6	80.5	95.4	95.7	75.8	70.9	97.9	77.3	**15**
16	1934	—	—	88.6	76.1	85.2	80.0	82.9	92.9	90.8	95.3	102.1	86.3	74.7	93.7	91.5	**16**
17	1935	59.0	57.5	82.6	107.8	99.4	83.1	87.8	95.4	92.9	102.0	105.9	89.2	94.2	100.4	92.4	**17**
18	1936	99.6	83.7	90.1	122.3	102.2	86.4	95.1	94.9	91.1	103.1	107.6	91.0	83.9	82.8	86.9	**18**
19	1937	117.4	79.6	111.6	130.3	100.5	96.2	97.9	92.3	95.4	109.4	109.7	99.0	105.1	88.7	96.3	**19**
20	1938	125.8	116.9	109.6	70.8	99.7	99.0	98.4	97.3	98.1	103.2	102.3	96.3	90.9	95.3	97.7	**20**
21	1939	100.0	100.0	100.0	100.0	100.0	100.0	100.0	100.0	100.0	100.0	100.0	100.0	100.0	100.0	100.0	**21**
22	1940	—	—	—	—	—	—	—	—	103.2	103.6	103.9	101.4	105.7	108.7	104.1	**22**
23	1941	—	—	—	—	—	—	108.1	105.1	108.1	122.5	111.0	105.0	127.6	105.6	118.3	**23**
24	1942	—	—	—	—	—	—	119.0	106.9	118.2	77.2	81.0	117.9	134.6	99.3	141.5	**24**
25	1943	—	—	—	—	—	—	133.2	112.2	128.9	102.5	85.3	127.1	127.9	97.0	163.9	**25**
26	1944	—	—	—	—	—	—	135.7	111.0	136.5	120.7	88.8	132.4	146.9	104.1	174.6	**26**
27	1945	—	—	—	—	—	—	135.8	110.2	144.2	106.0	85.2	135.1	155.5	104.7	184.0	**27**
28	1946	—	—	—	—	—	—	131.1	106.8	162.3	89.1	75.7	151.8	184.2	106.8	209.9	**28**
29	1947	—	—	—	—	—	—	123.6	98.3	186.1	123.0	73.7	175.0	157.4	100.3	234.8	**29**

TABLE 20—CONTINUED

No.	Year	Cement A	Cement B	Cement C	Chemicals A	Chemicals B	Chemicals C	Clay Construction Products A	Clay Construction Products B	Clay Construction Products C	Coke A	Coke B	Coke C	Confectionery A	Confectionery B	Confectionery C	No.
1	1919	66.2	43.2	68.5	40.3	30.0	—	109.1	70.2	84.1	88.6	49.1	72.1	—	—	—	**1**
2	1920	80.5	44.5	84.8	49.6	49.6	—	119.7	71.6	101.7	99.9	50.8	—	—	—	—	**2**
3	1921	79.4	51.2	70.3	31.5	43.4	—	100.2	70.6	86.8	54.8	58.9	78.9	—	—	—	**3**
4	1922	93.5	56.5	84.5	42.9	43.5	—	130.6	73.5	80.9	83.4	69.4	—	—	—	—	**4**
5	1923	111.5	55.6	78.4	54.1	47.0	63.9	169.8	80.4	97.9	118.5	77.8	97.2	—	—	—	**5**
6	1924	120.9	56.9	80.5	48.3	45.9	66.7	162.1	76.1	100.0	96.3	81.1	—	—	—	—	**6**
7	1925	130.0	61.7	80.9	53.9	51.2	67.3	178.5	82.2	97.7	115.2	82.6	81.2	80.9	47.7	79.3	**7**
8	1926	133.1	62.0	78.2	59.8	61.1	71.0	180.8	83.0	98.4	126.4	89.7	—	92.0	52.2	80.3	**8**
9	1927	139.1	64.7	78.1	61.4	64.2	73.7	176.1	85.8	99.3	115.5	86.7	78.8	91.1	54.1	82.3	**9**
10	1928	142.3	67.8	76.8	67.1	65.9	74.0	166.8	90.5	100.1	122.1	98.5	—	87.5	53.1	81.2	**10**
11	1929	138.1	71.7	80.2	82.0	72.1	74.4	162.6	88.0	96.6	135.1	92.8	70.6	91.2	53.8	81.1	**11**
12	1930	130.8	74.8	79.3	71.1	72.6	74.6	118.5	88.9	98.0	110.1	86.1	—	88.3	61.2	85.6	**12**
13	1931	100.3	85.7	80.8	63.9	81.3	75.7	77.4	91.8	87.5	77.0	75.6	66.8	75.0	62.6	85.6	**13**
14	1932	61.9	83.4	66.7	54.9	85.6	71.0	36.3	79.8	71.4	50.4	66.3	—	69.1	67.9	78.9	**14**
15	1933	51.4	84.4	72.1	65.3	86.7	70.1	41.1	87.8	67.5	63.3	74.3	56.1	72.6	73.1	81.0	**15**
16	1934	62.8	86.0	88.1	66.9	75.9	76.8	43.6	78.6	80.4	72.5	73.9	—	82.2	83.2	93.8	**16**
17	1935	61.6	80.9	87.0	76.5	84.2	79.1	58.4	84.3	83.0	79.6	85.0	70.9	89.3	88.6	94.7	**17**
18	1936	91.9	92.1	84.3	88.4	88.5	82.5	88.0	84.7	83.5	104.1	92.3	—	97.8	91.1	88.0	**18**
19	1937	95.0	89.1	101.0	100.1	91.3	95.5	98.4	88.2	95.7	117.0	94.0	81.8	98.3	88.2	95.0	**19**
20	1938	85.8	92.2	101.4	78.9	89.6	100.0	71.9	86.8	96.4	73.6	87.9	—	95.4	94.1	97.5	**20**
21	1939	100.0	100.0	100.0	100.0	100.0	100.0	100.0	100.0	100.0	100.0	100.0	100.0	100.0	100.0	100.0	**21**
22	1940	106.5	100.4	101.6	—	—	—	92.4	104.5	93.4	128.0	104.4	99.6	107.5	107.4	101.6	**22**
23	1941	134.3	108.3	108.6	—	—	—	103.2	102.3	100.3	146.6	105.3	100.0	121.4	113.0	109.4	**23**
24	1942	148.2	108.4	118.6	—	—	—	79.9	94.6	108.8	158.3	106.2	106.8	121.9	112.9	122.2	**24**
25	1943	108.4	94.7	126.1	—	—	—	48.3	77.9	120.0	159.0	98.4	113.5	126.4	109.1	136.0	**25**
26	1944	73.7	83.8	131.6	—	—	—	44.8	80.4	125.5	164.1	103.1	118.6	140.0	111.2	148.8	**26**
27	1945	83.3	90.1	135.8	—	—	—	51.0	84.2	133.3	147.9	100.5	130.4	132.8	111.6	159.5	**27**
28	1946	134.1	108.7	149.7	—	—	—	98.1	100.0	157.0	128.0	97.0	162.2	128.5	111.9	179.1	**28**
29	1947	151.8	110.8	168.9	—	—	—	106.3	99.8	173.4	160.6	105.2	177.5	137.0	100.6	203.8	**29**

TABLE 20—CONTINUED

No.	Year	Cotton Goods			Fertilizers			Flour			Footwear			Furniture and Finished Lumber Products			No.
		A	B	C	A	B	C	A	B	C	A	B	C	A	B	C	
1	1919	81.0	58.2	91.0	97.2	51.2	95.9	122.4	55.9	82.0	76.4	64.3	96.6	75.9	68.4	83.1	**1**
2	1920	80.1	61.3	123.4	102.3	42.7	—	100.7	51.2	95.9	71.8	66.6	116.0	66.1	56.6	104.1	**2**
3	1921	74.4	56.7	89.1	69.7	58.0	95.8	106.3	62.8	89.8	65.1	63.2	108.3	62.1	69.6	104.0	**3**
4	1922	86.3	65.0	84.7	79.4	49.1	—	110.7	64.4	82.8	73.9	67.1	112.1	82.5	71.5	96.4	**4**
5	1923	94.7	65.0	97.1	88.0	65.2	87.1	111.6	66.2	87.2	79.5	62.9	107.8	94.6	72.4	100.7	**5**
6	1924	80.3	65.2	95.5	90.6	73.4	89.9	114.1	71.5	91.2	71.3	63.9	108.3	101.7	81.2	104.6	**6**
7	1925	92.5	65.9	89.9	94.2	66.7	90.2	109.5	72.0	92.0	73.1	62.8	105.6	116.9	84.2	104.5	**7**
8	1926	94.4	62.9	84.3	97.6	65.3	93.9	110.6	75.9	93.4	76.3	68.4	109.1	127.0	86.3	105.2	**8**
9	1927	99.7	60.9	83.0	94.3	70.6	94.8	109.5	77.2	93.3	83.5	73.8	108.3	127.0	87.6	105.8	**9**
10	1928	89.4	65.5	83.2	109.9	77.2	90.9	110.7	81.4	95.1	83.3	77.6	107.6	125.1	89.7	105.7	**10**
11	1929	95.1	68.5	83.2	111.1	74.1	85.7	110.4	87.0	97.4	86.8	77.7	108.4	137.7	94.1	106.8	**11**
12	1930	70.6	66.2	83.4	110.0	78.6	88.3	108.9	91.7	95.6	72.1	75.7	104.1	96.8	91.9	105.0	**12**
13	1931	69.8	64.3	72.2	82.0	86.8	92.3	102.8	96.8	90.6	72.9	73.5	89.6	74.1	90.6	99.1	**13**
14	1932	64.4	70.2	61.4	56.4	87.9	80.8	94.8	94.0	80.7	72.1	79.4	81.3	50.4	91.1	85.5	**14**
15	1933	80.9	74.7	71.2	63.1	83.0	68.7	90.0	93.6	82.7	81.7	88.0	83.4	53.4	86.7	79.7	**15**
16	1934	72.0	79.0	97.0	70.3	85.4	92.0	90.9	93.1	95.4	83.0	89.6	99.7	59.6	95.5	92.5	**16**
17	1935	76.2	85.0	96.5	77.4	90.5	92.0	90.4	90.8	95.9	89.4	97.0	101.7	77.8	94.8	89.3	**17**
18	1936	96.2	93.5	94.6	88.2	89.5	83.5	94.9	87.5	91.2	97.2	103.7	99.8	94.1	91.5	90.0	**18**
19	1937	100.8	93.5	106.0	108.6	89.1	90.5	93.4	83.8	95.4	95.6	95.7	104.2	103.2	92.4	99.5	**19**
20	1938	79.9	93.7	101.8	98.9	98.6	95.3	96.6	92.6	96.8	91.5	99.0	102.2	81.5	98.2	101.4	**20**
21	1939	100.0	100.0	100.0	100.0	100.0	100.0	100.0	100.0	100.0	100.0	100.0	100.0	100.0	100.0	100.0	**21**
22	1940	—	—	—	106.9	104.7	105.6	96.5	99.8	101.0	95.4	104.1	103.7	—	—	—	**22**
23	1941	—	—	—	119.1	100.8	116.7	99.9	99.9	106.7	118.4	108.5	116.1	—	—	—	**23**
24	1942	—	—	—	129.0	91.0	135.5	103.7	95.7	120.0	115.0	107.0	134.1	—	—	—	**24**
25	1943	—	—	—	148.6	84.0	154.0	122.1	89.3	133.8	105.8	108.3	145.3	—	—	—	**25**
26	1944	—	—	—	156.2	89.0	172.5	124.8	83.3	141.6	101.0	106.1	155.6	—	—	—	**26**
27	1945	—	—	—	171.2	96.0	181.9	131.5	83.4	149.2	105.3	111.3	166.8	—	—	—	**27**
28	1946	—	—	—	192.8	103.8	199.4	122.6	79.5	167.2	118.4	111.2	189.5	—	—	—	**28**
29	1947	—	—	—	194.9	102.7	223.9	139.1	82.5	192.6	110.1	97.1	206.4	—	—	—	**29**

TABLE 20—CONTINUED

No.	Year	Glass Products A	Glass Products B	Glass Products C	Ice Cream A	Ice Cream B	Ice Cream C	Iron and Steel A	Iron and Steel B	Iron and Steel C	Knit Goods A	Knit Goods B	Knit Goods C	Leather A	Leather B	Leather C	No.
1	1919	50.7	33.8	66.0	57.5	39.7	86.3	67.4	37.5	62.0	44.6	46.0	64.2	91.7	47.0	79.6	1
2	1920	60.0	38.4	80.8	64.0	42.8	—	83.4	47.6	76.4	—	—	81.5	75.7	44.6	94.0	2
3	1921	40.7	38.5	73.0	63.9	41.5	105.7	38.5	43.4	62.4	47.8	52.4	72.0	74.1	57.9	79.5	3
4	1922	63.1	49.5	65.3	69.8	42.0	—	67.8	55.6	55.1	—	—	69.6	92.1	58.8	73.3	4
5	1923	67.5	48.0	72.4	74.9	42.1	105.2	85.0	53.6	68.6	58.1	53.6	77.2	99.4	62.2	81.5	5
6	1924	63.2	49.4	74.6	73.6	40.3	103.4	71.2	54.4	76.8	—	—	81.0	84.9	62.5	85.0	6
7	1925	68.7	51.8	74.0	81.2	46.0	109.3	85.6	61.8	74.4	60.5	59.7	82.7	85.4	61.2	83.2	7
8	1926	80.0	57.3	73.3	80.5	46.9	114.1	91.6	63.5	74.4	—	—	85.8	87.0	62.8	86.6	8
9	1927	76.4	60.1	72.4	84.0	50.1	113.9	86.1	64.4	75.4	62.5	58.0	86.7	91.1	66.9	87.9	9
10	1928	74.0	57.7	72.5	85.4	50.3	115.4	99.1	72.7	76.9	—	—	88.1	89.4	68.1	87.7	10
11	1929	76.5	55.9	72.7	93.1	54.6	114.4	108.7	73.1	76.7	73.3	61.3	87.5	88.0	65.9	83.7	11
12	1930	63.3	58.3	75.2	88.5	57.2	114.3	80.0	69.0	78.8	—	—	89.1	77.4	66.2	85.4	12
13	1931	57.0	67.6	77.7	76.8	59.4	113.4	52.3	67.1	71.5	68.7	75.8	82.0	68.3	64.0	81.8	13
14	1932	44.7	70.8	71.0	57.3	53.3	100.3	28.8	69.9	69.2	—	—	77.1	61.6	71.2	75.1	14
15	1933	58.0	79.9	70.5	55.4	58.8	98.9	47.5	75.2	66.8	74.6	83.3	73.3	74.1	74.6	76.4	15
16	1934	66.2	75.4	79.5	67.5	66.2	105.8	53.2	73.9	79.6	—	—	94.6	80.6	81.5	89.4	16
17	1935	83.5	86.3	83.7	75.7	69.9	101.7	69.6	79.2	81.5	81.6	89.3	100.2	90.0	84.7	92.3	17
18	1936	90.6	85.6	87.3	89.6	76.9	97.1	98.0	81.7	80.8	—	—	96.9	93.1	84.3	92.7	18
19	1937	109.5	91.8	96.4	99.8	81.0	99.5	108.6	83.0	97.6	87.2	88.7	100.7	92.7	86.2	100.4	19
20	1938	74.2	87.2	99.6	96.4	89.4	101.5	60.9	84.9	99.7	—	—	103.2	81.3	93.4	100.3	20
21	1939	100.0	100.0	100.0	100.0	100.0	100.0	100.0	100.0	100.0	100.0	100.0	100.0	100.0	100.0	100.0	21
22	1940	111.5	103.4	104.0	101.1	99.0	102.9	—	—	—	—	—	—	93.8	101.2	102.5	22
23	1941	139.0	104.6	111.5	119.5	101.2	107.7	—	—	—	—	—	—	122.4	110.2	111.9	23
24	1942	126.7	92.5	119.1	143.2	106.6	117.2	—	—	—	—	—	—	132.3	120.1	128.3	24
25	1943	142.6	87.5	126.4	141.3	107.9	130.2	—	—	—	—	—	—	117.1	114.2	137.2	25
26	1944	158.2	91.2	131.0	150.4	113.9	139.1	—	—	—	—	—	—	114.3	118.0	146.3	26
27	1945	158.2	97.6	134.7	165.7	128.1	145.6	—	—	—	—	—	—	113.4	116.3	152.4	27
28	1946	194.1	98.1	155.0	227.6	152.4	160.3	—	—	—	—	—	—	111.9	112.3	169.5	28
29	1947	205.1	102.3	177.9	199.0	124.0	180.2	—	—	—	—	—	—	117.0	112.8	195.3	29

TABLE 20—Continued

No.	Year	Lumber and Timber Products			Newspaper and Periodical Printing and Publishing			Nonferrous Metals: Primary Smelters and Refiners			Nonferrous Metals: Alloyers, Rolling Mills, Foundries			Paints and Varnishes			No.
		A	B	C	A	B	C	A	B	C	A	B	C	A	B	C	
1	1919	134.6	79.0	116.7	55.4	43.7	57.5	87.6	45.6	82.6	47.5	35.1	70.3	48.3	53.0	66.5	1
2	1920	130.2	75.7	—	59.9	51.9	77.7	85.5	42.7	—	—	—	—	52.2	46.7	84.5	2
3	1921	107.4	84.4	100.2	57.8	51.8	78.9	52.4	54.8	74.9	27.5	38.4	66.9	42.7	57.2	78.2	3
4	1922	124.0	67.6	—	69.2	59.4	79.9	72.1	51.0	—	—	—	—	56.9	67.2	72.4	4
5	1923	143.9	71.4	95.9	76.7	63.2	81.8	101.2	58.8	85.3	70.2	59.9	76.3	65.0	65.2	75.2	5
6	1924	139.4	72.7	97.7	80.3	64.9	85.3	111.1	65.4	—	—	—	—	67.9	62.8	75.6	6
7	1925	148.0	76.5	95.9	85.1	69.0	89.0	116.7	71.4	83.6	80.5	70.6	79.6	74.9	63.6	75.5	7
8	1926	142.2	76.4	97.9	97.3	77.5	92.1	123.5	76.3	—	—	—	—	78.2	59.0	78.4	8
9	1927	134.4	79.4	99.2	96.5	75.7	91.5	122.0	80.5	84.2	78.2	67.6	79.8	83.3	67.0	81.1	9
10	1928	130.0	78.2	99.0	101.0	78.6	93.9	127.7	83.9	—	—	—	—	91.7	72.6	79.7	10
11	1929	140.3	82.5	100.6	107.0	77.4	94.6	138.3	89.5	90.8	125.9	92.9	83.6	95.1	71.7	79.9	11
12	1930	100.3	78.5	99.9	101.0	74.4	93.5	110.9	85.3	—	—	—	—	77.6	73.1	82.9	12
13	1931	64.1	90.7	89.7	91.8	75.4	93.5	74.4	96.1	83.6	66.5	103.9	83.3	67.2	76.5	84.2	13
14	1932	39.1	79.6	70.5	80.5	74.3	86.1	42.3	80.4	71.1	—	—	76.7	52.7	70.5	77.8	14
15	1933	53.7	86.1	73.6	75.9	75.3	81.7	49.8	88.5	68.6	48.5	82.9	72.5	57.5	70.8	73.5	15
16	1934	60.3	89.6	91.8	86.3	85.4	91.1	57.8	85.1	82.2	—	—	80.1	67.3	76.6	82.0	16
17	1935	75.9	90.9	89.0	93.9	92.1	95.5	71.0	76.2	76.0	68.9	79.7	81.9	83.0	85.9	83.6	17
18	1936	95.1	85.0	84.9	103.1	93.6	96.3	88.9	80.5	83.9	—	—	84.1	96.8	90.0	84.9	18
19	1937	101.8	82.4	90.4	108.6	93.1	95.9	108.0	87.6	99.8	104.9	92.7	98.9	104.2	91.2	93.9	19
20	1938	86.1	87.6	92.9	98.4	92.7	97.9	81.6	84.7	98.3	—	—	104.0	85.6	90.7	98.1	20
21	1939[a]	100.0	100.0	100.0	100.0	100.0	100.0	100.0	100.0	100.0	100.0	100.0	100.0	100.0	100.0	100.0	21

TABLE 20—Continued

No.	Year	Paper			Pulp			Petroleum Refining			Planing Mill Products			No.
		A	B	C	A	B	C	A	B	C	A	B	C	
1	1919	49.7	45.8	70.6	47.3	41.4	69.8	28.0	25.5	63.7	94.5	63.3	89.1	**1**
2	1920	57.2	48.6	91.4	52.6	41.4	88.3	33.7	—	—	—	—	122.8	**2**
3	1921	43.7	49.5	81.4	38.6	39.6	76.7	34.4	29.0	67.3	113.2	88.3	108.2	**3**
4	1922	56.7	59.1	74.9	47.6	43.9	69.0	39.2	—	—	—	—	102.0	**4**
5	1923	64.1	63.9	85.2	51.3	44.1	76.6	45.7	36.9	65.6	132.4	75.4	109.7	**5**
6	1924	62.4	65.6	89.1	50.0	46.7	82.4	50.6	43.7	64.6	—	—	112.9	**6**
7	1925	71.9	69.9	88.0	53.8	47.8	83.7	58.8	48.2	67.0	151.7	80.6	112.6	**7**
8	1926	76.4	70.3	87.3	59.8	51.6	85.3	61.9	46.0	66.4	—	—	115.1	**8**
9	1927	77.8	74.5	87.5	59.2	54.8	88.3	65.9	49.1	66.1	119.4	75.3	114.9	**9**
10	1928	80.7	77.4	88.1	62.0	60.4	91.5	73.1	57.0	67.0	—	—	114.4	**10**
11	1929	86.2	76.8	87.7	67.3	64.1	94.1	79.0	51.7	67.0	122.5	86.8	119.3	**11**
12	1930	80.6	76.9	88.0	64.1	65.8	92.3	74.3	49.4	68.8	—	—	118.3	**12**
13	1931	73.3	87.3	86.8	60.4	77.7	88.9	71.1	60.3	71.1	59.7	79.0	112.0	**13**
14	1932	62.3	87.1	75.9	51.7	76.3	76.5	64.9	64.0	68.4	—	—	91.9	**14**
15	1933	70.6	89.5	72.1	59.4	77.5	71.4	68.6	69.0	70.5	36.3	81.6	84.7	**15**
16	1934	68.7	83.6	84.3	61.8	77.9	82.0	71.4	69.8	78.9	—	—	93.5	**16**
17	1935	79.7	89.2	86.6	69.0	80.5	82.6	77.5	76.4	84.3	55.4	83.4	91.7	**17**
18	1936	90.3	93.5	87.4	80.2	83.8	85.3	86.0	81.5	86.4	—	—	93.4	**18**
19	1937	95.0	93.3	97.8	93.2	89.6	97.6	95.6	86.4	98.9	83.5	85.5	100.3	**19**
20	1938	84.3	94.7	100.4	84.4	93.8	100.2	94.2	91.5	101.7	—	—	102.6	**20**
21	1939[a]	100.0	100.0	100.0	100.0	100.0	100.0	100.0	100.0	100.0	100.0	100.0	100.0	**21**

TABLE 20—Continued

No.	Year	Rayon and Allied Products A	B	C	Rubber Tires and Inner Tubes A	B	C	Rubber Goods Other than Tires and Tubes A	B	C	Silk and Rayon Goods A	B	C	Slaughtering and Meat Packing A	B	C	No.
1	1919	—	—	—	—	—	—	—	—	—	35.8	27.1	87.8	86.8	58.8	83.3	1
2	1920	—	—	—	—	—	—	—	—	—	22.8	18.3	109.1	80.4	62.1	93.0	2
3	1921	—	—	—	31.2	23.5	63.0	75.3	78.8	70.9	31.6	25.4	97.5	75.6	71.9	86.5	3
4	1922	—	—	—	47.5	26.8	62.5	—	—	71.8	38.9	31.3	88.9	82.7	76.3	78.3	4
5	1923	9.6	23.5	66.9	52.1	30.2	70.1	100.0	75.1	77.0	41.7	31.3	102.0	93.7	74.0	79.1	5
6	1924	9.8	23.3	72.6	57.1	34.7	72.8	—	—	73.4	40.0	32.3	104.9	96.1	79.4	80.8	6
7	1925	13.6	25.3	71.3	72.3	39.5	73.5	93.9	71.1	74.8	50.9	35.8	107.5	89.8	78.0	83.2	7
8	1926	16.6	32.7	—	74.6	40.9	73.5	—	—	76.3	49.6	37.1	112.3	92.2	81.2	84.6	8
9	1927	19.8	28.2	68.0	82.1	44.9	73.3	113.6	82.9	79.4	53.1	39.6	111.9	92.1	79.8	84.1	9
10	1928	25.5	30.7	—	100.4	50.3	73.2	115.1	78.9	77.1	56.4	41.0	109.0	93.9	79.8	83.8	10
11	1929	31.9	30.4	71.1	97.3	50.5	73.5	110.9	78.4	79.2	61.8	43.3	103.2	95.3	79.1	83.2	11
12	1930	34.0	38.2	81.4	76.1	57.8	75.5	90.9	83.2	81.2	52.7	43.0	99.1	92.7	81.3	83.9	12
13	1931	41.5	45.6	70.0	69.7	71.9	72.5	72.4	83.1	79.3	54.9	49.6	94.2	91.3	88.9	79.8	13
14	1932	38.2	46.8	60.5	60.7	77.6	66.0	66.9	96.0	78.3	45.5	55.2	81.8	86.7	89.3	67.9	14
15	1933	60.5	60.7	64.5	68.9	76.9	68.1	77.3	93.5	74.8	44.2	47.2	84.7	92.1	91.6	68.9	15
16	1934	58.8	62.2	78.6	78.8	79.4	82.0	84.7	101.8	87.1	47.5	52.0	104.6	93.8	81.7	82.4	16
17	1935	70.9	67.8	80.7	84.9	86.5	89.0	84.6	98.3	89.9	66.6	65.9	102.4	78.8	82.2	87.8	17
18	1936	78.5	72.7	81.7	98.9	88.4	92.1	98.9	100.2	90.4	71.1	73.8	97.5	92.4	86.2	85.7	18
19	1937	92.0	79.4	94.0	95.0	88.5	100.5	99.6	96.2	100.6	71.4	73.7	103.5	89.2	83.8	98.4	19
20	1938	77.1	87.2	98.2	69.7	92.1	100.1	72.0	91.7	100.0	72.6	87.9	99.6	94.8	94.0	100.6	20
21	1939	100.0	100.0	100.0	100.0	100.0	100.0	100.0	100.0	100.0	100.0	100.0	100.0	100.0	100.0	100.0	21
22	1940	123.0	112.6	105.2	—	—	—	—	—	—	—	—	—	—	—	—	22
23	1941	153.4	132.0	113.3	—	—	—	—	—	—	—	—	—	—	—	—	23
24	1942	170.8	147.8	127.3	—	—	—	—	—	—	—	—	—	—	—	—	24
25	1943	179.1	145.0	136.2	—	—	—	—	—	—	—	—	—	—	—	—	25
26	1944	195.7	153.5	140.9	—	—	—	—	—	—	—	—	—	—	—	—	26
27	1945	212.3	163.7	146.7	—	—	—	—	—	—	—	—	—	—	—	—	27
28	1946	227.9	176.4	163.3	—	—	—	—	—	—	—	—	—	—	—	—	28
29	1947	258.2	196.8	189.2	—	—	—	—	—	—	—	—	—	—	—	—	29

TABLE 20—CONTINUED

No.	Year	Tobacco Products: Cigars			Tobacco Products: Cigarettes			Tobacco Products: Chewing and Smoking Tobacco, Snuff			Woolen and Worsted Goods			No.
		A	B	C	A	B	C	A	B	C	A	B	C	
1	1919	143.6	45.0	82.7	29.4	24.4	79.6	123.4	68.0	55.3	96.8	62.7	78.2	1
2	1920	161.0	50.2	—	26.3	22.6	—	120.1	65.9	—	86.9	68.7	103.8	2
3	1921	136.4	43.9	86.1	28.9	30.5	73.2	112.7	63.9	60.7	94.8	64.1	84.8	3
4	1922	135.7	44.7	—	30.9	34.6	—	122.1	68.3	—	101.3	64.3	81.2	4
5	1923	137.6	45.4	87.7	36.9	43.2	75.7	120.2	64.9	62.1	122.6	66.8	87.2	5
6	1924	131.5	47.5	—	40.2	47.9	—	120.6	66.1	62.1	102.2	68.1	95.5	6
7	1925	127.5	47.6	—	45.5	54.0	—	120.5	71.0	64.6	106.0	73.4	94.9	7
8	1926	127.4	50.3	—	51.0	63.7	—	119.5	73.1	63.8	99.0	73.7	92.0	8
9	1927	128.3	49.1	85.6	55.3	60.9	79.3	115.4	75.8	65.5	100.1	72.4	90.2	9
10	1928	125.2	50.6	—	60.2	60.7	—	112.4	75.1	65.1	94.9	72.8	89.4	10
11	1929	127.9	55.2	84.9	67.8	78.8	83.0	111.0	82.0	67.2	95.6	70.7	87.1	11
12	1930	115.6	54.4	80.7	68.5	83.0	74.5	108.2	77.4	64.8	70.3	71.2	90.1	12
13	1931	104.7	63.7	81.9	64.8	85.3	68.7	108.1	82.3	67.7	77.2	77.9	85.1	13
14	1932	86.1	57.9	77.5	59.0	87.7	63.9	101.1	85.5	66.4	64.0	82.3	73.5	14
15	1933	83.8	62.6	80.5	63.6	96.4	74.5	99.6	96.9	74.2	82.7	86.3	76.3	15
16	1934	88.0	69.7	87.2	72.0	79.8	68.7	100.7	88.8	75.4	70.0	95.1	97.8	16
17	1935	90.2	83.1	90.1	77.5	88.6	79.7	99.8	97.8	81.9	109.3	99.5	95.0	17
18	1936	99.2	86.0	89.4	87.9	102.7	91.5	101.3	101.4	85.4	103.1	97.8	96.8	18
19	1937	102.0	87.1	93.6	94.1	95.9	98.4	99.1	94.3	89.9	97.6	96.2	109.4	19
20	1938	96.4	92.8	98.4	95.1	97.1	99.0	100.6	98.2	94.6	70.6	90.4	104.0	20
21	1939	100.0	100.0	100.0	100.0	100.0	100.0	100.0	100.0	100.0	100.0	100.0	100.0	21
22	1940	100.7	100.4	103.4	—	—	—	—	—	—	—	—	—	22
23	1941	108.2	102.0	110.1	—	—	—	—	—	—	—	—	—	23
24	1942	112.5	104.0	122.0	—	—	—	—	—	—	—	—	—	24
25	1943	103.4	106.3	143.6	—	—	—	—	—	—	—	—	—	25
26	1944	100.3	117.7	163.0	—	—	—	—	—	—	—	—	—	26
27	1945	101.5	131.6	177.2	—	—	—	—	—	—	—	—	—	27
28	1946	108.6	127.0	199.4	—	—	—	—	—	—	—	—	—	28
29	1947	104.6	124.1	211.9	—	—	—	—	—	—	—	—	—	29

a. No data available for 1940–1947.

Source: Bureau of Labor Statistics.

TABLE 21

Major State Child Labor Standards, 1949

A—Law covering children in any gainful occupation
B—Law covering any gainful occupation except agriculture and domestic service (in Colorado and Wisconsin only, agriculture exempted)
C—Law covering specified industries and establishments

State	Coverage of the Law	Basic Minimum Age for Employment during School Hours	Employment or Age Certificate Required up to Age Indicated	Maximum Work Time: Daily Hours	Weekly Hours	Days per Week	For Boys under:	For Girls under:	Night Work Prohibited: For Boys under:	For Girls under:
Alabama	B	16	17[a]	8	40	6	16	16	16	16
Arizona	A	14	16	8	48	—	16	18	16	18
Arkansas	A	14	16	8	48	6	16	16	18	18
California	A	15	18	8	48	6	18	18	18	18
Colorado	B	14	16	8	48	—	16	16	16	16
Connecticut	B	16	18	8	48	6	18	18	18	18
Delaware	B	14	16	8	48	6	16	16	16	16
District of Columbia	A	14	18	8	48	6	18	18	18	18
Florida	C	16	18	8	40	6	16	16	18	18
Georgia	B	16	18	8	40	—	16	16	16	16
Idaho	A	14	—	9	54	—	16	16	16	16
Illinois	B	16	16	8	48	6	16	16	16	16
Indiana	B	14	18	8	48	6	16	18	16	18
Iowa	C	14	16	8	48	—	16	16	16	16
Kansas	A	14	16	8	48	—	16	16	16	16
Kentucky	C	16	18	8	40	6	18	18	17	17
Louisiana	B	16	18	8	44	6	18	18	18	18
Maine	A	16	16	8	48	6	16	16	—	—
Maryland	C	16	18	8	40	6	16	16	16	16
Massachusetts	B	16	21	8	48	6	16	16	18	21
Michigan	B	14	18	10	48	6	18	18	17	17
Minnesota	C	14	16	8	48	—	16	16	16	16
Mississippi	C	14	—	8	44	—	16	16	16	16
Missouri	B	14	16	8	48	6	16	16	16	16
Montana	C	16	18	8	48	—	18	18	—	—
Nebraska	A	14	16	8	48	—	16	16	16	16
Nevada	A	14	18	8	48	—	16	18	18[b]	18[b]
New Hampshire	C	14	16	10	48	—	18	18	16	16
New Jersey	A	16	18	8	40	6	18	18	18	18
New Mexico	A	14	16	8	44	—	16	16	16	16
New York	A	16	18	8	44	6	16	16	18	21
North Carolina	B	16	18	8	40	6	16	16	18	18
North Dakota	A	14	16	8	48	6	16	16	16	16
Ohio	A	16	18	8	48	6	18	21	18	21
Oklahoma	C	14	18	8	48	—	16	16	16	18
Oregon	A	14	18	8	44	6	18	18	16	16
Pennsylvania	B	16	18	8	44	6	18	18	16	18
Rhode Island	B	16	16	8	40	—	16	16	17	17
South Carolina	B	16	16	10	55	—	—	—	16	16
South Dakota	C	14	16	10	54	—	16	16	14	14
Tennessee	B	16	16	8	40	6	18	18	17	17
Texas	C	15	15	8	48	—	15	15	15	15
Utah	A	16	18	8	44	6	18	18	16	18
Vermont	A	14	16	8	48	6	16	16	16	16
Virginia	B	16	18	8	40	6	16	16	17	17
Washington	C	14	18	8	—	6	18	18	18	18
West Virginia	B	16	16	8	40	6	16	16	16	16
Wisconsin	B	16	18	8	40[c]	6	18	18	16	16
Wyoming	B	—[d]	[e]	8	48	6	16	16	16	16

a. For mines and quarries, 18 and 19.
b. For messengers.
c. For children under age 16, twenty-four.
d. No minimum age provision, but children required to attend school are prohibited from employment during school hours.
e. Certificates required for minors between 14 and 16 in occupations in which employment is prohibited under 16.

Sources: State Child-Labor Standards, Bulletin No. 98, Bureau of Labor Standards, 1949; "State Labor Legislation Enacted in 1949," *Monthly Labor Review,* January 1950; *Legislative Report,* U.S. Department of Labor, April 15, 1950.

TABLE 22

Types of State Labor Laws for Women, January 1, 1950

W—Law covering women only
A—Law covering all workers
Y—Law covering all workers under age 21

State [a]	Hours Limit		Day of Rest	Meal Periods	Night Work		Occupational Limitations			Minimum-Wage Laws	Industrial Home-work Laws	Equal-Pay Laws	Employment before and after Childbirth
	Daily Hours	Weekly Hours			Prohibited	Limited	Mining	Sale of Liquors	Other Limitations				
Alabama	—	—	—	—	—	—	W	—	—	—	—	—	—
Arizona	8	48	W	—	Y	—	W	—	W	W–Y	—	—	—
Arkansas	8	48	W	W	—	—	W	—	—	W	—	—	—
California	8	48	A	W	W	—	—	W	—	W–Y	A	W	—
Colorado	8	48	W	W	—	—	W	Y	—	W–Y	W–Y	—	—
Connecticut	8	48	A	—	W	—	—	W	—	A	A	W	W
Delaware	10	55	W	W	W	—	—	Y	—	—	—	—	—
District of Columbia	8	48	W	W	Y	—	—	—	—	W–Y	—	—	—
Florida	—	—	—	—	—	—	—	Y	—	—	—	—	—
Georgia	10A	60A	—	—	—	—	—	—	—	—	—	—	—
Idaho	9	—	—	—	—	—	—	—	—	—	—	—	—
Illinois	8	48	A	W	—	—	W	W	—	W–Y	A	W	—
Indiana	—	—	—	A	W	—	W	—	—	—	A	—	—
Iowa	—	—	—	—	—	—	—	—	—	—	—	—	—
Kansas	8	48	W	W	W	—	—	—	—	W–Y	—	—	—
Kentucky	10	60	—	W	Y	—	—	W	—	W–Y	—	—	—
Louisiana	8	48	W	W	—	—	—	W	W	W	—	—	—
Maine	9	50	—	W	—	—	—	—	—	W–Y	A	W	—
Maryland	10	60	—	W	—	W	W	Y	—	—	A	—	—
Massachusetts	9	48	A	W	W	—	—	Y	—	A	A	W	W
Michigan	9	54	—	—	—	—	—	W	W	—	A	W	—
Minnesota	—	54	—	—	—	—	—	—	W	W–Y	—	—	—
Mississippi	10A	60A	—	—	—	—	—	—	—	—	—	—	—
Missouri	9	54	—	—	—	—	W	—	W	—	A	—	W
Montana	8	48	—	—	—	—	—	Y	—	—	—	W	—
Nebraska	9	54	—	A	W	—	—	—	—	—	—	—	—
Nevada	8	48	W	W	—	—	—	—	—	W	—	—	—
New Hampshire	10	48	A	—	—	W	—	—	—	A	—	W	—
New Jersey	10	54	W	A	W	—	—	—	—	W–Y	A	—	—
New Mexico	8	48	—	W	—	W	—	—	—	—	—	—	—
New York	8	48	A	A	W	—	W	—	W	A	A	W	W
North Carolina	9	48	W	W	—	—	—	—	—	—	—	—	—
North Dakota	8½	48	W	W	W	—	—	—	—	W–Y	—	—	—
Ohio	8	48	W	W	W [b]	—	W	W	W	W–Y	A	—	—
Oklahoma	9	54	—	—	—	—	W	—	—	W	—	—	—
Oregon	8	44	W	W	—	—	—	—	—	W–Y	W–Y	—	—
Pennsylvania	10	48	W	W	Y	—	W	W	W	W–Y	A	W	—
Rhode Island	9	48	—	W	Y	—	—	—	—	A	A	W	—
South Carolina	10A	55A	W	—	W	—	—	Y	—	—	—	—	—
South Dakota	10	54	—	—	—	—	—	—	—	W	—	—	—
Tennessee	10	50	—	—	—	—	—	—	—	—	A	—	—
Texas	9	54	—	—	—	—	—	—	—	—	A	—	—
Utah	8	48	W	W	—	W	W	—	—	W–Y	W–Y	—	—
Vermont	9	50	—	—	—	—	—	—	—	—	—	—	W
Virginia	9	48	—	—	W [c]	—	W	—	—	—	—	—	—
Washington	8	—	—	W	W	—	W	—	W	W–Y	—	W	W
West Virginia	—	—	—	W	—	—	—	—	—	—	A	—	—
Wisconsin	9	50	A	W	W	—	W	—	W	W–Y	A	—	—
Wyoming	8	48	—	—	—	—	W	—	—	—	—	—	—
Total number	43	42	23	28	20	4	17	15	10	27	21	12	6

a. For states with different legal maximum-hour standards for different industries, the law establishing the lowest maximum hours was selected for this table.
b. Females under 21.
c. Girl messengers only (under 21).

Source: Women's Bureau.

TABLE 23

State Minimum-Wage Laws, 1950

State	Occupations and Industries: Covered	Occupations and Industries: Exceptions	Employees Covered by Law: Covered	Employees Covered by Law: Exceptions
Arizona	Any occupation	Domestic service; farm labor	Women; minors of either sex under 21	Special licenses for handicapped
Arkansas	Industrial occupations	Cotton factories; gathering of fruits or farm products; railroads	Women and girls	
California	Any occupation	——	Women; minors (girls under 21, boys under 18)	Special licenses for handicapped Special wage for apprentice or learner
Colorado	Any occupation	——	Women; minors (either sex under 18)	Special licenses for handicapped
Connecticut	Any sweatshop occupation	Domestic service; farm labor	All persons	"
District of Columbia	Any occupation	Domestic service	Women; minors (of either sex under 18)	Special licenses for handicapped, learners or apprentices for fixed period
Illinois	Any occupation	Domestic service; farm labor	Women; minors (females under 18 and males under 21)	Special licenses for handicapped
Kansas	Any occupation	——	Women; minors (females under 18 and males under 21)	
Kentucky	Any occupation	Domestic service; farm labor; person, firm or corporation subject to regulation by state public service commission	Women and minors	Special licenses for handicapped
Louisiana	Any occupation	Domestic service; farm labor; municipalities having population of 10,000 or less	Women and girls	"
Maine	Packing fish or fish products in oil, mustard or tomato sauce	——	Women; minors (of either sex under 21)	Special rates for learners and apprentices
Massachusetts	Any occupation	Domestic service; farm labor	All persons	Special licenses for handicapped
Minnesota	Any occupation	——	Women; minors (of either sex under 21)	"
Nevada	Private employment	Domestic service; state, county, city or town employees	Women and girls	"
New Hampshire	Any occupation	Domestic service; farm labor	All persons	"
New Jersey	Any occupation	Domestic service; farm labor	Women; minors (of either sex under 21)	"
New York	Any occupation	Domestic service; farm labor	All persons	"
North Dakota	Any occupation	Agriculture; domestic service	Women; minors (of either sex under 18)	"

TABLE 23—CONTINUED

State	Occupations and Industries: Covered	Occupations and Industries: Exceptions	Employees Covered by Law: Covered	Employees Covered by Law: Exceptions
Ohio	Any occupation	Domestic service; farm labor	Women; minors (of either sex under 21)	Special licenses for handicapped
Oklahoma	Any occupation	Agriculture; horticulture	Women	"
Oregon	Any occupation	—	Women; minors (of either sex under 18)	"
Pennsylvania	Any occupation	Domestic service; service in a religious community or charitable institution; farm labor; newsboys; railroads	Women; minors (of either sex under 21)	"
Rhode Island	Any occupation	Domestic service; farm labor	All persons	"
South Dakota	Any factory, workshop, mechanical or mercantile establishment, laundry, hotel, restaurant or packing house	—	Any woman over 14	Special licenses for handicapped, apprentices, learners
Utah	Any occupation	—	Women; minors (females under 21, males under 18)	Special licenses for handicapped, apprentices and learners for specified period
Washington	Any occupation	—	Women; minors (of either sex under 18)	Special licenses for handicapped
Wisconsin	Any occupation	—	Women; minors (of either sex under 21)	Any woman or minor unable to earn the living wage may obtain license fixing a lower wage

Sources: State Minimum-Wage Laws and Orders, Bulletin No. 191, Women's Bureau, 1942, and *State Minimum-Wage Laws and Orders, July 1, 1942–January 1949,* Bulletin No. 227, 1949.

TABLE 24

EMPLOYMENT STATUS OF MALE WORLD WAR II VETERANS IN THE CIVILIAN NONINSTITUTIONAL POPULATION, NOVEMBER 1945–JUNE 1950

(In Thousands)

Month	Total Male Veterans of World War II [a]	Civilian Labor Force: Total in Civilian Labor Force	Civilian Labor Force: Employed: Total	Civilian Labor Force: Employed: In Agriculture	Civilian Labor Force: Employed: In Nonagricultural Industries	Civilian Labor Force: Unemployed	Not in Labor Force: Total Not in Labor Force	Not in Labor Force: In School	Not in Labor Force: Other
1945									
November	5,600	3,830	3,310	300	3,010	520	1,770	170	1,600
December	7,020	4,990	4,240	360	3,880	750	2,030	230	1,800
1946									
January	8,580	6,410	5,570	430	5,140	840	2,170	290	1,880
February	9,600	7,440	6,380	520	5,860	1,060	2,160	420	1,740
March	10,410	8,410	7,200	660	6,540	1,210	2,000	540	1,460
April	11,080	9,240	8,250	770	7,480	990	1,840	540	1,300
May	11,520	9,830	8,900	860	8,040	930	1,690	570	1,120
June	11,890	10,380	9,400	930	8,470	980	1,510	480	1,030
July	12,280	10,810	9,880	890	8,990	930	1,470	460	1,010
August	12,580	10,950	10,100	830	9,270	850	1,630	480	1,150
September	12,790	11,230	10,400	830	9,570	830	1,560	760	800
October	12,810	11,150	10,390	820	9,570	760	1,660	1,160	500
November	13,030	11,380	10,680	770	9,910	700	1,650	1,100	550
December	13,160	11,450	10,610	690	9,920	840	1,710	1,110	600
1947									
January	13,390	11,600	10,700	720	9,980	900	1,790	1,190	600
February	13,470	11,810	10,810	800	10,010	1,000	1,660	1,190	470
March	13,480	11,920	11,070	830	10,240	850	1,560	1,180	380
April	13,630	12,170	11,310	880	10,430	860	1,460	1,070	390
May	13,720	12,340	11,700	990	10,710	640	1,380	1,050	330
June	13,818	12,758	12,035	1,095	10,940	724	1,060	642	418
July	13,866	12,816	12,044	1,108	10,936	772	1,050	581	469
August	13,918	12,842	12,155	1,032	11,122	687	1,076	495	581
September	13,954	12,666	12,080	994	11,085	586	1,288	758	530
October	13,994	12,652	12,173	939	11,234	479	1,342	1,010	332
November	14,127	12,760	12,247	884	11,363	513	1,367	1,035	332
December	14,137	12,749	12,213	838	11,374	536	1,388	965	422
1948									
January	14,175	12,681	12,068	852	11,217	612	1,494	1,117	377
February	14,219	12,808	12,106	862	11,244	702	1,411	1,097	315
March	14,231	12,796	12,113	904	11,208	683	1,435	1,141	294
April	14,272	12,883	12,262	911	11,351	621	1,389	1,095	294
May	14,329	12,919	12,410	944	11,467	508	1,411	1,112	299
June	14,326	13,208	12,723	991	11,732	485	1,119	721	398
July	14,321	13,433	12,918	996	11,922	515	887	546	342
August	14,341	13,456	12,964	971	11,994	491	886	452	433
September	14,351	13,367	12,923	921	12,002	444	984	513	471
October	14,375	13,267	12,879	884	11,995	388	1,108	864	245
November	14,395	13,287	12,850	855	11,995	437	1,108	836	272
December	14,430	13,241	12,760	836	11,924	481	1,188	906	283
1949									
January	14,402	13,175	12,437	850	11,587	738	1,227	910	318
February	14,419	13,175	12,352	845	11,507	823	1,244	971	274
March	14,436	13,309	12,395	921	11,473	915	1,127	862	265
April	14,443	13,332	12,519	945	11,574	813	1,112	825	287
May	14,470	13,419	12,572	1,000	11,572	847	1,051	794	257
June	14,489	13,600	12,708	1,001	11,706	893	889	576	313
July	14,514	13,733	12,729	1,013	11,716	1,004	781	427	354
August	14,509	13,680	12,844	1,049	11,795	830	828	416	413
September	14,539	13,613	12,861	991	11,870	752	926	469	458
October	14,558	13,532	12,654	925	11,729	878	1,026	768	259
November	14,581	13,593	12,810	944	11,866	783	988	720	268
December	14,590	13,545	12,814	925	11,888	732	1,045	739	306
1950									
January	14,605	13,559	12,570	880	11,691	988	1,047	730	318
February	14,622	13,610	12,508	787	11,721	1,102	1,013	730	283
March	14,636	13,596	12,629	834	11,795	967	1,039	728	312
April	14,636	13,623	12,778	923	11,854	846	1,013	745	268
May	14,638	13,682	13,036	979	12,057	646	956	749	207
June	14,638	13,811	13,272	961	12,310	540	827	534	293

a. In continental United States and not in institutions.

Source: "Monthly Report on the Labor Force," Bureau of the Census, December 1948 and June 1950.

TABLE 25

PERCENTAGE OF UNEMPLOYED MALE WORLD WAR II VETERANS AND OTHER MALES IN THE LABOR FORCE, BY AGE GROUP, NOVEMBER 1945–JUNE 1950

Year and Month	20–24 Years		25–34 Years		35–44 Years	
	Veterans	Other Males	Veterans	Other Males	Veterans	Other Males
1945						
November	15.6	4.1	13.2	2.4	12.0	1.7
December	17.9	5.2	14.6	2.5	12.5	2.0
1946						
January	17.8	6.4	12.6	3.6	7.5	2.7
February	21.8	7.6	12.9	3.4	7.9	3.1
March	21.7	4.4	12.9	3.2	8.0	3.1
April	15.7	4.3	9.7	2.4	4.7	3.0
May	14.4	4.5	7.3	3.1	6.2	3.1
June	14.6	6.7	6.7	2.5	8.0	2.2
July	13.8	4.1	6.1	2.0	6.4	1.8
August	11.7	6.1	5.6	1.6	6.1	1.9
September	11.8	4.1	5.2	2.0	4.7	2.0
October	10.2	4.0	5.2	2.0	4.0	2.3
November	8.3	5.0	4.8	1.9	2.7	2.1
December	9.7	4.9	5.6	1.9	4.5	2.1
1947						
January	10.9	6.1	5.2	2.6	5.0	2.8
February	13.4	6.9	5.7	2.7	5.4	2.5
March	11.5	5.5	4.5	2.2	5.3	2.2
April	10.4	4.6	4.4	2.7	5.7	2.8
May	8.3	4.3	3.4	2.5	3.0	1.7
June	10.5	6.9	3.1	1.6	3.6	1.7
July	9.8	3.8	3.8	2.6	3.3	2.0
August	8.1	4.8	3.6	2.1	3.9	1.8
September	5.3	4.3	4.3	2.2	2.7	1.7
October	5.8	3.6	2.6	1.9	2.9	1.7
November	6.9	4.0	2.5	1.7	2.5	1.5
December	6.4	4.5	3.1	1.5	2.7	1.6
1948						
January	7.5	7.1	3.1	2.3	3.8	1.9
February	9.4	7.9	3.6	2.4	3.8	2.8
March	9.4	10.1	3.3	2.3	3.9	2.5
April	8.1	5.6	3.3	2.7	3.2	2.2
May	7.1	4.6	2.5	2.0	3.0	1.7
June	7.0	3.8	2.1	1.7	2.4	1.4
July	6.0	4.9	2.6	1.7	3.4	1.7
August	5.1	4.3	3.1	1.6	1.6	1.8
September	4.5	4.3	2.5	1.6	3.1	1.6
October	4.8	3.9	1.9	1.8	2.5	1.5
November	5.0	3.1	2.4	2.4	2.4	1.3
December	5.7	5.4	2.5	2.2	3.0	1.8
1949						
January	8.6	7.8	4.1	3.8	4.5	2.5
February	9.8	11.4	4.7	3.8	5.1	3.8
March	11.2	8.1	5.4	4.1	4.4	3.7
April	9.8	7.1	4.8	3.5	4.1	3.4
May	10.7	8.7	4.8	3.9	5.1	3.2
June	10.7	10.0	5.4	3.6	4.4	2.9
July	13.2	12.2	6.0	3.9	3.8	4.2
August	10.9	9.7	4.5	4.1	4.1	4.0
September	8.9	8.2	4.6	3.7	4.0	4.1
October	10.9	10.2	5.8	5.7	3.3	4.6
November	8.8	7.7	5.1	3.9	4.4	4.1
December	8.1	9.2	4.7	4.9	4.2	4.5
1950						
January	11.1	13.8	6.6	7.5	4.7	4.7
February	13.4	14.0	6.9	5.8	6.1	5.0
March	11.0	12.4	6.2	6.6	6.0	4.6
April	10.4	7.4	5.1	5.6	5.2	3.9
May	7.1	7.5	4.2	4.5	4.0	3.2
June	7.4	7.1	3.2	4.6	2.8	2.6

Source: Unpublished tabulation of data collected for "Monthly Report on the Labor Force," Bureau of the Census.

TABLE 26

Veterans Enrolled in Readjustment Programs of Veterans Administration, 1945–1950

(In Thousands)

End of Month	World War II Veteran Population	Veterans in All Programs: Number	Veterans in All Programs: Percentage of World War II Veterans	Veterans in Education and Training [a]: All	School	On Job	On Farm [b]	Veterans Claiming Readjustment Allowances: All	Unemployment [c]	Self-Employment
1945										
June.......	2,469	81	3.3	37	30	7	—	44	32	12
December...	8,333	632	7.6	131	104	27	—	501	480	21
1946										
June.......	12,687	3,126	24.6	1,023	665	358	—	2,103	1,781	322
December...	13,928	3,550	25.5	2,392	1,679	713	—	1,158	988	170
1947										
June.......	14,361	3,030	21.1	2,075	1,184	700	191	955	713	242
December...	14,745	3,342	22.7	2,802	1,934	640	228	540	465	75
1948										
June.......	14,914	2,369	15.9	1,892	1,080	521	291	477	372	105
December...	15,058	2,903	19.3	2,533	1,761	468	304	370	331	39
1949										
June.......	15,182	2,427	16.0	1,811	1,081	390	340	616	548	68
December...	15,294	2,539	16.6	2,474	1,806	321	347	65	63	2
1950										
June.......	15,386	1,647	10.7	1,616	1,020	234	362	31	29	2

a. Under Vocational Rehabilitation Act (Public Law 16) and Servicemen's Readjustment Act (Public Law 346).
b. Veterans in institutional on-the-farm training before January 1947 are included in figures for veterans in school.
c. Average weekly number of continued claims filed during month.

Source: Veterans Administration.

TABLE 27

Number of Beneficiaries and Amount of Benefits under Selected Social Insurance and Related Programs, by Specified Period, 1940–1949

(In Thousands)

No.	Year and Month	Total	Retirement, Disability, and Survivor Programs: Monthly Retirement and Disability Benefits [a]: Social Security Act	Railroad Retirement Act	Civil Service Commission [b]	Veterans Administration	Survivor Benefits: Monthly: Social Security Act [c]	Railroad Retirement Act [d]	Civil Service Commission [b]	Veterans Administration [e]	Lump-sum [f]: Social Security Act	Other [g]	Temporary Disability Benefits [h]: State Laws [i]	Railroad Unemployment Insurance Act [j]	Unemployment Insurance Programs: State Unemployment Insurance Laws [i]	Servicemen's Readjustment Act [k]	Railroad Unemployment Insurance Act [j]	Readjustment Allowances to Self-Employed Veterans [l]	No.
	Number of Beneficiaries																		
1	1948																		1
2	December	—	1,394.7	226.1	135.1	2,296.1	919.9	113.1	4.6	963.5	15.9	10.3	23.3	38.2	939.4	330.7	42.0	39.2	2
3	1949																		3
4	January	—	1,422.9	227.0	136.8	2,295.4	928.9	114.4	5.4	972.5	15.3	11.8	23.7	37.0	1,212.3	495.1	64.1	37.7	4
5	February	—	1,454.1	227.9	138.0	2,297.4	939.4	115.9	6.2	977.0	15.6	10.2	24.2	34.7	1,466.0	634.0	82.9	51.6	5
6	March	—	1,489.1	229.4	139.2	2,302.2	952.8	117.6	7.2	979.9	21.0	6.4	26.4	34.9	1,788.0	688.4	110.4	64.1	6
7	April	—	1,516.3	230.9	140.1	2,305.6	964.1	119.3	8.0	981.8	17.8	4.1	28.7	31.1	1,598.3	624.7	133.6	68.4	7
8	May	—	1,542.5	232.6	141.2	2,309.2	974.6	120.6	8.6	987.5	17.5	21.5	30.0	28.1	1,718.3	552.7	76.3	71.3	8
9	June	—	1,568.9	234.2	143.2	2,313.5	985.4	121.9	9.4	959.7	17.7	13.5	31.0	29.5	1,809.0	548.1	77.8	68.7	9
10	July	—	1,588.2	235.1	143.9	2,321.3	989.2	122.8	9.7	961.7	15.3	9.0	28.7	24.6	1,717.4	606.4	80.1	60.2	10
11	August	—	1,615.8	236.6	145.2	2,324.8	997.8	123.6	10.3	963.2	17.9	11.1	30.0	37.5	1,951.7	218.3	127.3	48.2	11
12	September	—	1,636.6	237.6	146.7	2,326.6	1,008.4	124.8	11.0	964.6	16.7	10.5	28.6	36.0	1,738.0	95.2	126.6	5.8	12
13	October	—	1,656.5	239.1	148.0	2,333.1	1,017.4	125.8	11.7	967.2	15.4	11.2	28.8	35.3	1,527.1	64.2	180.3	3.7	13
14	November	—	1,683.4	240.1	149.4	2,336.8	1,026.9	127.0	12.2	969.0	16.2	10.2	27.7	38.2	1,698.0	60.4	219.1	2.7	14
15	December	—	1,706.5	241.6	151.1	2,343.0	1,036.3	128.4	12.8	970.7	15.7	10.6	28.2	36.0	1,892.0	62.8	166.6	2.3	15
	Amount of Benefits [m]																		
16	1940	$1,188,702	$21,074	$114,166	$62,019	$317,851	$7,784	$1,448	—	$105,696	$11,736	$12,267	—	—	$518,700	—	$15,961	—	16
17	1941	1,085,488	55,141	119,912	64,933	320,561	25,454	1,559	—	111,799	13,328	13,943	—	—	344,321	—	14,537	—	17
18	1942	1,130,721	80,305	122,806	68,115	325,265	41,702	1,603	—	111,193	15,038	14,342	—	—	344,084	—	6,268	—	18
19	1943	921,465	97,257	125,795	72,961	331,350	57,763	1,704	—	116,133	17,830	17,255	$2,857	—	79,643	—	917	—	19
20	1944	1,119,686	119,009	129,707	78,081	456,279	76,942	1,765	—	144,302	22,146	19,238	5,035	—	62,385	$4,113	582	$102	20
21	1945	2,067,434	157,391	137,140	85,742	697,830	104,231	1,772	—	254,238	26,135	23,431	4,669	—	445,866	114,955	2,359	11,675	21
22	1946	5,151,594	230,285	149,188	96,418	1,268,984	130,139	1,817	—	333,640	27,267	30,610	4,761	—	1,094,850	1,491,294	39,917	252,424	22
23	1947	4,698,642	299,830	177,053	108,691	1,676,029	153,109	19,283	—	382,515	29,517	33,115	22,025	$11,368	776,164	772,368	39,401	198,174	23
24	1948	4,502,775	366,887	208,642	134,886	1,711,182	176,736	36,011	$918	413,912	32,315	32,140	26,272	30,843	793,265	426,569	28,599	83,598	24
25	1949	5,669,013	454,483	240,893	161,426	1,692,215	201,369	39,252	4,317	477,406	33,158	31,770	31,552	30,103	1,737,279	386,635	103,596	43,559	25

Table 27—Continued

Retirement, Disability, and Survivor Programs

No.	Year and Month	Total	Monthly Retirement and Disability Benefits [a]: Social Security Act	Monthly Retirement and Disability Benefits [a]: Railroad Retirement Act	Monthly Retirement and Disability Benefits [a]: Civil Service Commission [b]	Monthly Retirement and Disability Benefits [a]: Veterans Administration	Survivor Benefits, Monthly: Social Security Act [c]	Survivor Benefits, Monthly: Railroad Retirement Act [d]	Survivor Benefits, Monthly: Civil Service Commission [b]	Survivor Benefits, Monthly: Veterans Administration [e]	Survivor Benefits, Lump-sum [f]: Social Security Act	Survivor Benefits, Lump-sum [f]: Other [g]	Temporary Disability Benefits [h]: State Laws [i]	Temporary Disability Benefits [h]: Railroad Unemployment Insurance Act [j]	Unemployment Insurance Programs: State Unemployment Insurance Laws [i]	Unemployment Insurance Programs: Servicemen's Readjustment Act [k]	Unemployment Insurance Programs: Railroad Unemployment Insurance Act [j]	Readjustment Allowances to Self-Employed Veterans [l]	No.
	Amount of Benefits [m]—Continued																		
26	1948																		26
27	December	$390,428	$31,188	$18,819	$12,700	$145,545	$14,684	$2,847	$212	$39,178	$2,612	$2,539	$2,329	$3,475	$79,966	$27,997	$2,698	$3,639	27
28	1949																		28
29	January	426,024	31,900	18,893	12,530	144,985	14,854	2,879	208	39,203	2,509	2,712	2,169	3,204	103,011	39,849	4,059	3,059	29
30	February	441,590	32,688	18,977	12,719	138,706	15,049	2,916	250	38,990	2,571	2,533	2,099	2,772	115,268	47,103	4,998	3,951	30
31	March	501,858	33,556	19,092	12,846	140,283	15,297	2,959	279	39,749	3,410	2,274	2,634	3,153	152,204	60,766	7,648	5,708	31
32	April	477,092	34,246	19,208	12,942	141,261	15,504	3,002	304	39,216	2,914	1,787	2,659	2,715	136,558	50,423	8,905	5,448	32
33	May	485,046	34,928	19,335	12,931	142,639	15,703	3,036	315	40,207	2,842	4,182	2,912	2,554	146,712	44,618	5,414	6,718	33
34	June	491,115	35,615	19,461	13,067	139,513	15,904	3,071	337	40,022	2,893	3,011	3,003	2,608	154,695	45,797	5,542	6,576	34
35	July	482,323	36,139	19,532	13,156	136,308	15,993	3,097	365	39,554	2,501	2,196	2,687	2,071	148,767	48,938	5,553	5,466	35
36	August	493,469	36,869	19,641	13,756	141,983	16,167	3,120	402	40,767	2,944	2,602	3,074	3,364	170,629	24,135	9,107	4,909	36
37	September	454,638	37,410	19,720	15,759	138,180	16,365	3,152	430	39,606	2,754	2,570	2,786	3,217	154,067	8,775	8,983	864	37
38	October	440,135	37,911	19,838	13,856	141,459	16,540	3,182	470	39,761	2,539	2,725	2,719	3,284	135,707	5,462	14,298	384	38
39	November	460,196	38,600	19,913	13,990	141,535	16,719	3,215	469	39,924	2,670	2,413	2,717	3,462	152,179	5,291	16,839	260	39
40	December	479,506	39,188	20,034	13,874	145,363	16,887	3,252	488	40,407	2,610	2,767	2,776	3,372	170,573	5,474	12,225	216	40

a. Under the Social Security Act, old-age retirement benefits (primary and wife's benefits and benefits to children of primary beneficiaries), partly estimated. Under the other three systems, benefits for age and disability.

b. Data for civil service retirement and disability fund (including Alaska Railroad and Canal Zone funds, integrated since July 1949 with principal fund); includes payments to Canal Zone construction-period workers administered by the Commission. Through June 1948, retirement and disability benefits include payments to survivors under joint and survivor elections; beginning July 1948, payments under survivor provisions shown as survivor benefits.

c. Widow's, widow's current, parent's and child's benefits. Partly estimated.

d. Annuities to widows under joint and survivor elections; twelve-month death-benefit annuities to widows and next of kin, and, beginning February 1947, widow's, widow's current, parent's and child's benefits in current-payment status.

e. Payments to widows, parents and children of deceased veterans.

f. Number of decedents on whose account lump-sum payments were made.

g. Payments under the Railroad Retirement Act and federal civil service and veterans programs.

h. Compensation for temporary disability payable in Rhode Island beginning April 1943, in California beginning December 1946, in New Jersey beginning January 1949, and under the Railroad Unemployment Insurance Act beginning July 1947. Excludes benefits under private plans in California and New Jersey.

i. Represents average weekly number of beneficiaries.

j. Represents average number of beneficiaries in a fourteen-day registration period.

k. Readjustment allowances to unemployed veterans; from 1 to 2 per cent of number and amount shown represents allowances for illness and disability after establishment of unemployment rights. Number represents average weekly number of continued claims.

l. Number and amount of claims paid under the Servicemen's Readjustment Act.

m. Payments: amounts certified, under the Social Security Act, the Railroad Retirement Act and the Railroad Unemployment Insurance Act; disbursements, for Veterans Administration programs except the readjustment allowance program; checks issued, under the state unemployment insurance and temporary disability laws and under the Servicemen's Readjustment Act; for civil service programs, disbursements through June 1949 and authorizations beginning July 1949. Data for all programs except those of the Civil Service Commission are adjusted on annual basis only; Civil Service Commission data adjusted monthly.

Source: Social Security Bulletin, March 1950, p. 19.

TABLE 28

BENEFITS IN CURRENT-PAYMENT STATUS, PAYMENTS CERTIFIED, AND WORKERS WITH WAGE CREDITS UNDER OASI, 1946–1949

Item	Fiscal Year 1946–1947	1947–1948	1948–1949
Benefits in current-payment status (end of period):			
Number	1,832,285	2,162,693	2,554,248
Primary	797,927	968,682	1,180,909
Wife's	245,364	296,711	359,840
Child's	499,246	556,834	614,714
Widow's	146,124	188,612	236,394
Widow's current	134,673	140,807	149,724
Parent's	8,951	11,047	12,667
Total monthly amount	$35,071,472	$42,391,324	$51,520,000
Primary	19,722,150	24,344,534	30,369,096
Wife's	3,206,007	3,948,153	4,898,101
Child's	6,328,004	7,175,060	8,043,794
Widow's	2,965,620	3,865,451	4,897,656
Widow's current	2,730,446	2,908,578	3,137,870
Parent's	119,245	149,548	173,483
Average monthly amount:			
Primary	$24.72	$25.13	$25.72
Wife's	13.07	13.31	13.61
Child's	12.68	12.89	13.09
Widow's	20.30	20.49	20.72
Widow's current	20.27	20.66	20.96
Parent's	13.32	13.54	13.70
Payments certified during period:			
Monthly benefits	$406,252,135	$499,314,611	$594,744,288
Primary	225,415,715	284,588,746	346,376,498
Supplementary	39,418,950	49,633,683	59,972,453
Survivor	141,417,470	165,092,182	188,395,337
Lump-sum payments	28,514,685	31,281,156	32,249,231
1939 and 1946 amendments	28,501,375	31,280,024	32,248,926
1935 act	13,310	1,132	305
Additional benefits under Section 210 (included in above figures)	$2,899,058	$3,495,918	$3,582,431
Monthly benefits	1,254,119	2,340,766	2,903,915
Lump-sum payments	1,644,939	1,155,151	678,516
Estimated number of living workers with wage credits (midpoint of period — January 1): [a]			
Total	74,800,000	76,900,000	79,100,000
Fully insured	35,100,000	36,800,000	38,300,000
Currently but not fully insured	6,400,000	6,200,000	5,100,000
Uninsured	33,200,000	33,900,000	35,700,000

a. Not adjusted to reflect changes in insured status arising from (1) combined earnings under coordinated survivor provisions of the old-age and survivors insurance and railroad retirement programs, and (2) veterans deemed to be fully insured only under Section 210 of Title II of the Social Security Act, as amended in 1946.

Source: Annual Report, 1949, Federal Security Agency, 1950, p. 205.

TABLE 29

PERCENTAGE DISTRIBUTION OF BENEFICIARY FAMILIES UNDER OASI BY MONTHLY AMOUNT OF FAMILY BENEFIT IN CURRENT-PAYMENT STATUS, FOR EACH SPECIFIED FAMILY GROUP IN RECEIPT OF BENEFITS, END OF 1949 [a]

No.	Monthly Family Benefit Amount	Retired Worker Only		Retired Worker and Wife	Retired Worker and 1 Child	Aged Widow	Widowed Mother and Children			Children Only				No.
		Male	Female				1 Child	2 Children	3 or More Children	1 Child	2 Children	3 Children	4 or More Children	
1	Total number [b] ..	686,600	185,700	390,300	15,000	261,200	78,300	44,200	26,200	105,800	48,600	19,000	24,500	**1**
2	Total per cent....	100.0	100.0	100.0	100.0	100.0	100.0	100.0	100.0	100.0	100.0	100.0	100.0	**2**
3	Less than $10.00..	—	—	—	—	0.9 [c]	—	—	—	3.7 [d]	—	—	—	**3**
4	$10.00–14.99	12.1 [e]	27.7 [f]	—	—	15.6	4.0	—	—	65.1	10.3	0.7 [d]	0.1 [d]	**4**
5	15.00–19.99	7.6	14.8	8.8 [g]	6.7 [h]	30.1	3.4	4.1	0.1 [d]	26.4	7.6	10.1	0.2 [d]	**5**
6	20.00–24.99	24.3	31.9	4.1	4.4	27.2	4.5	2.8	7.6	4.8 [i]	23.9	5.1	11.5	**6**
7	25.00–29.99	22.7	17.1	4.5	4.9	15.2	14.6	2.6	3.1	—	23.9	5.9	4.8	**7**
8	30.00–34.99	16.1	5.4	13.4	14.8	11.1 [j]	18.2	3.2	4.0	—	20.9	17.7	4.8	**8**
9	35.00–39.99	10.2	1.9	15.9	18.9	—	16.4	9.3	3.8	—	9.3	18.5	5.2	**9**
10	40.00–44.99	6.5	1.1	14.0	15.1	—	16.4	12.7	7.3	—	4.1	15.0	8.3	**10**
11	45.00–49.99	0.5 [k]	[k, l]	12.1	12.9	—	10.8	13.3	12.4	—	0.1 [k]	13.6	14.0	**11**
12	50.00–54.99	—	—	9.9	9.4	—	8.7	11.9	12.5	—	—	8.2	13.0	**12**
13	55.00–59.99	—	—	7.3	6.5	—	3.1 [m]	13.7	10.5	—	—	3.2	10.7	**13**
14	60.00–64.99	—	—	5.9	3.9	—	—	9.9	10.5	—	—	1.6	8.8	**14**
15	65.00–69.99	—	—	3.9 [n]	2.6 [n]	—	—	7.0	10.6	—	—	0.4 [n]	8.1	**15**
16	70.00–74.99	—	—	—	—	—	—	5.7	7.0	—	—	—	5.1	**16**
17	75.00–79.99	—	—	—	—	—	—	3.9 [o]	4.8	—	—	—	3.1	**17**
18	80.00–84.99	—	—	—	—	—	—	—	3.2	—	—	—	1.3	**18**
19	85.00	—	—	—	—	—	—	—	2.5	—	—	—	1.1	**19**
20	Average monthly amount per family	$26.50	$20.60	$41.40	$40.70	$20.80	$36.50	$50.40	$54.00	$13.50	$26.60	$37.50	$49.60	**20**

a. Based on 20 per cent sample; average benefits shown to the nearest 10 cents.
b. Families with retired worker, wife and child; retired worker and two or more children; widowed mother only; or one or two aged parents not shown because too few cases in sample.
c. Widow's benefit reduced to less than $10 by primary benefit to which widow was concurrently entitled.
d. Family benefit is less than minimum amount because one or more additional family members were entitled to benefits that were being withheld at end of 1949.
e. 5.6 per cent at $10 minimum.
f. 13.2 per cent at $10 minimum.
g. 5.2 per cent at $15 minimum.
h. 3.6 per cent at $15 minimum.
i. $22.60 maximum possible in 1949.
j. $33.90 maximum possible in 1949.
k. $45.20 maximum possible in 1949.
l. Less than 0.05 per cent.
m. $56.50 maximum possible in 1949.
n. $67.80 maximum possible in 1949.
o. $79.10 maximum possible in 1949.

Source: Bureau of Old-Age and Survivors Insurance.

TABLE 30

Summary of Data on Unemployment Insurance Operations, 1938–1949

No.	Item	1938	1939	1940	1941	1942	1943	1944	1945	1946	1947	1948	1949	No.
1	Covered employment and wages:													1
2	Estimated workers with wage credits (in thousands)	27,500	30,100	31,900	37,600	43,000	44,000	43,000	43,000	45,500	45,300	45,600	44,400	2
3	Average monthly employment (in thousands)	19,929	21,378	23,096	26,814	29,349	30,828	30,044	28,407	30,235	32,277	33,088	31,695	3
4	Total wages in covered employment (in millions)	$26,200	$29,069	$32,450	$42,146	$54,796	$66,117	$69,139	$66,642	$73,403	$86,595	$96,095	$93,863	4
5	Taxable wages in covered employment (in millions)	$25,665	$28,411	$30,107	$38,677	$49,721	$59,034	$60,655	$58,545	$63,691	$72,981	$78,536	$76,268	5
6	Subject employers as of December 31 (in thousands)	—	807	843	896	877	876	885	943	1,223	1,338	1,418	1,454	6
7	Claim and benefit activities:[a]													7
8	Total number of initial claims (in thousands)	9,565	9,765	11,140	8,527	6,324	1,884	1,503	6,030	9,828	9,724	10,918	17,660	8
9	New claims (in thousands)	—	—	7,328	5,435	4,250	1,296	1,067	4,862	6,988	6,159	6,585	10,789	9
10	Additional claims (in thousands)	—	—	—	—	—	589	436	1,169	2,838	3,565	4,333	6,871	10
11	Estimated number of different beneficiaries (in thousands)	—	4,336	5,043	3,311	2,680	633	523	2,861	4,461	3,984	4,008	7,364	11
12	Average weekly number of beneficiaries (in thousands)	732	799	982	621	541	115	79	462	1,150	852	821	1,666	12
13	Weeks compensated, all unemployment (in thousands)	38,076	41,554	51,084	32,295	28,158	6,004	4,124	24,261	59,915	44,325	42,695	86,638	13
14	Average weekly benefit amount for total unemployment	$10.94	$10.66	$10.56	$11.06	$12.66	$13.84	$15.90	$18.77	$18.50	$17.83	$19.03	$20.48	14
15	Average actual duration of benefits (in weeks)[b]	—	—	9.9	9.4	10.0	9.0	7.7	8.5	13.4	11.1	10.7	11.8	15

TABLE 30—Continued

No.	Item	1938	1939	1940	1941	1942	1943	1944	1945	1946	1947	1948	1949	No.
16	Ratio of persons exhausting benefits to first payments (per cent)[c]	—	59.6	50.6	45.6	34.9	25.5	20.2	19.2	38.3	30.7	27.5	29.1	**16**
17	Total benefits paid (in millions)[d]	$393.8	$429.3	$518.7	$344.3	$344.1	$79.6	$62.4	$445.9	$1,094.9	$775.1	$989.9	$1,736.0	**17**
18	Interstate benefits paid (in millions)	—	—	$24.2	$21.1	$20.8	$6.8	$4.6	$19.1	$89.9	$39.0	$33.8	$73.4	**18**
19	Ratio of benefits to collections (per cent)	74.3	54.6	60.7	34.2	30.2	6.0	4.7	38.4	120.1	70.7	79.0	175.9	**19**
20	Ratio of benefits to taxable wages (per cent)[e]	2.2	1.5	1.7	0.9	0.7	0.1	0.1	0.8	1.7	1.1	1.0	2.3	**20**
21	Financial data:													**21**
22	Average rate of employer contributions (per cent):													**22**
23	For the United States	2.75	2.72	2.69	2.58	2.17	2.09	1.92	1.72	1.43	1.41	1.24	1.3	**23**
24	For states operating under experience rating	2.74	2.09	2.29	2.17	1.81	1.85	1.73	1.68	1.38	1.40	1.24	1.3	**24**
25	Number of states with experience rating in effect	1	1	4	17	34	40	42	45	45	50	51	51	**25**
26	Estimated reduction in revenue as result of experience rating (in millions)[f]	0	$4	$7	$54	$269	$369	$485	$586	$821	$984	$1,150	$1,058	**26**
27	Collections (in millions)[g]	$819	$825	$854	$1,006	$1,139	$1,325	$1,317	$1,162	$912	$1,096	$1,000	$987	**27**
28	Interest (in millions)	$21	$32	$42	$53	$68	$82	$102	$127	$130	$139	$155	$156	**28**
29	Funds available for benefits, as of December 31 (in billions)	$1.1	$1.5	$1.8	$2.5	$3.4	$4.7	$6.1	$6.9	$6.9	$7.3	$7.6	$7.0	**29**

a. Benefits first become payable as follows: 1936, 1 state (Wisconsin); 1938, 30 states; 1939, 20 states.

b. Computed by dividing weeks compensated for all types of unemployment by the number of first payments during the year.

c. Ratios for 1940–1947 computed by dividing exhaustions for the calendar year by first payments for twelve-month period ending September 30 of same year.

d. Excludes reconversion unemployment benefits paid to summer, 1947, 1948, 1949.

e. "Taxable wages" used here are wages under $3,000. For some states in some years, taxable wages were not in fact identical with wages under $3,000.

f. Includes voluntary contributions and effect of war-risk contributions in 1943, 1944, 1945 and 1946.

g. Includes collections subsequently transferred to railroad unemployment insurance account.

Sources: Data for 1938–1946 from *Recommendations for Social Security Legislation,* S.Doc. 208, 80th Cong., 2d sess., Advisory Council on Social Security to the Senate Committee on Finance, p. 220; for 1947–1949, from Bureau of Employment Security.

TABLE 31

FINANCIAL ASPECTS OF UNEMPLOYMENT INSURANCE, BY STATE, JUNE 30, 1949[a] SELECTED DATA ON

No.	Region and State	Month and Year Benefits First Payable	Average Employer Contribution Rates, Fiscal Year Ended June 30, 1949[b] (Per Cent)	Amounts as of June 30, 1949 (In Thousands): Cumulative Contributions and Interest[c]	Amounts as of June 30, 1949 (In Thousands): Cumulative Benefits Paid[d]	Amounts as of June 30, 1949 (In Thousands): Funds Available for Benefits[e]	Amount of Benefits[f] Paid for Each $1 Collected as of June 30, 1949: Since Benefits First Payable	Amount of Benefits[f] Paid for Each $1 Collected as of June 30, 1949: Fiscal Year Ended June 30, 1949	Ratio of Benefits[f] to Taxable Wages,[g] Fiscal Year Ended June 30, 1949	Funds Available on June 30, 1949, as Percentage of Taxable Wages	Percentage of Employed Covered Workers Who Could Be Paid Benefits for Maximum Duration out of Funds Available on June 30, 1949: Under State Formula[h]	Percentage of Employed Covered Workers Who Could Be Paid Benefits for Maximum Duration out of Funds Available on June 30, 1949: Under Uniform-Benefit Formula[i]	No.
1	Total	—	1.2	$13,396,098[j]	$6,088,032	$7,308,065[j]	$0.54[k]	$1.21	1.5	9.3	48.7	38.2	1
2	Region I:												2
3	Connecticut	Jan. 1938	0.6	286,075	110,883	175,191	0.45	3.83	1.9	11.0	49.0	44.1	3
4	Maine	"	1.7	78,113	37,474	40,639	0.54	1.27	2.1	10.3	83.8	42.1	4
5	Massachusetts	"	1.3	471,864	327,840	144,024	0.83	1.82	2.4	4.4	18.5	16.9	5
6	New Hampshire	"	1.4	46,498	21,609	24,889	0.56	1.80	2.4	8.4	43.8	33.1	6
7	Rhode Island	"	1.4	125,354[j]	91,628	33,726[j]	0.85	3.27	4.7	6.2	24.6	24.4	7
8	Vermont	"	1.5	24,672	8,681	15,991	0.41	1.17	1.8	11.3	63.7	42.2	8
9	Region II:												9
10	Delaware	Jan. 1939	0.6	23,192	8,054	15,138	0.48	0.84	0.5	7.1	32.1	28.7	10
11	New Jersey	"	1.3	780,090[j]	335,733	444,357[j]	0.52	1.28	2.0	13.4	62.9	56.1	11
12	New York	Jan. 1938	1.5	2,140,697	1,193,346	947,351	0.63	1.69	2.4	8.7	36.5	35.5	12
13	Pennsylvania	"	0.9	1,117,321	491,344	625,977	0.51	1.12	1.0	8.7	41.2	33.9	13
14	Region III:												14
15	District of Columbia..	"	0.6	64,581	19,356	45,226	0.38	1.32	0.7	9.3	57.7	37.3	15
16	Maryland	"	1.2	224,631	100,491	124,140	0.51	1.21	1.5	10.0	40.8	35.5	16
17	North Carolina	"	1.5	207,157	52,566	154,591	0.29	0.64	1.0	12.1	89.2	54.9	17
18	Virginia	"	0.7	127,710	45,085	82,625	0.42	1.22	0.9	7.9	65.8	32.7	18
19	West Virginia	"	1.3	149,082	57,305	91,778	0.45	0.55	0.8	9.0	56.3	37.8	19
20	Region IV:												20
21	Kentucky	Jan. 1939	1.6	158,311	41,648	116,663	0.33	0.68	1.2	14.2	92.4	56.6	21
22	Michigan	July 1938	1.9	728,244	431,317	296,927	0.69	0.63	1.2	6.9	37.8	29.4	22
23	Ohio	Jan. 1939	0.7	773,033	218,608	554,425	0.36	0.94	0.7	10.2	42.7	40.7	23
24	Region V:												24
25	Illinois	July 1939	1.0	907,545	401,264	506,281	0.59	1.12	1.2	8.4	37.6	37.2	25
26	Indiana	Apr. 1938	0.7	312,003	121,329	190,674	0.47	1.22	0.8	8.4	57.9	35.6	26
27	Minnesota	Jan. 1938	1.1	193,742	69,489	124,253	0.41	0.65	0.7	10.1	50.2	38.3	27
28	Wisconsin	July 1936	0.7	276,378	57,585	218,793	0.26[k]	0.93	0.6	12.2	53.8	51.1	28
29	Region VI:												29
30	Alabama	Jan. 1938	1.0	131,921	71,074	60,847	0.62	1.03	1.4	6.8	43.3	25.8	30
31	Florida	Jan. 1939	0.9	121,129	46,536	74,592	0.45	1.01	1.0	9.2	87.5	36.7	31
32	Georgia	"	1.1	147,778	45,405	102,374	0.38	0.83	0.9	10.0	83.3	38.8	32
33	Mississippi	Apr. 1938	1.3	62,723	19,165	43,558	0.34	0.88	1.5	13.9	104.0	50.4	33
34	South Carolina	July 1938	1.2	76,596	23,954	52,642	0.38	1.01	1.3	8.5	52.9	31.8	34
35	Tennessee	Jan. 1938	1.4	182,080	80,868	101,213	0.50	1.20	1.7	9.8	69.1	42.5	35
36	Region VII:												36
37	Iowa	July 1938	1.3	$120,068	$31,562	$88,506	$0.31	$0.40	0.5	11.3	66.0	48.3	37
38	Kansas	Jan. 1939	1.2	94,127	31,003	63,124	0.41	0.52	0.7	11.5	75.6	51.5	38

TABLE 31—CONTINUED

No.	Region and State	Month and Year Benefits First Payable	Average Employer Contribution Rates, Fiscal Year Ended June 30, 1949 [b] (Per Cent)	Amounts as of June 30, 1949 (In Thousands): Cumulative Contributions and Interest [c]	Cumulative Benefits Paid [d]	Funds Available for Benefits [e]	Amount of Benefits [f] Paid for Each $1 Collected as of June 30, 1949: Since Benefits First Payable	Fiscal Year Ended June 30, 1949	Ratio of Benefits [f] to Taxable Wages,[g] Fiscal Year Ended June 30, 1949	Funds Available on June 30, 1949, as Percentage of Taxable Wages	Percentage of Employed Covered Workers Who Could Be Paid Benefits for Maximum Duration out of Funds Available on June 30, 1949: Under State Formula [h]	Under Uniform-Benefit Formula [i]	No.
39	Missouri	Jan. 1939	1.4	286,983	102,725	184,258	0.45	0.67	1.0	10.5	68.8	42.3	39
40	Nebraska	"	0.6	45,728	11,639	34,089	0.34	0.65	0.4	9.8	61.5	38.5	40
41	North Dakota	"	1.8	12,321	3,574	8,747	0.38	0.38	0.7	9.1	56.0	35.6	41
42	South Dakota	"	1.0	11,790	2,508	9,282	0.29	0.48	0.5	8.3	52.7	33.8	42
43	Region VIII:												43
44	Arkansas	"	1.6	62,064	24,164	37,900	0.46	0.81	1.3	9.6	64.3	32.7	44
45	Louisiana	Jan. 1938	1.8	167,670	66,726	100,944	0.45	0.64	1.2	11.0	55.7	42.9	45
46	New Mexico	Dec. 1938	1.9	26,065	5,973	20,092	0.27	0.30	0.6	10.2	64.8	39.2	46
47	Oklahoma	"	1.3	89,160	41,356	47,804	0.60	0.65	0.8	7.6	43.3	34.2	47
48	Texas	Jan. 1938	1.0	286,751	77,519	209,232	0.32	0.31	0.3	8.0	46.2	33.9	48
49	Region IX:												49
50	Colorado	Jan. 1939	1.0	70,606	16,151	54,454	0.29	0.34	0.4	12.0	73.4	48.3	50
51	Idaho	Sept. 1938	2.0	36,606	12,120	24,486	0.39	0.53	1.1	11.9	73.1	46.1	51
52	Montana	July 1939	1.8	42,619	12,947	29,672	0.39	0.48	0.9	13.3	95.5	56.1	52
53	Utah	Jan. 1938	1.2	53,818	21,258	32,560	0.45	1.24	1.5	11.5	56.5	46.2	53
54	Wyoming	Jan. 1939	1.3	17,248	4,881	12,367	0.36	0.35	0.4	9.2	49.6	38.1	54
55	Region X:												55
56	Arizona	Jan. 1938	1.5	40,863	12,525	28,338	0.35	0.64	0.9	10.9	118.6	46.8	56
57	California	"	1.8	1,495,875 [j]	858,627	637,247 [j]	0.65	1.86	3.2	9.7	42.8	42.0	57
58	Nevada	Jan. 1939	1.6	20,229	6,882	13,347	0.40	0.92	1.5	13.7	57.9	58.4	58
59	Oregon	Jan. 1938	1.7	145,584	63,189	82,395	0.49	0.93	1.6	10.1	48.4	41.4	59
60	Washington	Jan. 1939	2.0	287,412	140,800	146,612	0.56	0.96	1.9	10.9	54.2	45.0	60
61	Territories:												61
62	Alaska	"	1.4	15,726	5,560	10,166	0.41	1.62	2.5	11.6	69.0	66.3	62
63	Hawaii	"	1.1	28,263	4,705	23,558	0.21	1.02	1.2	10.7	58.0	41.3	63

a. Based on data reported by state agencies.

b. Preliminary estimates; excludes effect of voluntary contributions from employers.

c. Represents contributions, penalties and interest from employers; interest earned by state accounts in unemployment trust fund and reported by the Treasury; and contributions from employees. Also includes the excess of contributions on wages earned by railroad workers through June 30, 1939 over the amounts transferred to the railroad unemployment insurance account, and refund of $41 million by the federal government to 13 states, Alaska and Hawaii, collected on payrolls for 1936 under Title IX of the Social Security Act.

d. Adjusted for voided benefit checks. Includes benefits paid to railroad workers through June 30, 1939; excludes reconversion unemployment benefits for seamen.

e. Represents sum of balances at end of month in state clearing account, and benefit-payment account, and in state unemployment trust fund account in the Treasury.

f. Excludes reconversion unemployment benefits for seamen.

g. Wages of $3,000 or less. For some states for years in which taxable wages were not identical with wages of $3,000 or less, estimate was used.

h. Employed covered workers during average month in 1948; maximum duration under laws enacted by September 1, 1949 (except for Alaska, Arizona, Maryland, North Dakota and Wyoming, where the percentages do not reflect the recent amendments on dependents allowances); average weekly payment equal to average weekly benefit in the state during April–June 1949; all claimants assumed to be eligible for and receiving the maximum number of weeks of benefits payable under the state law (for Michigan and Wisconsin, claimants assumed to have only one base-period employer).

i. Employed covered workers during average month in 1948; uniform duration of 26 weeks and a weekly benefit rate of 1/20 of high-quarter earnings — $5 minimum, $25 maximum (or schedule with dependents allowance resulting in same average weekly benefit amount); all claimants assumed to draw benefits for 26 weeks. Average weekly benefit amount derived from distribution of high-quarter earning of eligible claimants.

j. Excludes $200,000 in California, $50,000,000 in New Jersey, and $28,968,681 in Rhode Island, withdrawn for payment of temporary disability benefits.

k. Ratio for Wisconsin based on benefits and collections since January 1, 1938.

Source: Social Security Bulletin, October 1949, p. 36.

TABLE 32

SIZE OF FIRMS COVERED BY STATE UNEMPLOYMENT INSURANCE LAWS, SEPTEMBER 1949

State	Minimum Number of Workers	Minimum Period of Time	Added Conditions (Payroll)	Alternative Conditions (Workers or Payroll)
Alabama	8	20 weeks	—	—
Alaska	1	At any time	—	—
Arizona	3	20 weeks	—	—
Arkansas	1	10 days	—	—
California	1	At any time	$100 in any quarter	—
Colorado	8	20 weeks	—	—
Connecticut	4	13 weeks	—	—
Delaware	1	20 weeks	—	—
District of Columbia	1	At any time	—	—
Florida	8	20 weeks	—	—
Georgia	8	20 weeks	—	—
Hawaii	1	At any time	—	—
Idaho	1	At any time	$75 in any quarter	—
Illinois	6	20 weeks	—	—
Indiana	8[a]	20 weeks	—	—
Iowa	8	15 weeks	—	—
Kansas	8	20 weeks	—	25 in 1 week
Kentucky	4	3 quarters of preceding year	$50 per quarter for each worker	8 in 20 weeks
Louisiana	4	20 weeks	—	—
Maine	8	20 weeks	—	—
Maryland	1	At any time	—	—
Massachusetts	1	20 weeks	—	—
Michigan	8	20 weeks	—	—
Minnesota	1[b]	20 weeks	—	[b]
Mississippi	8	20 weeks	—	—
Missouri	8	20 weeks	—	—
Montana	1	20 weeks	—	$500 in a calendar year
Nebraska	8	20 weeks	—	$10,000 in any quarter
Nevada	1	At any time	$225 in any quarter	—
New Hampshire	4	20 weeks	—	—
New Jersey	4	20 weeks	—	—
New Mexico	1	At any time	$450 in any quarter	2 or more in 13 weeks[a]
New York	4	15 days	—	—
North Carolina	8[a]	20 weeks	—	—
North Dakota	8	20 weeks	—	—
Ohio	3	At any time	—	—
Oklahoma	8	20 weeks	—	—
Oregon	4	6 weeks	$500 in same quarter	—
Pennsylvania	1	At any time	—	—
Rhode Island	4	20 weeks	—	—
South Carolina	8	20 weeks	—	—
South Dakota	8	20 weeks	—	—
Tennessee	8	20 weeks	—	—
Texas	8	20 weeks	—	—
Utah	1	At any time	$140 in any quarter	—
Vermont	8	20 weeks	—	—
Virginia	8	20 weeks	—	—
Washington	1	At any time	—	—
West Virginia	8	20 weeks	—	—
Wisconsin	6	18 weeks	—	$6,000 in any year or $10,000 in any quarter[c]
Wyoming	1	At any time	$500 in any year	—

a. Workers whose services are covered by another state through election under a reciprocal-coverage agreement are included for purposes of determining employer liability.

b. Employers of less than 8 (not subject to the federal unemployment tax act) outside the corporate limits of a city, village or borough of 10,000 population or more are not liable for contributions.

c. Not counting more than $1,000 wages per employee in applying the test of $10,000 per quarter.

Source: Comparison of State Unemployment Insurance Laws as of September 1949, Bureau of Employment Security, 1949, p. 2.

TABLE 33

SELECTED DATA RELATING TO THE WEEKLY BENEFIT AMOUNT UNDER UNEMPLOYMENT INSURANCE, BY STATE, 1938–1949

No.	State	Average Weekly Payment for Total Unemployment[a] in: 1938[e]	1939[e]	1940	1941	1944	1945	1946	1947	1948	1949	Percentage of Weeks of Total Unemployment Compensated during 1949 at:[b] Less than $5.00	$5.00–9.99	$10.00–14.99	$15.00–17.99	$18.00–19.99	$20.00–24.99	$25.00 or More	Maximum[b, d]	Minimum[e]	
1	United States	$10.94	$10.66	$10.56	$11.06	$15.90	$18.77	$18.50	$17.83	$19.03	$20.48	0.1	2.7	10.3	9.1	8.1	39.8	29.8	60.0	1.9	1
2	Alabama	7.63	7.15	6.52	7.16	11.64	16.72	16.57	14.65	15.40	16.50	1.0	8.4	18.5	12.1	8.8	51.3	—	51.3	1.0	2
3	Alaska	—	15.06	14.67	14.24	14.21	15.57	16.03	21.79	23.45	23.85	—	0.7	3.3	3.0	1.9	3.9	87.2	87.2	0.4	3
4	Arizona	11.79	11.19	10.96	11.02	14.43	14.70	14.39	16.08	18.79	20.11	—	2.4	5.6	6.2	5.1	80.7	—	80.7	0.2	4
5	Arkansas[e]	—	6.66	6.36	6.84	11.15	13.24	12.61	13.75	15.97	16.57	—	9.6	22.0	17.8	10.3	40.3	—	39.1	2.3	5
6	California	9.72	10.99	13.98	14.57	18.22	19.40	19.03	18.75	21.35	22.79	—	—	5.1	4.1	3.7	27.6	59.4	59.4	1.3	6
7	Colorado[e]	—	10.79	10.51	10.21	13.36	13.58	13.89	14.53	15.54	17.99	—	3.8	12.3	45.8	3.8	34.3	—	64.3	0.9	7
8	Connecticut	10.62	10.04	9.98	10.65	18.87	20.84	21.08	19.56	20.21	21.72	—	4.9	8.0	8.3	6.8	72.0	—	54.6	3.9	8
9	Delaware[e]	—	8.41	8.96	9.08	14.76	16.69	16.25	14.95	15.42	18.69	—	6.6	13.8	9.9	25.8	13.6	30.2	51.2	2.1	9
10	District of Columbia.	8.81	8.58	9.71	12.20	17.78	17.78	17.14	16.46	16.99	17.67	—	4.1	14.9	16.3	9.8	54.9	—	54.9	1.2	10
11	Florida	—	8.68	9.72	10.24	12.96	13.99	14.02	13.53	13.78	13.85	—	5.0	21.6	73.4	—	—	—	73.4	0.4	11
12	Georgia	—	6.38	6.56	7.47	10.54	15.94	15.20	13.32	13.64	14.68	1.8	11.2	21.7	22.7	42.5	—	—	42.5	1.8	12
13	Hawaii	—	8.96	8.24	7.36	19.57	21.25	21.86	19.87	21.01	21.48	—	2.4	8.7	9.0	7.3	21.1	51.3	51.3	0.3	13
14	Idaho	10.73	11.21	11.24	11.19	12.40	13.70	15.45	15.99	18.45	18.89	—	—	8.1	11.0	7.7	73.2	—	73.2	1.4	14
15	Illinois	—	12.90	12.92	13.17	17.55	18.95	18.67	18.23	18.50	18.95	—	—	8.5	6.6	5.3	79.6	—	79.6	2.0	15
16	Indiana	12.42	11.06	10.97	11.51	16.10	16.38	18.66	17.00	17.68	18.48	—	2.0	9.0	8.6	6.1	74.3	—	74.3	[f]	16
17	Iowa[e]	9.30	9.08	9.50	9.37	11.59	16.25	15.80	14.55	15.98	17.56	—	7.1	12.8	9.8	6.5	63.8	—	62.7	0.8	17
18	Kansas[e]	—	10.25	9.30	9.57	13.42	15.37	15.09	14.56	15.28	17.86	—	6.0	14.3	10.0	39.7	8.5	21.4	58.0	1.0	18
19	Kentucky[g]	—	8.45	7.88	7.56	10.50	12.43	12.09	10.98	12.76	15.59	—	12.2	26.4	16.9	12.6	31.9	—	32.1	3.3	19
20	Louisiana	8.41	8.33	8.02	9.65	14.46	16.48	15.76	13.93	15.30	20.62	0.1	4.7	10.8	9.5	8.8	16.8	49.5	51.3	0.6	20
21	Maine[e]	8.94	7.64	6.65	7.06	10.49	15.83	15.86	13.48	14.91	15.99	—	18.1	24.6	9.8	10.7	33.5	3.3	18.5	5.2	21
22	Maryland	10.21	9.31	8.96	11.04	17.43	19.24	18.97	18.07	18.70	21.25	—	3.5	12.4	9.5	7.2	19.2	48.2	48.2	0.3	22
23	Massachusetts	10.62	9.93	10.09	10.44	16.21	19.19	20.86	21.85	22.41	23.39	—	1.7	4.6	5.2	4.7	14.3	69.6	69.6	0.3	23
24	Michigan[e]	13.49	13.30	12.56	12.76	19.03	20.70	20.37	19.77	20.34	22.68	—	1.0	2.1	2.2	2.1	92.6	—	89.1	0.5	24
25	Minnesota[e]	10.41	11.14	10.24	10.61	14.28	17.18	16.70	14.98	15.30	16.72	—	4.8	27.2	12.5	13.4	38.7	3.3	28.5	1.8	25
26	Mississippi	5.89	5.64	6.03	7.58	11.16	12.90	12.85	12.15	13.56	14.60	2.6	14.7	29.0	15.8	8.1	29.7	—	29.7	1.2	26
27	Missouri	—	8.68	9.09	9.60	15.27	16.75	16.40	16.40	16.20	17.17	0.4	3.4	14.9	13.0	8.7	59.5	—	59.5	0	27
28	Montana[e]	—	11.20	10.89	11.00	12.34	13.05	13.35	14.24	16.01	17.31	—	6.0	12.8	10.3	32.6	38.2	—	64.8	2.1	28
29	Nebraska[e]	—	8.67	9.28	9.21	12.65	16.31	16.17	14.92	15.12	16.26	—	4.2	17.9	12.6	51.7	13.5	—	63.2	0.3	29
30	Nevada[e]	—	12.94	13.22	13.30	14.75	17.17	18.09	18.85	20.04	21.66	—	1.0	4.3	4.5	4.7	66.2	19.3	80.6	0.5	30

TABLE 33—Continued

No.	State	Average Weekly Payment for Total Unemployment[a] in: 1938[c]	1939[c]	1940	1941	1944	1945	1946	1947	1948	1949	Percentage of Weeks of Total Unemployment Compensated during 1949 at:[b] Less than $5.00	$5.00–9.99	$10.00–14.99	$15.00–17.99	$18.00–19.99	$20.00–24.99	$25.00 or More	Maximum[b, d]	Minimum[e]	No.
31	New Hampshire[e]	$9.28	$8.80	$8.82	$8.65	$11.14	$13.38	$13.61	$15.42	$15.55	$18.24	—	12.1	19.3	12.7	8.6	27.5	19.9	25.9	3.2	**31**
32	New Jersey	—	9.68	9.46	11.26	16.41	20.27	20.39	19.51	19.91	20.73	—	1.1	4.8	5.3	4.5	84.2	—	78.9	1.1	**32**
33	New Mexico	9.22	10.14	9.16	8.89	11.66	12.67	13.41	13.85	17.05	17.96	—	4.7	13.0	10.0	8.4	64.0	—	64.0	0.7	**33**
34	New York[h]	12.04	12.88	11.58	11.69	16.17	19.48	19.36	18.77	20.72	22.77	—	—	9.0	8.3	6.2	18.2	58.3	54.7	2.7	**34**
35	North Carolina[e]	[i]	5.81	4.68	5.90	7.91	12.66	11.94	11.35	11.45	14.06	1.2	20.9	35.4	20.0	9.1	11.0	2.4	6.5	1.2	**35**
36	North Dakota	—	9.45	9.54	9.69	12.10	14.56	16.87	17.39	18.05	18.83	[f]	3.5	8.6	9.4	4.6	73.9	—	73.9	0.6	**36**
37	Ohio[e]	—	10.25	10.28	10.14	14.44	18.84	18.72	17.27	17.77	20.38	—	0.5	6.9	10.6	10.1	58.4	13.5	63.4	0.1	**37**
38	Oklahoma[e]	10.57	10.15	9.84	10.07	14.69	17.43	16.69	16.09	16.59	17.08	—	4.7	10.0	8.4	57.8	19.2	—	67.9	1.4	**38**
39	Oregon[e]	11.95	11.90	12.43	12.52	14.32	16.82	16.88	15.94	16.91	19.09	—	—	11.0	17.7	9.6	47.9	13.8	47.4	1.9	**39**
40	Pennsylvania[e]	11.18	11.67	10.90	11.02	15.18	17.87	18.15	17.13	17.36	19.43	—	3.2	10.2	8.9	6.5	52.4	18.8	66.3	0.7	**40**
41	Rhode Island	9.63	9.99	10.54	10.69	16.44	17.35	17.36	18.90	21.34	22.31	—	—	8.2	5.4	4.7	14.9	66.7	66.7	3.6	**41**
42	South Carolina	6.71	6.28	6.71	7.30	11.15	11.89	14.10	13.92	15.41	17.41	[f]	6.1	14.3	12.7	9.8	57.0	—	57.0	0.9	**42**
43	South Dakota	—	9.11	7.24	7.45	9.50	11.21	13.59	13.59	16.37	17.58	—	5.7	13.6	11.6	5.7	63.3	—	63.3	1.0	**43**
44	Tennessee[e]	7.27	7.21	7.48	8.12	11.45	13.15	13.38	12.85	13.50	14.84	—	15.8	23.0	14.7	33.6	12.9	—	43.8	3.1	**44**
45	Texas[e]	9.23	8.43	8.07	8.11	11.55	15.44	15.64	13.74	13.93	15.28	—	9.2	15.3	11.3	60.6	3.5	—	63.8	1.8	**45**
46	Utah	11.37	10.32	11.11	12.26	18.88	22.76	23.35	22.82	23.10	23.75	—	0.2	2.0	3.7	1.9	9.9	82.3	82.3	[f]	**46**
47	Vermont[e]	9.39	9.23	9.08	9.52	12.29	16.55	16.85	16.84	16.89	19.30	—	2.3	14.4	16.0	12.0	33.5	21.8	33.1	0.2	**47**
48	Virginia	8.08	7.88	7.68	8.03	11.13	12.81	12.97	12.35	14.22	16.22	—	10.5	20.5	14.5	9.1	45.5	—	45.5	2.1	**48**
49	Washington	—	11.82	12.62	12.65	13.91	21.07	20.94	19.14	18.38	20.28	—	—	21.1	9.4	6.9	16.8	45.8	45.8	9.3	**49**
50	West Virginia[e]	10.83	8.44	8.00	9.60	14.42	16.00	16.03	15.27	15.74	17.42	—	8.2	20.8	14.8	11.8	33.9	10.5	37.1	4.0	**50**
51	Wisconsin[e]	10.57	10.05	11.02	11.19	14.25	17.81	17.67	16.44	18.35	21.53	—	0.4	9.8	12.1	8.2	43.8	25.6	47.7	0.3	**51**
52	Wyoming[e]	—	13.84	13.16	13.21	15.13	18.02	18.89	18.52	18.62	20.65	—	1.3	4.5	4.5	4.2	54.7	30.8	80.2	0.4	**52**

a. Includes cost-of-living adjustment and dependents allowances; as of December 31, 1949, cost-of-living adjustment was paid in Utah, and dependents allowances were paid in Alaska, Arizona, Connecticut, District of Columbia, Maryland, Massachusetts, Michigan, Nevada, North Dakota and Ohio.

b. Based on payments for full basic weekly benefit rate only; excludes dependents allowances, residual payments, and payments reduced because of receipt of benefits under other programs.

c. Average computed from date benefits were first payable.

d. Percentage represents payments at maximum under old and new laws for states that changed their maximum benefit amounts during 1949.

e. Minimum weekly benefit amount changed by law during 1949. Percentages based on payments made under old and new benefit provisions.

f. Less than 0.05 per cent.

g. Changes in state law during 1948 affected 1949 data. Percentages based on payments made under old and new benefit provisions.

h. Percentages based on data that include payments for "less than total unemployment."

i. Data not available.

Sources: 1938–1947 data from *Recommendations for Social Security Legislation,* S.Doc. 208, 80th Cong., 2d sess., Advisory Council on Social Security to the Senate Committee on Finance, p. 227; 1948 data from *Social Security Yearbook, 1948,* Social Security Administration, 1950, p. 28; 1949 data from *Social Security Bulletin,* September 1950, p. 44; proportion of benefits paid at minimum rate from *Labor Market and Employment Security,* Bureau of Employment Security, Statistical Supplement, June 1950, p. 18.

TABLE 34

Benefit Provisions for Total Unemployment in State Laws as of December 1949

No.	State	Fraction or Percentage of Wages Specified [a]	Minimum Weekly Benefit [b]	Maximum Weekly Benefit [b]	Qualifying Formula [c]	Wage Credits Required [d]: For Minimum: High Quarter	For Minimum: Base Period	For Maximum: High Quarter	For Maximum: Base Period	No.
1	High-quarter-wage formula:									1
2	Alabama	1/26	$4.00	$20.00	30 x wba	$75.01	$120.00	$507.01	$600.00	2
3	Alaska	1/20 + d.a.	8.00–10.00	25.00–40.00	Flat	37.50	150.00	480.01	480.01	3
4	Arizona	1/20 + d.a.	5.00– 7.00	20.00–26.00	30 x wba [c, e]	37.50	150.00	380.01	600.00	4
5	Arkansas	1/20–1/26	7.00	22.00	30 x wba	52.50	210.00	572.00	660.00	5
6	California	1/20–1/23	10.00	25.00	30 x wba [f]	75.00	300.00	580.00	750.00	6
7	Colorado	1/25	7.00	22.75	30 x wba	52.50	210.00	562.51	682.50	7
8	Connecticut	1/26 + d.a.	8.00–11.00	24.00–36.00	Flat [c]	60.00	240.00	611.00	611.00	8
9	Delaware	1/25	7.00	25.00	30 x wba	52.50	210.00	612.51	750.00	9
10	District of Columbia	1/23 + d.a.	6.00– 7.00	20.00 [b]	25 x wba to $250	37.50	150.00	437.01	437.01	10
11	Florida	1/18–1/24	5.00	15.00	30 x wba [c]	37.50	150.00	345.01	450.00	11
12	Georgia	1/23–1/26	4.00	18.00	25, 30, 40, x wba [c, e]	48.00	100.00	455.01	720.00	12
13	Hawaii	1/25	5.00	25.00	30 x wba	37.50	150.00	600.01	750.00	13
14	Idaho	1/19–1/24	10.00	20.00	25–37 x wba [c]	150.00	250.00	475.01	745.00	14
15	Illinois	1/20	10.00	25.00	Flat +	75.00	300.00	490.01	490.01	15
16	Indiana	1/25	5.00	20.00	Flat [c]	75.00	250.00	475.01	475.01	16
17	Iowa	1/20	5.00	22.50	20 x wba	25.00	100.00	450.00	450.00	17
18	Kansas	1/25	5.00	27.00 [g]	Flat [c]	25.00	100.00	600.01	600.01	18
19	Louisiana	1/20	5.00	25.00	30 x wba	37.50	150.00	480.01	750.00	19
20	Maryland	1/26 + d.a.	6.00– 8.00	25.00–33.00	30 x wba	156.00	180.00	637.00	750.00	20
21	Massachusetts	1/20 + d.a.	6.00– 8.00	25.00 [b]	Flat	37.50	150.00	480.00	480.00	21
22	Mississippi	1/26	3.00	20.00	30 x wba [e]	22.50	90.00	494.01	600.00	22
23	Missouri	1/25	.50 [h]	20.00	40 x wba [c]	2.50	20.00	487.51	800.00	23
24	Montana	1/22	7.00	20.00	30 x wba	52.50	210.00	422.23	600.00	24
25	Nebraska	1/25	6.00	20.00	Flat	75.00	300.00	450.01	450.01	25
26	Nevada	1/25 + d.a.	8.00–11.00	25.00–37.00	30 x wba [e]	60.00	240.00	600.01	750.00	26
27	New Jersey	1/22	9.00	22.00	30 x wba	67.50	270.00	462.01	660.00	27
28	New Mexico	1/26	5.00	20.00	30 x wba	78.00	150.00	494.01	600.00	28
29	New York	1/23	10.00	26.00	30 x wba	100.00	300.00	586.00	780.00	29
30	North Dakota	1/23 + d.a.	5.00– 7.00	20.00–26.00	28 x wba	35.00	140.00	437.01	560.00	30
31	Ohio	1/17–1/24 + d.a.	10.00–12.50	25.00–30.00	14 weeks	80.00	240.00	581.00	581.00	31
32	Oklahoma	1/20	6.00	22.00	20 x wba	30.00	120.00	420.01	420.01	32
33	Pennsylvania	1/25	8.00	25.00	30 x wba	60.00	240.00	613.00	750.00	33
34	Rhode Island	1/20	10.00	25.00	Flat	25.00	100.00	490.00	490.00	34
35	South Carolina	1/20	5.00	20.00	30 x wba [e]	100.00	150.00	400.00	600.00	35
36	South Dakota	1/20–1/23	6.00	20.00	Flat	60.00	125.00	450.00	450.00	36
37	Tennessee	1/21–1/26	5.00	20.00	25, 30 x wba [i]	50.00	125.00	494.01	600.00	37
38	Texas	1/26	7.00	20.00	Flat [c]	50.00	200.00	494.01	494.01	38

TABLE 34—CONTINUED

No.	State	Fraction or Percentage of Wages Specified [a]	Minimum Weekly Benefit [b]	Maximum Weekly Benefit [b]	Qualifying Formula [c]	Wage Credits Required [d]: For Minimum: High Quarter	For Minimum: Base Period	For Maximum: High Quarter	For Maximum: Base Period	No.
39	Utah [j]	1/20 plus cost-of-living allowances	$5.00– 7.00	$17.00–25.00	19 weeks [k] and 16 per cent of average state wage	$88.00	$352.00	$380.00	$555.38 [l]	39
40	Vermont	1/18–1/26	6.00	25.00	30 x wba	50.00	180.00	650.00	750.00	40
41	Virginia	1/25	5.00	20.00	20, 25 x wba [i]	25.00	100.00	475.01	500.00	41
42	Wyoming	1/20 + d.a.	7.00–10.00	25.00–31.00	25 x wba	70.00	175.00	480.20	625.00	42
43	Annual-wage formula:									43
44	Kentucky	2.3–1.1 per cent	7.00	20.00	Schedule	—	300.00	—	1,755.00	44
45	Maine	2.0–0.85	6.00	25.00	Schedule	—	300.00	—	2,950.00	45
46	Minnesota	3.3–0.91	10.00	25.00	Schedule	—	300.00	—	2,750.00	46
47	New Hampshire	3.0–1.25	6.00	25.00	Schedule	—	200.00	—	2,000.00	47
48	North Carolina	3.0–1.0	6.00	25.00	Schedule	—	262.00	—	2,500.00	48
49	Oregon	3.75–0.96	15.00	25.00	Schedule	—	400.00	—	2,600.00	49
50	Washington	1.7–1.2	10.00	25.00	Schedule	—	600.00	—	2,100.00	50
51	West Virginia	2.7–1.0	8.00	25.00	Schedule	—	300.00	—	2,500.00	51
52	Average-weekly-wage formula:									52
53	Michigan	67–64 per cent + d.a.	6.00– 7.00	24.00–32.00	14 weeks [k]	—	112.14 [l]	—	588.14 [l]	53
54	Wisconsin	68–51	9.00	26.00	14 weeks [k]	—	168.00 [l]	—	700.14 [l]	54

a. The fraction of high-quarter wages applies between the minimum and maximum amounts. When state uses a weighted table, approximate fractions are figured at midpoint of brackets between minimum and maximum. When dependents allowances are provided, the fraction applies to the basic benefit amount. With annual-wage formula, fraction is minimum and maximum percentage used in any wage bracket. Dependents allowances abbreviated as d.a.

b. When two amounts are given, higher includes dependents allowance except in Utah (see note j). Higher figure for minimum benefit amount includes allowance for one dependent; for maximum benefit amount, includes allowance for maximum number of dependents. The District of Columbia pays the same maximum with or without dependents. Maximum augmented payment to individual with dependents not shown for Massachusetts.

c. Based on wages or employment in a specified prior period — two years in Missouri and one year in all other states. States footnoted require wages in at least two quarters; Missouri, three quarters. Weekly benefit amount abbreviated as wba.

d. See also Appendix Table 35 for wage credits required for maximum duration.

e. If claimant failed to receive qualifying wage for weekly benefit amount computed on high-quarter wages but received qualifying wages in next lower bracket, he is eligible for lower weekly benefit.

f. Base-period wages equal to $1\frac{1}{3}$ times high-quarter wages or 30 times wba, whichever is less, but not less than $300.

g. One-half average state weekly wage; for 1950, $27.

h. If weekly benefit is less than $3, total benefits are payable in $3 weekly amounts.

i. Minimum number of weeks applies to minimum weekly benefit only. Same step-down provision as described in note e.

j. The normal rates are minimum $5, maximum $20, currently increased 20 per cent (to next higher dollar) with increase in the consumers' price index. Minimum earnings required for minimum benefits are those now applicable for benefit years beginning July 3, 1949, to April 1, 1950.

k. Weeks of employment at $8.01 or more (Michigan); with average wage of $12 or more (Wisconsin); at least 16 hours or 2 full days (Utah).

l. Figured as 14 times minimum and maximum average weekly wage brackets (Michigan and Wisconsin); 19 times average weekly wage in high quarter, assuming 13 weeks' work in the quarter (Utah).

Source: Social Security Bulletin, December 1949, p. 4.

TABLE 35

Duration of Unemployment Insurance Benefits in a Benefit Year under State Laws, December 1949

State and Type of Formula	Proportion of Wages in Four-Quarter Base Period	Minimum Potential Benefits [a]		Maximum Potential Benefits			
						Wage Credits Required [a]	
		Amount	Weeks	Amount [b]	Weeks	High Quarter	Base Period
Uniform Potential Duration for All Eligible Claimants							
Arizona	——	$60.00	12	$240–312	12	$380.01	$600.00
Georgia	——	64.00	16	288	16	455.01	720.00
Hawaii	——	100.00	20	500	20	600.01	750.00
Kentucky	——	154.00	22	440	22	438.75 [c]	1,755.00
Maine	——	120.00	20	500	20	737.50 [c]	2,950.00
Mississippi	——	48.00	16	320	16	494.01	600.00
Montana	——	126.00	18	360	18	422.23	600.00
New Hampshire	——	138.00	23	575	23	500.00 [c]	2,000.00
New York	——	260.00	26 [d]	676	26 [d]	586.00	780.00
North Carolina	——	120.00	20	500	20	625.00 [c]	2,500.00
North Dakota	——	100.00	20	400–520	20	437.01	560.00
South Carolina	——	90.00	18	360	18	400.00	600.00
Tennessee	——	100.00	20	400	20	494.01	600.00
Vermont	——	120.00	20	500	20	650.00	750.00
West Virginia	——	184.00	23	575	23	625.00 [c]	2,500.00
Maximum Potential Duration Varying with Wage Credits							
Alabama	1/3	$40.00	10	$400	20	$507.01	$1,198.50
Alaska	1/3	64.00	8 [e]	625	25	480.01	1,872.01
Arkansas	1/3	70.00	10	352	16	572.00	990.01
California	1/2	150.00	12+ [a]	650	26	580.00	1,298.01
Colorado	1/3	70.00	10	455	20	562.51	1,365.00
Connecticut	1/4	70.00	6+ [a]	624–936	26	620.00 [f]	2,480.00
Delaware	1/4	77.00	11 [e]	650	26	649.51	2,598.01
District of Columbia	1/2	75.00	10+ [a]	400	20	437.01	798.01
Florida	1/4	38.00	7+	240	16	345.01	956.01
Idaho	40–22 per cent	100.00	10	400	20	475.01	1,820.00
Illinois	47–33 per cent	140.00	10 [e]	650	26	493.75 [f]	1,975.00
Indiana	1/4	62.00	6+ [a]	400	20	475.01	1,600.00
Iowa	1/3	33.33	6+	450	20	450.00	1,350.00
Kansas	1/3	34.00	6+	540	20	600.01	1,500.00
Louisiana	1/3	50.00	10	500	20	480.01	1,497.01
Maryland	1/4	45.00	7+	650–858	26	858.00 [f]	3,432.00
Massachusetts	3/10	45.00	5+ [a]	575– [b]	23	480.00	1,913.34
Michigan	2/3 weeks of employment	56.00	9+	480–640	20	546.13 [g]	1,260.30 [g]
Minnesota	47–23 per cent	140.00	14	625	25	687.50 [c]	2,750.00
Missouri	1/4 in 8 quarters	5.00	1+ [h]	400	20	487.51	1,600.00
Nebraska	1/3	102.00	8+ [a]	400	20	450.01	1,185.00
Nevada	1/3	80.00	10	650–962	26	600.01	1,947.01
New Jersey	1/3	90.00	10 [e]	572	26	462.01	1,713.01
New Mexico	2/5	60.00	12	400	20	494.01	997.51
Ohio	2/3	160.00	12+ [a]	650–780	26	581.00	973.51
Oklahoma	1/3	40.00	6+	484	22	420.01	1,449.01
Oregon	1/4	100.00	6+	650	26	650.00 [c]	2,600.00
Pennsylvania	3/10	72.00	9	600	24	613.00	2,057.00
Rhode Island	52–27 per cent	52.00	5+	650	26	600.00 [f]	2,400.00
South Dakota	48–22 per cent	60.00	6+ [a]	400	20	450.00	1,800.00
Texas	1/5	40.00	5+	480	24	600.00 [f]	2,400.00
Utah	Schedule in percentage of average state wages [i]	150.00 [i]	15 [i]	500	20 [i]	550.00 [f]	2,200.00 [i]
Virginia	1/4	30.00	6	320	16	475.01	1,240.01
Washington	25–31 per cent	150.00	15	650	26	525.00 [c]	2,100.00
Wisconsin	2/3 weeks of employment	85.50	9+	689	26+	650.13 [g]	2,000.40 [g]
Wyoming	1/4	42.00	6	500–620	20	487.51 [f]	1,950.01

a. Maximum potential benefits for claimants with minimum qualifying wages. (See Table 34 for qualifying wages.) In states noted, weeks for claimants with minimum weekly benefit will be greater than figure here for claimants whose weekly benefit is higher than the minimum because qualifying wages are concentrated largely or wholly in high quarter; see Table 34 for minimum weekly benefit and divide into minimum potential benefits. In Arizona, Connecticut, the District of Columbia, Massachusetts, Michigan, Nevada, North Dakota, Ohio and Wyoming, dependents allowances, being outside the duration formula, may add to potential benefits for claimants with minimum qualifying wages.

b. When two amounts are given, higher includes maximum dependents allowances: same maximum with or without dependents allowances in Alaska and District of Columbia; no maximum augmented benefit given for Massachusetts since augmented weekly benefit is practically unlimited.

c. Annual-wage formula; amount shown for high quarter is ¼ of required base-period wages.

d. Converted from days of unemployment.

e. Statutory minimum.

f. Amount shown is ¼ of base-period wages. To obtain maximum potential annual benefits, claimant must have more than four times high-quarter wages necessary for maximum weekly benefit; see Table 34.

g. Figures given are based on highest average weekly wage in schedule ($42.01). High-quarter figure assumes 13 weeks of employment; base-period figure assumes the 30 weeks required for maximum duration.

h. A claimant eligible for the minimum benefit amount may draw all benefits due in one and a fraction weeks because when benefits are 50 cents to $3 a week, total benefits are paid at rate of $3 a week.

i. Maximum potential benefits of $150 for 16 per cent of average state wages to $500 for 100 per cent are not increased by cost-of-living allowance that raises weekly benefits; hence, weeks of duration are reduced. Statutory minimum is 15 weeks. Qualifying wages shown are for benefit years beginning on and after April 1, 1950, based on 1949 average wages.

Source: Social Security Bulletin, December 1949, p. 17.

TABLE 36

Summary of Disqualification Provisions under State Unemployment Insurance Laws for Three Major Causes,[a] September 1949

State	Voluntary Leaving: Number of Weeks Disqualified	Voluntary Leaving: Benefits Reduced or Canceled	Discharge for Misconduct: Number of Weeks Disqualified	Discharge for Misconduct: Benefits Reduced or Canceled	Refusal of Suitable Work: Number of Weeks Disqualified	Refusal of Suitable Work: Benefits Reduced or Canceled
Alabama	Duration	Partial cancellation	W+3–6	Mandatory	Duration	Mandatory
Alaska	W+1–5	—	W+1–5	—	W+1–5	—
Arizona	W+4	Mandatory	W+4	Mandatory	W+1–5	—
Arkansas	10	—	10	—	10	—
California	1–5	—	1–5	—	1–5	—
Colorado	W+1–20	Mandatory	W+1–20	Mandatory	W+1–20	Mandatory
Connecticut	W+4	—	W+4	—	W+4	—
Delaware	Duration	—	Duration	—	Duration	—
District of Columbia	W+3	—	W+1–4	—	W+3	—
Florida	W+1–12 and duration+	—	W+1–12 and duration+	—	W+1–5 and duration+	Optional
Georgia	W+2–8	Mandatory	W+3–10	Mandatory	W+2–8	Mandatory
Hawaii	W+2–7	—	W+2–7	—	W+2–7	—
Idaho	6	—	6	—	6	—
Illinois	W+6	—	W+6	—	W+6	—
Indiana	W+5	Mandatory	W+5	Mandatory	W+5	Mandatory
Iowa	Duration+	Cancellation	2–9	Mandatory	Duration	—
Kansas	W+1–9	—	W+1–9	—	W+1–9	—
Kentucky	1–16	—	1–16	—	1–16	—
Louisiana	W+1–6	—	W+1–6	—	W+1–6	—
Maine	W+1–5	Mandatory	W+1–9	Mandatory	W+1–5	Mandatory
Maryland	Duration+	—	W+1–9	—	Duration+	—
Massachusetts	Duration	—	Duration	—	W+1–4	Optional
Michigan	Duration	Partial cancellation	Duration	Partial cancellation	Duration	Partial cancellation
Minnesota	3–7	—	3–7	—	W+3	—
Mississippi	W+1–12	—	W+1–12	—	W+1–12	—
Missouri	Duration+	—	Duration+	—	Duration+	—
Montana	1–5	—	1–9	—	W+1–5	—
Nebraska	W+1–5	—	W+1–5	—	Duration+	Cancellation
Nevada	W+1–15	—	W+1–15	—	W+1–15	—
New Hampshire	Duration+	—	W+3	Mandatory	W+3	—
New Jersey	W+3	—	W+3	—	W+3	—
New Mexico	W+1–13	Mandatory	W+1–13	Mandatory	W+1–13	Mandatory
New York	6	—	7	—	Duration	—
North Carolina	4–12	Mandatory	5–12	Mandatory	4–12	Mandatory
North Dakota	W+1–7	—	W+1–10	—	W+1–7	—
Ohio	W+4	Mandatory	W+4	Mandatory	Duration	—
Oklahoma	W+2	—	W+3	—	W+2	—
Oregon	W+4	—	W+4–8	—	W+4	—
Pennsylvania	Duration	—	Duration	—	Duration	—
Rhode Island	W+3	—	W+1–10	—	W+1–3	Optional
South Carolina	W+1–5	Optional	W+1–18	—	W+1–5	Optional
South Dakota	1–5	—	1–10	—	1–10	—
Tennessee	W+1–5	—	W+1–9	—	W+1–5	—
Texas	1–24	Mandatory	1–24	Mandatory	1–12	Mandatory
Utah	W+1–5	—	W+1–9	—	W+1–5	—
Vermont	W+1–9	—	W+1 or more	—	W+6	—
Virginia	5	Mandatory	5–9	Mandatory	6–9	Mandatory
Washington	5	—	5	—	5	—
West Virginia	W+6	Mandatory	W+6	Mandatory	W+4 or more	Mandatory
Wisconsin	W+4	Partial cancellation	W+3	Partial cancellation	Duration+	—
Wyoming	W+1–5	Mandatory	W+1–5	—	W+1–5	Mandatory

a. "W+" means week in which the disqualifying act occurred plus indicated number of weeks following. "Duration" means that the disqualification is for the duration of the unemployment due to or following the act, and "duration+" indicates that the disqualification lasts until the individual earns a specified amount or works a given time. "Mandatory" indicates a reduction to be applied in every case; "optional," one in the discretion of the state agency.

Source: Comparison of State Unemployment Insurance Laws as of September 1949, Bureau of Employment Security, 1949, p. 67.

TABLE 37

Estimated Average Annual Benefit Costs and State Unemployment Reserves as Percentage of Taxable Wages[a] at End of a Ten-Year Cycle with Uniform Contribution Rate of 1.2 Per Cent and $40 Maximum Benefit Formula[b]

		Percentage of Taxable Wages			
		Assuming 2 to 5 Million Unemployed		Assuming 2 to 10 Million Unemployed	
State	Reserves as of June 30, 1948	Cost of Average Annual Benefits	Reserves at End 10-Year Cycle with Contribution Rate of 1.2 Per Cent	Cost of Average Annual Benefits	Reserves at End 10-Year Cycle with Contribution Rate of 1.2 Per Cent
Average	8.3	1.7	4.4	2.0	1.1
Alabama	5.8	1.9	−0.3	2.2	−3.9
Alaska	10.3	1.5	9.1	1.8	5.8
Arizona	9.3	1.6	6.8	1.9	3.4
Arkansas	9.2	1.6	6.6	1.9	3.3
California	10.6	2.3	0.6	2.7	−3.8
Colorado	8.6	1.4	8.1	1.6	5.9
Connecticut	10.8	1.5	9.7	1.8	6.4
Delaware	6.6	1.3	6.8	1.5	4.6
District of Columbia	8.5	0.8	14.6	0.9	13.5
Florida	7.1	1.5	5.2	1.8	1.9
Georgia	8.5	1.1	10.3	1.3	9.1
Hawaii	9.6	0.8	15.9	0.9	14.8
Idaho	10.8	1.4	10.8	1.6	8.6
Illinois	6.9	1.6	3.9	1.9	0.6
Indiana	7.2	1.5	5.3	1.8	2.0
Iowa	8.1	1.4	7.5	1.6	5.4
Kansas	8.5	1.7	4.7	2.0	1.4
Kentucky	12.3	1.5	11.4	1.8	8.1
Louisiana	9.4	1.7	5.8	2.0	2.5
Maine	9.1	2.1	0.2	2.5	−3.4
Maryland	9.5	1.7	5.9	2.0	2.6
Massachusetts	5.2	1.9	−1.5	2.2	−4.8
Michigan	5.1	1.9	−1.6	2.2	−4.9
Minnesota	8.7	1.4	8.2	1.6	6.0
Mississippi	10.8	1.3	11.8	1.5	9.7
Missouri	8.4	1.9	2.4	2.2	−0.9
Montana	12.0	1.5	11.1	1.8	7.7
Nebraska	7.3	1.1	9.9	1.3	7.5
Nevada	13.4	1.5	12.8	1.8	9.8
New Hampshire	9.0	1.6	6.4	1.9	3.1
New Jersey	13.3	2.1	6.0	2.5	1.9
New Mexico	8.9	1.1	10.8	1.3	9.6
New York	8.2	2.1	−0.1	2.5	−4.8
North Carolina	10.3	1.1	13.5	1.3	11.2
North Dakota	5.6	1.3	5.6	1.5	3.4
Ohio	9.2	1.3	9.9	1.5	7.7
Oklahoma	5.9	1.5	3.8	1.8	0.4
Oregon	8.7	1.6	6.0	1.9	2.7
Pennsylvania	7.9	1.6	5.1	1.9	1.8
Rhode Island	8.4	2.5	−4.8	2.9	−8.6
South Carolina	7.9	1.1	10.6	1.3	8.4
South Dakota	5.7	1.1	7.9	1.3	5.7
Tennessee	8.8	1.6	6.1	1.9	2.8
Texas	6.1	1.3	6.2	1.5	4.0
Utah	11.2	1.6	9.0	1.9	5.7
Vermont	9.7	1.4	9.4	1.6	7.2
Virginia	7.0	1.1	9.5	1.3	7.3
Washington	10.4	2.3	0.4	2.7	−4.0
West Virginia	7.3	1.6	4.4	1.9	1.1
Wisconsin	10.3	0.8	17.1	0.9	15.6
Wyoming	8.5	1.3	9.1	1.5	6.9

a. "Taxable wages" have been increased to take account of the Council's recommendations for extension of coverage and for an increase in the maximum tax base to $4,200 a year.

b. Weekly benefits equal, on the average, to 50 per cent of previous weekly earnings calculated on wages up to $80 a week. Minimum duration of 13 weeks and a maximum duration of 26 weeks, with the further assumption that a week of employment or twice the benefit amount would be required for each additional week of benefits between 13 and 26 weeks.

Source: Recommendations for Social Security Legislation, S.Doc. 208, 80th Cong., 2d sess., Advisory Council on Social Security to the Senate Committee on Finance, p. 198.

TABLE 38

SPECIAL TYPES OF PUBLIC ASSISTANCE UNDER PLANS APPROVED BY THE SOCIAL SECURITY ADMINISTRATION, BY PROGRAM AND STATE, JUNE 1949 AND FISCAL YEAR 1948–1949

State	Old-Age Assistance: Number of Recipients, June	Old-Age Assistance: Payments to Recipients: Average Payment, June	Old-Age Assistance: Payments to Recipients: Total, in Thousands, Fiscal Year	Aid to Dependent Children: Number of Recipients, June: Families	Aid to Dependent Children: Number of Recipients, June: Children	Aid to Dependent Children: Payments to Recipients: Average Payment per Family, June	Aid to Dependent Children: Payments to Recipients: Total, in Thousands, Fiscal Year	Aid to the Blind: Number of Recipients, June	Aid to the Blind: Payments to Recipients: Average Payment, June	Aid to the Blind: Payments to Recipients: Total, in Thousands, Fiscal Year
1946–1947	2,271,007	$36.06	$910,330	396,098	1,009,360	$61.76	$254,415	62,085	$37.88	$25,810
1947–1948	2,367,597	38.18	1,037,554	449,154	1,145,816	66.21	325,696	65,797	41.18	30,531
1948–1949	2,625,594	43.60	1,259,445	536,714	1,365,715	72.71	414,138	71,196	46.50	36,458
Alabama	73,344	22.61	18,063	13,194	35,949	36.28	5,105	1,287	25.02	344
Alaska	1,497	55.97	855	450	1,078	69.64	164	a	a	a
Arizona	11,316	54.86	6,710	3,158	8,930	92.70	2,686	787	63.07	533
Arkansas	55,242	20.95	12,583	11,458	29,517	37.17	4,511	1,752	24.64	482
California	245,294	70.55	163,340	24,160	53,898	113.70	26,891	9,004	82.54	7,757
Colorado	47,104	67.08	40,952	5,052	13,748	76.61	4,756	387	55.79	253
Connecticut	16,846	54.01	10,206	3,499	8,493	100.38	3,674	182	47.77	91
Delaware	1,509	28.06	468	526	1,556	72.69	390	158	37.16	58
District of Columbia	2,629	41.67	1,285	1,753	5,311	79.75	1,542	240	43.86	120
Florida	64,946	40.19	29,245	22,342	54,706	41.95	9,745	3,094	42.21	1,472
Georgia	93,962	20.54	21,630	12,316	31,739	40.85	4,879	2,546	25.75	704
Hawaii	2,306	35.33	912	2,081	6,184	92.20	1,821	93	38.75	39
Idaho	10,473	46.57	5,684	2,089	5,277	94.97	2,214	203	51.56	123
Illinois	126,417	44.87	63,965	25,003	63,509	101.27	26,706	4,553	46.87	2,425
Indiana	49,938	35.22	20,504	9,331	23,068	55.93	5,575	1,841	37.60	808
Iowa	48,465	48.08	26,672	4,652	11,920	62.78	3,350	1,200	52.88	722
Kansas	37,275	50.10	18,742	5,130	13,242	82.80	4,722	767	52.14	437
Kentucky	59,182	20.83	13,051	19,027	47,875	38.43	7,379	2,068	22.13	497
Louisiana	118,239	47.05	61,587	24,323	63,104	59.08	13,167	1,673	42.31	791
Maine	13,714	41.34	5,740	3,414	9,419	81.21	2,819	659	42.11	287
Maryland	11,786	36.88	5,028	5,297	16,040	82.95	5,070	470	40.83	217
Massachusetts	93,230	61.13	64,915	11,790	28,754	112.84	14,421	1,367	60.65	896
Michigan	94,632	42.88	46,278	24,841	57,494	86.05	22,745	1,668	45.83	852
Minnesota	55,060	47.15	29,230	7,566	19,180	69.17	5,964	1,057	55.26	688
Mississippi	58,051	18.80	10,895	8,194	22,172	26.49	2,270	2,520	25.79	717
Missouri	123,883	42.57	59,168	23,762	60,549	53.50	13,826	b	b	b
Montana	11,128	44.93	5,722	2,120	5,447	72.42	1,665	479	46.23	249
Nebraska	23,767	42.00	11,815	3,342	7,978	84.01	3,197	550	49.85	306
Nevada	2,420	54.05	1,441	b	b	b	b	b	b	b
New Hampshire	7,111	43.48	3,513	1,433	3,622	87.47	1,325	313	46.77	167
New Jersey	23,653	47.80	12,389	5,154	13,361	84.20	4,814	686	53.04	372
New Mexico	9,416	34.22	3,669	4,963	12,727	52.53	2,893	444	38.19	190
New York	116,465	52.74	71,630	53,106	123,126	107.20	62,708	3,768	59.46	2,574
North Carolina	54,278	21.55	11,943	12,178	34,314	41.48	5,026	3,661	30.09	1,219
North Dakota	8,770	46.56	4,636	1,723	4,630	97.97	1,882	119	45.99	63
Ohio	125,638	46.72	67,105	12,482	33,864	61.92	9,745	3,635	44.79	1,822
Oklahoma	100,415	52.10	59,403	24,140	61,103	52.20	14,285	2,656	53.18	1,597
Oregon	22,980	48.21	12,684	3,244	8,160	107.48	3,713	383	55.66	249
Pennsylvania	87,785	40.01	40,924	46,098	119,196	91.34	45,382	b	b	b
Rhode Island	9,653	45.04	4,854	3,249	8,040	85.77	2,906	158	51.05	86
South Carolina	37,674	24.70	9,787	7,690	21,914	35.51	2,743	1,408	28.73	428
South Dakota	11,979	38.02	5,205	2,033	5,006	55.36	1,164	215	34.57	83
Tennessee	59,751	27.15	17,648	18,943	51,005	48.14	9,880	2,259	36.13	890
Texas	215,723	34.23	83,930	16,912	46,942	47.18	8,685	6,046	38.58	2,622
Utah	10,058	50.27	5,895	3,311	8,407	106.68	4,046	201	54.53	123
Vermont	6,562	32.13	2,701	940	2,554	48.36	500	185	35.67	88
Virginia	17,952	20.28	4,030	6,618	18,792	44.15	3,079	1,399	27.47	410
Washington	69,133	67.11	49,257	11,047	26,079	135.44	13,222	717	77.59	615
West Virginia	23,539	21.35	5,673	12,803	34,622	43.53	5,915	911	25.02	256
Wisconsin	49,316	41.60	23,237	8,308	20,843	95.17	8,465	1,334	45.38	672
Wyoming	4,088	55.63	2,647	469	1,271	97.11	505	93	55.46	65

a. Alaska does not administer aid to the blind. b. No approved plan in operation.

Source: Annual Report, 1949, Federal Security Agency, 1950, p. 210.

TABLE 39

Estimated Number of Work Injuries, by Industry Group and Type of Disability, 1936–1949

No.	Industry Group and Type of Disability	1936	1937	1938	1939	1940	1941	1942	1943	1944	1945	1946	1947	1948	1949	No.
1	Agriculture,[a] total	264,600	270,500	267,400	257,300	270,400	270,400	283,700	311,900	311,900	305,600	323,600	298,000	304,000	340,000	1
2	Fatalities	5,500	4,500	4,400	4,300	4,500	4,500	4,500	4,800	4,800	4,500	4,500	4,300	4,400	4,300	2
3	Permanent total	b	b	b	c	c	c	400	400	400	400	400	400	400	400	3
4	Permanent partial	6,100	13,500	13,000	13,000	13,900	13,900	14,200	15,600	15,600	15,300	16,200	14,900	15,200	15,200	4
5	Temporary total	253,000	252,500	250,000	240,000	252,000	252,000	264,600	291,100	291,100	285,400	302,500	278,400	284,000	320,100	5
6	Mining and quarrying,[d] total	103,100	107,800	82,000	91,000	86,500	97,100	102,700	96,400	92,100	82,100	83,800	92,900	87,200	70,000	6
7	Fatalities	1,700	1,900	1,700	1,600	1,800	1,900	2,000	2,000	1,700	1,500	1,300	1,500	1,400	1,000	7
8	Permanent total	b	b	b	c	c	c	200	200	200	200	200	200	200	100	8
9	Permanent partial	3,400	3,300	2,500	2,700	2,900	3,700	4,500	4,200	4,000	3,600	3,700	4,100	3,700	3,000	9
10	Temporary total	98,000	102,600	77,800	86,700	81,800	91,500	96,000	90,000	86,200	76,800	78,600	87,100	81,900	65,900	10
11	Construction,[e] total	283,900	391,700	292,200	404,700	453,800	495,500	349,500	260,100	99,600	112,200	131,800	151,700	193,000	183,000	11
12	Fatalities	2,700	3,700	2,600	3,600	4,100	4,100	3,300	2,500	1,100	1,700	2,200	2,400	2,100	2,100	12
13	Permanent total	b	b	b	c	b	c	300	200	100	100	300	300	300	300	13
14	Permanent partial	15,400	20,600	14,600	18,100	20,900	21,800	17,100	12,800	3,600	3,400	3,400	4,300	7,800	7,300	14
15	Temporary total	265,800	367,400	275,000	383,000	428,800	469,600	328,800	244,600	94,800	107,000	125,900	144,700	182,800	173,300	15
16	Manufacturing,[f] total	311,600	364,400	220,800	286,200	316,000	452,700	635,200	802,500	786,900	591,600	541,500	539,000	469,200	381,000	16
17	Fatalities	2,100	2,500	1,900	1,600	1,900	2,400	2,500	3,100	2,900	2,700	2,500	2,700	2,600	2,300	17
18	Permanent total	b	b	b	c	c	c	300	300	300	300	200	300	200	200	18
19	Permanent partial	21,200	27,900	14,000	17,600	18,600	25,300	27,000	34,100	35,400	30,700	28,200	27,200	23,700	19,200	19
20	Temporary total	288,300	334,000	204,900	267,000	295,500	425,000	605,400	765,000	748,300	557,900	510,600	508,900	442,700	359,300	20
21	Public utilities, total	13,700	16,500	16,300	21,000	21,000	21,000	21,000	19,700	19,300	20,300	25,500	27,700	27,400	27,000	21
22	Fatalities	300	300	500	500	500	500	500	400	400	400	400	400	400	400	22
23	Permanent total	b	b	b	c	c	c	g	g	g	g	g	g	g	g	23
24	Permanent partial	400	700	700	500	500	500	500	500	500	600	600	600	600	600	24
25	Temporary total	13,000	15,500	15,100	20,000	20,000	20,000	20,000	18,800	18,400	19,300	24,500	26,700	26,400	26,000	25
26	Trade,[e] total	133,000	241,200	201,500	200,800	244,600	297,100	284,200	268,400	273,800	296,400	333,100	360,600	347,300	329,000	26
27	Fatalities	600	2,800	1,800	1,800	1,900	1,600	1,200	1,100	700	1,200	1,400	1,500	1,500	1,500	27
28	Permanent total	b	b	b	c	c	c	100	100	100	100	100	100	100	100	28
29	Permanent partial	1,700	32,000	39,700	39,000	8,700	7,500	7,000	6,600	6,000	7,100	8,000	8,600	8,400	7,900	29
30	Temporary total	130,700	206,400	160,000	160,000	234,000	288,000	275,900	260,600	267,000	288,000	323,600	350,400	337,300	319,500	30
31	Railroads,[h] total	37,800	40,100	30,300	34,500	33,700	48,200	60,800	85,400	92,400	94,100	76,000	71,900	62,900	46,000	31
32	Fatalities	800	800	600	800	700	1,100	1,100	1,300	1,200	1,100	800	800	700	500	32
33	Permanent total	b	b	b	c	c	c	200	200	300	400	300	300	300	200	33
34	Permanent partial	1,200	1,400	1,500	1,700	1,700	3,300	4,200	5,900	6,400	6,500	5,300	5,000	4,400	3,200	34
35	Temporary total	35,800	37,900	28,200	32,000	31,300	43,800	55,300	78,000	84,500	86,100	69,600	65,800	57,500	42,100	35
36	Miscellaneous transportation,[e] total	27,500	42,400	52,900	54,400	129,300	130,300	136,900	146,000	135,100	139,900	132,800	135,200	132,600	126,000	36
37	Fatalities	600	800	700	800	900	1,200	1,200	1,300	900	1,000	900	900	800	800	37
38	Permanent total	b	b	b	c	c	c	100	100	100	100	100	100	100	100	38
39	Permanent partial	1,100	2,200	1,000	1,600	3,400	3,600	3,800	4,100	4,100	4,200	7,600	7,400	6,300	6,000	39
40	Temporary total	25,800	39,400	51,200	52,000	125,000	125,500	131,800	140,500	130,000	134,600	124,200	126,800	125,400	119,100	40
41	Service, government and miscellaneous industries,[e] total	232,000	363,400	212,200	253,600	334,400	367,900	393,700	423,600	419,300	378,100	407,900	382,000	360,300	368,000	41
42	Fatalities	1,700	2,300	2,200	1,400	1,800	1,900	1,800	1,900	2,200	2,400	2,500	2,500	2,200	2,100	42
43	Permanent total	b	b	b	c	c	c	200	200	200	200	200	200	200	200	43
44	Permanent partial	15,700	25,100	11,900	15,200	19,000	21,000	22,500	24,200	18,800	16,700	19,400	17,900	16,600	17,000	44
45	Temporary total	214,600	336,000	198,100	237,000	313,600	345,000	369,200	397,300	398,100	358,800	385,800	361,400	341,300	348,700	45

a. Based on fragmentary data.
b. Permanent total included in permanent partial.
c. Permanent total included in fatalities.
d. Based largely on Bureau of Mines data.
e. Based on small sample studies.
f. Based on comprehensive surveys.
g. Fewer than 50.
h. Based on Interstate Commerce Commission data.

Sources: *Handbook of Labor Statistics,* 1947 edition, Bulletin No. 916, Bureau of Labor Statistics, p. 164; *Work Injuries in the United States during 1948,* Bulletin No. 975, p. 2; and "Work Injuries Decline in 1949," Bureau of Labor Statistics, mimeographed.

TABLE 40

Injury Rates in Selected Industries, 1941–1949

(Number of Disabling Injuries per Million Man-Hours Worked)

Industry	1941	1942	1943	1944	1945	1946	1947	1948	1949
Manufacturing									
Total [a]	18.1	19.9	20.0	18.4	18.6	19.9	18.8	17.2	15.0
Apparel and other finished textile products:	—	—	—	—	—	—	—	6.8[b]	6.5
Clothing, men's and boys'	6.7	7.7	7.6	9.2	8.4	7.6	7.0	7.1	6.0
Chemicals and allied products:	—	—	—	—	—	—	—	10.8[b]	9.4
Drugs, toiletries and insecticides	9.0	15.4	18.5	18.6	14.9	14.2	12.0	10.7	9.6
Explosives	5.7	6.4	5.3	5.3	3.6	5.7	5.3	4.3	1.8
Fertilizers	27.7	32.0	32.6	33.7	35.5	33.0	31.6	27.3	21.6
Paints, varnishes and colors	14.8	17.4	19.0	18.3	17.6	18.6	17.3	15.4	11.3
Soap and glycerin	10.9	10.3	11.4	15.0	11.6	10.7	9.4	7.5	7.1
Synthetic textile fibers	9.6	8.4	10.5	9.0	8.9	6.8	5.8	5.4	3.6
Electrical machinery, equipment and supplies:	—	—	—	—	—	—	—	8.0[b]	6.5
Radios and phonographs	6.2	5.9	7.9	9.2	6.8	7.4	6.2	5.5	4.4
Food products:	—	—	—	—	—	—	—	20.9[b]	18.9
Baking	15.0	16.2	20.5	20.2	18.6	18.1	18.1	16.3	14.8
Canning and preserving	30.0	33.0	25.3	28.9	27.2	30.7	27.3	21.1	20.8
Confectionery	16.1	15.2	19.4	19.0	18.1	17.4	16.1	16.7	12.8
Flour, feed and grain mill products	21.8	24.9	30.2	31.1	27.6	26.6	27.1	21.6	18.1
Slaughtering and meat packing	30.9	44.8	47.6	35.9	32.4	35.7	29.9	24.6	23.2
Sugar refining	28.2	31.4	29.9	31.6	30.3	33.6	32.8	29.7	23.4
Furniture and finished lumber products:	—	—	—	—	—	—	—	25.7[b]	22.8
Furniture metal	21.4	23.0	30.7	30.2	21.2	21.1	19.6	17.4	15.2
Morticians' supplies	13.6	17.2	21.3	17.8	18.7	24.7	25.0	20.0	16.7
Office, store and restaurant fixtures	21.7	18.2	27.1	21.0	26.3	27.9	23.9	15.3	17.1
Iron and steel and their products:	—	—	—	—	—	—	—	19.5[b]	15.6
Cutlery and edge tools	20.7	24.5	25.9	28.1	26.0	23.0	23.6	20.3	14.0
Fabricated structural steel	35.7	40.7	34.7	35.7	27.6	29.3	27.3	26.0	22.2
Forgings, iron and steel	44.5	38.0	40.8	37.7	32.5	31.2	28.4	24.0	18.3
Hardware	19.4	24.3	20.2	20.0	16.6	13.8	16.0	13.1	11.3
Heating equipment, not elsewhere classified	29.6	33.7	36.3	42.8	33.8	36.0	34.3	27.2	21.5
Iron and steel	10.2	10.4	10.0	9.9	8.7	9.5	8.2	7.4	6.8
Ornamental metalwork	18.4	30.2	31.9	32.4	26.2	23.1	27.8	20.6	21.2
Plumbers' supplies	17.7	20.1	21.9	20.8	16.4	20.2	23.3	18.8	16.2
Stamped and pressed metal products, not elsewhere classified	29.1	20.6	28.8	27.4	22.2	22.7	23.4	21.6	14.0
Tin cans and other tinware	21.0	20.3	17.3	19.7	17.3	17.1	18.6	14.7	12.2
Tools, except edge tools	24.9	24.3	25.5	25.5	22.8	24.8	23.7	19.3	16.9
Wire and wire products	19.0	21.6	21.4	23.2	23.1	23.7	21.5	20.4	17.2
Leather and leather products:	—	—	—	—	—	—	—	11.2[b]	10.2
Boots and shoes, not rubber	7.6	9.0	11.8	12.3	10.8	10.8	9.6	8.4	7.8
Leather	26.6	30.2	29.4	29.2	28.4	34.9	29.4	27.4	23.8
Lumber and timber basic products:	—	—	—	—	—	—	—	58.6[b]	55.5
Logging	96.3	89.6	82.2	85.4	92.0	80.4	102.8	91.8	92.2
Machinery, except electrical:	—	—	—	—	—	—	—	17.5[b]	14.2
Agricultural machinery and tractors	25.7	18.3	19.9	24.0	23.5	25.5	23.4	21.9	17.1
Construction and mining machinery	29.4	28.4	29.5	28.4	25.9	27.5	28.5	24.6	19.6
Food products machinery	24.3	18.3	27.2	27.3	20.8	25.0	24.6	19.8	15.0
Metalworking machinery	20.0	21.8	19.2	16.9	15.8	15.8	15.5	14.1	11.4
Special-industry machinery, not elsewhere classified	23.2	25.2	24.6	22.6	20.9	22.7	21.4	20.2	17.6
Textile machinery	15.8	18.3	14.6	17.3	14.1	18.0	18.4	20.9	13.6
Printing and publishing:	—	—	—	—	—	—	—	9.2[b]	8.2
Book and job printing	8.2	10.5	10.5	9.9	8.5	8.9	9.4	8.8	7.5
Bookbinding	6.5	8.6	13.6	12.7	4.2	10.3	10.0	13.3	11.1
News and periodical	7.6	8.5	8.3	8.0	7.8	8.9	9.3	8.9	8.8
Rubber products:	—	—	—	—	—	—	—	11.1[b]	9.7
Rubber boots and shoes	12.6	8.6	10.7	12.4	12.5	11.4	9.8	6.3	7.1
Rubber tires and tubes	13.0	11.9	14.5	15.5	13.5	12.9	10.5	7.7	5.9

TABLE 40—Continued

(Number of Disabling Injuries per Million Man-Hours Worked)

Industry	1941	1942	1943	1944	1945	1946	1947	1948	1949
Manufacturing—Continued									
Stone, clay and glass products:	—	—	—	—	—	—	—	22.1[b]	19.6
Structural clay products	38.2	47.1	42.9	43.9	41.8	44.9	43.9	37.9	36.8
Concrete, gypsum and plaster products	46.7	48.4	40.8	28.7	27.0	32.7	36.1	28.7	25.5
Cut stone and cut-stone products	33.4	33.4	33.0	32.9	27.6	42.7	36.8	38.0	36.6
Glass	17.4	20.5	20.2	18.0	15.7	17.5	15.8	15.0	12.9
Pottery and related products	17.8	15.5	19.5	17.9	18.5	22.5	21.1	18.0	15.8
Textile and textile mill products:	—	—	—	—	—	—	—	11.7[b]	10.1
Carpets, rugs and other floor coverings	12.9	14.1	17.1	11.0	12.8	17.8	17.9	16.8	14.8
Cotton yarn and textiles	15.2	16.3	16.7	16.5	15.1	14.0	12.2	10.8	9.8
Dyeing and finishing textiles	17.7	24.8	23.6	24.5	19.5	21.7	19.2	16.5	14.8
Knit goods	6.5	7.7	8.3	8.1	7.7	8.2	6.9	7.1	5.6
Rayon and other synthetic silk textiles	11.4	11.5	13.9	13.3	14.2	12.0	10.4	9.2	6.9
Woolen and worsted textiles	15.5	17.9	19.8	20.2	20.1	22.3	18.6	14.8	13.3
Transportation equipment:	—	—	—	—	—	—	—	12.3[b]	10.1
Motor vehicles	9.3	11.3	13.6	14.4	13.0	10.8	8.4	7.3	6.7
Motor vehicle parts	21.2	31.9	22.0	25.8	20.1	17.9	17.6	13.2	10.8
Railroad equipment	17.8	17.4	25.0	21.3	20.1	19.0	17.9	18.1	13.4
Shipbuilding	26.4	33.1	31.5	23.6	23.3	20.7	25.2	26.8	26.1
Miscellaneous manufacturing:	—	—	—	—	—	—	—	12.3[b]	10.3
Tobacco products	6.2	6.5	9.2	12.3	9.9	9.3	7.5	8.3	7.5
Nonmanufacturing									
Construction:	—	—	—	—	—	—	—	36.7[b]	39.8
Building construction	41.8	36.2	25.4	30.6	30.9	35.4	38.7	39.0	40.8
Heavy engineering	68.0	37.4	24.5	21.5	28.1	46.7	41.8	39.2	41.8
Highway construction	55.9	38.6	31.8	36.0	35.8	50.5	46.8	43.3	45.5
Communications:									
Telephone (wire and radio)	2.7	2.9	3.2	3.4	3.0	2.9	3.0	2.6	2.3
Transportation:	—	—	—	—	—	—	—	23.9[b]	21.0
Streetcar	15.5	19.8	26.5	26.7	26.6	25.4	22.0	20.7	14.3
Bus	13.3	15.3	18.8	20.4	22.8	19.6	15.9	13.8	13.8
Streetcar and bus	11.6	13.6	18.1	22.3	26.3	22.6	22.3	20.5	17.3
Trucking and hauling	34.8	34.8	41.4	38.3	37.5	35.6	38.2	30.7	27.9
Warehousing and storage	51.9	38.2	32.2	37.5	34.3	34.8	33.5	26.6	31.2
Heat, light and power:	—	—	—	—	—	—	—	17.1[b]	15.8
Electric light and power	11.1	9.5	11.8	12.0	13.0	14.8	16.4	15.2	13.7
Gas	14.3	14.7	16.0	16.1	17.7	24.5	23.0	22.6	22.1
Waterworks	19.9	10.9	13.7	21.3	22.2	18.0	21.0	25.1	27.3
Personal services:	—	—	—	—	—	—	—	10.2[b]	9.0
Dry cleaning	5.7	5.2	5.0	5.8	5.8	5.3	5.5	6.3	4.9
Laundries	7.3	8.9	9.9	8.3	8.1	8.9	8.0	7.8	6.7
Laundry and dry cleaning	5.9	10.1	9.1	8.8	6.4	8.3	8.4	9.2	7.4
Amusements and related services	10.4	6.9	6.9	8.4	13.4	8.3	7.5	8.4	10.6
Medical and other professional services	13.1	6.0	5.3	4.8	4.6	4.5	3.7	5.3	4.0
Miscellaneous personal services	2.9	3.7	2.5	3.7	4.3	6.9	7.5	6.6	5.1
Business services:	—	—	—	—	—	—	—	4.4[b]	4.1
Banks and other financial agencies	2.3	3.5	2.7	3.6	3.0	2.9	2.7	2.2	2.4
Insurance	3.0	2.2	2.7	1.6	2.8	3.1	2.0	2.1	2.1
Real estate	13.8	10.6	8.9	6.7	6.9	5.3	4.9	7.0	5.9
Educational services	16.4	8.0	16.8	10.4	8.0	7.8	8.0	8.3	7.6
Trade:	—	—	—	—	—	—	—	15.1[b]	12.9
Retail, general merchandise	6.9	6.7	6.0	8.0	6.1	15.6	5.8	5.5	5.1
Retail automobiles	16.5	15.3	12.5	17.5	13.6	8.0	18.6	16.3	14.3
Filling stations	15.6	12.9	7.7	7.2	5.8	8.8	10.6	10.0	4.8
Retail apparel and accessories	4.3	5.4	6.5	2.5	2.2	3.8	4.7	4.2	4.4

a. Weighted average.
b. Weighted averages for each class of industry, including categories other than those listed. Averages available only for 1948 and 1949.

Sources: Handbook of Labor Statistics, 1947 edition, Bulletin No. 916, Bureau of Labor Statistics, p. 166; *Work Injuries in the United States during 1948,* Bulletin No. 975, pp. 8–12; and Bureau of Labor Statistics press release, September 21, 1950.

TABLE 41

Injury Rates in Selected Mining and Related Industries, 1910–1949

No.	Year	Coal Mining[a]			Metallic and Nonmetallic Mining			Quarrying and Related Industries			Coke Ovens			No.
		Number of Men Working, in Thousands	Rate per Million Man-Hours Worked		Number of Men Working, in Thousands	Rate per Million Man-Hours Worked		Number of Men Working, in Thousands	Rate per Million Man-Hours Worked		Number of Men Working, in Thousands	Rate per Million Man-Hours Worked		
			Killed	Injured		Killed	Injured		Killed	Injured		Killed	Injured	
1	1910	725	2.0	—	—	—	—	—	—	—	—	—	—	1
2	1911	728	1.9	—	166	—	—	111	0.8	22.7	—	—	—	2
3	1912	723	1.7	—	169	—	—	113	0.8	24.9	—	—	—	3
4	1913	748	1.8	—	191	—	—	106	0.8	31.6	—	—	—	4
5	1914	763	1.8	—	158	—	—	88	0.9	40.9	—	—	—	5
6	1915	734	1.7	—	152	—	—	101	0.6	41.8	—	—	—	6
7	1916	721	1.5	—	205	—	—	91	0.8	62.5	31	0.5	55.0	7
8	1917	757	1.7	—	191	—	—	82	0.6	65.9	32	0.8	67.6	8
9	1918	762	1.6	—	183	—	—	68	0.8	52.4	32	0.7	77.8	9
10	1919	777	1.8	—	145	—	—	76	0.7	51.3	28	0.7	51.0	10
11	1920	785	1.6	—	137	—	—	86	0.8	51.8	28	0.6	39.7	11
12	1921	823	1.7	—	94	—	—	77	0.7	62.2	16	0.4	45.5	12
13	1922	845	2.0	—	106	—	—	80	0.7	61.2	19	0.6	32.5	13
14	1923	862	1.8	—	123	—	—	92	0.6	62.7	24	0.7	38.9	14
15	1924	780	2.0	—	123	—	—	94	0.6	62.4	20	0.5	31.7	15
16	1925	749	1.9	—	127	—	—	92	0.6	60.7	23	0.5	27.8	16
17	1926	759	1.9	—	128	—	—	81	0.7	57.3	23	0.8	31.2	17
18	1927	759	1.8	—	120	—	—	92	0.6	58.6	21	0.4	22.1	18
19	1928	683	1.9	—	114	—	—	88	0.5	47.0	19	0.3	18.7	19
20	1929	654	1.9	—	119	—	—	86	0.6	46.3	22	0.4	20.9	20
21	1930	644	1.9	90.7	103	—	—	81	0.6	39.8	20	0.5	18.3	21
22	1931	590	1.7	88.3	81	1.1	58.8	69	0.5	40.6	16	0.2	12.0	22
23	1932	528	1.7	80.5	53	1.2	54.5	57	0.3	38.1	12	0.6	9.6	23
24	1933	523	1.3	74.6	57	1.0	63.0	62	0.7	41.4	14	0.3	10.4	24
25	1934	566	1.4	76.6	67	1.0	68.0	64	0.6	41.2	15	0.3	12.0	25
26	1935	565	1.5	77.4	158	1.0	63.4	73	0.5	37.7	16	0.2	7.9	26
27	1936	585	1.4	72.9	101	1.0	72.5	80	0.6	38.9	18	0.5	9.3	27
28	1937	590	1.6	72.6	118	0.9	76.8	84	0.5	40.1	20	0.2	10.8	28
29	1938	542	1.6	71.4	103	0.8	64.3	77	0.6	37.6	14	0.2	7.7	29
30	1939	539	1.4	68.1	112	0.8	64.7	79	0.3	36.2	17	0.2	9.0	30
31	1940	533	1.6	68.8	120	1.0	63.9	80	0.5	35.2	20	0.3	10.1	31
32	1941	547	1.4	66.3	125	0.9	62.1	86	0.4	39.7	23	0.2	13.2	32
33	1942	531	1.4	65.4	112	0.9	55.6	84	0.6	35.1	24	0.2	14.0	33
34	1943	487	1.4	62.4	101	0.9	55.5	70	0.5	33.5	26	0.2	14.0	34
35	1944	454	1.2	59.1	82	0.8	53.9	58	0.6	34.3	25	0.2	14.2	35
36	1945	438	1.1	59.6	72	0.7	48.7	58	0.4	32.4	23	0.3	13.0	36
37	1946	463	1.1	62.9	77	0.7	55.4	70	0.4	32.4	21	0.1	14.0	37
38	1947	490	1.2	60.7	83	0.7	51.7	75	0.4	32.0	24	0.2	14.0	38
39	1948	507	1.1	59.5	83	0.6	46.5	77	0.4	27.9	25	0.3	13.1	39
40	1949	483	0.9	58.1	83	0.5	45.5	80	0.4	26.0	25	0.1	11.0	40

a. For coal mines from 1930 on, hours worked are in terms of portal-to-portal time; for earlier years, in terms of time spent at the face of the mine, which is on the average about 90 per cent of portal-to-portal time.

Source: Bureau of Mines.

TABLE 42

INJURY RATES AMONG WORKERS ON STEAM RAILWAYS, 1922–1949

Year	Number of Train-Service and Non-train Accidents per Million Man-Hours Worked	
	Killed [a]	Injured
1922	0.41	27.4
1923	0.44	31.2
1924	0.36	27.8
1925	0.37	26.6
1926	0.38	24.4
1927	0.36	19.8
1928	0.32	16.6
1929	0.35	14.2
1930	0.28	9.7
1931	0.24	7.8
1932	0.27	7.6
1933	0.27	7.2
1934	0.26	7.4
1935	0.28	7.1
1936	0.30	8.4
1937	0.28	8.7
1938	0.24	7.1
1939	0.23	7.0
1940	0.24	7.0
1941	0.28	8.7
1942	0.31	10.6
1943	0.30	12.4
1944	0.28	12.3
1945	0.26	12.4
1946	0.21	11.1
1947	0.23	10.4
1948	0.19	9.1
1949	0.16	7.7

a. Includes those who died subsequently.

Source: For 1922–1943, *Summary and Analysis of Accidents on Steam Railways in the United States, Subject to Interstate Commerce Act, Calendar Year 1943,* Accident Bulletin No. 112, Bureau of Transport Economics and Statistics, Interstate Commerce Commission, Table 17, p. 6; for 1944–46, *Calendar Year 1946,* Bulletin No. 115, Table 16, p. 6; for 1947, *Calendar Year 1947,* Bulletin No. 116, Table 16, p. 6; for 1948, *Calendar Year 1948,* Bulletin No. 117, Table 16, p. 7; for 1949, *Calendar Year 1949,* Bulletin No. 118, Table 16, p. 6.

TABLE 43

COMPANIES AND PLANTS WITH THE BEST RECORD OF PREVENTION OF WORK INJURIES IN SELECTED INDUSTRIES, 1950

No.	Industry	Company, Plant, Location	Injury-Free: Man-Hours	Injury-Free: Man-Years	Injuries Avoided	Man-Days Saved	No.
1	Textile	E. I. du Pont de Nemours and Co., Martinsville Plant, Martinsville, Virginia	28,132,583	14,066	218	17,161	1
2	Communication	Southwestern Bell Telephone Co., St. Louis, Missouri	18,624,242	9,312	38	2,235	1
3	Chemicals	E. I. du Pont de Nemours and Co., Spruance Rayon Plant, Richmond, Virginia	17,222,643	8,611	100	13,089	3
4	Automobile	General Motors Corp., A. C. Sparkplug Div.	15,071,464	7,536	72	7,536	4
5	Electrical equipment		15,039,298	7,520	64	5,565	5
6	Tobacco	Bayuk Cigars, Inc., Philadelphia, Pennsylvania	14,314,436	7,157	82	3,292	6
7	Machinery	General Time Instruments Corp., Westclox Division, LaSalle, Illinois	11,114,600	5,557	96	6,335	7
8	Iron and steel products (misc.)	E. I. du Pont de Nemours and Co., Remington Arms Co., Ilion, New York	9,069,485	4,534	117	8,163	8
9	Steel	Republic Steel Corp., Truscon Steel Co., Youngstown, Ohio	7,799,615	3,900	36	10,062	9
10	Foundry	Union Carbide & Carbon Co., Haynes Stellite Division, Kokomo, Indiana	7,407,010	3,704	98	10,370	10
11	Petroleum	Standard Oil Co. (Indiana), Wood River Refinery	6,879,296	3,440	69	5,779	11
12	Rubber	Dominion Rubber Co., Ltd., St. Jerome Factory, Montreal, Canada	6,411,303	3,206	45	4,488	12
13	Sheet metal	Remington Arms Co., Bridgeport Plant, Bridgeport, Connecticut	6,087,165	3,044	52	4,383	13
14	Aircraft manufacturing	North American Aviation, Inc., Los Angeles, California	5,932,234	2,966	25	3,619	14
15	Printing and publishing	Westinghouse Electric Corporation, Printing Plant, Trafford, Pennsylvania	5,379,446	2,690	37	1,345	15
16	Railroad equipment	General Motors Corp., Electro-Motive Div., Cleveland, Ohio	5,294,960	2,647	30	4,871	16
17	Leather	General Shoe Corp., Atlanta, Georgia	5,086,861	2,543	68	2,543	17
18	Meat packing	Wilson and Co., Inc., Los Angeles, California	5,051,451	2,526	57	2,728	18
19	Nonferrous metals and their products	Aluminum Company of America, Alcoa, Tennessee	4,955,909	2,478	68	8,276	19
20	Construction	E. I. du Pont de Nemours and Co., Bell Construction Unit, Belle, West Virginia	4,428,629	2,214	86	12,046	20
21	Glass	Anchor Hocking Glass Co., Plant No. 6, Salem, New Jersey	4,340,957	2,170	32	1,953	21
22	Electric utilities	Fall River Electric Light Co., Fall River, Massachusetts	4,337,640	2,169	52	8,502	22
23	Service	Brunswick Laundry Co., Jersey City, New Jersey	4,174,257	2,087	36	793	23
24	Food	Peter Cailler Kohler Swiss Chocolates Co., Fulton, New York	3,904,841	1,952	51	3,397	24
25	Cement	Universal Atlas Cement Co., Northampton Plant, Northampton, Pennsylvania	3,700,000	1,850	18	6,993	25
26	Paper and pulp	Hollingsworth and Whitney Co., Waterville, Maine	3,343,598	1,672	39	3,511	26
27	Gas utilities	Hope Natural Gas & Subsidiary Companies, Clarksburg, West Virginia	3,167,788	1,584	51	2,503	27
28	Woodworking	The Mengel Co., Fourth St. Plant, Louisville, Kentucky	3,077,620	1,539	58	2,708	28
29	Clay products	Harbison-Walker Refractories Co., Fulton, Missouri	2,582,542	1,291	62	3,771	29
30	Air transport	United Air Lines, Chicago, Illinois	2,433,088	1,217	35	2,798	30
31	Shipbuilding	Philadelphia Naval Shipyards, Naval Base, Philadelphia, Pennsylvania	2,005,972	1,003	14	1,845	31
32	Transit	New Orleans Public Service, Inc., New Orleans, Louisiana	1,935,772	968	27	1,684	32
33	Quarry	Michigan Limestone and Chemical Co., Rogers City, Michigan	1,809,965	905	33	3,620	33
34	Mining	Oliver Iron Mining Co., Rouchleau Open Pit Mines, Virginia, Minnesota	1,546,211	773	40	5,025	34
35	Marine	Erie Railroad, Marine Dept., Jersey City, New Jersey	1,525,140	763	29	2,089	35
36	Lumbering	Koppers Company, Wood Preserving Division, Houston, Texas	1,128,357	564	53	5,405	36
37	Total		244,316,378	122,158	2,088	190,483	37

Source: Derived from *Accident Facts,* 1951 edition, National Safety Council, Chicago, pp. 35, 42; item 8 from p. 36.

TABLE 44

MAXIMUM ALLOWABLE CONCENTRATION VALUES OF HARMFUL SUBSTANCES REPORTED BY 24 STATES AND 3 CITIES, 1947

Substance	Number Reporting Established MAC[a] Values	MAC[a] Value
		(*ppm*)[b]
Acetic acid	3	10
Acetone	14	200–1,000
Acrylonitrile	12	20
Ammonia	21	100
Amyl acetate	20	100–400
Aniline	22	5
Arsine	22	1
Benzene	25	75–100
n-Butanol	16	25–300
n-Butyl acetate	19	100–400
Carbon disulphide	23	15–20
Carbon monoxide	27	100
Carbon tetrachloride	26	50–100
Chloroform	10	100
l-Chloro-1-nitropropane	4	20
Cyclohexane	3	400
o-Dichlorobenzene	21	75
1, 1-Dichloroethane	4	100
1, 2-Dichloroethane	16	100
Dichlorethyl ether	13	15
Dimethylaniline	11	5
Ethyl alcohol	10	100–1,000
Ethyl bromide	6	400–1,700
Fluorine (HF)	24	3
Formaldehyde	22	10–20
Gasoline	20	500–1,000
Hydrogen chloride	24	10
Hydrogen cyanide	25	20
Hydrogen fluoride	25	3
Hydrogen selenide	3	0.1
Hydrogen sulphide	26	20
Methanol	24	100–300
Methyl chloride	11	100–500
Monochlorbenzene	16	75
Mononitrotoluene	9	5
Naphtha (petroleum)	15	500–5,000
Nitrobenzene	19	1–5
Nitrogen oxide	25	10–40
Phosgene	23	1
Phosphine	19	1–2
iso-Propyl ether	3	500
Styrene	12	400
Sulphur dioxide	25	3–23
Tetrachlorethylene	22	200
Toluene	24	200
Trichloroethylene	26	200
Turpentine	21	100–700
Xylene	22	100–200
Toxic dusts and fumes		(*Mg/m*^{3})[c]
Asbestos	17	5[d]
Barium peroxide	6	0.5
Cadmium	24	0.1
Chlorodiphenyls	13	0.1
Chromic acid	23	0.1
Dinitrotoluene	7	1.5
Lead	26	0.15
Mercury	22	0.1
Tetranitromethylaniline	10	1.5
Trinitrotoluene	11	1.5
Zinc oxide	21	15.0

a. Maximum allowable concentration.
b. Parts of substance per million parts of air by volume.
c. Milligrams of substance per cubic meter of air.
d. Millions of particles of substance per cubic foot of air.

Source: Adapted from J. J. Bloomfield, "Codes for the Prevention and Control of Occupational Diseases," *Health in Industry,* Transactions Bulletin No. 8, Industrial Hygiene Foundation, 1946, Tables III and IV, pp. 76–78.

TABLE 45

THRESHOLD LIMIT VALUES OF HARMFUL SUBSTANCES ADOPTED AT MEETING OF AMERICAN CONFERENCE OF GOVERNMENTAL INDUSTRIAL HYGIENISTS AT CHICAGO, APRIL 1950

Gases and Vapors

(*Parts of Substance per Million Parts of Air by Volume*)

Substance	Value	Substance	Value
Acetaldehyde	200	Gasoline	500
Acetic acid	10		
Acetic anhydride	5	Heptane	500
Acetone	500	Hexane	500
Acrolein	0.5	Hydrogen chloride	5
Acrylonitrile	20	Hydrogen cyanide	10
Ammonia	100	Hydrogen fluoride	3
Amyl acetate	200	Hydrogen selenide	0.05
Isoamyl alcohol	100	Hydrogen sulphide	20
Aniline	5		
Arsine	0.05	Iodine	1
		Isophorone	25
Benzene (benzol)	35		
Bromine	1	Mesityl oxide	50
1, 3-Butadiene	1,000	Methanol	200
n-Butanol	100	Methyl acetate	200
2-Butanone	250	Methyl bromide	20
n-Butyl acetate	200	Methyl butanone	100
Butyl cellosolve[a] (2-Butoxyethanol)	200	Methyl cellosolve[a] (2-methoxyethanol)	25
		Methyl cellosolve[a] acetate	25
Carbon dioxide	5,000	Methyl chloride	100
Carbon disulphide	20	Methylcyclohexane	500
Carbon monoxide	100	Methylcyclohexanol	100
Carbon tetrachloride	50	Methylcyclohexanone	100
Cellosolve[a] (2-Ethoxyethanol)	200	Methyl formate	100
Cellosolve[a] acetate	100	Methyl iso-butyl ketone	100
Chlorine	1		
Chlorobenzene	75	Naphtha (coal tar)	200
2-Chlorobutadiene	25	Naphtha (petroleum)	500
Chloroform	100	Nickel carbonyl	1
1-Chloro-1-nitropropane	20	Nitrobenzene	1
Cyclohexane	400	Nitroethane	100
Cyclohexanol	100	Nitrogen oxides (other than N_2O)	25
Cyclohexanone	100	Nitroglycerin	0.5
Cyclohexene	400	Nitromethane	100
Cyclopropane (propene)	400	2-Nitropropane	50
		Nitrotoluene	5
o-Dichlorobenzene	50		
Dichlorodifluoromethane	1,000	Octane	500
1, 1-Dichloroethane	100	Ozone	1
1, 2-Dichloroethane (ethylene dichloride)	75		
1, 2-Dichloroethylene	200	Pentane	1,000
Dichloroethyl ether	15	Pentanone (methyl propanone)	200
Dichloromethane	500	Phosgene	1
Dichloromonofluoromethane	1,000	Phosphine	0.05
1, 1-Dichloro-1-nitroethane	10	Phosphorus trichloride	0.5
1,2-Dichloropropane (propylene dichloride)	75	Isopropyl alcohol	400
Dichlorotetrafluoroethane	1,000	Propyl acetate	200
Dimethylaniline	5	Isopropyl ether	500
Dimethylsulphate	1		
Dioxane	100	Stibine	0.1
		Stoddard solvent	500
Ethyl acetate	400	Styrene monomer	200
Ethyl alcohol	1,000	Sulphur chloride	1
Ethyl benzene	200	Sulphur dioxide	10
Ethyl bromide	200		
Ethyl chloride	1,000	1, 1, 2, 2-Tetrachloroethane	5
Ethylene chlorohydrin	5	Tetrachloroethylene	100
Ethylene oxide	100	Toluene	200
Ethyl ether	400	Toluidine	5
Ethyl formate	100	Trichloroethylene	100
Ethyl silicate	100	Turpentine	100
		Vinyl chloride	500
Fluorotrichloromethane	1,000		
Formaldehyde	5	Xylene	200

TABLE 45—Continued

Toxic Dusts, Fumes and Mists

(Milligrams per Cubic Meter of Air)

Substance	Value	Substance	Value
Antimony	0.5	Magnesium oxide fume	15
Arsenic	0.5	Manganese	6
		Mercury	0.1
Barium	0.5		
		Pentachloronaphthalene	0.5
Cadmium	0.1	Pentachlorophenol	0.5
Chlorodiphenyl	1	Phosphorus (yellow)	0.1
Chromic acid and chromates as CrO_3	0.1	Phosphorus pentachloride	1
Cyanide as CN	5	Phosphorus pentasulphide	1
Dinitrotoluene	1.5	Selenium, as Se	0.1
o-Dinitrocresol	0.2	Sulphuric acid	1.0
		Tellurium	0.1
Fluoride	2.5	Tetryl	1.5
		Trichloronaphthalene	5
Iron oxide fume	15	Trinitrotoluene	1.5
Lead	0.15	Zinc oxide fume	15

Mineral Dusts

(Millions of Particles per Cubic Foot of Air)

Substance	Value	Substance	Value
Alundum	50	Talc	20
Asbestos	5		
		Silica	
Carborundum	50	high (above 50% free SiO_2)	5
		medium (5 to 50% free SiO_2)	20
Dust (nuisance, no free silica)	50	low (below 5% free SiO_2)	50
		Slate (below 5% free SiO_2)	50
Mica (below 5% free silica)	50	Soapstone (below 5% free SiO_2)	20
		Total dust (below 5% free SiO_2)	50
Portland cement	50		

Radiations

(Material or Radiation)

Substance	Value	Substance	Value
Gamma (roentgens per week)	0.3	Roentgen ray (roentgens per week)	0.3
Radon (curies per cubic meter)	10^{-8}		
Thoron (curies per cubic meter)	10^{-8}		

a. Trade name.

Source: Archives of Industrial Hygiene and Occupational Medicine, July 1950, Vol. II, pp. 98–100.

TABLE 46

SUMMARY OF STATUTORY COVERAGE PROVISIONS UNDER WORKMEN'S COMPENSATION LAWS, JANUARY 1950

Jurisdiction	Employments Covered [a]		Exceptions [b]	Special Coverage Provisions [a]
	Private	Public		
Alabama	Elective as to all employments having 8 or more employees *	Voluntary as to county, city, town, village, or school district	Farm labor, domestic servants and casual employees	Voluntary as to employers of less than 8, except farmers
Arizona	Compulsory as to all employers having 3 or more workmen or operatives regularly employed. Employee may reject *	Compulsory as to state and each county, city, town, municipal corporation and school district. Includes volunteer fire departments	Farm labor "not employed in the use of machinery." Domestic servants and casual employees	Voluntary as to employers of agricultural workers or domestic servants
Arkansas	Compulsory as to all employers having 5 or more employees *	Voluntary as to state and political subdivisions	Farm labor, domestic servants, casual workers, public charities, vendors or distributors of newspapers and other publications	Voluntary as to excluded employments. Compulsory for building or building repair work, if contractor employs 2 or more employees at any one time. Compulsory for contractor employing one or more where he subcontracts
California	Compulsory as to all employments *	Compulsory as to all public employments except clerks serving without renumeration. Includes fire fighters in certain instances	Farm labor, domestic servants (unless employed by one employer for over 52 hours a week), newspaper vendors, charity workers and casual employees	Voluntary as to excluded employments. Agricultural employers are presumed to have accepted act in absence of positive rejection unless payroll does not exceed $500. Special compensation benefits are provided for civilian defense workers
Colorado	Elective as to employments having 4 or more employees *	Compulsory as to all public employments except elective officials. Covers volunteer firemen	Farm labor, domestic servants and casual employees	Voluntary as to excluded employments
Connecticut	Elective as to employments having 3 or more employees *	Elective as to state and all public corporations having 3 or more employees	Casual employees and outworkers [c]	Voluntary as to employers having less than 3 employees
Delaware	Compulsory as to employments having 3 or more employees. (Elective for occupational diseases) *	Elective as to state and certain counties, cities and towns	Farm labor, domestic servants and casual employees	Voluntary as to employers of less than 3 employees
District of Columbia	Compulsory as to all employments	Compulsory for all employments, except officers or employees of the United States, or state or foreign governments	Domestic workers are not included. Farm labor is included	
Florida	Elective as to employments having 3 or more employees *	Elective as to state, political subdivisions and public and quasi-public corporations	Domestic servants, casual employees, farm labor, professional athletes, independent contractors, turpentine labor and employees of common carriers	Voluntary as to excluded employments
Georgia	Elective as to employments having 10 or more employees *	Compulsory as to state, municipal corporations and political subdivisions	Farm labor, domestic servants, charitable employees and employees of common carriers	Voluntary as to excluded employments
Idaho	Compulsory as to all employments *	Compulsory as to all public employments except judges of election, clerks of election, and jurors	Farm labor, domestic servants, casual employees, employees of charitable organizations, employment not for pecuniary gain, and airmen	Voluntary as to excluded employments
Illinois	Compulsory as to enumerated "extra-hazardous" employments. (Elective for occupational diseases) *	Compulsory as to all public employments except officials and members of fire departments in cities of 200,000 or more	Farm labor, totally blind persons, and persons not in usual course of employer's business	Voluntary as to excluded employments[d]

TABLE 46—CONTINUED

Jurisdiction	Employments Covered [a] Private	Public	Exceptions [b]	Special Coverage Provisions [a]
Indiana	Elective as to all employments *	Compulsory as to state, all municipal corporations and all political subdivisions	Farm labor, domestic servants, casual workers, and railroad employees engaged in train service	Compulsory as to coal mining. Voluntary as to excluded employments
Iowa	Elective as to all employments *	Compulsory as to all public employments, except officials and firemen and policemen entitled to pension fund. Covers highway safety patrol and conservation officers	Farm labor, domestic servants, clerical employees, casual workers, and those not in the course of the employer's business	Compulsory as to the operation of coal mines or the production of coal for sale
Kansas	Elective as to "especially dangerous employments" enumerated where 5 or more employees are employed continually for one month before accident *	Elective as to county, city, school district, drainage district and other public and quasi-public corporations engaged in hazardous employments. Voluntary as to nonhazardous employments	Farm labor and those not in usual course of employer's business	All mines and building work covered regardless of number of employees. Voluntary as to excluded and nonhazardous employments
Kentucky	Compulsory as to employments having 3 or more as defined; elective as to others [e]	Compulsory as to all municipal corporations and all districts of the state in hazardous occupations	Domestic servants, farm labor, steam railroads and common carriers. See code for definitions of hazardous employment	Operators of threshing machines are specifically covered. Voluntary as to excluded employments
Louisiana	Elective as to hazardous employments enumerated or decided by court to be hazardous	Compulsory as to all public employments except officials	None	Voluntary as to nonhazardous employments
Maine	Elective as to all employments having more than 5 regular employees *	Compulsory as to state, counties, cities, and quasi-municipal corporations	Farm labor, domestic servants, logging operations, maritime employees in interstate or foreign commerce, and casual employment	Voluntary as to logging operations, agricultural or domestic service, and employments with 5 or less regular employees
Maryland	Compulsory as to enumerated "extrahazardous" employments for gain *	Compulsory as to state, county, city or municipality engaged in extrahazardous work in which workmen are engaged for wages, unless equal or more beneficial provision is otherwise made	Farm labor, domestic servants, and country blacksmiths, wheelwrights or similar rural employments, and employees not engaged in extrahazardous employments	Voluntary as to excluded and nonhazardous employments
Massachusetts	Compulsory as to employments having 4 or more employees *	Compulsory as to state; elective as to counties and cities	Persons not in the usual course of employer's business; masters and seamen; employees of carriers subject to Interstate Commerce Act; domestic service; farm labor, family in household of employer, and persons in religious. charitable and educational institutions other than laborers, workmen and mechanics	Elective as to employers of 3 or less. Voluntary as to farm labor and domestic service
Michigan	Compulsory as to all employers having 4 or more employees *	Compulsory as to all public employments	Farm labor, domestic servants, casual workers and employers subject to federal employer liability law	Voluntary as to employers of 3 or less, farm labor and domestic service
Minnesota	Compulsory as to all employments. Includes executive officers in some instances *	Compulsory as to all public employments	Farm labor, domestic servants, steam railroads and casual employees	Commercial threshing and baling specifically included. Voluntary as to farm labor and domestic service

TABLE 46—CONTINUED

Jurisdiction	Employments Covered [a] Private	Public	Exceptions [b]	Special Coverage Provisions [a]
Mississippi	Compulsory as to all employers having 8 or more workmen or operatives regularly employed * [f]	Public service corporations	Domestic servants, farmers, farm labor	Voluntary as to exempted employers
Missouri	Elective as to all employments having more than 10 employees. (Elective for occupational diseases) *	Voluntary as to all public employments. Special provision for firemen	Farm labor, domestic servants, casual employments, employees whose average annual earnings exceed $3,600, and those exclusively covered by federal law	Voluntary as to excluded employees, except employees receiving more than $3,600 a year and employees exclusively covered by federal law. Where 10 or less are regularly employed in hazardous occupation, commission may require an employer to elect
Montana	Elective as to employers engaged in hazardous occupations *	Compulsory as to all public employments engaged in hazardous occupations, including public contractors	Farm labor, domestic servants, agricultural employments and railroad employments	Voluntary as to nonhazardous employments and farm labor
Nebraska	Elective as to all employments *	Elective as to all employments except officials elected or appointed for fixed terms [d]	Farm labor, domestic servants and casual employees	Voluntary as to farm labor and domestic service, 4 or more specified
Nevada	Elective as to all employments *	Compulsory as to all employments including public contractors	Farm labor, domestic servants and casual employees	Voluntary as to farm labor and domestic service. Compulsory for employer with 2 or more employees
New Hampshire	Compulsory as to all employments and employers having 5 or more employees *	Voluntary as to counties, towns, cities, school districts, and for workmen designated by employer	Farm labor, domestic servants and casual employments	Governor and council may award compensation to employees of state not exceeding amount under act
New Jersey	Elective as to all employments *	Compulsory as to all public employments except elected officials or retired employees, including volunteer firemen	Casual workers and vendors of newspapers	Employers of farm labor and domestic servants are not required to carry insurance
New Mexico	Elective as to extra-hazardous employments having 4 or more employees *	Elective as to state and each county, city, town, school district, drainage, irrigation or conservancy district, and public institution and administrative board employing workmen in any extrahazardous occupation	Farm or ranch labor, domestic servants and casual employees	Numerical exception does not apply to structural work 10 feet above ground. Voluntary as to nonhazardous employments, farm labor, domestic service, and where less than 4 are employed
New York	Compulsory as to enumerated "hazardous" employments and all other employments having 4 or more workmen or operatives *	Compulsory as to any employment by the state and any employment by a subdivision of the state when engaged in hazardous occupations enumerated. Voluntary as to municipal corporations in nonhazardous employments. Also volunteer firemen	Farm labor, domestic servants (working less than 40 hours a week in municipalities of 40,000 or less), volunteer workers, members of the clergy, or persons engaged in teaching or nonmanual capacity in a religious or educational institution	Executive officers may be covered by employer's election
North Carolina	Elective as to employments in which 5 or more employees are regularly employed *	Compulsory as to public employments and public and quasi-public corporations except elective officials and certain firemen	Farm labor, domestic servants, sawmills and logging operators having less than 15 employees, and railroad employees	Voluntary as to casual employees, farm labor, domestic servants, and employers having less than 5 employees
North Dakota	Compulsory as to all employments *	Compulsory as to all public employments	Farm labor, domestic servants, casual workers, illegal enterprises or occupations, executive officers receiving more than $2,400 a year, and common carriers by steam railroad	Voluntary as to excluded employments

TABLE 46—CONTINUED

Jurisdiction	Employments Covered[a] — Private	Employments Covered[a] — Public	Exceptions[b]	Special Coverage Provisions[a]
Ohio	Compulsory as to all employments regularly having 3 or more employees *	Compulsory as to state, county, city, township, incorporated village and school district except elective officials	Casual employees	Voluntary as to employments having less than 3 employees
Oklahoma	Compulsory as to hazardous employments having 2 or more workmen *	Compulsory as to state, county, city or municipality when employing workmen in hazardous employments except where equivalent schemes are in force	Agriculture, horticulture, dairy and stock raising, and railroads engaged in interstate commerce	If insured, presumed to be hazardous
Oregon	Elective as to enumerated hazardous employments and occupations found hazardous by commission *	Compulsory as to state, departments, city or town (except those having over 100,000 population), and other political subdivisions engaged in hazardous occupations. Voluntary as to nonhazardous occupations	Farm labor	Voluntary as to farming and nonhazardous employments
Pennsylvania	Elective as to all employments *	Compulsory as to all public employments	Farm labor, domestic servants, industrial homework and casual employees	Voluntary as to farm labor and domestic service
Rhode Island	Elective as to all employments having more than 3 employees *	Compulsory as to state; elective as to cities or towns	Farm labor, domestic servants, casual employees, and employees receiving over $3,000 a year	Voluntary as to farm labor, domestic service, and employers having 3 or less employees
South Carolina	Elective as to all employments having 15 or more regular employees *	Compulsory as to all public employments except elective and appointive officials	Casual employees, persons engaged in selling agricultural products, farm labor, sawmills, manufacturers of shipping containers, logging operations, production of turpentine, steam laundries, rock quarries, sand mines, oil mills, domestic servants, railroads, express companies, and state and county fair associations	Voluntary as to excluded employments
South Dakota	Elective as to all employments *	Compulsory as to all public employments except elected or appointed officials	Farm labor, domestic servants and casual employees	Compulsory as to threshing machines and other farm machinery operated for profit. Voluntary as to farm labor and domestic service
Tennessee	Elective as to all employments having 5 or more employees *	Voluntary as to state and political subdivisions	Farm labor, domestic servants, casual employees, and employees of interstate common carriers	Voluntary as to employers of less than 5
Texas	Elective as to all employments having 3 or more employees *	Compulsory as to employees of State Highway Department	Farm and ranch labor, domestic servants, railways used as common carriers, and employees not in usual course of employer's business	None
Utah	Compulsory as to all employments having 2 or more employees *	Compulsory as to all public employments	Farm labor, domestic servants and casual employees	Voluntary as to farm labor, domestic service
Vermont	Elective as to all employments for gain having more than 7 employees *	Compulsory as to State Department of Highways. Elective as to towns, school districts, fire districts and villages, except elective officials and employees receiving more than $2,000 a year	Casual employees, domestic servants, and employees receiving more than $2,000 a year. State treasurer, state auditor and commissioner may award compensation in certain classes	Voluntary as to employers with 7 or less employees, employments not for pecuniary gain, and employees receiving more than $2,000 a year

TABLE 46—CONTINUED

Jurisdiction	Employments Covered [a]: Private	Employments Covered [a]: Public	Exceptions [b]	Special Coverage Provisions [a]
Virginia	Compulsory as to all employments having 7 or more employees *	Compulsory as to all public employments except administrative officers and employees elected or appointed for definite terms	Casual employees, horticultural and farm laborers, domestic servants and employees of steam railroads	Forest wardens covered by statute
Washington	Compulsory as to "hazardous employments" *	Compulsory as to state, county, any municipality or other taxing district when engaged in extrahazardous work, unless other provision is made for injured employees	Railroad employees and employments not extrahazardous	Voluntary as to employments not extrahazardous
West Virginia	Elective as to all employments *	Compulsory as to state and all government agencies or departments, except elective or appointive officials	Farm labor and domestic servants	Voluntary coverage for casual employees for not more than 3
Wisconsin	Compulsory as to all employments having 3 or more employees *	Compulsory as to state, county, city, town, village, school districts, and sewer districts, drainage districts and other public and quasi-public corporations and metropolitan transit authorities	Farm labor, domestic servants and employees not in usual course of employer's business	Voluntary as to excluded employments and employers having less than 3 employees
Wyoming	Compulsory as to enumerated "extrahazardous" occupations conducted for gain *	Compulsory as to state, county, and municipal corporations when engaged in "extrahazardous" work	Domestic servants, ranch, farm, agricultural or horticultural labor, clerical workers and stock raising	Power farms with less than 5 workmen may voluntarily come under coverage
Federal Employees' Compensation Act	All civil employees, including employees of wholly owned instrumentalities, commissioned officers in the Public Health Service, enlisted reserves under certain conditions, and persons performing activities of civilian employees but not paid therefor			
Longshoremen's and Harbor Workers' Act	All employees in maritime employment on navigable waters of the U.S., including drydocks	Officers and employees of United States or foreign governments are not covered	Master or crew of any vessel and persons unloading or repairing vessels of less than 18 tons	

* See "Exceptions."

a. Compensation laws are classified as compulsory or elective. A compulsory law requires every employer to accept the act and pay the compensation specified. An elective act is one in which the employer has the option of either accepting or rejecting the act, but if he rejects it he loses the customary common-law defenses (assumed risk of the employee, negligence of fellow servants and contributory negligence). In most states, workers in excepted or excluded employments may be brought under coverage of the act through voluntary action of the employer. In other states, such action of the employer must be concurred in by the employees.

b. Applying to private employments only. The exceptions for public employments are given under "Employments Covered — Public."

c. An outworker is one to whom articles are given for cleaning, repair, etc., in his home.

d. The law states that it is elective as to private employments of a nonhazardous nature. However, as there are no provisions in the law abrogating the employer's defenses in case he does not accept the act, it is considered, in this table, to be a voluntary one. State Supreme Court rules all public employees subject to the act without right of rejection.

e. Supreme Court decision invalidated.

f. Nonprofit charitable, fraternal, cultural or religious corporations or associations excluded.

Note: State courts vary in decisions whether minimum number of persons must be employed within the state.

Source: Analysis of Provisions of Workmen's Compensation Laws and Discussion of Coverage, prepared by the Insurance Department of the Chamber of Commerce of the United States, Washington, D.C., January 1950, Chart IV(a), pp. 28–31.

TABLE 47

Minimum and Maximum Benefits for Widows and Children in Death Cases under Workmen's Compensation Laws, September 1950

No.	State	Maximum Percentage of Wages: Widow Only	Maximum Percentage of Wages: Widow plus Children	Maximum Period *	Limit of Payments per Week: Minimum	Limit of Payments per Week: Maximum	Total Maximum Stated in Law	No.
1	Alabama	35	65	300 weeks [a]	$5.00 [b]	$21.00	$8,400	1
2	Alaska	—	—	—	—	—	9,000 [c]	2
3	Arizona	35	66⅔	Widowhood, or to children until 18 or marriage or to children over 18 if incapable of self-support	—	153.85	—	3
4	Arkansas	35	65	450 weeks	7.00	25.00	8,000	4
5	California	61¾	61¾	240 weeks	9.75	30.00	7,500 [d]	5
6	Colorado	50	50	312 weeks [a]	10.00	22.75	7,098	6
7	Connecticut	50	50	312 weeks; thereafter reduced payments to children until 18 [e]	9.00	32.00	—	7
8	Delaware	30	65	312 weeks; thereafter to children until 16	10.00	15.00–32.50 [f]	—	8
9	District of Columbia	35	66⅔	Widowhood, or to children until 18 [g]	6.30	13.38–35.00 [f]	—	9
10	Florida	35	60	350 weeks	8.00 [b]	22.00	—	10
11	Georgia	[h]	[h]	300 weeks [a]	—	20.40	—	11
12	Hawaii	40	66⅔	Widowhood, or to children until 18 [i]	4.80	21.00–35.00 [f]	7,500 [j]	12
13	Idaho	45	55	400 weeks; thereafter to children until 18 [k]	10.00 [b]	15.60	—	13
14	Illinois	50	65	—	11.25	22.50–30.00 [f]	8,500 [l]	14
15	Indiana	55	55	350 weeks [a]	12.10 [b]	23.10	10,000	15
16	Iowa	60	60	300 weeks [a]	12.00 [b]	24.00	—	16
17	Kansas	—	—	—	—	20.00	5,000 [l]	17
18	Kentucky	65	65	400 weeks [a]	7.00	23.00	8,500	18
19	Louisiana	32½	65	300 weeks [a]	3.00 [b]	30.00	—	19
20	Maine	66⅔	66⅔	300 weeks [a]	9.00	24.00	6,000	20
21	Maryland	66⅔	66⅔	500 weeks [a]	12.00 [b]	20.00	7,500	21
22	Massachusetts	—	—	400 weeks,[a] thereafter to children until 18	—	20.00 [m]	10,000 [n]	22
23	Michigan	66⅔	66⅔	400 weeks [a]	11.00–19.00	24.00–32.00 [f]	—	23
24	Minnesota	40	66⅔	Widowhood, or to children until 18 or over 18 if physically or mentally incapacitated	15.00 [b]	30.00	10,000 [o]	24
25	Mississippi	35	66⅔	450 weeks	10.00	25.00 [p]	8,600	25
26	Missouri	66⅔	66⅔	—	8.00	25.00	12,000	26
27	Montana	50	66⅔	500 weeks [a]	13.00	20.00–26.00 [f]	—	27
28	Nebraska	66⅔	66⅔	325 weeks [a]	11.00 [b]	22.00	—	28
29	Nevada	40	80	Widowhood, or to children until 18	—	13.85–27.70 [f]	—	29
30	New Hampshire	66⅔	66⅔	300 weeks [l]	15.00	25.00	7,500	30
31	New Jersey	35	60	300 weeks,[a] thereafter to children until 18	10.00	30.00	—	31
32	New Mexico	40	60	300 weeks [a]	12.00	25.00	—	32
33	New York	40	66⅔	Widowhood, or to children until 18 or over 18 if blind or crippled	7.20	21.00–35.00 [f]	—	33
34	North Carolina	60	60	350 weeks [a]	8.00	24.00	6,000	34
35	North Dakota	45 [q]	75 [q]	Widowhood, or to children until 18	11.25	15.75–26.25 [f]	—	35
36	Ohio	66⅔	66⅔	416 weeks [a]	—	30.00	8,000	36

TABLE 47—CONTINUED

No.	State	Maximum Percentage of Wages: Widow Only	Maximum Percentage of Wages: Widow plus Children	Maximum Period *	Limit of Payments per Week: Minimum	Limit of Payments per Week: Maximum	Total Maximum Stated in Law	No.
37	Oklahoma	No death benefits		——	——	——	——	37
38	Oregon	—	—	Widowhood, or to children until 18	——	$16.15–35.77 [f]	——	38
39	Pennsylvania	44	66⅔	300 weeks,[a] thereafter reduced payments to children until 16	$9.35	15.00–25.00 [f]	——	39
40	Puerto Rico	—	—	——	——	——	$3,500	40
41	Rhode Island	60	60	600 weeks [a]	12.00	16.00–20.00 [f]	——	41
42	South Carolina	60	60	350 weeks [a]	5.00	25.00	6,000	42
43	South Dakota	50	50 [r]	——	——	——	5,000 [r]	43
44	Tennessee	35	60	400 weeks [a]	10.00 [s]	25.00	7,500	44
45	Texas	60	60	360 weeks [a]	9.00	25.00	9,000	45
46	Utah	60	60	313 weeks [a]	15.00	25.00 [t]	8,000 [u]	46
47	Vermont	40	50	260 weeks [a]	12.00	25.00	6,500	47
48	Virginia	60	60	300 weeks [a]	6.00	20.00	6,600	48
49	Washington	—	—	Widowhood, or to children until 18	——	17.31 [v]	——	49
50	West Virginia	—	—	Widowhood, or to children until 18	——	11.54 [w]	——	50
51	Wisconsin	50	50 [x]	400 weeks, widow only; additional weeks for children under 16, depending on age of child [y]	10.00	23.25	9,300 Widow only [y]	51
52	Wyoming	—	—	Widowhood, or to children until 18 or until 21 if mentally or physically incapacitated	——	20.19 [z]	5,200 [z]	52
	United States:							
53	Civil employees	45	75	Widowhood, or to children until 18 [g]	15.57	121.15	——	53
54	Longshoremen	35	66⅔	Widowhood, or to children until 18 [g]	6.30	13.38–35.00 [f]	——	54

* A few laws also provide lump sums payable to widow upon remarriage.
a. Less period of disability payments, if any.
b. Actual wage, if less.
c. Includes additional benefits for dependents or members of family.
d. $6,000, except in case of surviving widow and one or more dependent children. Less disability payments, if disability occurred between 9/19/47 and 9/30/49 and death occurred more than twelve months after injury. If disability occurs on or after 10/1/49 no deduction is made.
e. Less period of disability payments, if death occurs more than two years after injury.
f. According to number of dependents.
g. May be continued beyond age 18 if incapable of self-support.
h. 85 per cent of compensation provided for total disability.
i. Continues for 104 weeks thereafter if child is unmarried and incapable of self-support.
j. In case death occurs after period of disability, total is $10,500 for disability and death payments.
k. Less period of disability payments, if any. In case of incapacitated unmarried child, payments are made for 400 weeks after he becomes 18.
l. Less disability payments, if any.
m. Plus $5 a week for each child under 18 or over 18 if physically or mentally incapacitated from earning.
n. Except that benefits continue to children until they become 18. Payments continue also to a child over 18 physically or mentally incapacitated and to a widow during periods in which such child or widow is not in fact self-supporting.
o. Less disability payments, if any. After maximum death benefits are paid to widow with a dependent child, she is entitled to additional compensation from a special fund, maximum $20, until youngest child is 18 or total payments amount to $2,500.
p. In addition to an immediate lump-sum payment of $100 to widow.
q. In addition, flat sum of $300 to widow and $100 for each dependent child up to maximum $600 at the time of death.
r. Death benefits equal four times average annual earnings of employee, minimum benefits $2,400, maximum $5,000, payable at same intervals as wages or weekly, plus $10 a month for each child (not to exceed five) under 18; total payments not to exceed $7,500. Less disability payments, if any.
s. Actual wage, if less, minimum $8.
t. Plus 5 per cent for each dependent child (up to five).
u. Plus $356.25 for each child (up to five) or maximum $9,781.25.
v. Plus $4.62 a week for youngest or only child; $3.46 for the next or second youngest child; $2.31 for each additional child; total payments may not exceed $32.31 a week.
w. Plus $4.62 a week for each child and $3.46 for each invalid child as long as he remains an invalid.
x. Plus specified percentage according to age of child.
y. A child one year of age or under would receive a sum equal to the average annual earnings of the deceased employee; for children in each successive yearly age group the amount allowed would be reduced by one-fifteenth part of such earnings, with no allowance for any child 16 years of age or over unless such child is physically or mentally incapacitated from earning. Maximum for children under 16, 780 weeks. Total amount payable to children and widow may not be in excess of $20,000.
z. In addition, $4.85 a week for each child under 18, with maximum for all children of $6,350.

Source: State Workmen's Compensation Laws as of September 1950, Bulletin No. 125, Bureau of Labor Standards, Table 4, pp. 13–15.

TABLE 48

Minimum and Maximum Benefits for Temporary Total Disability under Workmen's Compensation Laws, September 1950

No.	State	Maximum Percentage of Wages	Maximum Period	Limit of Payments per Week: Minimum	Limit of Payments per Week: Maximum	Total Maximum Stated in Law	No.
1	Alabama	65[a]	300 weeks	$5.00[b]	$21.00	——	1
2	Alaska	65	Period of disability	——	——	——	2
3	Arizona	65[c]	433 weeks	——	150.00	——	3
4	Arkansas	65	450 weeks	7.00	25.00	$8,000	4
5	California	61¾	240 weeks	9.75	30.00	7,200	5
6	Colorado	50	Period of disability	10.00	22.75	——	6
7	Connecticut	50	624 weeks	9.00	32.00	——	7
8	Delaware	60	Period of disability	8.00[b]	25.00	——	8
9	District of Columbia	66⅔	Period of disability	12.00[b]	35.00[d]	11,000	9
10	Florida	60	350 weeks	8.00[b]	22.00	——	10
11	Georgia	50	350 weeks	7.00[b]	24.00	8,400	11
12	Hawaii	66⅔	Period of disability	8.00[b]	35.00	10,500	12
13	Idaho	60[e]	400 weeks; thereafter $8 a week	10.00	17.00[f]	——	13
14	Illinois	65	Period of disability	11.25	22.50[g]	8,500	14
15	Indiana	55	500 weeks	12.10[b]	23.10	7,500	15
16	Iowa	60	300 weeks	12.00[b]	24.00	——	16
17	Kansas	60	416 weeks	7.00	20.00	——	17
18	Kentucky	65	520 weeks	7.00	24.00	10,000	18
19	Louisiana	65	300 weeks	3.00[b]	30.00	——	19
20	Maine	66⅔	500 weeks	12.00	24.00	9,000	20
21	Maryland	66⅔	312 weeks	12.00[b]	28.00	4,500	21
22	Massachusetts	66⅔	Period of disability	18.00[h]	30.00[i]	10,000	22
23	Michigan	66⅔	500 weeks	11.00[j]	24.00[k]	[l]	23
24	Minnesota	66⅔	300 weeks	15.00[b]	30.00	——	24
25	Mississippi	66⅔	450 weeks[m]	10.00	25.00	8,600[m]	25
26	Missouri	66⅔	400 weeks	8.00[b]	25.00	——	26
27	Montana	66⅔	300 weeks	13.00	20.00[n]	——	27
28	Nebraska	66⅔	300 weeks; thereafter 45 per cent of wages for life, maximum $16, minimum $8 (or actual wage, if less)	11.00[b]	22.00	——	28
29	Nevada	80	433 weeks	——	24.23[o]	——	29
30	New Hampshire	66⅔	300 weeks	10.00[b]	30.00	7,500	30
31	New Jersey	66⅔	300 weeks	10.00	30.00[p]	——	31
32	New Mexico	60	550 weeks	12.00[b]	25.00	——	32
33	New York	66⅔	Period of disability	12.00[b]	32.00	6,500	33
34	North Carolina	60	400 weeks	8.00	24.00	6,000	34
35	North Dakota	66⅔	Period of disability	9.00	20.00[q]	——	35

TABLE 48—CONTINUED

No.	State	Maximum Percentage of Wages	Maximum Period	Limit of Payments per Week: Minimum	Limit of Payments per Week: Maximum	Total Maximum Stated in Law	No.
36	Ohio	66⅔	312 weeks	$10.00[b]	$30.00	$6,000	**36**
37	Oklahoma	66⅔	300 weeks; may be extended to 500 weeks	15.00[b]	25.00	——	**37**
38	Oregon	66⅔	Period of disability	17.31[r]	21.92[s]	——	**38**
39	Pennsylvania	66⅔	500 weeks	12.50[t]	25.00	12,500	**39**
40	Puerto Rico	50	104 weeks	3.00	15.00	——	**40**
41	Rhode Island	60	1,000 weeks	15.00	28.00	14,000	**41**
42	South Carolina	60	500 weeks	5.00	25.00	6,000	**42**
43	South Dakota	55	312 weeks	10.00[b]	25.00	——	**43**
44	Tennessee	60	300 weeks	10.00[t]	25.00	——	**44**
45	Texas	60	401 weeks	9.00	25.00	——	**45**
46	Utah	60	313 weeks	15.00[b]	25.00[u]	9,750	**46**
47	Vermont	50	260 weeks	12.00[b]	25.00	——	**47**
48	Virginia	60	500 weeks	6.00	20.00	7,800	**48**
49	Washington	—	Period of disability	——	20.77[v]	——	**49**
50	West Virginia	66⅔	156 weeks	15.00	25.00	——	**50**
51	Wisconsin	70	Period of disability	8.75	32.55[d]	——	**51**
52	Wyoming	—	Period of disability	——	20.19[w]	——	**52**
	United States:						
53	Civil employees	75[x]	Period of disability	25.96[b]	121.15	——	**53**
54	Longshoremen	66⅔	Period of disability	12.00[b]	35.00[d]	11,000	**54**

a. For worker without dependents, 55 per cent; plus 5 per cent for dependent wife and 5 per cent for each dependent child under 18 subject to maximum 65 per cent.
b. Actual wage if less.
c. Plus $10 a month for total dependents residing in the United States.
d. Additional compensation for maintenance during vocational rehabilitation.
e. For worker without dependents, 55 per cent.
f. $20 for married employee, plus $2 a week for each dependent child under 18, maximum $28, minimum $10.
g. $24 if employee has two children under 18; $27, if three children; and $30, if four or more children.
h. Actual wages if less, but minimum shall not be less than $10 a week if employee's number of normal working hours are 15 or more a week.
i. $2.50 added to weekly compensation for each total dependent, but aggregate of such amounts limited to weekly wage.
j. For worker with no dependents; for worker with one dependent, $13; with two dependents, $15; with three dependents, $17; with four dependents, $19; with five or more dependents, $21.
k. For worker without dependents; with one dependent, $26; with two dependents, $28; with three dependents, $30; with four dependents, $32; with five or more dependents, $34.
l. Not to exceed 500 times total weekly amount payable.
m. 450 weeks or $8,600, whichever is less.
n. $22 if employee has one dependent; $23, if two dependents; $24, if three dependents; $25, if four dependents; and $26, if five or more dependents.
o. For worker without dependents; with one dependent, $27.69; with two dependents, $32.31; with three or more dependents, $34.62.
p. Effective January 1, 1951; $25 before that date.
q. Plus $2 a week for each dependent child under 18, and $5 for dependent spouse, maximum $37.
r. For unmarried workman. For married workman, $21.92. Actual wage, if less.
s. For unmarried workman. For married workman without children, $25.38; if he has one child under 18, $28.08; if two children, $33.46; if three children, $36.92; if four or more children, $40.38.
t. Actual wage if less, but not less than $8.
u. Plus 5 per cent for each dependent child (not to exceed five) under 18 years.
v. For unmarried workman. Same amount for married workman with wife and no children; with wife and one child, $25.38 a week; with wife and two children, $28.85 a week; and $2.31 for each additional child, but total payments shall not exceed $35.77 a week.
w. For married workman $25.96; plus $3.75 for each dependent child under 18 with total maximum weekly payments of $40.38.
x. For worker with dependents, applies to monthly pay up to $420; on monthly pay over $420, 66⅔ per cent. For worker without dependents, 66⅔ per cent of entire monthly pay.

Source: State Workmen's Compensation Laws as of September 1950, Bulletin No. 125, Bureau of Labor Standards, Table 7, pp. 26–28.

TABLE 49

Waiting Period under Workmen's Compensation Laws, September 1950

No Waiting Period	1 to 6 Days	7 Days unless Otherwise Indicated	Compensation Paid for Waiting Period if Disability Lasts Specified Time
Oregon	Alaska (1 day)	Alabama[a]	Arizona (2 weeks)
	Delaware (3 days)	Arizona	Arkansas (4 weeks)
	Florida (4 days)	Arkansas[b]	California (49 days)
	Hawaii (5 days)[c]	California	Colorado (6 weeks)
	Illinois (6 days)[d]	Colorado[e]	Connecticut (2 weeks)
	Maryland (3 days)	Connecticut	District of Columbia (7 weeks)
	Mississippi (5 days)	District of Columbia	Hawaii (21 days)
	Missouri (3 days)	Georgia	Idaho (4 weeks and 1 day)
	Nevada (5 days)	Idaho	Illinois (28 days)[d]
	North Dakota (5 days)	Indiana	Indiana (28 days)
	Oklahoma (5 days)	Iowa[f]	Iowa[f, g]
	Rhode Island (3 days)	Kansas	Kentucky (3 weeks)
	South Carolina (3 days)	Kentucky	Louisiana (6 weeks)
	Utah (3 days)	Louisiana	Maine (28 days)
	Washington (3 days)	Maine	Massachusetts (8 days)
	Wisconsin (3 days)	Massachusetts	Michigan (4 weeks)
	Wyoming (3 days)[d]	Michigan[h]	Minnesota (4 weeks)
	United States:	Minnesota[a]	Mississippi (14 days)
	Civil employees (3 days)[i]	Montana	Missouri (4 weeks)
	Puerto Rico (5 days)	Nebraska	Montana (3 weeks)[j]
		New Hampshire	Nebraska (6 weeks)
		New Jersey	Nevada (5 days)
		New Mexico	New Hampshire (1 week)
		New York	New Jersey (4 weeks)
		North Carolina	New York (35 days)
		Ohio[k]	North Carolina (28 days)
		Pennsylvania	North Dakota (5 days)
		South Dakota	Puerto Rico (4 weeks)
		Tennessee	Rhode Island (2 weeks)
		Texas	South Carolina (14 days)
		Vermont	South Dakota (6 weeks)
		Virginia	Tennessee (4 weeks)
		West Virginia	Texas (4 weeks)
		United States:	Vermont (28 days)
		Longshoremen	Virginia (6 weeks)
			West Virginia (21 days)
			Wisconsin (10 days)
			Wyoming (8 days)
			United States:
			Civil employees (21 days)
			Longshoremen (7 weeks)

a. Applies only to temporary disability.
b. No compensation allowed for first 7 days of disability, but if disability extends beyond such period, compensation begins on the ninth day of disability.
c. For total disability. No waiting period in case of partial disability.
d. Applies only to temporary total disability.
e. Thirty days in case of occupational disease, but payable from date of disability if disability lasts 60 days or more.
f. No waiting period in case of permanent partial disability.
g. If compensation extends beyond fourth, fifth, or sixth week after injury, compensation for such fourth, fifth, or sixth week is increased by one third.
h. If death results from injury, compensation is payable from date of injury.
i. Waiting period does not apply to permanent disability.
j. Period doubled if injured has no dependent residing in the United States.
k. Also, no compensation allowed for the first week of total disability, whenever it may occur.

Source: State Workmen's Compensation Laws as of September 1950, Bulletin No. 125, Bureau of Labor Standards, Table 12, pp. 41–42.

TABLE 50

STATUTORY PROVISIONS RELATING TO MEDICAL BENEFITS UNDER WORKMEN'S COMPENSATION LAWS, SEPTEMBER 1950

State	Full Benefits: By Statute	Full Benefits: By Administrative Authority [a]
Arizona	[b]	[b]
Arkansas [c]	—	X [d]
California	X	—
Connecticut	X	—
Delaware	—	X [d]
District of Columbia	X	—
Florida	—	X [j]
Hawaii	X	—
Idaho [k]	X	—
Illinois [m]	X	—
Indiana	—	X [d]
Maine	—	X [p]
Maryland	—	X
Massachusetts	X	—
Minnesota	X	—
Mississippi	X	—
Missouri	—	X [p]
Nebraska	X	—
New Hampshire	—	X [d]
New Jersey	—	X [j]
New Mexico	—	X [w]
New York	X	—
North Carolina [x]	—	X [d]
North Dakota	X	—
Ohio	—	X
Oklahoma	—	X [d]
Oregon	—	X [j]
Puerto Rico	X	—
Rhode Island	—	X [j]
South Carolina	—	X [d]
Utah [y]	—	X [j]
Washington	X	—
Wisconsin	X	—
Wyoming	—	X [z]
United States:		
Civil employees	X	—
Longshoremen	X	—

State	Limited Benefits: Period	Limited Benefits: Amount
Alabama	90 days	$500
Alaska	1 year	—
Colorado	6 months	1,000 [e]
Georgia	10 weeks [f]	500 [g]
Iowa	—	1,500 [h]
Kansas	120 days	100 [i]
Kentucky	—	2,500
Louisiana	—	500
Michigan	6 months [l]	—
Montana	9 months	1,000
Nevada	6 months [n]	[o]
Pennsylvania	90 days	225 [q]
South Dakota	20 weeks	200 [r]
Tennessee	6 months	800
Texas	4 weeks [s]	—
Vermont	90 days [t]	750 [t]
Virginia	60 days [u]	—
West Virginia	—	1,600 [v]

a. After an initial period or amount (given in the notes) the administrative agency may extend the time or amount indefinitely.
b. Full medical aid, in the judgment of the Arizona Industrial Commission, is authorized through a combination of the medical care and rehabilitation provisions of the law. Medical benefits for occupational diseases are payable for total disability, maximum $500, and for partial disability due to listed diseases, $250.
c. In case of silicosis or asbestosis, 90-day limit; may be extended 90 days.
d. After period specified, as follows: Arkansas, 6 months; Delaware, 30 days; Indiana, 180 days; New Hampshire, 90 days; North Carolina, 10 weeks; Oklahoma, 60 days; South Carolina, 10 weeks.
e. For occupational diseases, limit is $500.
f. Period may be extended.
g. Board may permit additional $250.
h. $1,000 maximum for hospital service and supplies and $500 for medical and surgical services.
i. Commissioner may extend to $750.
j. After expenditure of specified amounts as follows: Florida, $1,000; New Jersey, $100; Oregon, $250; Rhode Island, $300 or $500 depending upon circumstances; Utah, $1,000.
k. In case of occupational disease, 90-day limit; may be extended 90 days.
l. Commission may extend three additional 6-month periods.
m. Limited to 6 months in case of silicosis or asbestosis.
n. May be extended an additional year.
o. Limits hospital and medical benefits in cases of silicosis to $750.
p. After specified time and amount as follows: Maine, 30 days and $100; Missouri, 90 days and $750.
q. Hospital services also allowed for 90 days, maximum $225.
r. Also hospital benefits not to exceed $500.
s. May be extended to 91 days. Hospital services may be extended for not more than 180 days.
t. Also hospital charges for 90 days, but amount expended for services and supplies shall not exceed $750.
u. Additional services not to exceed 180 days.
v. Additional $800 may be authorized. $800 may also be paid for vocational rehabilitation. No allowance for medical treatment for silicosis.
w. After expenditure of $700, district court, which has jurisdiction over claims for compensation, may order additional services as appear reasonably necessary upon application of employee.
x. Medical benefits for occupational disease are unlimited, except that in the case of silicosis or asbestosis, treatment is limited to 3 years, with maximum expenditure of $1,000 a year.
y. In case of occupational diseases, benefits are payable only for total disability, maximum $1,000 plus $500 in special cases.
z. After expenditure of $165 for medical treatment and $165 for hospital care, court may authorize additional $220 for medical treatment and $330 for hospital treatment; such services may be further extended to 6-month periods with no limit on number of such extensions.

Source: State Workmen's Compensation Laws as of September 1950, Bulletin No. 125, Bureau of Labor Standards, Table 10, pp. 37–38.

TABLE 51

Estimated Consumer Expenditures for Medical Services and Earnings Losses from Nonoccupational Total Disability, Compared with Indemnities Paid by Voluntary and Government Agencies, 1949

(Dollar Figures in Millions)

No.	Risks	Losses: Entire Population	Losses: Wage and Salary Workers	Total Indemnities: Entire Population	Total Indemnities: Wage and Salary Workers	Percentage of Loss Indemnified: Entire Population	Percentage of Loss Indemnified: Wage and Salary Workers	Type of Protection — Commercial: Entire Population	Commercial: Wage and Salary Workers	Blue Cross, Blue Shield and Related: Entire Population	Blue Cross, Blue Shield and Related: Wage and Salary Workers	Other Nonprofit: Entire Population	Other Nonprofit: Wage and Salary Workers	Industrial: Wage and Salary Workers [b]	State and Local: Wage and Salary Workers [b]	Federal [a]: Entire Population	Federal [a]: Wage and Salary Workers [b]	No.
1	Total	$24,922 [c]	$18,400 [c]	$1,863	$1,628	7.5	8.8	$617 [d]	$523	$401 [e]	$361	$15	$12	$118	$64	$648	$550	1
2	Total medical expenditures	9,372 [f]	6,500	1,122	954	12.0	14.7	276	221	401	361	15	12	80	10	340	270	2
3	Hospital	1,800	1,400	861	726	47.8	51.9	174	139	315	284	5	4	30	2	335 [g]	267 [g]	3
4	Surgical	1,450	1,050	188	161	13.0	15.3	91	73	71	64	3	2	20	1	2	1	4
5	All other medical	6,122	4,050	73	67	1.2	1.7	11	9	15	13	7	6	30	7	3	2	5
6	Earnings loss	15,550 [h]	11,900	741	674	4.8	5.7	341	302	—	—	—	—	38	54	308	280	6
7	Temporary disability	4,250	3,600	281	260	6.6	7.2	211	190	—	—	—	—	8	32	30	30	7
8	Permanent disability	9,500	7,000	432	392	4.5	5.6	102	90	—	—	—	—	30	22	278	250	8
9	Accidental death and dismemberment	1,800 [i]	1,300 [j]	28 [k]	22	1.6	1.7	28	22	—	—	—	—	—	—	—	—	9

a. Excludes medical expenditures for the armed forces and dependents of men in the armed forces, also payments and medical care services for service-connected cases among veterans.
b. Exclusive of sick leave, which has been subtracted from the total estimated earnings loss.
c. Includes a small fraction of losses incidental to accidental death and dismemberment.
d. *Spectator Casualty Insurance by States,* 1950 edition, p. 238 ($539 million paid through accident and health insurance contracts), and *Life Insurance Fact Book,* 1950, p. 36 ($78 million paid under life insurance contracts as cash benefits for permanent total disability). Only payment of cash benefits included, not the value of waived premiums.
e. Duplication of payments included in both Blue Cross and Blue Shield plans eliminated wherever such duplication was known to have occurred.
f. Based on the assumption that on the average consumers spent 5 per cent of their expendable income for payment of medical care directly or through prepayment or insurance.
g. No attempt is made to split hospital cost into surgical and medical, since patients hospitalized in veterans facilities or at Veterans Administration expense receive all the medical services provided in a hospital — perhaps 40 to 50 per cent of the cost is for services that in private hospitals are rendered by physicians and surgeons who must be paid separately.
h. Exclusive of partial disability, except for a negligible fraction included with accidental death and dismemberment.
i. *Accident Facts,* 1950 edition, National Safety Council, Chicago, p. 13.
j. Does not include payments made under life insurance policies.
k. Includes miscellaneous other benefits not included elsewhere.

Source: Estimated by Barkev S. Sanders.

TABLE 52

ENROLLMENT OF BLUE CROSS PLANS, BY STATE, JUNE 30, 1950

State	Number Enrolled, in Thousands	Percentage of Population	State	Number Enrolled, in Thousands	Percentage of Population
Rhode Island	556	70.9	Indiana	615	15.6
District of Columbia	445	57.8	Arizona	115	15.5
Delaware	178	56.0	Virginia	485	14.9
Connecticut	994	49.6	Tennessee	441	13.4
New York	6,152	41.6	Nebraska	169	12.8
Pennsylvania	4,191	40.0	California	1,283	12.3
Ohio	3,161	39.8	Alabama	368	12.1
Massachusetts	1,835	39.3	North Dakota	71	11.5
Minnesota	1,033	34.7	West Virginia	228	11.4
Colorado	439	33.6	Kentucky	309	10.6
Maryland	767	33.2	Utah	72	10.5
Missouri	1,298	32.9	Florida	260	9.5
Michigan	1,880	29.5	Louisiana	249	9.3
New Jersey	1,411	29.4	Idaho	50	8.5
Maine	262	28.8	Texas	589	7.8
New Hampshire–Vermont	256	28.1	South Carolina	132	6.3
Illinois	2,213	25.5	Oregon	84	5.5
Wisconsin	751	21.9	Washington	100	4.3
Kansas	396	21.0	Georgia	140	4.1
Wyoming	56	19.9	Mississippi	72	3.3
Iowa–South Dakota	649	19.8	New Mexico	22	3.2
Montana	114	19.3	Arkansas	39	2.0
North Carolina	630	15.7			
Oklahoma	348	15.7	Continental United States	35,909	24.0

Source: Enrollment figures obtained from the Blue Cross Commission; population based on preliminary census figures for April 1, 1950; computed and arranged by Barkev S. Sanders.

TABLE 53

Membership of Labor Unions, by Affiliation, 1897–1949 [a]

(In Thousands)

Year	All Unions	American Federation of Labor	Congress of Industrial Organizations	Independent or Unaffiliated Unions
1897....	440	265	——	175
1898....	467	278	——	189
1899....	550	349	——	201
1900....	791	548	——	243
1901....	1,058	788	——	270
1902....	1,335	1,024	——	311
1903....	1,824	1,466	——	358
1904....	2,067	1,676	——	391
1905....	1,918	1,494	——	424
1906....	1,892	1,454	——	438
1907....	2,077	1,539	——	538
1908....	2,092	1,587	——	505
1909....	1,965	1,483	——	482
1910....	2,116	1,562	——	554
1911....	2,318	1,762	——	556
1912....	2,405	1,770	——	635
1913....	2,661	1,996	——	665
1914....	2,647	2,021	——	626
1915....	2,560	1,946	——	614
1916....	2,722	2,073	——	649
1917....	2,976	2,371	——	605
1918....	3,368	2,726	——	642
1919....	4,046	3,260	——	786
1920....	5,034	4,079	——	955
1921....	4,722	3,907	——	815
1922....	3,950	3,196	——	754
1923....	3,629	2,926	——	703
1924....	3,549	2,866	——	683
1925....	3,566	2,877	——	689
1926....	3,592	2,804	——	788
1927....	3,600	2,813	——	787
1928....	3,567	2,896	——	671
1929....	3,625	2,934	——	691
1930....	3,632	2,961	——	671
1931....	3,526	2,890	——	636
1932....	3,226	2,532	——	694
1933....	2,857	2,127	——	730
1934....	3,249	2,608	——	641
1935....	3,728	3,045	——	683
1936....	4,164	3,422	——	742
1937....	7,218	2,861	3,718	639
1938....	8,265	3,623	4,038	604
1939....	8,980	4,006	4,000	974
1940....	8,944	4,247	3,625	1,072
1941....	10,489	4,569	5,000	920
1942....	10,762	5,483	4,195	1,084
1943....	13,642	6,564	5,285	1,793
1944....	14,621	6,807	5,935	1,879
1945....	14,796	6,931	6,000	1,865
1946....	14,974	7,152	6,000	1,822
1947....	15,414	7,578	6,000	1,836
1948 [b]...	14–16,000	7,221	n.a.	1,800–2,500
1949 [b]...	14–16,000	7,241	n.a.	1,800–2,500

a. Includes membership outside continental United States, primarily in Canada, of international unions whose headquarters and principal activities are in the United States. According to the Thirty-eighth Annual Report on Labour Organization in Canada, published by the Canadian Department of Labor, 675,044 Canadian workers were members of "international" unions in 1948. According to the Bureau of Labor Statistics (*Brief History of the American Labor Movement*, p. 16), these membership series are "based upon reports and statements issued by the trade union organizations in their official journals, reports, or convention proceedings. . . . 'Union membership' is defined differently by the various unions and the data are, therefore, not strictly comparable. The trend series, however, reasonably reflects year-to-year changes within each major union group."

b. There are no firm estimates of union membership for these years, although the Secretary of Labor has referred to a total membership of 15.5 million on several occasions. The AFL membership shown here represents a minimum estimate (based on per capita payments); membership may actually exceed 8 million. CIO membership is probably under 4 million.

Sources: Data for 1897–1946 from *Brief History of the American Labor Movement*, Bureau of Labor Statistics, October 1947, pp. 17–19; estimates for 1947 from *Approximate Trade Union Membership, Autumn of 1947*, Bureau of Labor Statistics, December 1947; estimates for 1948 and 1949 supplied by the Department of Labor.

TABLE 54

NATIONAL AND INTERNATIONAL UNIONS, 1950

Union	Affiliation	Membership
Actors and Artists of America, Associated	AFL	40,000
Air Line Dispatchers Ass'n	AFL	500
Air Line Pilots Ass'n, Int'l	AFL	6,100[a]
Architects and Draftsmen's Unions, Int'l Federation of Technical Engineers	AFL	6,000
Asbestos Workers, Int'l Ass'n of Heat and Frost Insulators and	AFL	6,000
Associated Unions of America	Ind.	6,600
Automobile, Aircraft and Agricultural Implement Workers of America, Int'l Union, United	CIO	947,600
Automobile Workers of America, Int'l Union, United	AFL	54,200[a]
Bakery and Confectionery Workers' Int'l Union of America	AFL	170,000
Barbers and Beauty Culturists Union of America	CIO	[b]
Barbers, Hairdressers, Cosmetologists, and Proprietors' Int'l Union of America, Journeymen	AFL	60,900
Bill Posters, Billers and Distributors, Int'l Alliance of	AFL	1,600[a]
Blacksmiths, Drop Forgers and Helpers, Int'l Bro. of	AFL	24,000
Boilermakers, Iron Ship Builders and Helpers of America, Int'l Bro. of	AFL	150,000[a]
Bookbinders, Int'l Bro. of	AFL	47,000
Brewery, Flour, Cereal, Soft Drink and Distillery Workers of America, Int'l Union of United	CIO	50,000
Brick and Clay Workers of America, United	AFL	23,000
Bricklayers, Masons and Plasterers Int'l Union of America	AFL	65,000
Bridge, Structural and Ornamental Iron Workers, Int'l Ass'n of	AFL	105,400[a]
Broadcast Engineers and Technicians, National Ass'n of	Ind.	2,400
Broom and Whisk Makers' Union, Int'l	AFL	500[a]
Building Service Employees' Int'l Union	AFL	173,000
Carpenters and Joiners of America, United Bro. of	AFL	735,000
Cement, Lime and Gypsum Workers Int'l Union, United	AFL	33,200
Chemical Workers Union, Int'l	AFL	130,000
Christian Labor Ass'n of the United States of America	Ind.	[b]
Cigar Makers' Int'l Union of America	AFL	11,200
Cleaning and Dye House Workers, Int'l Ass'n of	AFL	18,300
Clothing Workers of America, Amalgamated	CIO	375,000
Communications Ass'n, American	Ind.	[b]
Communications Workers of America	CIO	240,000
Coopers' Int'l Union of North America	AFL	5,000
Diamond Workers' Protective Union of America	AFL	500
Die Sinkers Conference, Int'l	Ind.	3,500
Distillery, Rectifying and Wine Workers' Int'l Union of America	AFL	33,800
Electrical, Radio and Machine Workers, Int'l Union of	CIO	[b]
Electrical, Radio and Machine Workers of America, United	Ind.	[b]
Electrical Workers, Int'l Bro. of	AFL	450,000
Elevator Constructors, Int'l Union of	AFL	10,300
Engineers, Int'l Union of Operating	AFL	150,000[a]
Engineers, Architects and Scientists, Nat'l Professional Ass'n	Ind.	1,420
Engravers and Sketchmakers, Friendly Society of	Ind.	500
Farm Labor Union, Nat'l	AFL	17,500
Federal Employees, Nat'l Federation of	Ind.	93,000
Fire Fighters, Int'l Ass'n of	AFL	68,000
Firemen and Oilers, Int'l Bro. of	AFL	58,000[a]
Flight Engineers' Int'l Ass'n	AFL	650
Food, Tobacco, Agricultural and Allied Workers Union of America	Ind.	[b]
Foreman's Ass'n of America	Ind.	19,600
Foundry and Metal Employes, Int'l Bro. of	Ind.	2,500
Fur and Leather Workers' Union of U.S. and Canada, Int'l	Ind.	100,000
Furniture Workers of America, United	CIO	45,000
Garment Workers of America, United	AFL	40,000
Garment Workers' Union, Int'l Ladies'	AFL	423,000[c]
Gas, Coke and Chemical Workers of America, United	CIO	50,100
Glass Bottle Blowers Ass'n of the U.S. and Canada	AFL	35,000
Glass, Ceramic and Silica Sand Workers of America, Federation of	CIO	34,000
Glass Cutters' League of America, Window	AFL	1,600

TABLE 54—CONTINUED

Union	Affiliation	Membership
Glass Workers' Union, American Flint	AFL	26,100
Glove Workers' Union of America, Int'l	AFL	3,000
Government Employees, American Federation of	AFL	46,000
Grain Millers, American Federation of	AFL	35,000
Granite Cutters' Int'l Ass'n of America, The	AFL	4,000
Guard Workers of America, Int'l Union, United Plant	Ind.	7,000
Guards Union of America, Int'l	Ind.	9,000
Guards' and Watchmen's Ass'n, Int'l	Ind.	60
Handbag, Luggage, Belt and Novelty Workers' Union, Int'l	AFL	35,000
Hatters, Cap and Millinery Workers Int'l Union, United	AFL	32,000[a]
Hod Carriers', Building and Common Laborers' Union of America, Int'l	AFL	267,500[a]
Horseshoers of the U.S. and Canada, Int'l Union of Journeymen	AFL	200
Hosiery Workers, American Federation of	Ind.	[b]
Hotel and Restaurant Employees and Bartenders Int'l Union	AFL	400,000
Independent Unions, Allied	Ind.[d]	70
Industrial Trades Union of America	Ind.	10,000
Industrial Workers of the World	Ind.	16,000
Jewelry Workers' Union, Int'l	AFL	14,000
Lace Operatives of America, Amalgamated	Ind.	4,000
Lathers, Int'l Union of Wood, Wire and Metal	AFL	12,000
Laundry Workers' Int'l Union	AFL	88,000
Leather Workers Int'l Union, United	AFL	3,500
Letter Carriers, Nat'l Ass'n of	AFL	90,000
Letter Carriers' Ass'n, Nat'l Rural	Ind.	33,100
Life Insurance Agents, Int'l Union of	Ind.	1,900
Lithographers of America, Amalgamated	CIO	24,100
Locomotive Engineers, Bro. of	Ind.	79,700
Locomotive Firemen and Enginemen, Bro. of	Ind.	102,900
Longshoremen's Ass'n, Int'l	AFL	55,400
Longshoremen's and Warehousemen's Union, Int'l	CIO	65,000
Machine Printers Beneficial Ass'n of the U.S.	Ind.	1,000
Machinists, Int'l Ass'n of	Ind.	581,900
Mailers Union, Int'l	Ind.	2,600
Maintenance of Way Employes, Bro. of	AFL	171,400
Marble, Slate and Stone Polishers, Rubbers and Sawyers, Tile and Marble Setters Helpers and Terrazzo Helpers, Int'l Ass'n of	AFL	5,000
Marine Cooks and Stewards, Nat'l Union of	CIO	6,000
Marine Engineers' Beneficial Ass'n, Nat'l	CIO	13,500
Marine Firemen, Oilers, Watertenders and Wipers Ass'n, Pacific Coast	Ind.	6,300
Marine and Shipbuilding Workers of America, Industrial Union of	CIO	86,600
Maritime Union of America, Nat'l	CIO	45,700
Masters, Mates and Pilots of America, Nat'l Organization	AFL	7,700[a]
Meat Cutters and Butcher Workmen of North America, Amalgamated	AFL	175,000
Mechanics Educational Society of America	Ind.	[b]
Mechanics and Foremen of Naval Shore Establishments, Nat'l Ass'n of Master	AFL	500
Messengers, The Nat'l Ass'n of Special Delivery	AFL	2,200
Metal Engravers and Marking Device Workers Union, Int'l	Ind.	600
Metal Polishers, Buffers, Platers and Helpers Int'l Union	AFL	18,000
Mine, Mill and Smelter Workers, Int'l Union of	Ind.	91,400
Mine Workers of America, Int'l Progressive	Ind.	27,900
Mine Workers of America, United	Ind.	600,000
Molders and Foundry Workers Union of North America, Int'l	AFL	88,000
Motion Picture Salesmen of America, Colosseum of	Ind.	1,000[c]
Musicians, American Federation of	AFL	237,000
Newspaper Guild, American	CIO	25,000
Newspaper and Mail Deliverers' Union of New York and Vicinity	Ind.	[b]
Office Employes' Int'l Union	AFL	40,000
Office and Professional Workers of America, United	Ind.	[b]
Oil Workers Int'l Union	CIO	77,900[c]
Optical and Instrument Workers of America, United	CIO	[b]
Packinghouse Workers, Nat'l Bro. of	Ind.[d]	[b]
Packinghouse Workers of America, United	CIO	84,000

TABLE 54—CONTINUED

Union	Affiliation	Membership
Painters, Decorators and Paperhangers of America, Bro. of	AFL	178,000
Paper Makers, Int'l Bro. of	AFL	59,000
Paperworkers of America, United	CIO	39,000
Pattern Makers' League of North America	AFL	11,000[a]
Paving Cutters' Union of the United States and Canada	Ind.	200
Petroleum Workers, Independent Union of	Ind.	3,800
Photo-Engravers' Union of North America, Int'l	AFL	12,800
Plasterers' and Cement Finishers' Int'l Ass'n of the U.S. and Canada, Operative	AFL	32,000
Plate Printers, Die Stampers and Engravers' Union of North America, Int'l	AFL	1,300
Playthings, Jewelry and Novelty Workers Int'l Union	CIO	35,300
Plumbing and Pipe Fitting Industry of the U.S. and Canada, United Ass'n of Journeymen and Apprentices of the	AFL	180,000
Pocketbook Workers Union — New York	Ind.	[b]
Post Office Clerks, Nat'l Federation of	AFL	88,000
Post Office Clerks, United Nat'l Ass'n of	Ind.	35,000
Post Office Maintenance Employees, Nat'l Ass'n of	Ind.	7,500
Post Office Motor Vehicle Employees, Nat'l Federation of	Ind.	4,600
Post Office and Railway Mail Service Mail Handlers, Nat'l Ass'n of	AFL	1,500
Postal Employees, Nat'l Alliance of	Ind.	18,000
Postal Supervisors, Nat'l Ass'n of	AFL	14,000
Postal Transport Ass'n, Nat'l	AFL	27,600
Postmasters of the U.S., Nat'l League of District	Ind.	25,000
Potters, Nat'l Bro. of Operative	AFL	30,200
Printing Pressmen and Assistants' Union of North America, Int'l	AFL	75,000
Protection Ass'n, Plant	Ind.	[b]
Public Workers of America, United	Ind.	[b]
Pulp, Sulphite and Paper Mill Workers, Int'l Bro. of	AFL	120,000
Radio Ass'n, American	CIO	1,600
Radio and Television Directors Guild	AFL	500
Railroad Signalmen of America, Bro. of	AFL	12,900
Railroad Telegraphers, The Order of	AFL	57,500
Railroad Trainmen, Bro. of	Ind.	210,600
Railroad Yardmasters of America	AFL	3,600
Railroad Yardmasters of North America, Inc	Ind.	[b]
Railway Carmen of America, Bro.	AFL	145,500
Railway Conductors of America, Order of	Ind.	37,600
Railway Patrolmen's Int'l Union	AFL	3,000
Railway and Steamship Clerks, Freight Handlers, Express and Station Employes, Bro. of	AFL	350,000[c]
Railway Supervisors Ass'n, Inc., The American	Ind.	6,500
Railway Trainmen and Locomotive Firemen, Inc., Ass'n of Colored	Ind.	[b]
Retail Clerks Int'l Ass'n	AFL	200,000
Retail, Wholesale and Department Store Union	CIO	65,000
Roofers, Damp and Waterproof Workers Ass'n, United Slate, Tile and Composition	AFL	13,400
Rubber, Cork, Linoleum and Plastic Workers of America, United	CIO	150,100
Salaried Unions, Nat'l Federation of	Ind.	27,000
Seafarers' Int'l Union of North America	AFL	45,000[a]
Sheet Metal Workers' Int'l Ass'n	AFL	50,000
Shoe and Allied Craftsmen, Bro. of	Ind.	7,000
Shoe Workers of America, United	CIO	67,000
Shoe Workers Union, Boot and	AFL	50,000
Shoeworkers Protective Ass'n, Lewiston-Auburn	Ind.	3,500
Siderographers, Int'l Ass'n of	AFL	55
Sleeping Car Porters, Bro. of	AFL	10,600
Spinners Union, Int'l	AFL	500[a]
Stage Employes and Moving Picture Machine Operators of the U.S. and Canada, Int'l Alliance of Theatrical	AFL	56,000
State, City, Town and County Employees, Federation of	Ind.	15,000
State, County and Municipal Employees, American Federation of	AFL	90,000
Steelworkers of America, United	CIO	960,700[c]
Stereotypers' and Electrotypers' Union of North America, Int'l	AFL	11,500
Stone and Allied Products Workers of America, United	CIO	[b]
Stone Cutters' Ass'n of North America, Journeymen	AFL	1,900
Stove Mounters Int'l Union of North America	AFL	20,000

TABLE 54—CONTINUED

Union	Affiliation	Membership
Street, Electric Railway and Motor Coach Employes of America, Amalgamated Ass'n of	AFL	115,000
Switchmen's Union of North America	AFL	8,900
Taxicab Drivers and Employees, Independent Union of Milwaukee	Ind.[d]	800
Teachers, American Federation of	AFL	50,000
Teachers of Slavic and East European Languages, American Ass'n of	Ind.	500
Teamsters, Chauffeurs, Warehousemen and Helpers of America, Int'l Bro. of	AFL	1,103,000
Telegraphers' Union, Commercial	AFL	26,800
Texas Unions, Federated Independent	Ind.	750
Textile Workers of America, United	AFL	87,000
Textile Workers Union of America	CIO	373,800
Tobacco Workers Int'l Union	AFL	34,400
Tool and Die Craftsmen, The Society of	Ind.	[b]
Train Dispatchers Ass'n, American	Ind.	4,200
Trainmen of America, Colored	Ind.	470
Transport Service Employees of America, United	CIO	[b]
Transport Workers Union of America	CIO	[b]
Transportation Association, Int'l	Ind.	2,900
Typographical Union, Int'l	AFL	95,700[c]
Upholsterers' Int'l Union of North America	AFL	50,000
Utility Workers of New England, Inc., Bro. of	Ind.	6,000
Utility Workers Union of America	CIO	75,000
Wall Paper Craftsmen and Workers of North America, United	AFL	4,300
Watch Workers Union, American	Ind.	8,800
Watchmen's Ass'n, Independent	Ind.	2,500
Welders of America, Nat'l Union, United	Ind.	400
Wire Weavers Protective Ass'n, American	AFL	355
Woodworkers of America, Int'l	CIO	90,000

a. Per capita average annual membership as published in the convention proceedings of the American Federation of Labor.
b. Not available.
c. Data appearing in the union's journal or reports.
d. Affiliated with the Confederated Unions of America.

Source: Directory of Labor Unions in the United States, 1950, Bulletin No. 980, Bureau of Labor Statistics, 1950.

TABLE 55

Proportion of Wage Earners under Union Agreements, by Industry, 1946

80–100 Per Cent	60–79 Per Cent	40–59 Per Cent	20–39 Per Cent	1–19 Per Cent
		Manufacturing Industries		
Agricultural equipment Aircraft and parts Aluminum Automobiles and parts Breweries Carpets and rugs, wool Cement Clocks and watches Clothing, men's Clothing, women's Electrical machinery Furs and fur garments Glass and glassware Leather tanning Meat packing Newspaper printing and publishing Nonferrous metals and products Rayon yarn Rubber Shipbuilding Steel, basic Sugar	Book and job printing and publishing Canning and preserving foods Coal products Dyeing and finishing textiles Gloves, leather Machinery, except agricultural equipment and electrical machinery Millinery and hats Paper and pulp Petroleum refining Railroad equipment Steel products Tobacco Woolen and worsted textiles	Baking Chemicals, excluding rayon yarn Flour and other grain products Furniture Hosiery Jewelry and silverware Knit goods Leather, luggage, handbags, novelties Lumber Paper products Pottery, including chinaware Shoes, cut stock and findings Stone and clay products, except pottery	Beverages, nonalcoholic Confectionery products Cotton textiles Dairy products Silk and rayon textiles	None
		Nonmanufacturing Industries		
Actors and musicians Airline pilots and mechanics Bus and streetcar Coal mining Construction Longshoring Maritime Metal mining Motion-picture production Railroads Telegraph Trucking, local and intercity	Radio technicians Theater — stage hands, motion-picture operators	Bus lines, intercity Light and power Newspaper offices Telephone	Barber shops Building service and maintenance Cleaning, dyeing Crude petroleum and natural gas Fishing Hotels, restaurants Laundries Nonmetallic mining and quarrying Taxicabs	Agriculture [a] Beauty shops Clerical and professional, excluding transportation, communication, theaters and newspapers Retail and wholesale trade

a. Less than one per cent.

Source: Extent of Collective Bargaining and Union Recognition, 1946, Bulletin No. 909, Bureau of Labor Statistics, 1947, p. 2.

TABLE 56

Proportion of All Workers under Agreements Who Were Covered by Agreements with Associations and Groups of Employers, by Industry, 1947

80–100 Per Cent	60–79 Per Cent	40–59 Per Cent	20–39 Per Cent
Clothing, men's	Baking	Building service and maintenance	Beverages, nonalcoholic
Clothing, women's	Book and job printing and publishing	Leather products, other	Hosiery
Coal mining	Canning and preserving foods	Newspaper and periodical printing and publishing	Hotels and restaurants
Laundry and cleaning and dyeing	Construction		Jewelry and silverware
Longshoring	Dyeing and finishing textiles		Lumber
Maritime	Glass and glassware		Shoes, cut stock and findings
Shipbuilding and boat building [a]	Malt liquors		Trade
	Pottery and related products		
	Trucking and warehousing		

1–19 Per Cent [b]

- Clerical and professional, excluding transportation, communication, theaters, and newspapers
- Cotton textiles
- Confectionery products
- Dairy products
- Electrical machinery, equipment and appliances
- Flour and other grain products
- Furniture
- Knit goods, except hosiery
- Leather (tanned, curried and finished)
- Machinery and machine tools
- Meat packing
- Metal mining
- Newspaper offices
- Nonferrous metals and products, except jewelry and silverware
- Nonmetallic mining and quarrying
- Paper and pulp
- Paper products
- Petroleum refining
- Railroad equipment
- Rayon and allied products
- Silk and rayon textiles
- Steel products
- Stone and clay products, other
- Sugar, beet and cane
- Tobacco manufactures
- Woolen and worsted textiles

a. During World War II most of the industry was covered by tripartite zone standard agreements, signed by representatives of unions, employers and certain government agencies. The principal association agreement other than the zone standard agreements is between the Pacific Coast Shipbuilders and the Metal Trades Department of the AFL, covering yards organized by AFL unions.

b. A number of additional industries have less than one half of one per cent of their workers covered by agreements with associations and groups of employers.

Source: Collective Bargaining with Associations and Groups of Employers, Bulletin No. 897, Bureau of Labor Statistics, 1947, p. 3.

TABLE 57

Area of Bargaining with Associations or Groups of Employers, by Industry, 1947

Local-Area Bargaining (Within a City, County or Metropolitan Area)	Regional Bargaining	Industry-wide or National Bargaining
Baking	Canning and preserving foods [a]	Coal mining
Beverages, nonalcoholic	Dyeing and finishing textiles [a]	Elevator installation and repair
Book and job printing and publishing	Fishing	Glass and glassware
Building service and maintenance	Hosiery	Installation of automatic sprinklers
Clothing, men's [b]	Leather (tanned, curried, and finished) [a]	Pottery and related products
Clothing, women's [b]	Longshoring [a]	Stoves
Confectionery products	Lumber [a]	Wallpaper
Construction	Maritime	
Cotton textiles	Metal mining	
Dairy products	Nonferrous metals and products, except jewelry and silverware [a]	
Furniture [b]	Paper and pulp	
Hotel and restaurant	Shoes, cut stock and findings [a]	
Jewelry and silverware		
Knit goods		
Laundry and cleaning and dyeing		
Leather products, other		
Malt liquors		
Meat packing		
Newspaper printing and publishing		
Paper products, except wallpaper		
Silk and rayon textiles		
Steel products, except stoves [b]		
Tobacco		
Trade [b]		
Trucking and warehousing [b]		

a. There also is some bargaining on a city, county and/or metropolitan area basis.
b. There also is some bargaining on a regional and/or industry-wide basis.

Source: Adapted from *Collective Bargaining with Associations and Groups of Employers,* Bulletin No. 897, Bureau of Labor Statistics, 1947, p. 3.

TABLE 58

Prevalence of Various Provisions in Union-Management Agreements Signed between September 1947 [a] and July 1948 [b]

General Provisions

Provision	Percentage of Contracts
Union security [e]	
Membership requirements:	
Closed shop	5
Union shop	30
Covering all employees	25
Exempting certain employees	5
Maintenance of membership	15
Clause to be negotiated when legally permissible	3–4
Checkoff:	
Coverage:	
Union dues	75
Initiation fees	30
Assessments	15
Fines and other levies	3–4
Duration of authorization:	
Revocable at any time	10
Irrevocable for definite period	50
Duration of contract	
1 year or less	75
More than 1 but less than 2 years	10
2 years or more	15
Strikes and lockouts	
No-strike, no-lockout clause included	80
Absolute ban on work stoppages	55
No exceptions	50
Exceptions (enforcement of agreement or arbitration award, or when wage renegotiations are deadlocked)	5
Conditional pledges (strikes permitted only on unsettled grievances not subject to arbitration)	25
Limitations on union liability	55
In agreements with no-strike clause	50
In agreements without no-strike clause	5
Coupled with required union actions against strikes	40
Management and union rights	
Management rights referred to	60
Listing of specific rights	45
General statement only	15
Company rules referred to	30
Safety provision included	55
General type:	
Joint safety committee	10
Company consideration of union recommendations	10
Company to comply with state regulations	10
Miscellaneous requirements:	
Company to furnish protective clothing and safety equipment	20
Company to maintain first-aid equipment and personnel	5
Physical examinations (on hiring and often at regular intervals after)	15
Bulletin boards open to unions	60
Restrictions on production work by supervisors	25
Discrimination because of race, creed, color, national origin, or sex outlawed	10
Discrimination because of union activities banned	40
Union pledge against intimidation or coercion because of nonmembership	15

Wages and Hours

Provision	Percentage of Contracts
Wages	
Wage reopening:	
Not permitted within 1 year	70
Permitted within 1 year	30
At any time	10
At specified time or under certain conditions	20
Automatic general wage adjustment provided	2–3
Reporting and call-back pay:	
Minimum payment for workers reporting	75–80
No payment if lack of work beyond company control	25
No payment if employee refuses reasonable work	15
Special pay arrangement for call-in or call-back outside regular hours	40
Weekly wage guarantees	5
Rates on temporary transfer:	
Regular rate if transferred to lower-rated jobs for company's convenience	45–50
No time limit	38–42
Time limit (after which rate of new job payable)	7–8
Higher rate if transferred to higher-rated job	40
Immediately	30
After certain period on new job	10
Wage progression plans specified	15–20
Automatic, regular increases to maximum	8–10
Solely on merit	5–7
Automatic at first, then on merit basis	2–3
Hiring progression plans provided [d]	20

TABLE 58—CONTINUED

Wages and Hours—Continued

Provision	Percentage of Contracts
Expenses paid by company:	
Expenses necessitated by job (travel, moving, etc.)	10
Uniforms and tools	15
Jury duty	5–10
Hours and overtime	
Daily work schedule:	
Less than 8 hours	5–10
8 hours	65–70
More than 8 hours	1–5
Weekly work schedule:	
Less than 40 hours	5–10
40 hours	45–50
More than 40 hours	10–15
Daily overtime premium payable	90
After 8 hours work	80
After other number of hours	10
Weekly overtime premium payable	75[e]
After 40 hours	65–70
After work week longer than 40 hours	5
After work week shorter than 40 hours	1–2
Premium rates provided for:	
Saturday work	35–40
Sunday work	55–60
Sixth-day work	15–20
Seventh-day work	15–25
Shift differentials	65
Method of calculation:	
Flat cents-per-hour	50
Related to salary	10
Other	5
Differences between shifts:	
Third-shift bonus larger than second-shift	35
Uniform bonus for all late shifts.	25
Differential for any work "at night"	5

Fringe Issues

Provision	Percentage of Contracts
Vacations	
Type of provision:	
Uniform vacation	10
Vacation related to length of service	85
Amount of vacation:	
Less than 1 year's service:	
Less than 1 week	10–15
1 week	10–15
2 weeks	1–5
After 1 year's service:	
1 week	75–80
2 weeks	15–20
3 weeks	1–5
After 2 years' service:	
1 week	55–60
Between 1 and 2 weeks	10–15
2 weeks	25–30
3 weeks	1–5
After 3 years' service:	
1 week	45–50
Between 1 and 2 weeks	10–15
2 weeks	35–40
3 weeks	1–5
After 4 years' service:	
1 week	40–45
Between 1 and 2 weeks	10–15
2 weeks	40–45
3 weeks	1–5
After 5 years' service:	
1 week	5–10
2 weeks	85–90
3 weeks	1–5
For long-service employees:	
3 weeks after 10 years	1–5
3 weeks after 15 years	10–15
3 weeks after 20 years	5–10
No reference to amount of vacation	5–10
Vacation pay:	
Straight-time rates	70
Percentage of earnings[f]	15–20
Work requirements for vacation eligibility	40–45
Minimum amount or percentage of time worked	30–35
Top limit on absences	10–15
Holidays	
Number of holidays:	
Less than 6	5
6	60–65
More than 6	25
Pay for holidays:	
Pay for all specified holidays	55–60
Pay for some holidays only	10–15
No statement on holiday practice.	1–5
No reference to holiday pay	20–25
Number of paid holidays:	
Less than 6	15–20
6	40–45
More than 6	15–20
Eligibility for holiday pay:	
Work day before and day after holiday required	45
Only regular employees eligible	30
Employee benefits	
Paid sick leave provided	20
Amount of leave:	
1 week or less a year	5
Between 1 and 3 weeks a year	5
Between 3 and 13 weeks	5–10
Other	1–5
Waiting period:	
Required	5
Not required	15
Funeral leave with pay provided	10
Health and welfare plans provided	30
Coverage:	
Life insurance	15–20
Hospitalization	15–20
Nonoccupational sickness and accident benefits	10–15
Surgical expenses	10–15
Comprehensive programs	10

TABLE 58—Continued

Provision	Percentage of Contracts
Fringe Issues—Continued	
Financing:	
Employer	15
Employer-employee	5
Not specified	10
Hiring, Firing and Promotion	
Hiring	
Rehiring:	
In reverse order of layoff	95–100
Preference to laid-off over new employees for jobs in other seniority units	10
Loss of seniority and rehiring rights:	
If employee fails to return on recall	65–70
After layoff of specified period	50–55
Uniform length	40
Less than 1 year	5
1 year	20
More than 1 year	15
Variable length according to service	10
New hiring:	
Probationary period set	75
Specific statement that company has full right to discharge during probation	50
Discharge	
Clauses concerning discharges included	75
Reference to cause for discharge included	60
Blanket rule: no discharge except for "just cause"	50
Specific list of offenses warranting discharge	10
Discharge appeal procedures:	
Appeal must be filed within specified period (usually 2 to 5 days)	50
Usual grievance procedure shortened or separate, brief procedure provided	15
Retroactive pay for time lost and reinstatement explicitly guaranteed if discharge reversed	40
Separation pay provided	10
Layoff	
Notice of layoff required	80
Pay in lieu of notice	15–20
Layoff pay guaranteed on temporary severance	5
Work sharing provided	25
Initiation:	
Before layoff of any regular employees	10–15
After layoff of short-service employees	10–15
Work week reduction limited	15
Promotion	
All employees given preference over outsiders for jobs in other seniority units	10
Union participation:	
Before selection	5–10
After selection (through grievance procedure)	95–100
Posting of vacancies provided	35
Bids must be submitted within specified time	30
Less than 5 days	7–8
5 days	15
More than 5 days	7–8
Bids accepted in advance of job openings	5
Seniority in layoff and promotion	
Layoffs:	
Seniority governs	70–75
Seniority given equal weight with other factors	1–5
Seniority secondary, used only if other factors equal	15–20
No reference to layoffs	5–10
Promotions:	
Seniority governs	35–40
Seniority given equal weight with other factors	5–10
Seniority secondary, used only if other factors equal	30–35
No reference to promotions	25–30
Bumping of less senior employees on other jobs	30
Union representatives assigned top seniority	25
Grievance Procedures	
Grievance procedure	
Grievance presentation at first step in procedure:	
By union representative	40–45
Steward alone	20–25
Employee and steward	15–20
Employee with or through steward	1–5
By employee, with option of union aid	30–35
Employee with or without steward	5–10
Employee and/or steward	5–10
Employee alone	10–15
No reference	10–15
Time limits set:	
Between occurrence and initial presentation of grievance	25
15 days or less	15
More than 15 days	10

TABLE 58—Continued

Provision	Percentage of Contracts	Provision	Percentage of Contracts
Grievance Procedures—Continued			
On processing at subsequent steps.	50	Arbitration of grievances	
On over-all procedure (exclusive of arbitration)	1–5	Arbitration provided	85–90
Written presentation of grievance required	65	On request of either party	85
Before grievance considered	10	If both parties agree	1–5
Only if no settlement after oral presentation at first step	45	Tenure of arbitrator:	
After second step	10	Temporary ("ad hoc")	85
Grievance pay for union representative:		Permanent	5
Provided for all grievance work	25	Arbitrator or board:	
Provided with limitation	15	Single arbitrator	40
Explicitly prohibited	5	Board of arbitrators	50
Grievance work must take place outside working hours (except in emergencies)	5	3 members	40
No reference	50	5 members	5–10
		7 or more members	1–5
		Selection of temporary arbitrator:	
		Mutual agreement	65
		If no agreement, then appointed by impartial agency	50
		Appointed by impartial agency	20

a. After Labor-Management Relations Act of 1947 became fully effective.

b. Summarized from *Basic Patterns in Collective Bargaining Contracts,* Bureau of National Affairs, Washington, D.C., 1948. ". . . based on detailed analysis of a broad sampling of agreements, supplemented and tempered by experienced examination of the many thousands of contracts received annually by the staff of *Collective Bargaining Negotiations and Contracts.* Three fourths of the contracts surveyed are in manufacturing industries, a fourth in nonmanufacturing." p. 15:25. It should be noted that the percentages shown reflect only specific references in contracts; frequently agreements fail to cover something that is carried out in practice.

c. Union security provisions were particularly affected by the Labor-Management Relations Act of 1947; union security clauses, especially closed-shop provisions, were more prevalent before passage of that act.

d. Automatic advancement from below-normal beginning rate to normal rate.

e. Omission of provision in 25 per cent of contracts probably due to fact that Fair Labor Standards Act covers situation.

f. Usually 2 per cent of annual earnings per vacation week.

TABLE 59

WORK STOPPAGES, BY MAJOR ISSUES INVOLVED, 1935–1950

Major Issues and Period	Work Stoppages: Number	Work Stoppages: Percentage of Total for Year	Workers Involved: Number	Workers Involved: Percentage of Total for Year	Man-Days Idle: Number	Man-Days Idle: Percentage of Total for Year
All issues:						
1935	2,003	100.0	1,100,000	100.0	14,900,000	100.0
1936	2,156	100.0	710,000	100.0	11,400,000	100.0
1937	4,720	100.0	1,950,000	100.0	30,800,000	100.0
1938	2,772	100.0	688,000	100.0	8,930,000	100.0
1939	2,639	100.0	1,180,000	100.0	18,500,000	100.0
1940	2,493	100.0	573,000	100.0	6,680,000	100.0
1941	4,314	100.0	2,360,000	100.0	23,000,000	100.0
1942	3,026	100.0	852,000	100.0	4,740,000	100.0
1943	3,734	100.0	1,970,000	100.0	13,300,000	100.0
1944	4,958	100.0	2,130,000	100.0	8,880,000	100.0
1945	4,616	100.0	3,070,000	100.0	24,400,000	100.0
1946	4,990	100.0	4,940,000	100.0	124,000,000	100.0
1947	3,693	100.0	2,170,000	100.0	34,600,000	100.0
1948	3,419	100.0	1,960,000	100.0	34,100,000	100.0
1949	3,606	100.0	3,030,000	100.0	50,500,000	100.0
1950	4,843	100.0	2,410,000	100.0	38,800,000	100.0
Wages and hours: [a]						
1935	760	37.9	663,000	60.2	6,400,000	42.9
1936	756	35.1	251,000	35.3	3,690,000	32.2
1937	1,410	29.9	436,000	22.4	4,840,000	15.7
1938	776	28.0	252,000	36.7	3,110,000	34.8
1939	699	26.5	352,000	29.9	3,310,000	17.9
1940	753	30.2	235,000	41.0	3,090,000	46.3
1941	1,535	35.6	1,110,000	46.9	10,400,000	45.4
1942	1,423	46.8	429,000	50.4	2,070,000	43.5
1943	1,906	51.0	1,220,000	61.9	10,700,000	80.4
1944	2,146	43.3	810,000	38.1	3,380,000	38.0
1945	1,956	42.4	1,340,000	43.7	10,800,000	44.4
1946	2,238	44.9	3,710,000	75.1	101,000,000	81.9
1947	1,707	46.3	805,000	37.2	15,200,000	43.9
1948	1,737	50.8	1,210,000	61.9	25,200,000	73.9
1949	1,682	46.6	1,540,000	51.0	39,800,000	78.7
1950	2,559	52.8	1,460,000	60.7	32,500,000	83.8
Union organization, wages and hours:						
1935 to 1941	a	a	a	a	a	a
1942	531	17.5	104,000	12.2	1,240,000	26.1
1943	232	6.2	57,300	2.9	272,000	2.0
1944	247	5.0	66,100	3.1	496,000	5.6
1945	366	7.9	158,000	5.1	2,120,000	8.7
1946	914	18.3	439,000	8.9	16,600,000	13.4
1947	559	15.1	840,000	38.8	15,200,000	43.9
1948	322	9.4	128,000	6.5	4,390,000	12.9
1949	216	6.0	43,100	1.4	1,010,000	2.0
1950	270	5.6	53,700	2.2	789,000	2.0
Union organization: [a]						
1935	945	47.2	288,000	26.1	7,050,000	42.3
1936	1,083	50.2	365,000	51.4	6,880,000	60.2
1937	2,728	57.8	1,160,000	59.8	23,600,000	76.4
1938	1,385	50.0	224,000	32.6	3,960,000	44.4
1939	1,411	53.5	641,000	54.4	13,800,000	74.7
1940	1,243	49.9	190,000	33.1	2,730,000	40.8
1941	2,138	49.5	744,000	31.5	10,100,000	43.8
1942	412	13.7	87,000	10.2	407,000	8.6
1943	353	9.5	169,000	8.6	471,000	3.5
1944	561	11.3	329,000	15.5	1,540,000	17.3
1945	580	12.6	513,000	16.7	5,050,000	20.7
1946	703	14.1	129,000	2.6	2,190,000	1.8
1947	543	14.7	91,000	4.2	1,790,000	5.1
1948	458	13.4	99,800	5.1	1,590,000	4.7
1949	565	15.7	38,400	1.3	736,000	1.5
1950	649	13.4	76,200	3.2	1,560,000	4.0
Other working conditions: [b]						
1935	298	14.9	151,000	13.7	1,470,000	9.8
1936	317	14.7	94,000	13.3	865,000	7.6
1937	582	12.3	347,000	17.8	2,430,000	7.9
1938	611	22.0	211,000	30.7	1,860,000	20.8
1939	529	20.0	185,000	15.7	1,370,000	7.4
1940	497	19.9	148,000	25.9	859,000	12.9
1941	641	14.9	512,000	21.6	2,490,000	10.8
1942	497	16.4	158,000	18.5	590,000	12.6
1943	1,094	29.3	462,000	23.5	1,400,000	10.6
1944	1,800	36.3	807,000	37.9	2,580,000	29.1
1945	1,510	32.7	888,000	29.0	5,020,000	20.6
1946	879	17.6	425,000	8.6	2,500,000	2.0
1947	695	18.8	387,000	17.8	1,580,000	4.6
1948	736	21.5	383,000	19.6	1,740,000	5.1
1949	903	25.0	1,330,000	43.8	8,580,000	17.0
1950	1,065	22.0	746,000	30.9	3,450,000	8.9
Interunion or intraunion matters:						
1935 to 1941	b	b	b	b	b	b
1942	173	5.6	74,300	8.7	434,000	9.2
1943	149	4.0	61,100	3.1	463,000	3.5
1944	204	4.1	115,000	5.4	886,000	10.0
1945	194	4.2	169,000	5.5	1,350,000	5.6
1946	246	4.9	236,000	4.8	1,140,000	0.9
1947	159	4.3	32,000	1.5	845,000	2.4
1948	130	3.8	128,000	6.6	1,080,000	3.2
1949	208	5.8	66,800	2.2	398,000	0.8
1950	255	5.3	65,800	2.7	419,000	1.1

a. For the years 1935 to 1941, stoppages primarily over union organization matters but also involving wage and hour issues were classified under "union organization."

b. For the years 1935 to 1941 the stoppages primarily over interunion or intraunion matters (jurisdictional and rival-union disputes) were classified under "other working conditions."

Sources: For 1935–1947, *Handbook of Labor Statistics,* 1947 edition, Bulletin No. 916, Bureau of Labor Statistics, 1948, Table E-5, p. 138; for 1948, *Work Stoppages Caused by Labor-Management Disputes in 1948,* Bulletin No. 963, 1949, p. 10; for 1949, "Work Stoppages in 1949," April 2, 1950, mimeographed; for 1950, "Work Stoppages in 1950," April 18, 1951, mimeographed.

TABLE 60

Work Stoppages, 1881–1950

Year	Work Stoppages		Workers Involved		Man-Days Idle		
	Number	Average Duration, in Calendar Days	Number, in Thousands [a]	Percentage of Total Employed [b]	Number, in Thousands	Percentage of Estimated Working Time [c]	Per Worker Involved
1881	477	d	130	d	d	d	d
1882	476	d	159	d	d	d	d
1883	506	d	170	d	d	d	d
1884	485	d	165	d	d	d	d
1885	695	d	258	d	d	d	d
1886	1,572	d	610	d	d	d	d
1887	1,503	d	439	d	d	d	d
1888	946	d	163	d	d	d	d
1889	1,111	d	260	d	d	d	d
1890	1,897	d	373	4.2	d	d	d
1891	1,786	d	330	3.6	d	d	d
1892	1,359	d	239	2.5	d	d	d
1893	1,375	d	288	3.2	d	d	d
1894	1,404	d	690	8.3	d	d	d
1895	1,255	d	407	4.4	d	d	d
1896	1,066	d	249	2.8	d	d	d
1897	1,110	d	416	4.3	d	d	d
1898	1,098	d	263	2.6	d	d	d
1899	1,838	d	432	3.9	d	d	d
1900	1,839	d	568	4.9	d	d	d
1901	3,012	d	564	4.6	d	d	d
1902	3,240	d	692	5.4	d	d	d
1903	3,648	d	788	5.9	d	d	d
1904	2,419	d	574	4.3	d	d	d
1905	2,186	d	302	2.1	d	d	d
1906–1913	d	d	d	d	d	d	d
1914	1,204	d	d	d	d	d	d
1915	1,593	d	d	d	d	d	d
1916[a]	3,789	d	1,600	8.4	d	d	d
1917	4,450	d	1,230	6.3	d	d	d
1918	3,353	d	1,240	6.2	d	d	d
1919	3,630	d	4,160	20.8	d	d	d
1920	3,411	d	1,460	7.2	d	d	d
1921	2,385	d	1,100	6.4	d	d	d
1922	1,112	d	1,610	8.7	d	d	d
1923	1,553	d	757	3.5	d	d	d
1924	1,249	d	655	3.1	d	d	d
1925	1,301	d	428	2.0	d	d	d
1926	1,035	d	330	1.5	d	d	d
1927	707	26.5	330	1.4	26,000	0.37	79.5
1928	604	27.6	314	1.3	12,600	0.17	40.2
1929	921	22.6	289	1.2	5,350	0.07	18.5
1930	637	22.3	183	0.8	3,320	0.05	18.1
1931	810	18.8	342	1.6	6,890	0.11	20.2
1932	841	19.6	324	1.8	10,500	0.23	32.4
1933	1,695	16.9	1,170	6.3	16,900	0.36	14.4
1934	1,856	19.5	1,470	7.2	19,600	0.38	13.4
1935	2,014	23.8	1,120	5.2	15,500	0.29	13.8
1936	2,172	23.3	789	3.1	13,900	0.21	17.6
1937	4,740	20.3	1,860	7.2	28,400	0.43	15.3
1938	2,772	23.6	688	2.8	9,150	0.15	13.3
1939	2,613	23.4	1,170	4.7	17,800	0.28	15.2
1940	2,508	20.9	577	2.3	6,700	0.10	11.6
1941	4,288	18.3	2,360	8.4	23,000	0.32	9.8
1942	2,968	11.7	840	2.8	4,180	0.05	5.0
1943	3,752	5.0	1,980	6.9	13,500	0.15	6.8
1944	4,956	5.6	2,120	7.0	8,720	0.09	4.1
1945	4,750	9.9	3,470	12.2	38,000	0.47	11.0
1946	4,985	24.2	4,600	14.5	116,000	1.43	25.2
1947	3,693	25.6	2,170	6.5	34,600	0.41	15.9
1948	3,419	21.8	1,960	5.5	34,100	0.37	17.4
1949	3,606	22.5	3,030	9.0	50,500	0.59	16.7
1950	4,843	19.2	2,410	6.9	38,800	0.44	16.1

a. The exact number of workers involved in some strikes that occurred from 1916 to 1926 is not known. The missing information is for the smaller disputes, however, and it is believed that the totals given here are approximate.

b. "Total employed workers" as used here refers to all workers except those in occupations and professions in which there is little if any union organization or in which strikes rarely, if ever, occur. In most industries it includes all wage and salary workers except those in executive, managerial or high supervisory positions or those performing professional work the nature of which makes union organization or group action impracticable. It excludes all self-employed, domestic workers, agricultural wage workers on farms employing fewer than six, all federal and state government employees, and officials (both elected and appointed) in local governments.

c. Estimated working time was computed for purposes of this table by multiplying the average number of employed workers each year by the prevailing number of days worked per employee in that year.

d. No information available.

Sources: Publications of the Bureau of Labor Statistics, as follows: data for 1881–1915 from ***Strikes in 1941,*** **Bulletin No. 711, 1942, Table 1, p. 2; for 1916–1949, from** ***Work Stoppages Caused by Labor-Management Disputes in 1949,*** **Bulletin No. 1003, 1950, Table 1, p. 1; for 1950, from "Work Stoppages in 1950," April 18, 1951, mimeographed.**

TABLE 61

WORK STOPPAGES IN SELECTED INDUSTRY GROUPS, 1942–1946 [a]

Industry Group	Percentage of Employed Workers [b] Involved					Percentage of Available Working Time [b] Lost				
	1942	1943	1944	1945	1946	1942	1943	1944	1945	1946
All industries	2.8	6.9	7.0	12.2	14.5	0.05	0.15	0.09	0.47	1.43
Manufacturing:										
Iron and steel and their products	6.0	20.4	20.3	26.4	54.1	0.07	0.14	0.22	0.81	5.81
Electrical machinery	3.6	4.7	4.4	18.4	40.1	0.03	0.04	0.05	0.74	7.30
Machinery (except electrical)	4.3	5.0	10.8	20.0	20.5	0.03	0.04	0.13	0.91	4.51
Transportation equipment (except automobiles)	3.7	6.9	14.4	23.4	10.8	0.03	0.05	0.12	0.55	1.68
Automobiles and automobile equipment	8.4	26.8	50.5	75.9	21.7	0.04	0.20	0.58	4.08	7.81
Nonferrous metals and their products	7.6	11.2	10.8	18.8	18.2	0.07	0.07	0.10	0.52	3.91
Lumber and timber basic products	3.2	2.4	8.4	11.9	2.6	0.08	0.04	0.19	1.61	0.60
Furniture and finished lumber products	4.2	3.1	4.5	5.9	10.0	0.15	0.04	0.07	0.36	1.36
Stone, clay and glass products	9.0	7.6	10.4	17.2	7.1	0.24	0.13	0.18	1.19	1.02
Textile mill products	7.2	4.4	4.6	9.3	3.8	0.14	0.10	0.13	0.44	0.39
Apparel and other finished products made from fabrics and similar materials	2.8	6.4	1.5	1.7	2.1	0.08	0.08	0.02	0.07	0.19
Leather and leather products	7.5	8.2	7.1	14.9	7.2	0.25	0.17	0.11	0.25	0.42
Food and kindred products	3.0	2.7	3.1	7.4	13.4	0.08	0.03	0.05	0.30	0.70
Tobacco manufactures	3.8	27.3	7.8	18.0	4.3	0.10	0.38	0.21	1.12	1.02
Paper and allied products	4.5	6.8	4.8	8.2	5.1	0.10	0.10	0.12	0.36	0.57
Printing, publishing and allied products	2.4	0.6	0.7	3.7	3.2	0.07	0.01	0.01	0.22	0.28
Chemicals and allied products	5.1	2.9	3.9	7.2	7.9	0.07	0.03	0.06	0.25	0.77
Products of petroleum and coal	2.9	3.2	6.6	34.2	2.5	0.03	0.04	0.06	1.07	0.24
Rubber products	10.1	46.8	18.5	127.3 [c]	39.1	0.08	0.44	0.18	2.61	1.26
Miscellaneous manufacturing industries	1.9	2.4	1.4	5.0	4.9	0.07	0.04	0.02	0.37	0.51
Nonmanufacturing:										
Mining	10.5	86.2	34.3	89.8	120.1 [c]	0.31	4.25	0.56	2.88	10.35
Construction	1.9	3.4	3.5	5.8	10.3	0.04	0.04	0.06	0.20	0.40
Trade	[d]	[d]	0.5	0.6	0.9	[d]	[d]	0.01	0.02	0.05
Transportation, communication and other public utilities	[d]	[d]	2.0	4.4	27.1	[d]	[d]	0.03	0.15	0.94

a. Work stoppages are classified by industry on the basis of normal or peacetime products or services of the firms involved. Many of the firms manufactured other products and did other types of work during the war. Data are not available for several nonmanufacturing industries where the impact of work stoppages was very small.

b. See footnotes b and c to Appendix Table 60.

c. The number of workers involved was greater than total employment in the industry since many participated in more than one stoppage during the year and were counted separately each time.

d. Not available.

Sources: The following publications of the Bureau of Labor Statistics: *Strikes in 1942,* Bulletin No. 741, Table 4, p. 6; *Strikes in 1943,* Bulletin No. 782, Table 3, p. 5; *Strikes and Lockouts in 1944,* Bulletin No. 833, Table 3, p. 5; *Work Stoppages Caused by Labor-Management Disputes in 1945,* Table 4, p. 9; and *Work Stoppages Caused by Labor-Management Disputes in 1946,* Table 3, p. 13.

TABLE 62

Work Stoppages Involving 10,000 or More Workers, 1935–1950

Business and Location	Union or Unions Involved	Beginning Date	Approximate Duration, in Calendar Days	Approximate Number of Workers Involved
1935:				
Shirt manufacturers, New York, New Jersey, Pennsylvania and Connecticut	Amalgamated Clothing Workers (AFL)	Jan. 21	11	15,000
Trucking companies, New York City	Brotherhood of Teamsters (AFL)	Jan. 28	1	20,000
Cotton dress companies, Chicago, Ill.	International Ladies' Garment Workers' Union (AFL)	Feb. 20	50	10,000
Dress manufacturers, New York, New Jersey, Pennsylvania and Connecticut	International Ladies' Garment Workers' Union (AFL)	April 9	8	17,000
Lumber industry, Washington and Oregon	Sawmill and Timber Workers (AFL)	May 6	104	32,000
General strike, Terre Haute, Ind.	General strike (AFL unions)	July 22	2	26,000
Dress manufacturers, New York City	International Ladies' Garment Workers' Union (AFL)	Sept. 3	9	10,000
Bituminous coal mines, 23 states	United Mine Workers (AFL)	Sept. 23	6	366,000
Bituminous coal mines, Alabama	United Mine Workers (AFL)	Sept. 23	56	20,000
1936:				
Millinery companies, New York City	United Hatters, Cap and Millinery Workers (AFL)	Feb. 4	7	20,000
Goodyear Tire & Rubber Co., Akron, Ohio	United Rubber Workers (AFL)	Feb. 17	34	14,000
Realty owners, New York City	Building Service Employees (AFL)	Mar. 1	15	36,000
Barber shops, New York City	The Journeymen Barbers (AFL)	Apr. 27	71	20,000
Goodyear Tire & Rubber Co., Akron, Ohio	United Rubber Workers (AFL)	June 10	1	12,000
Painting contractors, New York City	Brotherhood of Painters (AFL)	Aug. 27	9	10,000
Maritime industry, Pacific Coast	International Longshoremen's Association (AFL), Marine Engineers' Beneficial Association (ind.), Masters, Mates and Pilots (AFL), Marine Firemen, Oilers, Watertenders and Wipers Association (ind.), Marine Cooks and Stewards (AFL), American Radio Telegraphists Association (ind.), and Sailors Union of the Pacific (ind.)	Oct. 30	98	37,000
Maritime industry, Atlantic and Gulf Coasts	International Seamen's Union (AFL)	Nov. 1	85	20,000
1937:				
General Motors Corp., 6 states	United Automobile Workers (CIO)	Jan. 1	42	48,000
B. F. Goodrich Co., Akron, Ohio	United Rubber Workers (CIO)	Jan. 28	3	10,000
Shirt manufacturers, New York, New Jersey, Connecticut and Pennsylvania	Amalgamated Clothing Workers (CIO)	Feb. 16	10	12,000
Shoe manufacturers, Massachusetts	United Shoe and Leather Workers (CIO)	Feb. 23	9	11,500
Firestone Tire & Rubber Co., Akron, Ohio	United Rubber Workers (CIO)	Mar. 3	59	10,500
Chrysler Corp., Detroit, Mich.	United Automobile Workers (CIO)	Mar. 8	30	63,000
Hudson Motor Car Co., Detroit, Mich.	United Automobile Workers (CIO)	Mar. 8	34	10,000
General Motors Corp., Flint, Mich.	United Automobile Workers (CIO)	Mar. 8	1	13,000
General Motors Corp., Flint, Mich.	United Automobile Workers (CIO)	Apr. 1	3	14,000
Bituminous coal mines, Alabama	United Mine Workers (CIO)	Apr. 2	43	15,000
Caterpillar Tractor Co., Peoria, Ill.	Amalgamated Association of Iron, Steel and Tin Workers (CIO-SWOC)	Apr. 6	3	11,000
Anthracite mines, Pennsylvania	United Mine Workers (CIO)	May 3	23	15,000
Jones and Laughlin Steel Corp., Aliquippa and Pittsburgh, Pa.	Steel Workers Organizing Committee (CIO)	May 12	3	25,000
Independent steel companies, Republic, Youngstown Sheet & Tube, Inland, and Bethlehem	Steel Workers Organizing Committee (CIO)	May 26	64	92,000
General strike, Lansing, Mich.	United Automobile Workers (CIO)	June 7	1	15,000
General Motors Corp., Detroit, Mich.	United Automobile Workers (CIO)	June 8	8	11,000
Shipyards, New York and New Jersey	Industrial Union of Marine and Shipbuilding Workers (CIO)	June 11	69	15,000
Captive coal mines, Pennsylvania and West Virginia	United Mine Workers (CIO)	June 14	45	10,000
Trucking companies, Philadelphia, Pa.	Brotherhood of Teamsters (AFL)	July 2	2	20,000
Cloak manufacturers, New York and New Jersey	International Ladies' Garment Workers' Union (CIO)	July 8	5	12,000
Bituminous coal mines, Illinois	Progressive Mine Workers (ind.)	July 31	28	16,000
Chrysler Corp., Detroit, Mich.	United Automobile Workers (CIO) and Independent Association of Chrysler Employees (ind.)	Aug. 4	4	10,000
Silk manufacturers, New York, New Jersey and Pennsylvania	Textile Workers Organizing Committee (CIO)	Aug. 9	23	31,000
Painting contractors, New York City	Brotherhood of Painters (AFL)	Aug. 26	20	13,000
Hudson Motor Car Co., Detroit, Mich.	United Automobile Workers (CIO)	Nov. 9	1	10,500
Goodyear Tire & Rubber Co., Akron, Ohio	United Rubber Workers (CIO)	Nov. 19	3	13,500
1938:				
Hosiery mills, New York, New Jersey and Pennsylvania	American Federation of Hosiery Workers (CIO)	Feb. 28	4	21,000
Trucking companies, New Jersey and New York City	Brotherhood of Teamsters (AFL)	Sept. 15	19	18,000
1939:				
Chrysler Corp., Detroit, Mich.	United Automobile Workers (CIO)	Feb. 22	2	10,000
Bituminous coal mines, 23 states	United Mine Workers (CIO)	Apr. 1	48	330,000
Bituminous coal mines, Harlan County, Ky.	United Mine Workers (CIO)	May 19	62	14,000

TABLE 62—CONTINUED

Business and Location	Union or Unions Involved	Beginning Date	Approximate Duration, in Calendar Days	Approximate Number of Workers Involved
1939 — Continued				
Briggs Manufacturing Co., Detroit, Mich.	United Automobile Workers (CIO)	May 22	17	15,000
WPA projects, 38 states	Workers Alliance (ind.)	July 5	16	123,000
Building and construction industry, Philadelphia, Pa.	Philadelphia Building Trades Council and Plumbers and Steamfitters (AFL)	Aug. 29	10	15,000
Chrysler Corp., Detroit, Mich.	United Automobile Workers (CIO)	Oct. 6	55	50,000
Cotton growers, California	Cannery, Agricultural, Packing and Allied Workers (CIO)	Oct. 9	53	15,000
1940:				
Clothing industry, New York	International Ladies' Garment Workers' Union (AFL)	July 11	2	15,000
Painting contractors, New York, Connecticut and District of Columbia	Brotherhood of Painters (AFL)	Aug. 26	32	15,000
Building and construction industry, St. Louis, Mo.	St. Louis Building and Construction Trades Council (AFL)	Oct. 25	4	15,000
Lumber companies, Oregon and Washington	Lumber and Sawmill Workers (AFL)	Dec. 2	15	12,000
1941:				
International Harvester Co., Illinois and Indiana	Farm Equipment Organizing Committee (CIO)	Jan. 17	73	16,000
Bethlehem Steel Corp., Lackawanna, N. Y.	Steel Workers Organizing Committee (CIO)	Feb. 27	2	12,000
Bethlehem Steel Corp., Bethlehem, Pa.	Steel Workers Organizing Committee (CIO)	Mar. 24	4	10,000
Bethlehem Steep Corp., Johnstown, Pa.	Steel Workers Organizing Committee (CIO)	Mar. 28	3	10,000
Bituminous coal mines, Illinois	Progressive Mine Workers (AFL)	Apr. 1	15	15,000
Bituminous coal mines, Alabama, Illinois and Iowa	United Mine Workers (CIO)	Apr. 1	44	49,000
Bituminous coal mines, 14 states	United Mine Workers (CIO)	Apr. 1	30	269,000
Ford Motor Co., Dearborn, Mich.	United Automobile Workers (CIO)	Apr. 1	11	85,000
Lumber industry, Washington	International Woodworkers (CIO)	May 9	37	12,000
Building and construction industry, Detroit, Mich., and vicinity	Detroit Building Trades Council (AFL)	May 9	9	15,000
General Motors Corp., Flint, Saginaw and Detroit, Mich.	United Automobile Workers (CIO)	May 15	2	40,000
Anthracite mines, Pennsylvania	United Mine Workers (CIO)	May 19	1	91,000
Ravenna Ordnance Plant, Ravenna, Ohio	Hod Carriers, Building and Common Laborers (AFL)	May 21	3	10,000
North American Aviation Inc., Inglewood, Calif.	United Automobile Workers (CIO)	June 5	5	11,000
Building and construction industry, New York City	Greater New York City Building and Construction Trades Council (AFL)	June 27	5	30,000
Building and construction industry, New York City	Electrical Workers (AFL)— supported by other AFL unions	July 29	12	28,000
Missouri ordnance plants	AFL Building and Construction Trades Council	Aug. 2	9	16,000
Federal Shipbuilding & Drydock Co., Kearny, N. J.	Industrial Union of Marine and Shipbuilding Workers (CIO)	Aug. 7	18	15,500
Bituminous coal mines, Alabama	United Mine Workers (CIO)	Sept. 2	6	22,000
Anthracite mines, Pennsylvania	United Mine Workers (CIO)	Sept. 9	30	26,000
Captive coal mines, 6 states	United Mine Workers (CIO)	Sept. 14	[a]	53,000
Tennessee Coal, Iron & R. R. Co., Alabama	Steel Workers Organizing Committee (CIO)	Sept. 27	2	15,000
Chrysler Corp., Detroit, Mich.	United Automobile Workers (CIO)	Sept. 30	1	19,000
Carnegie-Illinois Steel Corp., Gary, Ind.	Steel Workers Organizing Committee (CIO)	Oct. 5	2	17,500
B. F. Goodrich Co., Akron, Ohio	United Rubber Workers (CIO)	Oct. 7	1	16,000
Shipyards, California and Washington	United Welders and Burners (dissident members of various AFL Craft Unions)	Oct. 17	20	12,000
Bituminous coal mines, Alabama	United Mine Workers (CIO)	Oct. 20	5	20,000
Ford Motor Co., Dearborn, Mich.	United Automobile Workers (CIO)	Nov. 7	1	20,000
Bituminous coal mines, 6 states	United Mine Workers (CIO)	Nov. 17	6	115,000
1942:				
Textile mills, New Bedford, Mass.	United Textile Workers (AFL)	Feb. 23	1	13,000
Textile mills, Fall River, Mass.	Textile Workers Union (CIO) and American Federation of Textile Operators (ind.)	Mar. 24	14	16,000
Yellow Truck & Coach Mfg. Co., Pontiac, Mich.	United Automobile Workers (CIO)	June 25	2	12,000
Western Cartridge Co. and East Alton Mfg. Co., East Alton, Ill.	Chemical Workers' Union No. 22574 (AFL)	Sept. 8	4	10,500
Alabama Drydock & Shipbuilding Co., Mobile, Ala.	Industrial Union of Marine and Shipbuilding Workers (CIO)	Sept. 17	3	12,000
Western Cartridge Co. and East Alton Mfg. Co., East Alton, Ill.	Molders and Foundry Workers (AFL)	Oct. 10	3	11,000
1943:				
Anthracite mines, Pennsylvania	United Mine Workers (ind.)	Jan. 4	18	20,000
Dress manufacturers, New York, New Jersey, Pennsylvania and Connecticut	International Ladies' Garment Workers' Union (AFL)	Jan. 26	2	16,000

TABLE 62—CONTINUED

Business and Location	Union or Unions Involved	Beginning Date	Approximate Duration, in Calendar Days	Approximate Number of Workers Involved
1943 — Continued				
Bituminous coal mines, industry-wide	United Mine Workers (ind.)	Apr. 26	b	360,000
Anthracite mines, Pennsylvania	United Mine Workers (ind.)	May 1	c	74,000
Chrysler Corp., Detroit, Mich.	United Automobile Workers (CIO)	May 20	4	27,000
Goodyear Tire & Rubber Co., Firestone Tire & Rubber Co., General Tire, and B. F. Goodrich Co., Akron, Ohio	United Rubber Workers (CIO)	May 22	6	49,000
Packard Motor Car Co., Detroit, Mich.	United Automobile Workers (CIO)	June 2	6	24,000
Ladies' clothing industry, New York City	International Ladies' Garment Workers' Union (AFL)	June 24	2	15,000
Cramp Shipbuilding Co., Philadelphia, Pa.	Industrial Union of Marine and Shipbuilding Workers (CIO)	Oct. 15	3	17,000
Steel industry, 10 states	United Steelworkers (CIO)	Dec. 25	3	134,000
1944:				
Cramp Shipbuilding Co., Philadelphia, Pa.	Industrial Union of Marine and Shipbuilding Workers (CIO)	Jan. 5	5	14,000
Automotive machinery and other metalworking companies	Mechanics Educational Society of America (ind.)	Feb. 4	4	19,000
Briggs Manufacturing Co., Detroit, Mich.	United Automobile Workers (CIO)	Feb. 25	2	11,000
Garwood Manufacturing Co., Briggs Manufacturing Co., Hudson Motor Car Co., Murray Corp., and Packard Motor Car Co., Detroit, Mich.	Foremen's Association of America (ind.)	May 1	19	55,000
Chrysler Corp., Detroit, Mich.	United Automobile Workers (CIO)	May 16	8	11,000
Northwest lumber industry, Washington, Oregon and Montana	Lumber and Sawmill Workers (AFL) and International Woodworkers (CIO)	May 19	14	30,000
Ford Motor Co., Ypsilanti, Mich.	United Automobile Workers (CIO)	July 15	2	25,000
Wright Aeronautical Corp., New Jersey	United Automobile Workers (CIO)	Aug. 7	4	10,000
Electric Boat Co., Groton, Conn.	Shipbuilding and Marine Engineers' Union (ind.)	Aug. 14	4	10,000
Bituminous coal mines, Kentucky, Pennsylvania and West Virginia	United Clerical, Technical, and Supervisory Employees, District 50, United Mine Workers (ind.)	Aug. 17	d	30,000
Ford Motor Co., Ypsilanti, Mich.	United Automobile Workers (CIO)	Sept. 7	3	19,000
Todd-Houston Shipbuilding Corp., Houston, Tex.	Brotherhood of Boilermakers (AFL)	Sept. 11	2	11,000
Pratt & Whitney Corp., Kansas City, Mo.	Machinists (AFL)	Oct. 2	1	13,000
Automotive and ordnance plants, Detroit area	United Automobile Workers	Oct. 4	2	50,000
Packard Motor Car Co., Detroit, Mich.	United Automobile Workers (CIO)	Nov. 3	14	28,000
Wright Aeronautical Corp., New Jersey	Wright Aircraft Supervisory Association (ind.)	Nov. 13	3	23,000
1945:				
Chrysler Corp., Dodge main, and DeSoto plants, Detroit and Hamtramck, Mich.	United Automobile Workers (CIO)	Feb. 23	11	16,000
Briggs Manufacturing Co., Detroit and Hamtramck, Mich.	United Automobile Workers (CIO)	Mar. 1	10	11,000
A. C. Spark Plug Division of General Motors, Flint, Mich.	United Automobile Workers (CIO)	Mar. 26	3	11,000
Hudson Motor Car Co., Detroit, Mich.	United Automobile Workers (CIO)	Mar. 28	4	13,000
Bituminous coal mines, 13 states	United Mine Workers (ind.)	Apr. 3	13	100,000
B. F. Goodrich Co., Akron, Ohio	Foremen's Association of America (ind.)	Apr. 5	3	16,000
Packard Motor Car Co., Detroit, Mich.	United Automobile Workers (CIO)	Apr. 9	6	12,000
B. F. Goodrich Co., Akron, Ohio	United Rubber Workers (CIO)	Apr. 20	4	15,000
Anthracite mines, Pennsylvania	United Mine Workers (ind.)	May 1	20	63,000
Bituminous coal mines, 12 states	United Mine Workers (ind.)	May 1	3	64,000
32 bituminous coal mines, Pennsylvania and West Virginia	United Clerical, Technical, and Supervisory Employees, District 50, United Mine Workers (ind.)	May 14	18	10,000
Chrysler Corp., Ford Motor Co., Packard Motor Car Co., Budd Wheel Co., Detroit and Dearborn, Mich.	United Automobile Workers (CIO) and AFL Building Trades	June 14	17	47,000
Libby-Owens-Ford Glass Co. and Pittsburgh Plate Glass Co., Illinois, Louisiana, Ohio, Oklahoma and West Virginia	Federation of Glass, Ceramic and Silica Sand Workers (CIO)	June 15	20	16,000
Goodyear Tire & Rubber Co., Akron, Ohio.	United Rubber Workers (CIO)	June 16	20	21,000
Trucking companies, Chicago, Ill., and East Chicago, Ind.	Chicago Truck Drivers, Chauffeurs, and Helpers (ind.) and Brotherhood of Teamsters (AFL)	June 16	10	10,000
Firestone Tire & Rubber Co., Akron, Ohio.	United Rubber Workers (CIO)	July 1	14	17,000
Wright Aeronautical Corp., Paterson, East Paterson, Fair Lawn and Wood Ridge, N. J.	United Automobile Workers (CIO)	July 20	8	24,000
Chrysler Corp., Chicago, Ill.	United Automobile Workers (CIO)	July 25	4	19,000
Wright Aeronautical Corp., Lockland, Ohio.	United Automobile Workers (CIO)	Aug. 3	5	27,000
Consolidated Steel Corp., Orange, Tex.	AFL Craft Unions	Sept. 1	6	11,000
Goodyear Tire & Rubber Co., Akron, Ohio.	United Rubber Workers (CIO)	Sept. 3	1	16,000
B. F. Goodrich Co., Akron, Ohio	Foremen's Association of America (ind.)	Sept. 4	22	14,000
Westinghouse Electric Corp., Maryland, Massachusetts, New Jersey, New York, Ohio and Pennsylvania	Federation of Westinghouse Independent Salaried Unions (ind.)	Sept. 10	19	40,000

TABLE 62—Continued

Business and Location	Union or Unions Involved	Beginning Date	Approximate Duration, in Calendar Days	Approximate Number of Workers Involved
1945 — Continued				
Oil refineries, 20 states	Oil Workers (CIO)	Sept. 17	20	43,000
Bituminous coal mines, 8 states	United Clerical, Technical, and Supervisory Employees, District 50, United Mine Workers (ind.)	Sept. 21	30	209,000 [e]
Midtown realty owners, New York City	Building Service Employees (AFL)	Sept. 24	6	15,000
New York Shipbuilding Corp., Camden, N. J.	Industrial Union of Marine and Shipbuilding Workers (CIO)	Sept. 24	4	17,000
Northwest lumber industry, California, Idaho, Montana, Oregon and Washington	Lumber and Sawmill Workers (AFL)	Sept. 24	[f]	44,000
Textile printing companies, Connecticut, New Jersey, New York, Pennsylvania and Rhode Island	Federation of Dyers, Finishers, Printers, and Bleachers (CIO)	Sept. 27	13	16,000
Consolidated Steel Corp., Los Angeles, Calif.	Operating Engineers (AFL) and Machinists (AFL)	Oct. 1	3	10,000
General Motors Corp., Frigidaire Division, Dayton, Ohio	United Electrical Workers (CIO)	Oct. 1	6	12,000
New York Shipping Association, New York City, Hoboken and Newark, N. J.	International Longshoremen's Association (AFL)	Oct. 1	19	30,000
Libby-Owens-Ford Glass Co. and Pittsburgh Plate Glass Co., 7 states	Federation of Glass, Ceramic, and Silica Sand Workers (CIO)	Oct. 16	102	13,000
Firestone Tire & Rubber Co., Akron, Ohio	United Rubber Workers (CIO)	Oct. 29	—	15,000
Machine shops, shipyards, etc., San Francisco Bay area, Calif.	Machinists (AFL) and United Steelworkers (CIO)	Oct. 29	140	37,000
Textile mills, Connecticut, Maine, Massachusetts, New Hampshire and Rhode Island	Textile Workers Union (CIO)	Nov. 1	133	18,000
Goodyear Tire & Rubber Co., Akron, Ohio.	United Rubber Workers (CIO)	Nov. 6	2	15,000
Midwest Truck Operators Association, 21 states	Brotherhood of Teamsters (AFL)	Nov. 12	81	10,000
Leather manufacturers, 15 states	Fur and Leather Workers Union (CIO)	Nov. 15	1	25,000
Illinois Bell Telephone Co., Illinois and Indiana	Illinois Telephone Traffic Union (ind.)	Nov. 19	6	14,000
General Motors Corp., 11 states	United Automobile Workers (CIO)	Nov. 21	[g]	200,000
Steamship and stevedoring companies, Pacific, Atlantic and Gulf ports	Maritime Unions (CIO)	Dec. 3	1	13,000
1946:				
Western Electric Co., New Jersey and New York	Western Electric Employees Association — affiliated with National Federation of Telephone Workers (ind.)	Jan. 3	65	24,000
Western Electric Co., nation-wide	Association of Communication Equipment Workers — affiliated with National Federation of Telephone Workers (ind.)	Jan. 9	7	142,000
Electrical manufacturing: General Motors, General Electric and Westinghouse plants.	United Electrical Workers (CIO)	Jan. 15	[h]	174,000
Meatpacking industry, several states	Packinghouse Workers (CIO) and Amalgamated Meat Cutters (AFL)	Jan. 16	19	93,000
Steel, industry-wide	United Steelworkers of America (CIO)	Jan. 21	[i]	750,000
International Harvester Co., Illinois, Indiana, Iowa and New York	United Farm Equipment and Metal Workers (CIO)	Jan. 21	86	29,000
Caterpillar Tractor Co., Peoria, Ill.	United Farm Equipment and Metal Workers (CIO)	Jan. 29	29	17,000
American Brass Co., and Chase Brass Co., Connecticut and N. Y.	International Union of Mine, Mill and Smelter Workers (CIO)	Feb. 4	[j]	16,000
Philadelphia Transit Co.	Transport Workers Union (CIO)	Feb. 11	2	10,000
Allis-Chalmers, 7 plants in 6 states	United Automobile Workers (CIO), United Farm Equipment and Metal Workers (CIO), United Electrical Workers (CIO) and CIO Industrial Union, 1424	Mar. 14	[k]	25,000
Bituminous coal mines, industry-wide	United Mine Workers (AFL after Jan. 1946)	Apr. 1	59	340,000
Port of Philadelphia	CIO and AFL unions in support of the United Harbor Workers (District 50, United Mine Workers, AFL)	Apr. 5	6	18,000
Briggs Manufacturing Co., Detroit, Mich.	United Automobile Workers (CIO)	May 3	1	11,000
Railroad industry, nation-wide	Brotherhood of Locomotive Engineers and Brotherhood of Railroad Trainmen (ind.)	May 23	2	350,000
City of Rochester, N. Y.	AFL and CIO Unions — general sympathy strike	May 28	1	20,000
Anthracite mines, Pennsylvania	United Mine Workers (AFL)	May 31	8	75,000
Association of General Contractors of America, Cincinnati, Ohio	Hod Carriers, Building and Common Laborers (AFL)	June 3	2	10,000
Railway Express Co., New York City and Hudson County, N. J.	Brotherhood of Railway and Steamship Clerks, Freight Handlers, Express and Station Employees (AFL)	June 27	5	12,000

TABLE 62—CONTINUED

Business and Location	Union or Unions Involved	Beginning Date	Approximate Duration, in Calendar Days	Approximate Number of Workers Involved
1946 — Continued				
Motion-picture studios, Los Angeles (Hollywood), Calif.	Conference of Studio Unions (comprising AFL craft affiliates)	July 1	2	14,000
New York City and other Atlantic ports	Seafarers' International Union (AFL) and its affiliated Sailors Union of the Pacific (supported by other AFL unions), National Maritime Union (CIO)	July 10	4	11,500
Waterfront Employers' Asssociation San Francisco, Long Beach, and Los Angeles, Calif.	International Longshoremen's and Warehousemen's Union (CIO)	July 31	1	12,000
Building and construction industry, Buffalo, N. Y.	Allied Building Trades Council (AFL)	Aug. 12	11	18,000
General Motors Corp. — Fisher Body Plant, Truck and Coach Division, Pontiac Motor Division	United Automobile Workers (CIO)	Aug. 14	1	11,000
Commercial and industrial construction, Cuyahoga, Geauga and Lake Counties, Ohio	Building Trades (AFL)	Aug. 29	2	24,000
Trucking companies, New York City area and New Jersey	Brotherhood of Teamsters (AFL)	Sept. 1	m	31,000
Maritime industry, unlicensed personnel — Atlantic, Gulf and Pacific Coast ports	Seafarers' International Union (AFL) and its affiliate, Sailors Union of the Pacific, National Maritime Union (CIO), Marine Cooks and Stewards (CIO), and Marine Firemen, Oilers, Watertenders and Wipers Association (ind.), supported by other AFL Unions	Sept. 5	17	132,000
Hudson Motor Car Co., Detroit, Mich.	United Automobile Workers (CIO)	Sept. 11	1	12,000
Maritime industry, licensed personnel — Atlantic, Gulf and Pacific Coast ports; longshoremen on Pacific Coast	Marine Engineers Beneficial Association (CIO), Masters, Mates and Pilots (AFL), International Longshoremen's and Warehousemen's Union (CIO)	Oct. 1	n	142,000
Transcontinental & Western Air, Inc. (Trans World Airline)	Air Line Pilots Association (AFL)	Oct. 21	26	13,000
Bituminous coal mines, industry-wide [o]	United Mine Workers (AFL)	Nov. 21	17	335,000 [o]
General strike, Oakland, Calif.	Retail Clerks' Int'l Association (AFL) in original dispute. AFL unions participated in general sympathy strike	Dec. 3	2	50,000
1947:				
Hudson Motor Car Company, Detroit, Mich.	United Automobile Workers (CIO)	Jan. 27	2	14,000
Telephone industry, nation-wide	National Federation of Telephone Workers (ind.)	Apr. 7	44 [p]	370,000
State-wide demonstration, Iowa	Various unions (AFL & CIO)	Apr. 21	1	100,000
Inland Steel Co., East Chicago, Ind., and Chicago Heights, Ill.	United Steelworkers (CIO)	May 1	7	14,000
Construction industry, Detroit, Mich., area.	Building trades unions (AFL)	May 1	47 [q]	19,000
Construction industry, Lehigh Valley area, Pennsylvania	Building trades unions (AFL)	May 1	38 [r]	10,000
Metal trades industries, Washington State.	Metal Trades Council (AFL) and International Association of Machinists (ind.).	May 16	4	10,000
Remington Rand, Inc., New York and Michigan	International Association of Machinists (ind.) and United Electrical, Radio, and Machine Workers (CIO) beginning June 18	May 26	70 [s]	15,000
Construction industry, Philadelphia, Pa., area	Building trades unions (AFL)	June 5	13	15,000
Bituminous coal mines, Indiana and southwestern Pennsylvania	United Mine Workers (AFL)	June 6	t	18,000
Hudson Motor Car Co., Detroit, Mich.	United Automobile Workers (CIO)	June 11	2	16,000
Bituminous coal mines, industry-wide	United Mine Workers (AFL)	June 23	u	343,000
Shipyards, Atlantic and Gulf Coasts and San Pedro, Calif.	International Union of Marine and Shipbuilding Workers (CIO)	June 26	v	50,000
Union Railroad and Carnegie Illinois Steel Corp., Pittsburgh, Pa., area	Railroad Trainmen (ind.) and Locomotive Engineers (ind.)	Sept. 5	9	23,000 [w]
Railway Express Agency, Inc., New York City and near-by New Jersey	Teamsters (AFL)	Sept. 19	25	10,000
1948:				
Timbermen and sawmill workers, western Pennsylvania and Maryland, and northern West Virginia	United Construction Workers, affiliated with District 50, UMWA (ind.)	Jan. 3	28 [x]	11,000
Women's garment manufacturers, Los Angeles, Calif.	International Ladies' Garment Workers' Union (AFL)	Feb. 17	y	10,000
Bituminous coal strike, nation-wide	United Mine Workers (ind.)	Mar. 15	40	320,000
Meat-packing plants, 20 states	United Packinghouse Workers (CIO)	Mar. 16	67 [z]	83,000
Hudson Motor Car Co., Detroit, Mich.	United Automobile Workers (CIO)	Mar. 22	2	13,000
Anthracite mines, Pennsylvania	United Mine Workers (ind.)	Apr. 6	8 [aa]	30,000

TABLE 62—Continued

Business and Location	Union or Unions Involved	Beginning Date	Approximate Duration, in Calendar Days	Approximate Number of Workers Involved
1948 — Continued				
Goodyear Tire & Rubber Co. (Plants 1 and 2), Akron, Ohio	United Rubber, Cork, Linoleum, & Plastic Workers (CIO)	Apr. 7	4	10,000
Caterpillar Tractor Co., Peoria, Ill.	United Farm Equipment & Metal Workers (CIO); United Automobile Workers (CIO); United Automobile Workers (AFL)	Apr. 8	35	20,000
Boeing Airplane Co., Seattle, Wash.	Aero Mechanics, affiliated with International Association of Machinists (ind.)	Apr. 22	142 [bb]	18,000
Chrysler Corp., Detroit, Mich., Evansville, Ind., and Maywood, Calif.	United Automobile Workers (CIO)	May 12	17	75,000
International Harvester Co., 10 plants in New York, Indiana, Illinois and Kentucky	United Farm Equipment and Metal Workers (CIO)	June 29 [cc]	2	34,000
"Captive" coal mines, 5 states	United Mine Workers (ind.)	July 6	9	42,000
Bituminous coal mines, scattered locations	United Mine Workers (ind.)	July 6	9	40,000
International Harvester Co., Indiana, Illinois, Ohio and Tennessee	United Automobile Workers (CIO)	Aug. 17	16	23,000
Truckers' strike, New York and northern New Jersey	International Brotherhood of Teamsters (AFL)	Sept. 1	[dd]	16,000
Maritime industry, west coast	International Longshoremen's and Warehousemen's Union (CIO); Marine Cooks & Stewards (CIO); Marine Engineers Beneficial Association (CIO); Marine Firemen, Oilers, Watertenders & Wipers Association (ind.); Radio Officers' Union (ind.)	Sept. 2	93	28,000
Oil companies, California	Oil Workers International Union (CIO)	Sept. 4	[ee]	17,000
Briggs Manufacturing Co., Detroit, Mich.	United Plant Guard Workers (ind.)	Sept. 8	16	25,000
Chrysler Corp., Detroit, Mich	United Automobile Workers (CIO)	Nov. 9	4	13,000
Shipping operators, east coast	International Longshoremen's Association (AFL)	Nov. 10	18	45,000
1949:				
Philadelphia Transportation Co., Philadelphia, Pa.	Transport Workers Union (CIO)	Feb. 11	10	11,000
Anthracite and bituminous coal mines, area east of the Mississippi River	United Mine Workers (ind.)	Mar. 14	13	365,000
Wabash Railroad Co., Mo., Ill., Ind., Ohio, Mich., Iowa	Bro. of Locomotive Engineers (ind.); Bro. of Locomotive Firemen & Enginemen (ind.); Bro. of Railroad Trainmen (ind.); Order of Railway Conductors of America (ind.)	Mar. 15	8	10,000
Hudson Motor Car Co., Detroit, Mich.	United Automobile Workers (CIO)	Mar. 17	1	13,000
Taxicab companies, New York, N. Y.	United Mine Workers, District 50 (ind.)	April 1	8	16,000
Philco Corporation, Philadelphia and Croydon, Pa.	United Electrical, Radio and Machine Workers (CIO) [ff]	May 2	5	10,000
Ford Motor Co., Detroit, Mich., and Dearborn, Mich.	United Automobile Workers (CIO)	May 5	25	62,000
Master Builders Ass'n, Washington, D.C., area	Hod Carriers (AFL); Carpenters and Joiners (AFL)	June 1	39	13,000
Tri-State Lumbermen's Ass'n, Md., Pa. and W. Va.	United Construction Workers, UMWA, District 50 (ind.)	June 10	58	10,000
Anthracite and bituminous coal mines, nation-wide	United Mine Workers (ind.)	June 13	7	385,000
Briggs Mfg. Co., Detroit, Mich.	United Automobile Workers (CIO)	June 14	3	29,000
Distributors Ass'n of Northern California, San Francisco and Bay Area, Calif.	Int'l Longshoremen's and Warehousemen's Union (CIO)	June 16	107	11,000
Associated General Contractors of Minnesota, construction in Minneapolis and St. Paul, Minn.	AFL Building Trades	June 22	35	20,000
Chrysler Corporation, Detroit, Mich.	United Automobile Workers (CIO)	Aug. 13	6	17,000
The B. F. Goodrich Co., Ohio, Pa., Tenn., Ala., Okla., Mich., Calif.	United Rubber, Cork, Linoleum and Plastic Workers (CIO)	Aug. 27	35	15,000
Missouri-Pacific Railroad, 9 western states	Bro. of Locomotive Engineers (ind.); Bro. of Locomotive Firemen & Enginemen (ind.); Bro. of Railroad Trainmen (ind.); Order of Railway Conductors (ind.)	Sept. 9	44	27,000
Anthracite and bituminous coal mines, nation-wide	United Mine Workers (ind.)	Sept. 19	54 [gg]	400,000
Basic steel companies, and some fabricating companies, nation-wide	United Steelworkers (CIO)	Oct. 1	[hh]	500,000
1950:				
Chrysler Corp. (25 plants), Ark., Calif., Del., Ga., Ind., Kan., Mich.	United Automobile Workers (CIO)	Jan. 25	102	95,000
Bituminous coal mines, Illinois	Progressive Mine Workers (ind.)	Feb. 15	15	10,000
Apartment houses, New York, N. Y.	Building Service Employees (AFL)	Apr. 27	4	12,000
Construction industry, Buffalo area, N. Y.	Building trades unions (AFL)	May 1	40 [ii]	12,000
Construction industry, Denver area, Colo.	Building trades unions (AFL)	May 1	80 [jj]	10,000

TABLE 62—CONTINUED

Business and Location	Union or Unions Involved	Beginning Date	Approximate Duration, in Calendar Days	Approximate Number of Workers Involved
Pennsylvania R. R. (west of Harrisburg); N. Y. Central R. R. (west of Buffalo); Southern Railway Co.; Atchison, Topeka & Santa Fe R. R.; Union Pacific R.R. (affected operations in 27 states)	Brotherhood of Locomotive Firemen & Enginemen (ind.)	May 10	7	175,000
Construction industry, state-wide, Utah	Building trades unions (AFL)	June 2	6	12,000
Bituminous coal mines, Kentucky and Tennessee	United Mine Workers (ind.)	June 15	5	13,000
Chicago, Rock Island & Pacific R. R.; Great Northern Rwy. Co.; Chicago Great Western Rwy. Co.; Denver & Rio Grande Western R. R. Co.; Western Pacific R. R. Co. (affected operations in 33 states)	Switchmen's Union (AFL)	June 25	14	59,000
Construction industry, Los Angeles and San Diego counties, Calif.	United Brotherhood of Carpenters & Joiners (AFL)	July 10	36	40,000
Kaiser-Frazer Corp., Willow Run, Mich.	United Automobile Workers (CIO)	July 20	1	12,000
The Studebaker Corp., South Bend, Ind.	United Automobile Workers (CIO)	July 24	3	20,000
Briggs Mfg. Co., Detroit, Mich.	United Automobile Workers (CIO)	Aug. 1	2	12,000
Tennessee Coal, Iron & R. R. Co., Birmingham area, Ala.	United Steelworkers (CIO)	Aug. 12	7	15,000
International Harvester Co. plants in Illinois, Indiana, Kentucky, Ohio and Tennessee	Farm Equipment Workers, UE (ind.); United Automobile Workers (CIO); Int'l Ass'n of Machinists (ind.)	Aug. 16	86 [kk]	52,000
General Electric Co. plants in Indiana, Massachusetts, New Jersey, New York, Ohio, Pennsylvania, Rhode Island, and West Virginia	Int'l Union of Electrical, Radio & Machine Workers (CIO)	Aug. 29	18	40,000
Deere & Co. (7 plants), Illinois and Iowa.	United Automobile Workers (CIO)	Sept. 1	111	13,000
National Ass'n of Mfrs. of Pressed & Blown Glassware, Illinois, Indiana, New Jersey, New York, Ohio, Pennsylvania, and West Virginia	American Flint Glass Workers' Union (CIO)	Sept. 5	17	11,500
Hudson Motor Car Co., Detroit, Mich.	United Automobile Workers (CIO)	Sept. 26	4	15,000
Associated and Independent Farmers, San Joaquin Valley, Calif.	National Farm Labor Union (AFL)	Oct. 5	13	13,000
Western Electric Co., nation-wide; Michigan Bell Telephone Co., Michigan	Communications Workers (CIO)	Nov. 9	11	80,000 [ll]
Railroad terminals, 16 cities	Brotherhood of Railroad Trainmen (ind.).	Dec. 13	3	10,000

a. Intermittent idleness for total of 18 days during September, October and November.
b. Average per worker was 20 days. Includes intermittent stoppages April through November.
c. Average per worker was 21 days. Includes intermittent stoppages May through November.
d. Stoppage began August 17; however, majority of workers did not become idle until September.
e. About 45,000 workers were idle by September 30. The remainder became idle during October.
f. Settlements reached with a few companies before December 1945. Majority of agreements signed by late December, with most of the remaining settlements occurring at some time in the following three months.
g. Agreement reached on March 13, 1946; ratification by local unions, together with plant production problems, delayed reopening of most plants until late in the month. A few plants continued idle into April.
h. General Motors Corp. (Electrical Division) settled on February 9, General Electric Co. on March 14, and Westinghouse Electric and Manufacturing Co. on May 10.
i. Settlement on February 15, 1946 with U.S. Steel Corp., followed by agreements with other large basic steel companies within four days, resulted in the return to work of approximately 450,000 employees. Virtually all the remaining 300,000 workers went back to their jobs at various dates during the next two months as additional settlements were reached.
j. Chase Brass Co. settled on April 6, American Brass Co. on May 19.
k. Duration of stoppages at various plants as follows: LaPorte, Indiana, March 14–October 12; Norwood, Ohio, March 19–September 28; Pittsburgh, Pennsylvania, March 22–September 16; Springfield, Illinois, April 16–September 18; Hyde Park (Boston), Massachusetts, April 30–December 8; LaCross, Wisconsin, April 30–October 24; West Allis, Wisconsin, April 30, 1946–March 23, 1947.
l. Majority of employees resumed work August 1; some idleness continued through August 1 in Los Angeles area.
m. Some settlements were reached on September 17. Virtually all other employers settled in the following six weeks.
n. MEBA and MMP on East and Gulf Coasts signed agreements on October 22 and October 26, respectively. West Coast stoppage continued until November 23.
o. This figure does not include some 7,500 anthracite miners who were idle for two days during this period following an erroneous report that their president had been jailed.
p. Major portion of strike ended by May 20, some companies settled earlier and several not until the last week in May.
q. Settlements involving substantial numbers of workers were reached May 29, June 16 and July 14.
r. Stoppage terminated by June 7 for all trades except electricians and roofers, who remained out until June 24.
s. Electrical workers settled July 28, machinists August 3.
t. Most workers idle not more than three working days.
u. Between June 23 and 27, more than 200,000 stopped work, allegedly in protest against passage of the Labor-Management Relations Act by Congress. June 28–July 7 was the scheduled industry-wide vacation period. On June 30 the mines, operated by the government since May 1946, were returned to private control. After the scheduled vacation, most miners were idle from July 8 to 11 until contracts with operators were signed and ratified.
v. About 25,000 stopped work June 26; an additional 25,000 went out July 1. Some companies settled during July, August and September. Agreement covering most Bethlehem Steel yards was reached by November 7. The last plants to settle were the Patapsco Scrap Corp. (a subsidiary of Bethlehem Steel) at Fairfield, Maryland (November 16), and the San Pedro, California, plant of Bethlehem Steel (December 24).
w. About 1,900 employees of the Union Railroad (a subsidiary of U.S. Steel Corp. servicing steel plants) were involved in the dispute, and about 21,000 steelworkers in closely integrated operations were made idle.
x. By late January approximately 8,000 workers had returned; others returned about two weeks later.
y. Most workers idle two days; 3,000 workers for five days; 500 idle for approximately two months.
z. Settlements reached with Swift, Armour and Cudahy plants on May 21. Stoppage continued at Wilson plants until June 5.
aa. Some workers out only two or three days.
bb. Total length of stoppage; some workers returned to their jobs during strike and company also hired replacements.
cc. Approximately 2,000 workers at Auburn, New York, went out on June 15 and remained out until June 30.
dd. Approximately 10,000 New York truck drivers and helpers idled September 1, with the New Jersey workers going out on September 7. On September 18, individual companies began to sign separate agreements with the union.

TABLE 62—Continued

ee. First settlements with individual companies were reached about November 4; other settlements later in November. About 1,600 employees of one company still on strike at the end of December.

ff. The UERMWA was expelled from the CIO in November 1949. The local union representing Philco employees voted to affiliate with the newly chartered International Union of Electrical Workers, CIO.

gg. Approximately 400,000 anthracite and bituminous coal miners were idle from September 19 to October 3. On that date all anthracite miners and approximately 20,000 bituminous coal miners employed in mines west of the Mississippi were ordered back to work. On November 9 the remaining miners returned to work during a three-week truce. Following the truce, about 300,000 bituminous coal miners were idle on December 1 and 2. The strike continued intermittently to March 5, 1950.

hh. First major settlement occurred on October 31 with Bethlehem Steel Co., involving approximately 80,000 workers. Other settlements with major companies were reached through November 11. By December 1 only 45,000 workers were still on strike.

ii. Fifteen of the unions involved reached agreement by May 8; Asbestos Workers on May 14; Plasterers and Lathers on May 16; Plumbers on May 29; Bricklayers on June 9.

jj. Some trades working on projects outside of Denver terminated stoppage on May 31; in Denver, Teamsters and Operating Engineers on June 2; Laborers on June 9; Cement Finishers about June 25; Carpenters did not reach agreement until July 19.

kk. The larger segments of the stoppage did not begin until August 18. However, 600 machinists (IAM) at the Louisville, Kentucky, plant stopped work on August 16, closing the plant. The FEUE (ind.) settled September 18; the IAM (ind.) October 1; and the UAW (CIO) on November 4, subject to ratification by the union members on November 8.

ll. A larger number of workers were idle for less than a full shift as the result of the intermittent picketing technique used by the Communications Workers of America in this stoppage.

Sources: The following publications of the Bureau of Labor Statistics: for 1935–1947, *Handbook of Labor Statistics,* 1947 edition, Bulletin No. 916, Table E-9, pp. 146–49; for 1948, *Work Stoppages Caused by Labor-Management Disputes in 1948,* Bulletin No. 963, Table 4, p. 8; for 1949, "Review of Labor-Management Disputes in 1949," mimeographed; for 1950, "Review of Labor-Management Disputes in 1950," January 9, 1951, mimeographed (corrected October 1, 1951).

TABLE 63

Workers in Total Population, by Sex and Age, 1900–1949

No.	Sex and Age	Number, in Thousands: Gainful Workers 1900	1920	1930	Number, in Thousands: Labor Force [a] 1930	1940	1944	1949	Percentage of Total Population: Gainful Workers 1900	1920	1930	Percentage of Total Population: Labor Force [a] 1930	1940	1944	1949	No.
1	Total, 14 years and over	28,282	41,236	48,595	47,404	54,740	65,150	62,183	55.0	55.7	54.5	53.2	54.1	64.5	57.0	1
2	14–19	4,136	4,650	4,457	4,386	4,300	7,752	4,472	45.2	40.2	32.0	31.4	29.2	50.9	36.1	2
3	20–24	4,533	5,941	7,153	7,063	7,900	9,137	7,276	61.6	64.0	65.7	64.9	68.2	75.9	62.7	3
4	25–44	12,584	19,029	22,344	21,902	25,480	28,194	28,421	58.9	60.8	61.7	60.5	64.2	67.8	63.6	4
5	45–64	5,823	9,922	12,434	12,015	14,840	17,328	18,982	55.8	58.3	58.0	56.0	56.9	61.5	62.0	5
6	65 and over	1,203	1,692	2,207	2,038	2,220	2,740	3,035	39.0	34.3	33.2	30.7	24.6	24.5	26.9	6
7	Male, 14 years and over	23,168	32,806	37,916	37,008	40,900	46,510	44,120	87.7	86.6	84.1	82.1	80.9	92.0	83.2	7
8	14–19	2,905	3,009	2,865	2,795	2,840	5,022	2,795	63.6	52.4	41.1	40.0	38.4	61.0	45.7	8
9	20–24	3,339	4,129	4,803	4,747	5,080	5,814	4,678	91.7	91.2	89.9	88.8	89.3	97.5	87.1	9
10	25–44	10,734	15,606	17,792	17,498	18,980	20,059	20,320	96.3	97.4	97.4	95.8	96.4	98.0	96.7	10
11	45–64	5,123	8,567	10,516	10,173	12,090	13,255	13,869	93.3	94.0	94.0	91.0	90.4	92.8	91.8	11
12	65 and over	1,064	1,494	1,940	1,795	1,910	2,360	2,459	68.3	60.2	58.3	53.9	43.3	49.6	46.1	12
13	Female, 14 years and over	5,114	8,430	10,579	10,396	13,840	18,640	18,063	20.4	23.3	24.3	23.6	27.4	36.9	32.1	13
14	14–19	1,231	1,641	1,592	1,591	1,460	2,730	1,677	26.8	28.2	22.8	22.8	19.9	39.0	26.6	14
15	20–24	1,194	1,812	2,350	2,316	2,820	3,323	2,598	32.1	38.1	42.4	41.8	47.8	54.7	44.6	15
16	25–44	1,850	3,423	4,552	4,404	6,500	8,135	8,101	18.1	22.4	25.4	24.6	32.5	38.6	40.0	16
17	45–64	700	1,355	1,918	1,842	2,750	4,072	5,113	14.1	17.1	18.7	18.0	21.6	29.8	33.0	17
18	65 and over	139	197	267	243	310	380	576	9.1	8.0	8.1	7.3	6.7	7.4	9.6	18

a. End of March or beginning of April of each year. For 1944 and 1949, age distribution of persons in armed forces estimated.

Sources: For 1900–1930, Sixteenth Census (1940), *Population — Comparative Occupation Statistics for the United States, 1870–1940,* p. 13; for 1940, "Monthly Report on the Labor Force," *Current Population Reports,* Series P-57, Bureau of the Census; for 1944, "Labor Force, Employment and Unemployment in the United States, 1940 to 1946," *Current Population Reports,* Series P-50, No. 2, Bureau of the Census; for 1949, "Monthly Report on the Labor Force."

TABLE 64

Population and Labor Force, by Sex, Monthly, 1940–1950

(In Thousands)

Year and Month	Noninstitutional Population 14 Years and Over			Labor Force (Including Armed Forces)			Civilian Labor Force (Excluding Armed Forces)		
	Total	Male	Female	Total	Male	Female	Total	Male	Female
1940									
March	99,930	49,790	50,140	54,740	40,900	13,840	54,460	40,620	13,840
April	99,950	49,800	50,150	55,140	41,130	14,010	54,870	40,860	14,010
May	100,040	49,840	50,200	55,880	41,590	14,290	55,590	41,300	14,290
June	100,160	49,900	50,260	57,640	42,680	14,960	57,330	42,370	14,960
July	100,260	49,930	50,330	58,310	43,460	14,850	58,000	43,150	14,850
August	100,330	49,940	50,390	58,010	43,270	14,740	57,670	42,930	14,740
September	100,480	50,030	50,450	56,780	42,160	14,620	56,330	41,710	14,620
October	100,590	50,080	50,510	56,350	42,080	14,270	55,830	41,560	14,270
November	100,680	50,120	50,560	55,570	41,980	13,590	54,960	41,370	13,590
December	100,780	50,160	50,620	55,150	41,760	13,390	54,460	41,070	13,390
Annual average	100,230	49,930	50,300	56,030	41,870	14,160	55,640	41,480	14,160
1941									
January	100,870	50,200	50,670	54,730	41,570	13,160	53,990	40,830	13,160
February	100,950	50,240	50,710	54,740	41,530	13,210	53,870	40,660	13,210
March	101,030	50,270	50,760	54,700	41,530	13,170	53,660	40,490	13,170
April	101,110	50,300	50,810	56,240	42,300	13,940	54,980	41,050	13,930
May	101,210	50,350	50,860	57,420	42,560	14,860	55,970	41,110	14,860
June	101,310	50,390	50,920	59,660	44,070	15,590	58,120	42,540	15,580
July	101,410	50,440	50,970	59,910	44,400	15,510	58,260	42,760	15,500
August	101,510	50,490	51,020	59,860	44,290	15,570	58,130	42,560	15,570
September	101,620	50,540	51,080	58,770	43,240	15,530	56,950	41,430	15,520
October	101,710	50,580	51,130	57,790	42,480	15,310	55,950	40,640	15,310
November	101,840	50,650	51,190	57,540	42,450	15,090	55,650	40,570	15,080
December	101,910	50,680	51,230	57,260	42,510	14,750	55,330	40,580	14,750
Annual average	101,370	50,420	50,950	57,380	42,740	14,640	55,910	41,270	14,640
1942									
January	101,990	50,700	51,290	56,510	42,330	14,180	54,540	40,360	14,180
February	102,200	50,870	51,330	57,140	42,780	14,360	54,880	40,520	14,360
March	102,300	50,910	51,390	57,820	43,130	14,690	55,260	40,580	14,680
April	102,250	50,810	51,440	58,740	43,270	15,470	55,880	40,420	15,460
May	102,340	50,860	51,480	59,670	43,720	15,950	56,500	40,560	15,940
June	102,200	50,690	51,510	61,820	44,940	16,880	58,340	41,470	16,870
July	102,460	50,890	51,570	62,180	45,500	16,680	58,400	41,730	16,670
August	102,550	50,950	51,600	62,110	45,450	16,660	57,900	41,260	16,640
September	102,660	51,020	51,640	61,110	44,350	16,760	56,500	39,760	16,740
October	102,770	51,050	51,720	61,820	44,620	17,200	56,800	39,610	17,190
November	102,810	51,030	51,780	61,900	44,660	17,240	56,240	39,030	17,210
December	103,010	51,180	51,830	61,970	44,610	17,360	55,680	38,350	17,330
Annual average	102,460	50,910	51,550	60,230	44,110	16,120	56,410	40,300	16,110
1943									
January	103,050	51,170	51,880	61,630	44,450	17,180	54,700	37,560	17,140
February	103,210	51,280	51,930	61,990	44,530	17,460	54,560	37,160	17,400
March	103,190	51,230	51,960	62,170	44,530	17,640	54,340	36,770	17,570
April	103,260	51,260	52,000	63,160	44,970	18,190	54,860	36,760	18,100
May	103,350	51,320	52,030	64,680	45,530	19,150	56,080	37,040	19,040
June	103,280	51,210	52,070	66,410	46,260	20,150	57,580	37,550	20,030
July	103,520	51,400	52,120	66,850	46,820	20,030	57,680	37,770	19,910
August	103,780	51,570	52,210	66,690	46,900	19,790	57,160	37,500	19,660
September	103,760	51,520	52,240	65,730	46,030	19,700	56,030	36,470	19,560
October	103,810	51,520	52,290	64,980	45,790	19,190	55,110	36,060	19,050
November	103,920	51,590	52,330	64,600	45,780	18,820	54,550	35,880	18,670
December	103,950	51,580	52,370	64,000	45,600	18,400	53,770	35,530	18,240
Annual average	103,510	51,390	52,120	64,410	45,600	18,810	55,540	36,840	18,700

TABLE 64—CONTINUED

Year and Month	Noninstitutional Population 14 Years and Over			Labor Force (Including Armed Forces)			Civilian Labor Force (Excluding Armed Forces)		
	Total	Male	Female	Total	Male	Female	Total	Male	Female
1944									
January	104,050	51,650	52,400	63,680	45,610	18,070	53,370	35,460	17,910
February	104,180	51,700	52,480	63,530	45,670	17,860	53,010	35,330	17,680
March	104,220	51,720	52,500	63,900	45,710	18,190	53,210	35,200	18,010
April	104,300	51,760	52,540	65,150	46,510	18,640	54,220	35,770	18,450
May	104,360	51,790	52,570	66,430	46,660	19,770	55,270	35,690	19,580
June	104,440	51,820	52,620	67,970	47,430	20,540	56,640	36,300	20,340
July	104,520	51,860	52,660	68,140	47,500	20,640	56,660	36,230	20,430
August	104,600	51,900	52,700	67,260	47,420	19,840	55,640	36,020	19,620
September	104,680	51,930	52,750	66,790	46,750	20,040	55,090	35,280	19,810
October	104,780	51,980	52,800	66,740	46,620	20,120	54,970	35,090	19,880
November	104,810	51,910	52,900	66,060	46,290	19,770	54,270	34,750	19,520
December	104,900	51,950	52,950	65,030	46,030	19,000	53,210	34,460	18,750
Annual average	104,480	51,830	52,650	65,890	46,520	19,370	54,630	35,460	19,170
1945									
January	104,960	51,980	52,980	64,600	45,940	18,660	52,770	34,360	18,410
February	105,020	51,980	53,040	65,240	46,020	19,220	53,340	34,370	18,970
March	105,090	52,000	53,090	65,790	46,230	19,560	53,820	34,520	19,300
April	105,150	52,020	53,130	66,250	46,410	19,840	54,180	34,610	19,570
May	105,230	52,050	53,180	66,500	46,420	20,080	54,370	34,560	19,810
June	105,290	52,070	53,220	67,590	47,030	20,560	55,460	35,170	20,290
July	105,390	52,120	53,270	67,450	47,100	20,350	55,350	35,270	20,080
August	105,460	52,150	53,310	66,470	46,870	19,600	54,460	35,130	19,330
September	105,560	52,190	53,370	64,770	45,850	18,920	53,050	34,400	18,650
October	105,640	52,230	53,410	63,770	45,010	18,760	53,170	34,650	18,520
November	105,800	52,300	53,500	62,410	44,040	18,370	53,190	35,030	18,160
December	105,880	52,340	53,540	60,920	43,560	17,360	53,130	35,950	17,180
Annual average	105,370	52,120	53,250	65,140	45,870	19,270	53,860	34,830	19,030
1946									
January	105,950	52,360	53,590	59,490	43,220	16,270	53,320	37,160	16,160
February	106,020	52,390	53,630	59,130	43,020	16,110	53,890	37,890	16,000
March	106,070	52,410	53,660	59,630	43,240	16,390	55,160	38,870	16,290
April	106,140	52,450	53,690	60,300	43,630	16,670	56,450	39,860	16,590
May	106,200	52,470	53,730	60,570	43,820	16,750	57,160	40,480	16,680
June	106,210	52,460	53,750	62,000	44,670	17,330	58,930	41,660	17,270
July	106,360	52,540	53,820	62,820	45,370	17,450	60,110	42,710	17,400
August	106,470	52,580	53,890	62,200	44,990	17,210	59,750	42,580	17,170
September	106,630	52,650	53,980	61,340	44,040	17,300	59,120	41,850	17,270
October	106,760	52,700	54,060	61,160	43,970	17,190	58,990	41,820	17,170
November	106,840	52,730	54,110	60,980	43,940	17,040	58,970	41,950	17,020
December	106,940	52,790	54,150	60,320	43,860	16,460	58,430	41,990	16,440
Annual average	106,370	52,540	53,830	60,820	43,980	16,840	57,520	40,740	16,780
1947									
January	106,970	52,790	54,180	59,510	43,560	15,950	57,790	41,860	15,930
February	107,060	52,830	54,230	59,630	43,700	15,930	58,010	42,100	15,910
March	107,190	52,820	54,370	59,960	43,990	15,970	58,390	42.440	15,950
April	107,260	52,840	54,420	60,650	44,310	16,340	59,120	42,800	16,320
May	107,330	52,870	54,460	61,760	44,620	17,140	60,290	43,170	17,120
June	107,407	52,901	54,506	64,007	45,839	18,168	62,609	44,460	18,149
July	107,504	52,943	54,561	64,035	46,213	17,822	62,664	44,861	17,803
August	107,590	52,978	54,612	63,017	45,874	17,143	61,665	44,540	17,125
September	107,675	53,014	54,661	62,130	44,881	17,249	60,784	43,551	17,233
October	107,755	53,045	54,710	62,219	44,754	17,465	60,892	43,443	17,449
November	107,839	53,080	54,759	61,510	44,426	17,084	60,216	43,148	17,068
December	107,918	53,113	54,805	60,870	44,156	16,714	59,590	42,892	16,698
Annual average	107,458	52,935	54,523	61,608	44,694	16,915	60,168	43,272	16,896

TABLE 64—CONTINUED

Year and Month	Noninstitutional Population 14 Years and Over			Labor Force (Including Armed Forces)			Civilian Labor Force (Excluding Armed Forces)		
	Total	Male	Female	Total	Male	Female	Total	Male	Female
1948									
January	107,979	53,135	54,844	60,455	44,071	16,384	59,214	42,846	16,368
February	108,050	53,161	54,889	61,004	44,236	16,768	59,778	43,026	16,752
March	108,124	53,190	54,934	61,005	44,228	16,777	59,769	43,009	16,760
April	108,173	53,204	59,969	61,760	44,589	17,171	60,524	43,369	17,155
May	108,262	53,241	55,021	61,660	44,519	17,141	60,422	43,298	17,124
June	108,346	53,275	55,071	64,740	46,039	18,701	63,479	44,794	18,685
July	108,597	53,436	55,161	65,135	46,715	18,420	63,842	45,437	18,405
August	108,660	53,461	55,199	64,511	46,525	17,986	63,186	45,215	17,971
September	108,753	53,501	55,252	63,578	45,453	18,125	62,212	44,101	18,111
October	108,853	53,546	55,307	63,166	45,229	17,937	61,775	43,851	17,924
November	108,948	53,587	55,361	63,138	45,182	17,956	61,724	43,782	17,942
December	109,036	53,624	55,412	62,828	45,012	17,816	61,375	43,573	17,802
Annual average	108,482	53,364	55,118	62,748	45,150	17,598	61,442	43,858	17,583
1949									
January	109,117	53,658	55,459	61,546	44,614	16,932	60,078	43,161	16,917
February	109,195	53,689	55,506	61,896	44,721	17,175	60,388	43,229	17,159
March	109,290	53,730	55,560	62,305	45,000	17,305	60,814	43,525	17,289
April	109,373	53,764	55,609	62,327	45,143	17,184	60,835	43,668	17,167
May	109,458	53,799	55,659	63,452	45,337	18,115	61,983	43,886	18,097
June	109,547	53,837	55,710	64,866	46,282	18,584	63,398	44,832	18,566
July	109,664	53,898	55,766	65,278	46,712	18,566	63,815	45,267	18,548
August	109,760	53,939	55,821	65,105	46,613	18,492	63,637	45,163	18,474
September	109,860	53,984	55,876	64,222	45,759	18,463	62,763	44,319	18,444
October	109,975	54,036	55,939	64,021	45,413	18,608	62,576	43,988	18,588
November	110,063	54,075	55,988	64,363	45,515	18,848	62,927	44,099	18,828
December	110,169	54,121	56,048	63,475	45,174	18,301	62,045	43,765	18,280
Annual average	109,623	53,878	55,745	63,571	45,524	18,048	62,105	44,075	18,030
1950									
January	110,256	54,160	56,096	62,835	45,102	17,733	61,427	43,715	17,712
February	110,344	54,196	56,148	63,003	45,115	17,888	61,637	43,769	17,868
March	110,442	54,238	56,204	63,021	45,204	17,817	61,675	43,879	17,796
April	110,536	54,279	56,257	63,513	45,429	18,084	62,183	44,120	18,063
May	110,608	54,308	56,300	64,108	45,614	18,494	62,788	44,316	18,472
June	110,703	54,350	56,353	66,177	46,718	19,459	64,866	45,429	19.437
July	110,806	54,395	56,411	65,742	47,000	18,742	64,427	45,708	18,719
August	110,924	54,427	56,497	66,204	47,132	19,072	64,867	45,818	19,049
September	111,030	54,473	56,557	65,020	46,155	18,865	63,567	44,726	18,841
October	111,141	54,522	56,619	65,438	45,978	19,460	63,704	44,268	19,436
November	111,234	54,558	56,676	65,453	45,934	19,519	63,512	44,019	19,493
December	111,329	54,600	56,729	64,674	45,644	19,030	62,538	43,535	19,003
Annual average	110,779	54,376	56,404	64,599	45,919	18,680	63,099	44,442	18,657

Source: "Monthly Report on the Labor Force," *Current Population Reports,* Series P-57, Bureau of the Census.

TABLE 65

PERSONS NOT IN THE LABOR FORCE, BY SEX AND AGE, MONTHLY, 1941–1950

(In Thousands)

Year and Month	Male: Total, 14 Years and Over	Male: 14 to 19 Years	Male: 20 to 24 Years	Male: 25 to 44 Years	Male: 45 to 64 Years	Male: 65 Years and Over	Female: Total, 14 Years and Over	Female: 14 to 19 Years	Female: 20 to 24 Years	Female: 25 to 44 Years	Female: 45 to 64 Years	Female: 65 Years and Over
1941												
October	8,100	4,180	350	240	900	2,430	35,820	5,110	2,970	13,520	9,930	4,290
November	8,200	4,190	390	260	900	2,460	36,100	5,180	2,960	13,550	10,070	4,340
December	8,170	4,180	410	240	890	2,450	36,480	5,250	2,970	13,660	10,180	4,420
1942												
January	8,370	4,270	460	260	910	2,470	37,110	5,440	3,100	13,850	10,270	4,450
February	8,090	4,140	410	260	860	2,420	36,970	5,450	3,070	13,830	10,190	4,430
March	7,780	3,940	390	260	850	2,340	36,700	5,400	3,000	13,740	10,030	4,530
April	7,540	3,730	350	250	800	2,410	35,970	5,240	3,110	13,360	9,880	4,380
May	7,140	3,390	320	230	710	2,490	35,530	5,060	3,180	13,200	9,740	4,350
June	5,750	2,170	220	220	690	2,450	34,630	4,300	3,080	13,240	9,630	4,380
July	5,390	1,770	180	230	700	2,510	34,890	4,080	3,110	13,590	9,740	4,370
August	5,500	1,920	180	200	750	2,450	34,940	4,220	3,110	13,550	9,720	4,340
September	6,670	3,140	260	170	730	2,370	34,880	4,610	3,020	13,350	9,570	4,330
October	6,430	3,050	280	160	700	2,240	34,520	4,590	2,930	13,070	9,630	4,300
November	6,370	3,020	280	210	670	2,190	34,540	4,630	3,010	12,910	9,600	4,390
December	6,570	3,130	240	220	700	2,280	34,470	4,630	3,030	12,890	9,610	4,310
Annual average	6,800	3,140	300	220	760	2,380	35,430	4,810	3,060	13,380	9,800	4,380
1943												
January	6,720	3,250	260	220	710	2,280	34,700	4,760	3,040	12,910	9,660	4,330
February	6,750	3,310	230	180	730	2,300	34,470	4,650	2,930	12,820	9,730	4,340
March	6,700	3,260	240	190	720	2,290	34,320	4,700	2,950	12,670	9,600	4,400
April	6,290	3,050	180	200	600	2,260	33,810	4,470	3,040	12,500	9,440	4,360
May	5,790	2,670	130	150	610	2,230	32,880	4,290	2,910	11,950	9,400	4,330
June	4,950	1,790	100	130	710	2,220	31,920	3,530	2,800	11,910	9,340	4,340
July	4,580	1,470	90	160	600	2,260	32,090	3,270	2,800	12,310	9,380	4,330
August	4,670	1,590	80	160	600	2,240	32,420	3,460	2,870	12,300	9,470	4,320
September	5,490	2,380	80	160	620	2,250	32,540	3,770	2,780	12,310	9,350	4,330
October	5,730	2,600	80	180	600	2,270	33,100	4,030	2,870	12,470	9,380	4,350
November	5,810	2,510	90	190	730	2,290	33,510	4,200	2,720	12,530	9,530	4,530
December	5,980	2,650	100	170	740	2,320	33,970	4,290	2,750	12,700	9,610	4,620
Annual average	5,790	2,540	140	170	670	2,270	33,310	4,120	2,870	12,450	9,490	4,380
1944												
January	6,040	2,650	100	190	750	2,350	34,330	4,420	2,820	12,810	9,670	4,610
February	6,030	2,710	90	170	750	2,310	34,620	4,500	2,800	12,960	9,730	4,630
March	6,010	2,670	110	170	750	2,310	34,310	4,390	2,740	12,890	9,670	4,620
April	5,250	2,000	100	170	710	2,270	33,900	4,200	2,730	12,770	9,590	4,610
May	5,130	2,000	110	200	670	2,150	32,800	4,090	2,770	12,280	9,170	4,490
June	4,390	1,320	80	190	660	2,140	32,080	3,560	2,690	12,220	9,180	4,430
July	4,360	1,280	80	220	660	2,120	32,020	3,350	2,670	12,410	9,160	4,430
August	4,480	1,380	80	210	640	2,170	32,860	3,520	2,760	12,740	9,380	4,460
September	5,180	2,070	70	210	650	2,180	32,710	3,870	2,650	12,510	9,210	4,470
October	5,360	2,230	90	220	670	2,150	32,680	3,950	2,670	12,470	9,170	4,420
November	5,620	2,470	90	190	680	2,190	33,130	4,110	2,700	12,580	9,240	4,500
December	5,920	2,620	110	190	710	2,290	33,950	4,160	2,790	12,810	9,600	4,590
Annual average	5,310	2,120	100	190	690	2,210	33,280	4,010	2,730	12,620	9,400	4,520
1945												
January	6,040	2,710	120	210	710	2,290	34,320	4,320	2,770	12,950	9,670	4,610
February	5,960	2,610	110	230	720	2,290	33,820	4,230	2,710	12,790	9,480	4,610
March	5,770	2,480	110	230	680	2,270	33,530	4,180	2,710	12,640	9,390	4,610
April	5,610	2,230	140	250	690	2,300	33,290	4,100	2,690	12,540	9,340	4,620
May	5,630	2,290	140	230	690	2,280	33,100	4,070	2,730	12,430	9,270	4,600
June	5,040	1,660	140	260	720	2,260	32,660	3,610	2,700	12,490	9,260	4,600
July	5,020	1,570	150	330	760	2,210	32,920	3,440	2,770	12,590	9,510	4,610
August	5,280	1,770	160	330	800	2,220	33,710	3,590	2,820	13,000	9,640	4,660
September	6,340	2,700	190	390	830	2,230	34,450	4,200	2,830	13,090	9,680	4,650
October	7,220	2,940	400	750	890	2,240	34,650	4,300	2,840	13,080	9,760	4,670
November	8,260	3,070	620	1,410	870	2,290	35,130	4,320	2,910	13,360	9,800	4,740
December	8,780	3,190	910	1,400	970	2,310	36,180	4,540	3,090	13,760	10,040	4,750
Annual average	6,250	2,430	260	510	780	2,270	33,980	4,080	2,800	12,890	9,570	4,640

TABLE 65—CONTINUED

Year and Month	Male: Total, 14 Years and Over	14 to 19 Years	20 to 24 Years	25 to 44 Years	45 to 64 Years	65 Years and Over	Female: Total, 14 Years and Over	14 to 19 Years	20 to 24 Years	25 to 44 Years	45 to 64 Years	65 Years and Over
1946												
January	9,140	3,360	1,010	1,420	930	2,420	37,320	4,750	3,250	14,190	10,340	4,790
February	9,370	3,500	1,140	1,320	920	2,490	37,520	4,850	3,200	14,300	10,380	4,790
March	9,170	3,490	1,120	1,140	930	2,490	37,270	4,820	3,190	14,110	10,330	4,820
April	8,820	3,410	1,130	980	870	2,430	37,020	4,770	3,190	13,990	10,230	4,840
May	8,650	3,310	1,030	900	960	2,450	36,980	4,750	3,270	13,890	10,260	4,810
June	7,790	2,680	940	780	920	2,470	36,420	4,320	3,260	13,860	10,170	4,810
July	7,170	2,190	910	750	850	2,470	36,370	3,980	3,290	13,980	10,340	4,780
August	7,590	2,370	960	790	1,010	2,460	36,680	4,030	3,260	14,320	10,250	4,820
September	8,610	3,380	1,010	700	990	2,530	36,680	4,380	3,280	14,040	10,150	4,830
October	8,730	3,420	1,060	680	1,010	2,560	36,870	4,460	3,290	14,030	10,180	4,910
November	8,790	3,410	1,140	650	1,010	2,580	37,070	4,490	3,280	14,260	10,130	4,910
December	8,930	3,480	1,150	690	1,050	2,560	37,690	4,590	3,350	14,410	10,390	4,950
Annual average	8,560	3,170	1,050	900	950	2,490	36,990	4,520	3,260	14,110	10,260	4,840
1947												
January	9,230	3,660	1,180	700	1,040	2,650	38,230	4,750	3,470	14,540	10,510	4,960
February	9,130	3,630	1,100	710	1,080	2,610	38,300	4,790	3,370	14,710	10,410	5,020
March	8,830	3,500	1,030	690	1,020	2,590	38,400	4,870	3,360	14,760	10,410	5,000
April	8,530	3,350	970	690	970	2,550	38,080	4,750	3,380	14,560	10,400	4,990
May	8,250	3,080	920	660	1,050	2,540	37,320	4,660	3,280	14,250	10,130	5,000
June	7,062	2,207	691	606	1,030	2,527	36,337	3,983	3,232	14,129	9,992	5,003
July	6,730	1,933	659	616	1,014	2,509	36,739	3,850	3,300	14,402	10,167	5,020
August	7,104	2,213	652	668	1,008	2,565	37,469	4,117	3,361	14,491	10,460	5,040
September	8,132	3,071	858	616	978	2,612	37,412	4,448	3,346	14,191	10,435	4,990
October	8,290	3,233	926	601	948	2,582	37,245	4,423	3,247	14,119	10,419	5,035
November	8,655	3,341	937	661	1,059	2,657	37,675	4,513	3,347	14,318	10,427	5,069
December	8,956	3,485	964	696	1,120	2,690	38,091	4,500	3,415	14,621	10,494	5,060
Annual average	8,241	3,059	901	660	1,026	2,423	37,578	4,471	3,342	14,424	10,350	5,015
1948												
January	9,063	3,532	1,040	718	1,024	2,749	38,461	4,636	3,352	14,765	10,568	5,141
February	8,925	3,452	1,001	700	1,031	2,739	38,121	4,577	3,344	14,573	10,510	5,119
March	8,962	3,391	1,051	679	1,044	2,797	38,157	4,559	3,349	14,622	10,523	5,103
April	8,616	3,179	1,047	645	989	2,756	37,798	4,582	3,322	14,489	10,336	5,069
May	8,723	3,252	1,040	670	1,030	2,730	37,879	4,618	3,252	14,518	10,438	5,052
June	7,235	2,151	784	633	961	2,706	36,370	3,779	3,160	14,130	10,237	5,063
July	6,720	1,815	583	590	979	2,752	36,742	3,709	3,257	14,497	10,282	5,097
August	6,936	2,105	543	612	1,010	2,672	37,213	3,944	3,290	14,440	10,435	5,105
September	8,048	3,039	660	626	1,036	2,688	37,128	4,308	3,228	14,163	10,299	5,131
October	8,316	3,230	823	614	1,025	2,625	37,369	4,366	3,273	14,258	10,304	5,170
November	8,405	3,301	819	576	1,074	2,635	37,405	4,393	3,261	14,248	10,350	5,154
December	8,612	3,341	852	647	1,103	2,671	37,596	4,367	3,330	14,333	10,397	5,168
Annual average	8,213	2,982	854	642	1,025	2,710	37,520	4,319	3,285	14,420	10,390	5,114
1949												
January	9,044	3,435	920	703	1,187	2,800	38,527	4,597	3,500	14,577	10,632	5,221
February	8,968	3,393	930	665	1,157	2,824	38,330	4,498	3,454	14,500	10,688	5,190
March	8,730	3,343	845	590	1,154	2,798	38,255	4,448	3,327	14,580	10,620	5,280
April	8,621	3,216	805	631	1,191	2,780	38,425	4,571	3,446	14,591	10,554	5,263
May	8,461	2,934	758	663	1,224	2,781	37,545	4,371	3,245	14,262	10,430	5,238
June	7,557	2,336	578	641	1,230	2,773	37,126	3,925	3,179	14,294	10,467	5,262
July	7,185	2,080	469	674	1,210	2,757	37,200	3,820	3,126	14,425	10,552	5,279
August	7,326	2,206	485	642	1,206	2,787	37,329	3,935	3,160	14,476	10,501	5,257
September	8,226	3,037	617	683	1,147	2,743	37,412	4,197	3,158	14,389	10,449	5,220
October	8,622	3,278	785	681	1,176	2,704	37,331	4,241	3,143	14,385	10,317	5,246
November	8,560	3,228	730	717	1,158	2,728	37,141	4,385	3,112	14,261	10,222	5,261
December	8,947	3,390	775	712	1,273	2,797	37,747	4,390	3,143	14,550	10,346	5,320
Annual average	8,354	2,998	725	667	1,193	2,773	37,497	4,272	3,249	14,441	10,481	5,253
1950												
January	9,057	3,457	751	759	1,256	2,835	38,363	4,611	3,171	14,708	10,480	5,392
February	9,082	3,448	736	732	1,295	2,873	38,260	4,528	3,184	14,700	10,478	5,369
March	9,035	3,451	730	717	1,305	2,833	38,388	4,652	3,264	14,640	10,450	5,383
April	8,851	3,337	695	707	1,236	2,875	38,173	4,619	3,230	14,537	10,399	5,388
May	8,694	3,251	726	686	1,177	2,856	37,806	4,473	3,203	14,390	10,304	5,436
June	7,632	2,311	593	656	1,187	2,886	36,894	3,963	3,164	14,149	10,230	5,388
July	7,395	2,121	462	655	1,250	2,907	37,669	3,910	3,314	14,520	10,505	5,421
August	7,294	2,116	439	671	1,179	2,888	37,424	3,941	3,148	14,372	10,534	5,430
September	8,318	3,047	551	613	1,200	2,907	37,694	4,300	3,006	14,468	10,464	5,455
October	8,544	3,070	669	665	1,163	2,977	37,160	4,171	2,968	14,269	10,300	5,453
November	8,624	3,196	651	618	1,207	2,953	37,158	4,263	3,013	14,136	10,296	5,449
December	8,957	3,308	664	660	1,266	3,061	37,700	4,319	2,966	14,446	10,460	5,510
Annual average	8,457	3,010	639	679	1,227	2,904	37,724	4,313	3,136	14,444	10,408	5,423

Sources: "Monthly Report on the Labor Force," *Current Population Reports,* Series P-57, Bureau of the Census; "Annual Report on the Labor Force," *Current Population Reports,* Series P-50, Bureau of the Census.

TABLE 66

Civilian Labor Force, by Sex and Age, Monthly, 1941–1950

(In Thousands)

Year and Month	Male: Total, 14 Years and Over	Male: 14 to 19 Years	Male: 20 to 24 Years	Male: 25 to 44 Years	Male: 45 to 64 Years	Male: 65 Years and Over	Female: Total, 14 Years and Over	Female: 14 to 19 Years	Female: 20 to 24 Years	Female: 25 to 44 Years	Female: 45 to 64 Years	Female: 65 Years and Over
1941												
October	40,640	3,250	4,470	18,250	12,540	2,130	15,310	2,090	2,940	6,730	3,160	390
November	40,570	3,300	4,190	18,580	12,410	2,090	15,080	2,030	2,960	6,710	3,010	370
December	40,580	3,180	4,360	18,470	12,490	2,080	14,750	1,950	2,950	6,620	2,910	320
1942												
January	40,360	2,990	4,310	18,380	12,590	2,090	14,180	1,730	2,800	6,470	2,880	300
February	40,520	3,140	4,280	18,430	12,550	2,120	14,360	1,740	2,860	6,500	2,940	320
March	40,580	3,280	4,300	18,230	12,580	2,190	14,680	1,820	2,820	6,570	3,130	340
April	40,420	3,390	4,050	18,070	12,740	2,170	15,460	1,910	2,820	7,020	3,330	380
May	40,560	3,720	3,940	18,070	12,740	2,090	15,940	2,140	2,800	7,160	3,440	400
June	41,470	4,860	3,860	17,810	12,780	2,160	16,870	2,890	2,920	7,140	3,560	360
July	41,730	5,130	3,820	17,760	12,900	2,120	16,670	3,070	2,890	6,820	3,500	390
August	41,260	5,060	3,690	17,620	12,740	2,150	16,640	2,980	2,890	6,870	3,490	410
September	39,760	3,860	3,430	17,520	12,750	2,200	16,740	2,600	2,990	7,100	3,630	420
October	39,610	3,860	3,340	17,140	12,910	2,360	17,190	2,520	3,060	7,430	3,700	480
November	39,030	3,850	2,980	17,010	12,810	2,380	17,210	2,510	2,940	7,520	3,750	490
December	38,350	3,750	2,750	16,740	12,810	2,300	17,330	2,510	3,020	7,600	3,690	510
Annual average	40,300	3,910	3,730	17,730	12,740	2,190	16,110	2,370	2,900	7,020	3,420	400
1943												
January	37,560	3,520	2,510	16,270	12,980	2,280	17,140	2,310	2,940	7,640	3,730	520
February	37,160	3,470	2,390	16,110	12,920	2,270	17,400	2,360	3,060	7,760	3,680	540
March	36,770	3,350	2,130	16,010	12,990	2,290	17,570	2,340	3,050	7,920	3,790	470
April	36,760	3,350	2,040	15,840	13,190	2,340	18,100	2,580	2,930	8,080	4,010	500
May	37,040	3,790	1,940	15,820	13,140	2,350	19,040	2,780	3,080	8,650	4,010	520
June	37,550	4,640	1,940	15,640	12,980	2,350	20,030	3,580	3,190	8,700	4,060	500
July	37,770	4,620	2,100	15,510	13,180	2,360	19,910	3,820	3,180	8,320	4,070	520
August	37,500	4,640	1,830	15,480	13,210	2,340	19,660	3,650	3,140	8,350	3,990	530
September	36,470	3,920	1,800	15,350	13,090	2,310	19,560	3,290	3,240	8,360	4,140	530
October	36,060	3,150	1,910	15,420	13,220	2,360	19,050	2,980	3,130	8,250	4,160	530
November	35,880	3,150	1,900	15,470	13,050	2,310	18,670	2,790	3,260	8,180	4,030	410
December	35,530	2,960	1,850	15,420	13,020	2,280	18,240	2,690	3,220	8,030	3,960	340
Annual average	36,840	3,710	2,030	15,700	13,080	2,320	18,700	2,930	3,120	8,190	3,970	490
1944												
January	35,460	2,830	1,890	15,430	13,040	2,270	17,910	2,540	3,150	7,940	3,930	350
February	35,330	2,790	1,890	15,290	13,060	2,300	17,680	2,460	3,180	7,810	3,890	340
March	35,200	2,840	1,850	15,130	13,070	2,310	18,010	2,560	3,230	7,890	3,970	360
April	35,770	3,500	1,810	14,990	13,110	2,360	18,450	2,730	3,240	8,030	4,070	380
May	35,690	3,470	1,730	14,830	13,170	2,490	19,580	2,830	3,190	8,540	4,510	510
June	36,300	4,130	1,710	14,760	13,200	2,500	20,340	3,360	3,270	8,670	4,520	580
July	36,230	4,160	1,670	14,660	13,210	2,530	20,430	3,560	3,290	8,430	4,560	590
August	36,020	4,030	1,620	14,630	13,250	2,490	19,620	3,370	3,200	8,120	4,360	570
September	35,280	3,360	1,640	14,540	13,250	2,490	19,810	3,010	3,300	8,370	4,560	570
October	35,090	3,220	1,620	14,480	13,240	2,530	19,880	2,920	3,280	8,430	4,620	630
November	34,750	2,990	1,620	14,440	13,220	2,480	19,520	2,760	3,270	8,360	4,570	560
December	34,460	2,850	1,590	14,420	13,210	2,390	18,750	2,700	3,180	8,150	4,240	480
Annual average	35,460	3,350	1,720	14,800	13,170	2,420	19,170	2,900	3,230	8,220	4,320	500
1945												
January	34,360	2,760	1,580	14,390	13,240	2,390	18,410	2,530	3,190	8,030	4,190	470
February	34,370	2,830	1,580	14,330	13,230	2,400	18,970	2,610	3,250	8,230	4,400	480
March	34,520	2,940	1,590	14,280	13,280	2,430	19,300	2,650	3,250	8,400	4,510	490
April	34,610	3,190	1,550	14,170	13,290	2,410	19,570	2,720	3,270	8,510	4,580	490
May	34,560	3,120	1,570	14,130	13,310	2,430	19,810	2,740	3,230	8,640	4,680	520
June	35,170	3,720	1,620	14,080	13,290	2,460	20,290	3,200	3,260	8,590	4,710	530
July	35,270	3,770	1,620	14,090	13,270	2,520	20,080	3,350	3,200	8,520	4,480	530
August	35,130	3,540	1,560	14,260	13,250	2,520	19,330	3,190	3,140	8,140	4,380	480
September	34,400	2,620	1,530	14,490	13,240	2,520	18,650	2,570	3,140	8,080	4,360	500
October	34,650	2,400	1,640	14,880	13,210	2,520	18,520	2,460	3,130	8,120	4,310	500
November	35,030	2,290	1,880	15,110	13,270	2,480	18,160	2,430	3,070	7,890	4,310	460
December	35,950	2,220	2,090	15,980	13,190	2,470	17,180	2,200	2,910	7,530	4,080	460
Annual average	34,830	2,950	1,650	14,510	13,260	2,460	19,030	2,720	3,180	8,230	4,410	490

TABLE 66—Continued

Year and Month	Male: Total, 14 Years and Over	Male: 14 to 19 Years	Male: 20 to 24 Years	Male: 25 to 44 Years	Male: 45 to 64 Years	Male: 65 Years and Over	Female: Total, 14 Years and Over	Female: 14 to 19 Years	Female: 20 to 24 Years	Female: 25 to 44 Years	Female: 45 to 64 Years	Female: 65 Years and Over
1946												
January	37,160	2,150	2,570	16,810	13,260	2,370	16,160	1,980	2,770	7,160	3,820	430
February	37,890	2,100	2,850	17,350	13,280	2,310	16,000	1,880	2,830	7,050	3,810	430
March	38,870	2,160	3,200	17,900	13,300	2,310	16,290	1,890	2,840	7,280	3,870	410
April	39,860	2,270	3,470	18,360	13,380	2,380	16,590	1,930	2,830	7,420	4,000	410
May	40,480	2,450	3,730	18,620	13,310	2,370	16,680	1,940	2,770	7,550	3,970	450
June	41,660	3,130	3,920	18,900	13,360	2,350	17,270	2,360	2,770	7,600	4,090	450
July	42,710	3,690	4,090	19,110	13,460	2,360	17,400	2,690	2,750	7,520	3,950	490
August	42,580	3,590	4,150	19,140	13,320	2,380	17,170	2,640	2,790	7,210	4,060	470
September	41,850	2,650	4,180	19,310	13,370	2,340	17,270	2,270	2,780	7,530	4,200	490
October	41,820	2,620	4,140	19,360	13,380	2,320	17,170	2,170	2,770	7,580	4,210	440
November	41,950	2,670	4,130	19,460	13,380	2,310	17,020	2,130	2,770	7,390	4,280	450
December	41,990	2,630	4,200	19,460	13,360	2,340	16,440	2,020	2,700	7,250	4,050	420
Annual average	40,740	2,680	3,720	18,650	13,350	2,340	16,780	2,160	2,780	7,370	4,020	450
1947												
January	41,860	2,500	4,210	19,490	13,400	2,260	15,930	1,850	2,570	7,140	3,950	420
February	42,100	2,470	4,370	19,570	13,370	2,320	15,910	1,790	2,670	6,990	4,080	380
March	42,440	2,590	4,480	19,590	13,440	2,340	15,950	1,720	2,710	6,990	4,110	420
April	42,800	2,760	4,540	19,610	13,500	2,390	16,320	1,820	2,690	7,220	4,150	440
May	43,170	3,000	4,650	19,660	13,450	2,410	17,120	1,900	2,790	7,560	4,430	440
June	44,460	3,950	4,863	19,746	13,478	2,424	18,149	2,560	2,838	7,703	4,603	444
July	44,861	4,223	4,901	19,768	13,513	2,456	17,803	2,681	2,767	7,456	4,455	443
August	44,540	3,952	4,911	19,728	13,539	2,412	17,125	2,405	2,703	7,391	4,187	439
September	43,551	3,069	4,711	19,802	13,587	2,382	17,233	2,059	2,712	7,722	4,237	504
October	43,443	2,902	4,649	19,840	13,630	2,422	17,449	2,074	2,807	7,816	4,277	475
November	43,148	2,816	4,643	19,793	13,536	2,360	17,068	1,973	2,701	7,641	4,296	457
December	42,892	2,649	4,625	19,787	13,491	2,338	16,698	1,971	2,628	7,362	4,255	483
Annual average	43,272	3,074	4,629	19,699	13,494	2,376	16,896	2,067	2,716	7,416	4,253	445
1948												
January	42,846	2,607	4,559	19,794	13,601	2,285	16,368	1,825	2,686	7,243	4,202	411
February	43,026	2,699	4,600	19,817	13,610	2,304	16,752	1,873	2,691	7,456	4,285	446
March	43,009	2,739	4,558	19,843	13,612	2,255	16,760	1,877	2,680	7,432	4,298	475
April	43,369	2,940	4,558	19,898	13,675	2,301	17,155	1,844	2,703	7,588	4,506	515
May	43,298	2,886	4,551	19,871	13,653	2,338	17,124	1,796	2,768	7,582	4,431	548
June	44,794	4,028	4,762	19,895	13,739	2,372	18,685	2,622	2,858	7,996	4,658	552
July	45,437	4,337	4,952	20,022	13,783	2,346	18,405	2,682	2,742	7,783	4,674	535
August	45,215	4,097	4,936	19,978	13,765	2,440	17,971	2,440	2,699	7,744	4,546	543
September	44,101	3,154	4,792	19,961	13,777	2,438	18,111	2,070	2,755	8,046	4,708	534
October	43,851	2,950	4,618	19,984	13,783	2,516	17,924	2,004	2,703	7,976	4,729	513
November	43,782	2,857	4,621	20,033	13,755	2,519	17,942	1,972	2,709	8,007	4,711	546
December	43,573	2,775	4,578	19,986	13,739	2,497	17,802	1,995	2,630	7,944	4,687	547
Annual average	43,858	3,173	4,674	19,923	13,706	2,384	17,583	2,083	2,719	7,732	4,537	514
1949												
January	43,161	2,648	4,519	19,953	13,667	2,375	16,917	1,758	2,452	7,724	4,475	508
February	43,229	2,655	4,497	20,005	13,715	2,360	17,159	1,850	2,493	7,821	4,446	551
March	43,525	2,688	4,595	20,113	13,732	2,398	17,289	1,897	2,611	7,766	4,540	478
April	43,668	2,789	4,637	20,101	13,714	2,425	17,167	1,767	2,484	7,778	4,632	509
May	43,886	2,968	4,684	20,101	13,699	2,436	18,097	1,961	2,676	8,131	4,781	549
June	44,832	3,727	4,818	20,128	13,706	2,454	18,566	2,400	2,735	8,123	4,770	539
July	45,267	3,977	4,932	20,148	13,752	2,459	18,548	2,500	2,778	8,017	4,726	527
August	45,163	3,851	4,900	20,204	13,769	2,441	18,474	2,379	2,735	7,988	4,805	568
September	44,319	3,017	4,768	20,189	13,844	2,501	18,444	2,116	2,728	8,096	4,881	623
October	43,988	2,779	4,599	20,215	13,837	2,560	18,588	2,069	2,737	8,122	5,040	619
November	44,099	2,855	4,628	20,207	13,869	2,544	18,828	2,024	2,757	8,267	5,161	619
December	43,765	2,693	4,594	20,212	13,775	2,493	18,280	1,916	2,719	7,998	5,067	581
Annual average	44,075	3,054	4,681	20,132	13,756	2,454	18,030	2,053	2,659	7,986	4,777	556
1950												
January	43,715	2,655	4,603	20,192	13,804	2,463	17,712	1,694	2,681	7,862	4,952	523
February	43,769	2,680	4,626	20,246	13,780	2,434	17,868	1,774	2,660	7,896	4,979	561
March	43,879	2,670	4,647	20,288	13,786	2,490	17,796	1,646	2,573	7,977	5,034	565
April	44,120	2,795	4,678	20,320	13,869	2,459	18,603	1,676	2,598	8,101	5,113	576
May	44,316	2,897	4,638	20,355	13,944	2,483	18,472	1,821	2,616	8,264	5,230	540
June	45,429	3,870	4,741	20,403	13,950	2,465	19,437	2,328	2,647	8,528	5,329	604
July	45,708	4,062	4,865	20,421	13,905	2,457	18,719	2,378	2,489	8,481	5,082	589
August	45,818	4,073	4,871	20,423	13,978	2,473	19,049	2,348	2,655	8,371	5,078	596
September	44,726	3,113	4,711	20,457	13,972	2,474	18,841	1,989	2,790	8,294	5,176	593
October	44,268	3,060	4,473	20,294	14,020	2,421	19,436	2,116	2,819	8,517	5,366	617
November	44,019	2,895	4,408	20,272	13,985	2,459	19,493	2,025	2,767	8,668	5,393	641
December	43,535	2,746	4,318	20,170	13,938	2,364	19,003	1,966	2,805	8,379	5,255	599
Annual average	44,442	3,126	4,632	20,320	13,911	2,454	18,657	1,980	2,675	8,253	5,166	584

Sources: "Monthly Report on the Labor Force," *Current Population Reports,* Series P-57, Bureau of the Census; "Annu Report on the Labor Force," *Current Population Reports,* Series P-50, Bureau of the Census.

TABLE 67

APPLICATIONS FOR SOCIAL SECURITY ACCOUNT NUMBERS, MONTHLY, 1937–1950 [a]

(In Thousands)

Month	1937	1938	1939	1940	1941	1942	1943	1944	1945	1946	1947	1948	1949	1950
January	5,987	692	434	459	544	451	770	304	245	186	210	203	175	130
February	1,177	501	339	340	408	378	547	277	248	189	160	152	131	131
March	1,631	508	371	337	392	383	530	330	277	220	149	145	127	158
April	1,021	488	359	361	430	433	683	307	224	190	164	203	170	155
May	1,026	452	369	335	599	699	618	344	251	242	234	195	166	182
June	2,253	496	502	433	802	803	806	731	492	339	340	371	280	438
July	1,908	560	496	502	760	1,050	1,194	526	372	326	302	413	320	299
August	1,592	619	549	514	797	651	558	388	342	375	292	227	195	277
September	1,063	528	503	445	524	587	465	373	200	234	215	217	240	302
October	964	547	615	511	590	784	617	311	207	228	272	253	172	—
November	713	457	538	462	416	536	448	287	254	274	205	188	146	—
December	690	474	503	496	423	626	450	357	212	204	188	187	220	—

a. Unadjusted figures. For 1937–1940, by calendar month; from 1941 on, by operating month, which includes either four or five weeks and ends on the last Friday of each month.

Source: Bureau of Old-Age and Survivors Insurance.

TABLE 68

Applications for Social Security Account Numbers, by Sex and Age, 1938–1949 [a]

(*In Thousands*)

Year and Sex	Total	Under 20 Years	20 to 24 Years	25 to 34 Years	35 to 44 Years	45 to 54 Years	55 to 64 Years	65 Years and Over	Un-known
1938									
Total	5,786	1,465	1,103	1,243	833	595	344	176	27
Men	3,680	877	668	749	528	420	267	156	15
Women	2,106	588	435	493	305	175	77	20	12
1939									
Total	5,945	1,985	1,103	1,126	762	519	296	145	8
Men	3,523	1,137	650	619	432	335	218	124	6
Women	2,423	848	453	507	330	184	78	21	2
1940									
Total	5,227	2,138	866	851	617	422	231	99	4
Men	3,080	1,264	499	450	341	270	168	85	3
Women	2,147	873	367	401	276	152	63	14	1
1941									
Total	6,678	3,174	932	961	760	498	260	91	1
Men	3,701	1,886	473	423	361	293	185	79	1
Women	2,976	1,288	459	537	398	206	75	12	0
1942									
Total	7,637	3,721	712	947	987	742	383	144	1
Men	3,547	2,013	226	266	336	342	241	122	1
Women	4,090	1,707	486	681	651	400	142	22	0
1943									
Total	7,297	3,634	577	876	917	711	402	178	1
Men	2,846	1,830	108	155	216	218	183	135	1
Women	4,451	1,804	469	721	701	493	220	43	0
1944									
Total	4,529	2,445	389	518	476	365	230	105	1
Men	1,826	1,213	97	109	116	115	100	74	0
Women	2,702	1,232	292	408	360	250	129	30	0
1945									
Total	3,321	1,852	317	402	313	231	142	65	0
Men	1,506	923	132	161	99	80	65	46	0
Women	1,816	929	185	240	214	151	77	19	0
1946									
Total	3,022	1,600	383	396	290	193	116	45	1
Men	1,432	747	236	195	99	70	53	31	0
Women	1,590	853	147	201	191	124	62	14	0
1947									
Total	2,728	1,620	293	269	240	170	99	36	0
Men	1,299	801	172	114	76	62	47	25	0
Women	1,429	819	121	155	164	108	51	10	0
1948									
Total	2,720	1,771	238	225	216	153	86	30	0
Men	1,305	912	123	90	64	53	40	22	0
Women	1,415	858	115	135	152	100	46	9	0
1949									
Total	2,340	1,518	209	198	192	130	69	23	0
Men	1,113	773	104	82	60	46	32	16	0
Women	1,226	745	105	116	132	84	37	7	0

a. Because of a slight lag between the time of receipt of applications and final processing, these data are not reconcilable with those in Appendix Table 67.

Source: Bureau of Old-Age and Survivors Insurance.

TABLE 69

Employment Status of Civilian Labor Force, Monthly, 1940–1950

(In Thousands)

Year and Month	Total Employment			Employment in Agriculture			Employment in Nonagricultural Industries: Self-Employed and Family Workers			Employment in Nonagricultural Industries: Wage and Salary Workers		
	Both Sexes	Male	Female	Both Sexes	Male	Female	Both Sexes	Male	Female	Both Sexes	Male	Female
1940												
March	46,100	34,180	11,920	8,750	8,050	700	5,040	3,940	1,100	32,310	22,190	10,120
April	46,640	34,640	12,000	9,410	8,440	970	5,210	4,050	1,160	32,020	22,150	9,870
May	47,600	35,490	12,110	10,450	9,020	1,430	5,540	4,280	1,260	31,610	22,190	9,420
June	49,020	36,620	12,400	11,520	9,300	2,220	5,950	4,610	1,340	31,550	22,710	8,840
July	48,850	36,880	11,970	10,980	9,490	1,490	6,630	5,040	1,590	31,240	22,350	8,890
August	48,930	36,990	11,940	10,320	9,010	1,310	6,330	4,680	1,650	32,280	23,300	8,980
September	49,480	36,900	12,580	10,790	8,950	1,840	6,400	4,820	1,580	32,290	23,130	9,160
October	48,590	36,360	12,230	10,020	8,610	1,410	5,730	4,280	1,450	32,840	23,470	9,370
November	47,700	36,030	11,670	8,490	8,060	430	5,830	4,290	1,540	33,380	23,680	9,700
December	47,550	35,880	11,670	8,150	7,680	470	5,600	4,030	1,570	33,800	24,170	9,630
Annual average [a]	47,520	35,550	11,970	9,540	8,450	1,090	5,690	4,320	1,370	32,290	22,780	9,510
1941												
January	46,580	35,270	11,310	7,720	7,360	360	5,940	4,400	1,540	32,920	23,510	9,410
February	46,940	35,520	11,420	7,690	7,320	370	5,890	4,450	1,440	33,360	23,750	9,610
March	47,160	35,580	11,580	7,890	7,510	380	5,890	4,430	1,460	33,380	23,640	9,740
April	48,600	36,360	12,240	8,950	7,920	1,030	5,840	4,490	1,350	33,810	23,950	9,860
May	50,310	37,080	13,230	9,970	8,150	1,820	5,940	4,520	1,420	34,400	24,410	9,990
June	51,930	38,350	13,580	10,780	8,660	2,120	6,080	4,640	1,440	35,070	25,050	10,020
July	52,260	38,760	13,500	10,340	8,560	1,780	6,210	4,680	1,530	35,710	25,520	10,190
August	52,510	38,790	13,720	9,840	8,150	1,690	6,180	4,680	1,500	36,490	25,960	10,530
September	52,270	38,290	13,980	9,900	7,890	2,010	6,130	4,630	1,500	36,240	25,770	10,470
October	52,110	38,160	13,950	9,450	7,700	1,750	6,040	4,580	1,460	36,620	25,880	10,740
November	51,850	38,020	13,830	8,820	7,530	1,290	5,930	4,460	1,470	37,100	26,030	11,070
December	51,710	38,030	13,680	7,810	7,130	680	5,960	4,470	1,490	37,940	26,430	11,510
Annual average	50,350	37,350	13,000	9,100	7,830	1,270	6,000	4,530	1,470	35,250	24,990	10,260
1942												
January	50,220	37,340	12,880	7,590	7,030	560	5,810	4,350	1,460	36,820	25,960	10,860
February	50,840	37,630	13,210	7,840	7,160	680	5,880	4,430	1,450	37,120	26,040	11,080
March	51,680	38,080	13,600	8,110	7,310	800	5,850	4,340	1,510	37,720	26,430	11,290
April	52,830	38,380	14,450	9,130	7,670	1,460	5,750	4,190	1,560	37,950	26,520	11,430
May	53,910	38,990	14,920	9,900	7,800	2,100	5,720	4,080	1,640	38,290	27,110	11,180
June	55,450	39,700	15,750	11,150	8,280	2,870	5,800	4,110	1,690	38,500	27,310	11,190
July	55,570	40,010	15,560	10,510	8,310	2,200	5,750	4,060	1,690	39,310	27,640	11,670
August	55,710	39,850	15,860	10,260	8,180	2,080	5,770	4,030	1,740	39,680	27,640	12,040
September	54,820	38,740	16,080	9,500	7,490	2,010	5,650	3,970	1,680	39,670	27,280	12,390
October	55,190	38,660	16,530	10,170	7,810	2,360	5,360	3,740	1,620	39,660	27,110	12,550
November	54,610	38,070	16,540	8,880	7,240	1,640	5,320	3,760	1,560	40,410	27,070	13,340
December	54,160	37,500	16,660	7,910	6,850	1,060	5,240	3,680	1,560	41,010	26,970	14,040
Annual average	53,750	38,580	15,170	9,250	7,600	1,650	5,660	4,060	1,600	38,840	26,920	11,920
1943												
January	53,220	36,720	16,500	7,680	6,590	1,090	5,160	3,600	1,560	40,380	26,530	13,850
February	53,140	36,370	16,770	7,680	6,600	1,080	5,200	3,640	1,560	40,260	26,130	14,130
March	53,220	36,160	17,060	7,890	6,720	1,170	5,240	3,660	1,580	40,090	25,780	14,310
April	53,850	36,250	17,600	8,780	7,040	1,740	5,210	3,670	1,540	39,860	25,540	14,320
May	55,130	36,530	18,600	10,090	7,490	2,600	5,050	3,550	1,500	39,990	25,490	14,500
June	56,280	36,880	19,400	10,970	7,850	3,120	5,080	3,570	1,510	40,230	25,460	14,770
July	56,290	37,020	19,270	10,380	7,720	2,660	5,160	3,550	1,610	40,750	25,750	15,000
August	56,110	36,980	19,130	10,420	7,730	2,690	5,210	3,630	1,580	40,480	25,620	14,860
September	55,160	36,040	19,120	10,020	7,260	2,760	5,240	3,660	1,580	39,900	25,120	14,780
October	54,330	35,660	18,670	9,210	7,030	2,180	5,250	3,660	1,590	39,870	24,970	14,900
November	53,840	35,540	18,300	8,450	6,810	1,640	5,010	3,510	1,500	40,380	25,220	15,160
December	53,080	35,120	17,960	7,450	6,410	1,040	5,010	3,530	1,480	40,620	25,180	15,440
Annual average	54,470	36,270	18,200	9,080	7,100	1,980	5,150	3,600	1,550	40,240	25,570	14,670

TABLE 69—Continued

Year and Month	Total Employment			Employment in Agriculture			Employment in Nonagricultural Industries: Self-Employed and Family Workers			Employment in Nonagricultural Industries: Wage and Salary Workers		
	Both Sexes	Male	Female	Both Sexes	Male	Female	Both Sexes	Male	Female	Both Sexes	Male	Female
1944												
January	52,560	35,000	17,560	7,300	6,320	980	5,020	3,540	1,480	40,240	25,140	15,100
February	52,320	34,950	17,370	7,310	6,480	830	5,030	3,540	1,490	39,980	24,930	15,050
March	52,520	34,840	17,680	7,610	6,670	940	5,090	3,560	1,530	39,820	24,610	15,210
April	53,590	35,410	18,180	8,340	7,070	1,270	5,080	3,540	1,540	40,170	24,800	15,370
May	54,540	35,350	19,190	9,830	7,480	2,350	5,010	3,490	1,520	39,700	24,380	15,320
June	55,760	35,850	19,910	10,800	7,780	3,020	5,090	3,570	1,520	39,870	24,500	15,370
July	55,770	35,790	19,980	10,540	7,730	2,810	5,200	3,640	1,560	40,030	24,420	15,610
August	54,960	35,660	19,300	9,310	7,220	2,090	5,280	3,710	1,570	40,370	24,730	15,640
September	54,490	34,960	19,530	9,670	7,140	2,530	5,250	3,680	1,570	39,570	24,140	15,430
October	54,530	34,870	19,660	9,850	7,180	2,670	5,160	3,640	1,520	39,520	24,050	15,470
November	53,770	34,490	19,280	9,120	6,800	2,320	5,060	3,560	1,500	39,590	24,130	15,460
December	52,710	34,180	18,530	7,760	6,370	1,390	5,190	3,640	1,550	39,760	24,170	15,590
Annual average	53,960	35,110	18,850	8,950	7,020	1,930	5,120	3,590	1,530	39,890	24,500	15,390
1945												
January	52,140	34,020	18,120	7,250	6,190	1,060	5,100	3,550	1,550	39,790	24,280	15,510
February	52,700	34,040	18,660	7,430	6,150	1,280	5,200	3,580	1,620	40,070	24,310	15,760
March	53,230	34,200	19,030	8,100	6,450	1,650	5,190	3,570	1,620	39,940	24,180	15,760
April	53,650	34,340	19,310	8,700	6,770	1,930	5,330	3,650	1,680	39,620	23,920	15,700
May	53,840	34,270	19,570	8,960	6,740	2,220	5,480	3,730	1,750	39,400	23,800	15,600
June	54,570	34,710	19,860	10,220	7,290	2,930	5,480	3,760	1,720	38,870	23,660	15,210
July	54,400	34,790	19,610	9,900	7,190	2,710	5,350	3,710	1,640	39,150	23,890	15,260
August	53,630	34,700	18,930	9,090	6,930	2,160	5,360	3,750	1,610	39,180	24,020	15,160
September	51,400	33,470	17,930	8,840	6,700	2,140	5,460	3,850	1,610	37,100	22,920	14,180
October	51,610	33,710	17,900	8,810	6,620	2,190	5,480	3,940	1,540	37,320	23,150	14,170
November	51,450	33,820	17,630	8,380	6,310	2,070	5,390	3,950	1,440	37,680	23,560	14,120
December	51,160	34,450	16,710	7,160	5,960	1,200	5,400	3,950	1,450	38,600	24,540	14,060
Annual average	52,820	34,210	18,610	8,580	6,610	1,970	5,350	3,750	1,600	38,890	23,850	15,040
1946												
January	51,020	35,390	15,630	6,720	5,840	880	5,350	4,010	1,340	38,950	25,540	13,410
February	51,240	35,750	15,490	6,940	6,010	930	5,380	4,060	1,320	38,920	25,680	13,240
March	52,460	36,680	15,780	7,530	6,370	1,160	5,480	4,150	1,330	39,450	26,160	13,290
April	54,120	37,990	16,130	8,170	6,810	1,360	5,570	4,260	1,310	40,380	26,920	13,460
May	54,850	38,590	16,260	8,880	7,100	1,780	5,720	4,360	1,360	40,250	27,130	13,120
June	56,360	39,650	16,710	10,010	7,610	2,400	5,960	4,540	1,420	40,390	27,500	12,890
July	57,840	40,950	16,890	9,970	7,810	2,160	6,310	4,800	1,510	41,560	28,340	13,220
August	57,690	40,980	16,710	9,140	7,320	1,820	6,430	4,940	1,490	42,120	28,720	13,400
September	57,050	40,270	16,780	8,750	6,790	1,960	6,550	5,080	1,470	41,750	28,400	13,350
October	57,030	40,270	16,760	8,620	6,770	1,850	6,520	5,100	1,420	41,890	28,400	13,490
November	57,040	40,430	16,610	7,900	6,380	1,520	6,570	5,110	1,460	42,570	28,940	13,630
December	56,310	40,300	16,010	7,210	6,290	920	6,440	4,980	1,460	42,660	29,030	13,630
Annual average	55,250	38,940	16,310	8,320	6,760	1,560	6,020	4,610	1,410	40,910	27,570	13,340
1947												
January	55,390	39,910	15,480	6,500	5,850	650	6,460	4,990	1,470	42,430	29,070	13,360
February	55,520	40,090	15,430	6,920	6,260	660	6,380	4,920	1,460	42,220	28,910	13,310
March	56,060	40,590	15,470	7,240	6,560	680	6,460	4,950	1,510	42,360	29,080	13,280
April	56,700	40,900	15,800	7,860	6,930	930	6,340	4,880	1,460	42,500	29,090	13,410
May	58,330	41,750	16,580	8,960	7,410	1,550	6,550	4,990	1,560	42,820	29,350	13,470
June	60,055	42,753	17,302	10,377	8,024	2,353	6,626	5,064	1,562	43,052	29,666	13,386
July	60,079	43,071	17,008	10,066	8,134	1,932	6,523	4,963	1,560	43,492	29,975	13,517
August	59,569	43,022	16,547	8,975	7,570	1,405	6,431	4,930	1,501	44,161	30,520	13,641
September	58,872	42,158	16,714	8,727	6,955	1,772	6,472	5,035	1,437	43,674	30,168	13,506
October	59,204	42,260	16,944	8,622	6,920	1,702	6,452	5,067	1,385	44,132	30,273	13,859
November	58,595	41,972	16,623	7,985	6,649	1,336	6,367	4,984	1,383	44,242	30,339	13,903
December	57,947	41,653	16,294	6,962	6,169	793	6,591	5,073	1,518	44,392	30,410	13,982
Annual average	58,021	41,677	16,344	8,270	6,955	1,314	6,470	4,980	1,490	43,290	29,740	13,550

TABLE 69—Continued

Year and Month	Total Employment			Employment in Agriculture			Employment in Nonagricultural Industries: Self-Employed and Family Workers			Employment in Nonagricultural Industries: Wage and Salary Workers		
	Both Sexes	Male	Female	Both Sexes	Male	Female	Both Sexes	Male	Female	Both Sexes	Male	Female
1948												
January	57,149	41,273	15,876	7,060	6,254	806	6,418	5,000	1,418	43,672	30,019	13,653
February	57,139	41,137	16,002	6,771	6,091	680	6,378	4,949	1,429	43,991	30,097	13,894
March	57,329	41,244	16,085	6,847	6,181	666	6,352	4,915	1,437	44,131	30,148	13,983
April	58,330	41,801	16,529	7,448	6,450	998	6,588	5,097	1,491	44,295	30,255	14,040
May	58,660	42,058	16,602	7,861	6,673	1,188	6,458	5,034	1,424	44,341	30,352	13,989
June	61,296	43,420	17,876	9,396	7,257	2,139	6,528	5,084	1,444	45,372	31,078	14,294
July	61,615	43,989	17,626	9,163	7,356	1,807	6,713	5,071	1,642	45,739	31,562	14,176
August	61,245	43,889	17,356	8,444	7,053	1,391	6,703	5,080	1,623	46,097	31,756	14,341
September	60,312	42,850	17,462	8,723	6,890	1,833	6,663	5,059	1,604	44,928	30,901	14,027
October	60,134	42,763	17,371	8,627	6,747	1,880	6,585	5,008	1,577	44,921	31,008	13,913
November	59,893	42,551	17,342	7,961	6,472	1,489	6,488	4,940	1,548	45,443	31,139	14,304
December	59,434	42,162	17,272	7,375	6,171	1,204	6,601	5,003	1,598	45,458	30,988	14,470
Annual average	59,378	42,428	16,950	7,973	6,633	1,340	6,540	5,020	1,520	44,866	30,775	14,090
1949												
January	57,414	41,150	16,264	6,763	5,957	806	6,452	4,961	1,491	44,200	30,233	13,967
February	57,168	40,812	16,356	6,993	6,123	870	6,453	4,939	1,514	43,720	29,750	13,970
March	57,647	41,092	16,555	7,393	6,470	923	6,457	4,959	1,498	43,797	29,663	14,134
April	57,819	41,463	16,356	7,820	6,749	1,071	6,554	5,000	1,554	43,445	29,714	13,731
May	58,694	41,521	17,173	8,974	7,109	1,865	6,493	4,880	1,513	43,327	29,531	13,796
June	59,619	42,223	17,386	9,696	7,438	2,258	6,618	5,061	1,557	43,306	29,735	13,571
July	59,720	42,422	17,298	9,647	7,623	2,024	6,590	4,941	1,649	43,483	29,858	13,625
August	59,947	42,644	17,303	8,507	7,095	1,412	6,656	5,075	1,581	44,785	30,474	14,311
September	59,411	42,085	17,326	8,158	6,565	1,593	6,667	5,029	1,638	44,586	30,491	14,095
October	59,001	41,426	17,575	7,710	6,302	1,408	6,705	5,043	1,662	44,586	30,081	14,505
November	59,518	41,783	17,735	7,878	6,299	1,579	6,780	5,129	1,651	44,861	30,356	14,505
December	58,556	41,293	17,263	6,773	5,924	849	6,916	5,161	1,755	44,867	30,208	14,659
Annual average	58,710	41,660	17,049	8,026	6,638	1,388	6,604	5,015	1,589	44,080	30,008	14,072
1950												
January	56,947	40,453	16,494	6,198	5,573	625	6,542	4,936	1,606	44,207	29,944	14,263
February	56,953	40,343	16,610	6,223	5,645	578	6,577	4,992	1,585	44,155	29,707	14,448
March	57,551	40,877	16,675	6,675	5,987	688	6,399	4,881	1,518	44,478	30,009	14,469
April	58,668	41,492	17,176	7,195	6,272	923	6,441	4,967	1,474	45,032	30,254	14,778
May	59,731	42,186	17,545	8,062	6,589	1,473	6,498	5,031	1,467	45,171	30,565	14,606
June	61,482	43,229	18,253	9,046	7,013	2,033	6,543	5,029	1,514	45,893	31,187	14,706
July	61,214	43,582	17,632	8,440	6,977	1,463	6,893	5,324	1,569	45,882	31,282	14,600
August	62,367	44,154	18,213	8,160	6,699	1,461	6,472	4,948	1,524	47,736	32,507	15,229
September	61,226	43,244	17,982	7,811	6,367	1,444	6,318	4,897	1,421	47,097	31,981	15,116
October	61,764	43,096	18,668	8,491	6,589	1,902	6,372	4,928	1,444	46,900	31,578	15,322
November	61,271	42,710	18,561	7,551	6,156	1,395	6,377	4,834	1,543	47,345	31,721	15,624
December	60,308	42,076	18,232	6,234	5,491	743	6,244	4,735	1,509	47,831	31,850	19,981
Annual average	59,957	42,287	17,670	7,507	6,280	1,227	6,473	4,959	1,514	45,977	31,049	14,929

a. Estimated for 12 months.

Sources: "Monthly Report on the Labor Force," *Current Population Reports,* Series P-57, Bureau of the Census; "Annual Report on the Labor Force," *Current Population Reports,* Series P-50, Bureau of the Census.

TABLE 70

EMPLOYEES IN NONAGRICULTURAL ESTABLISHMENTS, BY INDUSTRY DIVISION, ANNUAL AVERAGE, 1929–1950 [a]

(In Millions)

Period	Total	Manu-facturing	Mining	Contract Con-struction	Trans-portation and Public Utilities	Trade	Finance	Services	Govern-ment [b]
1929	31.9	10.4	1.0	1.5	3.9	5.8	1.3	5.0	2.9
1930	30.0	9.3	0.9	1.4	3.7	5.5	1.3	4.8	3.1
1931	27.0	7.9	0.8	1.2	3.2	5.1	1.3	4.5	3.2
1932	23.8	6.7	0.7	0.9	2.8	4.5	1.2	4.0	3.1
1933	24.3	7.2	0.7	0.7	2.6	4.4	1.1	3.9	3.6
1934	27.5	8.4	0.8	0.8	2.7	5.0	1.2	4.2	4.5
1935	28.9	8.9	0.8	0.9	2.7	5.2	1.2	4.4	4.8
1936	31.9	9.6	0.9	1.1	2.9	5.6	1.2	4.7	5.8
1937	33.1	10.6	1.0	1.1	3.1	6.0	1.3	4.9	5.2
1938	31.5	9.1	0.9	1.1	2.8	5.9	1.3	4.7	5.8
1939	33.0	10.0	0.8	1.2	2.9	6.1	1.3	4.9	5.8
1940	34.8	10.9	0.9	1.3	3.0	6.5	1.3	5.2	5.7
1941	38.2	13.1	1.0	1.8	3.2	6.9	1.4	5.2	5.6
1942	40.7	15.3	1.0	2.1	3.4	6.8	1.4	5.3	5.6
1943	42.2	17.4	0.9	1.6	3.5	6.6	1.3	5.1	5.8
1944	41.5	17.0	0.9	1.1	3.7	6.6	1.3	5.0	5.7
1945	39.8	15.2	0.8	1.1	3.8	6.9	1.3	5.0	5.7
1946	41.4	14.5	0.9	1.7	4.0	8.1	1.5	5.2	5.3
1947	43.2	15.2	0.9	2.1	4.0	8.6	1.6	5.5	5.1
1948	44.3	15.3	1.0	2.3	4.1	8.8	1.6	5.6	5.2
1949	42.8	14.2	0.9	2.1	3.9	8.7	1.6	5.6	5.5
1950	44.3	15.0	0.9	2.3	3.9	8.9	1.7	5.9	5.6

a. Full-time employment equivalent, excluding armed forces, but including work relief.
b. Federal (excluding armed forces), state and local, including government enterprises and work relief.

Source: Survey of Current Business, National Income Supplement, 1951 edition, pp. 180–81.

TABLE 71

Employees in Manufacturing Establishments, by Industry, Monthly, 1939–1950 [a]

(*In Thousands*)

No.	Industry [b] and Year	January	February	March	April	May	June	July	August	September	October	November	December	No.
	All manufacturing													
1	1939	9,535	9,671	9,787	9,787	9,732	9,775	9,817	10,117	10,489	10,780	10,746	10,694	1
2	1940	10,453	10,475	10,439	10,343	10,298	10,353	10,411	10,830	11,182	11,405	11,523	11,647	2
3	1941	11,603	11,874	12,113	12,394	12,648	12,967	13,275	13,540	13,784	13,847	13,821	13,817	3
4	1942	13,740	13,971	14,184	14,391	14,576	14,791	15,143	15,519	15,800	15,956	16,128	16,415	4
5	1943	16,570	16,816	17,037	17,129	17,181	17,431	17,618	17,736	17,696	17,777	17,858	17,722	5
6	1944	17,587	17,581	17,447	17,235	17,105	17,116	17,091	17,085	16,888	16,758	16,695	16,747	6
7	1945	16,753	16,801	16,728	16,528	16,292	16,061	15,693	15,343	13,414	13,307	13,367	13,331	7
8	1946	13,524	12,798	13,510	14,147	14,235	14,493	14,681	15,062	15,245	15,303	15,541	15,642	8
9	1947	15,677	15,783	15,826	15,750	15,569	15,672	15,580	15,962	16,175	16,209	16,256	16,354	9
10	1948	16,267	16,183	16,269	15,950	15,892	16,115	16,172	16,441	16,697	16,597	16,455	16,278	10
11	1949	14,782	14,649	14,475	14,177	13,877	13,884	13,757	14,114	14,312	13,892	13,807	14,031	11
12	1950	13,980	13,997	14,103	14,162	14,413	14,666	14,777	15,450	15,685	15,827	15,758	15,765	12
	Durable goods													
13	1939	4,066	4,118	4,171	4,210	4,203	4,230	4,179	4,233	4,473	4,736	4,808	4,858	13
14	1940	4,755	4,725	4,724	4,716	4,741	4,779	4,746	4,922	5,158	5,350	5,493	5,590	14
15	1941	5,645	5,792	5,937	6,132	6,314	6,515	6,668	6,733	6,906	7,021	7,068	7,094	15
16	1942	7,134	7,270	7,432	7,612	7,803	8,026	8,265	8,517	8,692	8,910	9,114	9,367	16
17	1943	9,561	9,768	9,967	10,086	10,168	10,344	10,464	10,518	10,544	10,663	10,764	10,713	17
18	1944	10,643	10,620	10,528	10,387	10,294	10,258	10,186	10,131	9,952	9,833	9,772	9,796	18
19	1945	9,842	9,869	9,806	9,652	9,453	9,189	8,883	8,548	6,729	6,617	6,641	6,492	19
20	1946	6,615	5,758	6,370	6,962	7,057	7,230	7,383	7,580	7,698	7,751	7,865	7,887	20
21	1947	7,949	8,030	8,071	8,068	7,962	8,050	7,874	7,987	8,070	8,126	8,194	8,274	21
22	1948	8,250	8,167	8,258	8,164	8,114	8,122	8,165	8,188	8,294	8,318	8,299	8,228	22
23	1949	8,044	7,923	7,819	7,656	7,441	7,392	7,255	7,302	7,409	6,986	7,050	7,303	23
24	1950	7,342	7,324	7,418	7,548	7,809	7,964	7,978	8,294	8,423	8,618	8,658	8,701	24
	Nondurable goods													
25	1939	5,469	5,553	5,616	5,577	5,529	5,545	5,638	5,884	6,016	6,044	5,938	5,836	25
26	1940	5,698	5,750	5,715	5,627	5,557	5,574	5,665	5,908	6,024	6,055	6,030	6,057	26
27	1941	5,958	6,082	6,176	6,262	6,334	6,452	6,607	6,807	6,878	6,826	6,753	6,723	27
28	1942	6,606	6,701	6,752	6,779	6,773	6,765	6,878	7,002	7,108	7,046	7,014	7,048	28
29	1943	7,009	7,048	7,070	7,043	7,013	7,087	7,154	7,218	7,152	7,114	7,094	7,009	29
30	1944	6,944	6,961	6,919	6,848	6,811	6,858	6,905	6,954	6,936	6,925	6,923	6,951	30
31	1945	6,911	6,932	6,922	6,876	6,839	6,872	6,810	6,795	6,685	6,690	6,726	6,839	31
32	1946	6,909	7,040	7,140	7,185	7,178	7,263	7,298	7,482	7,547	7,552	7,676	7,755	32
33	1947	7,728	7,753	7,755	7,682	7,607	7,622	7,706	7,975	8,105	8,083	8,062	8,080	33
34	1948	8,011	8,016	8,011	7,786	7,778	7,993	8,007	8,253	8,403	8,279	8,156	8,050	34
35	1949	6,738	6,726	6,656	6,521	6,436	6,492	6,502	6,819	6,903	6,906	6,757	6,728	35
36	1950	6,638	6,673	6,685	6,614	6,604	6,702	6,799	7,156	7,262	7,209	7,100	7,064	36

TABLE 71—Continued

No.	Industry [b] and Year	January	February	March	April	May	June	July	August	September	October	November	December	No.
	Iron and steel and their products (D) [b]													
37	1939	1,078	1,093	1,109	1,114	1,111	1,115	1,114	1,146	1,194	1,298	1,340	1,337	**37**
38	1940	1,305	1,286	1,256	1,239	1,242	1,271	1,301	1,348	1,380	1,420	1,451	1,478	**38**
39	1941	1,489	1,523	1,551	1,581	1,620	1,667	1,699	1,721	1,732	1,729	1,724	1,727	**39**
40	1942	1,742	1,767	1,788	1,803	1,815	1,836	1,849	1,858	1,862	1,879	1,901	1,940	**40**
41	1943	1,983	2,007	2,030	2,037	2,031	2,036	2,035	2,040	2,039	2,051	2,066	2,057	**41**
42	1944	2,048	2,049	2,031	2,012	2,006	2,018	2,019	2,023	2,002	1,990	1,983	1,997	**42**
43	1945	2,013	2,037	2,041	2,025	2,012	1,964	1,896	1,819	1,527	1,529	1,544	1,584	**43**
44	1946	1,608	1,140	1,567	1,659	1,648	1,678	1,722	1,772	1,800	1,788	1,832	1,820	**44**
45	1947	1,856	1,865	1,875	1,875	1,861	1,871	1,854	1,884	1,892	1,896	1,908	1,922	**45**
46	1948	1,925	1,920	1,929	1,897	1,894	1,904	1,897	1,928	1,945	1,955	1,952	1,936	**46**
	Electrical machinery (D)													
47	1939	328	329	332	332	334	340	346	354	372	397	404	398	**47**
48	1940	387	382	382	385	389	395	399	414	426	440	451	464	**48**
49	1941	471	490	506	527	551	571	591	608	617	622	626	631	**49**
50	1942	628	640	651	661	665	673	690	715	739	768	792	814	**50**
51	1943	833	858	886	893	898	911	926	929	940	954	967	968	**51**
52	1944	972	982	983	979	975	979	973	969	961	951	940	935	**52**
53	1945	936	941	945	936	930	920	892	870	642	673	683	678	**53**
54	1946	665	482	518	616	672	694	703	722	743	762	775	785	**54**
55	1947	785	791	789	745	731	759	742	745	752	763	772	773	**55**
56	1948	767	763	756	742	717	726	714	716	725	731	735	730	**56**
57	1949	834	818	795	770	746	725	712	712	734	753	750	762	**57**
58	1950	762	772	779	791	800	810	817	853	872	915	928	932	**58**
	Machinery, except electrical (D)													
59	1939	647	666	678	683	682	682	680	681	689	710	736	751	**59**
60	1940	760	774	782	787	786	790	792	799	805	819	847	878	**60**
61	1941	908	930	958	1,015	1,050	1,084	1,108	1,124	1,134	1,145	1,153	1,173	**61**
62	1942	1,196	1,226	1,256	1,279	1,295	1,324	1,345	1,370	1,387	1,418	1,445	1,474	**62**
63	1943	1,502	1,529	1,554	1,568	1,583	1,600	1,605	1,607	1,606	1,616	1,626	1,622	**63**
64	1944	1,622	1,610	1,597	1,563	1,554	1,561	1,550	1,538	1,520	1,508	1,499	1,513	**64**
65	1945	1,533	1,545	1,542	1,527	1,511	1,502	1,475	1,439	1,251	1,241	1,248	1,254	**65**
66	1946	1,291	1,165	1,217	1,296	1,341	1,375	1,399	1,428	1,453	1,479	1,504	1,516	**66**
67	1947	1,532	1,540	1,552	1,565	1,561	1,558	1,519	1,552	1,560	1,565	1,569	1,589	**67**
68	1948	1,583	1,591	1,587	1,562	1,568	1,577	1,571	1,564	1,569	1,569	1,563	1,561	**68**
69	1949	1,481	1,458	1,431	1,385	1,327	1,285	1,241	1,229	1,236	1,223	1,209	1,232	**69**
70	1950	1,238	1,261	1,283	1,307	1,328	1,347	1,343	1,374	1,368	1,426	1,458	1,491	**70**

TABLE 71—Continued

No.	Industry [b] and Year	January	February	March	April	May	June	July	August	September	October	November	December	No.
	Transportation equipment, except automobiles (D)													
71	1939	154	165	168	176	186	192	194	194	203	216	228	242	**71**
72	1940	247	258	269	273	284	295	313	337	357	383	407	431	**72**
73	1941	459	485	510	546	579	623	676	716	783	850	902	967	**73**
74	1942	1,074	1,197	1,301	1,428	1,545	1,667	1,816	1,967	2,081	2,203	2,314	2,443	**74**
75	1943	2,554	2,666	2,768	2,843	2,898	2,989	3,051	3,066	3,087	3,141	3,183	3,168	**75**
76	1944	3,131	3,125	3,087	3,043	2,988	2,932	2,882	2,831	2,749	2,700	2,667	2,660	**76**
77	1945	2,651	2,620	2,549	2,455	2,309	2,139	2,023	1,886	1,052	894	783	732	**77**
78	1946	706	635	620	656	642	629	624	613	598	597	602	611	**78**
79	1947	614	611	608	612	598	594	527	530	540	552	578	591	**79**
80	1948	598	589	589	589	565	562	561	542	572	583	588	585	**80**
81	1949	473	473	472	474	476	448	443	417	430	419	414	411	**81**
82	1950	400	402	401	402	407	412	413	439	452	471	492	513	**82**
	Automobiles (D)													
83	1939	495	487	486	479	447	440	379	355	474	511	487	549	**83**
84	1940	539	528	533	524	515	496	408	426	544	604	631	634	**84**
85	1941	632	643	655	664	677	686	655	584	649	675	685	638	**85**
86	1942	575	512	497	506	544	574	608	634	662	684	709	738	**86**
87	1943	761	778	789	796	807	828	850	872	898	919	932	931	**87**
88	1944	929	923	912	899	886	874	864	867	856	839	834	841	**88**
89	1945	856	859	856	852	825	800	769	718	582	618	691	507	**89**
90	1946	548	552	592	809	789	822	863	894	939	925	920	905	**90**
91	1947	899	938	942	957	899	939	941	926	960	964	961	983	**91**
92	1948	989	914	985	979	964	918	984	953	985	982	973	985	**92**
93	1949	794	772	776	778	727	776	799	807	810	789	697	708	**93**
94	1950	797	690	699	720	862	893	884	908	913	923	878	884	**94**
	Nonferrous metals and their products (D) [b]													
95	1939	267	270	273	273	272	269	267	276	289	311	316	317	**95**
96	1940	310	306	304	301	301	304	306	324	340	355	367	371	**96**
97	1941	374	384	390	396	400	407	412	419	423	429	428	427	**97**
98	1942	430	436	443	441	445	451	457	466	471	477	484	493	**98**
99	1943	500	506	506	509	512	522	528	534	538	548	554	546	**99**
100	1944	545	541	532	520	517	515	509	507	499	490	487	488	**100**
101	1945	492	501	508	509	510	499	476	468	385	386	401	406	**101**
102	1946	412	355	389	414	424	443	462	477	482	489	495	500	**102**
103	1947	502	506	504	498	486	475	462	463	468	472	479	482	**103**
104	1948	473	478	482	475	467	469	457	465	469	473	474	468	**104**

TABLE 71—CONTINUED

No.	Industry [b] and Year	January	February	March	April	May	June	July	August	September	October	November	December	No.
	Lumber and timber basic products (D)													
105	1939	423	423	425	444	458	467	470	484	490	503	502	486	**105**
106	1940	462	458	460	465	474	475	478	502	515	522	525	519	**106**
107	1941	513	523	535	552	564	585	617	634	639	642	620	611	**107**
108	1942	597	599	602	607	614	625	636	645	628	616	608	598	**108**
109	1943	572	569	578	587	592	605	614	612	592	588	587	575	**109**
110	1944	561	561	564	560	565	572	583	588	573	567	569	563	**110**
111	1945	559	560	557	547	553	553	549	547	527	498	505	517	**111**
112	1946	538	547	564	591	613	636	648	677	679	693	707	705	**112**
113	1947	707	715	731	750	780	798	793	821	821	827	828	829	**113**
114	1948	816	813	827	833	851	881	912	930	930	918	908	875	**114**
115	1949	726	714	719	719	733	747	736	747	743	750	751	746	**115**
116	1950	702	713	728	753	784	803	812	845	853	849	840	817	**116**
	Furniture and finished lumber products (D)													
117	1939	356	366	370	367	369	374	379	388	400	416	419	412	**117**
118	1940	398	393	392	387	389	390	386	400	414	423	424	426	**118**
119	1941	416	426	432	437	446	457	467	474	473	472	473	470	**119**
120	1942	456	461	461	450	446	442	436	432	432	435	430	434	**120**
121	1943	430	432	433	429	425	427	430	433	426	429	431	428	**121**
122	1944	425	422	419	412	409	413	414	416	407	405	406	410	**122**
123	1945	413	418	418	414	415	419	414	411	381	386	403	422	**123**
124	1946	437	448	456	465	466	480	485	500	503	511	522	533	**124**
125	1947	542	552	554	546	537	541	534	549	557	565	573	578	**125**
126	1948	580	581	576	561	548	550	542	552	558	562	562	549	**126**
127	1949	325	320	316	311	301	298	295	305	319	327	326	332	**127**
128	1950	333	341	344	347	348	349	350	367	376	378	376	373	**128**
	Stone, clay and glass products (D)													
129	1939	318	319	330	342	344	351	350	355	362	374	376	366	**129**
130	1940	347	340	346	355	361	363	363	372	377	384	390	389	**130**
131	1941	383	388	400	414	427	435	443	453	456	457	457	450	**131**
132	1942	436	432	433	437	434	434	428	430	430	430	431	433	**132**
133	1943	426	423	423	424	422	426	425	425	418	417	418	418	**133**
134	1944	410	407	403	399	394	394	392	392	385	383	387	389	**134**
135	1945	389	388	390	387	388	393	389	390	382	392	383	392	**135**
136	1946	410	434	447	456	462	473	477	497	501	507	508	512	**136**
137	1947	512	512	516	520	509	515	502	517	520	522	526	527	**137**
138	1948	520	518	527	526	530	535	527	538	541	545	544	539	**138**
139	1949	504	498	492	484	482	478	469	480	482	478	477	479	**139**
140	1950	469	475	478	489	501	511	512	532	532	544	551	547	**140**

TABLE 71—CONTINUED

No.	Industry [b] and Year	January	February	March	April	May	June	July	August	September	October	November	December	No.
	Textile mill products and other fiber manufactures (ND)													
141	1939	1,209	1,223	1,217	1,190	1,189	1,181	1,202	1,234	1,243	1,308	1,328	1,291	**141**
142	1940	1,258	1,251	1,193	1,166	1,150	1,134	1,163	1,192	1,219	1,257	1,289	1,308	**142**
143	1941	1,302	1,328	1,342	1,357	1,377	1,394	1,406	1,407	1,399	1,402	1,400	1,402	**143**
144	1942	1,388	1,389	1,390	1,394	1,387	1,385	1,379	1,368	1,357	1,361	1,366	1,380	**144**
145	1943	1,368	1,373	1,370	1,356	1,332	1,340	1,327	1,311	1,291	1,294	1,298	1,296	**145**
146	1944	1,272	1,277	1,267	1,245	1,230	1,226	1,211	1,204	1,197	1,195	1,202	1,214	**146**
147	1945	1,209	1,200	1,192	1,170	1,160	1,166	1,146	1,142	1,143	1,147	1,154	1,207	**147**
148	1946	1,224	1,258	1,280	1,290	1,295	1,312	1,299	1,315	1,332	1,398	1,369	1,384	**148**
149	1947	1,388	1,395	1,388	1,368	1,342	1,325	1,305	1,320	1,341	1,368	1,391	1,409	**149**
150	1948	1,413	1,428	1,435	1,425	1,416	1,418	1,364	1,397	1,384	1,371	1,368	1,357	**150**
151	1949	1,288	1,279	1,240	1,188	1,175	1,170	1,145	1,179	1,220	1,256	1,272	1,275	**151**
152	1950	1,265	1,273	1,272	1,261	1,252	1,264	1,250	1,316	1,347	1,357	1,356	1,350	**152**
	Apparel and other finished textile products (ND)													
153	1939	834	899	928	905	865	848	831	923	949	952	907	888	**153**
154	1940	880	931	949	896	855	825	813	906	945	943	935	938	**154**
155	1941	934	991	1,016	1,016	1,008	997	1,004	1,060	1,078	1,066	1,039	1,028	**155**
156	1942	1,011	1,070	1,090	1,087	1,072	1,104	1,015	1,072	1,074	1,079	1,063	1,064	**156**
157	1943	1,077	1,103	1,121	1,117	1,093	1,085	1,072	1,073	1,056	1,060	1,058	1,047	**157**
158	1944	1,047	1,058	1,064	1,046	1,038	1,055	1,031	1,057	1,054	1,069	1,068	1,069	**158**
159	1945	1,056	1,062	1,066	1,053	1,038	1,033	982	1,009	1,017	1,036	1,040	1,049	**159**
160	1946	1,063	1,099	1,119	1,119	1,109	1,127	1,091	1,136	1,153	1,166	1,159	1,174	**160**
161	1947	1,187	1,217	1,220	1,167	1,137	1,141	1,141	1,222	1,251	1,287	1,277	1,305	**161**
162	1948	1,311	1,333	1,334	1,268	1,247	1,263	1,235	1,329	1,348	1,353	1,338	1,324	**162**
163	1949	1,129	1,171	1,166	1,121	1,070	1,073	1,055	1,155	1,198	1,199	1,146	1,159	**163**
164	1950	1,146	1,180	1,174	1,119	1,091	1,093	1,097	1,208	1,218	1,221	1,179	1,186	**164**
	Leather and leather products (ND)													
165	1939	378	395	400	387	363	370	392	398	391	386	369	371	**165**
166	1940	381	388	383	368	343	346	367	373	374	376	370	383	**166**
167	1941	392	405	412	409	402	412	424	425	419	418	412	419	**167**
168	1942	415	422	429	423	417	413	410	402	392	393	400	402	**168**
169	1943	402	400	397	380	383	380	377	372	361	361	362	359	**169**
170	1944	357	360	360	358	355	356	355	353	351	352	354	356	**170**
171	1945	356	356	355	352	351	355	352	353	343	353	360	370	**171**
172	1946	380	393	408	405	408	412	411	412	416	415	420	428	**172**
173	1947	429	430	430	424	411	414	417	429	435	438	442	446	**173**
174	1948	445	448	442	418	414	419	421	429	425	421	408	409	**174**
175	1949	396	400	399	389	373	380	383	397	395	390	373	385	**175**
176	1950	388	395	396	379	374	382	390	409	411	406	398	396	**176**

TABLE 71—CONTINUED

No.	Industry [b] and Year	January	February	March	April	May	June	July	August	September	October	November	December	No.
	Food (ND)													
177	1939	1,104	1,082	1,093	1,111	1,135	1,182	1,244	1,337	1,370	1,272	1,207	1,172	**177**
178	1940	1,126	1,122	1,122	1,130	1,144	1,202	1,248	1,329	1,337	1,291	1,227	1,211	**178**
179	1941	1,151	1,138	1,149	1,178	1,211	1,273	1,358	1,460	1,490	1,413	1,364	1,331	**179**
180	1942	1,290	1,280	1,265	1,273	1,291	1,337	1,444	1,518	1,606	1,490	1,430	1,410	**180**
181	1943	1,360	1,338	1,330	1,325	1,338	1,387	1,464	1,548	1,552	1,489	1,456	1,430	**181**
182	1944	1,397	1,392	1,386	1,387	1,395	1,434	1,516	1,549	1,553	1,507	1,477	1,461	**182**
183	1945	1,426	1,419	1,404	1,404	1,406	1,428	1,485	1,496	1,567	1,504	1,479	1,478	**183**
184	1946	1,469	1,477	1,477	1,475	1,470	1,480	1,570	1,647	1,640	1,570	1,635	1,648	**184**
185	1947	1,612	1,585	1,588	1,609	1,622	1,666	1,785	1,922	1,964	1,833	1,769	1,735	**185**
186	1948	1,688	1,658	1,655	1,562	1,610	1,786	1,903	1,957	2,069	1,931	1,840	1,787	**186**
187	1949	1,439	1,414	1,406	1,410	1,436	1,501	1,585	1,718	1,703	1,631	1,540	1,491	**187**
188	1950	1,432	1,409	1,420	1,432	1,461	1,519	1,617	1,718	1,739	1,643	1,572	1,528	**188**
	Tobacco manufactures (ND)													
189	1939	99	104	99	103	105	106	107	109	109	110	108	107	**189**
190	1940	97	101	104	104	102	106	103	105	107	108	108	106	**190**
191	1941	100	104	103	104	106	107	107	107	105	109	111	110	**191**
192	1942	104	107	106	105	102	104	105	108	109	110	111	111	**192**
193	1943	108	106	105	105	102	101	101	100	100	101	102	102	**193**
194	1944	100	99	94	95	94	95	95	94	95	96	97	98	**194**
195	1945	95	95	95	95	93	93	91	92	96	99	96	94	**195**
196	1946	93	94	94	98	98	99	98	99	100	102	104	105	**196**
197	1947	104	103	100	95	96	97	97	99	100	103	104	102	**197**
198	1948	101	101	100	99	97	98	96	99	101	103	103	100	**198**
199	1949	96	95	92	90	90	91	89	98	101	99	95	93	**199**
200	1950	92	88	85	83	83	82	82	89	96	96	91	90	**200**
	Paper and allied products (ND)													
201	1939	305	306	311	309	310	310	312	319	328	344	344	339	**201**
202	1940	330	326	325	324	331	333	334	336	338	339	342	343	**202**
203	1941	338	343	350	357	364	373	380	387	392	394	395	396	**203**
204	1942	390	389	389	388	382	375	365	361	361	365	370	376	**204**
205	1943	378	383	384	385	387	393	394	395	389	392	396	396	**205**
206	1944	395	394	393	389	387	387	389	387	381	383	386	390	**206**
207	1945	388	390	389	385	384	389	386	386	387	397	402	412	**207**
208	1946	420	427	433	440	444	449	446	452	454	460	468	472	**208**
209	1947	473	475	475	473	470	470	462	469	470	476	479	484	**209**
210	1948	482	479	480	476	476	477	476	479	487	491	493	491	**210**
211	1949	463	456	451	442	437	434	429	436	448	456	458	455	**211**
212	1950	451	453	455	458	459	467	465	479	488	491	499	501	**212**

TABLE 71—CONTINUED

No.	Industry [b] and Year	January	February	March	April	May	June	July	August	September	October	November	December	No.
	Printing, publishing and allied industries (ND)													
213	1939	558	557	559	558	560	555	556	557	564	566	567	573	**213**
214	1940	564	563	562	559	560	555	556	559	559	566	568	573	**214**
215	1941	564	564	564	565	567	563	572	573	576	583	583	591	**215**
216	1942	578	570	562	558	553	548	548	545	544	552	561	567	**216**
217	1943	554	557	549	541	540	545	552	550	541	548	557	558	**217**
218	1944	555	556	555	550	545	549	551	547	541	549	551	555	**218**
219	1945	552	555	555	553	556	562	563	568	571	587	600	609	**219**
220	1946	617	631	640	647	648	656	662	667	671	682	690	700	**220**
221	1947	696	700	699	702	703	705	706	710	713	720	726	732	**221**
222	1948	726	724	722	718	718	719	716	720	725	735	734	738	**222**
223	1949	729	726	723	722	725	725	716	719	728	735	734	738	**223**
224	1950	730	732	734	735	736	739	739	741	746	754	758	762	**224**
	Chemicals and allied products (ND)													
225	1939	412	414	425	427	413	399	400	396	431	449	447	444	**225**
226	1940	442	444	451	455	445	440	445	457	476	494	501	502	**226**
227	1941	507	519	532	550	553	561	571	586	607	625	633	641	**227**
228	1942	662	689	719	744	756	771	783	793	817	831	839	840	**228**
229	1943	853	865	875	885	878	885	885	883	881	884	872	833	**229**
230	1944	834	842	819	803	792	783	786	794	803	812	819	834	**230**
231	1945	847	864	869	869	860	854	828	784	707	690	690	690	**231**
232	1946	692	695	703	705	694	695	692	702	718	729	744	749	**232**
233	1947	756	761	765	764	761	748	752	750	763	773	777	778	**233**
234	1948	774	773	773	767	759	762	751	775	785	789	790	788	**234**
235	1949	700	693	691	675	654	642	630	636	654	665	661	661	**235**
236	1950	658	665	671	675	671	670	669	684	701	720	720	723	**236**
	Products of petroleum and coal (ND)													
237	1939	142	140	142	142	144	147	147	150	152	155	154	151	**237**
238	1940	149	149	150	150	151	154	155	158	159	159	160	158	**238**
239	1941	157	157	158	158	161	165	168	169	169	168	168	168	**239**
240	1942	166	167	169	170	170	172	173	173	172	169	168	168	**240**
241	1943	167	166	166	166	169	170	172	174	172	173	173	173	**241**
242	1944	172	174	175	178	183	185	187	188	187	187	188	188	**242**
243	1945	188	190	192	193	193	195	197	198	193	192	202	202	**243**
244	1946	207	204	212	214	216	219	223	226	225	225	222	224	**244**
245	1947	225	225	227	227	232	235	237	238	238	237	239	237	**245**
246	1948	238	237	238	238	242	245	247	246	245	240	242	240	**246**
247	1949	247	246	245	246	246	246	246	247	247	241	244	243	**247**
248	1950	242	242	241	234	236	239	241	254	251	252	254	254	**248**

TABLE 71—CONTINUED

No.	Industry[b] and Year	January	February	March	April	May	June	July	August	September	October	November	December	No.
	Rubber products (ND)													
249	1939	143	144	146	145	145	143	142	148	154	164	166	164	**249**
250	1940	159	156	154	151	149	149	150	153	158	163	166	170	**250**
251	1941	172	176	179	183	186	193	194	195	195	196	196	194	**251**
252	1942	178	176	177	172	172	177	185	191	196	202	208	215	**252**
253	1943	220	222	224	224	225	229	234	236	237	237	242	244	**253**
254	1944	247	249	251	246	246	245	245	246	244	245	248	251	**254**
255	1945	254	254	254	250	246	243	240	236	208	229	237	247	**255**
256	1946	253	255	261	262	262	265	256	264	270	277	281	282	**256**
257	1947	280	279	277	274	262	257	250	252	252	257	259	261	**257**
258	1948	259	257	253	246	243	243	240	245	246	248	249	246	**258**
259	1949	251	246	243	238	233	230	224	227	209	234	234	235	**259**
260	1950	234	236	237	238	241	247	249	258	265	269	273	274	**260**
	Miscellaneous industries (ND)													
261	1939	285	289	296	300	300	304	305	313	325	338	341	336	**261**
262	1940	312	319	322	324	327	330	331	340	352	359	364	365	**262**
263	1941	341	357	371	385	399	414	423	438	448	452	452	443	**263**
264	1942	424	442	456	465	471	469	471	471	480	494	498	515	**264**
265	1943	522	535	549	559	566	572	576	576	572	575	578	571	**265**
266	1944	568	560	555	551	546	543	539	535	530	530	533	535	**266**
267	1945	540	547	551	552	552	554	540	531	453	456	466	481	**267**
268	1946	491	506	520	530	534	549	550	552	568	578	581	589	**268**
269	1947	578	583	586	579	571	564	554	564	578	591	599	590	**269**
270	1948	574	578	579	569	566	563	558	577	582	597	591	570	**270**
271	1949	439	434	426	414	404	403	384	417	439	457	456	438	**271**
272	1950	420	429	433	435	434	439	430	471	493	510	509	498	**272**
	Metallic industries, 1949													
273	Ordnance and accessories	28	28	28	27	26	25	24	23	23	23	22	22	**273**
274	Primary metal industries	1,257	1,245	1,229	1,195	1,158	1,135	1,095	1,092	1,097	703	887	1,114	**274**
275	Fabricated metal products, except ordnance, machinery and transportation equipment	932	917	890	867	843	836	826	843	863	829	820	841	**275**
276	Instruments and related products	251	246	245	242	238	236	231	230	233	235	234	234	**276**

a. Estimates include all full- and part-time wage and salary workers in manufacturing industries who worked or received pay during the pay period ending nearest the 15th of the month.

b. The classification of industries in 1949 differs from that in the preceding years. The most important changes were made in the classification of metal industries: the distinction between "iron and steel and their products" and "nonferrous metals and their products" has been replaced by the distinction between "primary metal industries" and "fabricated metal products, except ordnance, machinery and transportation equipment." Also, two new groups of metal industries have been formed: "ordnance and accessories" and "instruments and related products." The data for the four groups in 1949 are shown at the bottom of the table.

Source: Monthly Labor Review, Bureau of Labor Statistics.

TABLE 72

Pattern of Seasonal Variation in Employment before World War II

(Deviation from Lowest Level during Year, in Thousands)

Industry	January	February	March	April	May	June	July	August	September	October	November	December
Agriculture												
Hired labor	0	0	150	400	650	1,050	1,450	1,250	1,250	1,300	850	400
Family labor	0	0	100	300	500	900	1,250	900	850	750	200	100
Mining												
Bituminous coal	43	41	38	11	9	7	0	10	21	26	36	40
Anthracite	21	22	14	13	14	7	2	0	14	21	22	22
Metals	1	1	1	1	1	1	0	1	1	2	2	2
Quarrying	0	0	3	9	12	13	14	15	15	14	11	5
Crude petroleum	0	0	1	3	5	6	8	8	5	7	6	5
Manufacturing												
Durable goods												
Iron and steel	0	17	22	23	21	16	2	11	18	22	16	7
Machinery	0	10	16	17	13	10	2	4	14	20	13	8
Transportation equipment	0	77	83	91	88	56	36	47	34	66	61	55
Railroad repair shops	2	3	4	3	1	1	0	2	5	9	9	7
Nonferrous metals	13	17	14	11	6	3	0	6	14	23	27	20
Lumber	5	4	13	28	35	42	43	51	59	61	51	29
Stone, glass, clay	0	5	15	27	34	36	27	33	34	31	27	18
Nondurable goods												
Textile	76	86	80	59	38	23	0	6	30	58	69	76
Apparel	28	56	68	55	33	19	0	26	45	47	28	26
Leather	13	20	22	14	6	0	10	21	23	19	6	3
Food	15	11	10	19	23	59	108	170	224	153	86	49
Tobacco	0	7	7	4	6	8	6	6	10	13	13	10
Paper and printing	9	9	9	6	5	2	0	1	6	12	15	16
Chemicals	25	27	31	30	12	5	6	9	24	31	31	29
Building construction												
Bad years	0	0	75	225	375	525	600	675	675	600	450	225
Active years	0	0	125	375	625	875	1,000	1,125	1,125	1,000	750	375
Transportation and utilities												
Steam railroads	0	0	12	40	70	83	97	101	97	97	61	14
Electric railroads	0	0	1	2	3	4	6	5	4	4	2	1
Telephone	5	2	1	2	3	4	7	7	7	4	1	0
Electric light and power	2	0	0	2	5	6	8	11	11	11	9	6
Trade												
Wholesale	13	10	6	5	2	0	5	11	21	27	27	27
Retail	117	54	81	158	180	176	23	0	162	252	279	589
Warehousing	4	3	1	0	0	1	2	9	18	26	18	11
Service industries	2	2	8	29	50	65	67	67	83	64	48	36

Source: Derived from the Calendar of the American Labor Market in W. S. Woytinsky, *Seasonal Variations in Employment in the United States,* Committee on Social Security, Social Science Research Council, Washington, 1939, pp. 75, 79, 82, 86, 88, 90.

TABLE 73

NUMBER OF ESTABLISHMENTS (REPORTING UNITS) COVERED BY OASI, BY INDUSTRY AND SIZE OF REPORTING UNIT, FIRST QUARTER OF 1948

No.	Industry [a]	Total	Size of Reporting Unit (Number of Employees) [b] 0–3	4–7	8–19	20–49	50–99	100–499	500–999	1,000 or More	No.
1	All industries	2,734,152	1,565,765	563,758	359,342	149,030	50,536	38,351	4,391	2,979	1
2	Agriculture	13,488	8,289	2,981	1,670	434	79	35	0	0	2
3	Mining	28,602	10,211	6,148	5,932	3,240	1,373	1,365	234	99	3
4	Contract construction	216,186	111,909	52,315	33,792	12,229	3,666	2,089	142	44	4
5	Manufacturing	271,107	73,397	52,894	59,425	40,922	19,558	20,076	2,788	2,047	5
6	Ordnance and accessories	113	29	10	27	22	9	4	3	9	6
7	Food and kindred products	37,414	9,455	7,802	9,001	5,825	2,643	2,348	221	119	7
8	Tobacco manufactures	1,067	452	148	141	91	61	131	23	20	8
9	Textile mill products	9,188	1,113	897	1,740	1,641	1,153	1,974	415	255	9
10	Apparel and other finished products made from fabrics and similar materials	32,731	6,799	4,792	7,469	7,694	3,410	2,410	133	24	10
11	Lumber and wood products, except furniture	42,392	12,766	11,170	10,431	4,723	1,908	1,302	80	12	11
12	Furniture and fixtures	9,947	2,931	1,883	2,196	1,473	696	683	57	28	12
13	Paper and allied products	4,150	407	386	770	926	604	859	137	61	13
14	Printing, publishing and allied industries	30,924	11,838	7,355	6,098	3,238	1,229	981	109	76	14
15	Chemicals and allied products	11,063	2,850	1,924	2,380	1,741	970	966	126	106	15
16	Products of petroleum and coal	1,415	240	170	251	246	176	234	41	57	16
17	Rubber products	1,030	200	126	199	137	88	168	56	56	17
18	Leather and leather products	5,695	1,134	783	1,157	999	612	868	114	28	18
19	Stone, clay and glass products	11,379	3,575	2,407	2,236	1,465	709	826	99	62	19
20	Blast furnaces, steel works and rolling mills	375	12	13	18	24	31	94	42	121	20
21	Iron and steel foundries	1,968	162	136	274	449	370	467	72	38	21
22	Smelting and refining of nonferrous metals and alloys	404	65	45	86	57	41	68	26	16	22
23	Rolling, drawing and alloying of nonferrous metals	327	36	37	53	61	34	54	16	36	23
24	Nonferrous foundries	1,787	436	337	436	315	119	119	16	9	24
25	Other metal industries	1,120	160	155	227	202	120	196	37	23	25
26	Metal products	17,166	4,534	3,033	3,638	2,666	1,362	1,533	258	122	26
27	Machinery	19,457	5,276	3,557	4,279	2,760	1,345	1,651	311	278	27
28	Electrical machinery, equipment and supplies	4,560	951	649	860	715	408	662	154	161	28
29	Motor vehicles and motor vehicle equipment	2,107	384	346	384	355	168	241	75	154	29
30	Aircraft and parts	396	77	61	70	60	43	43	14	28	30
31	Ship and boat building and repairing	1,494	517	285	250	176	93	121	17	35	31
32	Railroad equipment	317	43	49	71	69	19	34	8	24	32
33	Motorcycles, bicycles and parts	132	33	18	29	18	12	12	5	5	33
34	Other transportation equipment	315	85	69	74	49	30	7	1	0	34
35	Professional and scientific instruments	3,412	951	633	756	476	227	277	41	51	35
36	Miscellaneous manufacturing industries	17,282	5,906	3,578	3,824	2,249	868	743	81	33	36
37	Wholesale trade	248,066	113,358	57,563	47,501	20,608	5,937	2,883	161	55	37
38	Retail trade	944,009	558,622	224,364	113,425	34,345	8,325	4,253	388	287	38
39	Department stores	6,561	218	463	1,607	2,042	1,030	890	166	145	39
40	Mail-order houses, general merchandise	240	51	52	45	36	12	15	4	25	40
41	Limited-price variety stores	14,588	4,696	2,581	2,827	2,887	1,089	496	11	1	41
42	Dry goods stores	11,772	6,783	2,871	1,515	475	84	42	2	0	42
[illegible]	[illegible]	29,053	19,656	6,169	2,478	584	117	47	0	2	43

TABLE 73—CONTINUED

No.	Industry [a]	Total	Size of Reporting Unit (Number of Employees) [b] 0–3	4–7	8–19	20–49	50–99	100–499	500–999	1,000 or More	No.
	Retail trade—Continued										
44	Grocery stores, with and without meat	125,380	92,068	23,638	6,918	1,787	436	377	85	71	44
45	Meat and seafood markets	18,450	14,228	3,030	958	193	35	6	0	0	45
46	Fruit stores and vegetable markets	7,024	5,466	1,091	371	80	9	7	0	0	46
47	Candy, confectionery and nut stores	10,820	7,086	2,370	1,003	249	69	41	1	1	47
48	Dairy products stores and milk dealers	12,366	5,354	2,832	2,251	1,123	434	350	18	4	48
49	Liquor stores	12,613	10,223	1,893	407	79	10	1	0	0	49
50	Miscellaneous retail food	25,601	14,554	7,009	3,240	623	102	69	3	1	50
51	Motor vehicle dealers — new and used cars	35,614	6,877	9,690	12,348	5,457	1,045	197	0	0	51
52	Motor vehicle dealers — used cars only	8,197	5,384	1,896	773	127	14	3	0	0	52
53	Accessory, tire and battery dealers	13,905	8,068	3,386	1,867	426	89	61	7	1	53
54	Automotive dealers, not elsewhere classified	1,123	588	268	190	62	11	4	0	0	54
55	Men's and boys' clothing and furnishings stores	14,090	7,942	3,312	1,954	618	173	89	0	2	55
56	Women's ready-to-wear stores	20,652	9,741	4,945	3,865	1,425	424	222	23	7	56
57	Women's accessory and specialty stores	8,263	4,910	1,971	1,000	288	70	24	0	0	57
58	Children's specialty and infants' wear shops	2,911	2,034	556	234	77	10	0	0	0	58
59	Family clothing stores and clothing stores not further described	5,739	2,671	1,469	1,067	360	99	57	10	6	59
60	Shoe stores	13,498	6,836	3,774	2,147	607	85	47	2	0	60
61	Custom tailors	3,009	1,884	621	367	112	23	2	0	0	61
62	Other clothing	3,781	2,507	743	400	99	23	9	0	0	62
63	Furniture, home furnishings and equipment	30,679	15,959	7,962	4,792	1,489	297	173	6	1	63
64	Drug stores	44,207	20,741	15,493	6,322	1,269	241	115	18	8	64
65	Hardware and farm implements	32,526	18,960	9,000	3,820	615	93	36	1	1	65
66	Paint, glass and wallpaper stores	6,031	3,427	1,619	808	154	19	4	0	0	66
67	Electrical and gas household appliance stores and radio dealers	19,095	11,954	4,533	2,004	472	105	26	1	0	67
68	Second-hand stores, not elsewhere classified	1,725	1,418	235	62	9	1	0	0	0	68
69	Farm and garden supply stores	10,456	6,123	2,733	1,202	303	60	34	1	0	69
70	Fuel and ice dealers	19,195	10,177	4,864	3,079	835	180	59	1	0	70
71	Retail trade, not elsewhere classified	69,366	45,618	14,646	6,840	1,740	370	142	7	3	71
72	Eating and drinking places	222,619	119,877	61,985	31,514	7,247	1,393	576	20	7	72
73	Retail filling stations	82,860	64,543	14,664	3,150	396	73	32	1	1	73
74	Public utilities	102,791	49,236	21,189	16,750	8,643	3,423	2,852	377	321	74
75	Interstate railroads	20	11	1	6	1	0	1	0	0	75
76	Local railways and bus lines	1,974	573	346	377	287	158	179	25	29	76
77	Trucking and warehousing for hire	59,692	32,822	12,283	8,548	3,972	1,357	687	21	2	77
78	Bus lines other than city and suburban	1,714	531	300	352	247	142	130	10	2	78
79	Air transportation (common carrier)	644	111	110	137	110	68	71	21	16	79
80	Taxicabs	11,487	5,461	2,603	2,132	877	246	143	15	10	80
81	Pipeline transportation, except natural gas	369	70	81	67	57	47	39	4	4	81
82	Highway passenger transportation, not elsewhere classified	1,963	1,153	436	268	85	15	6	0	0	82
83	Miscellaneous transportation, unclassified	11	5	2	4	0	0	0	0	0	83
84	Water transportation	2,022	616	345	350	283	141	213	36	38	84
85	Services allied to transportation, not elsewhere classified	7,378	3,432	1,644	1,271	508	213	240	50	20	85
86	Communication: telephone, telegraph and related services	8,868	2,814	1,927	1,763	1,110	481	552	103	118	86
87	Utilities: electric and gas	4,504	543	603	1,137	977	510	563	90	81	87
88	Local utilities and local public services, not elsewhere classified	2,145	1,094	508	338	129	45	28	2	1	88

TABLE 73—CONTINUED

No.	Industry [a]	Total	Size of Reporting Unit (Number of Employees) [b] 0–3	4–7	8–19	20–49	50–99	100–499	500–999	1,000 or More	No.
89	Finance	226,181	155,851	35,702	21,572	8,432	2,550	1,846	147	81	**89**
90	Banks and trust companies	16,280	2,899	5,507	4,968	1,788	581	459	47	31	**90**
91	Security dealers and investment banking	4,698	2,373	948	751	381	165	78	1	1	**91**
92	Credit agencies, other than banks	15,589	8,393	4,316	2,081	577	147	73	2	0	**92**
93	Investment trusts and investment companies	933	686	148	67	23	5	3	1	0	**93**
94	Finance agencies, not elsewhere classified	615	360	121	83	27	12	11	0	1	**94**
95	Insurance carriers	15,552	6,134	2,450	2,909	2,421	754	752	85	47	**95**
96	Insurance agents, brokers and services	28,181	20,743	4,568	2,006	593	163	107	1	0	**96**
97	Real estate	143,405	113,666	17,460	8,625	2,592	704	347	10	1	**97**
98	Holding companies, except real estate holding companies	928	597	184	82	30	19	16	0	0	**98**
99	Service industries	631,668	444,903	102,355	56,113	19,632	5,534	2,933	153	45	**99**
100	Hotels	22,461	10,119	5,169	3,855	1,728	744	751	76	19	**100**
101	Rooming and boarding houses	8,299	6,832	1,042	346	60	9	10	0	0	**101**
102	Camps	6,646	4,892	1,213	448	79	13	1	0	0	**102**
103	Other lodging places	110	62	19	11	10	8	0	0	0	**103**
104	Laundries and laundry services	14,877	5,313	2,334	2,520	2,599	1,374	727	6	4	**104**
105	Cleaning and dyeing plants	11,843	3,026	3,492	3,557	1,365	302	100	1	0	**105**
106	Photographic studios, including commercial photography	7,752	5,466	1,434	615	175	45	17	0	0	**106**
107	Barber and beauty shops	72,855	61,924	8,704	1,864	312	42	8	1	0	**107**
108	Shoe repair shops and shoeshine parlors, including hat cleaning	10,080	8,345	1,308	363	55	9	0	0	0	**108**
109	Funeral service, including crematories	10,863	7,482	2,447	801	116	12	5	0	0	**109**
110	Cleaning, pressing, alteration, and garment repair shops	29,263	20,418	6,228	2,180	377	55	5	0	0	**110**
111	Other personal services	4,644	3,365	863	288	108	10	10	0	0	**111**
112	Business services, not elsewhere classified	53,955	31,864	10,788	7,136	2,865	792	467	34	9	**112**
113	Employment agencies and commercial and trade schools	4,805	2,350	1,198	879	276	71	30	1	0	**113**
114	Automobile repair services and garages	65,164	45,542	13,167	5,358	951	115	30	1	0	**114**
115	Miscellaneous repair services and hand trades	35,111	24,831	6,663	2,867	616	101	29	3	1	**115**
116	Motion pictures	14,155	3,104	3,288	4,794	2,284	494	169	13	9	**116**
117	Amusement and recreation and related services, not elsewhere classified	35,143	17,157	8,335	6,518	2,433	526	171	3	0	**117**
118	Medical and other health services	111,536	99,084	8,261	2,910	904	252	121	3	1	**118**
119	Law offices and related services	45,505	40,594	3,451	1,157	222	55	26	0	0	**119**
120	Educational institutions and agencies	3,626	2,047	815	498	189	57	19	1	0	**120**
121	Other professional and social service agencies and institutions	13,143	7,828	2,823	1,634	607	143	101	6	1	**121**
122	Nonprofit membership organizations	49,480	32,941	9,294	5,501	1,298	305	136	4	1	**122**
123	Private households	352	317	19	13	3	0	0	0	0	**123**
124	Not elsewhere classified	8,923	7,329	1,047	426	86	18	16	1	0	**124**
125	Unclassified	43,131	32,660	7,200	2,736	459	73	3	0	0	**125**

a. Data for manufacturing industries are classified according to the Standard Industrial Classification Manual prepared by the Bureau of the Budget in 1945. Data for nonmanufacturing industries are classified according to the Social Security Industrial Classification Code, prepared by the Federal Security Agency, 1942.

b. A reporting unit is an establishment or a group of establishments of the same firm engaged in the same activity and located in the same area, generally the same county. Size of reporting unit is measured by the number of persons employed in the unit during the pay period ending nearest the middle of March 1948. Although figures are shown to the last digit for tabulating purposes, they should not be considered accurate to the last digit. Figures in this table may differ slightly from similar data in other tables because of computing procedures.

Source: First quarter 1948 employer tabulations, Bureau of Old-Age and Survivors Insurance, based on employers' reports of taxable wages.

TABLE 74

ESTIMATED NUMBER OF EMPLOYEES IN ESTABLISHMENTS COVERED BY OASI, BY INDUSTRY AND SIZE OF REPORTING UNIT, FIRST QUARTER OF 1948 [a]

No.	Industry [b]	Total	Size of Reporting Unit (Number of Employees) [c] 0–3	4–7	8–19	20–49	50–99	100–499	500–999	1,000 or More	No.
1	All industries	35,805,000	2,571,375	2,887,474	4,266,023	4,493,342	3,465,788	7,619,322	3,012,380	7,489,296	1
2	Agriculture	70,481	13,392	14,898	18,711	12,346	5,501	5,633	—	—	2
3	Mining	955,034	17,325	32,228	73,350	99,795	94,763	294,793	161,603	181,177	3
4	Contract construction	2,030,360	194,516	269,305	398,363	366,603	250,743	381,156	97,828	71,846	4
5	Manufacturing	15,198,057	132,066	280,113	740,557	1,274,744	1,359,890	4,181,769	1,920,772	5,308,146	5
6	Ordnance and accessories	29,896	47	42	298	746	597	1,517	1,994	24,655	6
7	Food and kindred products	1,384,067	17,575	41,377	112,191	179,975	184,697	459,346	149,222	239,684	7
8	Tobacco manufactures	103,114	757	784	1,760	2,886	4,262	32,311	15,661	44,693	8
9	Textile mill products	1,396,127	2,011	4,861	22,863	52,017	81,875	452,001	283,406	497,093	9
10	Apparel and other finished products made from fabrics and similar materials	1,189,992	11,689	26,111	97,026	242,231	234,025	450,940	86,061	41,909	10
11	Lumber and wood products, except furniture	800,870	23,199	59,138	128,123	143,745	131,133	243,500	53,369	18,663	11
12	Furniture and fixtures	356,351	5,282	9,869	27,011	46,395	48,446	137,736	37,401	44,211	12
13	Paper and allied products	462,781	784	2,101	10,115	29,706	42,440	176,946	93,152	107,537	13
14	Printing, publishing and allied industries	720,746	21,528	38,692	73,672	98,749	83,968	193,263	76,268	134,606	14
15	Chemicals and allied products	703,493	5,051	9,859	29,554	55,048	67,408	200,441	88,340	247,792	15
16	Products of petroleum and coal	249,661	465	944	3,334	7,802	12,524	54,604	27,697	142,291	16
17	Rubber products	252,443	326	640	2,505	4,394	6,336	37,353	40,141	160,748	17
18	Leather and leather products	415,972	1,979	4,217	14,777	31,828	42,776	191,949	76,963	51,483	18
19	Stone, clay and glass products	506,370	6,607	12,663	27,367	45,447	49,805	178,425	66,892	119,164	19
20	Blast furnaces, steel works and rolling mills	597,429	24	88	236	795	2,165	25,522	28,571	540,028	20
21	Iron and steel foundries	262,991	321	766	3,696	14,727	25,725	103,590	49,701	64,465	21
22	Smelting and refining of nonferrous metals and alloys	70,040	127	229	1,091	1,798	2,893	15,990	19,069	28,843	22
23	Rolling, drawing and alloying of nonferrous metals	106,834	78	205	641	1,902	2,559	12,991	10,505	77,953	23
24	Nonferrous foundries	75,916	796	1,773	5,497	9,556	8,037	22,912	11,225	16,120	24
25	Other metal industries	176,893	311	902	3,139	7,546	11,217	63,781	37,241	52,756	25
26	Metal products	945,207	7,066	16,270	45,169	82,323	92,603	299,665	167,872	234,239	26
27	Machinery	1,550,071	9,371	18,774	53,107	86,579	94,362	361,090	218,305	708,483	27
28	Electrical machinery, equipment and supplies	858,103	1,710	3,388	10,654	22,606	28,935	151,960	107,906	530,944	28
29	Motor vehicles and motor vehicle equipment	780,866	700	1,804	4,842	11,182	11,984	55,238	54,846	640,270	29
30	Aircraft and parts	204,031	117	301	834	1,834	2,859	10,443	10,602	177,041	30
31	Ship and boat building and repairing	165,168	896	1,447	3,067	5,474	6,375	25,732	12,063	110,114	31
32	Railroad equipment	87,052	77	264	936	2,214	1,273	9,195	5,995	67,098	32
33	Motorcycles, bicycles and parts	17,718	45	101	337	578	859	3,021	4,016	8,761	33

TABLE 74—Continued

No.	Industry [b]	Total	Size of Reporting Unit (Number of Employees) [c] 0–3	4–7	8–19	20–49	50–99	100–499	500–999	1,000 or More	No.
	Manufacturing—Continued										
34	Other transportation equipment	6,650	138	349	850	1,496	2,058	1,033	726	—	34
35	Professional and scientific instruments	264,068	1,680	3,335	9,310	14,433	15,759	61,488	30,457	127,606	35
36	Miscellaneous manufacturing industries	457,137	10,309	18,819	46,555	68,732	59,935	147,786	56,105	48,896	36
37	Wholesale trade	2,799,573	197,594	299,789	571,730	618,137	402,370	509,671	103,873	96,409	37
38	Retail trade	6,722,442	963,160	1,145,531	1,315,360	1,008,585	561,624	790,934	266,122	671,126	38
39	Department stores	820,433	305	2,694	21,808	64,962	71,402	181,785	113,644	363,833	39
40	Mail-order houses, general merchandise	73,943	86	262	515	1,209	884	3,088	2,159	65,740	40
41	Limited-price variety stores	312,177	8,427	13,620	35,867	90,280	72,989	83,028	6,963	1,003	41
42	Dry goods stores	72,422	11,595	14,614	17,655	13,909	5,785	7,128	1,736	—	42
43	Other retail general merchandise	130,133	32,747	30,722	28,473	16,804	7,510	7,866	—	6,010	43
44	Grocery stores, with and without meat	720,779	151,534	116,099	77,681	52,200	29,893	79,119	59,040	155,213	44
45	Meat and seafood markets	56,680	22,626	14,965	10,621	5,339	2,388	741	—	—	45
46	Fruit stores and vegetable markets	22,095	8,596	5,361	4,177	2,126	633	1,202	—	—	46
47	Candy, confectionery and nut stores	57,352	11,772	11,995	11,403	7,280	4,721	8,286	501	1,394	47
48	Dairy products stores and milk dealers	201,525	9,246	14,839	27,012	34,618	29,816	66,308	12,712	6,974	48
49	Liquor stores	32,890	16,219	9,201	4,410	2,269	669	122	—	—	49
50	Miscellaneous retail food	138,544	25,600	36,102	36,309	18,026	6,572	12,988	1,900	1,047	50
51	Motor vehicle dealers — new and used cars	476,485	14,034	52,828	153,324	159,448	68,772	28,079	—	—	51
52	Motor vehicle dealers — used cars only	32,171	9,106	9,533	8,753	3,412	913	454	—	—	52
53	Accessory, tire and battery dealers	90,335	14,231	17,383	21,793	11,791	5,919	13,232	4,872	1,114	53
54	Automotive dealers, not elsewhere classified	7,555	972	1,344	2,177	1,838	754	470	—	—	54
55	Men's and boys' clothing and furnishings stores	102,082	14,160	17,082	22,545	18,382	11,845	15,684	—	2,384	55
56	Women's ready-to-wear stores	228,326	17,354	26,074	46,307	41,470	28,817	42,252	16,066	9,986	56
57	Women's accessory and specialty stores	47,660	8,523	9,975	11,461	8,219	4,694	4,788	—	—	57
58	Children's specialty and infants' wear shops	11,703	3,428	2,798	2,618	2,220	639	—	—	—	58
59	Family clothing stores and clothing stores not further described	69,751	4,789	7,673	12,559	10,493	6,937	10,907	6,648	9,745	59
60	Shoe stores	90,347	12,903	19,549	24,600	17,400	5,814	8,797	1,284	—	60
61	Custom tailors	15,666	3,067	3,235	4,262	3,230	1,594	278	—	—	61
62	Other clothing	33,457	3,964	3,790	4,553	2,883	1,593	1,676	—	—	62
63	Furniture, home furnishings and equipment	227,644	28,141	41,243	55,851	43,665	20,178	33,028	3,620	1,918	63
64	Drug stores	297,215	40,511	81,787	72,093	36,428	16,149	23,128	12,605	14,514	64
65	Hardware and farm implements	154,722	33,952	45,833	42,771	17,330	6,154	6,783	762	1,137	65
66	Paint, glass and wallpaper stores	29,429	5,983	8,368	9,137	4,163	1,198	580	—	—	66
67	Electrical and gas household appliance stores and radio dealers	91,918	20,283	22,973	22,701	13,950	7,013	4,385	613	—	67

TABLE 74—Continued

No.	Industry [b]	Total	Size of Reporting Unit (Number of Employees) [c] 0–3	4–7	8–19	20–49	50–99	100–499	500–999	1,000 or More	No.
	Retail trade—Continued										
68	Second-hand stores, not elsewhere classified	4,340	2,166	1,152	690	239	93	—	—	—	68
69	Farm and garden supply stores	58,437	10,656	13,954	13,676	8,836	3,906	6,735	674	—	69
70	Fuel and ice dealers	124,577	17,342	25,005	35,503	23,961	12,137	9,851	778	—	70
71	Retail trade, not elsewhere classified	337,677	75,072	74,341	78,051	50,659	24,825	24,781	5,896	4,052	71
72	Eating and drinking places	1,326,646	215,354	317,689	359,719	208,095	93,620	97,949	13,141	21,079	72
73	Retail filling stations	240,327	108,418	71,448	34,285	11,451	4,798	5,436	508	3,983	73
74	Public utilities	2,616,765	82,694	108,885	201,086	264,832	236,379	577,081	259,650	886,158	74
75	Interstate railroads	517	17	6	76	28	—	390	—	—	75
76	Local railways and bus lines	157,214	1,120	1,855	4,690	8,904	11,108	40,743	17,392	71,402	76
77	Trucking and warehousing for hire	564,068	54,593	62,704	101,906	120,506	92,480	115,914	13,587	2,378	77
78	Bus lines other than city and suburban	58,778	952	1,561	4,471	7,629	9,924	25,693	6,416	2,132	78
79	Air transportation (common carrier)	76,295	211	581	1,637	3,426	4,685	14,472	15,643	35,640	79
80	Taxicabs	151,007	8,936	13,374	25,059	25,945	16,985	28,155	9,844	22,709	80
81	Pipeline transportation, except natural gas	23,393	124	404	729	1,794	3,224	8,298	2,719	6,101	81
82	Highway passenger transportation, not elsewhere classified	12,069	1,988	2,223	3,151	2,306	1,035	1,366	—	—	82
83	Miscellaneous transportation, unclassified	66	10	11	45	—	—	—	—	—	83
84	Water transportation	184,566	1,055	1,788	4,408	8,973	9,913	48,490	25,723	84,216	84
85	Services allied to transportation, not elsewhere classified	186,938	5,896	8,449	14,928	15,633	14,906	50,329	33,257	43,540	85
86	Communication: telephone, telegraph and related services	686,829	4,890	10,083	21,329	34,777	33,491	116,418	69,368	396,473	86
87	Utilities: electric and gas	491,409	993	3,260	14,622	30,873	35,585	121,492	64,112	220,472	87
88	Local utilities and local public services, not elsewhere classified	23,616	1,909	2,586	4,035	4,038	3,043	5,321	1,589	1,095	88
89	Finance	1,740,995	233,349	182,787	255,937	252,189	173,839	353,906	99,882	189,106	89
90	Banks and trust companies	388,705	6,630	29,744	59,744	52,937	40,371	92,026	32,520	74,733	90
91	Security dealers and investment banking	57,890	3,996	4,934	8,943	12,101	11,450	14,287	830	1,349	91
92	Credit agencies, other than banks	101,444	14,904	22,243	23,795	17,159	9,909	12,290	1,144	—	92
93	Investment trusts and investment companies	4,832	1,045	750	822	752	315	378	770	—	93
94	Finance agencies, not elsewhere classified	7,318	583	596	1,020	863	804	1,713	—	1,739	94
95	Insurance carriers	503,530	10,396	13,093	37,472	74,471	51,401	149,876	57,277	109,544	95
96	Insurance agents, brokers and services	127,210	31,520	23,021	22,915	17,316	11,124	20,739	575	—	96
97	Real estate	541,879	163,259	87,510	100,307	75,682	47,237	59,377	6,766	1,741	97
98	Holding companies, except real estate holding companies	8,187	1,016	896	919	908	1,228	3,220	—	—	98

TABLE 74—CONTINUED

No.	Industry [b]	Total	Size of Reporting Unit (Number of Employees) [c] 0–3	4–7	8–19	20–49	50–99	100–499	500–999	1,000 or More	No.
99	Service industries	3,527,290	682,230	516,962	660,109	584,491	374,917	521,201	102,052	85,328	**99**
100	Hotels	420,729	17,245	26,569	45,845	52,083	51,629	147,108	51,801	28,449	**100**
101	Rooming and boarding houses	22,170	9,571	5,001	3,730	1,751	612	1,505	—	—	**101**
102	Camps	21,810	7,558	5,987	5,081	2,246	833	105	—	—	**102**
103	Other lodging places	1,109	92	95	130	269	523	—	—	—	**103**
104	Laundries and laundry services	359,806	9,161	12,182	32,155	83,615	94,185	120,294	3,881	4,333	**104**
105	Cleaning and dyeing plants	144,232	5,654	18,983	42,559	40,094	20,080	16,101	761	—	**105**
106	Photographic studios, including commercial photography	34,140	8,853	7,170	7,243	5,243	3,009	2,622	—	—	**106**
107	Barber and beauty shops	172,040	95,950	42,057	20,579	8,893	2,781	1,249	531	—	**107**
108	Shoe repair shops and shoeshine parlors, including hat cleaning	24,856	12,302	6,477	4,072	1,507	498	—	—	—	**108**
109	Funeral service, including crematories	38,494	12,716	12,197	8,671	3,277	832	801	—	—	**109**
110	Cleaning, pressing, alteration, and garment repair shops	103,538	33,242	31,209	24,131	10,513	3,609	834	—	—	**110**
111	Other personal services	18,784	5,626	4,221	3,288	3,119	661	1,879	—	—	**111**
112	Business services, not elsewhere classified	457,593	52,388	55,287	85,689	84,757	54,246	81,775	23,182	20,269	**112**
113	Employment agencies and commercial and trade schools	40,310	4,140	6,156	10,371	7,893	4,743	6,304	703	—	**113**
114	Automobile repair services and garages	241,631	75,510	66,141	59,863	26,553	7,620	5,357	587	—	**114**
115	Miscellaneous repair services and hand trades	137,389	39,261	33,225	32,452	17,450	6,659	4,920	2,106	1,316	**115**
116	Motion pictures	250,586	5,849	17,762	60,751	67,191	32,769	32,145	7,888	26,231	**116**
117	Amusement and recreation and related services, not elsewhere classified	290,608	29,043	43,543	78,840	72,371	34,801	30,136	1,874	—	**117**
118	Medical and other health services	275,713	134,820	40,581	33,383	27,086	17,042	19,326	1,580	1,895	**118**
119	Law offices and related services	98,532	54,758	16,967	12,966	6,348	3,788	3,705	—	—	**119**
120	Educational institutions and agencies	26,506	3,343	4,184	5,711	5,711	3,910	3,079	568	—	**120**
121	Other professional and social service agencies and institutions	97,713	12,932	14,279	18,862	18,114	9,723	18,230	4,117	1,456	**121**
122	Nonprofit membership organizations	248,341	51,832	46,629	63,600	38,338	20,364	23,726	2,473	1,379	**122**
123	Private households	660	384	60	147	69	—	—	—	—	**123**
124	Not elsewhere classified	26,658	9,800	5,165	4,792	2,607	1,073	2,623	598	—	**124**
125	Unclassified	117,345	45,249	31,811	26,028	9,013	4,689	555	—	—	**125**

a. Represents estimated employment during pay period ending nearest middle of March 1948 for employers who reported taxable wages under the OASI program for January–March 1948. Although figures are shown to the last digit for tabulating purposes, they should not be considered accurate to the last digit.

b. Data for manufacturing industries are classified according to the Standard Industrial Classification Manual prepared by the Bureau of the Budget in 1945. Data for nonmanufacturing industries are classified according to the Social Security Industrial Classification Codes, prepared by the Federal Security Agency in 1942.

c. A reporting unit is an establishment or a group of establishments of the same firm engaged in the same activity and located in the same area, generally the same county. Size of reporting unit is measured by the number of persons employed in the unit during the pay period ending nearest middle of March 1948.

Source: First quarter 1948 employer tabulations, Bureau of Old-Age and Survivors Insurance, based on employers' reports of taxable wages.

TABLE 75

ESTIMATED NUMBER OF EMPLOYERS (FIRMS) AND EMPLOYEES COVERED BY OASI, BY SIZE OF FIRM, SELECTED PERIODS, 1938–1948

Size of Firm (Number of Employees)	1938 Jan.–March	1939 July–Sept.	1940 July–Sept.	1942 July–Sept.	1945 Jan.–March	1946 Jan.–March	1947 Jan.–March	1948 Jan.–March
	Number, in Thousands							
Employers								
Total	1,880.0	2,065.0	2,167.0	2,119.0	2,001.0	2,280.0	2,487.0	2,590.0
0	30.5	33.4	31.9	36.6	23.3	29.2	40.4	42.4
1–3	1,132.6	1,213.3	1,235.2	1,287.2	1,174.3	1,288.0	1,415.7	1,488.5
4–7	364.4	411.4	447.9	402.4	404.0	482.1	519.6	537.2
8–19	204.0	232.8	259.8	222.4	233.4	293.3	314.8	325.0
20–49	90.0	104.2	115.6	95.7	100.5	115.9	121.6	122.3
50–99	30.1	35.7	39.3	34.4	34.0	38.1	39.6	39.3
100–999	26.6	32.1	35.0	36.9	28.7	30.8	32.2	32.3
100–499	23.9	28.8	31.4	a	25.6	27.7	28.9	29.0
500–999	2.7	3.3	3.6	a	3.2	3.1	3.3	3.3
1,000 or more	1.9	2.2	2.4	3.3	2.8	2.7	3.0	2.9
1,000–9,999	1.8	2.0	2.2	a	2.6	2.5	2.8	2.7
10,000 or more	0.1	0.1	0.1	a	0.2	0.2	0.2	0.2
Employees								
Total	23,288	26,794	28,916	34,178	32,803	32,483	35,057	35,805
0	0	0	0	0	0	0	0	0
1–3	1,815	1,902	1,905	2,126	1,949	2,194	2,382	2,497
4–7	1,808	1,967	2,087	2,020	2,078	2,507	2,650	2,739
8–19	2,346	2,571	2,784	2,568	2,759	3,496	3,704	3,832
20–49	2,609	2,918	3,142	2,825	3,018	3,483	3,599	3,662
50–99	1,994	2,281	2,435	2,287	2,322	2,611	2,676	2,690
100–999	6,355	7,425	7,872	9,350	7,502	7,738	8,051	8,060
100–499	4,572	5,341	5,666	a	5,269	5,581	5,782	5,779
500–999	1,783	2,085	2,206	a	2,233	2,157	2,269	2,281
1,000 or more	6,361	7,729	8,691	13,002	13,177	10,454	11,995	12,325
1,000–9,999	4,060	4,783	5,220	a	6,554	6,183	6,794	6,812
10,000 or more	2,301	2,946	3,470	a	6,623	4,270	5,201	5,513
	Percentage Distribution							
Employers								
Total	100.0	100.0	100.0	100.0	100.0	100.0	100.0	100.0
0	1.6	1.6	1.5	1.7	1.2	1.3	1.6	1.6
1–3	60.2	58.8	57.0	60.7	58.7	56.5	56.9	57.6
4–7	19.4	19.9	20.7	19.0	20.2	21.1	20.9	20.7
8–19	10.9	11.3	12.0	10.5	11.7	12.9	12.7	12.6
20–49	4.8	5.0	5.3	4.5	5.0	5.1	4.9	4.7
50–99	1.6	1.7	1.8	1.6	1.7	1.7	1.8	1.5
100–999	1.4	1.6	1.6	1.7	1.4	1.3	1.3	1.2
100–499	1.3	1.4	1.4	a	1.3	1.2	1.2	1.1
500–999	0.1	0.2	0.2	a	0.2	0.1	0.1	0.1
1,000 or more	0.1	0.1	0.1	0.2	0.1	0.1	0.1	0.1
1,000–9,999	0.1	0.1	0.1	a	0.1	0.1	0.1	0.1
10,000 or more	b	b	b	a	b	b	b	b
Employees								
Total	100.0	100.0	100.0	100.0	100.0	100.0	100.0	100.0
0	0	0	0	0	0	0	0	0
1–3	7.8	7.1	6.6	6.2	5.9	6.8	6.8	7.0
4–7	7.8	7.3	7.2	5.9	6.3	7.7	7.6	7.6
8–19	10.1	9.6	9.6	7.5	8.4	10.8	10.6	10.7
20–49	11.2	10.9	10.9	8.3	9.2	10.7	10.3	10.2
50–99	8.6	8.5	8.4	6.7	7.1	8.0	7.6	7.5
100–999	27.3	27.7	27.2	27.4	22.9	23.8	23.0	22.5
100–499	19.6	19.9	19.6	a	16.1	17.2	16.5	16.1
500–999	7.7	7.8	7.6	a	6.8	6.6	6.5	6.4
1,000 or more	27.3	28.8	30.0	38.0	40.2	32.3	34.2	34.4
1,000–9,999	17.4	17.9	18.1	a	20.0	19.1	19.4	19.0
10,000 or more	9.9	11.0	12.0	a	20.2	13.2	14.8	15.4

a. Data not available.
b. Less than 0.05 per cent.

Source: Bureau of Old-Age and Survivors Insurance.

TABLE 76

WORKERS WITH WAGE CREDITS UNDER OASI, BY SEX AND AGE, 1937–1947

Sex and Age	1937	1938	1939	1940	1941	1942	1943	1944	1945	1946	1947 [a]
	Number, in Thousands										
Total	32,904	31,822	33,751	35,393	40,976	46,363	47,656	46,296	46,392	48,845	48,900
Under 20	3,277	2,582	2,858	2,963	4,393	6,176	7,237	6,907	6,314	5,626	5,200
20–24	6,303	5,972	6,261	6,482	7,338	7,390	6,327	5,673	5,909	7,477	7,650
25–29	5,481	5,330	5,551	5,795	6,439	6,303	5,747	5,267	5,571	6,779	6,800
30–34	4,414	4,485	4,671	4,905	5,384	5,949	5,720	5,435	5,495	6,043	6,000
35–39	3,689	3,624	3,793	3,930	4,543	5,153	5,377	5,199	5,288	5,400	5,450
40–44	3,055	3,103	3,079	3,342	3,678	4,336	4,648	4,797	4,623	4,654	4,750
45–49	2,580	2,524	2,595	2,706	3,143	3,589	3,994	3,980	4,061	3,843	3,950
50–54	1,918	1,971	2,034	2,147	2,412	2,932	3,224	3,298	3,275	3,246	3,200
55–59	1,308	1,322	1,416	1,483	1,756	2,143	2,473	2,560	2,577	2,495	2,600
60–64	782	812	859	931	1,088	1,362	1,599	1,738	1,757	1,784	1,800
65 and over [b]...	97	97	634	709	802	1,030	1,310	1,442	1,522	1,498	1,500
Median age	32	32	32	33	32	33	34	35	35	34	34
Male	23,811	22,891	24,360	25,572	29,370	31,838	30,124	28,101	28,825	32,182	32,800
Under 20	2,020	1,552	1,744	1,821	2,769	3,683	3,987	3,632	3,345	2,935	2,800
20–24	4,021	3,709	3,932	4,072	4,562	4,235	2,815	1,968	2,298	4,077	4,450
25–29	3,797	3,671	3,859	4,029	4,465	4,142	3,303	2,728	3,055	4,374	4,500
30–34	3,237	3,267	3,382	3,546	3,857	4,131	3,659	3,348	3,502	4,190	4,200
35–39	2,776	2,724	2,824	2,922	3,331	3,619	3,518	3,322	3,486	3,684	3,750
40–44	2,387	2,399	2,346	2,550	2,769	3,123	3,153	3,235	3,150	3,188	3,250
45–49	2,091	2,020	2,073	2,151	2,479	2,708	2,834	2,778	2,840	2,690	2,750
50–54	1,606	1,637	1,688	1,770	1,973	2,319	2,415	2,428	2,409	2,393	2,350
55–59	1,110	1,123	1,198	1,265	1,494	1,779	1,959	1,986	1,984	1,923	2,000
60–64	681	704	743	807	947	1,170	1,321	1,417	1,429	1,440	1,450
65 and over [b]...	85	85	571	639	724	929	1,160	1,259	1,327	1,288	1,300
Median age	33	34	34	34	34	35	37	39	38	36	36
Female	9,093	8,931	9,391	9,821	11,606	14,525	17,532	18,195	17,567	16,663	16,100
Under 20	1,257	1,030	1,114	1,142	1,624	2,493	3,250	3,275	2,969	2,691	2,400
20–24	2,282	2,263	2,329	2,410	2,776	3,155	3,512	3,705	3,611	3,400	3,200
25–29	1,684	1,659	1,692	1,766	1,974	2,161	2,444	2,539	2,516	2,405	2,300
30–34	1,177	1,218	1,289	1,359	1,527	1,818	2,061	2,087	1,993	1,853	1,800
35–39	913	900	969	1,008	1,212	1,534	1,859	1,877	1,802	1,716	1,700
40–44	668	704	733	792	909	1,213	1,495	1,562	1,473	1,466	1,500
45–49	489	504	522	555	664	881	1,160	1,202	1,221	1,153	1,200
50–54	312	334	346	377	439	613	809	870	866	853	850
55–59	198	199	218	218	262	364	514	574	593	572	600
60–64	101	108	116	124	141	192	278	321	328	344	350
65 and over [b]...	12	12	63	70	78	101	150	183	195	210	200
Median age	28	29	29	29	29	29	29	29	29	30	30

TABLE 76—CONTINUED

Sex and Age	1937	1938	1939	1940	1941	1942	1943	1944	1945	1946	1947[a]
				Percentage Distribution							
Total	100.0	100.0	100.0	100.0	100.0	100.0	100.0	100.0	100.0	100.0	100.0
Under 20	10.0	8.1	8.5	8.4	10.7	13.3	15.2	14.9	13.6	11.5	10.6
20–24	19.2	18.8	18.6	18.3	17.9	15.9	13.3	12.3	12.7	15.3	15.6
25–29	16.7	16.7	16.4	16.4	15.7	13.6	12.1	11.4	12.0	13.9	13.9
30–34	13.4	14.1	13.8	13.9	13.1	12.8	12.0	11.7	11.8	12.4	12.3
35–39	11.2	11.4	11.2	11.1	11.1	11.1	11.3	11.2	11.4	11.1	11.1
40–44	9.3	9.8	9.1	9.4	9.0	9.4	9.8	10.4	10.0	9.5	9.7
45–49	7.8	7.9	7.7	7.6	7.7	7.7	8.4	8.6	8.8	7.9	8.1
50–54	5.8	6.2	6.0	6.1	5.9	6.3	6.8	7.1	7.1	6.6	6.5
55–59	4.0	4.2	4.2	4.2	4.3	4.6	5.2	5.5	5.6	5.1	5.3
60–64	2.4	2.6	2.5	2.6	2.7	2.9	3.4	3.8	3.8	3.7	3.7
65 and over[b]...	0.3	0.3	1.9	2.0	2.0	2.2	2.7	3.1	3.3	3.1	3.1
Male	100.0	100.0	100.0	100.0	100.0	100.0	100.0	100.0	100.0	100.0	100.0
Under 20	8.5	6.8	7.2	7.1	9.4	11.6	13.2	12.9	11.6	9.1	8.5
20–24	16.9	16.2	16.1	15.9	15.5	13.3	9.3	7.0	8.0	12.7	13.6
25–29	15.9	16.0	15.8	15.8	15.2	13.0	11.0	9.7	10.6	13.6	13.7
30–34	13.6	14.3	13.9	13.9	13.1	13.0	12.1	11.9	12.1	13.0	12.8
35–39	11.7	11.9	11.6	11.4	11.3	11.4	11.7	11.8	12.1	11.4	11.4
40–44	10.0	10.5	9.6	10.0	9.4	9.8	10.5	11.5	10.9	9.9	9.9
45–49	8.8	8.8	8.5	8.4	8.4	8.5	9.4	9.9	9.9	8.4	8.4
50–54	6.7	7.2	6.9	6.9	6.7	7.3	8.0	8.6	8.4	7.4	7.2
55–59	4.7	4.9	4.9	4.9	5.1	5.6	6.5	7.1	6.9	6.0	6.1
60–64	2.9	3.1	3.1	3.2	3.2	3.7	4.4	5.0	5.0	4.5	4.4
65 and over[b]...	0.4	0.4	2.3	2.5	2.5	2.9	3.9	4.5	4.6	4.0	4.0
Female	100.0	100.0	100.0	100.0	100.0	100.0	100.0	100.0	100.0	100.0	100.0
Under 20	13.8	11.5	11.9	11.6	14.0	17.2	18.5	18.0	16.9	16.1	14.9
20–24	25.1	25.3	24.8	24.5	23.9	21.7	20.0	20.4	20.6	20.4	19.9
25–29	18.5	18.6	18.0	18.0	17.0	14.9	13.9	14.0	14.3	14.4	14.3
30–34	12.9	13.6	13.7	13.8	13.2	12.5	11.8	11.5	11.3	11.1	11.2
35–39	10.0	10.1	10.3	10.3	10.4	10.6	10.6	10.3	10.3	10.3	10.6
40–44	7.3	7.9	7.8	8.1	7.8	8.4	8.5	8.6	8.4	8.8	9.3
45–49	5.4	5.6	5.6	5.7	5.7	6.1	6.6	6.6	7.0	6.9	7.5
50–54	3.4	3.7	3.7	3.8	3.8	4.2	4.6	4.8	4.9	5.1	5.3
55–59	2.2	2.2	2.3	2.2	2.3	2.5	2.9	3.2	3.4	3.4	3.7
60–64	1.1	1.2	1.2	1.3	1.2	1.3	1.6	1.8	1.9	2.1	2.2
65 and over[b]...	0.1	0.1	0.7	0.7	0.7	0.7	0.9	1.0	1.1	1.3	1.2

a. Preliminary.
b. For 1937 and 1938, represents workers aged 65 only; wages of workers over 65 years of age were not taxable in those years.
Source: Handbook of Old-Age and Survivors Insurance Statistics, 1947, Bureau of Old-Age and Survivors Insurance, 1950, p. 46.

TABLE 77

PERCENTAGE OF NEW ENTRANTS AMONG WORKERS WITH WAGE CREDITS UNDER OASI, BY SEX AND AGE, 1940, 1944 AND 1947

Age	Male 1940	Male 1944	Male 1947 [a]	Female 1940	Female 1944	Female 1947 [a]
All ages	10.0	7.3	4.1	14.4	15.5	8.1
Under 20	46.2	33.4	25.8	49.1	36.7	29.5
20–24	12.1	6.9	4.7	11.8	9.6	4.0
25–29	6.3	2.9	2.1	8.8	9.3	3.6
30–44	5.9	2.5	1.2	9.6	10.9	4.8
45–59	6.2	3.2	1.4	8.7	13.1	5.0
60–64	6.8	4.5	1.6	7.5	15.8	4.4
65 and over	8.4	7.2	2.1	8.0	14.7	3.7

a. Preliminary.

Source: Bureau of Old-Age and Survivors Insurance.

TABLE 78

PERCENTAGE DISTRIBUTION, BY NUMBER OF QUARTERS IN COVERED EMPLOYMENT, OF WORKERS WITH WAGE CREDITS UNDER OASI, CLASSIFIED BY SEX AND AGE, 1944 AND 1946

Age	Male Total	Male Quarters Employed 1	Male 2	Male 3	Male 4	Female Total	Female Quarters Employed 1	Female 2	Female 3	Female 4
1944										
All ages	100.0	12.3	10.7	10.3	66.6	100.0	16.7	16.0	14.5	52.9
Under 20	100.0	25.1	25.3	21.1	28.4	100.0	21.9	23.0	19.8	35.4
20–24	100.0	25.7	17.1	14.1	43.1	100.0	16.0	15.6	14.4	54.0
25–29	100.0	15.7	12.2	10.6	61.5	100.0	17.3	15.6	14.2	52.9
30–34	100.0	11.4	8.4	8.1	72.1	100.0	15.9	15.2	13.9	54.9
35–39	100.0	8.6	7.3	7.9	76.3	100.0	14.5	13.5	13.1	58.9
40–44	100.0	6.8	6.3	7.6	79.3	100.0	14.3	13.0	12.2	60.4
45–49	100.0	6.4	6.4	7.5	79.6	100.0	13.8	12.7	11.6	61.9
50–54	100.0	6.5	6.4	7.4	79.7	100.0	14.5	12.3	12.1	61.1
55–59	100.0	6.7	6.5	7.5	79.3	100.0	14.6[a]	12.9[a]	11.5[a]	61.0
60–64	100.0	8.0	7.5	8.7	75.8	100.0	15.6[a]	13.7[a]	10.6[a]	60.1
65–69	100.0	10.8[a]	9.4[a]	9.8[a]	69.9	100.0	16.3[a]	14.8[a]	10.4[a]	58.5[a]
70–74	100.0	13.6[a]	10.9[a]	11.2[a]	64.3	100.0	15.8[a]	13.2[a]	13.2[a]	57.9[a]
75 and over	100.0	15.2[a]	12.0[a]	10.4[a]	62.4[a]	100.0	20.0[a]	20.0[a]	10.0[a]	50.0[a]
1946										
All ages	100.0	12.8	12.7	13.4	61.1	100.0	18.1	16.7	14.6	50.7
Under 20	100.0	30.4	27.6	17.4	24.6	100.0	23.5	24.0	18.3	34.1
20–24	100.0	20.9	22.1	21.4	35.6	100.0	18.4	17.7	14.9	49.0
25–29	100.0	12.6	14.2	17.5	55.7	100.0	20.0	17.3	15.2	47.5
30–34	100.0	9.8	10.7	13.2	66.3	100.0	18.9	16.2	14.7	50.2
35–39	100.0	8.6	8.6	10.8	72.0	100.0	16.0	14.5	13.6	55.8
40–44	100.0	7.7	7.4	9.3	75.6	100.0	14.7	13.2	12.2	59.8
45–49	100.0	7.9	7.4	8.8	75.9	100.0	14.0	11.8	12.5	61.8
50–54	100.0	7.3	7.3	9.0	76.4	100.0	14.0	12.0	11.9	62.1
55–59	100.0	8.4	7.2	8.7	75.7	100.0	13.4[a]	11.7[a]	12.4[a]	62.5
60–64	100.0	8.7	7.6	9.8	73.8	100.0	12.8[a]	11.3[a]	11.3[a]	64.6
65–69	100.0	11.9[a]	10.8[a]	11.2[a]	66.1	100.0	13.4[a]	12.8[a]	11.4[a]	62.4[a]
70 and over	100.0	14.8[a]	12.9[a]	11.6[a]	60.7	100.0	14.5[a]	12.9[a]	11.3[a]	61.3[a]

a. Fewer than 100 persons in sample.

Source: Bureau of Old-Age and Survivors Insurance.

TABLE 79

PERCENTAGE DISTRIBUTION, BY NUMBER OF QUARTERS IN COVERED EMPLOYMENT, OF NEW ENTRANTS AND OTHER WORKERS WITH WAGE CREDITS UNDER OASI, CLASSIFIED BY SEX AND AGE, 1944

	Male					Female				
		Quarters Employed					Quarters Employed			
Age	Total	1	2	3	4	Total	1	2	3	4
	Workers without Previous Wage Credits									
All ages	100.0	40.8	31.1	18.4	9.7	100.0	39.9	32.0	18.8	9.4
Under 15	100.0	49.5	32.7	14.2	3.7	100.0	56.3	30.3	11.6	1.8
15–19	100.0	36.0	34.1	21.0	8.8	100.0	37.5	34.4	21.1	7.0
20–24	100.0	50.8	27.6	13.3	8.3	100.0	39.8	31.9	17.8	10.4
25–29	100.0	50.4	27.9	12.5	9.1	100.0	41.6	31.4	16.0	11.0
30–34	100.0	46.6	27.3	16.1	10.1	100.0	39.6	30.5	18.5	11.4
35–39	100.0	43.2	28.6	16.3	11.8	100.0	40.4	29.4	18.2	12.1
40–44	100.0	43.8	26.7	15.9	13.6	100.0	40.2	31.2	16.7	11.9
45–49	100.0	38.8	28.0	18.1	15.1	100.0	40.7	29.2	18.5	11.6
50–54	100.0	39.7	26.6	18.5	15.2	100.0	40.0	27.6	19.3	13.1
55–59	100.0	38.1	27.7	19.0	15.2	100.0	42.1	28.2	17.3	12.4
60–64	100.0	39.8	26.7	19.2	14.2	100.0	43.1	30.5	15.9	10.5
65–69	100.0	40.9	25.1	19.7	14.3	100.0	46.8	30.2	11.8	11.2
70–74	100.0	39.2	25.8	21.8	13.1	100.0	38.4	24.9	20.0	16.8
75 and over....	100.0	42.1	26.7	15.6	15.6	100.0	a	a	a	a
	Workers with Previous Wage Credits									
All ages	100.0	10.2	9.3	11.0	69.5	100.0	12.5	13.3	15.0	59.2
Under 15	100.0	26.3	25.4	21.8	26.4	100.0	25.9	28.5	22.9	22.7
15–19	100.0	18.2	21.2	22.5	38.2	100.0	12.0	16.8	20.1	51.1
20–24	100.0	23.9	16.5	15.2	44.4	100.0	13.5	14.2	15.3	57.0
25–29	100.0	14.7	11.9	11.8	61.7	100.0	14.8	14.2	15.2	55.8
30–34	100.0	10.6	8.2	9.2	72.0	100.0	13.2	13.4	14.7	58.7
35–39	100.0	7.9	6.9	8.8	76.3	100.0	11.5	11.7	13.8	62.9
40–44	100.0	5.8	5.9	8.7	79.5	100.0	11.1	11.0	13.1	64.8
45–49	100.0	5.4	6.0	8.7	79.9	100.0	10.1	10.5	12.6	66.8
50–54	100.0	5.6	5.9	8.6	79.9	100.0	10.7	10.2	12.6	66.5
55–59	100.0	5.7	5.9	8.7	79.6	100.0	10.0	10.3	12.5	67.2
60–64	100.0	6.7	6.7	9.8	76.8	100.0	10.5	10.5	12.3	66.8
65–69	100.0	9.0	8.6	10.7	71.7	100.0	11.8	11.7	11.7	64.8
70–74	100.0	11.6	11.1	14.0	63.3	100.0	13.1	12.6	14.0	60.4
75 and over....	100.0	13.2	12.1	13.0	61.7	100.0	14.9	14.9	13.7	56.4

a. Not computed; base includes fewer than 100 persons.

Source: Bureau of Old-Age and Survivors Insurance.

TABLE 80

Percentage of Workers with Wage Credits under OASI Who Did Not Receive Wage Credits in the Following Year, by Sex and Age, 1940–1945

Sex and Age	1940	1941	1942	1943	1944	1945
Total [a]	11.4	12.9	18.6	18.6	16.6	18.3
Under 20	12.7	11.8	18.9	25.6	23.0	25.0
20–24	14.5	20.2	32.8	29.8	23.8	22.4
25–29	11.6	16.3	23.8	21.7	20.7	19.3
30–34	9.8	11.3	18.9	17.2	14.7	16.3
35–39	9.0	9.0	13.0	14.5	13.0	15.4
40–44	9.1	8.4	11.2	10.9	11.7	14.5
45–49	9.1	7.9	9.8	11.2	11.5	14.7
50–54	9.5	8.9	10.2	12.0	11.4	14.6
55–59	10.2	9.4	10.9	12.2	11.9	14.5
60–64	12.7	10.9	12.5	12.9	12.8	16.2
65–69	22.3	18.8	17.6	18.3	17.1	24.1
70 and over	27.6	24.3	21.8	23.6	24.3	29.6
Male [a]	9.8	11.3	19.3	18.5	14.6	14.9
Under 20	11.9	11.4	23.2	33.9	28.4	30.1
20–24	12.9	20.7	43.1	42.3	28.1	16.3
25–29	9.2	14.2	25.0	20.4	19.2	12.1
30–34	7.9	8.6	18.7	16.0	11.2	11.0
35–39	7.6	7.0	12.1	12.0	9.9	11.3
40–44	7.9	7.0	9.8	8.6	8.0	11.0
45–49	8.1	6.6	8.6	9.2	8.6	11.5
50–54	8.5	7.8	9.1	9.9	9.0	11.8
55–59	9.5	8.3	9.6	10.9	9.8	12.4
60–64	12.2	10.1	11.9	11.6	11.4	14.8
65–69	22.0	18.3	17.0	17.4	16.2	23.5
70 and over	27.4	24.2	22.0	23.1	23.6	29.5
Female [a]	15.4	16.9	17.0	18.7	19.7	23.8
Under 20	14.1	12.4	12.6	15.5	17.0	19.3
20–24	17.3	19.6	19.0	19.8	21.5	26.1
25–29	16.7	20.5	21.4	21.7	22.3	28.1
30–34	14.2	17.7	18.7	19.8	20.5	25.8
35–39	12.8	14.4	14.8	18.0	19.0	23.2
40–44	12.8	12.4	14.0	17.7	18.3	21.8
45–49	13.4	13.0	13.8	17.6	18.2	21.9
50–54	13.6	13.7	15.0	19.1	18.7	22.0
55–59	15.0	15.5	15.8	19.2	18.8	21.2
60–64	16.4	15.7	16.2	19.6	18.9	22.2
65–69	25.1	22.6	22.7	24.2	22.0	27.5
70 and over	29.5	25.1	19.9	28.6	31.0	30.2

a. Excludes persons whose age was not reported.

Source: Bureau of Old-Age and Survivors Insurance.

WORKERS WITH WAGE CREDITS UNDER OASI, BY NUMBER OF EMPLOYERS, SEX, RACE AND AGE, 1944 (A 3 PER CENT SAMPLE)

No.	Sex, Race and Age	Total	Number of Employers: 1	2 or More	2	3	4	5 or More	5	6	7	8	9 or More	No.
	All Workers													
1	Total	1,352,289	900,714	451,575	257,086	99,322	44,345	50,822	21,662	11,783	6,715	3,982	6,680	1
2	Under 14	3,976	3,276	700	518	117	41	24	13	6	3	a	2	2
3	14–15	27,564	18,784	8,780	5,712	1,859	711	498	280	106	52	30	30	3
4	16–17	81,859	42,439	39,420	21,469	9,597	4,287	4,067	1,959	1,000	507	286	315	4
5	18–19	87,592	46,240	41,352	22,124	10,015	4,530	4,683	2,161	1,102	672	297	451	5
6	20	36,350	20,721	15,629	8,190	3,657	1,743	2,039	911	456	263	177	232	6
7	21–24	128,627	78,070	50,557	27,251	11,569	5,457	6,280	2,750	1,474	849	474	733	7
8	25 and over	984,272	689,917	294,355	171,433	62,294	27,501	33,127	13,559	7,606	4,357	2,710	4,895	8
9	Unknown	2,049	1,267	782	389	214	75	104	29	33	12	8	22	9
10	Male	822,045	538,713	283,332	152,191	62,455	29,893	38,793	15,474	8,914	5,317	3,265	5,823	10
11	Under 14	3,335	2,725	610	455	103	33	19	12	3	3	a	1	11
12	14–15	18,471	12,025	6,446	4,031	1,429	564	422	240	85	44	24	29	12
13	16–17	46,237	21,804	24,433	12,281	6,123	2,966	3,063	1,416	758	394	229	266	13
14	18–19	37,542	19,353	18,189	8,697	4,440	2,260	2,792	1,212	636	429	197	318	14
15	20	11,336	5,861	5,475	2,393	1,278	737	1,067	418	232	157	107	153	15
16	21–24	45,870	25,467	20,403	9,409	4,638	2,554	3,802	1,475	857	556	326	588	16
17	25 and over	657,535	450,442	207,093	114,590	44,255	20,718	27,530	10,674	6,312	3,723	2,374	4,447	17
18	Unknown	1,719	1,036	683	335	189	61	98	27	31	11	8	21	18
19	Female	530,244	362,001	168,243	104,895	36,867	14,452	12,029	6,188	2,869	1,398	717	857	19
20	Under 14	641	551	90	63	14	8	5	1	3	a	a	1	20
21	14–15	9,093	6,759	2,334	1,681	430	147	76	40	21	8	6	1	21
22	16–17	35,622	20,635	14,987	9,188	3,474	1,321	1,004	543	242	113	57	49	22
23	18–19	50,050	26,887	23,163	13,427	5,575	2,270	1,891	949	466	243	100	133	23
24	20	25,014	14,860	10,154	5,797	2,379	1,006	972	493	224	106	70	79	24
25	21–24	82,757	52,603	30,154	17,842	6,931	2,903	2,478	1,275	617	293	148	145	25
26	25 and over	326,737	239,475	87,262	56,843	18,039	6,783	5,597	2,885	1,294	634	336	448	26
27	Unknown	330	231	99	54	25	14	6	2	2	1	a	1	27
	White Workers													
28	White total	1,221,155	828,857	392,298	228,819	85,823	37,129	40,527	17,677	9,425	5,289	3,132	5,004	28
29	Under 14	3,454	2,897	557	417	90	32	18	10	4	2	a	2	29
30	14–15	25,033	17,271	7,762	5,137	1,646	580	399	230	86	40	22	21	30
31	16–17	74,891	39,143	35,748	19,794	8,725	3,795	3,434	1,716	855	408	229	226	31
32	18–19	78,623	42,289	36,334	19,964	8,776	3,882	3,712	1,741	875	529	222	345	32
33	20	32,158	18,794	13,364	7,231	3,120	1,435	1,578	730	343	210	137	158	33
34	21–24	113,373	70,962	42,411	23,670	9,691	4,435	4,615	2,116	1,062	624	351	462	34
35	25 and over	891,983	636,456	255,527	152,287	53,613	22,919	26,708	11,118	6,179	3,469	2,164	3,778	35
36	Unknown	1,640	1,045	595	319	162	51	63	16	21	7	7	12	36
37	White male	739,227	495,740	243,487	134,700	53,532	24,829	30,426	12,474	7,060	4,106	2,526	4,260	37
38	Under 14	2,877	2,402	475	359	78	25	13	9	1	2	a	1	38
39	14–15	16,559	10,949	5,610	3,579	1,249	450	332	193	68	33	18	20	39
40	16–17	41,573	19,895	21,678	11,118	5,465	2,574	2,521	1,220	632	308	175	186	40
41	18–19	32,755	17,520	15,235	7,598	3,744	1,838	2,055	920	463	312	135	225	41
42	20	9,410	5,089	4,321	1,999	1,020	576	726	291	158	115	74	88	42
43	21–24	38,673	22,565	16,108	7,831	3,714	1,967	2,596	1,065	589	375	229	338	43
44	25 and over	596,007	416,462	179,545	101,939	38,123	17,359	22,124	8,761	5,129	2,955	1,888	3,391	44
45	Unknown	1,373	858	515	277	139	40	59	15	20	6	7	11	45

TABLE 81—Continued

No.	Sex, Race and Age	Total	1	2 or More	2	3	4	5 or More	5	6	7	8	9 or More	No.
			Number of Employers											
						White Workers—Continued								
46	White female	481,928	333,117	148,811	94,119	32,291	12,300	10,101	5,203	2,365	1,183	606	744	46
47	Under 14	577	495	82	58	12	7	5	1	3	a	a	1	47
48	14–15	8,474	6,322	2,152	1,558	397	130	67	37	18	7	4	1	48
49	16–17	33,318	19,248	14,070	8,676	3,260	1,221	913	496	223	100	54	40	49
50	18–19	45,868	24,769	21,099	12,366	5,032	2,044	1,657	821	412	217	87	120	50
51	20	22,748	13,705	9,043	5,232	2,100	859	852	439	185	95	63	70	51
52	21–24	74,700	48,397	26,303	15,839	5,977	2,468	2,019	1,051	473	249	122	124	52
53	25 and over.......	295,976	219,994	75,982	50,348	15,490	5,560	4,584	2,357	1,050	514	276	387	53
54	Unknown	267	187	80	42	23	11	4	1	1	1	a	1	54
						Negro Workers								
55	Negro total	131,134	71,857	59,277	28,267	13,499	7,216	10,295	3,985	2,358	1,426	850	1,676	55
56	Under 14	522	379	143	101	27	9	6	3	2	1	a	a	56
57	14–15	2,531	1,513	1,018	575	213	131	99	50	20	12	8	9	57
58	16–17	6,968	3,296	3,672	1,675	872	492	633	243	145	99	57	89	58
59	18–19	8,969	3,951	5,018	2,160	1,239	648	971	420	227	143	75	106	59
60	20	4,192	1,927	2,265	959	537	308	461	181	113	53	40	74	60
61	21–24	15,254	7,108	8,146	3,581	1,878	1,022	1,665	634	412	225	123	271	61
62	25 and over.......	92,289	53,461	38,828	19,146	8,681	4,582	6,419	2,441	1,427	888	546	1,117	62
63	Unknown	409	222	187	70	52	24	41	13	12	5	1	10	63
64	Negro male	82,818	42,973	39,845	17,491	8,923	5,064	8,367	3,000	1,854	1,211	739	1,563	64
65	Under 14	458	323	135	96	25	8	6	3	2	1	a	a	65
66	14–15	1,912	1,076	836	452	180	114	90	47	17	11	6	9	66
67	16–17	4,664	1,909	2,755	1,163	658	392	542	196	126	86	54	80	67
68	18–19	4,787	1,833	2,954	1,099	696	422	737	292	173	117	62	93	68
69	20	1,926	772	1,154	394	258	161	341	127	74	42	33	65	69
70	21–24	7,197	2,902	4,295	1,578	924	587	1,206	410	268	181	97	250	70
71	25 and over.......	61,528	33,980	27,548	12,651	6,132	3,359	5,406	1,913	1,183	768	486	1,056	71
72	Unknown	346	178	168	58	50	21	39	12	11	5	1	10	72
73	Negro female	48,316	28,884	19,432	10,776	4,576	2,152	1,928	985	504	215	111	113	73
74	Under 14	64	56	8	5	2	1	a	a	a	a	a	a	74
75	14–15	619	437	182	123	33	17	9	3	3	1	2	a	75
76	16–17	2,304	1,387	917	512	214	100	91	47	19	13	3	9	76
77	18–19	4,182	2,118	2,064	1,061	543	226	234	128	54	26	13	13	77
78	20	2,266	1,155	1,111	565	279	147	120	54	39	11	7	9	78
79	21–24	8,057	4,206	3,851	2,003	954	435	459	224	144	44	26	21	79
80	25 and over.......	30,761	19,481	11,280	6,495	2,549	1,223	1,013	528	244	120	60	61	80
81	Unknown	63	44	19	12	2	3	2	1	1	a	a	a	81

a. Sample did not include any workers.

Source: Handbook of Old-Age and Survivors Insurance Statistics, 1944, Bureau of Old-Age and Survivors Insurance, 1947, p. 84.

TABLE 82

PERCENTAGE OF SINGLE-INDUSTRY WORKERS AMONG PERSONS WITH WAGE CREDITS UNDER OASI, BY NUMBER OF EMPLOYERS, SEX AND AGE, 1944

Sex and Age	Total	Number of Employers: 1	2	3	4	5	6	7	8	9 or More
Male	69.0	100.0	15.2	6.7	4.0	3.5	2.7[a]	1.6[a]	2.0[a]	1.4[a]
Under 14	85.7	100.0	28.2[a]	11.4[a]	11.1[a]	[b]	[b]	[b]	[b]	[b]
14–15	67.1	100.0	11.7	4.1[a]	1.0[a]	1.2[a]	[b]	[b]	[b]	[b]
16–17	48.9	100.0	7.2	1.4[a]	0.5[a]	0.4[a]	[b]	[b]	[b]	[b]
18–19	53.6	100.0	7.5	2.3[a]	0.9[a]	1.0[a]	0.5[a]	[b]	[b]	[b]
20	52.9	100.0	10.4[a]	3.0[a]	2.0[a]	[b]	1.1[a]	[b]	[b]	[b]
21–24	58.9	100.0	11.8	4.2[a]	2.9[a]	1.8[a]	1.1[a]	[b]	0.9[a]	0.5[a]
25 and over	72.2	100.0	17.0	8.4	5.1	4.7	3.6[a]	2.3[a]	2.7[a]	1.7[a]
Female	71.7	100.0	14.6	5.6	3.1[a]	2.8	2.8[a]	2.3[a]	2.6[a]	1.8[a]
Under 14	89.6	100.0	40.0[a]	[b]	[b]	[b]	[b]	[b]	[b]	[b]
14–15	77.0	100.0	18.8	4.1[a]	1.9[a]	[b]	[b]	[b]	[b]	[b]
16–17	61.1	100.0	12.1	2.7[a]	1.1[a]	[b]	[b]	[b]	[b]	[b]
18–19	56.3	100.0	8.6	2.3[a]	0.4[a]	0.3[a]	1.1[a]	[b]	3.3[a]	[b]
20	61.4	100.0	11.0	2.3[a]	2.4[a]	0.6[a]	[b]	2.9[a]	[b]	[b]
21–24	66.4	100.0	11.4	4.0[a]	2.3[a]	2.1[a]	1.8[a]	1.3[a]	5.0[a]	[b]
25 and over	77.2	100.0	17.7	8.2	4.8	4.9[a]	5.0[a]	3.8[a]	2.8[a]	3.3[a]

a. Fewer than 100 persons in sample. b. No workers in sample.

Source: Bureau of Old-Age and Survivors Insurance.

TABLE 83

NUMBER AND PERCENTAGE OF WOMEN AMONG WORKERS WITH WAGE CREDITS UNDER OASI, BY INDUSTRY, 1939, 1944 AND 1946

Industry	1939		1944		1946 [a]	
	Number, in Thousands	Percentage of Total	Number, in Thousands	Percentage of Total	Number, in Thousands	Percentage of Total
All industries	9,391	27.8	18,195	39.4	16,695	34.0
Mining	25	2.4	47	4.3	47	4.0
Contract construction	38	1.9	100	6.1	90	3.3
Manufacturing	3,592	27.7	8,094	36.7	6,164	31.3
Ordnance and accessories	b	b	252	41.9	31	21.1
Food and kindred products	574	28.4	914	37.0	757	33.0
Tobacco manufactures	96	60.0	91	68.9	89	63.6
Textile mill products	680	44.3	831	51.8	805	47.1
Apparel and other finished products made from fabrics and similar materials	821	69.6	1,085	77.0	1,222	72.9
Lumber and timber basic products	16	3.0	68	8.1	97	8.2
Furniture and finished lumber products	76	15.2	186	31.5	84	20.5
Paper and allied products	94	26.7	199	37.8	192	33.2
Printing, publishing and allied industries	188	25.6	279	39.9	305	35.3
Chemicals and allied products	117	18.8	316	31.4	220	25.6
Products of petroleum and coal	16	6.8	39	15.1	31	11.0
Rubber products	37	23.7	138	42.9	103	30.0
Leather and leather products	207	43.5	250	55.8	273	50.8
Stone, clay and glass products	72	14.6	147	28.4	141	21.4
Primary metals industry	116	8.5	509	23.7	129	9.0
Transportation equipment	b	b	1,062	28.5	237	14.5
Fabricated metal products	b	b	b	b	258	22.0
Electrical machinery	136	32.4	679	50.5	488	42.8
Machinery, except electrical	87	10.4	410	24.8	287	17.0
Transportation, communication and other public utilities	365	18.4	652	25.0	833	26.0
Trucking and warehousing for hire	27	5.6	69	10.0	62	8.1
Communication: telephone, telegraph and related services	241	54.0	388	75.9	580	70.0
Utilities: electric and gas	59	12.2	73	19.3	75	15.2
Wholesale trade	379	22.8	940	32.7	841	27.1
Full-service and limited-function wholesalers	b	b	513	33.8	514	28.4
Wholesale distributors, other than full-service and limited-function wholesalers	b	b	427	31.6	327	25.4
Retail trade	2,501	42.5	4,813	57.4	4,964	49.7
Retail general merchandise	1,165	69.1	1,807	79.8	1,806	73.9
Retail food and liquor stores	197	19.6	563	40.5	548	33.7
Retail automotive	35	7.7	54	14.1	72	11.4
Retail apparel and accessories	365	61.4	558	71.4	578	67.6
Eating and drinking places	509	44.6	1,220	61.9	1,276	55.6
Retail filling stations	—	—	—	—	23	6.6
Finance, insurance and real estate	462	32.0	846	50.7	934	45.7
Banks and trust companies	30	29.4	218	56.9	218	51.9
Security dealers and investment banking	20	23.3	21	44.7	25	32.9
Insurance carriers	153	40.4	225	52.8	286	50.2
Insurance agents, brokers and services	47	58.8	73	70.9	91	62.8
Real estate	108	25.0	192	37.6	192	32.9
Service industries	1,340	38.1	2,170	50.1	2,350	45.3
Hotels, rooming houses, camps and other lodging places	268	44.7	434	58.7	457	53.6
Personal services	463	55.1	785	65.8	856	62.3
Business services, not elsewhere classified	140	34.5	204	43.4	215	35.8
Automobile repair services and garages	b	b	26	13.0	29	9.2
Motion pictures	62	27.4	132	39.9	146	38.3
Amusement and recreation and related services, not elsewhere classified	62	16.2	87	19.7	89	17.1
Medical and other health services	153	80.5	246	85.4	295	83.3
Other professional and social service agencies and institutions	9	16.7	39	32.8	22	17.7
Nonprofit membership organizations	58	31.4	92	35.9	93	32.6

a. Manufacturing industries differ in content from corresponding industries shown in previous year. Data are preliminary.
b. Not available.

Source: Bureau of Old-Age and Survivors Insurance.

TABLE 84

NUMBER AND PERCENTAGE OF WOMEN AMONG WORKERS WITH WAGE CREDITS IN FOUR QUARTERS AND LESS THAN FOUR QUARTERS UNDER OASI, BY INDUSTRY, 1944 AND 1946

Industry	1944				1946[a]			
	Four Quarters		Less than Four Quarters		Four Quarters		Less than Four Quarters	
	Number, in Thousands	Percentage of Total	Number, in Thousands	Percentage of Total	Number, in Thousands	Percentage of Total	Number, in Thousands	Percentage of Total
All industries	9,622	33.9	8,573	48.1	8,464	29.9	8,231	39.5
Mining	27	3.4	20	6.9	30	3.6	17	5.0
Contract construction	45	5.2	55	7.1	43	3.3	47	3.3
Manufacturing	4,672	32.0	3,422	46.1	3,418	27.7	2,746	37.2
Ordnance and accessories	147	36.8	105	52.2	17	19.8	14	23.0
Food and kindred products	333	28.7	581	44.4	290	24.8	467	41.6
Tobacco manufactures	56	65.9	35	74.5	55	61.1	34	68.0
Textile mill products	520	47.4	311	61.2	513	43.9	292	54.1
Apparel and other finished products made from fabrics and similar materials	662	73.7	423	82.6	662	70.4	560	76.1
Lumber and timber basic products	26	6.4	42	9.6	44	8.2	53	8.2
Furniture and finished lumber products	95	26.8	91	38.6	41	17.3	43	24.9
Paper and allied products	113	32.9	86	47.0	111	29.0	81	41.3
Printing, publishing and allied industries	163	34.0	116	52.7	178	31.1	127	43.8
Chemicals and allied products	178	26.6	138	41.2	134	22.8	86	31.9
Products of petroleum and coal	26	12.8	13	23.2	20	9.0	11	18.0
Rubber products	81	37.7	57	53.3	65	26.4	38	39.2
Leather and leather products	153	50.5	97	66.9	167	47.2	106	57.9
Stone, clay and glass products	84	24.9	63	35.0	82	19.8	59	24.0
Primary metals industry	309	19.3	200	36.8	77	7.4	52	13.6
Transportation equipment	727	24.3	465	43.4	126	12.7	111	17.3
Fabricated metal products	[b]	[b]	[b]	[b]	143	18.9	115	27.5
Electrical machinery	435	45.5	244	63.0	293	39.2	195	49.6
Machinery, except electrical	255	21.0	155	35.7	170	14.4	117	25.8
Transportation, communication and other public utilities	437	24.9	215	25.3	537	25.5	296	26.9
Trucking and warehousing for hire	39	9.6	30	10.6	31	7.2	31	9.3
Communication: telephone, telegraph and related services	275	72.2	113	86.9	380	68.6	200	72.7
Utilities: electric and gas	53	17.3	20	27.8	55	14.4	20	17.9
Wholesale trade	540	29.3	400	38.9	475	24.3	366	31.9
Full-service and limited-function wholesalers	279	29.6	234	40.6	275	24.7	239	34.1
Wholesale distributors, other than full-service and limited-function wholesalers	261	29.0	166	36.8	200	23.9	127	28.4
Retail trade	2,070	50.3	2,743	64.2	2,100	43.5	2,864	51.1
Retail general merchandise	763	75.0	1,044	83.7	770	69.2	1,036	77.8
Retail food and liquor stores	259	36.0	304	45.2	251	29.3	297	38.6
Retail automotive	31	12.9	23	16.1	37	9.9	35	13.5
Retail apparel and accessories	290	66.5	268	77.7	293	63.6	285	72.3
Eating and drinking places	448	52.2	772	69.4	439	46.8	837	61.7
Retail filling stations	—	—	—	—	12	7.7	11	5.8
Finance, insurance and real estate	573	46.7	273	62.0	604	43.0	330	51.6
Banks and trust companies	157	53.2	61	69.3	159	49.7	59	59.0
Security dealers and investment banking	15	35.7	6	—	20	32.8	5	33.3
Insurance carriers	163	48.8	62	67.4	183	45.3	103	62.0
Insurance agents, brokers and services	51	68.9	22	75.9	56	61.5	35	64.8
Real estate	108	32.8	84	46.4	109	30.2	83	37.4
Service industries	971	44.5	1,199	55.7	1,025	41.0	1,325	49.3
Hotels, rooming houses, camps and other lodging places	152	48.3	282	66.5	165	47.3	292	58.1
Personal services	345	57.3	440	74.5	357	54.3	499	69.6
Business services, not elsewhere classified	103	37.0	101	52.6	114	32.9	101	39.8
Automobile repair services and garages	[c]	[c]	[c]	[c]	14	8.5	15	9.9
Motion pictures	56	34.4	76	45.2	58	32.6	88	43.3
Amusement and recreation and related services, not elsewhere classified	31	19.3	56	19.9	30	16.7	59	17.4
Medical and other health services	126	84.6	120	83.3	137	83.5	158	83.2
Other professional and social service agencies and institutions	[c]	[c]	[c]	[c]	11	16.9	11	18.6
Nonprofit membership organizations	52	33.3	40	40.0	53	29.0	40	39.2

a. Manufacturing industries differ in content from corresponding industries shown in previous years. Data are preliminary.
b. Not available.
c. Number of workers too small to be included.

Source: Bureau of Old-Age and Survivors Insurance.

TABLE 85

PERCENTAGE DISTRIBUTION, BY NUMBER OF QUARTERS IN COVERED EMPLOYMENT, OF WORKERS WITH WAGE CREDITS UNDER OASI AT SOME TIME IN 1937–1946[a]

No.	Quarters Employed	Male						Female						No.
		Total	Under 25 Years	25–44 Years	45–64 Years	65 Years and Over	Unreported	Total	Under 25 Years	25–44 Years	45–64 Years	65 Years and Over	Unreported	
1	Total	100.0	100.0	100.0	100.0	100.0	100.0	100.0	100.0	100.0	100.0	100.0	100.0	**1**
2	1	6.3	9.5	4.2	4.4	7.5	66.2	9.3	10.1	8.0	10.2	12.9	68.2	**2**
3	2	4.9	9.5	3.4	3.5	5.6	9.7	7.7	9.7	6.6	7.6	8.5	8.0[b]	**3**
4	3	4.2	7.9	3.1	3.2	4.5	5.0	6.1	7.5	5.4	5.7	7.0	4.6[b]	**4**
5	4	3.8	7.3	2.9	2.8	4.2	2.2	5.2	6.2	4.8	4.7	5.2	1.9[b]	**5**
6	5	3.4	7.0	2.5	2.3	3.0	1.1[b]	4.5	5.9	4.0	3.9	4.4	1.5[b]	**6**
7	6	3.3	6.9	2.4	2.1	3.7	1.1[b]	4.2	5.6	3.7	3.6	3.9	0.9[b]	**7**
8	7	3.1	6.6	2.3	2.0	3.1	0.9[b]	4.0	5.5	3.5	3.2	3.3	1.4[b]	**8**
9	8	3.1	6.5	2.2	1.9	3.2	0.8[b]	3.7	4.7	3.3	3.0	3.3	0.4[b]	**9**
10	9	2.9	6.1	2.2	1.8	2.8	0.7[b]	3.5	4.7	3.1	3.0	2.9	1.1[b]	**10**
11	10	2.8	5.6	2.2	1.7	2.7	0.6[b]	3.4	4.6	3.0	2.9	2.5	0.6[b]	**11**
12	11	2.7	5.0	2.2	1.7	2.7	0.7[b]	3.4	4.4	3.0	2.8	3.0	0.5[b]	**12**
13	12	2.5	4.2	2.1	1.7	2.7	0.7[b]	3.1	3.7	2.9	2.6	3.0	1.3[b]	**13**
14	13	2.3	3.4	2.2	1.8	2.5	0.9[b]	3.0	3.9	2.8	2.5	2.3	0.5[b]	**14**
15	14	2.3	2.9	2.2	1.9	2.5	0.6[b]	3.0	3.7	2.8	2.4	2.4	0.9[b]	**15**
16	15	2.1	2.3	2.2	1.8	2.3	0.7[b]	2.8	3.5	2.6	2.5	2.0	1.3[b]	**16**
17	16	2.1	1.9	2.3	1.9	2.5	1.3[b]	2.6	2.8	2.6	2.4	1.9	1.2[b]	**17**
18	17	2.0	1.5	2.2	1.9	2.2	0.4[b]	2.4	2.6	2.4	2.3	1.8	1.2[b]	**18**
19	18	1.9	1.3	2.2	1.8	1.9	0.4[b]	2.3	2.5	2.4	1.9	1.8	0.3[b]	**19**
20	19	1.8	1.0	2.3	1.8	1.8	0.4[b]	1.9	1.8	2.1	1.5	1.3[b]	0.1[b]	**20**
21	20	1.8	0.8	2.2	1.7	1.8	0.4[b]	1.7	1.4	2.0	1.4	1.5[b]	0.6[b]	**21**
22	21	1.7	0.6	2.3	1.6	1.7	0.4[b]	1.5	1.2	1.9	1.3	1.0[b]	0.4[b]	**22**
23	22	1.7	0.5	2.4	1.7	1.4	0.4[b]	1.5	1.2	1.9	1.3	1.1[b]	0.3[b]	**23**
24	23	1.7	0.4	2.3	1.5	1.4	0.4[b]	1.3	0.8	1.6	1.2	1.3[b]	0.1[b]	**24**
25	24	1.6	0.3	2.3	1.5	1.6	0.5[b]	1.2	0.6	1.6	1.2	0.7[b]	0.2[b]	**25**
26	25	1.5	0.2	2.3	1.4	1.4	0.3[b]	1.1	0.5	1.5	1.1	1.2[b]	0.4[b]	**26**
27	26	1.5	0.2	2.2	1.4	1.2	0.2[b]	1.0	0.4	1.4	1.0	1.0[b]	0.1[b]	**27**
28	27	1.4	0.1	2.1	1.3	1.2	0.3[b]	0.9	0.2	1.4	0.9	1.0[b]	0.3[b]	**28**
29	28	1.5	0.1[b]	2.2	1.6	1.5	0.3[b]	0.9	0.1	1.3	1.1	1.0[b]	0.3[b]	**29**
30	29	1.3	0.1[b]	2.0	1.3	1.3	0.3[b]	0.8	0.1[b]	1.2	0.9	0.7[b]	0.1[b]	**30**
31	30	1.3	[b, c]	1.8	1.4	1.3	0.2[b]	0.8	0.1[b]	1.2	0.8	0.8[b]	0.1[b]	**31**
32	31	1.2	[b, c]	1.8	1.3	1.3	0.3[b]	0.7	0.1[b]	1.1	0.8	0.9[b]	0.1[b]	**32**
33	32	1.3	[b, c]	1.7	1.4	2.3	0.3[b]	0.7	[b, c]	1.0	0.8	1.3[b]	[c]	**33**
34	33	1.2	[b, c]	1.6	1.4	1.1	0.1[b]	0.7	[b, c]	1.0	0.8	0.7[b]	0.2[b]	**34**
35	34	1.2	[b, c]	1.6	1.5	1.0	0.1[b]	0.6	[b, c]	1.0	0.8	0.5[b]	0.1[b]	**35**
36	35	1.3	[b, c]	1.6	1.7	1.4	0.2[b]	0.7	[b, c]	1.0	0.9	0.7[b]	[c]	**36**
37	36	1.4	[b, c]	1.8	2.0	1.6	0.2[b]	0.7	[b, c]	1.0	1.0	1.0[b]	0.1[b]	**37**
38	37	1.4	[b, c]	1.7	2.0	1.5	0.2[b]	0.7	[b, c]	1.0	1.0	1.0[b]	0.1[b]	**38**
39	38	1.7	[b, c]	2.1	2.7	1.5	0.1[b]	0.8	[b, c]	1.1	1.2	1.1[b]	0.2[b]	**39**
40	39	2.8	[b, c]	3.1	4.9	2.4	0.3[b]	1.2	[b, c]	1.4	2.4	1.8	0.1[b]	**40**
41	40	11.8	[b, c]	11.5	22.8	8.7	0.2[b]	4.0	[b, c]	4.4	9.1	6.2	0.3[b]	**41**

a. Age as of birthday in 1946. b. Fewer than 100 persons in sample. c. Less than 0.05 per cent.

Source: Bureau of Old-Age and Survivors Insurance.

TABLE 86

NUMBER AND PERCENTAGE OF NEGROES AMONG WORKERS WITH WAGE CREDITS UNDER OASI, BY INDUSTRY, 1939, 1944 AND 1946

Industry	1939		1944		1946 [a]	
	Number, in Thousands	Percentage of Total	Number, in Thousands	Percentage of Total	Number, in Thousands	Percentage of Total
All industries	2,415	7.2	4,489	9.7	4,594	9.4
Mining	62	5.8	67	6.2	66	5.7
Metal mining	b	b	7	4.9 [c]	5	4.3 [c]
Bituminous and other soft-coal mining	b	b	42	8.8	45	7.9
Nonmetallic mining and quarrying	b	b	14	13.3	14	11.0
Contract construction	224	11.3	231	14.2	318	11.9
Building construction — general contractors	b	b	72	14.1	139	14.2
General contractors, other than building	b	b	75	16.4	95	15.4
Construction — special-trade contractors	b	b	84	12.8	84	7.8
Manufacturing	739	5.7	1,956	8.9	1,714	8.8
Food and kindred products	123	6.1	290	11.8	283	12.6
Tobacco manufactures	40	25.0	33	25.3	36	26.6
Textile mill products	40	2.6	76	4.8	79	4.7
Apparel and other finished products made from fabrics and similar materials	39	3.3	127	9.1	141	8.6
Lumber and wood products, except furniture	142	27.0	237	28.4	292	25.0
Furniture and fixtures	39	7.9	85	14.5	39	9.7
Paper and allied products	12	3.5	47	9.0	42	7.5
Printing, publishing and allied industries	12	1.7	29	4.2	36	4.3
Chemicals and allied products	83	13.3	126	12.7	110	13.1
Products of petroleum and coal	10	4.4	19	7.5	21	7.5
Rubber products	5	3.4	28	8.7	24	6.9
Leather and leather products	6	1.3	25	5.6	27	5.1
Stone, clay and glass products	38	7.8	40	7.8	59	9.1
Primary metal industries	89	6.5	209	9.8	177	12.6
Fabricated metal products, except ordnance, machinery and transportation equipment	b	b	b	b	74	6.4
Machinery, except electrical	11	3.3	58	3.5	53	3.2
Electrical machinery, equipment and supplies	3	0.7	58	4.3	43	3.9
Transportation equipment	b	b	319	7.8	117	7.3
Transportation, communication and other public utilities	133	6.7	223	8.6	232	7.4
Interstate railroads, local railways and bus lines	4	2.9	8	4.1 [c]	10	4.9
Trucking and warehousing for hire	62	12.8	96	14.3	93	12.9
Other transportation, except water transportation	6	3.8	16	5.5	18	4.9
Water transportation	11	20.1	18	6.1	23	9.7
Services allied to transportation, not elsewhere classified	b	b	61	26.2	44	22.9
Communication: telephone, telegraph and related services	6	1.3	7	1.4 [c]	12	1.6
Utilities: electric and gas	17	3.5	15	4.0	18	4.1
Local utilities and local public services, not elsewhere classified	b	b	2	7.1 [c]	14	6.7
Wholesale and retail trade	580	7.0	1,079	9.3	1,120	8.4
Full-service and limited-function wholesalers	b	b	193	12.8	203	11.4
Wholesale distributors, other than full-service and limited-function wholesalers	b	b	91	6.8	80	6.4
Wholesale and retail trade combined, not elsewhere classified	b	b	39	10.6	49	11.3
Retail general merchandise	40	2.4	97	4.3	103	4.3
Retail food and liquor stores	54	5.4	79	5.7	83	5.2
Retail automotive	36	8.0	34	8.8	45	7.3
Retail apparel and accessories	22	3.7	47	6.0	52	6.2
Retail trade, not elsewhere classified	b	b	131	9.6	131	7.5
Eating and drinking places	120	10.5	343	17.5	341	15.1
Retail filling stations	b	b	25	12.0	33	9.7
Finance, insurance and real estate	93	6.4	124	7.5	140	6.9
Insurance carriers	18	4.8	15	4.0	21	4.0
Real estate	60	13.9	82	18.1	91	16.7
Service industries	389	11.1	687	16.0	766	15.0
Hotels, rooming houses, camps and other lodging places	118	19.7	192	26.1	211	25.2
Personal services	129	15.3	295	25.0	339	25.1
Business services, not elsewhere classified	12	3.0	23	5.0	29	4.8
Automobile repair services and garages	b	b	26	13.2	30	9.8
Miscellaneous repair services and hand trades	b	b	10	7.6	9	4.8 [c]
Motion pictures	12	5.4	22	6.5	26	6.8
Amusement and recreation and related services, not elsewhere classified	42	11.0	56	12.7	60	11.8
Medical and other health services	14	7.4	25	8.7	30	8.7
Nonprofit membership organizations	7	3.9	20	8.0	22	7.7

a. All nonwhite workers. Manufacturing industries in 1946 differ in content from corresponding industries shown for other years.
b. Not available. c. Fewer than 100 persons in sample.

Source: Bureau of Old-Age and Survivors Insurance.

TABLE 87

Percentage Distribution of All and of Negro Workers with Wage Credits under OASI, by State and Region, 1939, 1944 and 1946

State and Region	1939				1944				1946			
	All Workers		Negroes		All Workers		Negroes		All Workers		Negroes	
	Male	Female	Male	Female	Male	Female	Male	Female	Male	Female	Male	Female
United States, total....	100.0	100.0	100.0	100.0	100.0	100.0	100.0	100.0	100.0	100.0	100.0	100.0
New England	8.0	9.8	1.1	1.2	7.1	7.9	1.2	1.6	7.2	8.2	1.4	1.8
Maine	0.7	0.8	a	0.1	0.7	0.6	a	a	0.6	0.6	a	a
New Hampshire ...	0.5	0.6	a	a	0.3	0.4	a	a	0.4	0.4	a	a
Vermont	0.3	0.2	a	a	0.2	0.2	a	a	0.2	0.2	a	a
Massachusetts	4.0	5.1	0.5	0.6	3.5	4.1	0.6	0.8	3.7	4.3	0.6	0.9
Rhode Island	0.7	1.1	0.2	0.1	0.6	0.8	0.1	0.1	0.6	0.8	0.2	0.1
Connecticut	1.8	2.0	0.4	0.4	1.8	1.8	0.5	0.7	1.7	1.9	0.6	0.8
Middle Atlantic	25.7	28.5	13.0	17.3	23.8	24.5	15.5	21.6	24.8	25.6	17.3	22.8
New York	13.1	15.9	5.7	9.1	12.0	13.4	6.5	11.8	12.8	14.4	8.4	13.7
New Jersey	3.8	4.4	2.7	3.2	3.8	3.8	3.5	4.0	3.6	3.7	3.0	4.1
Pennsylvania	8.8	8.2	4.6	5.0	8.0	7.3	5.5	5.8	8.4	7.5	5.9	5.0
East North Central....	22.9	21.9	11.8	13.1	23.8	23.0	16.6	19.6	23.3	21.8	17.5	18.4
Ohio	6.1	5.5	3.5	2.7	6.4	6.0	4.5	4.9	6.2	5.5	4.8	4.1
Indiana	2.7	2.5	1.4	1.2	2.8	2.9	1.7	1.8	2.7	2.6	1.7	1.4
Illinois	7.3	7.9	4.1	7.2	6.9	7.2	6.0	8.4	7.1	7.5	6.6	9.6
Michigan	4.6	3.9	2.6	1.9	5.4	4.7	4.1	4.2	5.1	4.1	4.1	3.1
Wisconsin	2.2	2.1	0.2	0.1	2.3	2.2	0.3	0.3	2.2	2.1	0.3	0.2
West North Central...	7.4	7.8	3.1	3.7	7.1	8.0	3.5	4.8	7.3	7.9	3.4	4.4
Minnesota	1.6	1.8	0.1	0.1	1.5	1.6	0.1	0.1	1.7	1.8	0.2	0.2
Iowa	1.3	1.3	0.2	0.3	1.2	1.3	0.2	0.3	1.2	1.3	0.2	0.2
Missouri	2.6	2.9	2.1	2.8	2.4	3.0	2.5	3.4	2.5	2.9	2.3	3.3
North Dakota	0.2	0.2	a	a	0.2	0.2	a	a	0.2	0.2	a	a
South Dakota	0.2	0.2	a	a	0.2	0.2	a	a	0.2	0.2	a	a
Nebraska	0.6	0.6	0.2	0.2	0.6	0.7	0.2	0.3	0.6	0.7	0.2	0.2
Kansas	0.9	0.8	0.5	0.3	1.0	1.0	0.5	0.7	0.9	0.8	0.5	0.5
South Atlantic	11.8	11.5	36.7	42.3	11.5	11.8	28.8	24.7	11.7	11.6	29.2	26.3
Delaware	0.3	0.3	0.4	0.9	0.4	0.3	0.6	0.4	0.3	0.2	0.4	0.4
Maryland	1.5	1.5	3.3	4.3	1.6	1.6	3.2	3.7	1.5	1.5	3.2	3.2
District of Columbia.	0.6	0.7	2.3	2.6	0.5	0.7	1.8	2.4	0.6	0.7	2.1	2.4
Virginia	1.7	1.6	5.6	8.4	1.6	1.6	4.4	3.9	1.7	1.6	4.6	4.4
West Virginia	1.5	0.7	1.7	0.5	1.3	0.8	1.1	0.3	1.3	0.8	1.0	0.4
North Carolina	2.0	2.5	6.2	11.4	1.8	2.2	4.7	4.0	1.9	2.2	4.9	4.9
South Carolina	1.1	1.0	4.5	2.4	1.0	1.0	3.4	1.6	1.0	1.0	3.4	1.8
Georgia	1.7	1.9	7.2	6.5	1.8	2.0	5.8	4.5	1.8	1.9	5.4	4.6
Florida	1.4	1.3	5.5	5.3	1.5	1.6	3.8	3.9	1.6	1.7	4.2	4.2
East South Central....	5.1	3.9	16.5	10.0	5.5	4.9	14.1	10.0	5.1	4.7	13.1	9.4
Kentucky	1.4	1.0	2.1	1.6	1.3	1.1	1.7	1.4	1.3	1.0	1.4	1.1
Tennessee	1.5	1.5	4.0	3.4	1.8	1.9	3.5	3.4	1.6	1.8	3.3	3.3
Alabama	1.4	0.9	6.2	3.2	1.7	1.3	5.7	3.3	1.5	1.2	5.2	3.1
Mississippi	0.8	0.5	4.2	1.8	0.7	0.6	3.2	1.9	0.7	0.7	3.2	1.9
West South Central...	7.5	5.4	16.2	10.9	7.6	6.9	14.8	11.6	7.5	6.6	13.7	11.1
Arkansas	0.8	0.5	2.6	1.3	0.8	0.6	2.2	1.0	0.7	0.6	1.8	1.1
Louisiana	1.5	1.0	6.0	4.3	1.5	1.2	5.3	3.9	1.4	1.1	4.6	3.8
Oklahoma	1.1	0.8	0.8	0.5	1.1	1.1	0.8	0.9	1.1	1.0	0.8	0.6
Texas	4.1	3.1	6.8	4.8	4.2	4.0	6.5	5.8	4.3	3.9	6.5	5.6
Mountain	2.8	2.1	0.4	0.4	2.7	2.1	0.3	0.3	2.7	2.5	0.4	0.5
Montana	0.4	0.3	a	a	0.3	0.2	a	a	0.3	0.3	a	a
Idaho	0.4	0.2	a	a	0.3	0.2	a	a	0.3	0.3	a	a
Wyoming	0.2	0.1	a	a	0.2	0.1	a	a	0.1	0.1	a	a
Colorado	0.7	0.7	0.1	0.2	0.7	0.7	0.1	0.1	0.8	0.8	0.1	0.2
New Mexico	0.3	0.2	0.1	0.1	0.2	0.2	0.1	0.1	0.3	0.2	a	0.1
Arizona	0.3	0.2	0.2	0.1	0.4	0.3	0.1	0.1	0.4	0.3	0.2	0.1
Utah	0.4	0.3	a	a	0.4	0.3	a	a	0.4	0.4	a	a
Nevada	0.1	0.1	a	a	0.2	0.1	a	a	0.1	0.1	0.1	0.1
Pacific	8.4	8.8	1.1	1.4	10.8	11.0	4.9	5.4	10.1	10.6	3.8	5.4
Washington	1.4	1.4	0.1	0.1	2.0	1.8	0.5	0.5	1.6	1.5	0.2	0.3
Oregon	0.9	0.9	a	0.1	1.0	1.1	0.2	0.2	1.0	1.0	0.1	0.2
California	6.1	6.5	1.0	1.2	7.8	8.1	4.2	4.7	7.5	8.1	3.5	4.9
Alaska	0.1	a	a	a	0.1	a	a	a	0.1	a	a	a
Hawaii	0.3	0.3	a	a	0.3	0.2	a	a	0.3	0.2	a	a

a. Less than 0.05 per cent.

Source: Bureau of Old-Age and Survivors Insurance.

TABLE 88

NUMBER AND PERCENTAGE OF NEGROES AMONG WORKERS WITH WAGE CREDITS UNDER OASI, BY STATE, 1939, 1944 AND 1946

State [a]	1939		1944		1946 [b]	
	Number, in Thousands	Percentage of Total	Number, in Thousands	Percentage of Total	Number, in Thousands	Percentage of Total
United States, total	2,415	7.2	4,489	9.7	4,594	9.4
Alabama	139	31.4	215	30.3	208	30.2
Arizona	4	3.9	6	3.8	7	4.0
Arkansas	55	24.2	81	24.7	72	21.3
California	26	1.2	191	5.2	185	4.9
Colorado	3	1.2	6	1.9	7	1.8
Connecticut	10	1.6	26	3.2	16	3.5
Delaware	12	14.0	24	15.1	20	15.8
District of Columbia	56	25.6	92	32.5	98	30.1
Florida	131	27.4	177	25.4	197	24.5
Georgia	169	28.1	238	27.7	241	27.1
Hawaii	[c]	[c]	1	0.5	[c]	[c]
Idaho	[c]	[c]	1	0.9	[c]	[c]
Illinois	113	4.5	309	9.5	347	9.7
Indiana	36	4.0	78	6.0	73	5.5
Iowa	5	1.1	9	1.7	9	1.5
Kansas	10	3.4	26	5.8	23	5.3
Kentucky	48	11.4	71	12.5	59	10.1
Louisiana	138	30.3	215	33.7	201	32.2
Maine	1	0.4	1	0.2	1	0.4
Maryland	83	15.9	154	20.8	145	20.0
Massachusetts	12	0.8	31	1.8	34	1.8
Michigan	59	4.0	189	7.9	173	7.4
Minnesota	2	0.4	5	0.7	9	1.1
Mississippi	91	37.9	122	37.9	126	36.0
Missouri	55	6.3	124	10.3	121	9.3
Montana	[c]	[c]	1	0.4	1	0.4
Nebraska	4	1.9	9	3.3	10	3.3
Nevada	[c]	[c]	2	3.3	2	4.0
New Hampshire	1	0.6	[c]	[c]	1	0.3
New Jersey	67	5.0	164	9.3	152	8.5
New Mexico	2	2.6	4	3.9	2	1.9
New York	151	3.2	379	6.5	473	7.2
North Carolina	171	23.7	199	21.9	225	22.7
Ohio	82	4.1	212	7.3	211	7.2
Oklahoma	18	5.1	38	7.3	32	6.3
Oregon	1	0.3	9	1.9	5	1.1
Pennsylvania	113	3.9	249	6.9	260	6.5
Rhode Island	4	1.4	6	1.9	7	2.0
South Carolina	101	28.5	123	27.2	134	28.0
Tennessee	95	18.3	155	18.4	150	18.2
Texas	157	12.0	282	14.7	284	13.8
Utah	[c]	[c]	2	1.0	2	1.2
Vermont	1	1.2	[c]	[c]	1	0.5
Virginia	146	26.0	190	25.6	207	25.2
Washington	2	0.4	22	2.5	12	1.6
West Virginia	37	8.7	36	7.1	36	6.5
Wisconsin	4	0.6	14	1.4	14	1.3
Wyoming	[c]	[c]	1	1.6	1	1.5

a. States with fewer than 500 Negroes with wage credits are omitted.
b. All nonwhite workers.
c. Fewer than 500 workers.

Source: Bureau of Old-Age and Survivors Insurance.

TABLE 89

PERCENTAGE DISTRIBUTION OF WHITE AND OF NEGRO WORKERS WITH WAGE CREDITS UNDER OASI, BY NUMBER OF QUARTERS IN COVERED EMPLOYMENT, 1944 AND 1946

Race and Age	1944					1946				
		Quarters Employed					Quarters Employed			
	Total	1	2	3	4	Total	1	2	3	4
Male										
White	100.0	12.0	10.4	10.0	67.6	100.0	12.4	12.5	13.2	62.0
Under 20	100.0	25.0	25.3	21.2	28.4	100.0	30.4	27.8	17.4	24.3
20–24	100.0	26.5	16.9	13.7	42.9	100.0	20.7	22.2	21.6	35.4
25–29	100.0	15.4	11.9	10.3	62.4	100.0	12.1	14.0	17.4	56.6
30–34	100.0	11.0	8.0	7.7	73.3	100.0	9.4	10.3	13.0	67.3
35–39	100.0	8.3	6.9	7.5	77.3	100.0	8.2	8.3	10.5	73.0
40–44	100.0	6.5	6.1	7.2	80.3	100.0	7.3	7.1	9.1	76.5
45–49	100.0	6.1	6.2	7.2	80.4	100.0	7.8	7.1	8.4	76.8
50–54	100.0	6.2	6.1	7.2	80.5	100.0	6.9	7.1	8.8	77.2
55–59	100.0	6.4	6.3	7.3	80.0	100.0	8.1	6.9	8.6	76.4
60–64	100.0	7.7	7.3	8.6	76.4	100.0	8.5	7.4	9.7	74.4
65–69	100.0	10.6	9.2	9.7	70.5	100.0	11.5	10.8	11.3	66.4
70 and over	100.0	13.8	11.1	10.9	64.2	100.0	14.3	12.7	11.6	61.3
Negro	100.0	15.3	13.6	13.1	58.0	100.0	16.1	15.0	15.1	53.9
Under 20	100.0	26.0	24.8	20.4	28.7	100.0	30.4	25.2	17.8	26.5
20–24	100.0	21.3	18.2	16.2	44.3	100.0	22.5	21.2	19.6	36.6
25–29	100.0	17.2	14.5	13.3	55.0	100.0	16.8	16.8	18.8	47.7
30–34	100.0	14.2	11.8	11.5	62.5	100.0	13.2	13.9	15.2	57.7
35–39	100.0	11.3	10.4	11.0	67.2	100.0	12.5	10.7	13.5	63.3
40–44	100.0	9.7	8.3	10.9	71.1	100.0	11.2	10.6	11.2	67.1
45–49	100.0	9.3	8.5	10.5	71.7	100.0	9.4	10.4	12.2	68.0
50–54	100.0	9.8	9.8	9.8	70.5	100.0	11.2	9.7	11.2	67.9
55–59	100.0	11.9	9.7	9.7	68.7	100.0	12.4	11.6	10.1	65.9
60–64	100.0	12.9	10.6	10.6	65.9	100.0	12.9	11.8	11.8	63.5
65–69	100.0	14.3	14.3	11.9	59.5	100.0	17.0	10.6	10.6	61.7
70 and over	100.0	17.4	13.0	13.0	56.5	100.0	23.1	15.4	11.5	50.0
Female										
White	100.0	15.9	15.3	14.2	54.6	100.0	17.4	16.2	14.4	52.0
Under 20	100.0	20.8	22.4	19.9	36.9	100.0	22.4	23.6	18.6	35.3
20–24	100.0	14.9	14.7	14.1	56.4	100.0	17.3	16.9	14.7	51.0
25–29	100.0	16.4	14.9	13.8	55.0	100.0	19.3	16.9	15.0	48.7
30–34	100.0	15.3	14.6	13.6	56.5	100.0	18.6	15.7	14.2	51.5
35–39	100.0	13.9	12.8	12.7	60.5	100.0	15.7	14.0	13.5	56.9
40–44	100.0	13.7	12.5	12.0	61.9	100.0	14.0	12.9	11.9	61.3
45–49	100.0	13.3	12.3	11.3	63.1	100.0	13.6	11.4	12.2	62.8
50–54	100.0	14.0	11.9	11.9	62.1	100.0	13.8	11.7	11.7	62.8
55–59	100.0	14.2	12.8	11.3	61.7	100.0	13.3	11.5	12.2	63.1
60–64	100.0	15.2	13.6	10.4	60.8	100.0	12.7	11.1	11.1	65.1
65–69	100.0	16.2	14.6	10.0	59.2	100.0	13.2	12.5	11.1	63.2
70 and over	100.0	17.4	15.2	13.0	54.3	100.0	14.0	12.3	10.5	63.2
Negro	100.0	24.8	22.1	16.8	36.2	100.0	25.2	21.5	16.3	37.0
Under 20	100.0	35.8	30.1	17.5	16.7	100.0	39.5	29.1	14.5	16.9
20–24	100.0	25.9	24.2	18.0	31.8	100.0	28.6	25.1	17.0	29.3
25–29	100.0	24.3	21.3	17.3	37.0	100.0	25.6	21.0	16.4	37.0
30–34	100.0	20.6	19.8	16.6	43.1	100.0	21.2	19.4	18.4	41.0
35–39	100.0	20.2	19.1	16.5	44.1	100.0	18.7	19.2	14.8	47.3
40–44	100.0	21.3	18.4	14.9	45.4	100.0	22.4	17.2	15.7	44.8
45–49	100.0	21.0	18.5	14.8	45.7	100.0	19.8	16.0	16.0	48.1
50–54	100.0	22.4	18.4	14.3	44.9	100.0	17.0	17.0	14.9	51.1
55–59	100.0	23.1	15.4	15.4	46.2	100.0	16.7	16.7	16.7	50.0
60–64	100.0	25.0	16.7	16.7	41.7	100.0	15.4	15.4	15.4	53.8
65–69	100.0	20.0	20.0	20.0	40.0	100.0	20.0	20.0	20.0	40.0
70 and over	100.0	a	a	a	100.0	100.0	20.0	20.0	20.0	40.0

a. No workers in sample.

Source: Bureau of Old-Age and Survivors Insurance.

TABLE 90

PERCENTAGE OF NEGROES AMONG WORKERS WITH WAGE CREDITS UNDER OASI, BY NUMBER OF QUARTERS IN COVERED EMPLOYMENT, 1944 AND 1946

	1944					1946				
		Quarters Employed					Quarters Employed			
Sex and Age	Total	1	2	3	4	Total	1	2	3	4
Male	10.1	12.5	12.8	12.8	8.7	9.7	12.2	11.4	10.9	8.5
Under 20	11.2	11.6	11.0	10.8	11.3	10.5	10.5	9.6	10.7	11.4
20–24	15.9	13.0	17.1	18.3	16.4	10.9	11.8	10.5	10.0	11.2
25–29	12.4	13.3	14.3	15.6	11.1	10.3	13.7	12.1	11.0	8.8
30–34	11.1	13.9	15.5	15.8	9.6	10.6	14.3	13.7	12.1	9.1
35–39	10.1	13.2	14.7	14.3	8.8	10.8	15.6	13.4	13.4	9.4
40–44	10.5	15.2	13.9	15.0	9.2	10.0	14.3	14.2	12.0	8.8
45–49	9.2	13.5	12.2	12.7	8.2	10.2	12.1	14.2	14.1	9.1
50–54	7.5	11.5	11.6	10.2	6.5	8.1	12.3	10.8	10.0	7.1
55–59	6.7	11.6	10.0	8.8	5.8	6.6	9.9	10.6	7.5	5.7
60–64	6.0	9.3	8.9	7.5	5.1	5.8	9.0	9.1	6.9	4.9
65–69	5.2	7.4	8.1	6.0	4.4	5.8	8.4	5.7	5.7	5.3
70 and over	5.0	6.8	6.1	5.3	4.3	5.4	7.9	6.8	6.2	4.2
Unreported	20.1	20.9	24.8	26.5	17.7	21.3	14.3	23.0	19.7	23.1
Female	9.1	13.5	12.6	10.6	6.1	8.7	12.1	11.2	9.7	6.3
Under 20	7.5	12.1	9.9	6.6	3.5	6.4	10.7	7.8	5.0	3.1
20–24	9.6	15.5	14.8	11.9	5.5	9.1	14.2	13.0	10.4	5.3
25–29	11.8	16.6	16.2	14.4	8.1	10.9	13.9	13.1	11.9	8.4
30–34	12.1	15.7	15.7	14.6	9.4	11.7	13.0	14.1	14.6	9.3
35–39	10.0	14.0	14.1	12.5	7.4	10.5	12.2	13.9	11.6	8.8
40–44	9.0	13.5	13.0	11.1	6.6	9.1	14.0	11.7	11.6	6.6
45–49	6.8	10.4	9.6	8.9	4.8	7.0	9.8	9.5	8.9	5.5
50–54	5.7	8.6	8.0	7.0	4.2	5.4	6.8	7.9	6.8	4.3
55–59	4.5	7.5	5.3	5.5	3.4	4.2	5.7	6.6	5.5	3.1
60–64	3.7	5.7	5.0	4.4	2.7	3.8	5.2	4.2	4.3	3.4
65–69	3.3	5.4	5.7	4.1	1.9	3.1	6.3	3.8	3.7	2.1
70 and over	3.2	5.7	2.9	3.4	2.4	7.8	10.1	14.7	12.3	4.8
Unreported	19.1	24.6	22.2	20.0	15.4	25.0	20.0	30.8	22.2	25.7

Source: Bureau of Old-Age and Survivors Insurance.

TABLE 91

Monthly Labor Turnover Rates in Manufacturing Industries, 1930–1950

(Per 100 Employees)

Year	Jan.	Feb.	March	Apr.	May	June	July	Aug.	Sept.	Oct.	Nov.	Dec.
					Accessions							
1930	3.9	3.9	4.1	3.6	3.3	2.9	2.5	2.7	3.3	2.6	2.0	2.1
1931	3.0	2.8	3.7	3.1	2.8	2.4	3.0	2.6	3.6	2.7	3.6	3.3
1932	4.1	2.7	2.7	2.8	2.6	2.7	3.0	4.2	4.0	3.7	3.1	3.1
1933	3.5	2.6	2.2	4.9	7.2	10.2	9.5	8.6	5.5	4.0	3.7	3.4
1934	5.8	6.7	6.3	5.2	4.2	3.6	3.7	3.2	3.6	4.1	4.3	6.1
1935	6.3	4.2	3.8	3.6	3.0	3.2	4.2	4.6	4.9	5.2	3.6	3.3
1936	3.6	2.9	4.0	4.5	4.0	4.5	4.9	4.7	5.1	4.8	4.6	4.4
1937	4.6	4.7	4.7	4.0	3.6	3.7	3.4	3.4	3.8	2.8	1.8	2.1
1938	3.8	3.1	3.1	2.6	2.8	3.4	4.8	5.3	4.5	5.2	4.2	3.2
1939	4.1	3.1	3.3	2.9	3.3	3.9	4.2	5.1	6.2	5.9	4.1	2.8
1940	3.7	3.0	2.9	3.0	3.4	4.8	4.8	6.6	6.2	5.5	4.6	4.1
1941	5.5	4.9	5.6	6.0	6.0	6.3	6.0	5.4	5.2	4.9	3.9	4.8
1942	6.9	6.0	7.0	7.1	7.3	8.3	8.3	7.9	9.2	8.7	8.1	6.9
1943	8.3	7.9	8.3	7.4	7.2	8.4	7.8	7.6	7.7	7.2	6.6	5.2
1944	6.5	5.5	5.8	5.5	6.4	7.6	6.3	6.3	6.1	6.0	6.1	5.1
1945	7.0	5.0	4.9	4.7	5.0	5.9	5.8	5.9	7.4	8.7	8.6	7.9
1946	8.5	6.8	7.1	6.7	6.1	6.7	7.4	7.0	7.1	6.8	5.7	4.3
1947	6.0	5.0	5.1	5.1	4.8	5.5	4.9	5.3	5.9	5.5	4.8	3.6
1948	4.6	3.4	4.0	4.0	4.1	5.7	4.7	5.0	5.1	4.5	3.9	2.7
1949	3.2	2.9	3.0	2.9	3.5	4.4	3.5	4.4	4.1	3.7	3.3	3.2
1950	3.6	3.2	3.6	3.5	4.4	4.8	4.7	6.6	5.7	5.2	4.0	3.1
					All Separations							
1930	5.1	4.7	5.4	5.2	5.2	5.3	5.8	5.7	5.0	4.5	3.9	3.8
1931	2.9	2.7	2.9	3.4	3.8	5.1	4.7	3.7	5.6	6.2	3.9	3.4
1932	3.3	3.3	4.4	5.7	5.1	5.6	5.2	3.8	4.5	3.5	3.4	4.1
1933	3.6	4.4	4.6	2.8	2.4	2.5	3.5	3.4	4.3	4.6	4.8	4.7
1934	3.4	2.9	3.2	3.4	4.9	4.6	3.8	4.5	5.1	5.3	4.5	3.4
1935	3.0	2.8	3.2	3.7	4.4	4.5	3.7	3.8	3.2	3.1	3.5	3.8
1936	3.6	3.1	2.9	3.3	3.3	3.3	3.2	4.7	3.3	3.2	3.0	3.4
1937	3.4	2.8	3.2	3.1	3.4	4.0	3.5	4.0	4.6	5.7	6.9	8.5
1938	6.1	4.4	4.5	4.5	4.6	4.4	3.8	3.1	3.6	3.3	3.1	3.9
1939	3.2	2.6	3.2	3.5	3.5	3.3	3.4	3.0	2.8	2.9	2.9	3.5
1940	3.4	3.6	3.5	3.7	3.8	3.4	3.3	3.0	3.2	3.2	3.1	3.2
1941	3.4	3.2	3.4	3.9	3.9	3.7	4.2	4.1	4.5	4.1	3.5	4.7
1942	5.1	4.8	5.4	6.1	6.5	6.5	6.7	7.1	8.1	7.9	7.1	6.4
1943	7.1	7.1	7.7	7.5	6.7	7.1	7.6	8.3	8.1	7.0	6.4	6.6
1944	6.7	7.6	7.4	6.8	7.1	7.1	6.6	7.8	7.6	6.4	6.0	5.7
1945	6.2	6.0	6.8	6.6	7.0	7.9	7.7	17.9	12.0	8.6	7.1	5.9
1946	6.8	6.3	6.6	6.3	6.3	5.7	5.8	6.6	6.9	6.3	4.9	4.5
1947	4.9	4.5	4.9	5.2	5.4	4.7	4.6	5.3	5.9	5.0	4.0	3.7
1948	4.3	4.2	4.5	4.7	4.3	4.5	4.4	5.1	5.4	4.5	4.1	4.3
1949	4.6	4.1	4.8	4.8	5.2	4.3	3.8	4.0	4.2	4.1	4.0	3.2
1950	3.1	3.0	2.9	2.8	3.1	3.0	4.9	4.2	4.9	4.3	3.8	3.6

TABLE 91—CONTINUED

Year	Jan.	Feb.	March	Apr.	May	June	July	Aug.	Sept.	Oct.	Nov.	Dec.
					Voluntary Quits							
1930	1.8	1.6	1.9	2.1	2.0	1.8	1.3	1.4	1.5	1.3	0.9	0.8
1931	0.7	0.7	0.9	1.1	1.1	1.0	1.1	1.0	1.1	1.0	0.7	0.7
1932	0.7	0.7	0.9	0.9	0.7	0.7	0.6	0.7	0.8	0.6	0.5	0.6
1933	0.6	0.5	0.5	0.6	0.8	1.0	1.2	1.2	1.6	0.9	0.8	0.7
1934	0.9	0.8	0.9	1.1	1.0	0.9	0.7	0.7	1.5	0.7	0.6	0.6
1935	0.8	0.7	0.7	0.9	1.2	0.8	0.9	0.9	1.0	0.9	0.8	0.7
1936	0.7	0.7	0.9	1.2	1.1	1.1	1.1	1.2	1.6	1.3	1.1	1.0
1937	1.3	1.2	1.4	1.4	1.4	1.9	1.2	1.2	1.0	1.0	0.7	0.6
1938	0.5	0.5	0.6	0.6	0.6	0.6	0.6	0.6	0.8	0.8	0.6	0.6
1939	0.8	0.6	0.8	0.8	0.7	0.7	0.7	0.8	1.1	0.9	0.8	0.7
1940	0.7	0.7	0.8	0.8	0.9	0.9	1.0	1.2	1.6	1.5	1.2	1.1
1941	1.3	1.3	1.7	2.1	2.2	2.1	2.3	2.5	2.8	2.1	1.6	1.8
1942	2.4	2.4	3.0	3.6	3.8	3.9	4.0	4.3	5.2	4.7	4.2	3.7
1943	4.5	4.7	5.4	5.4	4.8	5.2	5.6	6.3	6.3	5.2	4.5	4.4
1944	4.6	4.6	5.0	4.9	5.3	5.4	5.0	6.2	6.1	5.0	4.6	4.3
1945	4.6	4.3	5.0	4.8	4.8	5.1	5.2	6.2	6.7	5.6	4.7	4.0
1946	4.3	3.9	4.2	4.3	4.2	4.0	4.6	5.3	5.3	4.7	3.7	3.0
1947	3.5	3.2	3.5	3.7	3.5	3.1	3.1	4.0	4.5	3.6	2.7	2.3
1948	2.6	2.5	2.8	3.0	2.8	2.9	2.9	3.4	3.9	2.8	2.2	1.7
1949	1.7	1.4	1.6	1.7	1.6	1.5	1.4	1.8	2.1	1.5	1.2	0.9
1950	1.1	1.0	1.2	1.3	1.6	1.7	1.8	2.9	3.4	2.7	2.1	1.7
					Layoffs, Discharges and Other Separations							
1930	3.3	3.1	3.5	3.1	3.2	3.5	4.5	4.3	3.5	3.2	3.0	3.0
1931	2.2	2.0	2.0	2.3	2.7	4.1	3.6	2.7	4.5	5.2	3.2	2.7
1932	2.6	2.6	3.5	4.8	4.4	4.9	4.6	3.1	3.7	2.9	2.9	3.5
1933	3.0	3.9	4.1	2.2	1.6	1.5	2.3	2.2	2.7	3.7	4.0	4.0
1934	2.5	2.1	2.3	2.3	3.9	3.7	3.1	3.8	3.6	4.6	3.9	2.8
1935	2.2	2.1	2.5	2.8	3.2	3.7	2.8	2.9	2.2	2.2	2.7	3.1
1936	2.9	2.4	2.0	2.1	2.2	2.2	2.1	3.5	1.7	1.9	1.9	2.4
1937	2.1	1.6	1.8	1.7	2.0	2.1	2.3	2.8	3.0	4.7	6.2	7.9
1938	5.6	3.9	3.9	3.9	4.0	3.8	2.6	1.9	2.0	2.5	2.5	3.3
1939	2.4	2.0	2.4	2.7	2.8	2.6	2.7	2.2	2.7	2.0	2.1	2.8
1940	2.7	2.9	2.7	2.9	2.9	2.5	2.3	1.8	1.6	1.7	1.9	2.1
1941	2.1	1.9	1.7	1.8	1.7	1.6	1.9	1.6	1.7	2.0	1.9	2.9
1942	2.7	2.0	2.4	2.5	2.7	2.6	2.7	2.8	2.9	3.2	2.9	2.7
1943	2.6	2.4	2.3	2.1	1.9	1.9	2.0	2.0	1.8	1.8	1.9	2.2
1944	2.1	3.0	2.4	1.9	1.8	1.7	1.6	1.6	1.5	1.4	1.4	1.4
1945	1.6	1.7	1.8	1.8	2.2	2.8	2.5	11.7	5.3	3.0	2.4	1.9
1946	2.5	2.4	2.4	2.0	2.1	1.7	1.2	1.3	1.6	1.6	1.2	1.5
1947	1.4	1.3	1.4	1.5	1.9	1.6	1.5	1.3	1.4	1.4	1.3	1.4
1948	1.7	1.7	1.7	1.7	1.5	1.6	1.5	1.7	1.5	1.7	1.9	2.6
1949	2.9	2.7	3.2	3.1	3.6	2.8	2.4	2.2	2.1	2.6	2.8	2.3
1950	2.0	2.0	1.7	1.5	1.5	1.3	2.1	1.3	1.5	1.6	1.7	1.9

Sources: Handbook of Labor Statistics, 1947 edition, Bulletin No. 916, p. 42, and *Labor Turnover Report,* December 1950 (February 15, 1951), Bureau of Labor Statistics.

TABLE 92

NUMBER OF MULTI-INDUSTRY AND MULTI-EMPLOYER WORKERS WITH WAGE CREDITS UNDER OASI, BY LAST INDUSTRY, 1944

(In Thousands)

Last Industry	All Workers	Multi-industry Workers	Multi-employer Workers
Total	46,296	13,867	15,463
Agriculture, forestry and fishing	120	43	48
Mining	1,090	252	343
Metal mining	134	28	35
Anthracite mining	93	9	17
Bituminous and other soft-coal mining	500	82	140
Crude-petroleum and natural-gas production	261	101	116
Nonmetallic mining and quarrying	102	32	35
Contract construction	1,636	843	931
Building construction — general contractors	509	275	306
General contractors, other than building	459	234	247
Construction — special-trade contractors	668	334	378
Manufacturing	22,028	5,741	6,249
Ordnance and accessories	601	166	169
Food and kindred products	2,471	766	826
Tobacco manufactures	132	32	39
Textile mill products	1,605	277	338
Apparel and other finished products made from fabrics and similar materials	1,410	393	478
Lumber and timber basic products	840	265	317
Furniture and finished lumber products	590	190	199
Paper and allied products	526	140	148
Printing, publishing and allied industries	699	202	226
Chemicals and allied products	1,005	291	298
Products of petroleum and coal	259	65	70
Rubber products	322	84	85
Leather and leather products	448	105	120
Stone, clay and glass products	517	142	147
Iron and steel and their products	2,145	537	558
Transportation equipment, except automobiles	3,726	844	933
Nonferrous metals and their products	613	167	174
Electrical machinery	1,344	320	335
Machinery, except electrical	1,651	453	473
Automobiles and automobile equipment	452	104	106
Miscellaneous manufacturing industries	672	198	209
Transportation, communication and other public utilities	2,607	883	1,005
Railways and bus lines	186	44	46
Trucking and warehousing for hire	688	303	339
Other transportation, except water transportation	295	100	115
Water transportation	287	153	186
Services allied to transportation, not elsewhere classified	235	127	143
Communication: telephone, telegraph and related services	511	84	98
Utilities: electric and gas	379	66	71
Local utilities and local public services, not elsewhere classified	26	6	7
Wholesale and retail trade	11,629	3,800	4,310
Full-service and limited-function wholesalers	1,520	527	558
Wholesale distributors, other than full-service or limited-function wholesalers	1,351	369	380
Wholesale and retail trade combined, not elsewhere classified	370	130	138
Retail general merchandise	2,265	702	753
Retail food and liquor stores	1,391	430	483
Retail automotive	384	135	145
Retail apparel and accessories	781	250	280
Retail trade, not elsewhere classified	1,392	466	512
Eating and drinking places	1,971	707	969
Retail filling stations	204	84	90

TABLE 92—CONTINUED

Last Industry	All Workers	Multi-industry Workers	Multi-employer Workers
Finance, insurance and real estate	1,668	442	491
Banks and trust companies	383	80	84
Security dealers and investment banking	47	10	11
Finance agencies, not elsewhere classified	82	25	28
Insurance carriers	426	93	98
Insurance agents, brokers and services	103	27	30
Real estate	510	176	208
Real estate, insurance, loans, law offices: any combination	57	13	14
Holding companies, except real estate holding companies	60	18	18
Service industries	4,332	1,504	1,716
Hotels, rooming houses, camps and other lodging places	739	269	314
Personal service	1,193	362	438
Business services, not elsewhere classified	470	167	181
Employment agencies and commercial and trade schools	53	16	18
Automobile repair services and garages	200	86	91
Miscellaneous repair services and hand trades	127	54	56
Motion pictures	331	130	148
Amusement and recreation and related services, not elsewhere classified	442	180	201
Medical and other health services	288	62	74
Law offices and related services	88	22	29
Educational institutions and services	26	7	7
Other professional and social service agencies and institutions	119	48	51
Nonprofit membership organizations	256	101	108
Establishments not elsewhere classified	32	11	12
Unclassified	1,154	348	360

Source: Bureau of Old-Age and Survivors Insurance.

TABLE 93

Estimates of Unemployment, 1929–1940

(In Thousands)

Year	American Federation of Labor	Congress of Industrial Organizations	National Industrial Conference Board	Robert Nathan	Alexander Hamilton Institute	Labor Research Association [a]	Cleveland Trust	National Research League [b]	Daniel Carson
1929......	1,864	1,831	429	1,752	3,456	—	—	1,250	1,910
1930......	4,735	4,710	2,896	4,646	6,929	—	4,124	—	4,825
1931......	8,568	8,322	7,037	8,118	10,939	—	8,777	9,800	8,725
1932......	12,870	12,120	11,385	11,639	14,727	16,783	13,416	12,880	13,100
1933......	13,271	12,643	11,842	11,942	14,394	16,138	14,098	16,750	13,700
1934......	11,424	10,845	9,761	9,998	12,419	16,824	12,130	15,110	12,115
1935......	10,652	10,050	9,092	9,102	11,629	16,658	—	14,950	11,240
1936......	9,395	8,756	7,386	7,723	10,009	14,751	—	—	10,000
1937......	8,282	8,109	6,403	6,856	8,366	14,825	—	—	9,235
1938......	10,836	11,030	9,796	9,865	11,934	16,368	—	—	—
1939......	9,979	10,813	8,786	9,835	10,696	—	—	—	—
1940......	9,104	10,276	7,607	9,552	9,379	—	—	—	—

a. Estimates as of November, except 1938, which is as of April.
b. Estimates as of January, except 1929, which is as of September.

Source: Bureau of Labor Statistics.

TABLE 94

Estimated Unemployment, by Month, 1940–1950 [a]

(In Thousands)

Month	1940	1941	1942	1943	1944	1945	1946	1947	1948	1949	1950
January	—	7,410	4,320	1,480	810	630	2,300	2,400	2,065	2,664	4,480
February	—	6,930	4,040	1,420	690	640	2,650	2,490	2,639	3,221	4,684
March	8,360 [a]	6,500	3,580	1,120	690	590	2,700	2,330	2,440	3,167	4,123
April	8,230	6,380	3,050	1,010	630	530	2,330	2,420	2,193	3,016	3,515
May	7,990	5,660	2,590	950	730	530	2,310	1,960	1,761	3,289	3,057
June	8,310	6,190	2,890	1,300	880	890	2,570	2,555	2,184	3,778	3,384
July	9,150	6,000	2,830	1,390	890	950	2,270	2,584	2,227	4,095	3,213
August	8,740	5,620	2,190	1,050	680	830	2,060	2,096	1,941	3,689	2,500
September	6,850	4,680	1,680	870	600	1,650	2,070	1,912	1,899	3,351	2,341
October	7,240	3,840	1,610	780	440	1,560	1,960	1,687	1,642	3,576	1,940
November	7,260	3,800	1,630	710	500	1,740	1,930	1,621	1,831	3,409	2,240
December	6,910	3,620	1,520	690	500	1,970	2,120	1,643	1,941	3,489	2,229
Annual average	8,120 [b]	5,560	2,660	1,070	670	1,040	2,270	2,140	2,060	3,395	3,142

a. For census survey week: week including the 8th of the month, except for March 1940, when survey covered week ending March 30.
b. Annual average for 1940 includes allowance for January and February.

Source: Bureau of the Census.

TABLE 95

Insured Unemployment, Weekly Figures, July 1945–December 1950 [a]

(In Thousands)

Week Ended		Insured Unemployment: Under All Programs	Under State Unemployment Insurance Programs	Under Veterans Unemployment Allowance Program [b]	Under Railroad Unemployment Insurance Program
1945					
July	7	288	244	43	1
	14	291	247	43	1
	21	301	255	45	1
	28	306	258	47	1
August	4	310	264	45	1
	11	258	210	47	1
	18	425	364	60	1
	25	626	560	64	2
September	1	922	846	74	2
	8	1,200	1,105	92	3
	15	1,325	1,217	104	4
	22	1,439	1,321	113	5
	29	1,571	1,446	119	6
October	6	1,594	1,450	137	7
	13	1,655	1,479	168	8
	20	1,686	1,482	194	10
	27	1,741	1,501	229	11
November	3	1,760	1,502	247	11
	10	1,787	1,489	287	11
	17	1,865	1,511	342	12
	24	2,026	1,594	419	13
December	1	2,165	1,626	526	13
	8	2,236	1,620	602	14
	15	2,236	1,615	606	15
	22	2,168	1,529	622	17
	29	2,348	1,578	751	19
1946					
January	5	2,720	1,831	867	22
	12	2,781	1,814	943	24
	19	2,887	1,825	1,033	29
	26	3,119	1,892	1,191	36
February	2	3,195	1,862	1,291	42
	9	3,325	1,883	1,396	46
	16	3,426	1,862	1,516	48
	23	3,609	1,907	1,652	50
March	2	3,662	1,912	1,698	52
	9	3,655	1,897	1,707	51
	16	3,609	1,814	1,747	48
	23	3,577	1,744	1,784	49
	30	3,462	1,628	1,782	52
April	6	3,406	1,586	1,765	55
	13	3,381	1,568	1,761	52
	20	3,349	1,546	1,750	53
	27	3,308	1,509	1,737	62
May	4	3,302	1,475	1,762	65
	11	3,273	1,454	1,752	67
	18	3,323	1,497	1,748	78
	25	3,300	1,487	1,728	85
June	1	3,296	1,450	1,759	87
	8	3,267	1,420	1,770	77
	15	3,232	1,406	1,764	62
	22	3,130	1,345	1,734	51
	29	2,927	1,242	1,639	46
July	6	3,024	1,273	1,702	48
	13	3,073	1,281	1,745	48
	20	2,956	1,212	1,694	50
	27	2,900	1,176	1,673	50
1946—Continued					
August	3	2,821	1,125	1,645	51
	10	2,782	1,087	1,644	51
	17	2,748	1,048	1,650	51
	24	2,694	1,014	1,633	47
	31	2,542	939	1,554	50
September	7	2,561	955	1,556	51
	14	2,501	959	1,491	51
	21	2,305	925	1,329	52
	28	2,169	911	1,205	53
October	5	2,082	918	1,110	54
	12	2,039	922	1,061	56
	19	1,990	912	1,020	57
	26	1,918	891	970	56
November	2	1,850	862	931	57
	9	1,799	845	896	59
	16	1,858	876	925	57
	23	1,803	848	896	59
	30	1,912	916	925	71
December	7	2,012	940	992	80
	14	2,010	935	996	78
	21	1,867	855	935	77
	28	2,039	950	1,006	83
1947					
January	4	2,344	1,110	1,150	83
	11	2,369	1,127	1,157	84
	18	2,353	1,118	1,151	84
	25	2,360	1,122	1,157	81
February	1	2,350	1,124	1,145	80
	8	2,296	1,104	1,113	79
	15	2,354	1,156	1,119	79
	22	2,373	1,171	1,124	78
March	1	2,323	1,151	1,095	77
	8	2,302	1,148	1,078	76
	15	2,250	1,130	1,048	73
	22	2,171	1,106	1,004	70
	29	2,103	1,079	957	67
April	5	2,060	1,080	914	65
	12	2,074	1,125	887	62
	19	2,062	1,144	859	59
	26	2,014	1,143	817	54
May	3	1,970	1,134	785	51
	10	1,944	1,140	757	47
	17	1,927	1,154	730	43
	24	1,842	1,120	681	41
	31	1,891	1,160	690	40
June	7	1,883	1,149	697	38
	14	1,922	1,179	708	35
	21	1,905	1,164	710	32
	28	1,828	1,107	689	32
July	5	1,927	1,157	733	37
	12	1,969	1,171	758	41
	19	1,978	1,173	765	41
	26	1,916	1,137	741	38
August	2	1,886	1,115	733	38
	9	1,842	1,079	727	36
	16	1,799	1,039	723	38
	23	1,742	995	712	35
	30	1,617	915	667	36

TABLE 95—Continued

Week Ended		Insured Unemployment: Under All Programs	Under State Unemployment Insurance Programs	Under Veterans Unemployment Allowance Program[b]	Under Railroad Unemployment Insurance Program
1947—Continued					
September	6	1,597	905	655	38
	13	1,536	874	624	38
	20	1,425	835	551	38
	27	1,309	787	479	43
October	4	1,248	767	434	47
	11	1,188	735	404	50
	18	1,203	752	404	47
	25	1,190	750	400	40
November	1	1,155	728	388	40
	8	1,134	711	382	41
	15	1,186	744	402	40
	22	1,170	725	403	43
	29	1,225	756	423	46
December	6	1,299	786	466	47
	13	1,302	782	473	47
	20	1,247	744	454	49
	27	1,340	802	483	54
1948					
January	3	1,569	945	568	56
	10	1,641	990	594	57
	17	1,623	973	594	56
	24	1,649	981	612	55
	31	1,696	1,009	633	54
February	7	1,724	1,032	638	54
	14	1,841	1,116	674	51
	21	1,845	1,123	670	52
	28	1,801	1,098	650	52
March	6	1,790	1,092	648	51
	13	1,754	1,073	633	49
	20	1,722	1,067	607	49
	27	1,691	1,053	582	56
April	3	1,675	1,048	564	63
	10	1,695	1,088	539	69
	17	1,715	1,120	522	74
	24	1,659	1,100	489	69
May	1	1,618	1,099	463	57
	8	1,584	1,098	442	44
	15	1,520	1,069	415	36
	22	1,482	1,059	391	32
	29	1,356	967	358	31
June	5	1,438	1,043	366	29
	12	1,450	1,049	374	27
	19	1,417	1,018	374	25
	26	1,410	1,006	382	23
July	3	1,342	953	365	23
	10	1,454	1,032	397	26
	17	1,463	1,035	403	25
	24	1,421	1,001	394	26
	31	1,378	964	388	26
August	7	1,366	952	388	27
	14	1,363	942	395	26
	21	1,330	913	392	25
	28	1,289	883	382	24
September	4	1,200	813	362	25
	11	1,227	843	359	25
	18	1,204	853	326	24
	25	1,114	816	274	24
October	2	1,071	801	246	24
	9	1,032	777	231	24
	16	1,081	822	235	24
	23	1,106	846	236	24
	30	1,074	821	229	24
1948—Continued					
November	6	1,109	850	233	26
	13	1,221	940	255	27
	20	1,249	958	260	31
	27	1,344	1,028	281	35
December	4	1,455	1,105	313	38
	11	1,493	1,122	329	42
	18	1,549	1,157	345	48
	25	1,679	1,246	378	55
1949					
January	1	1,935	1,425	445	65
	8	2,108	1,546	493	69
	15	2,195	1,603	520	72
	22	2,279	1,652	552	75
	29	2,373	1,705	590	78
February	5	2,470	1,774	615	80
	12	2,544	1,821	639	83
	19	2,549	1,813	644	93
	26	2,712	1,935	679	98
March	5	2,732	1,946	684	103
	12	2,728	1,945	680	103
	19	2,735	1,940	674	121
	26	2,742	1,928	667	147
April	2	2,681	1,896	642	142
	9	2,684	1,936	620	128
	16	2,692	1,983	599	109
	23	2,695	2,021	584	90
	30	2,666	2,001	575	90
May	7	2,643	2,009	557	76
	14	2,655	2,045	540	70
	21	2,674	2,071	535	68
	28	2,608	2,015	518	75
June	4	2,648	2,048	526	73
	11	2,657	2,046	545	66
	18	2,721	2,085	563	72
	25	2,734	2,069	586	79
July	2	2,663	1,994	583	87
	9	2,824	2,110	611	103
	16	2,915	2,185	627	104
	23	2,843	2,145	589	109
	30	2,732	2,122	501	109
August	6	2,496	2,139	245	112
	13	2,438	2,182	141	114
	20	2,374	2,148	114	112
	27	2,303	2,092	106	106
September	3	2,172	1,961	98	113
	10	2,150	1,937	93	120
	17	2,119	1,909	83	127
	24	2,051	1,845	72	134
October	1	2,005	1,776	64	165
	8	1,994	1,749	60	185
	15	2,101	1,840	61	200
	22	2,174	1,911	62	201
	29	2,186	1,922	60	204
November	5	2,065	1,796	57	212
	12	2,261	2,007	60	194
	19	2,311	2,062	59	189
	26	2,458	2,214	65	181
December	3	2,516	2,288	65	163
	10	2,425	2,211	63	151
	17	2,350	2,144	59	147
	24	2,347	2,130	59	158
	31	2,451	2,227	61	163

TABLE 95—Continued

Week Ended		Insured Unemployment: Under All Programs	Under State Unemployment Insurance Programs	Under Veterans Unemployment Allowance Program[b]	Under Railroad Unemployment Insurance Program
1950					
January	7....	2,604	2,376	64	164
	14....	2,611	2,385	65	161
	21....	2,610	2,391	65	154
	28....	2,589	2,371	65	153
February	4....	2,593	2,377	64	152
	11....	2,548	2,334	63	151
	18....	2,495	2,276	62	158
	25....	2,545	2,317	62	166
March	4....	2,497	2,286	61	150
	11....	2,417	2,205	60	151
	18....	2,310	2,125	57	128
	25....	2,197	2,030	56	110
April	1....	2,067	1,915	54	99
	8....	2,051	1,911	50	90
	15....	2,093	1,964	47	81
	22....	2,030	1,912	44	73
	29....	1,955	1,848	42	65
May	6....	1,892	1,792	39	61
	13....	1,837	1,737	37	64
	20....	1,775	1,671	34	71
	27....	1,696	1,601	32	63
June	3....	1,654	1,578	29	47
	10....	1,638	1,569	29	40
	17....	1,605	1,543	27	35
	24....	1,556	1,497	26	33
1950—Continued					
July	1....	1,501	1,418	27	56
	8....	1,560	1,459	26	74
	15....	1,550	1,464	27	59
	22....	1,437	1,361	26	50
	29....	1,337	1,269	24	44
August	5....	1,255	1,191	23	41
	12....	1,178	1,119	21	38
	19....	1,117	1,063	20	35
	26....	1,062	1,010	18	34
September	2....	984	933	17	34
	9....	954	907	15	32
	16....	906	862	14	31
	23....	858	816	11	31
	30....	825	781	9	34
October	7....	785	744	8	34
	14....	820	779	7	34
	21....	838	799	6	32
	28....	829	795	6	28
November	4....	853	818	5	29
	11....	889	855	5	29
	18....	887	850	5	32
	25....	971	931	5	35
December	2....	1,057	1,016	5	36
	9....	1,059	1,016	6	37
	16....	1,058	1,014	6	39
	23....	1,083	1,032	6	45
	30....	1,176	1,124	6	47

a. Continental United States; includes insured partial and part-total unemployment.
b. Includes individuals filing claims under disability proviso; such claims amount to less than one per cent of total.

Source: Bureau of Employment Security.

TABLE 96

PERCENTAGE UNEMPLOYED, BY SEX AND AGE, MONTHLY, 1941–1950 [a]

Year and Month	Male: Total, 14 Years and Over	Male: 14 to 19 Years	Male: 20 to 24 Years	Male: 25 to 44 Years	Male: 45 to 64 Years	Male: 65 Years and Over	Female: Total, 14 Years and Over	Female: 14 to 19 Years	Female: 20 to 24 Years	Female: 25 to 44 Years	Female: 45 to 64 Years	Female: 65 Years and Over
1941												
October	6.1	10.2	6.7	4.6	7.1	5.6	8.9	16.3	9.5	7.3	7.6	2.6
November	6.3	10.0	7.4	4.8	7.2	5.7	8.3	14.3	8.1	7.2	7.6	2.7
December	6.3	10.1	5.7	5.0	7.4	6.7	7.2	13.3	7.1	5.6	7.2	6.2
1942												
January	7.5	12.7	7.6	5.6	8.8	8.1	9.2	17.3	9.3	7.4	8.7	3.3
February	7.1	11.8	6.5	5.3	8.7	8.0	8.0	14.4	8.4	6.6	7.5	3.1
March	6.2	8.5	5.6	4.4	7.9	8.2	7.4	14.3	7.4	6.1	6.4	2.9
April	5.0	6.2	4.7	3.5	6.8	6.0	6.5	8.9	6.7	6.1	6.3	2.6
May	3.9	4.8	3.6	2.7	5.2	4.8	6.4	9.8	6.8	6.4	4.6	—
June	4.3	8.2	4.4	2.6	4.9	4.6	6.6	13.1	6.5	5.5	4.5	—
July	4.1	10.5	3.7	2.1	4.4	4.2	6.6	13.4	6.2	5.0	4.8	2.6
August	3.4	7.5	3.0	2.0	3.8	4.2	4.7	8.0	5.5	3.8	3.4	—
September	2.6	4.4	3.2	1.6	3.0	3.2	3.9	5.4	3.3	3.7	4.1	2.4
October	2.4	3.9	2.4	1.4	3.0	3.4	3.8	5.2	3.6	3.1	4.9	2.1
November	2.4	3.6	2.3	1.4	3.4	3.4	3.9	4.4	4.4	3.4	4.3	2.0
December	2.2	3.5	2.2	1.1	3.0	3.9	3.9	4.8	3.6	3.3	4.6	3.9
Annual average	4.3	7.2	4.3	2.9	5.2	5.0	5.8	9.7	5.9	5.0	5.3	2.5
1943												
January	2.2	4.3	2.8	1.2	2.8	3.1	3.7	4.8	4.4	2.6	4.8	3.8
February	2.1	3.4	2.9	1.0	2.5	4.8	3.6	5.1	3.9	3.1	3.5	3.7
March	1.6	3.3	0.9	1.0	1.8	3.9	2.9	4.7	2.6	2.5	2.9	2.1
April	1.4	3.3	1.5	0.8	1.2	3.4	2.8	5.8	1.7	3.0	1.5	—
May	1.4	2.6	1.5	0.9	1.4	2.1	2.3	4.0	1.9	2.1	2.0	1.9
June	1.8	6.9	2.6	0.6	1.2	2.6	3.1	7.5	1.6	2.4	2.5	—
July	2.0	8.4	2.8	0.6	1.1	2.1	3.2	7.6	2.2	2.0	2.7	—
August	1.4	4.1	2.7	0.6	1.0	1.7	2.7	5.2	2.2	2.2	2.2	—
September	1.2	2.0	4.4	0.8	0.8	1.7	2.2	4.0	2.2	1.9	1.9	—
October	1.1	2.2	2.6	0.7	0.8	2.5	2.0	3.4	1.3	2.2	1.4	—
November	0.9	1.9	1.6	0.7	0.8	1.3	2.0	3.6	2.1	1.7	1.5	—
December	1.2	3.0	2.2	0.8	0.9	1.3	1.5	2.2	1.9	1.2	1.5	—
Annual average	1.5	4.0	2.5	0.8	1.4	2.6	2.7	4.8	2.2	2.3	2.3	2.0
1946												
January	4.8	6.0	13.6	5.2	2.5	3.4	3.3	4.0	1.8	3.5	1.8	—
February	5.6	5.7	17.2	5.8	3.1	4.8	3.2	4.2	1.8	3.1	2.1	—
March	5.6	5.1	16.9	6.0	2.6	5.2	3.1	2.6	2.2	3.0	2.1	—
April	4.7	4.8	12.7	4.8	2.6	3.8	2.8	4.7	1.6	2.3	2.0	—
May	4.7	6.9	12.1	4.5	2.8	2.5	2.5	4.1	1.7	1.8	1.8	—
June	4.8	9.3	12.8	4.0	3.0	2.6	3.2	7.6	1.7	2.4	1.7	—
July	4.1	6.0	11.5	3.5	2.5	2.5	2.9	6.7	1.3	2.3	1.5	—
August	3.8	6.1	10.4	3.3	2.1	1.7	2.7	4.9	1.2	2.1	2.0	2.1
September	3.8	6.8	10.0	3.2	2.3	2.1	2.8	4.0	1.3	2.5	2.4	2.0
October	3.7	6.9	8.7	3.2	2.4	2.6	2.4	3.7	1.2	1.7	2.6	—
November	3.6	7.5	7.5	2.9	2.9	2.2	2.4	4.7	1.2	1.9	1.9	—
December	4.0	9.9	8.6	3.3	2.8	1.7	2.6	5.0	1.5	2.1	1.7	—
Annual average	4.4	7.1	11.6	4.1	2.6	2.6	2.8	4.6	1.5	2.3	2.0	2.2
1947												
January	4.6	11.6	9.7	3.7	3.6	2.2	2.8	4.9	4.7	2.2	2.0	—
February	4.8	9.7	11.9	3.8	3.4	2.6	3.0	5.6	3.7	2.9	2.0	—
March	4.4	9.3	10.0	3.2	3.3	3.4	3.0	5.2	3.7	3.0	1.7	2.4
April	4.4	10.1	9.0	3.6	3.1	3.8	3.2	6.6	3.3	2.8	2.4	2.3
May	3.3	7.3	7.3	2.5	2.3	2.1	3.2	6.8	3.9	2.4	2.5	2.3
June	3.8	11.2	9.6	2.3	2.2	2.0	4.7	14.1	5.7	2.7	2.2	2.5
July	4.0	10.6	8.4	2.8	2.4	1.9	4.5	10.7	5.0	3.3	2.5	1.6
August	3.4	7.5	7.3	2.6	2.1	2.6	3.4	6.4	4.4	2.8	2.1	1.8
September	3.2	9.1	5.1	2.7	2.0	2.6	3.0	5.3	4.0	2.4	2.4	2.8
October	2.7	7.1	5.2	2.2	1.8	2.4	2.9	5.4	3.8	2.4	2.0	2.7
November	2.7	7.4	6.2	2.0	1.7	2.4	2.6	4.7	2.5	2.6	1.9	0.6
December	2.9	7.6	5.9	2.2	2.0	2.4	2.4	5.2	3.2	1.8	1.7	2.1
Annual average	3.7	9.1	7.9	2.8	2.5	2.5	3.2	7.1	4.0	2.6	2.1	1.8

TABLE 96—CONTINUED

Year and Month	Male: Total, 14 Years and Over	Male: 14 to 19 Years	Male: 20 to 24 Years	Male: 25 to 44 Years	Male: 45 to 64 Years	Male: 65 Years and Over	Female: Total, 14 Years and Over	Female: 14 to 19 Years	Female: 20 to 24 Years	Female: 25 to 44 Years	Female: 45 to 64 Years	Female: 65 Years and Over
1948												
January	3.7	9.8	7.4	2.6	2.8	3.5	3.0	5.8	3.1	2.8	2.4	0.7
February	4.4	8.0	9.0	3.1	3.4	3.8	4.5	8.3	4.9	3.9	3.6	2.7
March	4.1	10.7	9.6	2.9	2.7	3.9	4.0	7.4	5.4	3.4	3.0	3.2
April	3.6	7.8	7.5	2.8	2.7	3.0	3.6	7.8	4.1	3.2	2.8	0.6
May	2.9	6.0	6.5	2.2	2.0	2.8	3.0	5.1	4.4	2.6	2.2	1.6
June	3.1	10.4	6.2	1.8	1.8	2.4	4.3	13.0	3.9	2.9	2.6	0.9
July	3.2	9.3	5.7	2.2	2.0	2.2	4.2	10.4	5.3	2.8	2.7	1.7
August	2.9	6.8	4.9	2.2	2.3	2.4	3.4	5.6	3.9	3.2	2.5	2.6
September	2.8	6.5	4.5	2.1	2.5	2.8	3.6	6.5	3.7	3.5	2.5	1.9
October	2.5	5.9	4.5	1.8	2.0	2.8	3.1	4.5	4.0	2.9	2.4	1.9
November	2.8	6.6	4.4	2.0	2.6	2.9	3.3	6.3	4.1	3.2	2.0	2.7
December	3.2	7.0	5.6	2.2	3.0	3.8	3.0	4.9	3.8	2.6	2.4	3.5
Annual average	3.3	8.2	6.3	2.3	2.5	3.0	3.6	7.3	4.2	3.1	2.6	1.9
1949												
January	4.6	11.1	8.3	3.5	3.9	4.3	3.8	8.4	3.9	3.4	2.9	2.4
February	5.6	11.2	10.3	4.3	4.8	6.0	4.7	9.8	6.2	4.0	3.3	1.6
March	5.6	11.7	10.1	4.4	4.6	5.6	4.2	8.9	5.4	3.6	3.0	2.1
April	5.0	10.6	8.9	4.0	4.1	5.3	4.7	8.9	5.8	4.6	3.1	1.8
May	5.4	12.3	10.0	4.1	3.6	5.2	5.1	10.4	5.8	4.5	3.7	3.1
June	5.8	16.2	10.4	4.1	4.0	5.0	6.4	16.0	6.8	5.1	3.7	3.5
July	6.3	13.1	12.8	4.8	4.5	4.7	6.7	14.8	6.7	5.7	4.5	4.7
August	5.6	11.3	10.4	4.2	4.4	4.8	6.3	10.4	8.6	5.9	4.0	4.8
September	5.0	9.7	8.7	4.2	4.1	4.6	6.1	12.7	8.5	4.9	3.8	5.1
October	5.8	11.2	10.6	5.1	4.6	3.9	5.4	9.2	7.8	5.1	3.5	3.4
November	5.3	11.3	8.4	4.5	4.3	4.5	5.8	11.1	7.2	5.3	4.0	4.4
December	5.6	13.2	8.6	4.6	5.0	4.5	5.6	10.2	7.0	4.9	4.1	5.2
Annual average	5.5	12.0	9.8	4.3	4.4	4.8	5.4	11.1	6.7	4.8	3.6	3.6
1950												
January	7.5	18.3	12.2	5.8	6.4	6.3	6.9	11.5	9.2	5.9	6.1	2.9
February	7.8	17.4	13.7	6.0	6.9	6.7	7.0	11.7	9.3	6.3	5.8	3.4
March	6.8	12.9	11.6	5.7	6.0	5.5	6.3	12.2	6.3	6.1	4.9	4.8
April	6.0	11.6	9.0	4.8	5.7	5.0	4.9	7.4	6.2	4.6	4.1	3.6
May	4.8	11.2	7.3	3.9	4.2	3.9	5.0	9.4	6.5	4.7	3.4	3.5
June	4.8	14.4	7.3	3.1	3.1	4.7	6.1	16.1	7.3	4.4	4.2	1.8
July	4.7	10.6	7.3	3.7	3.6	3.9	5.8	14.6	6.5	4.5	3.9	2.2
August	3.6	7.4	6.0	2.8	3.0	3.6	4.4	7.8	4.6	4.1	3.3	3.2
September	3.3	7.7	6.1	2.4	2.7	4.0	4.6	9.2	6.3	3.9	3.2	2.2
October	2.6	6.1	3.3	2.0	2.5	3.4	4.0	6.9	4.7	3.2	3.7	3.1
November	3.0	6.4	4.4	2.3	2.6	3.8	4.8	7.9	4.4	4.9	3.8	3.6
December	3.4	7.9	4.4	2.6	3.1	4.1	4.1	7.8	4.3	3.6	3.4	3.2
Annual average	4.9	10.8	7.7	3.7	4.2	4.6	5.3	10.3	6.3	4.7	4.1	3.1

a. Estimates for 1944-1945 omitted because total unemployment was so low that estimates were subject to very high percentage sampling error.

Source: Computed from *Current Population Reports,* Series P-50, Bureau of the Census.

TABLE 97

Percentage Distribution of All Workers and of Four-Quarter Workers under OASI, by Annual Wage Credits, 1937–1948

A. All Workers

Annual Wage Credits	1937	1938	1939	1940	1941	1942	1943	1944	1945	1946	1947	1948
					Both Sexes							
Total	100.0	100.0	100.0	100.0	100.0	100.0	100.0	100.0	100.0	100.0	100.0	100.0
$1–199	21.7	25.0	23.6	22.7	21.1	20.7	19.1	17.9	18.7	16.0	13.4	12.3
200–399	10.5	11.4	10.9	10.7	10.5	10.5	9.8	8.9	9.8	9.1	7.9	7.0
400–599	9.5	10.1	9.7	9.3	8.5	8.0	7.1	6.6	6.9	6.8	6.1	5.6
600–799	10.3	10.1	10.0	10.1	8.8	7.2	6.0	5.6	5.5	5.7	5.1	4.7
800–999	9.4	9.0	9.0	8.7	8.2	7.1	5.8	5.2	5.0	5.2	4.5	4.1
1,000–1,199	8.1	7.5	7.6	7.4	7.0	6.4	5.6	5.2	5.1	5.1	4.5	4.0
1,200–1,399	7.1	6.4	6.8	6.6	6.2	5.5	5.2	5.2	5.2	5.2	4.7	4.1
1,400–1,599	5.8	4.9	5.4	5.6	5.6	4.8	4.7	4.8	5.0	5.3	4.7	4.2
1,600–1,799	4.3	3.5	4.1	4.4	4.8	4.4	4.2	4.3	4.5	5.1	4.7	4.3
1,800–1,999	3.4	3.0	3.3	3.7	4.2	4.1	4.0	4.1	4.2	4.9	4.8	4.5
2,000–2,199	2.4	2.1	2.3	2.6	3.4	3.7	3.7	3.8	3.8	4.4	4.6	4.4
2,200–2,399	1.6	1.4	1.5	1.8	2.5	3.1	3.5	3.5	3.5	4.1	4.3	4.3
2,400–2,599	1.2	1.1	1.2	1.3	1.9	2.7	3.2	3.3	3.2	3.6	4.0	4.1
2,600–2,799	0.9	0.9	0.9	1.0	1.5	2.2	2.9	3.1	3.0	3.2	3.9	4.0
2,800–2,999	0.7	0.7	0.6	0.8	1.1	1.9	2.7	3.0	2.8	2.8	3.6	3.8
3,000 [a]	3.1	2.9	3.1	3.4	4.6	7.7	12.5	15.5	13.7	13.3	19.2	24.8
					Male							
Total	100.0	100.0	100.0	100.0	100.0	100.0	100.0	100.0	100.0	100.0	100.0	100.0
$1–199	18.5	21.9	20.6	19.4	17.4	15.7	15.4	14.5	16.2	12.7	10.3	9.2
200–399	9.1	10.0	9.7	9.4	9.0	8.6	7.8	6.7	8.4	7.3	6.1	5.5
400–599	7.8	8.6	8.2	7.7	7.2	6.8	5.6	5.0	5.7	5.7	5.0	4.5
600–799	8.3	8.6	8.2	8.2	7.0	6.1	4.6	4.2	4.3	4.8	4.2	3.7
800–999	8.7	8.5	8.2	7.8	6.8	5.7	4.2	3.7	3.6	4.3	3.6	3.2
1,000–1,199	8.7	8.2	8.1	7.8	6.8	5.5	4.0	3.7	3.5	4.2	3.5	3.1
1,200–1,399	8.4	7.5	7.9	7.7	6.9	5.4	4.0	3.7	3.6	4.3	3.7	3.2
1,400–1,599	7.2	6.0	6.7	6.9	6.8	5.4	4.1	3.7	3.7	4.6	3.7	3.2
1,600–1,799	5.6	4.5	5.3	5.6	6.2	5.4	4.1	3.8	3.7	4.6	3.8	3.3
1,800–1,999	4.4	3.9	4.3	4.9	5.5	5.4	4.5	4.1	4.1	5.1	4.2	3.6
2,000–2,199	3.2	2.8	3.0	3.5	4.6	5.0	4.7	4.3	4.3	5.0	4.5	3.9
2,200–2,399	2.1	1.9	2.0	2.4	3.5	4.4	4.7	4.4	4.4	5.0	4.6	4.2
2,400–2,599	1.6	1.5	1.6	1.8	2.6	3.8	4.5	4.5	4.5	4.8	4.8	4.4
2,600–2,799	1.2	1.2	1.2	1.4	2.0	3.2	4.2	4.5	4.4	4.4	5.0	4.7
2,800–2,999	0.9	0.9	0.8	1.0	1.5	2.7	4.1	4.5	4.2	3.9	4.8	4.8
3,000 [a]	4.2	4.0	4.2	4.6	6.2	11.0	19.3	24.6	21.4	19.3	28.2	35.3
					Female							
Total	100.0	100.0	100.0	100.0	100.0	100.0	100.0	100.0	100.0	100.0	100.0	100.0
$1–199	30.0	32.9	31.3	31.2	30.6	31.6	25.6	23.3	22.7	22.3	20.1	18.5
200–399	14.1	14.9	14.0	13.9	14.4	14.5	13.3	12.2	12.0	12.7	11.3	10.3
400–599	14.0	13.9	13.6	13.5	11.8	10.5	9.7	9.1	8.8	8.9	8.4	8.0
600–799	15.5	13.9	14.7	14.9	13.3	9.7	8.4	7.7	7.5	7.5	6.9	6.5
800–999	11.4	10.2	11.2	10.9	11.6	10.3	8.4	7.5	7.4	6.9	6.2	5.7
1,000–1,199	6.5	5.8	6.3	6.5	7.5	8.4	8.4	7.7	7.8	6.8	6.2	5.6
1,200–1,399	3.6	3.5	3.9	3.9	4.5	5.7	7.3	7.5	7.8	7.0	6.5	5.9
1,400–1,599	2.0	2.0	2.0	2.2	2.7	3.6	5.7	6.4	7.2	6.8	6.6	6.1
1,600–1,799	1.0	1.0	1.0	1.1	1.4	2.2	4.2	5.1	5.7	6.0	6.4	6.1
1,800–1,999	0.7	0.7	0.7	0.7	0.8	1.4	3.1	4.0	4.4	4.7	5.8	6.1
2,000–2,199	0.4	0.4	0.4	0.4	0.4	0.7	2.1	3.0	3.0	3.3	4.7	5.5
2,200–2,399	0.2	0.2	0.2	0.2	0.2	0.4	1.4	2.1	1.9	2.3	3.5	4.4
2,400–2,599	0.2	0.2	0.1	0.1	0.2	0.2	0.9	1.5	1.2	1.5	2.4	3.4
2,600–2,799	0.1	0.1	0.1	0.1	0.1	0.1	5.0	1.0	0.8	1.0	1.6	2.4
2,800–2,999	0.1	0.1	0.1	0.1	0.1	0.1	0.3	0.7	0.5	0.6	1.0	1.7
3,000 [a]	0.3	0.3	0.4	0.3	0.3	0.4	0.7	1.4	1.1	1.7	2.4	3.8

TABLE 97—CONTINUED

B. Four-Quarter Workers

Annual Wage Credits	1938	1939	1940	1941	1942	1943	1944	1945	1946	1947	1948
					Both Sexes						
Total	100.0	100.0	100.0	100.0	100.0	100.0	100.0	100.0	100.0	100.0	100.0
$1–199	2.8	2.5	2.1	1.4	1.0	0.8	0.7	0.8	0.5	0.3	0.3
200–399	6.4	5.6	5.2	3.8	2.9	2.3	2.1	2.2	1.5	1.3	1.1
400–599	10.9	9.9	9.1	6.6	4.8	3.6	3.3	3.3	2.6	2.0	1.7
600–799	13.5	12.9	13.0	10.5	7.2	4.9	4.3	4.2	3.4	2.8	2.3
800–999	13.3	12.8	12.2	11.2	9.1	6.5	5.4	5.1	4.4	3.5	3.0
1,000–1,199	11.5	11.3	10.9	10.1	9.0	7.4	6.4	6.3	5.5	4.4	3.6
1,200–1,399	9.8	10.4	10.0	9.4	8.2	7.4	7.1	7.1	6.7	5.4	4.6
1,400–1,599	7.6	8.3	8.6	8.7	7.5	7.0	6.8	7.3	7.5	5.9	5.2
1,600–1,799	5.4	6.4	6.7	7.6	7.1	6.4	6.4	6.7	7.6	6.4	5.6
1,800–1,999	4.6	5.1	5.7	6.7	6.9	6.2	6.1	6.5	7.7	6.7	6.1
2,000–2,199	3.3	3.6	4.0	5.5	6.1	6.0	5.8	6.0	7.1	6.6	6.2
2,200–2,399	2.2	2.3	2.8	4.1	5.3	5.7	5.5	5.6	6.6	6.4	6.1
2,400–2,599	1.7	1.9	2.0	3.1	4.6	5.3	5.3	5.4	6.0	6.1	5.9
2,600–2,799	1.4	1.4	1.5	2.3	3.8	4.8	5.0	5.1	5.4	5.9	5.8
2,800–2,999	1.0	0.9	1.1	1.7	3.2	4.5	4.8	4.7	4.6	5.4	5.5
3,000 [b]	4.5	4.8	5.1	7.3	13.2	21.2	25.0	23.8	22.8	30.8	37.1
					Male						
Total	100.0	100.0	100.0	100.0	100.0	100.0	100.0	100.0	100.0	100.0	100.0
$1–199	2.1	1.9	1.5	1.0	0.7	0.6	6.0	0.6	0.4	0.3	0.2
200–399	4.4	4.1	3.8	2.7	1.9	1.5	1.4	1.4	1.0	0.8	0.6
400–599	7.8	6.9	6.1	4.5	2.9	2.2	2.0	2.0	1.6	1.3	1.1
600–799	10.4	9.3	9.2	6.7	4.0	2.8	2.5	2.4	2.0	1.7	1.5
800–999	11.9	10.7	10.1	8.1	5.2	3.4	2.8	2.7	2.6	2.1	1.9
1,000–1,199	12.1	11.5	10.9	9.0	6.4	4.1	3.5	3.3	3.4	2.7	2.1
1,200–1,399	11.2	11.7	11.1	9.7	7.1	4.6	4.1	4.0	4.3	3.5	2.7
1,400–1,599	9.0	10.0	10.2	9.9	7.6	5.2	4.5	4.6	5.3	4.0	3.4
1,600–1,799	6.7	8.0	8.4	9.2	8.1	5.6	4.9	4.9	6.0	4.5	3.8
1,800–1,999	5.9	6.5	7.2	8.4	8.4	6.3	5.5	5.7	7.1	5.4	4.4
2,000–2,199	4.2	4.6	5.2	7.0	7.8	6.8	5.9	6.3	7.4	6.0	5.1
2,200–2,399	2.9	3.0	3.6	5.2	6.9	7.0	6.2	6.7	7.6	6.4	5.5
2,400–2,599	2.2	2.4	2.6	4.0	6.1	6.9	6.5	6.9	7.4	6.7	5.9
2,600–2,799	1.8	1.8	2.0	3.0	5.1	6.5	6.6	6.9	6.9	7.1	6.3
2,800–2,999	1.3	1.1	1.5	2.3	4.3	6.3	6.6	6.6	6.1	6.7	6.5
3,000 [b]	5.9	6.2	6.7	9.4	17.7	30.2	36.5	35.0	31.0	40.8	48.9
					Female						
Total	100.0	100.0	100.0	100.0	100.0	100.0	100.0	100.0	100.0	100.0	100.0
$1–199	4.6	4.0	3.8	2.7	2.1	1.4	1.1	1.1	0.9	0.8	0.5
200–399	12.0	10.0	9.4	7.1	5.7	4.1	3.6	3.7	2.9	2.4	2.2
400–599	19.7	18.5	17.8	13.3	9.9	6.6	5.9	5.8	4.8	3.9	3.3
600–799	22.4	23.3	24.1	22.2	15.8	9.6	8.0	7.6	6.7	5.4	4.3
800–999	17.3	18.6	18.3	20.9	20.2	13.1	10.4	9.9	8.7	6.9	6.0
1,000–1,199	9.9	10.7	11.0	13.7	16.4	14.7	12.2	12.2	10.7	8.7	7.6
1,200–1,399	6.0	6.5	6.6	8.4	11.4	13.5	12.8	13.2	12.4	10.3	9.2
1,400–1,599	3.4	3.5	3.8	5.0	7.3	10.9	11.4	12.5	12.6	11.3	9.8
1,600–1,799	1.6	1.7	1.8	2.6	4.5	8.3	9.2	10.2	11.3	11.4	10.3
1,800–1,999	1.2	1.2	1.2	1.5	2.8	6.0	7.4	7.9	9.1	10.6	10.3
2,000–2,199	0.6	0.6	0.6	0.8	1.5	4.2	5.5	5.5	6.4	8.6	9.2
2,200–2,399	0.3	0.3	0.4	0.4	0.8	2.8	4.0	3.6	4.4	6.3	7.6
2,400–2,599	0.3	0.2	0.2	0.3	0.5	1.8	2.8	2.3	2.8	4.4	6.0
2,600–2,799	0.2	0.2	0.2	0.2	0.3	1.1	2.0	1.5	1.9	2.9	4.3
2,800–2,999	0.1	0.1	0.1	0.1	0.2	0.7	1.3	0.9	1.2	1.8	2.7
3,000 [b]	0.4	0.7	0.5	0.6	0.7	1.3	2.5	2.0	3.2	4.4	6.5

a. For 1937, 1938 and 1939, represents wage credits of $3,000 or more; for those years earnings up to $3,000 from each employer in year were credited.

b. For 1938 and 1939, represents wage credits of $3,000 or more; for those years earnings up to $3,000 from each employer in year were credited.

Source: Bureau of Old-Age and Survivors Insurance.

TABLE 98

Decile Annual Wage Credits of Workers under OASI, by Number of Quarters in Covered Employment, 1937–1948

Year	Number of Workers, in Thousands	First Decile	Second Decile	Third Decile	Fourth Decile	Median	Sixth Decile	Seventh Decile	Eighth Decile	Ninth Decile
					All Workers					
1937	32,904	$80	$175	$335	$525	$720	$930	$1,180	$1,485	$1,950
1938	31,822	75	150	270	465	665	865	1,100	1,405	1,915
1939	33,751	85	170	310	505	700	910	1,165	1,470	1,950
1940	35,393	85	175	330	530	730	945	1,215	1,545	2,040
1941	40,976	95	190	370	595	825	1,080	1,390	1,770	2,340
1942	46,363	95	190	375	620	900	1,190	1,590	2,055	2,755
1943	47,656	105	210	425	720	1,065	1,450	1,910	2,455	3,160
1944	46,296	110	235	490	830	1,210	1,615	2,090	2,685	3,325
1945	46,392	105	220	440	760	1,145	1,530	1,965	2,535	3,215
1946	49,096	120	275	535	870	1,260	1,640	2,050	2,535	3,250
1947	48,900	150	350	700	1,125	1,575	1,975	2,450	2,950	3,500
1948	49,100	160	425	825	1,300	1,780	2,250	2,750	3,250	3,800
					Four-Quarter Workers [a]					
1938	20,002	$420	$610	$760	$905	$1,070	$1,250	$1,465	$1,775	$2,280
1939	21,376	440	625	790	950	1,110	1,290	1,505	1,795	2,305
1940	22,649	470	670	825	985	1,170	1,370	1,590	1,890	2,405
1941	25,328	560	765	945	1,130	1,340	1,565	1,825	2,150	2,710
1942	26,624	645	895	1,115	1,350	1,610	1,895	2,220	2,620	3,210
1943	27,741	750	1,050	1,330	1,615	1,930	2,270	2,640	3,060	—
1944	28,344	785	1,130	1,415	1,720	2,050	2,415	2,790	3,205	—
1945	26,634	780	1,150	1,430	1,720	2,005	2,375	2,750	3,155	—
1946	28,300	890	1,270	1,550	1,810	2,070	2,360	2,700	3,110	—
1947	30,400	1,010	1,400	1,725	2,040	2,350	2,670	3,000	—	—
1948	32,900	1,100	1,525	1,875	2,200	2,525	2,900	3,250	—	—
					Three-Quarter Workers [a]					
1938	3,617	$90	$180	$260	$340	$430	$525	$645	$810	$1,120
1939	3,729	80	160	230	290	365	455	550	680	955
1940	3,880	120	230	315	400	490	600	730	920	1,240
1941	5,074	125	230	315	395	480	580	700	875	1,175
1942	6,093	165	285	390	495	610	740	905	1,130	1,520
1943	6,151	180	300	415	540	680	835	1,035	1,320	1,780
1944	5,536	185	310	420	540	680	840	1,050	1,330	1,805
1945	5,929	220	370	510	660	835	1,045	1,280	1,585	2,030
1946	6,800	255	410	560	705	860	1,030	1,235	1,500	1,925
1947	6,600	260	420	570	730	880	1,080	1,300	1,550	2,100
1948	5,000	250	390	525	700	790	950	1,125	1,350	1,750
					Two-Quarter Workers [a]					
1938	3,724	$35	$70	$100	$135	$170	$215	$290	$370	$530
1939	4,036	35	65	100	130	165	205	260	340	460
1940	4,090	35	70	105	145	180	225	280	360	505
1941	5,228	40	80	125	165	210	255	320	410	565
1942	6,477	50	100	150	210	265	330	415	535	740
1943	6,546	55	100	160	215	280	360	460	610	860
1944	5,914	55	100	160	220	285	370	470	620	875
1945	5,918	60	110	175	240	310	400	515	670	950
1946	6,900	70	140	210	280	360	450	565	715	950
1947	5,900	75	150	220	300	380	460	580	690	920
1948	5,500	75	150	220	300	380	460	600	725	975

a. Data by number of quarters employed not available for 1937.

Source: Bureau of Old-Age and Survivors Insurance.

TABLE 99

Decile Annual Wage Credits of Male Workers under OASI, by Age, 1939, 1944, 1946 and 1948

Year of Employment and Age	Number of Workers, in Thousands[a]	First Decile	Second Decile	Third Decile	Fourth Decile	Median	Sixth Decile	Seventh Decile	Eighth Decile	Ninth Decile
1939										
All ages[b]	24,360	$65	$190	$385	$630	$870	$1,115	$1,370	$1,675	$2,160
15–19	1,710	15	40	65	90	140	190	260	380	580
20–24	3,932	40	125	220	350	505	660	825	1,010	1,265
25–29	3,859	80	240	450	670	870	1,070	1,265	1,470	1,780
30–34	3,382	115	340	610	865	1,110	1,325	1,545	1,810	2,220
35–39	2,824	125	370	670	955	1,210	1,450	1,705	2,015	2,545
40–44	2,346	135	400	700	1,020	1,275	1,515	1,790	2,140	2,800
45–49	2,073	130	390	715	1,010	1,255	1,500	1,780	2,130	2,820
50–54	1,688	120	360	660	940	1,190	1,415	1,680	2,025	2,740
55–59	1,198	100	300	580	835	1,090	1,320	1,570	1,925	2,630
60–64	743	90	270	525	775	1,010	1,230	1,470	1,815	2,505
65–69	386	75	230	445	690	910	1,125	1,355	1,675	2,330
70 and over	185	80	245	460	695	900	1,110	1,330	1,670	2,495
1944										
All ages[b]	28,101	120	360	775	1,310	1,820	2,290	2,740	3,170	—
15–19	3,299	30	95	150	215	310	425	590	795	1,225
20–24	1,968	45	130	220	450	750	1,115	1,530	2,030	2,675
25–29	2,728	120	355	760	1,250	1,730	2,190	2,640	3,075	—
30–34	3,348	195	645	1,250	1,850	2,305	2,705	3,040	—	—
35–39	3,322	300	910	1,545	2,065	2,470	2,830	3,155	—	—
40–44	3,235	390	1,070	1,650	2,120	2,505	2,840	3,175	—	—
45–49	2,778	405	1,080	1,630	2,075	2,445	2,800	3,115	—	—
50–54	2,428	390	1,040	1,560	2,005	2,370	2,705	3,045	—	—
55–59	1,986	360	960	1,455	1,850	2,195	2,530	2,880	3,240	—
60–64	1,417	260	720	1,210	1,575	1,915	2,240	2,570	2,990	3,420
65–69	795	165	490	875	1,255	1,570	1,900	2,250	2,670	3,195
70 and over	464	90	270	540	885	1,210	1,500	1,845	2,285	2,975
1946										
All ages[b]	32,182	130	395	765	1,235	1,670	2,070	2,475	2,945	3,440
15–19	2,935	25	70	120	180	265	370	505	720	1,120
20–24	4,077	70	210	370	560	790	1,050	1,355	1,710	2,180
25–29	4,374	155	465	820	1,185	1,505	1,815	2,125	2,470	2,970
30–34	4,190	265	715	1,200	1,640	1,990	2,325	2,650	3,040	—
35–39	3,684	310	870	1,420	1,865	2,235	2,585	2,930	3,275	—
40–44	3,188	350	980	1,570	2,020	2,385	2,720	3,085	—	—
45–49	2,690	330	910	1,520	1,980	2,345	2,700	3,055	—	—
50–54	2,393	355	970	1,560	1,975	2,315	2,650	3,055	—	—
55–59	1,923	295	860	1,445	1,870	2,205	2,525	2,870	3,260	—
60–64	1,440	270	755	1,290	1,685	2,000	2,305	2,655	3,080	—
65–69	1,288	160	475	875	1,300	1,640	1,960	2,300	2,710	3,320
70 and over		95	290	580	940	1,310	1,635	1,990	2,450	3,135
1948										
All ages	33,000	225	625	1,210	1,800	2,120	2,950	3,120	—	—
Under 20	2,900	70	120	190	260	375	540	760	1,100	1,660
20–24	4,450	180	400	700	1,040	1,440	1,830	2,210	2,600	3,100
25–29	4,500	300	800	1,280	1,870	2,280	2,620	2,950	3,260	—
30–34	4,200	400	1,180	1,830	2,370	2,760	3,080	—	—	—
35–39	3,750	490	1,280	1,980	2,500	2,900	3,220	—	—	—
40–44	3,300	520	1,320	2,030	2,580	2,990	3,300	—	—	—
45–49	2,750	500	1,280	1,980	2,530	2,945	3,260	—	—	—
50–54	2,400	500	1,275	1,970	2,520	2,930	3,250	—	—	—
55–59	1,950	400	1,150	1,860	2,360	2,760	3,200	—	—	—
60–64	1,500	360	1,000	1,630	2,125	2,525	2,900	3,225	—	—
65–69	1,300	200	675	1,200	1,680	2,070	2,475	2,860	3,250	—
70 and over		180	460	880	1,330	1,720	2,100	2,500	3,010	—

a. Workers with unreported age distributed proportionately among the known ages.
b. Totals include workers under 15 years of age.

Source: Bureau of Old-Age and Survivors Insurance.

TABLE 100

DECILE ANNUAL WAGE CREDITS OF FEMALE WORKERS UNDER OASI, BY AGE, 1939, 1944, 1946 AND 1948

Year of Employment and Age	Number of Workers, in Thousands[a]	First Decile	Second Decile	Third Decile	Fourth Decile	Median	Sixth Decile	Seventh Decile	Eighth Decile	Ninth Decile
1939										
All ages[b]	9,391	$25	$70	$160	$315	$455	$595	$735	$885	$1,130
15–19	1,109	12	35	60	90	130	190	270	385	550
20–24	2,329	30	95	180	295	420	540	660	780	930
25–29	1,692	40	120	250	390	530	665	790	930	1,130
30–34	1,289	45	130	270	430	585	725	865	1,050	1,310
35–39	969	45	130	270	430	580	715	875	1,070	1,375
40–44	733	45	130	280	445	590	710	860	1,065	1,410
45–49	522	40	125	285	435	575	700	840	1,035	1,390
50–54	346	40	120	270	425	560	685	820	1,010	1,375
55–59	218	35	110	250	405	540	665	795	970	1,330
60–64	116	35	110	250	390	530	650	775	945	1,290
65–69	48	35	110	240	370	510	635	750	925	1,270
70 and over......	15	30	100	220	350	490	630	750	950	1,360
1944										
All ages[b]	18,195	55	160	295	490	740	1,010	1,255	1,550	1,990
15–19	3,168	30	95	145	215	315	445	630	875	1,225
20–24	3,705	60	180	350	585	825	1,065	1,300	1,545	1,910
25–29	2,539	60	180	360	580	835	1,115	1,370	1,660	2,065
30–34	2,087	70	210	385	610	865	1,130	1,410	1,720	2,095
35–39	1,877	80	235	440	690	970	1,220	1,490	1,805	2,215
40–44	1,562	80	235	450	710	965	1,225	1,485	1,790	2,225
45–49	1,202	80	240	455	710	960	1,200	1,445	1,765	2,230
50–54	870	75	225	430	670	910	1,140	1,365	1,650	2,070
55–59	574	70	210	400	625	870	1,080	1,275	1,535	1,970
60–64	321	60	185	360	555	785	980	1,185	1,440	1,795
65–69	135	55	160	305	485	730	935	1,125	1,390	1,765
70 and over......	48	40	120	235	405	595	810	1,020	1,285	1,725
1946										
All ages[b]	16,663	55	170	310	510	750	1,035	1,330	1,625	2,010
15–19	2,691	35	100	150	220	320	455	640	895	1,260
20–24	3,400	60	180	325	530	770	1,045	1,300	1,555	1,840
25–29	2,405	60	175	320	510	760	1,050	1,350	1,655	2,010
30–34	1,853	65	190	350	560	815	1,110	1,405	1,720	2,110
35–39	1,716	75	230	420	660	950	1,230	1,520	1,830	2,265
40–44	1,466	85	250	460	735	1,045	1,320	1,595	1,900	2,350
45–49	1,153	85	260	500	780	1,065	1,325	1,590	1,905	2,360
50–54	853	85	255	490	785	1,070	1,325	1,565	1,850	2,280
55–59	572	85	250	485	760	1,035	1,270	1,510	1,795	2,205
60–64	344	90	265	510	765	1,005	1,230	1,435	1,685	2,100
65–69	210	80	240	440	690	915	1,140	1,330	1,580	1,970
70 and over......		60	180	325	550	810	1,040	1,275	1,560	2,070
1948										
All ages[b]	16,100	100	230	410	680	1,050	1,360	1,680	2,030	2,460
Under 20	2,300	60	120	180	220	300	390	520	750	1,050
20–24	3,150	100	240	440	720	1,040	1,370	1,640	1,940	2,220
25–29	2,250	100	240	450	730	1,060	1,420	1,770	2,080	2,470
30–34	1,850	105	250	470	760	1,100	1,440	1,780	2,120	2,560
35–39	1,700	110	290	540	860	1,210	1,550	1,900	2,260	2,710
40–44	1,550	140	330	610	990	1,320	1,640	1,960	2,330	2,790
45–49	1,200	140	340	630	990	1,300	1,620	1,930	2,290	2,740
50–54	900	140	360	670	1,020	1,320	1,605	1,900	2,240	2,700
55–59	600	140	360	650	980	1,280	1,560	1,830	2,150	2,610
60–64	350	130	340	620	940	1,210	1,470	1,730	2,050	2,530
65–69	250	120	280	540	800	1,080	1,320	1,580	1,880	2,350
70 and over.......		110	210	440	760	1,040	1,300	1,580	1,860	2,320

a. Workers with unreported age distributed proportionately among the known ages; estimates for 1946 are preliminary.
b. Totals include workers under 15 years of age.

Source: Bureau of Old-Age and Survivors Insurance.

TABLE 101

DECILE ANNUAL WAGE CREDITS OF MEN AND WOMEN WITH FOUR QUARTERS IN EMPLOYMENT UNDER OASI, BY AGE, 1946

Age	Number of Workers, in Thousands[a]	First Decile	Second Decile	Third Decile	Fourth Decile	Median	Sixth Decile	Seventh Decile	Eighth Decile	Ninth Decile
				Male Four-Quarter Workers						
All ages[b]	19,806	$1,150	$1,585	$1,905	$2,170	$2,435	$2,720	$3,060	—	—
15–19	706	310	450	570	695	845	1,010	1,215	$1,480	$1,880
20–24	1,455	845	1,125	1,350	1,550	1,725	1,910	2,110	2,365	2,770
25–29	2,451	1,170	1,495	1,750	1,955	2,155	2,360	2,595	2,905	3,270
30–34	2,800	1,390	1,780	2,065	2,300	2,535	2,780	3,050	—	—
35–39	2,675	1,460	1,880	2,185	2,465	2,720	2,980	3,235	—	—
40–44	2,434	1,480	1,945	2,270	2,545	2,805	3,100	—	—	—
45–49	2,059	1,445	1,895	2,230	2,505	2,780	3,065	—	—	—
50–54	1,845	1,450	1,875	2,175	2,455	2,710	2,985	3,275	—	—
55–59	1,468	1,370	1,795	2,090	2,340	2,605	2,880	3,185	—	—
60–64	1,071	1,280	1,650	1,920	2,160	2,400	2,660	2,980	3,325	—
65–69	535	1,095	1,430	1,700	1,940	2,165	2,415	2,715	3,140	—
70 and over......	292	805	1,230	1,480	1,710	1,940	2,185	2,525	2,980	3,470
				Female Four-Quarter Workers						
All ages[b]	8,464	645	915	1,115	1,290	1,450	1,610	1,785	2,010	2,355
15–19	916	340	500	660	820	960	1,105	1,260	1,430	1,650
20–24	1,669	730	985	1,160	1,310	1,440	1,565	1,695	1,850	2,075
25–29	1,141	740	1,010	1,205	1,370	1,530	1,690	1,850	2,035	2,315
30–34	933	725	995	1,215	1,375	1,545	1,710	1,885	2,105	2,445
35–39	961	725	1,020	1,215	1,395	1,570	1,740	1,945	2,195	2,590
40–44	800	730	1,030	1,235	1,415	1,585	1,770	1,985	2,240	2,640
45–49	714	735	995	1,215	1,385	1,555	1,745	1,950	2,230	2,690
50–54	533	750	1,010	1,210	1,380	1,530	1,690	1,890	2,145	2,600
55–59	359	700	970	1,150	1,300	1,470	1,645	1,835	2,080	2,565
60–64	223	665	890	1,080	1,240	1,380	1,530	1,705	1,935	2,360
65–69	93	625	860	1,025	1,175	1,310	1,440	1,615	1,860	2,240
70 and over......	38	435	730	930	1,090	1,250	1,425	1,605	1,880	2,380

a. Preliminary, workers with unreported age distributed proportionately among the known ages.
b. Totals include workers under 15 years of age.

Source: Bureau of Old-Age and Survivors Insurance.

TABLE 102

DECILE ANNUAL WAGE CREDITS OF WORKERS UNDER OASI, BY SEX, RACE AND AGE, 1937, 1939, 1944 AND 1946

Year of Employment and Age	Number of Workers, in Thousands[a]	First Decile	Second Decile	Third Decile	Fourth Decile	Median	Sixth Decile	Seventh Decile	Eighth Decile	Ninth Decile
A. White Male										
1937										
All ages[b]	21,868	$100	$260	$500	$750	$980	$1,205	$1,440	$1,750	$2,300
15-19	1,820	15	50	85	125	180	255	365	515	735
20-24	3,687	65	190	330	490	640	800	950	1,120	1,350
25-29	3,452	140	375	600	800	990	1,070	1,240	1,445	1,740
30-34	2,941	190	500	770	1,010	1,220	1,425	1,635	1,890	2,300
35-39	2,502	190	530	830	1,095	1,320	1,550	1,790	2,090	2,680
40-44	2,191	190	530	860	1,125	1,360	1,590	1,820	2,120	2,850
45-49	1,946	185	510	820	1,090	1,320	1,550	1,805	2,140	2,900
50-54	1,508	170	470	770	1,010	1,240	1,470	1,715	2,070	2,800
55-59	1,046	140	400	670	930	1,160	1,375	1,620	1,960	2,700
60-64	648	120	360	615	840	1,060	1,270	1,510	1,840	2,500
65 and over[c].....	78	35	110	210	340	485	650	860	1,130	1,590
1939										
All ages[b]	22,345	75	225	445	705	950	1,185	1,430	1,750	2,235
15-19	1,577	13	40	70	105	150	200	265	395	595
20-24	3,593	45	140	250	390	550	710	860	1,035	1,280
25-29	3,489	95	290	525	750	945	1,125	1,305	1,510	1,805
30-34	3,065	135	405	710	970	1,190	1,385	1,605	1,860	2,275
35-39	2,551	155	460	790	1,070	1,310	1,540	1,790	2,090	2,640
40-44	2,145	155	470	825	1,110	1,360	1,590	1,865	2,210	2,890
45-49	1,928	150	450	790	1,080	1,325	1,555	1,830	2,180	2,920
50-54	1,583	135	410	725	1,000	1,240	1,470	1,730	2,080	2,805
55-59	1,130	110	335	635	900	1,140	1,360	1,615	1,970	2,700
60-64	709	95	290	555	810	1,035	1,265	1,500	1,855	2,545
65-69	367	90	265	505	745	965	1,170	1,390	1,740	2,405
70 and over......	177	90	265	500	740	935	1,140	1,365	1,720	2,580
1944										
All ages[b]	25,270	135	400	865	1,450	1,965	2,420	2,845	3,255	—
15-19	2,932	35	125	165	225	310	435	600	810	1,240
20-24	1,654	45	135	225	480	835	1,220	1,655	2,160	2,770
25-29	2,390	135	405	870	1,430	1,895	2,345	2,780	3,185	—
30-34	2,975	225	750	1,465	2,050	2,460	2,825	3,140	—	—
35-39	2,987	350	1,080	1,750	2,230	2,620	2,940	3,245	—	—
40-44	2,896	460	1,255	1,840	2,280	2,630	2,945	3,245	—	—
45-49	2,520	475	1,210	1,780	2,215	2,570	2,900	3,200	—	—
50-54	2,245	455	1,140	1,695	2,115	2,465	2,790	3,100	—	—
55-59	1,852	410	1,050	1,550	1,945	2,275	2,600	2,950	3,290	—
60-64	1,332	295	795	1,270	1,640	1,970	2,285	2,625	3,025	—
65-69	753	175	520	920	1,310	1,615	1,940	2,290	2,705	3,230
70 and over......	441	95	290	575	930	1,250	1,550	1,890	2,335	3,030
1946										
All ages[b]	29,260	145	440	840	1,330	1,780	2,175	2,575	3,025	—
15-19	2,487	25	80	135	200	285	395	535	750	1,170
20-24	3,644	75	225	395	590	825	1,095	1,405	1,750	2,205
25-29	3,949	205	530	900	1,265	1,595	1,900	2,190	2,540	3,040
30-34	3,778	295	810	1,350	1,770	2,110	2,420	2,745	3,115	—
35-39	3,316	375	1,000	1,585	2,025	2,370	2,700	3,030	—	—
40-44	2,899	420	1,125	1,740	2,165	2,515	2,840	3,185	—	—
45-49	2,436	380	1,040	1,675	2,125	2,475	2,820	3,160	—	—
50-54	2,219	405	1,085	1,675	2,075	2,420	2,745	3,075	—	—
55-59	1,810	340	950	1,545	1,950	2,280	2,605	2,940	3,320	—
60-64	1,367	310	820	1,365	1,765	2,060	2,370	2,700	3,115	—
65-69	762	170	500	920	1,345	1,685	2,005	2,350	2,750	3,360
70 and over......	455	105	310	605	985	1,365	1,685	2,030	2,490	3,180

TABLE 102—CONTINUED

Year of Employment and Age	Number of Workers, in Thousands[a]	First Decile	Second Decile	Third Decile	Fourth Decile	Median	Sixth Decile	Seventh Decile	Eighth Decile	Ninth Decile
					B. White Female					
1937										
All ages[b]	8,698	$35	$105	$205	$330	$460	$590	$730	$890	$1,190
15–19	1,219	12	35	65	100	155	230	335	460	640
20–24	2,210	35	110	210	315	420	540	660	780	920
25–29	1,601	50	150	285	420	555	685	810	970	1,160
30–34	1,111	55	165	300	455	600	735	880	1,060	1,330
35–39	855	55	160	300	440	590	730	880	1,080	1,390
40–44	633	60	170	305	450	590	720	860	1,060	1,410
45–49	467	60	170	305	450	580	700	840	1,020	1,390
50–54	299	55	160	305	440	570	690	820	1,005	1,370
55–59	190	50	150	280	415	550	670	790	980	1,330
60–64	97	50	145	275	410	530	655	770	940	1,270
65 and over[c].....	11	25	80	120	205	300	410	530	690	910
1939										
All ages[b]	8,991	35	100	190	330	470	610	740	905	1,150
15–19	1,084	10	30	55	90	130	190	270	390	555
20–24	2,259	35	105	195	310	440	555	665	785	945
25–29	1,610	50	145	270	415	555	685	805	945	1,145
30–34	1,216	55	165	295	455	610	740	890	1,070	1,320
35–39	910	55	165	295	460	610	750	900	1,110	1,410
40–44	694	55	165	295	460	605	730	880	1,090	1,420
45–49	498	55	165	295	455	590	715	855	1,050	1,410
50–54	332	55	160	285	445	580	695	835	1,030	1,395
55–59	211	50	155	270	420	555	680	810	990	1,350
60–64	112	50	155	265	410	550	665	790	950	1,320
65–69	46	50	155	260	390	530	650	770	930	1,270
70 and over......	15	40	120	230	370	510	640	765	975	1,400
1944										
All ages[b]	16,537	60	175	330	540	790	1,060	1,310	1,595	2,010
15–19	2,931	35	105	165	225	330	480	670	920	1,265
20–24	3,350	70	210	410	650	910	1,135	1,350	1,585	1,925
25–29	2,239	70	215	410	645	930	1,190	1,435	1,720	2,115
30–34	1,834	75	230	430	680	965	1,215	1,470	1,780	2,175
35–39	1,689	85	255	480	760	1,035	1,290	1,550	1,850	2,250
40–44	1,421	85	260	490	770	1,030	1,285	1,530	1,840	2,245
45–49	1,121	85	255	485	750	1,015	1,240	1,480	1,785	2,235
50–54	821	80	245	450	700	950	1,170	1,400	1,675	2,105
55–59	548	75	220	420	645	890	1,095	1,310	1,570	1,975
60–64	309	65	190	370	580	810	1,010	1,200	1,445	1,860
65–69	130	55	165	310	510	750	950	1,140	1,415	1,780
70 and over......	46	45	135	245	415	610	825	1,030	1,305	1,725
1946										
All ages[b]	15,242	60	185	330	545	805	1,095	1,380	1,670	2,060
15–19	2,466	35	110	170	250	350	485	680	930	1,300
20–24	3,092	70	205	370	585	840	1,115	1,355	1,590	1,870
25–29	2,142	65	190	350	565	830	1,130	1,415	1,705	2,050
30–34	1,640	70	210	370	605	890	1,185	1,480	1,780	2,155
35–39	1,539	80	245	450	710	1,020	1,300	1,580	1,890	2,320
40–44	1,338	90	270	505	805	1,100	1,385	1,650	1,950	2,390
45–49	1,075	95	280	530	840	1,120	1,370	1,630	1,940	2,405
50–54	811	90	265	520	815	1,110	1,360	1,590	1,880	2,295
55–59	550	90	265	505	790	1,065	1,290	1,530	1,825	2,230
60–64	332	95	280	520	785	1,025	1,260	1,450	1,710	2,100
65–69	144	85	250	455	715	935	1,155	1,350	1,600	1,995
70 and over......	57	70	205	350	590	850	1,080	1,315	1,595	2,100

TABLE 102—CONTINUED

Year of Employment and Age	Number of Workers, in Thousands[a]	First Decile	Second Decile	Third Decile	Fourth Decile	Median	Sixth Decile	Seventh Decile	Eighth Decile	Ninth Decile
C. Negro Male										
1937										
All ages[b]	1,943	$25	$65	$130	$210	$330	$470	$630	$820	$1,150
15–19	146	7	20	35	50	70	100	150	210	335
20–24	334	15	45	80	120	180	270	370	500	720
25–29	345	25	80	140	230	330	440	570	720	950
30–34	296	35	100	200	315	430	560	700	880	1,170
35–39	274	40	120	220	350	490	630	780	990	1,280
40–44	196	40	120	230	370	510	665	830	1,050	1,340
45–49	145	35	110	220	350	500	650	810	1,035	1,320
50–54	98	35	100	205	340	480	630	790	990	1,290
55–59	64	30	90	185	300	440	590	750	960	1,230
60–64	33	25	80	170	280	410	560	710	920	1,180
65 and over[c].....	7	12	35	60	100	150	230	350	590	850
1939										
All ages[b]	2,015	20	60	120	205	315	445	585	760	1,055
15–19	133	—	—	—	—	—	—	—	215	330
20–24	339	15	40	70	120	180	250	345	465	635
25–29	370	20	65	135	210	310	420	530	670	885
30–34	317	35	100	180	295	410	530	655	820	1,080
35–39	273	40	115	210	335	465	595	745	945	1,230
40–44	201	40	120	220	360	500	640	800	1,010	1,285
45–49	145	35	105	200	340	485	630	800	1,020	1,300
50–54	105	30	95	185	315	455	610	770	985	1,265
55–59	68	30	90	175	290	425	570	735	950	1,230
60–64	34	30	85	170	280	410	550	710	910	1,170
65–69	19	20	60	125	195	310	450	605	790	1,070
70 and over......	8	20	60	125	200	310	430	595	750	1,010
1944										
All ages[b]	2,831	60	180	350	595	895	1,195	1,530	1,940	2,520
15–19	367	30	85	130	180	250	350	490	675	980
20–24	314	40	125	215	355	540	750	1,005	1,365	1,880
25–29	338	60	185	365	600	875	1,155	1,470	1,880	2,440
30–34	373	90	265	520	820	1,095	1,390	1,730	2,150	2,730
35–39	335	115	350	655	980	1,250	1,550	1,900	2,295	2,820
40–44	339	145	445	775	1,090	1,365	1,640	1,975	2,365	2,845
45–49	258	150	455	780	1,070	1,355	1,640	1,955	2,335	2,825
50–54	183	130	390	705	980	1,240	1,505	1,810	2,190	2,730
55–59	134	105	315	590	895	1,145	1,390	1,655	2,045	2,540
60–64	85	85	250	490	780	1,060	1,330	1,580	1,935	2,400
65–69	42	60	185	330	540	795	1,040	1,330	1,670	2,135
70 and over......	23	40	120	200	340	515	720	970	1,275	1,640
1946										
All ages[b]	3,141	65	195	380	625	915	1,220	1,520	1,855	2,300
15–19	291	25	70	120	180	245	350	495	680	1,030
20–24	448	40	125	210	350	520	725	970	1,270	1,665
25–29	453	70	215	390	610	860	1,130	1,390	1,690	2,085
30–34	447	100	305	545	825	1,090	1,360	1,625	1,935	2,375
35–39	401	115	345	660	980	1,270	1,520	1,790	2,085	2,510
40–44	322	135	405	700	1,050	1,350	1,605	1,895	2,190	2,590
45–49	278	135	410	750	1,080	1,380	1,630	1,910	2,230	2,625
50–54	196	120	360	680	1,020	1,340	1,640	1,875	2,130	2,510
55–59	129	90	275	560	900	1,220	1,480	1,745	2,090	2,510
60–64	85	90	275	500	785	1,030	1,300	1,595	1,900	2,260
65–69	47	75	230	455	710	980	1,245	1,470	1,780	2,135
70 and over......	26	40	125	210	390	570	790	1,080	1,360	1,835

TABLE 102—Continued

Year of Employment and Age	Number of Workers, in Thousands [a]	First Decile	Second Decile	Third Decile	Fourth Decile	Median	Sixth Decile	Seventh Decile	Eighth Decile	Ninth Decile
					D. Negro Female					
1937										
All ages [b]	395	$10	$30	$60	$105	$160	$235	$335	$450	$630
15–19	32	5	15	30	45	60	75	90	105	210
20–24	72	10	30	50	75	105	205	315	405	565
25–29	83	15	45	80	120	180	250	335	445	715
30–34	66	20	60	105	165	240	315	410	530	680
35–39	58	20	60	105	170	245	330	420	545	690
40–44	35	20	60	105	170	250	335	430	560	700
45–49	22	20	60	100	160	235	320	420	540	690
50–54	13	17	50	85	140	210	300	400	520	680
55–59	8	15	45	80	130	200	280	380	505	665
60–64	4	12	35	70	115	170	240	350	480	655
65 and over [c]	1	5	15	25	45	70	100	160	260	420
1939										
All ages [b]	400	10	40	70	120	190	270	370	500	665
15–19	26	—	—	—	—	—	—	—	—	215
20–24	70	8	25	50	80	110	160	220	320	470
25–29	82	18	50	90	140	195	270	360	475	635
30–34	73	25	70	120	180	250	340	445	560	710
35–39	59	25	70	125	190	280	370	475	590	740
40–44	39	25	70	125	190	280	370	470	590	735
45–49	24	25	70	120	185	255	355	460	580	730
50–54	14	20	65	110	175	245	335	445	585	730
55–59	7	18	55	95	150	215	300	400	545	715
60–64	4	18	55	95	150	210	295	400	515	680
65–69	2	15	45	70	110	165	225	315	435	610
70 and over	—	13	40	65	100	150	200	270	380	610
1944										
All ages [b]	1,658	35	100	145	225	335	485	675	930	1,290
15–19	237	15	45	70	115	150	205	265	430	695
20–24	355	30	85	135	190	280	405	580	810	1,180
25–29	300	35	105	170	245	370	530	725	975	1,400
30–34	253	40	125	195	310	460	630	835	1,085	1,475
35–39	188	45	140	230	345	490	670	870	1,110	1,460
40–44	141	40	125	195	315	470	650	850	1,085	1,415
45–49	81	45	140	220	330	475	645	850	1,085	1,420
50–54	49	45	130	205	310	450	610	790	1,005	1,320
55–59	26	40	115	185	285	420	600	815	1,030	1,305
60–64	12	30	90	160	245	365	530	730	955	1,230
65–69	5	25	70	115	180	260	410	625	865	1,090
70 and over	2	15	40	80	130	190	330	530	750	1,025
1946										
All ages [b]	1,453	35	105	170	245	375	545	750	1,010	1,340
15–19	167	15	45	70	115	150	205	290	465	725
20–24	311	25	80	130	190	265	400	580	830	1,175
25–29	262	35	105	165	260	385	535	750	1,020	1,350
30–34	217	45	140	220	345	515	680	860	1,110	1,405
35–39	182	55	160	260	395	555	750	965	1,190	1,495
40–44	134	45	130	225	360	515	705	935	1,225	1,545
45–49	81	50	150	255	410	585	745	950	1,225	1,495
50–54	47	55	165	280	425	590	785	985	1,240	1,520
55–59	24	50	150	235	370	560	720	925	1,155	1,450
60–64	13	40	125	195	370	510	635	795	1,115	1,445
65–69	5	55	160	260	320	380	535	725	940	1,225
70 and over	5	40	125	215	310	420	650	830	1,130	1,450

a. Workers with unreported age distributed proportionately among the known ages; estimates for 1946 are preliminary.
b. Totals include workers under 15 years of age.
c. Represents workers who attained age 65 during the year (workers over 65 years of age were excluded from coverage).

Source: Bureau of Old-Age and Survivors Insurance.

TABLE 103

DECILE ANNUAL WAGE CREDITS OF WORKERS UNDER OASI IN SPECIFIED AGE CLASSES AS PERCENTAGE OF RESPECTIVE DECILE FOR ALL AGES, BY SEX AND RACE, 1937, 1944 AND 1946

Year and Age	Male						Female					
	White			Negro			White			Negro		
	First Decile	Median	Ninth Decile	First Decile	Median	Ninth Decile	First Decile	Median	Ninth Decile	First Decile	Median	Ninth Decile
1937												
All ages	100.0	100.0	100.0	100.0	100.0	100.0	100.0	100.0	100.0	100.0	100.0	100.0
15–19	15.0	18.3	31.9	28.0	21.2	29.1	34.2	33.6	53.7	50.0	37.5	33.3
20–24	65.0	65.3	58.6	60.0	54.5	62.6	100.0	91.3	77.3	100.0	65.6	89.6
25–29	140.0	101.0	75.6	100.0	100.0	82.6	142.8	120.6	97.4	150.0	112.5	113.4
30–34	190.0	124.4	100.0	140.0	130.3	101.7	157.1	130.4	111.7	200.0	150.0	107.9
35–39	190.0	134.7	116.5	160.0	148.4	111.3	157.1	128.2	116.8	200.0	153.1	109.5
40–44	190.0	138.7	123.9	160.0	154.5	116.5	171.4	128.2	118.4	200.0	156.2	111.1
45–49	185.0	134.6	126.0	140.0	151.5	114.7	171.4	126.0	116.8	200.0	146.8	109.5
50–54	170.0	126.5	121.7	140.0	145.4	112.1	157.1	123.9	115.1	170.0	131.2	107.9
55–59	140.0	118.3	117.3	120.0	133.3	106.9	142.8	119.5	111.7	150.0	125.0	105.5
60–64	120.0	108.1	108.6	100.0	124.2	102.6	142.8	115.2	106.7	120.0	106.2	103.9
65 and over	35.0	49.4	69.1	48.0	45.4	73.9	71.4	65.2	76.4	50.0	43.7	66.6
1944												
All ages	100.0	100.0	100.0	100.0	100.0	100.0	100.0	100.0	100.0	100.0	100.0	100.0
15–19	25.9	15.7	—	50.0	27.9	38.8	58.3	41.7	62.9	42.8	44.7	53.8
20–24	33.3	42.4	—	66.6	60.3	74.6	116.6	115.1	95.7	85.8	83.5	91.4
25–29	100.0	96.4	—	100.0	97.7	96.8	116.6	117.7	105.2	100.0	110.4	108.5
30–34	166.6	125.1	—	150.0	122.3	108.3	125.0	122.1	108.2	114.2	137.3	114.3
35–39	259.2	133.3	—	191.6	139.6	111.9	141.6	131.0	111.9	128.4	146.2	113.1
40–44	340.7	133.8	—	241.6	152.5	112.9	141.6	130.3	111.6	114.2	140.2	109.6
45–49	351.8	130.7	—	250.0	151.3	112.1	141.6	128.4	111.1	128.4	141.7	110.0
50–54	337.0	125.4	—	216.6	138.5	108.3	133.3	120.2	104.7	128.4	134.3	102.3
55–59	303.7	115.7	—	175.0	127.9	100.7	125.0	112.6	98.2	114.2	125.3	101.1
60–64	218.5	100.2	—	141.6	118.4	95.2	108.3	102.5	92.5	85.8	108.9	95.3
65–69	129.6	82.1	—	100.0	88.8	84.7	91.7	94.9	88.5	71.6	77.6	84.4
70 and over	70.3	63.6	—	66.6	57.5	65.0	75.0	77.2	85.8	42.8	56.7	79.4
1946												
All ages	100.0	100.0	100.0	100.0	100.0	100.0	100.0	100.0	100.0	100.0	100.0	100.0
15–19	17.2	16.0	—	38.4	26.8	44.8	58.3	43.5	63.1	42.9	40.0	54.1
20–24	51.6	46.3	—	61.5	56.8	72.4	116.7	104.3	90.8	71.4	70.7	87.7
25–29	141.3	89.6	—	107.7	94.0	90.7	108.4	103.1	99.5	100.0	102.7	100.7
30–34	203.4	118.5	—	153.8	119.1	103.3	116.7	110.6	104.6	128.6	137.3	104.9
35–39	258.6	133.1	—	176.9	138.8	109.1	133.4	126.7	112.6	157.1	148.0	111.6
40–44	289.6	141.3	—	207.6	147.6	112.6	150.0	136.6	116.0	128.6	137.3	115.3
45–49	262.0	139.0	—	207.6	150.8	114.1	158.4	139.1	116.7	142.8	156.0	111.6
50–54	279.3	136.0	—	184.6	146.5	109.1	150.0	137.9	111.4	157.1	157.4	113.4
55–59	234.5	128.1	—	138.4	133.3	109.1	150.0	132.3	108.2	142.8	149.4	108.2
60–64	213.8	115.7	—	138.4	112.6	98.3	158.4	127.3	101.9	114.3	136.0	107.8
65–69	117.2	94.7	—	115.3	107.1	92.8	141.7	116.1	96.8	157.1	101.3	91.4
70 and over	72.4	76.7	—	61.5	62.3	79.8	116.7	105.6	101.9	114.3	112.0	108.2

Source: Derived from Appendix Table 102, A–D.

TABLE 104

Indexes of Decile Annual Wage Credits of Workers under OASI, by Sex and Number of Quarters in Covered Employment, 1937–1946

(1939 = 100)

Year	First Decile		Median		Ninth Decile	
	Male	Female	Male	Female	Male	Female
All Workers						
1937	115.3	140.0	104.5	95.6	100.0	98.3
1938	100.0	100.0	93.6	92.5	98.4	98.3
1939	100.0	100.0	100.0	100.0	100.0	100.0
1940	107.6	100.0	105.2	103.2	118.9	101.7
1941	130.6	120.0	122.9	106.6	141.7	108.5
1942	138.5	100.0	143.6	103.2	159.3	123.4
1943	153.7	180.0	181.6	138.5	159.5	154.9
1944	184.6	220.0	209.3	162.7	—	176.1
1945	146.3	220.0	188.5	165.8	—	169.2
1946	200.0	220.0	191.8	164.9	159.4	177.9
Four-Quarter Workers [a]						
1938	96.2	89.6	96.2	98.5	100.5	99.2
1939	100.0	100.0	100.0	100.0	100.0	100.0
1940	110.6	104.5	105.9	102.7	105.3	102.2
1941	129.4	120.8	121.7	113.5	117.5	109.4
1942	154.5	138.8	150.4	133.2	134.0	125.1
1943	189.4	161.2	186.3	163.6	—	157.7
1944	201.9	174.6	201.1	181.7	—	176.5
1945	207.7	176.1	198.5	182.4	—	167.4
1946	223.4	192.4	188.7	195.8	—	177.2
Three-Quarter Workers [a]						
1938	116.6	107.7	116.6	114.4	121.9	125.2
1939	100.0	100.0	100.0	100.0	100.0	100.0
1940	155.7	138.6	135.7	134.6	110.3	128.5
1941	155.7	138.6	135.7	134.6	128.6	118.4
1942	233.3	176.9	176.1	163.6	165.8	149.5
1943	233.3	230.7	204.6	194.6	202.4	197.4
1944	233.3	246.2	204.6	203.5	208.2	209.3
1945	277.8	315.3	254.7	243.7	224.1	249.7
1946	—	—	—	—	—	—
Two-Quarter Workers [a]						
1938	114.5	100.0	102.7	107.3	116.5	115.2
1939	100.0	100.0	100.0	100.0	100.0	100.0
1940	114.5	100.0	105.5	107.3	113.5	106.0
1941	128.6	120.0	129.7	121.6	126.2	115.2
1942	171.5	140.0	170.2	150.0	170.7	150.1
1943	185.6	160.0	183.6	164.2	200.0	187.9
1944	171.5	160.0	183.6	178.6	213.6	193.9
1945	200.0	180.0	205.5	172.1	224.2	204.6
1946	242.8	200.0	243.4	200.0	217.3	203.0

a. Data by number of quarters employed not available for 1937.

Source: Bureau of Old-Age and Survivors Insurance.

TABLE 105

Decile Annual Wage Credits of White Men and Women under OASI by State and Region, 1939 and 1946

State	Number of Workers, in Thousands	First Decile	Second Decile	Third Decile	Fourth Decile	Median	Sixth Decile	Seventh Decile	Eighth Decile	Ninth Decile
				A. White Male, 1939						
United States	22,345	$75	$225	$445	$705	$950	$1,185	$1,430	$1,750	$2,235
New England	1,917	100	300	550	780	975	1,170	1,380	1,650	2,140
Maine	174	45	140	260	430	625	810	910	1,050	1,665
New Hampshire	109	70	210	390	595	770	935	1,110	1,325	1,695
Vermont	63	40	115	230	400	625	825	1,030	1,260	1,710
Massachusetts	966	110	335	610	830	1,030	1,230	1,450	1,750	2,270
Rhode Island	177	110	335	565	770	940	1,095	1,280	1,540	1,975
Connecticut	428	140	420	715	950	1,135	1,310	1,500	1,755	2,225
Middle Atlantic	5,998	120	350	625	875	1,105	1,320	1,560	1,890	2,480
New York	3,080	115	345	620	885	1,125	1,370	1,645	2,010	2,700
New Jersey	876	120	360	645	910	1,150	1,370	1,605	1,920	2,420
Pennsylvania	2,041	115	345	620	855	1,060	1,250	1,450	1,710	2,185
East North Central	5,324	100	305	595	880	1,115	1,330	1,560	1,840	2,335
Ohio	1,406	110	330	630	920	1,155	1,370	1,600	1,870	2,330
Indiana	629	80	235	490	750	975	1,190	1,420	1,680	2,105
Illinois	1,706	110	330	620	890	1,125	1,350	1,590	1,915	2,535
Michigan	1,061	105	310	595	910	1,150	1,370	1,580	1,845	2,305
Wisconsin	523	80	240	505	805	1,040	1,255	1,470	1,710	2,135
West North Central	1,727	45	130	270	500	755	1,005	1,260	1,545	2,030
Minnesota	378	45	140	315	570	855	1,120	1,375	1,650	2,085
Iowa	318	35	110	235	445	695	930	1,170	1,420	1,860
Missouri	560	55	165	385	645	895	1,135	1,375	1,690	2,260
North Dakota	49	20	55	110	220	390	650	930	1,250	1,740
South Dakota	54	30	100	180	310	540	790	1,050	1,300	1,710
Nebraska	152	35	105	190	350	580	830	1,085	1,370	1,870
Kansas	217	35	105	190	350	590	845	1,110	1,395	1,830
South Atlantic	2,152	55	160	350	540	720	910	1,150	1,450	1,980
Delaware	53	95	290	545	805	1,030	1,285	1,520	1,865	2,520
Maryland	311	95	290	530	765	980	1,195	1,440	1,745	2,240
District of Columbia	109	100	295	575	860	1,160	1,460	1,795	2,165	2,860
Virginia	299	50	155	330	530	710	910	1,150	1,420	1,920
West Virginia	323	70	215	410	665	875	1,060	1,240	1,450	1,845
North Carolina	363	55	165	355	510	650	760	915	1,170	1,660
South Carolina	170	50	150	330	495	630	735	865	1,065	1,520
Georgia	282	40	120	250	430	605	750	945	1,280	1,910
Florida	242	35	100	180	320	500	705	965	1,310	1,870
East South Central	925	40	120	220	405	605	800	1,025	1,325	1,830
Kentucky	291	40	120	230	425	660	875	1,095	1,355	1,810
Tennessee	295	40	125	250	440	630	805	1,020	1,310	1,830
Alabama	232	40	125	255	440	620	790	1,020	1,355	1,865
Mississippi	108	20	60	120	200	355	545	780	1,110	1,680
West South Central	1,508	30	100	180	355	580	825	1,140	1,560	2,030
Arkansas	133	20	65	130	225	380	555	755	1,055	1,590
Louisiana	245	45	125	250	445	665	905	1,210	1,565	2,070
Oklahoma	256	30	100	190	370	630	885	1,180	1,560	1,980
Texas	874	30	95	185	350	575	840	1,180	1,600	2,070
Mountain	666	40	120	220	400	640	920	1,220	1,510	1,930
Montana	91	45	125	250	450	730	1,050	1,330	1,590	2,065
Idaho	86	30	90	160	280	470	710	1,010	1,350	1,760
Wyoming	45	45	140	270	475	740	1,055	1,345	1,600	1,960
Colorado	188	45	130	245	435	680	945	1,200	1,490	1,940
New Mexico	61	30	90	160	275	455	695	960	1,325	1,800
Arizona	79	40	120	230	420	680	960	1,275	1,620	1,995
Utah	86	40	120	230	430	700	970	1,230	1,490	1,885
Nevada	30	55	165	310	495	730	1,010	1,300	1,575	1,945
Pacific	2,018	65	195	405	685	970	1,250	1,500	1,810	2,260
Washington	336	65	195	405	695	985	1,235	1,455	1,750	2,180
Oregon	211	55	160	340	600	875	1,120	1,335	1,580	1,990
California	1,471	80	205	420	705	995	1,280	1,540	1,850	2,305
Alaska	27	80	230	335	460	615	805	1,065	1,410	2,000
Hawaii	83	20	60	125	275	460	650	850	1,120	1,575

TABLE 105—CONTINUED

State	Number of Workers, in Thousands	First Decile	Second Decile	Third Decile	Fourth Decile	Median	Sixth Decile	Seventh Decile	Eighth Decile	Ninth Decile
			B. White Female, 1939							
United States	8,991	$35	$100	$190	$330	$470	$610	$740	$905	$1,150
New England	918	60	150	255	415	550	665	765	880	1,070
Maine	77	15	55	110	195	325	450	575	685	835
New Hampshire	52	35	100	195	320	430	535	640	750	925
Vermont	22	13	50	100	185	290	415	540	680	865
Massachusetts	476	70	160	290	430	565	675	775	900	1,120
Rhode Island	103	75	170	315	450	565	660	730	820	985
Connecticut	189	80	190	360	530	660	760	850	965	1,160
Middle Atlantic	2,614	65	150	280	430	565	690	810	975	1,250
New York	1,463	75	170	310	460	610	740	880	1,060	1,375
New Jersey	399	65	150	275	405	530	655	770	915	1,150
Pennsylvania	751	55	140	235	380	495	610	730	855	1,055
East North Central	2,002	35	110	200	340	510	655	785	930	1,170
Ohio	508	40	120	205	350	515	670	795	945	1,175
Indiana	230	30	90	160	270	420	570	710	855	1,055
Illinois	717	60	145	250	400	560	700	820	970	1,220
Michigan	354	35	100	175	295	450	620	775	950	1,200
Wisconsin	193	32	95	170	290	450	610	740	880	1,080
West North Central	713	27	85	155	260	400	540	690	840	1,045
Minnesota	163	35	100	180	300	470	630	760	900	1,090
Iowa	123	15	60	110	210	330	465	610	750	960
Missouri	261	40	120	205	350	480	610	730	875	1,100
North Dakota	18	13	55	100	180	280	425	580	725	905
South Dakota	20	13	55	100	175	270	400	545	705	875
Nebraska	58	15	60	110	190	305	450	605	755	970
Kansas	70	12	50	90	155	250	370	520	685	915
South Atlantic	914	30	95	170	285	410	525	625	750	955
Delaware	21	25	85	155	265	405	540	690	890	1,170
Maryland	127	35	95	180	315	425	565	680	820	1,010
District of Columbia	54	60	150	255	445	635	815	965	1,210	1,510
Virginia	117	32	95	170	290	420	535	640	775	975
West Virginia	67	25	85	150	260	390	530	660	785	980
North Carolina	189	40	120	210	350	460	550	630	720	870
South Carolina	83	35	100	190	325	435	530	585	640	770
Georgia	151	32	95	170	290	415	520	600	705	910
Florida	105	12	45	80	140	210	315	450	610	850
East South Central	326	20	75	135	240	370	485	590	725	925
Kentucky	83	20	75	140	245	380	510	635	775	960
Tennessee	130	30	85	165	290	415	520	630	755	970
Alabama	72	15	60	110	210	340	460	560	685	890
Mississippi	41	12	40	90	155	250	360	470	585	780
West South Central	463	10	45	85	145	230	365	525	705	970
Arkansas	39	8	35	70	120	190	270	410	560	785
Louisiana	73	17	65	115	195	305	430	560	710	970
Oklahoma	77	12	50	95	160	255	405	585	790	1,040
Texas	274	10	45	85	145	230	360	510	700	980
Mountain	194	12	50	90	155	245	385	550	730	975
Montana	23	17	65	115	195	310	470	650	860	1,145
Idaho	23	8	35	70	120	190	270	410	620	865
Wyoming	10	12	50	90	150	240	365	510	680	900
Colorado	68	17	65	115	195	310	470	630	770	995
New Mexico	15	8	35	70	125	195	280	390	560	810
Arizona	19	15	60	110	180	295	440	615	820	1,070
Utah	30	8	35	70	125	195	310	465	630	850
Nevada	7	15	60	110	205	290	415	560	770	1,030
Pacific	816	20	75	135	250	405	590	785	980	1,250
Washington	127	15	60	110	210	350	560	760	940	1,190
Oregon	80	20	75	130	235	380	560	780	910	1,180
California	609	25	85	150	260	410	595	800	995	1,265
Alaska	4	8	35	70	120	185	260	370	615	900
Hawaii	27	8	35	65	110	160	220	315	455	750

TABLE 105—Continued

State	Number of Workers, in Thousands [a]	First Decile	Second Decile	Third Decile	Fourth Decile	Median	Sixth Decile	Seventh Decile	Eighth Decile	Ninth Decile
				C. White Male, 1946						
United States	29,260	$145	$440	$840	$1,330	$1,780	$2,175	$2,575	$3,025	—
New England	2,315	210	550	1,040	1,520	1,900	2,230	2,580	2,995	$3,435
Maine	205	95	280	510	790	1,180	1,590	1,950	2,350	2,945
New Hampshire	133	120	360	710	1,140	1,490	1,820	2,080	2,510	3,005
Vermont	75	125	370	630	1,025	1,440	1,750	2,020	2,360	2,830
Massachusetts	1,164	225	605	1,130	1,590	1,980	2,310	2,640	3,035	—
Rhode Island	196	225	570	1,090	1,550	1,930	2,215	2,550	2,990	3,500
Connecticut	542	320	810	1,360	1,820	2,160	2,490	2,820	3,340	—
Middle Atlantic	7,477	235	655	1,190	1,670	2,040	2,405	2,790	3,210	—
New York	3,866	235	635	1,165	1,650	2,085	2,470	2,905	3,345	—
New Jersey	1,072	250	700	1,270	1,780	2,185	2,550	2,930	3,320	—
Pennsylvania	2,539	235	655	1,220	1,640	1,970	2,270	2,590	2,965	3,375
East North Central	7,001	205	585	1,100	1,625	2,045	2,395	2,760	3,350	—
Ohio	1,861	220	635	1,175	1,660	2,065	2,410	2,730	3,130	—
Indiana	828	165	500	925	1,420	1,845	2,210	2,550	2,950	3,395
Illinois	2,098	210	565	1,125	1,680	2,110	2,505	2,890	3,290	—
Michigan	1,515	265	665	1,205	1,745	2,135	2,450	2,785	3,195	—
Wisconsin	699	150	450	885	1,415	1,865	2,240	2,550	2,910	3,310
West North Central	2,248	90	270	555	930	1,410	1,835	2,220	2,650	3,235
Minnesota	533	100	305	650	1,060	1,535	1,940	2,295	2,705	3,230
Iowa	395	90	270	525	850	1,320	1,745	2,120	2,500	3,085
Missouri	731	110	335	665	1,115	1,565	1,955	2,330	2,785	3,420
North Dakota	57	45	140	285	515	895	1,380	1,925	2,390	3,065
South Dakota	63	60	185	365	640	985	1,350	1,885	2,280	2,970
Nebraska	191	75	230	440	730	1,185	1,630	2,070	2,545	3,180
Kansas	278	70	205	420	765	1,200	1,635	2,085	2,545	3,125
South Atlantic	2,838	105	315	620	1,010	1,415	1,790	2,180	2,665	3,305
Delaware	73	290	695	1,210	1,775	2,095	2,440	2,995	3,500	—
Maryland	382	200	550	1,005	1,455	1,845	2,215	2,615	3,055	—
District of Columbia	139	130	385	810	1,305	1,915	2,415	2,930	3,375	—
Virginia	407	100	295	590	950	1,360	1,720	2,105	2,535	3,110
West Virginia	379	125	370	770	1,280	1,700	2,045	2,420	2,830	3,230
North Carolina	464	95	290	540	870	1,215	1,510	1,825	2,185	2,850
South Carolina	212	95	290	570	940	1,320	1,575	1,880	2,250	2,920
Georgia	396	80	235	455	760	1,140	1,560	1,950	2,450	3,280
Florida	386	85	260	465	760	1,160	1,570	2,045	2,600	3,200
East South Central	1,258	75	230	445	760	1,160	1,570	1,975	2,470	3,090
Kentucky	371	80	235	465	810	1,255	1,665	2,040	2,470	3,070
Tennessee	421	80	235	450	775	1,170	1,570	1,975	2,480	3,120
Alabama	325	85	250	465	760	1,180	1,585	2,010	2,510	3,115
Mississippi	141	60	185	350	600	920	1,260	1,705	2,340	3,190
West South Central	1,994	70	215	435	745	1,175	1,620	2,120	2,705	3,320
Arkansas	179	40	130	250	425	700	1,080	1,465	1,920	2,560
Louisiana	295	95	290	550	870	1,270	1,710	2,195	2,795	3,400
Oklahoma	324	75	225	445	780	1,215	1,685	2,115	2,640	3,200
Texas	1,196	75	225	445	780	1,215	1,685	2,240	2,815	3,360
Mountain	850	80	240	455	765	1,145	1,655	2,125	2,620	3,195
Montana	100	85	255	485	825	1,220	1,740	2,205	2,645	3,083
Idaho	97	80	240	455	770	1,220	1,740	2,225	2,700	3,320
Wyoming	47	85	260	455	730	1,200	1,810	2,370	2,880	3,365
Colorado	245	75	230	435	785	1,200	1,685	2,100	2,560	3,100
New Mexico	87	55	160	305	525	810	1,185	1,700	2,255	3,000
Arizona	112	90	270	510	825	1,170	1,590	2,090	2,560	3,265
Utah	122	85	250	490	800	1,205	1,720	2,190	2,740	3,310
Nevada	40	95	290	530	850	1,280	1,865	2,280	2,930	3,535
Pacific	3,162	135	410	760	1,220	1,720	2,190	2,645	3,100	—
Washington	514	130	385	720	1,165	1,640	2,125	2,535	2,990	3,430
Oregon	326	135	405	725	1,130	1,630	2,065	2,485	2,890	3,315
California	2,322	140	415	785	1,250	1,765	2,225	2,710	3,135	—
Alaska	22	165	500	750	1,060	1,445	2,000	2,730	3,320	—
Hawaii	95	85	260	485	890	1,360	1,805	2,255	2,900	3,255

TABLE 105—CONTINUED

State	Number of Workers, in Thousands [a]	First Decile	Second Decile	Third Decile	Fourth Decile	Median	Sixth Decile	Seventh Decile	Eighth Decile	Ninth Decile
				D. White Female, 1946						
United States	15,242	$60	$185	$330	$545	$805	$1,095	$1,380	$1,670	$2,060
New England	1,338	85	250	435	710	1,005	1,255	1,470	1,685	1,970
Maine	102	45	130	230	370	565	835	1,160	1,450	1,810
New Hampshire	66	60	180	315	505	825	1,095	1,340	1,590	1,850
Vermont	36	45	130	210	320	470	760	1,040	1,330	1,640
Massachusetts	707	90	265	460	730	1,005	1,245	1,450	1,650	1,940
Rhode Island	128	95	285	515	785	1,095	1,330	1,520	1,705	1,950
Connecticut	299	130	330	570	890	1,180	1,420	1,635	1,840	2,125
Middle Atlantic	3,950	85	255	465	745	1,025	1,295	1,540	1,820	2,220
New York	2,203	105	280	515	820	1,120	1,400	1,655	1,945	2,365
New Jersey	564	85	260	470	745	1,025	1,300	1,570	1,845	2,210
Pennsylvania	1,183	70	210	390	630	890	1,130	1,350	1,580	1,905
East North Central	3,398	65	200	355	570	845	1,145	1,425	1,715	2,080
Ohio	862	70	205	365	585	845	1,135	1,405	1,675	2,005
Indiana	420	55	160	280	460	700	1,020	1,295	1,575	1,910
Illinois	1,122	75	225	415	635	925	1,240	1,545	1,820	2,190
Michigan	646	70	205	360	575	850	1,150	1,460	1,780	2,160
Wisconsin	348	55	170	300	485	735	990	1,250	1,520	1,860
West North Central	1,261	45	140	260	410	625	880	1,165	1,445	1,785
Minnesota	295	55	170	290	470	690	960	1,205	1,495	1,800
Iowa	206	45	130	230	365	560	810	1,075	1,360	1,685
Missouri	444	55	170	290	475	725	1,010	1,285	1,545	1,875
North Dakota	33	40	115	195	300	475	705	995	1,225	1,630
South Dakota	40	35	110	185	280	435	650	900	1,225	1,600
Nebraska	109	50	145	240	350	520	740	1,035	1,360	1,690
Kansas	134	40	115	210	340	480	700	945	1,270	1,715
South Atlantic	1,568	55	160	280	470	720	985	1,250	1,525	1,870
Delaware	32	60	185	345	530	760	990	1,310	1,595	2,000
Maryland	197	65	195	355	610	850	1,135	1,380	1,670	2,020
District of Columbia	90	55	160	285	540	825	1,120	1,480	1,920	2,310
Virginia	209	55	165	275	435	680	975	1,265	1,560	1,925
West Virginia	133	50	150	250	390	620	880	1,160	1,485	1,820
North Carolina	302	65	190	360	570	825	1,075	1,285	1,490	1,765
South Carolina	133	45	140	270	475	715	1,000	1,220	1,425	1,700
Georgia	251	55	170	285	470	720	985	1,240	1,515	1,840
Florida	221	40	120	210	330	515	745	1,000	1,305	1,790
East South Central	651	40	130	230	380	600	865	1,125	1,420	1,770
Kentucky	158	40	135	240	385	575	865	1,105	1,370	1,725
Tennessee	253	50	140	255	425	655	910	1,165	1,465	1,810
Alabama	157	40	130	230	380	565	830	1,175	1,450	1,780
Mississippi	83	30	110	200	320	540	780	1,020	1,230	1,650
West South Central	940	35	110	190	305	470	700	990	1,335	1,790
Arkansas	86	22	70	125	210	330	535	770	1,050	1,435
Louisiana	129	40	120	195	320	470	715	990	1,345	1,840
Oklahoma	154	35	100	180	310	460	690	1,000	1,355	1,785
Texas	571	40	120	205	325	495	750	1,025	1,375	1,805
Mountain	403	40	115	190	295	450	655	910	1,240	1,700
Montana	44	40	120	200	320	470	680	905	1,235	1,740
Idaho	44	35	100	170	270	390	550	735	1,100	1,640
Wyoming	22	40	125	210	320	445	595	825	1,140	1,650
Colorado	131	35	100	180	305	470	725	1,020	1,340	1,735
New Mexico	35	30	85	150	240	360	550	765	1,045	1,425
Arizona	50	40	115	200	310	490	715	945	1,260	1,790
Utah	58	40	115	205	315	465	640	880	1,190	1,585
Nevada	19	35	105	185	305	450	640	980	1,370	1,850
Pacific	1,684	55	170	305	485	710	995	1,360	1,760	2,225
Washington	248	50	150	280	445	650	950	1,305	1,660	2,120
Oregon	159	50	150	260	410	610	870	1,205	1,520	2,000
California	1,277	60	180	310	500	745	1,025	1,400	1,800	2,280
Alaska	8	65	200	320	455	580	800	970	1,350	1,870
Hawaii	41	70	210	300	430	630	940	1,250	1,575	2,125

a. For 1946, preliminary.

Source: Bureau of Old-Age and Survivors Insurance.

TABLE 106

DECILE ANNUAL WAGE CREDITS OF NEGRO MEN AND WOMEN UNDER OASI, IN SELECTED STATES, 1939 AND 1946

A. 1939

State	Number of Workers, in Thousands	First Decile	Second Decile	Third Decile	Fourth Decile	Median	Sixth Decile	Seventh Decile	Eighth Decile	Ninth Decile
					Negro Male					
United States	2,015	$20	$60	$120	$205	$315	$445	$585	$760	$1,055
New York	114	50	145	285	445	610	780	955	1,155	1,400
New Jersey	54	30	85	170	285	435	615	815	1,020	1,320
Ohio	71	40	120	235	380	585	785	980	1,170	1,375
Illinois	84	40	120	235	380	565	760	955	1,160	1,375
Pennsylvania	93	55	155	300	470	665	855	1,020	1,190	1,380
Michigan	51	80	205	340	520	750	975	1,205	1,430	1,650
Missouri	44	25	75	150	250	370	540	705	865	1,070
Maryland	66	25	75	150	250	375	520	695	900	1,170
District of Columbia	46	40	115	225	360	495	630	775	930	1,240
Virginia	112	18	55	110	180	280	405	520	670	860
North Carolina	126	12	35	80	135	220	310	410	530	675
South Carolina	91	10	32	70	120	200	280	380	480	585
Georgia	143	10	32	70	120	195	270	375	485	620
Florida	110	10	32	70	120	200	285	395	510	660
Tennessee	81	20	60	125	210	320	430	550	670	790
Alabama	126	20	60	120	210	310	425	545	695	900
Mississippi	84	8	25	60	110	175	250	350	450	580
Arkansas	51	12	35	80	140	220	310	420	515	630
Louisiana	121	15	45	85	150	240	350	460	580	750
Texas	138	15	45	85	155	250	360	485	625	810
					Negro Female					
United States	400	$10	$40	$70	$120	$190	$270	$370	$500	$665
New York	37	35	95	170	305	430	545	650	740	855
New Jersey	13	12	35	80	140	215	310	425	550	715
Ohio	11	20	55	115	200	305	425	545	650	740
Illinois	29	20	60	125	210	320	430	530	620	745
Pennsylvania	20	35	100	180	320	430	525	610	680	775
Michigan	8	20	60	115	185	290	405	515	645	805
Missouri	11	17	55	110	175	275	370	455	535	650
Maryland	17	5	25	55	85	120	165	220	350	520
District of Columbia	10	40	115	225	360	490	620	685	740	875
Virginia	34	10	40	70	115	170	245	330	430	550
North Carolina	45	10	40	65	110	160	220	285	380	550
South Carolina	10	5	20	40	65	100	140	195	260	350
Georgia	26	8	35	50	95	135	180	235	315	430
Florida	21	5	20	45	75	110	155	205	280	420
Tennessee	14	10	40	70	115	170	240	305	390	505
Alabama	13	10	40	65	110	160	215	280	360	460
Mississippi	7	5	22	50	80	115	160	210	270	360
Arkansas	4	8	35	60	95	135	180	230	290	385
Louisiana	17	8	35	60	100	150	205	270	360	480
Texas	19	10	40	65	105	145	190	270	365	490

TABLE 106—CONTINUED

B. 1946

State	Number of Workers, in Thousands [a]	First Decile	Second Decile	Third Decile	Fourth Decile	Median	Sixth Decile	Seventh Decile	Eighth Decile	Ninth Decile
				Negro Male						
United States	3,141	$65	$195	$380	$625	$915	$1,220	$1,520	$1,855	$2,300
New York	268	115	345	590	870	1,180	1,540	1,860	2,170	2,600
New Jersey	93	115	350	615	900	1,215	1,515	1,850	2,205	2,635
Ohio	151	130	390	685	1,120	1,465	1,800	2,100	2,355	2,735
Illinois	207	110	325	630	1,010	1,390	1,745	2,020	2,295	2,650
Pennsylvania	185	125	375	690	1,010	1,370	1,660	1,900	2,175	2,510
Michigan	127	265	615	1,030	1,415	1,785	2,040	2,255	2,510	2,905
Missouri	74	55	170	350	580	920	1,265	1,545	1,845	2,220
Maryland	98	75	225	430	705	1,020	1,290	1,570	1,880	2,205
District of Columbia	64	70	210	370	690	925	1,245	1,580	1,875	2,230
Virginia	144	60	180	350	540	770	1,010	1,280	1,565	1,930
North Carolina	154	45	130	255	415	625	910	1,160	1,410	1,670
South Carolina	108	40	120	215	355	545	780	1,020	1,285	1,550
Georgia	172	40	120	235	405	630	870	1,120	1,360	1,630
Florida	135	50	150	270	440	645	895	1,190	1,490	1,810
Tennessee	102	60	175	325	535	770	1,055	1,325	1,560	1,880
Alabama	163	50	145	290	500	765	1,040	1,330	1,580	1,930
Mississippi	99	30	90	165	270	420	615	885	1,165	1,450
Arkansas	56	35	110	185	320	470	680	945	1,240	1,530
Louisiana	146	40	120	225	390	560	780	1,000	1,260	1,650
Texas	202	55	165	305	495	730	1,030	1,270	1,550	1,920
				Negro Female						
United States	1,453	$35	$105	$170	$245	$375	$545	$750	$1,010	$1,340
New York	200	55	160	270	455	670	900	1,145	1,360	1,620
New Jersey	59	40	120	210	330	495	705	1,020	1,300	1,650
Ohio	60	30	90	165	255	390	600	860	1,080	1,365
Illinois	137	50	150	260	410	585	790	1,035	1,265	1,550
Pennsylvania	74	40	115	205	330	505	705	945	1,165	1,390
Michigan	45	30	95	170	280	435	680	985	1,305	1,675
Missouri	47	25	80	140	215	305	480	680	875	1,130
Maryland	46	30	90	165	240	350	490	675	895	1,150
District of Columbia	34	35	105	185	325	485	680	920	1,180	1,425
Virginia	63	25	75	145	240	360	500	660	860	1,140
North Carolina	71	25	80	140	210	300	415	555	725	1,040
South Carolina	27	20	60	100	160	230	330	540	730	985
Georgia	68	13	40	80	130	235	395	555	745	975
Florida	62	20	60	110	170	250	340	480	655	895
Tennessee	48	25	70	100	190	285	405	545	725	950
Alabama	45	17	50	90	145	225	325	460	650	870
Mississippi	27	13	40	75	125	190	270	385	570	785
Arkansas	16	20	60	110	170	270	380	520	670	885
Louisiana	55	17	50	90	145	205	300	425	610	885
Texas	81	18	55	95	150	220	315	435	625	890

a. For 1946, preliminary.

Source: Bureau of Old-Age and Survivors Insurance.

TABLE 107

DECILE ANNUAL WAGE CREDITS OF NEGROES AS PERCENTAGE OF THOSE OF WHITE WORKERS UNDER OASI, IN SELECTED STATES, 1939 AND 1946

	1939						1946					
	First Decile		Median		Ninth Decile		First Decile		Median		Ninth Decile	
State	Male	Female	Male	Female	Male	Female	Male	Female	Male	Female	Male	Female
United States	26.6	28.5	33.1	40.4	47.2	57.8	44.8	58.3	51.4	46.5	—	65.0
New York	43.4	46.6	54.2	70.4	51.8	62.1	48.9	52.4	56.5	59.8	—	68.4
New Jersey	25.0	18.4	37.8	40.5	54.5	62.1	46.0	47.0	55.7	48.2	—	74.6
Ohio	36.3	50.0	50.6	59.2	59.0	62.9	59.0	42.8	70.9	46.2	—	68.0
Illinois	36.3	33.3	50.2	57.1	54.2	61.0	52.3	66.6	65.8	63.2	—	70.7
Pennsylvania	47.8	63.6	62.7	86.8	63.1	73.4	53.1	57.1	69.5	56.7	74.3	72.9
Michigan	76.1	57.1	65.2	64.4	71.5	67.0	100.0	42.8	83.6	51.1	—	77.5
Missouri	45.4	42.5	41.3	57.2	47.3	59.0	50.0	45.4	58.7	42.0	64.9	60.2
Maryland	26.3	14.2	38.2	28.2	52.2	51.4	37.5	46.1	55.2	41.1	—	56.9
District of Columbia.	40.0	66.7	42.6	77.1	43.3	57.9	53.8	63.6	48.3	58.7	—	61.6
Virginia	36.0	31.2	39.4	40.4	44.7	56.4	60.0	45.4	56.6	52.9	62.0	59.3
North Carolina	21.8	25.0	33.8	34.7	40.6	63.2	47.3	38.4	51.4	36.3	58.5	58.9
South Carolina	20.0	14.2	31.7	22.9	38.4	45.4	42.1	44.4	41.2	32.1	53.0	57.9
Georgia	25.0	25.0	32.2	32.5	32.4	47.2	50.0	23.6	55.2	32.6	49.6	52.9
Florida	28.5	41.6	40.0	52.3	35.2	49.4	58.8	50.0	55.6	48.5	56.5	50.0
Tennessee	50.0	33.3	50.8	40.9	43.2	52.0	75.0	50.0	65.8	43.5	60.2	52.4
Alabama	50.0	66.6	50.0	47.0	48.3	51.6	58.8	42.5	64.8	39.8	61.9	48.8
Mississippi	40.0	41.6	49.2	46.0	34.5	46.1	50.0	43.3	45.6	35.1	45.4	47.5
Arkansas	60.0	100.0	57.8	71.0	39.6	49.0	87.5	90.9	67.1	81.8	59.7	61.6
Louisiana	33.3	47.0	36.0	49.1	36.2	49.4	42.1	42.5	44.0	43.6	48.5	48.1
Texas	50.0	100.0	43.5	63.0	39.1	50.0	73.3	45.0	60.0	44.4	57.1	49.3

Sources: Derived from Appendix Tables 105 and 106.

TABLE 108

Average Annual Earnings per Full-Time Employee, by Industry, 1929–1950

(In Dollars)

No.	Industry	1929	1930	1931	1932	1933	1934	1935	1936	1937	1938	1939	1940	1941	1942	1943	1944	1945	1946	1947	1948	1949	1950	No.
1	All industries	1,421	1,380	1,292	1,136	1,064	1,109	1,153	1,199	1,270	1,238	1,269	1,306	1,450	1,719	1,964	2,120	2,207	2,368	2,598	2,809	2,866	3,024	1
2	Agriculture, forestry and fishing	455	429	352	272	253	288	328	358	411	401	403	415	503	649	863	1,013	1,138	1,223	1,311	1,375	1,349	1,365	2
3	Mining	1,526	1,424	1,221	1,016	990	1,108	1,154	1,263	1,366	1,282	1,367	1,388	1,579	1,795	2,162	2,499	2,621	2,719	3,113	3,387	3,203	3,436	3
4	Metal mining	1,616	1,542	1,297	1,055	1,046	1,122	1,247	1,383	1,626	1,455	1,518	1,610	1,771	2,045	2,333	2,458	2,551	2,636	3,000	3,327	3,411	3,541	4
5	Anthracite mining	1,728	1,750	1,602	1,452	1,435	1,500	1,414	1,408	1,388	1,315	1,406	1,306	1,466	1,761	2,119	2,525	2,685	2,890	3,125	3,420	2,896	3,107	5
6	Bituminous and other soft-coal mining	1,293	1,119	909	723	748	900	957	1,103	1,170	1,050	1,197	1,235	1,500	1,715	2,115	2,535	2,629	2,724	3,212	3,383	2,925	3,266	6
7	Crude petroleum and natural gas	2,019	1,980	1,890	1,600	1,427	1,472	1,558	1,594	1,734	1,734	1,684	1,714	1,779	1,934	2,299	2,601	2,762	2,819	3,157	3,584	3,735	3,834	7
8	Nonmetallic mining and quarrying	1,413	1,361	1,186	939	852	901	976	1,108	1,207	1,132	1,171	1,217	1,375	1,634	1,911	2,089	2,205	2,371	2,663	2,928	3,021	3,245	8
9	Contract construction	1,674	1,526	1,233	907	869	942	1,027	1,178	1,278	1,193	1,268	1,330	1,638	2,194	2,503	2,602	2,600	2,537	2,828	3,119	3,235	3,358	9
10	Manufacturing	1,543	1,488	1,369	1,150	1,086	1,153	1,216	1,287	1,376	1,296	1,363	1,432	1,653	2,023	2,349	2,517	2,517	2,517	2,793	3,039	3,093	3,303	10
11	Food and kindred products	1,503	1,489	1,451	1,303	1,204	1,221	1,253	1,290	1,351	1,331	1,372	1,385	1,472	1,650	1,878	2,044	2,170	2,385	2,669	2,853	2,926	3,071	11
12	Tobacco manufactures	979	985	908	787	725	750	778	817	883	870	916	1,000	1,117	1,240	1,431	1,580	1,676	1,779	1,950	2,040	2,089	2,258	12
13	Textile mill products	1,155	1,096	1,039	847	829	883	926	952	994	926	960	986	1,159	1,385	1,556	1,681	1,817	2,056	2,338	2,587	2,565	2,767	13
14	Apparel and other finished fabric products	1,361	1,265	1,162	941	900	987	1,016	1,013	1,025	999	1,025	1,022	1,159	1,330	1,595	1,788	1,943	2,192	2,327	2,435	2,383	2,492	14
15	Lumber and timber basic products	1,172	1,156	1,010	787	737	791	833	911	963	940	956	934	1,026	1,204	1,446	1,564	1,618	1,813	2,046	2,254	2,296	2,519	15
16	Furniture and finished lumber products	1,398	1,310	1,196	962	900	948	988	1,074	1,123	1,102	1,138	1,158	1,304	1,514	1,743	1,892	1,988	2,187	2,395	2,603	2,651	2,846	16
17	Paper and allied products	1,514	1,487	1,404	1,208	1,143	1,186	1,235	1,313	1,403	1,359	1,414	1,458	1,646	1,850	2,076	2,254	2,365	2,535	2,903	3,200	3,230	3,474	17
18	Printing, publishing and allied industries	2,010	2,011	1,943	1,740	1,599	1,644	1,698	1,702	1,722	1,697	1,718	1,764	1,852	1,973	2,156	2,376	2,576	2,862	3,210	3,495	3,653	3,798	18
19	Chemicals and allied products	1,673	1,647	1,608	1,419	1,312	1,341	1,385	1,455	1,559	1,621	1,611	1,723	1,893	2,131	2,386	2,608	2,670	2,765	3,119	3,389	3,529	3,763	19
20	Products of petroleum and coal	1,844	1,904	1,810	1,619	1,505	1,513	1,587	1,629	1,833	1,863	1,852	1,954	2,113	2,410	2,806	3,046	3,097	3,183	3,610	4,072	4,179	4,320	20
21	Rubber products	1,597	1,563	1,392	1,191	1,137	1,248	1,358	1,472	1,526	1,457	1,548	1,583	1,778	2,116	2,478	2,699	2,722	2,826	3,085	3,189	3,225	3,528	21
22	Leather and leather products	1,327	1,215	1,152	970	950	1,017	1,043	1,045	1,085	1,017	1,038	1,041	1,236	1,450	1,659	1,831	1,972	2,131	2,313	2,414	2,410	2,550	22
23	Stone, clay and glass products	1,557	1,525	1,386	1,167	1,071	1,088	1,171	1,262	1,357	1,303	1,359	1,393	1,554	1,771	2,024	2,174	2,249	2,380	2,672	2,925	3,014	3,263	23
24	Iron and steel and their products, including ordnance	1,740	1,640	1,410	1,044	1,073	1,166	1,295	1,446	1,591	1,359	1,549	1,643	1,923	2,284	2,637	2,781	2,792	2,696	3,063	3,360	3,390	3,628	24
25	Nonferrous metals and their products	1,665	1,554	1,455	1,177	1,132	1,209	1,277	1,361	1,492	1,402	1,521	1,594	1,824	2,235	2,581	2,724	2,735	2,717	2,969	3,248	3,271	3,617	25
26	Machinery, except electrical	1,827	1,748	1,521	1,311	1,260	1,345	1,425	1,550	1,693	1,534	1,681	1,813	2,144	2,629	2,857	2,975	2,930	2,862	3,112	3,431	3,478	3,757	26
27	Electrical machinery	1,655	1,658	1,461	1,182	1,203	1,282	1,364	1,478	1,616	1,527	1,601	1,688	1,919	2,287	2,466	2,578	2,584	2,615	2,876	3,154	3,247	3,369	27
28	Transportation equipment, except automobiles	1,747	1,728	1,590	1,463	1,310	1,317	1,381	1,496	1,614	1,589	1,667	1,764	2,160	2,695	2,982	3,188	3,175	2,971	3,146	3,601	3,600	3,753	28
29	Automobiles and automobile equipment	1,813	1,571	1,455	1,234	1,170	1,314	1,489	1,600	1,672	1,653	1,762	1,934	2,243	2,880	2,978	3,103	2,968	2,814	3,143	3,381	3,607	4,007	29
30	Miscellaneous	1,568	1,535	1,466	1,230	1,166	1,195	1,244	1,298	1,359	1,274	1,337	1,380	1,540	1,882	2,176	2,320	2,401	2,442	2,657	2,870	2,961	3,140	30
31	Wholesale and retail trade	1,597	1,568	1,497	1,318	1,187	1,232	1,281	1,299	1,356	1,357	1,365	1,391	1,491	1,626	1,796	1,965	2,135	2,403	2,661	2,867	2,936	3,082	31
32	Wholesale trade	2,164	2,113	2,017	1,748	1,541	1,618	1,712	1,724	1,767	1,760	1,773	1,834	2,024	2,254	2,489	2,670	2,806	3,079	3,379	3,625	2,671	3,900	32
33	Retail trade and automobile services	1,409	1,384	1,324	1,173	1,066	1,102	1,140	1,159	1,219	1,217	1,224	1,242	1,314	1,422	1,582	1,741	1,918	2,187	2,420	2,607	2,686	2,807	33
34	Finance, insurance and real estate	2,090	2,001	1,886	1,687	1,591	1,635	1,668	1,747	1,819	1,762	1,761	1,754	1,805	1,918	2,064	2,212	2,369	2,598	2,764	2,958	3,083	3,279	34
35	Transportation	1,642	1,610	1,549	1,373	1,334	1,393	1,492	1,582	1,644	1,676	1,723	1,754	1,888	2,181	2,489	2,678	2,733	2,948	3,147	3,442	3,557	3,684	35
36	Railroads	1,749	1,717	1,661	1,461	1,439	1,505	1,645	1,724	1,774	1,849	1,877	1,903	2,035	2,299	2,580	2,709	2,706	3,051	3,212	3,577	3,704	3,752	36
37	Local railways and bus lines	1,721	1,719	1,678	1,533	1,422	1,473	1,515	1,583	1,633	1,674	1,701	1,700	1,795	2,018	2,288	2,468	2,619	2,729	2,965	3,146	3,256	3,400	37
38	Highway passenger transportation, not elsewhere classified	1,328	1,308	1,135	921	833	959	1,023	1,106	1,220	1,236	1,303	1,320	1,473	1,960	2,270	2,446	2,570	2,648	2,707	2,766	2,764	2,869	38
39	Highway freight transportation and warehousing	1,298	1,269	1,230	1,179	1,172	1,207	1,264	1,328	1,408	1,456	1,521	1,551	1,630	1,863	2,147	2,374	2,545	2,752	3,063	3,355	3,557	3,812	39
40	Water transportation	1,272	1,218	1,146	1,038	1,066	1,054	1,092	1,375	1,541	1,294	1,553	1,648	1,854	2,729	3,388	3,624	3,583	3,415	3,747	4,006	4,137	4,413	40

TABLE 108—Continued

No.	Industry	1929	1930	1931	1932	1933	1934	1935	1936	1937	1938	1939	1940	1941	1942	1943	1944	1945	1946	1947	1948	1949	1950	No.
41	Air transportation (common carriers)	2,624	2,424	2,381	2,346	2,227	2,201	2,195	2,243	2,257	2,269	2,328	2,239	2,258	2,296	2,457	2,766	2,830	2,852	3,268	3,679	3,870	4,118	41
42	Pipeline transportation	1,927	1,802	1,794	1,691	1,443	1,521	1,575	1,609	1,822	1,909	1,930	1,928	2,099	2,298	2,720	3,038	3,240	3,259	3,750	4,100	4,172	4,296	42
43	Services allied to transportation	1,425	1,427	1,375	1,227	1,139	1,182	1,259	1,279	1,282	1,280	1,269	1,365	1,579	1,780	2,094	2,331	2,403	2,549	2,767	2,862	2,907	3,087	43
44	Communications and public utilities	1,474	1,497	1,514	1,438	1,351	1,426	1,486	1,522	1,601	1,674	1,692	1,718	1,766	1,881	2,075	2,248	2,425	2,567	2,792	3,002	3,151	3,319	44
45	Telephone, telegraph and related services	1,385	1,411	1,436	1,336	1,247	1,336	1,378	1,420	1,482	1,580	1,599	1,610	1,633	1,715	1,878	2,035	2,246	2,413	2,583	2,776	2,907	3,033	45
46	Radio broadcasting and television	2,513	2,624	2,732	2,740	2,510	2,198	2,089	2,223	2,361	2,497	2,427	2,554	2,581	2,714	2,929	3,333	3,515	3,972	4,073	4,234	4,469	4,698	46
47	Utilities: electric and gas	1,590	1,601	1,599	1,541	1,456	1,513	1,589	1,617	1,705	1,750	1,767	1,795	1,870	2,035	2,284	2,467	2,596	2,697	2,994	3,223	3,376	3,569	47
48	Local utilities and public services, not elsewhere classified	1,116	1,124	1,122	1,081	1,021	1,061	1,116	1,135	1,197	1,228	1,240	1,318	1,364	1,524	1,778	1,889	2,000	2,045	2,217	2,391	2,522	2,682	48
49	Services	1,069	1,058	1,002	914	850	852	868	893	932	938	943	949	1,016	1,131	1,337	1,519	1,669	1,870	2,002	2,111	2,168	2,214	49
50	Hotels and other lodging places	1,098	1,097	1,030	908	816	863	878	897	941	946	958	967	990	1,055	1,210	1,378	1,518	1,681	1,807	1,898	1,950	1,991	50
51	Personal services	1,219	1,200	1,136	996	889	905	915	940	978	992	1,008	1,019	1,054	1,169	1,346	1,513	1,655	1,859	1,989	2,116	2,188	2,256	51
52	Private households	701	650	560	477	442	455	467	487	536	506	520	533	578	678	876	1,079	1,236	1,328	1,379	1,412	1,409	1,414	52
53	Commercial and trade schools and employment agencies	1,650	1,778	1,625	1,500	1,364	1,417	1,400	1,471	1,526	1,500	1,529	1,625	1,833	2,175	2,520	2,714	2,571	2,520	2,903	3,147	3,270	3,462	53
54	Business services, not elsewhere classified	2,185	2,311	2,178	1,792	1,596	1,657	1,813	1,849	1,902	1,840	1,828	1,863	1,980	2,150	2,456	2,735	2,949	3,114	3,316	3,554	3,648	3,863	54
55	Miscellaneous repair services and hand trades	1,814	1,793	1,684	1,464	1,286	1,339	1,429	1,456	1,544	1,552	1,603	1,607	1,921	2,203	2,747	2,975	2,914	2,902	3,165	3,358	3,465	3,627	55
56	Motion pictures	2,169	2,175	2,179	1,959	1,891	1,844	1,892	1,896	1,972	1,942	1,971	1,948	2,016	2,124	2,250	2,379	2,567	2,978	3,031	2,911	2,920	2,919	56
57	Amusement and recreation, except motion pictures	1,273	1,268	1,244	1,218	1,185	1,190	1,193	1,232	1,269	1,270	1,277	1,263	1,267	1,305	1,430	1,628	1,838	2,116	2,247	2,289	2,363	2,432	57
58	Medical and other health services	925	931	916	865	809	799	828	850	876	898	907	923	948	1,008	1,102	1,206	1,333	1,529	1,765	1,898	1,995	2,107	58
59	Legal services	1,385	1,392	1,334	1,261	1,166	1,164	1,165	1,201	1,225	1,201	1,205	1,228	1,260	1,302	1,369	1,533	1,699	1,805	1,977	2,096	2,188	2,268	59
60	Engineering and other professional services, not elsewhere classified	2,314	2,027	1,897	1,714	1,619	1,609	1,600	1,759	1,774	1,909	1,973	1,902	2,245	2,641	3,063	3,237	3,258	3,280	3,495	3,745	3,922	4,144	60
61	Educational services, not elsewhere classified	1,313	1,329	1,323	1,279	1,189	1,175	1,163	1,180	1,211	1,228	1,234	1,241	1,263	1,342	1,481	1,579	1,654	1,811	2,006	2,205	2,332	2,420	61
62	Religious organizations	1,610	1,600	1,542	1,413	1,300	1,289	1,297	1,315	1,364	1,391	1,410	1,407	1,382	1,379	1,436	1,541	1,583	1,692	1,860	2,015	2,163	2,276	62
63	Nonprofit membership organizations, not elsewhere classified	1,758	1,730	1,701	1,637	1,567	1,558	1,537	1,572	1,590	1,625	1,634	1,675	1,778	1,962	2,200	2,455	2,667	2,986	3,279	3,530	3,717	3,905	63
64	Government and government enterprises	1,552	1,554	1,549	1,479	1,330	1,286	1,293	1,281	1,356	1,338	1,339	1,349	1,392	1,647	1,813	1,958	2,097	2,364	2,568	2,786	2,882	3,045	64
65	Federal — general government	1,571	1,513	1,577	1,528	1,226	1,187	1,189	1,115	1,193	1,153	1,143	1,139	1,240	1,650	1,820	1,972	2,113	2,464	2,755	2,935	2,974	3,249	65
66	Civilian, except work relief	1,924	1,763	1,895	1,823	1,673	1,718	1,757	1,895	1,799	1,830	1,842	1,893	1,968	2,220	2,622	2,670	2,640	2,732	2,986	3,176	3,335	3,552	66
67	Military	1,195	1,207	1,198	1,175	1,084	1,084	1,163	1,166	1,144	1,135	1,164	1,077	1,111	1,513	1,600	1,816	1,999	2,319	2,544	2,704	2,648	2,994	67
68	Work relief	—	—	—	—	954	971	839	931	1,007	991	939	883	889	965	1,064	—	—	—	—	—	—	—	68
69	Federal — government enterprises	1,903	1,907	1,913	1,791	1,577	1,635	1,780	1,869	1,851	1,811	1,820	1,826	1,870	1,988	2,270	2,344	2,379	2,727	2,718	3,029	3,118	3,211	69
70	State and local — general government	1,499	1,517	1,497	1,427	1,333	1,289	1,283	1,397	1,436	1,467	1,471	1,497	1,523	1,573	1,690	1,800	1,941	2,095	2,337	2,594	2,739	2,818	70
71	Public education	1,445	1,455	1,463	1,399	1,300	1,265	1,293	1,329	1,367	1,406	1,403	1,436	1,464	1,509	1,612	1,735	1,887	2,032	2,345	2,675	2,830	2,927	71
72	Nonschool, except work relief	1,549	1,576	1,541	1,479	1,413	1,391	1,425	1,457	1,493	1,517	1,530	1,552	1,574	1,628	1,756	1,855	1,986	2,144	2,331	2,536	2,674	2,741	72
73	Work relief	—	1,000	1,045	1,057	1,140	1,128	1,034	1,345	1,454	1,333	909	909	1,000	1,000	—	—	—	—	—	—	—	—	73
74	State and local — government enterprises	1,600	1,595	1,573	1,529	1,455	1,438	1,473	1,487	1,536	1,563	1,578	1,610	1,734	1,896	2,142	2,255	2,405	2,590	2,818	3,045	3,228	3,293	74

Source: Survey of Current Business, National Income Supplement, 1951 edition, pp. 184–85.

TABLE 109

AVERAGE ANNUAL WAGE CREDITS OF WORKERS UNDER OASI CLASSIFIED BY LAST INDUSTRY IN WHICH THEY WERE EMPLOYED, 1945[a]

Industry	Total	Male	Female
All industries	$1,321	$1,585	$887
Agriculture, forestry and fishing	993	1,088	643
Mining	1,819	1,847	1,199
Metal mining	1,736	1,774	1,079
Anthracite mining	2,030	2,036	1,452
Bituminous coal mining	1,944	1,965	1,085
Crude petroleum and natural gas	1,738	1,767	1,367
Nonmetallic mining and quarrying	1,397	1,425	1,015
Contract construction	1,411	1,435	996
General contractors, building construction	1,350	1,368	978
Other general contractors	1,259	1,278	966
Special-trade contractors	1,548	1,580	1,026
Manufacturing	1,467	1,724	1,003
Food	1,053	1,266	644
Tobacco	1,103	1,425	948
Textile mill products	1,203	1,486	926
Apparel, etc.	1,191	1,854	989
Lumber basic products	933	948	750
Furniture, etc.	1,189	1,347	799
Paper and allied products	1,391	1,677	916
Printing, publishing, etc.	1,504	1,820	1,015
Chemicals	1,578	1,795	1,084
Products of petroleum and coal	2,033	2,129	1,461
Rubber	1,587	1,857	1,113
Leather	1,268	1,662	933
Stone, clay and glass	1,377	1,533	962
Iron and steel	1,763	1,936	1,115
Transportation equipment, except automobiles	1,781	1,985	1,260
Nonferrous metals	1,701	1,894	1,159
Electrical machinery	1,601	2,018	1,164
Machinery, except electrical	1,844	2,025	1,239
Automobiles	1,884	2,053	1,320
Transportation, communication and other public utilities	1,537	1,658	1,194
Railways and bus lines	1,901	1,966	1,277
Trucking, etc.	1,325	1,357	1,013
Water transportation	1,818	1,839	1,337
Services allied to transportation	1,344	1,400	1,024
Telephone and telegraph	1,383	1,805	1,224
Electricity and gas	1,833	1,971	1,256
Local utilities and public services	1,477	1,539	1,088
Wholesale and retail trade	1,030	1,343	698
Wholesalers	1,377	1,557	996
Other wholesale distributors	1,547	1,707	1,150
Retail general merchandise	709	1,123	593
Retail food and liquor stores	1,009	1,218	688
Retail automotive	1,419	1,467	1,063
Retail apparel and accessories	981	1,416	800
Eating and drinking places	1,025	1,258	706
Retail filling stations	764	1,111	541
Finance, insurance and real estate	1,494	1,855	1,134
Banks and trust companies	1,538	2,016	1,204
Insurance carriers	1,669	2,166	1,226
Insurance agents	1,435	2,007	1,173
Real estate	1,221	1,463	827
Holding companies	1,705	2,062	1,306
Service industries	996	1,239	751
Hotels and lodging places	669	931	528
Personal services	927	1,362	694
Business services	1,344	1,588	1,005
Commercial schools, etc.	1,197	1,357	998
Automobile repair and garages	1,241	1,276	946
Repair services and hand trades	1,361	1,454	861
Motion pictures	964	1,187	651
Amusement, etc.	711	720	675
Medical and other health services	935	1,258	887
Legal services	1,302	1,667	1,211
Educational institutions and agencies	848	1,296	645
Other professional institutions and agencies	1,585	1,721	1,149
Nonprofit membership organizations	1,392	1,596	1,030

a. Based on one per cent sample.

Source: Handbook of Old-Age and Survivors Insurance Statistics, Employment, Wages and Insurance Status of Workers in Covered Employment, Social Security Administration, Federal Security Agency, Baltimore, 1946, pp. 102–03.

TABLE 110

DECILE ANNUAL WAGE CREDITS OF MEN AND WOMEN UNDER OASI, BY INDUSTRY, 1939, 1944 AND 1946

Industry	Number of Workers, in Thousands	First Decile	Second Decile	Third Decile	Fourth Decile	Median	Sixth Decile	Seventh Decile	Eighth Decile	Ninth Decile
		A. Male, 1939								
All industries	24,360	$65	$190	$385	$630	$870	$1,115	$1,370	$1,675	$2,160
Mining	1,036	95	285	505	730	925	1,095	1,270	1,500	1,865
Metal mining	142	140	425	720	975	1,180	1,330	1,470	1,655	1,950
Anthracite mining	86	240	555	820	960	1,065	1,170	1,290	1,460	1,740
Bituminous and other soft-coal mining	504	110	325	530	715	865	1,000	1,140	1,300	1,570
Crude-petroleum and natural-gas production	190	70	200	485	855	1,225	1,520	1,725	1,935	2,350
Nonmetallic mining and quarrying	114	25	80	180	325	485	670	895	1,185	1,620
Contract construction	1,942	25	75	130	235	390	590	850	1,200	1,720
Manufacturing	9,394	120	365	620	850	1,070	1,290	1,490	1,765	2,235
Food and kindred products	1,444	65	190	390	670	955	1,215	1,445	1,740	2,160
Tobacco manufactures	64	65	200	415	620	780	945	1,160	1,520	2,190
Textile mill products	854	135	405	555	680	775	900	1,060	1,270	1,660
Apparel and other finished products made from fabrics and similar materials	358	200	460	670	850	1,035	1,255	1,510	1,850	2,480
Lumber and timber basic products	516	30	85	190	320	450	570	755	1,050	1,425
Furniture and finished lumber products	425	85	260	440	610	760	920	1,100	1,335	1,705
Paper and allied products	258	255	630	870	1,035	1,165	1,290	1,450	1,695	2,165
Printing, publishing and allied industries	546	85	250	640	975	1,275	1,610	1,985	2,385	2,980
Chemicals and allied products	505	105	320	640	970	1,230	1,430	1,640	1,950	2,520
Products of petroleum and coal	221	220	720	1,135	1,410	1,630	1,780	1,950	2,170	2,640
Rubber products	119	290	625	885	1,105	1,290	1,480	1,670	1,905	2,295
Leather and leather products	269	210	455	650	790	925	1,065	1,210	1,400	1,760
Stone, clay and glass products	421	130	385	630	830	995	1,155	1,330	1,575	2,050
Iron and steel and their products	1,245	260	565	865	1,070	1,230	1,385	1,560	1,780	2,200
Nonferrous metals and their products	283	230	530	845	1,055	1,215	1,365	1,530	1,755	2,200
Electrical machinery	284	235	540	860	1,090	1,280	1,465	1,690	2,000	2,600
Machinery, except electrical	750	320	725	990	1,180	1,345	1,515	1,715	1,960	2,445
Automobiles and automobile equipment	395	350	710	1,030	1,210	1,365	1,520	1,660	1,815	2,105
Transportation, communication and other public utilities	1,623	75	225	515	860	1,220	1,485	1,725	1,985	2,430
Local railways and bus lines	152	860	1,240	1,425	1,550	1,665	1,760	1,860	1,990	2,200
Trucking and warehousing for hire	457	45	130	260	460	710	980	1,270	1,570	1,950
Other transportation, except water transportation	160	85	255	430	610	785	995	1,330	1,665	2,050
Water transportation	56	50	145	325	590	890	1,195	1,530	1,935	2,505
Communication: telephone, telegraph and related services	205	60	180	460	1,075	1,625	2,085	2,420	2,755	3,180
Utilities: electric and gas	425	195	715	1,170	1,410	1,590	1,760	1,940	2,160	2,565
Wholesale trade	1,281	50	155	340	610	885	1,165	1,465	1,870	2,570
Retail trade	3,378	45	140	255	440	645	855	1,095	1,380	1,850
Retail general merchandise	522	30	95	210	435	690	930	1,180	1,470	2,030
Retail food and liquor stores	809	35	110	230	390	590	805	1,015	1,315	1,730
Retail automotive	421	100	300	505	705	900	1,105	1,320	1,570	1,970
Retail apparel and accessories	229	50	155	340	600	850	1,105	1,380	1,720	2,310
Eating and drinking places	633	30	95	210	325	450	610	785	1,010	1,345
Finance, insurance and real estate	984	110	330	625	905	1,170	1,425	1,780	2,250	3,090
Banks and trust companies	72	190	575	865	1,140	1,360	1,600	1,920	2,395	3,235
Security dealers and investment banking	66	280	730	1,025	1,285	1,550	1,885	2,285	3,170	—
Insurance carriers	226	195	620	985	1,320	1,670	2,030	2,420	2,860	3,465
Insurance agents, brokers and services	33	250	655	975	1,310	1,640	2,035	2,525	3,220	—
Real estate	324	55	160	365	575	785	1,005	1,220	1,480	2,000
Service industries	2,178	35	110	230	390	580	800	1,065	1,400	2,005
Hotels, rooming houses, camps and other lodging places	332	25	75	155	260	370	515	690	920	1,300
Personal services	378	75	225	390	575	750	940	1,150	1,400	1,840
Business services, not elsewhere classified	266	50	145	265	525	830	1,160	1,535	2,020	3,040
Employment agencies and commercial and trade schools	13	30	95	205	375	595	860	1,210	1,680	2,500

TABLE 110—CONTINUED

Industry	Number of Workers, in Thousands	First Decile	Second Decile	Third Decile	Fourth Decile	Median	Sixth Decile	Seventh Decile	Eighth Decile	Ninth Decile
	A. Male, 1939—Continued									
Motion pictures	164	$45	$140	$250	$455	$705	$1,035	$1,480	$2,080	$3,015
Amusement and recreation and related services, not elsewhere classified	320	20	60	120	200	315	475	680	970	1,455
Medical and other health services	37	50	145	260	425	620	840	1,110	1,520	2,520
Other professional and social-service agencies and institutions	45	55	165	385	700	1,050	1,440	1,870	2,370	3,125
Nonprofit membership organizations	127	30	85	195	480	870	1,240	1,580	2,030	2,805
	B. Female, 1939									
All industries	9,391	$25	$70	$160	$315	$455	$595	$735	$885	$1,130
Mining	25	50	145	325	530	720	900	1,130	1,360	1,695
Contract construction	38	40	120	255	390	540	680	840	1,050	1,355
Manufacturing	3,592	45	135	280	410	520	630	745	870	1,060
Food and kindred products	574	15	40	80	130	190	300	475	695	960
Tobacco manufactures	96	80	240	380	480	565	645	725	795	915
Textile mill products	680	70	205	345	450	530	610	690	770	895
Apparel and other finished products made from fabrics and similar materials	821	45	140	310	425	510	590	675	785	975
Lumber and timber basic products	16	40	125	265	410	560	710	870	1,050	1,290
Furniture and finished lumber products	76	45	135	285	420	545	665	775	890	1,080
Paper and allied products	94	70	205	370	510	635	730	810	900	1,060
Printing, publishing and allied industries	188	50	150	330	530	680	805	935	1,115	1,420
Chemicals and allied products	117	80	245	460	645	775	885	990	1,165	1,440
Products of petroleum and coal	16	190	565	845	1,020	1,170	1,290	1,395	1,550	1,770
Rubber products	37	95	280	450	600	710	795	885	990	1,175
Leather and leather products	207	50	145	320	420	510	580	655	750	895
Stone, clay and glass products	72	85	255	420	575	700	780	880	1,000	1,215
Iron and steel and their products	116	95	280	480	635	745	840	950	1,080	1,305
Nonferrous metals and their products	60	90	270	470	640	745	830	900	1,010	1,190
Electrical machinery	136	70	205	350	525	670	790	900	1,030	1,230
Machinery, except electrical	87	120	355	580	730	845	930	1,045	1,185	1,390
Automobiles and automobile equipment	34	85	255	420	595	765	890	985	1,105	1,290
Transportation, communication and other public utilities	365	120	365	600	785	930	1,070	1,210	1,365	1,575
Trucking and warehousing for hire	27	40	125	260	430	590	735	890	1,070	1,330
Communication: telephone, telegraph and related services	241	140	420	645	815	955	1,090	1,225	1,380	1,575
Utilities: electric and gas	59	180	545	790	920	1,050	1,170	1,300	1,450	1,665
Wholesale trade	379	20	55	115	255	425	625	825	1,020	1,105
Retail trade	2,501	17	50	90	155	250	390	565	725	930
Retail general merchandise	1,165	13	40	75	130	195	340	550	715	910
Retail food and liquor stores	197	20	60	115	220	330	450	590	725	915
Retail automotive	35	55	165	350	520	665	780	900	1,065	1,295
Retail apparel and accessories	365	20	60	110	200	350	540	695	845	1,055
Eating and drinking places	509	15	45	85	145	225	300	395	520	710
Finance, insurance and real estate	462	95	280	475	645	790	920	945	1,215	1,455
Banks and trust companies	30	110	325	555	725	850	990	1,145	1,305	1,535
Security dealers and investment banking	20	145	440	745	945	1,095	1,235	1,370	1,530	1,820
Insurance carriers	153	155	470	700	830	925	1,010	1,125	1,260	1,490
Insurance agents, brokers and services	47	125	370	580	740	875	995	1,130	1,285	1,510
Real estate	108	50	145	270	390	510	615	730	890	1,220
Service industries	1,340	30	95	170	290	410	550	685	830	1,110
Hotels, rooming houses, camps and other lodging places	268	17	50	90	155	245	330	450	590	765
Personal services	463	40	115	210	315	430	535	650	750	900
Business services, not elsewhere classified	140	50	145	270	440	625	770	910	1,095	1,415
Motion pictures	62	30	90	165	270	400	545	710	925	1,300
Amusement and recreation and related services, not elsewhere classified	62	15	45	80	145	220	325	450	665	965
Medical and other health services	153	40	120	250	370	500	635	780	950	1,240
Other professional and social-service agencies and institutions	9	50	155	355	550	715	910	1,130	1,360	1,690
Nonprofit membership organizations	58	25	70	120	195	370	655	910	1,155	1,470

TABLE 110—Continued

Industry	Number of Workers, in Thousands	First Decile	Second Decile	Third Decile	Fourth Decile	Median	Sixth Decile	Seventh Decile	Eighth Decile	Ninth Decile
C. Male, 1944										
All industries	28,101	$120	$360	$775	$1,310	$1,820	$2,290	$2,740	$3,170	—
Mining	1,043	210	710	1,295	1,770	2,120	2,400	2,670	2,975	$3,275
Metal mining	127	320	780	1,290	1,730	2,045	2,250	2,460	2,705	3,040
Anthracite mining	92	780	1,520	1,885	2,070	2,210	2,360	2,550	2,770	3,110
Bituminous and other soft-coal mining	489	275	890	1,485	1,900	2,235	2,520	2,760	3,005	—
Crude-petroleum and natural-gas production	240	165	500	1,100	1,670	2,170	2,550	2,895	3,215	—
Nonmetallic mining and quarrying	95	90	265	530	865	1,180	1,495	1,870	2,320	2,995
Contract construction	1,536	90	265	540	920	1,380	1,920	2,435	3,025	—
Manufacturing	13,934	185	560	1,130	1,710	2,200	2,620	2,980	3,340	—
Ordnance and accessories	349	240	740	1,430	2,000	2,430	2,795	3,105	—	—
Food and kindred products	1,557	45	140	310	620	1,100	1,675	2,170	2,645	3,165
Tobacco manufactures	41	165	495	890	1,170	1,460	1,730	1,910	2,195	3,045
Textile mill products	774	180	545	965	1,235	1,460	1,735	2,050	2,430	2,965
Apparel and other finished products made from fabrics and similar materials	325	195	590	1,115	1,585	2,030	2,515	2,925	3,290	—
Lumber and timber basic products	772	40	120	245	430	660	930	1,255	1,740	2,500
Furniture and finished lumber products	404	95	290	595	970	1,320	1,655	2,045	2,470	3,105
Paper and allied products	327	160	480	1,020	1,565	1,915	2,230	2,550	2,910	3,380
Printing, publishing and allied industries	420	155	460	1,045	1,760	2,320	2,755	3,045	—	—
Chemicals and allied products	689	195	610	1,165	1,730	2,160	2,510	2,850	3,220	—
Products of petroleum and coal	220	390	1,240	2,030	2,465	2,820	3,080	—	—	—
Rubber products	184	240	770	1,395	1,975	2,435	2,870	3,195	—	—
Leather and leather products	198	195	595	1,060	1,435	1,785	2,085	2,405	2,765	3,190
Stone, clay and glass products	370	120	360	770	1,260	1,690	2,020	2,400	2,800	3,230
Iron and steel and their products	1,637	375	1,060	1,760	2,190	2,520	2,805	3,080	—	—
Transportation equipment, except automobiles	2,664	415	1,190	1,940	2,510	2,900	3,200	—	—	—
Nonferrous metals and their products	444	325	975	1,650	2,095	2,425	2,705	2,985	3,260	—
Electrical machinery	665	375	1,145	1,915	2,415	2,770	3,060	—	—	—
Machinery, except electrical	1,241	385	1,090	1,890	2,240	2,620	2,945	3,220	—	—
Automobiles and automobile equipment	322	380	1,260	2,070	2,615	2,930	3,155	—	—	—
Transportation, communication and other public utilities	1,955	150	455	955	1,485	1,930	2,310	2,630	3,025	—
Railways and bus lines	167	350	1,125	1,835	2,145	2,370	2,570	2,740	2,960	3,230
Trucking and warehousing for hire	619	75	225	490	830	1,260	1,725	2,150	2,570	3,105
Other transportation, except water transportation	240	230	580	1,030	1,420	1,785	2,170	2,505	2,880	3,320
Water transportation	274	280	720	1,175	1,605	1,985	2,365	2,820	3,195	—
Communication: telephone, telegraph and related services	123	320	1,390	2,340	2,760	3,075	—	—	—	—
Utilities: electric and gas	306	285	1,230	1,805	2,135	2,380	2,600	2,835	3,110	—
Wholesale trade	1,931	110	330	765	1,330	1,830	2,320	2,800	3,245	—
Full-service and limited-function wholesalers	1,007	105	310	660	1,160	1,605	2,040	2,520	3,035	—
Wholesale distributors, other than full-service and limited-function wholesalers	924	120	355	960	1,585	2,160	2,620	3,030	—	—
Retail trade	3,575	50	150	335	590	925	1,370	1,850	2,390	3,115
Retail general merchandise	458	35	110	230	410	720	1,215	1,710	2,340	3,210
Retail food and liquor stores	828	45	135	285	500	810	1,330	1,805	2,410	3,020
Retail automotive	330	115	340	675	1,110	1,535	1,960	2,355	2,810	3,355
Retail apparel and accessories	223	70	205	425	750	1,340	1,915	2,415	3,600	—
Eating and drinking places	751	55	160	365	590	850	1,155	1,540	2,030	2,660
Retail filling stations	185	45	140	305	470	685	1,000	1,400	1,875	2,630
Finance, insurance and real estate	822	195	580	1,175	1,605	2,070	2,550	3,015	—	—
Banks and trust companies	165	285	1,010	1,675	2,090	2,420	2,750	3,090	—	—
Security dealers and investment banking	26	305	980	1,680	2,245	2,885	3,230	—	—	—
Insurance carriers	201	345	1,250	2,020	2,565	2,940	3,240	—	—	—
Insurance agents, brokers and services	30	295	795	1,735	2,420	2,870	3,175	—	—	—
Real estate	318	125	370	710	1,070	1,380	1,645	1,980	2,490	3,255

TABLE 110—Continued

Industry	Number of Workers, in Thousands	First Decile	Second Decile	Third Decile	Fourth Decile	Median	Sixth Decile	Seventh Decile	Eighth Decile	Ninth Decile
	C. Male, 1944—Continued									
Service industries	2,162	$50	$150	$330	$615	$990	$1,445	$1,970	$2,580	$3,375
Hotels, rooming houses, camps and other lodging places	305	45	135	285	460	690	955	1,295	1,710	2,305
Personal services	408	100	295	565	910	1,250	1,595	1,985	2,420	3,070
Business services, not elsewhere classified	266	95	280	700	1,275	1,880	2,420	2,895	3,415	—
Employment agencies and commercial and trade schools	34	95	290	555	875	1,220	1,630	2,050	2,805	3,530
Automobile repair services and garages	174	90	270	495	800	1,160	1,535	1,890	2,285	2,950
Motion pictures	199	35	115	225	400	720	1,230	2,110	3,075	—
Amusement and recreation and related services, not elsewhere classified	355	15	45	90	165	260	475	860	1,410	2,210
Medical and other health services	42	70	205	370	590	885	1,315	1,775	2,460	3,460
Other professional and social-service agencies and institutions	80	135	410	785	1,365	2,040	2,660	3,225	—	—
Nonprofit membership organizations	164	75	225	600	1,155	1,695	2,200	2,765	3,240	—
	D. Female, 1944									
All industries	18,195	$55	$160	$295	$490	$740	$1,010	$1,255	$1,550	$1,990
Mining	47	90	270	510	760	1,030	1,335	1,625	1,880	2,225
Contract construction	100	50	150	310	500	735	1,015	1,310	1,615	2,065
Manufacturing	8,094	85	255	470	735	985	1,230	1,480	1,780	2,185
Ordnance and accessories	252	125	370	625	925	1,210	1,480	1,710	1,950	2,285
Food and kindred products	914	20	60	115	220	350	560	835	1,160	1,530
Tobacco manufactures	91	70	215	430	670	925	1,140	1,330	1,490	1,705
Textile mill products	831	90	275	490	710	910	1,060	1,210	1,380	1,600
Apparel and other finished products made from fabrics and similar materials	1,085	80	240	465	725	940	1,120	1,295	1,530	1,860
Lumber and timber basic products	68	35	105	210	280	395	610	860	1,160	1,625
Furniture and finished lumber products	186	45	140	290	450	650	870	1,130	1,405	1,720
Paper and allied products	199	65	200	375	600	850	1,055	1,265	1,470	1,720
Printing, publishing and allied industries	279	55	165	350	590	870	1,110	1,330	1,550	1,885
Chemicals and allied products	316	95	280	485	745	1,050	1,290	1,510	1,780	2,110
Products of petroleum and coal	39	280	570	790	1,110	1,350	1,535	1,750	2,015	2,450
Rubber products	138	110	330	570	840	1,150	1,410	1,655	1,925	2,255
Leather and leather products	250	80	235	430	670	870	1,050	1,225	1,420	1,670
Stone, clay and glass products	147	80	240	430	675	900	1,110	1,315	1,550	1,865
Iron and steel and their products	509	125	370	630	920	1,210	1,445	1,660	1,895	2,205
Transportation equipment, except automobiles	1,062	230	530	885	1,255	1,610	1,960	2,245	2,520	2,880
Nonferrous metals and their products	169	125	375	645	970	1,270	1,490	1,700	1,935	2,235
Electrical machinery	679	145	435	750	1,065	1,325	1,550	1,745	1,970	2,255
Machinery, except electrical	410	145	430	725	1,030	1,285	1,525	1,770	2,010	2,370
Automobiles and automobile equipment	130	230	520	860	1,245	1,570	1,830	2,080	2,335	2,705
Transportation, communication and other public utilities	652	125	370	625	890	1,120	1,315	1,525	1,775	2,090
Trucking and warehousing for hire	69	65	190	390	655	955	1,210	1,470	1,730	2,070
Communication: telephone, telegraph and related services	388	135	410	670	910	1,120	1,305	1,510	1,750	2,095
Utilities: electric and gas	73	240	525	855	1,090	1,290	1,450	1,615	1,815	2,070
Wholesale trade	940	70	215	400	660	935	1,210	1,430	1,690	2,070
Full-service and limited-function wholesalers	513	50	150	335	540	790	1,065	1,295	1,535	1,890
Wholesale distributors, other than full-service and limited-function wholesalers	427	90	265	510	835	1,130	1,375	1,585	1,855	2,230
Retail trade	4,813	20	65	125	240	365	550	780	1,050	1,400
Retail general merchandise	1,807	20	60	110	180	290	470	710	970	1,310
Retail food and liquor stores	563	40	115	210	320	465	635	840	1,095	1,425
Retail automotive	54	80	240	415	645	890	1,110	1,320	1,570	1,910
Retail apparel and accessories	558	35	105	185	330	530	780	1,030	1,295	1,650
Eating and drinking places	1,220	20	65	120	230	350	490	665	875	1,245

TABLE 110—Continued

Industry	Number of Workers, in Thousands [a]	First Decile	Second Decile	Third Decile	Fourth Decile	Median	Sixth Decile	Seventh Decile	Eighth Decile	Ninth Decile
D. Female, 1944—Continued										
Finance, insurance and real estate	846	$110	$330	$570	$845	$1,080	$1,290	$1,465	$1,655	$1,960
Banks and trust companies	218	210	465	735	970	1,165	1,315	1,465	1,650	1,900
Security dealers and investment banking	21	255	525	905	1,210	1,470	1,685	1,850	2,030	2,330
Insurance carriers	225	205	495	795	1,030	1,230	1,395	1,535	1,730	2,020
Insurance agents, brokers and services	73	110	330	590	880	1,130	1,340	1,500	1,680	1,960
Real estate	192	45	140	295	450	625	830	1,065	1,330	1,690
Service industries	2,170	35	110	200	325	500	720	965	1,255	1,645
Hotels, rooming houses, camps and other lodging places	434	18	55	110	215	320	455	640	885	1,185
Personal services	785	30	90	165	295	460	665	885	1,135	1,465
Business services, not elsewhere classified	204	45	135	285	490	755	1,055	1,335	1,620	2,020
Automobile repair services and garages	26	65	195	405	630	855	1,070	1,295	1,550	1,895
Motion pictures	132	25	70	125	220	325	520	790	1,150	1,730
Amusement and recreation and related services, not elsewhere classified	87	25	75	135	240	365	530	785	1,125	1,650
Medical and other health services	246	55	160	325	495	690	910	1,140	1,410	1,755
Other professional and social-service agencies and institutions	39	85	250	415	615	860	1,175	1,460	1,730	2,055
Nonprofit membership organizations	92	55	170	340	585	910	1,190	1,460	1,710	2,070
E. Male, 1946										
All industries	32,401	$130	$395	$765	$1,235	$1,670	$2,070	$2,475	$2,945	$3,440
Mining	1,123	270	765	1,330	1,795	2,125	2,420	2,690	2,975	3,290
Metal mining	120	340	790	1,250	1,650	1,935	2,185	2,425	2,760	3,160
Anthracite mining	91	635	1,565	2,080	2,380	2,555	2,710	2,890	3,105	—
Bituminous and other soft-coal mining	551	390	950	1,505	1,895	2,170	2,430	2,680	2,955	3,270
Crude-petroleum and natural-gas production	237	170	505	1,010	1,675	2,140	2,535	2,840	3,115	—
Nonmetallic mining and quarrying	124	120	360	750	1,170	1,540	1,925	2,250	2,720	3,235
Contract construction	2,632	85	260	520	820	1,225	1,650	2,125	2,700	3,355
Manufacturing [b]	13,559	200	570	1,050	1,525	1,910	2,240	2,570	2,995	3,435
Ordnance and accessories	116	390	895	1,490	1,845	2,135	2,370	2,670	2,995	3,325
Food and kindred products	1,535	90	270	565	990	1,510	1,980	2,390	2,840	3,350
Tobacco manufactures	51	115	340	680	1,230	1,535	1,800	2,130	2,510	3,070
Textile mill products	903	280	705	1,165	1,485	1,750	1,970	2,250	2,605	3,145
Apparel and other finished products made from fabrics and similar materials	455	125	375	820	1,350	1,890	2,420	2,970	3,435	—
Lumber and wood products, except furniture	1,092	45	135	305	505	750	1,045	1,400	1,845	2,480
Furniture and fixtures	326	135	405	730	1,110	1,430	1,750	2,085	2,500	3,055
Paper and allied products	387	265	675	1,260	1,715	2,040	2,345	2,650	3,055	—
Printing, publishing and allied industries	558	205	600	1,165	1,820	2,345	2,870	3,335	—	—
Chemicals and allied products	638	260	735	1,310	1,785	2,150	2,470	2,805	3,165	—
Products of petroleum and coal	252	615	1,485	2,115	2,480	2,750	3,025	—	—	—
Rubber products	240	430	1,100	1,675	2,060	2,390	2,710	2,995	3,295	—
Leather and leather products	264	220	585	1,125	1,510	1,805	2,100	2,420	2,795	3,255
Stone, clay and glass products	519	150	445	850	1,335	1,705	2,015	2,330	2,725	3,210
Primary metal industries	1,297	430	1,005	1,520	1,845	2,330	2,585	2,900	3,290	—
Transportation equipment	1,396	290	760	1,270	1,730	2,065	2,345	2,630	2,985	3,365
Fabricated metal products, except ordnance, machinery and transportation equipment	917	280	710	1,185	1,630	1,955	2,260	2,585	2,995	3,410
Electrical machinery, equipment and supplies	653	355	890	1,440	1,830	2,145	2,400	2,730	3,175	—
Machinery, except electrical	1,401	430	1,005	1,540	1,930	2,230	2,505	2,805	3,160	—
Professional, scientific and controlling instruments; photographic and optical goods; watches and clocks	204	460	1,065	1,610	1,995	2,325	2,630	2,980	3,300	—

TABLE 110—Continued

Industry	Number of Workers, in Thousands [a]	First Decile	Second Decile	Third Decile	Fourth Decile	Median	Sixth Decile	Seventh Decile	Eighth Decile	Ninth Decile
E. Male, 1946—Continued										
Transportation, communication and other public utilities	2,371	$175	$525	$990	$1,500	$1,945	$2,345	$2,720	$3,080	—
Railways and bus lines	200	760	1,520	2,020	2,345	2,565	2,750	2,930	3,090	—
Trucking and warehousing for hire	702	100	295	605	1,010	1,465	1,900	2,310	2,715	3,175
Other transportation, except water transportation	341	230	525	900	1,275	1,640	2,010	2,440	2,880	3,370
Water transportation	243	360	860	1,300	1,670	1,990	2,350	2,740	3,150	—
Communication: telephone, telegraph and related services	249	185	550	1,160	1,870	2,470	3,155	—	—	—
Utilities: electric and gas	420	395	1,080	1,730	2,145	2,450	2,720	2,960	3,190	—
Wholesale trade	2,257	160	480	950	1,475	1,915	2,330	2,785	3,290	—
Full-service and limited-function wholesalers	1,299	160	480	900	1,395	1,820	2,230	2,660	3,170	—
Wholesale distributors, other than full-service and limited-function wholesalers	958	160	480	1,020	1,570	2,045	2,470	2,940	3,440	—
Retail trade	5,023	85	255	460	750	1,145	1,560	2,000	2,530	3,235
Retail general merchandise	639	55	160	360	610	1,020	1,480	1,965	2,560	3,410
Retail food and liquor stores	1,080	80	245	450	750	1,205	1,650	2,105	2,615	3,290
Retail automotive	561	220	490	840	1,235	1,590	1,980	2,380	2,880	3,365
Retail apparel and accessories	277	85	250	520	970	1,555	2,115	2,670	3,280	—
Eating and drinking places	1,020	70	210	395	635	935	1,245	1,590	2,070	2,735
Retail filling stations	323	75	225	380	570	830	1,150	1,500	1,940	2,550
Finance, insurance and real estate	1,112	255	640	1,120	1,630	2,080	2,585	3,115	—	—
Banks and trust companies	202	380	940	1,560	2,080	2,495	2,900	3,255	—	—
Security dealers and investment banking	51	460	1,200	1,775	2,440	2,950	3,410	—	—	—
Insurance carriers	284	415	1,095	1,840	2,380	2,930	3,380	—	—	—
Insurance agents, brokers and services	54	310	550	1,025	1,600	2,110	2,680	3,385	—	—
Real estate	391	125	370	695	1,040	1,400	1,760	2,095	2,640	3,435
Service industries	2,838	70	210	390	680	1,080	1,520	2,010	2,630	3,425
Hotels, rooming houses, camps and other lodging places	395	45	135	290	440	660	970	1,305	1,725	2,395
Personal services	519	110	325	590	940	1,300	1,680	2,080	2,570	3,230
Business services, not elsewhere classified	386	110	325	690	1,160	1,675	2,220	2,840	3,375	—
Employment agencies and commercial and trade schools	26	120	365	585	890	1,260	1,570	2,095	2,805	3,365
Automobile repair services and garages	287	110	325	595	880	1,225	1,550	1,900	2,365	2,950
Motion pictures	235	40	125	240	440	805	1,440	2,240	3,190	—
Amusement and recreation and related services, not elsewhere classified	430	25	65	125	215	385	650	1,080	1,720	2,560
Medical and other health services	59	85	255	420	615	990	1,330	1,825	2,385	3,635
Other professional and social-service agencies and institutions	102	115	350	665	1,145	1,720	2,220	2,985	3,645	—
Nonprofit membership organizations	192	130	385	795	1,360	1,880	2,360	2,785	3,300	—
F. Female, 1946										
All industries	16,695	$55	$170	$310	$510	$750	$1,035	$1,330	$1,625	$2,010
Mining	47	135	405	810	1,140	1,405	1,660	1,940	2,200	2,580
Contract construction	90	75	225	430	640	900	1,200	1,500	1,890	2,405
Manufacturing [b]	6,164	75	230	430	705	995	1,250	1,485	1,725	2,060
Ordnance and accessories	31	125	370	670	950	1,285	1,545	1,710	1,900	2,105
Food and kindred products	757	25	80	145	260	435	695	1,030	1,380	1,760
Tobacco manufactures	89	100	305	560	820	1,065	1,250	1,390	1,605	1,990
Textile mill products	805	115	345	595	880	1,120	1,325	1,490	1,670	1,910
Apparel and other finished products made from fabrics and similar materials	1,222	75	220	395	650	920	1,150	1,370	1,655	2,120
Lumber and wood products, except furniture	97	40	120	290	450	700	915	1,140	1,455	1,890
Furniture and fixtures	84	70	215	365	545	765	1,040	1,270	1,525	1,830
Paper and allied products	192	85	250	455	715	990	1,250	1,465	1,670	1,890
Printing, publishing and allied industries	305	85	250	450	730	1,025	1,300	1,540	1,820	2,285
Chemicals and allied products	220	100	295	555	935	1,265	1,520	1,730	1,935	2,250
Products of petroleum and coal	31	210	480	845	1,320	1,580	1,855	2,095	2,375	2,755
Rubber products	103	115	340	640	1,005	1,315	1,575	1,785	2,000	2,285

TABLE 110—Continued

Industry	Number of Workers, in Thousands[a]	First Decile	Second Decile	Third Decile	Fourth Decile	Median	Sixth Decile	Seventh Decile	Eighth Decile	Ninth Decile
	F. Female, 1946—Continued									
Leather and leather products	273	$100	$295	$510	$820	$1,035	$1,230	$1,405	$1,620	$1,945
Stone, clay and glass products	141	105	320	555	790	1,085	1,325	1,520	1,750	2,045
Primary metal industries	129	105	320	610	985	1,310	1,545	1,740	1,945	2,200
Transportation equipment	237	105	315	635	960	1,280	1,585	1,830	2,070	2,350
Fabricated metal products, except ordnance, machinery and transportation equipment	258	90	275	510	800	1,085	1,340	1,570	1,800	2,060
Electrical machinery, equipment and supplies	488	120	355	605	915	1,200	1,415	1,610	1,785	2,085
Machinery, except electrical	287	135	400	675	990	1,275	1,520	1,720	1,920	2,225
Professional, scientific and controlling instruments; photographic and optical goods; watches and clocks	127	145	430	780	1,095	1,350	1,540	1,710	1,910	2,205
Transportation, communication and other public utilities	833	150	450	730	1,025	1,320	1,595	1,840	2,125	2,515
Trucking and warehousing for hire	62	55	170	340	605	840	1,110	1,400	1,760	2,110
Communication: telephone, telegraph and related services	580	220	480	760	1,050	1,355	1,630	1,890	2,190	2,590
Utilities: electric and gas	75	270	610	950	1,255	1,460	1,650	1,860	2,110	2,405
Wholesale trade	841	75	230	460	720	1,040	1,365	1,640	1,920	2,285
Full-service and limited-function wholesalers	514	70	205	370	615	885	1,220	1,530	1,830	2,225
Wholesale distributors, other than full-service and limited-function wholesalers	327	105	310	600	925	1,280	1,555	1,780	2,015	2,375
Retail trade	4,964	35	100	175	300	445	640	895	1,210	1,620
Retail general merchandise	1,806	25	70	140	260	385	590	885	1,200	1,590
Retail food and liquor stores	548	40	115	235	350	510	720	960	1,245	1,615
Retail automotive	72	90	275	475	735	1,015	1,265	1,485	1,885	2,295
Retail apparel and accessories	578	40	125	255	415	640	920	1,220	1,530	1,975
Eating and drinking places	1,276	25	70	135	250	365	505	685	915	1,280
Retail filling stations	23	70	210	320	450	660	945	1,240	1,615	2,100
Finance, insurance and real estate	934	125	370	620	885	1,175	1,415	1,635	1,885	2,210
Banks and trust companies	218	280	615	920	1,210	1,420	1,590	1,765	1,965	2,230
Security dealers and investment banking	25	415	985	1,390	1,680	1,905	2,105	2,300	2,525	2,890
Insurance carriers	286	140	415	680	950	1,250	1,455	1,655	1,870	2,200
Insurance agents, brokers and services	91	115	350	580	840	1,095	1,340	1,600	1,840	2,170
Real estate	192	50	155	340	520	715	950	1,215	1,520	1,995
Service industries	2,350	40	115	235	370	560	790	1,055	1,380	1,840
Hotels, rooming houses, camps and other lodging places	457	25	75	140	265	370	550	730	995	1,340
Personal services	856	35	110	220	350	525	730	960	1,220	1,600
Businesss services, not elsewhere classified	215	50	155	340	555	895	1,225	1,530	1,865	2,295
Automobile repair services and garages	29	50	145	325	490	700	1,015	1,275	1,495	1,950
Motion pictures	146	20	65	125	230	350	545	835	1,250	1,985
Amusement and recreation and related services, not elsewhere classified	89	25	75	145	275	410	605	840	1,195	1,770
Medical and other health services	295	70	215	370	545	750	995	1,245	1,530	1,905
Other professional and social-service agencies and institutions	22	70	210	460	630	1,025	1,380	1,675	2,085	2,560
Nonprofit membership organizations	93	65	195	410	650	960	1,290	1,575	1,870	2,350

a. For 1946, preliminary.
b. Differs in content from corresponding industries shown in previous years.

Source: Bureau of Old-Age and Survivors Insurance.

TABLE 111

Decile Annual Wage Credits of Men and Women with Four Quarters in Employment under OASI, by Industry, 1944 and 1946

Industry	Number of Workers, in Thousands	First Decile	Second Decile	Third Decile	Fourth Decile	Median	Sixth Decile	Seventh Decile	Eighth Decile	Ninth Decile
A. Male Four-Quarter Workers, 1944										
All industries	18,722	$1,040	$1,540	$1,940	$2,290	$2,595	$2,890	$3,200	—	—
Mining	775	1,335	1,775	2,055	2,285	2,490	2,690	2,910	$3,240	—
Metal mining	93	1,390	1,790	2,010	2,160	2,310	2,475	2,650	2,870	$3,275
Anthracite mining	79	1,640	1,910	2,070	2,185	2,315	2,465	2,635	2,865	3,285
Bituminous and other soft-coal mining	382	1,415	1,810	2,105	2,350	2,565	2,745	2,935	3,125	—
Crude-petroleum and natural-gas production	165	1,335	1,880	2,225	2,495	2,765	2,990	3,215	—	—
Nonmetallic mining and quarrying	56	825	1,110	1,350	1,580	1,850	2,130	2,420	2,865	3,260
Contract construction	816	1,050	1,490	1,870	2,220	2,565	2,910	3,270	—	—
Manufacturing	9,941	1,305	1,810	2,190	2,505	2,790	3,050	—	—	—
Ordnance and accessories	253	1,630	2,100	2,410	2,685	2,925	3,160	—	—	—
Food and kindred products	828	940	1,410	1,760	2,045	2,310	2,555	2,820	3,125	—
Tobacco manufactures	29	950	1,225	1,470	1,690	1,850	1,950	2,120	2,685	3,325
Textile mill products	577	985	1,235	1,415	1,595	1,815	2,050	2,330	2,670	3,165
Apparel and other finished products made from fabrics and similar materials	236	1,160	1,565	1,925	2,310	2,650	2,965	3,265	—	—
Lumber and timber basic products	378	565	795	985	1,185	1,425	1,720	2,080	2,500	3,095
Furniture and finished lumber products	259	915	1,210	1,450	1,700	1,955	2,230	2,530	2,920	3,410
Paper and allied products	230	1,305	1,670	1,930	2,170	2,395	2,620	2,870	3,200	—
Printing, publishing and allied industries	316	1,000	1,705	2,170	2,545	2,845	3,070	—	—	—
Chemicals and allied products	492	1,335	1,830	2,160	2,430	2,680	2,925	3,180	—	—
Products of petroleum and coal	177	1,880	2,300	2,630	2,890	3,095	—	—	—	—
Rubber products	134	1,505	2,045	2,400	2,745	3,015	—	—	—	—
Leather and leather products	150	1,105	1,430	1,715	1,955	2,180	2.420	2,660	2,990	3,390
Stone, clay and glass products	253	1,085	1,495	1,760	2,010	2,255	2,510	2,790	3,090	—
Iron and steel and their products	1,292	1,630	2,065	2,360	2,610	2,835	3,055	—	—	—
Transportation equipment, except automobiles	2,008	2,000	2,505	2,830	3,075	—	—	—	—	—
Nonferrous metals and their products	343	1,600	2,030	2,315	2,555	2,760	2,970	3,195	—	—
Electrical machinery	522	1,850	2,330	2,630	2,890	3,115	—	—	—	—
Machinery, except electrical	962	1,705	2,140	2,465	2,745	2,990	3,225	—	—	—
Automobiles and automobile equipment	257	1,930	2,475	2,790	2,995	3,195	—	—	—	—
Transportation, communication and other public utilities	1,319	1,135	1,630	1,980	2,260	2,510	2,740	3,026	—	—
Railways and bus lines	134	1,675	2,040	2,245	2,410	2,550	2,695	2,890	3,085	—
Trucking and warehousing for hire	366	825	1,205	1,570	1,865	2,155	2,430	2,680	3,030	—
Water transportation	156	1,295	1,765	2,120	2,405	2,790	3,110	—	—	—
Communication: telephone, telegraph and related services	106	1,760	2,470	2,800	3,065	—	—	—	—	—
Utilities: electric and gas	254	1,940	2,175	2,380	2,565	2,760	2,980	3,210	—	—
Wholesale trade	1,303	1,065	1,555	1,940	2,295	2,605	2,930	3,255	—	—
Full-service and limited-function wholesalers	664	915	1,380	1,715	2,035	2,355	2,695	3,045	—	—
Wholesale distributors, other than full-service and limited-function wholesalers	639	1,290	1,820	2,230	2,565	2,855	3,145	—	—	—
Retail trade	2,047	555	910	1,255	1,570	1,880	2,205	2,565	3,005	—
Retail general merchandise	254	455	785	1,165	1,490	1,820	2,175	2,585	3,140	—
Retail food and liquor stores	460	505	850	1,255	1,610	1,960	2,290	2,625	2,980	3,350
Retail automotive	210	935	1,360	1,700	1,995	2,265	2,540	2,865	3,220	—
Retail apparel and accessories	146	580	980	1,500	1,925	2,270	2,620	3,035	—	—
Eating and drinking places	410	580	850	1,090	1,330	1,595	1,885	2,210	2,590	3,160
Retail filling stations	92	545	795	1,070	1,325	1,565	1,845	2,180	2,610	3,205
Finance, insurance and real estate	655	960	1,445	1,840	2,235	2,630	3,000	3,359	—	—
Banks and trust companies	138	1,160	1,745	2,105	2,405	2,670	2,965	3,280	—	—
Security dealers and investment banking	27	1,360	1,905	2,410	2,945	3,270	—	—	—	—
Insurance carriers	171	1,390	2,160	2,645	2,950	3,200	—	—	—	—
Insurance agents, brokers and services	23	1,500	2,160	2,685	2,980	3,235	—	—	—	—
Real estate	221	730	1,120	1,385	1,590	1,825	2,105	2,515	3,082	—

TABLE 111—Continued

Industry	Number of Workers, in Thousands	First Decile	Second Decile	Third Decile	Fourth Decile	Median	Sixth Decile	Seventh Decile	Eighth Decile	Ninth Decile
A. Male Four-Quarter Workers, 1944—Continued										
Service industries	1,210	$600	$1,010	$1,350	$1,685	$2,035	$2,400	$2,830	$3,325	—
Hotels, rooming houses, camps and other lodging places	163	490	725	930	1,140	1,370	1,615	1,890	2,230	2,780
Personal services	257	730	1,110	1,400	1,655	1,910	2,185	2,485	2,870	3,390
Business services, not elsewhere classified	175	1,000	1,600	2,050	2,425	2,755	3,125	—	—	—
Automobile repair services and garages	100	840	1,185	1,470	1,720	1,940	2,150	2,430	2,860	3,260
Motion pictures	107	470	785	1,150	1,610	2,330	2,930	3,460	—	—
Amusement and recreation and related services, not elsewhere classified	130	270	495	790	1,100	1,380	1,670	2,050	2,550	3,409
Medical and other health services	23	555	860	1,205	1,505	1,830	2,230	2,805	3,440	—
Other professional and social-service agencies and institutions	49	1,265	1,925	2,430	2,880	3,280	—	—	—	—
Nonprofit membership organizations	104	680	1,305	1,755	2,190	2,620	3,025	—	—	—
B. Female Four-Quarter Workers, 1944										
All industries	9,622	$585	$850	$1,020	$1,190	$1,345	$1,510	$1,700	$1,950	$2,350
Mining	27	920	1,150	1,360	1,555	1,715	1,845	1,995	2,240	2,550
Contract construction	45	670	930	1,150	1,330	1,490	1,670	1,880	2,125	2,570
Manufacturing	4,672	790	1,010	1,190	1,345	1,500	1,680	1,890	2,130	2,505
Ordnance and accessories	147	1,000	1,250	1,435	1,600	1,740	1,870	2,030	2,245	2,550
Food and kindred products	333	555	760	925	1,065	1,210	1,360	1,505	1,660	1,925
Tobacco manufactures	56	730	915	1,070	1,210	1,330	1,430	1,530	1,650	1,880
Textile mill products	520	710	860	980	1,090	1,180	1,290	1,395	1,530	1,740
Apparel and other finished products made from fabrics and similar materials	662	730	910	1,040	1,150	1,270	1,405	1,570	1,805	2,115
Lumber and timber basic products	26	455	655	825	985	1,150	1,335	1,550	1,780	2,065
Furniture and finished lumber products	95	580	785	960	1,110	1,250	1,385	1,540	1,730	1,965
Paper and allied products	113	700	925	1,065	1,195	1,290	1,400	1,530	1,685	1,920
Printing, publishing and allied industries	163	655	895	1,065	1,215	1,340	1,465	1,620	1,825	2,250
Chemicals and allied products	178	810	1,100	1,290	1,430	1,560	1,710	1,875	2,065	2,335
Products of petroleum and coal	26	1,005	1,240	1,400	1,540	1,690	1,850	2,030	2,305	2,655
Rubber products	81	930	1,190	1,355	1,515	1,680	1,840	1,995	2,190	2,435
Leather and leather products	153	685	870	1,000	1,100	1,210	1,330	1,455	1,610	1,830
Stone, clay and glass products	84	765	955	1,105	1,235	1,360	1,485	1,625	1,820	2,110
Iron and steel and their products	309	960	1,215	1,375	1,515	1,665	1,810	1,955	2,135	2,440
Transportation equipment, except automobiles	646	1,290	1,620	1,875	2,085	2,255	2,410	2,600	2,815	3,070
Nonferrous metals and their products	105	985	1,240	1,390	1,535	1,685	1,830	1,975	2,160	2,450
Electrical machinery	435	1,020	1,260	1,435	1,580	1,720	1,850	1,995	2,170	2,440
Machinery, except electrical	255	985	1,235	1,430	1,595	1,740	1,880	2,050	2,270	2,610
Automobiles and automobile equipment	81	1,195	1,520	1,730	1,905	2,065	2,220	2,385	2,610	2,910
Transportation, communication and other public utilities	437	790	1,005	1,185	1,335	1,470	1,610	1,780	1,975	2,250
Trucking and warehousing for hire	39	780	1,030	1,220	1,375	1,530	1,685	1,850	2,030	2,360
Communication: telephone, telegraph and related services	275	780	985	1,145	1,290	1,425	1,565	1,745	1,960	2,235
Utilities: electric and gas	53	915	1,115	1,270	1,400	1,510	1,635	1,775	1,950	2,185
Wholesale trade	540	740	980	1,170	1,320	1,450	1,590	1,785	2,005	2,365
Full-service and limited-function wholesalers	279	680	900	1,070	1,230	1,365	1,490	1,640	1,845	2,200
Wholesale distributors, other than full-service and limited-function wholesalers	261	830	1,105	1,280	1,430	1,565	1,710	1,905	2,170	2,520
Retail trade	2,070	355	540	700	840	975	1,120	1,280	1,480	1,765
Retail general merchandise	763	310	500	670	815	950	1,070	1,210	1,390	1,710
Retail food and liquor stores	259	380	555	710	840	990	1,130	1,290	1,465	1,730
Retail automotive	31	625	895	1,065	1,210	1,345	1,495	1,665	1,860	2,225
Retail apparel and accessories	290	380	620	815	975	1,120	1,265	1,435	1,640	2,055
Eating and drinking places	448	385	530	640	750	870	1,005	1,170	1,380	1,660

TABLE 111—Continued

Industry	Number of Workers, in Thousands [a]	First Decile	Second Decile	Third Decile	Fourth Decile	Median	Sixth Decile	Seventh Decile	Eighth Decile	Ninth Decile
B. Female Four-Quarter Workers, 1944—Continued										
Finance, insurance and real estate	573	$705	$935	$1,120	$1,270	$1,395	$1,520	$1,655	$1,830	$2,130
Banks and trust companies	157	800	1,010	1,165	1,290	1,390	1,500	1,630	1,790	2,030
Security dealers and investment banking	15	845	1,130	1,290	1,425	1,550	1,680	1,805	1,955	2,230
Insurance carriers	163	845	1,060	1,210	1,330	1,435	1,550	1,685	1,865	2,170
Insurance agents, brokers and services	51	740	1,015	1,180	1,305	1,415	1,540	1,680	1,850	2,100
Real estate	108	450	630	790	940	1,085	1,235	1,405	1,610	1,990
Service industries	971	470	675	845	995	1,135	1,295	1,480	1,710	2,065
Hotels, rooming houses, camps and other lodging places	152	405	550	670	790	910	1,025	1,145	1,300	1,555
Personal services	345	490	670	810	945	1,055	1,185	1,345	1,540	1,810
Business services, not elsewhere classified	103	635	920	1,130	1,300	1,440	1,595	1,780	2,015	2,370
Motion pictures	56	285	455	675	870	1,040	1,230	1,510	1,830	2,310
Amusement and recreation and related services, not elsewhere classified	31	330	535	715	905	1,090	1,305	1,550	1,890	2,400
Medical and other health services	126	550	735	905	1,060	1,210	1,365	1,545	1,750	2,055
Nonprofit membership organizations	52	550	880	1,125	1,315	1,475	1,625	1,790	1,990	2,440
C. Male Four-Quarter Workers, 1946										
All industries	19,806	$1,150	$1,585	$1,905	$2,170	$2,435	$2,720	$3,060	—	—
Mining	798	1,480	1,875	2,130	2,350	2,550	2,740	2,950	$3,175	—
Metal mining	77	1,535	1,800	1,990	2,180	2,350	2,535	2,800	3,055	—
Anthracite mining	73	1,945	2,280	2,450	2,590	2,720	2,865	3,030	—	—
Bituminous and other soft-coal mining	416	1,500	1,870	2,110	2,310	2,505	2,690	2,890	3,125	—
Crude-petroleum and natural-gas production	157	1,465	1,965	2,315	2,580	2,765	2,950	3,135	—	—
Nonmetallic mining and quarrying	75	1,150	1,475	1,745	2,010	2,215	2,485	2,790	3,135	—
Contract construction	1,258	1,070	1,465	1,800	2,090	2,410	2,750	3,180	—	—
Manufacturing [b]	8,915	1,360	1,735	2,005	2,245	2,480	2,725	3,020	—	—
Ordnance and accessories	69	1,655	2,005	2,270	2,445	2,665	2,855	3,070	—	—
Food and kindred products	879	1,220	1,630	1,960	2,220	2,460	2,705	2,990	3,290	—
Tobacco manufactures	35	1,140	1,420	1,605	1,795	2,005	2,225	2,525	2,835	$3,280
Textile mill products	655	1,260	1,510	1,705	1,880	2,070	2,290	2,535	2,885	3,320
Apparel and other finished products made from fabrics and similar materials	279	1,360	1,810	2,175	2,565	2,925	3,255	—	—	—
Lumber and wood products, except furniture	495	730	970	1,205	1,410	1,640	1,900	2,205	2,550	3,125
Furniture and fixtures	196	1,120	1,385	1,610	1,835	2,045	2,305	2,580	2,930	3,305
Paper and allied products	272	1,500	1,830	2,065	2,285	2,510	2,720	3,025	—	—
Printing, publishing and allied industries	395	1,315	1,920	2,360	2,745	3,135	—	—	—	—
Chemicals and allied products	454	1,480	1,870	2,150	2,395	2,630	2,870	3,135	—	—
Products of petroleum and coal	202	2,020	2,390	2,620	2,840	3,050	—	—	—	—
Rubber products	181	1,685	2,025	2,305	2,565	2,775	3,010	—	—	—
Leather and leather products	187	1,245	1,560	1,800	2,015	2,235	2,470	2,745	3,080	—
Stone, clay and glass products	332	1,295	1,620	1,865	2,070	2,270	2,500	2,770	3,090	—
Primary metal industries	967	1,565	1,840	2,040	2,220	2,400	2,600	2,820	3,115	—
Transportation equipment	757	1,620	1,965	2,205	2,390	2,590	2,805	3,050	—	—
Fabricated metal products, except ordnance, machinery and transportation equipment	1,009	1,455	1,780	2,025	2,250	2,475	2,725	3,005	—	—
Electrical machinery, equipment and supplies	455	1,605	1,900	2,150	2,355	2,565	2,820	3,160	—	—
Machinery, except electrical	864	1,630	1,975	2,215	2,420	2,625	2,850	3,120	—	—
Professional, scientific and controlling instruments; photographic and optical goods; watches and clocks	232	1,645	2,035	2,305	2,545	2,810	3,065	—	—	—
Transportation, communication and other public utilities	1,568	1,295	1,750	2,075	2,355	2,610	2,865	3,105	—	—
Railways and bus lines	164	1,810	2,205	2,430	2,595	2,750	2,890	3,025	—	—
Trucking and warehousing for hire	401	1,045	1,485	1,840	2,110	2,355	2,585	2,850	3,120	—
Other transportation, except water transportation	215	1,200	1,545	1,830	2,090	2,375	2,665	2,950	3,270	—
Water transportation	158	1,335	1,710	2,025	2,300	2,570	2,870	3,190	—	—
Communication: telephone, telegraph and related services	174	1,560	2,090	2,580	3,100	—	—	—	—	—
Utilities: electric and gas	328	1,680	2,065	2,335	2,565	2,760	2,945	3,125	—	—

TABLE 111—CONTINUED

Industry	Number of Workers, in Thousands [a]	First Decile	Second Decile	Third Decile	Fourth Decile	Median	Sixth Decile	Seventh Decile	Eighth Decile	Ninth Decile
C. Male Four-Quarter Workers, 1946—Continued										
Wholesale trade	1,476	$1,285	$1,720	$2,050	$2,350	$2,655	$2,970	$3,315	—	—
Full-service and limited-function wholesalers	838	1,210	1,640	1,955	2,245	2,550	2,855	3,220	—	—
Wholesale distributors, other than full-service and limited-function wholesalers	638	1,410	1,855	2,185	2,480	2,805	3,135	—	—	—
Retail trade	2,724	745	1,195	1,520	1,825	2,095	2,410	2,765	3,170	—
Retail general merchandise	343	680	1,155	1,485	1,810	2,110	2,445	2,860	3,350	—
Retail food and liquor stores	607	650	1,155	1,545	1,875	2,170	2,480	2,790	3,215	—
Retail automotive	336	1,190	1,545	1,820	2,085	2,360	2,665	2,965	3,270	—
Retail apparel and accessories	168	720	1,420	1,890	2,230	2,640	3,035	—	—	—
Eating and drinking places	500	690	1,015	1,265	1,500	1,770	2,040	2,380	2,745	3,310
Retail filling stations	143	710	1,055	1,335	1,565	1,795	2,030	2,300	2,650	3,100
Finance, insurance and real estate	802	1,080	1,620	1,990	2,365	2,800	3,215	—	—	—
Banks and trust companies	161	1,340	1,875	2,240	2,580	2,920	3,250	—	—	—
Security dealers and investment banking	41	1,595	2,085	2,690	3,100	—	—	—	—	—
Insurance carriers	221	1,675	2,250	2,750	3,130	—	—	—	—	—
Insurance agents, brokers and services	35	1,305	1,830	2,310	2,760	3,230	—	—	—	—
Real estate	252	740	1,180	1,485	1,725	1,950	2,220	2,615	3,175	—
Service industries	1,476	755	1,190	1,525	1,850	2,175	2,545	2,970	3,420	—
Hotels, rooming houses, camps and other lodging places	184	525	785	1,045	1,250	1,490	1,730	2,030	2,425	3,050
Personal services	301	855	1,265	1,555	1,825	2,085	2,375	2,725	3,140	—
Business services, not elsewhere classified	233	1,105	1,640	2,030	2,430	2,830	3,180	—	—	—
Employment agencies and commercial and trade schools	14	820	1,225	1,550	1,950	2,400	2,685	3,040	—	—
Automobile repair services and garages	151	1,015	1,355	1,570	1,780	2,000	2,270	2,560	2,910	3,370
Motion pictures	120	500	955	1,530	1,985	2,610	3,205	—	—	—
Amusement and recreation and related services, not elsewhere classified	150	350	665	1,010	1,310	1,625	1,970	2,370	2,930	3,640
Medical and other health services	27	595	1,070	1,340	1,710	2,025	2,375	2,860	3,690	—
Other professional and social-service agencies and institutions	54	1,365	1,865	2,275	2,805	3,250	—	—	—	—
Nonprofit membership organizations	130	975	1,525	1,950	2,320	2,610	2,950	3,325	—	—
D. Female Four-Quarter Workers, 1946										
All industries	8,464	$645	$915	$1,115	$1,290	$1,450	$1,610	$1,785	$2,010	$2,355
Mining	30	1,100	1,345	1,525	1,705	1,885	2,070	2,230	2,435	2,800
Contract construction	43	830	1,085	1,280	1,470	1,690	1,890	2,070	2,420	2,885
Manufacturing [b]	3,418	845	1,090	1,260	1,405	1,535	1,675	1,830	2,025	2,345
Ordnance and accessories	17	1,015	1,280	1,475	1,620	1,715	1,825	1,975	2,150	2,385
Food and kindred products	290	655	910	1,105	1,270	1,410	1,550	1,695	1,870	2,140
Tobacco manufactures	55	805	1,040	1,190	1,295	1,375	1,500	1,650	1,860	2,185
Textile mill products	513	855	1,075	1,245	1,365	1,470	1,570	1,690	1,840	2,065
Apparel and other finished products made from fabrics and similar materials	662	800	1,000	1,150	1,285	1,420	1,585	1,780	2,045	2,525
Lumber and wood products, except furniture	44	705	890	1,030	1,170	1,350	1,515	1,710	1,940	2,230
Furniture and fixtures	41	705	950	1,110	1,260	1,405	1,525	1,665	1,835	2,110
Paper and allied products	111	845	1,070	1,245	1,370	1,490	1,610	1,720	1,840	2,045
Printing, publishing and allied industries	178	775	1,075	1,255	1,420	1,565	1,720	1,910	2,210	2,630
Chemicals and allied products	134	1,030	1,290	1,460	1,610	1,730	1,845	1,985	2,175	2,465
Products of petroleum and coal	20	1,350	1,545	1,730	1,900	2,055	2,210	2,395	2,655	2,930
Rubber products	65	1,045	1,280	1,485	1,635	1,770	1,900	2,035	2,210	2,415
Leather and leather products	167	830	1,020	1,165	1,285	1,390	1,510	1,670	1,870	2,170
Stone, clay and glass products	82	910	1,150	1,310	1,440	1,550	1,670	1,820	1,995	2,245
Primary metal industries	77	1,175	1,375	1,525	1,650	1,750	1,870	2,005	2,150	2,380
Transportation equipment	223	1,105	1,450	1,635	1,780	1,915	2,045	2,170	2,340	2,575
Fabricated metal products, except ordnance, machinery and transportation equipment	170	935	1,185	1,350	1,480	1,630	1,750	1,880	2,035	2,310
Electrical machinery, equipment and supplies	293	965	1,220	1,370	1,495	1,605	1,715	1,845	2,020	2,325
Machinery, except electrical	126	1,085	1,330	1,485	1,610	1,730	1,850	1,985	2,170	2,435
Professional, scientific and controlling instruments; photographic and optical goods; watches and clocks	150	1,030	1,290	1,450	1,570	1,690	1,810	1,940	2,120	2,375

TABLE 111—CONTINUED

Industry	Number of Workers, in Thousands[a]	First Decile	Second Decile	Third Decile	Fourth Decile	Median	Sixth Decile	Seventh Decile	Eighth Decile	Ninth Decile
D. Female Four-Quarter Workers, 1946—Continued										
Transportation, communication and other public utilities	537	$965	$1,260	$1,465	$1,645	$1,790	$1,965	$2,155	$2,395	$2,740
Trucking and warehousing for hire	31	760	985	1,195	1,375	1,580	1,770	1,920	2,105	2,445
Communication: telephone, telegraph and related services	380	970	1,270	1,485	1,660	1,825	2,010	2,210	2,460	2,810
Utilities: electric and gas	55	1,035	1,290	1,445	1,590	1,735	1,900	2,080	2,265	2,570
Wholesale trade	475	785	1,110	1,345	1,530	1,685	1,840	2,010	2,235	2,600
Full-service and limited-function wholesalers	275	710	1,015	1,265	1,450	1,610	1,785	1,950	2,170	2,575
Wholesale distributors, other than full-service and limited-function wholesalers	200	925	1,265	1,465	1,635	1,770	1,905	2,065	2,285	2,615
Retail trade	2,100	430	630	830	990	1,150	1,310	1,490	1,710	2,100
Retail general merchandise	770	405	620	845	1,010	1,160	1,305	1,470	1,685	2,040
Retail food and liquor stores	251	435	625	810	960	1,125	1,290	1,460	1,660	1,975
Retail automotive	37	965	1,170	1,310	1,445	1,615	1,835	2,070	2,285	2,615
Retail apparel and accessories	293	465	750	980	1,170	1,335	1,515	1,710	1,970	2,225
Eating and drinking places	439	435	580	700	825	950	1,090	1,245	1,450	1,760
Retail filling stations	12	430	700	1,005	1,180	1,380	1,620	1,820	2,010	2,655
Finance, insurance and real estate	604	765	1,085	1,290	1,450	1,590	1,735	1,905	2,105	2,430
Banks and trust companies	159	1,040	1,265	1,420	1,550	1,670	1,790	1,945	2,110	2,350
Security dealers and investment banking	20	1,390	1,655	1,815	1,990	2,135	2,285	2,440	2,675	3,035
Insurance carriers	183	905	1,205	1,360	1,490	1,625	1,755	1,910	2,100	2,410
Insurance agents, brokers and services	56	750	1,055	1,250	1,415	1,590	1,740	1,890	2,080	2,405
Real estate	109	390	645	830	1,030	1,205	1,405	1,595	1,870	2,445
Service industries	1,025	550	765	955	1,120	1,280	1,455	1,660	1,910	2,290
Hotels, rooming houses, camps and other lodging places	165	450	620	745	870	1,010	1,145	1,290	1,465	1,750
Personal services	357	570	755	900	1,045	1,170	1,310	1,470	1,690	2,020
Business services, not elsewhere classified	114	690	1,065	1,280	1,460	1,630	1,830	2,010	2,265	2,725
Automobile repair services and garages	14	570	910	1,130	1,265	1,360	1,490	1,775	1,940	2,150
Motion pictures	58	335	550	770	950	1,185	1,485	1,810	2,130	2,770
Amusement and recreation and related services, not elsewhere classified	30	455	685	850	1,050	1,225	1,440	1,685	2,060	2,930
Medical and other health services	137	645	885	1,085	1,235	1,380	1,565	1,750	1,925	2,235
Other professional and social-service agencies and institutions	11	966	1,275	1,445	1,620	1,885	2,070	2,335	2,550	3,245
Nonprofit membership organizations	53	640	970	1,230	1,430	1,620	1,790	1,985	2,300	2,720

a. For 1946, preliminary.
b. Differs in content from corresponding industries shown in previous years.
Source: Bureau of Old-Age and Survivors Insurance.

TABLE 112

Indexes of Decile Annual Wage Credits under OASI, by Industry Division, 1939, 1944 and 1946

(*All Industries = 100*)

A. All Workers, Classified by Sex, 1939, 1944 and 1946

Industry	First Decile		Median		Ninth Decile	
	Male	Female	Male	Female	Male	Female
1939						
All industries	100.0	100.0	100.0	100.0	100.0	100.0
Mining	146.1	200.0	106.3	158.2	86.3	150.0
Contract construction	38.4	160.0	44.8	118.6	79.6	119.9
Manufacturing	184.6	180.0	122.9	114.2	103.4	93.8
Transportation, communication and other public utilities	115.3	480.0	140.2	204.3	112.5	139.3
Wholesale trade	76.9	80.0	101.7	93.4	118.9	97.7
Retail trade	69.3	68.0	74.1	54.9	85.6	82.3
Finance, insurance and real estate	169.2	380.0	134.4	173.6	143.0	128.7
Service industries	53.8	120.0	66.6	90.1	92.8	98.2
1944						
All industries	100.0	100.0	100.0	100.0	100.0	100.0
Mining	175.0	163.6	116.4	139.1	—	111.8
Contract construction	75.0	90.9	75.8	99.3	—	103.7
Manufacturing	154.1	154.5	120.8	133.1	—	109.7
Transportation, communication and other public utilities	125.0	227.2	106.0	151.3	—	105.0
Wholesale trade	91.6	127.2	100.5	126.3	—	104.0
Retail trade	41.6	36.3	50.8	49.3	—	70.3
Finance, insurance and real estate	162.5	200.0	113.7	145.9	—	98.4
Service industries	41.6	63.6	54.3	67.5	—	82.6
1946						
All industries	100.0	100.0	100.0	100.0	100.0	100.0
Mining	207.6	245.4	127.2	187.3	95.6	128.3
Contract construction	65.3	136.3	73.3	120.0	97.5	119.6
Manufacturing	153.8	136.3	114.3	132.6	99.8	102.4
Transportation, communication and other public utilities	134.6	272.7	116.4	176.0	—	125.1
Wholesale trade	123.0	136.3	114.5	138.6	—	113.6
Retail trade	65.3	63.6	68.5	59.3	94.0	80.5
Finance, insurance and real estate	196.1	227.2	124.5	156.6	—	109.9
Service industries	53.8	72.7	64.7	74.6	99.5	91.5

TABLE 112—CONTINUED

B. All Workers, Classified by Race and Sex, 1946

Industry	Male First Decile	Male Median	Male Ninth Decile	Female First Decile	Female Median	Female Ninth Decile
White Workers						
All industries	100.0	100.0	100.0	100.0	100.0	100.0
Mining	186.6	120.4	—	135.5	171.9	80.2
Contract construction	66.6	74.4	—	106.5	114.9	118.3
Manufacturing	153.3	111.7	—	118.7	128.4	101.6
Transportation, communication and other public utilities	130.1	115.9	—	250.0	166.6	122.9
Wholesale trade	130.1	115.5	—	135.5	141.6	113.9
Retail trade	66.6	67.9	—	93.7	56.7	80.9
Finance, insurance and real estate	183.4	124.5	—	231.2	151.9	108.9
Service industries	46.5	65.1	—	93.7	77.6	95.1
Negro Workers						
All industries	100.0	100.0	100.0	100.0	100.0	100.0
Mining	226.6	198.9	122.3	—	—	—
Contract construction	86.7	75.7	93.0	—	—	—
Manufacturing	86.7	121.5	104.6	66.6	144.1	116.9
Transportation, communication and other public utilities	93.3	109.7	102.7	105.5	173.4	130.9
Wholesale trade	93.3	90.1	91.5	111.1	73.3	78.6
Retail trade	80.0	77.4	85.6	73.2	84.0	83.9
Finance, insurance and real estate	153.4	104.9	95.1	66.6	113.1	88.2
Service industries	106.5	75.2	93.3	77.7	86.6	84.6

C. Four-Quarter Workers, Classified by Sex, 1944 and 1946

Industry	First Decile Male	First Decile Female	Median Male	Median Female	Ninth Decile Male	Ninth Decile Female
1944						
All industries	100.0	100.0	100.0	100.0	100.0	100.0
Mining	128.3	157.2	95.9	127.5	—	108.5
Contract construction	100.9	114.5	98.8	110.7	—	109.3
Manufacturing	125.4	135.0	107.5	111.5	—	106.5
Transportation, communication and other public utilities	109.1	135.0	96.7	109.2	—	95.7
Wholesale trade	102.4	126.4	100.3	107.8	—	100.6
Retail trade	53.3	60.6	72.4	72.4	—	75.1
Finance, insurance and real estate	92.3	120.5	101.3	103.7	—	90.6
Service industries	57.6	80.3	78.4	84.3	—	87.8
1946						
All industries	100.0	100.0	100.0	100.0	100.0	100.0
Mining	128.6	170.5	104.7	130.0	—	118.8
Contract construction	93.0	128.6	98.9	116.5	—	122.5
Manufacturing	118.2	131.0	101.8	105.8	—	99.5
Transportation, communication and other public utilities	112.6	149.6	107.1	123.4	—	116.3
Wholesale trade	111.7	121.7	109.0	116.2	—	110.4
Retail trade	64.7	66.6	86.0	79.3	—	89.1
Finance, insurance and real estate	93.9	118.6	114.9	109.6	—	103.1
Service industries	65.6	85.2	89.3	88.2	—	97.2

Source: Bureau of Old-Age and Survivors Insurance.

TABLE 113

Types of Occupations in Manufacturing Industries and Indexes of Their Wages, 1945–1947

Type of Occupation	Occupational Index[a] Median	Occupational Index[a] Range (Middle Half of All Indexes)
Skilled	155	145–170
Occupations comprising the trades or crafts that normally require an extensive learning period under formal apprenticeship or equivalent arrangements. Within the limits of each trade or craft the work requires planning of projects, determination of sequence of operations, and responsibility for accuracy of final results. It also requires knowledge of use of characteristic tools, machine and measuring instruments, as well as knowledge of certain basic principles relating to materials and to standard computations. Depending upon the specific arrangement of production in an establishment, workers in these occupations may be used on varying assignments or in the more skilled phases of recurring operations.		
Semiskilled, group 1	135	125–145
Occupations that are limited in scope to part of a trade or to the operation of a specific machine or unit of equipment. Within the limits of the work there is opportunity for independent judgment based on extensive experience. The work requires care of the machine, knowledge when the work is or is not in accord with specifications, and making the necessary adjustments to assure accuracy. It also requires the use of relevant tools and measuring devices.		
Semiskilled, group 2	115	110–125
Occupations that involve highly repetitive operations, where the work sequence is wholly predetermined. The use of judgment is limited to recognition of when the work is not in accord with acceptable standards. When anything goes wrong, other, more skilled, workmen or supervisors are called upon to make the necessary adjustments. The learning process is generally short, and the major emphasis in learning is to aid the worker in producing an acceptable amount and quality of output.		
Unskilled, group 1	115	105–120
Occupations that involve handling of heavy objects or materials, such as in loading and unloading, in stacking, hoisting or hauling. The work in these occupations is arduous and is frequently performed under unpleasant conditions, because of exposure to weather, fumes, heat or unclean surroundings. These occupations also require some knowledge in the use of simple tools or equipment, such as hooks, shovels, wheelbarrows, crowbars, and various lifting devices.		
Unskilled, group 2	100	95–105
Occupations that comprise janitorial, protective and other light unskilled work, such as maintaining grounds in trim, clean and orderly appearance. Simple tools may be used, such as brooms, shovels, lawn mowers. The work is either inside or within easy reach of shelter.		

a. Data from 42 industries were used in the computation of the indexes. The number of industries from which pertinent data were available for each of the groups of occupations varied somewhat. The median wage rate for unskilled workers, group 2, is set at 100.

Source: Harry Ober, "Occupational Wage Differentials, 1907–1947," *Monthly Labor Review,* August 1948, p. 128.

TABLE 114

WAGE RATES IN SKILLED OCCUPATIONS AS PERCENTAGE OF AVERAGE WAGE RATES OF JANITORS AND HAND TRUCKERS IN MANUFACTURING INDUSTRIES, 1945–1947

Industry	Median Occupational Index
Aircraft engines and engine parts	151
Bakeries	152
Candy and chocolates	157
Chewing and smoking tobacco	162
Cigars	198
Cigarettes	181
Copper alloying, rolling and drawing	139
Cotton garments	191
Cotton textiles	148
Drugs and medicines	151
Electric light and power	166
Electroplating, plating and polishing	162
Fabricated structural steel	165
Ferrous foundries	147
Footwear, except house slippers and rubber footwear	218
Glassware	154
Hosiery, full-fashioned	189
Hosiery, seamless	175
Industrial chemicals	144
Iron and steel forgings	203
Iron and steel mills	170
Jewelry, costume	170
Jewelry, precious	230
Knit outerwear	193
Knit underwear	162
Leather tanning, currying and finishing	134
Machine tools	153
Machine tool accessories	161
Machinery	143
Meat packing (except the "Big Four")	143
Mechanical rubber goods	134
Metal furniture	140
Military tanks	144
Nonferrous foundries	160
Oil burners, hot water and heating apparatus and fittings	142
Paints, varnishes and lacquers	155
Paperboard containers and boxes	161
Paperboard mills	158
Perfumes and cosmetics	166
Power boilers and associated products	154
Pulp and paper mills	155
Radios, radio equipment (except tubes) and phonographs	146
Rayon and silk textiles	156
Sheet metal	202
Small arms	153
Soap and glycerin	134
Stamped and pressed metals	144
Stoves and ranges	165
Structural clay products	153
Textile dyeing and finishing	140
Tool and die jobbing shops	174
Women's and misses' dresses, blouses and waists	268
Women's and misses' suits and coats	293
Wood furniture, other than upholstered	147
Wood furniture, upholstered	192
Woolen and worsted textiles	145

Source: Harry Ober, "Occupational Wage Differentials, 1907–1947," *Monthly Labor Review,* August 1948 (unpublished table used as basis for text of paragraph 2, page 129).

TABLE 115

Wage Rates in Skilled Occupations in Manufacturing Industries as Percentage of Those in Unskilled, by Region, Selected Periods, 1907–1947

(Average Wage Rates for Representative Unskilled Occupations = 100)

Region [a]	Occupational Index: Median	Occupational Index: Range (Middle Half of All Indexes)
United States		
1907	205	180–280
1918–1919	175	150–225
1931–1932	180	160–220
1937–1940	165	150–190
1945–1947	155	145–170
Northeast		
1907	200	175–245
1918–1919	165	150–235
1931–1932	175	155–215
1937–1940	b	b
1945–1947	155	145–175
South		
1907	215	195–235
1918–1919	195	175–230
1931–1932	190	165–235
1937–1940	b	b
1945–1947	170	150–195
Middle West		
1907	190	170–250
1918–1919	175	145–235
1931–1932	170	150–215
1937–1940	b	b
1945–1947	150	140–165
Far West		
1907	185	165–200
1918–1919	170	160–195
1931–1932	160	145–170
1937–1940	b	b
1945–1947	145	140–165

a. *Northeast* — Connecticut, Maine, Massachusetts, New Hampshire, New Jersey, New York, Pennsylvania, Rhode Island, Vermont; *South* — Alabama, Arkansas, Delaware, District of Columbia, Florida, Georgia, Kentucky, Louisiana, Maryland, Mississippi, North Carolina, Oklahoma, South Carolina, Tennessee, Texas, Virginia, West Virginia; *Middle West* — Illinois, Indiana, Iowa, Kansas, Michigan, Minnesota, Missouri, Nebraska, North Dakota, Ohio, South Dakota, Wisconsin; *Far West* — Arizona, California, Colorado, Idaho, Montana, Nevada, New Mexico, Oregon, Utah, Washington, Wyoming.

b. Regional data for the period 1937–1940 insufficient to warrant presentation of separate regional indexes.

Source: Harry Ober, "Occupational Wage Differentials, 1907–1947," *Monthly Labor Review,* August 1948, p. 130.

TABLE 116

Percentage Ratios and Cents-per-Hour Differences between Union Wage Rates of Journeymen and Those of Laborers and Helpers in the Building Trades, 1907–1947

Year	Ratio (Per Cent)	Difference in Cents	Year	Ratio (Per Cent)	Difference in Cents	Year	Ratio (Per Cent)	Difference in Cents
1907	185	20	1921	168	42	1935	179	54
1908	188	21	1922	174	42	1936	175	53
1909	191	23	1923	180	49	1937	172	56
1910	192	25	1924	180	53	1938	170	60
1911	195	25	1925	181	54	1939	170	60
1912	197	26	1926	177	56	1940	169	61
1913	197	26	1927	180	60	1941	167	61
1914	199	27	1928	179	60	1942	160	61
1915	199	28	1929	179	60	1943	159	61
1916	199	29	1930	177	62	1944	158	61
1917	191	29	1931	179	64	1945	154	59
1918	183	30	1932	179	54	1946	147	59
1919	180	34	1933	182	54	1947	143	64
1920	166	41	1934	178	52			

Source: Harry Ober, "Occupational Wage Differentials, 1907–1947," *Monthly Labor Review,* August 1948, p. 130.

TABLE 117

PERCENTAGE RATIOS AND CENTS-PER-HOUR DIFFERENCES BETWEEN UNION WAGE RATES OF SKILLED WORKERS AND THOSE OF PRESS ASSISTANTS AND FEEDERS IN THE BOOK AND JOB PRINTING TRADES, 1907–1946

Year	Compositors, Hand	Electrotypers	Machine Operators	Machine Tenders	Photoengravers	Pressmen, Cylinder	Pressmen, Platen
			Percentage Ratio				
1907	163	168	186	—	—	168	140
1908	148	153	175	—	—	160	132
1909	146	151	179	—	—	171	134
1910	149	154	181	—	—	168	133
1911	147	157	176	—	—	165	131
1912	149	157	178	175	—	165	131
1913	147	156	179	174	—	163	130
1914	146	159	175	170	—	163	129
1915	146	161	175	169	—	162	128
1916	147	163	173	167	165	161	129
1917	143	160	168	163	171	157	129
1918	135	144	155	153	155	149	121
1919	128	128	145	146	141	140	116
1920	123	134	135	133	141	132	114
1921	130	143	141	142	139	135	118
1922	137	151	146	145	145	136	119
1923	125	144	133	132	131	131	111
1924	132	150	139	139	141	136	115
1925	124	142	132	132	137	131	110
1926	125	141	132	135	144	132	113
1927	126	141	136	134	149	130	113
1928	127	142	135	134	153	131	110
1929	126	144	136	134	153	132	111
1930	128	146	138	135	152	133	112
1931	127	148	138	135	151	132	111
1932	133	154	144	142	163	135	114
1933	134	155	145	143	171	136	114
1934	130	160	140	142	168	134	113
1935	130	159	139	140	174	133	111
1936	129	154	139	140	173	134	112
1937	128	149	136	137	167	132	111
1938	125	148	133	134	162	129	109
1939	125	148	133	134	163	130	109
1940	126	147	134	134	163	129	109
1941	127	149	133	134	162	129	109
1942	124	143	131	132	155	128	108
1943	124	142	131	132	152	127	108
1944	125	142	129	132	156	126	108
1945	125	143	129	132	157	126	108
1946	121	135	124	125	148	122	105

TABLE 117—CONTINUED

Year	Compositors, Hand	Electrotypers	Machine Operators	Machine Tenders	Photoengravers	Pressmen, Cylinder	Pressmen, Platen
	Cents-per-Hour Difference						
1907	15	17	21	—	—	17	10
1908	13	14	20	—	—	16	8
1909	13	14	21	—	—	19	9
1910	13	15	22	—	—	18	9
1911	13	16	22	—	—	18	9
1912	14	17	23	22	—	19	9
1913	14	17	23	22	—	19	9
1914	14	18	23	21	—	19	8
1915	14	19	23	22	—	19	9
1916	15	20	23	21	21	20	9
1917	14	20	22	21	25	19	9
1918	14	17	22	21	22	19	9
1919	13	14	22	22	20	19	7
1920	15	23	24	23	28	22	10
1921	22	32	30	31	28	25	13
1922	26	37	33	32	32	26	14
1923	20	34	26	25	24	25	8
1924	25	40	31	31	33	29	12
1925	21	35	27	27	32	26	8
1926	22	35	28	30	38	27	11
1927	23	36	31	30	43	26	12
1928	23	36	30	29	45	26	9
1929	23	38	31	29	46	27	10
1930	24	40	33	30	45	28	10
1931	24	42	33	30	45	28	10
1932	27	46	37	35	53	29	12
1933	27	43	36	34	56	28	11
1934	25	49	33	35	55	28	10
1935	25	49	33	33	62	27	9
1936	25	47	34	34	63	29	10
1937	25	44	33	33	60	29	10
1938	24	45	31	32	59	28	8
1939	25	46	32	33	60	29	9
1940	26	46	32	33	61	28	9
1941	26	48	32	33	60	28	9
1942	25	44	32	33	57	29	8
1943	26	45	33	34	55	29	9
1944	28	47	32	35	61	29	9
1945	27	48	31	36	63	29	8
1946	28	49	32	34	65	30	7

Source: Harry Ober, "Occupational Wage Differentials, 1907–1947," *Monthly Labor Review,* August 1948 (unpublished data compiled for preliminary draft of subject).

TABLE 118

Percentage Distribution of Working Population[a] Aged 14 Years and Over by Occupational Group, 1910–1940

Occupational Group	1910	1920	1930	1940
Total	100.0	100.0	100.0	100.0
Professional occupations	4.4	5.0	6.1	6.5
Proprietors (managers and officials)	23.0	22.3	19.9	17.8
Farmers (owners and tenants)	16.5	15.5	12.4	10.1
Wholesale and retail dealers	3.3	3.4	3.7	3.9
Other proprietors, managers and officials	3.2	3.4	3.8	3.7
Clerks and kindred workers	10.2	13.8	16.3	17.2
Skilled workers and foremen	11.7	13.5	12.9	11.7
Semiskilled workers	14.7	16.1	16.4	21.0
Semiskilled workers in manufacturing	9.8	10.6	9.4	[b]
Other semiskilled workers	4.9	5.5	7.0	[b]
Unskilled workers	36.0	29.4	28.4	25.9
Farm laborers	14.5	9.4	8.6	7.1
Laborers, except farm	14.7	14.6	12.9	10.7
Factory and building construction laborers	7.1	7.6	6.9	[b]
Other laborers	7.6	7.0	6.0	[b]
Servant classes	6.8	5.4	6.9	8.0

a. Gainful workers in 1910 to 1930; persons in the labor force in 1940.
b. Comparable figures for 1940 not available.

Source: Sixteenth Census (1940), *Population — Comparative Occupation Statistics for the United States, 1870 to 1940,* p. 187.

INDEX

The designation (t) or (f) following a page number indicates that the reference is to a table (t) or a chart or figure (f).